1979 Craftworker's Market

1979
Craftworker's
Market

Edited by
Lynne Lapin

Assisted by
Connie Achabal

Writer's Digest Books
Cincinnati, Ohio

Published by Writer's Digest Books, 9933 Alliance Rd., Cincinnati, Ohio 45242.

International Standard Serial Number 0161-0554
International Standard Book Number 0-911654-57-7

Printed and bound in the United States of America

Preface

National Endowment for the Arts' Acting Craft Coordinator, Eudorah Moore, says, "Crafts represent the most important art historical movement of this century." Others have called it a renaissance, a resurgence, a rebirth. Whatever name it goes by it still means just one thing—the craft field is exploding! In all areas of the country and Canada there's a growing movement to spurn the machine-made for the handmade. The number of craft markets contained in this book (3,000+) indicates the demand for crafts by the buying public.

We're excited to take part in this craft movement by offering the first edition of *Craftworker's Market*—over 600 pages of markets, professional advice, opportunities and services. Here in one book is the information the craftworker needs to sell his work to thousands of buyers throughout the US and Canada.

Craftworker's Market will help you grow and progress in your career as a professional craftworker. And *Craftworker's Market* will also grow and progress and will list even more markets and updated information on the markets herein. Your comments and suggestions on the book are most welcome.

— **Lynne Lapin**

Contents

The Profession 1

How to Use Your Craftworker's Market 1

The Craft Market Today 5

Working With the Retailer 9

Handling Your Business 13

Copyright and Patents 18

Packing Your Work for Shipping 22

Photographing Your Crafts 27

Promoting Yourself and Your Work 32

The Craft of Writing Craft Articles 35

Artist-Dealer Agreement 39

The Markets 41

Architectural & Interior Design Firms 41

Colleges & Universities 44

Companies & Manufacturers 53

Department Stores 62

Miscellaneous Markets 65

Professional Show Promoters 68

Shops & Galleries 73

Shows & Fairs 283

Writing Outlets 464

Opportunities and Services 469

Agents 469

Apprenticeships 472

Associations & Organizations 476

Courses 506

Publications of Interest 555

Glossary 567

Index 569

The Profession

How to Use Your Craftworker's Market

Craftworker's Market is divided into three major sections. The Profession describes what every selling craftworker needs to know— whether a fledgling or professional. Included is an overview of the markets today, business and legal concerns, how to package your work, the "ins" of getting free publicity, how to photograph your crafts, and an article on how to write about your creations. The Markets includes sections such as architectural firms, department stores, galleries and shops, shows and fairs, and other outlets actively seeking crafts to show and/or sell. All listings in this section are designed to provide you with needed information about the buyers and services; thus making it easy for the craftworker to decide who he wants to deal with. Opportunities and Services includes listings for craft agents, places offering financial or legal assistance, and schools giving college credit or courses in craftwork.

Below are two sample listings from The Markets section to show you what information is included in each listing. (Specific tips about the listings in a particular section are given at the beginning of each section.)

MARYLAND CRAFT FESTIVAL, Sugarloaf Mountain Works, Inc., Box 319, Poolesville MD 20837. (301)279-7551. Director: Deann Verdier. — who to contact Purpose: "to provide the ideal marketplace for the public to purchase unique, original arts and crafts directly from their creators and to provide the independent professional art and crafts people with a means to sell their goods." Estab. — year of first show 1977. Annual indoor show held 3 days in mid-October at the Maryland State Fairgrounds near Baltimore. Approximate attendance: 10,000

duration and time of show —

entry deadline and fees — paid. Entries accepted until 10 weeks before show date. Entry fee: $85/8x10 display area. Prejudging by 4 slides representative of work to be displayed; entry fee refunded for refused work. Work must be offered for sale; no commission. Craftworker must attend show; demonstrations encouraged. Registration limit: — number of exhibitors 175. Sponsor provides chairs at $1 each; electricity for demonstrations and lighting at $5/300 watts; tables at $3 each; and 24-hour security. "Maryland sales tax people will be present at the show to provide temporary sales tax licenses (free) to all who need them."

Acceptable Work: Considers batik; candlemaking; ceramics (none made from commercial molds); dollmaking ("only the very best"); glass art; jewelry; leatherworking; macrame; metalsmithing; mobiles; pottery; sculpture; soft sculpture; weaving; and woodcrafting. "All work must be completely finished."

Promotion: "We purchase advertising throughout the Baltimore metropolitan area in printed and broadcast media. The paid advertising is supplemented with a direct mail campaign to known art and craft buyers in the area plus much public relations work. B&w photos of artist's work and studio are helpful. Resumes are also helpful for public relations."

***

MINDSCAPE GALLERY AND STUDIO, INC., 1521 Sherman Ave., Evanston IL 60201. who to contact — (312)864-2660. Director: Ronald Isaacson. Craft — type of business shop/gallery/rental gallery. Estab. 1974. number of exhibitors — Represents 300 craftworkers. Price range: $5- — price range 3,000; bestsellers: $20-150. Works on consignment; 40% commission. Retail price set by — working terms joint agreement. Requires exclusive area representation. Reports in 2-4 weeks. Work may how to deliver work — be shipped or hand-delivered. Dealer pays insurance for exhibited work.

Acceptable Work: Considers batik; ceramics; wearables; blown and stained glass; jewelry; leatherworking; metalsmithing; pottery; soft sculpture; wall hangings; weavings; woodcrafting; and commissioned architectural works. Especially needs soft sculpture; sculptural — special needs ceramics; wall tapestry; weavings; and unusual jewelry, functional and sculptural. Finished and one-of-a-kind pieces; utilitarian and/or decorative.

Profile: "Artists are displayed with a grouping of — decription of business their work. The size of the display area is based on the amount of work on hand. Gallery space has 3,000 sq. ft. The gallery provides all display props and has a corner gallery with much window space and exposure. The premise of the gallery is to be a true reflection of what is happening in contemporary fine crafts and present it fairly for the public and artist alike." Located on the North Shore of Chicago, in the center of a major university town. Heaviest wholesale buying time; October-December and April-June; best selling time: October-December.

The following items will be helpful to you while using this book:

• Read each listing thoroughly. A market may only want to work with craftworkers from a certain region of the country, or they may only consider those artists who send a specified number of slides covering specific angles of the work. Also, take note that many of the listings do *not* want to receive unsolicited crafts in the mail — these buyers usually prefer to see the craftworker's resume or slides of the work first.

• A few of the categories in The Markets section are broken down geographically. While this was done for the ease of those who want to work with local markets only, it should be understood that many of the listings are willing to work with craftworkers from anywhere. Check these listings carefully for submission details.

• The year in which a show or business was established will give you some idea of its reliability — a gallery established in 1953 is less likely to fold than one founded last year. But, while the risk is greater when working with a new firm, the buyers are usually more open to new craftworkers.

• If you don't recognize a name or term you read in a listing, chances are it will be defined in the glossary at the back of the book. For example, SASE means self-addressed, stamped envelope — and this should be included with *all* correspondence with buyers.

• Information contained in the Profile subhead found in many listings will give you some idea of the type of atmosphere that the buyer sells under, the best selling times, who the customers are, and other information concerning the type of work you'll have to produce for that particular buyer. Occasionally you will come across a listing with a How To Break In or Sales Tip subhead in which buyers give tips on how to sell to their particular market.

• Another subhead to watch for is Promotion. This information will tell you if there are any special materials you can supply to the show or shop in order to get extra publicity. Also, the type of promotion used by the exhibit sponsor will indicate how well the show or shop is promoted — and thus give you some idea of how many persons you can expect to view your crafts.

• A firm, publication or organization may not be included in *Craftworker's Market* for any of the following reasons: (1) It asked to be omitted. (2) It did not return a questionnaire. (3) It does not buy crafts.

• If you know of a good market for crafts which is not included, please let us know. Send the name and address of the firm, what type of establishment it is (craft shop, gallery, kit manufacturer, show, etc.) and any other information you have. We will then contact them about a free listing in our next edition.

• Likewise, if you have any problems with a particular market listed in this book — they have not returned your material after requesting it, you have not been paid, etc. — contact us by letter telling the nature of the complaint and what you've done in an attempt to settle it yourself first.

Here are the Postal Service's two-letter state codes used in the addresses in this book:

STATE CODES

AK	Alaska	MT	Montana
AL	Alabama	NC	North Carolina
AR	Arkansas	ND	North Dakota
AZ	Arizona	NE	Nebraska
CA	California	NH	New Hampshire
CO	Colorado	NJ	New Jersey
CT	Connecticut	NM	New Mexico
DC	District of Columbia	NV	Nevada
DE	Delaware	NY	New York
FL	Florida	OH	Ohio
GA	Georgia	OK	Oklahoma
HI	Hawaii	OR	Oregon
IA	Iowa	PA	Pennsylvania
ID	Idaho	PR	Puerto Rico
IL	Illinois	RI	Rhode Island
IN	Indiana	SC	South Carolina
KS	Kansas	SD	South Dakota
KY	Kentucky	TN	Tennessee
LA	Louisiana	TX	Texas
MA	Massachusetts	UT	Utah
MD	Maryland	VA	Virginia
ME	Maine	VI	Virgin Islands
MI	Michigan	VT	Vermont
MN	Minnesota	WA	Washington
MO	Missouri	WI	Wisconsin
MS	Mississippi	WV	West Virginia
		WY	Wyoming

Now you can match your talents with the buyers listed in this book. After you've noted those you'd like to work with, be sure to read the listings carefully, follow the directions given by the buyers, and read the articles contained in The Profession for additional tips. In *Craftworker's Market,* we've done the research, all you have to do is contact the buyers.

The Craft Market Today

By Lynne Lapin

"I started making these miniature cannons about seven years ago, originally on a part-time basis, but now I'm interested in making a full-time living out of this. Where and how can I sell them?"

"I've been trying to sell my scarves for the last two years, but no one buys them. Oh sure, a few people take them on consignment, but then they don't sell and I end up getting them back six months later. People aren't buying crafts today are they?"

These cases aren't isolated. The craftsman's cannons are beautiful (they even shoot miniature ammunition), but he has no idea of where to market his work or how.

At the same time, the scarves the woman produces are silk tie-dyed. She knew where the markets were and how to approach them, but not *what* they were buying. If she had kept up with fashion trends she would have known that shops were only willing to take her scarves on consignment (if at all) because the market had virtually died about two years earlier. People just don't wear tie-dyed scarves today, as a brief glance through current women's and fashion publications would have indicated.

If you develop your talents until your workmanship is of consistent high quality, keep abreast of what is selling in the market, learn who is buying, know what your capacities are, and develop good business practices, there is definitely a market for your crafts.

In 1965 the handcrafts market was doing $65 million in retail sales; in 1974 it was up to $750 million, and by 1978 it was reported to have grown to a $1.6 billion industry.

Who Is Producing Crafts?

According to a survey by the National Endowment for the Arts (NEA) during the spring of 1978, there were between 250,000-350,000 craftworkers in the United States affiliated with some organization. And countless others involved with crafts are not affiliated with an organization.

Many of the nation's best craftworkers come from professional design training. But individuals earning an income from their crafts range from Dick Schnacke who left a 30-year engineering job to make primitive toys and develop his Appalachian industry into a prosperous livelihood — to the young couple who quit full-time jobs to support their family of four by making powder horns and rifles ornamented with scrimshaw.

"It was a family decision," said the scrimshaw artist. "We were getting so many orders that we decided we should either produce on a full-time basis or we wouldn't be able to fill all our orders. We sat down with our two girls and told them it would mean we would have less money to spend, at least for a while, but Daddy would be around a lot more." Without hesitation they chose for him to become a full-time craftworker.

Pat and Paul Wilson of Sault Ste. Marie, Michigan, work in stoneware. Pat explains that making a living by producing and selling crafts is possible today, "but only if you are truly self-disciplined. The hours are long and you had better love what you're doing or you simply won't make it. Chances are it will not be a living of $10,000 clear, but as demand and appreciation grow for what you are doing this can give you the guts to stick with it. Without demand or appreciation you need to accept a new alternative, or quit!"

But discipline is not enough. John Williams Zehring conducted a study of the career development patterns of the New England Craft Industry. He concluded that: "This work is 20% crafts (and you'd better be good!) and 80% business."

An interesting survey was conducted by the Vermont Interagency Crafts Council in 1977. Although the survey results were based on Vermont craftworkers, the conclusions give a good idea of who today's craftworkers are. For a copy of the survey write Vermont State Craft Center at Frog Hollow, Middlebury VT 05753.

Who's Buying?

The interest in crafts has transcended the bounds of "grandmother" and "4-H" handicrafts to become recognized as a valuable art form. Art collectors are taking advantage of this crafts renaissance; grandmothers and grandfathers are buying their grandchildren handmade toys; young couples are filling their homes with handcrafted pieces; and shops and galleries can't seem to find enough of the *right* crafts to keep their inventory complete. Although some craftworkers cry they can't find markets for their work, shops are also crying that they can't find what they need.

Pamela McGinley Scurry, owner of the Wicker Garden in New York City, says that although she gets a great many submissions by producers of calico pillows (which she has no market for), she is unable to find pillows with bright California-type colors for her customers. This is only one of many examples of how producing the right product for a particular retailer can open doors for the alert craftworker.

Outlets for crafts aren't restricted to shops and galleries specializing only in craft objects. Scurry's shop is primarily a Victorian wicker shop with pillows and other items sold as accessories. The Shops & Galleries section of this book contains a listing for the Wicker Garden as well as museum gift shops and galleries, banks, gift and stationery shops, plant stores, and mail order houses that also maintain retail outlets.

One of the more recent retailers of crafts is the department store. In the mid seventies a few New York stores, such as Saks Fifth Avenue, began handling limited craft objects. Now stores throughout the country are retailing handcrafts. Among the departments looking for items are accessories, gift, jewelry, housewares, home accessories, and even specialized craft departments.

Crafts for resale isn't the only interest department stores have in crafts. Retailers, such as Tiffany's and Macy's, have begun using crafts in their windows as props.

Manufacturers are a growing market for crafts. Reed & Barton, a well-known silver manufacturer, hired five craftworkers to design a collection of 28 necklaces, bracelets, pins and earrings ranging in price from $15-300. Spring Mills created a linen collection based on the hieroglyphs from King Tut's tomb. And fine china shops across the country are carrying table settings patterned after the work of contemporary craftworkers.

Mail order sales for craftworkers are also booming. Publications like *The Goodfellow Catalog of Wonderful Things* have emerged as a sort of "Sears Roebuck catalog where the consumer can find the work he/she's looking for," said Chris Weills, editor.

Not to be forgotten is the craft show or fair. From large wholesale events such as the Northeast Craft Fair at Rhinebeck, New York, to small local church sales, the craft show plays a vital role in the development of crafts. A survey conducted by *Craftworker's Market* of approximately 1,000 craftworkers indicated that they would advise adept craftworkers to begin selling their work in these shows (preferably those that are prescreened).

In addition to being a good starting ground, shows also allow crafts greater exposure than might otherwise be received. There are more customers that pass through a shopping mall than a gallery showing, for example. Demonstrations held at shows is one of the best tools possible for educating the general public to the meaning and purpose of crafts. The revenue generated by these shows isn't to be scoffed at either. The 1977 Northeast Craft Fair accepted 2,000 craftworkers who sold a total of $2 million worth of crafts.

One of the most important attributes of a craftworker seeking craft outlets is creativity. All you need is to keep your eyes and ears open for opportunities to market your work. Remembering our college days and the popularity of handicrafts with students, we wrote to various colleges resulting in the Colleges & Universities section of this book. Using your imagination, you'll be able to develop a long list of clients in your own area.

What Part is Government Playing?

The growing interest in crafts cannot help but have some effect on legislation concerning the crafts field. But, unfortunately, government action hasn't kept pace with the growing recognition of crafts by the public.

When asked what she felt the biggest obstacle facing the craftworker today was, Cynthia Hickok, fiber artist from Houston, said, "There are many but Uncle Sam and the IRS are among the greatest obstacles. The restrictions regarding deductions of home workshop space and being able to deduct only the cost of materials of artwork contributed to charity seem unfair."

The individual craftworker isn't alone in the fight to get better governmental legislation for crafts. Joan Mondale, potter and wife of the vice president, is one of the most active voices speaking out in favor of the arts. With this top-level support, government has begun pilot projects to help craftworkers increase sales.

Joel Solomon, administrator of the General Services Administration (GSA), has increased purchasing of arts and crafts for federal buildings. Even GSA shops, which furnish federal buildings, have begun carrying crafts.

The National Park Service began a program of buying crafts retailing from $3-35. This is expected to put hundreds of thousands of dollars in the pockets of American craftworkers.

Senators and congressmen, such as Rep. John Brademas (Indiana), are actively supporting the arts and related legislation. And percentage-for-arts legislation is cropping up as states and cities begin giving architects mandates that require them to include a specified percentage of crafts in each public building.

These steps are definitely a beginning, but to get more legislation for crafts passed it is important that craftworkers get their opinions known in Washington.

Senator James B. Pearson (Kansas) explained the method of expressing craftworker's views to the legislative bodies in this way: "In my opinion, the individual constituent letter is still the most effective and dynamic way of presenting a case to a member of Congress. . . . In my experience all congressional offices closely monitor the flow of mail, but certain types of mail, such as personally written letters, are much more likely to command the attention of legislators and individual staff members.

"With as diverse and talented a group as would be reached with the *Craftworker's Market*, I would guess that the motivation and eloquence required for individual letters could easily be tapped."

You can learn of various bills pending which relate to crafts by reading publications mentioned in the Publications of Interest section of this book.

Where Is the Craft Field Headed?

Today's craftworker is more than someone who produces woven shawls for warmth, makes silverware and pottery for everyday living, or thinks of metalworking only in terms of shoeing horses and adorning buildings. The craftworker of today is being recognized as an artist.

Craftworkers and craft retailers both agree the craft field has a promising future. Much of its growth can be traced directly to the increased exposure of the public to craft demonstrations at fairs, magazine articles about collecting and producing crafts, television shows about crafts, and general discussions on the subject. As the public learns more about this art form, their interest grows, sales increase, and more individuals decide to make a livelihood from crafts.

Colleges and universities are responding to the need for more qualified craftworkers by offering Master's programs in crafts. There are more than 200 such schools in the US today. Indicative of this promising growth is a $1,225,000 capital fund drive launched by The School of Arts & Crafts (Portland, Oregon) to develop a new campus expanding 7.26 acres. (Founded in 1906, The School of Arts & Crafts is said to be the oldest craft school in the country.)

It is difficult to predict exactly what types of crafts will be popular at a given time, or what the styles will be in upcoming seasons, but we can watch for indications.

Applications (1,600 were received) for the 1978 Northeast Craft Fair at Rhinebeck, New York, show an upswing in the number of craftworkers in the areas of stained glass, pewter work, "married metals," leather, traditional rugs (especially those dyed with natural colors) and soft sculpture. Knitting techniques were also growing. And since the Rhinebeck show is known by most as trend-setter, it is likely that these crafts will be seen more and more in 1979.

As with all else, styles and public demand will change periodically; but, if you keep abreast of what is happening by reading publications listed in the Publications of Interest section of this book, noting what is selling in stores, and reading materials related to your specific craft, you should be able to realize what the public wants (and thereby what the retailers are seeking). After all, the market is growing for those who are producing the *right* quality crafts, and who know where to sell them.

Working with the Retailer

By Loretta Holz

The methods you choose to sell your work depend on what you are selling and how you prefer to do the selling. If you make one-of-a-kind designer pieces, they are naturally more expensive, and, therefore, your markets are more limited. You will need to find galleries and specialty shops willing to handle these expensive items.

Or, if you design an item and repeatedly make copies to sell, these handmade production crafts will be less expensive than the one-of-a-kind items. Because of this price differential, the number of retailers who will accept your work is naturally much larger for production crafts.

Market Research

Large companies spend great amounts of money on research before introducing new products. You, too, will certainly find it worth your time and effort to find out what you can about potential markets before starting your sales campaign. And this research really needn't be expensive.

Through your research you should try to determine:

(1) What types of shops exist in your area that sell handcrafted items? Look not only for shops and galleries specializing in handcrafts, but also for gift shops, florists, boutiques and other retail businesses such as those found in the Shops & Galleries section of this book. While you can sell to shops by mail, you may want to start out with those in your area to learn first-hand how this marketing channel functions.

(2) Who are the typical customers of these shops, and who are the typical customers for your work? If, for example, you are selling wooden toys, it's important to remember that the typical customer who buys toys is not the child who plays with them, but the parents, grandparents and other relatives — probably female. While toys should certainly be fun for the child to play with, they should also appeal to the buyer.

(3) What price will the typical customer be willing to pay for a product like yours? In some wealthy areas price is no problem, but in most middle-class areas, while customers want to buy quality handmade items, there is a limit to what they are willing to spend on them.

(4) What is the competition doing? Look for others at craft shows who are making products like yours and see what they have that is selling well and at what prices. How will your items compare, and can you compete at their prices? If your work is unique, your potential market will be larger than if you are competing with other craftworkers who are making similar items— especially if they have been selling and building up a clientele for some time.

(5) Is the specific item you plan to produce salable? Once you've developed a product, find out if it will sell by testing it in the open market before building a large inventory. Take a booth at a craft show and watch customers' reaction to your new product.

(6) Are materials available to you in the quantities needed and at prices you can afford? Retailers will place orders and expect you to deliver, without taking into

Loretta Holz is author of several craft books, including How to Sell Your Art and Crafts *(Scribners), and has written more than 100 articles on crafts and related subjects for* Profitable Craft Merchandising, Woman's Day, Creative Crafts *and other nationally-known publications.*

consideration your supply problems.

One craftworker who did market research and came up with a best selling craft line is Dick Schnacke, founder and director of Mountain Craft Shop of Proctor, West Virginia. He sells to shops nationally and is said to be the largest producer of American folk toys. Schnacke noticed few handmade toys for sale at craft shops and shows in the early 1960s. He remembered the toys of his childhood — whimmydiddles, flipperdingers and whirlygigs as well as other simple fun items made from wood scraps and other inexpensive materials. These traditional toys could be produced quickly at very low cost, and with the "back to earth" movement, their rustic appearance would appeal to the customers. He knew that while children would enjoy playing with them, the adults buying them would be interested too. Schnacke made a few toys in 1963 and tested their salability at a craft show. He sold out, and since then his business has grown so rapidly that he now has production help and sells over $200,000 in toys annually.

Selling Through Shops and Galleries

Selling to shops has several advantages over selling through shows. (See the Shows & Fairs section of this book for a discussion of selling at shows.) To sell to shops, you usually don't have to travel like you do to get from show to show. You can live anywhere as long as you have access to the Postal Service or the United Parcel Service (UPS).

Instead of talking to individual customers who buy single items, you'll deal with a professional buyer who gives you quantity orders. Also, retailers offer more permanent displays for your work, unlike shows that run for only a few days. Customers can go home to think about large purchases and then return to buy the work. If they are happy with one purchase, they can return to make another. Also, customers tend to trust the prices and quality of items purchased in a shop more than those bought at a show which won't be there tomorrow if they have problems.

A disadvantage of selling through shops and galleries is that the profit on each item you sell may be less. Basically what you are doing is giving the shop the selling half of the retail price of the item. Despite this, many craftworkers increase production and work toward selling through shops and galleries, which provides more time for producing rather than producing *and* selling through shows.

The most obvious shop carrying crafts is one that specializes in handcrafted items. These are usually small shops run by an owner/manager who is often also a craftworker. Sometimes the manager operates the shop to sell his/her own work and supplements the supply with others' work.

Other small shops are run by people who appreciate handcrafted items. Some are nonprofit, like women's exchanges or shops connected with service organizations. These shops usually specialize in production items.

One-of-a-kind or limited editions are the bulk of the merchandise carried in a number of other shops. These shops are often called craft galleries, and frequently function like art galleries, giving feature space to works by a certain craftworker for a designated period of time.

There are also many shops that carry handmade work in addition to other merchandise. For example, some florists carry handmade plant holders. Fashionable clothing stores, often called boutiques, might feature handmade accessories. Gift shops often include handmade gifts.

Museum shops are also not to be overlooked. They are usually in business to provide funds for the museum they are affiliated with.

While *Craftworker's Market* carries thousands of listings of retail outlets in the US and Canada, it would be impossible for it to encompass all the possible outlets for your work. Look further by checking the Yellow Pages under Galleries and Gift

Shops. When you visit a new area, look for shops where your work might fit in. Other craftworkers can also tell you about shops that sell handcrafted merchandise, and these craftspeople will often be willing to tell you how reliable the shop is.

Other invaluable sources of information are various craft publications, like *The Craft Report*, *Craft Horizons* and *The Working Craftsman*, or regional publications such as *The Goodfellow Review of Crafts*. Also, if you produce one-of-a-kind designer crafts, you'll find an abundant market for your work among the various art galleries listed. Several art publications are included among the Publications of Interest listings in this book.

Membership in craft organizations, locally or nationally, is always a way of learning about new markets. The American Crafts Council (ACC) is the most widely known of these organizations. For others, and the address of the ACC, check out the Associations and Organizations section of this book.

Selling Arrangements

There are two basic methods of selling to stores: on consignment or on a wholesale basis (selling outright). When working on consignment, the shop manager takes your work on loan, and if it is sold while on display you will be paid for the sale—minus a commission paid to the shop. If your work doesn't sell, the shop has the option to return the work to you, or hold it until you request its return.

If you are just beginning to market your work, you'll probably find yourself working on consignment, because the shop manager won't be sure the items you're presenting will sell. He may be willing to give you a chance, but won't commit the store's money by buying the work outright. Once the retailer has been successful selling this type of item he may be very willing, in fact anxious, to buy on a wholesale basis.

When selling wholesale, the shop typically receives a larger percentage of the retail price. The typical portion received is usually 50%, but some shops will more than double the wholesale price to arrive at the retail price. You, the craftworker, set only the wholesale price, and then the manager can set the retail price he feels will sell the work.

Although you receive a larger percentage of the selling price when sold on consignment, you are taking more of a risk. The percentage taken by shops ranges from 10-50%. When work is sold, the shop subtracts its percentage and gives the remaining money to you.

One variation of the wholesale selling agreement is the guaranteed sale. Some shops agree to buy work as long as the craftworker promises to replace nonselling items with items more likely to sell. The nonsellers then once again become the property of the craftworker.

Some shops not only sell what you bring in, but they also take special, or custom, orders for you. This means extra work for the shop manager, but he may be willing to do so if it means added sales. The shop should write an order to be signed by the customer, and the manager should collect a deposit on all custom orders. If the customer doesn't pick up the order and pay the balance of the bill, the deposit is forfeited and hopefully the piece can be sold to someone else.

Dealing with Shop Managers

The best way to begin selling to shops is to speak in person to the manager. But call first for an appointment. Also, find out the shop's heaviest time for buying or consigning new work. If the manager isn't interested in new items at that particular time, it might be best to call back. If your work is seasonal be sure to call months in advance.

Decide on which terms you want to sell your work. Most craftworkers ask for "net 30 days," which means the shop should pay you within 30 days after delivery. Retail shops like to receive a discount for prompt payment. They prefer "2/10/net 30," which means they receive a 2% discount if they pay within 10 days of receiving your bill or invoice. Some craftworkers ask for COD (collection on delivery) or "net 10 days" (payment within 10 days), but shops generally don't find it convenient to pay this quickly.

If you want to sell on a wholesale basis, before you talk to the shop manager about your work get order forms from an office supply store. Look over the forms carefully to be sure you know how to complete them.

When working on consignment, it's a good idea for you to have a consignment agreement form. In some cases the shop manager may give you a list of rules that govern consignment selling in the shop, and he/she may ask you to complete a form on the items you will be leaving. Always get any agreements in writing.

You should also take samples of the work with you to the shop or gallery. Attach a label on each, stating the selling price you have in mind.

Collecting Your Money

After you've delivered your products to the retailer, your next concern is collecting your money. Most shops are honest, but some, especially if they are economically unsound, may be a problem. Keep a close watch if you are the least bit uncertain about a retailer.

Accurate records are vital in collecting money owed you. Always get a signed purchase order. If you deliver the items personally, be sure to get a signed receipt; or if you mail or ship work, keep a copy of the packing slip and all of your shipping receipts.

If you're working on consignment and don't receive a periodical report on how your work is selling, and don't receive payments for sold work, investigate.

If you work on a wholesale basis, send out an invoice the day you mail the items. After a month, if you haven't received payment, send a statement providing complete information about the bill due, including a request for payment. If after another month you don't receive payment, send a second statement marked "past due."

If all your methods of collecting your money fail, seek legal advice for your next step.

Handling Your Business

By Michael Scott

Paperwork, or recordkeeping, is the nemesis of most craftspeople. We'd much rather spend our time at the loom or the wheel or the bench. But once we've decided to produce craftwork for sale and enjoyment, keeping good and accurate records becomes an essential activity toward success.

Records fall into two basic categories:

1) The records required by government agencies, particularly tax collectors. Such records come under the heading of bookkeeping. They serve not only to keep us out of trouble at tax time, but allow us to take all the proper deductions and pay no more in taxes than the law requires.

2) The records which tell us at a glance where our business has been, where it is now, and where it is headed. Accurate inventory records, for example, are the guideposts which tell us what is selling and producing income, and what sits on the shelf forever and ties up our cash. That in turn dictates our production schedules and even the direction of our design and creative efforts.

Recordkeeping, then, is not simply paperwork, but a "tool" for keeping your business activity on an even keel. But what you get out of records is only as good as what you put into them. Haphazard recordkeeping can give the illusion that we know what we're doing, and that can be even more dangerous than not knowing what we're doing at all.

Many craftspeople blanch when they face the prospect of filling out yet another form. "I'm not in business," they say, "I make pots. Business is for General Motors, not for me."

But the moment you sell your first pot you're in business. *You* may not think so, but the Internal Revenue Service (IRS) certainly does. And they make the rules by which we all have to play.

Then there are craftspeople who wonder why they've worked so hard all year and have so little to show for it. They may simply not have kept records that show them where their time has been productively spent, and where it's been wasted.

An example: You've rented a booth at a craft show. Your sales were great. You've had a good show, right?

Perhaps! But then again, perhaps not. If the costs of going to that show (travel, motels, booth expenses, etc.) turn out to be greater than the sales you made, you might have been better off not going to that show at all, no matter how well your work sold.

The only way to know the true results of a show is by keeping accurate records of all the costs and balancing them against the income. Not to mention that all those costs are probably tax-deductible as a business expense.

Leaving everything up to memory can play costly tricks. If you sell to retail stores, prepare a card file, with a card for each customer. Record every contact, every sale, what you sold and on what terms, the customer's payment performance, and so on. All of this information gives you a complete history of the account at a glance. It tells you when to make another sales approach, what items to promote, what terms to offer. Or — in the case of slow payers or non-payers — whether to make another sales approach at all.

Michael Scott is editor of The Crafts Report *and author of* The Crafts Business Encyclopedia *(Harcourt Brace Jovanovich). He is currently president of the International Guild of Craft Journalists, Authors and Photographers.*

Many of the records you are required to keep, primarily for tax purposes, can be accomplished through simple bookkeeping. You need not be a mathematical wizard to do that, although neatness and attention to detail counts. Have an accountant set up a simple ledger on which you enter every transaction, every item of income and every item of expense. At least once a year (at tax time), your accountant will balance the books, assign the income and expense items to their proper categories, and prepare your tax returns. Without such simple records, you find yourself paying taxes far beyond what is required.

Bookkeeping serves another purpose. An accountant, trained in such matters, can easily spot some of the strong points and some of the weak points in your operation simply by studying the financial transactions revealed in your books of account. As a result, the accountant can often provide valuable advice on your future activities — how you might eliminate the weak spots, where to capitalize on your strengths, and so forth. The accountant might discover, for example, that you purchased materials in small quantities on a monthly basis, and suggest the possibility of buying less frequently but in larger quantities and thereby taking advantage of quantity discounts to save money. The bookkeeping records also tend to provide the sense of organization needed to retain all receipts in an orderly fashion.

One craftworker I know takes a notebook of lined paper along to every craft show. Inside the back cover of this book she pastes a brown manila envelope. Every time she spends money on that trip, even for so seemingly small an item as a phone call, the amount is entered in the book. All receipts are stuffed into the envelope — even the receipts for bridge tolls, and certainly the receipts for motels. She doesn't leave it up to memory to reconstruct at day's end, or at the end of the show, what her daily expenses were.

And when she gets home, all those little notebooks and envelopes of receipts go into a file drawer to be available for the accountant at tax time.

If the necessity ever arises for a tax examination by the IRS, it is essential to have such records available to substantiate your deductions. The more, the better. In fact, any expense item of more than $25 must be supported by a receipt. If you use a credit card, hold on to all those slips as well, and mark the reason for the expense in the space provided if you want to claim it as a tax deductible business expense.

Financial records related to taxes must be kept for at least three years beyond the date of the tax return if a tax examination becomes necessary. Some other documents — payroll records, for example — must be kept for as long as seven years, according to law.

For the other business records, common sense will dictate how long they should be kept. Contracts, cleared checks, correspondence, orders and the like should certainly be kept until all possibility of further need has vanished. To throw out a purchase order right after the goods have been shipped only invites trouble. What if there's a claim of error? How do you substantiate that what you have done is correct and as ordered?

Bookkeeping scares a lot of people. It's not the most exciting activity in the world — except, perhaps, to bookkeepers. But it need not be a scary activity, nor do you need an accountant to keep your books. An evening course at a nearby high school or college can serve as a painless introduction to the basic essentials. The forms are available at most good stationery supply stores, or from such mail order firms as Ideal System Co. (Box 1568, August GA 30903) or Dome Publishing Co. (Providence RI 02903).

Let's examine a few of the documents and records which commonly enter into a craftsperson's daily business activity.

Sales Tax

Most areas of the country impose a sales tax on all goods sold at retail. If you sell directly to the public, you are required to collect the appropriate sales tax and send it along to the tax collector. This requires a certificate from the particular local or state tax agency, as well as careful recordkeeping of your sales activities in dollar terms. When you go to a craft show in a locality where a sales tax is imposed but where you do not have the certificate, the situation is handled in one of two ways. Either the show management obtains a blanket certificate covering all exhibitors, or you get a temporary certificate. The rules are different in each locality. But in all cases, you must keep an accurate record of your sales volume. Where you are required to obtain your own certificate, you may find that the very first visitor at your booth, even before the show opens, is an agent of the local sales tax collector.

Since sales taxes are collected only when the product is sold to the ultimate consumer, a different situation applies when you sell at wholesale to a retailer or if you work on consignment. In that case you don't collect a sales tax, but the retailer does.

When you sell your work to a retailer, be sure to get his "sales tax exemption" or his "resale" number as your authority not to collect the sales tax. This information may be important to tax authorities.

On the other side of the coin, if you have your own "sales tax exemption" or "resale" number, you are not required to pay sales tax on the materials you buy from your supplier — clay, yarn, metal, wood, etc. — since you are not the ultimate consumer. The material will, after all, be incorporated in the production of an object which will be sold to a consumer and on which the sales tax will then be collected.

Be sure to give your resale or exemption number to your supplier when you place an order so that he won't charge you the sales tax. That may seem like no big deal, but when the sales taxes are up there around the 6% or 8% mark, the pennies mount up. If you buy $1,000 worth of raw materials, saving 8% translates into $80.

Your sales tax exemption does not apply to such items as stationery, packing supplies and other materials which do not become a part of the ultimate craft object you produce.

Inventory Records

Since your inventory — raw materials, work in process, and finished work — represents a considerable investment in time and money, a careful record of your inventory can have a profound effect on your cash flow, your profitability, your production schedules, even your tax situation.

An inventory control system, which is a daily record of everything that goes in and out of inventory, tells you how fast a given item is moving, what kind of work sits on the shelf and might be discontinued, how much you should produce to keep your inventory at sufficient levels to fill orders promptly, and so forth.

This can be a very simple system, a set of index cards or a loose leaf notebook. Each card or page should carry information on one particular item — how many pieces you made on what date, how many pieces you sold on what date, reorder quantity for your next production run, etc.

Since inventory represents an investment of time and money, good records tell you at a glance how often your inventory "turns over." This term is often misunderstood. "Turn over" doesn't mean only how much you sell, but how often you get your original investment back so that you can invest it in new inventory. Making

```
                                        INVENTORY
    10" plates -- Sunburst pattern
```

10" plates -- Sunburst pattern

Date		In	Out	Balance
3/1	Inventory			137
3/20	Prod. Run	100		237
4/3	Macy's		144	93
4/15	Prod. Run	250		343
6/10	Rhinebeck Fair		117	226

A simple system of in-dex cards — each card showing information on one particular item — can be set-up to keep a record of work moving in and out of inventory.

```
The Gift Boutique            Susan Smith
225 Main Street              Tableware Buyer
Big City, OH 41679           112-498-2222
```

PO Date	PO #	Qty	Item	Unit $$	Total $$	Ship Date	Bill Date	Date Paid
3/6/77	1217	144	Sunburst 10" Plates	2.95	424.80	4/30/77	5/1/77	6/9/77
4/4/77	1364	60	#7 Mugs	1.18	70.80	5/17/77	5/30/77	7/5/77
9/15/77	2410	48	Melior Plates 8"	2.50	120.00	10/28/77	10/30/77	12/6/77
11/1/77	2671	72	Sunburst 10" Plates	2.95	212.40	11/10/77	11/30/77	1/3/78

If you keep a card file on your retail outlets— recording each transaction— you can see at a glance the history of each account.

your money work effectively for you that way is the secret of success.

A practical example might explain this more clearly. Suppose you start out with $100 of your own money to produce 100 items which you sell for $1.25 each. You have taken in $125. This means your original $100 investment has come back and you've made a $25 profit. Now you can invest that same $100 to make another 100 items on which you again make $25. Each time that happens, your inventory "turns over."

If it happens once a year, your initial $100 investment produces a total profit of $25. It turned over only once. But if it happens once a month, your original $100, reinvested 12 times, produces a total profit of $300. It turned over 12 times. You've spent $1,200 on producing the work in inventory that year, but only $100 of that was "upfront money" out of your own pocket.

This is obviously a simplified explanation. In real life things are a little more complicated. But here's the point: with good inventory records, items that turn over slowly are easily spotted and can be discontinued, and items with a rapid turnover can be expanded. It focuses on your production and sales activity *in relation to your investment*.

Inventory records serve still another purpose. While the perpetual inventory is on paper, at least once a year it is advisable to take an actual physical inventory. You'll find that it rarely agrees with the paper inventory. There are discrepancies due to breakage, theft, error and other problems. This can tell you a lot about how you run your business. If breakage turns into a real problem, for example, you might want to revise your storage and handling procedures. Furthermore, inventory loss is usually a tax deductible business expense. Contact your accountant or the IRS for details.

Systems

Don't let the word "system" scare you. Your own telephone number index is a perfect example of a system at work. Your checkbook is another. Neither one is particularly complicated.

What we are concerned with here is the importance of systems. Not a particular system necessarily, but some sort of system that suits your style, keeps your affairs in good order, and enables you to plan ahead.

A simple system for keeping track of orders, for instance, helps you fill the orders properly. Without a system you either have to rummage all over the place to find the order, or trust to memory that you'll ship the right things to the right place at the right time. If you've shipped the wrong stuff to the wrong place at the wrong time, you'll spend a lot of time and effort correcting it. That can cost money and you might even lose a good customer.

The same principle applies to all your other management and production procedures. A system need not be complicated to be effective. In fact, the simpler the system, the better.

But a system is only as good as its execution. It is important that everyone who is involved in your operation, even if you're the only one, follows whatever system you devise to make things run smoothly and give you more time for your creative work.

Many craftspeople consider paperwork and office systems a bother and a waste of time. They'd rather spend their time at their craft instead of their desk. But since some sort of paperwork must be done, a simple system in the long run saves more time than it wastes.

Just take care not to get so bogged down with systems and recordkeeping that they become an end in themselves, rather than the means toward an end. That *is* a waste of time.

Copyright and Patents

By Michael Scott

1. What is copyright and what kind of protection does it give me? Copyright is legal protection for anything original that has been created. No one but the creator can reproduce the creation, distribute or display it publicly, or create derivative works without the permission of the creator. Infringement of a registered copyright allows the copyright owner to institute court proceedings against the individual infringing the copyright and then to collect damages should the court decide in the owner's favor.

Any of the rights given under copyright law can be assigned to anyone else by the copyright owner. For example, if you sell a work to a museum, the museum can only display the work; it cannot take photos of the work to sell in the gift shop. If you sell a retail store the right to sell one dozen of your originally designed and produced leather belts, the store can only sell that one dozen; it cannot ask another leather worker to make more of the belts. Or, if you sell a manufacturer the right to reproduce 1,000 of your pendants, it cannot make more than the 1,000 agreed upon; nor can it make derivative works such as reproducing the design on wallpaper.

If the copyright owner agrees to sell *all* rights to anyone, the purchaser is allowed to use the creation in any way he/she wants to without further payment or permission from the creator.

2. How do I go about getting a copyright on my work? Copyright protection begins from the moment that an orginal creation is completed. All the creator has to do is inform observers that the finished product is under copyright protection. This means putting a legal notice somewhere on the work itself. Normally, the notice must be given by using the symbol © or the word "Copyright" or the abbreviation "Copr.," together with the year the object was created and the name of the copyright owner. For example, "Copyright, 1979, Jane Doe." If space is at a real premium on the object, the full name can be replaced by an abbreviation by which the name will be recognized or a generally known alternative designation such as a monogram. Also, the year date does not have to be included on greeting cards, postcards, jewelry, toys, dolls or any useful articles.

Putting such notice on craftwork, however, might be a problem since some media do not always allow for easy display of the notice. While potters, jewelers and woodworkers might not find it difficult to engrave the proper notice on each copy of a copyrighted work, fiber artists may run into problems in making the notice an integral part of their work.

The basic rule is that the copyright notice must be affixed so that it can be easily seen. It can be engraved, glued or sewn to the front or back of the work. Even a securely affixed tag is acceptable under certain circumstances. But be sure the notice is not covered by a frame or does not appear on the underside of a heavy piece that can't be picked up; or isn't sewn to the top edge of a 12-foot high wall hanging where even 20/20 vision couldn't see it.

Copyright notice should be incorporated in every piece, including the first one. So if you design a pendant, be sure that all copies also have the copyright notice on them. While unintentional errors and omissions (leaving out the date, for example) do not automatically disqualify a work from being protected, it is much more difficult to prove the case in court, even if the proper documents were filed. Be sure to correct errors on subsequent copies of the work. And contact the Copyright Office to find out if the defective notice can be cured.

If you give permission for a copyrighted work to be used as an illustration in a book or magazine, be sure to require your own copyright notice (for example, printed under it). The publication's general copyright notice does *not* give you as complete protection against infringement as your own notice does.

The Register of Copyrights, which administers the copyright law, can furnish advice and information regarding specific problems.

   3.   OK. I have the copyright notice on my work. Now what do I do? You may now need to formally register your creation with the Copyright Office.

However, the craftworker need not run out and register every new creation he/she ever made, nor register all future creations. Evaluate each creation according to its worth. If it is determined that the future value of the creation might be substantial and/or that someone else might be tempted to reproduce the creation as his/her own, then registration should be made. For example, the craftworker might design a pendant that would sell for only about $5 each. Spending the money to register the design is worthwhile only if the design is unique and attractive enough to tempt imitation, especially if production techniques could allow mass production of the work. On the other hand, a handcrafted chandelier which takes you six months to make and sells for $5,000 is not likely to be copied. It may still be worth the $10 fee to be on the safe side, but the very nature of the work makes an infringement less likely.

Without registration, the creator of a work cannot bring suit against a copyright infringer. And if the creator waits to see if his work will be infringed and only then decides to register his work, a resulting court case could be tough. Also, attorney's fees will not be awarded to you if you haven't registered before the start of the infringement, even though you may win damages. Registration as soon as possible after creation helps solve a lot of potential problems. The longer you wait, the tougher it gets to prove creator status.

The cost for registering a work is $10. To register, write the Copyright Office and ask them to send you some forms for "Class VA — Visual Artists." The VA form should be submitted to the Copyright Office within three months after the work appears in public. With the form, you also have to send two copies of the actual work. An exception to the copies rule is when it is impractical to send actual copies of the work. Then it is permitted to substitute photographs of the work. Photos should definitely be sent for any three-dimensional objects, one-of-a-kind pieces, valuable objects, or anything fragile or extremely heavy. The photos can be taken with a Polaroid camera. If the photos are not acceptable, the Registrar at the Copyright Office will let you know. If you would prefer to deposit copies of the three-dimensional object instead of taking photos, you can request permission to do so from the Registrar.

The Class VA category for copyright is defined by the Copyright Office as follows: "This category consists of published (meaning when the work was first made public) and unpublished pictorial, graphic and sculptoral works, including two-dimensional and three-dimensional works of fine, graphic, and applied art, photographs, prints and art reproductions, maps, globes, charts, technical drawings, diagrams and models. Within this class are pictorial or graphic labels and advertisements, as well as works of artistic craftsmanship. The design of a useful article may be registerable in Class VA, but only if, and only to the extent that, such design incorporates pictorial, graphic or sculptoral features that can be identified separately from, and are capable of existing independently of, the utilitarian aspects of the article."

You cannot copyright an ordinary shape, like a circle. Thus a plain gold band with no decorative or design features — other than that it is round — most likely cannot be copyrighted. Nor is it likely that you can copyright an ordinary plate simply because it is blue and everyone else's is white. However, if that plate incorporates a design element which is your unique creation, it can be copyrighted. A good example is Robert Indiana's famous design of the word LOVE. While the letters L-O-V-E might in themselves not be unique enough to be copyrighted, the way they were combined by Indiana certainly made them copyrightable. Unfortunately, Indiana failed to copyright this piece and it was freely plagiarized by many opportunistic manufacturers.

4. Can an idea be copyrighted? No. The law very specifically states that work must exist in some tangible form that can be reproduced. If it exists only in your head, it cannot be copyrighted.

5. Are there any aesthetic requirements to registering a copyright? No. The Copyright Office exercises no artistic judgment. As long as the work is original (that is, you created it, as opposed to copying someone else's work), it can be registered for copyright. If your copyright is infringed, you will have to show in court that you exercised at least a small degree of creativity in making the work.

6. What is meant by "copying"? That's a ticklish question since it's a matter of case-by-case judicial interpretation when infringement suits are filed.

It is certainly conceivable that two craftworkers, quite independently of each other, could come up with similar work that reflects originality and creativity. Neither was copied from the other. Both could be copyrighted (all other requirements being met), and neither would be considered an infringement on the other.

But suppose a craftworker creates a unique work and someone else adopts it with only very minor alterations, e.g. putting a border around it. That would most likely be considered an infringement. The test for infringement is whether an ordinary observer looking at the two works would consider one to have been copied from the other.

7. Can I copyright work produced under a government grant? The copyright law specifically states that work produced for the US Government by an employee or officer of the government as part of his or her official duties cannot be copyrighted. Works created under a government grant by someone who is not a government employee can be copyrighted if Congress or the agency involved agrees to permit this based on the particular circumstances of each case.

8. If I sell my copyrighted craft to an individual and that individual in turn displays it to the public, isn't that an infringement of my copyright? Then, what if someone takes a picture of the work while it is on display? Is that also an infringement? An important new addition to the copyright law is the section regarding public display of a copyrighted work. The purchaser of a copyrighted work still has the right to display the object to people who are present in the same place as the object itself. If you sell your work to a museum, for example, the work can be put on display at the museum. However, it cannot be "displayed" through the use of films or television without your permission.

There's an important exception to the rights of the copyright owner. It is called the "fair use" doctrine which allows copyrighted work to be copied under limited circumstances without being an infringement. For example, if you have a copyrighted work on display at a gallery, it is not an infringement if a newspaper photographer takes a picture of the work and publishes it in connection with a review. Nor is it an infringement when a visitor to a craft show takes a snapshot of your booth display, even though it may include copyrighted work.

The thrust of the "fair use" doctrine is that such use does not detract from your ability to sell the work. If that newspaper photograph is later published without your permission in a book, for example, you have a good cause for complaint.

9. How long am I protected by copyright? A copyright registered after January 1, 1978 provides protection for the author's lifetime, plus 50 years. (Copyright law in effect before January 1, 1978 only allowed for a 28 year protection period, with an option to renew another 28 years after the first period was over, or for a total of 56 years. The new law extended the term for these copyrights from 56 to 75 years.) Now the only date that matters is the date of the author's death. (In the language of the law, the word "author" means anyone who has created a copyrightable work, such as a writer, a craftworker, a filmmaker, or a composer.)

10. What about work that I copyrighted before January 1, 1978 and which is currently in its 28 year term? The copyright still has to be renewed when the 28 year term expires. But instead of only getting another 28 year extension, the new law allows for an extended period of 47 years, for a new total of 75 years protection from the date of the first copyright registration.

11. What is the difference between copyright and patent? A copyright protects artistic creativity. A patent protects inventions and discoveries of a mechanical or utilitarian nature.

While a copyright is protected simply through using the proper "notice" and filing a copyright application, patents are much more difficult to obtain. They require the assistance of a patent lawyer and usually involve considerable sums of money for research, documentation, and legal work.

Patents fall into four categories: Mechanical, Process or Method, Composition of Materials, and Design.

A Mechanical Patent would cover your invention of a totally different kind of kiln. A Process Patent would apply to a new method of glazing. A Composition Patent protects a new glaze formula. And a Design Patent covers a new and original design or ornamentation for a functional object such as a lamp base, for example.

While copyrights are easy and inexpensive to obtain, the costs and problems of getting a patent should be weighed carefully against the potential income of the invention. A booklet on "General Information Concerning Patents" is available for 75c from the Superintendent of Documents, US Government Printing Office, Washington DC 20402.

12. If I need more information or help with copyright, where can I go? The Copyright Office (Register of Copyrights, Library of Congress, Washington DC 20559) has a free Copyright Information Kit that is useful. The kit contains a copy of the law, the regulations, the application forms, and numerous circulars about copyright and the operation of the Copyright Office. However, the Copyright Office does not provide legal advice or opinions. If you cannot afford the help of a lawyer, you might consider one of the volunteer lawyers for the arts groups that now exist in many parts of the country. To find the group nearest you, you can contact one of the following established organizations: Bay Area Lawyers for the Arts, 25 Taylor St., San Francisco CA 94102. Tel. (415)775-7200; Lawyers for the Creative Arts, 111 N. Wabash Ave., Chicago IL 60602. Tel. (312)263-6889; or Volunteer Lawyers for the Arts, 36 W. 44th St., New York NY 10036. Tel. (212)575-1150.

The Visual Artist's Guide to the New Copyright Law is available from the Graphic Artists Guild, 30 E. 20th St., Room 405, New York NY 10003. The pamphlet is updated regularly to cover new regulations and court decisions. Cost is $5.50.

Packing Your Work for Shipping

If a gallery, dealer, shop or art show is located a good distance from your home, you'll probably need to ship your work to the location. To do so means you need a sturdy container.

Containers can be purchased ready-made, but for the painter or sculptor shipping a great deal of work, the costs can be prohibitive. The following two pieces tell you how to make your own containers using only a few tools and a bit of common sense.

Two-Dimensional Work

All two-dimensional works should be wrapped in plastic sheeting to prevent water damage. If polyethylene rolls are unavailable, cheap plastic drop cloths are a good substitute.

Framed works, especially those with carved or raised corners, should be further protected. Newspaper, rolled up, is excellent for corner protection (Fig. 1). The ends of the rolled paper should be stapled to the back of the frame.

Remember to remove screw eyes, picture light brackets and other protruding objects which might damage other works.

When pictures with glass are shipped, it is important to tape the glass so that in the event of breakage it does not damage the work. Masking tape is strong enough to prevent pieces of glass from coming loose. Never use tape requiring water — it could damage the work.

First tape a large X on the glass. Then tape horizontal and vertical rows a couple of inches apart (Fig. 2). Do not overlap the frame. Works framed with Plexiglas need no tape because it is unbreakable.

A wooden box makes the most reliable crate. The frame of the crate should be about 2" larger than the picture on all sides. The same size is not good, because a diagonal shock can break a corner of a frame.

To build a crate, stack the work to be packed on a table so that you can measure the height, width and length to determine size of lumber needed.

The top (a) and bottom of the crate must be able to resist puncture. Museums usually recommend ¾ to ⅞" thick pine, but cheap boards are usually as good as the more expensive grades. Plywood is best. Cheap construction grade sheathing also works well, as does paper-faced ply-score. Masonite, which is brittle, should be used with trepidation because it can be punctured, and in any case ⅛" Masonite should never be considered. Construction grade board is adequate for the sides of the crate.

Cut lumber for sides (b) to size allowing 2" all the way around the work. Butt longer boards against shorter sides and nail together with 2½" rosin-coated box nails about 1½" apart.

Measure outside dimensions of frame sides and cut top and bottom. Nail bottom of crate to sides (1½" plaster board nails work well for this). The top of crate should be screwed on with either six or eight 1" flat head screws (Fig. 3).

If you wish to enforce corners of the crate, use 1x4" boards cut to width of two sides, top and bottom (c). These eight pieces should be nailed to board ends before crate assembly. Longer nails are required here — 3½" will do the trick. On the longer sides they should overlap enough to butt against the braces of the shorter sides which are flush to the end of the side.

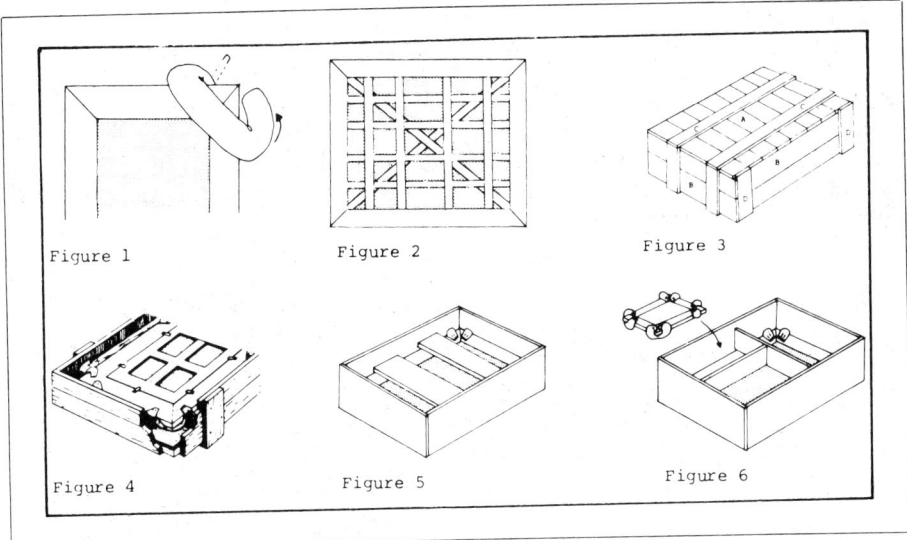

Figure 1   Figure 2   Figure 3

Figure 4   Figure 5   Figure 6

Be careful not to leave nail heads protruding into the crate. Bend into U shape rather than just turn, and hammer into sides.

If a crate is to be made deeper than width of lumber available, use two or more boards for sides, joining at corners using above procedures and nail two additional brace boards (d) along each of the four sides.

Once the sides and bottom of the crate are assembled, a sheet of corrugated cardboard should be placed in the bottom of the crate. Next, put in the painting. Then wedge strips of corrugated cardboard around the picture on all sides until the painting cannot move (Fig.4). If the sides of the crate are significantly higher than the painting, add an additional piece of cardboard and two or three boards across the inside of the crate (Fig. 5). This will prevent the painting from moving — the most common cause of damage.

If more than one painting is being shipped, a piece of corrugated cardboard must be placed between all paintings which are placed back to back and face to face.

If one or two small paintings are shipped along with large works, it is important to put the larger works in first and cushion them along the sides with strips of cardboard. Smaller works should be laid next to one another and stacked evenly. Cradling with board may be necessary to provide compartments for small pictures (Fig. 6).

When unframed graphic work is included in the crate, be sure to mark it clearly. Work has occasionally been mistaken for packing and discarded.

Finally, mark the box on at least two sides with appropriate cautions such as "Fine Art," "Fragile," "Handle with Care," "Glass."

Three-Dimensional Work

By Norman Holen

If a sculptured masterpiece is only a pile of earthen rubble when it reaches its destination for exhibition, no amount of insurance can make up for the artistic mastery and effort that went into it. To make sure that your sculpture arrives safely, try making and using one of the following three containers and packing methods.

The first container (drawing #1) holds up to 200 lbs. and is designed for shipping by express. A relatively easy crate to build, it is made of 2x2" pine boards and ⅜" plywood. To hold it together, #8 flat head wood screws should be used rather than nails, which may work loose. Also, metal corners prolong the crate's life. With all the supporting structure on the inside and a smooth exterior, collapsible handles should be attached to each end.

This 15¼x15¼x23" wooden container (based on drawing #3) carried the author's 32-lb. terra cotta sculpture, which sat on a one-inch piece of foam rubber on top of corrugated cardboard.

The second container (drawing #2) is similar to the first — designed for express shipping of objects up to 200 lbs. The primary difference, however, is that its lighter weight enables some sculpture to be shipped cheaper; some express companies offer reduced rates if total weight is under 100 lbs. Made of pine boards and Masonite panels, rather than plywood, this crate is somewhat more difficult to build than crate #1 and is not quite as sturdy.

Norman Holen has exhibited his works in one-man and group shows — including the National Gallery — all over the country and is now a professor of art at Augsburg College in Minneapolis.

When shipping by United Parcel Service (UPS) or first-class US Mail, which have respective maximum weights of 50 and 70 lbs., crate #3 is recommended. A box with the dimensions of 15x15x23 weighs only 13 pounds. This light-weight container is constructed of pine boards and ¼" plywood. The thin metal edging is attached with #6 pan head tapping screws or sheet metal screws, which extend through the metal and plywood walls into corner boards.

Construction materials for all three containers are available at most hardware stores and lumber yards.

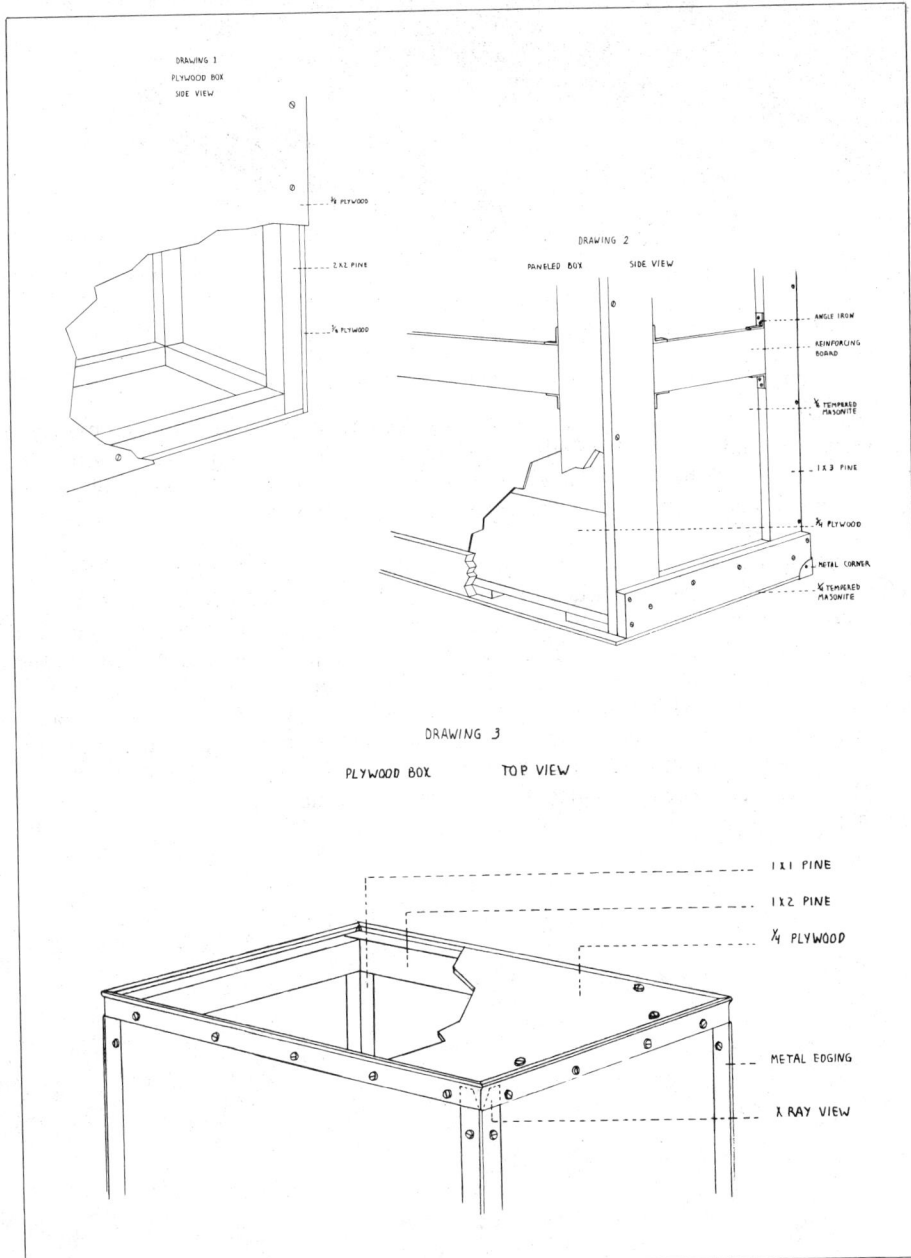

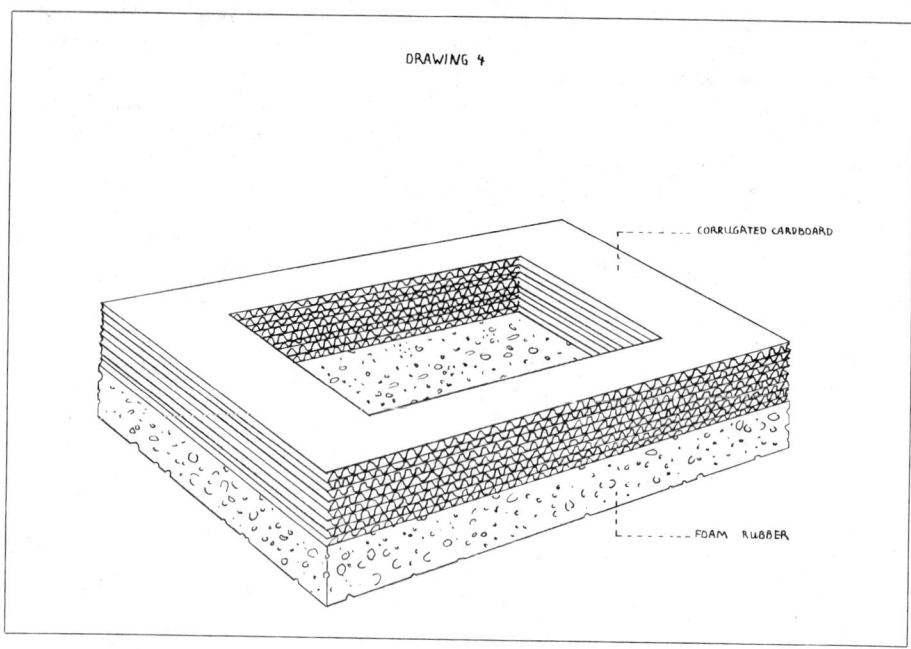

DRAWING 4

CORRUGATED CARDBOARD

FOAM RUBBER

After your container is built, you also need to pack it in a secure manner. Between one and one and a half inches of corrugated cardboard (drawing #4) around the base of the sculpture will keep it from sliding around should the box be overturned. Foam rubber under the cardboard also helps to absorb any shock the crate may suffer.

Crumpled newspaper is an excellent packing material. It holds the sculpture in place, packs and unpacks neatly and quickly, and can be used over and over again. You should have approximately five inches of tightly packed paper between the sculpture and container walls. The same amount of paper should also separate the sculpture from the roof of the box. If more than one sculpture is being crated, separate the objects with double-thickness cardboard before packing in six to eight inches of newspaper between objects; only small pieces should be crated together. For the light-weight container, polystyrene pieces may be used instead of paper.

If the sculpture is easily soiled, cover it with a plastic bag before packing in the newspaper.

Photographing Your Crafts

By Doug Long

Once you begin creating to sell, it isn't enough just to be an adept craftworker, you should also become a proficient photographer.

More than half of the listings in *Craftworker's Market* request you send slides or photos of your work so they can decide if it is the type they are interested in for their shop, gallery, show or firm.

If you send unsolicited work to galleries — as opposed to the photos they actually request — the work may get lost or may be disregarded. Also, if the dealer doesn't want the work — which was never requested in the first place — he is forced to repack and mail it back.

Basically you should learn to shoot both color and black and white shots of your creations in order to become a professional marketing craftworker.

Retailers and the jurors of prejudged shows usually want *color* slides or photos of the work you are interested in selling or exhibiting. The jurors also occasionally use photos of your booth.

Black and white photos, on the other hand, are used primarily for publicity purposes. They should include photos of actual work, of you with your work, and of you alone.

It is certainly possible to hire a professional photographer to take these shots for you, or sometimes to trade off work with a photographer. But in the long run, the least expensive and easiest thing is to do your own photography.

Equipment

It is important to start with the right basic tool: a 35mm single-lens reflex camera with built-in light meter. The most economical, good quality package is a camera-with-normal-lens by Pentax, Minolta, Yashica or Fugica, to name a few. These run about $150-175. Check the back pages of photography magazines or your local newspaper for the best deals. Looking for used equipment is not a bad idea if you can get a warranty on a camera in good condition.

Note that if your work is smaller than three or four feet high or wide, a normal (50mm-55mm) lens won't allow you to get the tight shots or details you need. An inexpensive solution is to get a set of screw-on close-up lenses that attach to the main lens. These are simply magnifying glasses (about $25 per set of three) of progressively greater strengths which are used individually or combined.

An expensive, but timesaving alternative to the normal lens and attachment close-ups is the macro close-up lens. By merely turning the barrel as you move closer to the subject, you can photograph a whole house, then its door and finally the nails that hold it together. Detail photos become a snap. Because it costs between $100-200, depending on the brand, I recommend you buy just the camera body and the macro close-up lens.

In addition to a camera and lens, a tripod is also virtually a necessity. If you have been hand-holding your camera to shoot your work and find many pictures out of focus, blurry, crooked or otherwise bizarre, the lack of a tripod is the likely

Doug Long, craft and art photographer since 1973, is principal photographer for major books by Charles Scribner and Son, Van Nostrand/Reinhold and Houghton-Mifflin Publications Co. He is also a photography columnist for The Crafts Report, *and has had work appear in numerous craft publications, including* Fiberarts, Craft Horizons *and* Ceramics Monthly.

The problem with this outdoor shot is obvious — it's hard to find the pot in the picture. This is the most typical fault of outdoor shots. Watch out for confusing backgrounds. Creature pot by Vanessa Obten.

This photo is an example of inadequate lighting, shallow depth of field and bad and confusing location and composition. More lighting would have allowed greater depth of field, and more care in setting up this shot would have improved it. Nail work by Barbara Spear.

These two shots show the work to its best advantage and are examples of successful craft photography. Above: Black velvet was used for the background with a strong directional light from right and a white card on left to bounce back a soft, diffuse light on dark side. Lens: 85mm with close-up lens attached; film: Panatomic-X, f11 at 1 sec. Possibly the camera was not quite square to the pieces and the lefthand sphere is slightly out of focus. The porcelain sculpture is by Naomi Cahana. Below: This is a classic table-top shot with a single piece of white background paper curving behind and under pots. Two 500-watt lights on background, one front light carefully placed for minimal reflections on high-glass glaze. White cards in front bounce additional light back onto pots. Lens: 85mm with close-up lens attached; film: Panatomic-X, f22 at ½ sec. Pottery by Doug Sassi.

cause. A brief sketch may suggest many reasons why so much craft photography is only fair to poor.

Craftwork is three dimensional. A good photo will get the width, height and the depth of the piece in focus; but when you put your camera close to the piece it is harder to achieve depth of focus (the range from the camera that appears in focus). So, you must use f-stops which give you more depth of focus (like f11, f16, and f22) and a slower shutter speed (⅛ or ¼ of a second). Since these speeds are too slow to hand-hold the camera (¹⁄₆₀ is usually the limit), the tripod is necessary.

Another reason to use a tripod is that it obliges you to slow down and view each shot critically through the viewfinder.

A reliable tripod will weigh 4-5 pounds or more, have both vertical and horizontal shooting positions, allow panning (rotating) movement, extend upward to your eye level, and cost $45-60. Skimping here might send your good camera to the floor (as happened to mine some years back), so take your camera along and test it in all positions.

To further steady the camera, buy a shutter release cable. It allows you to press the shutter without touching the camera.

Lighting

What kind of lighing is best? Daylight or indoor lights? Flash? Forget flash! Its light is usually harsh, ugly, and produces horrible shadows. It's a bad tool for sensitive craft work.

Daylight, on the other hand, is natural, free and abundant. It would seem ideal, except direct sunlight can wash out delicate colors and details and often produce harsh shadows too. But, if you choose to shoot outside, try it on an overcast day when the light is soft.

An alternative, using daylight, is to shoot the work indoors on a table next to a window. The camera is set up perpendicular to the direction of the light. White card or paper facing the window can then be used to bounce light back onto the otherwise dark side of the work.

My preferred choice is indoor lighting. It frees you from the vagaries of the weather and sun — especially important when time is short — and allows you to shoot when, where and for as long as you want. But its most valuable benefit to your photographs is the lighting control. The ability to examine and subtly adjust for the best light and shadow is an enormous advantage over other lighting methods.

I recommend getting three or four 250 or 500 watt bulbs called photofloods (available at photo stores for about $1.50 each), and put these into 10-inch reflector/socket units with hand clamps ($5-10 per unit). Ideally you should have three or four light stands ($10 each at the photo store, or make them yourself) to which you attach the lights, either singly or in pairs, depending upon what the piece requires. This gives you enough flexibility to shoot everything from five-foot square wall hangings to jewelry.

It is this flexibility of lighting that is one of the keys to good craft photography. Only by moving the lights around, exploring the possibilities, and seeing the changes with your own eyes, can you put as much as possible of that piece into a photograph.

Background

Beware of your number one enemy: confusing backgrounds. Especially when outdoors, craftworkers will painstakingly photograph a piece in a natural setting or against the siding of a house so distracting that the work is overwhelmed. Take care to find a compatible background.

To get the smooth, unbroken backgrounds you see in books and slide shows, use seamless background paper from art supply stores. Seamless paper comes in two sizes— the half roll (54"x36', about $8) and the full roll (107"x36', about $15) which is big enough to make a whole wall when you need one. The paper comes in white, greys, black and other various colors. I mostly stick with the neutral tones.

Fabrics make good backgrounds too, but not when they are creased or wrinkled. They absorb more shadows than paper, and can be used and stored easily. Felt and velvet are commonly used. (Black velvet is used specifically for eliminating shadows and often for jewelry.)

A typical shooting set-up of a pot, for example, will be on a table with a piece of seamless paper four or five feet long and three or four feet wide, taped at one end to the wall and dropping in a gentle curve to the front edge of the table. Place two lights in front, and one or two at the sides aimed at the shadows if too distracting. Try putting a light above the piece for top-lighting.

Film

What film to use? Remember that for color there's film for daylight and different film for indoor (tungsten) lights. Don't mix them or the light sources. That is, if you want to shoot indoors with lights, but during the day, pull the shades first or else you'll find a blue tint in the pictures. Vice versa, tungsten color film used outdoors will give you orange-tinted photos.

When outdoors use Kodachrome 64, indoors use Ektachrome Tungsten 50 (EPY) for color slides. You can get prints for your portfolio from slides.

For black and white prints use medium or slow-speed films. Medium-speed film (Kodak Plux-X and Ilford Pan F) is easier to use, but the slow-speed film (Kodak Panatomic-X and Ilford FP4) has finer grain for sharper prints.

Getting Ready to Shoot

Now for the final steps. Load the film, set the appropriate ASA (the film speed which is found on the film's carton) position on your light meter, move up close (6 inches or so) to the piece to get your light reading, then place the camera on the tripod to compose and focus the shot. Bracket your shots. That is, if your meter tells you that f16 requires ¼ second shutter speed, shoot at least four other frames: two f-stops above and below f16 as well. Later you can get down to just three brackets, but realize that film is a tool, an investment; don't hoard it, use it.

To learn more about photographing your crafts, get the easy-to-understand Petersen series of large-format paperback guides to photography at photo stores or write Petersen Publishing Co, 8490 Sunset Blvd., Los Angeles CA 90069.

Promoting Yourself and Your Work

Certainly you, as a craftworker, can sit around waiting "to be found," but if you ever want to achieve first rate sales, you're going to have to do more than just wait. You have to take steps toward promoting yourself.

There are many ways you can promote yourself at little or no cost. You should first prepare a kit for working with the markets. If you check the listings in this book, you'll discover many ask for bio sheets, resumes, business cards, labels to be placed on your work and/or photographs of you and your work.

So be prepared. Not only will these materials help you in working with the media and the retailer, but by passing the appropriate materials along to potential customers who might not have money to buy just then, you increase your potential sales.

Biographical or Resume Sheet

Most working people have had to design a resume to tell potential employers about their qualifications. As a craftworker, this is essentially what you should also do. Look at the outlets carrying your work as your employers. Not only do they want to know something about you before "hiring" you, but they also want to know about you and your work so they can answer questions asked by customers. All this relates heavily to the personal nature of crafts.

The resume will also help you work with reporters. Suppose someone from the media decides to do a write-up on you, what better way to fill in the gaps about your work in the craft field than to give him/her a resume for reference.

When writing your resume, stick to the facts. There are numerous formats for putting your particular information down on paper; but, the basic information should include the following:
- Personal data: name, address, phone number (of home and studio), media in which you work, and any other data you feel helpful, such as age, marital status, etc.
- Educational background: list schooling as it relates to crafts.
- Professional experience: list jobs you have held in the crafts field; exhibitions and shows you have participated in; publications you have written for; and galleries and shops you sell to or have exhibits in.
- Awards: list awards and honors you've received.
- Professional Organizations: include those to which you belong and any offices you have held or now hold.
- References: list two personal references along with the names and addresses of persons who have worked with you professionally. (It's always a good idea to ask a person ahead of time to be a reference.)

Try to keep your resume to one page of information. Most single-page resumes can be run off in a day's time by "quick" printers for approxmately $5 per 100. If you are extremely active in the crafts field you may want to only have a few resumes printed at a time. This way you can periodically update your sheet and have new ones made.

Business Cards/Labels

It's impossible to know just when you might run into someone who will help you in your craft career or who might be a potential buyer. So, it's a good idea to always have your name, address, phone number and area of specialization available in printed form.

Your resume gives this information, but it would be impractical to carry a handful of resumes everywhere you go. The best way to be prepared for this type of casual meeting is to have business cards printed. A plain, one-color business card can be printed for less than $10 per 100.

Pass the cards out to potential buyers of your work at shows and sales, as well as leaving them with retailers and other businesses you hope to be able to work with. And don't limit the cards to *buyers* of your work, distribute them to passers-by as well. They may get back to you for a purchase in the future.

Putting labels on your work is an inexpensive way to get yourself known and help improve sales. Design a tag that is distinctive and attractive, yet reflective of your personality or the nature of your crafts. Include copy telling about you and/or your work. Try to answer the questions you've most often been asked by buyers and viewers of your work.

While printed labels can be attached to most work, you may want to sew fabric labels to inconspicuous spots on soft items, such as clothing. Cards can be produced individually by hand, silkscreened or printed. The cost would be about the same as that of a business card, depending on the paper or material used.

For added benefits you may want to create a label that can double as a business card. If you do this, make certain your address and phone number can be easily removed by the retailer if he/she wishes to do so. (Although many shops and galleries may request that labels be placed on work, they don't want to encourage customers to leave the store and call the craftworker to attempt to get the work at discount.)

Publicity Release

When you feel you have something newsworthy, or something that may be of particular interest to the community, be sure to keep the local media informed by writing a press release.

The main keys to writing a publicity release are to keep it as brief as possible and to try to get all the important information near the beginning. An editor will usually cut copy from the bottom if he/she feels the piece is too long for its topic or if space requires a shorter piece.

And keep the media you are writing for in mind. Except on the editorial page and in a few columns, newspapers, for example, rarely editorialize. So remember that adjectives such as "beautiful" will quickly be cut. But, if you have a quote from a prestigious person who claimed this was the most beautiful design work he/she has seen, it may be left in because this makes it documented rather than your opinion of your work.

Type the press release on 8½x11 paper and be sure to double-space. At the top of the page note when the information is for release (for example: For Immediate Release); the name of the person the release is coming from; and an address and phone number where that person can be called for additional information for a possible feature story. Also, in two or three words under this information, tell what the release is about (for example: pottery show opens).

Photos

Many show sponsors and retailers request color slides or photos of a craftworker's work prior to working with him/her. It is wise to have quality color reproductions of your work. You should also have a few 8x10 or 5x7 black and white glossy photos of you working at your craft; pieces of your work; and photos of you alone. A good photo will make your press release extra appealing to the editor.

Remember too, action photos have the most appeal, and human interest is always a plus. (See "Photographing Your Crafts" for specifics on taking shots of your work.)

Contacting the Media

Never send material to a publication or the electronic media without addressing it to a specific name. Chances are, if you simply place the name of the publicaton on the envelope, it could end up in the billing department, and not arrive in the right hands until it is old news. To find the names and addresses of various editors, check *Ayers Guide to Periodicals* in your local library. This rule applies whether you're simply writing a letter to the press to get them interested in doing a story about you and your work, or sending an actual release.

It is preferable that first contacts be made by phone or letter, but at some point it is a good idea to meet the person you'll be working with face to face. People like to work with individuals they know; but be sure not to make a nuisance of yourself. A friendly attitude will be well-received, especially by the harried reporter who deals with a variety of "no comment" types each day.

To learn more about writing press releases, and other aspects of handling your public relations, read *How to Handle Your Own Public Relations* by H. Gordon Lewis (Nelson-Hall Inc., publishers). There is a section in the book written especially for the artist.

The Craft of Writing Craft Articles

By Nancy Jackson

You don't have to be an experienced writer to sell craft articles— just an innovative craftworker with a taste for detail work. You must provide clear, concise instructions and illustrations to accompany the original designs. And you must ensure that a reader can successfully complete the project and not have to ask, "Now why doesn't mine look like theirs?"

Craft editors are eager to receive new ideas and develop new sources of designs for their publications. More than 650 articles on crafts will be purchased from craftworkers and/or freelance writers in the next year by the publications listed in this book (see section on Writing Outlets). But while most of the publications listed here deal somewhat or wholly with the craft field, there are hundreds of other publications that always run at least one craft article each issue or periodically. An invaluable sourcebook for the person really interested in writing about crafts is the annual *Writer's Market* (A Writer's Digest Book). The book lists thousands of magazines; each listing includes the types of articles the editor buys and what is paid for them.

Pay for craft articles varies from a $5 rights-to-design fee to $300 for a full article— depending on the length, the placement within the publication (lead story or a half-column "somewhere in the back"), whether or not photographs and artwork are used, and how much staff time is required to double-check or rewrite the piece. After a few articles, editors learn to trust a writer to give precise instructions; staff time is cut, and the pay goes up.

Submitting Ideas

The first step in submitting ideas is to obtain copies of the publications you're interested in. Check libraries, newsstands, variety stores, craft supply stores and sewing centers. Note what kinds of crafts are found in the magazine and what it has covered in the last year. (Beware: If you do needlework, some publications only use their own designers or exclusive designs from yarn companies.)

Write a personal letter to the crafts editor (his/her name is on the masthead) about your project, and include a photograph (even a snapshot) and a self-addressed stamped envelope for return of your material and the editor's reply. You might want to mention your related experience — "I've been doing leatherwork for 14 years." *Never send unsolicited craft objects.*

If you get a go-ahead, find out if you need photographs (color or black and white), secure a copy of the editorial guidelines, and study the publication. Then get going. You could well be on your way toward a long relationship with the publication.

Be Original

Versatility is your greatest attribute. Craft publications are looking for new approaches, recycled items, easier techniques, or traditional crafts redone in contemporary materials.

Original, practical designs are the basis for good craft projects. (Floral designs

Nancy Jackson is a writer, editor, designer, photographer and craftworker, and has worked on hundreds of craft project instructions.

are always popular.) Thumb through magazines for ideas that may spark a design in an interesting medium, such as needlepoint "nostalgia" posters or stained glass candleholders. If you're stuck for an idea, look at themes in art, such as Early American, Art Deco, American Indian, Oriental or African — anything international.

But *don't steal*. Don't take a kit, revise the instructions and rephotograph (I've seen it happen!); don't accept someone else's techniques without trying them yourself. Although you should be well-informed about the "in" crafts, keep in mind that they are "out" very quickly. "If it's done all over the place," says one editor, "we don't want it."

Once you have a design idea, don't stop with one item. One wall hanging is not as exciting as half a dozen made of several colors in different sizes that can decorate a kitchen, bedroom, living room or mobile trailer. That way, you also increase the potential of the article from an idea to a full-color spread.

You may want to time yourself as you make the project so you'll know how long it will take to deliver the article. Quality counts. Use the best materials and be meticulous in your work. You want the reader to say, "I want to make one just like that."

Everybody Drops the Stitch You Slip

Keep the amount of required materials to a minimum, and select those that are readily available to readers. If you are using hard-to-find materials such as ostrich feathers, then list suppliers, but be sure they can accommodate mail orders and will deliver the proper items. Choose colors that will photograph well, work together, and look appealing.

Avoid costly materials. "To make these earth-tone vases, you need: a potter's wheel, a kiln . . ."—I'd stop right there. This is where you might substitute self-hardening clay.

The description of materials must be specific, down to the length of the nails, the width of the paintbrush, the dimensions of lumber, or the number of plies in yarn. Most publications prefer that you give the brand names for yarns so readers can match the colors. Contact the company to be sure it's not about to discontinue a certain color. *Keep track of how much you use.* The complaint I hear most often is that designers and craftspeople don't give exact amounts of materials, especially for needlework.

Check the publication's policy on brand names and switch to generic terms if necessary: Elmer's Glue is white glue; Plexiglas is sheet acrylic; Styrofoam is foamed plastic. Offer alternatives for materials readers may have at home— scraps of cloth for a patchwork play table or bread-dough flowers instead of ceramic ones for decorating a raffia breadbasket.

List every step as you make the project. *Be specific.* "Roll the dough into shape" is not as helpful as "Flatten the dough with a rolling pin until it is a uniform ¼-inch thick, and cut it into ½-inch strips. Connect the strips by pressing the end together until you have three four-foot strips, then braid them, as shown in Figure 1. . . ."

Be consistent. If you call something a lid, always call it a lid— don't switch to top. Include any tips, hints or special recipes that you find make the project easier, such as "thin-skinned oranges are the best for making pomanders," or "keep track of the acrylic pieces by marking them with a grease pencil— you can rub the marks off later."

Alert the reader to protection and caution; advise wearing rubber gloves for tie-dyeing or warn about the flammability of wax and the need for proper ventilation while working with plastics.

Offer suggestions for the practical use of finished crafts and alternatives for finishes, such as "You can simply sand it and coat the wood with polyurethane plastic, stain it, or paint it with two coats of enamel."

While writing the final copy, carefully follow the publication's style. You may want to include a history of the craft in the introduction, and books for further reference. Most instructions use the active imperative voice— "Fold the ends"; but many are more personal — "I made these unusual arrangements with bits and pieces I've collected through the years. . . ." How does the publication deal with measurements and abbreviations? Is the word "inches" spelled out, abbreviated, or are the symbols used?

When in doubt, use full sentences, but don't try for any prose award. The most important aspects of craft instructions are *clarity* and *accuracy*.

If you key illustrations to the text, mark them and follow the publication's style — "See Figure A"; "As shown in Ill. Two" — for textural references. You may find it handy to ask a friend who doesn't know about your craft to read the instructions for clarity.

Photographs

Good photographs are essential for craft articles. Many publications have their own facilities for photography and prefer to use their own models. In that case, you would send the items themselves, not pictures of them. Be sure to include a note such as "this side up" if it's needed. That way, when you receive the published article, you won't say, "They hung it upside down!"

If you can't take the photographs yourself, collaborate with a photographer; of course, the editor may be able to arrange for the photographs himself. But if you have access to good equipment, here are some guidelines:

• *All photographs must be in sharp focus and clearly show the object.* Most publications accept color as 35mm transparencies (slides). Black-and-white photos should be enlarged: 5 x 7 is a good size, but check first.

• *Take full advantage of your own home and place the crafts in a practical setting when possible.* Hang a macrame planter and place healthy plants in it. (There's nothing worse than a beautiful planter with droopy plants.) Create an interesting mood, but don't clutter the photograph with extraneous objects. Be careful — will that picture hanging on the wall show up as half a picture? Clear away materials with brand names if the publication does not endorse them. The outdoors is a great place to photograph crafts, and if you look through magazines, you'll find everything from leather belts cinching trees to stuffed animals on the rocks.

• *Shoot step-by-step photographs as you make the project — don't try to fake it.* Keep the camera at one distance from the project so you can take photos in the same scale. Compose the photos through the viewfinder. You'll usually only need to show hands completing various steps, or just that portion of the project illustrating the text. Don't rely on the art department to improve your photograph— it's too expensive. Be sure to clean hands and fingernails and remove jewelry that may detract from the clarity of the photograph.

Artwork

"Exploded" drawings and other helpful assemblage illustrations are usually completed by the art department to keep in style with the publication, but they need sketches to guide them. If you use a pattern for the design, submit it with your article and let the publication decide upon its use.

When drawing on graph paper, remember that blue doesn't reproduce easily with a copying machine, which makes it difficult for editors to disperse copies.

Draw over the lines with black, or request special paper from the magazine.

Design drawings must be exact, especially in needlepoint, where every stitch counts. Some editors find it useful to have the actual object so they can be sure — but don't send it unless it's requested.

Double-check measurements in the callouts (the labels and dimensions printed with the illustrations) to those given in the text and materials. This is an excellent checkpoint for yourself, as well. For example, you may have specified four 12-inch wood strips in the materials, but after drawing the illustrations, you may realize that two of them are actually supposed to be 14 inches. There is nothing more frustrating for the reader than numbers that don't match!

Follow Up

Proofread. Check spellings of craft materials — one word, hyphenated, two words? Use standard proofreader's symbols (found in most dictionaries) for marking corrections on the manuscript. *Keep your deadline.* Submit the entire manuscript and all illustrations at the same time with your name clearly marked on everything. Place 35mm transparencies in protective acetate sheaths (notebook-size plastic sheets available at photo shops). If you've been requested to send the craft items, pack them carefully, insure them, and be sure to send everything to one person.

If you have made an error, inevitably it will be found — if not by an editor, then by a reader — and you will hear about it. But if your project is made by one of the millions of amateur craftspeople who read these publications, you may receive some warm compliments. And that's what it's all about: to give others the skills to produce items on their own; to continue and enrich our crafts tradition; and most of all, to create with loving care.

Artist-Dealer Agreement

When working with a craft dealer, it is always a good idea to have a written contract that specifies the mutually-agreed upon terms. Verbal contracts can be forgotten or easily broken. The contract should specify exactly what the craftworker wants to get out of the agreement while taking into account the needs and desires of the dealer. The following contract — drawn up and used with permission of Artists Equity Association — is helpful for the craftworker to study to the extent that it points out items to be considered and who is responsible for what. However, keep in mind that the best contracts are those that are designed to meet individual needs. Legal advice on designing any contract should be a must before the craftworker enters into any agreement.

* * * *

It is hereby agreed between _____, the artist, address: _____ and _____, the dealer, address:_____ that the dealer shall exhibit the artist's work at the dealer's premises under the following conditions:

1. The works hereby consigned for exhibition and sale by the dealer as agent for the artist are enumerated, described, and priced at retail on the attached list. Such works are warranted by the artist: to be free of inherent vice, to be his/her own original creations, and to be the unencumbered property of the artist. They shall remain the property of the artist unless and until they are purchased by collectors or by the dealer.

2. The works here listed shall be exhibited by the dealer from _____(date) to and including _____(date). These works shall constitute a solo/part of a group (*choose either term*) exhibition. Such exhibitions shall be held approximately every _____ months.

3. Approximately_____ works on the attached list shall be hung during the exhibition period. The remainder shall be available for inspection by prospective purchasers. After the exhibition period, the artist's consigned works may be retained by the dealer for sale for a term of_____months. At the end of that period, they may be individually removed by the artist providing five days prior written notice has been given. Other works may be supplied as additions or replacements for works sold or removed from time to time by mutual written agreement of artist and dealer. The term for retention of works may be thereafter extended annually by mutual written agreement.

4. The artist will assist the dealer by: (*select appropriate responsibilities/eliminate inappropriate items*)
   a) crating and shipping works to the dealer,
   b) framing the works for exhibition,
   c) furnishing advice, cooperation, and assistance in advertising and publicizing the artist's work,
   d) furnishing data regarding prospective and existing collectors.

5. The dealer will pay the artist_____% of the retail sales price on any works sold. Notice of all sales, including the name and address of purchaser, will be

given to the artist at the conclusion of each month and payment of all monies due shall be made not more than thirty days after the receipt of payment by the dealer. The dealer assumes full risk of non-payment by the purchaser. However, if a work is returned in good condition by a client for credit, the dealer will make appropriate pro rata adjustments in future payments to the artist.

6. During the term of this agreement or any extension thereof and during the shipment to the artist of works from the dealer, the dealer shall cause all of the artist's works consigned to the dealer to be insured to the benefit of the artist against any and all loss in an amount equal to the artist's portion of the retail sales price.

7. No unsold works shall be removed from the dealer's premises and no discounts shall be permitted except by specific permission of the artist.

8. The artist shall have the right to inventory all consigned works at reasonable times and to obtain a full accounting for any works not present at the dealer's premises at such time.

9. The artist reserves all rights to the reproduction of works in any manner. This restriction shall be indicated by the dealer in writing on all sales invoices and memoranda. However, the artist will not withhold permission for the reproduction of such works for promotional purposes.

10. During the term of this agreement, the dealer will exclusively represent the artist in the following geographical area:

However, the artist takes the following exceptions to such exclusive representation (e.g.: *The artist reserves the right to sell works from his/her own studio. In this case, the artist will remit_____ % of the proceeds of such sales to the dealer*)

11. Costs of crating and shipping shall be absorbed as follows: (*Indicate responsibility of artist and/or dealer*)

12. Promotion and advertising costs shall be absorbed as follows: (*Indicate responsibility of artist and/or dealer*)

13. Costs of an exhibition opening in conjunction with the exhibition provided above shall be absorbed as follows: (*Indicate responsibility of artist and/or dealer*)

14. In the event that a dispute arises under this agreement involving the interpretation of any of the provisions herein which cannot be resolved by discussion between the artist and the dealer, both parties will submit such dispute to an arbitrator appointed by the American Arbitration Association, who shall decide the issue in accordance with the terms of the agreement and the laws of the State of _____. Costs in such cases shall be borne equally by both parties.

Artist_____ **Dealer** _____

Date _____ **Date** _____

The Markets

Architectural & Interior Design Firms

If the world's largest employer of architectural services — the US General Services Administration — is spearheading a campaign to bring crafts into their construction, remodeling and interior design plans, can the rest of industry be far behind?

When GSA completed work on the Alfred P. Murrah federal building in Oklahoma City, it contained $80,000 worth of handcrafted furnishings and accessories in media ranging from fiberworks to Plexiglas.

This is only one example of how percentage-for-arts legislation throughout the country is helping to increase the purchasing activity of architects in the craft field.

Privately, architects and interior designers are also incorporating crafts into their designs. The Holiday Inn in Richmond, Kentucky, was recently redecorated to emphasize the traditional aspects of the area, concentrating on Kentucky crafts for the interior design theme.

What does this craft renaissance in the building industry mean to you, the individual craftworker?

The architectural/interior design firms in this section will buy and commission more than 200 works from craftworkers during 1979. These range from exterior crafts such as stained glass, woodworking, and outdoor sculpture to wall hangings, pillows, furniture and desk accessories in a variety of media.

Your best bet when looking for an architectural firm to work with is to seek out those with an interior design department. In addition to the listings in this book, consult the yellow pages of the phone book for other companies and keep up with construction reports, found in the library, published by community building contractors' associations.

Call the head of the design department and make an appointment. If refused, don't be discouraged. Send slides or photos (include some black and white; they won't conflict with the client's personal color preferences) and a cover letter that says this is the type of work you do, these are your qualifications, these are your terms and your prices. Close by saying you will give them a call in a week or so to set up an appointment. Have your portfolio ready for personal interviews.

Not all architectural firms will report back to you immediately. Some will only contact you when they have a specific project for your craft. Every six months or so you should give them another call, reminding them of your work and bringing them up to date on your career.

Designing a brochure of your work and qualifications may well be worth the extra time and expense (approximately $250 for 500 1-page fold-out color brochures; exact estimates can be obtained from printers in your area). In addition to creating a professional impression a brochure can be easily filed away for future reference. Design Director A. Dewitt Day, A. Dewitt Day and Associates, tells us he keeps brochures on file for consideration of work for as long as 5 years.

You may also want to advertise in trade publications such as *Contract Interiors, The Designer, Decor, Interior Design, Interiors* or *Residential Interiors.* These publications will give you a reader's service card listing and send queries to you. Again your brochure will be an asset in responding to these.

Don't limit your architectural assignments exclusively to architectural and interior design firms. Call on the offices of some professionals— doctors, lawyers, etc. They are frequently interested in crafts not only for decorative purposes but as an investment.

Remember salesmanship is involved as well as your craft ability. Try to educate and convince; gallery showings or competition awards are always impressive. Make the rounds, get exposure, take advantage of the resurgence of crafts in the building industry.

ADI (ASHWORTH DESIGNS, INC.), 6044 E. Double Tree Ranch Rd., Scottsdale AZ 85253. (602)948-1980. Contact: Dean Ashworth. Architectural/landscape architectural firm specializing in residential, institutional and commercial customers; especially dental offices. Buys 100 craftworks and commissions 1-6 craft designs annually. Considers wall hangings; pillows; self-standing statutes; items for display on tables, etc.; umbrella stands; and one-of-a-kind furniture. Acceptable media include ceramics; fiber art; glass art; leatherworking; metal sculpture; pottery; and wood sculpture. Payment is made by cash within 45 days of acceptance. Send brochure of work and resume. SASE. Reports in 30 days maximum; keeps resume on file. "We [recently] designed a building that called for wood signage. Craftsperson was given free hand."

A. DEWITT DAY & ASSOCIATES LANDSCAPE ARCHITECTS & PLANNERS ASLA, 4566 Office Park Dr., Jackson MS 39206. (601)981-5524. Contact: A. Dewitt Day. Architectural firm. Designs 6+ interiors; buys 10-20 original craftworks; and commissions 1-2 craft designs annually. Considers wall hangings; self-standing statues; and display pieces for use in planning exteriors. Acceptable media include ceramics; some fiber art; glass art; metal sculpture; pottery; and wood sculpture. "The craftsman sets his price — I see if the project's budget can afford original artwork and how much." For past work has paid: $900 for wood sculpture for deck residential client; $17,000 for bronze work for a commercial client; $51,000 for stone work for a park; and $7,000 for steel work for a park. Mail resume; brochure of work with price list; and cover letter and slides of work. No samples returned. Reports to craftworker "only if I can sell their work to our clients or if we have projects where we can use their works." Keeps resume on file a maximum of 5 years. Recently commissioned a bronze sculpture to be completed for the Josh Halbert Gardens.
To Break In: "Include a brochure; price list; resume— anything that will help us sell your art to our clients."

DEZIGN HOUSE III, 1701 E-12 Park Centre W., Cleveland OH 44114. (216)621-7777. Director: Ray Elias. Private design studio working primarily in interior design work. Estab. 1962. Represents 75 craftworkers who do custom work in all crafts. Price range: $100-10,000. Requires exclusive area representation. Craftworkers who are experienced in interior design work are asked to make personal inquiries by letter first.

HIGH POINT GLASS & DECORATIVE CO., Box 101, High Point NC 27261. (919)882-4519. Contact: A. W. Klemme, Jr. Manufacturer. Clients are residential, institutional and churches. Commissions approximately 75 craft designs annually. Considers stained and leaded glass craft items. "Cost depends upon the amount of work required to produce the product." Send "letter with resume of abilities and pictures of work available." SASE. Reports as to interest in work; keeps resume on file 3-5 years. "We work with designers either at our studio or freelance."

INTRARC PLANNING CORP., 7370 NW 36th St., Miami FL 33166. Contact: John G. Dieckmann, ASID. Architectural/interior design firm specializing in residential, commercial and medical clients. Designs 10-20 interiors annually. Considers wall hangings; self-standing statues; ashtrays; desk accessories; and one-of-a-kind furniture. Acceptable media include metal sculpture; pottery; ceramics; and wood sculpture. Payment determined "by job budget allowance." Pays $10-200/assignment. Send cover letter and slides of work. SASE. Keeps resume on file for 1-2 years.
To Break In: "Contact designers, show examples of your work, and ask them for ideas or suggestions as to what you might be able to create for their needs — let them provide you with designs (originals) *they* can use."

JAMES A. MARTIS JR., ARCHITECTS, 28790 Chagrin Blvd. # 250, Cleveland OH 44122. (216)831-0757. Contact: James A. Martis Jr. Architectural firm specializing in residential, industrial and commercial clients. Designs 5-10 interiors; buys about 10 pieces of original craft work; and commissions about 10 craft designs annually. Considers wall hangings; pillows; self-standing statues; items for display; ashtrays; desk accessories; and one-of-a-kind furniture. Acceptable media include batik; ceramics; fiber art; glass art; metal sculpture; pottery; and wood sculpture. Payment determined by "competitive market price; what the creator feels the work is worth." Call to arrange interview, or send brochure of work. SASE. Reports in 1 week; keeps resume on file permanently. Working process: "discuss concept of, or objective of work; designer submits sketches; reviewed with client; contract [agreed upon] for execution."
To Break In: "Quality b&w single sheet flyer [should be] sent by mail to widest number of design professionals with a return mail card for response."

LIZA SHERMAN CORPORATE ART, 19 W. 55th St., New York NY 10019. (212)581-1638. Contact: Liza Sherman. Specializes in selling large quantities of posters and limited edition original prints to international business clients. Considers large, colorful abstract images or landscapes; weavings; and ethnic art. Maximum size: 18x24". Send samples. Clients are architects and space planners.

DUFFY B. STANLEY, ARCHITECT, 308 Bassett Tower, El Paso TX 79901. Contact: Duffy Stanley. Architectural firm specializing in institutional; commercial; and public clients. Designs 2-3 interiors annually. Acceptable media include glass art; leatherworking; metal sculpture; pottery; and wood sculpture. Mail resume and brochure of work.

TAPESTRY ASSOCIATES, 300 Central Park W., New York NY 10024. Director: Lee Naiman. Agent and consultant to architects and designers. Estab. 1970. Represents 12 craftworkers. Considers batik; wall hangings; and weavings. Fine one-of-a-kind designer pieces. Price range: $500 minimum; bestsellers: $1,000-2,000. Works on consignment; commission varies. Retail price set by joint agreement. Reports in 3 weeks. Work may be shipped or hand-delivered. "One work of each artist is usually on display." Customers are corporate and institutional.

HELENE WEISSNER DESIGNS, INC., 4330 NE 2nd Ave., Miami FL 33137. (305)573-6666. Works with local craft designers. Considers decorative wall hangings; pillows; self-standing statues; and items for display on tables, etc. Considers ashtrays, umbrella stands; desk accessories; and one-of-a-kind furniture. Acceptable media include batik; ceramics; glass art; metal sculpture; pottery; and wood sculpture. Send brochure of work. Keeps brochuresindefinitely.

Colleges & Universities

Imagine your work being exhibited in a gallery or shop with more than 50,000 affiliates. Then add another 585,000 possible viewers to include the area's population. And there you have it—the potential market for your work at Ohio State University in Columbus.

Ohio State has both a student activities center and gift shop where crafts are exhibited and sold. A growing number of the nation's more than 3,000 colleges and universities are beginning to expose their students to crafts. Other campus outlets include bookstores; college organizations sponsoring craftworkers for a percentage of sales; bulletin boards where ads can be placed; galleries; and shows and fairs.

Although jewelry and personal items for students are popular, the college market by no means restricts itself to specific media. This is a market for items ranging from smoking paraphernalia to children's toys; media range from glass to fibers.

The eventual owner of campus-bought crafts won't always be the student. Members of the surrounding college community also come to buy, and students purchase gifts to take home to their family and friends during holiday breaks. Your on-campus location will be a boost to the student's holiday shopping—especially as vacations usually seem to be preceded by hard-to-get-away exam times.

Items under $20 are reported to sell best on college campuses, but a few will handle those marked as high as $50. Keeping this in mind, you should prepare to exhibit at schools by producing in volume. A number of high-quality, reasonably-priced production pieces will certainly outsell expensive one-of-a-kind work.

If there is a campus near you that isn't listed here, don't despair. There are also colleges listed under the Shops & Galleries and Shows & Fairs sections. Many of the schools we've included had just begun taking crafts; so, chances are the school near you has also recently joined this on-campus craft movement.

You can learn of additional colleges and universities in your vicinity by checking *Comparative Guide to American Colleges* (Harper & Row, Publishers, Inc., 10 E. 53rd St., New York NY 10022) or *Barron's Profiles of American Colleges* (Barron's Educational Series, Inc., 113 Crossways Park Dr., Woodbury NY 11797). Both books can be found in most libraries.

Once you find the school you'd like to work with, call the Director of Student Activities and tell him/her you would be interested in promoting your work on his/her campus; offer to stop by and show your portfolio. Chances are you'll open doors to an entire new and exciting market for your crafts!

ADRIAN COLLEGE, Rush Union, Adrian MI 49221. (517)265-5161. Director of Student Activities: Aleta Nitschke. Student activities committee and homecoming committee sponsor craft shows; Rush Union has exhibit space for craftworkers and sponsors craftworkers for a percentage of sales; and student activities committee holds workshops in crafts. Considers batik; baskets; candlemaking; carvings; sculpture; ceramics; decoupage; glass art; jewelry; macrame; metalsmithing; mobiles; pottery; wall hangings; and weavings. Charges 10% commission on sold works. Craftworker sets retail price. Bestsellers: items under $10. Write explaining qualifications. "Potential gross per day is not more than $100. Student residents on campus number only 600."

AMERICAN INTERNATIONAL COLLEGE, 170 Wilbraham Rd., Springfield MA 01109. (413)737-5331. Coordinator of Student Activities: Betty Edgett. Student activities committee sponsors craftworkers for percentage of sales and has bulletin board where craftworkers can advertise. Considers baskets; candlemaking; carvings; sculpture; ceramics; children's toys; dolls; glass art; handbags and leather accessories; macrame; pottery; wall hangings; and weavings. Charges 15% commission on sold items. Craftworker sets retail price. Bestsellers: $2-15. Write with resume and illustrations of work, or call for interview. "I would like to see some of the outside craftspeople have workshops for our students."

ANTIOCH, Community Government, Yellow Springs OH 45387. (513)767-7331, ext. 600. Community Manager: Ron Williams. Community government has exhibit space for craftworkers; sponsors craftworkers for percentage of sales; and has bulletin board where craftworkers can advertise. "We have begun a community free concert program (for both Antioch and Yellow Springs community) which holds outdoor presentations of music, theater, dance, display arts, poetry, etc. Craftspeople are invited to set up and sell at these events for a small fee which goes toward the performing artists." Entry fee: $5. Bestsellers: $1-15. "Call in spring about free concert program schedule."

STEPHEN F. AUSTIN UNIVERSITY, Box 3056, SFA Station, Nacogdoches TX 75962. (713)569-3401. Craft Shop Director: Billie Elliott. Craft shop holds craft workshops and has bulletin board where craftworkers can advertise. "The craft shop is for all persons affiliated with the University. We provide free to low-priced materials and offer a variety of noncredit classes." Classes offered in batik; baskets; candlemaking; carvings and sculpture; ceramics; decoupage; furniture; handbags and leather accessories; jewelry; macrame; needlecrafts; pottery; wall hangings; and weavings. "We do not resale but always looking for employees." Write for personal interview.

AVERETT COLLEGE, 420 W. Main St., Danville VA 24541. (804)793-7811, ext. 214. Director of Student Activities: Sherry Stitt. Student Activities Association sponsors craft shows and craftworkers for a percentage of sales, holds craft workshops and has bulletin board where craftworkers can advertise. "What we would be interested in would be craftsmen to come to our campus once during the fall for a weekend or a day and once during the spring to show, sell and perhaps demonstrate their particular crafts." Considers batik; baskets; carvings; candlemaking; sculpture; decoupage; furniture; handbags and leather accessories; jewelry, macrame; metalsmithing; mobiles; needlecrafts; pottery; wall hangings; and weavings. Charges 15-20% mark-up on items purchased outright and sold in bookstore or gallery. Bestsellers: $2.50-40. Write with resume and illustration or samples or work.

BENNINGTON COLLEGE, Bennington VT 05201. (801)442-5401. Manager, College Bookstore: Josie Rahe. Bookstore has exhibit space and sponsors craftworkers for a percentage of sales. Considers all crafts. Craftworker sets retail price. Send resume or call for interview.

BERRY COLLEGE, Box T, Mt. Berry GA 30149. (404)232-5374. Director of Student Activities: W. Rufus Massey Jr. Academy art department sponsors craft shows and student activities has exhibit space for craftworkers. "Exhibit and sale outdoor in spring during Festival." Considers all crafts. Requests entry fee or gallery rental charge. Craftworker sets retail price. Write with illustration of work.

BRADFORD COLLEGE, S. Main St. Haverhill MA 01830. Associate Dean for Student Services: Joseph Forgiano. Student activities office sponsors craftworkers for percentage of sales. "Exhibition limited to 8x10 table; 1 craftworker per day allowed to sell; some demonstration work is appropriate and valuable; and most crafts will be purchased by students for presents and/or room decoration." Considers batik; baskets; candlemaking; carvings and sculpture; ceramics; children's toys; decoupage; glass art; handbags and leather accessories; macrame; mobiles; pottery; wall hangings; and weavings. Charges 15-25% commission on sold items. Craftworker sets retail price. Bestsellers: $20 maximum. Write with illustrations of work.

BRYANT COLLEGE, Smithfield RI 02917. (410)231-1200. Program coordinator: Anne-Marie Smith. Student Programming Board Director: Diane Studwell. Student affairs office and/or student programming board sponsors shows, has exhibit space for craftworkers and has bulletin board where craftworkers can advertise. "At present we have no history of craftspeople being at Bryant, so we are pressed to describe special requirements. We hope to have some type of crafts program soon — whether this will include space for workshops or space for an artist to display and sell his/her work will depend upon the space that we're given to work with. We have sponsored artists on a very small scale; that is, people have come to the campus to sell crafts, etc. There have been no fees involved." Considers candlemaking; ceramics; handbags and leather accessories; jewelry; macrame; metalsmithing; mobiles; pottery; smoking paraphernalia; wall hangings; and weavings. Write with resume or call for personal interview.

CATAWBA COLLEGE, Hoke Student Union, Salisbury NC 28144. (704)637-4412. Director of Student Activities: K. Ann Toney. College Union Board sponsors craft shows, has exhibit space for craftworkers and sponsors craftworkers for percentage of sales. "We have a Visiting Regional Artist Program in which we use 1 craftsman per month in our student union for 3 days. The craftsman is expected to demonstrate, display, and sell his craft. He also talks with students about his craft. We provide room and board plus $10/day to cover travel expenses." Considers all crafts. Craftworker sets retail price. Bestsellers: $1-25. Write with resume and illustrations of work; if possible, send sample.

CLEMSON UNIVERSITY, Clemson University Student Union, Program Office, Clemson SC 29631. (803)656-2461. Assistant Program Director: Bill Mandicott. University Union sponsors craft shows; has exhibit space for craftworkers; sponsors craftworkers for percentage of sales; and holds craft workshops. Considers baskets; candlemaking; carvings and sculpture; ceramics; decoupage; glass art; handbags and leather accessories; jewelry; macrame; metalsmithing; needlecrafts; pottery; wall hangings; and weavings. Charges 15% commission on sold items. Craftworker sets retail price. Best sellers: $2-10. Contact by mail, phone, and/or personal interview.

COLLEGE OF ST. CATHERINE, 2004 Randolph Ave., St. Paul MN 55105. (612)690-6000. Bookstore Manager: Sue Rasmussen. Student Activities Director: Gail Ward. Student clubs consign crafts for resale and sponsor craft shows; and bookstore consigns crafts for 1 semester at 20% commission. "Due to space limitations small craft items are preferable for the bookstore. Student clubs sponsoring craft sales are limited to 1-2 table spaces (3x6') in a lounge area." Considers baskets; candlemaking; carvings and sculpture; decoupage; glass art; handbags and leather accessories; jewelry; macrame; metalsmithing; mobiles; pottery; wall hangings; and weavings. Retail pricing negotiable. Maximum price of consignment crafts: $10. Bestsellers: $1-7. Write Student Activity Director with resume and illustrations of work. Call Bookstore Manager (612-690-6729) for personal interview.

DAKOTA STATE COLLEGE, Trojan Center, Madison SD 57042. (605)256-3551, ext. 221. Director of Housing and Activities: Robert J. Courtney. Coordinator of Student Activities: Kelly Johnson. Union Board sponsors craft shows, has exhibit space for craftworkers; sponsors craftworkers for percentage of sales and holds craft workshops. "We are interested in craft demonstrations as well as the sale of craft products." Considers all crafts. Charges 15% commission on sold items. Craftworker sets retail price. Write with resume, illustrations of work and samples.

FITCHBURG STATE COLLEGE CAMPUS CENTER, 160 Pearl St., Fitchburg MA 01420. (617)345-2024. Assistant Director, Campus Center: Victoria Angis. Campus Center sponsors craft shows, has exhibit space for craftworkers and holds craft workshops. "We sponsor non-credit craft classes and demonstrations for the college community taught by students and professional craftspeople. We sponsor an annual holiday craft sale in early December which is open to professional craftspeople." Considers batik; baskets; candlemaking; decoupage; glass art; handbags and leather accessories; jewelry; lapidary; macrame; metalsmithing; needlecrafts; pottery; wall hangings; weavings; copper enameling; wood carving; and sand painting. $25 table fee for craft sales. Craftworker sets retail price. Bestsellers: $1-20. Write with resume and illustrations of work.

FLORIDA TECHNOLOGICAL UNIVERSITY, Box 26000, Village Center, Orlando FL 32807. (305)275-2611. Program Director: Mark W. Glickman. Village Center Programming Department sponsors craft shows, has exhibit space for craftworkers and sponsors craftworkers for percentage of sales. "We like to sponsor individual craftspersons such as silversmiths; candlemakers; potters; etc., in our Village Center for 10% commission on sales. We have an annual craft fair." Considers all original crafts. $15 entry fee for annual craft fair; 10% commission in Village Center for sold items. Craftworker sets retail price. Bestsellers: $1-30. Write with photos or slides of work.

GOUCHER COLLEGE, Towson MD 21204. Director of Student Activities: Linda S. Wenick. Student Life consigns and buys crafts outright for resale; and sponsors craft shows and craftworkers for percentage of sales. Considers batik; baskets; carvings and sculpture; ceramics; decoupage; furniture; glass art; jewelry; macrame; needlecrafts; pottery; and weavings. Craftworker sets retail price. Write for personal interview with resume and illustrations of work.

HOOD COLLEGE, Frederick MD 21701. Director of Student Activities: Krys Kornmeir. Renaissance Chairperson: Karen Kerber. Renaissance sponsors a craft show and has bulletin board where craftworkers can advertise; student organizations sponsor craftworkers for percentage of sales. Considers batik; baskets; candlemaking; handbags and leather accessories; jewelry; macrame; pillows; pottery; smoking paraphernalia; wall hangings; and weaving. Charges 10% commission on sold items in sponsored sales; table space fee for Festival of the Arts, a craft show. Bestsellers: $1-15. Write with illustrations of work and send samples.

JUNIATA COLLEGE, Ellis College Center, Huntingdon PA 16652. (814)643-4310, ext. 84. Director of Programming: Wayne Justham. Fine Arts Committee sponsors craft shows, has exhibit space for craftworkers, sponsors craftworkers for percentage of sales, and holds craft workshops. "Basically we're interested in bringing quality craftsmen to the community to do one-man/woman shows, selling throughout the year. There are no specific requirements except that the artist be interested in talking with the public as well as selling to them. We are planning an arts and crafts festival where craftsmen may sell, exhibit, or demonstrate their craft." Considers all crafts. Charges $10-25 entry fee or gallery rental charge, or mutually agreeable terms. Craftworker sets retail price. Bestsellers: $2-50, any work in any price range is welcome, however. Write with illustrations of work, "then we will contact for interview."

KEENE STATE COLLEGE, L.P. Young Student Union, Keene NH 03431. (603)352-1909, ext. 214. President, Distaff Club: Chrystal Montgomery. Distaff Club sponsors craft show. Considers all crafts. Charges entry fee. Craftworker sets retail price. Bestsellers: $2-30. Write for personal interview.

KENYON COLLEGE, Gambier OH 43022. (614)427-2244, ext. 453. Assistant Dean of Students: Corlin Henderson. Craft Center has exhibit and work space for craftworkers creating in ceramics and fabrics, holds craft workshops and has bulletin board where craftworkers can advertise for percentage of sales. "Kenyon has just opened a craft shop on campus which has prospered during its opening weeks. It has been organized for student and community crafters, but we are interested in expanding our operation." Considers all handmade crafts. Charges 5% commission on sold items. Craftworker sets retail price. Bestsellers: $1-50. Contact by mail, phone, and/or personal interview. The college also sponsors craft fair sales and demonstrations twice annually.

KNOX COLLEGE, Box 79, Galesburg IL 61401. (309)343-0112. Director: Michael Murphy. Student Union Gallery sponsors craft shows, has exhibit space for craftworkers, sponsors craftworkers for percentage of sales and holds craft workshops. "Gallery/lounge in Student Union has large display area for various crafts. We are not in this for the sale of products, but rather for the display of quality goods. Sales, as a bi-product, though, are OK." Considers all crafts. Craftworker sets retail price. Bestsellers: $2-50. Contact by mail, phone, and/or personal interview.

LA ROCHE COLLEGE, 9000 Babcock Blvd., Pittsburgh PA 15237. (412)913-9333, ext. 122. Director, Student Activities: Regina S. Battaglia. The Student Activities Committee sponsors craft shows, has exhibit space for craftworkers, sponsors craftworkers for percentage of sales and has a bulletin board where craftworkers can advertise. Considers all crafts. Charges 5% commission on sold items. Craftworker sets retail price. Bestsellers: $1-25. Write with resume and illustrations of work.

LA SALLE COLLEGE, 20th Street and Cincy Avenue, Philadelphia PA 19141. (215)951-1374. Assistant Director, Student Life: Kathy Schrader. Student Life and Student Programming sponsor craft shows, have exhibit space for craftworkers and sponsor craftworkers for percentage of sales. Considers batik; baskets; candlemaking; ceramics; glass art; handbags and leather accessories; jewelry; macrame; needlecrafts; pottery; wall hangings; and weavings. Charges 20% commission on sold items. Craftworker sets retail price. Bestsellers: $5-50. Write with illustrations of work.

LAKELAND COLLEGE, Culture and Education Committee, Plymouth WI 53073. (414)565-1229. Culture and Education Chairperson: Peter Perkins. Culture and Education Committee has bulletin board where craftworkers can advertise and will possibly sponsor craft show and have exhibit space for craftworkers. Considers candlemaking; carvings and sculpture; glass art; ceramics; handbags and leather accessories; jewelry; macrame; metalsmithing; needlecrafts; pottery; smoking paraphernalia; and weavings. Craftworker sets retail price. Write with resume.

LAWRENCE UNIVERSITY, Wilson House, Appleton WI 54911. (414)739-3681, ext. 542. Associate Dean, Campus Activities: Tom Lonnquist. Campus Life and Art Department sponsor craft shows; art department and S. Mudd Library have exhibit space for craftworkers; Campus Life sponsors craftworkers (Christmas and spring term) for percentage of sales; and Union has bulletin board where craftworkers can advertise. "The Christmas Arts and Crafts Fair takes place in early December. The Celebrate Weekend is held around Mothers Day, spring term." Considers all crafts. Charges $15 entry fee. Craftworker sets retail price. Write with illustrations of work.

LOYOLA UNIVERSITY, 6363 St. Charles Ave., Box 20, New Orleans LA 70118. (504)865-3622. Program Director: Diane Gulick. Arts and Crafts Center consigns crafts for resale, sponsors craft shows, holds craft workshops and has bulletin board where craftworkers can advertise. Loyola Union Art Gallery Committee has exhibit space for craftworkers and sponsors craftworkers for percentage of sales along with Arts and Crafts Center. "We hold annual juried art shows; arts and crafts sales twice a year; and offer various crafts courses each semester." Considers all crafts. Charges 15% commission on sold items. Craftworker sets retail price. Bestsellers: $1-35. Write with resume and illustrations of work.

MARIETTA COLLEGE, Marietta OH 45750. (614)373-4643. Director, Campus Activities: Lew Yeager. Art Department sponsors craft shows and Student Center has exhibit space for craftworkers. "We have designated an 8x8 area in our Student Center for craftpersons to demonstrate, show and sell their creations. We have had a variety of such exhibits, some successful ($1,100 jewelry sales in 3 days) some not so successful ($200 macrame sales in 3 days). Our Art Department sponsors the annual Marietta College Crafts National competitive exhibition and is involved in the extensive Indian Summer Festival, a college/community show." Student Center considers all crafts. Charges 10% commission on sold items. Craftworker sets retail price. Bestsellers: $1-25. Write with resume.

MARION COLLEGE, Marion IN 46952. (317)674-6901. Book Store Manager: Nolan Hauser. Book store buys and consigns crafts for resale. Considers all crafts. Write with resume.

MARS HILL COLLEGE, Wren College Union, Mars Hill NC 28754. (704)689-1253. Chairperson, Outreach Committee: Susan Jordan. Wren College Union sponsors craft shows, holds craft workshops and has bulletin board where craftworkers can advertise. "Our craft shows seek to expose the culture of western North Carolina and the mountains. We use it as a form of bringing together students and community." Considers batik; baskets; decoupage; candlemaking; glass art; handbags and leather accessories; jewelry; macrame; metalsmithing; mobiles; needlecrafts; pillows; wall hangings; and weavings. Craftworker sets retail price. Bestsellers: $10 maximum. Write with resume.

MORAVIAN COLLEGE, Haupert Union Bldg., Bethlehem PA 18018. (215)865-0741. Union Director: Paty Eiffe. Art department buys crafts outright for resale; Haupert Union Program Board consigns crafts for resale, sponsors craft shows, has exhibit space for craftworkers, sponsors craftworkers for percentage of sales and holds craft workshops. "We usually set up a room to accommodate the needs of the craftsperson; however, we are not prepared to do any elaborate or specialized type of craft show but we are willing to try almost anthing once." Considers adult games; carvings and sculpture; ceramics; glass art; jewelry; mobiles; pillows; pottery; kites; posters; and woodworking. Selling terms negotiable. Craftworker sets retail price. Maximum price of consignment crafts: $40. Bestsellers: $2-15. Write with resume; illustrations of work; and samples.

MOUNT VERNON COLLEGE, Office of Student Activities, 2100 Foxhall Rd., Washington DC 20007. (202)331-3422. Director of Student Affairs: Gail Newman. Student Activities Office sponsors craft shows, has exhibit space for craftworkers and has bulletin board where craftworkers can advertise. "We have a small exhibit of crafts for sale at reasonable prices to girls of Mt. Vernon College." Considers candlemaking; ceramics; handbags and leather accessories; needlecrafts; wall hangings; and weavings. Craftworker sets retail price. Bestsellers: $3-25. Write with resume.

NEW HAMPSHIRE COLLEGE, 2500 N. River Rd., Manchester NH 03104. Director of the Hobby Shop: Andrea Banchik. Hobby Shop sponsors craft shows, has exhibit space for craftworkers, holds craft workshops and has bulletin board where craftworkers can advertise. "We are looking mainly for craftspeople to demonstrate and/or exhibit their crafts at the Hobby

Shop in return for free advertising. The Hobby Shop is an arts and crafts studio designed for recreational use by the students. We sponsor an annual Arts and Crafts Festival which includes competition and exhibit space for those outside the college community." Considers all crafts. Bestsellers: 50c-$10. Write with resume and request for personal interview.

NORTH PARK COLLEGE, Art Department, 5125 N. Spaulding, Box 21, Chicago IL 60625. Contact: Professor G. Bradley. Art department has exhibit space for craftworkers and holds ceramic workshops. Considers batik; ceramics; glass art; jewelry; leatherworking; metalsmithing; pottery; soft sculpture; weavings; and woodcrafting. Write with resume and slides of work.

NORTHERN KENTUCKY UNIVERSITY, University Center, Highland Heights KY 41076. Center Director: Bill Lamb. Bookstore buys crafts outright for resale; art department sponsors craft shows and has exhibit space for craftworkers; and University Center has exhibit space for craftworkers and sponsors craftworkers for percentage of sales. "We are interested in craftspeople who conduct workshops for students along with selling their wares." Considers adult games; batik; baskets; candlemaking; ceramics; dolls; handbags and leather accessories; jewelry; macrame; metalsmithing; mobiles; needlecrafts; pottery; wall hangings; and weavings. Craftworker sets retail price. Bestsellers: $3-12. Write with illustrations of work and request personal interview.

OHIO STATE UNIVERSITY, Earthtones, 1739 N. High St., Columbus OH 43210. (614)422-2325. Contact: Program Assistant to Program Director; Art Exhibit Coordinator; or Gift Shop (Earthtones) Supervisor. Earthtones consigns crafts for resale; Art Exhibits sponsors craft shows, has exhibit space for craftworkers and sponsors craftworkers for percentage of sales; and Creative Arts Program holds craft workshops. Considers all crafts marketable to college students and staff. Charges $5-12 entry fee for art/craft fair; 15% commission on sold items; 30% mark-up on items purchased outright. Craftworker sets retail price subject to sponsor agreement. Maximum price of consignment craft: $30. Bestsellers: $3-8. Write or call to set up personal interview.

PITTSBURG STATE UNIVERSITY, Student Union, Pittsburg KS 66762. (316)231-7000, ext. 276. Program Director: Mike Sullivan. Student Union Board sponsors craft shows and craftworkers for percentage of sales. "Craftperson is set up in lobby near 2 cafeterias. Traffic is high for approximately 6 hours." Considers adult games; batik; candlemaking; ceramics; decoupage; glass art; jewelry; macrame; mobiles; wall hangings; and weavings. Charges 20% commission on sold items. Craftworker sets retail price. Best sellers: $1-20. Write with resume, illustrations of work or samples.

QUEENS COLLEGE, Box 412, Charlotte NC 28274. Dean of Students: Diane Del Pizzo. Student government sponsors craft shows and craftworkers for percentage of sales and holds workshops. "Would consider offering student workshops for specific skills if exhibitors were interested." Considers candlemaking; carvings and sculpture; ceramics; glass art; jewelry; macrame; needlecrafts; pottery; wall hangings; and weavings. Charges 10% commission on sales under $100; 15% commission on sales over $100. Craftworker sets retail price. Bestsellers: $2-20. Write with resume, illustrations of work; and/or samples.

ST. ANDREWS PRESBYTERIAN COLLEGE, Laurinburg NC 28352. (919)276-3652, ext. 235. Chairman, Art Department: Anne Woodson. The Art Department, Art Guild, and the Special Events Committee sponsor craft shows and hold craft workshops. "There is a possibility that a craftsman could be hired to teach craft the month of January. We're open to the possibility of sponsoring a crafts festival and an annual workshop in one of the crafts." Considers all crafts. Bestsellers: $5-100. Write with resume and illustrations of work, or call or write for personal interview.

ST. CLOUD STATE UNIVERSITY, Atwood Center, Craft Center, St. Cloud MN 56301. (612)255-2202. Program Director: Patricia A. Krueger. Ward's University Bookstore consigns and buys crafts outright for resale. Program Board, Atwood Center, sponsors craft shows and has exhibit space for craftworkers. Craft Center, Atwood Center, sponsors craftworkers for percentage of sales and holds craft workshops. Craft Center, Art Department, has bulletin board where craftworkers can advertise. "We have 3 areas for participation, exhibits and workshops. Those selected to exhibit may sell work, but must be able to deal directly with buyers. We do not act as sales agents and do not take commission. Those hired as workshop instructors are paid either hourly or flat rate for workshop. Projects are separate, but may do both. 3 times per year art sales are held. Artists and crafters set up and sell work sidewalk style." Considers all crafts except decoupage. Charges registration fee for arts and crafts fair. Bookstore is private enterprise, contact separately. Craftworker sets retail price. Write with resume.

ST. FRANCIS COLLEGE, 1901 Spring St., Fort Wayne IN 46808. (219)432-3551. Chairman, Art Department: Mr. Papier. Art department has exhibit space for craftworkers, holds craft workshops and has bulletin board where craftworkers can advertise. Considers batik; ceramics; jewelry; macrame; metalsmithing; pillows; pottery; wall hangings; and weavings. Charges 20% commission on sold items. Craftworker sets retail price. Bestsellers: $10-50. Write for personal interview.

SAINT FRANCIS COLLEGE, JFK College Center, Loretto PA 15940. (814)742-7000, ext. 267. Director, Student Art: Donwick Peruso. Student Union Organization sponsors craft shows and craftworkers for percentage of sales and holds craft workshops. "Basically an artist in residence program. We provide space and table. Hours usually 10 a.m. - 4 p.m." Considers baskets; candlemaking; carvings and sculpture; glass art; handbags and leather accessories; jewelry; macrame; metalsmithing; pottery; wall hangings; and weavings. Charges 10% commission on sold items. Craftworker sets retail price. Bestsellers: $2-15. Write with resume and illustrations of work.

ST. MARY'S COLLEGE, Winona MN 55987. (507)452-4430. Director, College Center: Joseph P. Fleischman. Bookstore buys crafts outright for resale. College Center has exhibit space for craftworkers, sponsors craftworkers for percentage of sales and has bulletin board where craftworkers can advertise. "Quality should be adequate for gallery showing. Media should not be anything recycled." Considers batik; baskets; carvings and sculpture; ceramics; children's toys; dolls; furniture; glass art; handbags and leather accessories; jewelry; pottery; wall hangings; and weavings. Charges 10% commission on sold items. Craftworker sets retail price. Maximum price of consignment crafts: $15. Write with illustrations of work.

ST. MARY'S COLLEGE OF MARYLAND, St. Mary's City MD 20686. (301)994-1600. Director of Student Activities: John Nicholson. Bookstore and student government consign crafts for resale and have bulletin board where craftworkers can advertise. Student government sponsors craft shows. Considers adult games; carvings and sculpture; ceramics; jewelry; and weavings. Charges 15% commission on sold items. Craftworker sets retail price. Price of consignment crafts: $2.50-25. Bestsellers: $2.50-10. Write with illustration of work.

SETON HILL COLLEGE, Greensburg PA 15601. Harlan Gallery Director: Ray DeFazio. Art department has exhibit space for craftworkers. Considers batik; carvings and sculpture; ceramics; jewelry; lapidary; macrame; metalsmithing; pottery; wall hangings; and weaving. Craftworker sets retail price. Write with resume.

SOUTHERN ILLINOIS UNIVERSITY, Student Center, Craft Shop, Carbondale IL 62901. (618)453-3636. Arts and Crafts Coordinator: Kay M. Pick Zivkovich. SGAC Fine Arts Committee sponsors art and craft sales at $3-5/table space for shows. Craftworker sets retail prices. The student center craft shop holds workshops for SIU students, faculty, staff and alumni only; has bulletin board where craftspersons can advertise. Considers all general crafts; display cases are available in the student center for exhibitions. The Museum Art Gallery Association (MAGA) buys crafts for resale. MAGA also sponsors an annual craft fair during the fall season. Price range varies. Write with resume, describing specific field of interest.

SPRING ARBOR COLLEGE, Spring Arbor MI 49283. (517)750-1200. Assistant to Dean of Students: Mark Kendall. Campus bookstore buys crafts outright for resale. Art Department, Student Affairs and Student Government sponsor craft shows; Art Department and Student Affairs have exhibit space for craftworkers; Student Government sponsors craftworkers for percentage of sales and has bulletin board where craftworkers can advertise; and Student Affairs and Student Government hold craft workshops. "We'd be most interested in craft shows (sales) with workshops at designated times. In many cases, exhibitor will be charged no fee if he presents 1 or more workshops. Contact Student Affairs. The art department will sponsor certain shows. The bookstore will buy limited amounts of crafts." Considers baskets; candlemaking; carvings and sculpture; ceramics; decoupage; furniture; glass art; handbags and leather accessories; jewelry; lapidary; macrame; needlecrafts; pottery; wall hangings; weavings; crocheting; knitting; and quilting. Selling terms negotiable. Craftworker sets retail price. Maximum price of consignment crafts: $20. Bestsellers: $1-20. Write with resume, illustrations and samples of work or write or call for personal interview.

SUNY COLLEGE OF ENVIRONMENTAL SCIENCE AND FORESTRY, Syracuse Campus, Syracuse NY 13210. Assistant to Vice-President for Student Affairs: Catherin Glennon. College Activities Committee sponsors craft show, has exhibit space for craftworkers, holds craft workshops and has bulletin board where craftworkers can advertise. Considers baskets; ceramics; candlemaking; handbags and leather accessories; macrame; mobiles; needlecrafts; pillows; pottery; wall hangings; and weavings. Craftworker sets retail price. Bestsellers: $35 maximum. Write with illustrations and/or samples.

TEXAS CHRISTIAN UNIVERSITY, University Programs and Services, Ft. Worth TX 76129. Program Coordinator: Dottie Buchanan. University Programs and Services sponsors craft shows; University Programs and Services and Programming Council Committee sponsor craftworkers for percentage of sales. "Crafts Faire is near Christmas and there is a space charge, but during the year a craftsman may set up but must be sponsored by a Programming Council committee." Considers all crafts. Charges 10% commission on sold items for use of space. Craftworker sets retail price. Bestsellers: $1-35. Write with resume.

TRINITY COLLEGE, Colchester Ave., c/o Director Student Activities, Burlington VT 05401. (802)658-0337. Director Student Activities: Linda Ready. Student activities may sponsor craft shows, has exhibit space for craftworkers, may sponsor craftworkers for percentage of sales and has bulletin board where craftworkers can advertise. "The college encourages local craftpeople to come to campus to sell their crafts. Generally only 1 craftsperson is here at a time and we set them up at meal times in the lounge near the cafeteria." Considers crafts "that college students would like and could afford." Daily fee: $5. Craftworker sets retail price. Bestsellers: $15-20 maximum. Write with resume.

UNION COLLEGE, Carnegie Hall, Schenectady NY 12308 (518)370-6118. Coordinator of Student Activities: Lorraine T. Marra. College Center sponsors craftworkers for percentage of sales and has bulletin board where craftworkers can advertise. Considers ceramics; handbags and leather accessories; jewelry; macrame; mobiles; needlecrafts; pottery; and wall hangings. Space charge for 1 day: $20. Craftworker sets retail price. Bestsellers: $3-30. Write with resume and illustrations of work.

UNIVERSITY OF ALABAMA, Ferguson Center/Alabama Union, Box CQ, University AL 35486. (205)348-7525. Program Director: Patricia C. O'Neill. Union sponsors craft shows, has exhibit space for craftworkers, sponsors craftworkers for percentage of sales, has bulletin board where craftworkers can advertise and plans to hold craft workshops in the future. Considers batik; baskets; carvings and sculpture; ceramics; dolls; furniture; stained and leaded glass; jewelry; lapidary; macrame; mobiles; needlecrafts; pillows; pottery; wall hangings; and weavings. Charges 10-25% commission on sold items. Craftworker sets retail price. Write with resume or call for personal interview.

UNIVERSITY OF CENTRAL ARKANSAS, Box W, Conway AR 72032. (501)329-6793. Dean of Students: Robert C. Dawson. Student Center sponsors craftworkers for percentage of sales. Considers batik; candlemaking; carvings and sculpture; ceramics; glass art; handbags and leather accessories; jewelry; macrame; metalsmithing; pottery; wall hangings; and weavings. Charges 10% commission on sold works. Craftworker sets retail price. Bestsellers: $5-20. Write with resume and illustrations of work.

UNIVERSITY OF MAINE AT FARMINGTON, Activities Office, Farmington ME 04938. (207)778-3501. Chairman, Crafts and Exhibits Committee: Ruth Dutting. Crafts and Exhibits Committee sponsors craft shows, has exhibit space for craftworkers and holds craft workshops. "We have started this year holding workshops for small groups of students where we ask craftsmen to come demonstrate, instruct, and let students participate in making crafts." Considers all crafts. Rental charge: $2/table. Craftworker sets retail price. Write with illustrations of work or send samples.

UNIVERSITY OF NORTH CAROLINA, Chapel Hill, Campus Y, Y Bldg. 151-A, Chapel Hill NC 27514. (919)933-2084. Director: Edith M. Elliott. Campus Y sponsors a craft show the first weekend in December. Considers batik; baskets; candlemaking; carvings and sculpture; children's toys; dolls; glass art; handbags and leather accessories; jewelry; lapidary; macrame;

metalsmithing; mobiles; needlecrafts; pillows; pottery; wall hangings; and weavings. Charges 20% commission on sold items. Craftworker sets retail price. Bestsellers: $3-75. Write for applications before September 1.

UNIVERSITY OF SOUTHERN CALIFORNIA, YWCA, Craft Center, University Park, Los Angeles CA 90007. (213)741-6208. Coordinator, USC Craft Center: Jo Ann M. Fried. Craft Center sponsors 2 annual craft shows. "We have 2 craft fairs each year with approximately 100 craftspeople. Commercially-manufactured goods do not qualify. The show is several years old and quite successful." Considers all crafts. Entry fee: $40. Craftworker sets retail price. Write with resume and illustrations of work or call for application.

UNIVERSITY OF THE PACIFIC, University Center, Stockton CA 95211. (209)946-2171. University Center Director: Gary Kleemann. University Center sponsors crafts shows and has exhibit space for craftworkers. Sponsors 2 craft fairs (1 in early December and 1 in late April) per year and "allows occasional craftsmen to come sell their work in the University Center." Considers all crafts. Charges 10% commission on sold items. Craftworker sets retail price. Bestsellers: $2-15. Write with resume and illustrations of work.

VASSAR COLLEGE, College Center, Poughkeepsie NY 12601. (914)452-7000. Manager, College Center: Nanci Howe. College Center sponsors craft shows, has exhibit space for craftworkers, sponsors craftworkers for percentage of sales, holds weekly craft workshops, and has bulletin board where craftworkers can advertise. Considers all handmade crafts by artists or craftworkers. Charges 15% commission on sold items or $12-15 entry fee, depending on nature of event. Craftworker sets retail price. Bestsellers: $1-75. Write with resume for weekend craft sales. Write with illustrations of work, samples, and a request for personal interview for fairs and exhibits.

WESTERN MARYLAND COLLEGE, Westminster MD 21157. (301)876-3752. Director of College Activities: Joan M. Avey. Art department sponsors crafts shows and has exhibit space for craftworkers. College Activities sponsors craftworkers for percentage of sales and has bulletin board where craftworkers can advertise. "We sponsor a program with a working craftsman actually 'doing' his craft. Serves as demonstration in addition to sales." Considers all crafts. Charges 10% commission on sold items. Craftworker sets retail price. Bestsellers: $2-10. Write with illustrations of work.

WORCESTER POLYTECHNIC INSTITUTE, Worcester MA 01609. (617)753-1411, ext. 291. Associate Dean of Students: Bernard H. Brown. Student Affairs Office sponsors craft shows, has exhibit space for craftworkers, sponsors craftworkers for percentage of sales and holds craft workshops. "We have a January intersession period when we could have craftsmen do a 2-3 day workshop." Considers all crafts. Charges 10% commission on sold items. "We only sponsor craftworker if prices are reasonable for students." Bestsellers: $2-10. Write with resume and samples or call for personal interview.

WORCESTER STATE COLLEGE, 486 Chandler St., Worcester MA 01602. (617)752-7700. Director, Student Center and Student Activities: Paul M. Joseph. Student Center sponsors craft shows, has exhibit space for craftworkers, sponsors craftworkers for percentage of sales, holds craft workshops and has bulletin board where craftworkers can advertise. "One of the goals of our new Student Center is to provide an on-going exposure to crafts. We will probably start week-long craft demonstrations/sales and run 1 per month. We expect (would like) to rent 6x6 exhibit spaces by the day or week eventually." Considers all crafts. Craftworker sets retail price. Bestsellers: $1-25. Write with resume and illustrations of work.

XAVIER UNIVERSITY, Office of Student Development, Victory Pkwy., Cincinnati OH 45207. (513)745-3201. Assistant Dean of Student Development: Peggy Dillon. Student Development sponsors craft shows and craftworkers for percentage of sales. "We hold a craft show each year at Christmas. Since we are a small school we can only give each exhibitor about 12x9 space. We normally supply table and chairs; but people with their own set-up are welcome as long as the display is no larger than specified above." Considers all crafts. Entry fee: $10 or 10% commission on sold items. "We use a system of either a flat fee or a percentage." Craftworker sets retail price. Bestsellers: $2-10. Write with resume. Limited number of spaces available.

Companies & Manufacturers

"Crafts fulfill a need in each of us to personalize what comes into our lives. And as we become more and more industrialized, that need for handcrafted items will also increase."

If your motivation as a craftperson is based on Julie Shafler of Julie: Artisan's Gallery's philosophy above, then the last place you may want to look for markets for your crafts is the mass-producing markets of this section.

But if you are interested in making more than $500 for a weaving kit design or model, read on. The listings in this section will buy about 13,000 craft designs in the next year. Buyers range from miniature firms seeking actual handmade merchandise to jewelry manufacturers seeking prototypes.

There are markets for every type of craftworker here— from the ceramacist to the metal sculptor. And, as public interest in crafts grows there will be an increase in the number of items designed after original handicrafts, and a growing need for do-it-yourself craft kits.

Reed & Barton, for example, recently hired five craftspeople to develop a collection for mass production; fine china shops throughout the country are carrying dinnerware imitating handmade pottery; and Spring Mills developed a complete line of linens based on designs from King Tut's tomb.

The listings in this section have been designed to tell you who you should contact and by what means; how soon they'll report back to let you know if they're interested in your work; and by what means they pay [a design (one-time) payment; royalty; or royalty plus design fee].

Once you receive an assignment from a company or manufacturer it is always a good idea to get all dealings in writing. Handshakes and gentlemen's agreements are easier to obtain and more pleasant to work with; but a written agreement is the best way to avoid forgotten or broken promises.

Also, inquire as to whether your signature will appear on the product. Push for this as it is an excellent way to increase your exposure. Consumers who are pleased with the first piece they buy designed by you will watch for your future work— and so will other manufacturers. Some companies have policies against including signatures or names; others make information about the craftperson a standard item to be included— it gives the mass-produced piece a bit of personal appeal.

Don't limit yourself to the markets in this section. If you feel you have a product that would have mass market appeal, keep your eyes open for the right company to produce it. An excellent place to find potential manufacturers for your work is by browsing through gift and stationery shops. Write the producer of products similar to your own; ask if they would be interested in working with you and send photos of your work as samples.

You can also find companies by sending a press release to publications such as *Greetings*. Include a black and white photo, and ask the magazine to include your article in their New Product section.

A&A TROPHY MANUFACTURERS, 11523 Harry Hines, Dallas TX 75229. (214)241-3211. Contact: William P. Hess. Kit and jewelry manufacturer. Products are die cast in metal then painted, and include a 22" authentic ⅛" scale model of an oil derrick and a 7"-tall ¼" scale model pump jack. Buys about 500 designs annually. Payment determined by quantity and time it takes to develop. Send samples. Reports in 2 weeks.

AMERICAN MINIATURES, 102 2nd Ave. N., Mount Vernon IA 52314. (319)895-6371. President: Tim Morrissey. Manufacturer and distributor of miniature houses, furniture and accessories. Buys and sometimes commissions crafts to use as prototypes; and uses craftworkers to help with product distribution. Buys 10-20+ designs annually. Pays $100 minimum for furniture; $25-50 for accessory items. Products are of metal and wood. Works on 1"-1' scale. Call or write with samples. Reports in 2 weeks.

ANGELIQUE JEWELRY, 8400 Magnolia, Suite G, Santee CA 92071. (714)449-6050. Vice President: Jeff Elden. Manufacturer of fashion jewelry and gift items using ceramics, wood, feathers, beads and fabrics. Specializes in florals and natural themes. Especially needs "handcrafted looks, but must be able to be produced in some volume." Buys 50-100 original designs annually to use as prototypes. Pays $25 minimum or royalty for a group of jewelry designs. Send samples or photos.

C. J. BATES & SON, Rt. 9A, Chester CT 06412. (203)526-5381. Manager, National Accounts: Cliff Earley. Manufacturer of knitting needles; crochet hooks; embroidery hoops; and knitting and crochet accessories. Buys crafts in bulk for resale; and commissions and buys designs to use as prototypes. Uses 40-50 designs annually. Payment for knitting, crocheting and embroidery based on garment. Send resume. Reports in 1 week.

THE BEADERY, Box 178, Canonchet Rd., Hope Valley RI 02832. (401)539-2366. Vice President: W. Henry Wagner. "We package our parent company's craft items. Sell through mail, wholesalers, distributors and dealers. Also sell bulk beads and spooled wire. Produce craft kits consisting mainly of our product." Buys about 3 designs annually for mass production. Pays $8-11/hour for design ideas with instructions; $4-7/hour for variation creations. Write explaining qualifications, requesting personal interview. Include samples or actual work. Reports in 2 weeks.

Mary Chilton Ferguson, experienced cake decorator, earns a 5% royalty on sales of this cake saver kit, designed for Flo-Sculpt TM Studios, New York City. Vice President James Fobel will pay a minimum of $50 to persons designing a Flo-Sculpt TM project or teaching for the firm.

EMILE BERNAT & SONS CO., Depot and Mendon Streets, Uxbridge MA 01569. (617)278-2414; "no collect calls." Craft Design Coordinator: Sydelle Byer or Laurel Horvat. Manufacturer of latch hook rugs and pillows; quick stitch; needlepoint; and stitchery— both stamped canvases and kits. "Our needlework line is very varied and includes contemporary, traditional, florals, geometrics, etc. with emphasis on texture and dimension. We purchase designs of all types to be used as printed canvases or kits." Pays minimum $150, rugs; $75, pillows; $75, needlepoint. Payment determined by size and complexity. Write explaining qualifications and send slides and drawings of work. Reports in 2 weeks.

BERSTED'S HOBBY CRAFT INC., Box 40, Monmouth IL 61462. (309)734-7011. Sales Manager: Roger Bersted. Kit manufacturer and bulk supplies. Products are kits of plaster casting; papier mache; basketry; liquid rubber; and chair caning. Buys crafts in bulk for resale; commissions craftworkers; buys design outright; and sponsors Kiddy Kraft Klub craft show. Minimum payment is 5% of invoice price. Submit resume and sample; arrange personal interview. Reports in 2 weeks.

BGI CRAFTS INTERNATIONAL, 12821 Western Ave., Garden Grove CA 92641. (714)636-1570. President: Ilene Miller. Manufacturer of macrame and weaving supplies; porcelain beads; porcelain wind chimes; ceramic beads; and gift items. "We sell finished products, kits, and open stock." Buys and commissions "hundreds of designs annually" to use as prototypes, and buys crafts in bulk for resale. Payment varied; determined by originality and quality of workmanship. Write with samples for a personal interview. Reports in 3 weeks.

KEN BROWN STUDIO, Box 637 CW, Hugo OK 74743. (405)326-7544. Contact: Ken Brown. Studio of calligraphic art. Sells parchment reproductions of calligraphic art, ink drawings and decals. Line includes poems, quotations and religious prints. Interested in made-ups of prints. Commissions craftworkers who are familiar with the work. Buys 40-50 designs annually. Pays $20 minimum for memory boxes and plaques. Call for personal interview. Reports in 2 weeks.

CAROUSEL CRAFTS COMPANY, Box 42549, Houston TX 77042. National Sales Manager: H. Allen Bryant. Manufacturer of needlecraft kits. Buys crafts/designs to use as prototypes for products. "We review sample before purchasing design." Payment is negotiable. Submit resume, samples and/or actual work. Reports in 3 weeks.

CHOCOLATE AND VANILLA LTD., 460 W. 24th St., New York NY 10011. (212)675-6600. Contact: Peter Listro. Estab. 1977. Considers ceramics and woodcrafting. Special need for food reproduction in ceramics. Fine handmade production line items; utilitarian and/or decorative. Price range: (retail) $1-40; bestsellers: (retail) $2-10. Buys outright; pays royalty. Submit color slides. SASE. Reports in 2 weeks. Dealer pays insurance for exhibited work.
Profile: "We buy whimsical, unique, and functional items from craftworkers and resell to better gift and department stores on a national basis. We will also arrange for the limited manufacture of a sculptured item using the old world method and buy it outright or arrange a royalty for the craftworker; e.g. dinner bells, paperweights, magnets, pen holders, pencil sharpeners and bookends." Heaviest wholesale buying time: February-March and September-October; best selling time: January-February and November-December.

COLONIAL CRAFTSMEN, INC., Box 1644, Wayne NJ 07470. (201)696-7700. President: Robert Kunz. Manufacturer of wood craft kits; functional yet decorative designs. Buys and commissions designs to use as prototypes for products and orders demos or build-ups of products for use by dealers (furnishes raw materials). Pays $1-25 for tole painting and $10-50 for dollhouse assembly. Submit resume. "It is helpful for craftworker to be from local area." Reports as soon as possible.

CRAFTS LTD., 295 Melville Rd., Farmingdale NY 11735. (516)249-0949. Manager: Wiliam N. Alter. Manufactures 3-dimensional needlepoint kits. Buys imported crafts in bulk for resale and crafts/designs outright. Uses about 25 designs annually. Payment for original gifts is open. Submit resume, samples or actual work. Reports in 4 weeks.

CREATIVE PAPERS, 41 Main St., Jaffrey NH 03452. (603)532-8736. Director Design/Product: Lew Fifield. Publisher of greeting cards; note papers; and stationery. "Ours is a 2-dimensional product to which 3-dimensional art may be adapted, or an image of a 3-dimensional form reproduced. We have a fairly sophisticated 'museum quality' product line that is geared to better shops and department stores. Although we are not limited to any particular theme we are interested only in work that will appear to the more sophisticated or cultivated taste. Perhaps certain 3-D forms could be used as models for package or product design." Buys 200-300 2-dimensional designs and illustrations annually. Send photos of work. Reports in 6 weeks.

CUSTOM HOUSE OF NEEDLE ARTS AND DESIGN, INC., 76 Elm St., W. Townsend MA 01474. (617)597-6639. President: June S. Clark. Manufactures crewel embroidery kits silkscreened on linen. Buys and commissions designs. "We either purchase designs or work on royalty basis." Buys 10 designs annually. Rate of payment depends upon size and detail. Pays $25-100 or royalty of 5% of wholesale for embroidery designs and $15-50 for original design embroidery; must include yarn count and stitch instruction. Submit resume and samples. Reports in 2 weeks.

CUSTOM-FOAM CRAFTS, INC., Box 712, 1001 N. Rowe St., Ludington MI 49431. (616)843-3401. Vice President, Sales: Lorne Farley. "We manufacture all basic shapes of Styrofoam for the craft and floral industries. We also make complete project kits and have a new Foam Coater that should revolutionize the craft industry." Commissions craftworkers to evaluate products and possibly make kit prototypes. Commissions 10+ designs annually. Pays 2% royalty on sales of kits. Write with samples explaining qualifications. Reports in 3 weeks.

DESHANE MINIATURE GALLERIES, 6262 S. Jamestown, Tulsa OK 74136. (918)743-6711. Contact: Ann L. Nelson. Miniatures manufacturer. Produces decorative accessories for dollhouses and miniature rooms in wood, metal, paper, ceramics, clay, fabric, oil, and watercolor. "We do not specialize in a particular theme or style though we do have a number of Oriental items. All items must be 1"-1' scale." Buys crafts in bulk for resale; sometimes buys and commissions crafts. Pays 30% of wholesale price. Submit resume and samples. Reports in 3 weeks.

DESIGN DIVISION-REGENCY/CENTURY GREETINGS, 1500 W. Monroe, Chicago IL 60607. (312)666-8686. Art Director: David Cuthbertson. Publishers of all styles Christmas cards — full-color reproduction, mixed media. Buys designs to use as prototypes for one-of-a-kind card reproduction. Buys 50 designs annually. Pays $100 for any media; original returned. Submit resume. Reports in 3-4 weeks. "Format of designs should fit some standard rectangular size; prefer to work from slides of works."

FANTASY CREATIONS, 337 Glenn Ave., Lawrenceville NJ 08648. (709)883-7751. General Manager: Chomy Garces. Manufacturers accessories for dollhouses, mainly nursery items or toys in miniature (1"-1' scale) in bread dough and wood. Co-sponsors a miniature show, "Miniature Makers Society," and offers 2 seminars annually. Buys and commissions work. Buys about 200 designs annually. Pays $10-25 for dolls; 3 miniflowers for $1-3 each; and 30c-50c for foods. "We also use ½" scale for Christmas tree decorations; submit by August." Send resume, samples and/or actual work. Reports in 4 weeks.

FEDERAL SMALLWARES CORP., 85 5th Ave. (16th St.), New York NY 10003. Manufacturers "old fashioned" miniature furniture and accessories out of wood, metal, etc.; 1"-1' scale. Buys crafts in bulk for resale and buys work outright to use as prototypes for products. Pays 5% royalty. Submit resume. Reports in 2 weeks.

FITZGERALD ENTERPRISES, INC., 1610 E. 12th St., Oakland CA 94606. (415)533-3727. Merchandise Coordinator: Penny Brown. Craft wholesaler/manufacturer/publisher. Sells beads, cords, rings and other accessories for macrame and weaving and publishes books for the craft market. Buys crafts in bulk for resale; offers advice to craftworker; adds and promotes new ideas to the industry; and buys and commissions work. Minimum payment: $50. Submit resume, samples, actual work and/or arrange interview. Reports in 2 weeks.

FLO-SCULPT STUDIOS, INC., 8 W. 19th St., New York NY 10011. (212)675-8892. Vice President: James Fobel. Kit-manufacturer. "We are manufacturers of Flo-Sculpt (TM), which is a pre-mixed, non-toxic acrylic substance for making 3-D appliques. Flo-Sculpt is placed in a standard cake decorating bag with decorative tip and squeezed onto waxed paper. The designs air dry overnight and are then painted with acrylic, spray paint or enamel and then glued onto accessories, furniture, walls, etc. Anything you can do with cake decorating you can do with Flo-Sculpt — and it will be permanent. We make special kits that include the Flo-Sculpt, all tips, designs and materials necessary to complete any designated project." Buys crafts in bulk for resale, and "need teachers of Flo-Sculpt. Must be experienced cake decorators; send photos." Works on commission and buys work outright. Pays $50 minimum/Flo-Sculpt design project; $50 minimum/day for teacher. Payment determined by job. Write explaining qualifications. Reports in 3 weeks.

GALLO MANUFACTURING CO., 1312 N. Memorial Dr., Racine WI 53404. (414)633-4281. President: Michael S. Gallo. Manufactures woodcraft hobby kits. Buys crafts in bulk for resale and buys crafts/designs outright. Write for personal interview. Reports in 1 week.

GO FLY A KITE INC., 1434 3rd Ave., New York NY 10028. (212)988-8885. President: Andrea Bahadur. Manufactures, designs and imports kites. "We deal in kites and kite accessories on all levels from mass market $1.29 kites to handcrafted $500 kites in paper, cloth, plastic, bamboo, birch dowels, etc. Birds, butterflies, airplanes — or anything one would expect to see in the sky — are particularly popular." Buys crafts in bulk for resale and buys and commissions crafts/designs. Uses 20 single designs (30,000 pieces) annually. Payment varies. Submit resume, sample, actual work and/or arrange interview. Usually reports in 3 weeks.

GRAPHIC IDEAS, 3108 5th Ave., San Diego CA 92103. Art Director: Jill Timm. "We create new toys, crafts and products for other firms; also premiums, gifts and promotional items.

Sometimes we manufacture and sometimes we sell concept and idea. Whatever is created will need to be mass produced at a low cost. In the past we have produced a lot of paper items (card, calendar, games) but we are open to any good idea or product in any area." Buys 25-30 designs annually. Pays a $150 minimum for product ideas; $100 minimum for designs and illustrations; and sometimes 2-5% royalties. Submit resume, samples or photos. Reports in 4 weeks.

HOBE CIE. LTD., 138 S. Columbus Ave., Mt. Vernon NY 10553. (914)664-2640. Jewelry manufacturer. Commissions new product development. Uses 10,000 designs annually. Payment varies. Send samples and arrange interview. Reports in 4 weeks.

J. D. ENTERPRISES, 581 W. 10th St., Pittsburg CA 94565. (415)432-0300. Contact: Jim Dolhanyk. Manufactures wooden craft products, mostly tole boards and plaques. Specializes in redwood; heavy demand for Christmas items. "We manufacture wooden plaques for decoupage; tole; and decorating and are open for new ideas." Write and call. Reports "promptly."

JACQU MIN INC., 7601 Forsyth Blvd., St. Louis MO 63105. (314)726-0474. President: Jacqueline Schaefer. Manufactures miniature dollhouse accessories in wood, ceramics and tin pot metal. Submit resume and samples. Reports in 1 week.

JO-HAN MODELS, INC., 17255 Moran Ave., Detroit MI 48212. (313)366-2230. President: John Haenle Jr. Manufactures plastic scale model airplane and car kits and built-up promotional models for the automotive field. Submit resume. Reports in 1 week.

LAWBRE CO., 888 Tower Rd., Unit J, Mundelein IL 60060. (312)949-0031. Director of Marketing: Cathy Oldenburg. "We manufacture dollhouses; kits for flooring dollhouses; architectural pieces for outside; exterior and interior molding; hydrocal cement fireplaces; and circulars and straight staircases. Houses are made of 7-ply, ⅜" plywood; castings are of hydrocal cement; and all kinds of flooring. Houses are of various styles, 19th or 18th century, as are our fireplaces and architectural pieces." Buys crafts in bulk for resale; and buys and commissions designs. Uses 5 designs annually. Payment depends on item and skill or craftworker. Reports in 1 week.

LEISURE SUPPLIES INC., 675 W. Terrace Dr., San Dimas CA 91773. (213)335-0558. Vice President, Marketing: Dave Archibald. Kit manufacturer with macrame and weaving supplies. Buys crafts in bulk for resale; and buys and commissions designs to use as prototypes. Pays $25-200 depending on items produced. Write or call Jean Jenkins for personal interview. Reports as soon as possible.

LEWIS CORPORATION, 543 S. Vermont, Palatine IL 60067. (312)359-3900. President: John M. Lewis. Manufacturer and distributor. Estab. 1970. Represents 50-70 craftworkers. Considers leatherworking. Handmade production-line items; utilitarian and/or decorative. Price range: $1-2.50. Buys outright. Retail price set by joint agreement. Reports in 3 weeks. Work may be shipped or hand-delivered. Dealer pays shipping to shop. "Items are cataloged and sold nationally." Customers are mostly male; 16-30 years old. Best selling time: winter.

Plastic stencils, such as the one pictured, are in demand by Stencil-Magic, New York City kit manufacturer. During 1979 Stencil-Magic will buy and commission 10-15 custom stencil designs, paying $25-75.

LIFE-LIKE PRODUCTS INC., 1600 Union Ave., Baltimore MD 21211. Vice President, Marketing Services: Jay Kramer. Hobby/craft material manufacturer. Produces miniature trees and landscape materials. Buys and commissions designs to develop a line based on products. Submit resume and arrange interview. Reports in 1 week.

LOVE-BUILT TOYS AND CRAFTS, 2907 Lake Forest Rd., Box 5459, Tahoe City CA 95730. (916)583-1555. Contact: Dale C. Prohaska Jr. Sells patterns to make wooden toys. Buys designs for custom-made wooden toys to be reproduced in woodworking pattern. Also buys craft project lesson plans for grades K-12 using toy-making supplies. Pays $25+, depending on amount of work needed to complete the project.

MARV-PAUL INC., 1650 3rd Ave., New York NY 10028. (212)534-1012. Manager: Joe Block. Manufactures all-wood dollhouses (live smoke out of chimney, electric wiring, and plumbing included). Buys crafts in bulk for resale. Write with samples explaining qualifications. Reports in about 3 days.

MAXWELL HOUSE MINIATURES, 310 Hillcrest Dr., Edinboro PA 16412. (814)734-4594. Contact: Sandy or Pam Maxwell. Miniature doors and window manufacturer. Produces wood windows and doors in Victorian, Federal, Colonial and modern styles. Sponsors craft show "Maxwell House Miniature Show and Sale." Reports in 1 week.

MAXWELL INTERNATIONAL LTD., 1338 W. Washington Blvd., Venice CA 90291. Art Director: Victoria Waller. Kit manufacturer and yarn and cord supplier. Sells synthetic macrame cords; acrylic; poly-olefins; synthetic weaving and novelty yarns; cardboard weaving looms; kits; and modern and natural craft products. Buys and commissions designs to use as prototypes for possible kits. Offers opportunity to use yarns for salesman trade shows. Buys 50-100 designs annually. Pays $5/simple, small weaving; $50/large weaving; $5/small macrame item; $20/larger macrame hangers; $40/large macrame wall hangings. "In sample requirements include instructions and diagrams; we pay more accordingly. Not all samples require detailed instructions and diagram." Craftworkers must be from San Francisco or Los Angeles area. "We need most samples August-December, preparing for January trade show." Submit resume to arrange interview. Reports in 3-4 weeks.

ME ENTERPRISES, 2650 Country Club Dr., Glendora CA 91740. (213)335-2710. Managing Director: Allan Markowitz. Manufactures portable weaving looms, wind cords and yarns; imports jute; and wholesales wooden beads and metal rings. Buys and commissions designs to use as prototypes for customers who occasionally need made-ups. Buys 1-4 designs annually. Pays $25 minimum for macrame or weaving samplers. Craftworkers must be from local area. Call for interview. Reports in 3 weeks.

MINIATURE REFLECTIONS, 409 S. 1st, Evansville WI 53536. (608)882-4682. Contact: Patricia Diedrich. Manufactures needlepoint kits for miniature rugs; supplies miniature-making supplies; hardwoods; and books and magazines about period decorating and miniatures. Specializes in period styling such as Victorian and Colonial. "We do our own design work but are interested in expanding and working with craftpersons." Submit resume and photos. Reports as soon as possible.

MINIS BY ME, 606 David St., West Hempstead NY 11552. Contact: Marilyn Davidson or Elaine Fleischman. Work with miniature furniture and accessories. Specializes in modern designs mostly in Lucite and/or related materials. Also interested in dried flowers, macrame, metals, etc. Work should be finished completely, 1"-1' scale. Buys crafts in bulk for resale; supports cottage industry. Commissions 20-50 designs annually. Pay for assembly of items to our specifications based on minimum wage. Submit resume and sample. "Prefer local area craftworkers; must stick to minimum number items as per prior agreement." Reports in 2 weeks or as soon as possible.

STEPHEN A. MINTZ COMPANY, 705 Scottsdale Rd., Westminster MD 21157. (301)876-6323. Secretary/Treasurer: Stephen Allan Mintz. Manufacturer of fine quality aluminum and stainless steel toys and jewelry. Specializes in railroad and geometric toys. Buys and commissions designs to use as prototypes. Buys 4 designs annually. Payment depends on size of object. Submit resume. Reports in 3 weeks.

MISS BOUTIQUE INC., 112 W. 34th St., Rm. 710, New York NY 10001. (212)564-5168. President: Richard N. Bloch. Fashion firm. Manufactures a variety of children's items in natural fibers. Buys and commissions designs to use as prototypes. Uses 200 designs annually. Submit resume and actual work.

MORGAN LOOM FACTORY, Railroad Engine House, Guilford CT 06437. (203)453-6341. President: A. Licata. Kit manufacturer/loom manufacturer. Manufactures small hand looms and weaving kits. Buys and commissions designs to use as projects for weaving kits. Buys 4-6 designs annually. Pays maximum of $15 for made-up loom samples and maximum of $250 for weaving kit designs. Submit resume, samples and/or actual work. Reports in 2 weeks.

NASHCO PRODUCTS, INC., 1015 N. Main Ave., Scranton PA 18508. (717)347-4210. Order Department: Gladys Malko. Manufactures decorated and undecorated toleware items in steel sheet — black or raw. Specializes in trays, wastebaskets, umbrella stands, silent butlers and canisters. Buys 3-6 designs annually. Submit samples. Reports in 4 weeks.

NATCOL CRAFTS, INC., Box 299, Redlands CA 92373. (714)795-2407. National Sales Manager: Jason Ott. Manufacturer of candle molds, resin molds and products, liquid craft products, silk flowers, dough art and plaster molds. "We aim at producing whatever the consumer has a need for. Will consider any new product idea." Buys 5-10 prototypes annually. Also gives assistance to craftworkers in the form of direction, referrals and encouragement. Pays $50 minimum/mold design; $100 minimum or precentage/new product idea; $15-50/flower arrangement. Call or write for personal interview. Christmas craft projects must be submitted by August 1. Usually reports in 1 week; "varies with need or workload."

NICHOLAS PRESS, 132 Nassau St., New York NY 10038. Art Director: A. Goldson. Manufactures everyday greeting cards, seasonals, posters and notes. Style varies but specifically leans toward more modern design concept for Christmas lines. "Good possibility for buying designs to use as prototypes but have bought none to date. Since this is a new market for us, research and craftworkers themselves will have to aid us in defining proper minimum and maximum payment." Submit resume and samples, "also suggested price for designs and all other basic information." Reports in 4 weeks.

OCA CRAFTS CO., 852 Hawthrone Dr., Pittsburgh PA 15235. (412)241-7215. President: Jean Hennel. Manufactures OCA kits; silk-padded and painted pictures used for greeting cards; hanging pictures; fire screens; table tops; clothing; and purses. Buys and commissions designs to develop ancient Oriental art form found in museums. "Finished worked design/product prices higher according to design and size." Prices for design only are 5x7 sketch greeting card design, $2-5; 9x12-2'x2' design/sketch picture or table, $5-25; 2'x2'-3'x6' pictures for fireplace and regular screen, $25-100. "Craftworker must know art form and how it works." Submit resume. Reports in 2 weeks.

C. M. OFFRAY & SON INC., 261 Madison Ave., New York NY 10016. Creative Director: Ann Karas. Manufacturer and importer of woven edge fashion ribbons in polyester grosgrain, satin, velvet, jacquards, checks, plaids and polka dots. Colors and patterns updated seasonally to comply with fashion trends. Buys designs for new end uses for ribbons; only interested in original design concepts. Write for interview. Reports in 2 weeks.

HAZEL PEARSON HANDICRAFTS, 16017 E. Valley Blvd., Industry CA 91744. (213)968-4645. Product Manager: Ginny Ross. Manufactures all forms of needlework (crewel, applique, needlepoint, etc.), macrame, weaving and other miscellaneous craft kits. Buys and commissions designs to use as prototypes, in kits or in "how-to" books. Uses 250 designs annually. Pay $25-250 for prototype design, depending on what is purchased. Submit resume and photos. Reports in 1-4 weeks, depending on product or idea.

POLICH'S DESERT PRODUCTS AND MANUFACTURING, 9736 E. Apache Trail, Mesa AZ 85027. (602)986-9188. Contact: Carol or Don Polich. Manufactures ceramic beads for macrame and jewelry. Buys 50 designs annually. Pays minimum $25 for design. Submit resume and samples. Reports in 1 week.

REPLICA SEA CRAFT STUDIOS, Box 319, Staten Island NY 10304. (212)981-4190. Designer: Richard Surving. Manufacturer of model boat kits and model fish kits; supplies paper templates, plaster mesh and molding compound with kits. Fish are life-size (30''); boats are ½" - 1' scale. Commissions craftworkers to create build-ups for in-store promotion. "Kits and materials are provided free for craftspeople that are given commission. Handicapped people will be given preference and special assistance where necessary." We will need about 200 units in the next 6 months." Pays $100-300/model. Write with photos of work, explaining qualifications and requesting personal interview, or call for personal interview. "Applicants that seem to qualify must build 1 model from kit, as directed, before contract is given. Models take from 20-30 hours to build; the artist must be sensitive to boat or fish models." Reports in 2 weeks.

SELEXOR DISPLAYS INC., 1916 Park Ave., New York NY 10037. (212)368-7791. Director of Marketing: R. McCarthy. Manufactures trade show/showroom exhibits and displays constructed in wood, Plexiglas and miscellaneous materials. Commissions designs to use for customer requirements. "We counsel the craftworker in use of materials." Submit resume and samples; write for interview. Reports in 1 week.

STENCIL-MAGIC, 8 W. 19th St., New York NY 10011. (212)675-8892. Vice President: James Fobel. Manufactures pre-cut stencils, stencil patterns, stencil kits, brushes, paints, stencil paper, books and instructions. Buys and commissions crafts to use as prototypes; and buys crafts in bulk for resale. "Designs must work as stencils, meaning the designer must have knowledge of stencil bridges or registration marks." Buys and commissions 10-15 designs annually. Pays $25-75/custom stencil design. Payment determined by job. Write explaining qualifications. Reports in 3 weeks.

Replica Sea Craft Studios, Staten Island, New York, will provide free kits and materials to craftworkers working for them on a commission basis. In a 6-month period Designer Richard Surving predicts the kit manufacturing firm will need 200 units, bringing craft designers payments of $100-500. To be considered write with photos of work explaining qualifications and requesting personal interview, or call for interview. "Applicants that qualify must build 1 model from kit, as directed, before contract is given."

SYMMOGRAPHY, INC., Rt. 3, Box 32, Strawberry Plains TN 37871. (615)933-1331. President: Jim Bartram. Manufactures string art kits; oak reproduction tables; book racks; upholstered solid foam youth chairs; and ottomans. Buys and commissions designs to use as prototypes. "Ideas; designs; and new kits can be functional or decorative. We need simple designs for Plexiglas items or kits and small wood items to utilize oak scrap." Minimum payment is $50-100, negotiable. Submit resume. Reports in 1 week.

TEX-CRAFT CO. INC., 311 E. Park St., Moonachie NJ 07074. (201)440-2500. President: Arnold Epstein. Manufactures Schiffli embroidery emblems; sew on and iron on patches; iron on and embroidery initials; and belting design trimmings. Uses fabric, denim, cork, polyurethane, and velveteen in timely and age-old themes. Buys designs to use as design prototypes. Payment varies. Submit resume and samples. Reports in 2 weeks.

TEXTURED YARN ARTS, INC., 1329 Aloha St., Seattle WA 98109. General Manager: Gary Haldane. Manufactures cord and yarns for weaving, macrame and other craft uses. Buys and commissions designs to use as prototypes. "We welcome suggestions for craft yarns and cord." Buys 30 designs annually. Pays $25-100 for new weaving or macrame designs. Submit samples. Reports in 8 weeks.

THORENS MUSIC BOXES, Division of Elpa Marketing Industries, Inc., Box 1050, Thorens and Atlantic Ave., New Hyde Park NY 11040. (516)746-3002. Marketing Manager: Edwin Lesson. Manufactures and imports musical movements for music boxes, mounting movements in wood, glass, and brass cases, and in jewelry boxes, figurines, and picture frames. Buys designs to use as prototypes; buys crafts in bulk for resale; and hires local casemakers to help expand present gift line. Buys 6-8+ designs annually. Pays $50-150/box design. Submit resume and samples of actual work. Reports in 3 weeks.

E. J. TOWLE COMPANY, 760 Market St., San Francisco CA 94102. President: W.G. Lefort. Manufactures silver, gold, and gold-filled jewelry with particular emphasis on Northwest coast Indian designs and Hawaiian designs. Buys designs to use as prototypes. Buys 10-20 designs annually. Pay $75-200. Send resume and samples. Reports in 2 weeks.

BETTY WIITA DECORATOR CRAFTS, INC., 500 W. Chestnut St., Clayton NJ 08312. (609)881-2218. Designer: Betty Wiita. Manufactures dried flower kits with dried natural materials. Specializes in floral arrangements; candle rings; and wall hangings. Buys designs; looking for new ideas. Payment is negotiable. Submit resume and photos. Reports in 1 week.

YALEY ENTERPRISES, 145 Sylvester Rd., San Francisco CA 94080. (415)761-3428. President: Thomas Yaley. Manufactures candle crafting supplies, macrame supplies and bulk candle waxes. Buys designs. Call for personal interview. Reports in 2 weeks.

YE OLDE HUFF N PUFF, 4820 W. Whitehall Rd., Pennsylvania Furnace PA 16865. Contact: Shirley Koontz. Manufactures model railroad car kits, HO and O scale, wood with metal detail. Looking for ideas for new products in model railroading.

Department Stores

Department store merchandising usually brings to mind production-line items. It's evident when you see boxes of the same shirt being unpacked by store clerks. But the production-line stops — even in department stores — when it comes to craft merchandising.

More and more department stores are looking for quality, one-of-a-kind (and, of course, production) crafts ranging from batiks to jewelry. Their merchandising mix no longer calls for what they can only buy in bulk. As consumer demand for crafts continues to grow in the marketplace, department stores try to satisfy that demand by making crafts more readily available.

Department stores provide a double-edged market for the craftworker. Not only can you sell your work on a wholesale basis, but there are often opportunities for your crafts to be used for display purposes. Keep in mind, then, that sometimes your work might be considered by both a buyer and a display manager.

But be careful. Study your market. If you're making expensive items, don't contact the local five-and-ten-cent-store. Contact the expensive stores. If a local department store is already carrying crafts, watch for trends in the merchandise they're carrying.

At times you'll probably have the opportunity to sell your crafts to a department store chain. Chances are the buyer will want to put your work in most, if not all, of the stores. So be prepared to meet hefty orders.

Wholesaling your crafts to department stores can be demanding, but if you have your sights set on building your sales, don't ignore this lucrative market — this may be your department.

BROOKNEAL DEPARTMENT STORE, 101 Main St., Brookneal VA 24528. Vice President: Katharine R. Holt. Gift department buys (and sometimes consigns) dinnerware; handbags and leather accessories; jewelry; silverwork; wall hangings; and weavings. Handmade production lines only. Display department uses carvings, sculpture and wall hangings. Handmade production lines only. Retail price range: $3-50; set by store. Write with illustrations of work.

M. M. COHN CO., 510 Main St., Little Rock AR 72203. (501)374-3311, ext. 266. Gift and Dinnerware Buyer: Susan Deaton. Gift and dinnerware department buys and consigns baskets; dinnerware; pillows; pottery; silverwork; wall hangings; and weaving. One-of-a-kind and handmade production lines OK. Retail price range: $5-150; set by joint agreement. Submit resume and illustrations of work or arrange interview. "We try to appeal to a carriage trade apparel customer who is interested in both quality and uniqueness."

THE DUNLAP CO., 200 Greenleaf Ave., Ft. Worth TX 76107. (817)336-4985. Merchandise Manager, Home Furnishings: Russell Womack. Write with illustrations of work and resume.
Resale Items: Home furnishings department will consider baskets, carvings, sculpture, Christmas ornament, dinnerware, furniture, pillows, pottery, silverwork, wall hangings and weaving for resale. "For most items we need production work that can supply between 5 and 20 stores." Retail price range: $3-300; set by store "based on cost and item."
Props: Home furnishings department will consider buying baskets, carvings and sculpture, Christmas ornaments, handmade furniture, pillows, pottery and wall hangings. One-of-a-kind or handmade production lines OK.

THE FAIR, 315 Central Ave., Valley City ND 58072. General Merchandise Manager: R. Munkeby. Buys crafts outright; consigns crafts for resale; and sponsors craft shows.

GEORGE FILLEY DEPARTMENT STORE, 214 S. Main St., Victoria TX 77901. Contact: George Filley. Antique department buys baskets; carvings and sculpture; dinnerware; dolls; furniture; jewelry; pottery; silverwork; wall hangings; and weavings for resale. Display department considers handmade furniture and pottery for use as props. Store sets retail price. Send samples.

A. GOLDMANN'S & SONS, 930 W. Mitchell St., Milwaukee WI 53204. (414)645-9100. General Manager: Carl M. Brown. Art and needlework and housewares departments buy adult games; baskets; carvings; pillows; pottery; sculpture; wall hangings; and weavings for resale. Handmade production-line items only. Store sets retail price. "We could sell crafts up to $30 retail." Local craftworkers should call for interview or write with illustrations of their work.

HEMPWILL-WELLS CO., 13th & J Sts., Lubbock TX 79408. (806)763-3411 or 795-4333. Display Director: Mrs. Vern Wiggins. Display department buys Christmas ornaments; handmade furniture; and wall hangings for use as props. Particularly interested in spring on formulating plans for Christmas windows and interiors. Handmade production lines only. "Only large items are appropriate for our large display areas." Write with illustrations of work.

S.F. ISZARD CO., 150 N. Main St., Elmira NY 14902. (607)734-7171. Assistant General Merchandise Manager: Robert Hooker. Buys and consigns baskets; carvings and sculpture; Christmas ornaments; dinnerware; handbags and leather accessories; jewelry; pillows; pottery; and silverwork. One-of-a-kind and handmade production lines OK. Retail price range: $5-100; store sets retail price. Submit resume; illustrations of work; and arrange interview. "We are a 2-unit department store."

MAN CLOTHING & JEWELRY CO., 209 Main St., Man WV 25635. Ladies, furniture and jewelry departments buy baskets; carvings; sculpture; Christmas ornaments; dinnerware; furniture; handbags and leather accessories; jewelry; pillows; silverwork; wall hangings; and weavings for resale. Retail price set by joint agreement.

MERKEL'S DEPARTMENT STORE, 74-76 Margaret St., Plattsburgh NY 12901. Buyer: Deborah McNamee. Write with illustrations of work, send samples or call for interview. Store sets retail price.
Resale Items: Buys baskets; Christmas ornaments; dinnerware; dolls; handbags and leather accessories; jewelry; pillows; pottery; wall hangings; and weavings for resale. Will consider "anything that would be interesting for the store." Considers one-of-a-kind designer and production-line crafts.
Props: Considers one-of-a-kind crafts. Buys outright.

MOSTELLER'S INC., 19-27 N. Church St., West Chester PA 19380. (215)696-0582. General Merchandise Manager: James L. Mosteller. Advertising and Sales Promotion Manager: H. Harold Barnett. Write with resume and illustrations of work to arrange interview.
Resale Items: Home furnishings department will consider buying or consigning adult games; baskets; carvings and sculpture; Christmas ornaments; dinnerware; dolls; handbags and leather accessories; jewelry; pillows; silverwork; and wall hangings. One-of-a-kind designer, and production lines OK. Retail price range: $1-100; set by joint agreement. "Need gift type items especially at Christmas."
Props: Anthony D'Orazio, display manager. Considers buying or leasing baskets; carvings and sculpture; children's toys; Christmas ornaments; handmade furniture; pillows; pottery; and wall hangings. One-of-a-kind designer and production-line crafts OK.
Shows: Advertising and Sales Promotion department sponsors 1 show annually. "Hope to start smaller shows throughout the year." Write for prospectus.

PRIEHS DEPARTMENT STORE, 60-66 Macomb St., Mount Clemens MI 48043. (313)463-4567. General Manager: George W. Priehs. Write with resume and samples/illustrations of work.
Resale Items: Mrs. W. Cummings, buyer of hosiery, budget lingerie, candy, books, gifts, cards and stationery. Considers adult games; carvings; sculpture; children's toys; Christmas ornaments; dinnerware; dolls; furniture; jewelry; pillows; and silverwork. Handmade production-line items only. Prices set by store depending upon item's quality, workmanship and originality.
Props: Milo D'Oriole, display manager, store planning and development, and equipment buyer. Considers buying carvings; sculpture; Christmas ornaments; handmade furniture; and pottery.

SPURGEON MERCANTILE CO., 822 W. Washington Blvd., Chicago IL 60607. Buyer: Tom Bloyd. Arts & Crafts department buys adult games; children's toys; wall hangings; and weavings for resale. Buyer sets retail price. Call or write for interview.

THE VALLEY, 1423 Washington St., Box 111, Vicksburg MS 39180. (601)636-6121. General Manager: Ray L. Bolmes. Buys and consigns baskets; carvings and sculpture; dinnerware; dolls; furniture; jewelry; pillows; pottery; silverwork; wall hangings; and weavings. Display department uses baskets; carvings; sculpture; and handmade furniture. One-of-a-kind and handmade production lines OK. Store sets retail price. Write or call for interview.

WATKINS, INC., Box 89, Quanah TX 79252. (817)663-2261. General Manager: Douglas Jeffrey. Fabric department buys and consigns Christmas ornaments; dinnerware; pillows; wall hangings; and weaving for resale. Handmade production lines only. Retail price range: $2-30; set by store. Write with resume and samples.

WOODCHOP, 35 Main St., Warrenton VA 22186. Contact: Roy Anderson. Buys various crafts for resale. Handmade production lines and one-of-a-kind designer pieces OK. Retail price set by joint agreement. Write with resume and illustrations or samples of work.

Miscellaneous Markets

The markets for crafts is only as limited as your imagination. And, "on the whole it appears to be imagination unlimited amongst the successful craftsmen," said Bill Kocsis, owner of the Hobbit Gallery in Ogunquit, Maine.

The markets in this section, for example, invite craftworkers to sell their work at places ranging from a resort along Lake Erie to a theater lobby in Philadelphia. Other possibilities you may want to pursue on your own range from setting up a jewelry counter in a hair stylist studio to selling baskets to your neighborhood florist. The whole key to successful selling is creativity plus action. Welcome to a potpourri of craft markets.

BITTERSWEET FARM, 777 E. Main St., Branford CT 06405. (203)488-9126. Contact Bob Wallace. Estab. 1973. Over 50 rental working/selling studios and specialty shops available. Studios available for craftworkers working in batik; weaving; silkscreening; pewter; macrame; and calligraphy. Monthly rents from $50-250. Utilities included. Write. Reports in 2 weeks.

CALLE de CRAFTS-ARCADE OF ARTISANS, Oak Mill Mall, 7900 N. Milwaukee Ave., Niles IL 60648. (312)967-8860. Marketing Director: Marilynn Grais. Purpose: "to create a 'Montmarte' atmosphere at this unique mall featuring Old World shops. Space available on monthly basis for artisan to work and display their craft. Cooperative arrangements by groups of artists acceptable. Artists in group must demonstrate and work at space at least ⅓ of time space is rented." Fee: $40 per week for an 8x10 display area; no commission. Prejudging. Work may be offered for sale; each artist must have $15 Niles business license. Craftworker must attend show; demonstrations OK. "Artists may give classes in community room and charge a fee to registrants. Mall charges $10 for maintenance and clean-up of community room." Numbers of exhibitors limited to 20. Sponsor provides electricity for demonstrations and 24-hour security. Considers all crafts.
Sales Tip: "Old World crafts are popular. Viewing public is middle-aged and many of German, Polish and Italian extraction."
Promotion: "Oak Mill Mall sponsors visits by women's groups by the busload. Advertised by local print advertising and radio. Mall often gets TV coverage on special events."

CENTRAL MADISON COUNCIL, Box 71, Madison WI 53701. (608)255-5793. Coordinator: Janice Durand. "Madison will have available in the spring of 1979 a new downtown mall complete with special areas designed for the display and sale of handmade crafts. The Central Madison Council (a downtown business organization) will be responsible for sponsoring and programming craft sales in the area. Persons interested in arranging special outdoor craft show and sales should write for more information."

CONTEMPORARY ART WORKSHOP, 542 W. Grant Place, Chicago IL 60614. (312)525-9624. Administrative Director: Lynn Kearney. Estab. 1950. "Our Workshop is an amalgam of 30 artists with studios. We also have a nonprofit gallery and classes. We are what is known as a workshop/alternative space. The artists who have studios here must be professional, must show slides and a resume for consideration to have a studio or to show in our gallery. Studios range up to $150/month." Write for more information.

JOHN M. CUELENAERE LIBRARY, 125-12 St. E., Prince Albert, Saskatchewan Canada S6V 1B7. (306)763-8496. Head Librarian: Eleanor Acorn. Library. Estab. 1973. Considers all crafts that can be hung. Work is fastened to gallery wall and displayed for 4 weeks. Will put buyer in touch with seller. Work may be shipped or hand-delivered. Library pays insurance for exhibited work.

DEPARTMENT OF TOURISM, CITY OF PETERSBURG, Petersburg VA 23803. (804)733-7690. Director of Tourism: John Elliott. City government. Estab. 1850. Would like to represent 10 craftworkers. Considers all crafts; deals mainly with 19th century period. All styles;

utilitarian and/or decorative. Price range: $1-400; bestsellers: $1-15. Works mostly on consignment and buys some outright; commission is negotiable. Director sets retail price. Requires exclusive area representation. Reports in 2 weeks. Work may be shipped or hand-delivered. Heaviest wholesale buying time: spring; best selling time: spring-fall.

FARMINGTON VALLEY ARTS CENTER, Box 220, Avon Park N., Avon CT 06001. (203)678-1867. Executive Director: Betty Friedman. Provides studio rentals and workshops for craftworkers producing in batik; ceramics; glass art; jewelry; leatherworking; macrame; metalsmithing; needlecrafts; pottery; soft sculpture; weavings; and woodcrafting. Offers 18-22 subsidized studio spaces "in this community of artists at reasonable rates: $102.50 for 20x22 including all utilities. Also it is possible to supplement income through teaching in the Arts Center program of classes." Available to full-time professionals who are deeply committed to their work; will open their studios to the public a minimum of 10 hours per week on a regular basis; and will participate in Arts Center activities. To apply send resume, slides and a letter stating goals and reasons for wanting studio space; should be sent to the attention of the Director. Applications accepted at any time.

FRANKLIN STREET MALL, Tampa Downtown Development Authority, 512 N. Florida Ave., Tampa FL 33602. (813)229-6547. Mall Administrator: Reba F. Cook. Maintains a registry of craftspeople who set-up at the Mall. "Anyone coming into our area can obtain a temporary permit for the duration of their visit by contacting our office."

GALES CREEK ENTERPRISES OF OREGON LIMITED, Star Rt., Box 1318, Glenwood OR 97120. (503)357-3574. Manager: Paul V. Class. Streetcar museum. Estab. 1969. "We are an operating shop moving in the direction of the American Village Institute program concentrating on cottage industry. Our customers are mostly museums, restaurants, and cities who want quality exhibits and have the funding needed for this type of work. Each streetcar, body or complete tram is set on horses; stripped of all paint inside and out; rusted metal is removed and body prepared for new materials. Craftworkers then insert stained glass or inlay, carpenters' joinery, etc. Final painting is done by museum staff." Write for more information.

GCAH CRAFTS PROGRAM, 711-A Industrial Blvd., Gainesville GA 30501. (404)532-5406. Director: F. Thomas Gilmartin. State crafts program. Estab. 1978. Represented professional craftworkers in 35 North Georgia counties during first year. Considers all crafts plus native materials. All styles; utilitarian and/or decorative. Works by referral. Craftworker sets retail price.

GIBBES ART GALLERY SCHOOL, Carolina Art Association, 135 Meeting St., Charleston SC 29401. (803)577-7275. Registrar: Pamela Kerr Leonard. Interested in professional craftworkers applying for teaching positions. Emphasizes batik; ceramics; glass art; jewelry; needlecrafts; quilting; soft sculpture; and weaving. Offers introductory classes in 3 separate sessions (fall, spring, and summer) annually. Classes are taught at basic level for the general public. Also has a workshop program which offers a few classes in a specific area of concentration. Write for more information.

LOWER ADIRONDACK REGIONAL ARTS COUNCIL, Box 659, 184 Glen St., Glens Falls NY 12801. (518)798-1144. Arts and Crafts Coordinator: Eleanor Rowland. Offers part-time employment at $50/day to craftworkers in any craft medium. No special requirments. Write for more information.

NORTH POINT PIER, Box 73720, San Francisco CA 94119. (415)981-8030. Operations Manager: Nick Hoppe. "We are a specialty shopping center dealing primarily in crafts. There are 110 shops available and a large number are craft-workshops where the artisan is manufacturing his craft in full view of the public." Write for more information.

OLD SASH MILL, Box 1332, Santa Cruz CA 95060. (408)425-8331. Contact: Leland Zeidler. Craft Shopping Center. Estab. 1973. Represents 20 craftworkers. Considers batik; ceramics; clothing; glass art; jewelry; leatherworking; metalsmithing; wall hangings; weavings; and woodcrafting. One-of-a-kind designer pieces only; utilitarian and/or decorative. Price range: $5-1,000. Each business in the center has its own systems, methods and requirements. Write with SASE for a directory of shops, then write individual shops for further information.
Profile: "Authentic turn of the century sash mill structures with diverse representation of businesses in an attractive surrounding." Best selling time: summer and Christmas.

PERA'S SUMMER RESORT, Amusement Park, Lake Rd., Geneva on the Lake OH 44043. (216)466-8659. Contact: Martha Pera Woodward. Summer resort has locations for rent for craftworkers Memorial Day-Labor Day. Submit resume or actual work; call for interview. Reports in 2 weeks.

SUNBURY SHORES ARTS AND NATURE CENTER, INC., Box 100, St. Andrews, New Brunswick Canada E0G 2X0. (506)529-3386. Director: H. Kreiberg. Instructor positions for batik; ceramics; glass art; jewelry; leatherworking; macrame; metalsmithing; pottery; and weaving offered to craftworkers with Canadian citizenship or visa; stature and recognition in their chosen field; letters of recommendation; and references. Deadline for summer is fall of preceding year. Write to Director.

THUMB FUN AMUSEMENT PARK, Box 128, Hwy. 42, Fish Creek WI 54272. (414)868-3418. President: D. B. Butchart. "We are presently developing a craft area in our park where craftworkers will perform their craft during operating hours and sell their products. Space is available on lease and percentage. 1890's theme." Write for more information.

TOM R. TOPERZER VISUAL ARTS CONSULTANT, Box 68, Normal IL 61761. (309)452-7882. Contact: Tom R. Toperzer. Visual arts consultant. Clients are businesses and financial institutions. Estab. 1975. Price range: open. Works on consignment; 25% commission. Retail price set by joint agreement. Reports in 1 week. Work may be shipped or hand-delivered.
Acceptable Work: Considers batik; ceramics; glass art; jewelry; metalsmithing; pottery; quilting; soft sculpture; wall hangings; weavings; and woodcrafting. Especially needs wall pieces and fiber hangings. Primitive, finished and one-of-a-kind pieces; utilitarian and/or decorative.

UP COUNTRY CRAFTS CATALOG, Box 217, Pinedale CA 93650. (209)298-8690. Editor/Publisher: Carole Seligman. Estab. 1975. Wholesale and retail buyer catalog published 3 times annually and distributed via direct mail and through selected bookstore, health food and gift stores. "Submit photos of work and a jurying fee (this is the only charge to the advertiser). If work is not accepted the fee and photos are returned. If work is accepted the craftworker is assigned ¼, ⅓, or ½ page. We put the ad together from the information and photos provided." Write for brochure.

THE WALNUT STREET THEATRE GALLERY, 825 Walnut St., Philadelphia PA 19107. (215)574-3562. Coordinator: Dorothy Smallwood. Estab. 1972. Work displayed in 2 theatre lobbies; work may be offered for sale; 20% commission. Craftworker sets retail price. "Submit slides or photos plus educational information. Committee reviews work of craftworkers during the year." Dealer pays insurance for exhibited work.
Profile: "The Gallery includes craftworkers in most of our shows. We have approximately 6 shows annually running for 6 weeks with an average of 15 artists in each. We promote the show by press releases; opening reception; and special interviews on radio, TV, etc."

HELENE WURLITZER FOUNDATION OF NEW MEXICO, Box 545, Taos NM 87571. (505)758-2413. Executive Director: Henry A. Sauerwein Jr. Provides 12 rent-free and utilities-free studio-apartments in Taos, New Mexico; furnished (including linen) to persons engaged in creative work in all media. Arrangements are for a period of 3 months but a period can be shortened or lengthened to a year if conditions are mutually satisfactory. Write for information.

Professional Show Promoters

The Shows & Fairs section of this book has been designed to list shows held on a regular basis. But not all shows are held annually or regularly. This section, Professional Show Promoters, includes the names, addresses, entrance fees and other information about persons and organizations that regularly hold one-time-only shows.

Write to the show promoters who sponsor shows in your area, asking for a listing of upcoming shows. Also, as with all shows, you should search out other craftworkers who have exhibited with that show promoter previously, or consult *The Crafts Fair Guide*, published bimonthly.

AMERICAN CRAFTS EXPOSITIONS, Box 370, Farmington CT 06032. (203)224-8388. Directors: Rudy Kowalczyk and Denise Barile. Estab. 1972. Sponsors 6 civic center and outdoor shows annually in Boston, Massachusetts and Connecticut. Considers all quality crafts. Prejudging by slides. Entry fee: $50-100; no commission or awards. Write for additional information.

AMERICAN FAIRS, INC., 2131 Union St., San Francisco CA 94123. (415)346-6800. Contact: Michael J. Warfield or Sybil Douglas. Estab. 1972. Sponsors art and crafts shows in California, Arizona, Utah, Nevada and Oregon; 50 annually. Entry fee: $20-25; 10% sales commission. Write for more information. "Send photos of craft and display unit with SASE."

AMERICAN SOCIETY OF ARTISTS, INC., 700 N. Michigan Ave., Chicago IL 60611. (312)751-2500. Director, American Artisan Division: Judy A. Edborg. Estab. 1972. Sponsors about 20 mall, shopping center and outdoor shows annually in Illinois. Considers batik; candlemaking; ceramics; glass art; jewelry; leatherworking; macrame; metalsmithing; pottery; soft sculpture; tole painting; weaving; and woodcrafting. No machine-made, hobby crafts or kits. "Craft must meet high quality standard." Entries prejudged. Entry fee: $15-30; no commission. No awards at this time, but could change. Submit 4 slides/photos of work; 1 slide/photo of set-up; and SASE to receive information (applications) for shows. *Art and Craft Fair Bulletin* lists shows around the country presented by many different groups, available only to members.

ART ENTERPRISE, Box 231, Rackerby CA 95972. Contact: Manfred P. Schiedeck. Sponsors 60-80 enclosed mall shows annually in California, Oregon and Washington. Considers all crafts. "We insist on professional work, work habits, displays, and mannerisms." Entry fee varies; 10% commission. Write for additional information.

ART SHOWS BY MURRAY, 4808 Auburn Ave., Bethesda MD 20014. (301)656-1103. Contact: Murray F. Scher or Clara R. Craft. Estab. 1967. Sponsors about 30 enclosed mall and covered shopping center shows annually in Maryland, Virginia, Delaware, Pennsylvania and Washington DC. Considers batik; candlemaking; ceramics; decoupage; dollmaking; glass art; macrame; metalsmithing; pottery; tole painting; weaving; woodcrafting; and any craft that is original and handmade. No commercial molds or items made from kits. Craftworkers must be experienced adults having own set-ups. "All first entries must send slides or photos of their work and a photo or drawing of display." Entry fee: $15-55, depending on how many days and where show is held. No commission. Write or phone for additional information; "no letters or brochures will be sent unless medium is described."

ART-CRAFT ASSOCIATES, Millside Manor Arcade, Delran NJ 08075. (609)764-1600. Director: Gordon T. Gattone. Estab. 1970. Sponsors 35 enclosed shopping center and mall shows annually in 30 eastern states and California. Considers all crafts. Prejudging by slides or photos. Entry fee: $30-300; no commission or awards. Write or phone for application form and additional information.

ARTISTS CO-OP, Box 7112, South Lake Tahoe CA 95731. (916)544-4696 or (213)355-3766. Contact: Wayne Denney. Estab. 1972. Sponsors art and crafts fairs, Renaissance festivals and Western fairs in southern California and Lake Tahoe; 25 annually. Entries prejudged. Entry fee: $15-75; 15% maximum sales commission. Write for more information. SASE.

ARTS UNLIMITED, 149 Kalb Ave., Green Bay WI 54301. (414)437-5849. Contact: Nancy Hacker. Estab. 1974. Sponsors art and craft shows in Green Bay area. Entry fee: $10; no sales commission. Write with slides and resume for more information.

B.C. AND WESTERN CRAFT SHOWS, Box 11069, 1055 W. Georgia St., Vancouver, British Columbia Canada V6E 3P3. (604)688-6836. Contact: Mike Kovacsics or Robert Leblanc. Estab. 1976. Sponsors about 20 mall; exhibition; fair; and private shows annually in British Columbia, western Canada and the northwest coast. Considers all crafts. US craftworkers should check with customs and immigration for border crossing. Prejudging. Entry fee: $10-150 or 15-20% commission dependent on rental and license fees in each location. Occasional awards. Write for additional information; "a letter stating the limit of your traveling distance from home; description of craft and display; price range of product; estimated dollar value of stock you can display and travel with."

BETTY BALDWIN ARTIST'S SHOWPLACE, 18415 North Dr., Southfield MI 48076. (313)642-7905. Contact: Nate Baker. Estab. 1959. Sponsors craft and painting shows in Michigan and Ohio; 16 annually. Entries prejudged. Entry fee: $25; 20% sales commission. Write for more information.

CERMAK ROAD BUSINESS ASSOCIATION, 2130 S. 61st Ct., Cicero IL 60650. (312)863-2104. Contact: Norm Scaman. Estab. 1915. Sponsors crafts and painting shows in Berwyn and Cicero, Illinois. No prejudging. Entry fee: $15; no sales commission. Write for more information.

COASTAL CRAFTERS INC., 7737 Nellview Dr., Charleston Heights SC 29405. (803)552-3973. President: Pearl J. Marangelli. Estab. 1974. Sponsors 1 outdoor and about 20 mall shows annually in southeastern and northeastern states. Considers all crafts. Prejudging by 2 slides or photos of work and display. Entry fee: $30-70; no commission. Cash and ribbon awards at all shows. Write for additional information.

LINN COSTELLO CRAFT SHOWS, 55 Talcott Ave., Rockville CT 06066. (203)872-8093. Director: Linn Costello. Estab. 1975. Sponsors 8-10 mall shows annually in Massachusetts (Springfield, Hadley, and Holyoke) and Connecticut (Enfield and Vernon). Considers batik; candlemaking; decoupage; dollmaking; glass art; jewelry; leatherworking; macrame; metalsmithing; needlecrafts; pottery; soft sculpture; tole painting; weaving; and woodcrafting. "No imports; commercial kits; paintings on velvet; commercial molds; or paper or plastic flowers." Craftworkers must be 16 years of age with proper tax number according to state showing craft. Prejudging by slides or photos; jewelers must send samples. SASE. Entry fee: $10/day; no commission. No awards. Write for additional information.

CRAFT SHOWS AND PROMOTIONS, Drawer Q, Williamsburg VA 23185. (804)229-8232. Contact: Michael Makulowich. Estab. 1974. Considers all crafts. Write for additional information.

CRAFTPRODUCERS INCORPORATED, Box 92, Readsboro VT 05350. Director: Riki Moss. Estab. 1973. Sponsors 5 ski lodge and college shows annually in Vermont. Will not consider decoupage; tole painting; coin crafting; slate etching; or pressed flowers. Prejudging by 5 slides; a proportion of the shows are invitational. Entry fee: $60-80; no commission or awards. Write for additional information.

CREATIVE FAIRES LTD., Box 1688, Westhampton Beach NY 11978. (516)288-4263. Directors: Don Gaiti and Barbara Hope. Estab. 1974. Sponsors 4 civic arena shows annually (1 outdoor) in the metropolitan New York City area including Long Island and New Jersey. Considers all crafts. No kits or imports. "Works must be by an American artisan living and working in this country." Entries prejudged by 5 slides of work and 1 slide of booth display. Entry fee: $55-210; no commission; awards vary.

DOUBLE D ENTERPRISES, Box 232, Irwin PA 18642. (412)751-8122. Managers: Dot and Dave Davis. Estab. 1972. Sponsors 50-61 mall shows annually anywhere east of the Mississippi. Considers all crafts. "Our shows and sales are costumed." Entry fee: $25-60. Write for more information; request to be put on mailing list. SASE.

FREELANDS NATIONAL ARTS & CRAFTS SHOWS, 2918 Martel Dr., Dayton OH 45420. (513)254-2900. Director: Clarence Freeland. Estab. 1970. Sponsors arts and crafts shows in

Ohio, Florida, Pennsylvania and New York; 35 annually. Entries sometimes prejudged. Entry fee: $50-90; no sales commission. Write for entry blank. SASE. "Describe your art or craft."

GHETZLER PRODUCTIONS, 18570 Martinique Dr., Houston TX 77058. (713)333-4029. Contact: Lila Ghetzler. Estab. 1976. Sponsors 6 convention center shows annually in Texas. Considers all handmade crafts. $35 limit shows. Entry fee: $50/10x10 display area; no commission or awards. Write for additional information.

BEA GRIFFIN, 3608 Cinnabar Ave., Carson City NV 89701. (702)883-0968. Director: Bea Griffin. Estab. 1961. Sponsors outdoor and mall shows in San Francisco, Daly City, San Jose, and Salinas, California; and Carson City, Nevada. Considers all crafts except leather or jewelry in mall shows. Candles are not allowed in some shows. "No set-ups over 5'. Must charge sales tax." No prejudging but photographs appreciated. Entry fee: $20-25; 10% commission; awards vary.

JOHN AND DIANE GROMOSIAK, 1937 Wilene Dr., Dayton OH 45432. (513)429-1823. Show Director: John G. Gromosiak. Estab. 1970. Sponsors 25-30 mall shows annually in all areas. Considers batik; candlemaking; ceramics; decoupage; glass art; jewelry; leatherworking; macrame; metalsmithing; pottery; soft sculpture; tole painting; and woodcrafting. No kits. Prejudging by 3 slides or photos of work. Entry fee: $55-85. No commission or awards. Write for additional information.

JINX HARRIS SHOWS, INC., Rt. 1, Box 1535, Auburn NH 03032. (603)483-2742. President: Jinx Harris. Estab. 1959. Sponsors 70 shopping center shows annually in the northeastern US (New Hampshire to Maryland to West Virginia). Considers "any handmade craft — new or old"; no commercial molds, commercial findings in jewelry, sand terrariums or plastic/paper flowers. Craftworker must attend complete show — usually 4-day shows. Prejudging by slides or photos. Entry fee; $35-70/8x4 display area. No commission or awards. Write for application form and additional information.

HERBIE PRODUCTIONS, 10301 I-10 Service Rd., Suite B249, New Orleans LA 70127. (504)246-5476. Contact: Herb Gorden or Ronnie Marr. Estab. 1975. Sponsors 20 enclosed mall shows in the South, especially Louisiana. Considers all crafts. "The only requirement is professional work and working approach." Entries prejudged. Entry fee: $35; 10% commission. No awards. "Craftspeople may request to be put on our mailing list. This will mean we will direct current information to them."

J&R PRODUCTIONS, Box 46X, East Kingston NH 03827. (603)642-5073. Directors: Ron or June Richardson. Estab. 1974. Sponsors about 20 mall shows annually in New England. Considers all handmade crafts. No molds or kits. "Items must meet a high level of quality." Prejudging. Entry fee: $20 plus 10% commission or $40 flat fee. No awards. Write for additional information.

IRIS G. KLEIN, 9761 E. Bay Harbor Dr., Bay Harbor Island FL 33154. (305)864-8725. Contact: Iris G. Klein. Estab. 1961. Sponsors 9 outdoor fair, temple, organization, and shopping center shows annually in Florida and the Chicago area. Considers all original crafts; no kits. Craftworker must be over 18 years of age. Prejudging by slides or photos. No commission. Presents awards. Write for additional information.

MARY LEHNER, 1219 Elmart Lane, Richmond VA 23235. (804)231-1085. Arts and Crafts Coordinator: Mary Lehner. Estab. 1972. Sponsors about 12 enclosed mall shows annually on the eastern seaboard, mostly in Virginia. Considers all crafts. Jewelry and leatherwork by invitation only. Must be original work done by exhibitor; no kits or molds unless exhibitor created the kit or mold. No imports, agents, alcohol or small children. Must furnish own display material. Craftworker must be 21 or over; neatly groomed; and must attend exhibit for complete show. Prejudging by slides or photos; resume; and brochure; and SASE for new exhibitors. 90% of exhibitors are by invitation. Entry fee: $30-50; no commission or awards. Write for additional information.

NANCY MCGUIRE ART SHOWS, 11 Doris St., Unionville CT 06085. (203)673-5527. Director: Nancy McGuire. Estab. 1973. Sponsors 33 enclosed mall shows annually in New England (Connecticut, Massachusetts, Rhode Island, New York and New Hampshire). Considers all original crafts except beaded jewelry and clothing. Prejudging. Entry fee: $35; no commission. No awards. Write for additional information.

MARCHE ENTERPRISES, INC., Box 1571, Wheaton MD 20902. (301)681-7880. President: Marlene Mollerick. Estab. 1977. Sponsors 8-12 mall; shopping center; and National Guard Armory shows annually in suburban Washington DC. Considers all handcrafted original crafts. Excludes ceramics and candle from molds; beaded/feather flowers; strung beads; jewelry with commercial setting; dried flower arrangements; and Lucite/Plexiglas. Prejudging; new exhibitors must submit 4 slides or photos, including 1 of display. Entry fee: $20-40; no commission or awards. Write for additional information.

MERCHANT'S ASSOCIATION OF BROOKFIELD SQUARE SHOPPING CENTER, c/o Rosemary Roth, 2193 S. 84th, West Allis WI 53227. (414)321-5288. Estab. 1974. Sponsors 5 mall and shopping center shows annually at Brookfield, Wisconsin. Considers batik; ceramics; blown glass; jewelry; leatherworking; macrame; metalsmithing; creative stitchery; pottery; rosemaling; paper sculpture; soft sculpture; weaving; woodcrafting; and papier tole. All work must be original; no commercial kits, stencils, molds or patterns. Prejudging. Display area: 8x10. Entry fee: $35; no commission. Present awards. SASE.

MIDWEST ARTISTS ASSOCIATION, Box 454, Palos Heights IL 60463. Contact: John Basso. Estab. 1969. Sponsors 15 mall and shopping center shows annually in Illinois and Indiana. Considers all handmade crafts; no commercial items or parts. Craftworker must project professional image. Prejudging at first show. Entry fee: $15-45; no commission. Awards vary. Write for additional information.

CONSTANCE E. MORROW AND GRANT R. HARTSOCK, 2006 N. North St., Peoria IL 61604. Sponsors arts and crafts shows in Illinois. Entry fee: approximately $40; no commission. New entrants should send short resume and photos of work.

NATIONAL ARTISTS TOUR, 1122 Fox Valley Center, Aurora IL 60505. (312)851-3657. Contact: Robert E. Downs. Estab. 1974. Sponsors national art and craft shows; 30 annually. Entries prejudged. Entry fee: $5/day; 10% sales commission. Write for more information.

IRENE "RAE" PARTRIDGE, Rt. 4, 146 Park Dr., Barrington IL 60010. (312)639-5665. Contact: Irene "Rae" Partridge. Estab. 1966. Sponsors fine arts and selected craft shows in Chicago; 10-15 annually. Entries prejudged. Entry fee: $18-30; no sales commission. Write for more information.

PROVIDENCE ART CLUB EXHIBITIONS, 11 Thomas St., Providence RI 02903. Contact: Marjory Dalenius. Sponsors shows for New England artists; 3 seasonally (September-July). Some member-only shows.

RAINBOW ENTERPRISES, 1 Rose Ct., Narragansett RI 02882. (401)789-8260. Director: Andrea Kotula. Estab. 1972. Sponsors about 6 indoor/outdoor shows annually in New England. Considers batik; candlemaking; dollmaking; glass art; jewelry; leatherworking; macrame; metalsmithing; needlecrafts; pottery; soft sculpture; weaving; and woodcrafting. All crafts must be completely handmade; no manufactured settings. Prejudging by slides. Entry fee: $45-65; no commission or awards. Write or phone for additional information.

R&R PROMOTIONS, 4871 Brecksville Rd., Richfield OH 44286. (216)659-3318. Director: Carol Raab. Estab. 1975. Sponsors 15 mall; theater; and hall shows annually in Cleveland, Akron, and Canton, Ohio. Considers original crafts. Prejudging by slides or photos. Entry fee: $60-150. No commission or awards. Write for additional information.

R&S ASSOCIATES, Box 97, Bloomsbury NJ 08804. (201)454-3737. Contact: Raymond Roe. Estab. 1973. Sponsors arts, crafts, collectables, stamp and coin shows in malls on the East Coast. Entries prejudged. Entry fee: $30-100; no sales commission. Write for more information.

J.J. READEY PROMOTIONS, 615 S. "H" St., Lake Worth FL 33460. (305)582-6133. Director: J.J. Readey. Estab. 1974. Sponsors 40 mall; shopping center; and outdoor shows annually in Florida, Georgia, Alabama, Louisiana, and Tennessee. Considers all crafts. Prejudging by slides. Entry fee: $15-100; no commission. No awards. Write for additional information.

REITER PROMOTIONS, INC., Box 321, Chanhassen MN 55317. (612)445-1998. Contact: Arthur Reiter. Estab. 1973. Sponsors art, craft and fine art shows in Rochester and Duluth. Entry fee: $25-30; no sales commission. Write for more information.

SPECTRA PRODUCTIONS, INC., Box 333, Eagle ID 83616. (208)939-6426. President: Doug Fitzgerald. Estab. 1967. Sponsors 6 fairground shows annually in Boise, Idaho, and Eugene, Oregon. Considers all crafts. Prejudging. Entry fee: $35-140; no commission. Awards vary. Write for additional information.

JAY VIETS— CREATIVE PROMOTIONS, 19312 Collier St., Tarzana CA 91356. (213)705-1112. Contact: Peggy or Jay Viets. Estab. 1975. Sponsors crafts, sculpture and painting shows in Texas, Colorado, Louisiana, Arizona, New Mexico, California, Oregon, Utah, Montana, Washington, Idaho and Oklahoma; 52 annually. Entry fee: $25; 10% sales commission. Write for more information.

LYDIA WARD PRODUCTIONS, Rt. 1, Box 218, Bedford NY 10506. Director: Lydia Ward. Estab. 1967. Sponsors 6 county; civic center; and auditorium shows annually in New York City and Westchester and Greenwich, Connecticut. Considers all crafts; no kits, molds, or imports. Prejudging by 5 slides of work including 1 of display. Display area: 8x10. Entry fee: $35-135; no commission. No awards. Write for additional information.

Shops & Galleries

If the number of listings of shops and galleries looking for crafts is any kind of sales barometer, then you shouldn't have a dry year.

Since last year, the number of shops and galleries listed in this book has more than tripled. And the need for crafts among retailers is perhaps greater than ever before. The listings in this section include those shops and galleries that carry crafts exclusively, gift shops, art and craft stores, supply shops, museums— even coops and banks.

As with any other listing in this book, read the requirements carefully. For example, although many retailers accept all media, others are looking for specific items. Also, every listing tells you what the price range is of the goods currently being carried. This lets you know how your work fits in as far as price is concerned. In general, paying attention to details in the listings will make the task of selling your work an easier one.

There is no need for you to contact only those in your area. With a few good photos of your crafts (see Working With the Retailer and Photographing Your Crafts), almost any shop or gallery will consider your work.

Once you start using the listings in this section, you're likely to find several outlets for your crafts. Chances are you'll be flooded with orders!

Alabama

THE GREATER BIRMINGHAM ARTS ALLIANCE, Box 2152, Birmingham AL 35201. (205)251-1228. Director: Jack Horlacher. Nonprofit gallery. Estab. 1969. Represents 1 craftworker per month in one-man show. Considers glass art; jewelry; pottery; wall hangings, and weavings. One-of-a-kind designer pieces only. Price range: $15-500. Works on consignment; 25% commission. Craftworker sets retail price. Reports in 3 weeks. Gallery also sponsors a juried crafts exhibition in the fall.

THE H.A.S. BIN GIFT SHOPPE, Rt. 3, Phillipson Dr., Albertville AL 35950. Contact: Wanda Reed. Gift shop. Estab. 1977. Represents 30+ craftworkers. Considers ceramics; clothing; decoupage; dollmaking; jewelry; leatherworking; needlecrafts; quilting; tole painting; wall hangings; weavings; woodcrafting; and anything handmade. All styles; utilitarian and/or decorative. Price range: 50c-$50; bestsellers: $5-25. Works on consignment. Craftworker sets retail price, shop mark-up added to this. Requires exclusive area representation. Reports in 4 weeks; pays in 1 month. Work may be shipped or delivered in person. Dealer pays insurance on exhibited work and return shipping. "I keep the product for a few months and return it if it does not move." Best selling time: holidays.

THE LOLLIE SHOP, 2917 Linden Ave., Birmingham AL 35209. Contact: Christine Davis. Gift shop. Represents 30 craftworkers. Considers batik; candlemaking; ceramics; clothing; decoupage; dollmaking; glass art; jewelry; needlecrafts; pottery; quilting; tole painting; and woodcrafting. Especially needs baby gifts; good design stained glass ornaments; ceramic mobiles; and pottery. All styles; utilitarian and/or decorative. Price range: $1-250; "average sale runs about $20." Works on consignment; 30% commission. Craftworker sets retail price. Reports in 4 weeks. Write before mailing work. "I send a list of what has been sold to each person between the first and tenth of each month along with a check for their share."
Profile: Work is displayed on rustic shelves and by hanging items on the walls. "We carry stained glass ornaments and handcrafted items of good quality and plants and plant accessories as well as needlework supplies." Customers are in middle to high income bracket.

USS ALABAMA BATTLESHIP, Box 65, Mobile AL 36601. Manager: Alice Miller. Museum gift shop. Estab. 1964. Considers candlemaking; ceramics; decoupage; dollmaking; glass art; jewelry; wall hangings; weaving; and woodcrafting. Nautical theme preferred. Fine handmade production-line and one-of-a-kind items only; utilitarian and/or decorative. Price range: $5-60. Works on consignment; but prefers to buy outright. Shop sets retail price. Query.
Profile: "We buy mostly small items and sell in volume. We try to have something for everybody. We have 375,000 visitors a year." Best selling time: June-August.

WINDWARD CRAFTS, Rt. 1, Mentone AL 35894. (205)634-3819. Contact: Mildred Moerlins or Jill Howard. Estab. 1975. Represents 15-20 craftworkers. Considers batik; candlemaking; dollmaking; glass art; jewelry; leatherworking; metalsmithing; needlecrafts; pottery; quilting; soft sculpture; wall hangings; weavings; and woodcrafting. Finished, one-of-a-kind or handmade production items; utilitarian and/or decorative. Price range: $1-300; bestsellers: $2-20. Works on consignment and occasionally buys outright; 30% commission. Craftworker sets retail price. Write or query with color transparencies or b&w prints of work. Reports in 2 weeks. Dealer pays shipping from shop and insurance for exhibited work.
Profile: "Windward Crafts is an old 2-story log house which was originally a small inn for summer tourists. We are open only in the summer, with all items displayed all summer. Customers are a wide variety of people vacationing in the area."

Alaska

ALASKA CERAMIC SUPPLY, INC., 7901 Old Seward Hwy., Anchorage AK 99502. (907)344-2094. Manager, High Fire Division: Norma L. Nelson. Rental gallery/pottery classes/wholesale supply company. Estab. 1965. Represents up to 24 craftworkers in gallery. Considers ceramics; pottery; and soft sculpture. All styles; utilitarian and/or decorative. Price range: $10-800; bestsellers: $25-75. Works on consignment and buys outright; 25% commission. Retail price set by joint agreement. Rental gallery fee: $1/square foot. Reports in 1 week. Work may be shipped or delivered in person; dealer pays insurance on exhibited work.
Profile: "All one-time exhibits are displayed in a manner satisfactory to the craftsman and our High Fire Division manager. By being in conjunction with their supplier, our craftsmen are given special treatment, guidance, understanding, and their wares receive tender loving care. We treat amateurs and professionals alike, and we urge the professionals to help the others. Heaviest wholesale buying time: spring; best selling time: summer tourist season. "In Alaska, the interest in crafts during the last 5 years has tripled. The input of craftsmen from the other 49 states has helped tremendously. We are growing by leaps and bounds."

ALASKA NATIVE ARTS & CRAFTS, 425 "D" St., Anchorage AK 99501. (907)274-2932. Contact: Susan Fair. Estab. 1937. Represents hundreds of local craftworkers. Native art only. Primitive and finished one-of-a-kind items; utilitarian and/or decorative. Price range: $1.50-4,500; bestsellers: $40-110. Buys outright or on consignment; 20% commission. Retail price set by joint agreement. Heaviest wholesale buying time: winter; best selling time: summer. Shop is a native coop. Customers buy crafts for their artistic value and as an investment.

THE ART SHOP & STUDIO OF J. VAN HOESEN, Box 323, Haines AK 99827. Contact: Jack Van Hoesen. Summer gallery and studio. Estab. 1972. Represents 8-10 craftworkers. Works on consignment and buys outright; 30% commission. Retail price set by joint agreement. Reporting time varies according to season. Query first. Dealer pays insurance on exhibited work.
Acceptable Work: Considers jewelry; leatherworking; metalsmithing; pottery; and woodcrafting. All styles; utilitarian and/or decorative. "I am interested in Alaskan crafts or items oriented to the 'Last Frontier' motif. No trinkets please! I desire crafts not widely marketed in the state, but available only from the craftsperson directly and a very few other outlets (quality shops or galleries)."
Special Needs: Wants silver and woodcarving representative of the northwest coast Indian art. "I will consider some items of special quality or uniqueness for a traveling exhibit in the lower 48 states in conjunction with my own gallery shows of wildlife and nature paintings."
Profile: Open during summer only. "Items are usually grouped according to craftsman, but not always. A display blurb about the craftman is used, so the craftsman should submit a summary of his background and/or unique quality of his particular craft if not readily evident when viewing the items." Heaviest wholesale buying time: spring; best selling time: summer. "Most of my market is the summer tourists visiting the state of Alaska or residents who purchase uniquely Alaskan gifts to send elsewhere."

THE ARTWORKS, 3055 College Rd., Fairbanks AK 99701. (907)479-2563. Contact: Gloria Fischer. Craft shop/gallery. Estab. 1974. Represents 25-30 craftworkers. Considers batik; candlemaking; glass art; jewelry; metalsmithing; wall hangings; weavings; Eskimo and Indian crafts; and handbound blank books. All styles; utilitarian and/or decorative. Price range: $1-1,000; bestsellers: $5-50. Works on consignment and buys outright; 30% commission. Retail price set by joint agreement. Prefers exclusive area representation. Reports in 2 weeks. Ship or hand-deliver work. Shop pays insurance on exhibited work.
Profile: "Emphasis is on uncluttered display in order to show each piece to its best advantage. Work is not necessarily grouped by craftperson." Minimum display time: 6 weeks. Best selling time: summer and pre-Christmas months; heaviest wholesale buying time: spring and fall. Shop

is "located in a traditional log cabin, but nevertheless has a contemporary feel. Traditional native crafts are displayed side by side with contemporary pieces, all of which seem to blend harmoniously." Customers are primarily "in 20s and 30s, outdoors oriented, well-educated and have traveled widely. We're located near the University of Alaska."

DINJII ZHUU ENJIT MUSEUM, Box 42, Fort Yukon AK 99740. (907)662-2345. Coordinator: Virginia Alexander. Museum gift shop. Estab. 1976. Represents 10 craftworkers from the Yukon Flats area. Considers beadwork and birch bark baskets; specializes in Athabascan beadwork. Primitive and fine one-of-a-kind pieces only; utilitarian and/or decorative. Price range: $3-600; bestsellers: $3-50. Works on consignment; no commission. Craftworker sets retail price. Reports in 1 week. Ship or hand-deliver work.
Profile: "All items are on display in 1 room of the Museum. They are not in glass cases. We display them until they are sold or the artists ask for them back. It is the only gift shop in Fort Yukon." Best selling time: June-September. "Most of our customers are middle-aged or older tourists. They generally have a rather moderate income."

KAILL FINE CRAFTS, 4 Marine Way, Merchants Wharf, Juneau AK 99801. (907)586-2880. Contact: Anne Kaill. Estab. 1976. Represents 75 craftworkers. Considers batik; candlemaking; ceramics; dollmaking; glass art; jewelry; leatherworking; metalsmithing; pottery; quilting; soft sculpture; toys; wall hangings; weavings; and woodcrafting. Finished one-of-a-kind items OK; utilitarian and/or decorative. Price range: 65c-$2,000; bestsellers: $10-20 and $40-80. Buys outright or on consignment; 33⅓% commission. Retail price set by joint agreement. Requires exclusive area representation. All methods of contact OK. Reports in 2 weeks. "In Alaska, US Mail or air freight is our only means of shipment." Dealer pays insurance for exhibited work; negotiates shipping and in-transit insurance. "I rotate items and change the gallery weekly." Best selling time: Christmas.
Special Needs: Unusual, not necessarily expensive items, including kites, musical instruments, cards, prints, quilts and dolls.

OLD STORE GALLERY, Box 4-1160, Anchorage AK 99509. (907)274-0424. Owner: Don Parker. Manager: Sandy Mjolsnes. Gallery. Estab. 1974. Represents 90-100 artists and craftworkers. Considers batik; glass art; candlemaking; dollmaking; jewelry; metalsmithing; soft sculpture; wall hangings; weavings; woodcrafting; and especially needs stoneware and porcelain pottery. Fine one-of-a-kind and handmade production-line pieces; utilitarian and/or decorative. Price range: $1-1,500; bestsellers: $5-150. Works on consignment, but may consider buying outright "in selected cases." 30% commission on consigned work; 50% mark-up on items bought outright. Retail price set by craftworker, "although we may advise." Reports in 2 weeks. Work may be mailed to gallery, but "we need to screen mailed items first via slides or photos if the craftsman is new to us." Dealer pays return shipping to craftworker and insurance on exhibited work.
Profile: Heaviest wholesale buying time and best selling time: winter months preceding Christmas. "Our style in art is contemporary. We display our work on antique trunks and the like—old boxes, barrels. Our decor includes barn boards on the walls (genuinely aged), a used brick floor. We attempt to display what we have constantly." Customers are knowledgeable of the arts, with reasonably good to excellent incomes — "many artists patronize us."
To Break In: "It is a joy to meet a craftsman whose work is ready for display when it reaches us, who keeps good records, prices realistically, etc."

Arizona

THE CATALYST, 403 East St., Tucson AZ 85705. (602)622-3130. Contact: Shirl Christensen. Craft/gift shop. Estab. 1971. Represents 15 craftworkers. Considers jewelry; pottery; wall hangings; and weavings. One-of-a-kind designer pieces only. Price range: 10c-$340; bestsellers: 50c-$26. Buys outright. Shop sets retail price. Requires exclusive area representation. Reports in 2-4 weeks.
Profile: Best selling time: fall. Customers are homemakers, doctors, teachers, tradespeople, etc. with average to above par incomes.

COB-WEB HALL, Box 2035, Prescott AZ 86302. (602)445-2262. Contact: Dick or Beth Jorgensen. Gallery. Estab. 1962. Considers batik; ceramics; glass art; jewelry; leatherworking; metalsmithing; pottery; soft sculpture; woodcrafting; and limited clothing, needlecrafts, wall hangings and weavings. One-of-a-kind designer pieces only. Price range: $2-500; bestsellers: $10-50. Works on consignment and buys outright; 33⅓% commission. Craftworker sets retail price. Requires exclusive area representation. Reports in 4 weeks (sometimes a little longer). Gallery pays return shipping to craftworker.

COLORADO RIVER INDIAN TRIBES MUSEUM, Rt. 1, Box 23-B, Parker AZ 85344. (602)669-9211, ext. 213. Director: Charles A. Lamb. Museum gift shop/tribal museum. Estab. 1965. Represents about 50 craftworkers from the Mohave, Chemehuevi, Hopi and Navajo tribes of the Colorado River Indian Reservation. Price range: $6.25-9,000; bestsellers: $6-50. Works on consignment and buys outright; 20% commission. Retail price set by joint agreement. Reports as soon as possible. Work may be shipped or hand-delivered. Work is displayed 30 days.
Acceptable Work: Considers Indian-made ceramics; clothing; dollmaking; jewelry; leatherworking; pottery; woodcrafting; basketry; beadwork; Kachina carving; and rug weaving. Fine and primitive one-of-a-kind pieces; utilitarian and/or decorative.
Profile: "Publicity is sent out to dealers and other shops and customers on special orders only. We are owned and operated by Indian people, located on a reservation." Heaviest wholesale buying and best selling time: Christmas, Easter, Fourth of July and Thanksgiving.

FIVE NINETY THREE, Box 1425, 593 4th Ave., Yuma AZ 85364. (602)783-7977. Contact: Linda Lane. Craft, jewelry and jewelry supplies shop. Estab. 1973. Considers all crafts. Price range: $5-1,000; bestsellers: $5-75. Works on consignment and buys outright; 40% commission. Retail price set by joint agreement. Requires exclusive area representation. Submit slides and photos. SASE. Reports in 1 week.

THE FRANKLIN GALLERY, 105 N. Beaver, Flagstaff AZ 86001. (602)774-0183. Contact: David Franklin Menne. Gallery and frame shop. Estab. 1974. Represents 6-12 craftworkers. Considers bronze sculpture; pottery; and prints. One-of-a-kind designer pieces only; utilitarian and/or decorative. Especially needs bronze sculpture and prints. Bestsellers: $200-600. Works on consignment; 33⅓%commission. Retail price set by joint agreement. Reports in 3 weeks. Work may be shipped or hand-delivered. Work displayed a minimum of 90 days. Customers are 30-50 years old; middle to upper incomes. Best selling time: July-December.

THE FRONT ROOM, 215 W. Leroux, Prescott AZ 86301. (602)445-0249. Contact: Mara Gai Katz or Betty Miller. Gallery and craft vocational training school. Estab. 1976. Represents 25 craftworkers. "We work primarily with graduates of our program but will take some outside crafts on consignment." Considers ceramics; jewelry; metalsmithing; pottery; wall hangings; weavings; and woodcrafting. Fine one-of-a-kind and handmade production-line items; utilitarian and/or decorative. Price range: $5-400; bestsellers: $5-100. Works on consignment; 30% commission. Retail price set by joint agreement. Reports in 2 weeks. Dealer pays return shipping and insurance for exhibited work.
Profile: "We are located in a mixed community of many retired people and a good deal of college age students. We also have a large tourist trade." Best selling time: summer and Christmas.

GALLERY 3, 3819 N. 3rd St., Phoenix AZ 85012. (602)277-9540. Contact: Sherry Manorkian. Considers batik; ceramics; jewelry; pottery; sculpture; wall hangings; weavings; and woodcrafting. Specializes in contemporary and Southwest art. Works on consignment; 40% commission. Price range: $25-1,000, oils and acrylics; $25-500, graphics. Bestsellers: $150-400. Retail price set by joint agreement. Requires exclusive area representation. Query with samples. SASE. Gallery pays insurance on exhibited work. 2 months maximum exposure.

THE GATHERING, 24 W. Camelback Rd., Phoenix AZ 85013. (602)264-0580. Buyer: Jo Campbell. Craft gallery. Estab. 1975. Represents 15-25 Arizona craftworkers. Considers batik; clothing; needlecrafts; pottery; soft sculpture; tole painting; wall hangings; weavings; and woodcrafting. One-of-a-kind designer pieces only; utilitarian and/or decorative. Price range: $2.50-300; bestsellers: $20-75. Works on consignment and buys outright; 40% commission. Retail price set by joint agreement. Reports in 2 weeks. "Since we deal with Arizona residents, most of our people deliver to us." Gallery pays insurance on exhibited work.
Profile: "We decide the method of display depending on the work and the space available. Timing of show depends some on interest and season of year. During the Christmas season we have an area devoted to handcrafted Christmas decorations (as an example)." Best selling time: fall and winter. "We try to maintain a shop of high quality crafts but we also try to keep our items in a reasonable price range, so that clients other than collectors can afford to buy and enjoy a fine piece of work." Customers are primarily age 25-60 with incomes of $20,000+. "Our people are interested in good-looking, well-designed pieces. They have some knowledge of crafts, and we try to increase that knowledge by telling them a lot about what they're buying."
Special Needs: "We are interested in fiber baskets and handwoven clothing suitable for our Phoenix climate."
To Break In: "Be realistic, that both the gallery and the craftsmen have to make money to

benefit each other. The costs of running a gallery, including advertising, increase yearly. We want our craftsmen to realize a fair profit from their work, but we must realize a profit also."

GRA WUN JEWELERS, LTD., 7122 5th Ave., Scottsdale AZ 85251. Contact: Margaret Graves. Considers ceramics; jewelry; metalsmithing; and glass art. Price range: $14-75. Buys outright. Craftworker determines fee. Requires exclusive area representation. Send transparencies or b&w photos (12x12x24" or smaller) of work. Items displayed 1 week minimum.

THE HAND AND THE SPIRIT CRAFTS GALLERY, 4200 N. Marshall Way, Scottsdale AZ 85251. (602)946-4529. Partners: Joanne Rapp and Star Sacks. Gallery. Estab. 1972. Represents 30 craftworkers. Price range: 60c-$3,500; bestsellers: $20-175. Works on consignment and buys outright; 40% commission. Retail price set by joint agreement. Requires exclusive area representation. Jurying in July. Dealer pays return shipping and insurance for exhibited work.
Acceptable Work: Considers all crafts, contemporary and traditional, primarily American. All styles; utilitarian and/or decorative.
Profile: "Each piece is treated as an individual object. The gallery has complete space devoted to shows (lasting 1-2 months). They are 2 or more person or thematic shows." Heaviest wholesale buying time: fall; best selling time: winter and spring.

HOPI ARTS & CRAFTS COOPERATIVE GUILD, Box 37, Second Mesa AZ 86043. (602)734-2463. Co-managers: Mark Lormayestewa/Michael Kabotic. Estab. 1949. Represents 280 local craftworkers. Considers basketweaving; dollmaking; jewelry; painting; pottery; and weaving. Finished, one-of-a-kind and handmade production-line items; utilitarian and/or decorative. Price range: $5-3,000; bestsellers: $7-150. Buys outright; 40% commission. Retail price set by joint agreement. Requires exclusive area representation. Reports in 2 weeks. Dealer pays shipping from shop and insurance. Best selling time: summer. Customers are ages 50-60; they buy crafts for artistic value and gifts.

HUACHUCA HISTORICAL SOCIETY, Box 766, Fort Huachuca AZ 85613. (602)538-5736. Director: James P. Finley. Museum gift shop. Estab. 1977. Represents 6 craftworkers. Considers ceramics; jewelry; and art prints. One-of-a-kind designer pieces; utilitarian and/or decorative. price range: $7.50-60; bestsellers: $7.50-10. Works on consignment; 40% commission. Gallery sets retail price. Reports in 1 week. Hand-delivered work only. US government pays insurance for exhibited work. Heaviest wholesale buying time: spring; best selling time: summer.

KNOX CAMPBELL GALLERIES, 3015 N. Campbell Ave., Tucson AZ 85719. (602)793-2100. Administrator: Melody Sears. Considers some sculpture and woodcrafting. Specializes in Western art, but is interested in any theme. Works on consignment and buys outright; 40% commission. Price range: $85-2,000; bestsellers: $500-1,000. Retail price set by joint agreement. Requires exclusive area representation. Send slides of work or call or write for interview. SASE. 1 month minimum exposure.

LA GALERIA, Box 617, Sedona AZ 86336. (602)282-3580. Contact: Ernestine Nestler. Gallery/gift shop. Estab. 1960. Represents 8 craftworkers. Considers batik; ceramics; pottery; woodcarving; and wood sculpture. Fine one-of-a-kind pieces; utilitarian and/or decorative. Works on consignment and buys outright; 33⅓%commission. Retail price set by joint agreement. Requires exclusive area representation. Reports in 1-4 weeks. Return shipping is negotiable; dealer pays transit insurance if notified at time of shipment and dealer pays insurance for exhibited work.
Profile: "We are essentially an art gallery and we handle quality gift items as a special courtesy to our collectors."

MUSEUM OF NORTHERN ARIZONA, Rt. 4, Box 720, Flagstaff AZ 86001. (602)774-5211. Exhibits Coordinator: David Cross. Gift shop considers Navajo rugs; jewelry; and pottery (all Indian). Price range: $1-5,000. Buys outright. Sponsors 3 annual art competitions: Junior Indian Art; Hopi Craftsmen; Navajo Craftsmen.

THE PAVILION, 7150 Main St., Scottsdale AZ 85251. (602)994-9444. Contact: Bill Orovan. Craft shop/gallery/gift shop. Estab. 1972. Represents 35 craftworkers. Price range: $2.50-2,000. Works on consignment and buys outright; 40-50% commission. Craftworker sets retail price. Requires exclusive area representation. Reports as soon as possible. Work may be shipped or hand-delivered.
Acceptable Work: Considers ceramics; decoupage; glass art; metalsmithing; needlecrafts;

pottery; quilting; soft sculpture; wall hangings; weavings; and woodcrafting. All styles; utilitarian and/or decorative.

Profile: "We are a unique combination of craft gallery, gift shop and art gallery. Some of our displays are rather elaborate, others quite simple." Heaviest wholesale buying time: late summer-early winter; best selling time: late fall-spring.

THE PENDLETON SHOP, Box 233, Sedona AZ 86336. (602)282-3671. Contact: Mary Pendleton. Gift shop. Estab. 1958. Represents 8-10 craftworkers. Price range: 95c-$200. Works on consignment and buys outright; 33⅓-40% commission. Retail price set by joint agreement. Requires exclusive area representation. Reports as soon as possible. Work may be shipped or hand-delivered.

Acceptable Work: Considers candlemaking; ceramics; clothing; jewelry; leatherworking; needlecrafts; pottery; wall hangings; weavings; and woodcrafting. All styles; utilitarian and/or decorative.

Profile: "Consigned items get as much attention as purchased items. Customers are older, with upper income." Displays consigned work 3-6 months. Heaviest wholesale buying and best selling time: spring-fall.

PHOENIX ART MUSEUM SHOP, 1625 N. Central, Phoenix AZ 85004. (602)257-1222. Manager: Marsha Weiss. Museum gift shop. Estab. 1959. Represents 2-3 craftworkers. Price range: $1-200; bestsellers: $1-40. Buys outright. Gallery sets retail price. Reports in 2 weeks. Work may be shipped or hand-delivered. Dealer pays return shipping.

Acceptable Work: Considers clothing; glass art; jewelry; soft sculpture; and soleri bells. Especially needs soft sculpture. Fine one-of-a-kind and handmade production-line items; utilitarian and/or decorative.

Profile: "Work is displayed in cases with colorful backdrop for 6-12 months. Customers are winter tourists and local residents, 25-60 years old with an income of $25,000 per year." Heaviest wholesale buying time: January and July; best selling time: winter.

THE THOMPSON GALLERY, 2020 N. Central, Phoenix AZ 85004. (602)258-4412. Contact: John R. Thompson. Considers sculpture; pottery; and jewelry. Works on consignment; 40% commission. Prices from $100. Set by artist. Requires exclusive area representation. 2 weeks exposure.

VERDE VALLEY ART GALLERY, INC., Box 877, Jerome AZ 86331. (602)634-5466. Manager: Mrs. Billie R. Kellogg. Gallery/gift shop. Estab. 1977. Represents 20 craftworkers. Price range: $5-350; bestsellers: $5-30. Works on consignment; 33⅓%commission. Retail price set by joint agreement. Reports in 1 week. Work may be shipped or hand-delivered. Work displayed 30 days minimum.

Acceptable Work: Considers batik; ceramics; clothing; dollmaking; leatherworking; bead work; glass art; jewelry; metalsmithing; needlecrafts; pottery; wall hangings; weavings; woodcrafting; and macrame. Especially needs ceramic wind chimes that have accurate musical tones; soft sculpture; and wood-carved or wood-sculpted items. Fine one-of-a-kind and handmade production-line items; utilitarian and/or decorative.

Profile: Work is shown in "glass cases, wall space, shelving and other unique displays. Shop is located in an historic, bicentennial mining town." Best selling time: spring-Christmas.

YUMA ART CENTER, Box 1471, Yuma AZ 85364. (602)782-9261. Director: Laurel Meinig. Museum gift shop/rental gallery. Estab. 1962. Represents 20-30 Southwestern and southern California craftworkers. Price range: $1.50-200; bestsellers: $10-60. Works on consignment; 34% commission. Retail price set by joint agreement. Reports in 2 weeks. Work may be shipped if previously arranged. Dealer pays return shipping and insurance. Work is rotated weekly. Heaviest wholesale buying time and best selling time: October-May.

Acceptable Work: Considers batik; ceramics; glass art; jewelry; leatherworking; metalsmithing; pottery; soft sculpture; wall hangings; and weavings. One-of-a-kind designer pieces; utilitarian and/or decorative.

Arkansas

ARKANSAS ARTS CENTER ART RENTAL-PURCHASE GALLERY, Box 2137, Little Rock AR 72203. Director: Townsend Wolfe. "Open to regional artists from Arkansas, Louisiana, Missouri, Oklahoma, Texas, Tennessee and Mississippi who have had one or more works accepted for any regional or national juried exhibition." 20% commission. Exhibitor receives half rental fee. Submit 3 works for review.

THE COUNTRY CUPBOARD, 805 Parkway, Conway AR 72032. (501)327-6262. Manager: Carole Culpepper. Craft and gift shop. Estab. 1976. Represents about 20 craftworkers. Considers candlemaking; ceramics; dollmaking; needlecrafts; quilting; tole painting; wall hangings; weavings; and woodcrafting. All styles; utilitarian and/or decorative. Price range: $1-120; bestsellers: $1-15. Works on consignment; 25% commission. Retail price set by joint agreement. Work may be shipped or hand-delivered. Dealer pays insurance for exhibited work.
Profile: "New items are placed for a time in window, then worked into shop arrangement that pleases us. Left indefinitely if I like it." Best selling time: fall.

THE DULCIMER SHOPPE, Drawer E, Hwy. 14 N., Mountain View AR 72560. (501)269-8639. Contact: Lynn McSpadden. Estab. 1962. Represents 10-12 craftworkers. Considers dollmaking; dried arrangements; jewelry; pottery; shuckery; white oak baskets; and woodcrafting. Fine, one-of-a-kind and handmade production-line items; utilitarian and/or decorative. Price range: $1-200; bestsellers: $1-125. Buys outright. Shop sets retail price, usually twice wholesale. Prefers exclusive area representation. Query. Reports in 2-3 weeks. Dealer pays shipping to shop and in-transit insurance.
Profile: "We do woodcarving where visitors can watch." Heaviest wholesale buying time: March-August. Tourist customers.

MUSEUM SHOP OF THE ARKANSAS ARTS CENTER, McArthur Park, Little Rock AR 72203. Manager: Jeanne Kelley. Museum gift shop. Estab. 1962. Represents 5-6 craftworkers who are members of the American Designer Crafts Association. Price range: $8-200; bestsellers: $15-50. Works on consignment and buys outright; 30% commission. Retail price set by joint agreement. Work may be shipped or hand-delivered. Heaviest wholesale buying time: fall and spring; best selling time: fall, spring and Christmas.
Acceptable Work: Considers ceramics; dollmaking; glass art; jewelry; and pottery. Especially needs one-of-a-kind toys. One-of-a-kind designer pieces; utilitarian and/or decorative.

THE OZARK FOLK CENTER SALES SHOP, General Delivery, Mountain View AR 72560. (501)269-3851. Contact: Kay Blair. Estab. 1973. Represents 60 Ozark area craftworkers. Considers candlemaking; dollmaking; leatherworking; needlecrafts; pottery; quilting; wall hangings; weavings; and woodcrafting. Primitive and finished, one-of-a-kind and handmade production-line items OK; utilitarian and/or decorative. Price range: 35c-$500; bestsellers: 35c-$20. Buys outright. Gallery sets retail price. Query with transparencies or photos. Reports in 3 weeks.
Profile: "The period we are interested in is 1820-1920 Ozark. The merchandise is displayed in period settings at times and also on well-lighted display shelves or rustic 'islands.' Located in state park." Heaviest wholesale buying time: winter; best selling time: August and October.

OZARK FOOTHILLS CRAFT GUILD, Box 140, Mountain View AR 72560. (501)269-3896. Director: James H. Sanders. Craft shop. Estab. 1961. Represents 400 Arkansas craftworkers. Price range: 25c-$500; bestsellers: 25c-$25. Works on consignment and buys outright; 50% commission. Retail price set by joint agreement. Work may be shipped or hand-delivered. Dealer pays shipping and insurance.
Acceptable Work: Considers candlemaking; ceramics; clothing; dollmaking; glass art; jewelry; leatherworking; metalsmithing; needlecrafts; pottery; quilting; soft sculpture; tole painting; wall hangings; weavings; woodcrafting; baskets, soap-making products; and grains. All styles; utilitarian and/or decorative. Especially needs low-priced production crafts with good designs.
Profile: "Each object demands its own type of displaying, whether under glass display case, hung on a wall, framed on shelving units, on bales of hay, in baskets, over parallel dowel rods, hung in front of glass window, according to color, media, design and color compatability." Best selling and heaviest wholesale buying time: spring-fall.

SEVEN SPRINGS CRAFTS SHOP, Heber Springs AR 72543. (501)269-3896. Director: James H. Sanders III. Craft shop. Estab. 1962. Represents 100 craftworkers. Considers all crafts except batik. All styles; utilitarian and/or decorative. Price range: 25c-$200; bestsellers: 50c-$12. Works on consignment and buys outright; 50% commission. Craftworker sets retail price. Reports in 1 week. Work may be shipped or hand-delivered. Dealer pays shipping and insurance.
Profile: "Shop doesn't have much room for larger pieces." Display is on shelves; building is rustic. Customers are tourists and transients. Heaviest wholesale buying time: spring-summer; best selling time: spring-fall.

THE SPRING STREET POTTERY, 65 Spring St., Eureka Springs AR 72632. (501)253-9380. Manager: David J. Foddrell. Gallery. Estab. 1971. Represents 10 local craftworkers. Price range: $3.50-5,800; bestsellers: $9-75. Works on consignment; 20-50% commission. Retail price

set by joint agreement. Requires exclusive area representation. Reports in 1 week. Work may be shipped or hand-delivered. Dealer and craftworker share cost of shipping and insurance. Work is displayed 6 months minimum. Best selling time: summer and fall.
Acceptable Work: Considers wall hangings; weavings; and antiques. Fine one-of-a-kind and handmade production-line items; utilitarian and/or decorative.

THE STORE, ARKANSAS TERRITORIAL RESTORATION, Territorial Square, Little Rock AR 72201. (501)371-2348. Manager: Maxine Rowland. Museum gift shop. Estab. 1972. Represents 120 Arkansas craftworkers. Considers all crafts except clothing. All styles; utilitarian and/or decorative. Price range: 25c-$200; bestsellers: 50c-$20. Works on consignment; 25% commission. Retail price set by joint agreement. Reports in 2 months. Work may be shipped or hand-delivered. Displays work for 6 months. Best selling time: summer and Christmas.

"There has been a tremendous surge in the public's awareness; more and more people are becoming involved with crafts," said Down on the Farm (Moddus, Connecticut) owner Paul Simon. "We are always looking for new craftspeople." Down on the Farm has doubled its size since its 1977 opening and will be sponsoring an annual craft fair on the premises.

SUGAR CREEK CRAFT SHOP, Main St., Hardy AR 72542. Director: James H. Sanders III. Craft shop. Estab. 1962. Represents 125 craftworker members of the Ozark Foothills Craft Guild. Considers all crafts; all styles; utilitarian and/or decorative. Especially needs fiber toys; soft sculpture; batik; and screen-printed pieces. Price range: 25c-$250; bestsellers: 50c-$12. Works on consignment and buys outright; 50% commission. Craftworker sets retail price. Work may be shipped or hand-delivered. Dealer pays shipping to shop and insurance. Work is "displayed in a 2,500 square foot shop, year-round, on walls, shelves, under glass, in windows, until sold."
Profile: "All crafts must be made of natural materials (no synthetics)." Customers are middle-income tourists; 18-35 years old. Heaviest wholesale buying time: spring-summer; best selling time: summer.

SYLAMORE CREEK CRAFT SHOP, Box 140, Mountain View AR 72560. Director: James H. Sanders III. Cooperative craft shop. Estab. 1975. Represents 150 member craftworkers. Price range: 25c-$250; bestsellers: 25c-$12. Works on consignment and buys outright; 50% commission. Craftworker sets retail price. Reporting time varies. Work may be shipped or hand-delivered. Dealer pays return shipping on consigned work and insurance. Work is displayed "til sold on various retail display tools (counters, shelves, walls); hung, draped, arranged."
Acceptable Work: Considers all crafts except decoupage. All styles; utilitarian and/or decorative. Especially needs items that would sell within the price range of $2-12 wholesale.
Profile: Cooperatively ran. "All participating craftpersons must be within the guild's membership and approved in their given categories by the standards committee. $10 membership fee. Must be Arkansas resident and submit 5 articles in any given media." Heaviest buying and selling time: spring, summer and fall.

TRAIL OF TEARS CRAFTS CENTER, Blue Spring Rd., Eureka Springs AR 72632. Contact: W. Lowell Baker. Estab. 1972. Represents 10 local craftworkers. Considers glass art; jewelry;

wall hangings; and weavings. One-of-a-kind and handmade production-line items; utilitarian and/or decorative. Price range: $1.50-200. Buys outright. Gallery sets retail price. Call for interview. Reports in 2 weeks. Dealer pays shipping to shop and insurance. Items displayed continuously. Buys and sells most crafts in summer. Customers buy for artistic value and gifts.

WILDWOOD CARVERS, Drawer E, Hwy. 14 N., Mountain View AR 72560. (501)269-8237. Contact: Jon Thompson. Estab. 1976. Represents 15-20 craftworkers. Considers dollmaking; dried arrangements; wooden jewelry; shuckery; white oak baskets; and woodcarving. Finished, one-of-a-kind and handmade production-line items; utilitarian and/or decorative. Price range: $1-600; bestsellers: $1-125. Buys outright. Shop sets retail price, usually twice wholesale. Prefers exclusive area representation. Query with transparencies or photos. Reports in 1 week.
Profile: "We do woodcarving where visitors can watch." Heaviest wholesale buying time: March-August. Many tourist customers. Prefers Ozark craftworkers.

California

THE ADDED TOUCH, 1578 Atterdag Sq., Solvang CA 93463. Contact: Irene Parks. Gift shop. Estab. 1971. Represents 15-20 craftworkers. Considers ceramics; decoupage; porcelain figurines; glass art; jewelry; metalsmithing; woodcrafting; and Lucite and metal etchings. One-of-a-kind and handmade production-line items; utilitarian and/or decorative. Price range: $5-250; bestsellers: $5-50. Buys outright. Gallery sets retail price. Requires exclusive area representation. "Send pictures and SASE." Reports in 1-2 weeks. Work may be shipped or hand-delivered if notified in advance.
Profile: "We give all items in our shop the best care possible. Signs are always posted to cut down on handling, etc. We are a tourist area that draws from around the world. Heaviest wholesale buying time: spring-summer; best selling time: summer.

ADI GALLERY, 530 McAllister, San Francisco CA 94102. (415)621-0602. Contact: Stephen Foster. Gallery. Estab. 1968. Represents 250 artists, sculptors, weavers, printmakers and painters. Considers weavings and wall hangings. Fine one-of-a-kind decorative items only. Price range: $800-3,000, tapestries; bestsellers: $1,000-2,000. Works on consignment. Retail price set by joint agreement. Requires exclusive area representation. Send slides for preliminary viewing. Gallery pays insurance on exhibited work.
Profile: "Since we are a gallery, once we accept an artist, we take his/her work in our consigned inventory for an indefinite period of time. This is then shown to our clients by the owner or director. Corporate art consultants work with designers. There are commissions and fiberworks must work in large corporate spaces although we do have private collectors too."

AFTER THE GOLD RUSH, Box 999, Arnold CA 95223. (209)795-2593. Contact: Rene or Kim del Valle. Craft shop. Estab. 1978. Represents 25 craftworkers. Considers batik; candlemaking; ceramics; clothing; glass art; jewelry; leatherworking; metalsmithing; pottery; wall hangings; weavings; woodcrafting; and enamelcraft. Fine one-of-a-kind and handmade production-line items; utilitarian and/or decorative. Price range: $2-125; bestsellers: $10-20. Buys outright. Shop sets retail price. Reports in 1 week. Dealer pays shipping to shop, in-transit insurance and insurance for exhibited work. Customers are middle to upper-middle class, 24-40 years of age. Best selling time: summer and Christmas.

APPALACHIA: AMERICAN MOUNTAIN CRAFTS AND CULTURE, 340 Village Lane, Los Gatos CA 95030. (408)354-6700. Contact: Owen or Wendy Nagler. Craft shop/gallery/gift shop. Estab. 1976. Represents about 100 craftworkers who deal exclusively in Appalachian folk art and crafts. Considers ceramics; clothing; dollmaking; metalsmithing; needlecrafts; pottery; quilting; wall hangings; weavings; woodcrafting; broomcraft; basketry; and shuckcrafts. All styles; utilitarian and/or decorative. Price range: $1-400. Works on consignment and buys outright. Craftworker sets commission. Work may be shipped or hand-delivered. Dealer pays shipping to shop.
Profile: "The interior of the shop is designed to lend an authentic country atmosphere. There are informational signs about crafts and craftspeople." Customers are affluent. Best selling time: Christmas.

THE ARTIFACTRIE, 2120 Vine St., Berkeley CA 94709. (415)843-9440. Contact: Valerie Adams. Estab. 1967. Represents 2,000 craftworkers. Considers batik; candlemaking; ceramics; dollmaking; glass art; jewelry; leatherworking; needlecrafts; pottery; wall hangings; weavings; and woodcrafting. Finished, one-of-a-kind and handmade production-line items only; utilitarian and/or decorative. Price range: 10c-$5,000; bestsellers: $3-100. Buys outright or on consignment; 40% commission. Retail price set by joint agreement. Write. Reports in 1 week. Dealer pays insurance on exhibited work.

Profile: Each craftworker's work is displayed as a unit on redwood and glass fixtures with displays rotated weekly. Best selling time: holidays and summer; heaviest wholesale buying time: fall. Customers are upper-middle class from a fairly intellectual community. They buy crafts for appreciation of handmade goods.

ARTISANS' ALLEY, INC., 13271 Century Blvd., Garden Grove CA 92643. (714)530-7021, 530-8120. Floor Supervisor: Vivian Dearing. Artisans' coop. Estab. 1972. Represents 100-150 craftworkers. Considers all crafts. "Special need for wood, leather and scrimshaw." All styles; utilitarian and/or decorative. Price range: $1-2,500; bestsellers: $2-100. "Artisans join the Alley and rent booth space. Members often buy outright or take on consignment the works of others not wishing membership. Spaces rent from $10-75 per month." Craftworker sets retail price. Reports in 2 weeks. Shipping is negotiable; dealer pays insurance for exhibited work.

Profile: "We have 6,000 square feet of space; variety of crafts; and person to person involvement. Working in conjunction with the Garden Grove Artisans Guild, which operates an exhibit gallery and 2 classrooms; we have a fascinating cultural center for northern and central Orange County."

BARTEL INTERIOR DESIGN, 161 N. Larchmont Blvd., Los Angeles CA 90004. (213)466-7727. Contact: Vera M. Sweeney. Gift shop. Estab. 1969. Represents 6-10 craftworkers. Considers batik; ceramics; glass art; jewelry; and pottery. Handmade production-line items only; utilitarian and/or decorative. Price range: $5-300; bestsellers: $5-100. Buys outright. Gallery sets retail price. Requires exclusive area representation. Reports in 2 weeks. Work may be hand-delivered. Best selling time: fall; heaviest wholesale buying time: July and January.

BAZAAR DEL MUNDO GALLERY, 2754 Calhoun St., San Diego CA 92110. (714)296-3161. Contact: Diane Powers. Gallery. Estab. 1971. Represents 30-50 craftworkers. Considers batik; ceramics; clothing; jewelry; pottery; wall hangings; weavings; and ethnic folk art. All styles; utilitarian and/or decorative. Price range: $5-500; bestsellers: $20-100. Works on consignment and buys outright; 40% commission. Retail price set by joint agreement. Requires exclusive area representation. Reports in 2 weeks. Work may be shipped or hand-delivered. Dealer pays shipping for solicited work and insurance for exhibited work.

Profile: "We do approximately 6-8 shows a year in our gallery. Rather than shows that concentrate on themes, we emphasize one man shows along with our regular gallery stock of crafts. If we don't have enough of 1 craftsman's work to make a statement, we group his/her work by category. We are in an area where we get maximum tourist traffic (Old State Historic Park)." Best selling time: summer and Christmas.

BEAUX ARTS GIFT SHOP OF FRESNO ARTS CENTER, 3033 E. Yale, Fresno CA 93703. (209)237-2070. Manager: Ann Buchanan. Gift shop/rental gallery. Estab. 1973. Represents 100+ craftworkers. Considers batik; ceramics; glass art; jewelry; needlecrafts; pottery; soft sculpture; wall hangings; weavings; and woodcrafting. Primitive and fine pieces; utilitarian and/or decorative. Price range: $1-200. Works on consignment and buys outright; 33⅓% commission. Retail price set by joint agreement. Reports in 1-2 weeks. Work may be shipped or hand-delivered. Dealer pays shipping to shop and insurance. Best selling time: Christmas.

BROCKMAN GALLERY PRODUCTIONS, 4334 Degnan Blvd., Los Angeles CA 90008. (213)294-3766. Program Coordinator: Ms. Pat Johnson. Considers batik; ceramics; dollmaking; jewelry; leatherworking; metalsmithing; mobiles; pottery; prints; sculpture; wall hangings; weavings; and woodcrafting. Maximum size: 5x7. Paintings must be ready to hang. Works on consignment; 40% commission. Price range: $10-1,500; bestsellers: $15-75. Retail price set by joint agreement. Send slides or photos or call or write for interview. SASE. Gallery pays shipping from gallery and insurance for exhibited work. Work displayed for 3-week period.

CALIFORNIA ARTISTS AND CRAFTSMEN'S GUILD, 1131 State St., Santa Barbara CA 93101. (805)963-2424. Contact: Fran Doll. Coop/rental gallery. Estab. 1971. Represents 60 craftworkers. Price range: $3-600; bestsellers: $20-100. Works on consignment or booth space rental; 40% commission. Craftworkers sets retail price. Requires exclusive area representation. Write. Reports in 1 week. Best selling time: summer. Customers are young college students and married couples with good incomes.

CANYON GALLERY TWO, 974 N. La Cienega Blvd., Los Angeles CA 90069. (213)653-5090. Contact: Barbara Lichterman. Craft shop/gallery/gift shop. Estab. 1969. Represents 50 craftworkers. Considers ceramics; clothing; glass art; jewelry; leatherworking; metalsmithing;

pottery; and ethnic arts and crafts. All styles; utilitarian and/or decorative. Price range: $10-1,500; bestsellers: $25-100. Works on consignment; 50% commission. Retail price set by joint agreement. Requires exclusive area representation. Reports in 4 weeks. Work may be shipped or hand-delivered after pre-arrangement. Dealer pays return shipping and insurance for exhibited work. Displays consigned work 90 days.
Profile: "Do well with interior decorators. I require that arrangements for peak sales (December) be made by September."

CARMEL WORK CENTER SHOP, Box 3547, Carmel by the Sea CA 93921. Contact: Wes or Fritzie Bonenberger. Craft and gift shop. Estab. 1955. Represents 30 contemporary California craftworkers. Considers ceramics; glass art; and pottery. Especially needs hand blown glass, raku and crystaline glazed ceramics. Fine one-of-a-kind and handmade production items; utilitarian and/or decorative. Price range: $5-150; bestsellers: $5-50. Works on consignment and buys outright; 40% commission. Retail price set by joint agreement. Requires exclusive area representation. Reports in 2 weeks. Work may be shipped or hand-delivered. Dealer pays return shipping and insurance for exhibited work. Best selling time: summer.
To Break In: "We would appreciate more care by craftspeople to check individual pieces for glaze flaws, cracks, chips and finished, smooth bottoms. No time in shop to do more than check superficially. It's embarassing when a customer points out flaws."

CHOICE INCORPORATED, 101 Kansas St., Suite 433, San Francisco CA 94103. (415)431-1172. President: Audrey S. Jarach. Gallery. Estab. 1977. Represents 100 craftworkers. Considers batik; ceramics; glass art; metalsmithing; quilting; soft sculpture; wall hangings; weavings; and woodcrafting. Fine one-of-a-kind pieces only; decorative. Open price range. Works on consignment. Retail price set by joint agreement. Reports in 4 weeks. Work may be shipped or hand-delivered. Dealer pays insurance for exhibited work. Works on 90 day consignment and sells (wholesale) to interior designers, architects and corporate collectors.

COFFEE CANTATA, 2030 Union St., San Francisco CA 94118. (415)931-7043. Manager: Judy Honig. Gallery. Estab. 1967. Sponsors 1-person and group showings. Considers batik; quilting; soft sculpture; wall hangings; and weavings. Fine one-of-a-kind pieces only; decorative. Price range: $50-2,500; bestsellers: $50-375. "We only display art and take 30% commission on sales." Craftworker sets retail price. Bring work in personally for review. Dealer pays insurance for exhibited work.
Profile: Gallery is open 12-14 hours daily along with 100-seat restaurant. Displays work for 30 days. Customers are all ages; tourists and locals.

COMMON GROUND ARTISTS CO-OPERATIVE, 509 N. Harbor Blvd., Fullerton CA 92632. (714)879-0075. President: Mary Ann Taggart. Gallery. Estab. 1973. Represents 15 (preferably local) craftworkers. Considers all crafts except decoupage. Fine and primitive one-of-a-kind pieces; utilitarian and/or decorative. Price range: $3-600; bestsellers: $3-50. Works on consignment. Craftworker sets retail price. Rental gallery fee: $50/month. Books from 2 months to 1 year in advance. Work may be shipped or hand-delivered. Dealer pays insurance for exhibited work. Reports in 7-14 days.
Profile: Displays change every month. "Association artists take turns working in the gallery. We charge no percentage on works. We advertise in southern California publications and have monthly meet-the-artists open houses." Best selling time: Christmas.

THE COMPANY STORE, 93 S. Central Ave. #84, Campbell CA 95008. (408)866-0232. Manager: Debbie de Diego. Craft shop. Estab. 1977. Represents 65 craftworkers. Considers all crafts; especially needs glass art and metalworking. Fine one-of-a-kind and handmade production-line items; utilitarian and/or decorative. Price range: $1-350; bestsellers: $1-100. Works on consignment; 40% commission. Retail price set by craftworker. Reports in 2 weeks. Work may be shipped or hand-delivered.
Profile: Shop has "excess of 10,000 square feet for display," and is located in historical area. Best selling time: July-December.

COUNTRYWIDE CRAFTS, 3608 The Barnyard, Carmel CA 93923. (408)624-6511. Contact: Marion or Bill Williams. Gallery/gift shop. Estab. 1976. Represents 20-40 craftworkers. Considers ceramics; clothing; dollmaking; glass art; metalsmithing; needlecrafts; pottery; quilting; wall hangings; weavings; and woodcrafting. Especially needs wood turnings; wood carvings; and functional ceramics. Primitive and fine one-of-a-kind items. Price range: $1.60-400; bestsellers: $10-150. Buys outright and occasionally works on consignment; 40% commission. Retail price set by joint agreement. Requires exclusive area representation. Reports in 2 weeks. Deliver work personally by prior agreement only. Dealer pays insurance for exhibited work.

Profile: Gallery shows handcrafted pieces from all over America; nothing imported; mostly functional. Customers have high incomes. Best selling time: October-December; heaviest wholesale buying time: June-September.

THE CRAFT GALLERY, 126 San Jose Ave., Box 155, Capitola CA 95010. (408)475-4724. Contact: Carin Mudgett. Craft shop. Estab. 1970. Represents 100 craftworkers. Considers batik; candlemaking; ceramics; glass art; jewelry; leatherworking; metalsmithing; pottery; and woodcrafting. All styles; utilitarian only. Price range: $2-200. Works on consignment and buys outright; 40% commission. Craftworker sets retail price. Requires exclusive area representation. Reports in 3 weeks. Work may be shipped or hand-delivered. Dealer pays shipping and insurance for exhibited work.

CRAFT STREET, INC., 24164 Laguna Hills Mall, Laguna Hills CA 92653. (714)770-0144. Manager: Margaret Hogg. Rental gallery. Estab. 1977. Represents 75 craftworkers. Considers all crafts. Handmade production-line items only; utilitarian and/or decorative. Price range: $1-250; bestsellers: $10-25. Works on consignment; 22% commission. Craftworker sets retail price. Rental gallery fee: $500-850/year. Work may be shipped or hand-delivered.

Profile: Craftworker constructs own display. "We supply storage space and will stock for craftsmen." Best selling time: November-December.

CRAFTSMAN'S GALLERY OF CARMEL, Box 1249, Carmel CA 93921. (408)624-8850. Contact: Sammy Crum. Craft and gift shop. Estab. 1977. Represents 40-50 California craftworkers. Considers all crafts except clothing and quilting. Fine one-of-a-kind and handmade production-line items; utilitarian and/or decorative. Price range: $1-1,000; bestsellers: $5-75. Crafts shop is on a membership basis. "Artists pay a membership fee of $400/year for a 4x2 space; or $250 for a 2x2 space. They work 1-2 days a month or pay a $24 workshift fee and receive 80% of the retail price of their work." Craftworker sets retail price. Exclusive Carmel representation. Work may be shipped or hand-delivered. Dealer pays insurance for exhibited work.

Profile: "Members of the Gallery design and build their own display using natural motif. They also provide back stock to replace items as they are sold."

CUSTOM HANDWEAVERS, Allied Arts Guild, Arbor Road and Creek Drive, Menlo Park CA 94025. (415)325-0626. Contact: Kathy Davis. Craft shop. Estab. 1965. Represents 10 craftworkers. Considers ceramics; pottery; wall hangings; and weavings. Handmade production-line items only; utilitarian and/or decorative. Price range: $1-300; bestsellers: $5-30. Works on consignment; 40% commission. Retail price set by joint agreement. Reports in 1 week. Work may be hand-delivered. Dealer pays insurance for exhibited work. Best selling time: May-December.

DAVID, Glass Department, Ocean & Dolores, Carmel-by-the-Sea CA 93921. See Light Opera, San Francisco.

DORIS' CRAFT FAIR, Village Green Shopping Center, Santa Clara CA 95051. (408)243-0888. Contact: Doris Sato. Craft shop. Estab. 1976. Represents about 95 craftworkers. Considers all crafts except clothing. One-of-a-kind and handmade production-line items; utilitarian and/or decorative. Price range: $1-500. Works on consignment; 30% commission. Craftworker sets retail price. Reports in 2 weeks. Work may be shipped or hand-delivered.

Profile: Work is displayed "in group displays in various craft categories — soft sculpture, ceramics, woodworking, jewelry, etc." Heaviest wholesale buying time and best selling time: spring and fall.

DOVETAIL, 3027 Fillmore St., San Francisco CA 94123. (415)931-4949. Contact: Melva Christopherson or Carla Roth. Craft shop/gallery/gift shop. Estab. 1972. Represents 100-125 American craftworkers. Fine one-of-a-kind and handmade production-line items; mainly utilitarian but some decorative. Price range: $1-2,500; bestsellers: $5-30. Works on consignment and buys outright; 40% commission. Retail price set by joint agreement. Requires exclusive area representation within "our shopping area within San Francisco." Shipping negotiable; dealer pays all insurance. Unsold consigned pieces returned after 6 months.

Acceptable Work: Considers batik; ceramics; dollmaking; glass art; jewelry; leatherworking; pottery; quilting; soft sculpture; wall hangings; weavings; and woodcrafting. "We're interested in traditional or contemporary styles, no Eskimo or Indian crafts. Special emphasis placed on

wood. We're always looking for any new approach to handcrafted home furnishings."
Profile: "We specialize in hardwood furnishings. The beautiful furniture is a very dramatic background to the other handcrafted home accessories we sell." Customers are 20-50 years old and in the upper-middle to upper income bracket. Best selling time: Christmas and summer.

THE EMERSON GALLERY, 18676 Ventura Blvd., Tarzana CA 91356. (213)342-3777. Contact: Wayne LaCoin. Gallery. Estab. 1962. Represents 10 craftworkers. Considers batik; ceramics; glass art; metalsmithing; pottery; and woodcrafting. One-of-a-kind designer pieces only; utilitarian and/or decorative. Price range: $5-600; bestsellers: $5-200. Works on consignment; 40% commission. Retail price set by joint agreement. Requires exclusive area representation. Reports in 2 weeks. Hand-deliver work only. Work displayed 2 months. Best selling time: fall-spring.

BETH AND BILL ETGEN FINE JEWELRY, 3600 Whitney Ave., Sacramento CA 95821. (916)481-3912. Contact: Beth Etgen. Craft shop/gallery/jewelry shop. Estab. 1970. Represents 20 craftwomen. Considers jewelry and metalsmithing. "We now specialize in silver and gold jewelry by women artist jewelers. We need sterling silver prototypes or waxes suitable for molding and replicating in limited editions." Fine one-of-a-kind and handmade production-line items; utilitarian and/or decorative. Price range: $5-35; bestsellers: $5-20. Works on consignment; 50% commission. Retail price set by joint agreement. Reports in 1 week. "Don't send items, just photographs, slides or 3x5 prints. SASE. We can then correspond for samples." Dealer pays insurance for exhibited work.
Profile: "If work looks good we accept piece for display and advertise it in our monthly mailer to our clients. We also recommend helpful production ideas. We can produce a finished item from the wax model. We can make multiple copies for craftworkers to sell on their own also. Best selling time: November-December; May-June. Customers are mostly women interested in supporting women artists using jewelry as their expressive medium, ages 20-40; approximate income $12,000.

FAMILY AND FRIENDS, 900 N. Point St., San Francisco CA 94109. (415)885-1072. Manager: Terence Gockman. Craft shop. Estab. 1974. Represents 100 regional craftworkers. Considers one-of-a-kind ceramics and clothing; quilting and soft sculpture. Especially needs low-fire ceramics and porcelain of colorful design and colorful cotton clothing. Utilitarian and/or decorative. Price range: $1-250; bestsellers: $3-15. Works on consignment and buys outright; 33⅓%commission. Retail price set by joint agreement. Reports in 1 week. Work may be shipped or hand-delivered. Dealer pays insurance for exhibited work.
Profile: Best selling time: summer and Christmas; heaviest wholesale buying time: spring and fall.

FIBERWORKS, 1940 Bonita Ave., Berkeley CA 94704. Contact: Gallery Committee. Estab. 1973. Considers experimental artwork; prints; graphics; sketches; sculpture; and textile arts. The gallery is fiber-related, but not restricted to that area. Price range: $50-1,000 or more. Works on consignment; 30% commission. Craftworker sets minimum price. Send resume with slides or photos of work. Items displayed 2 weeks minimum. Mailing sent 6 times annually, with extra mailings for special shows. List includes about 9,000 names.

FIBROUS BEGINNINGS, 1733 N. Broadway, Walnut Creek CA 94596. (415)935-3611. Contact: Lynne Conley. Retailer of yarns, weaving and textile supplies and equipment. Estab. 1976. Represents 3 northern California craftworkers. Considers batik; clothing; needlecrafts; quilting; soft sculpture; wall hangings; weavings; baskets; and felting. One-of-a-kind designer and handmade production-line items; utilitarian and/or decorative. Price range: $5-250; bestsellers: $5-75. Works on consignment; 33⅓%commission. Craftworker sets retail price. Reports in 3 weeks. Work must be hand-delivered and craftworker must help hang show. Dealer pays insurance for exhibited work.
Profile: Shop schedules monthly shows featuring a wide range of finished textile items. "Nearly all customers are female, ages 12-85, primarily hobbyist, in an area that has one of the highest per capita incomes in northern California." Best selling time: Christmas.

FOO-FA-RAH, Box 323, Main St., North Fork CA 93643. (209)877-2922. Contact: Barbara Grigsby. Gift shop. Estab. 1975. Represents 100 craftworkers. Considers candlemaking; ceramics; decoupage; dollmaking; glass art; jewelry; leatherworking; metalsmithing; needlecrafts; pottery; quilting; tole painting; wall hangings; weavings; and woodcrafting. "Prefer mountain type, natural pieces"; utilitarian and/or decorative. Price range: 50c-$175; bestsellers:

$3-95. Works on consignment; 34% commission. Retail price set by joint agreement. Requires exclusive area representation. Reports in 4 weeks. Work may be shipped or hand-delivered.
Profile: "Crafts are sometimes displayed in a setting with other similar items. Utilitarian pieces are shown in settings indicating different uses. Try to change displays monthly. Handle more traditional 'mountain' than theme crafts. The work is top quality, and the shop stands behind it. My price range is such that gift buyers are encouraged and I can compete with regular gift shops. This is a small mountain town with many retireds and new young families moving in. Have a large tourist population in the summer from campers to summer home owners— close to resort area." Heaviest wholesale buying time: Christmas for summer tourist season; best selling time: Christmas and summer.
To Break In: "If you want to sell to Foo-Fa-Rah by mail, an accurate description, etc. of merchandise should be sent for me to review before it is agreed to be sent. Be able to supply at least 6 items to begin with on production-style crafts."

FORGE PATIO ART GALLERIE, ASSOCIATIONS, 3420 Mt. Diablo Blvd., LaFayette CA 94549. (415)284-1080. Contact: Barbara Speck. Gallery. Estab. 1972. Represents 25 Bay area artists and craftworkers. Considers batik; ceramics; glass art; pottery; wall hangings; and weavings. "We would like to carry some ceramic or wood jewelry — unique and different in design." Fine one-of-a-kind items only; utilitarian and/or decorative. Price range: $3-400; craft bestsellers average $20. Works on consignment; 40% commission. Craftworker sets retail price. Reports on first or second Tuesday of each month. Work may be hand-delivered or mail slides, photos and biography. Dealer pays insurance on exhibited work.
Profile: "The gallery is a showroom for 6 professional artists, which also exhibits works of Bay area craftsmen. We sell unique, one-of-a-kind items of local artists in a well-lighted, beautifully displayed gallery. It is located in the El Diablo Forge Guild — a complex of shops and restaurants, part of which was once an actual forge. Each month part of the gallery is devoted to featuring one of or a group of artists and/or craftsmen. The remainder of the gallery is always a representation of our affiliated artists and craftsmen." Best selling time: Christmas, spring and fall.

GALERIE DE TOURS, Box 4996, Carmel CA 93921. Contact: Robert J. Kaller. Gallery. Considers sculpture. "Those we represent must have some previous record. Recently, our gallery has handled works more in a historical vein." Price range: $500-75,000. 40-50% commission. Requires exclusive area representation. Charges commission on art sold in area after exclusive representation. Gallery pays insurance on exhibited work. 4 weeks minimum exposure.

GALLERY 8, International Center, Q-018, University of California at San Diego, La Jolla CA 92093. (714)452-3732. Co-director: Ruth Newmark. Estab. 1973. Represents 25+ craftworkers. Considers batik; ceramics; dollmaking; glass art; jewelry; leatherworking; needlecrafts; pottery; quilting; soft sculpture; wall hangings; weavings; woodcrafting; and baskets. Primitive and finished one-of-a-kind and handmade production-line items; utilitarian and/or decorative. Price range: $1-600; bestsellers: $15-30. Buys outright or on consignment; 33⅓% commission. Retail price set by gallery or joint agreement. Write. Reports in 2 weeks. Dealer pays shipping from shop and insurance for exhibited work.
Profile: Heaviest wholesale buying time: fall; best selling time: October-December. Primarily middle-aged, upper middle-class customers and some students and university staff; they buy crafts for artistic value or gifts.

GARDEN GROVE ARTISANS' GUILD, 13271 Century Blvd., Garden Grove CA 92643. Contact: Teri Obole. Considers sculpture and untraditional media. Send transparencies or photos of work. "All sales of exhibited work will be made through the Guild Hall cashier, with 20% retained to help defray overhead. Balance will be remitted to artist on the 10th of the following month."
Profile: "Our gallery maintains available space for one-man shows, or themed exhibits, for 1 or 2-month periods. Artists are expected to hang their own show and prepare a mailing list (we use their list in combination with our own) and price list. Artists living too far away to make this feasible need not send their own mailing list, but must pay a $50 hanging fee. Guild provides printing and postage for standard invitations and food for opening receptions. Artist provides wine and/or punch for reception and agrees to donate 1 work of art for drawing to help defray exhibit expenses. We enjoy good coverage from the local media. Therefore, it is important that we feature only quality art and that we have sufficient time to interview and photograph the artist with his work. If person-to-person interview is not feasible, artist must send ample public relations information and 10 b&w glossy photos for newspapers 4-8 weeks prior to exhibit's opening date."

GARENDO GALLERY, 12955 Ventura Blvd., Studio City CA 91604. (213)783-1861. President: Masako. Craft and gift shop. Estab. 1972. Represents 18 craftworkers. Considers batik; candlemaking; ceramics; clothing; glass art; jewelry; pottery; wall hangings; weavings; and woodcrafting. Fine or primitive one-of-a-kind items; utilitarian and/or decorative. Price range: $1-500. Works on consignment and buys outright; 50% commission. Retail price set by joint agreement. Requires exclusive area representation. Work may be shipped or hand-delivered. Best selling time: Christmas. Reports in 2-3 weeks.

GLAD HAND, 201½ Ave. I, Redondo Beach CA 90277. (213)540-2221. Contact: Boni Erickson. Craft shop. Estab. 1969. Represents 6 craftworkers. Considers ceramics; glass art; jewelry; pottery; wall hangings; and weavings. Fine one-of-a-kind and handmade production-line items; utilitarian and/or decorative. Price range: $15-600; bestsellers: $35-75. Works on consignment and buys outright; 33⅓% commission. Retail price set by joint agreement. Requires exclusive area representation for jewelry. Reports in 4 weeks. Work may be shipped or hand-delivered. Dealer pays insurance for exhibited work.
Profile: "Large collections are featured 1 month; small collections featured 2-3 months." Best selling time: spring and Christmas; heaviest wholesale buying time: spring-summer.

THE GUILD STORE, 1131 12th St., Sacramento CA 95814. (916)446-2395. Contact: Joel Bragdon. Craft shop. Estab. 1972. Represents 20 craftworkers. Considers all crafts except decoupage; dollmaking; and tole painting. Especially needs blown and leaded glass and leather. All styles; utilitarian and/or decorative. Price range: 25c-$500; bestsellers: $2-20. Works on consignment; 38% commission. "Most items in the store belong to Guild Store Coop members. Each member works in the store 1 day a week and pays a 16% commission on sales to the store." Craftworker sets retail price. Reports in 2 weeks. Work may be shipped or hand-delivered. "We like to keep consignment items in the store a maximum of 4 months." Best selling time: June-August and November-December.

HALLIE'S WEST GALLERY, 13045 Ventura Blvd., Studio City CA 91604. (213)986-3837. Contact: Hallie Katz. Gallery. Estab. 1976. Considers ceramics; clothing; glass art; jewelry; metalsmithing; soft sculpture; wall hangings; weavings; and woodcrafting. Fine one-of-a-kind and handmade production-line items only; utilitarian and/or decorative. Price range: $10-3,500; bestsellers: $25-250. Works on consignment; 40% commission. Retail price set by joint agreement. Work may be shipped or hand-delivered. Dealer pays return shipping and insurance for exhibited work.
Profile: "Work is displayed on pedestals and in acrylic dome showcases and cubes; arranged with other artist's work, grouped together when possible or necessary." Best selling time: winter-spring.

HIDE 'N' FREAK LEATHER WORKSHOP AND CRAFTS BAZAAR, 437 E. Main St., Ventura CA 93001. Contact: Dave. Craft and gift shop. Estab. 1970. Represents 10 craftworkers. Considers leatherworking. All styles; utilitarian and/or decorative. Price range: $3-150; bestsellers: $9-25. Buys outright. Gallery sets retail price. Work may be hand-delivered. Heaviest wholesale buying time: November; best selling time: December.

IRIS, 1894 Solano Ave., Berkeley CA 94707. (405)525-1043. Contact: Susan or Ira Klein. Craft shop. Estab. 1976. Represents 150 craftworkers. Considers all crafts except decoupage and tole painting. Fine one-of-a-kind and handmade production-line items; utilitarian and/or decorative. Price range: 5c-$890; bestsellers: 5c-$50. Works on consignment and buys outright; 40% commission. Retail price set by joint agreement. Reports in 1 week. Work may be shipped (UPS only) or hand-delivered. Dealer pays insurance for exhibited work. Work displayed for 3-month period.
Special Needs: Wants jewelry (rings, semi-precious stones with gold or silver settings); moustache and shaving mugs; wooden combs, pens and crochet hooks; glass goblets; coasters; and wooden dolls and toys.
Profile: Shop is decorated with wall-to-wall carpeting, spot and flourescent lighting and wooden fixtures. Display for consigned items is total responsibility of the craftworker. Strive to achieve creative displays, e.g., telephone booth changing room. Customers are primarily of a median income ($25,000/year) and are often U.C. Berkeley faculty and professionals. Heaviest wholesale buying time: fall-winter; best selling time: winter-Christmas.

I-YE-QUEE GIFT SHOP, Box 7, Hoopa CA 95546. Contact: Vivien Hailstone. Gift shop. Estab. 1951. Represents 6 northern California Indian craftworkers. Considers jewelry and pottery with contemporary American Indian design. All styles; utilitarian and/or decorative. Price range: $1-800; bestsellers: $3-200. Works on consignment and buys outright; 30% commission. Craftworker sets retail price. Reports in 2 weeks. Work may be shipped or hand-delivered. Dealer pays return shipping and insurance on exhibited work. Customers are mainly tourists. Heaviest wholesale buying time: May-June; best selling time: July-September.

KAURI SHELL GALLERY, 2126 Tydd St., Eureka CA 95501. (707)443-9586. Director: Geraldine Serpa. Gallery. Estab. 1977. Represents 20 craftwomen. Considers batik; clothing; jewelry; needlecrafts; quilting; soft sculpture; wall hangings; and weavings. Fine one-of-a-kind pieces only. Price range: $20-200; bestsellers: $20-100. Handles membership work only. Retail price set by craftworker. Reports in 4 weeks. "We are a women's gallery; we show only fine craft, mostly wall pieces."

KEFFELER'S JUBILANT JEWELRY, 9 Strawflower Center, Half Moon Bay CA 94019. (415)726-4223. Contact: Boyd or Toni Keffeler. Jewelry shop. "We specialize in fine handcrafted jewelry." Estab. 1975. Represents 15 craftworkers. Considers ceramics; glass art; jewelry; leatherworking; metalsmithing; and pottery. Fine one-of-a-kind and handmade production-line items; utilitarian and/or decorative. Price range: $3-500; bestsellers: $5-40. Works on consignment; 40% commission. Retail price set by joint agreement. Reports in 2 weeks. Work may be shipped or hand-delivered. Dealer pays return shipping.
Profile: "We're the only shop for handcrafts in our area. Our area is rural turning to suburban. All displays have been designed and built by us for best presentation and safety from theft." Displays work 60 days minimum. Best selling and heaviest consigning time: pre-Christmas.

KLEIN ART GALLERY, 332 N. Rodeo Dr., Beverly Hills CA 90210. (213)274-8955. Contact: David Klein. Considers sculpture. Maximum size: 30x40. Buys outright or on consignment; 40% commission. Bestsellers: $300-3,500. Retail price set by joint agreement. Sometimes requires exclusive area representation. Send photos of work or call or write for interview. SASE. 2-6 months exposure.

ESTHER LEWITTES DESIGN GALLERY, 8344 Melrose Ave., Los Angeles CA 90069. (213)655-7112. Contact: Esther Lewittes. Craft and gift shop. Estab. 1973. Represents 6 craftworkers. Considers ceramics; glass art; jewelry; metalsmithing; pottery; wall hangings; weavings; woodcrafting; and enamels. One-of-a-kind designer pieces only; utilitarian and/or decorative. Price range: $10-1,500; bestsellers: $10-1,000. Buys outright. Gallery sets retail price. Requires exclusive area representation. Reports in 1 week. Work may be shipped or hand-delivered. Dealer pays insurance for exhibited work. Heaviest wholesale buying time: "around Christmas"; best selling time: spring, fall and winter.

LIGHT OPERA, 900 N. Point #102, Ghirardelli Square, San Francisco CA 94109. (415)775-7665. Contact: Katy Stevens. Craft shop/gallery/gift shop. Estab. 1969. Represents 50-100 craftworkers. Considers ceramics; jewelry; and especially glass art. Fine one-of-a-kind and handmade production-line items; utilitarian and/or decorative. Price range: $1-10,000; bestsellers: $20-500. Buys outright. Gallery sets retail price. Send slides or arrange appointment before submitting work. Reports in 2 weeks. Dealer pays insurance for exhibited work.
Profile: "We have an area of the store which is a gallery space in which we have rotating shows for periods of 4-6 weeks. These shows focus on the work of a particular craftsman or craftsmen. The rest of the store displays various artists works — usually in groupings. We change our displays a good deal. We focus almost exclusively on art glass — blown, leaded, beveled, etc. We are known for our commitment to handmade glass works (especially western American, although we are interested in branching out to other areas and fine European glass)." Heaviest wholesale buying time: spring and fall; best selling time: summer and winter.

LIVING DESERT RESERVE, 47900 Portola Ave., Palm Desert CA 92260. (714)346-5694. Contact: June M. Sheffet. Museum gift shop. Estab. 1971. Considers jewelry; metalsmithing; pottery; woodcrafting; and stone paintings. "We are desert oriented." All styles; utilitarian and/or decorative. Price range: 10c-$15; bestsellers: $1.75-5. Buys outright. Retail price set by joint agreement. Requires exclusive area representation. Reports in 2 weeks. Work may be shipped or hand delivered. Dealer pays insurance for exhibited work. Most items displayed in cabinets. Best selling time: January-April; heaviest wholesale buying time: September-May.

LONGPRE GALLERY, 846 Foothill Blvd., La Canada CA 91011. Contact: Mrs. Longpre. Gallery. Estab. 1971. Represents 40+ craftworkers. Considers batik; jewelry; pottery; soft sculpture; tole painting; wall hangings; weavings; and woodcrafting. One-of-a-kind decorative designer pieces only. Price range: $20-20,000+. Works on consignment; 40% commission. Retail price set by joint agreement. Requires exclusive area representation. Reports in 2 weeks. High income customers.

Promotion: Public relations work is done "in conjunction with news release. Biography poster [distributed for] solo exhibit." Send photos or slides with biography.

THE MAD WOOFER, 716 Yarmouth Rd., Palos Verdes Estates CA 90274. (213)377-9775. Contact: Patrice J. Kennard. Craft shop/gallery/gift shop. Estab. 1976. Represents 10 craftworkers. Considers ceramics; dollmaking; glass art; jewelry; pottery; quilting; soft sculpture; wall hangings; weavings; and woodcrafting. Especially needs handmade gourmet cookware; fine jewelry; and children's toys. All styles; utilitarian and/or decorative. Price range: $5-500; bestsellers: $5-25. Works on consignment and buys outright; 40% commission. Retail price set by joint agreement. Reports in 2 weeks. Work may be shipped or hand-delivered. Dealer pays insurance for exhibited work.

Profile: "We use existing display to show work — or, if needed, we will set up something special." Displays consigned work 30 days. Customers are ages 18-45, well-to-do, and into "earthy" things. Heaviest wholesale buying time: summer-fall; best selling time: winter.

JUDAH MAGNES MUSEUM GIFT SHOP, 2911 Russell St., Berkeley CA 94607. Buyer: Arlene Sarver. Museum gift shop. Estab. 1974. Represents 25 craftworkers; "most are Jewish or are of Jewish interest but there are no restrictions." Considers ceramics; clothing; glass art; jewelry; metalsmithing; pottery; woodcrafting; cards; notepaper; paper dolls; prints; and books. All styles; utilitarian and/or decorative. Price range: 10c-$375. Works on consignment, buys outright and orders by catalog; 40% commission or craftworkers can set price they wish to receive. Retail price set by joint agreement. Reports in 1 week. Accepts items by mutual agreement and signed contract; don't send samples without permission.

Profile: "We have a large number of loyal customers. We sell often by mail order and wholesale to other shops." Best selling time: June-January.

MANOS MARAVILLOSAS, 1057 Rosecrans St., San Diego CA 92106. (714)222-5615. Contact: Joan Reynolds. Needlework shop. Estab. 1972. Represents 5-10 craftworkers. Considers clothing; dollmaking; needlecrafts; quilting; soft sculpture; wall hangings; and weavings. One-of-a-kind and handmade production-line items; utilitarian and/or decorative. Maximum price: $200; bestsellers: $5-35. Works on consignment; 33⅓% commission. Retail price set by joint agreement. Reports in 1 week. Work may be shipped or hand-delivered. Best selling time: summer and fall.

MANY HANDS CREATIVE ARTS COOPERATIVE, 6350 El Cajon Blvd., San Diego CA 92115. (714)287-7150. Contact: Members. Craft shop/gallery/gift shop. Represents 50 member craftworkers; "must live in San Diego County so they will be able to work in the shop about 12 hours per month to fulfill membership requirements." Considers all crafts. All styles; utilitarian and/or decorative. Price range: $1.25/finger puppet-$700/clock; bestsellers: under $10. Works on cooperative arrangement. "Due to our low overhead the craftsman receives about 95% of the retail price — it varies due to amount sold." Craftworker sets retail price. "Craftsmen should come into the store for an application for membership. We have a large turnover of craftsmen and need new craftsmen all the time. We accept new members through a jurying process. We would like to have more *serious* craftsmen apply."

Profile: "We are a cooperative with no manager. Craftsmen share all the work. The store is huge and we carry a tremendous variety of items in all price ranges. Due to our wide variety of craft items we attract all kinds of customers — students to very wealthy people. At Christmas time they bring their lists and do all their shopping in our store." Craftworkers may use floor, wall or shelf space throughout the store or set up own display for work.

Sales Tip: "Know your market. Accept the fact that 100 small inexpensive items will sell before 1 'good' piece. Be willing to experiment with new materials and techniques and grow. Don't keep making the same thing over and over. Take classes in design and art theory — not just how-to-do classes."

MENDOCINO ART CENTER GALLERY, Box 36, Mendocino CA 95460. (707)937-5818. Contact: Marjorie LeRay. Craft shop/gallery/rental gallery. Estab. 1959. Represents 30 craftworkers. Considers batik; ceramics; glass art; jewelry; metalsmithing; pottery; soft sculpture; wall hangings; weavings; and woodcrafting. Especially needs cereal bowls; serving dishes; and souffle dishes. Fine one-of-a-kind and handmade production-line items; utilitarian and/or decorative. Price range: $2-1,500; bestsellers: $2-200. Works on consignment and buys outright; 33⅓% commission. Retail price set by joint agreement. Send photos or slides. Reports in 3 weeks. Hand-delivered work only. Dealer pays insurance for exhibited work. "We ask to return or exchange unsold consignment items after 3-4 months."

Profile: Work is displayed in open shelf or wall displays; locked cases for small/precious items. Heaviest wholesale buying time: summer-fall; best selling time: August-January.

MOUNTAIN WEAVER, 334 N. Santa Cruz Ave., Los Gatos CA 95030. (408)354-8720. Contact: Jill Altmann. Craft shop. Estab. 1974. Considers batik; clothing; soft sculpture; wall hangings; weavings; and baskets. Primitive one-of-a-kind and handmade production-line items; utilitarian and/or decorative. Price range: $1.50 minimum. Works on consignment; 25% commission. Retail price set by joint agreement. Reports in 1 month. Work may be shipped or hand-delivered.

Profile: Customers are ages 19-40 of mid-upper middle class backgrounds— many art students from professional families. Heaviest wholesale buying time: Christmas (November-January); best selling time: October-March.

MUD IN YOUR EYE POTTERY STUDIO, (Incorporates The Art Affaire), 50 University Ave., Los Gatos CA 95030. Contact: Frank Howell. Estab. 1971. Represents 150 craftworkers. Considers candlemaking; glass art; jewelry; leatherworking; metalsmithing; pottery; and soft sculpture. Fine one-of-a-kind and handmade production-line items only; utilitarian and/or decorative. Price range: $2-150; bestsellers: under $30. Buys outright. Retail price set by joint agreement. Requires exclusive area representation. Reports in 2 weeks. Work may be shipped or hand-delivered. Customers are ages 25-40, and very oriented toward crafts. Best selling time: Christmas and summer; heaviest wholesale buying time: fall.

To Break In: "We deal with only those craftspeople willing and able to produce on a production basis. Establish prices that are based on research, not emotion or love of an item. Have invoices with name and address of craftsperson at top (a cheap rubber stamp is fine). Include packing slips with orders and have invoices *match* packing slips."

MY HOUSE GALLERY, 1143 Westwood Blvd., West Los Angeles CA 90024. (213)477-4073. Contact: Barry Axelrod. Craft shop/gallery/gift shop. Estab. 1976. Represents 75-80 craftworkers. Considers all crafts. Fine one-of-a-kind and handmade production-line items; utilitarian and/or decorative. Price range: $1-2,000. Works on consignment, buys outright and leases spaces; 50% commission. Craftworker sets retail price. Charges fee for exhibit space. Reports in 3 weeks. Dealer pays insurance for exhibited work.

Profile: "Shop is located in a very exclusive, very crowded retail area in walking distance from UCLA." Best selling time: holidays.

THE NEEDLE NOOK, 35157 Yucarpa Blvd., Yucarpa CA 92399. (714)797-3782. Needlepoint shop. Estab. 1977. Represents 10 craftworkers. Considers ceramics; clothing; needlecrafts; wall hangings; weavings; and especially needs quilting. Handmade production-line items only; utilitarian and/or decorative. Price range: $4-395; bestsellers: $10-30. Works on consignment and buys outright; 20% commission. Retail price set by joint agreement. Reports in 2 weeks. Work may be shipped or hand-delivered. Dealer pays return shipping and insurance for exhibited work. Work displayed until sold. Best selling time: fall.

NEW WORLD RESOURCE AND SUPPLY CO., 6578 Trigo Rd., Isla Vista CA 93017. (805)968-5329. Contact: Janice Emmrich. General store. Estab. 1969. Represents 15-20 craftworkers. Considers batik; candlemaking; ceramics; clothing; jewelry; leatherworking; needlecrafts; pottery; wall hangings; weavings; macrame; and beadwork. All styles; utilitarian and/or decorative. Price range: $3-400; bestsellers: $10. Works on consignment; 20% commission. Retail price set by joint agreement. Work may be shipped or hand-delivered.

Profile: "We try to talk the crafts up and display them favorably. We have a quite a hodge-podge of rural needs — crafts, housewares, on and on. Customers are half students and half country folks." Heaviest wholesale buying and best selling time: pre-Christmas.

ORLANDO GALLERY, 17037 Ventura Blvd., Encino CA 91316. (213)789-6012. Contact: Robert Gino. Gallery. Estab. 1960. Considers ceramics; glass art; jewelry; wall hangings; weavings; and woodcrafting. Fine and primitive one-of-a-kind pieces; utilitarian and/or decorative. Works on consignment; 40% commission. Retail price set by joint agreement. Requires exclusive area representation. Work may be shipped or hand-delivered. Dealer pays insurance for exhibited work. Reports in 3 weeks.

PACIFIC BASIN TEXTILE ARTS, 1659 San Pablo Ave., Berkeley CA 94702. (415)526-9836. Contact: Director. Considers batik; soft sculpture; weavings; and other fiber media. Craftworker

supplies and installs any special lights, stands or other special installation accessories. Works on consignment; 25% commission. Bestsellers: $25-300. Craftworker sets retail price. Write for interview. Gallery sponsors reception. 5-6 weeks exposure.
Promotion: Exhibit is listed on the Pacific Basin calendar and on the gallery's brochure distributed in the community. Press release is sent to all local papers and mailing list publications.

PALM SPRINGS DESERT MUSEUM SHOP, Box 2288, 101 Museum Dr., Palm Springs CA 92262. (714)325-7186. Contact: Marjorie Merwin. Museum gift shop. Estab. 1976. Represents 60 Western craftworkers. Considers ceramics; glass art; jewelry; and pottery. Fine one-of-a-kind and handmade production-line items; utilitarian and/or decorative. Price range: $4-75. Works on consignment and buys outright; commission varies. Retail price set by joint agreement. Requires exclusive area representation. Reports in 2 weeks. Work may be shipped if photos are hand-delivered by appointment first. Dealer pays return shipping and insurance. Best selling time: December-February and March-April; heaviest wholesale buying time: fall and January.

PHOENIX SHOP, Big Sur CA 93920. Manager: Alice Russell. Craft and gift shop. Estab. 1965. Represents 15 craftworkers. Considers batik; candlemaking; ceramics; clothing; dollmaking; glass art; jewelry; leatherworking; metalsmithing; pottery; quilting; soft sculpture; and woodcrafting. All styles; utilitarian and/or decorative. Price range: $5-400; bestsellers: $10-50. Works on consignment and buys outright; 40% commission. Retail price set by joint agreement. Requires exclusive area representation. Hand delivered work only. Dealer pays shipping to shop if outright purchase and insurance for exhibited work. Best selling time: summer.

PLACER COUNTY MUSEUM, 175 Fulweiler Ave., Auburn CA 95603. (916)885-9570. Contact: Cevera Ingraham. Museum gallery/gift shop. Estab. 1948. Represents 5-60 craftworkers. Considers dollmaking; glass art; needlecrafts; quilting; wall hangings; weavings; and woodcrafting. All styles; utilitarian and/or decorative. Price range: $3-7,000; bestsellers: $3-15. Works on consignment; commission varies. Retail price set by craftsworker. Reports in 4 weeks. Hand-delivered work only.
Profile: "Shop is located in the gold county in a historical museum." Best selling and heaviest wholesale buying time: summer.

THE PLEBIAN, 834 Kline St., La Jolla CA 92037. (714)454-1888. Contact: David or Marji Nightingale. Craft shop. Estab. 1968. Represents 20 craftworkers. Considers jewelry; metalsmithing; enamels; and cloisonne jewelry. Fine one-of-a-kind and handmade production-line items; utilitarian and/or decorative. Price range: $25-1,500; bestsellers: $25-150. Works on consignment; 30-33% commission. Craftworker sets retail price. Requires exclusive area representation. Submit photos or slides. SASE. Reports in 2 weeks. Work may be shipped or hand-delivered. Dealer pays insurance for exhibited work.
Special Needs: "We would like to carry more cloisonne enamels— either in jewelry or in small functional or non-functional art pieces (e.g., boxes). Also interested in small enameled pieces and metalsmithed items — functional or non-functional, unique jewelry in gold or silver."
Profile: "We have glass showcases (all with locks). Every item on display can be easily seen by the customers. If we have enough pieces by 1 craftsman we will feature them in a special case. We have been located in La Jolla 8 years, and have built a reputation of good, personal service. We own and operate our own business (no employees) and know many of our customers. La Jolla is a very wealthy area. It is also an area of summer and winter resorting with many tourists. Tourists come from everywhere, including Europe and Canada. We have a mailing list of 2,000+." Displays work 1-6 months. Heaviest wholesale buying time: late spring and late fall; best selling time: summer and Christmas.

POTTERS STUDIO, 1801 E. McKinley, Fresno CA 93703. (209)266-5508. Contact: Hazel Olsen. Gift shop. Estab. 1970. Represents 15-20 craftworkers. Considers ceramics; jewelry; pottery; wall hangings; and weavings. Fine one-of-a-kind and handmade production-line items; utilitarian and/or decorative. Price range: $2.50-300; bestsellers: $25-80. Works on consignment and buys outright; 40% commission. Craftworker sets retail price. Reports in 2 weeks. Work may be shipped or hand-delivered. Dealer pays shipping to shop. Best selling time: spring and fall.

PRISM CRESCENTS, 2047 Allston Way, Box 182, Berkeley CA 94704. (415)841-1155. Co-directors: John Beuttler and Glenn Cochran. Craft shop/gallery. Estab. 1974. Represents 100 craftworkers. Price range: $2.50-2,000. Works on consignment; 30-40% commission.

Craftworker sets retail price. Reports in 1 week. Payment upon request. Dealer pays insurance for exhibited work.

Acceptable Work: Considers batik; ceramics; glass art; jewelry; leatherworking; metalsmithing; needlecrafts; pottery; quilting; soft sculpture; wall hangings; weavings; and woodcrafting. "Special need for blown glass and jewelry." Fine one-of-a-kind and handmade production-line items; utilitarian and/or decorative.

Profile: "We are not just a shop or gallery but a group of independent artists/craftspeople that have created this retail outlet for our work. It is an open ongoing creation. Our customers are mostly people that like very high quality art/craft items." Best selling time: Christmas.

WAYNE RED-HORSE, 106-K St., Suite 1, Sacramento CA 95814. Contact: Wayne Red-Horse. Estab. 1972. Represents 10 Indian craftworkers. Considers all Indian-made crafts. Finished one-of-a-kind items only; utilitarian and/or decorative. Price range: $1-500; bestsellers: $3-90. Buys outright or on consignment; 33⅓% commission. Craftworker sets retail price. Write. Reports in 2 weeks. Dealer pays shipping from shop and insurance for exhibited work.

Profile: Heaviest wholesale buying time: summer. "We do custom orders and repairs." Mostly tourist customers; they buy crafts for gifts.

RIVERSIDE ART CENTER AND MUSEUM, 3425 7th St., Riverside CA 92501. (714)684-7111. Curator: Katie Miller. Members gallery: sales and rental. Represents 60-100 craftworkers. Considers batik; ceramics; glass; jewelry; metalsmithing; pottery; wall hangings; weavings; and woodcrafting. One-of-a-kind designer pieces only; utilitarian and/or decorative. Price range: 25c-$750; bestsellers: $2-250. Works on consignment; 33⅓% commission. Craftworker sets retail price. Work may be hand-delivered. Art Center pays insurance for exhibited work. Reports after jurying (third Tuesday of each month).

Profile: Crafts taken on consignment for 6 months. Craftworkers should "bring the best of their work to exhibit (not everything)." Best selling time: Christmas and spring.

ROBINSONS' RED DOOR GALLERY, 2840 Main St., Morro Bay CA 93442. Contact: Anita or Roger Robinson. Gallery. Estab. 1966. Represents 5 craftworkers. Considers ceramics; glass art; pottery; wall hangings; and weavings. One-of-a-kind designer pieces only; decorative and/or utilitarian. Price range: $4-750; bestsellers: $15-225. Works on consignment; 40% commission. Retail price set by joint agreement. Requires exclusive area representation. Reports in 3 weeks. Work may be shipped or hand-delivered. Dealer pays insurance for exhibited work.

Profile: "Some items by each artist or craftsman are always on display on a pedestal or whatever is appropriate. Our new building was especially designed as a gallery. We like to have new work about every 90 days to replace what has been sold and/or to rotate stock."

RUBICON GALLERY, 1st and Main Sts., Los Altos CA 94022. (415)984-4848. Director: Paul Klein. Considers sculpture. Buys outright or on consignment; 40-50% commission. Price range: $200-20,000, sculpture; bestsellers: $300-1,000. Retail price set by joint agreement. Prefers exclusive area representation. Send slides of work. SASE. Gallery pays shipping from gallery and insurance on exhibited work. 6-8 weeks exposure.

RUG CRAFTERS, 777 Bridgeway, Sausalito CA 94965. (415)332-0808. Manager: Donn Lorenzo. One of 3 craft shops. Estab. 1971. Represents 5 craftworkers. Considers wall hangings; weavings; rugs; and tapestries. Handmade production-line items only; utilitarian and/or decorative. Price range: $25-500; bestsellers: $45-120. Works on consignment; 40% commission. Retail price set by joint agreement. Reports in 2 weeks. Work may be shipped or hand-delivered. Dealer pays return shipping and insurance for exhibited work. Best selling time: June-December; heaviest wholesale buying time: May-September.

THE RUSTIC SHOPPE, Box 953, 45098 Main St., Mendocino CA 95460. (707)937-5787. Contact: Richard Huckins. Gift shop. Estab. 1975. Represents "hundreds" of craftworkers. Considers candlemaking; ceramics; jewelry; leatherworking; metalsmithing; pottery; and woodcrafting. Fine one-of-a-kind and handmade production-line items; utilitarian and/or decorative. Price range: 50c-$2,500; bestsellers: $1.50-30. Works on consignment and buys outright; 33⅓-40% commission. Gallery sets retail price if bought outright; craftworker sets retail price if on consignment. Requires exclusive area representation. Reporting time varies. Work may be shipped or hand-delivered. Dealer pays shipping and insurance for exhibited work. Best selling time: summer; heaviest wholesale buying time: March-December.

SAN JOSE ART LEAGUE CENTER, 482 S. 2nd St., San Jose CA 95113. (408)294-4545. Director: Dr. Delmar Kolb. Gallery. Estab. 1938. Represents California (primarily Santa Clara

County) craftworkers. Considers batik; ceramics; clothing; glass art; jewelry; leatherworking; metalsmithing; pottery; quilting; soft sculpture; wall hangings; weavings; woodcrafting; cast metals; assemblage; and stone carving. One-of-a-kind designer pieces only; utilitarian and/or decorative. Price range: $30-1,000; bestsellers: $30-300. Provides exhibit space; 25% commission. Craftworker sets retail price. Reports "as soon as possible." Work may be hand-delivered. Dealer pays insurance for some exhibited work. Plaster and ceramics excluded.
Profile: "Standard pedestal/platform and shelving [provided] for sculptural works; hanging or platform display method for textiles; and plastic bubbles and cases for jewelry and small items. Our tradition is 1 month shows. We are a nonprofit exhibit and workshop organization funded by donations."

SANDALMAKER, 1334 Westwood Blvd., Los Angeles CA 90024. (213)473-9549. Contact: Steve. Craft shop. Estab. 1963. Represents 4 craftworkers. Considers leatherworking; metalsmithing; and antique-type firearms. "We need a good, consistent line of ready-made, elegant, 'earthy' sandals." All styles; utilitarian. Price range: $2.50-150; bestsellers: $8.50-35. Works on consignment and buys outright; 34% commission. Retail price set by joint agreement. Reports in 1 week. Work may be shipped or hand-delivered by prior arrangement only. Dealer pays insurance for exhibited work.
Profile: "Display [work] on wall (hodge-podge); shelf (open); or, if really valuable, in display case. We do leather work in the shop; we occasionally make custom muzzle-loading rifles in the shop; we demonstrate our crafts and instruct those showing interest." Best selling time: summer and Christmas.
Sales Tip: "For maximum sales, items should look elegant and very finished, but should be semi-production-line work to keep the price at attractive levels. Craftspeople should be dependable above all — delivery dates should be realistic and abided by."

SANTA BARBARA MUSEUM OF ART SHOP, 1124 State St., Santa Barbara CA 93101. (805)963-4364. Manager: Douglas Bartoli. Considers contemporary ceramics; dollmaking; glass art; jewelry; leatherworking; metalsmithing; mobiles; needlecrafts; pottery; soft sculpture; tole painting; wall hangings; weavings; and woodcrafting. Price range: 50c-$1,000; bestsellers: 50c-$100. Buys outright or on consignment; 100% mark-up on consigned items. Gallery sets retail price. Requires exclusive area representation. Call or write for interview or send photos. Dealer pays shipping from shop and insurance for exhibited work. Items displayed 6-8 weeks.

SANTA BARBARA MUSEUM OF NATURAL HISTORY, 2559 Puesta Del Sol Rd., Santa Barbara CA 93105. (805)682-4711. Contact: Laurel Johnson. Museum gallery/gift shop. Estab. 1916. Craftworks which relate to natural history, anthropology, botany, astronomy, marine life, bird life or animal life. Considers batik; jewelry; metalsmithing; and woodcrafting. All styles; utilitarian and/or decorative. Price range: $1-100; bestsellers: $1-10. Works on consignment and buys outright; 30% commission. Retail price set by joint agreement. Reports in 3 weeks. Work may be shipped or hand-delivered.
Profile: "As our gift shop is still in planning stages we hope to have it ready within the next 5 years. In the meantime, crafts are displayed in the book shop. The museum building is Spanish in design, and set in a wooded area on Mission Creek in Santa Barbara. Customers are of all ages; numerous school groups, tours and visitors from all over. Interests tend toward natural history related subjects." Heaviest wholesale buying time: spring-summer; best selling time: summer and Christmas.

THE SEA, 525 N. Harbor Blvd., San Pedro CA 90731. (213)831-1694. Contact: Tery Ponce. Craft and gift shop. Estab. 1968. Represents 6 craftworkers. Considers ceramics; jewelry; metalsmithing; needlecrafts; pottery; soft sculpture; and woodcrafting. Must be nautical or dealing with the ocean. One-of-a-kind and handmade production-line items; utilitarian and/or decorative. Price range: 50c-$900; bestsellers: 50c-$25. Works on consignment and buys outright. Retail price set by joint agreement.
Profile: "Crafts are mostly nautical or shells from the sea or land." Best selling time: summer and Christmas.

SENSEMAYA, 1718 University Ave., Berkeley CA 94703. (415)843-0790. Contact: Diane Mason. Craft and gift shop. Estab. 1967. Represents 200-300 craftworkers. Considers all crafts except decoupage and tole painting. Especially needs current clothing styles and full ceramic dinner sets. Fine one-of-a-kind and handmade production-line items; utilitarian and/or decorative. Price range: $1-200; bestsellers: $1-60. Works on consignment and buys outright; 38-40% commission. Craftworker sets retail price. Reports in 4 weeks. Work may be shipped or hand-delivered. Dealer pays insurance for exhibited work. Work displayed 1-3 months.

Profile: "Newest items are always given window display and are placed in prime spaces in the store. Our shop has a warm, homey environment in which we are able to offer handmade goods at very reasonable prices." Heaviest wholesale buying time: May-December; best selling time: May, July and November-December (mostly Christmas).

THE SHOP, Box 133, Amador City CA 95601. (209)267-5438. Contact: Harold Dickey. Estab. 1968. Represents 7 craftworkers. Considers pottery; weaving; wood; and leather that is not tooled or stamped. Price range: $2-600; bestsellers: $4-125. Works on consignment; 40% commission. Requires exclusive area representation. Write. Reports in 1 week. Dealer usually pays shipping from shop; negotiates in-transit insurance. Related items are segregated. Best selling time: October-April.

SOME PLACE, 2990 Adeline St., Berkeley CA 94705. (415)843-7178. Contact: Jules Kliot. Craft shop. Estab. 1965. Considers contemporary and antique lace and textiles. Price range: $1-3,000; bestsellers: $1-250. Buys outright and works on consignment. Reports in 1 week.

SOMETHING SPECIAL IN SIERRA CITY, Box 174, Sierra City CA 96125. Contact: Eunice Banks. Craft shop/gallery/gift shop. Estab. 1976. Represents local and regional craftworkers. Considers candlemaking; ceramics; decoupage; glass art; jewelry; leatherworking; metalsmithing; pottery; tole painting; wall hangings; weavings; and woodcrafting. All styles; utilitarian and/or decorative. Price range: $1-200; bestsellers: $1-35. Works on consignment and buys outright; 40% commission. Retail price set by joint agreement. Reports in 2 weeks. Work may be hand-delivered. Dealer pays return shipping and insurance for exhibited work.

Profile: "We are high in the Sierra Nevada northern mining area on historic Highway 49. Interest in gold mining history is keen here as is fishing, hunting and backpacking. Local scene is what sells." Best selling time: summer and winter; heaviest wholesale buying time: spring and fall.

SOURCE GALLERY, 1099 Folsom St., San Francisco CA 94103. (415)621-0545. Gallery. Considers sculpture; soft sculpture; wall hangings; and weavings. Price range: $500 minimum, fiberworks. Works on consignment; 50% commission. Retail price set by joint agreement. Requires exclusive area representation. "Visit gallery to see if artwork is appropriate and compatible," then, query or call for interview; if out-of-town, send resume and slides. SASE. Gallery pays insurance on exhibited work and shipping from gallery unless work is specifically requested by artist at an earlier date. 6 weeks minimum exposure.

SPIEGL GALLERY AND GIFT SHOP, Box 1056, San Juan Bautista CA 95045. (408)623-4357. Contact: Frank Dungan. Gallery/gift shop. Estab. 1971. Represents 8 craftworkers. Considers ceramics; glass art; jewelry; leatherworking; metalsmithing; pottery; tole painting; wall hangings; weavings; and woodcrafting. Fine one-of-a-kind and handmade production-line items; utilitarian and/or decorative. Price range: $1-200; bestsellers: $1-25. Works on consignment and buys outright; 40% commission. Retail price set by joint agreement. Requires exclusive area representation. Work may be shipped or hand-delivered. Displays work for a minimum of 60 days.

THE STRAWBERRY PATCH, 407 Elizabeth St., Vacaville CA 95688. (707)448-3200. Contact: Janette Jones. Craft shop. Estab. 1976. Represents 25 craftworkers "who do country-type work (ginghams, calicos, quilts, patchwork pillows, dolls, baby items and kitchen crafts)." Considers dollmaking; glass art; needlecrafts; pottery; quilting; soft sculpture; tole painting; wall hangings; weavings; woodcrafting; oak reproductions; dried flower arrangements; and pressed flowers. Primitive handmade production-line pieces only; utilitarian and/or decorative. Price range: 50c-$500; bestsellers: $2.50-25. Works on consignment and buys outright; 30% commission. Retail price set by joint agreement. Reports in 2 weeks. Work may be shipped or hand-delivered. Dealer pays return shipping and insurance for exhibited work.

Profile: Work is displayed "in an old house setting with kitchen crafts in kitchen area with pot belly stove, baby area and bay windows with shelves. There is a strawberry theme throughout—lots of unusual nooks and crannies to display." Best selling time: Christmas; heaviest wholesale buying time: Easter, Christmas and Mother's Day.

THE STUDIO, 214 W. Ridgecrest Blvd., Ridgecrest CA 93555. (714)375-7970. Contact: Barbara Battles. Craft and gift shop. Estab. 1977. Represents 50 craftworkers. All styles; utilitarian and/or decorative. Price range: $1-50, with exception of quilts; bestsellers: $3-25. Works on consignment and sometimes buys outright; 33⅓% commission (also charges a $5 annual consign-

ment fee which handles paperwork; insurance; mailing; etc.). Retail price set by joint agreement. Reports in 3 weeks. Send photos and good description of items. Send minimum amount of items before sending large shipment. Dealer pays shipping to shop; return in-transit insurance; and insurance for exhibited work. Unsold consigned pieces returned after 1 year.
Acceptable Work: Considers batik; ceramics; decoupage; dollmaking; glass art; jewelry; leatherworking; metalsmithing; needlecrafts; pottery; quilting; soft sculpture; tole painting; wall hangings; weavings; and woodcrafting. "Special need for one-of-a-kind jewelry pieces."
Profile: "We are in a desert area that is growing rapidly." Customers are of middle to high income. Best selling time: September-December.

STUDIO SUENAGA, 1105 Camino Del Mar, Del Mar CA 92014. (714)755-7575. Contact: Nancy Suenaga. Jewelry shop. Estab. 1971. Considers jewelry. Fine one-of-a-kind designer pieces; decorative only. Price range: $3-4,000; bestsellers: $50-800. Works very little on consignment. Owner sets retail price and pays shipping and insurance.
Profile: "The shop is 2,000 square feet with a large inventory of custom designed pieces displayed on velvets, burl and grapevine wood. Nancy's own designs have won many awards from the California (Southern) Exposition." Customers are 20-60 years of age, mostly professional with average income of $15,000+. Heaviest wholesale buying time and bestselling time: Christmas.

STUDIOS WEST — ENCINITAS, 167 Saxony Rd., Encinitas CA 92024. (714)753-8186. Director: Ralph Ritchie. Gallery Manager: Tanya Vint. Studio/gallery/sculpture garden. Estab. 1969. "Most of the work shown is done by Studios West associated craftspersons with occasional invitational shows." Considers some pottery, and architectural and garden sculpture. One-of-a-kind fine crafts only. Price range: $10-5,000; bestsellers: $100-1,000. Buys outright (materials and facilities supplied by the Studio). "We rarely work on consignment; but when we do it's 20-50% [commission]." Retail price set by joint agreement. "Rarely respond [to inquiries] unless in-person visit or SASE." Best selling time: spring or Christmas for architectural work; April-May and August-October for other work. Customers are age 30 or older with above-average income.

SUNNYVALE CREATIVE ARTS CENTER, Box 607, Sunnyvale CA 94088. (408)735-5521. Creative Arts Coordinator: Linda Pedroncelli. Gallery. Estab. 1973. Represents San Francisco Bay craftworkers, sometimes other parts of California. Considers batik; ceramics; clothing; glass art; jewelry; leatherworking; metalsmithing; needlecrafts; pottery; quilting; soft sculpture; tole painting; wall hangings; weavings; and woodcrafting. Primitive and fine one-of-a-kind pieces; utilitarian and/or decorative. Price range: $3-1,000; bestsellers: $3-500. "We are purely an exhibit gallery, any sales are handled by craftworker and the buyer." Craftworker sets retail price. Hand-delivered work only.
Profile: "Works are displayed as part of a 1-3 man show or group show. Most shows run 3 weeks. Since the gallery is in the middle of the Creative Arts Center, which is part of a 4 building community center, we get a wide variety of people who would not normally go to a gallery."

SUNSHINE STORE, 905 Linden Ave., Carpinteria CA 93013. (805)684-1215. Contact: Sylvia Orton. Craft/gift shop. Estab. 1970. Represents 25-30 craftworkers. Considers all crafts. Fine and primitive one-of-a-kind and handmade production-line pieces; utilitarian and/or decorative. Price range: $1.98-175; bestsellers: $2.50-30. Works on consignment; 35% commission. Retail price set by joint agreement. Requires exclusive area representation. Reports in 4 weeks. Hand-delivered work preferable first time. Dealer pays insurance for exhibited work.
Profile: Shop "serves primarily tourists of all ages and incomes." Best selling time: summer and December.

SWEET EARTH SHOP, 609 High St., Auburn CA 95603. Contact: Suzanne Souza. Craft and gift shop. Estab. 1975. Represents 25 craftworkers. Considers batik; candlemaking; ceramics; glass art; jewelry; metalsmithing; pottery; wall hangings; weavings; woodcrafting; illustrated children's books; and illustrated cards. Primitive handmade production-line items only; utilitarian and/or decorative. Price range: 50c-$38; bestsellers: 50c-$30. Works on consignment and buys outright; 35% commission. Shop sets retail price if bought outright; craftworker sets retail price if on consignment. Work may be shipped or hand-delivered, but must have prior approval if shipped. Dealer pays return shipping and insurance for exhibited work. Reports "immediately."
Profile: This shop has "a large variety. We sell our own pottery as well as work by other craftspeople." Best selling time: Christmas; heaviest wholesale buying time: summer and fall.

THE TAMARIND TREE, 35 Miller Ave., Mill Valley CA 94941. (415)388-6066. Contact: Catherine Todhunter. Estab. 1971. Represents 50 craftworkers. Considers batik; candlemaking; ceramics; dollmaking; glass art; jewelry; leatherworking; metalsmithing; pottery; wall hangings; weavings; woodcrafting; and functional sculpture. All styles; utilitarian and/or decorative. Price range: 50c-$2; bestsellers: $5-20. Buys outright or on consignment; 40% commission. Retail price set by joint agreement. Requires exclusive area representation. Write or query with transparencies or photos. Reports in 2 weeks. Negotiates payment for shipping and insurance. Best selling and wholesale buying time: fall. Customers are ages 20-40.

TARBOX GALLERY, 1025 Prospect St., La Jolla CA 92037. (714)459-0442. Gallery. Estab. 1971. Represents 30 West Coast craftworkers. Considers batik; ceramics; glass art; jewelry; metalsmithing; wall hangings; and weavings. One-of-a-kind designer pieces only; utilitarian and/or decorative. Price range: $5-5,000. Works on consignment with new artists and buys outright from artists established in the gallery; 40% commission. Retail price set by joint agreement. Requires exclusive area representation. Reports in 1 month. Work may be shipped or hand-delivered on advance notice.
Profile: Best selling time: summer. "The gallery reflects the West Coast scene and is divided into 2 rooms: fine art and crafts. On displays there is some intermingling when effective." Customers are "tourists and local customers in moderate to good income bracket."

TEMPLE OF GOOD THINGS, 6241 W. 87th St., Los Angeles CA 90045. (213)670-3772. Contact: Louis Nusinow. Gift shop. Estab. 1969. Represents 25 craftworkers. Considers candlemaking; ceramics; glass art; jewelry; wall hangings; weavings; and woodcrafting. Primitive and fine one-of-a-kind pieces; utilitarian and/or decorative. Price range: $2-250; bestsellers: $5-150. Works on consignment and buys outright; 30-40% commission. Retail price set by joint agreement. Requires exclusive area representation. Reports in 4 weeks. Work may be shipped or hand-delivered. Dealer pays shipping to shop and insurance on exhibited work.
Profile: Best selling time: Christmas; heaviest wholesale buying time: fall. Customers are "7-85 years of age and are in middle to upper income."

TEXTILES BY DESIGN, 5519 College Ave., Oakland CA 94703. (415)654-1434. Contact: Mary Hendricks. Craft shop/gallery. Estab. 1977. Represents 15-25 craftworkers. Considers wall hangings; weavings; basketry; textile dolls and toys; and textile kitchen items and household items. Fine one-of-a-kind and handmade production-line items; utilitarian and/or decorative. Price range: $5-700; bestsellers: $10-40. Works on consignment; 45% commission. Retail price set by joint agreement. Reports in 1-2 weeks. Work may be shipped or hand-delivered. Dealer pays return shipping and insurance for exhibited work.
Profile: Best selling time: fall-early spring; heaviest wholesale buying time: fall and spring. "We are the only shop that we know of anywhere out here which specializes in handmade fiber arts. We handle nothing else and are *the* place to shop for textiles!"

TIDEPOOL GALLERY, 22762 Pacific Coast Hwy., Malibu CA 90265. (213)456-2551. Partner: Jan Greenberg. Gallery/gift shop. Estab. 1969. Represents 100-125 craftworkers whose work relates to the ocean in some way. Prefers California or Western craftworkers. Considers batik; candlemaking; ceramics; glass art; jewelry; needlecrafts; pottery; soft sculpture; wall hangings; weavings; and woodcrafting. All styles utilitarian and/or decorative. Price range: $20-250; bestsellers: $25-50. Works on consignment and buys outright; 33⅓% commission. Craftworker sets retail price. Requires exclusive area representation. Reports in 2 weeks. Work may be shipped or hand-delivered. Dealer pays insurance for exhibited work.
Profile: Work is displayed "for a period of 2 months, then removed and displayed again." Customers are all ages and incomes. Best selling time: summer-Christmas; heaviest wholesale buying time: Christmas, spring and fall.

TRITON MUSEUM OF ART, 1505 Warburton Ave., Santa Clara CA 95050. Acting Director: Jo Farb Hernandez. Works with sculptors; jewelers; and glass and textile artists. Features work of San Francisco Bay area and Santa Clara Valley artists, but will consider work of artists from other areas as well. 25% commission. Send resume and photos or slides.

UPPER ECHELON, 777 Bridgeway, Sausalito CA 94765. Buyer: Sandy Younglove. Gallery/shop. Estab. 1962. Represents 75 craftworkers. Considers batik; candles; ceramics; glass art; jewelry; metalsmithing; pottery; wall hangings; weavings; and woodcrafting. Fine one-of-a-kind and handmade production-line items; utilitarian and/or decorative. Price range: 65c-$200. Buys outright. Retail price set by joint agreement. Requires exclusive area representation. Reports in 2-3 weeks. Deliveries accepted on order only.

Special Needs: Hand thrown juicers, batter bowls and sugar and creamer sets.
Profile: This shop represents "some of the nation's finest crafts from the foremost craftspeople."
Best selling and heaviest wholesale buying time: spring-fall.

VALLEY ART GALLERY, 1641 Locust Ave., Walnut Creek CA 94596. (415)935-4311. Director: Dorothy Magoffin. Gallery/museum gift shop/rental gallery. Estab. 1941. Represents 40 craftworkers. Considers ceramics; glass art; jewelry; pottery; and woodcrafting. Fine one-of-a-kind and handmade production-line items; utilitarian and/or decorative. Price range: $2-75; bestsellers: $5-25. Works on consignment; 20% commission. Retail price set by craftworker. Work may be hand-delivered. Dealer pays insurance for exhibited work. Reports "immediately if it is something we can use." Best selling time: November-December.

VAN DOREN GALLERY, 10 Gold St., San Francisco CA 94133. (415)392-0434. Gallery. Considers contemporary sculpture. Maximum size: 10x15. Price range: $100-15,000. Set by joint agreement. 50% commission. Requires exclusive area representation. Sponsors openings. Send resume and color slides. Exhibited art insured. Shipping costs shared.

VENICE PLACE ARTS CENTER, 1023½ W. Washington Blvd., Venice CA 90291. (213)399-0574. Contact: Charles Jaeger. Craft shop/gallery. Estab. 1970. Represents 10 craftworkers. Considers ceramics; pottery; soft sculpture; sculpture; and paintings. Fine one-of-a-kind and handmade production-line items only. Retail price set by joint agreement. This is a "collection of galleries and studios around a central patio which is beautifully landscaped." Best selling time: December.

DON WAKEFIELD FLOWERS AND GIFTS, 900 Wilshire Blvd., Los Angeles CA 90017. (213)626-4431. Contact: Don Wakefield. Gift shop. Estab. 1951. Represents 12 craftworkers. Considers candlemaking; ceramics; decoupage; dollmaking; glass art; pottery; and tole painting. Fine one-of-a-kind and handmade production-line items only; utilitarian and/or decorative. Price range: $9-60. Works on consignment; 50% commission. Gallery sets retail price. Requires exclusive area representation. Reports within 10 days. Work may be shippe or hand-delivered. Dealer pays insurance for exhibited work.
Profile: Shop has "abundance of shoppers" in a very good location; average and above average incomes. Best selling time: Christmas.

WALNUT CREEK CIVIC ARTS GALLERY, 1641 Locust St., Walnut Creek CA 94596. (415)935-3300, ext. 257. Contact: Marvin Schenck. Museum/rental gallery. Estab. 1963. Price range: $50-2,000; bestsellers: $50-400. Works on consignment; 30% commission. Craftworker sets retail price. Reports in 4 weeks. Work may be shipped or hand-delivered. Western Association of Art Museums pays insurance.
Acceptable Work: Considers batik; ceramics; clothing; glass art; jewelry; leatherworking; metalsmithing; needlecrafts; pottery; quilting; soft sculpture; wall hangings; weavings; woodcrafting; and puppets. One-of-a-kind designer pieces only; utilitarian and/or decorative.
Profile: Work "can be hung, set down in position, cased in Plexiglas or put into a Plexiglas wall cabinet. The time period for the show is 6 weeks with a 2 week period for installation."

WALSER'S DECOR ENCOUNTER, 23825 Hawthorne Blvd., Torrance CA 90505. (213)373-4330. Contact: J.O. Walser Jr. Gallery/art supplier. Estab. 1975. Represents 2-3 craftworkers. Considers batik; candlemaking; ceramics; glass art; metalsmithing; needlecrafts; pottery; tole painting; wall hangings; weavings; and woodcrafting. Primitive and fine one-of-a-kind and handmade production-line items; utilitiarian and/or decorative. Price range: 50c-$300; bestsellers: $5-25. Works on consignment; 50% commission. Retail price set by joint agreement. Requires exclusive area representation. Reports in 2 weeks. Hand-delivered work only. Dealer shares payment for insurance on exhibited work. Work is taken on a 90-day consignment period and receives promotion through a monthly newsletter. Best selling time: summer and Christmas.

WESTWOOD CERAMIC SUPPLY COMPANY GALLERY, 14400 Lomitas Ave., City of Industry CA 91744. (213)330-0631. Director: Darrel Trzeciak. Considers glass art; pottery; and sculpture. Especially needs ceramics. Maximum size: 8x4'. Price range: $15-500, ceramics. Works on consignment; 20% commission. Craftworker sets retail price. Query or send slides or photos of work. SASE. Work displayed maximum 4 weeks.

WHOLLY COW, 813 State St., Santa Barbara CA 93101. (805)965-3545. Contact: Gina Lestrade. Estab. 1976. Represents 9 craftworkers. Considers leatherworking. Finished, one-of-a-kind and handmade production-line items only; utilitarian and/or decorative. Price range: $1-

125; bestsellers: $20-60. Buys outright and works on consignment; 35% commission. Retail price set by joint agreement. Query with transparencies or photos. Reports in 2 weeks. Shop pays shipping to shop and insurance.
Profile: Items displayed in groups and rearranged weekly. Best selling time: Christmas; heaviest wholesale buying time: spring-Christmas. Customers buy crafts for artistic value.

WHOOPSIE DAISY, Berth 77, Ports O Call, San Pedro CA 90731. Contact: Lou Acosta. Gift shop. Estab. 1972. Represents 25 craftworkers. Considers batik; ceramics; dollmaking; jewelry; metalsmithing; pottery; soft sculpture; wall hangings; weavings; and woodcrafting. Fine one-of-a-kind and handmade production-line items only; utilitarian and/or decorative. Price range: $1-300; bestsellers: $5-100. Works on consignment and buys outright; 40% commission. Retail price set by joint agreement. Reports in 4 weeks. Work may be shipped or hand-delivered. Dealer pays return shipping and insurance for exhibited work. Best selling time: summer; heaviest wholesale buying time: summer and Christmas.

YAB YUM, 4749½ Santa Cruz Ave., San Diego CA 92107. Contact: Milo Clark. Gift shop. Estab. 1969. Represents 20-30 craftworkers. Considers all crafts except decoupage; dollmaking; and tole painting. All styles; utilitarian and/or decorative. Price range: 50c-$1,000; bestsellers: 50c-$150. Works on consignment and buys outright; 40% commission. Craftworker sets retail price. Requires exclusive area representation. Reports in 1 week. Work may be shipped or hand-delivered. Dealer usually pays shipping and insurance.
Special Needs: Needs fresh ideas in wood; ceramics; weavings/fiber arts; and wall decor.
Profile: "Items are prominently displayed 80% of the time; featured 20% of the time." Best selling time: Christmas; heaviest wholesale buying time: spring and Christmas.

YARN AND WEAVERS THINGS, 1250 Howe Ave., Sacramento CA 95825. (916)929-6966. Contact: Edna Davidson. Craft shop. Estab. 1973. Represents 10 craftworkers. Considers batik; needlecrafts; soft sculpture; wall hangings; and weavings. One-of-a-kind designer pieces only; utilitarian and/or decorative. Works on consignment; 25% commission. Retail price set by joint agreement. Reports in 3 weeks. Dealer pays insurance for exhibited work.

YOUNG GALLERY, 100 Park Center Plaza, San Jose CA 95113. (408)295-2800. Director: Edna Young. Gallery shop. Estab. 1971. Represents 12-15 craftworkers. Considers ceramics; dollmaking; glass art; jewelry; and soft sculpture. Fine and primitive one-of-a-kind pieces; utilitarian and/or decorative. Price range: $20-3,500; bestsellers: $20-500. Works on consignment; 40-50% commission. Retail price set by joint agreement. Requires exclusive area representation. Reports in 2 weeks. Work may be shipped or hand-delivered. Dealer pays insurance for exhibited work.
Special Needs: Seeking jewelry; soft sculpture; glass ornaments; game items; fabrics; and handmade paper items.
Profile: Gallery draws high income people. Best selling time: December and June; heaviest wholesale buying time: October-December. Send biography with slides or photos and price list.

ZARA GALLERY, 553 Pacific Ave., San Francisco CA 94133. (415)788-8696. Director: Joseph Chowning. Considers ceramics; sculpture; and soft sculpture. Maximum size: 12' square. Work must be ready for exhibition. Primarily interested in figurative work. Price range: $150-30,000, sculpture; bestsellers: $500-5,000. Works on consignment; 33⅓-60% commission. Retail price set by joint agreement. Requires exclusive area representation. Send slides and resume. SASE. Gallery pays insurance. 4-5 weeks exposure.

Colorado

ALBATROSS GALLERY, 1708 15th St., Boulder CO 80302. (303)449-6807. Manager: Michelle Schonbrun. Craft shop/gallery. Estab. 1974. Represents 40 potters and weavers. Considers ceramics; pottery; soft sculpture; wall hangings; and weavings. All styles; utilitarian and/or decorative. Price range: $4-300; bestsellers: $25. Works on consignment; 40% commission. Craftworker sets retail price. Prefers exclusive area representation. Reports in 2-3 weeks. Dealer pays return shipping and insurance for exhibited work. Unsold consigned pieces returned after 6 months. "Average customer is 30-45 years old with approximate income of $25,000-35,000." Best selling time: November-December.

THE CREWEL ELEPHANT, 124 E. 13th St., Silverton CO 81433. Contact: William M. Howell. Craft and gift shop. Considers ceramics; clothing; needlecrafts; and quilting. Especially needs needlework with emphasis on traditions from all areas. All styles; utilitarian and/or decorative. Price range: $5-300; bestsellers: $2-30. Buys outright. Retail price set by joint agree-

ment. Requires exclusive area representation. Reports in 2 weeks. Work may be shipped or hand-delivered with prior contact. Dealer pays shipping and insurance for solicited work.
Profile: "We feature primarily embroidered items; our mail order section offers designs for needleworkers both traditional and original; we are interested in reproducible needlework designs and patterns." Heaviest wholesale buying time: winter; best selling time: summer.

THE ENCOUNTER, Box 136, Boulder CO 95006. (408)338-3431. Contact: Rachel or Walt Bachrach. Craft and gift shop. Estab. 1967. Represents 200-250 craftworkers. Considers all crafts except tole painting. All styles; utilitarian and/or decorative. Price range: 75c-$1,200; bestsellers: 75c-$600. Works on consignment; 33⅓% commission. Retail price set by joint agreement. Requires exclusive Boulder representation. Reports in 2 weeks if by mail, same day if in person. Work may be hand delivered by pre-arrangement only. Dealer pays insurance for exhibited work. Work displayed 60 days minimum. Best selling and heaviest wholesale buying time: Christmas.

THE GLASS LANTERN, LTD., 7777 E. Hampden, Denver CO 80231. (303)750-7636. Contact: Luce Shuler. Gallery/gift shop. Estab. 1971. Represents 12 craftworkers. Price range: $1.50-800; bestsellers: $4.50-350. Works on consignment and buys outright; 30% commission. Retail price set by joint agreement. Requires exclusive area representation. Reports in 2 weeks. "Must jury actual work in person." Work may be shipped or hand-delivered. Dealer pays insurance for exhibited work.
Acceptable Work: Considers stained and acid-etched and sandblasted glass. One-of-a-kind designer pieces; utilitarian and/or decorative.
Profile: The shop carries "all stained glass items, finished hangings, lamps and small suncatchers and all supplies for craftsmen." All items are immediately displayed and changed in location every 2-3 weeks. Best selling time: summer-winter.

THE GOLD AND SILVERSMITHS OF VAIL, Box 385, Vail CO 81657. (303)476-3131. Contact: Dan Telleen. Craft shop. Estab. 1970. Represents 5 craftworkers. Price range: $15-200; bestsellers: $60-125. Works on consignment; 40% commission. Retail price set by joint agreement. Requires exclusive area representation. Send slides or photos. Reports in 4 weeks. Work may be shipped or hand-delivered. Dealer pays insurance for exhibited work.
Acceptable Work: Considers jewelry and metalsmithing. One-of-a-kind designer and primitive pieces; utilitarian and/or decorative.
Special Needs: Especially needs sterling 14K gold earrings; custom polishing on a piece basis and fabricated construction on a custom basis in gold and silver.
Profile: Work is "displayed prominently in well-lighted glass display case. Customers are 25-40 year old professionals." Best selling and heaviest wholesale buying time: summer and winter.

GREEN RIVER, Box 10220, Aspen CO 81611. (303)925-5742. Partners: George Janecek or Judy Pollock. Estab. 1974. Represents 10 craftworkers. Price range: $1.50-2,000; bestsellers: $25-100. Works on consignment and buys outright; 33⅓% commission. Retail price set by joint agreement. Requires exclusive area representation. Reports in 2 weeks. Work may be shipped or hand-delivered.
Acceptable Work: Considers jewelry; leatherworking; metalsmithing; knife-making; buckles and antique guns. One-of-a-kind and handmade production-line items; utilitarian and/or decorative.
Profile: "Our best customers are doctors, dentists, lawyers and company presidents." Best selling and heaviest wholesale buying time: winter and summer.

GREENBAER METAL WORKS, c/o General Delivery, Placerville CO 81430. (303)728-3758. Contact: Mike Baer. Studio. Estab. 1978. Considers jewelry and metalsmithing. Primitive and fine one-of-a-kind pieces; utilitarian and/or decorative. Price range: $1-2,000; bestsellers: $1-4. Works on consignment, buys outright and trades; 25% commission. Retail price set by joint agreement. Reports in 2 weeks. Shipping is negotiable. Insurance for exhibited work set by joint agreement. Best selling time: summer and winter.

MONFORD STOP GALLERY, 609½ Main St., Alamosa CO 81101. (303)589-2702. Contact: Steve Crawford or David Montgomery. Craft shop/gallery. Estab. 1975. Represents 15 Colorado and northern New Mexico craftworkers. Price range: $1-250; bestsellers: $1-50. Works on consignment; 25% commission. Retail price set by joint agreement. Reporting time varies. Work may be shipped or hand-delivered. Dealer pays insurance for exhibited work. Shows run 10-14 days; consigned work is displayed until sold or reclaimed by artist.
Acceptable Work: Considers batik; candlemaking; ceramics; jewelry; leatherworking; soft sculpture; wall hangings; weavings; and woodcrafting. Especially needs pottery. One-of-a-kind

designer pieces; utilitarian and/or decorative.
Profile: "We have a jewelry display case, shelves for pottery and a gallery for hanging works. We combine a working studio with an outlet for other artists." Heaviest wholesale buying time: spring and fall; best selling time: fall-early winter.
Sales Tip: "Once a craftsman is known in an area for a certain kind of work (i.e., mugs, pitchers, bowls or ornamental work) he/she should at least keep up that area to a certain extent. Public opinion of 'the artist' is shaky, and an inconsistent output is bad for the artist and the gallery."

NATIONAL CARVERS MUSEUM, 14960 Woodcarver Rd., Monument CO 80132. (303)481-2656. Contact: Harry Meech. Museum gift shop. Estab. 1969. Represents 200 craftworkers. Considers woodcrafting. All styles; utilitarian and/or decorative. Price range: $2.50-2,500; bestsellers: $2.50-75. Works on consignment and buys outright; 30% commission. Retail price set by joint agreement. Reports in 3 weeks. Work may be shipped or hand-delivered. Dealer pays insurance for exhibited work. "This is a national museum exhibiting over 5,000 woodcarvings." Heaviest wholesale buying time: spring; best selling time: spring-summer.

ROCKY MOUNTAIN PARK CO., 4155 E. Jewell #603, Denver CO 80222. (303)757-0871. President: Ted James Jr. Gift shop. Estab. 1935. Represents 100 craftworkers. Price range: $2-100; bestsellers: $5-25. Works on consignment and buys outright; 50% commission. Retail price set by joint agreement. Reports in 1 week. Work may be shipped or hand-delivered. Dealer pays return shipping and insurance for exhibited work.
Acceptable Work: Considers ceramics; glass art; jewelry; leatherworking; metalsmithing; pottery; wall hangings; weavings; and woodcrafting. Handmade production-line items only; utilitarian and/or decorative.
Profile: "We are the only gift shop in Rocky Mountain National Park. We average 2 million visitors annually in the 4 months we are open." Heaviest wholesale buying time: winter; best selling time: summer. "Craftworker should be able to supply reorder merchandise quickly; in a 4 month operation, time is of utmost importance."

SEBASTIAN-MOORE GALLERY, 1411 Market St., Denver CO 80202. (303)534-5659. Contact: Christy Sebastian or Mimi Moore. Craft shop/gallery/rental gallery. Estab. 1977. Represents 20 craftworkers. Price range: $20-1,000; bestsellers: $15-75. Works on consignment; 40% commission. Craftworker sets retail price. Requires exclusive area representation. Reports in 2 weeks. Work may be shipped or hand-delivered. Dealer pays insurance for exhibited work. Displays work 6 weeks-3 months.
Acceptable Work: Considers ceramics; clothing; dollmaking; glass art; jewelry; metalsmithing; soft sculpture; wall hangings; weavings; and woodcrafting. Especially needs glass blowing and soft sculpture of non-pop images. Decorative one-of-a-kind designer pieces only.
Profile: "Work is displayed in glass exhibit cases, on pedestals and wall space; gallery is 4,500 square feet. Customers are 30-60 year old professional people and art related students and collectors." Displays work 6 weeks-3 months. Heaviest wholesale buying time: Christmas and summer; best selling time: October-December.

SELF EXPRESSIONS, 900 S. Clermont, Denver CO 80222. (303)756-0664. Owner: Joanne M. Bircher. Fiber supply shop/gallery/gift shop/classes. Estab. 1978. Represents 10 craftworkers. Price range: $10-400; bestsellers: $20-150. Works on consignment; 33⅓% commission. Retail price set by joint agreement. Reports in 2 weeks. Work may be shipped or hand-delivered. Dealer pays return shipping and insurance for exhibited work. Displays work 90-120 days.
Acceptable Work: Considers batik; clothing; needlecrafts; wood; pottery; stained glass; soft sculpture; wall hangings; basketry, weavings; and fiber basketry. Especially needs craft wearables; unusual woven hangings; and fiber craft pieces done in one or more technique, such as a wall hanging woven, macramed and coiled. Fine one-of-a-kind designer and handmade production-line items; utilitarian and/or decorative.
Profile: "We are situated on the first floor of a little old red house with a warm, rustic atmosphere. The front room displays a vast variety of natural and novelty fibers for weaving, basketry, macrame, stitchery, knitting and crochet, and a complete line of accessory supplies such as rustic treasures, rings, feathers, books, hooks, etc. Consignment items are displayed throughout the shop. In the back portion of the shop are 2 classrooms where our diverse selection of fiber classes are taught." Heaviest buying and selling time: Christmas.

SUN SIGN, 1738 Pearl, Boulder CO 80302. (303)444-4280. Contact: Jerry Hodge. Craft and gift shop. Estab. 1967. Represents 15 craftworkers. Price range: $10-500; bestsellers: $10-25. Works on consignment and buys outright; 45% commission. Retail price set by joint agreement.

Requires exclusive area representation. Reports as soon as possible. Dealer pays shipping and insurance for exhibited work. Displays work 3 months maximum.
Acceptable Work: Considers batik; ceramics; glass art; jewelry; metalsmithing; pottery; soft sculpture; wall hangings; weavings; and woodcrafting. All styles; utilitarian and/or decorative.
Profile: "Customers are 15-70 years old; other craftspeople, young professionals, tourists; with middle to upper incomes." Heaviest wholesale buying time: April-November; best selling time: summer and December.

SUTTON-HOO GOLDSMITH, 22 E. Bijou, Colorado Springs CO 80903. (303)471-7075. Contact: Charles Lamouaux or Diana Newell. Craft shop/gallery. Estab. 1972. Represents 15-20 craftworkers. Price range: $8-2,600; bestsellers: $8-500. Works on consignment and buys outright; 40% commission. Craftworker sets retail price on consigned items only. Requires exclusive area representation. Reports in 2-3 weeks. Work may be hand-delivered after showing slides or photos. Dealer pays shipping to shop and insurance.
Acceptable Work: Considers jewelry; metalsmithing; and pottery. Fine one-of-a-kind and handmade production-line items; utilitarian only.
Profile: Work is shown in lighted showcases. Consigned work displayed minimum 3 months. "We have largest display of handmade jewelry in Colorado." Customers are 35-50; middle income and up. Heaviest wholesale buying time: January, September and October; best selling time: September-December.

TAPESTRY, 2859 E. 3rd Ave., Denver CO 80206. (303)322-2441. Contact: Carolyn Fineran. Gallery. Estab. 1974. Represents 75-100 craftworkers. Price range: $10-3,000; bestsellers: $15-350. Works on consignment and buys outright; 40% commission. Retail price set by joint agreement. Requires exclusive area representation. Reports in 4 weeks. Work may be shipped or hand-delivered. Dealer pays return shipping and insurance for exhibited work. Displays consigned work 6 weeks.
Acceptable Work: Considers dollmaking; glass art; jewelry; leatherworking; needlecrafts; soft sculpture; wall hangings; and weavings. Especially needs soft sculpture (dolls, plants and animals); good, basic, well-priced jewelry; and wall hangings for commercial office space. Fine one-of-a-kind and handmade production-line items; utilitarian and/or decorative.
Profile: We "usually rotate displays monthly. Craft is treated as art; shop has elegant appeal; we do a lot with great soft sculpture. Customers are sophisticated professionals; upper-upper middle class, relatively affluent with a great sense of style." Heaviest wholesale buying time: June and August; best selling time: November-December.

THINGS FOR LIVING, Manna Square, 8101 E. Bellview St., Denver CO 80237 (303)377-9780. Craft shop/gallery/gift shop. Estab. 1974. Represents 100 American craftworkers. Considers batik; candlemaking; ceramics; glass art; jewelry; leatherworking; metalsmithing; needlecrafts; pottery; quilting; soft sculpture; wall hangings; weavings; and woodcrafting. "Open to all new ideas." Fine one-of-a-kind and handmade production-line items; utilitarian and/or decorative. Price range: $2-2,000; bestsellers: $2-75. Works on consignment and buys outright; 33⅓-40% commission. Retail price set by joint agreement. Requires exclusive area representation. Reports in 3 weeks. Shop pays shipping to shop; in-transit insurance; and insurance for exhibited work. Dealer and craftworker mutually set consignment time.
Profile: "We have a complete selection of items from all types of crafts; we do not specialize in only a few items." Best selling time: Christmas.

THE UNIQUE, 21½ E. Bijou St., Colorado Springs CO 80903. (303)473-9406. Manager: Zita Miller. Craft shop. Estab. 1966. Represents 50-60 craftworkers. Price range: $2-1,000; bestsellers: $2.50-200. Works on consignment and buys outright; 40% commission. Retail price set by joint agreement. Requires exclusive area representation. Reports in 2 weeks. Work may be shipped or hand-delivered. Dealer pays insurance for exhibited work.
Acceptable Work: Considers batik; candlemaking; clothing; dollmaking; glass art; jewelry; leatherworking; metalsmithing; needlecrafts; quilting; tole painting; wall hangings; weavings; woodcrafting; and Christmas ornaments. Especially needs textiles and ceramics. All styles; utilitarian and/or decorative.
Profile: "Works are usually displayed in groups with constant rearranging. Customers are college students, local people of all ages and incomes and summer tourists." Displays work minimum 90 days. Heaviest wholesale buying time: May-June and September-October; best selling time: Christmas and summer.

URIAH HEEPS, Box 1362, Aspen CO 81611. Contact: Tukey Koffend. "We are always looking for new jewelry — silver preferably." Price range: $10-2,000. 33% commission. Retail price set by joint agreement. Prefers exclusive area represntation. Send transparencies or photos. Dealer pays insurance for exhibited work; shipping costs shared. Openings sponsored and items displayed 6 weeks minimum. Located at Hotel Jerome in Aspen.

US CUSTOMS, 220 S. Mill, Aspen CO 81611. Contact: Maureen or Bruce Geiss. Craft shop. Represents 120 craftworkers. Works on consignment and buys outright; commission negotiable. Retail price set by joint agreement. Send slides or photos. Reports in 2 weeks. Requires exclusive area representaiton. Work may be shipped or hand-delivered. Dealer pays freight-in and insurance for exhibited work. Heaviest wholesale buying time: July and December; best selling time: December-March and July-September.
Acceptable Work: Considers batik; ceramics; glass art; jewelry; metals; stitchery and soft sculpture; woven hangings and accessories; wood objects; and furniture. Especially needs special wood furniture and architectural accessories; objects that are special or multiple. Utilitarian and/or decorative pieces.

THE WATER WHEEL, 429 Elk Ave., B11, Crested Butte CO 81224. (303)349-5626. Contact: Jill West. Craft shop/gallery. Estab. 1972. Represents 120 Rocky Mountain craftworkers. Price range: $2-250; bestsellers: $2-40. Works on consignment and buys outright; 33⅓% commission. Retail price set by joint agreement. Requires exclusive area representation. Reports in 2 weeks. Work may be shipped or hand-delivered. Shipping and insurance payment negotiated.
Acceptable Work: Considers batik; candlemaking; ceramics; glass art; jewelry; leatherworking; metalsmithing; pottery; quilting; wall hangings; weavings; and woodcrafting. Especially needs quilting. Fine one-of-a-kind and handmade production-line items; utilitarian and/or decorative.
Profile: "Customers are 95% tourists to Colorado with middle to upper incomes." Best selling and heaviest wholesale buying time: July-September and ski season.

WHICKERBILL CONTEMPORARY, 212 N. Tejon, Colorado Springs CO 80903. (303)633-0518. Contact: John Eastham. Gift shop. Estab. 1957. Represents 40 craftworkers. Maximum price: $100; bestsellers: $5-35. Buys outright. Craftworker sets retail price. Requires exclusive area representation. Reports in 2 weeks. Work may be shipped or hand-delivered. Dealer pays return shipping and insurance for exhibited work. Heaviest wholesale buying time: May-December; best selling time: summer and Christmas.
Acceptable Work: Considers candlemaking; ceramics; glass art; jewelry; pottery; and woodcrafting. One-of-a-kind and handmade production-line items; utilitarian and/or decorative.

Connecticut

ALENA JEWELERS-DESIGNERS, 12 E. Putnam Ave., Greenwich CT 06830. (203)869-0934. Contact: Mrs. Zinn. Jewelry store. Estab. 1974. Considers jewelry. "Most of our jewelry is gold; small amount of sterling; fine cloisonne enamels; and champleve enamels." Fine one-of-a-kind and handmade production-line items; utilitarian and/or decorative. Minimum price: $25; bestsellers: $35-200. Works on consignment and buys outright; 40% commission. Requires exclusive area representation. Reports in 2 weeks. Dealer pays return shipping; shipping to shop and transit insurance if outright purchase; and insurance for exhibited work.
Profile: "Our store is very spacious and elegant. We specialize in simple, unique non-arty designs." Customers are of all ages; fairly conservative; and in mid to upper income bracket. Best selling time: May-June; November-December.

APPALACHIAN HOUSE, 1591 Post Rd., Fairfield CT 06430. (203)259-6149. Co-manager: John and Dolores Potterton. Estab. 1974. Represents 300+ Appalachian craftsmen. Considers Appalachian crafts. All styles; utilitarian and/or decorative. Price range: 75c-$250; bestsellers: $2.25-15. Buys outright. Shop sets retail price. Write. Reports in 2 weeks. Dealer pays shipping and insurance for exhibited work.
Profile: Items displayed on rustic shelves and handmade wood units. Heaviest wholesale buying time: fall and spring. Best selling time: November-December. "Our retail mark-up is lower than average thanks to our volunteer staff, which keeps down overhead." Women customers age 20-55 with middle to upper-middle income. Has second store at 1875 Palmer Ave., Larchmont, New York.

THE ARGYLE CRAFT GALLERY, 40 Post Rd. E., Westport CT 06880. (203)226-1334. Contact: Helenita Mathias. Estab. 1975. Represents 35-50 craftworkers. Considers candlemaking, ceramics; glass art; metalsmithing; pottery; soft sculpture; wall hangings; and weavings. Especially needs flameware. Finished one-of-a-kind and handmade production-line items; utilitarian and/or decorative. Price range: $5-300; bestsellers: $5-75. Buys outright or on consignment; 33% commission. Retail price set by joint agreement. Requires exclusive area representation. Query with transparencies or photos, or mail work. Reports in 2 weeks. Dealer pays shipping and insurance for exhibited work. Heaviest wholesale buying time: fall and spring; best selling time: winter and summer. Affluent customers.

ARTISTS' MARKET, 319 Main Ave., Rt. 7, Norwalk CT 06851. (203)846-2550. Contact: Nancy or Jeffrey Price. Craft shop/gallery/frame shop. Estab. 1972. Represents 30-50 craftworkers who reside in the US, preferably New England or Northeast. Considers jewelry; blown and stained glass; and pottery. Fine one-of-a-kind and handmade production-line items; utilitarian and/or decorative. Price range: $3-250; bestsellers: $7.50-40. Buys outright. Usually requires exclusive area representation. Shipping payments are negotiable.
Profile: "We have very unusual crafts; high quality; and fair prices. We also combine the crafts gallery with art supplies; some fine craft supplies; and a gallery of framed and unframed limited edition graphics. Customers are generally 25-50 in age, averaging on the young side; mostly fairly affluent. We get a lot of New York executive families since we're only 1 hour from the city." Best selling time: fall-winter.

MOLLY BRODY MINIATURES, 177 W. State St., Westport CT 06880. (203)226-5116. Contact: Molly Brody. Miniature shop. Estab. 1969. Represents 200-300 craftworkers. Considers miniatures and dollhouses; size restriction 1"-1'. Special need for silversmith doing top quality sterling pieces. Fine one-of-a-kind and handmade production-line items; utilitarian and/or decorative. Price range: $1-1,200. Works on consignment and buys outright; 33⅓% commission. Retail price set by joint agreement. Requires exclusive area representation. Reports in 4 weeks. Shipping payments negotiable; dealer pays insurance on exhibited work.
Profile: "We put most of our merchandise behind glass for protection. Customers range from 6-91 years. Generally high middle income fanatics about collecting miniatures. The field of miniatures is growing every year. We see a 10 year period of high sales and expect to develop a million lifetime collectors nationally."

COPPERTONE WORKSHOP, Box 699, 17A Old Avon Village, Avon CT 06001. (203)677-2717. President: Melinda Coelho. Craft and art shop. Estab. 1974. Represents 9 craftworkers. All styles; utilitarian and/or decorative. Price range: $2-200; bestsellers: $5-50. Works on consignment and buys outright. Retail price set by joint agreement. Exclusive area representation depends on items. Dealer has shop insurance for exhibited work.
Acceptable Work: Considers batik; candlemaking; bisque; ceramics; glass art; jewelry; leatherworking; metalsmithing; pottery; soft sculpture; tole painting; wall hangings; weavings; and woodcrafting. "We have a super demand for anything made from copper, the color of copper or pewter. Jewelry is also a big seller." Customer's income is middle to upper class. Best selling time: Christmas and spring.

COQUI GALLERIES, 20 Church Lane, Westport CT 06880. (203)227-5234. Contact: Rona Cohen or Gayla Halbrecht. Gallery. Estab. 1977. Represents 100+ mostly contemporary American craftworkers; but would consider artists in other media in limited amounts. Considers ceramics; hand-woven articles including clothing; glass art; jewelry; metalsmithing; needlecraft; quilting; soft sculpture; weavings; wall hangings; and woodworking. "Special need for more macrame; unusual functional items; seasonal items; jewelry; and clothing (art to wear for fashion shows and special exhibits)." One-of-a-kind decorative items and quality production items; quality is stressed. Price range: $4-3,600; bestsellers: $15-60. Mostly works on consignment and buys some outright; 40% commission. Retail price set by joint agreement. Requires exclusive area representation. Reports as soon as possbile. Shipping payment negotiable; dealer pays insurance on exhibited work.
Profile: Exhibited items are displayed for 30 days. "We are the only gallery shop of its kind in the area. We are actually 2 galleries in 1 store — artisan gallery as above and separate design studio which specializes in interior design and commissions many works from artisan gallery for design clients (accessories, glass, furniture, etc.). We do monthly exhibits featuring well-recognized, as well as new, artisans. We do a great deal of PR on all exhibits. Customers are of all ages; highly educated; knowledgeable; and with huge disposable income." Best selling time: spring, fall and early summer.

COUNTRY BAZAAR, 451 Main St. S., Woodbury CT 06798. (203)263-2228. Contact: Jerry Madans. Antique and craft shop. Estab. 1968. Represents 6 craftworkers. Considers jewelry; metalsmithing; pottery; and woodcrafting. Primitive handmade production-line items; utilitarian and/or decorative. Price range: $1-100; bestsellers: $5-25. Works on consignment and buys outright; 33⅓% commission. Craftworker sets retail price. Reports in 2 weeks.

CURRENT CRAFTS, 3208 Whitney Ave., Mt. Carmel CT 06518. (203)288-9868. Contact: Robert L. Evans. Estab. 1961. Represents 300 craftworkers. Considers candlemaking; glass art; jewelry; leatherworking; metalsmithing; pottery; wall hangings; and woodcrafting. Finished one-of-a-kind and handmade production-line items; utilitarian and/or decorative. Price range: $1-200; bestsellers: $5-50. Buys outright. Shop sets retail price. Query with transparencies or photos. Reports in 30 days. Dealer pays shipping to shop and insurance for exhibited work. Heaviest wholesale buying time: spring and summer; best selling time: winter.

THE DOUGLAS GALLERY, INC., 1117 High Ridge Rd., Stamford CT 06905. (203)322-7233. Contact: Douglas Jayne. Considers sculpture. Maximum size: 5' square. Sculpture must have pedestal. Works on consignment; 33⅓% commission. Price range: $25-2,000; bestsellers: $150-800. Retail price set by joint agreement. Requires exclusive area representation. Send slides or photos of work. SASE. Gallery pays insurance for exhibited work. 2-6 months exposure.

DOWN ON THE FARM, LTD., Banner Rd., Moodus CT 06469. (203)873-9905. Contact: Joyce Simon. Craft shop/gallery. Estab. 1977. Represents 125+ craftworkers. Considers all crafts except decoupage and tole painting. Finished one-of-a-kind and handmade production-line items; utilitarian and/or decorative. Price range: $5-500; bestsellers: $12-75. Works on consignment with some outright buying; 40% commission. Craftworker sets retail price; "we reserve right to raise or lower within reasonable limitations." Requires exclusive area representation. Reports in 2 weeks. Dealer pays shipping and insurance. Consigned items displayed for 3 months.
Profile: "We are part of a larger craft center located on a working poultry farm. The center is housed in a restored chicken coop. We are in a country environment but close enough to major metro areas, New York and Boston. Besides the shop, the center houses studios; teaching space; and other related facilities. We will be adding another restored coop to the center in the near future. Customers are of all ages and interests with incomes ranging from $5,000 to over $75,000." Best selling time: summer and Christmas.

FARMINGTON VALLEY ARTS CENTER, INC., Box 220, Avon Park N., Avon CT 06001. (203)678-1867. Executive Director: Betty Friedman. Nonprofit gallery. Estab. 1974. Represents 2-4 craftworkers, occasionally more. Considers batik; clothing; glass art; jewelry; leatherworking; metalsmithing; needlecrafts; pottery; quilting; soft sculpture; weavings; wallhangings; woodcrafting; and sculpture. Fine one-of-a-kind and sometimes handmade production-line items; utilitarian and/or decorative. Price range: $10-500; bestsellers: $10-150. Works on consignment; 20% commission. Craftworker sets retail price. Reports in 4 weeks. Shipping payment is negotiable; gallery pays insurance on exhibited work.
Profile: "The gallery features work by outstanding artists/craftsmakers who are not normally shown in this area. In conjunction with the gallery approximately 20 artists maintain studios at the Arts Center; the majority of which function as small shops and galleries as well as work space. Classes, workshops and lectures are held at the Arts Center, often in conjunction with the special gallery exhibitions."

LUTA STUDIOS, Rt. 9A, Deep River CT 06417. (203)526-5812. Contact: Nancy Mazzoni. Estab. 1971. Represents 3-6 craftworkers. Considers all crafts. Finished, one-of-a-kind and production-line, handmade items; utilitarian and/or decorative. Price range: $1.50-350; bestsellers: $3.50-35. Works on consignment; 25% commission. Craftworker sets retail price. Write.
Profile: "Items displayed 8-12 weeks in gallery setting with spot lighting. Items moved after several weeks for optimum attention." Heaviest wholesale buying time: fall and spring. Best selling time: Christmas and summer. "High quality, well-displayed crafts; not like a hodge-podge gift shop." Customers age 25-35 with $18,000-35,000 income; they buy crafts for artistic value.

MYSTIC SEAPORT MUSEUM STORE, Mystic CT 06355. (203)536-8010. General Manager: Thomas H. Aageson. Museum gift shop. Estab. 1938. Represents 50-75 craftworkers. Considers candlemaking; ceramics; clothing; dollmaking; jewelry; metalsmithing; needlecrafts; pottery; quilting; soft sculpture; weavings; and wall hangings. "We are searching for work that represents the 19th century, either reproductions or adaptations. We also need items that reflect a maritime theme." All styles; utilitarian and/or decorative. Price range: $1-1,500. Works on consignment and buys outright; 40% commission. Craftworker sets retail price. Requires exclusive area representation. Reports in 2 weeks. Dealer pays shipping to shop if outright purchase, and insurance for exhibited work.
Profile: "The shop is an integral part of Mystic Seaport, a nonprofit museum. As an educational

institution we represent the 19th century and the country's maritime heritage. It is the country's largest maritime museum. Our museum store selections represent this period and/or nation's maritime heritage." Best selling time: summer.

PEYTON ORIGINALS, Box 124, Brookfield Center CT 06805. (203)775-0044. Contact: Paul or Elizabeth Peyton. Craft and gift shop/manufacturer of handcrafted gifts. Estab. 1970. Represents 3-4 craftworkers. Considers glass art; needlecrafts; pottery; and unusual candles. Finished handmade production-line items; utilitarian and/or decorative. Nothing over $25; bestsellers: $3-10. Buys outright; shop sets retail price. Dealer pays shipping to shop and insurance for exhibited work. Best selling season: October-December.

THE QUEST FOR HANDCRAFTS, Forty Boutiques Mall, Ridgeway Center, 2299 Summer St., Stamford CT 06905. (203)324-2260. Buyer: Ruth A. Schrauf. Craft shop. Estab. 1974. Represents 300 craftworkers who are professional in their work and shipping procedures. Considers baskets; batik; candlemaking; ceramics; clothing; dolls; glass art; jewelry; leatherworking; metalsmithing; pottery; soft sculpture; weavings; and wall hangings. Finished one-of-a-kind and handmade production-line items; utilitarian and/or decorative. Bestsellers: $3-300. Buys outright; 50% discount. Prefers exclusive area representation.
Profile: "Customers are all ages but those in the 30's are the largest buyers. They are interested in all arts, but pottery is the bestseller, and their income ranges from $18,000-60,000." Best selling time: June, August and December.

THE SHOP— GUILFORD HANDCRAFT CENTER, Box 221, Guilford CT 06437. (203)453-5947. Business Manager: Carol Hill. Craft shop. Estab. 1968. Represents 75-100 craftworkers. Considers batik; ceramics; clothing; glass art; jewelry; leatherworking; metalsmithing; pottery; quilting; soft sculpture; wall hangings; weavings; and woodcrafting. Fine one-of-a-kind and handmade production-line items; utilitarian and/or decorative. Price range: $2-250; bestsellers: $5-50. Works on consignment and buys outright; 25% commission. Craftworker sets retail price. Reports in 1 week. Dealer pays insurance for exhibited work; unsold consigned pieces returned after 2 quarters.
Profile: "This is a nonprofit school, exhibit and sales center. We show a wide range of work representing all geographic areas." Customers are varied by generally well-educated and upper-middle class. Best selling time: Christmas and summer months.

THE SILO, Upland Road, New Milford CT 06776. (203)355-0300. Contact: Ruth Henderson. Gallery/gift shop/country kitchen store. Estab. 1972. Represents 24+ craftworkers with production capabilty to handle orders and with high level of creativity and individuality in work. Considers batik; ceramics; decoupage; glass art; metalsmithing; needlecrafts; pottery; quilting; soft sculpture; weavings; wall hangings; and woodcrafting. Finished and primitive handmade production-line items; utilitarian and/or decorative. Price range: $4-2,000; bestsellers: $10-50. Works on consignment; buys outright; and selects work for special exhibitions. 40% commission. Retail price set by consultation. Prefers exclusive area representation. Reports in 4 weeks. Only items with prepaid receipt and return postage accepted.
Profile: "Arts and crafts selected for exhibition remain on exhibition for roughly 4 weeks; display technique is at the craftworker's discretion with approval of The Silo. The Silo has been described as bringing the best of Bloomingdale's and Bendel's to Connecticut. Customers are chiefly professionals; artists; writers; musicians; Broadway producers; fashion designers— the 'in' crowd of western Connecticut, chiefly New Yorkers who maintain second homes in the area."

SOCIETY OF CONNECTICUT CRAFTSMEN, Box 37, Rt. 9A, Deep River CT 06417. (203)526-5812. Contact: Nancy Mazzoni. Estab. 1935. Represents about 250 member craftworkers. Contact SCC for membership details. Considers batik; candlemaking; ceramics; dollmaking; glass art; leatherworking; metalsmithing; mobiles; needlecrafts; pottery; sculpture; tole paintings; wall hangings; weavings; and woodcrafting. Price range: $1.50 and up; bestsellers: $1.50-35. 25% commission. Craftworker sets retail price. Reports on jury review in spring and fall in *SCC Newsletter*.

THE SUNSHINE FACTORY, 142 New Haven Ave., Milford CT 06760. (203)878-9797. Contact: Chris or Muriel Swihura. Gallery/craft shop/plant shop/tea room. Estab. 1976. Represents 185-200 craftworkers. Price range: 50c-$400; bestsellers: $5-15. Works on consignment; 40% commission. Craftworker sets retail price. Requires exclusive Milford representation.

Reports in 1 week. Work may be shipped or hand-delivered, subject to our approval of samples. Dealer pays return shipping.

Acceptable Work: Considers batik; candlemaking; clothing; dollmaking; glass art; jewelry; leatherworking; metalsmithing; needlecrafts; pottery; quilting; soft sculpture; tole painting; wall hangings; weavings; woodcrafting; pressed flowers; dough work; sandcasting; and stationery. All styles; utilitarian and/or decorative.

Profile: "Craftwork is exhibited with the help of antiques and collectibles (oak pews, Vermont glass pie cases for jewelry, old sleds, old stoves and a jungle of ferns and greenery). We are in a large lovely old home with a tea room upstairs. We use our fireplace all winter and have established a very friendly atmosphere. We handle a great deal of customer orders. 60% of our customers are from out of town; most are women although we see more men every day."

UPSTAIRS POTTERY, 198 West St., Cromwell CT 06416. (203)635-0808. Contact: Helen Yaglowski. Craft shop. Estab. 1977. Represents 6 local stoneware potters using no molds. Considers pottery. Primitive and fine one-of-a-kind pieces; utilitarian and/or decorative. Price range: $1-75; bestsellers: $5-20. Works on consignment; 40% commission. Craftworker sets retail price. Reports in 1 month. Hand-delivered work only. Dealer pays insurance for exhibited work.

Profile: "It is the only full-time pottery shop in a large area. Our customers are in the late 20's, early 30's and are getting into the natural nonplastic material area, looking for things not mass-produced." Best selling time: Christmas.

VOLTAIRE'S SHOP AND GALLERY, Rt. 2, New Milford CT 06776. (203)354-4200. Manager: Mrs. P. Voltaire. Craft shop/gallery/gift shop. Estab. 1956. Represents 35-45 craftworkers. Considers batik; ceramics; clothing; glass art; jewelry; leatherworking; metalsmithing; pottery; soft sculpture; wall hangings; weavings; and woodcrafting. "Special need for metalcrafts of contemporary design (iron, brass, etc.) and lower priced production ceramics." Fine one-of-a-kind and handmade production-line items; utilitarian and/or decorative. Works on consignment and buys outright; 40% commission on consignments; 50% on purchases. Craftworker sets retail price. Requires exclusive area representation. Dealer pays shipping for purchased work; return shipping for consignment work; and insurance for exhibited work.

Profile: "We are known as a contemporary, 'good design' establishment. Many New Yorkers of above average incomes who have second homes in the area are our customers." Best selling time: Christmas and August.

WASHINGTON ART ASSOCIATION, Washington Depot CT 06794. (203)868-2878. Executive Secretary: Joan Talbot. Gallery. Estab. 1952. Represents about 60 craftworkers during the Christmas sale; 4-10 during the craft show. Considers all crafts. Fine one-of-a-kind and handmade production-line items; utilitarian and/or decorative. Price range: $1.50-1,000; bestsellers: $1.50-250. Works on consignment; 25% commission. Craftworker sets retail price. Sometimes charges $50/week per room for exhibit space; group shows have $5 entry fee.

Profile: "It is a nonprofit gallery run by volunteers. Usually crafts are invited for a 3-week exhibit. Work is selected by a committee except for open craft show at Christmas when work is taken on consignment." Wide range of customers. Best selling time: Christmas and August.

Delaware

GALLERY 18, Box 593, Nassau DE 19969. (302)684-4829. Contact: W.E. Reifsnyder. Craft shop/gallery/frame shop. Estab. 1969. Represents 2-3 craftworkers. Considers ceramics; glass art; jewelry; leatherworking; metalsmithing; wall hangings; and weavings. Fine one-of-a-kind and handmade production-line items; utilitarian and/or decorative. price range: $10-70; bestsellers: $10-50. Buys outright. Gallery sets retail price. Requires exclusive area representation. Reports in 2 weeks. Dealer pays insurance for exhibited work. Customers are middle-level executives and professionals, 30-60 years old. Best selling time: spring-fall.

GRASSROOTS HANDCRAFTS, 39 E. Main St., Newark DE 19711. (302)453-9751. Contact: Marilyn Barnekov or Vonna Taylor. Craft shop. Estab. 1975. Represents 75+ craftworkers. Considers batik; candlemaking; ceramics; clothing; glass art; jewelry; leatherworking; metalsmithing; pottery; quilting; wall hangings; weavings; and woodcrafting. One-of-a-kind and handmade production-line items; utilitarian and/or decorative. Bestsellers: $5-215. Takes some consignment but prefers buying outright; 30% commission. Retail price set by joint agreement. Requires exclusive area representation. Dealer pays shipping if buying work; and insurance for exhibited work.

Profile: "Shop does custom sewing, alterations, and handmade clothing. We are near a university but have customers of all ages from the community." Best selling time: Christmas.

The Silo, New Milford, Connecticut, exhibits the art and crafts of 2-3 craftworkers/artists at a time on a monthly basis. If a craftworker wishes to hold a workshop it can be arranged with owner, Ruth Henderson. She is always available to view and discuss work with the craftworker. — Photo by Joyshine.

WARE GALLERY, 1800 Breen Lane, Wilmington DE 19810. (302)475-4208. Contact: Dorothy Truman. Craft shop/gallery/gift shop. Estab. 1951. Represents 15-20 craftworkers. Considers batik; ceramics; dollmaking; glass art; jewelry; leatherworking; metalsmithing; needlecrafts; pottery; quilting; soft sculpture; wall hangings; weavings; and woodcrafting. Fine one-of-a-kind pieces; utilitarian and/or decorative. Price range: $5-250; bestsellers: $5-25. Works on consignment and buys outright; 32⅓% commission. Craftworker sets retail price. Requires exclusive area representation. Hand-delivered work only.
Profile: "Shop is uncrowded and well-lighted. Work is displayed in conjunction with paintings on walls." Best selling time: fall-spring.

WARE GALLERY, GIFTS, 2208 Millers Rd., Ardentown DE 19810. (302)475-9804. Contact: Joan Ware Colgan. Gallery/gift shop. Estab. 1950. Represents about 15 craftworkers, mostly local. Considers batik; ceramics; decoupage; glass art; jewelry; leatherworking; needlecrafts; pottery; soft sculpture; wall hangings; weavings; and woodcrafting. All styles; utilitarian and/or decorative. Price range: $1-100; bestsellers: $1-20. Works on consignment and sometimes buys outright; 25% commission. Craftworker sets retail price. Hand-delivered work only. Consigned pieces kept until sold or craftworker requests return. Best selling time: Christmas.

Florida

THE BANANA BOX AT YBOR SQUARE, 1901 N. 13th St., Tampa FL 33605. (813)247-6972. Contact: Bettie Perez. Gift and antique shop. Represents 12-15 craftworkers. All styles; utilitarian and/or decorative. Price range: $1.95-250; bestsellers: $1.95-50. Buys outright. Retail price set by joint agreement. Requires exclusive area representation on some items. Submit samples and SASE. Reports in 4 weeks.
Acceptable Work: Considers ceramics; glass art; jewelry; miniatures of all kinds; metalsmithing; pottery; woodcrafting; scrimshaw; rubbings; copper enameling; dolls; note cards; and books. "We have a special need for Spanish crafts since Ybor Square's history is Spanish. Also [has a need] for $15-40 marquetry; pewter animals and boxes; unusual mirrors; small furniture accents; shelves; stools; and clocks. We are inclined towards inspirational or works that have some meaning, both functional and artistic. Boxes of all types are a specialty with us — $1-10."
Profile: "We are in a unique historical area that is being restored. There is much interest in antiques; old art forms; collectibles; and art shows. We have a big tourist season; there's always an interest in Florida artists but some of my best sellers are from New England and California." Best selling time: fall-winter.

BOUNTY SHOP, 219 Atlantic Blvd., Atlantic Beach FL 32233. (904)246-7855. Contact: Connie McManus. Considers ceramics; sculpture; jewelry; metalsmithing; glass; leather; tie dying; and batik. Price range: $5-200. Retail price set by joint agreement. Send transparencies or photos.

CAVALIER GALLERY OF ART, INC., 167 Miracle Strip Pkwy., Ft. Walton Beach FL 32548. Contact: Mrs. M.B. See. Exhibits traditional and abstract sculpture. Usually buys outright, some consignment; 40% commission. Price range: $2-2,000. Retail price set by joint agreement. Send color transparencies or b&w photos of work. 2 weeks exposure for special showings.

CRAFTS AND THINGS, 317 Brevard Ave., Rockledge FL 32922. (305)636-6381. Contact: Thelma M. Murrell. Craft and gift shop. Estab. 1977. Represents 150 craftworkers. Fine one-of-a-kind and handmade production-line items; utilitarian and/or decorative. Price range: $1-500; bestsellers: $2-25. Works on consignment and buys outright; 33⅓% commission. Retail price set by joint agreement. Payment made by 10th of month following sales. Dealer pays return UPS shipping.
Acceptable Work: Considers batik; ceramics; clothing; decoupage; jewelry; needlecrafts; pottery; wall hangings; weavings; woodcrafting; and any unique, quality handmade items. "Quilts and infants clothing are always in great demand."
Profile: "We specialize in quality, handmade items." Unsold consigned pieces returned after 90 days. Customers are local residents and tourists visiting Cape Canaveral. Best selling time: Christmas.

A DIFFERENT DRUMMER, 194 Miracle Strip Pkwy. SE, Fort Walton Beach FL 32548. (904)243-1834. Contact: Karen Ward. Craft and gift shop. Estab. 1974. Represents 75-100 craftworkers. Considers candlemaking; ceramics; decoupage; dollmaking; glass art; jewelry; needlecrafts; pottery; quilting; soft sculpture; tole painting; wall hangings; weavings; and woodcrafting. Primitive handmade production-line items; utilitarian and/or decorative. Price range: 69c-$150; bestsellers: $3.50-30. Works on consignment; 40% commission. Retail price set by joint agreement. Requires exclusive area representation. Reports in 2 weeks. "Payment is made on the 10th of the month following the month of sale; articles must remain in shop at least 60 days." Dealer pays insurance for exhibited work.

Profile: "The shop is managed by a professional artist and craftswoman. Our summer tourist season brings traffic from all over the US. From November 1-January 1 we transform our shop into 'The Wonderful World of Christmas' which attracts all income levels and ages." Best selling time: Christmas and June-Labor Day.

FIBRATIONS WEAVING STUDIO AND GALLERY, 14115 S. Dixie Hwy., Suite D, Miami FL 33176. (305)233-0221. Contact: B. Clark. Craft shop/gallery/workshop/supply studio. Estab. 1973. Represents 12+ craftworkers. Price range: $5-500; bestsellers: $10-100. Works on consignment; 25% commission. Retail price set by joint agreement. Prefers exclusive area representation. Reports in 3-4 weeks. Dealer pays insurance for exhibited work; "we are protected against theft only."

Acceptable Work: Considers batik; clothing; dollmaking; glass art; quilting; soft sculpture; wall hangings; and weaving. "We have a special need for one of a kind clothing; tapestries; wall hangings; and decorative items." All styles; utilitarian and/or decorative.

Profile: "We have a workshop atmosphere combined with high quality displays." Customers are fellow craftsmen; fiber students; shop and gallery owners; decorators; tourists; and local upper middle class neighbors. Best selling time: November-January. Shop closed in August.

FORT LAUDERDALE MUSEUM OF THE ARTS GIFT SHOP, 426 E. Las Olas Blvd., Ft. Lauderdale FL 33301. (305)463-5184. Buys original art and crafts outright or on consignment; 33⅓% minnimum commission. Price range: 50c-$100 for such items as small booklets to African/pre-Columbian artifacts. Museum holds Annual Hortt Memorial Competition & Exhibition, with residents of Broward, Dade, Monroe and Palm Beach counties invited.

FRIENDS OF THE MUSEUM, INC., 1101 E. River Cove, Tampa FL 33604. (813)932-8719. Treasurer, Manager: Terri Garnhart. Museum gift shop. Estab. 1968. Represents 10 craftworkers. Considers batik; candlemaking; ceramics; decoupage; jewelry; leatl erw rking; needlecrafts; pottery; wall hangings; weavings; and woodcrafting. Fine one-of-a-kind pieces; utilitarian and/or decorative. Price range: $1-75; bestsellers: $2-10. Works on consignment and buys outright; 25-50% commission. Shop sets retail price. Reports in 4 weeks. Dealer pays for return shipping; return shipping insurance; and insurance for exhibited work.

Profile: "In comparison to other Museum shops our lines are much more varied; something for everyone at reasonable prices. Geared for children 6-12 years old with $1-2 to spend." Best selling time: summer.

GROVE HOUSE, INC., 3496 Main Hwy., Coconut Grove, Miami FL 33133. (305)445-5633. Executive Director: Thyrza Jacocks. Craft shop/gallery. Estab. 1960. Represents 200-400 Florida craftworkers. Considers batik; ceramics; dollmaking; glass art; metalsmithing; needlecrafts; pottery; quilting; soft sculpture; wall hangings; weavings; and woodcrafting. All styles; utilitarian and/or decorative. Price range: $5-1,500; bestsellers: $20-250. Works on consignment; 35% commission. Craftworker sets retail price. Reports in 2 weeks. Dealer pays return shipping and insurance for exhibited work.

Profile: "We are a nonprofit cooperative." Customers are middle income with large age spread. Best selling time: November-March.

HALIFAX HISTORICAL SOCIETY, INC., Box 5051, Daytona Beach FL 32018. (904)255-5976. President: Florence D. Nordquist. Museum gift shop. Estab. 1978. Considers candlemaking; dollmaking; needlecrafts; quilting; wall hangings; weavings; and any pioneer craft. Primitive and fine one-of-a-kind pieces; utilitarian and/or decorative. Minimum price: $2.50. Works on consignment; 40% commission. Retail price set by joint agreement. Requires exclusive area representation. Reports in 3 weeks. Prefers UPS.

Profile: "The store follows the general motif of a country store. All items are of a type that would interest collectors. We advertise in some national magazines and papers. We are in a tourist area." Best selling time: summer and winter.

HISTORICAL ASSOCIATION OF SOUTHERN FLORIDA, INC., 3280 S. Miami Ave., Miami FL 33129. (305)854-3289. Business Manager: Jane Martin. Museum gift shop. Estab. 1941. Represents 6 Florida craftworkers who "manufacture products dealing specifically with the history of south Florida as illustrated in our museum gallery displays." Considers jewelry; woodcrafting; and Seminole Indian crafts. Primitive handmade production-line items; utilitarian and/or decorative. Price range: $1-100; bestsellers: $2-10. Works on consignment; 50% commission. Retail price set by joint agreement. Reports in 1 month. Dealer pays shipping to shop. **Profile:** "Our present museum shop is small. Items are displayed in display cases; on the wall; book shelves; or whichever of these is appropriate." Customers are older members of the museum; school age tour groups; and tourists. Best selling time: December-April.

HOUSE OF FINE ART, INC., 9476 Harding Ave., Surfside FL 33154. (305)868-6870. Contact Iris G. Klein. Gallery/gift, frame and art supplies shop. Estab. 1961. Represents 10-12 craftworkers. Considers batik; candlemaking; ceramics; decoupage; dollmaking; glass art; pottery; soft sculpture; and woodcrafting. Fine one-of-a-kind and handmade production-line items; utilitarian and/or decorative. Price range: $2-75; bestsellers: $2-25. Works on consignment and buys outright; 40% commission. Retail price set by joint agreement. Requires exclusive area representation. Dealer and craftworker pay insurance for exhibited work. Customers are upper middle and upper class. Best selling time: winter.

HOWARD GALLERIES, LTD., 148 Pompano Fashion Sq., Pompano Beach FL 33062. (305)781-9481. President: H.B. Solomon. Considers sculpture. Maximum size: 48x36". Minimum price: $25; bestsellers: $100-300. Buys outright or on consignment. Retail price set by joint agreement. Requires exclusive area representation. Write for interview or send photos of work. SASE. Gallery pays shipping from gallery and insurance on exhibited work. 60 days minimum exposure.

JACKSONVILLE ART MUSEUM SHOP, 4160 Boulevard Center Dr., Jacksonville FL 32207. (904)398-8336. Contact: Ruth Hall. Estab. 1968. Considers most crafts; especially interested in well-made ceramic work. Primitive and finished one-of-a-kind and handmade production-line items; utilitarian and/or decorative. Price range: $2.50-75; bestsellers: $5-15. Buys outright or on consignment; 30% commission. Craftworker sets retail price. Write. Tries to report within 10 days. Dealer pays shipping from shop and insurance for exhibited work.
Profile: Best selling time: November-December. "We are a museum shop in a teaching institution and we seek items to stimulate classroom discussion."

LAMOUREUX DESIGNS, 191 NW 71st St., Miami FL 33150. Contact: E. Lamoureux. Estab. 1969. Represents 12 craftworkers. Considers crafts for mail order — stuffed toys; quilted items; and patterns. Price range: $10-100; bestsellers: $25+. Buys outright. Retail price set by joint agreement. Query. Reports in 10 days.

LOCH HAVEN ART CENTER SHOP, 2416 N. Mills Ave., Orlando FL 32803. (305)896-4231. Manager: Linda C. Swindler. Museum gift shop. Estab. 1969. Represents 2 craftworkers. Considers batik; jewelry; pottery; wall hangings; and weaving. Fine one-of-a-kind pieces; utilitarian and/or decorative. Price range: $1-100; bestsellers: $1-25. Works on consignment; 34% commission. Retail price set by joint agreement. Reports in 4 weeks. Dealer pays return shipping and insurance for exhibited work.
Profile: "We have an Artist-of-the-Month series which we use to exhibit selected artists on a monthly basis." Best selling time: Christmas.

MUSEUM OF ARTS AND SCIENCES, 1040 Museum Blvd., Daytona Beach FL 32014. (904)255-0285. Director: Gary Russell Libby. Gift shop. Buys crafts outright or on consignment. Price range: $1-30. No commission.

MUSEUM OF FINE ARTS SHOP, 255 Beach Drive N., St. Petersburg FL 33701. (813)896-2667. Shop Manager: Mrs. Edgar Andruss. Museum gift shop. Estab. 1965. Represents 4-5 craftworkers. Considers ceramics; glass art; and pottery. Fine one-of-a-kind pieces; utilitarian and/or decorative. Price range: $3.50-30. Works on consignment and buys outright; 40-50% commission. Shop sets retail price. Requires exclusive area representation. Customers are high income, age 45-60; "we are now trying to appeal to younger group." Best selling time: fall-winter.

PENSACOLA MUSEUM OF ART, 407 S. Jefferson St., Pensacola FL 32501. (904)432-6247. Director: Brigitte Huybregts. Museum gallery/gift shop. Estab. 1954. Represents 4 craftworkers. Considers batik; ceramics; dollmaking; glass art; jewelry; metalsmithing; needlecrafts; pottery; quilting; soft sculpture; wall hangings; weaving; and woodcrafting. One-of-a-kind pieces; utilitarian and/or decorative. Price range: $5-100; bestsellers: $10-30. Works on consignment and buys outright; 30% commission. Retail price set by joint agreement. Shipping

and in-transit insurance are negotiable; dealer pays insurance for exhibited work.
Profile: "We are located in a historic building — Old City Jail." Best selling time: Christmas.

THE PINK PETUNIA, 97 St. George St., St. Augustine FL 32084. (904)829-9363. Contact: Kay or G.H. Welborn. Craft and gift shop. Estab. 1968. Represents 40-60 craftworkers. Price range: 75c-$125; bestsellers: $3-75. Works on consignment and buys outright; 40% commission. Shop sets retail price if items are purchased outright; craftworker sets retail price for consigned items. Requires exclusive area representation. Reports as soon as possible. Dealer pays return shipping; in-transit insurance if returning purchases; and insurance for exhibited work.
Acceptable Work: Considers batik; candlemaking; decoupage; dollmaking; glass art; jewelry; needlecrafts; pottery; quilting; wall hangings; weavings; woodcrafting; macrame; woodblock prints; trapunta; enamels; and collages. All styles; utilitarian and/or decorative.
Profile: "We have just moved into larger quarters in what was once the Pan American Center complete with Hispanic garden and typical Spanish architecture. We feature exclusive and well-displayed crafts." Best selling time: spring and summer.

ROOFTOP GALLERY, Harbor House, 423 Front St., Key West FL 33040. (305)294-6863, 294-5892. Contact: Barbara Doremus. Gallery/gift shop. Estab. 1971. Represents 7-8 craftworkers. Considers jewelry; wall hangings; weavings; and woodcrafting. Fine one-of-a-kind and handmade production-line items; utilitarian and/or decorative. Price range: $5-250. Works on consignment and buys outright; 40% commission. Gallery sets retail price. Requires exclusive area representation. Reports in 2 weeks. Dealer pays shipping to shop.
Profile: "Rooftop will carry only items well-designed, well-made and sensibly priced. We have established over a period of 7 years a reputation for integrity and fairness in pricing plus an unusually select line of merchandise." Best selling time: December-April.

TEMPLE MOUND MUSEUM, Box 1449, Fort Walton Beach FL 32548. Curator: Mrs. Yulee W. Lazarus. Museum gift shop. Estab. 1962. Considers ceramics; decoupage; jewelry; leatherworking; needlecrafts; pottery; wall hangings; and weavings in Southeastern Indian designs. Primitive one-of-a-kind and handmade production-line items; utilitarian and/or decorative. Price range: 75c-$30; bestsellers: 75c-$15. Buys outright. Shop sets retail price. Requires exclusive area representation. Submit photos or description. Reports in 2 weeks. Dealer pays for shipping to shop. Best selling time: summer.

TUTTLES SEAHORSE SHELL SHOP, 342 Periwinkle Way, Sanibel Island FL 33957. Contact: Pauline and Bob Tuttle. Gift shop. Estab. 1960. Represents 10 local craftworkers. Considers candlemaking; ceramics; jewelry; wall hangings; and weavings as related to shell craft. All styles; utilitarian and/or decorative. Price range: 59c-$450; bestsellers: 59c-$50. Buys outright. Retail price set by joint agreement. Requires exclusive area representation. Reports daily. Hand delivered work only.
Profile: "We carry only locally made items. Every item must have seashells or be marine life related. The island is famous for shelling beaches." Customers are tourists. Best selling time: winter.

THE TWENTY FOUR COLLECTION, Box 24, Miami FL 33153. Gallery. Estab. 1975. Represents 10 craftworkers. Considers ceramics; clothing; glass art; jewelry; needlecrafts; soft sculpture; wall hangings; weavings; and woodcrafting. Primitive and fine one-of-a-kind pieces; utilitarian and/or decorative. Price range: $5-500; bestsellers: $5-200. Works on consignment and buys outright; 40% commission. Retail price set by joint agreement. Requires exclusive area representation. Reports in 2 weeks. Dealer pays shipping to shop and insurance for exhibited work. Best selling time: fall.

THE WEB, INC., 4135 Aurora St., Coral Gables FL 33146. (305)446-7731. President: Donna Keller. Craft, batik and weaving supplies, and equipment shop. Estab. 1975. Considers batik; clothing; quilting; soft sculpture; wall hangings; and weaving. All styles: utilitarian and/or decorative. Price range: $3-700; bestsellers: $3-80. Works on consignment; 25% commission. Retail price set by joint agreement. Reports in 1 week. Hand-delivered work only. Customers are 24-45 years of age; craft oriented; and with income of $10,000-50,000. Best selling time: November-December, March-April.

Georgia

AUTUMN LEAVES, 3-B Public Sq., Dahlonega GA 30533. (404)864-7305. Contact: Jan Campbell. Craft and gift shop. Estab. 1976. Represents 25 craftworkers. Price range: 25c-$100; bestsellers: 40c-$20. Works on consignment and buys outright; 30% commission. Gallery sets retail price. Requires exclusive area representation. Reports in 1 month. Work may be shipped or hand-delivered. Dealer pays return shipping and insurance for exhibited work. Displays work "as long as craftsman desires."

Acceptable Work: Considers tole painting; clothing; books; dollmaking; jewelry; leatherworking; metalsmithing; needlecrafts; quilting; and woodcarving. Especially needs men's items; woodcarvings; baskets; and silver jewelry. All styles; utilitarian and/or decorative.

Profile: Work is displayed "on shelves; jewelry in cases. Customers are from the college in town; tourists of all ages; steady traffic from Atlanta." Best selling and heaviest wholesale buying time: May-October.

BARCLAY GALLERY, 3994 Peachtree-Dunwoody Rd., Atlanta GA 30342. Director: S. Isla. Gallery. Estab. 1969. Considers ceramics; metalsmithing; pottery; soft sculpture; wall hangings; weavings; and woodcrafting. "Special need for designer wall hangings and sculpture." Fine one-of-a-kind designer pieces; utilitarian and/or decorative. Price range: $20-500; bestsellers: $20-250. Works on consignment; 50% commission. Retail price set by joint agreement. Requires exclusive area representation. "We keep inquiries on file for reference as need for new work arises. Good color slides should be submitted; color should be accurate. Person's hand in photo would give indication of size/scale. Composition of materials used would be helpful. Sign your work."

ELAINE COYNE GALLERIES, 943 S. Main, Stone Mountain GA 30083. (404)469-7907. Contact: Elaine Coyne. Craft shop. Estab. 1973. Represents 10 craftworkers. Price range: $1-200; bestsellers: $10-25. Works on consignment and buys outright; 35% commission. Gallery sets retail price. Requires exclusive area representation. Reports in 4 weeks. Work may be shipped or hand-delivered. Dealer pays insurance for exhibited work.

Acceptable Work: Considers ceramics; glass art; jewelry; leatherworking; metalsmithing; pottery; and soft sculpture. Especially needs leather bags; glass blowing; and pottery. Fine handmade production-line items; utilitarian and/or decorative.

Profile: "We like to display a series and then take custom orders, as well as sell displayed pieces. Shop is located in a beautiful little old town at the tip of Stone Mountain." Best selling and heaviest wholesale buying time: Christmas and summer.

THE DOLL HOUSE, INC., 375 Pharr Rd. NE, Atlanta GA 30305. (404)261-0691. Manager: Melissa Stuart, Doll house and furnishings store. Estab. 1973. Represents 20 craftworkers. Price range: $1-1,500; bestsellers: $1-400. Buys outright. Shop sets retail price. Reports in 1 week. Work may be shipped or hand-delivered. Dealer pays return shipping.

Acceptable Work: Considers ceramics; needlecrafts; miniature furniture in all finishes and styles; miniature china; moldings; windows; and electrical work. One-of-a-kind handmade production-line items; decorative only. Especially needs fine 18th century English reproductions (Hepplewhite, Chippendale, Duncan Phyfe, etc.), and fine Victorian pieces in rosewood, walnut and mahogany.

Profile: "Work is displayed in glass cases, dollhouse interiors and vignettes, etc. We sell only miniatures scaled exactly 1"-1'. We are the largest miniature store in the Southeast."

GEORGIA MOUNTAIN ARTS ASSOCIATION, Box 67, Tallulah Falls GA 30573. (404)965-6561. Manager: Lassie Bradshaw. Craft shop. Estab. 1967. Represents 75 craftworkers. Price range: $1-200; bestsellers: $10-200. Works on consignment and buys outright; 25% commission. Craftworker sets retail price. Work may be shipped or hand-delivered. Dealer pays shipping and insurance. Heaviest wholesale buying time: winter; best selling time: April-December.

Acceptable Work: Considers batik; jewelry; pottery; quilting; wall hangings; weavings; and woodcrafting. Primitive and handmade production-line items; utilitarian and/or decorative.

HOMEPLACE, 1676 S. Lumpkin St., Athens GA 30606. (404)549-0829. Contact: Barbara Fuller. Craft and gift shop. Estab. 1971. Represents 10 craftworkers. Price range: $5-75; bestsellers: $10-15. Works on consignment; 33⅓% commission. Retail price set by joint agreement. Requires exclusive area representation. Reports in 1 week. Work may be shipped or hand-delivered.

Acceptable Work: Considers ceramics; needlecrafts; pottery; quilting; wall hangings; weavings; and woodcrafting. Especially needs pottery; weavings; quilts; and homemade toys. Finished, one-of-a-kind and handmade production-line items; utilitarian and/or decorative.

Profile: "We have 5 rooms in a Victorian house, many white shelves, sometimes items are in windows. Customers are above average in income, from a university community, sophisticated in taste and well traveled." Heaviest wholesale buying time: fall; best selling time: pre-Christmas.

MARK OF THE POTTER, INC., Rt. 3, Clarkesville GA 30523. (404)947-3440. Contact: Glen or John LaRowe. Estab. 1968. Represents 30-40 craftworkers. Considers glass art; jewelry; pottery; some wall hangings; weavings; and woodcrafting. Finished, one-of-a-kind and hand-made production-line only; utilitarian and/or decorative. Price range: $2-300; bestsellers: $2-30. Buys outright. Retail price set by craftworker or joint agreement. Requires exclusive area representation. Query with transparencies or photos. Reports in 3 weeks. LaRowe pays shipping from shop to craftworker. Heaviest wholesale buying time: spring and late summer. Shop located in converted grist mill.

THE MUD DAUBER'S NEST, Box 361, 7001 Blackhawk Trail, Chatsworth GA 30705. (404)695-3797. Contact: Virginia Keese. Craft shop. Estab. 1975. Represents 75 craftworkers. Price range: $1-200; bestsellers: $1-20. Works on consignment and buys outright; 40% commission. Retail price set by joint agreement. Reports in 2 weeks. Work may be shipped or hand-delivered. Dealer pays return shipping. Displays work 60 days minimum.
Acceptable Work: Considers all crafts. Especially needs dolls; stuffed toys; hand puppets; and items for boys of all ages. Primitive handmade production-line items; utilitarian and/or decorative.
Profile: "I take the same care of other craftsmen's work as I do my own. The items are attrac-tively displayed." Best selling and heaviest wholesale buying time: spring, summer and fall.

STOREHOUSE, INC., 2737 Apple Valley Rd. NE, Atlanta GA 30319. (404)262-2926. Craft Buyer: Banks O. Godfrey Jr. Specialty store for contemporary home furnishings. Estab. 1969. Represents 35 craftworkers. Considers ceramics; glass art; pottery; wall hangings; weavings; and baskets. "Special need for more glass." All styles; utilitarian and/or decorative. Price range: $2-75; bestsellers: $5.50-50. Buys outright. Shop sets retail price. Requires exclusive area represen-tation. Reports in 1 week. Dealer pays shipping.
Profile: "We are a chain of 13 stores of contemporary home furnishings. Each store has a major department of crafts." Best selling time: fall.

STOREHOUSE, INC., 3106 Early St., Buckhead, Atlanta GA 30305. See above.

STOREHOUSE, INC., Lenox Square, Lower Level, Atlanta, GA. See above.

STOREHOUSE, INC., Northlake 2, next to Northlake Mall, Atlanta GA. See above.

STOREHOUSE, INC., 6277 Roswell Rd., Sandy Springs Plaza, Atlanta GA. See above.

WESTVILLE HISTORIC HANDICRAFTS, INC., Box 1850, Lumpkin GA 31815. Contact: Ron Slusarchuk. Considers ceramics; woodwork; metalsmithing; graphics; glass; needlecrafts; and leather. "I am interested only in traditional items, particularly those patterned after mid-19th century American— rural or primitive." Price range: $5-150. 30% commission. Items dis-played 6 weeks minimum.

Hawaii

BISHOP MUSEUM, Box 6037, Honolulu HI 96818. (808)847-3511. Manager: Sandi Gouveia. Museum gift shop. Estab. 1889. Represents 50 craftworkers whose work relates to Hawaii or its overlaying cultures. Price range: $1.40-800; bestsellers: $5-250. Works on consignment and buys outright; 40-50% commission. Retail price set by joint agreement. Reports in 3 weeks. Work may be shipped or hand-delivered.
Acceptable Work: Considers ceramics; dollmaking; jewelry; Hawaiian quilting; wall hangings; weavings; woodcrafting; basketry; and shell jewelry. All styles; utilitarian and/or decorative.
Profile: "If the items are accepted first orders are usually taken on consignment for 30 days. If successful, then items are bought outright after that."

FOLLOWING SEA, 1441 Kapiolani Blvd., Honolulu HI 96814. Contact: Michael Gibson. Represents about 250 craftworkers from 35 states. Considers ceramics; jewelry; metal; glass; leather; batik; wood; and weaving. Price range: $1-1,500. Buys mostly outright. 35-50% commis-sion. Craftworker sets retail price. Send transparencies or photos. Gallery pays shipping.
Profile: From early spring through fall, features one-man and group shows. Craftworkers juried year-round and selected works are offered for display and sale through 4-week show periods. Show schedule available. "We are endeavoring to develop one of the finest representations of contemporary American craftsmanship in the country, and a truly valid representation of each craft medium and each area of the country."

RARE DISCOVERY COLLECTABLES, 1050 Ala Moana Blvd., Honolulu HI 96814. (808)524-7119. Contact: Mark Izbicki. Craft shop/gallery. Estab. 1974. Represents 100 craftworkers. Price range: 50c-$6,000; bestsellers: $30-350. Works on consignment and buys outright; 40% commission. Retail price set by joint agreement. Reports in 2 weeks. Work may be shipped or hand-delivered. Dealer pays shipping and insurance.
Acceptable Work: Considers batik; candlemaking; ceramics; dollmaking; glass art; jewelry; leatherworking; metalsmithing; pottery; soft sculpture; wall hangings; weavings; and woodcrafting. Especially needs furniture and art glass. Fine one-of-a-kind and handmade production-line items; utilitarian and/or decorative.
Profile: "There is 300 square feet devoted to each craftsman. Customers are middle-upper class; 50% are tourists from all over the world." Shows last 45 days. Heaviest wholesale buying time: February, June, August and October; best selling time: December.

U.F.O. AND PLANTS, 94-875 Waipahu St., Waipahu HI 96797. (808)671-3343. Contact: Lynette L. Arakawa. Craft shop/art studio. Estab. 1976. Represents 5 craftworkers. Price range: 50c-$500; bestsellers: $10-30. Works on consignment and buys outright; 30% commission. Craftworker sets retail price. Reports in 2 weeks. Work may be shipped or hand-delivered. Displays work 90 days.
Acceptable Work: Considers batik, ceramics; clothing; glass art; jewelry; pottery; soft sculpture; wall hangings; weavings; and wood crafting. All styles; utilitarian and/or decorative.
Profile: "Shop has a home-grown Hawaiian atmosphere. It is a casual working studio-shop arrangement." Heaviest wholesale buying time: August-December; best selling time: spring and winter.

Idaho

BOISE GALLERY OF ART, Box 1505, Boise ID 83701. Contact: Beth Sellars. Gallery/museum gift shop. Estab. 1937. Represents 35 craftworkers. Price range: $2-100; bestsellers: $5-50. Works on consignment; 30% commission. Craftworker sets retail price. Reports in 2 weeks. Work may be shipped or hand-delivered. Dealer pays return shipping and insurance. Displays work 6 months. Heaviest wholesale buying time: fall; best selling time: winter.
Acceptable Work: Considers batik; ceramics; glass art; jewelry; leatherworking; metalsmithing; needlecrafts; pottery; quilting; wall hangings; weavings; and woodcrafting. Fine one-of-a-kind and handmade production-line items; utilitarian and/or decorative.

COUNTRY MANOR INTERIORS, Rt. 1, Box 139B, Marsing ID 83639. Contact Nancy C. Kueneman. Gift shop/interiors. Estab. 1975. Represents 10-20 craftworkers. Price range: $5-500; bestsellers: $5-50. Buys outright. Shop sets retail price. Requires exclusive area representation. Reports in 3 weeks. Accepts only approved items. Dealer pays return shipping and insurance for exhibited work.
Acceptable Work: Considers batik; ceramics; glass art; jewelry; metalsmithing; needlecrafts; pottery; wall hangings; weavings; table cloths; runners; and napkins. Fine one-of-a-kind and handmade production-line items; utilitarian and/or decorative. "I do not accept any crafts from new craftworkers unless I am contacted by mail beforehand. At the time I order crafts from a craftworker I do not want any items on an order substituted."
Profile: "I handle items not found in other design shops in this area; ones of unique design and quality." Customers are executives' wives, lawyers, doctors, and schoolteachers interested in furnishing their homes with quality design pieces; income level $15,000-30,000. Best selling time: late fall.

LAKESIDE GALLERY SCHOOL OF ART, 611 Lakeside Ave., Coeur d'Alene ID 83814. (208)664-9052. Manager: Opal Brooten. Gallery/gift shop. Estab. 1967. Represents 20 craftworkers. Price range of bestsellers: $5-150. Works on consignment; 40% commission. Craftworker sets retail price. Reports in 1 week. Work may be shipped or hand-delivered. Shows are 3-4 weeks; consignment work displayed 3 months maximum.
Acceptable Work: Considers batik; ceramics; dollmaking; jewelry; leatherworking; metalsmithing; pottery; wall hangings; and weavings. Primitive and fine one-of-a-kind pieces; utilitarian and/or decorative.
Profile: "Customers are in the middle income bracket; mostly young marrieds and 45-50 years old." Shows are 3-4 weeks; consignment work 3 months maximum. Best selling time: October-December.

Illinois

AMERICAN SOCIETY OF ARTISTS, INC., 700 N. Michigan Ave., Chicago IL 60611. (312)751-2500. American Artisan Director: Judy Edborg. Membership Chairman: Helen Del

Valle. Gallery/shop. Estab. 1972. Has membership of about 500 craftworkers and artists. Price range: $10-1,000; bestsellers: $15-200. Works on consignment; 25% commission. Retail price set by joint agreement. Reports in 1 week. Work may be shipped or hand-delivered only from members and only after pre-notification and agreement.
Acceptable Work: Considers batik; glass art; jewelry; leatherworking; metalsmithing; pottery; quilting; soft sculpture; tole painting; wall hangings; weavings; and woodcrafting. All styles; preferably decorative.
Profile: "We have continually changing exhibits of work by members from across the nation. Things are on a casual basis, i.e. when an artist is able to bring or ship work. We suggest size, type, etc. of work." Best selling time: Christmas.

AMISH FARM MARKET, Rt. 1, Box 191, Arthur IL 61911. Manager: Jonas M. Schrock. Estab. 1966. Represents 5 local Amish craftworkers. Considers clothing; dollmaking; needlecrafts; and woodcrafting. Handmade production-line items. Price range: 60c-$7.95; bestsellers: $1-2.50. Works on consignment; 20% commission. Retail price set by joint agreement. Requires exclusive area representation. Reports in 2 weeks. Hand-delivered work only. Best selling and heaviest wholesale buying time: summer.

THE ARKWRIGHT AND HIS FRIENDS, 5 Long Grove Rd., Rt. 2, Box 294-C, Long Grove IL 60047. (312)634-3130. Partners: Patricia Lewis or Joan Zasadil. Craft shop. Estab. 1976. Represents 200 craftworkers. Price range: $1.50-600; bestsellers: $30-100. Works on consignment; 40% commission. Craftworker sets retail price. Requires exclusive area representation. Reports in 1 week. Work may be shipped or hand-delivered. Dealer pays shipping to shop and insurance for exhibited work.
Acceptable Work: Considers batik; ceramics; dollmaking; glass art; jewelry; leatherworking; metalsmithing; needlecrafts; pottery; quilting; soft sculpture; wall hangings; weavings; and woodcrafting. All styles; utilitarian and/or decorative.
Profile: "We carry only handcrafts. We are located in a unique restored Antique Village which includes approximately 60 specialty shops and 6 restaurants." Heaviest wholesale buying time: spring and fall; best selling time: April-December.

ARTISAN SHOP AND GALLERY, 1515 Sheridan Rd., Plaza del Lago, Wilmette IL 60091. (312)251-3775. Director: Lila Goddard. Craft shop/gallery. Estab. 1968. Represents 400 craftworkers. Price range: $5,000 maximum; bestsellers: $300 maximum. Works on consignment (40% commission) and buys outright (50% discount). Retail price set by joint agreement. Requires exclusive area representation. Reports in 2 weeks. Work may be shipped or hand-delivered. Dealer pays return shipping and insurance for exhibited work.
Acceptable Work: Considers batik, ceramics; clothing; glass art; jewelry; quilting; soft sculpture; wall hangings; weavings; and wood crafting. Especially needs wall pieces— fiber, soft sculpture, art glass and unique Christmas ornaments. Fine, one-of-a-kind and handmade production-line pieces; utilitarian and/or decorative.

ARTIST EXHIBITION AND REGISTRY SERIES, 1712 2nd Ave., Rock Island IL 61201. (309)793-1213. Executive Director: Dianne Coffin. Gallery. Estab. 1977. Considers all crafts. "Gallery show, featuring 2-4 artists, changes monthly. Craftworker must attend opening show. Work may be offered for sale." Craftworker sets retail price. Dealer pays insurance for exhibited work.

ARTISTS IN WOOD, Box 284, Roselle IL 60172. (312)893-3144. President: Claude Michaelson. Gallery/gift shop. Estab. 1977. Represents 12 craftworkers who produce original wood carved items. All styles; utilitarian and/or decorative. Price range: $5-750. Works on consignment and buys outright; 40% commission. Retail price set by joint agreement. Reports in 2 weeks. Work may be shipped or hand-delivered. Dealer pays insurance for exhibited work.
Profile: "We are a complete wood gallery featuring only domestic carvings of all types and styles. Customers are in upper and upper middle income bracket." Displays work 30 days minimum. Heaviest wholesale buying time: spring and fall.

ARTS INTERNATIONAL LTD., 58 E. Walton St., Chicago IL 60611. (312)943-1793. Director of Artists Relations: David Oates. Considers sculpture. Maximum size: 48x36. Price range: $25-300; bestsellers: $35-125. Buys outright; 50% commission. Retail price set by joint agreement. Requires exclusive area representation. Query with samples. SASE. Gallery pays shipping from gallery and insurance on exhibited art.

COLLECTORS' SHOWROOM, 325 N. Wells, Chicago IL 60610. (312)644-3180. President: Ruth Friedland. Gallery. Estab. 1970. Represents 250 craftworkers. Price range: $50-25,000. Works on consignment; 50% commission. Retail price set by joint agreement. Reports in 4 weeks. Work may be shipped or hand-delivered. Dealer pays insurance for exhibited work. "We are specifically designed as an art form resource for architects and designers and corporate collectors."
Acceptable Work: Considers nonfunctional pottery and stone sculpture; soft sculpture; wall hangings; weavings; and wood. Fine one-of-a-kind pieces; decorative only. Especially needs art forms for corporate art programs.

THE COMSTOCK LODE, 450 Duane, Glen Ellyn IL 60137. (312)858-3230. Contact: Jean Weliver. Gallery. Estab. 1974. Represents 70 craftworkers. Price range: $2-400; bestsellers: $20-150. Works on consignment and buys outright; 25% commission. Retail price set by joint agreement. Reports in 2 weeks. Work may be shipped or hand-delivered. Dealer pays return shipping and insurance for exhibited work. Displays work 3-12 months.
Acceptable Work: Considers jewelry; especially needs rings. Fine one-of-a-kind and handmade production-line items; utilitarian and/or decorative.
Profile: "Work is locked in glass cases. Our shop has exceptional variety and quantity at reasonable prices. Customers are sophisticated; under 40; middle income; conservative." Heaviest wholesale buying time: fall; best selling time: October-June.

CONTEMPORARY ART WORKSHOP, 542 W. Grant Pl., Chicago IL 60614. (312)525-9624. Contact: Lynn Kearney. Gallery/art center. Estab. 1950. Represents 2-30 craftworkers. Considers ceramics; glass art; metalsmithing; soft sculpture; wall hangings; weavings; and woodcrafting. Fine one-of-a-kind pieces; utilitarian and/or decorative. Price range: $15-2,000. Works on consignment; 33⅓% commission. Retail price set by joint agreement. Reports in 4 weeks. Hand-delivered work only. Shows last 1 month. "We are a nonprofit art center and gallery started and run by artists." Best selling time: September-May.

THE CONTEMPORARY QUILT, 2863 N. Clark St., Chicago IL 60657. (312)528-0360. Craft and supply shop. Estab. 1972. Represents 15-20 craftworkers. Price range: $3-600; bestsellers: $3-300. Works on consignment and buys outright; 20-30% commission. Retail price set by joint agreement. Reports in 1 month. Work may be shipped or hand-delivered. Dealer pays return shipping and insurance on exhibited work. Displays work 3 months or more. Best selling time: Christmas.
Acceptable Work: Considers clothing; dollmaking; quilting; soft sculpture; and woodcrafting. One-of-a-kind and handmade production-line items; utilitarian and/or decorative.

CRAFT CLOCKS AND GIFTS, Rt. 82 and North Ave., Elmhurst IL 60126. Director: Ruth Hall Smith. Gift shop. Price range: $1-3,200; bestsellers: $1-250. Buys outright. Shop sets retail prices. "Always send a query first, preferably accompanied by photos." Reports in 3 weeks. Work may be shipped or hand-delivered.
Acceptable Work: Considers dollmaking; metalsmithing; needlecrafts; pottery; tole painting; woodcrafting; craft clocks; dollhouses; and miniatures.
Profile: Customers are all ages and in the middle income bracket. Heaviest wholesale buying time: late summer months; bestselling time: November-January.

CRAFT CONNECTION, LTD., 2555 N. Clark, Chicago IL 60614. (312)549-0899. President: Marcia Fensin. Gallery. Estab. 1977. Represents 60 craftworkers. Price range: $2-380; bestsellers: $3-25. Works on consignment and buys outright; 40% commission. Retail price set by joint agreement. Reports in 1 month. Work may be shipped or hand-delivered. Dealer pays shipping to shop and insurance for exhibited work.
Acceptable Work: Considers batik; ceramics; clothing; dollmaking; jewelry; pottery; quilting; soft sculpture; wall hangings; weavings; and woodcrafting. Fine handmade production-line items; utilitarian and/or decorative.
Profile: "Most craftspeople's items are displayed together. Names of maker on all; tagged with price and materials and cleaning methods if necessary. Customers are 18-35; mainly single with $12,000/year income."

CRAFT PRODUCTS COMPANIES, Rt. 83 and North Ave., Elmhurst IL 60126. Manager: Toni Barloga. See Craft Products Companies, St. Charles, Illinois.

CRAFT PRODUCTS COMPANIES, 2200 Dean St., St. Charles IL 60174. (312)584-9600. Vice President: Ruth Smith. Craft, gift and mail order shop/museum gallery. Estab. 1940. Price range: $1-4,000; bestsellers: $3.95-800. Buys outright. Retail price set by joint agreement. Requires exclusive area representation. Reports in 3 weeks. Work may be shipped or hand-delivered by previous arrangement. Payment for return shipping is negotiable. Dealer pays insurance for exhibited work.

Acceptable Work: Considers ceramics; dollmaking; glass art; metalsmithing; needlecrafts; tole painting; woodcrafting; and scaled $^1/_{12}$ miniatures of all kinds. Especially needs clockmakers; miniaturists and woodcrafters. Fine handmade production-line items; utilitarian and/or decorative.

Profile: "We display representative samples at all times, then order additional quantities as needed. We are currently looking for unusual miniatures and inexpensive to moderately-priced items for the holiday season."

CREATIVE GIFT STUDIO, INC., 411 Main St., Glen Ellyn IL 60137. (312)469-2317. Contact: Dale B. Atkins. Gift shop. Estab. 1962. Price range: $1-200; bestsellers; $5-50. Works on consignment and buys outright; 30% commission. Retail price set by joint agreement. Requires exclusive area representation. Reports in 2 weeks. Work may be shipped or hand-delivered by previous agreement. Dealer pays insurance for exhibited work.

Acceptable Work: Considers candles; ceramics; glass art; jewelry; leather products; pottery; tole painting; wall hangings; weavings; and woodcrafting. All styles; utilitarian and/or decorative.

Profile: Work is displayed "on counters, shelves, walls or windows, depending on size and type of article. Customers have income of $5,000-100,000 annually."

CREATIVELY YOURS STUDIO, 929 Alpine Rd., Rockford IL 61108. Contact: Liz Hill. Craft and gift shop. Estab. 1973. Represents 150 craftworkers. Price range: $1-200; bestsellers: $3.50-35. Works on consignment; 40% commission. Retail price set by joint agreement. Requires exclusive area representation. Reports in 3 weeks. Work may be shipped or hand-delivered. Dealer pays return shipping. Displays work 3 months.

Acceptable Work: Considers candlemaking; dollmaking; glass art; jewelry; leatherworking; metalsmithing; pottery; soft sculpture; tole painting; wall hangings; weavings; and woodcrafting. Especially needs tole painting; sculpture; candles; jewelry; and toys. Fine one-of-a-kind and handmade production-line items; utilitarian and/or decorative.

Profile: "We display an artist's work for up to 3 months, continually changing display of merchandise to focus on various crafts and seasons." Customers are women; middle and high middle income; 16-65 years old. Best selling and heaviest wholesale buying time: Christmas.

DYECO, Conover Square, Oregon IL 61061. (815)732-2411. Contact: D. Dean Dye. Series of craft/art/gift shops. Represents 8 craftworkers; "must be excellent in their field." Price range: $1-500; bestsellers: $4-50. Buys outright. Requires exclusive representation within 25 miles. Reports in 1 week. Work may be shipped or hand-delivered. Dealer pays return shipping. "We have 130,000 square feet of a former piano plant, remodeled into a mall of 31 very different shops."

Acceptable Work: Considers all crafts except quilting and tole painting. All styles; utilitarian and/or decorative.

EARTH GLASS STUDIO, INC., 7433 N. Harlem Ave., Niles IL 60648. (312)647-9470. President: Sandra Iussig Bohn. Craft shop/gallery/gift shop. Estab. 1972. Represents 10 craftworkers. Considers glass art. Fine one-of-a-kind and handmade production-line items; utilitarian and/or decorative. Price range: $5-800; bestsellers: $10-300. Works on consignment; 33⅓% commission. Retail price set by joint agreement. Reports in 3 weeks. Hand-delivered work only. Dealer pays insurance for exhibited work (theft and fire only). Best selling time: Christmas.

EVERYTHING CREATIVE BY SUSIE SELLS, 330 W. State St., Sycamore IL 60178. (815)895-3331. Contact: Sue Sells. Craft shop/department store/gift shop. Estab. 1970. Represents 50 craftworkers. Considers all crafts except clothing and leatherworking. All styles; utilitarian and/or decorative. Price range: $1-150; bestsellers: $5-50. Works on consignment and buys outright; 40% commission. Retail price set by joint agreement. Reports in 1 week. Work may be shipped or hand-delivered. Customers are 18-35 years old with higher than average income. Heaviest wholesale buying time: fall-spring.

FINE ARTS CENTER OF CLINTON, 119 W. Macon St., Clinton IL 61727. (217)935-5055. Director: Vera MacGillivray. Gallery. Estab. 1960. Price range:$10-250; bestsellers: $10-100. Works on consignment; 20% commission. Craftworker set retail price. Rental gallery fee: $15. Requires exclusive area representation. Reports in 2 weeks. Work may be shipped or hand-

delivered. Center pays return shipping and insurance for exhibited work. Displays work 1 month.
Acceptable Work: Considers batik; ceramics; decoupage; jewelry; metalsmithing; quilting; wall
hangings; weavings; and woodcrafting. Primitive and fine one-of-a-kind pieces; utilitarian
and/or decorative.
Profile: "Large exhibits are in the gallery; small exhibits in a large locked case." Heaviest
wholesale buying time: September-May; best selling time: October-December.

THE FIRE WORKS, 7637 N. Greenview, Chicago IL 60626. (312)465-8655. Contact: James
Zerwin. Concessionaire. Estab. 1972. Considers glass art. Fine one-of-a-kind and handmade
production-line items; decorative. Price range: $1.95-40; bestsellers: $4.95-12.95. Buys outright.
Gallery sets retail price. Reports in 10 days. Work may be shipped or hand-delivered. Dealer
pays insurance for exhibited work. Customers are female; 25-45 years old; with income under
$10,000/year. Best selling and heaviest wholesale buying time: Christmas, Mother's Day and
summer.

4 ARTS GALLERY, 1629 Oak Ave., Evanston IL 60201. Director: Sidney Zwick. Gallery.
Estab. 1962. Represents 10 craftworkers. Considers ceramics and pottery. Fine one-of-a-kind
pieces; utilitarian and/or decorative. Price range: $3-400; bestsellers: $10-150. Works on consignment; 40% commission. Craftworker sets retail price. Reports immediately if not interested;
longer if interested. Work may be shipped or hand-delivered. Dealer pays return shipping and insurance for exhibited work up to $50/item. All items are on continuous display.
Profile: "We display a combination of paintings and sculpture with crafts. Customers are middle
income; many students or people associated with Northwestern University." Best selling time:
Christmas and June.

GALLERY YOLANDA, 148 E. Ontario, Chicago IL 60611. (312)266-7608. Director: Yolanda
Kelley. Gallery. Estab. 1975. Represents 8-10 craftworkers. Price range: $40-12,000; bestsellers:
$40-6,000. Works on consignment and buys outright; 50% commission. Retail price set by joint
agreement. Reports as soon as possible. Work may be shipped or hand-delivered. Dealer pays insurance for exhibited work.
Acceptable Work: Considers ceramics; metalsmithing; soft sculpture; wall hangings; and wood
sculpture. Finished and one-of-a-kind pieces; utilitarian and/or decorative. Especially needs fine
art ceramics and soft sculpture.
Profile: "We have window displays and shows that last 1 month usually. Our gallery is unique
because it does not intimidate the browser or buyer; the artists are always welcome. It is in the
manner of a European Salon where visitors and buyers feel like welcome guests in my home."
Heaviest wholesale buying time: August-June; best selling time: fall-Christmas.

GIRAFFE, 212 W. Green, Urbana IL 61801. (217)344-7802. Contact William Makris. Estab.
1970. Represents 10 craftworkers. Considers candlemaking; jewelry; leatherworking; and
pottery. Finished one-of-a-kind and handmade production-line items; utilitarian and/or
decorative. Price range: $2-140; bestsellers: $10-50. Buys outright. Seller sets retail price. Requires exclusive area representation. Write. Reports in 2 weeks. Dealer pays shipping from shop.
Heaviest wholesale buying time: fall; best selling time: August-December. Customers are college
students; they buy crafts for artistic value.

ILLINOIS RAILWAY MUSEUM, Box 431, Union IL 60180. Contact: Book Store Manager.
Estab. 1953. Considers railroad-oriented crafts. Handmade production-line items; utilitarian
and/or decorative. Price range: $30 maximum; bestsellers: $3-15. Retail price set by joint agreement. Submit photos; description; and information. Reports in 4 weeks. Work may be shipped
or hand-delivered. Dealer pays insurance for exhibited work.
Profile: "We are situated in a depot built in 1851 and located as the center of interest in an
operating museum with 150 pieces of railroad equipment." Heaviest wholesale buying time:
spring; best selling time: summer.

JEANNINE'S CERAMICS, Rt. 4, Urbana IL 61801. (217)344-0640. Contact: Jeannine Baker.
Ceramic shop. Estab. 1970. Represents 15 craftworkers. Considers utilitarian and/or decorative
ceramics. Price range: 50c-$150; bestsellers: 50c-$30. Buys outright. Reports in 1 week. Work
may be shipped or hand-delivered. Best selling and heaviest wholesale buying time: fall.

JOLIET CERAMIC ARTS AND CRAFTS, INC., 64 N. Desplaines St., Joliet IL 60431.
(815)723-8616. Contact: Carol A. McGuire or Helen M. Petrilla. Craft and gift shop. Estab.
1966. Represents 300 Illinois and Indiana craftworkers. Price range: 25c-$600; bestsellers: $1-
300. Works on a special order basis. Retail price set by joint agreement. Reports in 1 week.

Heaviest wholesale buying time: September-December: best selling time: fall and Christmas.
Acceptable Work: Considers ceramics and pottery. Finished and handmade production-line items; utilitarian and/or decorative.

KOEHNLINE GALLERY, 7900 Nagle, Morton Grove IL 60053. (312)967-5120, ext. 396. Contact: Bernard Krule. Estab. 1972. Primarily handles fine art photography. Considers sculpture. Maximum size: 4x6. Price range: $15-3,000. Works on consignment. Send resume and slides or photos. Gallery pays insurance on exhibited work. Audience of 300 receives mailing with each show. 2 weeks minimum exposure.

THE LOOM ROOM, 451 Duane St., Glen Ellyn IL 60137. (312)858-8057. Contact: Gary R. Babbitt. Weaving and fiber supply store. Estab. 1977. Works on consignment and buys outright; 30% commission. Retail price set by joint agreement. Requires exclusive area representation. Reports in 2 weeks. Work may be shipped or hand-delivered. Dealer pays insurance for exhibited work. "All items are displayed with care and consideration for what they are."
Acceptable Work: Considers clothing; pottery; wood; wall hangings; functional weavings "and other handmade items of high quality." Fine one-of-a-kind and handmade production-line items; utilitarian and/or decorative.

MERRILL CHASE GALLERIES, LTD., 225 Fence Lane, Hillside IL 60162. (312)449-5100. Contact: Robert Chase. Considers sculpture. Buys outright and works on consignment. Price range: $15-65,000. Retail price set by joint agreement. Requires exclusive area representation. Send slides or photos. SASE. Gallery pays shipping to gallery and insurance on exhibited work.

MINDSCAPE GALLERY AND STUDIO, INC., 1521 Sherman Ave., Evanston IL 60201. (312)864-2660. Director: Ronald Isaacson. Craft shop/gallery/rental gallery. Estab. 1974. Represents 300 craftworkers. Price range: $5-3,000; bestsellers. $20-150. Works on consignment; 40% commission. Retail price set by joint agreement. Requires exclusive area representation. Juried gallery. For application send SASE. Reports in 2-4 weeks. Work may be shipped or hand-delivered. Dealer pays insurance for exhibited work.
Acceptable Work: Considers batik; ceramics; wearables; blown and stained glass; jewelry;

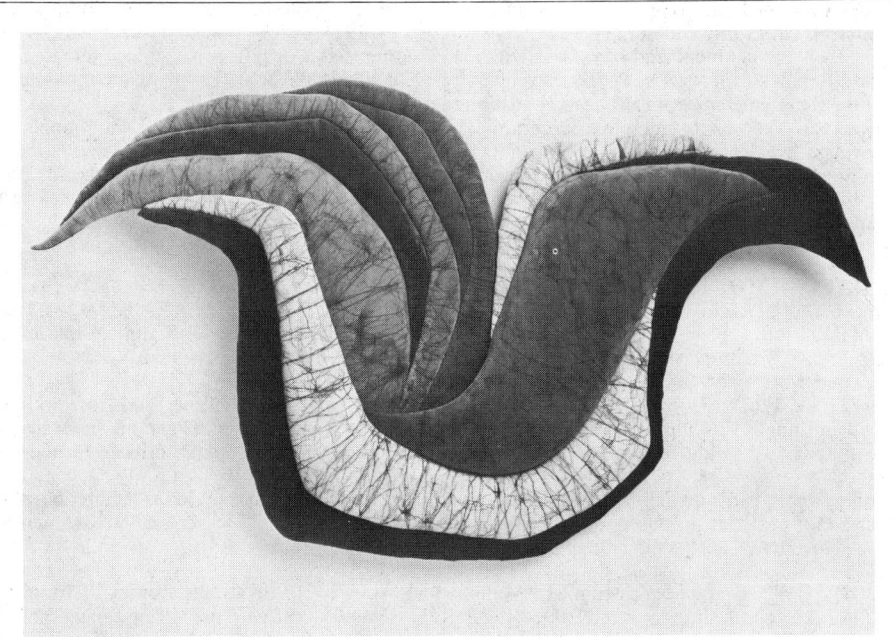

"The year of the textile is yet to come! We're promoting as much textile art as we possibly can," say the owners of Mindscape, Evanston, Illinois. This "Wondrous Bird," a soft sculpture batik on cotton velvet, is by Deborah Farber. — Photo by Uldis Saule.

leatherworking; metalsmithing; pottery; woodcrafting; and commissioned architectural works. Especially needs soft sculpture; sculptural ceramics; wall tapestry; weavings; and unusual jewelry, functional and sculptural. Fine one-of-a-kind pieces; utilitarian and/or decorative.
Profile: "Artists are displayed with a grouping of their work. The size of the display area is based on the amount of work on hand. Gallery space has 3,000 square feet. The gallery provides all display props and has a corner gallery with much window space and exposure. The premise of the gallery is to be a true reflection of what is happening in contemporary fine crafts and present it fairly for the public and artist alike." Located on the North Shore of Chicago, in the center of a major university town. Heaviest wholesale buying time: October-December and April-June; best selling time: October-December.

MOSTLY HANDMADE, INC., 508 Main St., Evanston IL 60202. (312)864-0845. Contact: Susan DePree, Mickey Nickels, Nancy Tucker or Rita Allison. Craft and gift shop. Estab. 1972. Represents 100-150 craftworkers. Price range: $1-400; bestsellers: $3-40. Works on consignment and buys outright; 40% commission. Reports in 2 weeks. Samples may be shipped or hand-delivered.
Acceptable Work: Considers ceramics; dollmaking; jewelry; toys; needlecrafts; quilting; and soft sculpture. Especially needs adult gifts priced at $10-30. One-of-a-kind and handmade production-line items; utilitarian and/or decorative.
Profile: "Displays change constantly as new merchandise comes in daily. Customers are male and female; 25-40. $15,000 and up income; looking for the unusual, noncommercial item." Displays work 1-3 months. Heaviest wholesale buying time: September-October; best selling time: October-December.

MUELLER'S WROUGHT IRON SHOP, 3632 N. Cicero, Chicago IL 60641. (312)286-2278. Buyer: Lynn Mueller. Gift shop. Estab. 1974. Represents 3-4 craftworkers. Considers metalsmithing; metal sculptures; and miscellaneous metal products. All styles; utilitarian and/or decorative. Price range: $5 minimum; best sellers: $15-250. Works on consignment; commission is negotiable. Retail price set by joint agreement. Reports in 2 weeks. Work may be shipped or hand-delivered. Dealer pays shipping to shop and insurance for exhibited work. "We specialize in wrought metals."

NATURAL SELECTION, 711 W. Belmont, Chicago IL 60657. (312)477-0203. Contact: K. Ishibashi. Craft, gift and home accessories shop. Estab. 1971. Price range of bestsellers: $2-100. Works on consignment and buys outright; 33⅓% commission. Retail price set by joint agreement. Reports in 4 weeks. Work may be shipped or hand-delivered. Payment on shipping is negotiable. Dealer pays insurance for exhibited work.
Acceptable Work: Considers batik; ceramics; jewelry; leatherworking; pottery; wall hangings; weavings; woodcrafting; and paper products. All styles; utilitarian and/or decorative.
Profile: "We try to give our shop a 'natural' look: very little plastic, mainly woods, fabrics, ceramics, etc. Customers are college educated; 20-45; good incomes." Best selling and heaviest wholesale buying time: spring and fall.

OCTAGON SHOP, 2603 Sheridan Rd., Evanston IL 60207. (312)685-5300. Managers: Stacey Greenberger or Janet Aliapolis. Craft and gift shop. Estab. 1971. Represents 20-30 craftworkers within 100 miles. Price range: $1.50-65; bestsellers: $1.50-20. Works on consignment and buys outright; 40% commission. Retail price set by joint agreement. Reports in 2 weeks. Hand-delivered work only.
Acceptable Work: Considers batik, ceramics; clothing; glass art; jewelry; leatherworking; metalsmithing; soft sculpture; wall hangings; and weavings. Especially needs glass paper weights and glass bowls. Fine one-of-a-kind and handmade production-line items; utilitarian and/or decorative.
Profile: Work is displayed in closed cases, on walls and on stands on the floor. "Shop does not operate for profit; it is housed in the Evanston Art Center building." Heaviest wholesale buying time: November; best selling time: November-December.

OLDE TOWN GALLERY, Main St., Mahomet IL 61853. (217)586-3211. Contact: Charlotte Williamson. Craft shop/gallery. Estab. 1977. Represents 30 craftworkers. Price range: $2.50-350; bestsellers: $11-50. Works on consignment and buys outright; 33⅓% commission. Retail price set by joint agreement. Reports in 2 weeks. Work may be shipped or hand-delivered. Displays work 9 months.
Acceptable Work: Considers clothing; dollmaking; glass art; jewelry; metalsmithing; needlecrafts; pottery; quilting; soft sculpture; wall hangings; weavings; and woodcrafting.

Especially needs soft sculpture and stitchery pieces. All styles; utilitarian and/or decorative.
Profile: "Work is always out on display in its category. We are a community fine arts center; we rent space to artists who work and teach at the gallery and help keep shop as part of rent. There is usually an artist working for customers to see." Heaviest wholesale buying time: late summer-early fall; best selling time: November-December.

PEORIA ART GUILD, 1831 N. Knoxville, Peoria IL 61603. (309)685-7522. Contact: P. Atterberry. Gallery. Estab. 1878. Represents 200-250 local and regional craftworkers. Price range: $3-1,000; bestsellers: $5-150. Works on consignment; 30% commission. Retail price set by craftworker. Reports in 2 weeks. Work may be shipped or hand-delivered. Dealer pays insurance for exhibited work.
Acceptable Work: Considers ceramics; glass art; jewelry; pottery; soft sculpture; wall hangings; weavings; and woodcrafting. Fine one-of-a-kind pieces; utilitarian and/or decorative.
Profile: "Non-wall pieces are displayed in an area separate from wall pieces. We do not jury individual pieces for placement in the Guild, rather the representation of a particular artist is decided by a committee. We are a nonprofit, all volunteer community arts center. Our customers range from university students to professional people." Best selling time: Christmas and late fall.

PRAIRIE HOUSE, 213 S. 6th, Springfield IL 62701. (217)544-2094. Contact: Edith Myers. Considers only "superior crafts . . . no 'craftsy' types." Price range: $5-1,000. Works on consignment with one-of-a-kind items; 40% commission. Craftworker sets retail price. Requires exclusive Springfield representation. Shop pays return shipping and insurance for exhibited work.

PRESTIGE GALLERIES INC., 3909 W. Howard St., Skokie IL 60076. (312)679-2555. Vice President: Louis Schutz. Considers glass art; metalsmithing; and sculpture. Maximum size: 5' square. Specializes in traditional romantic (i.e. mother with child) and representational works. Price range: $10-10,000, contemporary work; $50-5,000, sculpture. Bestsellers: $500-10,000. Buys outright or on consignment; 33⅓% commission. Retail price set by joint agreement. Requires exclusive area representation. Send slides or photos of work. 3 weeks minimum exposure.

RAMNAD CORPORATION-D/B/A PINK FLAMINGO, 228 E. Main St., Barrington IL 60010. (312)381-7760. President: Marian Ring. Gallery/gift shop. Estab. 1977. Represents 20 craftworkers. Price range: $5-1,500; bestsellers: $15-50. Buys outright. Gallery sets retail price. Requires exclusive area representation. Reports in 2 weeks. Work may be shipped or hand-delivered. Shipping payment is negotiable. Dealer pays insurance for exhibited work.
Acceptable Work: Considers clothing; glass art; soft sculpture; and clothing accessories. Especially needs custom furniture and home accessories. All styles; utilitarian and/or decorative.
Profile: "Work receives a 10-day window display, if merited. We will take custom orders from customers for artists in the same medium." Heaviest wholesale buying time: August-November; best selling time: December.

THE RED BARN, 202 Franklin, Fisher IL 61843. (217)897-1556. Contact: Ella Brake. Craft and gift shop. Estab. 1972. Represents 6 craftworkers. Considers candlemaking; ceramics; decoupage; leatherworking; tole painting; wall hangings; and weavings. All styles: utilitarian and/or decorative. Price range: 29c-$85; bestsellers: 29c-$10. Works on consignment and buys outright; 20% commission. Retail price set by joint agreement. Reports in 2 weeks. Work may be shipped or hand-delivered. Dealer pays return shipping and insurance for exhibited work. Displays work 1-2 months. Best selling and heaviest wholesale buying time: Christmas.

THE RED GERANIUM, 7131 N. Melvina Ave., Chicago IL 60646. Contact: Mildred Armato. Gallery/gift shop. Estab. 1967. Represents 30 craftworkers. Price range: $5-50; bestsellers: $3.50 minimum. Works on consignment and buys outright; 40% commission. Craftworker sets retail price. Work may be shipped or hand-delivered. Dealer pays in-transit insurance and insurance for exhibited work. Displays work 6 months. Customers are young to middle-aged; intellectual; middle to upper income. Heaviest wholesale buying time: February-April; best selling time: May-October.
Acceptable Work: Considers ceramics; clothing; jewelry; pottery; soft sculpture; wall hangings; weavings; and woodcrafting. Primitive and fine one-of-a-kind pieces; utilitarian and/or decorative.

THE RED OAK, Bishop Hill St., Bishop Hill IL 61419. (309)927-3539. Contact: Janet S. Arter. Gift shop. Estab. 1970. Represents 75 craftworkers. Price range: $5-150; bestsellers: $5-25. Works on consignment; 34% commission. Retail price set by joint agreement. Requires exclusive

area representation. Reports in 1 week. Work may be shipped or hand-delivered. Dealer pays return shipping.
Acceptable Work: Considers clothing; dollmaking; jewelry; leatherworking; metalsmithing; needlecrafts; quilting; tole painting; wall hangings; weavings; and woodcrafting. Especially needs quilts; woodwork; and enamelware. Primitive and fine handmade production-line items; utilitarian and/or decorative.
Profile: "Customers are greatly varied. We have a large tourist trade as we're located in a state park but we have a large area trade as well." Best selling and heaviest wholesale buying time: summer-fall.

S AND A CERAMICS, 3315 N. Harlem, Chicago IL 60634. (312)736-3351. Contact: Mrs. Ann Izzo. Gift shop/ceramic studio. Estab. 1960. Represents 50 craftworkers. Considers ceramics; decoupage; and dollmaking. Handmade production-line items. Price range: $5-500; bestsellers: $40-125. Works on consignment and buys outright; 50% commission. Retail price set by joint agreement. Reports in 3-5 days. Hand-delivered work only. Work is displayed in large window and on shelves.

THE SIDE STREET, 434 Franklin St., Waukegan IL 60085. (312)623-5155. Contact: Arva L. Wallace. Craft gift shop. Estab. 1969. Represents over 200 craftworkers. Considers all crafts except tole painting. Utilitarian and/or decorative. Price range: 50c-$100; bestsellers: $3-25. Works on consignment; 40% commission. Retail price set by joint agreement. Requires exclusive area representation. Reports in 1 week. Work may be shipped or hand-delivered. Dealer pays return shipping. Displays work 60 days minimum.
Special Needs: "Good unusual jewelry in the price range from $5-25 retail (some a little higher); $50 top limit."
Profile: "There is no limit on the type of craft. Baby things and toys are big sellers; also afghans and all knits, pillows, prints and pottery." Best selling and heaviest wholesale buying time: October-December and June.

SPERTUS MUSEUM OF JUDAICA, MUSEUM STORE, 618 S. Michigan Ave., Chicago IL 60605. (312)922-9012. Manager: Suzanne MacDonald. Museum gallery/gift shop. Estab. 1972. Represents 30-50 Israeli artists. Price range: $4.50-1,250; bestsellers: $20-200. Works on consignment and buys outright; 50% commission. Retail price set by joint agreement. Reports in 3 weeks. Work may be shipped or hand-delivered by previous consent. Dealer pays insurance for exhibited work. Displays work 2-6 months.
Acceptable Work: Considers batik; ceramics; jewelry; pottery; wall hangings; and weavings. Fine one-of-a-kind pieces; utilitarian and/or decorative.
Profile: "Exhibits change about every 2 months. We specialize in Israeli and Judaica items. Customers are students, museum visitors, conventioneers and tourists; 75% Jewish." Heaviest wholesale buying time: winter; best selling time: fall and spring.

SPRINGFIELD ART ASSOCIATION, 700 N. 4th St., Springfield IL 62702. (217)523-2631. Executive Director: William Bealmer. Museum gallery/rental gallery. Estab. 1933. Represents 200 craftworkers. Price range: $10-300. Works on consignment; 30% commission. Craftworker sets retail price. Reports in 3 weeks. Work may be shipped or hand-delivered. Dealer pays insurance for exhibited work. Work is featured for 2 weeks. Best selling time: September-January and April-June.
Acceptable Work: Considers batik; ceramics; glass art; jewelry; leatherworking; pottery; soft sculpture; wall hangings; and weavings. Especially needs ceramics and textiles. Finished and one-of-a-kind pieces; utilitarian and/or decorative.

SUBURBAN FINE ARTS CENTER, 472 Park Ave., Highland Park IL 60035. (312)432-1888. Contact: Receptionist. Nonprofit gallery and school. Estab. 1970. Represents 1-10 Chicago area craftworkers per show. Price range: $20-1,200; best sellers: $20-250. Exhibits work; commission varies. Retail price set by joint agreement. Hand-delivered work only.
Acceptable Work: Considers batik; ceramics; quilting; soft sculpture; wall hangings; and weavings. Fine one-of-a-kind pieces; utilitarian and/or decorative.
Profile: "We have a very nice professional looking space; are located in the North Shore area with a sophisticated audience; we are very easy to deal with and take a small percentage in relation to other galleries." Best selling time: Christmas. "Traditionally we have an exclusively crafts exhibit at Christmas time."

SUNSHINE UNLIMITED, INC., 1937 W. 95th St., Chicago IL 60643. (312)239-1166. Contact: Vivian J. Barry, Carol Foley, Therese Usher, Geri O'Malley or Carlie Nelson. Gift and plant shop. Estab. 1975. Represents 50 craftworkers. Price range: $1-150; bestsellers: $5-30. Works on consignment and buys outright; 33⅓% commission. Retail price set by joint agreement. Reports in 2 weeks. Work may be shipped or hand-delivered.

Acceptable Work: Considers candlemaking; ceramics; clothing; decoupage; dollmaking; glass art; jewelry; needlecrafts; pottery; quilting; soft sculpture; tole painting; wall hangings; weavings; and woodcrafting. Especially needs items for home and children. Handmade production-line items; utilitarian and/or decorative.

Profile: Customers are 25-65 years of age, upper middle class, and appreciators of unusual items. Work is displayed for 90 days. Heaviest wholesale buying time: early fall; best selling time: Christmas.

TOWER GALLERY, 300 N. State St., Chicago IL 60610. (312)222-1117. Contact: Seena Swibel. Craft shop. Estab. 1970. Represents 50 craftworkers. Price range: $2-300; bestsellers: $8-75. Works on consignment and buys outright; 40% commission. Retail price set by joint agreement. Reports in 4 weeks. Hand-delivered work only. Dealer pays insurance for exhibited work.

Acceptable Work: Considers batik; candlemaking; ceramics; glass art; jewelry; leatherworking; metalsmithing; needlecrafts; pottery; soft sculpture; wall hangings; weavings; and woodcrafting. Handmade production-line items, utilitarian and/or decorative.

Profile: "Shop has 3 windows; items are prominently displayed. Customers are all ages; upper middle income." Displays work 1 month. Heaviest wholesale buying time: fall; best selling time: Christmas.

THE UNIVERSITY GALLERY OF CHICAGO STATE UNIVERSITY, Department of Art, 95th and King Dr., Chicago IL 60628. (312)995-2192. Director: Robert Weitz. Gallery. Estab. 1976. Has 2 craft exhibition shows per year. Price range: $75-1,800; bestsellers: $75-400. Works on consignment via contract for exhibition purposes; 20-25% commission. Retail price set by joint agreement. Reports in 3 weeks. Work may be shipped or hand-delivered. Dealer pays return shipping and insurance for exhibited work.

Acceptable Work: Considers batik; ceramics; jewelry; needlecrafts; pottery; quilting; soft sculpture; wall hangings; and weavings. Especially needs ceramics and fiber. Primitive and fine one-of-a-kind pieces: utilitarian and/or decorative.

Profile: "We are an urban university in a middle-class neighborhood. Our customers are students, faculty, administrators and people of our south side community. But our exhibits often attract the attention of the Chicago public at-large. Craftworker is given advertising poster/mailers for his/her exhibit and a reception. Often craftworker is asked to lecture for a fee. Work is on display for 1 month."

WEAVING WORKSHOP, 3352 N. Halsted, Chicago IL 60657. (312)929-5776. Contact: Barbara diMauro. Estab. 1970. Represents 10 craftworkers. Considers glass art; leatherwork; rugs; and tapestries. Especially needs utilitarian crafts. Finished, one-of-a-kind items OK; utilitarian and/or decorative. Price range: $5-1,000; bestsellers: $5-150. Works on consignment; 25% commission. Retail price set by joint agreement. Write. Reports in 3 weeks. Dealer pays shipping from shop and insurance for exhibited work. Heaviest wholesale buying time: fall. Customers, ages 25-40, buy crafts for unusual gifts.

Indiana

THE ALLIANCE MUSEUM SHOP, Indianapolis Museum of Art, 1200 W. 38th St., Indianapolis IN 46208. (317)923-1331. Buyer: Thelma Battersby. Museum shop. Estab. 1975. Represents 200 craftworkers. Works on consignment and buys outright; 30% commission. Craftworker sets retail price on consigned work; shop sets retail price if bought outright. Reports in 1 week to 10 days. Work may be shipped or hand-delivered. Dealer pays return shipping and insurance for exhibited work. Best selling and heaviest wholesale buying time: fall.

Acceptable Work: Considers batik; ceramics; decoupage; glass art; jewelry; metalsmithing; needlecrafts; pottery; quilting; soft sculpture; wall hangings; weavings; and woodcrafting. All styles; utilitarian and/or decorative.

ART CENTER MUSEUM SHOP, 120 S. St. Joseph St., South Bend IN 46601. (219)284-9102. Manager: Helen Geglio. Museum gift shop. Estab. 1960. Represents 15-20 craftworkers; northern Indiana residents have first priority. Considers ceramics; glass art; jewelry; metalsmithing; needlecrafts; pottery; quilting; soft sculpture; weavings; wall hangings; and woodcrafting. All styles; utilitarian and/or decorative. Price range: $1-500; bestsellers: $5-50. Works on consignment (6 month contract) and buys outright; 30% commission. Craftworker sets retail price to include 30% commission. Reports in 2 weeks. Dealer pays return shipping and insurance on exhibited work.

Profile: "We are located in a new, exciting civic center designed by Philip Johnson. The shop is at the entrance to the Art Center complex and the gallery exhibition space." Best selling time: summer and Christmas.

BY HAND — A GALLERY FOR MIND OVER METAL, Box 313, Nashville IN 47448. (312)988-6778. Manager: John Albach. Craft gallery. Estab. 1973. Represents 5-6 craftworkers. Price range: 25c-$1,000; bestsellers: $8-50. Works on consignment; 25-35% commission. Retail price set by joint agreement. Requires exclusive area representation. Reports in 3 weeks. Work may be shipped or hand-delivered. Dealer pays shipping to shop.
Acceptable Work: Considers batik; candlemaking; clothing; decoupage; dollmaking; glass art; metalsmithing; needlecrafts; pottery; quilting; woodcrafting; handcrafted stationery; cards; and especially jewelry. All styles; utilitarian and/or decorative.
Profile: "Items are displayed in groupings of like media and subject. One room is exclusively cloth items and doll beds, etc. Jewelry and sculpture dominate the entry room. Batik, glass and sculpture are combined in our largest room." Heaviest wholesale buying time: early June and September; best selling time: late summer-fall.

COMMON PLACE, 302 Washington, Columbus IN 47201. (812)376-9915. Contact: Bill Mitchell. Gallery. Estab. 1974. Represents 100 craftworkers. Price range: 75c-$300; bestsellers: $1.50-50. Works on consignment and (occasionally) buys outright; 30% commission. Craftworker sets retail price. Reports in 2 weeks. Work may be shipped or hand-delivered. Dealer pays shipping for exhibited work. Displays work 3 months-1 year.
Acceptable Work: Considers batik; candlemaking; ceramics; clothing; dollmaking; glass art; jewelry; leatherworking; metalsmithing; needlecrafts; pottery; quilting; wall hangings; weavings; and woodcrafting. Fine one-of-a-kind and handmade production-line items; utilitarian and/or decorative.
Profile: "Work is displayed in glass cubes on pedestals, in jewelry cases, hanging onwalls and rafters and on counters. This is a nonprofit organization. All profits from sales are returned to the community through programs of The Commons and The Columbus Service League, who are joint sponsors of the shop." Heaviest wholesale buying time; September-October; best selling time: November-December.

FLOYD COUNTY MUSEUM, 201 E. Spring St., New Albany IN 47150. (812)944-7336. Director: Carol Tobe. Gallery/museum gift shop. Estab. 1971. Represents 15 craftworkers. Price range: $3-100; bestsellers: $3-25. Works on consignment; 25% commission. Craftworker sets retail price. Requires exclusive New Albany representation. Send inquiry or slides. Reports in 2 weeks. Work may be shipped or hand-delivered after acceptance. Dealer pays shipping and insurance for exhibited work. Best selling time: fall-winter.
Acceptable Work: Considers batik; dollmaking; glass art; jewelry; metalsmithing; pottery; soft sculpture; wall hangings; weavings; handbuilt ceramics; and original prints. Fine one-of-a-kind and handmade production-line items; utilitarian and/or decorative.

FORT OUIATENON BLOCKHOUSE TRADING POST, 909 South St., Lafayette IN 47901. (317)742-8411. Buyer: Robert McIntyre. Museum gift shop. Estab. 1969. Represents 5-10 18th century fur trade era craftworkers. Price range: $1-25; bestsellers: $1-12.50. Works on consignment and buys outright; 20% commission. Retail price set by joint agreement. Reports in 3 weeks. Work may be shipped or hand-delivered.
Acceptable Work: Considers candlemaking; clothing; dollmaking; glass art; jewelry; leatherworking; metalsmithing; needlecrafts; pottery; quilting; wall hangings; weavings; and woodcrafting. All styles; utilitarian and/or decorative.
Profile: "We are located in a reconstructed blockhouse, patterned after the structures from the French fur trade era in Indiana (18th century). The fort specializes in replica items from the fur trade era." Heaviest wholesale buying time: April-September; best selling time: September or October.

FORT WAYNE MUSEUM OF ART GIFT SHOP, 1202 W. Wayne St., Fort Wayne IN 46804. Director: John Krushenick. Museum gift shop. Estab. 1894. Price range: 49c-$150; bestsellers: $1.50-30. Works on consignment and buys outright; 50% commission. Retail price set by joint agreement. Reports in 2 weeks. Work may be shipped or hand-delivered. Displays work 6-12 months. Best selling and heaviest wholesale buying time: September-May.
Acceptable Work: Considers ceramics; glass art; jewelry; metalsmithing; pottery; woodcrafting; note cards; blank books; and sculpture.

GOURLEY'S OLDE SHOPPE, 2242 Cragmont, Madison IN 47250. (812)273-1697. Contact: Helen Gourley. Museum gallery. Estab. 1966. Represents 20-25 craftworkers. Price range: 50c-$500. Works on consignment; 20% commission. Craftworker sets retail price. Requires exclusive area representation. Work may be hand-delivered. "We have a living museum of antiques and crafts, displayed together."
Acceptable Work: Considers candlemaking; decoupage; needlecrafts; tole painting; wall hangings; weavings; and woodcrafting.

THE KATHY KAY SHOP, The Lumberyard Mall, 141 E. 1st St. SW, Carmel IN 46032. Contact: Kathleen Budd. Children's gift shop. Estab. 1973. Represents 20 craftworkers. Price range: $2-200; bestsellers: $4-35. Works on consignment and buys outright; 40% commission. Craftworker sets retail price. Requires exclusive area representation. Reports in 2 weeks. Work may be shipped or hand-delivered. Dealer pays insurance for exhibited work. Exhibits work 3-6 months.
Acceptable Work: Considers all crafts; anything pertaining to children. All styles; utilitarian and/or decorative.
Profile: "In our shop we have a large volume of baby gifts. Comments from customers, 'Looks like Saks Fifth Avenue,' 'Shops like these are usually found in New York.' We have a reputation for high quality merchandise." Heaviest wholesale buying time: spring and fall; best selling time: Christmas.

THE MUSEUM SHOP, 202 N. Alabama, Indianapolis IN 46204. (317)633-5007. Contact: Mrs. J.E. Burns Jr. Museum gift shop. Estab. 1970. Represents 10-12 craftworkers who make items as they were done in the 18th and 19th centuries. Price range: 10c-$350; bestsellers: 10c-$15. Works on consignment and buys outright; 34% commission. Retail price set by joint agreement. Reports in 3 weeks. Work may be shipped or hand-delivered. Dealer pays return shipping and insurance for exhibited work.
Acceptable Work: Considers candlemaking; ceramics; dollmaking; jewelry; metalsmithing; needlecrafts; pottery; quilting; tole painting; and woodcrafting. All styles; utilitarian and/or decorative.
Profile: "Work is displayed with similar items and items used with, i.e. candle holders with candles. We try to display the best craftwork reflecting what people would have used and made in Indiana prior to 1910." Best selling time: Christmas and summer.

NEW HARMONY GALLERY OF CONTEMPORARY ART, Owen Block, Main St., New Harmony IN 47631. (812)682-3156. Director: John P. Begley. Gallery. Estab. 1975. Represents 40 craftworkers who live within a 200-mile radius of New Harmony or with prior connections to this area. Price range: $5-1,000; bestsellers: $15-50. Works on consignment; 30% commission. Retail price set by joint agreement. Reports in 4 weeks. Work may be shipped or hand-delivered with prior consent. Dealer pays return shipping and insurance for exhibited work.
Acceptable Work: Considers ceramics; glass art; jewelry; metalsmithing; soft sculpture; wall hangings; weavings and woodcrafting. Fine utilitarian and/or decorative pieces.
Profile: "The gallery has 1 room with constantly rotating exhibitions of individual or small groups of artists. In addition, we keep a consignment room with pieces by artists we represent constantly on display." Best selling time: summer-fall.

STATION GALLERY, 422 E. Goldsboro, Crown Point IN 46307. (219)663-8770. Contact: Rita Mayer. Gallery/frame shop. Estab. 1972. Represents 100+ craftworkers. Considers batik; dollmaking; glass art; jewelry; metalsmithing; pottery; wall hangings; weavings; and woodcrafting. Fine one-of-a-kind and handmade production-line items; utilitarian and/or decorative. Price range: $5-150; bestsellers: $5-30. Works on consignment and sometimes buys outright. Craftworker sets retail price. Requires exclusive area representation. Reports in 4 weeks. Dealer pays return shipping.
Profile: "We are located in an old train station." Customers are middle to upper income professionals in mid 20's-50's. Best selling time: April-December.

TIPPECANOE COUNTY HISTORICAL ASSOCIATION, FOWLER HOUSE MUSEUM, 909 South St., Layfayette IN 47901. (317)742-8411. Buyer: Fern Martin. Museum gift shop. Estab. 1971. Represents 5-10 19th century/Victorian craftworkers. Price range: $1-25; bestsellers: $1-12.50. Works on consignment and buys outright; 20% commission. Retail price set by joint agreement. Reports in 3 weeks. Work may be shipped or hand-delivered.
Acceptable Work: Considers candlemaking; accessories; dollmaking; glass art; jewelry; leatherworking; metalsmithing; needlecrafts; pottery; quilting; wall hangings; weavings; and woodcrafting. All styles; utilitarian and/or decorative.

Profile: "Representative items are on display at all times. The museum is housed in a mansion dating from the 1850s." Customers range from pre-schoolers to Senior Citizens interested in things historic; income varies." Best selling and heaviest wholesale buying time: Christmas.

TRILOGY GALLERY INC., Box 642, Nashville IN 47448. (812)988-4030. Vice President: Donn Stoffer. Gallery. Estab. 1973. Considers all quality crafts. Price range: $3-1,500; bestsellers: $15-100. Works on consignment and buys outright; 33% commission. Craftworker sets retail price. Requires exclusive area representation. Arrange interview. Reports in 2 weeks. Dealer pays insurance for exhibited work.

VILLAGE CRAFTSMAN, 605 Washington St., Columbus IN 47201. (812)376-9156. Manager: Tom Browning. Craft shop. Estab. 1972. Represents 7 craftworkers. Price range: $10-1,000; bestsellers: $10-100. Works on consignment; 20-40% commission. Retail price set by joint agreement. Requires exclusive area representation. Reports in 2 weeks. Work may be shipped or hand-delivered. Dealer pays insurance for exhibited work.
Acceptable Work: Considers candlemaking; clothing (leather); glass art; jewelry; leatherworking; metalsmithing; pottery; and woodcrafting. Especially needs hardwood products and pottery. Finished and one-of-a-kind pieces; utilitarian and/or decorative.
Profile: Work is "either highlighted or blended with other pieces, depending on what care it needs. Jewelry is in glass, stainable items are put out of reach." Best selling and heaviest wholesale buying time: May-Christmas.

WAYNE COUNTY HISTORICAL MUSEUM, 1150 N. A St., Richmond IN 47374. Director: Stephen R. Williams. Museum gift shop. Estab. 1929. Represents 8 craftworkers. Price range: 25c-$15; bestsellers: 25c-$10. Works on consignment and buys outright; 20% commission. Retail price set by joint agreement. Reports in 2 weeks. Work may be shipped or hand-delivered. Dealer pays shipping to shop and insurance for exhibited work.
Acceptable Work: Considers candlemaking; clothing; dollmaking; glass art; jewelry; metalsmithing; needlecrafts; wall hangings; weavings; and woodcrafting. Especially needs blacksmithing; woodworking; weavings; and various doll types. All styles; utilitarian and/or decorative.
Profile: "Most items are located in glass display cases in the entrance area to the Museum." Heaviest wholesale buying time: early spring and mid-summer; best selling time: spring-early fall.

WINTHROP GALLERY, 5228 Winthrop Ave., Indianapolis IN 46220. (317)283-1147. Contact: Herman W. Kapherr. Considers sculpture. Handles mainly 19th and 20th century American art. Buys outright. Price range: $25-3,000.

WOODSY JUNCTION, Box 242, Rt. 5, New Castle IN 42362. (317)822-4744. Contact: Terry Yuncker. Museum gift and craft shop. Estab. 1976. Represents 60 craftworkers. Considers batik; dollmaking; glass art; leatherworking; metalsmithing; pottery; and especially woodcrafting. Primitive one-of-a-kind and handmade production-line items; utilitarian and/or decorative. Price range: 50c-$1,850; bestsellers: $1.99-9.95. Works on consignment and buys outright; 50% commission. Retail price set by joint agreement. Requires exclusive area representation. Reports in 3 weeks. "Just drop us a line plus a sample or photo or work." Return shipping depends upon quantity and item.
Profile: "Willing to put in most anything for variety and uniqueness to keep everyone interested." Best selling time: spring and fall.

Iowa

BLUE GRASS ART AND HOBBY CENTER, Box 206C, E. Telegraph Rd., Blue Grass IA 52726. (319)381-3111. Manager: LuElla Schroder. Gift shop/china-glass studio. Estab. 1950. Represents 3 craftworkers. Price range: 50c-$500; bestsellers: 50c-$275. Buys outright. Gallery sets retail price. Considers ceramics; glass art; jewelry; and china-painted porcelain.
Profile: "We carry exclusively glass, porcelain and china supplies. No one carries or teaches this full line in our area. We mail-order to all states." Best selling time: June-July and November-December.

CORNERHOUSE GALLERY AND FRAME, 2753 1st Ave. SE, Cedar Rapids IA 52402. (319)365-4348. Director: Janelle V. McClain. Gallery/frame shop. Estab. 1976. Represents 50 craftworkers. Price range: $5-500; bestsellers: $5-150. Works on consignment and buys outright; 40% commission. Gallery sets retail price. Requires exclusive area representation. Reports in 3 weeks. Work may be shipped or hand-delivered. Dealer pays insurance.

Acceptable Work: Considers batik; glass art; pottery; wall hangings; weavings; and woodcrafting. Fine one-of-a-kind and handmade production-line items; utilitarian and/or decorative. Especially needs pottery and Christmas ornaments.

Profile: "Each work is displayed so as to benefit it most with sufficient space. Displays are rotated once a month with special showings of individual artists' work. We are located in a large turn-of-the-century house emphasizing a comfortable, relaxed, artistic atmosphere." Heaviest wholesale buying time: fall; best selling time: winter-spring.

COTHRAN'S ART GALLERIES, 1100 19th Ave. SW, Cedar Rapids IA 52404. (319)365-5332. Contact: Sidney or Nancy Cothran. Gallery. Estab. 1976. Represents 80 craftworkers. Price range: $3-600; bestsellers: items up to $50. Works on consignment; 40% commission. Craftworker sets retail price. Requires exclusive area representation. Reports in 2 weeks. Work may be shipped or hand-delivered. Dealer pays return shipping and insurance for exhibited work.

Acceptable Work: Considers batik; candlemaking; dollmaking; glass art; jewelry; metalsmithing; needlecrafts; pottery; soft sculpture; wall hangings; weavings; and woodcrafting. Fine one-of-a-kind and handmade production-line items; utilitarian and/or decorative.

Profile: "We have a reputation for quality work. Customers are 20-50; middle to upper class and willing to pay for quality work. Send 3-5 slides of work for approval or stop by our galleries with work." Displays work 6 months minimum. Best selling and heaviest wholesale buying time: summer and Christmas.

COTHRAN'S ART GALLERIES, 99 16th Ave. SW, Czech Village IA 52404. See above.

CUSTOM CRAFTS, 3499 W. 4th St., Waterloo IA 50701. (319)236-1743. Contact: Ruth Moore. Craft and gift shop. Estab. 1972. Represents 3 craftworkers. Price range: $1-200; bestsellers: $5-100. Works on consignment; 30% commission. Retail price set by joint agreement. Reports in 1 week. Work may be shipped or hand-delivered.

Acceptable Work: Considers ceramics; decoupage; dollmaking; jewelry; needlecrafts; pottery; quilting; wall hangings; and weavings. Especially needs stained glass lamp shades and windows. All styles; utilitarian and/or decorative.

Profile: "Work is displayed to best advantage; customers are young adults with varied income. Displays work 3 months. Best selling and heaviest wholesale buying time: fall.

FIBER TO FABRIC SHOP, 232½ Main St., Ames IA 50010. (515)232-5331. Manager: Rosemary Boles. Weaving/spinning supply shop. Estab. 1970. Represents 2 craftworkers. Price range: $1-200; bestsellers: $5-50. Works on consignment; 30% commission. Craftworker sets retail price. Reports in 4 weeks. Work may be shipped or hand-delivered. Dealer pays insurance for exhibited work. Displays work 3-4 months.

Acceptable Work: Considers wall hangings; weavings; and handspun yarns. Primitive one-of-a-kind and handmade production-line items; utilitarian and/or decorative. Especially needs woven artwork in the $50 price range.

Profile: "Wall hangings and weavings are displayed in a prominent area. Customers are college students and faculty and spouses with middle income." Best selling time: fall and holiday season.

FOURTH STREET ARTISTS GALLERY, INC., 473 W. 4th St., Dubuque IA 52001. (319)556-9363. Manager: Randall Mesch. Craft shop/gallery/gift shop. Estab. 1973. Represents 100 craftworkers. Price range: 75c-$250; bestsellers: 75c-$30. Works on consignment; 30% commission. Craftworker sets retail price. Reports in 2 weeks. Work may be shipped or hand-delivered.

Acceptable Work: Considers all crafts except decoupage and tole painting. All styles; utilitarian and/or decorative.

Profile: "Work is well-displayed and kept until sold or reclaimed by artist. We are located in a charming remodeled old house near the number one tourist attraction in Dubuque — the 4th Street cablecar. Our best customers are tourists from Chicago." Best selling time: Christmas.

GENEVA'S GIFT SHOPPE, 111 W. Bremer Ave., Waverly IA 50677. (319)352-3281. Shopkeeper: Geneva Liebau. Craft and gift shop. Estab. 1974. Represents 125 craftworkers. Price range: $1-350; bestsellers: $2-25. Works on consignment and buys outright; 33⅓% commission. Retail price set by joint agreement. Requires exclusive area representation. Reports in 4 weeks. Work may be shipped or hand-delivered. Dealer pays fire and theft insurance for exhibited work. Displays work 3 months. Customers are mostly female. Best selling time: Christmas.

Acceptable Work: Considers batik; candlemaking; ceramics; clothing; decoupage; dollmaking; glass art; jewelry; leatherworking; metalsmithing; needlecrafts; pottery; quilting; soft sculpture;

tole painting; wall hangings; weavings; woodcrafting; baskets; and macrame. All styles; utilitarian and/or decorative.

GRANNY'S ATTIC, 222 5th St., West Des Moines IA 50265. (515)255-7088. Contact: Fran Schiers. Gift shop. Estab. 1973. Represents 400 craftworkers. Price range: $1-500; bestsellers: $1-30. Works on consignment; 50% commission. Retail price set by joint agreement. Reports in 4 weeks. Work may be shipped or hand-deliverd.
Acceptable Work: Considers ceramics; clothing; decoupage; dollmaking; glass art; jewelry; leatherworking; metalsmithing; needlecrafts; pottery; quilting; tole painting; wall hangings; weavings; and woodcrafting. Especially needs painted china; children's furniture; wooden toys; and handmade furniture. Fine one-of-a-kind and handmade production-line items; utilitarian and/or decorative.
Profile: "Jewelry is shown in glass showcase, delicate items are marked 'do not handle.' Shop is a mixture of old and new." Heaviest wholesale buying time: Easter and September; best selling time: summer and Christmas.

All work sold at Fourth Street Artists Gallery, Inc. Dubueque, Iowa, is juried as to quality of craftsmanship, design quality, originality and taste. A nonprofit corporation, The Gallery was organized to help interested area artists present their work to the public.— Photo by Russel Nash.

JAN'S GALLERY, 203 5th St., West Des Moines IA 50265. (515)277-6734. President: Jan Shotwell. Gallery. Estab. 1970. Represents 30-35 craftworkers. Price range: $5-500; bestsellers: $5-250. Works on consignment; 40% commission. Retail price set by joint agreement. Requires exclusive area representation. Reports in 1-2 weeks. Work may be shipped or hand-delivered. Dealer pays return shipping and insurance.
Acceptable Work: Considers batik; ceramics; glass art; jewelry; metalsmithing; pottery; soft sculpture; wall hangings; and weavings. Fine one-of-a-kind pieces only; utilitarian and/or decorative.
Profile: "I have 2 store front windows and 2 gallery rooms, 1 with shelving, etc. All work is displayed but I rotate windows and rearrange items every 2-3 weeks. I also have a leasing program for businesses and professional offices." Best selling time: pre-Christmas.

THE OCTAGON ART CENTER SHOP, 232½ Main St., Ames IA 50010. (515)232-5331. Contact: Shop Manager. Considers ceramics; jewelry; needlecrafts; glass; leather; tie dye; batik; wood; and toys. Price range: 50c-$150. Buys outright or on consignment; 30% commission. Craftworker sets retail price. "We primarily feature local and area artists' work, but we also actively seek quality handcrafts from other parts of the country."

THE POT SHOP/ART GALLERY, Rt. 1, US Hwy. 169 S., Humboldt IA 50548. (515)332-4210. Contact: Hiram or JoAnne Shouse. Gallery/gift shop. Estab. 1977. Represents 15 craftworkers. Considers all crafts. All styles; utilitarian and/or decorative. Price range: $1-300; bestsellers: $4-40. Works on consignment and buys outright; 25% commission on consignment; 40% outright purchase. Craftworker sets retail price. Requires exclusive area representation. Reports in 1 week after end of each month. Work may be shipped or hand-delivered. Dealer pays return shipping and insurance for exhibited work.
Profile: "We try to feature 1 craftsman at a time in special displays. We try to work with the

craftsman in his 'off' season if he attends shows and fairs." Heaviest wholesale buying time: early spring and early fall.

Kansas

BARRY'S ORIGINALS, Abilene KS 67410. (913)263-1575, after 5 p.m. Contact: Barry L. West. Gallery. Estab. 1971. Represents 5-6 Kansas craftworkers. Price range: $1-50; bestsellers: $1-10. 33% commission. Retail price set by joint agreement. Reports in 4 weeks. Work may be hand-delivered. Dealer pays return shipping and insurance for exhibited work.
Acceptable Work: Considers glass art; jewelry; metalsmithing; and pottery. All styles; utilitarian and/or decorative.
Profile: "The shop is located in Old Abilene Town, an early western setting adjacent to Eisenhower presidential library which provides excellent foot traffic." Best selling time: March-September and December.

CHEROKEE STRIP LIVING MUSEUM, Box 230, Arkansas City KS 67005. (316)442-6750. Curator: Herbert Marshall. Gallery/museum gift shop. Estab. 1966. Represents 12 craftworkers. Price range: $2.50-500; bestsellers: $10. Works on consignment; 20% commission. Curator sets retail price. Requires exclusive area representation. Reports in 2 weeks. Hand-delivered work only. Dealer pays insurance for exhibited work.
Acceptable Work: Considers ceramics; jewelry; leatherworking; pottery; wall hangings; and weavings. Primitive one-of-a-kind pieces; utilitarian and/or decorative.
Profile: "Items are very well taken care of and they are not handled by the visitor. Shop is connected to a historical museum and customers are very cultural minded." Heaviest wholesale buying time: spring; best selling time: summer.

CRAFTS INCREDIBLE, INC., 7217 Mission Rd., Prairie Village KS 66208. (913)362-9430. Contact: Irene L. Marsh or Donna or Claude Adam. Craft shop/gallery/gift shop. Estab. 1967. Represents 175 American craftworkers. Price range: 30c-$750; bestsellers: $4-35. Works on consignment and buys outright; 40% commission. Craftworker sets retail price on consigned work; gallery sets retail price on work bought outright. Requires exclusive area representation. Reports in 2 weeks. Work may be shipped or hand-delivered. Dealer pays return shipping and insurance for exhibited work.
Acceptable Work: Considers all crafts except clothing. All styles; utilitarian and/or decorative.
Profile: "Our displays are done in a vignet manner according to type of item ... i.e. kitchen items grouped in one area, children oriented items in another. Giving each item dignity is stressed. Customers are middle to upper class women. We look for craftsmen who are proud of their work and show it through care for their product in packing, inventory, correct receipts and listings as well as printed tags or biographies and a continued interest in the locations in which they place their work." Heaviest wholesale buying time: fall; best selling time: Christmas.

EARTH TO STONE, Box 61, Cawker City KS 67430. (913)781-4369. Contact: Barbara or Charles Stevens. Consignment gallery. Estab. 1977. Represents 10-12 craftworkers. Price range: $1-350; bestsellers: $1-25. Works on consignment; 33⅓% commission. Craftworker sets retail price. Reports in 4 weeks. Work may be shipped or hand-delivered.
Acceptable Work: Considers all crafts except decoupage. All styles; utilitarian and/or decorative. Especially needs themes of wildlife or anything dealing with the outdoors.
Profile: "We have both hanging space and shelf space. Art pieces are kept on display in gallery until picked up by artist. Each artist has a 60-day consignment period, and 60 days after consignment termination to pick up pieces." Heaviest wholesale buying time: spring and fall; best selling time: summer and Christmas.

FREDONIA ARTS COUNCIL, INC., Box 355, Fredonia KS 66736. Contact: Director. Interested in craftworkers exhibiting work in the Council's gallery. Works with sculptors; ceramists; weavers; and other craftworkers. Submit slides of work and resume. February 28 deadline for following September-May season.

THE MATCH BOX, 112 E. 11th St., Box 896, Hays KS 67601. Contact: Helen Ginthner. Gift shop. Estab. 1973. Represents 30 craftworkers. Price range: $3-150; bestsellers: $10-40. Works on consignment and buys outright; 33⅓% commission. Craftworker sets retail price. Requires exclusive area representation. Reports as soon as possible. Work may be shipped or hand-delivered. Dealer pays insurance for exhibited work.
Acceptable Work: Considers clothing; decoupage; glass art; jewelry; needlecrafts; pottery; quilting; tole painting; wall hangings; weavings; and woodcrafting. Primitive handmade items; utilitarian and/or decorative.

Profile: "Work is displayed as attractively as possible." Displays work 6-8 months. Heaviest wholesale buying time: fall and Christmas; best selling time: Christmas.

PRAIRIE FLOWER CRAFTS, Pioneer St., Alden KS 67512. (316)534-2405. Contact: Sara Fair Sleeper. Craft shop. Estab. 1970. Represents 2 craftworkers. Considers all crafts. All styles; utilitarian and/or decorative. Especially needs work with sunflower designs (state flower). Price range: $1-800; bestsellers: $5-100. Works on consignment and buys outright; 30% commission. Craftworker sets retail price. Reports in 4 weeks. Hand-delivered work only.
Profile: "When an item is consigned to our shop, the artist records when, what and price of item and records same when taking it out of the shop." Best selling time: fall and before Christmas.

SIGN OF THE ACORN, 4816 E. Douglas, Wichita KS 67208. Contact: Mary Leedom or Mary Ann Ranney. Considers ceramics; sculpture; glass; weavings; and wall hangings. Price range: $5-1,200. 35% commission. Craftworker sets retail price. Requires exclusive area representation. Charges commission on crafts sold in area after exclusive representation. Gallery pays shipping to craftworker and insurance for exhibited work. Items displayed 4 weeks minimum.

THE SPINSTER SHOP, 124 S. Main, Lindsborg KS 67456. Contact: Marlysue Esping. Craft shop/gallery/gift shop. Estab. 1973. Represents 5-10 craftworkers. Considers batik; needlecrafts; quilting; soft sculpture; wall hangings; weavings; macrame; basketry; and any fiber arts. All styles; utilitarian and/or decorative. Price range: $3-350; bestsellers: up to $60. Works on consignment; 30% commission. Retail price set by joint agreement. Reports in 2 weeks. Dealer pays return shipping; return transit insurance; and insurance for exhibited work.
Profile: "Family owned and operated by working, experienced craftsperson." Best selling time: fall and spring.

SUNSHINE HOLLOW, 217 N. Broadway, Protection KS 67127. Contact: Dawna Selzer. Gift shop. Estab. 1977. Represents 50 craftworkers. Considers all crafts. Fine handmade production-line items; utilitarian and/or decorative. Price range: $2.50-150; bestsellers: $2-20. Works on consignment; 25% commission. Gallery sets retail price. Reports in 2 weeks. Work may be shipped or hand-delivered.
Profile: "I try to have things that are unusual for this area. I like everything in my shop to get special treatment." Heaviest wholesale buying time: spring and fall; best selling time: winter (September-December).

THE TALENT TREE, 213 Delaware, Suite B-4, Leavenworth KS 66048. (913)651-7833. Contact: Jay Loftus. Craft shop. Estab. 1977. Represents 75 craftworkers. Considers all crafts; utilitarian and/or decorative. Price range: 35c-$500; bestsellers: $10-200. Works on consignment. Craftworker sets retail price. Call for an appointment. Work may be shipped or hand-delivered.
Profile: Work is displayed on wall space, shelves and from ceiling hangers. Displays work 60 days. Heaviest wholesale buying time: fall; best selling time: fall and winter.

TOPEKA PUBLIC LIBRARY GALLERY OF FINE ARTS, 1515 W. 10th, Topeka KS 66604. (913)233-2040. Director: Larry D. Peters. Gallery. Estab. 1975. Represents 40 craftworkers. Gallery is not specifically for sales. Price range: $20-600; bestsellers: $20-60. Items sold only after exhibition. Craftworker sets retail price. Rental gallery fee: 20%. Work may be shipped or hand-delivered. Gallery pays insurance for exhibited work. Exhibits work 1 month.
Acceptable Work: Considers batik; ceramics; glass art; jewelry; metalsmithing; pottery; quilting; soft sculpture; wall hangings; weavings; and woodcrafting. Fine one-of-a-kind pieces; utilitarian and/or decorative.
Profile: "We exhibit with some emphasis on each individual piece. All small items are under glass for protection. Customers are middle class and mostly middle aged." Shows are in April.

Kentucky
APOLLOS ART, Main, Box 74, Gamaliel KY 42140. (502)457-2642. Contact: Mrs. Clyde England. Studio. Estab. 1975. Represents 5 craftworkers. Price range: $1-150; bestsellers: $1-8. Works on consignment; 25% commission. Retail price set by joint agreement. Reports in 2 weeks. Work may be shipped or hand-delivered. Dealer pays insurance for exhibited work.
Acceptable Work: Considers clothing; needlecrafts; quilting; wall hangings; and weavings. Fine, one-of-a-kind and handmade production-line items; utilitarian and/or decorative.
Profile: "I change displays frequently. My shop is in my home, but I display in local business

places, state parks, etc. Customers range from age 20-70; high school and college students; some retired and on fixed incomes." Heaviest wholesale buying time: Christmas and fall; best selling time: Christmas and spring.

BENCHMARK GALLERY, Box 422, Berea KY 40403. (606)986-9413. Manager: Daphne Osolnik. Craft and gift shop. Estab. 1972. Represents 100+ American craftworkers. Price range: $1-1,500; bestsellers: from under $5 to as high as $50. Buys outright and occasionally works on consignment; 33⅓% commission. Requests exclusive area representation "when possible; it is a small place." Reports in 4 weeks on consigned items. Dealer pays return shipping and insurance (break-in and fire) for exhibited work.
Acceptable Work: Considers candlemaking; batik; ceramics; dollmaking; baskets; glass art; jewelry; leatherworking; metalsmithing; needlecrafts; pottery; enamels; quilting; wall hangings; weavings; woodcrafting; and prints. All styles; utilitarian and/or decorative.
Profile: "An individual show can be arranged for a week or 2. Craftworker should plan to stay, demonstrate and sell. 20% commission."

COFFETREES AT STEWART'S, 501 River City Mall, Louisville KY 40202. (502)584-3261. Contact: Rod Beck. Estab. 1973. Repreents 200+ Kentucky craftworkers. Considers batik; candlemaking; dollmaking; jewelry; leatherworking; hand-forged iron; pewter work; pottery; quilting; soft sculpture; wall hangings; weavings; woodcrafting; and wooden toys. Finished, one-of-a-kind and handmade production-line items only; utilitarian and/or decorative. Price range: 50c-$2,500; bestsellers: $5-40. Buys outright or on consignment; 40% commission. Retail price set by joint agreement. Prefers exclusive area representation. Write. Dealer pays shipping from shop and insurance on exhibited work.

THE CURIOUSITY SHOP, Railroad St., Midway KY 40347. (606)846-4884. Contact: Enzina Mastrippolito. Estab. 1973. Represents 50 craftworkers. Considers batik; candlemaking; ceramics; dollmaking; pottery; and soft sculpture. All styles; utilitarian and/or decorative. Price range: $1.50-36; bestsellers: $1.50-7. Buys outright or on consignment; 33⅓% commission. Retail price set by joint agreement. Write. Reports in 2 weeks. Dealer pays shipping from shop and insurance for exhibited work.
Profile: Items displayed 3-6 months. Heaviest wholesale buying time: spring and fall; best selling time: summer and winter. "This is the only gallery in central Kentucky besides the Guild Gallery to feature original contemporary crafts."

DOWNSTAIRS DOWNTOWN, 224½ W. Walnut St., Louisville KY 40202. (502)583-6202. Manager: Joann Ryan. Estab. 1973. Represents 50 craftworkers. Considers batik; candlemaking; dollmaking; glass art; jewelry; leatherworking; metalsmithing; pottery; quilting; soft sculpture; wall hangings; weavings; and woodcrafting. Finished one-of-a-kind and handmade production-line items; utilitarian and/or decorative. Price range: $2.30-500; bestsellers: $2.30-150. Works on consignment; 40% commission. Craftworker sets retail price. Write. Reports in 3 weeks. Dealer pays return shipping and insurance for exhibited work.
Profile: "Crafts remain in shop until sold, unless it's more than 1 year and hasn't moved." Best selling time: Christmas and May (Derby time). "High quality shop with unusual entrance; more of a gallery atmosphere than a craft shop." Customers age 18-55 with $15,000+ income; they buy crafts for artistic value, for gifts or for originality.

EDGEMONT YARN SERVICE, INC., Rt. 5, Box 132, Maysville KY 41056. (606)564-3193. President: Jean Adair. Craft and supply shop. Estab. 1960. Represents 2 craftworkers. Considers jewelry; metalsmithing; and needlecrafts. Price range: 10c-$500. Works on consignment; 5% commission plus material cost. Reports the day after inquiry. "We are located in an historic town established in 1783. Our shop is in a house built in 1824." Best selling time: Christmas.

EMERGENCY WORKSHOP, Box 8, Barbourville KY 40906. (606)546-4622. Director: Liz Hollinde. Gallery/wholesaler. Estab. 1966. Represents 50 craftworkers with basic emergency needs. Shop gives cash advances to people needing emergency funds who then produce crafts and receive retail credit to repay debt. Price range: $1-150; bestsellers: $2-60. Buys outright. Reporting time varies. Work may be shipped or hand-delivered. Dealer pays return shipping and insurance for exhibited work.
Acceptable Work: Considers dollmaking; quilting; woodcrafting; pieced table clothes; dresses; skirts; and corn shuck placemats. Primitive and fine handmade production-line items; utilitarian and/or decorative.
Profile: "When a craft is brought in or made in the shop, it becomes the property of Emergency

Fund. We attempt to sell it at the fair retail price and proceeds revert to the fund. Customers are families whose income is less than $300/month." Heaviest wholesale buying time: fall-winter; best selling time: spring-summer.

THE GALLERY, 487 High St., Hazard KY 41701. (606)436-5102. Contact: Audrey C. Rogers. Craft and gift shop. Estab. 1976. Represents 30-40 Appalachian craftworkers. Price range: $2-400; bestsellers: $10-200. Works on consignment and buys outright; 40% commission. Retail price set by joint agreement. Reports in 4 weeks. Work may be hand-delivered or shipped. Dealer pays insurance for exhibited work. Best selling and heaviest wholesale buying time: summer and fall.
Acceptable Work: Considers candlemaking; ceramics; clothing; dollmaking; jewelry; leatherworking; pottery; quilting; wall hangings; weavings; and woodcrafting. All styles; utilitarian and/or decorative.

KENTUCKY HILLS INDUSTRIES, INC., Box 186, Pine Knot KY 42635. (606)354-2813. Manager: Smith G. Ross. Craft shop. Estab. 1946. Represents 58 craftworkers. Apply for membership in Kentucky Hills Industries. Price range: $1-1,200; bestsellers: $1-25. Buys outright. Retail price set by joint agreement. Reports in 1 week. Hand-delivered work only.
Acceptable Work: Considers dollmaking; needlecrafts; pottery; woodcrafting; cornshuck; basketmaking; and handweaving. Especially needs "any craft that has a tie with the past, graceful in design and indigenous to the area." Primitive handmade production-line items; utilitarian and/or decorative.
Profile: "For the most part we handle only items that have utility and those that harken back to the early days. We sell mostly to young homemakers." Heaviest wholesale buying time: summer; best selling time: summer and fall.

LOG HOUSE SALES ROOM, #778, Berea College, Berea KY 40404. (606)986-9341. Manager: Haley Robinson. Gift shop. Represents 100 craftworkers. Price range of bestsellers: under $10. Buys outright. Gallery sets retail price. Work may be shipped or hand-delivered. "We handle mostly Appalachian handmade crafts and Berea College student craft items." Best selling and heaviest wholesale buying time: fall and spring.
Acceptable Work: Considers candlemaking; ceramics; jewelry; leatherworking; metalsmithing; needlecrafts; pottery; quilting; wall hangings; weavings; and woodcrafting. Handmade production-line items; utilitarian only.

LOUISVILLE SCHOOL OF ART GALLERY, 100 Park Rd., Anchorage KY 40223. (502)245-8836. Gallery. Estab. 1909. Represents 3 craftworkers. Price range: $20-1,000; bestsellers: $20-1,000. 15% commission. Craftworker sets retail price. Submit slides. Reports in 6-10 weeks. Hand-delivered work only. School pays insurance for exhibited work. Gallery provides news releases and mailed invitations. Best selling time: September-June.
Acceptable Work: Considers ceramics; jewelry; metalsmithing; pottery; quilting; soft sculpture; wall hangings and weavings.

ONE STEP UP GIFTS, 323 Romany Rd., Lexington KY 40502. (606)269-1345. Contact: Shirley Jeter. Gift shop. Estab. 1973. Represents 150-200 craftworkers. Considers all crafts. Fine one-of-a-kind and handmade production-line items; utilitarian and/or decorative. Price range: 50c-$660; bestsellers: $1.50-15. Buys outright. Reports in 2 weeks. Work may be shipped or hand-delivered. Dealer pays insurance for exhibited work.
Profile: "We specialize in unusual well-made and functional handcrafted gifts. We look for items not available in other shops. We accent reasonable prices and quality workmanship as well as uniqueness and practicality. Customers are 20-50; middle to upper income." Heaviest wholesale buying time: fall; best selling time: fall and winter.

OWENSBORO AREA MUSEUM, 2829 S. Griffith Ave., Owensboro KY 42301. (502)683-0296. Director: Joe Ford. Museum gift shop. Estab. 1969. Price range: 10c-$25; bestsellers: 25c-$20. Buys outright. Gallery sets retail price. Reports in 1 week. Best selling time: before Christmas.
Acceptable Work: Considers candlemaking; ceramics; jewelry; needlecrafts; pottery; quilting; wall hangings; weavings; and woodcrafting. Primitive handmade production-line items; utilitarian and/or decorative.

OWENSBORO MUSEUM OF FINE ART, 901 Frederica St., Owensboro KY 42301. (502)685-4978. Administrative Director: Mary Bryan Hood. Museum gift shop/gallery. Estab. 1977.

Represents Midwestern or Southern craftworkers. Considers all crafts. Works on consignment; 30% commission. Craftworker sets retail price. "Submit slides or photographs and a resume listing education, exhibition record and awards."

Profile: "We are only the second fine art museum to be formed in the state of Kentucky. We promote regional artists in 2 ways. First, we offer an opportunity for exhibitions in our galleries; and secondly, we offer an opportunity for sales through our Gift Shoppe."

THE UNFINISHED UNIVERSE, 505 E. High St., Lexington KY 40508. (606)252-3289. Partners: Joel Evans, Patrick White and Ricka White. Craft shop/gallery/antique shop. Estab. 1973. Represents 5 craftworkers. Price range: $1-3,000; bestsellers: $5-60. Works on consignment and buys outright; 20% commission. Retail price set by joint agreement. Reports in 1-2 weeks. Work may be shipped or hand-delivered. Displays work a maximum of 2-3 months. Customers are all ages and types from "college students to architects to jewel collectors, middle class families, etc."

Acceptable Work: Considers batik; candlemaking; ceramics; clothing; pottery; quilting; wall hangings; weavings; and woodcrafting. "We specialize in custom woodworking designs. Anything from a traditional table to an indoor cat playground."

THE UPSTAIRS GALLERY, 114 Main St., Berea KY 40403. (606)986-9293. Contact: Frankye or Warren A. May. Gallery/gift shop. Estab. 1977. Represents 28-30 craftworkers. Price range: $3-2,000; bestsellers: $10-200. Works on wholesale and/or consignment; 20% commission. Craftworker sets retail price. Requires exclusive area representation. Reports in 4 weeks. Work may be hand-delivered. Dealer pays return shipping and insurance for exhibited work.

Acceptable Work: Considers batik; ceramics; handmade toys; pottery; weavings; woodcrafting; and handmade furniture. Finished, one-of-a-kind and handmade production-line items; utilitarian and/or decorative.

Profile: "Since our gallery features the woodworking of owner Warren May, we are set up so that we don't have to make a living off another person's work. We feel that our other craftsmen's work makes us special and we feel great loyalty to their work and strive to represent them well." Best selling time: fall and spring.

Louisiana

ALROD ENTERPRISES, 728 Toulouse, New Orleans LA 70130. (504)522-6106. Contact: Al Willis or Rod Reeves. Craft and gift shop. Estab. 1972. Represents 150 craftworkers. Price range: $1-300; bestsellers: $1.99-20. Works on consignment and buys outright; 50% commission. Shop sets retail price. Requires exclusive area representation. Reports in 1 week. Work may be shipped or hand-delivered. Dealer pays return shipping and insurance for exhibited work.

Acceptable Work: Considers clothing; decoupage; dollmaking; jewelry; needlecrafts; pottery; quilting; tole painting; wall hangings; weavings; and woodcrafting. All styles; utilitarian and/or decorative. Especially needs items for boys.

Profile: "All merchandise is prominently displayed a long as it is in the shop. Customers are middle to upper income."

CALICO COTTAGE GIFTS AND INTERIORS, 1200 N. Pine St., De Ridder LA 70634. Contact: Manette Porter. Craft and gift shop. Estab. 1976. Represents 15 craftworkers. Price range: $2.50-350; bestsellers: $6-25. Works on consignment and buys outright; 50% commission. Retail price set by joint agreement. Requires exclusive area representation. Reports in 3 weeks. Work may be shipped or hand-delivered. Dealer pays insurance for exhibited work.

Acceptable Work: Considers ceramics; dollmaking; needlecrafts; quilting; soft sculpture; tole painting; wall hangings; weavings; and woodcrafting. Finished, one-of-a-kind and handmade production-line items; utilitarian and/or decorative.

Profile: Work is "included in decorative color coordinated display and changed about once a week. We display to show how items would look in the home. Customers are 18-75; young marrieds to grandmothers." Best selling and heaviest wholesale buying time: Christmas.

CHITIMACHA CRAFT, Rt. 2, Box 224, Jeanerette LA 70544. (318)923-7547. Contact: Faye Stouff. Craft shop. Estab. 1970. Represents 3 craftworkers. Considers pine needle and cane reed baskets and some beadwork. Handmade production-line items; decorative only. Price range: $2-300; bestsellers: $7-40. Works on consignment; no commission. Retail price set by joint agreement. Reports in 1 week. Work may be shipped or hand-delivered. "We have only handmade articles by members of the tribe; customers are all ages."

THE COUNTRY ART STORE, Box 459, Hwy. 90, Roanoke LA 70581. (318)753-2588. Contact: Sue Lewis. Art supply store/gallery. Estab. 1977. Represents 10 craftworkers. Considers

dollmaking; jewelry; needlecrafts; pottery; wall hangings; and weavings. One-of-a-kind pieces; utilitarian and/or decorative. Price range: $10-250; bestsellers: $30-70. Works on consignment; 10% commission. Craftworker sets retail price. Reports in 2 weeks. Work may be shipped or hand-delivered. Dealer pays insurance for exhibited work.
Profile: "All pieces are displayed 90 days in the best possible location. We are located in a community of 600 on a state highway. Most people are surprised when they see what we have on display. The village is 10 blocks long, 2 blocks wide and surrounded by soybean fields. One never expects to see an art shop." Heaviest wholesale buying time: fall; best selling time: winter.

THE CRAFT ALLIANCE, 1075 Dalzell, Shreveport LA 71104. (318)222-1780. Director: Roger Runge. Gallery/art center. Estab. 1972. Represents about 10 craftworkers — members of the Craft Alliance at one time. Price range: $5-500; bestsellers: $5-45. Works on consignment; 25% commission. Craftworker sets retail price. Reports in 1-2 weeks. Hand-delivered work only.
Acceptable Work: Considers batik; jewelry; pottery; soft sculpture; wall hangings; and weavings. Fine one-of-a-kind and handmade production-line items; utilitarian and/or decorative.
Profile: "Gallery space: usually has one-man show for 3-4 weeks. Sales area: typical display on shelves, counters, etc. All work is mixed in together. Since we are a nonprofit organization, the gallery shows are concerned more with exhibition of contemporary crafts, exposure, and education rather than sales." Best selling time: Christmas and February-May.

LAFAYETTE NATURAL HISTORY MUSEUM AND PLANETARIUM, 637 Girard Park Dr., Lafayette LA 70503. (318)233-6611. Director: Beverly D. Latimer. Museum gift shop. Estab. 1969. Represents 10 craftworkers. Price range: 25c-$50; bestsellers: 25c-$10. Works on consignment and buys outright; 30% commission. Gallery sets retail price. Reports in 2 weeks. Dealer pays shipping to shop and insurance.
Acceptable Work: Considers dollmaking; jewelry; pottery; quilting; and woodcrafting. Especially needs Louisiana crafts. All styles; utilitarian and/or decorative.
Profile: The "shop is very small; large items are seldom handled. Customers are young school children to adults. Craftsmen should submit color slides or photos of their work, their selling price and availability." Best selling and heaviest wholesale buying time: Christmas.

LOOM ROOM, INC., 623 Royal St., New Orleans LA 70130. (504)522-7101. President: Glenna Geisert. Craft and gift shop. Estab. 1975. Represents 50 craftworkers. Considers hand-woven wall hangings and rugs. One-of-a-kind and handmade production-line items; utilitarian and/or decorative. Price range: $1.35-250; bestsellers: $20-35. Buys outright. Reports in 1-2 weeks. Work may be shipped or hand-delivered by pre-arrangement. Dealer pays shipping and insurance for exhibited work. Displays work 1-2 months.
Profile: "We specialize in functional hand weavings. Customers are young adults and professional people. 75% of our business is tourist and convention business." Best selling and heaviest wholesale buying time: spring and fall.

LOUISIANA CRAFTS COUNCIL, 139 Broadway, New Orleans LA 70118. (504)861-8267. Manager: Lynne Higbee. Craft shop/gallery. Estab. 1961. Represents 30 craftworkers. Price range: $4.50-1,000; bestsellers: $6-45. Works on consignment; 25% commission. Craftworker sets retail price. Work may be shipped or hand-delivered.
Acceptable Work: Considers batik; ceramics; clothing; blown glass; jewelry; leatherworking; metalsmithing; needlecrafts; pottery; quilting; soft sculpture; wall hangings; weavings; and woodcrafting. Fine one-of-a-kind pieces; utilitarian and/or decorative.
Profile: "Craft items must pass a standards committee for quality; displayed on shelves and walls. We are a nonprofit organization which assists craftsmen with low commissions and free publicity." Displays work 6 months. Best selling time: fall and winter.

CAMILLE MAHER ANTIQUES AND GIFTS, 5408 Magazine St., New Orleans LA 70015. (504)897-6849. Contact: Camile Maher. Gift and antique shop. Estab. 1974. Represents 40-50 craftworkers. Price range: $3-350; bestsellers: $5-50. Works on consignment and buys outright; 33⅓%commission. Gallery sets retail price. Requires exclusive area representation. Reports in 1-2 weeks with SASE. Work may be shipped or hand-delivered. Dealer pays shipping on requested material.
Acceptable Work: Considers ceramics; decoupage; dollmaking; jewelry; metalsmithing; needlecrafts; pottery; quilting; soft sculpture; tole painting; wall hangings; weavings; woodcrafting; paintings; prints; and soft toys. All styles; utilitarian and/or decorative.
Profile: Shop is "in a quaint old Victorian cottage crammed with a melange of old things, handcrafted items, with a surprise here and there of something very modern, like soft sculpture.

Customers tell me they like the mix of nostalgia and new." Best selling and heaviest wholesale buying time: Christmas.

To Break In: "Please send full description of item you make: materials, size, etc. Also send a picture or two with SASE for return of pictures. Send your final price and SASE for reply."

SPORTS ART, 633 Toulouse St., New Orleans LA 70130. Contact: J. Peter Eaves. Considers traditional sculpture. Specializes in wildlife, hunting and fishing themes. Price range: $20-10,000. 30% commission. Retail price set by joint agreement. Exhibited art insured. Mailings sent with each show.

2 + 2 LTD. GALLERY, 5163 General DeGaulle, New Orleans LA 70114. (504)394-5265. Director: Lou Eckert. Gallery/frame shop. Estab. 1972. Represents 20-25 craftworkers. Price range: $3-150; bestsellers: $5-25. Works on consignment; 40% commission. Craftworker sets retail price. Requires exclusive area representation. Reports in 4 weeks. Work may be shipped or hand-delivered.

Acceptable Work: Considers dollmaking; glass art; pottery; soft sculpture; wall hangings; weavings; and woodcrafting. Fine one-of-a-kind pieces only; utilitarian and/or decorative. Especially needs pottery; unusual ceramic pieces; soft sculpture; pillows; and one-of-a-kind wooden toys.

Profile: "Work is displayed artfully according to the type of item. We switch displays monthly; some are stored and redisplayed throughout the year. Customers are suburban oil families with an income of $20,000-30,000." Heaviest wholesale buying time: early spring and early fall; best selling time: spring and fall.

USL UNION CRAFT SHOP, Box 4, 2611 USL, Lafayette LA 70504. (318)233-3850. Director: Mike Flaherty. Craft shop/gallery. Estab. 1970. Teaches workshops and has gallery shows 4 times per semester. Considers batik; ceramics; jewelry; leatherworking; and pottery. Reports in 4 weeks. Work may be shipped or hand-delivered. Dealer pays insurance. Shows last for 3 weeks. "Customers are students of this campus; minimal income."

Maine

ABACUS GALLERY, Box 3, Boothbay Harbor ME 04538. (207)633-3166. Contact: Dana Heacock or Sal Scaglione. Craft shop/gallery. Estab. 1971. Represents 100 craftworkers. Price range: 50c-$500; bestsellers: 50c-$50. Works on consignment and buys outright; 40% commission. Shop sets retail price. Requires exclusive area representation.

Acceptable Work: Considers batik; glass art; jewelry; metalsmithing; pottery; quilting; soft sculpture; wall hangings; weavings; and woodcrafting. Fine one-of-a-kind and handmade production-line items; utilitarian and/or decorative.

ACADIAN CRAFTS ASSOCIATION, 29 St. Catherine St., Madawaska ME 04756. (207)728-3295. Manager: Theresa Violette. Wholesale/mail order shop. Estab. 1970. Represents 40-70 St. John Valley women craftworkers. Considers clothing. Fine and handmade production-line items; utilitarian only. Price range: $18-57. Buys outright. Retail price set by joint agreement. Reports in 2 weeks. Hand-delivered work only. Dealer pays shipping to shop and in-transit insurance. Heaviest wholesale buying time: summer; best selling time: fall.

BAY STUDIO CRAFTS, 3 Belmont Ave., Belfast ME 04915. Contact: Frances Armington. Craft shop. Estab. 1976. Represents 100 craftworkers. Price range: 79c-$100; bestsellers: $1.50-20. Works on consignment and buys outright; 33⅓% commission. Craftworker sets retail price. Requires exclusive area representation. Reports in 4 weeks. Work may be shipped or hand-delivered with previous approval. Dealer pays shipping to shop, in-transit insurance and insurance for exhibited work if on consignment. Heaviest wholesale buying time: spring and fall; best selling time: summer and pre-Christmas.

Acceptable Work: Considers candlemaking; ceramics; clothing; decoupage; dollmaking; glass art; jewelry; leatherworking; metalsmithing; needlecrafts; pottery; tole painting; woodcrafting; and macrame. Handmade production-line items; utilitarian and/or decorative.

CAKEWALK: A HANDWORKS GALLERY, Box 187, Rockport ME 04856. Contact: Ms. Rickey Mullen. Craft shop/gallery. Estab. 1976. Represents 40 craftworkers. Price range: $2.50-600; bestsellers: $10-50. Works on consignment and buys outright; 33% commission. Retail price set by joint agreement. Reports in 2 weeks. Work may be shipped or hand-delivered. Return shipping paid by dealer if work was solicited. Dealer pays insurance for exhibited work.

Acceptable Work: Considers batik; candlemaking; clothing; dollmaking; glass art; jewelry;

metalsmithing; pottery; quilting; soft sculpture; wall hangings; weavings; and woodcrafting. All styles; utilitarian and/or decorative.

Profile: "Display is a combination of shop and gallery. Some work is lined up on shelves; other work is highlighted in displays mixing media. Changes every several months. I highlight both production and one-of-a-kind." Heaviest wholesale buying time: spring; best selling time: summer.

THE DANCING DEER, 10-12-D Mt. Desert St., Bar Harbor ME 04609. Owners: Paul DeVore and Gail Gutradt. Estab. 1974. Represents 50 craftworkers. Price range: 25c-$50; bestsellers: 25c-$20. Buys outright. Retail price set by shop. Reports in 2 weeks. Work may be shipped or hand-delivered.

Acceptable Work: Considers batik; candlemaking; ceramics; dollmaking; glass art; jewelry; metalsmithing; needlecrafts; pottery; small quilts; woodcrafting; beads; cards; stationery; posters; mobiles; and wind chimes. Primitive and fine handmade production-line items; utilitarian and/or decorative.

Profile: Roomy retail shop "where we highlight items to their best advantage. We emphasize delightful handmade items of high quality." Heaviest wholesale buying time: February-April; best selling time: summer. "Our season runs from May 15-October 15, so we order early to give craftworkers lead time." Customers are primarily tourists, middle to upper income. "They're interested in nature, hiking, sailing, camping, etc. Many vacationers are doing their Christmas shopping." Winter off-season address: 64 Wendell St., Cambridge MA 02138.

EASTERN MAINE CRAFTS COOP, Box 22, Steuben ME 04680. (207)546-2269. Secretary/Treasurer: Peter Weil. Craft shop located in Milbridge, Maine. Estab. 1973. Represents 10 eastern Maine craftworkers. Price range: $3-150; bestsellers: $3-50. Works on consignment; 40% commission. Craftworker sets retail price. Reports in 2 weeks. Work may be shipped or hand-delivered. Dealer pays insurance for exhibited work.

Acceptable Work: Considers batik; ceramics; glass art; jewelry; metalsmithing; pottery; wall hangings; and weavings. Especially needs glass, pewter and wood. Fine one-of-a-kind and handmade production-line items; utilitarian and/or decorative.

Profile: "Member and consigned items are displayed constantly; special exhibit items displayed 2-3 weeks in central location of gallery. Customers are tourists and summer residents age 30 and up; above average income and education." Open June-September.

ESPECIALLY MAINE, US Rt. 1, Arundel ME 04046. (207)985-3749. Gift and mail order shop. Estab. 1974. Represents 30 craftworkers. Price range: 50c-$450. Buys outright. Gallery sets retail price. Requires exclusive area representation. Work may be shipped or hand-delivered. Dealer pays shipping and insurance for exhibited work. Best selling and heaviest wholesale buying time: fall.

Acceptable Work: Considers candlemaking; ceramics; clothing; glass art; jewelry; leatherworking; metalsmithing; needlecrafts; and pottery. Fine handmade production-line items; utilitarian and/or decorative.

WILLIAM A. FARNSWORTH LIBRARY AND ART MUSEUM, Box 466, Rockland ME 04841. (207)596-6457. Director: Marius B. Peladeau. Museum gift shop. Estab. 1948. Exclusive representation of crafts by the alumni of Haystack Mountain School. Considers all crafts. All styles; utilitarian and/or decorative. Price range: under $50; bestsellers: under $25. Works on consignment; 40% commission. Craftworker sets retail price. Work is "displayed in Museum Shop sales area; breakable pieces in cases or behind glass". Best selling and heaviest wholesale buying time: summer.

THE GAMEKEEPER, INC., Box 1016, Bangor ME 04401. (207)947-8806. President: Gwethalyn M. Phillips. Game and toy shop. Estab. 1977. Considers toys in any medium. One-of-a-kind and handmade production-line items. Price range: $1.50-650; bestsellers: $2-50. Buys outright. Gallery sets retail price. Reports in 1 week. Work may be shipped with previous approval. Dealer pays shipping to shop and insurance for exhibited work.

Profile: "We specialize in high quality games (mostly for adults) and a few toys. We mix manufactured goods with handcrafted goods." Heaviest wholesale buying time: September-October; best selling time: Christmas.

HANDCRAFTERS GALLERY, 18 Exchange St., Portland ME 04101. Contact: Peter or Gail Kahn. Craft shop. Estab. 1973. Represents 100 craftworkers. Bestsellers: $25. Buys outright. Gallery sets retail price. Requires exclusive area representation. Work may be shipped or hand-delivered.

Acceptable Work: Considers ceramics; clothing; glass art; jewelry; pottery; soft sculpture; wall hangings; and weavings. All styles; utilitarian and/or decorative.

HERITAGE METALCRAFT, INC., Rt. 202, S. Windham ME 04082. (207)892-6739. President: Wayne R. Holmquist. Craft shop. Estab. 1967. Represents craftworkers who work in forged, cast or hammered copper metal items. Price range: $2.50-2,000; bestsellers: $5-100. Buys outright. Gallery sets retail price. Reports in 1 week. "Send catalog, pictures, description, pricing, packaging and normal shipping method. If production item, give time requirements for reorders and state volume available per year and on what basis." Work may be shipped or hand-delivered.
Acceptable Work: Considers decorative and functional metalcraft only. 90% are handmade production-line items; 10% are one-of-a-kind.
Profile: "We operate craft store, mail order and wholesale to dealers throughout US and Canada. Customers are mostly home owners." Heaviest wholesale buying time: June and December; best selling time: Christmas.

HERON POINT GALLERY, Rt. 2, Brunswick ME 04011. Director: Nell Burbank. Gallery. Estab. 1975. Represents 10-20 craftworkers. Price range: $1.25-200; bestsellers: $2.50-20. Works on consignment and buys outright; 25% commission. Retail price set by joint agreement. Reports in 1 week. Work may be shipped or hand-delivered. Dealer pays shipping to shop.
Acceptable Work: Considers batik; ceramics; glass art; jewelry; metalsmithing; needlecrafts; pottery; wall hangings; weavings; sculpture; cards; and notes. Fine one-of-a-kind pieces; utilitarian and/or decorative.
Profile: Gallery is "well lighted and uncrowded. The location has a view of Quohog Bay, sculpture terrace with woods background." Displays work 4-6 weeks. Heaviest wholesale buying time: spring; best selling time: summer.

HOBBIT HOUSE, Shore Rd., Ogunquit ME 03907. (207)646-9427. Contact: Ruth or Bill Kocsis. Gift shop. Estab. 1972. Represents 80 craftworkers. Price range: $1-200; bestsellers: $1-150. Buys outright. Gallery sets retail price. Requires exclusive area representation. Reporting time varies. Work may be shipped or hand-delivered. Dealer pays shipping.
Acceptable Work: Considers decoupage; dollmaking; glass art; jewelry; leatherworking; metalcraft; needlecrafts; pottery; quilting; wall hangings; woodcrafting; and internal carvings in Plexiglas. Especially needs blown glass; paper weights; and procelain bells. Fine one-of-a-kind pieces; utilitarian and/or decorative.
Profile: "All items are displayed to the best advantage possible, space limitations considered. Customers are teenagers to the elderly; middle income. We have repeat sales to those who are always interested in the newest, most novel and imaginative in handcrafts." Heaviest wholesale buying time: spring and winter; best selling time: summer.

H-O-M-E, INC., Rt. 1 Orland ME 04472. (207)469-7961. Marketing Manager: Arleen Coley. Cooperative craft shop. Estab. 1970. Represents 500 Maine craftworkers. Considers all crafts; utilitarian and/or decorative. Price range: 50c-$300; bestsellers: 50c-$75. Works on consignment; 30% commission. Retail price set by joint agreement. Reports immediately. Work may be shipped or hand-delivered with previous approval. Dealer pays insurance for exhibited work. Displays work 6 months.
Profile: "The h-o-m-e craft shops were established as an outlet for low income people to subsidize their income through the sale of crafts. h-o-m-e is a cooperative. There is a membership fee of $5 yearly." Heaviest wholesale buying time: prior to summer and Christmas; best selling time: summer and Christmas. Also holds annual craft fair in August.

THE ISLAND STORE, Spruce Head Island ME 04859. (207)594-7475. Contact: Erika E. Pilver. General store/gift and craft shop. Represents 24 craftworkers. Price range: 99c-$75; bestsellers: $1.50-5. Works on consignment and buys outright; 33⅓% commission. Gallery sets retail price on crafts bought outright; craftworker sets retail price on consignment work. Reports in 1 week. Work may be shipped or hand-delivered. Dealer pays insurance for exhibited work.
Acceptable Work: Considers batik; candlemaking; decoupage; glass art; jewelry; leatherworking; metalsmithing; and needlecrafts. Fine one-of-a-kind and handmade production-line items; utilitarian and/or decorative.
Profile: "Displays are changed several times a season. Location is right on the shore in a fishing village. Customers are a few retired 'summer people' who sometimes purchase designer items and many tourists who purchase inexpensive items for gifts." Heaviest wholesale buying time: spring; best selling time: summer.

JANE-GRAY SHOPPE, Rt. 2, Box 206, Dexter ME 04930. Contact: Jane Gilbert. Gift and antique shop. Estab. 1977. Represents 6 craftworkers. Price range: $1-150; bestsellers: $1-20. Works on consignment; 20% commission. Retail price set by joint agreement. Reports in 3 weeks. Work may be shipped or hand-delivered. Dealer pays shipping to shop and insurance for exhibited work.
Acceptable Work: Considers decoupage; dollmaking; jewelry; needlecrafts; quilting; and woodcrafting. Primitive one-of-a-kind pieces; utilitarian and/or decorative.
Profile: "Items are treated with respect and kept as long as craftsman wants, or left to my discretion." Heaviest wholesale buying time: spring-summer; best selling time: summer.

THE LAMP POST CRAFT SHOP, 335 Penobscot Ave., Millinocket ME 04462. (207)723-4225. Contact: Ronald or Susan Legere. Craft shop. Estab. 1974. Represents 54 craftworkers. Works on consignment; 25% commission. Retail price set by joint agreement. Requires exclusive area representation. Reports in 3 weeks. Work may be shipped or hand-delivered. Dealer pays insurance. Heaviest wholesale buying time: fall and spring; best selling time: fall.
Acceptable Work: Considers ceramics; clothings; decoupage; dollmaking; glass art; jewelry; leatherworking; pottery; quilting; tole painting; and woodcrafting. One-of-a-kind pieces; utilitarian and/or decorative.

THE LUBEC CRAFTS COUNCIL, INC., The Wharf Shop, Water St., Lubec ME 04652. (207)733-4701. Contact: Robert O. Voight. Estab. 1970. Represents 30 craftworkers. Considers candlemaking; glass art; jewelry; leatherworking; metalsmithing; pottery; wall hangings; weavings; and woodcrafting. Finished, one-of-a-kind items only; utilitarian and/or decorative. Price range: $2-300; bestsellers: $5-25. Buys outright; 20% commission. Retail price set by joint agreement. Write. Reports in 4 weeks. Council pays shipping from shop and insurance for exhibited artwork. Best selling time: summer.

MAINE CRAFT STORE, Blue Hill ME 04614. (207)374-5645. Contact: Rufus A. Candage. Craft shop. Estab. 1974. Represents 150 craftworkers. Price range: 10c-$500; bestsellers: $2.25-50. Works on consignment; 30% commission. Craftworker sets retail price. Reports in 4 weeks. Work may be shipped or hand-delivered. Best selling and heaviest wholesale buying time: summer.
Acceptable Work: Considers all crafts except tole painting. All styles; utilitarian and/or decorative.

MAPLE HILL POTTERY CRAFT GALLERY, RFD 3, Auburn ME 04210. (207)782-8768. Contact: Nancy Lee. Craft shop/gallery. Estab. 1974. Represents 50 craftworkers. Price range: 75c-$600; bestsellers: $4.50-60. Craft shop buys outright. Gallery pieces taken on consignment; 40% commission. Craftworker sets retail price. Requires exclusive area representation. Reports in 2 weeks. Work may be shipped or hand-delivered. Dealer pays shipping to shop on purchased work and insurance for exhibited work.
Acceptable Work: Considers fiber work such as weaving, clothing, wall hangings, soft sculpture and quilting; jewelry; and ceramics. Especially interested in jewelry in the $18-60 range. Finished, one-of-a-kind and handmade production-line items; utilitarian and/or decorative.
Profile: "An artist's work is grouped together and great effort is made to create the best environment for it. I use pedestals for the 3-dimensional pieces, Plexiglas caps over these when the work needs to be protected. The work is hung on muslin-covered walls." Heaviest wholesale buying time: February-July; best selling time: summer.

THE MARKETPLACE, INC., 107 Exchange St., Portland ME 04111. (207)774-1376. President: Ellen M. Higgins. Craft and gift shop. Estab. 1972. Represents 75-100 northern New England craftworkers. Price range: $1-500; bestsellers: $1-15. Buys outright. Retail price set by joint agreement. Requires exclusive area representation. Reports in 2 weeks. Work may be shipped or hand-delivered. Dealer pays insurance for exhibited work.
Acceptable Work: Considers batik; candlemaking; ceramics; clothing; dollmaking; glass art; jewelry; metalsmithing; pottery; soft sculpture; wall hangings; weavings; and woodcrafting. Miniatures in 1"-1' scale is a specialty. Fine one-of-a-kind and handmade production-line items; utilitarian and/or decorative.
Profile: "A body of work gets displayed together but we try to mix media which allows a double display. Our shop is 3,000 square feet broken up into architectural areas and full of articles of every media chosen for excellence of design and execution." Heaviest wholesale buying time: May-December. Best selling time: summer and pre-Christmas.

GEORGE MARSHALL MUSEUM STORE, 140 Lindsay Rd., York ME 03909. (207)363-4974. Director: Rachel Grieg. Museum gift shop. Estab. 1972. Represents 75 New England craftworkers. Considers all crafts. Fine, one-of-a-kind and handmade production-line items; utilitarian and/or decorative. Price range: $2.50-500; bestsellers: $5-20. Works on consignment; 33⅛% commission. Retail price set by joint agreement. Requires exclusive area representation. Reports in 2 weeks. Work may be shipped or hand-delivered. Dealer pays insurance for exhibited work.
Profile: Store is located "in an historic area at the wharf on pitaturesque York River. Customers are a combination of year-round resident, summer residents and tourists." Heaviest wholesale buying time: spring; best selling time: summer.

MUSEUM SHOP, BOWDOIN COLLEGE MUSEUM OF ART, Walker Art Building, Brunswick ME 04011. (207)725-8731, ext. 275. Contact: Lynn C. Yanok or Mary L. Poppe. Museum gift shop. Estab. 1961. Represents several craftworkers. Price range: $1-50; bestsellers: $5-25. Buys outright and occasionally accepts consignment; commission is negotiable. Retail price set by joint agreement or by museum staff. Requires exclusive area representation. Reports in 10 days. Work may be shipped or hand-delivered by advance agreement only. Dealer pays shipping to shop.
Acceptable Work: Considers ceramics; decoupage; glass art; jewelry; metalsmithing; and pottery. Especially needs work "in the reproduction of objects from our permanent collection—but only with exclusive distribution rights and without large minimum order requirements." All styles; utilitarian and/or decorative.
Profile: "Items generally turn over quickly enough so that no rotation or retirement period is necessary." Heaviest wholesale buying time: Christmas, commencement and summer.

PINE TREE KILN, Rt. 1, West Sullivan ME 04689. (207)422-3377. Contact: Ruth Vibert. Craft shop/gallery/gift shop. Estab. 1948. Represents 15-20 craftworkers. Price range: $1.75-350; bestsellers: $5-30. Works on consignment and buys outright; 33⅓% commission. Craftworker sets retail price. Reports in 2 weeks. Work may be shipped or hand-delivered. Dealer pays shipping to shop.
Acceptable Work: Considers batik; candlemaking; ceramics; glass art; jewelry; leatherworking; metalsmithing; pottery; wall hangings; weavings; and woodcrafting. Especially needs leather; woven wall hangings; and jewelry. One-of-a-kind and handmade production-line items; utilitarian and/or decorative.
Profile: "We display a craftsman's work all together in one place, identified as his work. We show work as long as it continues to sell. The shop is a handsome converted barn; has been going for 30 years and has an old, regular and loyal clientele. Customers are from old, well-established, wealthy summer colonies." Heaviest wholesale buying time: spring-early summer; best selling time: June-October.

PLUM DANDY, RFD # 2, Box 50, Wells ME 04090. (207)646-9093. Contact: Linda Haydock. Estab. 1974. Considers batik; basketweaving; candlemaking; ceramics; Christmas items; dollmaking; fiberwork; glass art; jewelry; metalsmithing; needlecrafts; silkscreening; and soft sculpture. Especially needs stoneware pottery with no wheel rings. "We need a potter to provide dinnerware sets and customer special orders within 6-8 weeks." Finished, one-of-a-kind and handmade production-line items; utilitarian and/or decorative. Price range: 15c-$175; bestsellers: 50c-$38. Buys outright or occasionally on consignment; 30% commission. Shop sets retail price. Requires exclusive area representation in York County. Query with transparencies or photos, price list and SASE. "We return items which don't meet our standards." Reports in 1 week (longer in July-August). Dealer pays insurance for exhibited work; negotiates payment for shipping and in-transit insurance.
Profile: Items displayed maximum 6 months (consignment). Heaviest wholesale buying time: late spring; best selling time: July-September. Shop offers largest wall hangings selection from northern Boston to Portland. Customers are ages 25-50 with upper-lower to middle incomes, interested in home decoration and plants.

THE PUMPKIN PATCH, Box 178, Searsport ME 04974. (207)548-6047. Contact: Robert F. Sommer. Craft and antique shop. Estab. 1974. Represents 10 Maine craftworkers. Price range: $2-100; bestsellers: $5-30. Buys outright. Retail price set by joint agreement. Reports in 1 week. Work may be shipped or hand-delivered. Dealer pays shipping to shop and insurance.
Acceptable Work: Considers candlemaking; clothing; dollmaking; glass art; jewelry; metalsmithing; pottery; quilting; wall hangings; weavings; woodcrafting; and graphics. All styles; utilitarian and/or decorative.

Profile: "Displays are constantly changed, integrating handworks and antiques. Each craftsman is highlighted in his own setting with background information on the artist, object and skill. Shop is an old sea captain's house and in a quaint coastal community." Heaviest wholesale buying time: May-July; best selling time: May-October.

RICKER BLACKSMITH SHOP, Campbell Hill, Cherryfield ME 04622. (207)546-7954. Contact: George A. Brace. Blacksmith shop. Estab. 1801. Represents 1 craftworker who works in metal or wrought iron. One-of-a-kind and handmade production-line items; utilitarian and/or decorative. Price range: $5-200; bestsellers: $5-60. Exhibits work; does not buy or consign. Work may be shipped or hand-delivered.
Profile: "This is the oldest family-run blacksmith shop in the East. It has been in our family since 1801." Best selling time: summer and fall.

THE SEA CRAFTERS, Box 770, Ocean Ave., Kennebunkport ME 04046. (207)967-2059. Contact: W.J. Berey. Gift shop. Estab. 1966. Represents 35-45 craftworkers. Price range: $1-500; bestsellers: $5-25. Works on consignment and buys outright; 33⅓% commission. Retail price set by joint agreement. Requires exclusive area representation. Reports in 2 weeks. Work may be shipped or hand-delivered. Dealer pays shipping and insurance for exhibited work.
Acceptable Work: Considers ceramics; decoupage; dollmaking; glass art; jewelry; leatherworking; metalsmithing; needlecrafts; pottery; soft sculpture; and woodcrafting. No shell work. Primitive and fine pieces; utilitarian and/or decorative.
Profile: "Items are generally displayed with related merchandise; period of display as agreed with craftsman, usually during tourist season of June-September. We specialize in merchandise with a nautical theme, primarily useful or decorative items for the home. We normally display over 1,750 items ranging from jewelry to large furniture, all shown in our 1785 colonial building featuring original hand hewn post and beam construction." Heaviest wholesale buying time: spring-summer; best selling time: July-August.

SHERRYMIKE POTTERY/GALLERY, 19 Pleasant St., Hallowell ME 04347. (207)622-1906. Contact: Adele Nichols. Craft shop/gallery. Estab. 1960. Represents 90+ craftworkers, mostly from Maine. Fine one-of-a-kind and handmade production-line items; utilitarian and/or decorative. Price range: $1.50-325; bestsellers: $2-20. Buys outright. Craftworker sets retail price. Requires exclusive area representation. Reports in 1 week. Dealer pays insurance for exhibited work. Best selling time: summer-Christmas.
Acceptable Work: Considers batik; candlemaking; ceramics; dollmaking; glass art; jewelry; leatherworking; metalsmithing; pottery; soft sculpture; wall hangings; weavings; and woodcrafting. "Pottery is always big; weaving sales have increased; and jewelry is a steady."

STRONG CRAFT GALLERY, Bar Harbor Rd., Ellsworth ME 04605. (207)667-2595. Contact: Roslyn Strong. Craft gallery. Estab. 1970. Represents 200 craftworkers. Price range: $1.25-300; bestsellers: $4-85. Works on consignment and buys outright; 33⅓% commission. Retail price set by joint agreement. Requires exclusive area representation. Reports in 2 weeks. Work may be shipped or hand-delivered. Dealer pays return shipping and insurance for exhibited work. Displays work 2-6 weeks. Heaviest wholesale buying time: spring; best selling time: summer.
Acceptable Work: Considers glass art; jewelry; leatherworking; metalsmithing; pottery; soft sculpture; wall hangings; weavings; and woodcrafting. Fine, one-of-a-kind and handmade production-line items; utilitarian and/or decorative.

SWAMP JOHN'S, Perkins Cove, Ogunquit ME 03907. (207)646-9414. Contact: Thomas Young. Craft shop. Estab. 1970. Represents 10-12 craftworkers. Considers jewelry and leatherworking. Fine, one-of-a-kind and handmade production-line items; utiliarian only. Price range: $15-900; bestsellers: $25-100. Buys outright. Gallery sets retail price. Requires exclusive area representation. Work may be shipped or hand-delivered. Dealer pays shipping and insurance for exhibited work.
Profile: "Since most everything is bought outright, it is usually displayed until it sells. Everything is displayed attractively; jewelry in exotic hardwood cases and in a manner to make it appealing to the consumer. We carry exclusive works from the other shops in our area." Heaviest wholesale buying time: March-April; best selling time: summer.

TOMTEGARD, INC., SCANDINAVIAN DESIGN INTERIORS, Central St., Rockport ME 04856. Contact: Doris Nuesse or Marcia Sims. Furniture and accessory store. Estab. 1974. Represents 5 New England craftworkers. Price range: $3-150; bestsellers: $3-90. Works on consignment and buys outright; 33⅓% commission. Retail price set by joint agreement. Requires exclusive area representation. Reports as soon as possible. Work may be shipped or hand-·

delivered. Dealer pays insurance for exhibited work.

Acceptable Work: Considers ceramics; pottery; wall hangings; weavings; woodcrafting; and furniture. Fine, one-of-a-kind and handmade production-line items only; utilitarian and/or decorative.

Profile: "We are a modern design shop specializing in the 'Scandinavian look' on the Maine Coast." Displays work 6-12 months. The average customer is 35-60 years old. Heaviest wholesale buying time: spring; best selling time: summer.

YANKEE ARTISAN, 119 Front St., Bath ME 04530. (207)443-6215. Craft shop. Estab. 1970. Represents 100 Maine craftworkers. Considers batik; candlemaking; ceramics; clothing; dollmaking; jewelry; leatherworking; needlecrafts; pottery; quilting; soft sculpture; wall hangings; weavings; and woodcrafting. One-of-a-kind and handmade production-line items; utilitarian and/or decorative. Price range: 25c-$150; bestsellers: 25c-$55. Works on consignment. Retail price set by joint agreement. Hand-delivered work only. Unsold consigned pieces returned after 6 months.

Profile: "We're located in historic district on downtown waterfront." Best selling time: July-August and December.

Maryland

APPALACHIANA, 10400 Old Georgetown Rd., Bethesda MD 20014. (301)530-6770. President: Joan A. Farrell. Vice President: Ann S. Powell. Craft shop. Estab. 1970. Represents 300 craftworkers. Price range: $1-400; best sellers: $1-30. Buys outright; 40% commission. Retail price set by shop. Reports in 2 weeks. Work may be shipped or hand-delivered. Dealer pays insurance on exhibited work.

Acceptable Work: Considers ceramics; candles; jewelry; metalsmithing; pottery; quilts; wall hangings; weavings; and woodcrafting. All styles; utilitarian and/or decorative.

Profile: "Volume and diversity make our shop unique." Heaviest wholesale buying time: fall; best selling time: fall-Christmas.

ARTS/OBJECTS, 1004 Reisterstown Rd., Baltimore MD 21208. (301)484-5355. Owners: Irvin and Nita Borenstein. "Mini-department store." Estab. 1961. Represents 75-100 craftworkers. Price range: $1-500; bestsellers: $15-100. Buys outright. Retail price set by joint agreement; "we must make 100% mark-up." Requires exclusive area representation. Reports in 2 weeks. Work may be shipped or hand-delivered; dealer pays insurance on exhibited work.

Acceptable Work: Considers batik; ceramics; metalsmithing; glass; pottery; quilts; soft sculpture; weavings; and wall hangings. "Special need for one-of-a-kind art pieces. All styles: utilitarian and/or decorative.

Profile: "We are a mini-department store. We have an art gallery, but we also show crafts mixed with commercially-made items. We do custom floral (silk, dried, paper) and use many containers. In addition, we have an interior design studio which uses many one-of-a-kind 'art pieces.' " Heaviest wholesale buying time: fall, preparing for Christmas; best selling time: Christmas season. Customers are "high income, well-educated, sophisticated. They expect the finest and most unusual."

BALTIMORE MUSEUM OF ART, Art Museum Dr., Baltimore MD 21218. (301)396-6338. Manager: Margaret Baker. Museum gallery/gift shop. Represents 10-12 craftworkers. Price range: 25c-$150; bestsellers: $1-25. Works on consignment; 40% commission. Retail price set by joint agreement. Reports in 1 week. Work may be shipped or hand-delivered.

Acceptable Work: Considers batik; ceramics; decoupage; dollmaking; jewelry; needlecrafts; pottery; quilting; soft sculpture; wall hangings; weavings; and woodcrafting. Primitive and fine one-of-a-kind pieces; utilitarian and/or decorative. "We're always looking for craftworkers who will carry out an idea based on some item from our collection. I usually spy a talent, then ask to use his talent in our direction."

Profile: "A large percentage of our gifts are items based on the Museum's collection, exclusive to us. We stock a large selection of art books, re-inforcing our collection." Small items displayed in locked cases, larger items on wall shelves out of customers' reach. Heaviest wholesale buying time: September-October; best selling time: fall-Christmas.

BECKY'S COUNTRY NOOK, Frederick County Square, Frederick MD 21701. (301)663-1155. Owner: Becky Higginbotham. Craft shop "representing craftworkers on a wholesale and retail basis." Estab. 1975. Represents 125 craftworkers. Price range: 50c-$60; bestsellers: $1.50-30. Works on consignment and buys outright; 40% commission. Retail price set by joint agreement. Reports in 2 weeks. Work may be shipped or hand-delivered; dealer pays insurance on exhibited work.

Acceptable Work: Considers clothing; decoupage; dollmaking; glass art; needlecrafts; pottery;

quilting; soft sculpture; tole painting; wall hangings; weavings; woodcrafting; and Christmas ornaments. "Everything must be of a country or traditional nature." Handmade production-line items; utilitarian and/or decorative.
Profile: "We handle everything of traditional/country nature, from corsages and Christmas ornaments to quilts and furniture. Items are displayed as best to give a country, homey overall look to the shop." Heaviest wholesale buying time: spring-summer; best selling time: October-December.

CALICO CAT, 2137 Gwynn Oak Ave., Baltimore MD 21207. (301)944-2450. Co-owner: Bruni Obriecht. Gallery and gift shop. Estab. 1968. Represents 200 craftworkers. Price range $1-350; bestsellers: $5-30. Works on consignment and buys outright; 30% commission. Retail price set by craftworker. Reports in 3 weeks. Query first.
Acceptable Work: Considers candles; clothing; decoupage; dollmaking; glass art; jewelry; pottery; quilting; and woodcrafting. All styles; utilitarian only.
Profile: Crafts displayed together, apart from the gallery. Also sponsors craft demonstrations. Best selling and heaviest wholesale buying time: Christmas season.

THE CRAFT GALLERY LTD., White Flint, Kensington MD 20795. (301)770-6990. Contact: Marvin Wies. Craft shop/gallery. Estab. 1969. Represents 200 North and South American craftworkers. Considers batik; ceramics; glass art; jewelry; leatherworking; metalsmithing; pottery; soft sculpture and woodcrafting. Fine one-of-a-kind and handmade production-line items; utilitarian and/or decorative. Price range: $1-$1,000; bestsellers: $1-50. Buys outright. Shop sets retail price; "we will discuss retail prices with craftsperson." Dealer pays shipping to shop.
Profile: "We're in a 125 store shopping mall catering to mostly college educated, government employees and professionals. Heaviest wholesale buying time: summer; best selling time: fall-Christmas.

THE EIGHT HANDS AT THE FARM WOMEN'S MARKET, 7155 Wisconsin Ave., Bethesda MD 20160. (301)052-9600. Vice President/Publicity: Jacqui Melpolder. Craft shop and gallery. Estab. 1966. Represents 40 craftworkers. Price range 75c-$250; bestsellers: $5-75. Works on consigment and buys outright; 33⅓% commission. Reports in 2 weeks. Work may be shipped or hand-delivered.
Acceptable Work: Considers batik; ceramics; clothing; dollmaking; glass art; jewelry; leatherworking; metalsmithing; needlecrafts; pottery; and woodcrafting. "Would like more variety in printmaking— we have batik, woodblock and lithographs now." All styles; utilitarian and/or decorative.
Profile: Jewelry and metalwork are displayed in locked cases; all other items are shown on open shelves and wall displays. Heaviest wholesale buying time: June; best selling time: fall. "Our customers range from US Senators to national news personalities to small children; with most being in the middle to upper income bracket."

FAVORITE THINGS, York & Monktur Rds., Hereford MD 21111. (301)472-2466. Owner: Betsy Swann. Specialty shop, emphasizing dollhouses and miniatures. Estab. 1973. Represents 10-15 craftworkers. Price range: $1.50-700; bestsellers: $1.50-100. Works on consignment and buys outright; 33% commission. Retail price set by joint agreement. Requires exclusive area representation. Reports in 2 weeks. Work may be shipped or hand-delivered.
Acceptable Work: Considers ceramics; clothing; dollmaking; jewelry; pottery; soft sculpture; and especially, dollhouses and miniatures. Primitive and fine handmade production-line items; utilitarian and/or decorative.
Profile: "Whimsey, variety and quality make our shop unique." Heaviest wholesale buying and best selling time: pre-Christmas. Most customers are in the upper and middle to upper income bracket.

GALLERY ON THE PARK, 1111 Sligo Creek Pkwy., Takoma Park MD 20012. (301)270-6633. Owners: Jack and Vaughn Hammond. Craft shop/gallery. Estab. 1973. Represents 40-50 craftworkers. Price range: $1-100; bestsellers: $1-50. Works on consignment and buys outright; 33% commission. Retail price set by joint agreement. "We'll be happy to answer inquiries, but we rarely order or accept items we have not seen and approved in person. Call for an appointment; bring a representative sampling of work and/or photos; be organized; have a price list and order forms. And, don't promise what can't be delivered." Reports in 2 weeks.
Acceptable Work: Considers batik; candlemaking; handcrafted ceramics; glass art; jewelry; leatherworking; metalsmithing; pottery; soft sculpture; weavings; wall hangings; and woodcraf-

ting. "We're always looking for items with circus motif." Fine one-of-a-kind and handmade production-line items; utilitarian and/or decorative.
Profile: "We display craft items grouped by artist's name. Minimum display time: 30 days; 60 maximum on consignment items. Our warm, relaxed atmosphere and reasonable prices make our shop unique." Heaviest wholesale buying time: fall and winter. "Our customers are mostly moderate income. Many are repeat customers, the majority having little knowledge of crafts/art, but are interested in learning."

THE GOODY SHOPPE, 4806 Olympia Ave., Beltsville MD 20705. (301)937-3979. Contact: Robert P. Gooding. Craft shop. Estab. 1962. Represents craftworkers who are knowledgeable in rare woods. Considers all crafts of rare wood. Fine one-of-a-kind and handmade production-line items. Price range: $2.50-10; bestsellers: $3-10. Works on consignment and buys outright. Retail price set by joint agreement. Reports in 1 week. Dealer pays insurance for exhibited work.
Profile: "We are unique in selling rare wood jewelry in quantity. We take items on consignment for 60 days." Shop is closed January-February. Customers are mostly women.

THE GREAT CHASE, 4949 Allan Rd., Chevy Chase MD 20016. (301)656-6228. Owners: Frances and Edward Garfinkle. See The Tifanee Tree, Chevy Chase, Maryland.

HANDS OF MAN, 1709 Reisterstown Rd., Baltimore MD 21208. (301)484-2114. President: Edie Brown. Vice President: Phyllis Attman. Craft shop. Estab. 1971. Represents 200 craftworkers. Price range: $2-500; bestsellers: $10-30. Works on consignment and buys outright; 40% commission. Retail price set by shop. Reporting time varies according to season. Work may be shipped or hand-delivered; dealer pays insurance on exhibited work.
Acceptable Work: Considers batik; ceramics; glass art; jewelry; leatherworking; metalsmithing; pottery; soft sculpture; wall hangings; weavings; and woodcrafting. All styles; utilitarian and/or decorative.
Profile: "We represent many craftworkers, and we're in a large area with 5 other shops. Our traffic flow is good, and our display is also excellent, though it changes constantly." Best selling time: Christmas, "but there's a steady flow throughout the year." Shop located in an upper income area.

HOLDEN GALLERY, 10408 Montgomery Ave., Kensington MD 20795. (301)933-6506. Owner: Charles Holden. Gallery. Estab. 1976. Represents 3-4 craftworkers from the Washington DC, Baltimore and Richmond, Virginia, area. Price range: $3-200; bestsellers: $15-75. Works on consignment and buys outright; 40% commission. Retail price set by joint agreement. Charges $150/month for exhibit space. Reports in 2 weeks. Work may be shipped or hand-delivered; dealer pays insurance on exhibited work.
Acceptable Work: Considers batik; ceramics; glass art; jewelry; metalsmithing; pottery; wall hangings; and weavings. Fine one-of-a-kind and handmade production-line items; utilitarian and/or decorative.
Profile: "Gallery shows in uncrowded condition for a period of 1 month. We feel that once the art is in the gallery, it's the craftworker's responsibility to help sell their work." Customers are 24-45, and in the upper income bracket.

LAWYERS ARTSHOP, 1106 Cathedral St., Baltimore MD 21201. (301)837-0820. General Manager: Doris Pierce. Considers sculpture related to law and the legal profession (i.e., showing lawyers, judges, courts, lawyer-client scenes, law offices, courtroom scenes, etc.). Price range: $25-100; bestsellers: $25-40. Buys outright. Retail price set by joint agreement. Query with samples or photos of work. SASE. Gallery pays shipping from gallery.

LEATHER STUFF, Upper Level-Valley Mall, Hagerstown MD 21740. (717)762-3776. Proprietor: Timothy Scott. Craft shop. Estab. 1975. Represents 7-10 craftworkers. Considers all leatherworking and belt buckles. Handmade production-line items; utilitarian and/or decorative. Price range: $5-18; bestsellers: $10 belts and wallets. Buys outright. Retail price set by shop. Work may be shipped or hand-delivered.
Profile: "We buy wholesale and display appropriately to sell." Best selling time: Christmas. Customers are ages 20-35.

MARSON LTD., 6 Shawan Rd., Cockeysville MD 21030. (301)666-7161. Owners: A.G. Marsiglia and S. Gamson. Gallery. Estab. 1971. Currently emphasizes oriental art. Considers batik and prints. Fine one-of-a-kind items; decorative. Price range: $5-3,500; bestsellers: $5-125. Buys outright. Work may be shipped or hand-delivered; dealer pays insurance on exhibited work.

Profile: "We specialize in original oriental art and have over 1,000 shows annually, through traveling sales representatives at universities, museums and art centers. Each piece of art is individually matted and the opening covered with Mylar. It's also labelled with the artist's name, country of origin, birth date, medium, title and price." Best selling time: fall.

POTTER'S GUILD OF BALTO, INC., 201 Homeland Ave., Baltimore MD 21212. (301)433-9738. President: Lee Novak. Gallery. Estab. 1955. Represents 50 Baltimore craftworkers. Specializes in pottery. One-of-a-kind items; utilitarian and/or decorative. Price range: $1-200; bestsellers: $4-50. "We accept members who are professional potters, willing to volunteer some time towards the maintenance and operation of the guild." Retail price set by craftworker.
Profile: "Work is done by individual professional craftworkers. We're a guild whose members exchange ideas, attend many workshops, teach and try to improve/promote the craft." Displays change monthly, "except during Christmas when it runs from November-December." Best selling time: Christmas. "Many students and educators are customers, most from middle to upper income."

A.D. SMULL GALLERY, 10419 Armory Ave., Kensington MD 20795. (301)946-6262. Director: A.D. Smull. Gallery. Estab. 1976. Considers fibers; soft sculpture; fantasy clothing; painted fabrics; weaving; and off loom sculpture. Price range: $25-1,500; bestsellers: $25-300. Works on consignment and buys outright sometimes; 40% commission. Retail price set by joint agreement. Requires exclusive area representation during show. Contact dealer with query, slides and photos; and arrange interview. SASE. Reports in 2 weeks. Dealer pays return shipping; in-transit insurance; and insurance for exhibited work. Work must be offered for sale. Work usually displayed 4-6 weeks.

THE STORE LTD., Village of Cross Keys, Baltimore MD 21210. (301)323-2350. Owner: Betty Cooke. Design store. Estab. 1965. Represents 10 craftworkers. Bestsellers: $50-200. Works on consignment and buys outright; 33⅓% commission. Retail price set by joint agreement. Work may be shipped or hand-delivered; dealer pays insurance on exhibited work.
Acceptable Work: "We represent all materials — fabric, metal, clay, wood, leather, glass, etc. Our items are primarily utilitarian; i.e.: clothing, gourmet utensils, toys, boxes. The standards for our store are high for design, style and workmanship."

THE TIFANEE TREE, 4949 Allan Rd., Chevy Chase MD 20016. (301)656-6228. Owners: Frances and Edward Garfinkle. Craft and gift shop. Estab. 1970. Represents 200-250 craftworkers. Price range: 50c-$1,500; bestsellers: $5-100. Works on consignment and buys outright; 40% commission. Retail price set by craftworker. Requires exclusive area representation. Reports in 3 weeks. Work may be shipped or hand-delivered; dealer pays insurance on exhibited work.
Acceptable Work: Considers candlemaking; ceramics; dollmaking; glass art; jewelry; metalsmithing; pottery; soft sculpture; wall hangings; weaving; and woodcrafting. Fine one-of-a-kind and handmade production-line items; utilitarian and/or decorative.
Profile: "We are known for fantasy and whimsy, with the emphasis on the very unique and high quality." Displays emphasize the craftworker, and last periods of 4-6 weeks. Heaviest wholesale buying time: fall-Christmas; best selling time: Christmas. "Customers are 25-50, professional people ($25,000 income) with an overall sophisticated taste."

THE TOMLINSON CRAFT COLLECTION, 711 W. 40th St., Baltimore MD 21211. (301)338-1555. Contact: Ginny Tomlinson. Craft shop/gallery. Estab. 1971. Represents 400 craftworkers. Price range: $15-500; bestsellers: $3-50. Buys outright. Retail price set by joint agreement. Reports as soon as possible. Work may be shipped or hand-delivered by previous consent. Dealer pays return shipping and insurance for exhibited work. Heaviest wholesale buying time: April-May and November-December; best selling time: December.
Acceptable Work: Considers batik; candles; ceramics; clothing; glass art; jewelry; leatherworking; metalsmithing; pottery; quilting; soft sculpture; wall hangings; weavings; and woodcrafting. Fine one-of-a-kind and handmade production-line items; utilitarian and/or decorative.

THE VILLAGE LEATHER SHOP, 6417 Windsor Mill Rd., Woodlawn MD 21207. (301)944-7671. Owner: Hank Yeatman. Craft shop. Estab. 1970. Represents 2 craftworkers. Considers jewelry and leatherworking; especially needs handmade buckles. All styles; utilitarian and/or decorative. Price range: $2-500; bestsellers: $5-125. Works on consignment and buys outright; 10-20% commission. Retail price set by joint agreement. Reports in 2 weeks. Work may be shipped or hand-delivered; dealer pays insurance on exhibited work.

Profile: Shop is in a rustic setting. Heaviest wholesale buying time: summer and fall; best selling time: summer, fall and Christmas. Customers are "in the 25-50 range, middle to upper middle class."

Massachusetts

ALI BABA, 99 Mt. Auburn St., Harvard Square, Cambridge MA 02138. Contact: Anne Brinton or Frank Cullen (617)547-9098. Museum style gift shop. Estab. 1975. Represents 20 craftworkers. One-of-a-kind and production-line items; utilitarian or decorative. Price range $5-75; bestsellers: $5-30. Retail price set by joint agreement. Requires exclusive area representation on most items. Shipping by UPS only. Ali Baba pays shipping on goods purchased outright by shop.
Acceptable Work: Open to any moderately-priced work in any media (including polymers and other less traditional substances) except as noted below, that evoke specific cultures, historic styles, or are replicas of museum pieces. These can be jewelry, sculptures, house gifts, greeting cards, etc. No animal slaughter products (leather, fur, bone, ivory, scrimshaw, shells, feathers, bone ash or human life support products in critical supply such as coral).
Profile: New and expanding shop. Spin off of well-established craft store in same high volume area. Prefer hard-line goods to soft lines but are not rigid. Heavy female clientele, well educated. Fashion lead market area.

ARABIS, Contemporary American Design, 122 North St., Pittsfield MA 01201. (413)443-0531. Owner: Robert Silberg. Craft shop and gallery. Estab. 1976. Represents 150 craftworkers. Price range: 50c-$1,000; bestsellers: 50c-$150. Works on consignment and buys outright; 30% commission. Retail price set by joint agreement. Reports in 4 weeks. Work may be shipped or hand-delivered; dealer pays insurance on exhibited work.
Acceptable Work: Considers batik; candlemaking; ceramics; dollmaking; glass art; jewelry; leatherworking; metalsmithing; pottery; soft sculpture; wall hangings; weaving; woodcrafting; and hand-printed or design greeting cards. Fine one-of-a-kind and handmade production-line items; utilitarian and/or decorative.
Profile: "Shop is owned by producing craftworkers with over 12 years retailing experience. We're very concerned with proper displaying of our objects. Shows run 6 weeks, and are promoted through extensive newspaper ads and mailings sent out to collectors." Heaviest wholesale buying: spring and fall; best selling time: summer, fall and Christmas. "Most of our customers are tourists with a strong interest in the arts."

ARTISAN'S COOPERATIVE, Faneuil Hall, Quincy Market, Boston MA. See Artisan's Cooperative, Chadds Ford, Pennsylvania.

ARTISAN'S COOPERATIVE, Straight Wharf, Nantucket Island MA 02554. See Artisan's Cooperative, Chadds Ford, Pennsylvania.

AYN'S SHUTTLE SHOP, Box 1207, Lake Ave., Oak Bluffs-Martha's Vineyard MA 02557. (617)693-0134. Owner: Ann Chase. Craft and gift shop. Estab. 1955. Represents 40+ craftworkers. Price range: $2-150; bestsellers: $2-30. Works on consignment; 25% commission. Retail price set by joint agreement. Reports in 2 weeks. Work may be shipped or hand-delivered; dealer pays insurance on exhibited work.
Acceptable Work: Considers batik; ceramics; dollmaking; glass art; jewelry; leatherworking; metalsmithing; needlecrafts; pottery; tole painting; wall hangings; weaving; and woodcrafting. "We're always looking for something new; e.g., I'd like some more pottery, dinnerware sets, unusual note paper and something for the men. It would be best in earth-tone colors, with samples on display for orders." Fine handmade production-line items; utilitarian and/or decorative.
Profile: "We're the only handicraft shop in this area; we're well established and business increases every year. All items are in full view. I've found that several items of the same craft displayed together sell better than having several types mixed together." Heaviest wholesale buying time: spring-summer; best selling time: summer. Customers are primarily tourists "who want something different than what's at home. If they like it, they'll buy it regardless of income."

BOSTON ATHENAEUM GALLERY, 10½ Beacon St., Boston MA 02108. (617)227-0270. Considers ceramics; decoupage; glass art; jewelry; mobiles; needlecrafts; pottery; sculpture; soft sculpture; wall hangings; and weavings. Price range: $25-10,000+. No commission. Retail price set by craftworker. All methods of contact OK. SASE. 1 month exposure.

BOSTON BAKED BEADS, 64 Wendell St., Cambridge MA 02138. Owners: Paul DeVore and Gail Gutradt. Craft and gift shop. Estab. 1974. Represents 50 craftworkers. Considers cards and

stationery; posters; mobiles; and, especially, beads. Primitive and fine handmade production-line items; utilitarian and/or decorative. Price range: 25c-$50; bestsellers: 25c-$20. Buys outright. Retail price set by shop. Reports in 2 weeks. Work may be shipped or hand-delivered.
Profile: "We specialize in handcrafted beads— about 100 varieties. Customers are encouraged to create their own jewelry in the store." Heaviest wholesale buying: February-April. "Our customers are mainly young families." Open October-April. May-September address is 12-D Mt. Desert St., Bar Harbor ME 04609.

CARDS AND SHARDS, 45 S. Main St., Cohasset MA 02025. (617)383-0729. Buyer-Manager: Bob Fesler. Gift shop. Estab. 1966. Price range: $3-250; bestsellers: $4-25. Works on consignment and buys outright; 40% commission. Retail price set by joint agreement. Requires exclusive area representation. Reporting times vary according to season. Work may be shipped or hand-delivered, if agreed upon in advance. Craftworker pays insurance on exhibited consignment work.
Acceptable Work: Considers ceramics; glass art; jewelry; metalsmithing; pottery; tole painting; wall hangings; weaving; and woodcrafting. All styles; utilitarian and/or decorative.
Profile: Has special displays and advance promotion. Exhibition lasts 3-4 weeks. Best selling and heaviest wholesale buying time: spring, summer and fall. Shop located in an affluent community.

CAT'S CRADLE, 244 Commercial St., Provincetown MA 02657. Contact: Alice Foley. Craft shop. Estab. 1976. Represents 40 craftworkers. "Specializes in pottery but has some other media as well. Unique clay work of any type, especially that which relates to Provincetown clientele or seashore. No gimmickry or tourist pieces." One-of-a-kind and production-line items; utilitarian and/or decorative. Price range: up to $200; bestsellers: $10-50. Works some on consignment and buys outright; 30% commission. Retail price set by joint agreement. Requires exclusive area representation. Shipping by UPS only. Dealer pays shipping on outright purchases by shop. Shop is in center of town in second oldest house in Provincetown. Customers are tourists. Best selling time: summer.

COSS GALLERY, Box 1360, Nantucket MA 02554. Contact: Carol Jepson. Gallery. Estab. 1972. Represents 8 craftworkers. Price range: $10-800; bestsellers: $10-60. Works on consignment; 40% commission. Retail price set by joint agreement. Requires exclusive area representation. Reports in 2 weeks. Work may be shipped or hand-delivered.
Acceptable Work: Considers jewelry and metalsmithing; especially needs cloisonne and original seashore designs. Fine one-of-a-kind and handmade production-line items; utilitarian and/or decorative.
Profile: "Small items are displayed under glass; from June-September. Customers average 40-60 years old; mostly have income in excess of $60,000." Best selling time: summer.

CRAFT CENTER, 25 Sagamore Rd., Worcester MA 01605. (617)753-8183. Director: Angelo Randazzo. Craft shop and gallery. Estab. 1951. Represents 50 craftworkers. Price range: $6-300; bestsellers: $16-75. Works on consignment and buys outright; 40% commission. Retail price set by craftworker. Requires exclusive area representation. "Call for an appointment to show your work." Reports in 2 weeks. Work may be shipped or hand-delivered; dealer pays insurance on exhibited work.
Acceptable Work: Considers ceramics; glass art; jewelry; metalsmithing; pottery; soft sculpture; wall hangings; weaving; and woodcrafting. Wants functional stoneware pottery, small wooden objects and "any gift item for men." Fine one-of-a-kind and handmade production-line items; utilitarian and/or decorative.
Profile: Displays work in cases and on shelves for at least 1 month. Best selling and heaviest wholesale buying time: fall. "We're also a craft school, plus we sponsor major craft exhibitions in our gallery." Customers are middle to upper income.

DANFORTH MUSEUM SHOP, 123 Union Ave., Framingham MA 01701. (617)620-0050. Chairman: Elaine Marks. Museum gift shop. Estab. 1975. Represents 100 craftworkers. Considers ceramics; glass art; jewelry; and pottery. Primitive and fine one-of-a-kind items; utilitarian and/or decorative. Price range: $3-250; bestsellers: $8-50. Works on consignment; 35% commission. Retail price set by craftworker. Report time varies according to season. Work may be shipped or hand-delivered.
Profile: "Located inside the museum, the shop has display cases, shelves and bins." Best selling time: winter. "Customers are middle and upper income people with art and craft interests."

DODGE HOUSE ART GALLERY, 426 Main St., Chatham MA 02633. (617)945-1231. Contact: H. Latham Kent. Gallery. Estab. 1968. Represents 25 craftworkers. Considers ceramics;

glass art; and pottery. Especially needs "small, realistic sculptures." Fine one-of-a-kind pieces; utilitarian and/or decorative. Price range: $10-500; bestsellers: $10-150. Works on consignment; 33⅓% commission. Retail price set by joint agreement. Requires exclusive area representation. Reports in 1 week. Work may be shipped or hand-delivered; craftworker pays insurance on exhibited work.

Profile: "Items are displayed in an antique setting. The gallery is housed in a 1750 homestead. We specialize in fine quality, original artwork sensibly priced." Best selling time: June-Labor Day. "Our customers appreciate traditional artwork."

FOLKLORICA, 259 Marlborough St., Apt. 6, Boston MA 02116. (617)262-9347 or 367-1201, and (413)298-4436. Contact: Ellen or Don Gross. Folk art gallery and jewelry emporium. Estab. 1973. Represents about 20 craftworkers. Has stores in Boston and Stockbridge; Boston store open year-round, Stockbridge store open summers only. Considers jewelry; ceramics; glass; and wall hangings. Especially needs unusual jewelry; small wall hangings; ceramics; and glass; with a "very primitive art deco or antique look, or an oriental feel." All styles; utilitarian and/or decorative. Price range: $5-150; bestsellers: $10-60. Works on consignment and buys outright; 33⅓-50% commission. Retail price set by joint agreement. Requires exclusive area representation. Reports in 1-2 weeks. Work may be hand-delivered; dealer pays insurance on exhibited work.

Profile: "Our merchandise is unusual and prices are very reasonable. Work is displayed to enhance the visual beauty of each piece." Heaviest wholesale buying time: November, May and June; best selling time: December, July and August. "Sophisticated upper middle-class clientele, 20-50 years old."

DANIEL FRISHMAN GALLERY, 933 Main St., Osterville MA 02655. Contact: Daniel Frishman. Considers sculpture and pottery. Price range: $10-10,000. 40% commission. Retail price set by joint agreement. Gallery may share shipping expenses. Requires exclusive area representation. Commission taken on any art sold locally after showing. Send transparencies or photos. Exhibited art insured. Sponsors openings. Open annually June-September. Winter address: 14 Castle Heights Rd., Andover MA 01810.

GALLERY OF WORLD ART INC., 745 Beacon St., Newton Centre MA 02159. (617)332-1800. Art Director: Susan Morrill. Considers sculpture. Maximum size: 72" square. Specializes in contemporary, realistic art. Works on consignment; 40% commission. Retail price set by joint agreement. Requires exclusive area representation. Arrange interview to show slides on larger work, samples on small. "Any artist interested in showing work should first come to the gallery and see in his own mind if his work fits in. If that is not possible, we will make suggestions."

THE GOLDSMITH, 5 Edgell Rd., Framingham MA 01701. (617)879-3996. Manager: Ann Frey. Estab. 1972. Represents 200 craftworkers. Considers batik; candlemaking; leatherworking; metalsmithing; pottery; and woodcrafting. Especially needs jewelry. Handmade production-line primitive and finished items; utiliarian and/or decorative. Price range: $1-100; bestsellers: $5-25. Buys outright. Gallery sets retail price. Requires exclusive area representation. Write. Reports in 2 weeks. Gallery pays shipping to shop and insurance.

Profile: Heaviest wholesale buying time: fall. Customers are college girls and upper-middle class women; they buy crafts for gifts.

GRANDMOTHER'S TRUNK, 75 Great Rd., Maynard MA 01754. (617)897-9811. Propritor: Debbie Regan. Craft, gift and antique shop located on Powder Hill Road. Estab. 1974. Represents 10 craftworkers. Price range: 50c-$100; bestsellers: 50c-$30. Works on consignment and buys outright; 33⅓% commission. Retail price set by joint agreement. Reports in 3 weeks; "please enclose SASE and photos of work." Work may be shipped or hand-delivered; dealer pays insurance on exhibited work.

Acceptable Work: Considers ceramics; clothing; dolls; doll clothes; glass art; jewelry; needlecrafts; pottery; quilting; tole painting; wall hangings; weavings; woodcrafting; prints; and small furniture. All styles; utilitarian and/or decorative.

Special Needs: "We're always looking for left-handed products (e.g., cards, aprons, mustache mugs) at reasonable prices. Also, crafts depicting horses, trains and antique cars are in demand, as are miniatures and doll furniture."

Profile: "Crafts are grouped and displayed to harmonize with the furniture and antiques we sell. Usual display time is 90 days." Best selling time: fall-winter. "Being situated next to Concord and near various large corporations gives us a clientele from other regions and countries, in addition to regular, local customers."

THE HANDCRAFTER, Whalers Wharf, 237-241 Commercial, Princeton MA 02657. (617)487-1966. Owner: Dale Elmer. Craft and gift shop, plus summer shops rented to craftworkers. Estab. 1963. Represents 40+ craftworkers. Price range: $2-350; bestsellers: $2-30. Works on consignment and buys outright; 33⅓% commission. Retail price set by joint agreement. Reports in 2 weeks. Work may be shipped or hand-delivered if a prior agreement has been made; dealer pays insurance on exhibited work.

Acceptable Work: Considers candlemaking; ceramics; glass art; jewelry; leatherworking; metalsmithing; pottery; and woodcrafting. Crafts must reflect sea themes; e.g., whales, fish, sailboats, lighthouses, seagulls. No scrimshaw. All styles; utilitarian and/or decorative.

Profile: "What makes us unusual is our location — on the beach, adjacent to the National Seashore, and in the center of a historical town (where the Mayflower Compact was made in the harbor) — and the fact that there are 40 artists and craftworkers producing and selling in our shop." Size: 10,000 square feet. Display time: 1-4 months, depending upon sales. Heaviest wholesale buying time: April 15-July 15; best selling time: May 15-September 15. "This town has a rich heritage of working artists and craftworkers, as well as galleries, ranging from average to excellent, so our customers are quite knowledgeable."

Forty artists and craftworkers produce and sell in The Handcrafter. Located in the historic town of Provincetown, Massachusetts, the shop enjoys a large volume of tourists and knowledgable customers.

HANDSCAPES, Box 733, Dennis Port MA 02639. (617)394-6657. Contact: Diane L. Thibault. Gift shop. Estab. 1975. Represents 100 craftworkers. Price range: $1.25-100; bestsellers: $2-18. Works occasionally on consignment but mostly buys outright; 40% commission. Retail price set by joint agreement. Requires exclusive area representation. Reports in 2-3 days. Work may be shipped or hand-delivered, if a prior contract has been made. Dealer pays insurance on exhibited work.

Acceptable Work: Considers batik; candlemaking; dollmaking; glass art; jewelry; leatherworking; metalsmithing; pottery; quilting; wall hangings; weavings; and woodcrafting. Fine one-of-a-kind and handmade production-line items; utilitarian and/or decorative.

Profile: "Although we have a gallery section, more and more gallery and shop items are being intermingled. This is to break down artificial barriers and assumptions; e.g. that price equals art. A $12 bowl can be as beautiful as a $3,500 wood sculpture, and we may have them displayed side by side." Heaviest wholesale buying time: winter; best selling time: summer. "This being a tourist area, 85% of our business is between July 1-October 1. However, we're open year-round. The bulk of our customers are middle income families who are shopping for a 'souvenir' of Cape Cod. As such, our shop has educational value since most of our customers don't come looking for quality crafts, but many end up buying them."

HANDWORKS, Winter St., Box 371, Edgartown MA 02539. (617)693-9215. Owners: John and Claudia Bradford. Craft and gift shop. Estab. 1972. Represents 100 craftworkers. Price range: $2-95; bestsellers: $5-15. Works on consignment and buys outright at 50% discount; 40% commission. On consignment items, craftworker sets retail price. Requires exclusive area representation. Reporting time varies according to season. Work may be shipped or hand-delivered, if prearranged agreement has been made.

Profile: "We mix commercial items with crafts, and they're displayed harmoniously." Heaviest wholesale buying time: spring; best selling time: summer. Customers are "tourists and island residents, 20's and 30's, middle income and up, looking for the unusual at reasonable prices."

HIGH STREET OF BOSTON, Box 161, Chestnut Hill MA 02167. Owner: William Hunter. Gift shop. Estab. 1972. Represents 50+ craftworkers. Price range: up to $200; bestsellers: up to $20. Works on consignment and buys outright; 34% commission. Retail price set by shop. Requires exclusive area representation. Reports "as soon as possible." Work may be shipped or hand-delivered.

Acceptable Work: Considers batik; candlemaking; ceramics; clothing; decoupage; dollmaking; glass art; jewelry; leatherworking; metalsmithing; needlecrafts; pottery; quilting; soft sculpture; tole painting; wall hangings; weavings; woodcrafting; and paintings. All styles; utilitarian and/or decorative.

Profile: "All work is original." Heaviest wholesale buying time: spring and summer; best selling time: summer and fall. "Customers are of discriminating taste, they appreciate the sea, nature and quality."

IMAGE GALLERY, Main St., Stockbridge MA 01262. Director: Clemens Kalischer. Gallery. Estab. 1965. Price range: $20-5,000. Works on consignment; 35% commission. Retail price set by joint agreement. Requires exclusive area representation. Reports in 4 weeks. Work may be shipped or hand-delivered. Exhibitions last 4-6 weeks.

Acceptable Work: Considers ceramics; glass; jewelry; metalsmithing; fiber sculpture; wall hangings; and wood. Fine one-of-a-kind pieces suitable for an art gallery only.

JOURNEYMAN, INC., 55 Boylston St., Harvard Square, Cambridge MA 02138. (617)876-0170. Contact: Frank Cullen, Donald McNeilly or Margaret Bailey. Contemporary craft shop. Estab. 1971. Represents over 100 craftworkers. Mostly production-line, some one-of-a-kind items; utilitarian and/or decorative. Price range: $5-200; bestsellers: $10-40. Retail price is set by joint agreement. Requires exclusive area representation. Shipping by UPS only. Journeyman pays shipping to shop if outright purchase; and pays insurance on exhibited work.

Acceptable Work: "We keep the largest selections of silver and pottery in our area thus emphasize those 2 media. We also sell blown glass; stain glass mirrors; low-line gold jewelry; and handmade lampshades. We do not use or sell *any* products that are the result of the slaughter of animals. This means leather; fur; bone; scrimshaw; ivory; shells; feathers; etc. For potters and glass blowers this means no bone ash. In stain glass or pottery hangings, no leather thongs. Also please don't use human life support products that are in critical supply (coral)."

Profile: Very prominent location. Fashion lead market. Customers are mostly women; average 30 years old; upper middle income; well-educated; professionals. Many out-of-staters. Best selling time: Christmas.

LEATHER SHED, 199 N. Pleasant St., Amherst MA 01002. Contact: Donald W. Muller. Estab. 1965. Represents 75 craftworkers. Considers ceramics; glass art; jewelry; leatherworking; metalsmithing; and pottery. Finished, one-of-a-kind and handmade production-line items OK;

utilitarian and/or decorative. Price range: $10-200; bestsellers: $10-100. Buys outright. Retail price set by joint agreement. Requires exclusive area representation. Mail artwork. Reports in 2 weeks. Shop pays shipping from shop and insurance. Best buying and selling time: fall. Customers are college students and faculty.

LEVERETT CRAFTSMEN & ARTISTS INC., Montague Rd., Leverett MA 01054. (413)549-6871. Salesroom Manager: Cathy Abrams. Craft shop and museum gallery; also rents studio space for classes/workshops. Estab. 1966. Represents 80-90 craftworkers, most living within a 40-mile radius. Price range: 75c-$500; bestsellers: $4.50-140. Works on consignment; 30% commission. Retail price set by craftworker, with guidance of the salesroom manager when requested. Reports after "all work has passed our jury." Work may be shipped or hand-delivered; dealer pays insurance on exhibited work.
Acceptable Work: Considers batik; ceramics; dollmaking; glass art; jewelry; leatherworking; metalsmithing; needlecrafts; pottery; quilting; soft sculpture; wall hangings; weavings; and woodcrafting. All styles; utilitarian and/or decorative.
Profile: "Salesrooms have a gallery flavor. As a nonprofit, educational organization, salesrooms are also exhibition spaces. Special monthly exhibits are in a separate gallery." Juries held 6 times per year. Best selling time: August-December. "People who buy things are aged 30-55, professional or university, with an income of over $20,000. Art lovers, with less income, also purchase select items for themselves."

LITTLETON GALLERY, Box 202, 225 Great Rd., Littleton MA 01460. (617)486-4969. Co-owner: Evalyn Wood. Gallery, craft and gift shop, and rental gallery. Estab. 1973. Represents 200 craftworkers and artists. Price range: $5-300; bestsellers: $10-25. Works on consignment and buys outright; 33% commission. Retail price set by joint agreement. Requires exclusive area representation. Reports in 1 week; "we have a jury system consisting of 3 partners and we all decide." Work may be shipped or hand-delivered.
Acceptable Work: Considers batik; candlemaking; clothing; decoupage; glass art; jewelry; leatherworking; needlecrafts; pottery; quilting; soft sculpture; wall hangings; weavings; cards; and woodcrafting. Fine one-of-a-kind pieces; utilitarian and/or decorative.
Profile: Has featured artist showings and conducts craft classes. "Items are displayed at our discretion for 3 months or longer after the show." Heaviest wholesale buying time: summer; best selling time: Christmas. Customers are primarily women, "young homemakers, secretaries, professional people."

LONDON VENTURERS CO., 2 Dock Sq., Rockport MA 01966. (617)546-7161. Owner: J. Manera. Gallery. Estab. 1968. Represents 12 craftworkers. Considers glass art; jewelry; wall hangings; and weavings. Fine one-of-a-kind pieces only; utilitarian and/or decorative. Price range: $1-2,000; bestsellers: $10-200. Works on consignment and buys outright; 40% commission. Retail price set by gallery. Requires exclusive area representation. Reports in 2 weeks. Craftworker pays insurance on exhibited work.
Profile: Best selling and heaviest wholesale buying time: summer. Customers are "30-40 years old, married and in the $20,000+ income bracket. They buy crafts for their artistic value."

MASSACHUSETTS AUDUBON SOCIETY GIFT SHOP, S. Great Rd., Lincoln MA 01773. (617)259-9500. Manager/Buyer: Mrs. George K. Lewis. Nonprofit organization gift shop. Estab. 1960. Price range: 50c-$750; bestsellers: $2.50-100. Works occasionally on consignment, but mostly buys outright. Retail price set by joint agreement. Requires exclusive area representation. Work may be shipped or hand-delivered.
Acceptable Work: Considers batik; ceramics; decoupage; glass art; jewelry; metalsmithing; pottery; wall hangings; and weavings. "All crafts must, in some way, be nature-oriented." All styles; utilitarian and/or decorative.
Profile: "We're located in a solar experiment building, which attracts great attention. Also, we've developed a wide reputation for exceptional crafts." Heaviest wholesale buying time: early spring-early fall; best selling time: April-June, September-December. 'Most customers are environmentally aware."

MacIVOR REDDIE GALLERY, Art Institute of Boston, 700 Beacon St., Boston MA 02215. (617)262-1223. Gallery Committee Member: Sissy Willis. College gallery. Estab. 1912. Represents 1-6 craftworkers. Price range: $10-2,500; bestsellers: $10-250. Works on consignment; no commission. Retail price set by craftworker. Reports in 4 weeks. Work should be hand-delivered; dealer pays insurance on exhibited work.
Acceptable Work: Considers batik; candlemaking; ceramics; clothing; decoupage; dollmaking;

glass art; jewelry; leatherworking; metalsmithing; needlecrafts; pottery; quilting; soft sculpture; tole painting; wall hangings; weavings; and woodcrafting. Fine one-of-a-kind and handmade production-line items; utilitarian and/or decorative.

Profile: Nonprofit gallery with free admission, "exhibiting virtually every form of visual art expression. Shows run for a month, and are both group and individual showings." Best selling time: winter of the academic year.

MUSEUM OF AFRO AMERICAN HISTORY, Dudley Station, Box 5, Boston MA 02119. (617)445-7400 or 723-8863. President: Byron Rushing. Museum gallery and gift shop. Estab. 1967. Represents African and Afro American craftworkers with an emphasis upon New England, South Carolina, Georgia, Louisiana, Haiti and Ethiopian sources. Price range: 50c-$150; bestsellers: 50c-$25. Works on consignment and buys outright; 50% commission. Retail price set by gallery. Requires exclusive area representation. Reports in 3 weeks. Work may be shipped or hand-delivered; museum pays insurance on exhibited work.

Acceptable Work: Considers dollmaking; quilting; soft sculpture; wall hangings; weavings; basketry; and woodcrafting. Primitive and fine one-of-a-kind pieces; utilitarian. "We specialize in Afro American crafts that have some connection with the year-round history exhibit program."

Profile: Crafts displayed in gallery atmosphere. Showing times vary from 1-12 months. Heaviest wholesale buying time: fall; best selling time: winter, May and June. Customers come from all races; lower and middle income.

PADDLEWICKER, 17 Church St., Lenox MA 01240. (413)637-3179. Contact: Joni Frankel. Craft shop and gallery. Estab. 1971. Represents Berkshire area craftworkers, "although we will consider craftworkers from Massachusetts proper, New York, New Hampshire and Vermont if they have quality items." Price range: $3-100; bestsellers: $3-26. Works on consignment and buys outright; 30-40% commission. Retail price set by joint agreement. Requires exclusive area representation. Reports in 4 weeks. Work may be shipped or hand-delivered.

Acceptable Work: Considers batik cards; candlemaking; ceramics; dollmaking; glass art; jewelry; needlecrafts; pottery; quilting; soft sculpture; wall hangings; weavings; woodcrafting; paintings; and sculpture. Fine one-of-a-kind and handmade production-line items; utilitarian and/or decorative.

Profile: Crafts are displayed on shelves or behind glass, possibly in a special exhibit. Crafts are shown for a maximum of 3 months. "We concentrate on work by local artisans, emphasizing quality items at a reasonable price." Heaviest wholesale buying time: spring; best selling time: summer. Customers are "both locals and New York tourists, anywhere in the $12,000-25,000+ income bracket."

PERCEPTIONS, INC., 75 Main St., Concord MA 01742. (617)369-6797. Craft shop and gallery. Estab. 1972. Represents 150 craftworkers. Price range: $1-1,200; bestsellers: $1-200. Works on consignment and buys outright; 33⅓% commission. Retail price set by craftworker. Requires exclusive area representation. Reports in 2 weeks. Work may be shipped or hand-delivered; dealer pays insurance on exhibited work.

Acceptable Work: Considers batik; ceramics; clothing; glass art; jewelry; leatherworking; metalsmithing; pottery; soft sculpture; wall hangings; weavings; woodcrafting; and prints. "We're always interested in seeing new designs in all categories, particularly weavings and jewelry." Fine one-of-a-kind and handmade production-line items; uilitarian and/or decorative.

Profile: "Each piece is given plenty of space, rotating as possible. We're unique because there is no other contemporary craft shop in this area." Heaviest wholesale buying time: "we order at major craft fairs"; best selling time: Christmas. Customers are "liberal, affluent and relatively young."

PETERSHAM CRAFT CENTER & CRAFT SHOP, Rt. 32, Petersham MA 07366. (617)724-3275. Shop Chairman: Hope W. Streeter. Gallery, craft and gift shop. Estab. 1954. Represents 40+ craftworkers. Price range: 50c-$350; bestsellers: $1-25. Works on consignment and buys outright; 25% commission. Retail price set by joint agreement. Reports in 2 weeks. Work may be shipped or hand-delivered.

Acceptable Work: Considers ceramics; clothing; decoupage; dollmaking; jewelry; needlecrafts; pottery; quilting; wall hangings; weavings; and woodcrafting. Especially needs "interesting toys; woven placemats; clothing; and useful pottery." Primitive and fine one-of-a-kind pieces; utilitarian and/or decorative.

Profile: Crafts are displayed for 6 months, then returned if not sold. Shop is run by volunteers, who also conduct arts and crafts classes. Best selling time: summer and fall.

POOR RICHARD'S GALLERY, 77 Rocky Neck Ave., East Gloucester MA 01930. (617)283-6861. Contact: Richard or Nancy Korb. Considers batik; glass art; metalsmithing; mobiles; pottery; and sculpture. Maximum size: 2x3. Specializes "to some degree" in New England marine themes. Buys outright or works on consignment; 40% commission. Price range: $5-300. Craftworker sets retail price. Requires exclusive area representation. Send slides or photos of work. SASE. Gallery pays shipping from gallery and insurance on exhibited work. Work is exhibited from May 30-October 30.

QUITTACUS WORKSHOP ORIGINALS, 477 Bedford St., Lakeville MA 02346. (617)947-4172. President: Arthur. Treasurer: Maureen. Estab. 1972. Represents 12 craftworkers. Considers ceramics; glass art; jewelry; metalsmithing; pottery; and woodcrafting. Finished handmade production-line items; utilitarian and/or decorative. Price range: $5-75; bestsellers: $12-20. Buys outright. Shop sets retail price. Write. Reports in 2 weeks. Dealer pays shipping. Best selling time: fall; heaviest wholesale buying time: spring and summer.

THE SNEAK BOX STUDIO, Box 55, Concord MA 01742. (617)369-8312. Contact: Charles F. Murphy. Represents 10 craftworkers. Considers decoys and bird carvings, but may accept any medium if subject pertains to wildfowl or birds. Finished one-of-a-kind and handmade production-line items; utilitarian and/or decorative. Price range: $1-1,000; bestsellers: $20-500. Buys outright or on consignment. Craftworker sets his price and studio then sets retail price. Requires exclusive area representation. Write or query with transparencies or color photos. Reports in 1 week.
Profile: Consigns items for 12 weeks minimum. All items displayed and many photographed and added to mail order literature. Customers are mostly collectors.

SOUTHERN BERKSHIRE LEATHER WORKS, 9 Railroad St., Great Barrington MA 01230. (413)528-4884. Contact: Steven Cline. Craft shop. Estab. 1973. Represents 12 craftworkers. Price range: $1.50-200; bestsellers: $1.50-45. Buys outright. Retail price set by joint agreement. Requires exclusive area representation. Reports in 2 weeks. Work may be shipped or hand-delivered. Dealer pays shipping to shop. Displays work indefinitely.
Acceptable Work: Considers jewelry; leatherworking; metalsmithing; and woodcrafting. Finished, one-of-a-kind and handmade production-line items; utilitarian and/or decorative.
Profile: "The interior is made of 100-150 year old barn wood, unusually and expertly designed and constructed. The way it offsets craftwork is very successful." Best selling and heaviest wholesale buying time: summer and pre-Christmas.

THE SPECTRUM OF AMERICAN ARTISTS AND CRAFTSMEN, INC., 369 Old King's Hwy., Brewster MA 02631. (617)385-3322. President: Addison H. Pratt Jr. Craft shop/gallery. Estab. 1966. Represents 225 craftworkers and artists. Price range: 75c-$1,500. Works on consignment and buys outright; commission varies. Retail price set by joint agreement on consigned items. Reports in 2 weeks. No work should be sent without prior agreement.
Acceptable Work: Considers batik; candlemaking; ceramics; dollmaking; glass art; jewelry; leatherworking; metalsmithing; needlecrafts; pottery; soft sculpture; wall hangings; weavings; and woodcrafting. Fine one-of-a-kind and handmade production-line items; utilitarian and/or decorative.
Profile: "Crafts receive prominent display in a spacious atmosphere." Heaviest wholesale buying time: "early in the year"; best selling time: summer. Customers are primarily tourists.
Sales Tip: "An appointment to show your work is absolutely necessary. Early in the year is the best time. We do not view work during the height of our season."

THE SPECTRUM OF AMERICAN ARTISTS AND CRAFTSMEN, INC., 433 Main St., Hyannis MA 02601. See above.

STORROWTON VILLAGE MUSEUM, 1305 Memorial Ave., West Springfield MA 01089. (413)736-0632. Director: June Cook. Museum gift shop. Estab. 1970. Represents 10-25 craftworkers. Price range: 50c-$100; bestsellers: 50c-$30. Works on consignment and buys outright; 35% commission. Retail price set by craftworker; however, advisory board juries all articles for price and appropriateness. For special events, charges $5/64 square feet for exhibit space. Reports in 4 weeks. Work may be shipped or hand-delivered.
Acceptable Work: Considers candlemaking; ceramics; clothing; dollmaking; glass art; jewelry; leatherworking; metalsmithing; needlecrafts; pottery; quilting; tole painting; and woodcrafting. All crafts must be early American orientation; "no plastic." Especially needs blown glass, tin and pottery in the $5-10 price range. All styles; utilitarian and/or decorative.

Profile: Located in a colonial village shopping area. Display is "in the old-style village motif." Displays work 30 days. Heaviest wholesale buying and best selling time: summer.

SUTTER'S MILL, 233 Main St., Northampton MA 01060. (413)586-1470. Owner: John Sutter. Craft and gift shop. Estab. 1968. Represents 20 craftworkers. Considers ceramics; glass art; jewelry; pottery; and woodcrafting. Specializes in custom-designed jewelry and settings. Fine one-of-a-kind and handmade production-line items; utilitarian and/or decorative. Price range: $5-1,500. Buys work outright. Retail price set by joint agreement. Requires exclusive area representation. Reports in 2 weeks. Work may be shipped or hand-delivered; dealer pays insurance on exhibited work. Best selling time: Christmas.

VLADA, Box 721, Stockbridge MA 01262. (413)298-3656. Contact: Vlada. Craft and gift shop. Estab. 1970. Represents 20 craftworkers. Price range: $2.50-250. Works on consignment; 33⅓% commission. Retail price set by joint agreement. Work may be shipped or hand-delivered, if a prior agreement has been made.
Acceptable Work: Considers batik; weaving; candlemaking; clothing; jewelry; leatherworking; pottery; and soft sculpture ("will take other things if they appeal"). Especially needs "interesting and well-made summer dresses, tops and skirts." Fine one-of-a-kind and handmade production-line items; utilitarian and/or decorative.
Profile: "We're a small shop dealing in unusual and well-made clothes, accessories and crafts. Display time agreed upon receipt of crafts." Heaviest wholesale buying time: spring-early summer; best selling time: summer and pre-Christmas. Customers are a "wide range of tourists and local people who come to New England's summer 'cultural' area."

WISTARIAHURST MUSEUM, 238 Cabot St., Holyoke MA 01040. (413)536-6771. Director: Marie Quirk. Museum gallery. Represents 4 craftworkers. Exhibition mainly, although items may be priced for sale. Retail price set by craftworker. Does not charge for exhibit space, but a donation is desired. Reports in 3 weeks. "For exhibition, items must be seen to ascertain the standards needed for museum display." Museum pays insurance on exhibited items.
Acceptable Work: Considers batik; ceramics; dollmaking; glass art; metalsmithing; pottery; quilting; paintings; prints; and textiles. "We're always interested in scheduling a craft exhibit of quality, well-designed pieces." Fine one-of-a-kind items; utilitarian and/or decorative.
Profile: "Items appropriate for hanging are hung in the gallery. Small items are shown in locked cases. Other large items are exhibited on standards and tables." Best selling time: summer, fall and Christmas. "The gallery is located in a Victorian mansion on an estate, and the architectural features attract much attention. Many groups schedule meetings and special programs at the museum, and many ethnic groups also participate in exhibits and programs."

WOMENCRAFTS INC., Box 190, Provincetown MA 02651. Contact: A.E. Picoff or V. Walker. Craft and gift shop. Estab. 1976. Represents 150 women craftworkers. Price range: 50c-$500; bestsellers: $1-30. Works on consignment and buys outright; 40% commission. Retail price set by joint agreement. Requires exclusive area representation. Work may be shipped or hand-delivered; dealer pays insurance on exhibited work.
Acceptable Work: Considers batik; candlemaking; ceramics; clothing; decoupage; dollmaking; glass art; jewelry; leatherworking; metalsmithing; needlecrafts; pottery; quilting; soft sculpture; wall hangings; weavings; woodcrafting; and silkscreened t-shirts. Especially needs items that retail under $10. All styles; utilitarian and/or decorative.
Profile: Heaviest wholesale buying time: spring and summer; best selling time: summer. Customers are primarily tourists and feminists.

WONDERFUL THINGS INC., 232 Stockbridge Rd., Great Barrington MA 01230. (413)528-2473. President: William Tanguay. Gallery, craft and gift shop. Estab. 1973. Represents 300+ craftworkers, "most are, naturally, from the Northeast because of the fairs we visit." Price range 1c-$500; bestsellers: $5-150. Works on consignment and buys outright; 25-35% commission. Retail price set by joint agreement. Reports in 4 weeks maximum. Work may be shipped or hand-delivered if prior agreement has been made. Dealer pays insurance on exhibited work.
Acceptable Work: Considers batik; candlemaking; ceramics; clothing; miniatures; decoupage; dollmaking; glass art; jewelry; leatherworking; metalsmithing; needlecrafts; pottery; quilting; soft sculpture; tole painting; wall hangings; weavings; and woodcrafting. All styles; utilitarian and/or decorative.
Profile: "We're a total craft center, selling everything from supplies to finished crafts. There are 7 rooms for living, 8 rooms for working and 10 rooms for selling 30,000+ items— we're really like 6 shops in one 8,000-foot location." Best selling time: July-December. "We're growing at a rate of 25% yearly because we appeal to anyone with an interest in or appreciation of crafts."

WORCESTER ART MUSEUM, 55 Salisbury St., Worcester MA 01608. Contact: Barbara Saltiel. Gift shop buys cards, crafts and jewelry outright.

Michigan

THE ART GLASS ALCOVE, 105 Butler St., Saugatuck MI 49453. (616)857-3431. Owner: Andrea Eming. Gift shop. Estab. 1972. Represents 35-40 craftworkers. Price range: 75c-$400; bestsellers: $3.50-25. Works on consignment and buys outright; 33⅓%commission. Retail price set by shop. Requires exclusive area representation. Reports in 2 weeks. Work may be shipped or hand-delivered.
Acceptable Work: Considers batik; candlemaking; ceramics; glass art; jewelry; leatherworking; metalsmithing; pottery; wall hangings; weavings; woodcrafting; prints; and cards. "I'd like to strengthen my metalsmithing area." Primitive handmade production-line items; utilitarian and/or decorative.
Profile: "Our shop is designed with virtually no poor display areas — our main shelving is pigeon-holed, so it lends itself to our creating special themes. We try to use as much of nature as possible: driftwood, rocks, crates, rope. We usually allow items to be displayed 3-4 weeks before changing them." Heaviest wholesale buying time: spring; best selling time: summer. "We're located in a resort town so we get all kinds of people, from the penniless student to the yacht owner. Primarily, though, we deal with vacationers with a set amount of money to spend."

ARTISANS GALLERY, 107 Howard, Petoskey MI 49770. (616)347-6466. Contact: Russell or Frances Secrest. Craft shop. Estab. 1970. Represents 100 craftworkers. Price range: $2-1,000; bestsellers: $2.50-50. Buys outright. Retail price set by joint agreement. Reports in 1 week. Work may be shipped or hand-delivered. Best selling time: summer. "Customers are moderately conservative."
Acceptable Work: Considers batik; candlemaking; ceramics; glass art; jewelry; leatherworking; metalsmithing; needlecrafts; pottery; soft sculpture; wall hangings; weavings; and woodcrafting. Fine one-of-a-kind and handmade production-line items; utilitarian only.

CLASSICAL GLASS, Liberty Plaza, Ann Arbor MI. Owners: Richard and Sandra Marks. See Marks Studio/Gallery, Tecumseh, Michigan.

THE CLAY GALLERY, Stone Village Art Center, 1701 Probert Rd., Jackson MI 49203. (517)789-7913. Director: Sandra Beaman. Gallery. Estab. 1977. Represents 10 craftworkers. Considers clay medium only: ceramics, sculpture and wall hangings. Fine one-of-a-kind and handmade production-line items; utilitarian and/or decorative. Bestsellers: $3-800. Works on consignment; 20% commission. Retail price set by joint agreement. Reports in 4 weeks; send slides, which will then be viewed by a jury. Work may be shipped or hand-delivered.
Profile: Each craftworker has his/her own display of 25-150 items. "We're a large gallery with a ceramic library for reference and slide lectures on participating craftworkers and their work." Best selling time: Christmas, spring and fall. Customers are "aged 20-40, middle to lower income, professional people with cultural interests."

CRANBROOK INSTITUTE OF SCIENCE, 500 Lone Pine Rd., Bloomfield Hills MI 48013. (313)645-3226. Bookshop Manager: Gloria B. Esau. Museum gift shop. Estab. 1931. Represents 1-2 craftworkers. Price range: $2.50-300; bestsellers: $1-20. Works on consignment and buys outright; commission negotiable. Retail price set by bookshop manager. Reports in 3 weeks. Work may be shipped or hand-delivered.
Acceptable Work: Considers jewelry; metalsmithing; needlecrafts; pottery; Eskimo sculpture; and porcupine quill baskets. Primitive and fine one-of-a-kind pieces; utilitarian and/or decorative. Especially needs natural history note paper; any crafts pertaining to science; and authentic American Indian material.
Profile: Nonprofit organization. Display time "depends on the material and how it is selling." Heaviest wholesale buying and best selling time: autumn and spring.

DETROIT ARTISTS MARKET, 1452 Randolph St., Detroit MI 48226. (313)962-0337. Gallery Manager: Margaret Conzelman. Gallery. Represents 175-200 craftworkers from the 60-mile radius of Detroit. Price range: $2-100; bestsellers: $5-45. Works on consignment; 25-30% commission. Work may be shipped or hand-delivered; however, work will not be shipped back, it must be claimed in person.
Acceptable Work: Considers batik; ceramics; jewelry; metalsmithing; soft sculpture; wall hangings; weavings; blown glass; woven pillows; placemats; skirts; stoles; scarves; and throws. Fine one-of-a-kind pieces; utilitarian and/or decorative.
Profile: "Established during the Depression, the shop is nonprofit and run by a board of direc-

tors. Its sole purpose is to give local artists and craftworkers a place to exhibit and sell their work." Best selling time: November-January. "Customers are primarily young business people, in their early 20's and 30's." Work is submitted to a jury; if accepted, it is shown on a rotating basis.

DISCOVERY, Saugatuck MI 49453. Contact: Peggy Boyce. Cooperative craft shop. Estab. 1972. Represents 6-8 local craftworkers. Price range: $2.50-250; bestsellers: $2.50-10. Takes some items on consignment; 35% commission. Retail price set by joint agreement. Work may be shipped or hand-delivered.
Acceptable Work: Considers batik; candlemaking; ceramics; clothing; dollmaking; glass art; jewelry; leatherworking; needlecrafts; pottery; wall hangings; weavings; and woodcrafting. Fine handmade production-line items; utilitarian and/or decorative.
Profile: "Everything must be handmade. Because of our coop arrangement, the customer has a chance to meet the artist. Items are displayed throughout the shop and moved frequently. If an item does not sell in one season, it can be held-over into the next if the craftworker desires." Best selling time: summer. Located in a resort area, where most customers are tourists.

HUGUETTE FISHER GALLERY INC., 752 Pine St., Muskegon MI 49440. (616)722-4773. President: Huguette Fisher. Gallery, gift shop and custom framing. Estab. 1974. Represents 20-25 craftworkers. Price range: $10-500; bestsellers: $10-150. Works on consignment and buys outright; 40% commission. Retail price set by joint agreement. Reports in 4 weeks. Work may be shipped or hand-delivered; dealer pays insurance on exhibited work.
Acceptable Work: Considers batik; ceramics; glass art; jewelry; soft sculpture; wall hangings; weavings; and woodcrafting. "Ceramic and raku should be used as sculptures for the home and wall reliefs." Primitive and fine one-of-a-kind pieces; decorative only.
Profile: "We're the only 'fine art' gallery in Muskegon. With our displays, we work out a theme several times a year." Heaviest wholesale buying time: fall and winter; best selling time: spring, summer and Christmas. "Our customers are middle to lower income, many are professionals; in addition, we do work with offices and buildings."

FRANKENMUTH HISTORICAL MUSEUM, 613 S. Main, Frankenmuth MI 48734. (517)652-9701. Director: Carl R. Hansen. Museum gift shop. Estab. 1973. Represents 6 craftworkers. Considers ceramics; jewelry; leatherworking; pottery; and woodcrafting. Primitive handmade production-line items; utilitarian. Price range: 75c-$100; bestsellers: 75c-$30. Works on consignment; 25% commission. Retail price set by joint agreement. Reports in 1 week. Work may be shipped or hand-delivered.
Profile: Indefinite display time. Heaviest wholesale buying time: spring-fall; best selling time: summer and fall.

GALLERIA INTERNAZIONALE, LTD., 1911 Wieneke Rd., Saginaw MI 48603. (517)799-1982. President: Luciana Weiss. Gallery. Estab. 1974. Represents 100+ craftworkers. Considers jewelry; pottery; soft sculpture; wall hangings; weavings; and woodcrafting. Primitive and fine one-of-a-kind pieces; utilitarian and/or decorative. Works on consignment and buys outright; 40% commission. Retail price set by joint agreement. Requires exclusive area representation. Reports in 4 weeks. Work may be shipped or hand-delivered. Work displayed for 3-month period.

THE GALLERY SHOP, 230 E. Fulton, Grand Rapids MI 49502. (616)459-9272. Craft Buyer: Mrs. R.E. Lee Gunning. Museum gift shop. Estab. 1962. Represents 50 craftworkers. Price range: $1-250; bestsellers: $10-35. Buys outright. Requires exclusive area representation. Reports in 2 weeks. Work may be shipped or hand-delivered; Grand Rapids Art Museum pays insurance on exhibited work.
Acceptable Work: Considers batik; candlemaking; ceramics; decoupage; dollmaking; glass art; jewelry; leatherworking; metalsmithing; needlecrafts; pottery; soft sculpture; wall hangings; weavings; and woodcrafting. All styles; utilitarian and/or decorative.
Profile: "We're a small shop, and we change arrangements frequently. We usually try to have all art types represented." Heaviest wholesale buying time: February-September; best selling time: September-December.

THE HOOT OWL, 10 W. Silver Lake Rd. N., Traverse City MI 49684. (616)947-9494. Contact: Helen Gould. Craft shop/gallery. Estab. 1967. Represents 12-15 craftworkers. Considers ceramics; dollmaking; glass art; jewelry; metalsmithing; pottery; wall hangings; weavings; and woodcrafting. All styles; utilitarian and/or decorative. Price range: $5-50; bestsellers: $8-25. Works on consignment and buys outright; 40% commission. Retail price set by joint agreement.

Requires exclusive area representation. Reports in 2 weeks. Dealer pays insurance for exhibited work.
Profile: "We are located in an old lakeside inn whose interior was designed by a former student and friend of Frank Lloyd Wright. We give time and thought to display. Fragile items may be placed out of reach of children but we do not restrict customer's handling items. Customers are mostly professional, middle class; many are involved with the National Music Camp at Interlochen 5 miles away." Heaviest wholesale buying time: spring, in some cases consignment in June. "We are a summer shop."

INDIAN HILLS TRADING CO., Indian Hills Reservation, Box 546, Petoskey MI 49770. (616)347-3789. Owner: Victor S. Kishigo. Trading post. Estab. 1970. Represents craftworkers from 50 North American Indian tribes. Considers all Indian arts, particularly pottery. Needs quill boxes; Black Ash bracelets; beadwork; woodcarvings; and featherwork. All styles; utilitarian and/or decorative. Price range: $3-3,700; bestsellers: $10-150. Buys outright, trades and works on consignment; 33% commission. Retail price set by shop. Reports in 1 week. Work may be shipped or hand-delivered; dealer pays insurance on exhibited consignment items.
Profile: "Indian Hills is owned and operated by a full-blooded Ottawa Indian. We not only sell the best quality Indian art, but also raw materials and craft supplies for the Indian craftworker. Catalog available for 50c." Heaviest wholesale buying time: late winter-early spring; best selling time: summer.

IRON COUNTY MUSEUM, Box 472, Caspian MI 49915. (906)265-2617. Curator: Marcia Bernhardt. Office Manager: Audrey Ridolphi. Museum gift shop. Estab. 1968. Represents 6-7 craftworkers on the average; during the Ferrous Frolics Festival, represents 25+. Works on consignment; 10% commission. Retail price set by craftworker. Charges $1 plus 10% commission for exhibit space during the Ferrous Frolics. Reports in 2 weeks. Work should be hand-delivered.
Acceptable Work: Considers candlemaking; decoupage; dollmaking; jewelry; metalsmithing; pottery; quilting; wall hangings; weavings; woodcrafting; and rosemaling. Wants pioneer crafts. "We'd like to develop a low-price range line of crafts — e.g., candles, old-fashioned cards, weavings, etc." Primitive one-of-a-kind pieces; utilitarian and/or decorative.
Profile: Crafts are displayed in glass cases. "Our principle business is our museum on pioneer life. It's located on a 5½ acre tract and consists of 9 buildings, most of which are circa 1890." Heaviest wholesale buying and best selling time: summer. Ferrous Frolics held the third weekend in July, preceded by a week long art show featuring 1 outstanding local artist. For the Frolics, tables are set up outdoors and artists sell their own work.

KALAMAZOO NATURE CENTER, 7000 N. Westnedge, Kalamazoo MI 49007. (616)381-1574. Shop Buyer: Janet Duffield. Museum gift shop. Estab. 1960. Represents 6 craftworkers. Price range: $1-50; bestsellers: $1-15. Works on consignment; 50% commission. Retail price set by joint agreement. Reports in 2 weeks. Work may be shipped or hand-delivered; dealer pays insurance on exhibited work.
Acceptable Work: Considers candlemaking; dollmaking; leatherworking; metalsmithing; needlecrafts; pottery; quilting; tole painting; wall hangings; weavings; woodcrafting; and homespun crafts. All work must be natural history, outdoor or environmentally oriented. Primitive one-of-a-kind and handmade production-line items; utilitarian and/or decorative.
Profile: Work shown in glass cases. Displays work 6 months. Heaviest wholesale buying and best selling time: fall, Christmas and spring. "Customers are families with a strong interest in the outdoors and the environment."

LAKEWINDS GALLERY, 405 Phoenix, South Haven MI 49090. Chairman: Steve French. Cooperative gallery. Estab. 1976. Represents 10 southwest Michigan craftworkers. Price range: $15-200; bestsellers: $15-100. Handles crafts of cooperative members only. Retail price set by craftworker. "Each member assumes an equal share of the rent."
Acceptable Work: Considers batik; ceramics; jewelry; needlecrafts; pottery; soft sculpture; wall hangings; weavings; paintings; and photographs. Fine one-of-a-kind pieces; utilitarian and/or decorative.
Profile: "Our shop is a cooperative gallery put together by and for area artists for the exhibition and sale of their work. Each member arranges their work in an agreeable manner amidst the other members' work, and is responsible for maintenance and rotation of stock." Best selling time: May-September and Christmas.

LEAVES 'N' WEAVES, 211 Washington, Grand Haven MI 49417. (616)846-4880. Owner: Nancy Vander Vere. Craft and gift shop. Estab. 1973. Represents 12 craftworkers. Price range: $5-100; bestsellers: $5-30. Works on consignment and buys outright; 33% commission. "We handle items on consignment first; then, if it sells, we buy outright." Retail price set by craftworker. Requires exclusive area representation. "Call before coming to shop." Reports in 1 week. Work may be shipped or hand-delivered; dealer pays insurance on exhibited work.

Acceptable Work: Considers candlemaking; glass art; needlecrafts; pottery; soft sculpture; wall hangings; weavings; woodcrafting; and macrame. Primitive and fine one-of-a-kind pieces; utilitarian and/or decorative.

Profile: "We have a large upstairs plant shop, and the handcrafted items are integrated there. There are also some handcrafted items on the first floor, which is a contemporary gift shop." Customers are age 20-50, professional people with "interests revolving around the outdoors and Lake Michigan."

LOOM ROOM GIFT SHOP, 5165 S. Shore Dr., Whitehall MI 49461. (616)894-8171. Owners: Cal and Alice Steele. Gift shop. Estab. 1946. Represents 3 craftworkers. Price range: $2-150; bestsellers: $3.98-15.98. Works on consignment and buys outright; 40% commission. Retail price set up joint agreement. Reports in 2 weeks. Work may be shipped ("UPS only") or hand-delivered; craftworker pays insurance on exhibited consignment work.

Acceptable Work: Considers candlemaking; ceramics; jewelry; wall hangings; weavings; and paintings. Needs all pottery; fruit and vegetable ceramics; men's jewelry; hand-loomed shawls, towels, rugs and macrame. All styles; utilitarian and/or decorative.

Profile: "Our displays are carefully thought out and clean, however items can be touched in our store. We took over the store in 1976, and we intend to help good artists and craftworkers who can give us quality, fair-priced articles." Heaviest wholesale buying time: spring; best selling time: summer. "Customers are primarily tourists — summer sunbells, fall hunters and winter lovers."

McKENDREE COLLABORATIVE, 1443 Wealthy SE, Grand Rapids MI 49506. (616)458-0267. Contact: Mona Erickson. Craft shop. Estab. 1974. Represents 4 craftworkers. Considers glass art; jewelry; leatherworking; and metalsmithing. Fine one-of-a-kind and handmade production-line items; utilitarian and/or decorative. Price range: $15-500; bestsellers: $15-60. Buys outright. Retail price set by craftworker. Reports in 2 weeks. Work may be shipped or hand-delivered.

Profile: "We have 900 square feet of display area; included are 6 antique showcases. We're unique in our area in providing handcrafted goods in a broad price range." Heaviest wholesale buying time: fall; best selling time: holidays.

MARKS STUDIO/GALLERY, 302 E. Chicago, Tecumseh MI 49286. (517)423-5858. Owners: Richard and Sandra Marks. Craft shop and gallery. Estab. 1972. Represents 8 Midwestern and East Coast craftworkers. Considers jewelry; metalsmithing; and glass art; especially glown and stained glass. Fine one-of-a-kind and handmade production-line items; utilitarian and/or decorative. Price range: $1-1,250; bestsellers: $10-200. Works on consignment and buys outright; 33⅓%commission. Retail price set by joint agreement. Requires exclusive area representation. Reports in 3 weeks. Work may be hand-delivered; dealer pays insurance on exhibited work.

Profile: "Our gallery is a working stained glass studio." Items displayed for 60 days. Heaviest wholesale buying time: fall; best selling time: fall and spring. "Our customers are very art aware."

MINIATURES BY ELNORA, 2301 N. 5th St., Niles MI 49120. (616)471-3844. Owner: Elsie Snyder. Miniature and toy shop. Estab. 1972. Represents 20+ craftworkers. Price range 20c-$300. Works on consignment and buys outright; 40% commission. Retail price set by joint agreement. Requires exclusive area representation. Reports in 1 week. Work may be shipped or hand-delivered; dealer pays insurance on exhibited work.

Acceptable Work: Considers various craft types in miniature — ceramics; decoupage; dollmaking; glass art; jewelry; leatherworking; needlecrafts; pottery; quilting; soft sculpture; tole painting; wall hangings; weavings; woodcrafting; paintings; and sculpture. All crafts should be dollhouse size, 1"-1' scale. Looking for art nouveau glass; porcelain; and silver work. All styles; utilitarian and/or decorative.

Profile: "Our shop is unique in that all items are scaled to dollhouses, except for the merchandise in the toy and doll room. We want to introduce original works as they become available, and to take these items to craft, miniature and doll shows." Best selling time: holidays and winter. "Many customers are collectors, with an income of $20,000+. We handle antique laces, ribbons and trims for miniature making and dolls. Because we handle so many supplies, this makes us interesting to both the crafter and the collector."

MURIEL ORIGINALS, 1047 Michigan Ave., Benzonia MI 49616. (616)882-7203. Owner: Murial Trapp. Interior decoration shop. Estab. 1948. Represents 4 craftworkers. Considers original jewelry and pottery. "We handle only our own pots." All styles; utiliarian and/or decorative. Price range: $1.50-250; bestsellers: $10-20. Works on consignment; 33% commission. Best selling time: summer.

PARK WEST GALLERIES, 24151 Telegraph, Southfield MI 48075. (313)354-2343. Contact: Dr. Albert Scaglione. Considers contemporary sculpture. Buys work outright. Prefers exclusive representation in area. Gallery pays insurance on exhibited work.

PONTIAC ART CENTER, 47 Williams St., Pontiac MI 48053. (313)333-7849. Executive Director: Ian R. Lyons. Art center, museum gallery and gift shop. Estab. 1964. Represents 35 craftworkers. Price range: 50c-$2,000; bestsellers: $35-150. Works on consignment; 25% commission. Retail price set by joint agreement. Reports in 2 weeks. Work may be shipped or hand-delivered; dealer pays insurance on exhibited work.
Acceptable Work: Considers ceramics; dollmaking; glass art; jewelry; metalsmithing; needlecrafts; pottery; soft sculpture; and tole painting. "No 'kitch,' only serious work." Primitive and fine one-of-a-kind pieces; utilitarian and/or decorative.
Profile: "We're the major art center for North Oakland County, so it's important that our crafts are the highest quality in both design and technique." Sponsors art and craft classes. Items are displayed in cases, and on counters, pedestals and walls. Display time ranges from 2-6 months. Heaviest wholesale buying time: fall; best selling time: Christmas.

REEDCRAFT WEAVERS, 153 N. Michigan, Beulah MI 49617. (616)882-5575. Contact: Lewis Small. Estab. 1940. Represents 5 craftworkers. Considers candlemaking; jewelry; needlecrafts; and wall hangings. Especially needs woven towels; napkins; and lunch cloths. Finished handmade production-line items only; utilitarian and/or decorative. Price range: 20c-$26; bestsellers: $1.35-26. Buys outright or on consignment; 50% commission. Shop sets retail price. Requires exclusive area representation. Write. Reports in 1 week.
Profile: Items shown in glass cases and hanging displays. Best selling time: summer; heaviest wholesale buying time: spring. Shop located in "barn"; daily handweaving demonstration. Customers are tourists with middle to upper incomes.

THE SIGN OF THE COPPER LANTERN, Box 899A, Royal Oak MI 48068. (313)545-7872. Owner: Peg Smith. Craft and gift shop. Estab. 1972. Represents 50-70 Michigan craftworkers. Price range: $1-500; bestsellers: $5-35. Works on consignment (33⅓% commission) and buys outright, (50%). Retail price set by joint agreement. Requires exclusive area representation. Reports in 3 weeks. Work may be shipped or hand-delivered, "but only if we have committed to purchase and agreed upon when and where delivery is to happen." Dealer pays shipping and insurance on exhibited work.
Acceptable Work: Considers most professional crafts, including batik; candlemaking; ceramics; glass art; jewelry; metalsmithing; pottery; wall hangings; and woodcrafting. Needs "good metal workers, especially in copper," and unusual toys. "We also encourage our craftworkers to devise kits, when it fits their discipline." All styles; utilitarian and/or decorative.
Profile: Owns 2 stores, a seasonal summer store on Main Street in Mackinaw City, Michigan, and a year-round store on Woodward in Berkley, Michigan. "We run our stores like gift shops. The commercial lines of little-known book publishers, small classic imported toys and the Rock Shop (Michigan minerals only) are the only other things we show besides Michigan art work." Uses gallery-type spotlighting plus general window and store displays. Maximum display time: 3 months. Heaviest wholesale buying time: spring and late summer; best selling time: summer in the Mackinaw store, October-December in the Berkley store. "Our greatest customer volume is women, age 25-50. Of all our customers 70% are from southeastern Michigan, 20% from the balance of the state, and 10% are regular customers from throughout the US."

SUNFLOWER SHOP, 116 E. Main, Northville MI 48167. (313)349-1425. Owner: Marie Bonamici. Gallery and gift shop. Estab. 1970. Represents 6-8 professional craftworkers. Considers jewelry; pottery; wall hangings; weavings; and prints. All styles; utilitarian and/or decorative. Price range: $2-495; bestsellers: $20-150. Works on consignment and buys outright; 33⅓% commission. Retail price set by shop. Requires exclusive area representation. Reports in 3 weeks. Hand-delivered work only. Dealer pays insurance on exhibited work.
Profile: Heaviest wholesale buying time: August-September; best selling time: November-December. Customers are middle to upper income with an interest in art. "We deal with many professional people and collectors."

Minnesota

BROOKLYN CENTER COMMUNITY CENTER, 6301 Shingle Creek Pkwy., Brooklyn Center MN 55430. (612)561-5448. Contact: Kathy Flesher. "Our small gallery is available without charge to local artists/craftsmen. It is a small portion of a complete community center operation. We would be interested in showing traveling shows." Craftworkers sets retail price. Call or write. 2 weeks exposure.

THE CANDLING MILL, 400 Sibley St., St. Paul MN 55101. (612)226-9891. President: Sherry Castvold. Gift and speciality shop. Estab. 1972. Represents 4 craftworkers. Considers only candlemaking and candle-related crafts. One-of-a-kind and handmade production-line items; utilitiarian and/or decorative. Price range: $1-65; bestsellers: $10-25. Works on consignment and buys outright. Retail price set by joint agreement. Requires limited area representation. Reports in 1-2 weeks. Dealer pays return shipping and insurance for exhibited work. Best selling time: Christmas.

ENDION STATION, 208½ W. Superior, Duluth MN 55802. (218)727-3534. Owners: Michael and Patricia Spencer. Craft shop and gallery. Estab. 1971. Represents 20 craftworkers. Price range: $1-200; bestsellers: $1-50. Works on consignment and buys outright; 30% commission. Retail price set by joint agreement. Reports in 2 weeks. Work may be shipped or hand-delivered. Dealer pays insurance on exhibited work.
Acceptable Work: Considers batik; ceramics; glass art; jewelry; leatherworking; pottery; quilting; soft sculpture; wall hangings; weavings; and woodcrafting. All styles; utilitarian and/or decorative.
Profile: Work is grouped by exhibitor. Heaviest wholesale buying time: September-October; best selling time: October-December. Customers are women age 12-45 with lower to upper-middle income; they buy crafts for their usefulness and for gifts.

THE HONEYCOMB, Rt. 2, Lewiston MN 55952. (507)523-3642. Contact: Mrs. Clifford Babcock. Estab. 1973. Represents 50 craftworkers. Considers candlemaking; ceramics; decoupage; dollmaking; glass art; jewelry; needlecrafts; quilting; wall hangings; weavings; and woodcrafting. Finished, one-of-a-kind and handmade production-line items OK; utilitarian and/or decorative. Price range: $1-50; bestsellers: $2-10. Works on consignment. Shops sets retail price. Write. Reports in 1 week. Dealer pays insurance for exhibited work. Best selling time: pre-Christmas season and summer. Customers are ages 30-50 with middle incomes.

KALICO KORNER, 101 S. Broadway, Box 94, Alden MN 56009. (501)874-3458. President: Lucy Stiehl. Treasurer: Shirley Phinney. Secretary: Lois Hemmingsen. Craft and gift shop. Estab. 1974. Represents 100-150 craftworkers. Price range: $1.50-50; besetllers: $2.50-25. Works on consignment. "Craftworker sets his price; we add 30%. He always gets the amount he sets. He should keep in mind ours is added so item isn't over-priced." Reports in 3 weeks. Work may be shipped or hand-delivered.
Acceptable Work: Considers candlemaking; ceramics; children's clothing; decoupage; dollmaking; jewelry; needlecrafts; pottery; quilting; soft sculpture; tole painting; wall hangings; weavings; and woodcrafting. Especially needs moderately priced holiday items; handmade toys; and ceramics. Primitive handmade production-line items; utilitarian and/or decorative.
Profile: "We have an ideal location in a small town atmosphere. Crafts are displayed with antiques, with better pieces kept under glass." Best selling time: fall-winter. Customers are both tourists and residents of the surrounding rural area.

LUMBERTOWN USA, Box 387, Brainered MN 56401. President: Peg Madden. Restoration town. Estab. 1954. Represents 3 craftworkers practicing Midwestern crafts of the 1870's. Considers clothing; glass art; quilting; and woodcrafting. Primitive one-of-a-kind and handmade production-line items; utilitarian and/or decorative. Price range: 25c-$150. Works on consignment; 40% commission. Retail price set by joint agreement. Work may be shipped or hand-delivered; craftworker pays insurance on exhibited work.
Profile: "Lumbertown USA is a genuine restoration and replica of an 1870 lumbertown." Season runs May 25-September 15. Customers are older tourists with middle incomes.

MAD MONEY BOUTIQUE, c/o Sun Bay, Moose Lake MN 55767. (218)485-4958. Owner: Sheri Sundby. Craft shop and gallery. Estab. 1973. Price range: $2-275; bestsellers: $4-30. Works on consignment and buys outright; 33⅓% commission. Retail price set by joint agreement. Reports in 2 weeks. Work may be shipped or hand-delivered. Dealer pays insurance on exhibited work.
Acceptable Work: Considers ceramics; clothing; dollmaking; jewelry; leatherworking;

metalsmithing; pottery; soft sculpture; tole painting; wall hangings; weavings; and woodcrafting. Fine one-of-a-kind and handmade production-line items; utilitarian and/or decorative.

Profile: "This shop is in northern Minnesota, a very unusual area. Our purpose is to present well-designed crafts and fine arts. The reaction over the years has been continuously supportive and complimentary, and the customers always comment on the unique visual treatment of the merchandise." Heaviest wholesale buying time: spring and summer; best selling time: late spring, summer and fall. "Customers are generally tourists or summer residence dwellers; professors, naturalists, administrators. They're often repeat customers who bring their guests to share what they've found 'in the middle of nowhere.' "

MINNESOTA LANDSCAPE ARBORETUM GIFT SHOP, 3675 Arboretum Dr., Chaska MN 55318. (612)443-2460. Manager: Lenore Johnson. Gift shop. Estab. 1974. Represents 15 craftworkers. Price range: 50c-$200; bestsellers: $1-45. Works on consignment and buys outright; 40% commission. Retail price set by joint agreement. Reports in 1 week. Work should be hand-delivered for consideration. "Our system of ordering, payments and invoicing is sometimes a problem because it's regulated by the University of Minnesota and we must conform to their statutes."

Acceptable Work: Considers batik; ceramics; glass art; jewelry; leatherworking; metalsmithing; pottery; wall hangings; weavings; and woodcrafting. Fine one-of-a-kind and handmade production-line items; utilitarian and/or decorative.

Profile: "We handle only nature-related items and try to have pieces that can't be found in mainline gift shops or department stores." Work is hung on walls and displayed in cases. Heaviest wholesale buying and best selling time: summer and fall. "Customers are mostly people who are interested in gardening, plants, animals and nature. During the summer we get many one-time customers. Some of our best buyers are arboretum members."

NORMANDALE COLLEGE GALLERY, 9700 France Ave. S., Bloomington MN 55431. (612)831-5001. Contact: J. Jack Bean. Considers graphics; pottery; jewelry; weaving; and glass enameling. Retail price set by craftworker. Prices range: $15+. Send resume and slides or photos. Gallery pays shipping.

PLAINS ART MUSEUM, Box 37, Moorhead MN 56560. (218)236-7171. Director: James O'Rourke. Museum gallery. Estab. 1960. Represents 20 craftworkers. Price range: 50c-$200; bestsellers: 50c-$15. Works on consignment; 50% commission. Retail price set by joint agreement. Reports in 4 weeks. Work may be shipped or hand-delivered. Heaviest wholesale buying and best selling time: fall and winter.

Acceptable Work: Considers batik; ceramics; clothing; dollmaking; glass art; jewelry; leatherworking; metalsmithing; pottery; soft sculpture; wall hangings; weavings; and woodcrafting. Fine handmade production-line items; utilitarian and/or decorative.

SANDEEN'S SCANDINAVIAN GIFT AND ART SHOP, 1315 White Bear Ave., St. Paul MN 55106. (612)776-7012. Contact: Gail Sandeen. Gift shop. Estab. 1956. Price range: 59c-$385; bestsellers: $1-30. Buys outright. Shop sets retail price. Work may be shipped or hand-delivered.

Acceptable Work: Considers candlemaking; ceramics; clothing; dollmaking; glass art; jewelry; metalsmithing; needlecrafts; pottery; wall hangings; weavings; woodcrafting; rosemaling; and dalmalning. "We specialize in Scandinavian and European style crafts. We are always looking for unusual and well made unfinished woodenware items suitable for decoration by rosemaling or dalmalning. Always open for new lines of artwork or giftware which is Scandinavian." Heaviest wholesale buying and best selling time: September-December.

STONEFLOWER, 1694 Grand Ave., St. Paul MN 55105. (612)699-0535. President: Nan Bolstad. Craft shop and gallery. Estab. 1972. Represents 40 craftworkers. Price range: 50c-$350; bestsellers: $3.50-25. Works on consignment and buys outright; 40% commission. Retail price set by craftworker. Requires exclusive area representation. Reports "as soon as possible, if a SASE is enclosed." Work may be shipped or hand-delivered. Dealer pays insurance on exhibited work.

Acceptable Work: Considers batik; clothing; glass art; jewelry; pottery; wall hangings; weavings; woodcrafting; silkscreened cards and stationery. Fine one-of-a-kind and handmade production-line items; utilitarian only.

Profile: Work is shown on a wall display area and wooden shelves. Consigned items must be left 3 months minimum. Heaviest wholesale buying time: April, September and October; best selling time: October-December. Customers are age 19-35 from 4 surrounding colleges and a middle class, professional neighborhood. Most have double incomes, and buy crafts for gifts.

3 ROOMS UP, 4316 Upton Ave. S., Minneapolis MN 55410. (612)926-1774. Partner: Patricia Burrets. Craft shop and gallery. Estab. 1971. Represents 125 local craftworkers. Price range: $1-150; bestsellers: $1.50-40. Works on consignment; 34% commission. Retail price set by joint agreement. Queries are answered "immediately; works are juried every 2 weeks, after which time we report." Work may be shipped or hand-delivered.
Acceptable Work: Considers batik; dollmaking; glass art; jewelry; metalsmithing; pottery; soft sculpture; wall hangings; weavings; woodcrafting; graphics; embossings; prints; trapunto; and basketry. All styles; utilitarian and/or decorative.
Profile: "Our shop emphasizes quality craft/artwork at moderate prices. We have 4-5 shows/year, featuring 1 or more artists working in 1 medium. We're always looking for new things, well done, to show at reasonable prices." Works often grouped together by genre or color. All framed and finished pieces are hung. New items are displayed for a trial period of 3-6 months. Accepts consignments "at any time"; best selling time: fall-Christmas. Customers are primarily women, age 20-50, middle to upper-middle class.

TIDEPOOL GALLERY, 3907 W. 50th St., Edina MN 55424. (612)926-1351. Manager: Bayle Greenberg. Gift shop. Estab. 1973. Represents 12-15 craftworkers. Price range: $2-135; bestsellers: $5-50. Works on consignment and buys outright; 33⅓% commission. Retail price set by joint agreement. Reports in 1 week. Work may be shipped or hand-delivered; dealer pays insurance on exhibited work.
Acceptable Work: Considers batik; candlemaking; ceramics; glass art; jewelry; metalsmithing; needlecrafts; pottery; soft sculpture; wall hangings; weavings; woodcrafting; wind chimes; pictures; flower arrangements; boxes; mirrors; and sand paintings. All crafts must relate to the ocean, and preferably made from shell, coral, driftwood or sand. Fine one-of-a-kind and hand-made production-line items; utilitarian and/or decorative.
Profile: "We deal exclusively in seashells, coral and sea-inspired crafts. We're the only shop of this kind in the upper Midwest; we're a branch of Tidepool Gallery, Malibu, California. Depending on the item, work is shown on center aisle tables, rough-hewn shelves or on the walls. Displays are changed every 2-3 weeks. Heaviest wholesale buying time: fall-Christmas; best selling time: fall-Christmas and April-June.

UP NORTH HANDCRAFTS/LADY SLIPPER DESIGNS, 314 Houston Ave., Crookston MN 56716. (218)281-3720. Shop Manager: Lisa Schumacher. Gallery, wholesale handcraft distributor and craft/gift shop. Estab. 1973. Represents 150 rural Minnesota craftworkers. Price range: $1-200; bestsellers: $1-25. Buys outright; 30% commission on gallery sales. Retail price set by craftworker. Reports in 6 weeks. Work may be shipped or hand-delivered. Insurance by arrangement.
Acceptable Work: Considers batik; ceramics; dollmaking; glass art; jewelry; leatherworking; metalsmithing; needlecrafts; pottery; quilting; soft sculpture; tole painting; wall hangings; weavings; and woodcrafting. "We always need $5 and under items." All styles; utilitarian and/or decorative.
Profile: "In the gallery, exhibits last 2-3 weeks; may be 1 artist or a group show." Heaviest buying time: spring for retail store; spring, summer and early fall for wholesaling. Best selling time: summer for retail; fall for wholesale. "Our wholesale accounts vary from large department stores to small gift shops — accounts are scattered all over the country." Retail shop customers are primarily visitors to Itasca State Park.

WINDSOR GALLERY, 5019 France Ave. S., Minneapolis MN 55410. (612)927-6041. Owner: S.J. Long. Gallery. Estab. 1961. Represents 3 craftworkers. Considers batik; soft sculpture; wall hangings; and weavings. Fine one-of-a-kind and handmade production-line items; decorative. Price range: $10-300; bestsellers: $10-100. Works on consignment; 33% commission. Retail price set by craftworker. Requires exclusive area representation. Reports in 2 weeks. Work may be shipped or hand-delivered; dealer pays insurance on exhibited work.
Profile: Work is displayed for 3 weeks minimum. Best selling time: fall-winter. Customers are age 25-50, upper income.

THE WINONA COUNTY HISTORICAL SOCIETY MUSEUM SHOP, 160 Johnson St., Winona MN 55987. (507)454-2723. Director: William D. Gernes. Craft and museum gift shop. Estab. 1976. Represents 60 craftworkers. "We have some responsibility to represent current trends, but more importantly we offer the traditional crafts of the Upper Mississippi Valley and the ethnic crafts of our area immigrant groups— Germans, Poles, Swedes, Norwegians and Luxemburgers." Price range: 35c-$150; bestsellers: 75c-$10. Works on consignment; 33⅓% commission. Retail price set by joint agreement. Requires exclusive area representation for craftworkers not from the immediate area. Reports in 3 weeks. Work may be shipped or hand-delivered.

Acceptable Work: Considers dollmaking; leatherworking; metalsmithing; needlecrafts; pottery; quilting; wall hangings; weavings; woodcrafting; wrought iron; stationery; ethnic Christmas ornaments; and rosemaling. Primitive handmade production-line items; utilitarian and/or decorative.

Profile: "We're the sole retailer of quality crafts in the city and are given added stability by our association with the Winona County Historical Society. Our shop sells traditional crafts exemplifying crafts' continuing role in the upper Midwest's development." Displays employ old-fashioned store fixtures, wicker baby buggies and steamer trunks. Maximum display time, 1 year. Customers are vacationers and gift buyers, income $15,000-30,000, with an interest in history and handicrafts.

Mississippi

COTTONLANDIA FOUNDATION, Box 1635, Greenwood MS 38930. (601)453-0925. Contact: Peggy H. McCormick. Gallery/museum gift shop. Estab. 1969. Price range: $1 and up. Buys outright. Retail price set by joint agreement. Reports in 1 week. Work may be shipped or hand-delivered.

Acceptable Work: Considers batik; ceramics; glass art; jewelry; leatherworking; needlecrafts; pottery; quilting; wall hangings; and weavings. Primitive and fine one-of-a-kind pieces; utilitarian and/or decorative.

Profile: "Pictures are hung on rods and cams; 3D work in on tables and stands in gallery; shop display is informal on shelving. Shop features cotton-related items." Displays gallery work 8 weeks. Heaviest wholesale buying time: spring and fall; best selling time: summer and Christmas.

SERENDIPITY, 516 Linden St., Corinth MS 38834. (601)287-5173. Contact: Mary H. Kennedy or Margaret Mathis. Craft shop. Estab. 1976. Represents 140 craftworkers. Price range: $1-450; bestsellers: $5-125. Works on consignment; 30% commission. Craftworker sets retail price. Reports in 4 weeks. Dealer pays return shipping; in-transit insurance; and insurance for exhibited work.

Acceptable Work: Considers ceramics; decoupage; dollmaking; jewelry; needlecrafts; pottery; quilting; tole painting; woodcrafting; and religious books. "Special need for wood products; baby gifts; and kitchen items."

Profile: "The shop is in a lovely old home with appropriate items in each room." All ranges of customers. Heaviest wholesale buying time and best selling time: fall.

Located in a lovely old home in Corinth, Mississippi, Serendipity uses antiques and appropriate room settings to display ceramics, decoupage, dollmaking, jewelry, needlecrafts, pottery, quilting, tole painting, and woodcrafting. — Photo by Terry Wood Photography.

THE WHISTLE SHOP, Box 884, Ocean Springs MS 39564. Director: Willis White. Considers sculpture; jewelry; and metalsmithing. "The artist sets his price (from $2-2,500), and we increase it to provide a 33⅓% commission on sales." Payments made monthly. Material may be taken out at any time— no time requirements. Prefers, but does not require, exclusive representation.

WOODVILLE MUSEUM OF SOUTHERN DECORATIVE ARTS, Box 328, Woodville MS 39669. (601)888-6809. Contact: Ernesto Caldeira. Museum gift shop. Estab. 1976. Represents 10-50 craftworkers. Considers all crafts. All styles; utilitarian and/or decorative. Price range: 50c-$75; bestsellers: $1-5. Works on consignment; 25-50% commission. Craftworker sets retail price. Work may be shipped or hand-delivered. Museum pays insurance for exhibited work.
Profile: We are the "only museum shop in southwestern Mississippi; are located on the court house square". Heaviest wholesale buying time: early spring; best selling time: March-April and September-December.

Missouri

BARRY'S: A UNIQUE ALTERNATIVE, Hillbilly Junction Mall, Branson MO 65616. (417)334-0711. Director: Barry Oelschlaeger. Gallery, craft and gift shop. Estab. 1977. Represents 20 craftworkers. Price range: $25-500; bestsellers: $25-250. Works on consignment; 30% commission. Retail price set by joint agreement. Requires exclusive area representation. Reports in 3 weeks. Work may be shipped or hand-delivered; dealer pays insurance on exhibited work.
Acceptable Work: Considers batik; clothing; glass art; jewelry; metalsmithing; pottery; soft sculpture; wall hangings; weavings; and woodcrafting. All styles; utilitarian and/or decorative.
Profile: Work is displayed for as long as the dealer possesses it. Heaviest wholesale buying time: spring and summer; best selling time: spring, summer and fall. "Most customers earn $25,000+."

BITS & PIECES INC, 230½ Nichols Rd., Kansas City MO 64112. (816)561-7686. Owner: Jacqueline Schulz. Miniatures and dollhouse shop. Estab. 1971. Represents 35 craftworkers. Considers all types of miniatures. All styles; 1 inch scale. Price range: 25c-$3,000; bestsellers: $2-50. Buys outright. Retail price set by shop. Reports in 2 weeks. Work may be shipped or hand-delivered. Heaviest wholesale buying and best selling time: fall. "We build and furnish dollhouses and rooms on a 1 inch equals 1 foot scale."

CALIFORNIA CLOTHING, CO., 620 S. Main, St. Charles MO 63301. Owner: Stephanie Preninger. Shop for handmade and recycled clothing. Estab. 1975. Represents 10 craftworkers. Considers clothing and jewelry. "No macrame or leather." All styles; utilitarian and/or decorative. Price range: $1-50; best sellers: $5-20. Works on consignment; 25% commission. Retail price set by joint agreement. Reports in 2 weeks. Work may be shipped or hand-delivered.
Profile: "This shop is the only one of its kind in a tourist area of historical buildings and other attractions." Clothes must be appropriate to the season. Displays work 3 months. Best selling time: fall. Customers are "college girls, young working women and housewives, age 17-35. They're interested in flattering quality clothing rather than the bizarre."

CRAFT ALLIANCE GALLERY, 6640 Delmar Blvd., St. Louis MO 63130. (314)725-1151. Gallery Director: Dorothy Farley. Gallery. Estab. 1964. Represents 65 craftworkers. Price range: $2.50-3,000; bestsellers: $12-75. Works on consignment; 33⅓% commission. Only work by juried member artists is shown. Work is juried twice annually. Retail price set by craftworker. Reports in 1 week. Work may be shipped or hand-delivered; dealer pays insurance on exhibited work.
Acceptable Work: Considers batik; ceramics; clothing; glass art; jewelry; metalsmithing; stitchery; pottery; soft sculpture; wall hangings; enamels; weavings; and woodcrafting. "Work must represent contemporary American craft-art." Fine one-of-a-kind and handmade production-line items (limited edition); utilitarian and/or decorative.
Profile: Nonprofit gallery with standards and policies determined by member-artists. "Part of it is gallery-like, another part is shop-like in its displays." Best selling time: November-December. Customers are age 18-65.

CUSTOM HOUSE, 701 S. Main St., St. Charles MO 63301. (314)723-6433. Owner: Duane Thornton. Craft shop. Estab. 1971. Price range: $10-2,000; bestsellers: $100-700. Works on consignment; 30% commission. Retail price set by joint agreement. Requires exclusive area representation. Reports in 1 week. Initially, work should be hand-delivered.
Acceptable Work: Considers jewelry; quilting; woodcrafting; clocks; and custom built furniture. Primitive and fine one-of-a-kind pieces; utilitarian and/or decorative.

Profile: "Our shop features only handmade, original items and customers can also place order of their own design. Displays are constantly changing; if customer response is negative, items are removed, usually after 8 weeks." Heaviest wholesale buying time: June-October; best selling time: June-December.

FEATHER YOUR NEST, 324 N. Main St., Hannibal MO 63401. (314)248-0381. Owner: Carolyn L. Dickey. Craft shop and gallery. Estab. 1977. Represents 14 craftworkers. Price range: $4-120; bestsellers: $5-35. Works on consignment and buys outright; 30% commission. Retail price set by joint agreement. Requires exclusive area representation. Reports in 2 weeks. Work should be mailed or shipped.
Acceptable Work: Considers batik; candlemaking; ceramics; clothing; jewelry; leatherworking; metalsmithing; pottery; quilting; soft sculpture; wall hangings; weavings; woodcrafting; toys; and blown and stained glass. Fine one-of-a-kind and handmade production-line items; utilitarian and/or decorative.
Profile: "We prefer contemporarily designed crafts, although we do deal with some replica/traditional crafts. We feature specific craftworkers on a rotation basis, with a back-up of regular stock items. In this area, we're the only shop emphasizing contemporary crafts." Heaviest wholesale buying time: early spring and late fall; best selling time: summer and Christmas. Customers are "young professional family types, age 20-35, $12,000-50,000 annual income."

THE RALPH FOSTER MUSEUM, The School of the Ozarks, Point Lookout MO 65726. (417)334-6411. Director: Marvin E. Tong, Jr. Museum gallery/gift shop. Estab. 1933. Represents 6 craftworkers; Ozarks region of Missouri, Arkansas and Oklahoma craftworkers preferred. Price range: $3-100; bestsellers: $3-25. Buys outright. Retail price set by joint agreement. Rental gallery fee: $30/$100. Reports in 2 weeks. Work may be shipped or hand-delivered. Displays work 30 days maximum.
Acceptable Work: Considers ceramics; decoupage; dollmaking; jewelry; leatherworking; metalsmithing; needlecrafts; pottery; quilting; woodcrafting; and native Ozarks crafts. Especially needs inexpensive woodcarvings; metalwork; ceramics; jewelry; native Ozarks crafts such as baskets; split hickory chairs; ceramics; and cast iron. All styles; utilitarian and/or decorative.
Profile: "We are the only museum in the area that is a legitimate museum with no admission charge; 240,000 visitors in 1977. May through August visitors are young married couples interested in the Ozarks and its crafts. September to October visitors are older retired couples on tours of the Ozarks." Heaviest wholesale buying time: March-April; best selling time: May-October.
To Break In: "Visit buyer with selection of samples, have price list available and be able to supply on a regular basis."

THE GATHERING, 919 W. 44th St., Kansas City MO 64111. (816)931-9393. Contact: Carolyn Cameron or Willie Morgan. Gallery. Estab. 1976. Price range: $1.50-500; bestsellers: up to $100. Works on consignment; 40% commission. Query with slides; submit actual pieces if possible. SASE. Reports in 2 weeks. Dealer pays return shipping and insurance for exhibited work.
Acceptable Work: Considers ceramics; metal; wood; glass; and fiber (weaving, stitchery, paint on silk or fabric, batik, quilted/stuffed sculptural and wall pieces). "Special emphasis on fiber." Fine one-of-a-kind pieces; utilitarian and/or decorative.
Profile: "We are dealing with tomorrow's market in this area of the country. Seeking to improve the understanding of the artist/craftsman and to give exposure to those persons working in those fields."

THE GLASS WORKBENCH, INC., 515 S. Main St., St. Charles MO 63301. (314)723-3557. President: Joanne Bishop. Craft shop. Estab. 1975. Represents 4 craftworkers. Considers stained glass art. Fine one-of-a-kind and handmade production-line items; utilitarian and/or decorative. Price range: $2.50-500; bestsellers: $2.50-65. Buys outright.
Profile: "We primarily handle our own design items. Classes, kits and craft supplies are also available for the stained glass beginner." Heaviest wholesale buying time: fall; best selling time: Christmas.

GRANDMA'S FOLLY, 401 S. Main St., St. Charles MO 63301. (314)724-5656. Owner: C. Thompson. Children's gift shop. Estab. 1974. Represents 75 craftworkers. Price range: 50c-$125; bestsellers: $2.50-20. Works on consignment and buys outright; 40% commission. Retail price set by joint agreement. Requires exclusive representation within a 10 mile radius. Reports in 4 weeks. Work may be shipped or hand-delivered; dealer pays insurance on exhibited work and return shipping.

Acceptable Work: Considers clothing; dollmaking; needlecrafts; quilting; wall hangings; weavings; and woodcrafting — "anything to wear or play with related to children." Needs all types of clothing and toys. Fine one-of-a-kind and handmade production-line items; utilitarian and/or decorative.

Profile: "We specialize in items for special little people." Work displayed for 30 days; "longer, if it seems necessary." Heaviest wholesale buying time: fall; best selling time: October-November. Customers are mothers, grandmothers and young women.

HOBBY SHOP, 209 E. Main, Union MO 63084. (314)583-5251. Contact: Ervin J. Aholt. Craft shop. Represents 2 craftworkers. Price range: $1-25; bestsellers $3-10. Works on consignment; 20% commission. Retail price set by joint agreement. Reports in 1 week. Work may be shipped or hand-delivered. Displays work 30 days maximum. Best selling and heaviest wholesale buying time: fall.

Acceptable Work: Considers candlemaking; decoupage; dollmaking; jewelry; leatherworking; needlecrafts; tole painting; wall hangings; weavings; and woodcrafting. Fine one-of-a-kind pieces; utilitarian and/or decorative.

MISSOURI RIVER TRADING COMPANY, 719 S. Main, St. Charles MO 63301. (314)946-3167. Contact: Ron Stanley. Craft shop. Estab. 1977. Represents 2 craftworkers. Price range: $5-200; bestsellers: $5-50. Works on consignment and buys outright; 50% commission. Retail price set by joint agreement. Requires exclusive area representation. Reports in 1 week. Work may be shipped or hand-delivered. Dealer pays return shipping. Best selling time: summer.

Acceptable Work: Considers candlemaking and jewelry. Finished and handmade production-line items; utilitarian and/or decorative. Especially needs any item with a Western theme.

MORGIE'S, 524 S. Main St., St. Charles MO 63301. (314)723-3468. Manager: Morgie Felt. Craft and gift shop. Estab. 1977. Represents 40 craftworkers. Price range: 99c-$125; bestsellers: $1.99-60. Works on consignment and buys outright; 40% commission. Retail price set by joint agreement. Requires exclusive area representation. Work may be shipped or hand-delivered. Dealer pays insurance for exhibited work.

Acceptable Work: Considers ceramics; clothing; decoupage; dollmaking; glass art; jewelry; needlecrafts; pottery; quilting; soft sculpture; tole painting; wall hangings; weavings; metalworking and woodcrafting. Utilitarian and/or decorative.

Profile: "Items are shown in a casual grouping; some under glass. We are located in a courtyard by a gazebo overlooking the Missouri River. Customers are tourists and residents; interested in history." Best selling time: summer-Chirstmas.

MUSEUM OF ANTHROPOLOGY SALES DESK, UNIVERSITY OF MISSOURI-COLUMBIA, 104 Swallow Hall, University of Missouri, Columbia MO 65201. (314)882-3764. Director: Dr. Lawrence H. Feldman. Museum gift shop. Estab. 1973. Price range: 50c-$60; bestsellers: 50c-$20. Works on consignment and buys outright; commission varies. Gallery sets retail price. Reports in 1-2 weeks. Work may be shipped or hand-delivered. Dealer pays shipping to shop and insurance for exhibited work.

Acceptable Work: Considers ceramics; clothing; pottery; wall hangings; weavings; and woodcrafting. "We need items used around the home, among peasant cultures." One-of-a-kind and handmade production-line items; utilitarian.

Profile: "Items are put in a locked display case. Customers are college students with poverty level income and somewhat better-off University staff and occasional tourists." Best selling time: July-August and November-December.

THE NATURE LOFT, 624 S. Main, St. Charles MO 63301. (314)724-0809. Contact: Jack Swindle. Craft and gift shop. Estab. 1973. Represents 6 craftworkers. Price range: $1-200; bestsellers: $3-35. Works on consignment and buys outright; 40% commission. Retail price set by joint agreement. Reports in 2 weeks. Work may be shipped or hand-delivered. Dealer pays insurance for exhibited work. Heaviest wholesale buying time: spring and fall; best selling time: summer and winter.

Acceptable Work: Considers jewelry; leatherworking; pottery; and woodcrafting. Handmade production-line items; utilitarian and/or decorative.

OLD COUNTRY STORE AND MUSEUM, Rt. 1, Milo MO 64767. (417)876-6280. Contact: Mrs. John A. Logan. Craft museum gift shop. Estab. 1975. Represents local craftworkers. Price range: $1-300; bestsellers: $1-75. Works on consignment and buys outright; 25% commission. Retail price set by joint agreement. Hand-delivered work only.

Acceptable Work: Considers ceramics; dollmaking; metalsmithing; barn wood picture frames; dollhouses; dollhouse furniture; and miniatures. Fine one-of-a-kind and handmade production-line items; utilitarian and/or decorative.

Profile: "My store not only sells staple groceries and picnic items, but also used books, miniature 3-D scenes, dolls, doll cradles, doll beds, dollhouses, dollhouse furniture and miniatures. Everything but the books and groceries is made right here in the community and there is no other store nearby that does that." Heaviest wholesale buying time: April; best selling time: May-October.

OLD MILL CRAFTS, Rt. 1, Box 6, Augusta MO 63332. (314)228-4496. Contact: Betty Bade. Craft and antique shop. Estab. 1976. Represents 10 craftworkers. Considers all crafts. One-of-a-kind and handmade production-line items; utilitarian and/or decorative. Price range: 10c-$150; bestsellers: $1.50-50. Works on consignment; 30% commission. Craftworker sets retail price. Requires exclusive area representation. Work may be shipped or hand-delivered. "We are located in a barn that was once an old mill." Best selling time: fall.

ONE MANZ FAMILY ARTS AND CRAFTS, 918 Westwood Mini Mall, Caruthersville MO 63830. (314)333-1324. Contact: Charles Manz. Craft shop. Estab. 1977. Represents 10 craftworkers. Price range: 50c-$15; bestsellers: $2-8.50. Works on consignment; 20% commission. Retail price set by joint agreement. Reports in 4 weeks. Hand-delivered work only. Dealer pays insurance for exhibited work.

Acceptable Work: Considers batik; candlemaking; decoupage; dollmaking; jewelry; leatherworking; metalsmithing; needlecrafts; quilting; wall hangings; weavings; woodcrafting; and especially needs tole painting.

Profile: Craftworker may display work as long as he wants. Customers are "from 15-65; from lawyers to welfare." Best selling and heaviest wholesale buying time: Christmas.

QUILT COUNTRY, 13426 Clayton Rd., Masons Woods Village, St. Louis MO 63131. (816)238-1540. See below.

QUILT COUNTRY ENTERPRISES, INC., 616 Ward Pkwy., Kansas City MO 64112. (816)561-3311. President: Mary Alys Corcoran. Quilt shop. Estab. 1974. Represents 100 quilt craftworkers. Considers clothing, quilting and wall hangings; all quilted. All styles; utilitarian and/or decorative. Price range: $1-3,000; bestsellers: $100-500. Buys outright. Reports in 2 weeks. Dealer pays insurance for exhibited work.

Profile: "Quilt Country in Kansas City offers the largest selection of quilts for sale anywhere. Our calico fabric selection is also extensive and we have a complete line of supplies for the do-it-yourself person."

RAACH'S PLAZA GALLERY INC., 630 W. 50th, Kansas City MO 64112. (816)753-2047. President: F.A. Raach. Considers batik; ceramics; glass art; jewelry; mobiles; pottery; sculpture; soft sculpture; wall hangings; weavings; and woodcrafting. Price range: $10-10,000; bestsellers: $100-500. Works on consignment; 33⅓% commission. Gallery sets retail price. Requires exclusive area representation. Query with slides of work. SASE.

J. ROACH GALLERIES, 26 N. 9th St., Columbia MO 65201. (314)449-8717. Contact: Jay Roach. Craft shop/gallery/gift shop. Estab. 1974. Represents 90-100 craftworkers. Price range: $3.50-1,000; bestsellers: $10-400. Buys outright. Craftworker sets retail price. Requires exclusive area representation. Work may be shipped or hand-delivered. Dealer pays insurance for exhibited work.

Acceptable Work: Considers ceramics; glass art; jewelry; metalsmithing; pottery; wall hangings; and weavings. Especially needs "nice and well-priced mirrors with etched glass designs in corner or around border." Finished and handmade production-line items; utilitarian and/or decorative.

Profile: "There are 3 colleges here; customers are college students with some money; and housewives and working women 30-45 years old. We really like to have the arrangement with our craftspeople that whatever does not sell in a reasonable amount of time can be exchanged for credit or for other merchandise." Best selling time: December.

ST. CHARLES ARTISTS GUILD, 1535 First Capitol Dr., St. Charles MO 63301. President. Serena Boschert. Gallery. Estab. 1966. Represents 70 craftworkers. "We are a nonprofit organization; members set values on their work; 20% is donated to the guild." Price range: $1-

1,000; bestsellers: $1-100. Craftworker sets retail price. Membership fee: $18/year. Work may be shipped or hand-delivered.

Acceptable Work: Considers batik; ceramics; decoupage; pottery; soft sculpture; tole painting; wall hangings; and weavings.

Profile: "One room is set aside where any member can exhibit frequently. Two other rooms feature special shows and exhibits, usually on a monthly basis. Customers are tourists from all over US and town people interested in crafts and fine art for their home. Average customer will spend $10-25." Best selling time: summer and pre-Christmas.

MARTIN SCHWEIG GALLERY, 4657 Maryland Ave., St. Louis MO 63108. (314)361-3000. Director: Lauretta Schumacher. Gallery. Estab. 1950s. Exhibits work for 3 week periods.33⅓% commission. Retail price set by joint agreement. Reports as soon as possible. Hand-delivered work only.

Acceptable Work: Considers batik; ceramics; dollmaking; jewelry; pottery; soft sculpture; wall hangings; weavings; and woodcrafting. Primitive and fine one-of-a-kind pieces; utilitarian and/or decorative.

Profile: "No display cases are available; walls are used for hanging and pedestals are available. Media coverage is given." Best selling time: fall and spring.

SERMON-ANDERSON, INC., 10815 Winner Rd., Independence MO 64052. (816)252-9192. Buyers: P. Tomas and R.T. Sermon. Gallery/gift, furniture and design shop. Represents traditional craftworkers. Price range: $1-10,000; bestsellers: $5-200. 20-33% commission. Retail price set by joint agreement. Reports in 2 weeks. Work may be shipped or hand-delivered. Dealer pays insurance for exhibited work.

Acceptable Work: Considers batik; candlemaking; ceramics; clothing; decoupage; glass art; jewelry; metalsmithing; needlecrafts; pottery; quilting; wall hangings; weavings; and woodcrafting. All styles; utilitarian and/or decorative.

Profile: "We maintain 26 rooms of display; these are rooms complete as in home or office, with furniture, furnishings, accessories and backgrounds as well. We also have a country store where smaller, inexpensive items are displayed in proper atmosphere. We also have a courtyard opened seasonally." Heaviest wholesale buying time: fall; best selling time: all seasons except summer.

SILVER DOLLAR CITY, INC., Marvel Cave Park, MO 65616. (417)338-2611. Product Manager: John Switt. Theme park with crafts in several shops. Estab. 1960. Represents 200 craftworkers with crafts representing 1880 theme. Price range: 15c-$5,000. Buys outright. Shops set retail price. Reports in 2 weeks. Work may be shipped or hand-delivered. Heaviest wholesale buying time: November-March; best selling time: April-October.

Acceptable Work: Considers candlemaking; dollmaking; glass art; jewelry; leatherworking; metalsmithing; needlecrafts; pottery; wall hangings; weavings; and woodcrafting. Handmade production-line items; utilitarian and/or decorative.

THE STUFFED STOCKING, 616 S. Main St., St. Charles MO 63301. (314)946-7714. Director: Beverly Jean Klug. Craft shop/gallery. Estab. 1969. Represents over 500 craftworkers. Price range: 50c-$500. Works on consignment; 40% commission. Retail price set by joint agreement. Requires exclusive area representation. "Do not send samples; send nonreturnable photo." Reports once a month. Work may be shipped or hand-delivered.

Acceptable Work: Considers batik; decoupage; dollmaking; glass art; jewelry; leatherworking; metalsmithing; needlecrafts; pottery; quilting; soft sculpture; tole painting; wall hangings; weavings; and woodcrafting. Major emphasis on quilts. Finished, one-of-a-kind and handmade production-line items; utilitarian and/or decorative.

Profile: "The Stuffed Stocking is located in the only historical district in the St. Louis area. Some 30 shops, restaurants and galleries are located on a cobblestone street with gas lights and a park along the Missouri River. Customers are upper income women in the $30,000 bracket. The shop maintains a card index and does mailings." Heaviest wholesale buying time: July-December; best selling time: summer-Christmas.

THE UNUSUAL SHOP, Rt. 4, Box 176, Festus MO 63028. (314)937-0410. Contact: Judy Jackson. Gift shop. Estab. 1976. Represents 6-8 craftworkers. Price range: $1-150; bestsellers: $3-10. Works on consignment; 40% commission. Gallery sets retail price. Reports in 2 weeks. Work may be shipped or hand-delivered; "contact us before shipping." Dealer pays return shipping and insurance for exhibited work.

Acceptable Work: Considers candlemaking; clothing; dollmaking; jewelry; needlecrafts; quilting; soft sculpture; tole painting; woodcrafting; hand-painted china; and antiques. Especially needs miniatures; baby gifts; gifts useful to older people; and things of interest to men. One-of-a-

kind and handmade production-line items; utilitarian and/or decorative.
Profile: "The shop has an unusual atmosphere created by antiques, original Ben Franklin stove that is used daily in winter." Displays work 3 months minimum. Best selling time: spring and fall.

VILLAGE MINIATURES, 910 Clayton Rd., Ballwin MO 63011. (314)527-4020. Partner: Shirley Franz. Collector's miniature shop. Estab. 1972. Represents 130 craftworkers. Considers dollhouse 1"-1' miniatures. One-of-a-kind and handmade production-line items. Especially needs handcrafted furniture and unusual accessories. Price range: 25c-$1,125; bestsellers: $1.50-50. Works on consignment and buys outright; 40% commission. Craftworker sets retail price. Requires exclusive area representation. Reports in 2 weeks. Work may be shipped or hand-delivered. Dealer pays return shipping and insurance for exhibited work.
Profile: "We display work in miniature room settings of different periods. Items are displayed as long as they are popular. We are the only exclusively miniature shop in greater St. Louis area and are located in a 70-year-old restored dairy barn." Heaviest wholesale buying time: August-December; best selling time: October-December.

THE WEAVERS' STORE, 110 N. 10th St., Columbia MO 65201. (314)442-5413. Contact: Barbara Overby. Gallery/weaving supplies. Estab. 1977. Represents 5 fiber artists. Price range: $1-700. Works on consignment; 30% commission. Retail price set by joint agreement. Reports in 3 weeks. Work may be shipped or hand-delivered. Dealer pays shipping to shop. Main gallery shows last 2-4 weeks.
Acceptable Work: Considers batik; clothing; needlecrafts; soft sculpture; wall hangings; and weavings. Fine one-of-a-kind and handmade production-line items; utilitarian and/or decorative.
Profile: Gallery provides publicity with shows; "we try to sell only fiber arts, no kit work."

Montana

DOUG ALLARD'S FLATHEAD INDIAN TRADING POST, Box 464, St. Ignatius MT 59865. (406)745-2951. Contact: Doug Allard. Craft shop/gallery/gift shop/museum. Estab. 1974. Represents hundreds of Indian craftworkers. Price range: 5c-$650; bestsellers: $15-63. Buys outright. Gallery sets retail price. Reports in 3 weeks. Hand-delivered work only.
Acceptable Work: Considers decoupage; dollmaking; jewelry; pottery; quilting; woodcrafting; and beadwork. Especially needs Indian-made beadwork using 13/0 cut beads. One-of-a-kind pieces.
Profile: "Customers are all ages; tourists and locals." Heaviest wholesale buying time: April, May and November; best selling time: summer.

THE ART GALLERY, 13 S. Willson, Bozeman MT 59715. (406)587-0092. Contact: Anita Kristensen. Gallery/gift shop. Estab. 1977. Represents 24 craftworkers whose work deals with Western wildlife or scenery typical of the Montana area. Price range: $10-1,000 (no limit); bestsellers: $15-150. Works on consignment and buys outright; 40% commission. Retail price set by joint agreement. Reports in 1 week. Work may be shipped or hand-delivered only if approved. Dealer pays insurance for exhibited work. Displays work 1 year maximum.
Acceptable Work: Considers glass art; jewelry; metalsmithing; and woodcrafting. Especially needs small, inexpensive items ($5-15 retail); impulse items. Fine one-of-a-kind pieces; utilitarian and/or decorative.
Profile: "Items are grouped whenever possible; the shop is tiny and I am very select in buying; all items accepted are on display at all times. I am the only gallery in this city which imports the works of nationally recognized artists." Heaviest wholesale buying time: fall and spring.

ART UNLIMITED, 431 2nd St., Whitefish MT 59937. (208)862-5155. Contact: Laurie Carlson. Art supply and gift shop. Estab. 1975. Represents 7 craftworkers. Price range: $1.50-125; bestsellers: $7 minimum. Buys outright. Retail price set by joint agreement. Requires exclusive area representation. Work may be shipped or hand-delivered. Dealer pays insurance.
Acceptable Work: Considers ceramics; jewelry; pottery; wall hangings; weavings; and macrame. Especially needs interesting gift ideas that are indicative of the Montana area in the $7-15 price range. Finished, one-of-a-kind and handmade production-line items; utilitarian and/or decorative.
Profile: "We teach everything we sell and try to give a personal touch." Best selling and heaviest wholesale buying time: summer and Christmas.

ARTIFACTS GALLERIES, LTD., Box 1989, Bozeman MT 59715. (406)586-3755. Director: Patricia Noteboom. Craft shop/gallery. Estab. 1978. Represents 20-30 craftworkers. Price range: $4-500; bestsellers; $10-40. Works some on consignment and buys outright; 40% commission. Shows on consignment. Craftworker sets retail price. Requires exclusive representation within 50 miles. Reports in 1 week. Work may be shipped or hand-delivered. Dealer pays return shipping if work has been requested and insurance for exhibited work.

Acceptable Work: Considers batik; ceramics; clothing; glass art; jewelry; metalsmithing; pottery; quilting; soft sculpture; wall hangings; weavings; and woodcrafting. Contemporary styles; utilitarian and/or decorative.

Profile: "The gallery has been designed with specific units for glass which are lighted; jewelry displayed in cases; ceramics on cubes, shelves, etc: wearables on mannequins or on wall surfaces; hangings suspended from gridwork ceiling. Displays are changed frequently. We have genuine interest and concern for craft and craftspeople." Displays consigned work 3 months; gallery shows 1 month. Heaviest wholesale buying time: March/April and August/September; best selling time: June-August and November-December.

BITTERROOT POTTERY, Rt. 1, Box 74, Victor MT 59875. (406)961-3307. Contact: Peggy Steffes. Craft shop/pottery studio. Estab. 1972. Represents 2 craftworkers. Price range: $1-200; bestsellers: $15-35. Buys outright; 35% commission. Craftworker sets retail price. Reports in 1 week. Work may be hand-delivered. Best selling and heaviest wholesale buying time: August, October and November.

Acceptable Work: Considers pottery; wall hangings; and weavings. Fine one-of-a-kind and handmade production-line items; utilitarian and/or decorative.

FLATHEAD LAKE GALLERIES, Corner Lake and Grand, Box 272, Bigfork MT 59911. (406)837-6633. Contact: Richard Ettinger. Estab. 1963. Represents 20 craftworkers. Considers ceramics; jewelry; leatherworking; and pottery. Finished, one-of-a-kind and handmade production-line items; utilitarian and/or decorative. Price range: $2-200; bestsellers: $25-50. Buys outright; 50% mark-up. Retail price set by joint agreement. Query with transparencies or photos. Reports in 3 weeks. Dealer pays shipping from shop and insurance for exhibited work. Heaviest wholesale buying time: spring; best selling time: June-September. Customers buy crafts for artistic value and for gifts.

HOCKADAY CENTER FOR THE ARTS GIFT SHOP, Box 83, Kalispell MT 59901. (406)755-5268. Director: John Brice. Considers pottery and weaving. Prices are $4+. Most items taken on consignment; 33⅓% commission. 40% discount for items purchased outright. Also sponsors annual outdoor art festival and sale. Write for more information.

THE MAGIC MUSHROOM GALLERY, Box 8375, Missoula MT 59801. (406)549-9322. Buyer: Kaye Caskey. Gallery/gift shop. Estab. 1970. Represents 100 craftworkers. Price range: $5-500; bestsellers: $5-100. Buys outright. Gallery sets retail price. Requires exclusive area representation. Reports in 2 weeks. Work may be shipped or hand-delivered.

Acceptable Work: Considers batik; ceramics; dollmaking; glass art; jewelry; metalsmithing; pottery; quilting; soft sculpture; wall hangings; weavings; and woodcrafting. All styles; utilitarian and/or decorative. Especially needs soft sculpture and jewelry.

Profile: "Customers are college students to housewives; mill workers to doctors. Best customers are lawyers, doctors, professional women and business people." Heaviest wholesale buying time: fall; best selling time: Christmas.

POTS 'N STUFF, Box 613, Ronan MT 59864. (406)676-2500. Contact: Donna L. Aadsen. Craft shop/gift shop. Estab. 1976. Represents 3 craftworkers. Price range: $5-100; bestsellers: $5-50. Buys outright. Gallery sets retail price. Requires exclusive area representation. Reports in 4 weeks. Work may be hand-delivered. Dealer pays insurance for exhibited work.

Acceptable Work: Considers candlemaking; ceramics; pottery; and macrame. Finished, one-of-a-kind and handmade production-line items; utilitarian and/or decorative.

Profile: "This is the only exclusive gift and macrame shop in our area. Customers are from all age groups and all social and economic groups." Heaviest wholesale buying time: summer; best selling time: Christmas.

J. K. RALSTON MUSEUM AND ART CENTER GIFT SHOP, Box 50, Sidney MT 59270. (406)482-3500. Director: Linda K. Mann. Considers ceramics and sculpture. Price range: $5-200. Works on consignment; 25% commission.

WESTERN HERITAGE GALLERY, 4289 N. Montana Ave., Helena MT 59601. (406)442-4154. Manager: Bernadine H. Wright. Craft shop/gallery. Estab. 1976. Represents 22 craftworkers of Indian extraction. Price range: $2.50-600; bestsellers: $10-50. Works on consignment; 25% commission. Gallery sets retail price. Requires exclusive area representation. Reports in 1 week. Work may be shipped or hand-delivered. Dealer pays return shipping and insurance for exhibited work.

Acceptable Work: Considers ceramics; glass art; jewelry; metalsmithing; pottery; wall hangings; and weavings. Primitive one-of-a-kind pieces; utilitarian and/or decorative.

Profile: Shop provides advertising. Displays work 3 months. "Customers are all ages; Indians; middle class; many are collectors of Indian art." Heaviest wholesale buying time: spring/summer; best selling time: summer.

YELLOWSTONE ART CENTER, 401 N. 27th St., Billings MT 59101. (406)259-1869. Manager: Katherine H. Haughey. Museum gift shop. Estab. 1967. Represents 10-12 craftworkers. Price range: $2.50-100; bestsellers: $2.50-60. Works on consignment and buys outright; 25% commission. Craftworker sets retail price. Reports in 1 month. Work may be shipped or hand-delivered. Dealer pays shipping to shop and insurance for exhibited work.

Acceptable Work: Considers ceramics; glass art; jewelry; pottery. Fine one-of-a-kind and handmade production-line items; utilitarian and/or decorative.

Profile: "Pottery is displayed on shelves; jewelry in cases. Customers are college age through early 40's; middle income." Displays work 1 year. Heaviest wholesale buying time: February-November; best selling time: December.

Nebraska

GRANDMA'S HOUSE, 403 10th St., Gothenburg NE 69138. (308)537-7333. Contact: Valerie Brooks, Aileene Hirsch or Sharon Tinlin. Craft, gift and antique shop. Estab. 1976. Represents 20 craftworkers. Price range: $1-80; bestsellers: $5-25. Works on consignment: 30% commission. Gallery sets retail price. Reports in 4 weeks. Work may be shipped or hand-delivered. Dealer pays return shipping.

Acceptable Work: Considers glass art; leatherworking; needlecrafts; pottery; quilting; tole painting; wall hangings; weavings; woodcrafting; and macrame. Fine one-of-a-kind pieces; utilitarian and/or decorative.

Profile: "Our items are displayed in a 100 year old home in a nostalgic fashion. We have 5 rooms set up. We are located in the home of the original Pony Express Station. We have something for everyone, from dolls to very old antiques. One of our handcrafters makes wood items from native walnut. We strive to carry the unusual but yet useful enough to give as gifts or use in your home."

THE PEDDLERS, 111 W. Mission, Bellevue NE 68005. Contact: Judy Bender. Considers ceramics; sculpture; jewelry; metalsmithing; needlecrafts; macrame; glass; leather; tie dye; and batik. Price range: $20-500. 30% commission. Send transparencies or photos. Items displayed 10 weeks minimum.

WEST NEBRASKA ARTS CENTER, Box 62, Scottsbluff NE 69361. (308)632-2226. Executive Director: Robert S. Hill. Gallery. Estab. 1966. Represents 2 craftworkers. Price range: $30-500; bestsellers: $30-200. Works on consignment; 35% commission. Craftworker sets retail price. Reports in 4 weeks. Work may be hand-delivered or shipped. Dealer pays insurance for exhibited work. Displays work 2-4 weeks.

Acceptable Work: Considers batik; ceramics; pottery; soft sculpture; wall hangings; and weavings. Especially needs pottery; fiber; mixed media; and sculpture. Fine one-of-a-kind pieces; utilitarian and/or decorative.

Profile: "Items are displayed as part of a 1-3 person exhibit. We are part of a nonprofit Arts Center located in the extreme western part of Nebraska. Customers are 30-70; have $20,000 and up income; newly interested in the arts; usually community minded; female." Best selling time: winter.

Nevada

GREEN APPLE GALLERY, 4800 Maryland Pkwy., #F, Las Vegas NV 89104. (702)736-6604. Contact: Peg Bolen. Gallery. Estab. 1974. Represents 5-6 craftworkers. Price range: $25-1,000; bestsellers: $50-250. Works on consignment and buys outright; 40% commission. Retail price set by joint agreement. Requires exclusive area representation. Reports in 4 weeks. Work may be shipped or hand-delivered. Shipping payment is negotiable. Dealer pays insurance for exhibited work. Best selling time: fall-winter.

Acceptable Work: Considers batik; ceramics; dollmaking; glass art; metalsmithing; needlecrafts; pottery; soft sculpture; wall hangings; weavings; and woodcrafting. Fine one-of-a-kind pieces; utilitarian and/or decorative.

IN THE CHILDREN'S ROOM, 4800 S. Maryland Pkwy., Las Vegas NV 89109. (702)736-6604. Contact Joanne Lefever. Gift shop. Considers any craft pertaining to children, birth to 12 years. Works on consignment and buys outright. Send slides, photos, and/or price sheets.

THE SHOP AT THE GALLERY (NEVADA ART GALLERY), 643 Ralston St., Reno NV 89503. (702)322-5626. Manager: Mimi Lohse. Gallery/gift shop. Estab. 1976. Prefers local craftworkers. Price range: $1-500; bestsellers: $5-30. Works on consignment and buys outright; 33⅓% commission. Craftworker sets retail price. Reports in 1 week. Work may be shipped or hand-delivered by prior consent. Dealer pays shipping to shop and insurance for exhibited work. Heaviest wholesale buying time: pre-Christmas and January; best selling time: Christmas.
Acceptable Work: Considers ceramics; clothing; glass art; jewelry; leatherworking; pottery; quilting; soft sculpture; wall hangings; weavings; and woodcrafting. Fine one-of-a-kind and handmade production-line items; utilitarian and/or decorative.

New Hampshire

ACORN, Rt. 1, Box 165 B, Newport NH 03773. (603)863-2528. Contact: Linda or David Perkins. Craft shop. Estab. 1977. Represents 10 craftworkers. Price range: 10c-$2,000; bestsellers: $3-75. Works on consignment and buys outright; 33⅓% commission. Reports in 4 weeks. Work may be shipped or hand-delivered. Dealer pays shipping to shop and insurance for exhibited work.
Acceptable Work: Considers glass art; jewelry; leatherworking; needlecrafts; pottery; wall hangings; weavings; woodcrafting; wooden toys; and metal sculpture. All styles; utilitarian and/or decorative.
Profile: "We have a rustic format; barnboard display cases and open shelves; wall and ceiling space." Displays work 6 months. Heaviest wholesale buying time: spring; best selling time: summer.

ARTISAN'S WORKSHOP, Main St., New London NH 03257. (603)526-4227. Manager: Muffin Bushueff. Art/craft shop. Estab. 1975. Represents 30-40 northern New England craftworkers. Price range: $2-150; bestsellers: $2-25. Works on consignment and buys outright; 33⅓% comission. Retail price set by joint agreement. Reports in 2 weeks. Work may be shipped or hand-delivered. Dealer pays return shipping and insurance for exhibited work. Heaviest wholesale buying time: spring-autumn; best selling time: summer and winter.
Acceptable Work: Considers batik; candlemaking; glass art; jewelry; leatherworking; pottery; and woodcrafting. Especially needs blown glass; pottery; batik (smaller items); serigraphs; woodcuts; and unusual, moderately-priced utilitarian pieces of wood and stone. Finished, one-of-a-kind and handmade production-line items; utilitarian and/or decorative.

AYOTTES' DESIGNERY, Box 287, Center Sandwich NH 03227. Contact: Robert Ayotte. Craft shop/handweaving studio. Estab. 1958. Represents 30 craftworkers; preferably from northern New England. Price range: $1-500; bestsellers: $40 maximum. Buys outright. Requires exclusive area representation. Reports in 1 month. Work may be shipped or hand-delivered.
Acceptable Work: Considers candlemaking; glass art; jewelry; leatherworking; metalsmithing; pottery; woodcrafting; and black iron work. Fine one-of-a-kind and handmade production-line items; utilitarian and/or decorative.
Profile: "We have been in business for 20 years and have established a reputation and repeat clientele. We pride ourselves on quality craftsmanship and unique designs in our own handweaving. Our customers come from all over the world. Heaviest wholesale buying time: spring; best selling time: July-August.

BERNIER STUDIO, Rt. 25, Wentworth NH 03282. (603)764-5720. Manager: Carol Ann Bernier. Craft and gift shop. Estab. 1966. Represents 50 craftworkers. Price range: $2-350; bestsellers: $5-25. Buys outright. Retail price set by joint agreement. Requires exclusive area representation. Reports in 4 weeks. Work may be shipped or hand-delivered. Dealer pays shipping to shop and insurance for exhibited work. Heaviest wholesale buying time: spring; best selling time: summer.
Acceptable Work: Considers ceramics; clothing; dollmaking; glass art; jewelry; metalsmithing; pottery; and woodcrafting.

CHOCORUA POTTERS, Box 51, Chocorua NH 03817. Contact: Bob Solar. Gallery. Estab. 1972. Represents 5 craftworkers. Considers ceramics and pottery. All styles; utilitarian and/or decorative. Price range: $1-100; bestsellers: $3-30. Works on consignment and buys outright; 30% commission. Retail price set by joint agreement. Requires exclusive area representation.

Reports in 1 week. Work may be shipped or hand-delivered. Dealer pays insurance for exhibited work.
Profile: "We are a studio-gallery located in an 1840 barn. Stoneware pottery is made on the premises, with additional work of other artists on display." Heaviest wholesale buying time: April-June; best selling time: June-November.

THE GOLDEN TOAD, 35 Amherst St., Milford NH 03055. (603)673-4307. Contact: Sandy Hammond. Craft shop/gallery. Estab. 1972. Represents 100-150 East Coast craftworkers. Price range: $1-300; bestsellers: $10-20. Buys outright. Requires exclusive area representation. Reports in 2 weeks. Work may be shipped or hand-delivered. Dealer pays shipping to shop.
Acceptable Work: Considers batik; candlemaking; dollmaking; glass art; jewelry; leatherworking; metalsmithing; pottery; soft sculpture; wall hangings; weavings; and woodcrafting. Especially needs items men would like. Primitive handmade production-line items; utilitarian and/or decorative.
Profile: "Customers are middle class to upper middle class; educated; with incomes of $20,000 and up." Displays work 3 months. Heaviest wholesale buying time: early fall; best selling time: Christmas and summer.

THE GUILD OF STRAWBERRY BANKE, 93 State St., Portsmouth NH 03801. (603)438-8004. Director of Merchandise: Carol Olson. Museum gift shop. Estab. 1965. Represents 100 craftworkers. Price range: $3-250; bestsellers: $5-35. Buys outright. Retail price set by joint agreement. Reports immediately. Work may be shipped or hand-delivered. Dealer pays shipping to shop.
Acceptable Work: Considers candlemaking; ceramics; decoupage; dollmaking; glass art; needlecrafts; pottery; quilting; tole painting; and woodcrafting. All styles; utilitarian and/or decorative.
Profile: "We have 3 shops; if an item does not sell in one shop, it is moved to another shop. Our average customer is between 30 and 50; high middle to high income." Heaviest wholesale buying time: spring; best selling time: August-September and November.

HAPPY HANDS CRAFT SHOPPE, 253 S. Main St., Concord NH 03301. (603)224-9775. Partners: Phyllis Cross and Pauline Boutwell. Craft shop. Estab. 1976. Represents 40-50 craftworkers. Considers all crafts. All styles; utilitarian and/or decorative. Price range: 30c-$75; bestsellers: $6-18. Works on consignment; 25% commission. Craftworker sets retail price. Reporting time varies. Work may be shipped only with permission or hand-delivered.
Profile: "Our customers are all ages; since we sell craft supplies." Best selling time: Christmas and winter.

KIRK-LAMOTHE GALLERY, Main St., Walpole NH 03608. (603)756-3234. Contact: Anne Lamothe. Craft shop/gallery. Estab. 1971. Represents 40 New England craftworkers. Price range: 50c-$500; bestsellers: 50c-$175. Works on consignment; 33⅓% commission. Retail price set by joint agreement. Work may be shipped or hand-delivered. Dealer pays return shipping and insurance for exhibited work. Displays work 6 months.
Acceptable Work: Considers decoupage; dollmaking; jewelry; leatherworking; metalsmithing; needlecrafts; pottery; quilting; soft sculpture; and woodcrafting. Especially needs jewelry. Fine one-of-a-kind and handmade production-line items; utilitarian and/or decorative.
Profile: "We combine crafts, paintings and antique glass and china. Customers are upper middle class." Heaviest wholesale buying time: fall; best selling time: Christmas.

LEAGUE OF NEW HAMPSHIRE CRAFTSMEN, 205 N. Main St., Concord NH 03301. Director: Merle D. Walker. Craft shop. Estab. 1932. Represents an unlimited number of craftworkers; must be state juried members of the League who meet residency requirements. Considers all crafts except candlemaking and ceramics. All styles; utilitarian and/or decorative. Price range: $1-1,000; bestsellers: $10-150. Works on consignment and buys outright; 33⅓% commission. Craftworker sets retail price.
Profile: "We are constantly working on new methods of displaying objects to encourage appreciation in the consumer. Buyers are obviously mostly middle years, middle incomes and have a developed appreciation level of the crafts." Heaviest wholesale buying time: spring-summer; best selling time: August and December.

LEAGUE OF NEW HAMPSHIRE CRAFTSMEN, HANOVER SHOP, 13 Lebanon St., Hanover NH 03755. (603)643-5050. Manager: Jane MacKinnon. Craft and gift shop. Estab. 1933. Represents 2,000 New Hampshire craftworkers. Considers all crafts except candlemaking.

One-of-a-kind and handmade production-line items; utilitarian and/or decorative. Price range: 15c-$800; bestsellers: 15c-$25. Works on consignment and buys outright; 40% commission. Craftworker sets retail price. Reports in 2 weeks after local jurying. Work may be shipped or hand-delivered. Shop pays return shipping and insurance for exhibited work. Best selling time: fall.

LEAGUE OF NEW HAMPSHIRE CRAFTSMEN, Wolfeboro Arts and Crafts, Rt. 28, Wolfeboro NH 03894. (603)569-3489. Manager: Sally Allen. Craft shop. Craftworkers must meet residential requirements. Considers all crafts. All styles; utilitarian and/or decorative. Price range: 10c-$650. Works on consignment. Craftworker sets retail price. Work may be shipped or hand-delivered. Best selling time: summer and fall.

New Jersey

ART LEASE AND SALES GALLERY, Friends of New Jersey State Museum, 205 W. State St., Trenton NJ 08625. (609)394-5310. Contact: Carol Rosenthal or Ann Gips. Museum/rental gallery. Estab. 1972. Represents 35-40 craftworkers. Price range: $4.50-1,000; bestsellers: $35-100. Works on consignment; 40% commission. Craftworker sets retail price. Reporting time varies. Work may be shipped or hand-delivered. Dealer pays insurance for exhibited work. Displays work 6 months maximum.
Acceptable Work: Considers batik; ceramics; jewelry; metalsmithing; needlecrafts; pottery; quilting; soft sculpture; wall hangings; and weavings. Especially needs hand woven items; and jewelry. Fine one-of-a-kind pieces; utilitarian and/or decorative.
Profile: We display work in enclosed cases. Our customers are in their early 20's to early 70's with the largest concentration in the 35-55 age group. They have interest in the fine and performing arts. Income is approximately $8,000-100,000 annually." Displays work 6 months. Heaviest consignment time: October and November; best selling time: mid-November to January.

THE ARTISAN'S GALLERY, 161 Main St., Ridgefield Park NJ 07660. Contact: Paul or Janet Sisko. Considers ceramics; jewelry; metalsmithing; glass; leather, enamels; wall hangings; macrame; and stitchery. Price range: $1-3,000; bestsellers: up to $30. 50% mark-up on crafts bought outright. Craftworker sets retail price. Requires exclusive area representation. Send transparencies or photos. Items displayed 4 weeks minimum. Openings sponsored.

THE BEA HIVE, 504 Cedar Lane, Teaneck NJ 07666. (201)836-1366. Contact: Bea Westin or Naomi Koncius. Craft and gift shop. Estab. 1975. Represents 50-100 craftworkers. Price range: $3.50-300; bestsellers: $10-30. Buys outright. Retail price set by joint agreement. Requires exclusive area representation. Reports in 2 weeks. Work may be shipped or hand-delivered. Dealer pays insurance for exhibited work.
Acceptable Work: Considers batik; candlemaking; ceramics; glass art; jewelry; leatherworking; metalsmithing; pottery; quilting; soft sculpture; wall hangings; weavings; and woodcrafting. Especially needs personalized items in baby gifts, name plaques, and gifts for men, etc. Fine one-of-a-kind and handmade production-line items; utilitarian and/or decorative.
Profile: "We display work in 2 large windows. New merchandise is displayed in the window and inside the shop. Windows are changed once a month completely, although new things are added every few days." Heaviest wholesale buying time: September-December and April, May and June; best selling time: Christmas.

BEARPAW LEATHER SHOP, 36 Main St., Clinton NJ 08809. (201)735-7351. Contact: Rod Gries. Craft shop. Estab. 1972. Represents 40 craftworkers. Considers leatherworking. Fine one-of-a-kind and handmade production-line items; utilitarian and/or decorative. Especially needs bags and wallets; designer art pieces are always welcome. Price range: $2-750; bestsellers: $20-100. Buys outright. Reports in 2-3 weeks. Work may be shipped or hand-delivered. Dealer pays shipping to shop.
Profile: "I will keep something until I sell it. Bearpaw is full of antiques and beautiful display cases. If I could sum up the shop in one word, it would be 'comfortable.' Customers are 27-35; quality is their main interst; income of $12,000-30,000." Heaviest wholesale buying time: June-September; best selling time: October-December.

BEAUTIFUL THINGS, 1838 E. 2nd St., Scotch Plains NJ 07076. (201)322-1817. Contact: Paula Gollhardt Leighton. Craft and gift shop. Estab. 1973. Represents 75-100 craftworkers. Price range: $2-300; bestsellers: $10-35. Buys outright. Gallery sets retail price. Reports in 4 weeks. Work may be shipped or hand-delivered. Dealer pays shipping to shop.
Acceptable Work: Considers dollmaking; glass art; jewelry; leatherworking; pottery; soft sculp-

ture; and woodcrafting. Especially needs gift items to sell for under $20; and production pottery items like juice squeezers and ladles. Fine one-of-a-kind and handmade production-line items; utilitarian and/or decorative.

Profile: "We feature our own jewelry; we have high quality and good taste with a total price range; we also mix crafts with some commercial items and some imported." Heaviest wholesale buying time: late summer and fall; best selling time: Christmas.

BEAUTIFUL THINGS, 3452 Springfield Ave., Summit NJ 07901. See above.

BY HAND FINE CRAFT GALLERY, 211 Kings Hwy. E, Haddonfield NJ 08033. (609)429-2550. Contact: Arlene R. Ludin. Craft gallery. Estab. 1976. Represents 120 craftworkers. Price range: $3-3,000; bestsellers: $10-250. Works on consignment and buys outright; 30-40% commission. Retail price set by joint agreement. Reports in 2 weeks. Work may be shipped or hand-delivered. Dealer pays insurance for exhibited work. Shows are 2 weeks.
Acceptable Work: Considers batik; ceramics; glass art; leatherworking; metalsmithing; pottery; soft sculpture; wall hangings; weavings; and woodcrafting. Fine one-of-a-kind and handmade production-line items; utilitarian and/or decorative.
Profile: "Items purchased are held until sold and constantly moved. Each piece is given as important a place as possible. The look of the gallery changes constantly. Customers are mostly women; interested in the arts; most are 25-40 years old; upper middle income." Heaviest wholesale buying time: September and March; best selling time: December, April and August.

CABIN CREEK QUILTS, 195 Nassau St., Princeton NJ 08540. (609)921-1278. See Cabin Creek Quilts, Cabin Creek, West Virginia.

CLINTON HISTORIAL MUSEUM VILLAGE, Box 5005, 56 Main St., Clinton NJ 08809. (201)735-4101. Director: Gloria Lazor. Museum gift shop. Estab. 1965. Represents 5 craftworkers. Price range: $1-200; bestsellers: $1-10. Works on consignment; 40% commission. Gallery sets retail price. Reports in 4 weeks. Hand-delivered work only. Dealer pays insurance for exhibited work. Displays work 3 months. Customers are family groups; 30-45 with an income of $15,000. Heaviest wholesale buying time: spring; best selling time: summer.
Acceptable Work: Considers candlemaking; ceramics; decoupage; dollmaking; glass art; jewelry; metalsmithing; needlecrafts; pottery; quilting; and woodcrafting. Primitive one-of-a-kind and handmade production-line items; utilitarian and/or decorative.

CRAFTSMAN'S CORNER, Morris County Mall, Cedar Knolls NJ 07927. (201)267-4556. Contact: Harriet Rost or Jan Schlosser. Craft shop. Represents 50 American craftworkers. Considers batik; glass art; jewelry; leatherworking; metalsmithing; pottery; wall hangings; weavings; and woodcrafting. Fine one-of-a-kind and handmade production-line items; utilitarian and/or decorative. Price range: $5-200; bestsellers: $5-50. Works on consignment and buys outright; 40% commission. Retail price set by joint agreement. Requires exclusive area representation. Dealer pays shipping to shop and insurance for exhibited work.
Profile: "Most of our jewelry is displayed attached to a cork wall so our customers try them on. We have a sincere interest in our craftworkers and customers." Best selling time: spring and Christmas.

CRAFTWORKS, 12 N. Van Brunt St., Englewood NJ 07631. (201)567-3881. Contact: Raye Cooke or Lorraine Cilluffo. Craft shop/pottery studio. Estab. 1975. Price range: $3-300; bestsellers: $10-25. Works on consignment and buys outright; 30% commission. Craftworker sets retail price. Requires exclusive area representation. Reports in 3 weeks. Work may be shipped or hand-delivered. Dealer pays shipping and insurance for exhibited work.
Acceptable Work: Considers batik; ceramics; glass art; jewelry; pottery; soft sculpture; wall hangings; weavings; and woodcrafting. One-of-a-kind and handmade production-line items; utilitarian and/or decorative.
Profile: "Work is displayed to its best advantage; like styles or shapes grouped together; functional displayed separately; displays change monthly." Heaviest wholesale buying time: fall and late winter; best selling time: spring and late fall.

THE CRAFTY LADY SHOP, 2 West Shore Trail, Lake Mohawk, Sparta NJ 07871. President: Victoria Cardella. Craft and gift shop. Estab. 1977. Represents 20 craftrworkers. Price range: 50c-$100; bestsellers: $1-80. Works on consignment and buys outright; 30% commission. Craftworker sets retail price. Reports at end of month. Work may be shipped or hand-delivered. Dealer pays return shipping and insurance for exhibited work.

Acceptable Work: Considers all crafts. Especially needs craftworkers who make collector items from paper weights to unusual candle holders to miniatures. All styles; utilitarian and/or decorative.

Profile: "Most items are placed on tables or decorative barrels and draped over old chairs and dresses. I am located in White Deer Plaza next to the Lake Mohawk boardwalk. Its an area that attracts vacationers." Best selling and heaviest wholesale buying time: Christmas and summer.

DEXTERITY, LTD., 26 Church St., Montclair NJ 07042. (201)746-5370. Contact: Shirley Zafirau. Craft shop. Estab. 1974. Represents 250 craftworkers. Price range: $1.25-250. Buys outright. Gallery sets retail price. Requires exclusive area representation. Reports in 3-4 weeks. Dealer pays shipping to shop.

Acceptable Work: Considers all crafts. Finished, one-of-a-kind and handmade production-line items; utilitarian and/or decorative.

Profile: We offer a large "selection of the best in crafts we can find; we offer service and beautifully packaged gifts; people react verbally to the visual impact of our display, shop and atmosphere. We would like advance notice of price increases and an opportunity to place orders at the old prices." Heaviest wholesale buying time: September-November; best selling time: November 15-December 31.

DOUBLETREE GALLERY, 5 Alvin Place, Upper Montclair NJ 07043. (201)783-5022. Contact: Lisa Suss. Gallery/coop. Estab. 1972. Represents coop members. Price range: $1.50-1,500; bestsellers: $4-32. Works on consignment; 34% commission. Craftworker sets retail price. Reports in 2 weeks. Work may be hand-delivered. Dealer pays insurance for exhibited work. Displays work 4-6 weeks for shows.

Acceptable Work: Considers batik; ceramics; clothing; dollmaking; glass art; jewelry; leatherworking; metalsmithing; pottery; quilting; soft sculpture; wall hangings; weavings; and woodcrafting. Finished, one-of-a-kind and handmade production-line items; utilitarian and/or decorative.

Profile: "Customers are affluent professionals; and most have some knowledge of art and/or crafts." Heaviest wholesale buying time: fall; best selling time: fall and spring.

EARTH AND FIRE CERAMIC STUDIO AND GALLERY, 20 Morris St., Morristown NJ 07960. (201)455-9368. Contact: Michael Feno or Sy Shames. Gallery/ceramic studio. Estab. 1969. Represents 2 craftworkers. Considers ceramics and pottery. Fine one-of-a-kind and handmade production-line items; utilitarian and/or decorative. Price range: $12-600; bestsellers: $18-90. Works on consignment. Craftworker sets retail price.

Profile: "Our items are displayed beautifully in a very elegant, uncrowded manner. We show unusual slab constructed pottery and one-of-a-kind ceramic objects." Best selling time: spring to Christmas.

GALLERY 2W0, 34 Washington Ave., Westwood NJ 07675. (201)666-1696. Contact: Joyce Kaplan. Craft shop/gallery. Estab. 1967. Represents 7-8 craftworkers. Price range: $10-500. Works on consignment; 40% commission. Retail price set by joint agreement. Requires exclusive area representation. Reports in 2 weeks. Work may be shipped or hand-delivered. Dealer pays insurance for exhibited work. Heaviest wholesale buying time: fall; best selling time: fall and spring.

Acceptable Work: Considers batik; pottery; soft sculpture; wall hangings; weavings; and woodcrafting. Finished, one-of-a-kind pieces; utilitarian and/or decorative.

GRANNY'S LOFT, INC., 31 S. Finley Ave., Basking Ridge NJ 07920. Contact: Phyllis Wallace. Estab. 1976. Represents 30-40 craftworkers. Price range: $1.67-375; bestsellers: $2.50-25. Works on consignment; 40% commission. Retail price set by joint agreement. Requires exclusive area representation. "Contract covering insurance, etc. is issued at time of consignment. Consignee is covered for 90 day period and has option to renew contract or remove items from premises." Work may be shipped or hand-delivered. Return shipping depends on contract arrangements. Dealer pays insurance for exhibited work.

Acceptable Work: Considers candlemaking; ceramics; clothing; decoupage; dollmaking; glass art; jewelry; needlecrafts; pottery; quilting; wall hangings; weavings; woodcrafting; macrame and pottery combination; lamps; and shell mirrors. One-of-a-kind and handmade production line items; utilitarian and/or decorative. "Specifically I am looking for a double weaving process which I found in Arizona. It is used as chair seats and wall hangings. I have not seen it in this area and do not really know the process. It has a quilted look. I am also most interested in anything exceptional with a horse motif."

Profile: "Displays are ever changing, depending on seasonal changes. Customers are mostly young marrieds in upper income bracket." Heaviest wholesale buying time: late summer-fall; best selling time: September-January.

HAND FEATS, 40 Main St., Madison NJ 07940. (201)822-1616. Manager: Kathy Mangina. Craft shop. Estab. 1970. Price range: $2-600. Works on consignment and buys outright; 34% commission. Retail price set by joint agreement. Reports in 2 weeks. Work may be shipped or hand-delivered.
Acceptable Work: Considers batik; candlemaking; ceramics; clothing; glass art; jewelry; leatherworking; metalsmithing; pottery; and woodcrafting. All styles; utilitarian and/or decorative.
Profile: "In our area there aren't any shops quite as diversified as ours. We deal with leather boots, shoes, jewelry and crafts, a combination that makes for a really pleasurable shopping experience." Heaviest wholesale buying time: fall; best selling time: Christmas.

HANDMAIDS, 39 Maple St., Summit NJ 07901. Contact: Peggy McNamara. Craft shop. Estab. 1975. Represents 300-500 craftworkers. Considers all crafts except decoupage and tole painting. All styles; utilitarian and/or decorative. Price range: $2-300. Works on consignment and buys outright; 40% commission. Retail price set by joint agreement. Requires exclusive area representation. Best selling time: Christmas.

In three years Handmaids, Summit, New Jersey, has grown from 180 square feet of space to 1,800 square feet and increased their representation of craftworkers from 75 to more than 500 from Maine to California. Handmaids schedules a minimum of six shows annually and is planning to produce a special order catalog.

HOUSE OF BERNARD, 353 Millburn Ave., Millburn NJ 07041. (201)376-8088. Contact: Berry or Shirley Bernard. Estab. 1961. Represents 60 out-of-town craftworkers. Considers batik; ceramics; jewelry; metalsmithing; pottery; wall hangings; and weaving. Primitive and finished, one-of-a-kind and handmade production-line items OK; utilitarian and/or decorative. Price range: $1-thousands of dollars; bestsellers: $5-50. Buys outright. Retail price set by joint agreement. Requires exclusive area representation. Write. Reports in 2 weeks. Dealer pays shipping to shop and insurance for exhibited work. Best selling time: Christmas. Customers are ages 20-50 with $20,000+ incomes and are informed about art.

JEAN JOHNSON MINIATURES, Allenwood General Store, Allenwood-Lakewood Rd., Allenwood NJ 08720. (201)223-4747. Contact: Jean Johnson. Miniature shop. Estab. 1973. Represents 125 craftworkers. Price range: 50c-$1,000; bestsellers: $3-125. Works on consignment and buys outright; 20% commission. Retail price set by joint agreement. Reports in 4 weeks. Work may be shipped or hand-delivered. Dealer pays insurance for exhibited work. "We display work in the shop and at miniature shows in 5 states." Best selling time: Christmas.
Acceptable Work: Considers miniatures in ceramics; clothing; dollmaking; glass art; metalsmithing; needlecrafts; pottery; quilting; tole painting; woodcrafting; and room settings. All styles; decorative only. Especially needs Victorian, heavily-detailed miniatures.

KAKIE'S GOLDMINE, Church Rd., Sicklerville NJ 08081. Contact: Katharine Cusack. Estab. 1976. Represents 6 craftworkers. Considers dollmaking; glass art; metalsmithing; needlecrafts; pottery; quilting; weavings; and woodcrafting. Especially needs jewelry; wall hangings; and unusual handbags. Finished handmade production-line items only; utilitarian and/or decorative. Price range: 29c-$9.95; bestsellers: 89c-$7.95. Works on consignment; 25% commission. Retail price set by joint agreement. Write. Reports in 1 week. Dealer pays shipping from shop and insurance on exhibited work.
Profile: Rotates crafts monthly. Heaviest wholesale buying time: Christmas and May. Customers are young marrieds with $12,000-15,000 incomes and interest in home and children.

KORNBLUTH GALLERY, 7-21 Fairlawn Ave., Fair Lawn NJ 07410. (201)791-3374. Contact: Lillian Kornbluth. Gallery. Estab. 1959. Represents 20 craftworkers. Price range: $25-2,500; bestsellers: $200-300 maximum. Works on consignment; 40% commission. Craftworker sets retail price. Requires exclusive area representation. Work may be shipped or hand-delivered. Dealer pays insurance for exhibited work. "We amalgamate fine, expensive paintings and sculpture with fine crafts." Best selling time: December and June.
Acceptable Work: Considers batik; ceramics; glass art; jewelry; metalsmithing; needlecrafts; pottery; soft sculpture; wall hangings; weavings; and woodcrafting. Especially needs sculptural wall hangings. Finished, one-of-a-kind and handmade production-line items; utilitarian and/or decorative.

MARY ANNE MARINACCIO DOLL HOUSE FURNITURE AND ACCESSORIES, Box 83, Adelphia Rd., Rt. 524, Adelphia NJ 07710. (201)431-2942. Contact: Mary Anne Marinaccio. Craft and gift shop. Estab. 1969. Represents 6 craftworkers. Considers dollmaking and dollhouse furniture and accessories. 1"-1' scale. Handmade production-line items; utilitarian and/or decorative. Price range: 50c-$500. Works on consignment; 30-50% commission. Retail price set by joint agreement. Reporting time varies. Work may be shipped or hand-delivered.

MORRIS MUSEUM SHOP, Box 125, Convent Station NJ 07961. (201)538-0454. Contact: Judith Chapin or Claire Cain. Museum gift shop. Represents 6 craftworkers. Price range: 10c-$95; bestsellers: 10c-$8. Works on consignment and buys outright; commission varies. Retail price set by joint agreement. Requires exclusive area representation. Reports in 2 weeks. Work may be shipped or hand-delivered. Dealer pays shipping to shop and in-transit insurance. Displays work 6-12 months.
Acceptable Work: Considers batik; ceramics; dollmaking; glass art; jewelry; pottery; needlecraft; wall hangings; weavings; and woodcrafting. Especially needs batik hangings; weavings; boxes; miniatures; and animals in pottery, ceramics or wood. All styles; utilitarian and/or decorative.
Profile: "We try to display each craft item to its best advantage; also find changing display periodically, that is, shifting location, helps items to sell. We are a family museum with exhibits for young and old, in both arts and sciences. Approximate income of customers: $5,000-200,000." Heaviest wholesale buying time: fall and spring; best selling time: fall.

ONLY ORIGINALS, 759 Somerset St., Watchung NJ 07060. (201)756-7475. Contact: Dot Kenney. Craft shop/gallery. Estab. 1970. Represents 10 craftworkers. Price range: $5-200; bestsellers: $10-35. Works on consignment; 30% commission. Retail price set by joint agreement. Requires exclusive area representation. Reports in 4 weeks. Work may be shipped or hand-delivered. Dealer pays return shipping and insurance for exhibited work.
Acceptable Work: Considers batik; ceramics; jewelry; pottery; wall hangings; weavings.

Especially needs mobiles, wall hangings and sculpture. One-of-a-kind pieces; utilitarian and/or decorative.

Profile: "Work is displayed in wall displays and shelf displays. Customers are middle-aged; with above average income." Displays work 6-8 weeks. Heaviest wholesale buying time: spring; best selling time: fall.

PAULA'S PLACE, 1 W. Main St., Marlton NJ 08053. (609)983-6880. Contact: Paula Vallen. Craft shop. Estab. 1974. Represents 80 craftworkers. Price range: $5-250; bestsellers: $15-40. Works on consignment and buys outright; 33⅓% commission. Retail price set by joint agreement. Requires exclusive area representation. Reports in 4 weeks. Work may be shipped or hand-delivered. Dealer pays shipping and insurance. Displays work 3-4 weeks.

Acceptable Work: Considers batik; ceramics; clothing; glass art; jewelry; leatherworking; pottery; quilting; soft sculpture; wall hangings; weavings; and woodcrafting. Especially needs wall hangings; soft sculpture; and functional pottery in large, interesting pieces. Fine one-of-a-kind and handmade production-line items; utilitarian and/or decorative.

Profile: "Work is displayed in special section with sign denoting exhibit; announcements are sent to customers and advertising done in local papers. Customers are in late 20's to mid 30's; middle class; $15,000-25,000 income." Heaviest wholesale buying time: summer; best selling time: fall.

To Break In: "Visit shop if possible, see if your craft fits in; send information, pictures and prices."

THE PEDDLERS CELLAR, 6 Hilltop Rd., Mendham NJ 07945. (201)543-2406. Contact: Ginny Hardy. Gift shop. Estab. 1970. Represents 200 craftworkers. Price range: 50c-$600; bestsellers: $1.50-20. Works on consignment and buys outright; 40% commission. Retail price set by joint agreement. Do not send samples unless requested. If interested reports in 2 weeks. Work may be shipped or hand-delivered. Dealer pays return shipping.

Acceptable Work: Considers all crafts except batik; metalsmithing; and soft sculpture. Especially needs dolls, baby and children's items. Primitive handmade production-line items; utilitarian and/or decorative.

Profile: Customers are "women; married; age 19-70; and interested in doing crafts themselves". Heaviest wholesale buying time: late summer; best selling time: Christmas.

PETERS VALLEY CRAFTSMEN, Star Route, Layton NJ 07851. (201)948-5202. Contact: Molly Mechem. Craft shop/gallery. Estab. 1969. Represents 100 regional craftworkers. Price range: $1-750; bestsellers: $15-175. Works on consignment; 33⅓% commission. Retail price set by joint agreement. Work may be shipped or hand-delivered. Dealer pays insurance for exhibited work.

Acceptable Work: Considers batik; .ceramics; clothing; glass art; jewelry; leatherworking; metalsmithing; pottery; soft sculpture; wall hangings; weavings; and woodworking. Especially needs contemporary quilting, soft sculpture and production furniture. Fine one-of-a-kind and handmade production-line items; utilitarian and/or decorative.

Profile: "We are located in a national park and are part of a crafts community with craft studios open to the public. Customers are 18-55; middle to upper income; interested in crafts." Displays work 90 days. Best selling time: summer.

WILLIAM RIS GALLERIES, 9725 Second Ave., Stone Harbor NJ 08247. See William Ris Galleries, Camp Hill, Pennsylvania.

THE SUNSHINE SHOPPE, 55 W. Shore Ave., Dumont NJ 07628. (201)387-0909. Contact: Doris Gripenburg or Gail Meyers. Craft shop. Estab. 1976. Represents 45 craftworkers. Price range: 59c-$35; bestsellers: 59c-$10. Works on consignment; 40% commission. Retail price set by joint agreement. Reports in 2 weeks. Contacts craftworker after 2 months of no sales to lower price or take back merchandise. Work may be shipped or hand-delivered. Dealer pays return shipping and insurance for exhibited work.

Acceptable Work: Considers candlemaking; decoupage; glass art; jewelry; needlecrafts; soft sculpture; tole painting; wall hangings; weavings; woodcrafting; miniatures, wood toys; and Christmas decorations. Especially needs Christmas ornaments and miniatures. Fine handmade production-line items; utilitarian and/or decorative.

Profile: "We are a very small store (but growing rapidly) and seek a variety of colorful, small items for display." Heaviest wholesale buying time: Christmas and spring; best selling time: Christmas.

TOOL AND TALENT, 229 Raritan Ave., Highland Park NJ 08904. (201)246-0878. Contact: Roselee Borow. Craft shop/gallery/gift shop. Estab. 1973. Represents 150 craftworkers. Price range: 35c-$1,500; bestsellers: $5-50. Works on consignment and buys outright; 40% commission. Retail price set by joint agreement. Requires exclusive area representation. Reports in 1 month. Work may be shipped or hand-delivered. Dealer pays shipping to shop and insurance for exhibited work. Displays work 3 months.

Acceptable Work: Considers batik; ceramics; glass art; jewelry; leatherworking; metalsmithing; pottery; soft sculpture; wall hangings; weavings; and woodcrafting. Especially needs furniture, sterling silver jewelry in the $10-30 range; and soft sculpture. Fine one-of-a-kind and handmade production-line items; utilitarian and/or decorative.

Profile: "We have a lovely gallery with excellent window and interior displays. We do advertising at Christmas and various gift seasons." Heaviest wholesale buying time: spring and summer; best selling time: winter through June.

UNIVERSAL GALLERIES, INC., Millside Manor Arcade, Delran NJ 08075. (609)764-1601. Estab. 1978. Sponsors 24 shows annually for members only. Membership is free to quality exhibitors. $65 exhibit fee. No commission. Limited space. Write or phone for membership application.

VITTI ARTISANS GALLERY, 594 Valley Rd., Upper Montclair NJ 07043. (201)746-1715. Contact: Vitti Stein. Estab. 1974. Represents 40-60 craftworkers. Considers all crafts; especially needs jewelry and glass art. Finished, one-of-a-kind and handmade production-line items only; utilitarian and/or decorative. Price range: $4-1,600; bestsellers: $15-500. Buys outright or on consignment; 40% commission. Craftworker sets retail price. Requires exclusive city representation. Query with transparencies or photos. Reports in 3 weeks. Dealer pays insurance for exhibited work. Heaviest wholesale buying time: fall, winter and spring. Closed during August.

THE WALL GALLERY, 55 Summit Ave., Summit NJ 07901. (201)273-5552. President: Muriel S. Bloom. Craft shop/gallery. Estab. 1975. Represents 150 craftworkers. Price range: $10-500. Works on consignment and buys outright; 40% commission. Craftworker sets retail price. Requires exclusive area representation. Reports first of the month. Work may be shipped or hand-delivered. Payment for return shipping is negotiable. Dealer pays insurance for exhibited work. Displays work 6 months minimum.

Acceptable Work: Considers (only for wall) batiks; ceramics; weavings; embroideries; metalsmithing; rugs; glass art; woodcrafting; soft sculpture; and other wall hangings. Primitive and fine one-of-a-kind pieces; decorative only.

Profile: "Work is displayed immediately on receipt. Our stock is from all over the world." Best selling time: winter and spring.

WHALE'S TALE, 312 Washington Mall, Cape May NJ 08204. (609)884-4808. Contact: Hilary Russell. Estab. 1974. Represents 20 craftworkers. Considers batik; candlemaking; ceramics; dollmaking; glass art; jewelry; pottery; soft sculpture; wall hangings; weavings; and woodcrafting. Finished one-of-a-kind and handmade production-line items; utilitarian and/or decorative. Price range: $2-160; bestsellers: $2-20. Buys outright or on consignment; 40% commission. Retail price set by joint agreement. Requires exclusive area representation. Query with transparencies or photos. Reports in 2 weeks. Dealer pays shipping and insurance.

Profile: "Display structures are versatile and we're able to build them around the work displayed." Most crafts displayed 1 month. Heaviest wholesale buying time: spring and summer; best selling time: summer and fall. "A large number of 25-35 year olds who appreciate the work of serious craftspeople (as opposed to hobbyists) pass through shop in summer."

WHEATON VILLAGE, Glasstown Rd., Millville NJ 08332. (609)825-6800. Merchandising Manager: Ben Weston. Craft shop/museum gallery/museum gift shop. Estab. 1970. Represents 12-20 craftworkers. Price range: $1-700; bestsellers: $5-15. Buys outright. Retail price set by joint agreement. Work may be shipped or hand-delivered.

Acceptable Work: Considers candlemaking; ceramics; clothing; dollmaking; glass art; jewelry; leatherworking; metalsmithing; needlecrafts; pottery; quilting; tole painting; wall hangings; weavings; woodcrafting; and reproductions of 19th century (especially glass). Primitive one-of-a-kind and handmade production-line items; utilitarian and/or decorative.

Profile: "Shops are part of a reconstructed 19th century museum village." Heaviest wholesale buying time: spring and summer; best selling time: summer and fall.

THE YELLOW DOOR, 24 Washington Ave., Tenafly NJ 07670. Contact: Betty Turino. Estab. 1973. Represents 375-400 craftworkers. Considers batik; candlemaking; ceramics; glass art; jewelry; leatherworking; metalsmithing; pottery; soft sculpture; wall hangings; weavings; and woodcrafting. Finished one-of-a-kind and handmade production-line items; utilitarian and/or decorative. Price range: $2.50-1,500; best sellers: $6.50-55. Buys outright or on consignment; 40% commission. Gallery sets retail price. Requires exclusive area representation. Write. Dealer pays shipping to shop and insurance on exhibited work.

Profile: Items displayed 3-4 weeks. Heaviest wholesale buying time: Christmas; best selling time: December. Customers are 30-55, urban-oriented and affluent.

New Mexico

ARTISTS' CO-OP GALLERY, 125 W. Palace Ave., Santa Fe NM 87501. (505)988-2582. Gallery/rental gallery. Estab. 1972. Represents 10 Santa Fe craftworkers. Price range: $2.98-600. Works on consignment; 15% commission. Craftworker sets retail price. Reports in 10 days. Work may be shipped or hand-delivered.

Acceptable Work: Considers batik; ceramics; needlecrafts; pottery; quilting; soft sculpture; wall hangings; weavings; woodcrafting; and raku. Especially needs wall hangings (multi-media). Fine one-of-a-kind pieces; utilitarian and/or decorative.

Profile: "We are a cooperative; artist owned and run. Each show last 3 weeks; 1 or 2 man shows are for 2 weeks. Customers are from US and foreign nations." Best selling time: June - December.

AVANTAOS, Box 2886, Taos NM 87571. (505)758-9583. Director: Ron Davis. Craft shop/gallery. Estab. 1977. Represents 15 craftworkers. Price range: $5-300; bestsellers: $30-40. Works on consignment; 35% commission. Retail price set by joint agreement. Reports in 2 weeks. "We pay insurance for work we ship to craftworker and insurance for exhibited work."

Acceptable Work: Considers batik; ceramics; jewelry; leatherworking; metalsmithing; pottery; soft sculpture; wall hangings; and weaving. Special need for contemporary sculpture." Fine one-of-a kind pieces; utilitarian and/or decorative.

Profile: "We are a comtemporary gallery on Taos Plaza; we handle both arts and crafts. We are open every evening in summer. We use as much individual exposure of work as possible." Customers are 40-60 years of age and usually from large cities. Heaviest wholesale buying time: March-April; best selling time: May-October.

BLAIR GALLERIES LTD., Box 2342, Santa Fe NM 87501. Contact: Joseph Burgess. Considers sculpture. Price range: $150-25,000. Retail price set by craftworker. Requires exclusive area representation; charges commission on art sold in area after show. Gallery pays insurance on exhibited work. Sponsors openings. Mailing for each new show goes to 1,500 individuals. 2 weeks minimum exposure.

BLUE DOOR GALLERY/GIFT SHOP, Drawer N, Taos NM 87571. (505)758-2233. Contact: Jay Slinde or LaVonne Moynihan. Gallery/gift shop. Estab. 1972. Represents 50 craftworkers. Price range: $5-4,000; bestsellers; $20-200. Works on consignment and buys outright; 33⅓% commission. Retail price set by joint agreement. Reports in 2 weeks. Work may be shipped or hand-delivered.

Acceptable Work: Considers batik; ceramics; clothing; dollmaking; jewelry; needlecrafts; pottery; tole painting; wall hangings; weaving; antiques; and sand paintings. Especially needs weavings. All styles; utilitarian and/or decorative.

Profile: "Maximum display time is indefinite; we show work in open and locked cases, on walls and shelves; we have 5 rooms." Heaviest wholesale buying time: spring and fall; best selling time: summer and fall.

CASA BLANCA WEAVERS, 1926 Broadway SE, Albuquerque NM 87102. (505)242-1827. Contact: Carlos Aceves. Craft shop. Estab. 1936. Represents 9 craftworkers. Considers wall hangings and weavings. Fine, one-of-a-kind and handmade production-line items; utilitarian and/or decorative. Price range: $3.50-900; bestsellers: $3.50-300. Works on consignment and buys outright; 25% commission. Retail price set by joint agreement. Requires exclusive area representation. Reports in 2 weeks. Work may be shipped. Dealer pays return shipping and insurance for exhibited work. Heaviest wholesale buying time: summer; best selling time: summer and fall.

CASA DE COLORES, 652 Canyon Rd., Santa Fe NM 87501. Contact: Karen DeMott or Jan Johnson. Studio/gallery. Estab. 1978. Represents 5 craftworkers. Price range: $10-500. Works on consignment and buys outright; 30-40% commission. Retail price set by joint agreement. Requires exclusive area representation. Reports in 3 weeks. Work may be shipped or hand-delivered. Dealer pays insurance for exhibited work.

Acceptable Work: Considers batik; jewelry; soft sculpture; pottery; sculpture; wall hangings;

weavings; and silk screening. Fine and one-of-a-kind pieces; utilitarian and/or decorative. **Profile:** "Work is displayed on open shelves, closed cases and in wall displays. Customers are tourists; all ages; middle to upper income." Heaviest wholesale buying time: spring; best selling time: summer. "Mail slides and photos and description of materials and prices."

CLAY AND FIBER GALLERY, Box 439, Taos NM 87571. (505)758-8093. Contact: Art or Mark Adair. Craft shop/gallery. Estab. 1974. Represents 60-75 craftworkers. Price range: $3-1,500; bestsellers: $10-500. Works on consignment and buys outright; 40% commission. Craftworker sets retail price. Requires exclusive area representation. Reports in 1 week. Work may be shipped or hand-delivered upon request from gallery. Shipping payment is negotiable. Dealer pays insurance for exhibited work. Work is displayed "on walls and shelves and pedestals by agreement with artist". Best selling and heaviest wholesale buying time: summer.
Acceptable Work: Considers batik; ceramics; clothing; glass art; jewelry; pottery; quilting; soft sculpture; wall hangings; weavings; and woodcrafting. Fine one-of-a-kind and handmade production-line items; utilitarian and/or decorative.

THE CONTEMPORARY CRAFTSMAN, 112 Don Gaspar, Santa Fe NM 87501. (505)988-1001. Director: Jane Gann. Gallery. Estab. 1976. Represents 120 craftworkers. Price range: $3-1,200; bestsellers: $3-700. Works on consignment and buys outright; 34% commission. Retail price set by joint agreement. Reports in 2 weeks. Work may be shipped or hand-delivered by prior arrangement. Dealer pays return shipping and insurance for exhibited work.
Acceptable Work: Considers batik; ceramics; clothing; dollmaking; glass art; jewelry; leatherworking; metalsmithing; needlecrafts; pottery; quilting; soft sculpture; wall hangings; weavings; woodcrafting; furniture; baskets; and stained glass. Fine one-of-a-kind and handmade production-line items; utilitarian and/or decorative.
Profile: "Items are displayed depending on the nature of the work. We use shelves, pedestals, glass display cases and wall space. We display them with integrity and concern for the individual piece. We make a concerted effort to educate people about the fine quality of work in New Mexico and the rest of the country." Heaviest wholesale buying time: spring - fall; best selling time: June - Christmas.

DEL SOL, INC., La Fonda Hotel, Shelby and Water Streets, Santa Fe NM 87501. (505)983-3927. Contact: Celina Garcia. Craft shop/gift shop. Estab. 1976. Represents 20 craftworkers. Price range: $1-300; bestsellers: $6-150. Works on consignment and buys outright; commission varies. Gallery sets retail price. Reports in 3 weeks. Work may be shipped or hand-delivered. "We display work on shelves, hung on walls and in niches in the wall." Best selling time: summer.
Acceptable Work: Considers batik; candlemaking; ceramics; decoupage; dollmaking; glass art; hand blown glass; silver; brass; copper art; jewelry; leatherworking; metalsmithing; needlecrafts; pottery; quilting; wall hangings; weavings; and woodcrafting. All styles; utilitarian and/or decorative.

DEWEY-KOFRON GALLERY, 112 E. Palace Ave., Santa Fe NM 87501. (505)982-8478. Contact: Ray Dewey. Arts/crafts gallery. Estab. 1976. Represents 30 craftworkers whose work relates to Indian and contemporary Southwest and New Mexico folk art. Price range: $20-15,000; bestsellers; $300-1,500. Works on consignment and buys outright; 33⅓% commission. Retail price set by joint agreement. Requires exclusive area representation. Reports in 2 weeks. Work may be shipped or hand-delivered. Dealer pays return shipping.
Acceptable Work: Considers jewelry; metalsmithing; pottery; wall hangings; weavings; and woodcrafting. Primitive and fine one-of-a-kind pieces; utilitarian and/or decorative.
Profile: "We display our work in enclosed cases and on wall space. We are selective and limited in what we show and have an excellent location near Santa Fe Plaza. Customers are from out of state (80%); aged 24-55; basically collectors; have over $20,000 per year income." Heaviest wholesale buying time: December - June; best selling time: June - December.

DE VARGAS ARTS AND CRAFTS FAIR, Box 205, Santa Fe NM 81501 (505)988-1110. Contact: Jane Dunn. Gallery/rental gallery/art promotion shop. Estab. 1974. Represents 75-100 craftworkers. Price range: $5-12,000; bestsellers: $15-250. Works on consignment and buys outright; 20-40% commission. Retail price set by joint agreement. Work may be shipped or hand-delivered. Dealer pays limited insurance for exhibited work. Heaviest wholesale buying time: fall and summer; best selling time: Christmas and summer.
Acceptable Work: Considers batik; candlemaking; ceramics; clothing; dollmaking; glass art; jewelry; leatherworking; metalsmithing; needlecrafts; pottery; wall hangings; weavings; and woodcrafting. Fine one-of-a-kind pieces; utilitarian and/or decorative.

EL GRINGO, Box 2356, Taos NM 87571. (505)758-8311. Contact: C.H. Burlingame. Craft shop/gallery/gift shop. Estab. 1972. Represents 15 craftworkers. Price range: $5-100; bestsellers: $5-8. Works on consignment and buys outright; 40% commission. Retail price set by joint agreement. Reports in 1 week. Dealer pays return shipping.
Acceptable Work: Considers glass art; jewelry; leatherworking; metalsmithing; pottery; woodcrafting; statuary, and ojos (God's eyes). Special need for pottery. Fine handmade production-line items; utilitarian and/or decorative.
Profile: "Work is enclosed in jewelry cases, placed on pedestals or shelves. Our store is in a good location. We stay open long hours in the summer (8:30 a.m. to 10 p.m.) 7 days a week." Customers are all tourists of upper middle income. Heaviest wholesale buying time: spring and summer; best selling time: summer.

EL RINCON, Box Q, Taos NM 87501. (505)758-9188. Contact: Rowena Myers Martinez. Craft shop/gift shop/museum gallery. Estab. 1970. Represents 35 craftworkers. Price range: $5-1,800; bestsellers: $20-75. Buys outright. Gallery sets retail price. Reports in 1 week. Hand-delivered work only.
Acceptable Work: Considers dollmaking; jewelry; pottery; wall hangings; weavings; woodcrafting; tin craft; and beadwork. All styles; utilitarian and/or decorative.
Profile: "We are a museum of Indian and Spanish Colonial cultural items. Work is displayed in showcases, on shelves and wallspace." Heaviest wholesale buying time: summer; best selling time: summer and fall.

GUIYERMO GALLERIES, 1825 San Mateo Blvd. NE, Albuquerque NM 87110. (505)265-2597. Curator: Mr. G. McDonald. Considers sculpture. Maximum size: 48x30x48". Sculpture must have pedestals. Price range: $10-50, sculpture. Works on consignment; 33⅓% commission. Gallery sets retail price. Requires exclusive area representation. Send photos of work. SASE.

HAND MADE USA, INC., 526 Coronado Center, Albuquerque NM 87110. (505)883-5861. President: Don Byrne. Craft shop. Estab. 1976. Represents 110 craftworkers. Considers all crafts. All styles; utilitarian and/or decorative. Price range: $1-1,000; bestsellers: $5.95-200. Works on consignment and operates as a high volume coop with a basic booth fee and percentage; 23% commission. Craftworker sets retail price. Reports each month. Work may be shipped or hand-delivered. Dealer pays insurance for exhibited work.
Profile: "Each craftsman has his own display booth, arranged the way he likes his craft displayed." Best selling time: summer, fall and Christmas.

HAND MAIDEN, El Centro Mall, 102 E. Water St., Santa Fe NM 87501. (505)982-8368. Contact: Kathe Brogan. Craft shop/gift shop. Estab. 1971. Represents 15 Southwestern craftworkers. Price range: $2-150; bestsellers: $10-40. Buys outright. Gallery sets retail price. Reports in 2 weeks. Work may be shipped or hand-delivered. Dealer pays shipping to shop and insurance for exhibited work.
Acceptable Work: Considers candlemaking; ceramics; leatherworking; pottery; and woodcrafting. Especially needs utilitarian stoneware; pottery and soft leather bags. All styles; utilitarian.
Profile: "We display work on open shelves and walls and in glass cases; customers are tourists." Heaviest wholesale buying time: spring; best selling time: summer.

HARBINGER-HUNTRESS STAINED GLASS, 109 Washington Ave., Santa Fe NM 87501. (505)983-1866. Contact: Cherie Huntress. Glass gallery/custom order studio. Estab. 1971. Represents 5-6 craftworkers. Considers glass art. Fine one-of-a-kind and handmade production-line items; utilitarian and/or decorative. Price range: $15-1,500; bestsellers: $20-50. Works on consignment; 33⅓% commission. Retail price set by joint agreement. Reports in 5 weeks. Work may be shipped or hand-delivered. Dealer pays shipping to shop.
Profile: Work is "back lit; shown in hanging displays; customers are home owners; builders; restaurant owners; municipalities; and churches". Best selling and heaviest wholesale buying time: summer.

HILL'S GALLERY OF CONTEMPORARY CRAFTS, 110 W. San Francisco, Santa Fe NM 87501. (505)982-2549. Director: Anne Schleider. Craft shop/gallery. Estab. 1970. Represents 35 craftworkers. Price range: $4.50-1,800; bestsellers: $15-900. Works on consignment and buys outright; 40% commission to gallery. Retail price set by joint agreement. Requires exclusive Santa Fe representation. Reports as soon as possible. Work may be shipped or hand-delivered. Dealer shares cost of shipping and pays insurance for exhibited work. Displays are changed monthly. Best selling and heaviest wholesale buying time: summer.

Acceptable Work: Considers ceramics; clothing; dollmaking; glass art; pottery; soft sculpture; wall hangings; weavings; and woodcrafting. Fine one-of-a-kind and handmade production-line items; utilitarian and/or decorative.

HOUSE AND TABLE, 20 Sena Plaza, Santa Fe NM 87501. (505)982-5265. Contact: Robert Olds. Craft shop/gift shop. Estab. 1967. Represents 6 craftworkers. Price range: $2-150; bestsellers: $5-25. Works on consignment and buys outright; 40% commission. Retail price set by joint agreement. Reports in 1 week. Work may be shipped or hand-delivered. Dealer pays shipping to shop after agreeing to buy and insurance for exhibited work. Heaviest wholesale buying time: spring; best selling time: summer.
Acceptable Work: Considers ceramics; clothing; metalsmithing; pottery; soft sculpture; wall hangings; weavings; woodcraftings; and furniture. Primitive one-of-a-kind and handmade production-line items; utilitarian and/or decorative.

JELLYBEANS, 602 Canyon Rd., Santa Fe NM 87501. (505)988-5227. Contact: Rebecca Carter. Needlework shop. Estab. 1974. Represents 100 craftworkers. Price range: $1-500; bestsellers: $15-40. Buys outright. Gallery sets retail price. Requires exclusive area representation. Reports in 2 weeks. Work may be shipped or hand-delivered by previous arrangement. Dealer pays shipping to shop.
Acceptable Work: Considers needlecrafts. Finished, one-of-a-kind and handmade production-line items; utilitarian and/or decorative. Especially needs more Southwestern designs.
Profile: "Most of our designs are handpainted. Designs and supplies are the best quality. Customers are locals and tourists; middle to upper income." Best selling time: summer.

LA PALOMA GALLERY, Box 3037, Taos NM 87571. (505)758-2921. Contact: Jane Mohon. Craft shop/gallery. Estab. 1977. Represents 10 craftworkers. Price range: $5-600; bestsellers: $10-50. Works on consignment and buys outright; 40% commission. Retail price set by joint agreement. Requires exclusive area representation. Reports in 2 weeks. Work may be shipped or hand-delivered.
Acceptable Work: Considers ceramics; glass art; jewelry; metalsmithing; pottery; wall hangings; weavings; woodcrafting; and mounted butterflies in glass cases. Primitive and fine one-of-a-kind pieces; utilitarian and/or decorative.
Profile: "We display work on display stands, shelves and enclosed cases and walls." Heaviest wholesale buying time: spring and summer; best selling time: summer.

LAS NOVEDADES, Box 1162, E. Kit Carson Rd., Taos NM 87571. (505)758-4439. Contact: Angie Martinez. Gift shop. Estab. 1969. Represents 5 craftworkers. Price range: $12-25; bestsellers: $12 maximum. Works on consignment and buys outright; 50% commission. Craftworker sets retail price. Reports in 1 week. Work may be shipped or hand-delivered. Dealer pays insurance for exhibited work. Heaviest wholesale buying time: May and June; best selling time: July, August and September.
Acceptable Work: Considers jewelry; leatherworking; metalsmithing; pottery. Primitive and handmade production-line items; utilitarian and/or decorative.

THE LEATHER GALLERY, 108 Old Santa Fe Trail, Santa Fe NM 87501. (505)982-2993. Contact: Don Bush. Craft shop. Estab. 1977. Represents 10-12 Southwestern craftworkers. Price range: $2-350; bestsellers: $10-60. Works on consignment and buys outright; 40% commission. Shop sets retail price. Requires exclusive area representation. Reports as soon as possible. Hand-delivered work only. Dealer pays return shipping and insurance for exhibited work.
Acceptable Work: Considers leatherworking. Fine one-of-a-kind and handmade production-line items; utilitarian and/or decorative. Especially needs soft bags, belts and unusual designs.
Profile: "Items are displayed with proper lighting against exotic wood background." Customers are tourists. Heaviest wholesale buying time: spring and pre-Christmas; best selling time: summer and Christmas.

THE MARKET, Box 1111, Taos NM 87571. (505)758-3195. Contact: Peggy Williamson or Jo Livingston. Craft shop/gallery. Estab. 1966. Represents 60 Southwestern craftworkers. Price range: $2-4,500. Works on consignment and buys outright. Requires exclusive area representation. Reports in 1 week. Dealer pays insurance for exhibited work.
Acceptable Work: Considers ceramics; glass art; jewelry; metalsmithing; pottery; wall hangings; weavings; and woodcrafting. Fine one-of-a-kind and handmade production-line items; utilitarian and/or decorative.

MAXWELL MUSEUM GIFT SHOP, University of New Mexico, Albuquerque NM 87131. (505)277-4404. Manager: Beverly J. Barsook. Museum gift shop. Estab. 1968. Considers authentic American Indian crafts only. One-of-a-kind and handmade production-line items; utilitarian and/or decorative. Price range: $10-1,500; bestsellers: $20-500. Works on consignment and buys outright; 50% commission. Retail price set by joint agreement. Work may be shipped with permission and hand-delivered by prior appointment. Dealer pays return shipping and insurance for exhibited work. "Customers are primarily college students and adults traveling." Best selling time: Chrismas and summer.

THE MELTING POINT GLASSWORKS AND POTTERY, 821 Canyon Rd., Santa Fe NM 87501. (505)988-2662. Contact: Daphne Morrissey. Craft shop/gallery. Estab. 1976. Represents 10 craftworkers. Price range: $3-500; bestsellers: $4-75. Works on consignment; 40% commission. Craftworker sets retail price. Reports in 4 weeks. Hand-delivered work only. Dealer pays insurance for exhibited work.
Acceptable Work: Considers ceramics; glass art; and pottery. Fine one-of-a-kind and handmade production-line items; utilitarian and/or decorative.
Profile: "We are fortunate to have our studios on the premises. Work is fully lighted and displayed on shelves, not overcrowded." Best selling and heaviest wholesale buying time: summer.

THE MUSEUM SHOP AT THE INTERNATIONAL FOLK ART MUSEUM, Box 2087, Santa Fe NM 87501. (505)982-3016. Buyer: Liz Buchan. Museum gift and craft shop. Estab. 1952. Represents 10-20 American craftworkers. Price range: $2-200; bestsellers: $5-30. Works on consignment and buys outright; commission varies. Retail price set by joint agreement. Reports immediately after personal appointment. Work may be shipped or hand-delivered. Dealer pays insurance for exhibited work.
Acceptable Work: Considers batik; ceramics; dollmaking; glass art; jewelry; metalsmithing; needlecrafts; pottery; wall hangings; weavings; woodcrafting; baskets; and toys. Only folk art, Spanish Colonial and local crafts based on a folk tradition. One-of-a-kind pieces; utilitarian and/or decorative.
Profile: Work is displayed in "glass enclosed cases, open shelves and securely locked storage closets and bins". Customers are tourists; collectors; school groups; people doing research; and local residents. Best selling time and heaviest wholesale buying time: summer.

MUSEUM SHOP — PALACE OF THE GOVERNOR, Box 2087, Santa Fe NM 87501. (505)982-3016. Buyer: Liz Buchanan. Museum gift shop. Estab. 1964. Represents over 100 Indian and Spanish-American craftworkers. Price range: 75c-$3,500; bestsellers: $10-400. Buys outright. Retail price set by joint agreement. Reports in 3 weeks. Work may be shipped or hand-delivered upon agreement to buy. Dealer pays insurance for exhibited work. Displays work 3-12 months.
Acceptable Work: Considers dollmaking; jewelry; needlecrafts; pottery; wall hangings; weavings; woodcrafting; and pottery figures. Primitive and one-of-a-kind pieces; utilitarian and/or decorative.
Profile: Work is displayed in "enclosed cases, walls; we have burglar alarms and museum guards. We are located in an historic city and building. We deal with craftsmen whose backgrounds are more ancient than the city". Best selling and heaviest wholesale buying time: summer.

NEW MEXICO ART LEAGUE, 3401 Juan Tabo NE, Albuquerque NM 87111. (505)293-5034. Director: Jean Rosenburg. Gallery. Estab. 1929. Represents 14 New Mexico craftworkers. Price range: $5-1,000; bestsellers: $45-100. Works on consignment; 33⅓% commission. Craftworker sets retail price. Reports in 2 weeks. Work may be shipped or hand-delivered. Displays work 1 month minimum. Best selling time: summer.
Acceptable Work: Considers ceramics; metalsmithing; pottery; wall hangings; weavings; and woodcrafting. Fine one-of-a-kind pieces; utilitarian and/or decorative.

1 OF A KIND, 706 Canyon Rd., Santa Fe NM 87501. (505)988-4867. President: Jim Livermore. Craft shop. Estab. 1976. Represents 12 member craftworkers. Price range: $2-300; bestsellers: $5-30. 10% commission. Craftworker sets retail price. Reports in 4 weeks. Work may be hand delivered.
Acceptable Work: Considers all crafts except decoupage; soft sculpture; and tole painting. Primitive and fine one-of-a-kind pieces; utilitarian and/or decorative.
Profile: Work is displayed on "walls, in display cases and on shelves. One coop member is in charge of display. There is no middle man between craftsman and customer". Best selling time: summer.

THE OWL'S NEST, Box 1726, The Plaza North, Taos NM 87501. (505)758-4478. Manager: Fran Smith. Craft shop/gallery/gift shop. Estab. 1972. Represents 18-20 craftworkers. Price range: 50c-$2,700; bestsellers: under $50. Works on consignment and buys outright; 35% commission. Craftworker sets retail price. Requires exclusive area representation. Reports in 1 week. Hand-delivered work only (initially).
Acceptable Work: Considers batik; stained glass art; jewelry; metalsmithing; pottery; soft sculpture; wall hangings; weavings; woodcrafting; furniture; lamps; hand painted tiles; rugs; sand painting; baskets; and handmade cards and stationery. Fine one-of-a-kind pieces; utilitarian and/or decorative.
Profile: "Work is displayed on counters, open shelves, locked cases and walls." Heaviest wholesale buying time: spring; best selling time: summer.

PACKARD'S INDIAN TRADING CO., 61 Old Santa Fe Trail, Santa Fe NM 87501. Contact: Al R. Packard. Indian arts and crafts shop. Estab. 1929. Represents 200 craftworkers. Price range: $10-10,000; bestsellers: $100-200. Buys outright. Shop sets retail price. Requires exclusive area representation in some cases. Reports in 2 weeks. Work may be shipped or hand-delivered. Dealer pays shipping to shop if work is ordered and insurance for exhibited work.
Acceptable Work: Considers only Indian jewelry; leatherworking; pottery; wall hangings; Navajo weavings; woodcrafting; and beading. Primitive and fine one-of-a-kind pieces; utilitarian and/or decorative.
Profile: "It's a real trading post. Work is displayed in enclosed glass cases, on walls and shelves." Heaviest wholesale buying time: winter; best selling time: summer and Christmas.

PEDDLER'S CART GALLERY, 7602 Menaul NE, Albuquerque NM 87110. (505)298-2770. Contact: Helen Sanchez. Gallery. Estab. 1965. Represents 100 craftworkers. Price range: $1.50-125; bestsellers: $1.50-40. Works on consignment and buys outright; 40% commission. Retail price set by joint agreement. Reports in 4 weeks. Work may be hand-delivered. Dealer pays shipping to shop and insurance for exhibited work.
Acceptable Work: Considers ceramics; jewelery; pottery; tole painting; wall hangings; weavings; and woodcrafting. Fine one-of-a-kind pieces; utilitarian and/or decorative.
Profile: "Customers are individualistic; represent the upper income group; aged 22-70." Heaviest wholesale buying time: late summer; best selling time: Christmas.

POPOVI DA INDIAN ARTS & CRAFTS, Rt. 5, Box 309, San Ildefonso Pueblo, Santa Fe NM 87501. (505)455-2456. Contact: Anita Da. Estab. 1949. Represents 100 Southwestern Indian craftworkers. Considers beadwork; dollmaking; jewelry; leatherworking; metalsmithing; needlecrafts; pottery; sand painting; sculpture; wall hangings; weavings; and woodcrafting. One-of-a-kind primitive and finished items; utilitarian and/or decorative. Price range: $9-5,000; bestsellers: $10-200. Buys outright or occasionally on consignment; 10-20% commission. Retail price set by joint agreement. Requires exclusive area representation. Call for interview. Dealer pays insurance for exhibited work. Heaviest wholesale buying time: April-September. Customers are tourists; they buy crafts for artistic value and gifts.

PRIMITIVES AND CONTEMPORARIES, 601 Canyon Rd., Santa Fe NM 87501. (505)983-8068. Contact: Jerilou Mayans. Craft shop/gallery. Estab. 1976. Represents 25 craftworkers. Price range: $10-500; bestsellers: $30-150. Works on consignment and buys outright; 40% commission. Retail price set by joint agreement. Requires exclusive area representation. Query first. Reports in 2 weeks; enclose SASE. Dealer pays return shipping and insurance for exhibited work. Displays work 3 months.
Acceptable Work: Considers batik; dollmaking; quilting; wall hangings; weavings; and woodcrafting. Primitive and fine one-of-a-kind pieces; utilitarian and/or decorative.
Profile: "Special items are displayed in the front window. Attention is given to floor displays using plants and furniture. Information about craftsperson is mounted next to items. Press releases are issued weekly." Best selling time: summer and fall.

QUIVIRA SHOP, 114 Old Santa Fe Trail, Box 1941, Santa Fe NM 87501. (505)983-7852. Manager: Larry Torres. Indian arts and crafts shop. Estab. 1971. Represents 100 American Indian craftworkers. Price range: $10 minimum; bestsellers: $10-250. Buys outright. Retail price set by joint agreement. Reporting time varies. Hand-delivered work only. Dealer pays return shipping and insurance for exhibited work. Work is displayed "in enclosed glass cases and on walls". Best selling time: March-November.
Acceptable Work: Considers only Indian dollmaking (kachinas); jewelry; pottery; wall hangings; weavings; and beadwork. Fine one-of-a-kind pieces; utilitarian and/or decorative.

RETURN, Box 53, Taos NM 87501. (505)758-3993. Contact: Charlotte Hopper. Gallery. Estab. 1976. Represents 36 craftworkers. "Southwestern mystical theme centered on northern New Mexico artists but also looking at artists from other regions with compatible new age consciousness." Considers all crafts, "mainly interested in refined workmanship and theme compatibility." All styles; utilitarian and/or decorative. Price range: $2.50-8,725; bestsellers: $30-150. Works on consignment; 40% commission. Retail price set by joint agreement. Reports in 2 weeks. Dealer pays return shipping; in-transit insurance; and insurance for exhibited work.
Profile: "Display environment created by the artists to emulate nature and ancient Indian civilization of Chaco Canyon. Extensive rock work, fine wood work, stained glass in decor. A museum quality in environment and work." Customers are successful young business people to older fine arts and crafts collectors. Best selling time: summer.

Emulating the ancient Indian civilization of Chaco Canyon and nature, Return (Taos, New Mexico) has used extensive rock work, fine woodwork, and stained glass in its interior. The shop emphasizes a Southwestern mystical theme and new age consciousness, and is looking for crafts of refined workmanship and theme compatibility.

RUYBALID'S INDIAN SHOP AND SANTA FE ARTS AND CRAFTS, 113-117 E. Palace, Santa Fe NM 87501. (505)982-0525. Contact: Victor Ruybalid. Craft and gift shop. Estab. 1957. Represents 3 craftworkers. Price range: $1-2,500; bestsellers: $35-2,500. Buys outright. Gallery sets retail price. Reports immediately. Work may be shipped or hand-delivered for approval.
Acceptable Work: Considers ceramics; dollmaking; glass art; jewelry; leatherworking; metalsmithing; needlecrafts; pottery; wall hangings; weavings; woodcrafting; ojos; and rugs. Primitive and fine one-of-a-kind pieces; utilitarian and/or decorative.
Profile: "We are one of the older dealers of Indian jewelry and are located in an historic adobe building." Best selling and heaviest wholesale buying time: summer.

SCHELU ARTISANS, 401-B San Felipe NW, Old Town, Albuquerque NM 87104. (505)765-5869. Contact: Doris Lusk. Gallery. Estab. 1973. Represents 100 craftworkers. Price range: $2.50-600; bestsellers: $14-250. Works on consignment and buys outright; 40% commission.

Retail price set by joint agreement. Reports in 2 weeks. Work may be shipped or hand-delivered. Dealer pays insurance for exhibited work. Displays work 1 month minimum.
Acceptable Work: Considers batik; ceramics; jewelry; metalsmithing; pottery; soft sculpture; wall hangings; weavings; and woodcrafting. Especially needs wall hangings; pottery; jewelry; and decorator pieces. All styles; utilitarian and/or decorative.
Profile: "We display work depending on item; on pedestals and on wall space. Displays and work are moved and rotated frequently to inspire sales. We show mostly Southwestern style of work; offer customers decorating service and custom orders." Heaviest wholesale buying time: spring and September-October; best selling time: summer and Christmas.

SHALAKO SHOP, INC., Box 970, Community Center, Los Alamos NM 87544. (505)662-2539. Contact: Edward B. Grothus. Estab. 1957. Represents 2 craftworkers. Considers candlemaking; ceramics; glass art; jewelry; leatherworking; metalsmithing; needlecrafts; pottery; wall hangings; weavings; woodcrafting; works in copper, brass and tile; and ecological and futuristic crafts. Primitive and finished one-of-a-kind and handmade production-line items; utilitarian and/or decorative. Price range: 50c-$1,500; bestsellers; $50. Buys outright or occasionally on consignment; 33⅓% commission. Retail price set by joint agreement. Arrange appointment. Negotiates payment for shipping and insurance. Heaviest buying and selling time: Christmas. Customers buy crafts for gifts.

SHOP OF THE RAINBOW MAN, INC., 107 E. Palace, Santa Fe NM 87501. (505)982-0791. Contact: Gwen Windus. Craft shop/gallery/gift shop. Estab. 1945. Represents 6 craftworkers. Price range: $6.50-475; bestsellers; $100-300. Buys outright. Retail price set by joint agreement. Reports in 1 day. Work may be shipped or hand-delivered.
Acceptable Work: Considers ceramics; dollmaking; glass art; jewelry; woodcrafting; sandpaintings; and tiles. Finished and handmade production-line items; utilitarian and/or decorative.
Profile: "We display work in show cases, windows and hanging on walls; our customers are all ages, interests and incomes." Heaviest wholesale buying time: spring; best selling time: summer.

SOUTHWESTERN INDIAN ARTS, Box 1892, Taos Indian Pueblo, Taos NM 87571. Contact: Tony or Ann Reyna. Estab: Shop #1 at Taos Indian Reservation, 1950; Shop #2 at the Kachina Lodge, 1960. Represents 25 Indian craftworkers. Considers jewelry; drums; rugs; paintings; beadwork; carvings; baskets; and pottery. Finished, one-of-a-kind handmade items OK; utilitarian and/or decorative. Price range: $10-2,000; bestsellers: $10-350. Buys outright. Retail price set by joint agreement. Write. Reports in 2 weeks. Dealer pays insurance for exhibited work.
Profile: Best selling time: March-June. Shop is Indian-owned and operated. Tourist customers buy crafts for artistic value. No mail orders.

STREETS OF TAOS, 200 Canyon Rd., Santa Fe NM 87501. (505)983-8268. Contact: Hilda Street. Craft shop/gallery/gift shop/trading post. Estab. 1947. Represents 16 craftworkers. Price range: $20-2,000; bestsellers: $100-1,000. Buys outright. Gallery sets retail price. Reports in 1 week. Work may be shipped or hand-delivered. Shipping payment is negotiable. Work is displayed in showcases, on walls and tables. Heaviest wholesale buying time: spring; best selling time: summer.
Acceptable Work: Considers clothing; jewelry; pottery; and woodcrafting. Primitive and fine one-of-a-kind items; utilitarian and/or decorative. Especially needs unusual handmade shirts and Indian made jewelry.

THE STUDIO GALLERY, 3529 Constitution NE, Albuquerque NM 87106. (505)262-0672. Contact: Tom W. Thomason. Gallery. Estab. 1962. Represents 25 craftworkers. Price range: 50c-$3,200; bestsellers; 50c-$350. Works on consignment; 40% commission. Craftworker sets retail price. Reports in 2 weeks. Work may be shipped or hand-delivered. Dealer pays insurance for exhibited work. Displays work 3 months minimum.
Acceptable Work: Considers all crafts except decoupage and tole painting. Especially needs good leather and fiber. Fine one-of-a-kind and handmade production-line items; utilitarian and/or decorative.
Profile: "We try to individually display each piece. Customers are in late 30's; income of $20,000 and up; interested in contemporary work." Best selling time: summer and Christmas.

SUNRISE OF SANTA FE, 111 Old Santa Fe Trail, Santa Fe NM 87501. (505)982-2993. President: Don Bush. Gallery. Estab. 1976. Represents 35 New Mexico, Arizona and Colorado jewelry craftworkers. Considers jewelry. Fine one-of-a-kind and handmade production-line items; decorative only. Price range: $10-1,500; bestsellers: $30-150. Works on consignment and buys outright; 40% commission. Retail price set by joint agreement. Requires exclusive area representation. Reports as soon as possible. Hand-delivered work only. Dealer pays return shipping and insurance for exhibited work.

Profile: "Work is displayed in handcrafted wood cases using natural materials (woods, cork, minerals, etc.) for background." Customers are 25-45 years old; middle to upper income; 20% of business is local; 50% tourists. Heaviest wholesale buying time: spring and summer; best selling time: spring through fall.

THE TRADING COMPANY, Box TTT, Taos NM 87571. (505)758-4582. Contact: Thelma Dodson. Trading company. Estab. 1978. Represents 10-15 craftworkers. Price range: $3-8,000. Arrangements with craftworkers vary. Retail price set by joint agreement. Reports in 2 weeks. Work may be shipped or hand-delivered. Dealer pays return shipping.

Acceptable Work: Considers batik; ceramics; clothing; dollmaking; glass art; jewelry; leatherworking; metalsmithing; needlecrafts; pottery; quilting; tole painting; wall hangings; weavings; woodcrafting; beading; and rugs. Primitive, finished and one-of-a-kind pieces; utilitarian and/or decorative.

Profile: "We display work in enclosed showcases, on walls, shelves and tables. We'll trade anything: artifacts, antiques and crafts." Heaviest wholesale buying time: spring and summer; best selling time: spring, summer and fall.

WHATSMENOT?, 703 Canyon Rd., Santa Fe NM 87501. (505)988-4241. Craft shop. Estab. 1976. Represents 6-7 craftworkers. Price range: $2-200; bestsellers: $30-50. Works on consignment and buys outright; 30% commission. Craftworker sets retail price. Reports same day. Work may be shipped or hand-delivered. Dealer pays insurance for exhibited work.

Acceptable Work: Considers batik; candlemaking; ceramics; glass art; jewelry; leatherworking; pottery; wall hangings; weavings; and woodcrafting. Primitive and fine one-of-a-kind pieces; utilitarian and/or decorative.

Profile: "Work is displayed in enclosed cases, open counters, tables and wall space." Heaviest wholesale buying time: early spring; best selling time: May-September.

THE WHEELWRIGHT MUSEUM, Box 5153, Santa Fe NM 87502. (505)982-4636. Director: Steven Tremper. Museum gallery. Considers ceramics; dollmaking; jewelry; metalsmithing; pottery; sculpture; and weavings. Maximum size: 6x8'. Historical and contemporary Indian art only. Price range: $50-1,500. Works on consignment; 30% commission. Artist sets retail price. Query, send samples or call or write for interview. No samples returned. Museum pays shipping from gallery and insurance. Exhibition department handles installation. 1-2 months exposure.

WINONA TRADING POST, 211-213 Galisteo St., Box 324, Santa Fe NM 87501. (505)988-4811. Contact: Pierre Bovis. Estab. 1965. Represents 100+ Indian craftworkers. Considers beadwork; jewelry; pottery; and quillwork. One-of-a-kind primitive and finished items only; utilitarian and/or decorative. Minimum price: $10. Buys outright or on consignment; 25% commission. Retail price set by joint agreement. Requires exclusive area representation. Write. Reports in 1 week. Dealer pays shipping from shop.

New York

ALL BY HAND, 7810 3rd Ave., Brooklyn NY 11209. (212)745-8904. Contact: Lou Gaita. Craft shop. Estab. 1976. Represents 25 craftworkers. Considers ceramics; glass art; jewelry; leatherworking; pottery; and woodcrafting. Hand-made production-line items only; utilitarian and/or decorative. Price range: $1-350; bestsellers: $10-25. Buys outright. Gallery sets retail price. Reports in 2 weeks. Work may be shipped or hand-delivered. Dealer pays shipping. "Do not send unsolicited samples unless they are not to be returned; always include a packing slip." Best selling time: Christmas; heaviest wholesale buying time: summer.

ALNICO GALLERY, 123 Prince St., New York NY 10012. (212)228-6586. Contact: Director. Gallery. Considers contemporary crafts. Price range: $100-3,000. "Artist-run gallery maintained by artist paid dues; 15% commission." Submit slides or photos and resume or call for interview.

ALONZO GALLERY, INC., 30 W. 57th St., New York NY 10019. (212)586-2500. Director: Jack Alonzo. Considers sculpture; wall hangings; and weavings. Maximum height: 9'. Art must be ready to exhibit. Specializes in abstracts with some literal work. Price range: $25-12,000; bestsellers: $50-1,000. Works on consignment; 50% commission. Retail price set by joint agreement. Requires exclusive area representation. Send slides of work or call for interview. SASE. 3-4 weeks exposure.

ARC EN CIEL STAINED GLASS, 1885 Palmer Ave., Larchmont NY 10538. (914)834-2616. Contact: Richard Cronk and Doris Goldfischer. Craft shop/gallery/gift shop/manufacturer and school of stained glass. Estab. 1975. Represents stained glass and blown glass craftworkers. Considers glass art and stained glass. Fine one-of-a-kind and handmade production line items; utilitarian and/or decorative. Price range: $10-15,000; bestsellers: $10-800. Works on consignment and buys outright; 40% commission. Retail price set by joint agreement. Dealer pays for insurance on exhibited work. Best selling time: fall-Christmas.

THE ARTISAN, 114 E. Noyes Blvd., Sherrill NY 13461. Contact: Rosamond Bennati or Carol Weimer. Craft and gift shop. Estab. 1976. Represents 30-40 craftworkers. Price range: $2-50; bestsellers: $2-25. Buys outright. Retail price set by joint agreement. Requires exclusive area representation. Reports in 2 weeks. Work may be shipped or hand-delivered.
Acceptable Work: Considers batik; candlemaking; dollmaking; glass art; jewelry; leatherworking; pottery; tole painting; wall hangings; weavings; and woodcrafting. Utilitarian and/or decorative.
Profile: "Our place of display changes about once a month. We will display on consignment about 3 months and then discontinue or buy outright." Best selling time: summer and Christmas; heaviest wholesale buying time: spring and fall.

ARTISAN HOUSE, 80 Main St., Northport NY 11768. (516)261-3800. Contact: G. Jackier. Craft shop/gallery. Estab. 1972. Represents 400 craftworkers. Price range: $1-250; bestsellers: $1-40. Works on consignment and buys outright; 40% commission. Retail price set by joint agreement. Requires exclusive area representation. Reports in 2 weeks. Work may be shipped or hand-delivered. Dealer pays shipping to shop and insurance for exhibited work. Displays consignment work at least 3 months. Best selling time: Christmas and summer.
Acceptable Work: Considers batik; candlemaking; clothing; glass art; jewelry; leatherworking; metalsmithing; pottery; soft sculpture; wall hangings; weavings; woodcrafting; graphics; wooden toys; handmade cards; and basketry. All styles; utilitarian and/or decorative.

ARTPARK STORE, Box 371, Lewistown NY 14094. (716)754-8250. Manager: Joan McDonough. Craft shop/gallery. Estab. 1974. Usually represents artists-in-residence. Price range: $5-500; bestsellers: $5-100. Works on consignment; commission varies. Craftworker sets retail price. Reports in 2 weeks. Work may be shipped or hand-delivered. Dealer pays return shipping and insurance for exhibited work.
Acceptable Work: Considers batik; clothing; dollmaking; glass art; jewelry; leatherworking; metalsmithing; pottery; soft sculpture; wall hangings; weavings; and woodcrafting. All styles; utilitarian and/or decorative.
Profile: "Artists work grouped together, will not be placed next to another working in the same medium. Length of time is flexible, payment in 30 days." Only open in summer; heaviest wholesale buying time: spring.

ARTWORKS, 208 W. State St., Olean NY 14760. (716)372-1740. Contact: Bette Hestle. Craft shop/gallery. Estab. 1973. Represents 15-20 craftworkers. Price range: $1.65-200; bestsellers: $3-25. Buys outright. Retail price set by joint agreement. Work may be shipped or hand-delivered. Dealer pays return shipping and insurance for exhibited work. Best selling and buying time: fall.
Acceptable Work: Considers batik; candlemaking; clothing; dollmaking; glass art; jewelry; leatherworking; metalsmithing; pottery; wall hangings; weavings; and woodcrafting. Fine one-of-a-kind and handmade production-line items; utilitarian and/or decorative.

"B. RUGGED", 345 Lafayette St., New York NY 10012. (212)226-2933. Contact: Susanna Cuyler. Craft shop/rugmaking workshop. Estab. 1976. Considers hooked and knotted rugs; fine one-of-a-kind designer pieces; utilitarian only. Price range: $10-1,000; bestsellers: $25-300. Works on consignment and does custom orders; 25% commission. Retail price set by joint agreement. Reports as soon as possible. Work may be shipped or hand-delivered.
Special Needs: Customer-designed rug patterns; original drawings; children's art; and personalized original hooked and knotted rugs.
Profile: "I want to sell other craftsmen's hooked and knotted rugs on my low commission to get at more of the infinite design possibilities inherent in the medium." Best selling time: winter; heaviest wholesale buying time: spring and fall.

BALDWIN POTTERY INC., 540 La Guardia Place, New York NY 10012. (212)475-7236. President: Judith Baldwin. Estab. 1960. Represents 12 craftworkers. Primitive or finished ceramics OK; utilitarian and/or decorative. Price range: $3-150; bestsellers: $3-50. Buys outright. Craftworker sets retail price. Requires exclusive area representation. Write or call. Reports in 2 weeks. Negotiates payment for shipping and insurance.

Profile: Window and central display area provided. "Try not to keep old merchandise (have sales or exchange these for new items)." Customers are ages 20-40, middle-class.

BARBARA BARRON FIBRE CREATIONS, 125 Walt Whitman Rd., Huntington Station NY 11746. (516)549-4242. President: Barbara Barron. Craft studio. Estab. 1973. Represents 6 fiber artists only. Price range: $1.50-2,100; bestsellers: $1.50-100. Works on consignment and buys outright; 40% commission. Retail price set by joint agreement. Requires exclusive area representation. Reports in 2 weeks. Work may be shipped or hand-delivered. Dealer pays return shipping and insurance for exhibited work. Best selling time: fall.

Acceptable Work: Considers batik; needlecrafts; quilting; soft sculpture; wall hangings; and weavings. Fine one-of-a-kind and handmade production-line items; utilitarian and/or decorative. Especially needs macrame; wall hangings; soft sculpture; quilting; weaving; and pillows.

BEAUTIFUL WOODS INC., 230 E. 59th St., New York NY 10022. (212)759-7246. Contact: Renee Levy. Designer showroom. Estab. 1977. Represents 2-3 craftworkers. Considers woodcrafting. "Special need for quality wall sculptures from wood; mirrors with wood; and crafts combining wood and other elements." Fine one-of-a-kind pieces; utilitarian and/or decorative. Price range: $75-7,000; bestsellers: $400-2,500. Works on consignment and buys outright; 25-50% commission. Requires exclusive area representation. Reports in 1 week. Dealer pays shipping and in-transit insurance.

Profile: "We sell wholesale to decorators and architects and are the only showroom in New York handling fine wood furniture for the designer trade."

BEDFORD/DOWNING GLASS, 202 E. 83rd St., New York NY 10028. (212)861-2634. Contact: Ingo Williams. Craft shop. Estab. 1972. Represents 3-4 craftworkers who work in leaded glass. Considers glass art only. Fine one-of-a-kind and handmade production-line items; utilitarian and/or decorative. Price range: $15-600; bestsellers: $15-300. Works on consignment; 25% commission. Gallery sets retail price. Reports in 1 week. Work may be shipped or hand-delivered. Work is "displayed in living room style." Best selling and buying time: spring and fall.

THE BEE SKEP, Rt. 2, Bee Skep Lane, Granville NY 12832. (518)632-5313. Contact: Carol L. Liedtke. Craft and gift shop. Estab. 1975. Represents 60 craftworkers. Price range: 15c-$155; bestsellers: $2-20. Works on consignment and buys outright; 40% commission. Gallery sets retail price. Reports in 4 weeks. Work may be shipped or hand-delivered.

Acceptable Work: Considers batik; candlemaking; ceramics; decoupage; dollmaking; glass art; jewelry; leatherworking; metalsmithing; needlecrafts; pottery; quilting; soft sculpture; tole painting; wall hangings; weavings; woodcrafting; quilling; tinsel art; fused glass; and Christmas ornaments. All styles; utilitarian and/or decorative

Profile: Work is in "glass display cases, shelves, small items in baskets. At least 1 year of displaying time. The Bee Skep is set in a wooded valley where visiting customers view a spectacular waterfall and stream." Heaviest wholesale buying time: early spring and late summer; best selling time: summer, fall and holidays.

BELLARDO LTD., 100 Christopher SE, New York NY 10014. (212)675-2668. Contact: Paul Bellardo. Gallery. Estab. 1967. Represents 50 craftworkers. Price range: $24-3,500; bestsellers: $45-300. Works on consignment and buys outright; 50% commission. Retail price set by joint agreement. Requires exclusive area representation. Reports in 2 weeks. Work may be shipped or hand-delivered. Dealer pays shipping and insurance for exhibited work.

Acceptable Work: Considers ceramics; glass art; jewelry; leatherworking; metalsmithing; pottery; wall hangings; and weavings. One-of-a-kind designer pieces only; utilitarian and/or decorative.

Profile: Displays individuals and groups "in or out of the main windows for as long as the shop wishes to show the artist's work". Heaviest wholesale buying time: September; best selling time: November-December.

BENSON GALLERY, Bridgehampton NY 11932. (516)537-0598. Director: Elaine Benson. Estab. 1966. Represents 2-3 craftworkers. Considers all crafts. Price range: $25-10,000; bestsellers: up to $250. Works on consignment; 40% commission. Retail price set by gallery or joint agreement. Requires exclusive area representation. Query with transparencies or photos. Reports in 1-2 weeks. Dealer pays insurance for exhibited work. Items exhibited for 2-week periods during May-September.

WESLEY BERGEN, 65 W. 55th St., New York NY 10019. (212)246-6279. Contact: Wesley Bergen. Considers jewelry and metalsmithing. Price range: $10-5,000. Retail price set by joint agreement. Dealer pays insurance for exhibited work. Openings sponsored. Advanced designs only. Submit color transparencies or b&w photos.

ALLEN BROOK THINGS UNLIMITED, 133 Main St., Port Washington NY 11050. (510)883-0019. Contact: Connie or Mal Chapman. Craft shop/gallery/gift shop. Estab. 1977. Represents 15 craftworkers. Price range: $1.25-750; bestsellers: $2.50-25. Works on consignment and buys outright; commission varies. Retail price set by joint agreement. Reports as soon as possible. Dealer pays insurance for exhibited work.
Acceptable Work: Considers candlemaking; ceramics; clothing; decoupage; glass art; jewelry; leatherworking; needlecrafts; pottery; quilting; wall hangings; weavings; and woodcrafting. All styles; utilitarian and/or decorative. Especially needs good, basic design in $5 price range.
Profile: "Contact us with pictures, samples (nonreturnables) and a plan for us to actually see your line. We like to buy small items outright; expensive art on consignment." Customers are young, above average intelligence, middle to upper middle class. Heaviest wholesale buying time: November and summer; best selling time: Christmas and late spring.

CANDLESTOCK, 16 Mill Hill Rd., Woodstock NY 12498. (914)679-8711. Contact: Barbara Moss. Candle shop. Estab. 1970. Represents 25 craftworkers. Considers candlemaking; ceramics; glass art; and pottery. One-of-a-kind and handmade production-line items; utilitarian and/or decorative. Price range: 25c-$200; bestsellers: $5-20. Buys outright. Gallery sets retail price. Requires exclusive area representation. Reports in 1 week. Work may be shipped or hand-delivered. Dealer pays insurance for exhibited work.
Profile: "Each item gets very special, loving care." Heaviest wholesale buying time: May-December; best selling time: August-December.

CERAMIC STUDIO'S, 144 W. 27th St., 5th Flr., New York NY 10001. (212)691-1470. Contact: Randi Feldman or Tobias Weissman. Gallery/rental gallery. Estab. 1977. Represents 6 craftworkers. Considers all crafts for gallery showing. Craftworker sets retail price. Rental gallery charge is dependent on the length and type of exhibit.

CLAY CRAFTS COMMUNITY, 222 W. 79th St., New York NY 10024. (212)595-2222. Contact: Deena Kolbert. Craft shop. Estab. 1972. Represents 24 craftworkers. Price range: $4-800; bestsellers: under $25. Works on consignment; 50% commission. Retail price set by joint agreement. Send slides. Reports monthly. Hand-delivered work only.
Acceptable Work: Considers all crafts, primarily ceramics. Fine one-of-a-kind and handmade production-line items; utilitarian and/or decorative.
Profile: "Exhibits are rearranged monthly. Customers are middle class and multi-ethnic. Please do not come in without appointment." Best selling time: Christmas and other holidays.

THE CLAY POT, 162 7th Ave., Brooklyn NY 11215. (212)788-6564. Contact: Robert Silberberg. Craft shop. Estab. 1968. Represents 70 craftworkers. Price range: 75c-$150; bestsellers: 25c-$75. Buys outright. Craftworker sets retail price. Requires exclusive area representation. Reports in 4 weeks. Work may be shipped or hand-delivered. Dealer pays shipping to shop.
Acceptable Work: Considers candlemaking; ceramics; glass art; jewelry; leatherworking; metalsmithing; pottery; wall hangings; weavings; and handcrafted greeting cards. Fine handmade production-line items only; utilitarian and/or decorative. Museum quality work.
Profile: "We serve the 4 million population of Brooklyn with quality production items. Customers are upwardly mobile New Yorkers, aware and interested in identifying with the objects around them." Heaviest wholesale buying time: spring and fall.

CLEAR LIGHT STUDIO, 10852 Main St., Clarence NY 14031. (716)633-7967. Contact: Donna Ioviero or Bill Jobling. Craft shop/gallery. Estab. 1977. Price range: $2.50-175; bestsellers: $7-45. Works on consignment; 25% commission. Requires exclusive area representation. Reports in 2 weeks. Work may be shipped or hand-delivered only by prior arrangement. Dealer pays return shipping.
Acceptable Work: Considers batik; candlemaking; clothing; glass art; jewelry; metalsmithing; pottery; and soft sculpture. Primitive and fine one-of-a-kind designer pieces; utilitarian and/or decorative.
Profile: "We have only 4 shows per year, usually on weekends. Customers are all ages, middle and upper class." Heaviest wholesale buying time: Christmas; best selling time: summer and Christmas.

CLOUDS, 1 Mill Hill Rd., Woodstock NY 12498. Director: Robert Orsini. Craft shop/gallery. Estab. 1974. Represents 80-100 craftworkers. Considers jewelry and leatherworking. Fine one-of-a-kind and handmade production-line items; utilitarian and/or decorative. Price range: $2.50-1,000; average sale is $30-50. Works on consignment and buys outright; 40% commission. Craftworker sets retail price. Requires exclusive area representation. Work may be shipped or hand-delivered. Dealer pays insurance for exhibited work.
Profile: Shop "is specifically American contemporary; on a gallery level more than a shop. Customer is 30 years or older; income $20,000 and up." Heaviest wholesale buying time: fall and winter; best selling time: Christmas and August.

COLLECTORS SHOP, Corning Glass Center, Centerway, Corning NY 14830. (607)974-8276. Director: John P. Fox Jr. Museum gift shop. Estab. 1951. Represents 20 craftworkers. Considers glass art. One-of-a-kind and handmade production-line items; utilitarian and/or decorative. Price range: $10-250; bestsellers: $40. Buys outright. Gallery sets retail price. Reports in 3 weeks. Work may be shipped or hand-delivered. Dealer pays shipping.
Profile: Shows items on a "large back-lighted display designed for glass. Shop is devoted to the best in glass design." Heaviest wholesale buying time: early spring; best selling time: summer.

A COMBINED EFFORT, 56 S. Main St., Sayville NY 11782. (516)589-9583. Contact: Victor A. Wilson. Craft shop/gallery. Estab. 1976. Represents 125 craftworkers. Price range: $3.50-250; bestsellers: $3.50-50. Works on consignment; 40% commission. Craftworker sets retail price. Requires exclusive area representation. Reports in 1 week. Work may be shipped or hand-delivered. Dealer pays shipping and insurance for exhibited work.
Acceptable Work: Considers batik; candlemaking; glass art; jewelry; leatherworking; metalsmithing; pottery; wall hangings; weavings; woodcrafting; macrame; and basketry. One-of-a-kind designer pieces; utilitarian and/or decorative.
Profile: "We are a large shop. Therefore, almost all our pieces are displayed at the same time. Time period is usually 60 days. The way that we display our crafts gives the shop a true gallery feeling." Best selling time: summer and Christmas; heaviest wholesale buying time: summer and fall.

CONTEMPORARY ART GLASS GALLERY, 806 Madison Ave., New York NY 10021. (212)879-4655. Director: Douglas Heller. Gallery. Estab. 1973. Represents 20 studio glass artists. One-of-a-kind designer pieces only; utilitarian and/or decorative. Price range: $30-1,600; bestsellers: $35-400. Works on consignment; 40% commission. Retail price set by joint agreement. Requires exclusive area representation. Reports in 3 weeks. Work may be shipped or hand-delivered. Dealer pays return shipping and insurance for exhibited work.
Profile: Items are displayed in "well lit show cases; shop has knowledgeable sales help." Customers are middle to high income group who have well-developed tastes; serious collectors. Best selling time: October-June.

THE COUNTRY GALLERY, Main St., Verona NY 13478. (315)363-2179. Director: Bette McBain. Gallery/gift shop. Estab. 1973. Represents 35-50 craftworkers "but we are expanding." Price range: $5-1,000; bestsellers: $8-200. Works on consignment for first order and buys outright; 33⅓% commission. Gallery sets retail price when work is purchased outright; craftworker sets retail price on consigned items. Requires exclusive area representation. Reports in 2 weeks. Work may be shipped or hand-delivered. Dealer shares shipping costs and pays insurance for exhibited work.
Acceptable Work: Considers batik; glass art; jewelry; leatherworking; needlecrafts; pottery; soft sculpture; tole painting; wall hangings; weavings; and silk screen. Especially needs pottery; glass art; wall hangings; weavings; needlecrafts; and soft sculpture. Fine one-of-a-kind and handmade production-line items; utilitarian and/or decorative.
Profile: "Work is beautifully displayed; gallery provides some individual shows and advertising. Building goes back to the Civil War period." Displays work 90 days. Heaviest wholesale buying time: spring to early December; best selling time: summer, fall and Christmas.

THE CRAFT BARN, Box 8, Florida NY 10921. (914)651-7949. Contact: Marjorie L. Zap. Craft shop. Estab. 1958. Represents 25 United States and countless international craftworkers. Price range: $1.50-200; bestsellers: $10-20. Buys outright. Requires exclusive area representation. Reports in 1 week. Work may be shipped or hand-delivered by prior arrangement. Dealer pays return shipping.
Acceptable Work: Considers candles; ceramics; clothing; glass art; jewelry; leatherworking; metalsmithing; pottery; and woodcrafting. Handmade production-line items; utilitarian and/or decorative.

Profile: Items are shown "in a 200-year-old barn. Direct importers of international traditional handcrafts. Gold and silver jewelry workshop with 2 full time craftspeople on staff." Customers' taste is basically traditional. Summer and Christmas shoppers will buy some higher priced one-of-a-kind crafts. Heaviest wholesale buying time: spring and late summer; best selling time: summer and Christmas.

CRAFT DESIGNS UNLIMITED, 548 La Guardia Place, New York NY 10012. (212)477-1690. Contact: Joel Waldman. Considers woven or textile crafts; especially needs woven art designs. Price range: $20-500; bestsellers: $50-250. Buys outright or on consignment; 25-50% commission. Retail price set by joint agreement. Call for interview. Reports in 1 week. Dealer pays insurance for exhibited work. Items displayed 3 weeks minimum. Gallery also distributes wholesale woven art designs to retailers.

CRAFT PEOPLE'S COOPERATIVE, 115 Park Ave., Rochester NY 14607. (716)271-7880. Treasurer: Ellen Saltzman. Craft shop/gallery. Estab. 1970. Represents 22 Rochester area craftworkers. Price range: $1.50-300; bestsellers: $4-30. Works on consignment with out-of-town craftworkers from western New York State; 30% commission. Members pay dues, work at running coop and pay 10% commission on sales. Retail price set by joint agreement. Reports in 3 weeks. Hand-delivered work only. Dealer pays insurance for exhibited work (liability, no theft or damage).
Acceptable Work: Considers batik; ceramics; clothing; dollmaking; glass; jewelry; leatherworking; metalsmithing; needlecrafts; quilting; soft sculpture; weavings; and woodcrafting. Fine one-of-a-kind and handmade production-line items; utilitarian and/or decorative. Especially needs leather; blown glass; wood (small items); clothing (one-of-a-kind adult and children); jewelry; and metalcrafts.
Profile: "Members share space as available; 1 or 2 person, or group shows; 12 per year. Consignment work is on display usually 3-6 months. Opportunities to do all aspects of work; group shows in local banks, colleges, etc. There is an invitational show once a year. All regular stock is removed and the show is hung gallery style." No new members accepted in November and December; best selling time: Christmas and late spring.

THE CRAFTS BARN, 61 Market St., Potsdam NY 13676. (315)265-9806. Manager: Jean E. Boismenu. Craft shop. Estab. 1970. Represents 20-30 craftworkers. Price range: $1-150; bestsellers: $1-35. Works on consignment and buys outright; 30% commission. Craftworker sets retail price. Reports in 7-10 days. Work may be shipped/or hand-delivered.
Acceptable Work: Considers batik; candlemaking; clothing; dollmaking; jewelry; leatherworking; metalsmithing; needlecrafts; pottery; quilting; wall hangings; weavings; woodcrafting; and original Indian basketry. One-of-a-kind and handmade production-line items; utilitarian and/or decorative. Especially needs items to sell to Olympic visitors to Lake Placid, New York: crafts indigenous to northern New York or related to winter sports.
Profile: "Items must meet approval of the Quality Control Board; then placed on display for a period of not less than 3 months. This is the only retail outlet for handcrafted articles in our area." Best selling time: summer and fall.

THE CRAFTSMAN'S GALLERY LTD., l6 Chase Rd., Scarsdale NY 10583. (914)725-4644. Contact: Sybil Robins or John Mucciolo. Craft Gallery. Estab. 1973. Price range: $10-2,000. Works on consignment; commission varies with price. Retail price set by joint agreement. Requires exclusive area representation. Send slides. SASE. Reports in 6 weeks. Work may be shipped or hand-delivered. Dealer pays insurance for exhibited work.
Acceptable Work: Considers batik; ceramics; glass art; jewelry; leatherworking; metalsmithing; pottery; quilting; soft sculpture; wall hangings; weavings; and woodcrafting. Fine one-of-a-kind handmade limited production items; itilitarian and/or decorative. Especially needs wood; blown glass; and fiber.
Profile: "Pieces are displayed as unique works of art for an agreed upon length of time, usually 5 weeks. Customers are 30-60, married, well-educated with income of $20,000 plus." Do not send unrequested material.

CRAFTSMEN CORNER, INC., 192 E. Main St., Mt. Kisco NY 10549. (914)666-2231. President: Mrs. Mullane. Treasurer: Mrs. Amuso. Craft and gift shop. Estab. 1973. Represents 125-135 craftworkers over the age of 55. Considers ceramics; dollmaking; jewelry; and knitted and crocheted items. Utilitarian and/or decorative. Price range: 50c-$125; bestsellers: 50c-$35. Works on consignment; 25% commission. Retail price set by joint agreement. Reports in 4 weeks. Hand-delivered work only. Dealer pays insurance for exhibited work.

Profile: Shop has "window displays; glass counters for jewelry and small items. All open shelves on wall and tables in center of store have articles draped and displayed." Heaviest retail selling time: September until Christmas and before Easter.

CREATIONS AND CRAFTS CO., 11 W. 37 St., New York NY 10018. (212)221-3299. President: A. Shah. Craft shop/store/gift shop. Estab. 1974. Represents 20 craftworkers. Price range: 50c-$500. Works on consignment and buys outright; 40% commission. Retail price set by joint agreement. Reports in 4 weeks. Work may be shipped or hand-delivered. Dealer pays return shipping and insurance for exhibited work. Heaviest buying and selling time: August-December.
Acceptable Work: Considers clothing; jewelry; leatherworking; needlecrafts; woodcrafting; beads; lapidary; and stones. All styles; utilitarian and/or decorative.

CREATIVE JEWELRY, 107 Tinker St., Woodstock NY 12498. (914)679-9223. Contact: Gus Pawelka. Estab. 1965. Represents 35 craftworkers. Finished one-of-a-kind and handmade production-line items; utilitarian and/or decorative. Price range: $5-1,000; bestsellers: $10-200. Buys outright. Shop sets retail price. Requires exclusive area representation. Write. Reports in 2 weeks. Dealer pays shipping to shop and in-transit insurance. Heaviest wholesale buying time: spring; best selling time: summer and Christmas.

CREATIVE WOMEN'S COLLECTIVE, 236 W. 27th St., 12th Flr., New York NY 10001. (212)924-0665. Organization of Women Artists. Estab. 1973. Represents 8 craftworker/members. Price range: 35c-$50; bestsellers: 35c-$12. Works on consignment. Retail price set by joint agreement. Reports in 2 weeks. Hand-delivered work only.
Acceptable Work: Considers jewelry; wall hangings; small textile items; weavings; silk-screened cards; macrame. Fine one-of-a-kind and handmade production-line items; utilitarian and/or decorative.
Profile: "We sell crafts only occasionally at fairs, exhibits, conferences and open houses or fund-raisers. The group specializes in producing work related to issues of the Women's Movement. We help other women's groups and others working for social change to produce graphics related to these issues." Best selling time: Christmas.

DESIGNS IN SILVER, ETCETERA, 230 E. Main St., Port Jefferson NY 11777. (516)928-2037. Contact: Charles Kohn. Estab. 1976. Represents 23 craftworkers. Considers candlemaking; ceramics; glass art; jewelry; leatherworking; metalsmithing; pottery; wall hangings; weavings; and woodcrafting. All styles; utilitarian and/or decorative. Price range: $1.75-500; bestsellers: $1.75-300. Buys outright and works on consignment; 40% commission. Retail price set by joint agreement. Requires exclusive area representation. Query with transparencies or photos. Reports as soon as inquiry is received. Dealer pays shipping from shop and insurance.
Profile: Items displayed 1 month minimum. Displays are on walls, windows, tables, pedestals and showcases. Each craft is treated independently as required. Crafts arrranged in museum-like atmosphere where everything can be viewed without distracting items surrounding them.

EAGER WEAVERS, 182 Jefferson Rd., Rochester NY 14623. (716)424-1051. Contact: Joseph DeSormeau. Craft shop. Estab. 1950. Represents 10-15 craftworkers. Considers clothing; needlecrafts; quilting; wall hangings; and weaving. Fine one-of-a-kind and handmade production-line items; utilitarian and/or decorative. Price range: $15-950; bestsellers: $15-298. Management sets retail price. Requires exclusive area representation. Reports in 2 weeks. Work may be hand-delivered. Dealer pays return shipping and insurance for exhibited work. Best selling time: summer and winter.

EARTHWORKS POTTERY, 251 W. 85th St., New York NY 10024. (212)874-8245. Contact: Claire DesBecker. Estab. 1971. Represents 20 craftworkers. Considers candlemaking; ceramics; clay jewelry; and pottery. Finished, one-of-a-kind and handmade production-line items only; utilitarian and/or deocrative. Price range: $2-200; bestsellers: $5-50. Buys outright or on consignment; 40% commission. Retail price set by joint agreement. Query with color transparencies or b&w prints. Reports in 1 week. Gallery pays insurance for exhibited work. Heaviest wholesale buying time: summer.

THE ELDER CRAFTSMEN, 850 Lexington Ave., New York NY 10021. (212)535-8030. Estab. 1955. Represents 500 age 60+ craftworkers. Considers decoupage, silver, and macrame jewelry; needlecrafts; and soft sculpture. Especially needs copper enamel dishes; ashtrays; inlaid wood boxes; picture frames; baby toys; gifts; sweaters; and quilts. Finished, one-of-a-kind and handmade production-line items only; utilitarian and/or decorative. Price range: $4-125;

bestsellers: $10-25. Works on consignment; 35% commission. Retail price set by joint agreement. Prefers exclusive area representation. Write or send samples or photos. Reports in 3 weeks. Items displayed 3 months minimum. Best selling time: September-December. "We make crafts to order."

ELECTRUM JEWELRY, 10 Main St., East Hampton NY 11937. (516)324-3232. Contact: Susan Kalman. Gallery. Estab. 1975. Represents 10-12 craftworkers. Considers jewelry. Fine one-of-a-kind and handmade production-line items; decorative only. Price range: $20-1,200; bestsellers: $20-350. Works on consignment and buys outright; 33⅓-50% commission. Requires exclusive area representation. Reports in 1 week. Work may be shipped or hand-delivered. Dealer pays shipping and insurance.
Profile: Shop uses "non-commercial display methods, refined promotion and selling techniques. Period of display is usually through summer. Jewelry making and designing is done by the owners; a lot of precious gems used as well as metal only. Only gold and sterling used." Best selling time: summer and Christmas.

FIBERFOLK, LTD., 49 Edward St., Buffalo NY 14202. (716)842-0199. Contact: Dianne Baker or Sheila Brodnick. Craft shop/gallery. Estab. 1974. Represents 6-10 fiber craftworkers. Price range: $1.50-300; bestsellers: $15. Works on consignment; 30% commission. Retail price set by joint agreement. Work may be hand-delivered.
Acceptable Work: Considers batik; clothing; jewelry; needlecrafts; wall hangings; weavings; pillows; basketry; crochet; and macrame. One-of-a-kind and handmade production-line items; utilitarian and/or decorative.
Profile: Work is displayed "on clothes racks and in windows on main street. The shop is a combination of supplies, finished products and craftsmen working at looms in a newly renovated section of a downtown city." Heaviest wholesale buying time: fall-winter.

FOCUS CRAFTS AND FURNISHINGS, INC., 4 Purchase St., Rye NY 10580. (914)961-3015. Contact: Ioan Tillman. Craft shop. Estab. 1970. Price range: $3-150. Buys outright. Gallery sets retail price. Work may be shipped or hand-delivered. Dealer pays shipping to shop.
Acceptable Work: Considers batik; candlemaking; ceramics; clothing; decoupage; glass art; pottery; quilting; wall hangings; weavings; and woodcrafting. Fine one-of-a-kind and handmade production-line items; utilitarian only.

FORMS AND FOLIAGE, LTD., Wold Road Park, Albany NY 12205. (518)458-1313. Contact: David Sofer or Martin Weber. Craft shop. Estab. 1975. Represents 250+ craftworkers from the northeastern US. Price range: $2-400; bestsellers: $20-40. Works some on consignment but mostly buys outright; 34% commission. Retail price set by joint agreement. Requires exclusive area representation. Send slides with a personal cover letter; make appointment before bringing work to store. Work may be shipped or hand-delivered. Dealer pays shipping to shop and insurance.
Acceptable Work: Considers batik; candlemaking; glass art; jewelry; leatherworking; pottery; wall hangings; weavings; and woodcrafting. Fine one-of-a-kind and handmade production-line items; utilitarian and/or decorative.
Profile: "Each artist's work is grouped together with identification of artist and state. Most customers have contemporary taste in home accessories, jewelry and art." Heaviest wholesale buying time: fall; best selling time: fall and summer.

GALERIE PAULA INSEL, 987 3rd Ave., New York NY 10022. (212)355-5740. Director: Paula Insel. Gallery. Price range: $25-1,000. Works on consignment. Retail price set by joint agreement. Reports in 2 weeks. Work may be shipped or hand-delivered. "Work is usually exhibited 2 weeks, then placed in other locations."
Acceptable Work: Considers ceramics; glass art; leatherworking; metalsmithing; needlecrafts; soft sculpture; wall hangings; weavings; and woodcrafting. All styles; utilitarian and/or decorative.

GALERIE INTERNATIONALE, 1095 Madison Ave., New York NY 10028. (212)861-7877. Manager: E.M. Martin. Considers batik; decoupage; glass art; pottery; sculpture. Buys outright or on consignment; 33⅓% commission. Retail price set by joint agreement. Send slides of work. SASE.

GALLERY 84 INC., 1046 Madison Ave., New York NY 10021. (212)628-4920. Director: Cecile Fine. Considers mobiles; sculpture; and wall hangings. Maximum size: 14'x54x60". 25% commission. Artist sets retail price. Query. Artist is requested to bring 3 works to be viewed to become member. SASE. 3 weeks maximum exposure.

GALLERY NORTH, Box 1145, Setauket NY 11733. (516)751-2676. Director: Elizabeth Goldberg. Assistant: Alexandra Randall. Gallery. Estab. 1965. Represents 50-100 craftworkers. Considers batik; ceramics, glass art; jewelry; pottery; wall hangings; weavings; and woodcrafting. Handmade production-line items only; utilitarian and/or decorative. Price range: $5-400; bestsellers: $5-50. Works on consignment; 33⅓% commission. Retail price set by joint agreement. Requires exclusive area representation. Reports in 1 month. Work may be shipped or hand-delivered. Dealer pays insurance for exhibited work. Customers are from the local area with modest incomes. Best selling time: October-December.

THE GALLERY SHOP, ALBRIGHT-KNOX ART GALLERY, 1285 Elmwood Ave., Buffalo NY 14222. (716)882-8700. Manager: Leta K. Stathacos. Museum gift shop. Estab. 1975. Represents 20 contemporary craftworkers. Considers contemporary-designed crafts. Designer pieces only; utilitarian and/or decorative. Price range: $1-250. Works on consignment and buys outright; 50% commission. Retail price set by joint agreement. Work may be shipped or hand-delivered. Dealer pays insurance for exhibited work upon receipt of items.
Special Needs: Seeking Christmas ornaments; playing cards; contemporary toys; and soft sculpture kits.
Profile: "We are a contemporary art museum. The shop makes every effort to display the items attractively. Information on the craft-artist is available." Best selling time: September-December.
Sales Tips: "I always like to 'test my market first,' so small quantities are a must to start off with. The most marketable item can be priced out of existence; common sense of business (reality) is important."

THE GALLERY SHOP AT THE JAMAICA ARTS CENTER, 161-04 Jamaica Ave., Jamaica NY 11432. (212)658-1770. Director: Carole Joyce McCully. Estab. 1976. Represents 50 craftworkers. Considers batik; jewelry; and ceramics. Primitive and finished one-of-a-kind and handmade production-line items; utilitarian and/or decorative. Price range: 50c-$300; bestsellers: $2.50-30. Buys outright or on consignment; 33⅓% commission. Craftworker sets retail price. Write. Reports in 2 weeks. Dealer pays shipping from shop and insurance for exhibited work. Work displayed in lighted cabinets, opera glass shelving and wall space. Best selling time: Christmas. Customers buy crafts for gifts.

GIFT HAUS, 5651 Main St., Williamsville NY 14221. (716)634-6888. Contact: Judith Nachbar. Gift shop. Estab. 1973. Represents 600-800 craftworkers. Considers all crafts; one-of-a-kind and handmade production-line items; utilitarian and/or decorative. Price range: 25c-$500; bestsellers: 89c-$150. Works on consignment and buys outright; 40% commission. Gallery sets retail price. Reports in 4-6 weeks. Work may be shipped or hand-delivered by prior arrangement. Dealer pays shipping to shop and insurance. Consigns for 6 months and changes windows at least every 3 weeks. Best selling time: 4th quarter.

GILLARY GALLERY, 62 Maiden Lane, Jericho NY 11753. (516)681-2015. Director: Sylvia R. Gillary. Considers ceramics; glass art; jewelry; pottery; and sculpture. Maximum size: 48x36". Specializes in modern, contemporary, realistic, impressionistic and primitive work. Statues must have pedestals. Price range: $150-2,000, sculpture; $10-500, jewelry; bestsellers: $150-300. Works on consignment; 40% commission. Retail price set by joint agreement. Query or call for interview. 6 weeks maximum exposure.

GLASS BALLET, LTD., 65 Main St., Westhampton Beach NY 11978. (516)288-4263. Contact: Don Gaiti. Craft shop/gallery/stained glass studio. Estab. 1975. Represents 45-50 craftworkers. Price range: $10-2,500; bestsellers: $15-150. Works on consignment and buys outright; 40% commission. Retail price set by joint agreement. Reports in 4 weeks. Work may be shipped or hand-delivered. Dealer pays return shipping and insurance for exhibited work.
Acceptable Work: Considers batik; candlemaking; ceramics; clothing; dollmaking; glass art; jewelry; leatherworking; metalsmithing; pottery; quilting; soft sculpture; tole painting; wall hangings; weavings; and woodcrafting. Fine one-of-a-kind and handmade production-line items; utilitarian and/or decorative.
Profile: Studio and gallery have 5 display rooms. Customers are 18-65, upper middle and upper class. Best selling time: summer; heaviest wholesale buying time: spring.

GLASS MASTERS, INC., 154 W. 18th St., New York NY 10011. (212)929-7978. Manager: Lili Lihn. Craft shop/gallery. Estab. 1972. Represents "a growing number of craftworkers who work in stained glass." Considers glass art only. Fine one-of-a-kind and handmade production-line items; utilitarian and/or decorative. Price range: $6-4,000; bestsellers: $65-300. Works on consignment and buys outright; 40% commission. Retail price is 50% plus any transportation costs. Reports in 1 month. Work may be shipped or hand-delivered. Dealer pays insurance for exhibited work.
Profile: "We are a supply store to stained glass artisans, and also have New York's only gallery devoted exclusively to the new stained glass art form." Best selling time: Christmas. "Please submit artwork by sending color slides through the mail. If we are intrigued by a specific artist we will ask to see one actual piece as an example of the artist's technique and craftmanship."

GRAHAM GALLERY, 1014 Madison Ave., New York NY 10021. (212)535-5767. Contact: Robert Graham or Terry Davis. Considers sculpture. Buys outright or on consignment; 40% commission. Price range: $100-100,000. Requires exclusive area representation. Query with slides or samples of work. SASE. 4 weeks exposure.

THE GRIST MILL GENERAL STORE ON THE RIVER, Warrensburg NY 12885. Contact: Nancy Fitler. Museum gift shop. Estab. 1976. Represents 12 craftworkers. Considers needlepoint (handmade aprons, purses, pillows, quilts, etc.); macrame; woodworks; and prints. Works on consignment and buys outright. Reports within a month.

HAND OF THE CRAFTSMAN, 58 S. Broadway, Nyack NY 10960. (914)358-6622. Contact: Janet Haber. Craft shop/gallery. Estab. 1971. Represents 70 craftworkers. Price range: $10-750; bestsellers: $25-175. Buys outright. Retail price set by joint agreement. Requires exclusive area representation. Reports in 1-2 weeks. Work may be shipped or hand-delivered. Dealer pays insurance for exhibited work.
Acceptable Work: Considers batik; candlemaking; ceramics; glass art; jewelry; leatherworking; metalsmithing; pottery; soft sculpture; and woodcrafting. Fine one-of-a-kind and handmade production-line items; utilitarian and/or decorative.
Special Needs: Seeks designer jewelry in silver and gold; handmade belt buckles; and bells in all media.
Profile: "As a shop with a growing reputation for fine crafts, we attempt to keep a cross section of each craftsman's work on permanent display. We are most interested in full-time designer craftsmen who can be relied upon to keep improving and producing." Best selling time: summer-December.

HANDCRAFTER'S COTTAGE, LTD., 733-A Middle Neck Rd., Great Neck NY 11024. (516)466-3647. President: Judy Ginsburg. Secretary: Loni Barocas. Craft shop. Estab. 1977. Represents 90 craftworkers. Price range: $5-600. Works on consignment; 40% commission. Retail price set by joint agreement. Requires exclusive area representation. Reports in 4 weeks. Work may be shipped or hand-delivered. Dealer pays return shipping and insurance for exhibited work.
Acceptable Work: Considers batik; candlemaking; ceramics; dollmaking; glass art; jewelry; leatherworking; metalsmithing; pottery; quilting; soft sculpture; wall hangings; weavings; and woodcrafting. Fine one-of-a-kind and handmade production-line items; utilitarian and/or decorative.
Profile: Work is "displayed in groups on natural shelves or crates and changed every 2 weeks." Customers include interior decorators.

HAVEN HOUSE, 4864 Ridge Rd., Lockport NY 14094. (716)434-5450. Contact: Mrs. G.H. Thompson. Gift shop. Estab. 1961. Represents 25 craftworkers. Considers candlemaking; dollmaking; and Christmas ornaments. Wants "finished-looking products. Looking for someone's own professional-looking ideas." Price range: $1-75. Buys outright. Gallery sets retail price. Reports as soon as possible. Samples may be shipped or hand-delivered. Dealer pays shipping.
Profile: "We have Early American antique furniture for display and sale. We also have a year round Christmas room." Best selling time: July-December.

HENRY HICKS GALLERY, 93 Atlantic Ave., Brooklyn NY 11201. (212)522-3693. Contact: President. Cooperative gallery. Estab. 1975. Represents 2-4 craftworkers. Price range: $25-2,000; bestsellers: $20-400. Juried shows; 10-20% commission. Retail price set by joint agreement. Rental gallery fee: $400/3-week period. Allow 3 months to prepare for a show. Work may be shipped or hand-delivered. Dealer pays insurance for exhibited work.

Acceptable Work: Considers ceramics; clothing; dollmaking; needlecrafts; quilting; soft sculpture; wall hangings; weavings; fabric art; and one-of-a-kind pillows. One-of-a-kind designer pieces only; utilitarian and/or decorative.

Profile: "We are a cooperative gallery. The individual craftsperson is responsible for choosing when to show and sell work and at what price." Customers are 20 years and up and are of middle and upper-class background. Best selling time: December.

THE HIRED HAND, 1324 Lexington Ave., New York NY 10028. (212)722-1355. Contact: Fran Stein. Craft and calico fabric shop. Estab. 1974. Represents 150 craftworkers. Price range: $1.50-75; bestsellers: $2-50. Works on consignment and buys outright; 40% commission. Retail price set by joint agreement. Reports in 1 week. Work may be shipped or hand-delivered. Dealer pays return shipping and insurance for exhibited work.

Acceptable Work: Considers dollmaking; needlecrafts; quilting; soft sculpture; and patchwork/applique. Primitive one-of-a-kind and handmade production-line items; utilitarian only.

Special Needs: Dolls; applique pillows; and crib quilts.

Profile: "We specialize in softwares and we sell quilting supplies. We try to things moderately for quick sales." Work displayed on shelves and plank walls. Best selling time: Christmas.

HOBBS PLACE, 25 Bridge St., Seneca Falls NY 13148. (315)568-5222. Contact: Howard R. Lainhart. Gallery/gift shop. Estab. 1976. Represents 4 craftworkers. Price range: $10-1,000; bestsellers: $65-100. Works on consignment and buys outright; 25-35% commission. Retail price set by joint agreement. Reports in 4 days. Work may be shipped or hand-delivered. Displays work in glass case. Best selling time: winter and summer.

Acceptable Work: Considers ceramics; decoupage; jewelry; leatherworking; pottery; wall hangings; weavings; woodcrafting; and hologram jewelry. All styles; utilitarian and/or decorative.

HORSE FEATHERS OF NYACK, 81 S. Broadway, Nyack NY 10960. (914)358-8880. Contact: Gordon Rauer. Craft shop/gift shop. Estab. 1973. Represents 15-20 craftworkers. Price range: $5-70; bestsellers: $10-40. Buys outright. Gallery sets retail price. Requires exclusive area representation. Reports as soon as possible. Work may be shipped or hand-delivered. Dealer pays shipping to shop and in-transit insurance. "We strongly prefer UPS." Best selling time: Christmas.

Acceptable Work: Considers ceramics; jewelry; leatherworking; and woodcrafting. Especially needs utilitarian pieces. All styles; utilitarian and/or decorative.

HUDSON VALLEY CRAFTS CO-OP, 15 N. Broadway, Irvington NY 10533. (914)591-8988. Contact: Chris Gordon. Craft shop coop. Estab. 1975. Represents 25 Westchester County area craftworkers. Price range: $1-200; bestsellers: $1-20. Works on consignment; 25% commission. Craftworker sets retail price. Reports in 4 weeks. Work may be hand-delivered.

Acceptable Work: Considers batik; candlemaking; ceramics; decoupage; dollmaking; glass art; jewelry; needlecrafts; pottery; quilting; wall hangings; weavings; woodcrafting; and plants. All styles; utilitarian and/or decorative.

Profile: "Shelf and showcase displays; items kept on display for 10 months; after 6 months shop has the option of reducing price by 25%." Best selling time: Christmas and Easter; heaviest wholesale buying time: fall.

ITHAC HOUSE GALLERY, 108 N. Plains St., Ithaca NY 14850. (607)272-1233. Contact: Sherry Hathaway. Gallery. Estab. 1969. Represents 11 craftworkers. Price range: $2.50-125; bestsellers: $5-125. Works on consignment; 30% commission. retail price set by joint agreement. Work may be shipped or hand-delivered by previous agreement. Best selling time: Christmas and spring.

Acceptable Work: Considers batik; ceramics; prints; soft sculpture; wall hangings; and weavings. One-of-a-kind designer pieces only; decorative.

JARO JEWELRY GALLERIES, INC., 955 Madison Ave., New York NY 10021. (212)734-5475. Contact: Jaro Parizek. Gallery. Estab. 1975. Represents 24 craftworkers who work in jewelry or small sculptures in precious metals. One-of-a-kind designer pieces only; utilitarian and/or decorative. Price range: $25-5,000; bestsellers: $35-1,500. Works on consignment; 50% commission. Retail price set by joint agreement. Requires exclusive area representation. Reports at end of month. Work may be shipped or hand-delivered. Best selling time: spring and fall.

JEWISH MUSEUM SHOP, 1109 5th Ave., New York NY 10028. (212)860-1866. Manager: Ceil Skydell. Museum gift shop. Represents 20 craftworkers. Price range: $3-200; bestsellers: $3-90. Buys outright. Retail price set by joint agreement. Reports in 2 weeks. Work may be shipped. Best selling time: Christmas and Hanuhkah.
Acceptable Work: Considers batik; ceramics; jewelry; metalsmithing; needlecrafts; pottery; soft sculpture; wall hangings; weavings; and woodcrafting. Especially needs Judaica. Fine handmade production-line items only; utilitarian and/or decorative.

JORICE DESIGNS, INC., 1057 2nd Ave., New York NY 10022. (212)752-0129. President: Maurice Mogulescu. Craft shop/gallery. Estab. 1976. Represents 40 craftworkers. Price range: $10-150; bestsellers: $10-65. Works on consignment and buys outright; 50% commission. Retail price set by joint agreement. Requires exclusive area representation. Reports in 2 weeks. Work may be shipped or hand-delivered. Dealer pays shipping and insurance for exhibited work.
Acceptable Work: Considers ceramics; glass art; pottery; wall hangings; weavings; woodcrafting; stained glass boxes; and mirrors. One-of-a-kind designer pieces; utilitarian and/or decorative.
Profile: "Send us 3 or 4 sample pieces with price list of typical pieces and photos of other pieces. If we like the work we will keep the samples and establish contact with the artist. If not we will return them at our expense." Best selling time: fall and Christmas; heaviest wholesale buying time: summer and fall.

J-P's GALLERY, 55 Deer Park Ave., Babylon NY 11702. (516)587-8129. Contact: J.P. Westpfahl. Craft shop/gallery/gift shop. Estab. 1977. Represents 38 craftworkers. Price range: $3-350; bestsellers: $3-25. Works on consignment and buys outright; commission varies. Craftworker sets retail price. Requires exclusive area representation. Reports in 4 weeks. Work may be shipped or hand-delivered. Dealer pays insurance for exhibited work.
Acceptable Work: Considers batik; ceramics; dollmaking; glass art; jewelry; leatherworking; metalsmithing; pottery; quilting; soft sculpture; wall hangings; weavings; and woodcrafting. Fine one-of-a-kind and handmade production-line items; utilitarian and/or decorative.
Profile: "We have special 2 week showings, publicity and mailing to customers." Best selling time: Christmas; heaviest wholesale buying time: pre-Christmas.

JULIE: ARTISANS' GALLERY, 687 Madison Ave., New York NY 10021. (212)688-2345. Contact: Julie. Craft gallery. Estab. 1973. Represents 100-200 craftworkers. Price range: $4-2,700. Works on consignment; negotiable commission. Gallery sets retail price. Reports in 2 weeks. Work may be shipped or hand-delivered. Dealer pays return shipping and insurance. "Write or phone for an appointment, or better yet, submit slides for viewing, stating price of each object." Best selling time: Christmas.
Acceptable Work: Considers all crafts except candlemaking; metalsmithing; and tole painting. Especially needs anything wearable and non-wearable of museum quality. Fine one-of-a-kind and handmade production-line items; utilitarian and/or decorative.

JUST ACCESSORIES, INC., 112 W. 34th St., Rm. 710, New York NY 10001. (212)564-5168. President: Richard N. Bloch. Gift shop. Estab. 1961. Represents 2-3 craftworkers. Fine handmade production-line items only; utilitarian and/or decorative. Price range: $15-60. Buys outright. Gallery sets retail price. Reports in 1 week. Work may be shipped or hand-delivered. Dealer pays return shipping and insurance for exhibited work. Best selling time: holidays.

KALEIDOSCOPE, 10 E. 4th St., Jamestown NY 14701. (716)488-4615. Contact: Wendy Chadwick-Case. Craft shop/gallery. Estab. 1974. Represents 50 craftworkers. Price range: $1-600; bestsellers: $5-50. Works on consignment and buys outright; 33⅓% commission. Craftworkers sets retail price. Reports in 2 weeks. Work may be shipped or hand-delivered.
Acceptable Work: Considers batik; ceramics; clothing; glass art; jewelry; leatherworking; metalsmithing; pottery; soft sculpture; wall hangings; weavings; woodcrafting and cards. All styles; utilitarian and/or decorative.
Profile: Items are on display for 3 months maximum. Customers are mostly female; 20-50 years of age. Best selling time: Christmas and summer; heaviest wholesale buying time: summer.

KIRKLAND ART CENTER, On the Park, Clinton NY 13323. (315)853-8871. Secretary: Sally Williams. Gallery/gift shop. Estab. 1960. Represents 12 craftworkers. Price range: 3c-$100; bestsellers: $1-10. Works on consignment and buys outright; 25% commission. Craftworker sets retail price on consigned items. Reports in 2 weeks. Work may be shipped or hand-delivered. Dealer pays insurance for exhibited work. Bring in work, send slides and resume or send illustrated catalog. Exhibits work 3 months before returning. Best selling time: Christmas.

Acceptable Work: Considers all crafts except candlemaking; clothing; and glass art. All styles; utilitarian and/or decorative.

THE KIVA: ARTISAN'S GALLERY, 37 Popham Rd., Scarsdale NY 10583. President: S. Bernstein. Treasurer: S. Herrmann. Gallery. Estab. 1977. Represents 25 craftworkers. Considers all crafts; especially needs fiber art, wall hangings, glass and ceramics. Fine one-of-a-kind designer pieces only; utilitarian and/or decorative. Price range: $8-8,500; bestsellers: $80-300. Works on consignment; 50% commission. Retail price set by joint agreement. Requires exclusive area representation. "Submit slides or photos and detailed description of work." Reports "as soon as possible." Work may be shipped or hand-delivered. Gallery pays return shipping and insurance on exhibited work.
Profile: Sculpture displayed on Lucite cubes; wearables on black forms. Displays work 4-6 weeks. "We are unique in design and works carried, as we do only unique, one-of-a-kind art including soft sculpture, wearable art and accessories, glass, etc." Customers are primarily of high incomes, "as we are in an affluent neighborhood."

KNOCK ON WOOD, 1601 Trumansburg Rd., Ithaca NY 14850. President: David Hoffman. Craft shop. Estab. 1974. Represents 10 craftworkers. Price range: $1-300; bestsellers: $1-65. Works on consignment and buys outright; 33% commission. Craftworker sets retail price. Reports in 4 weeks. Work may be shipped or hand-delivered. Dealer pays return shipping and insurance for exhibited work. Best selling time: Christmas; heaviest wholesale buying time: late fall.
Acceptable Work: Considers batik; ceramics; glass art; jewelry; leatherworking; metalsmithing; pottery; soft sculpture; wall hangings; weavings; and woodcrafting.
To Break In: "Develop a good catalog, either pictorial or with line drawings, with terms and prices set out clearly."

KRUGER GALLERY, 842 Madison Ave., New York NY 10021. (212)734-6436. President: Laura Kruger. Gallery. Estab. 1975. Considers jewelry. Price range: $15-5,000; bestsellers: $75-350. Works on consignment. Retail price set by joint agreement. Requires exclusive area representation during show. Submit photos and arrange interview. SASE. Reports in 2 weeks. Dealer pays return shipping and insurance for exhibited work.
Profile: Gallery sponsors regular one-man shows and provides openings and promotions. Shows run a minimum of 6 weeks with the possibility of becoming part of gallery's stable of craftworkers.

LA GALERIE ROUGE, Seneca Turnpike Nichols Plaza, New Hartford NY 13413. (315)724-1756. Contact: Rick Bianco. Gallery/art supplier. Estab. 1970. Represents 7 craftworkers. Price range: $2-150. Works on consignment; 30% commission. Retail price set by joint agreement. Requires exclusive area representation. Work may be hand-delivered and is displayed 30 days minimum. Best selling time: fall-Christmas.
Acceptable Work: Considers candlemaking; glass art; pottery; and silkscreening. One-of-a-kind and handmade production-line items; utilitarian and/or decorative.

JACK LEBOWITZ DESIGNS, 139-43 85 Dr., Jamaica NY 11435. (212)523-4123. President: Jack Lebowitz. Craft shop/gallery. Estab. 1963. Represents 10 craftworkers who work to Lebowitz's designs. Price range: $50-5,000; bestsellers: $50-2,000. Buys outright. Gallery sets retail price. Requires exclusive area representation. Work may be shipped or hand-delivered. Dealer pays insurance on exhibited work.
Acceptable Work: Considers ceramics; leatherworking; metalsmithing; pottery; soft sculpture; wall hangings; weavings; and woodcrafting. Fine one-of-a-kind designer pieces only; utilitarian and/or decorative.

THE LEE SHOP, 43 Greenwich Ave., New York NY 10014. (212)989-7215. Contact: Lee Erdberg. Craft shop. Estab. 1965. Represents 20 craftworkers. Considers leather garmets, bags and accessories. Price range: $15-350. Buys outright. Craftworker sets retail price. Requires exclusive area representation. Work may be shipped or hand-delivered. Special needs: leather goods. Best selling and buying time: autumn.
Sales Tip: "It would be helpful if craftworkers considered the retail price while working, so that they produce an item that has a viable price in the store."

LIMITED UNLIMITED, 8A S. Moger Ave., Mt. Kisco NY 10549. Contact: Thomas Carlaw. Handcrafted jewelry shop. Estab. 1971. Represents 25 craftworkers. Considers jewelry; fine one-of-a-kind and handmade production-line items. Price range: $3-450; bestsellers; $10-40. Buys outright. Gallery sets retail price. Reports in 1 week. Work may be shipped or hand-delivered. Dealer pays shipping and in-transit insurance. Best selling and heaviest wholesale buying time: Christmas and summer. Work displayed in glass cases.

LOVE AND LET LOVE, 1278 1st Ave., New York NY 10021. (212)288-0035. Crafts Dealer: Lourie Greenblatt. Considers ceramics; sculpture; jewelry; and metalsmithing. Price range: $5-200. Gallery sets retail price. Buys outright at 50% of retail price. Requires exclusive area representation. Gallery pays shipping costs.

LUMINERE CREATIONS, INC., 15 Charles St., New York NY 10014. (212)989-7858. President: Miss Shulman. Gallery/gift shop. Estab. 1969. Represents 30 craftworkers. Price range: $5-1,500; bestsellers: $10-50. Works on consignment but mostly buys outright; 40% commission. Gallery sets retail price. Requires exclusive area representation. Reports in 1-3 weeks. Work may be shipped or hand-delivered. Dealer pays return shipping and insurance for exhibited work.
Acceptable Work: Considers ceramics; glass art; metalsmithing; pottery; and especially needs wall treatments in mirror and glass from $20-50. Fine one-of-a-kind and handmade production-line items; utilitarian and/or decorative.
Profile: "Window and shelf display on all items for 2 weeks; inside store display another 2-6 weeks in scattered positions." Best selling time: September-December; heaviest wholesale buying time: September-October. Cosmopolitan customers.

THE MAD MONK, 500 6th Ave., New York NY 10011. (212)242-6678. Contact: Carl Monk. Craft shop. Estab. 1969. Represents 60 craftworkers. Considers ceramics and pottery. Fine one-of-a-kind and handmade production-line items; utilitarian and/or decorative. Price range: $1.50-3,000; bestsellers: $20. Buys outright. Retail price set by joint agreement. Reports in 1 week. Work may be shipped or hand-delivered. Dealer pays shipping to shop.
Profile: "We have 'Please Touch' signs. We are probably the only ceramics store in New York which buys pottery on a substantial scale. Heaviest wholesale buying time: pre-Christmas season; best selling time: Christmas season.

THE MAINE SCENE, 100 Johnson Terrace, Staten Island NY 10309. Contact: Joyce or Edward Collord. Craft shop/gallery/gift shop. Estab. 1967. Represents 10 craftworkers. Considers candlemaking; dollmaking; glass art; jewelry; metalsmithing; needlecrafts; pottery; quilting; wall hangings; weavings; and woodcrafting. Handmade production-line items; utilitarian and/or decorative. Price range: 50c-$75; bestsellers: $2.50-27. Works occasionally on consignment and buys outright; 40% commission. Retail price set by joint agreement. Reports in 1 week. Accepts mailed or shipped items with return postage included; dealer pays shipping to shop if outright purchase.

MARI GALLERIES OR WESTCHESTER, LTD., 133 E. Prospect Ave., Mamaroneck NY 10543. (914)698-0008. President: Carla Reuben. Gallery. Estab. 1966. Represents 6-10 craftworkers. Works on consignment; 40% commission. Craftworker sets retail price. Requires exclusive area representation. Write or call. Reports as soon as possible. Work may be shipped or hand-delivered. Dealer pays insurance for exhibited work.
Acceptable Work: Considers batik; ceramics; glass art; jewelry; pottery; soft sculpture; wall hangings; and weavings. Fine and primitive handmade production-line pieces; decorative only.
Profile: "Our gallery is set in a 200-year-old barn in the center of town— very contemporary and unique. Work is displayed for 5 weeks with appropriate flyers, publicity, etc." Fine art is on the main level, crafts on the uppper level, fine arts and/or crafts on lower level.

MINI MUNDUS SHOP, 970 Lexington, New York NY 10021. (212)288-5855. Contact: Kathryn Falk. Craft shop/gift shop with second location at 1030 Lexington Avenue. Estab. 1975. Represents 35 craftworkers. Price range: $1-500; bestsellers: $1-100. Works on consignment and buys outright; 33⅓% commission. Retail price set by joint agreement. Reports in 2 weeks. Work may be shipped or hand-delivered.
Acceptable Work: Miniatures in dollhouses; ceramics; dollmaking; glass art; needlecrafts; pottery; wall hangings; weavings; woodcrafting; and miniature furniture and accessories. Fine one-of-a-kind and hand-made production-line items only; utilitarian and/or decorative. 1"-1' scale.
Profile: "Work is displayed in glass cases. It is the only miniature shop in New York that carries a complete miniature line of furnishings and building and decorating parts." Best selling time: before Christmas.

THE MUSICAL MUSEUM, Deansboro NY 13328. (315)841-8774. Curator: Arthur H. Sanders. Musuem gallery/gift shop. Estab. 1948. Represents 2-6 craftworkers. Price range: 10c-$100; bestsellers: $6-10. Works on consignment and buys outright; 40-60% commission. Retail price set by joint agreement. Reports in 1 week. Work may be shipped or hand-delivered. Special needs: musical jewelry. Best selling time: summer and November; heaviest wholesale buying time: summer.
Acceptable Work: Considers all crafts with a musical motif except clothing, quilting and soft sculpture. Primitive one-of-a-kind pieces preferred; utilitarian.

MY SISTER, 10 E. 40th St., New York NY 10022. (212)868-3330. Contact: Ina Eckhaus. Boutique. Estab. 1973. Represents 8-10 craftworkers. Considers all accessories and jewelry; expecially needs unusual jewelry and knitted scarf and hat sets for adults and children. One-of-a-kind designer pieces; or other unusual decorative items. Price range: $10-200; bestsellers: $15-100. Works on consignment; commission varies. Retail price set by joint agreement. Arrange appointment to show work. Reports in 4 weeks. Work may be shipped or hand-delivered if previously arranged.
Profile: Items are "shown to all customers, usually in conjunction with other accessories that will show the item off to best advantage and [we] send notes to customers to promote items". Best selling and heaviest wholesale buying time: fall and winter. Customers are fashion-oriented, so "be aware of what women are wearing today."

NATURAL LEATHER, 203 Bleecker St., New York NY 10012. (212)533-6530. Contact: Phil or Dick. Craft shop. Estab. 1969. Represents 20-30 craftworkers. Considers leatherworking and metalsmithing. "Much of what we sell we make or buy from people we know. I buy about two-thirds of my stock." Handmade production-line items only; utilitarian and/or decorative. Price range: $5-400; bestsellers: $5-165. Buys outright. Gallery sets retail price. Reports in 2 weeks. Customers are about half tourists, and about half from Greenwich Village and New York City.

THE NIDDY NODDY, 416 Albany Post Rd., Croton-on-Hudson NY 10520. (914)271-9724. Contact: Irene Miller. Textile craft shop. Estab. 1966. Represents 12 craftworkers. Price range: $1.50-650. Works on consignment and buys outright; 33⅓ commission. Retail price set by joint agreement. Work may be shipped or hand-delivered. Dealer pays return shipping and insurance for exhibited work. Reports "immediately."
Acceptable Work: Considers batik; clothing; dollmaking; needlecrafts; quilting; and soft sculpture. All styles; utilitarian and/or decorative.

9 ARTISANS, INC., 142 7th Ave. S., New York NY 10014. (212)691-1695. Manager: Bertha Helmann. Cooperative craft shop/gallery. Estab. 1976. Represents 9-11 craftworker members. Price range: $4-1,200. Shows work of members only; does not buy or consign. Craftworker sets retail price. Requires exclusive area representation. Reports in 2 weeks.
Acceptable Work: Considers batik; glass art; leatherworking; pottery; soft sculpture; wall hangings; and weavings. Especially needs members working in wood, wrought iron and metal. One-of-a-kind designer pieces and handmade production-line items only; utilitarian and/or decorative.

OSAS ART SERVICES, 65 Worth St., Rm. 150, New York NY 10004. (212)433-4990. Art Services Coordinator: David McAllister. Gallery. Estab. 1978. Considers all crafts. All styles; utilitarian and/or decorative. Craftworker sets retail price. Reports in 1 week. Dealer pays insurance for exhibited work. Gallery is operated by City of New York. Sponsors monthly show.

OXFORD GALLERY, 267 Oxford St., Rochester NY 14607. (716)271-5885. Co-directors: Edythe Shedden and Glorya Mueller. Considers sculpture; soft sculpture; and wall hangings. Specializes in contemporary and ethnic arts. Price range: $75-10,000, sculpture; bestsellers: $100-1,000. Works on consignment; 40% commission. Retail price set by craftworker. Requires exclusive area representation. Call for interview. "We have an important 'letter of agreement' and we require an insurance release." 4-6 weeks exposure.

PARAFFINALIA, 122 Washington Ave., Endicott NY 13760. (607)754-0192. Contact: Donn or Jayne Kemp. Craft shop. Estab. 1972. Represents 15+ craftworkers. Price range: $2-300; bestsellers: $5-60. Works on consignment and buys outright; 30% commission. Craftworker sets retail price. Requires exclusive street representation. Work may be shipped or hand-delivered. Dealer pays shipping to shop and insurance for exhibited work if bought outright.
Acceptable Work: Considers ceramics; dollmaking; glass art; jewelry; leatherworking;

metalsmithing; pottery; wall hangings; weavings; and woodcrafting. Fine one-of-a-kind and hand-made production-line items; utilitarian and/or decorative.
Profile: "Item is displayed in best environment for work agreed to by craftsman and dealer. Usually work is displayed for up to 3 months; longer if there is big turnover." Heaviest wholesale buying time: fall; best selling time: Christmas and summer.

PERFORMERS' OUTLET, 222 E. 85th St., New York NY 10028. (212)249-8435. President: Jerald Thomas Young. Craft and gift shop. Represents 350 craftworkers. Estab. 1969. Price range: $5-70; bestsellers: $10-25. Works on consignment and buys outright; 50% commission. Retail price set by joint agreement. Write or call. Reports in 4 weeks. Work may be shipped or hand-delivered. Dealer pays shipping and insurance for exhibited work.
Acceptable Work: Considers batik; candlemaking; ceramics; decoupage; dollmaking; glass art; jewelry; needlecrafts; pottery; quilting; soft sculpture; wall hangings; weavings; and woodcrafting. All styles; utilitarian and/or decorative.
Profile: "We specialize in theatre people's art and craft work. Customers are middle to upper-middle class; 20-40 age range; well educated and well travelled." Best selling time: fall-Christmas; heaviest wholesale buying time: fall.

PHOENIX GALLERY, 30 W. 57th St., New York NY. 10019. (212)245-5095. Director: Gail Gelburd Kimler. Considers mobiles and sculpture. Specializes in contemporary art. Price range: $200-5,000. Works on consignment; 30% commission. Retail price set by joint agreement. Query.

PINCHPENNY GALLERY, 564 Lexington Ave., Mt Kisco NY 10549. (914)666-6525. President: Bertram J. Lange. Estab. 1966. Represents 3 craftworkers. Considers soft sculpture and woodcrafting; especially needs New England oriented woodworkings. Price range: $50-450. Buys outright. Retail price set by joint agreement. Requires exclusive area representation. Work may be shipped or hand-delivered. Best selling time: summer and November-December; heaviest wholesale buying time: early spring. Customers are primarily managerial and professional with incomes of $10,000-500,000.

POT-POURRI GALLERY OF AMERICAN CRAFTS, 85 N. Main St., Florida NY 10921. (914)651-7418. Contact: Louis or Dianne Mendez. Craft shop/gallery. Estab. 1968. Represents 125 craftworkers. Price range: 50c-$7,500; bestsellers: $150 maximum. Works on consignment and buys outright; 40% commission. Retail price set by joint agreement. Requires exclusive area representation. Make appointment to show work. Reports as soon as possible. Work may be shipped or hand-delivered. Dealer pays shipping and insurance for exhibited work.
Acceptable Work: Considers batik; candlemaking; ceramics; blown glass; jewelry; metalsmithing; pottery; soft sculpture; wall hangings; weavings; and woodcrafting.
Profile: "Special shows have approximately 6 weeks duration, otherwise no time limitation on displays; try to group items according to type." Best selling time: summer and Christmas; heaviest wholesale buying time: early spring and fall.

POTTERY & SOUTH 4TH, 177 W. 4th St., New York NY 10014. (212)675-7478. Contact: Randi Feldman, Ellen Richmond, Nancy Fern or Jerry Marshall. Estab. 1975. Coop. Represents 6 craftworkers. Price range: $5-200; bestsellers: $5-56. Works on consignment; 40% commission. Retail price set by joint agreement. Work may be hand-delivered.
Acceptable Work: Considers ceramics; pottery; wall hangings; weavings; and especially soft sculpture and jewelry. Fine one-of-a-kind and handmade production-line items; utilitarian and/or decorative.
Profile: "Items will be displayed along with a name card or biographical writing. Displays are changed or rotated around shop weekly. We are a coop, so our prices are reasonable. All members of coop work in shop, so customers and artists have direct interaction. Because we are located in Greenwich Village we get a large tourist traffic along with neighborhood customers."

THE QUEENS MUSEUM, New York City Bldg., Flushing Meadow Park, Flushing NY 11368. (212)592-2405. Contact: Barbara Sperber. Museum gift shop. Estab. 1972. Considers all crafts except clothing and tole painting. Fine one-of-a-kind pieces and handmade production line items; utilitarian and/or decorative. Bestsellers: $100 maximum. Works on consignment and buys outright; 40% commission. Retail price set by joint agreement. Work may be hand-delivered by pre-arrangement only. Dealer pays insurance for exhibited work. Items are exhibited for approximately 8 weeks.

RAINTREE BOOK AND ART SHOP, Fayetteville Mall, Fayetteville NY 13066. (315)657-5158. Contact: Achilles Nickles. Gallery. Estab. 1974. Represents 15 craftworkers. Considers all crafts except clothing; leatherworking; needlecrafts; and tole painting. Fine one-of-a-kind and handmade production-line items; utilitarian and/or decorative. Price range: $3.50-395. Works on consignment and buys outright; 40% commission. Retail price set by joint agreement. Requires exclusive area representation. Reports in 3-4 weeks. Work may be shipped or hand-delivered. Dealer pays return shipping. Buys/consigns most crafts in the summer for the fall and Christmas seasons.

ROADS GALLERIES, 400 E. 57th St., New York NY 10022. (212)486-1441. Contact: Louis Horwin. Estab. 1975. Represents 75 craftworkers. Considers batik; metalsmithing; soft sculpture; wall hangings; and weavings. Finished, one-of-a-kind and handmade production-line items only; decorative. Price range: $50-1,000; bestsellers: $150-300. Works on consignment; 50% commission. Retail price set by joint agreement. Mail slides or photos. Reports in 4 weeks. Dealer pays shipping from gallery and insurance for exhibited work.
Profile: "We sell office decorations to corporations. We show photos or slides to the customers; if there's interest, we have the item sent to us."

ROME HISTORICAL SOCIETY FT. STANWIX MUSEUM, 113 W. Court St., Rome NY 13440. (315)336-5870. Executive Director: Joseph G. Vincent. Gallery/gift shop. Estab. 1936. Represents 4 craftworkers. Price range: 10c-$100; bestsellers: $2-25. Works on consignment and on loans for exhibits; 25% commission. Retail price set by joint agreement. Reports in 1 day. Work may be shipped or hand-delivered. Dealer pays insurance for exhibited work. Heaviest wholesale buying time: spring; best selling time: spring-summer.
Acceptable Work: Considers clothing; decoupage; dollmaking; glass art; jewelry; leatherworking; metalsmithing; pottery; quilting; soft sculpture; tole painting; wall hangings; weavings; and woodcrafting. All styles; utilitarian and/or decorative.

ROSCOE CRAFT CENTER, Box 93, Roscoe NY 12776. (607)498-5500. Manager: Helen Orobello. Craft shop/gallery/gift shop. Estab. 1972. Represents 25-30 craftworkers. Price range: $1.25-500. Works on consignment and buys outright; 33⅓% commission. Retail price set by joint agreement. Requires exclusive area representation. Reports as soon as possible. Work may be shipped or hand-delivered. Dealer pays return shipping.
Acceptable Work: Considers all crafts except candlemaking and clothing. All styles; utilitarian and/or decorative.
Profile: Displays work in gallery 3-4 weeks; in gift shop for an indefinite period of time. Heaviest wholesale buying time: spring and fall; best selling time: summer and Christmas.

RHODA SANDE GALLERY, 61 E. 57th St., New York NY 10022. Director: R. Sande. Gallery. Estab. 1955. Considers soft sculpture; wall hangings; and weavings. Primitive and fine crafts; utilitarian and/or decorative. Price range: $500 minimum. Works on consignment; 50% commission. Retail price set by joint agreement. Requires exclusive area representation. Reports in 2 weeks.

1770 CRAFTS, 583 Little Britain Rd., Newburgh NY 12550. (914)564-1777. Manager: Gerald Parrish. Craft shop. Estab. 1970. Represents 6 craftworkers. Price range: $2-40; bestsellers: $25 maximum. Works on consignment; 25-30% commission. Retail price set by joint agreement. Reports in 2-3 weeks. Work may be hand-delivered. Dealer pays insurance for exhibited work. "We have large and varied inventory, take special orders and try to give personal attention to each person." Best selling time: fall and winter.
Acceptable Work: Considers batik; decoupage; tole painting; and woodcrafting. Fine and primitive one-of-a-kind pieces; utilitarian and/or decorative.

THE SHAKER MUSEUM, Shaker Museum Rd., Old Chatham NY 12136. (518)794-9105. Director: Peter Laskovski. Museum gift shop and bookstore. Estab. 1950. Represents 5+ craftworkers. Price range: 75c-$350; bestsellers: $2-25. Works on consignment and buys outright; 40% commission. Retail price set by joint agreement. Requires exclusive area representation. Reports in 2 weeks. Work may be shipped or hand-delivered. Dealer pays return shipping.
Acceptable Work: Considers candlemaking; ceramics; clothing; dollmaking; leatherworking; metalsmithing; needlecrafts; pottery; quilting; wall hangings; weavings; and woodcrafting. Emphasis on simple utilitarian items in the Shaker style. All styles; utilitarian only. Heaviest wholesale buying time: spring-summer; best selling time: summer.

THE SHOP, ADIRONDACK LAKES CENTER FOR THE ARTS, Box 101, Blue Mountain Lake NY 12812. (518)352-7715. Program Director: Sheila M. Hutt. Craft shop of art center. Estab. 1967. Represents 30 craftworkers. Price range: $5-400; bestsellers: $5-50. Works on consignment; 30% commission. Gallery sets retail price. Requires exclusive area representation within 25 miles. Reports in 3 weeks. Work may be shipped or hand-delivered by prior arrangement. Best selling time: May-October.

Acceptable Work: Considers ceramics; clothing; dollmaking; jewelry; metalsmithing; pottery; quilting; wall hangings; weavings; and especially needs batik, silver jewelry, soft sculpture and blown glass. Fine one-of-a-kind designer pieces only; utilitarian and/or decorative.

THE SHOP, ALBANY INSTITUTE OF HISTORY AND ART, 125 Washington Ave., Albany NY 12210. (518)465-1281. Manager: Mrs. R.H. Taylor. Museum gift shop. Estab. 1962. Represents 4-5 craftworkers. Price range: $2.50-50; bestsellers: $2.50-30. Works on consignment; 34% commission. Retail price set by joint agreement. Work may be hand-delivered. Dealer pays in-transit insurance.

Acceptable Work: Considers batik; ceramics; jewelry; glass art; pottery; quilting; tole painting; wall hangings; and weavings. One-of-a-kind designer pieces; utilitarian and/or decorative.

Profile: "Work is prominently displayed for 2-3 weeks. Customers are young business girls 25-30 years old and museum members 50-60 years old." Heaviest wholesale buying time: fall; best selling time: fall and Christmas.

A SHOW OF HANDS, 2310 Broadway, New York NY 10024. (212)874-9193. Managers: Lynn Bender and Valencia Saczynski. Craft shop. Estab. 1970. Represents 35 craftworkers. Price range: $1-1,000; bestsellers: $25-100. Works on consignment; 30% commission. Craftworker sets retail price. Reports in 4 weeks.

Acceptable Work: Considers batik; ceramics; clothing; dollmaking; glass art; jewelry; leatherworking; needlecrafts; pottery; quilting; wall hangings; weavings; marbelized paper; applique and stitchery in clothing and hangings; and mobiles. Fine one-of-a-kind and handmade production-line items only; utilitarian and/or decorative.

Profile: This is a "collective made up of very talented craftsmen who all feed into the direction and goals of the shop— setting policy and being part of how their work is displayed and sold. It gives a craftsman a chance to show new work and experiment with what sells." Best selling time: holidays and spring.

SIMPLY NATURAL, Rt. 23, Hermon NY 13652. Contact: Syd Gelbwaks. Craft shop. Estab. 1978. Price range: $10-250. Works on consignment; 40% commission. Retail price set by joint agreement. Reports in 3 weeks. Work may be shipped or hand-delivered. Dealer pays return shipping and insurance for exhibited work. Likes to display work "from March through October."

Acceptable Work: Considers clothing; pottery; quilting; wall hangings; weavings; handspun yarns and garments from handspun yarns. Primitive one-of-a-kind and handmade production-line items; utiltiarian and/or decorative.

SONNENBERG GARDENS, GARDEN GIFTS, 151 Charlotte St., Canandaigua NY 14424. (716)394-4922. Manager: Catherine Gifford. Gift shop at greenhouse location. Estab. 1973. Represents 5 craftworkers. Price range: 90c-$25; bestsellers: $1-7. Works on consignment and buys outright; 33⅓ commission. Craftworker sets retail price. Reports in 4 weeks. Work may be shipped or hand-delivered. Dealer pays return shipping and insurance for exhibited work.

Acceptable Work: Considers ceramics; glass art; jewelry; pottery; woodcrafting and items relative to plants, flowers and gardens that are not affected by temperature or humidity. All styles; utilitarian and/or decorative. Especially needs well designed, inexpensive useful containers for plants and flowers; flower holders; and wall hanging containers.

Profile: "Craft consignment shows rotate once a month and are promoted and advertised; purchased inventory is on general display." Heaviest wholesale buying time: April-July; best selling time: June-August.

SPOT ARTS AND CRAFTS SHOP, INC., 178 Front St., Owego NY 13827. (607)687-5705. Coordinator: Anita Zelle. Craft shop. Estab. 1973. Represents 100-150 craftworkers. Price range: 50c-$275; bestsellers: 50c-$45. Works on consignment; 25% commission. Craftworker sets retail price. Reports as soon as possible. Work may be shipped or hand-delivered if samples are okayed.

Acceptable Work: Considers all crafts. One-of-a-kind and hand-made production-line items; utilitarian and/or decorative.

Profile: "This is a store front shop on the Susquehanna River in 1880's brick row buildings. No other similar shop in geographic area that sells handmade items exclusively." Best selling time: fall and Christmas; heaviest wholesale buying time: summer.

THE SQUARE NAIL, 56 Glen St., Glens Falls NY 12801. (518)493-6215. Buyer: Joan Grishkot. Craft shop/gallery/gift shop. Estab. 1975. Represents 30 craftworkers. Considers ceramics; decoupage; dollmaking; jewelry; leatherworking; pottery; quilting; wall hangings; weavings; woodcrafting; corn husk dolls; eggery; and handmade silk flowers. One-of-a-kind and handmade production-line items; utilitarian and/or decorative. Price range: $3-400; bestsellers: $3-35. Works on consignment and buys outright; 30-40% commission. Retail price set by joint agreement. Requires exclusive area representation. Reports in 2 weeks. Dealer pays shipping to shop if outright purchase and insurance for exhibited work.
Profile: "The shop is located in oldest building in Glens Falls, a remodeled blacksmith shop. It is well lighted and well decorated. We serve mulled wine in winter, punch in summer." Customers are middle class to upper class. Best selling time: September-November 1.

THE STUDIO, INC., 15 Main St., Lake Placid NY 12946. (518)523-3589. Contact: Carter Lockwood. Estab. 1968. Represents 100-150 craftworkers. Considers non-abstract ceramics, decoupage, dollmaking, glass art, jewelry, metalsmithing, needlecrafts, pottery, quilting, tole painting, wall hangings, and woodcrafting. Especially needs figure skating and winter sports craft themes. Finished one-of-a-kind and handmade production-line items; utilitarian and/or decorative (likes nature themes). Price range: $2-2,000; bestsellers: $2-75. Buys outright or on consignment; 33⅓% commission. Retail price set by joint agreement. Requires exclusive area representation. Call for interview or send transparencies or photos. Reports in 1 week. Dealer pays shipping from shop; negotiates shipping to shop and insurance.
Profile: Consigned items displayed 6 months maximum. Heaviest wholesale buying time: spring; best selling time: summer and fall. Tourist customers ages 18+ with middle to upper incomes; they buy crafts for artistic value.

SUZUKI GALLERY, 38 E. 57th St., New York NY 10022. Director: Katsko Suzuki. Considers sculpture. Buys outright or on consignment: 33⅓-50% commission. Price range: $500-5,000, sculpture. Retail price set by joint agreement. Gallery pays shipping from gallery.

THREADBARE UNLIMITED, 289 Bleecker St., New York NY 10014. (212)675-2688. Contact: Sandy Lowe. Craft shop/gallery/craft school. Estab. 1971. Represents 15-25 craftworkers. Price range: $10-10,000; bestsellers: $60-200. Works on consignment; 40% commission. Retail price set by joint agreement. Work may be shipped or hand-delivered. Dealer pays insurance for exhibited work.
Acceptable Work: Considers batik; ceramics; clothing; leatherworking; needlecrafts; quilting; wall hangings; and weavings. All styles; utilitarian and/or decorative. Especially needs knitted and handwoven fashion.
Profile: Shop has "theme windows and interior display. We sell crafts that are both art and fashion; we also teach crafts."

THE THREE CROWNS, Box 144, Pittsford NY 14534. (716)586-5160. Contact: George Gordon. Craft shop. Estab. 1966. Represents 60 craftworkers with 4-6 years technical education. Price range: $2.50-125; bestsellers: $4-35. Works on consignment and buys outright; 33⅓% commission. Craftworker sets retail price. Requires exclusive area representation. Reports in 1 week. Work may be shipped or hand-delivered. Dealer pays insurance for exhibited work.
Acceptable Work: Considers batik; ceramics; glass art; jewelry; metalsmithing; pottery; hand woven textiles; woodcrafting; and copper enamel. Fine one-of-a-kind and handmade production-line items; utiltarian and/or decorative. Especially needs functional ceramics.
Profile: "Entire shop is rearranged at least every 3 months. There is ample space and only pieces of highest quality and design are offered; also services such as wrapping and delivery."

TODOROF GALLERIES, 311 Bryant St., Buffalo NY 14222. (716)886-4451. President: Arleen Solly. Craft shop/gallery. Estab. 1969. Represents 100 American craftworkers. Considers all crafts. All styles; utilitarian and/or decorative. Price range: $5-800. Works on consignment and buys outright; 40% commission. Craftworkers sets retail price. Requires exclusive area representation. Work may be shipped or hand-delivered. Dealer pays shipping and insurance.
Profile: "Customers are all types with a love and understanding for the crafts of our country." Heaviest wholesale buying time: fall; best selling time: Christmas.

A TOUCH OF WHIMSY, 210 Central Park S, New York NY 10019. (212)246-5320. President: Joan Rowland. Crafts gallery. Estab. 1973. Represents 150 craftworkers. Considers all crafts. Fine one-of-a-kind pieces; utilitarian and/or decorative. Price range: $10-2,500; bestsellers: $10-500. Works on consignment; 50% commission. Retail price set by joint agreement. Reports in 1 week. Work may be shipped or hand-delivered. Dealer pays insurance for exhibited work. Make appointment.
Profile: "We have special invitational events, often for 1 day only. We specialize in social and political satire." Best selling time: winter and spring.

TRIAS GALLERY, 49 W. 28th St., New York NY 10001. (212)689-1097. Director: Donald Mavros. Gallery. Estab. 1965. Represents East Coast craftworkers. Price range: $5-500; bestsellers: $5-80. Works on consignment; 30% commission. Gallery sets retail price. Reports in 4 weeks. Work may be hand-delivered.
Acceptable Work: Considers batik; ceramics; clothing; jewelry; and pottery. One-of-a-kind designer pieces; utilitarian and/or decorative.

TWO RIVERS GALLERY/ROBERSON CENTER FOR THE ARTS AND SCIENCES, 22 Front St., Binghamton NY 13905. (607)723-6921. Director: Mrs. Judith M. Carey. Craft shop/gallery/rental gallery. Represents 100 craftworkers. Price range: $2.25-400; bestsellers: $20-55. Works on consignment; 30% commission. Craftworker sets retail price. Show gallery fee: $75/show divided among artists exhibiting. Reports in 3 weeks. Work may be shipped or hand-delivered. Dealer pays return shipping and insurance for exhibited work.
Acceptable Work: Considers batik; ceramics; clothing; dollmaking; glass art; jewelry; leatherworking; quilting; soft sculpture; wall hangings; weavings; and woodcrafting. Especially needs clothing and ceramic sculpture. Fine one-of-a-kind and handmade production-line items; utilitarian and/or decorative.
Profile: Musuem has quality exhibit design; time period of display depends on artist, usually not more than 6 months; clientele is very sophisticated. Best selling time: Christmas and September.

THE UNCOMMON, 2079 S. Clinton Ave., Rochester NY 14618. (716)273-4981. Contact: Fran Becker. Gallery/gift shop. Estab. 1977. Represents 50-60 craftworkers. Considers candlemaking; ceramics; glass art; jewelry; metalsmithing; pottery; and woodcrafting. Fine one-of-a-kind and handmade production-line items; utilitarian and/or decorative (emphasis on utilitarian). Price range: $3-325; bestsellers: $5-60. Works on consignment; 40% commission. Craftworker sets retail price; gallery may advise adjustment. Requires exclusive area representation. Send slides; work is juried. Reports in 2 weeks. Dealer pays insurance for exhibited work.
Profile: "This is a craftsman-owned shop with careful selection of crafts exhibited. The presence of School for American Craftsmen in [the] community has increased awareness of crafts. Shop is located in middle to upper income area." Best selling time: Christmas and spring.

THE UNICORN CITY CORPORATION, 55 Greenwich Ave., New York NY 10014. (212)243-2017. Contact: Marty Proctor. Craft shop/gift shop. Estab. 1961. Represents 15 craftworkers. Price range: $5-1,800; bestsellers: $10-25. Works on consignment and buys outright; 50% commission. Gallery sets retail price. Requires exclusive area representation. Reports in 3 weeks. Work may be shipped. Best selling time: Christmas.
Acceptable Work: Considers batik; candlemaking; ceramics; dollmaking; glass art; jewelry; leatherworking; metalsmithing; pottery; soft sculpture; wall hangings; and weavings. Only uses unicorn designs. All styles; utilitarian and/or decorative.

VERZYL GALLERY, 377 Rt. 25A, Northport NY 11768. (516)261-8962. Director: June C. Verzyl. Considers ceramics; pottery; and sculpture. Works on consignment; 33⅓% commission. Minimum price: $100, sculpture; bestsellers: $200-800. Craftworker sets retail prices, but gallery will not exhibit work Verzyl feels is overpriced. "No exclusive representation, but we hope an artist will not overextend in the area. We welcome artists at any time during business hours." One-man shows are given 3 weeks exposure.

VILLAGE CRAFTS AND CURIOS, 17 Church St., Greenwich NY 12834. (518)692-2281. Contact: Helen A. Hoag. Craft shop/gallery. Estab. 1970. Represents 35-40 craftworkers. Price range: 60c-$560; bestsellers: 50c-$10. Works on consignment but usually buys outright; 30% commission. Retail price set by joint agreement. Requires exclusive area representation. Reports in 2 weeks. Work may be shipped or hand-delivered. Dealer pays shipping to shop and insurance for exhibited work.
Acceptable Work: Considers batik; candlemaking; dollmaking; glass art; jewelry; leatherwork-

ing; metalsmithing; needlecrafts; pottery; quilting; wall hangings; weavings; and woodcrafting. Especially needs enameling. All styles; utilitarian and/or decorative.

Profile: "We rotate displays at fairly close intervals. We try to be very careful in selection of crafts - color and placement are very important to us. We take only original designs." Heaviest wholesale buying time: February, June and October; best selling time: Christmas.

VILLAGE CRAFTSMEN, 219 W. Water, Elmira NY 14801. (607)732-5472. Contact: Julius or Carol Williams. Estab. 1973. Represents 50 craftworkers. Considers batik; ceramics; glass art; leatherworking; pottery; wall hangings; and weavings. Finished one-of-a-kind and handmade production-line items; utilitarian. Price range: $1.50-300; bestsellers: $1.50-20. Buys outright or on consignment; 33⅓% commission. Craftworker sets retail price. Query with transparencies or photos. Reports in 2 weeks. Dealer pays shipping from shop and insurance on exhibited work. Heaviest wholesale buying time: pre-Christmas.

THE VILLAGE SILVERSMITH, 149 Main St., Bellport NY 11713. (516)286-1660. Contact: Dwight Trujillo. Craft shop. Estab. 1970. Represents 5-8 craftworkers. Price range: $5-700; bestsellers: $5-50. Works on consignment and buys outright; 33⅓ commission. Retail price set by joint agreement. Requires exclusive area representation. Reports in 3 weeks. Work may be shipped or hand-delivered. Dealer pays return shipping and insurance for exhibited work.

Acceptable Work: Considers ceramics; glass art; jewelry; leatherworking; metalsmithing; wall hangings; weavings; and woodcrafting. All styles; utilitarian and/or decorative.

Profile: "All crafts are displayed in lighted cases and mingled with other craftsmen's work. We have wall and counter cases plus large front windows." Work is displayed 1-3 months. "We aim for the 18-40 age group when designing." Heaviest wholesale buying time: summer and winter; best selling time: spring and winter.

WARD-NASSE GALLERY, 178 & 131 Prince St., New York NY 10012. (212)925-6951 or 475-9125. Director: Harry Nasse. Exhibits all art, "whatever the artist membership votes in;" 2 years minimum exposure. Maximum size: 16' square. Art must be ready to exhibit. Price range: $3-3,000, sculpture; bestsellers: $100-300. Works on consignment; no commission. Artist sets retail price. Query. Gallery pays insurance for exhibited work. "This is an artist-run gallery and members vote in January and June to determine which artists are exhibited."

WAVE HILL CENTER FOR ENVIRONMENTAL STUDIES, 675 W. 252nd St., Bronx NY 10471. (212)549-2055. Director of Public Relations: Carol Robins. Museum gift shop. Estab. 1978. Considers all crafts relevant to the institution's programs; utilitarian and/or decorative.

Profile: "We're located in a former Hudson River estate manor house in a 28 acre public garden. Customers are adults of all ages and school children on field trips."

WEBB AND PARSONS, Bedford NY 10507. (914)234-9526. Director: Pat Parsons and William Webb. Gallery. Estab. 1970. Represents American and Canadian craftworkers. Considers all crafts. All styles; utilitarian and/or decorative. Price range: $1-5,000. Works on consignment; 40% commission. Retail price set by joint agreement. Send slides.

THE WHEELBARROW, 135 Main St., Cold Spring Harbor, Long Island NY 11724. (516)367-4604. Contact: Mrs. Mahan. Craft shop/gallery/gift shop. Estab. 1967. Represents 300 craftworkers. Considers all crafts except candlemaking. All styles; utilitarian and/or decorative. Price range: $1-300; bestsellers; $5-50. Works some on consignment and buys outright; commission negotiable. Shop sets retail price. Requires exclusive area representation. Insurance for exhibited work negotiable.

Profile: "We are in an historic area; our crafts are all American." Best selling time: Christmas.

THE WHIMSEY CRAFTSHOP AND GALLERY, Main St., Aurora NY 13026. (315)364-8486. Contact: Judith Erdely. Craft shop/gallery. Estab. 1971. Represents 30 craftworkers. Price range: 50c-$150; bestsellers: 50c-$25. Works on consignment and buys outright; 33⅓% commission. Retail price set by joint agreement. Reports in 2 weeks. Work may be shipped or hand-delivered. Dealer pays insurance for exhibited work.

Acceptable Work: Considers all crafts except ceramics. Especially needs quilts. One-of-a-kind designer pieces, handmade production-line items and primitive pieces; utilitarian and/or decorative.

Profile: "We hold special shows lasting from 1 weekend to 1 month. Unless it is a show, all work is dispersed throughout shop although larger works find their way to the top or other special areas." Heaviest wholesale buying time: summer and winter; best selling time: fall and spring.

THE WICKER GARDEN, INC., 1318 Madison Ave., New York NY 10028. (212)348-1166. President: Pamela McGinley Scurry. Gift shop. Estab. 1977. Represents 30 craftworkers. Price range: $3-300; bestsellers: $7.50-30. Buys outright. Shop sets retail price. Reports in 1 week. Work may be mailed or shipped. Dealer pays all shipping; in-transit insurance; and insurance for exhibited work.

Acceptable Work: Considers ceramics, dollmaking and quilting. Especially needs unusual, bright colored pillows, toys for boys, and children's things. Fine handmade production-line items; utilitarian and/or decorative.

Profile: "Work is displayed amidst antique Victorian wicker that is repaired to perfection and set in a bright garden atmosphere. The color is lime green and white. The shop and/or its items have been shown in 20 magazines during the past year. The accessories that complement the wicker are brightly colored pillows, quilts, baby toys, silk flowers, silkscreens, handpainted picnic baskets, aprons, pillows and umbrellas. The colors are lime green, lemon yellow, pure white, hot pinks, cornflower blue, pastels and lots of lace. Customers are 30-45 years of age, well-traveled, educated, upper-middle class and expect super quality for good price value."

WILKES GALLERY, INC., 101 Main St., Northport NY 11768. (516)261-4007. Contact: John or Jeannette Cuomo. Craft shop/gallery/gift shop. Estab. 1968. Represents 12-20 craftworkers. Price range: $2.50-100; bestsellers: $1.50-50. Works on consignment; 40% commission. Retail price set by joint agreement. Requires exclusive area representation. Work may be shipped or hand-delivered. Dealer pays insurance for exhibited work.

Acceptable Work: Considers batik; ceramics; decoupage; jewelry; leatherworking; metalsmithing; pottery; wall hangings; weavings; and woodcrafting. Especially needs work with a fishing or nautical theme. All styles; utilitarian and/or decorative.

Profile: Shop has "window displays as we are located on Main Street, with overwhelming walk by traffic; also additional items in several local newpapers announcing new crafts." Heaviest wholesale buying time: summer and November-December; best selling time: July-August.

WILL-O-THE-WICK, LTD., 1138 Lexington Ave., New York NY 10021. (212)535-1558. Contact: H. Cascante. Candle store. Estab. 1973. Represents 6 craftworkers. Considers candlemaking; utilitarian and/or decorative. Especially needs a wide range of novelty candles. Price range: $3-25; bestsellers: $5-18. Buys outright. Reports in 2 weeks. Work may be shipped or hand-delivered. Dealer pays insurance for exhibited work.

Profile: Items are placed immediately on display; no special time limit. Customers are in the middle and upper income brackets. Bestselling and heaviest wholesale buying time: fall.

To Break In: "Artists should do some research first. Find out from potential buyers what they want. Develop a line that is different, not a variation or copy of what many others are already doing."

WINDOW ON MAIN STREET, Box 575, Naples NY 14512. Manager: Judith Reifsnyder. Gallery. Estab. 1976. Represents 20 craftworkers. Price range: $3-1,000; bestsellers: $3-35. Works on consignment; 35% commission. Craftworker sets retail price. Reports in 4 weeks. Hand-delivered work only.

Acceptable Work: Considers ceramics; glass art; jewelry; metalsmithing; pottery; wall hangings; weavings; and woodcrafting. One-of-a-kind designer pieces; utilitarian and/or decorative.

Profile: "We're a cooperative gallery run by artists. Membership dues are $15 per year; a member may have a show and also keep work on display for the April-December season. We are located in an area of professional craftspeople and teachers." Best selling time: July, August and December.

WONDROUS THINGS, INC., Rt. 129, Croton-on-Hudson NY 10520. (914)271-3044. Contact any officer. Craft shop/gift shop. Estab. 1972. Represents 100 craftworkers. Price range: $3-165; bestsellers: $3-$15. Works on consignment and buys outright; 30% commission. Craftworker sets retail price. Reports in 4 weeks. Work may be shipped or hand-delivered after contracted.

Acceptable Work: Considers all crafts except clothing. Especially needs stained glass; leather; and wrought iron. Fine one-of-a-kind and handmade production-line items; utilitarian and/or decorative.

Profile: "We feature handmade gifts; we sell supplies and we give classes in silver jewelry, pottery, stained glass and watercolor painting."

THE WORKS GALLERY EAST, INC., 28 Jobs Lane, Southampton NY 11968. (516)283-1407. Contact: John Albano or Frank Pereira. Gallery. Estab. 1976. Represents 40-50 craftworkers. Price range: $20-2,000; bestsellers: $50-300. Works on consignment and buys outright; 40% commission. Retail price set by joint agreement. Requires exclusive area representation. Reports in 2-3 weeks. Work may be shipped or hand-delivered. Dealer pays shipping to shop and insurance for exhibited work. "Customers are extremely wealthy New Yorkers, 30-50 years of age, who appreciate good work." Heaviest wholesale buying time: early spring; best selling time: summer.

Acceptable Work: Considers batik; ceramics; glass art; jewelry; leatherworking; metalsmithing; pottery; quilting; soft sculpture; wall hangings; weavings; and woodcrafting. One-of-a-kind designer pieces; utilitarian and/or decorative.

North Carolina

ACT I, GALLERY, 111 E. Caswell St., Kinston NC 28501. (919)527-2517. Director: Pat Crawford. Associate Director: Steve Peeples. Craft shop/gallery. Estab. 1977. Represents 5 craftworkers. Price range: $3-500; bestsellers: $10-50. Works on consignment; 25% commission. Craftworker sets retail price. Reports in 2 weeks. Work may be shipped or hand-delivered. Dealer pays insurance for exhibited work.

Acceptable Work: Considers batik; ceramics; glass art; jewelry; leatherworking; metalsmithing; pottery; wall hangings; and weavings. Especially needs leatherworking; metalsmithing; batik; jewelry; and weavings. "We still encourage pottery and ceramics sales, but these are more easily available in our area." Fine one-of-a-kind pieces; utilitarian and/or decorative.

Profile: "Items are displayed on shelves within view from street. Featured items are placed in street windows." Best selling time: fall.

ARTS COUNCIL OF WILSON, INC. 205 Gray St., Wilson NC 27893. (919)291-4329. Executive Director: Vicky E. Bell. Craft shop/gallery. Estab. 1973. Represents 70 craftworkers. Considers all crafts. Primitive and fine one-of-a-kind; utilitarian and/or decorative. Price range: 50c-$150; bestsellers: $5-60. Works on consignment; 25% commission. Retail price set by joint agreement. Reports in 2 weeks. Work may be shipped or hand-delivered. Dealer pays return shipping. Displays work 6 months.

Profile: "Work is displayed in cases (jewelry and small items); on shelving; trunks; etc. Shop is housed in an art center; the center is in an old home and has galleries, artist studios, classrooms and offices. We have one- and two-man shows in our galleries." Best selling time: November, April and May.

BLUE RIDGE HEARTHSIDE CRAFTS, Box 1388, Boone NC 28607. (704)264-9078. General Manager: Joe Patelidas. Craft shop/wholesaler. Estab. 1968. Represents members only. Price range: 25c-$900; bestsellers: $15-30. Buys outright. Retail price set by joint agreement. Reports in 2 weeks. Work may be shipped or hand-delivered. Dealer pays shipping to shop and insurance for exhibited work. Best selling time: summer.

Acceptable Work: Considers batik; candlemaking; ceramics; dollmaking; glass art; jewelry; leatherworking; metalsmithing; needlecrafts; pottery; quilting; wall hangings; weavings; and woodcrafting. All styles.

BODYCRAFT GALLERIES, 409 West End Blvd., Winston Salem NC 27101. (919)722-4396. Contact: Tomi Melson or Bonnie Barger. Estab. 1976. Prejudging. 33⅓% commission. Sponsor pays insurance for exhibited work and pays return shipping.

Acceptable Work: Considers all wearable crafts. "Care instructions must be included on a detachable card. It really helps if the item can be cleaned, even if it's difficult. We have no objection to craftsmen using Vogue, McCall, etc. for basic garment patterns provided the item is unique in its treatment. Garments made from hand-woven cloth, for instance, are not disqualified by use of a professional pattern."

JOHN C. CAMPBELL FOLK SCHOOL, Rt. 1, Brasstown NC 28902. (704)837-2775. Manager: Gladys Rogers. Craft shop. Estab. 1925. Represents 55 craftworkers. Price range: 50c-$200; bestsellers: 50c-$80. Works on consignment and buys outright; 20% commission. Retail price set by joint agreement. Reports in 2 weeks. Hand-delivered work only.

Acceptable Work: Considers candlemaking; jewelry; leatherworking; metalsmithing; pottery; soft sculpture; wall hangings; weavings; and woodcrafting. Especially needs quilting and stitchery. All styles; utilitarian and/or decorative.

Profile: "We are in a rural mountain setting, located within a folk school." Heaviest wholesale buying time: winter; best selling time: summer.

CAROLINA MOUNTAIN ARTS & CRAFTS, Box 573, Murphy NC 28906. (704)644-5688. Contact: Manager. Estab. 1973. Represents 150 North Carolina, Tennessee and Georgia member craftworkers. Considers candlemaking; ceramics; decoupage; dollmaking; jewelry; leatherworking; metalsmithing; needlecrafts; pottery; macrame; quilting; tole painting; wall hangings; weavings; and woodcrafting. Price range: $1-200; bestsellers: $3-5. Works on consignment; 40% commission. Craftworker sets retail price. Write or visit shop. Reports in 2-3 weeks. Best selling time: Easter-Thanksgiving.

CAROLISTA JEWELRY DESIGNERS, 137 E. Rosemary St., Chapel Hill NC 27514 (summer: May-September, Box 201, Nags Head NC 27959). Contact: W. G. Baum. Estab. 1962. Considers ceramics; sculpture; tapestries; woven objects; glass; tie dye; and batik. Price range: $5-3,000. Work taken on consignment first year; often bought outright afterwards. 25-40% commission. Requires exclusive area representation. Send resume.

THE CRAFTY PEDDLERS, 122 W. Clay St., Mebane NC 27302. (919)563-2777. Contact: B. Kaye Smith. Craft shop. Estab. 1977. Represents 150 craftworkers. Primitive one-of-a-kind and handmade production-line items; utilitarian and/or decorative. Price range: $1-500; bestsellers: $2-40. Works on consignment and buys outright; 40% commission. Shop sets retail price. Reports in 2 weeks. "If inquiring by mail give description and price. When bringing items to store, please know ahead of time the price wanted for each item." Dealer pays insurance for exhibited work. Unsold consigned pieces returned after 6 months at craftworker's expense.
Acceptable Work: Considers ceramics; decoupage; jewelry; pottery; quilting; soft sculpture; tole painting; wall hangings; weavings; and woodcrafting. "We are in need of quality men's gift items (pipes, whimsical character plaques, sport statues). Woodcrafts have been very popular."
Profile: "We have over 1,000 square feet of floor space. Craftworkers occasionally present a special demonstration on pre-arranged days. Our shop motto: Handmade with love." Best selling time: May-December.

GALLERY 501 — MINT MUSEUM OF ART, Box 6011, Charlotte NC 28207. Manager: Jane Kessler. Museum gallery/rental gallery. Estab. 1960. Represents 20-30 craftworkers, preferably Southeastern. Price range: $5-200; bestsellers: $5-75. Works on consignment and buys outright; 30% commission. Craftworker sets retail price. Reports in 2 weeks. Dealer pays insurance for exhibited work.
Acceptable Work: Considers glass art; jewelry; leatherworking; pottery; quilting; wall hangings; weavings; and woodcrafting. Especially needs "production type pottery that still retains a uniqueness and innovativeness typical of the individual potter. I would like to see reasonably priced porcelain pieces." Fine one-of-a-kind and handmade production-line items; utilitarian and/or decorative.
Profile: "Items are placed on display shelves until sold or returned to artist. I like to carry whimsical pieces as well as very serious sculptural pieces." Heaviest wholesale buying time: early fall; best selling time: winter.

GOLDSBORO ART CENTER, Herman Park Center, 901-A E. Ash St. Goldsboro NC 27530. (919)736-3335. Gallery. Estab. 1971. Represents 90 craftworkers. Price range: $1-500; bestsellers: $5-50. Works on consignment; 20% commission. Craftworker sets retail price. Reports in 1 week. Work may be shipped or hand-delivered. Dealer pays return shipping and insurance for exhibited work.
Acceptable Work: Considers batik; dollmaking; jewelry; pottery; wall hangings; and weavings. Especially needs weavings and batik. Fine one-of-a-kind and handmade production-line items; utilitarian and/or decorative.
Profile: "We sell and exhibit only original art, no reproductions of any kind; we are completely nonprofit and we have classes and monthly exhibits." Best selling time: summer and Christmas.

GREEN HILL ART GALLERY, INC. 712 Summit Ave., Greensboro NC 27405. (919)273-6696. Executive Director: Mrs. John R. Beaman Jr. Nonprofit, educational facility. Gallery. Estab. 1974. Exhibits only original works of North Carolina artists. Considers all crafts, 2-D and 3-D. Group, educational, theme exhibitions; utilitarian and decorative. Price ranges: $10-900; bestsellers: $10-200. 25% commission. Craftworker sets price. Reports in 4 weeks. Work may be shipped or hand-delivered if selected to exhibit. Gallery insures all exhibits. Artists/craftsmen should submit slides and resume, slides returned within 20 days.

INDIAN MUSEUM OF THE CAROLINAS, 607 Turnpike Rd., Laurinburg NC 28352. (919)276-7294. Curator: Ruth Y. Wetmore. Museum gift shop. Estab. 1972. Represents 3-4 craftworkers; American Indian crafts only. Price range: 50c-$10; bestsellers: 50c-$1.50. Buys outright. Reports in 2 weeks. Museum sets retail price. Shipment is negotiated. Dealer pays insurance for exhibited work.

Acceptable Work: Considers dollmaking; jewelry, cornhusk dolls; and stone arrow points. Handmade production-line items; utilitarian and/or decorative.

Profile: "Our practice has been to hold a special exhibit, limited to 2-3 weeks in which items may be sold; or purchase crafts for sale in our museum shop." Best selling time: November and May.

THE JOLLY TROLLY, LTD., 325 S. Aspen St., Lincolnton NC 28092. (704)732-1703. Contact: Hugh or Mildred Sawyer. Gift shop. Estab. 1976. Represents 6 craftworkers. Price range: $2-75; bestsellers: $5-45. Works on consignment and buys outright; 55% commission. Retail price set by joint agreement. Requires exclusive area representation. Reports in 2 weeks. Work may be shipped or hand-delivered. Dealer pays insurance for exhibited work. Heaviest wholesale buying time: spring and summer; best selling time: fall and winter.

Acceptable Work: Considers ceramics; decoupage; pottery; wall hangings; weavings; and woodcrafting. Fine handmade production-line items; utilitarian and/or decorative.

KINSTON ARTS COUNCIL, 111 E. Caswell St., Kinston NC 28501. (919)527-2517. Director: Pat Crawford. Associate Director: Steve Peeples. Gallery/arts council. Estab. 1965. Represents 5-10 craftworkers. Price range: $4-75; bestsellers: $4-35. Works on consignment; 20% commission. Craftworker sets retail price. Reports in 2 weeks. Work may be shipped or hand-delivered. Dealer pays insurance for exhibited work.

Acceptable Work: Considers batik; candlemaking; ceramics; glass art; jewelry; leatherworking; metalsmithing; needlecrafts; pottery; quilting; soft sculpture; tole painting; wall hangings; weavings; and woodcrafting. Especially needs jewelry and metalsmithing. Fine one-of-a-kind pieces; utilitarian and/or decorative.

Profile: "All crafts are placed on shelves which are highly visible to the street and gallery. We handle only one-of-a-kind fine art crafts and, since we operate as an arts council, there is a ready made clientele in the people who use the building." Heaviest wholesale buying time: summer-fall; best selling time: fall-winter.

LITTLE ART GALLERY, North Hills Mall, Raleigh NC 27609. (919)787-6317. Contact: Ruth Green. Craft shop/gallery. Estab. 1968. Represents 50 craftworkers. Price range: $6-300; bestsellers: $15-50. Works on consignment and buys outright; 40% commission. Craftworker sets retail price. Reports in 1 week. Work may be shipped or hand-delivered. Dealer pays shipping.

Acceptable Work: Considers glass art; jewelry; pottery; wall hangings; and weavings. "I would like a good weaving exhibit on consignment. Most of the weavers will only sell, and I feel I have a market, if I can keep the work for 4-6 months." Fine one-of-a-kind and handmade production-line items; utilitarian and/or decorative.

Profile: "A show is up for 1 month. Work is on various walls and stands; our regular contributors remain up." Heaviest wholesale buying time: August; best selling time: Christmas.

MCNEAL GALLERY AND FRAMING, 1626 East Blvd., Charlotte NC 28203. (704)333-9201. Contact: Mark McNeal or Christie Taylor. Gallery. Estab. 1973. Represents 5 craftworkers. Price range: $10-2,500; bestsellers: $40-100. Works on consignment and buys outright; 33⅓-50% commission. Retail price set by joint agreement. Requires exclusive area representation. Reports in 2 weeks. Work may be shipped or hand-delivered. Dealer pays insurance.

Acceptable Work: Considers batik; ceramics; glass art; jewelry; leatherworking; metalsmithing; pottery; and woodcrafting. All styles; utilitarian and/or decorative.

Profile: "The main gallery is about 50'x50' broken into 4 quadrants. The adjoining 3 showrooms are 12'x20' making total gallery space 4,000 square feet." Best selling time: Christmas.

MACO CRAFTS, INC., Rt. 2, Box 1190, Franklin NC 28734. (704)524-7878. Manager: Betty Jo Warstler. Represents 350 local craftworkers. Considers quilts and furniture. Finished, one-of-a-kind and handmade production-line items only. Price range: $1-235; bestsellers: $5-235. Retail price set by joint agreement. "15% commission for craftsmen that work in the shop as volunteers 8 hours a month only." Write. Reports immediately. Dealer pays shipping to shop. Best selling time: summer and fall. Customers buy crafts to use as unusual gifts.

MIDLAND CRAFTERS, INC., Box 100, Pinehurst NC 28374. (919)295-6156. Contact: Mr. or Mrs. R.F. Stearn. Gallery/gift shop. Estab. 1960. Represents 1,500 craftworkers. Considers all crafts. All styles; utilitarian and/or decorative. Price range: 15c-$4,500; bestsellers: $2-30. Works on consignment and buys outright. Gallery sets retail price. Requires exclusive area representation. Reports in 1 week. Work may be shipped or hand-delivered. Dealer pays shipping to shop on purchased items.

Profile: "We're located in an old weaving mill. Display is our specialty with work of each crafter shown in lighted niche or grouped on counter." Heaviest wholesale buying time: late winter and early fall; best selling time: spring and late fall.

NECESSITIES, INC., 1308 Dixie Trail, Raleigh NC 27607. (919)781-5298. Contact: Becky W. Penny. Gallery/gift shop. Estab. 1975. Represents 10 craftworkers. Price range: $5-750; bestsellers: $5-150. Works on consignment and buys outright; 25% commission. Craftworker sets retail price. Reports in 1 week. Work may be shipped or hand-delivered. Dealer pays insurance for exhibited work. Displays work 3 months maximum. Best selling and heaviest wholesale buying time: fall and winter.
Acceptable Work: Considers batik; clothing; dollmaking; glass art; jewelry; metalsmithing; needlecrafts; pottery; wall hangings; weavings; and woodcrafting. Fine one-of-a-kind and handmade production-line items; utilitarian and/or decorative.

NEW MORNING GALLERY, 3½ Kitchen Place, Asheville NC 28803. (704)274-2831. Contact: John Cram. Craft shop/gallery. Estab. 1973. Represents 100 craftworkers. Price range: $2.50-850; bestsellers: $4.50-60. Works on consignment and buys outright; 40% commission. Craftworker sets retail price. Requires exclusive area representation. Reports in 1 week. Work may be shipped or hand-delivered with prior agreement. Dealer pays shipping to shop and insurance for exhibited work. Shows are 1 month or more.
Acceptable Work: Considers ceramics; glass art; jewelry; and pottery. Fine one-of-a-kind and handmade production-line items; utilitarian and/or decorative.
Profile: "We have an extensive display system of oak shelving and a wall oak glass case for art glass." Best selling time: summer and Christmas.

NORTH CAROLINA LEAGUE OF CREATIVE ARTS AND CRAFTS, INC., Box 10507, Winston-Salem NC 27108. (919)723-4800. President: Betty Place. Art and craft shop. Estab. 1975. Represents 200-250 artists and craftworkers. Price range: 75c-$800; bestsellers: $3-30. Works on consignment; 33⅓% commission. Retail price set by joint agreement. Work may be shipped or hand-delivered. Reports immediately. Dealer pays insurance for exhibited work. Work is displayed 3-6 months.
Acceptable Work: Considers all crafts except ceramics; patterns; and kits. Especially needs glass; leather, other than belts; weavings; and original stitchery. All styles; utilitarian and/or decorative.
Profile: "We are a total way of life for an artist or craftsperson to work. Resident craftworker pays on $20-30/month rent and takes 80% of sales." Heaviest wholesale buying time: summer and early fall; best selling time: March-June and October-December.

QUALLA ARTS AND CRAFTS MUTUAL, INC., Box 277, Cherokee NC 28719. (704)497-3103. Manager: Betty DuPree. Indian art and craft shop. Estab. 1946. Represents 250 Eastern Cherokee Indian craftworkers. Considers dollmaking; pottery; wall hangings; weavings; baskets; and beadwork. Primitive and fine work OK. Price range: $1.50-350. Shop sets retail price. "We are an Indian owned and operated coop." Reports in 10 days. Heaviest wholesale buying time: winter; best selling time: summer.

SNAGGY HOLLOW CRAFTSMEN, Box 393, Zirconia NC 28790. (704)693-4570. Contact: Jack Day. Craft shop. Estab. 1969. Represents 6 craftworkers. Price range: $1.50-60; bestsellers: $1.50-25. Works on consignment and buys outright; 34% commission. Retail price set by joint agreement. Reports in 1 week. Work may be shipped or hand-delivered. Dealer pays return shipping and insurance for exhibited work. Heaviest wholesale buying time: spring; best selling time: summer and fall.
Acceptable Work: Considers woodcrafting; and woodweaving (baskets, lamp shades, etc.) All styles; utilitarian and/or decorative.

STAINED GLASS ASSOCIATES, Box 1531, Raleigh NC 27602. (919)266-2493. Contact: Robert J. Wysocki. Craft shop/studio. Estab. 1958. Represents 5 craftworkers. Considers glass art; panels for individual residences and businesses. Fine one-of-a-kind pieces; utilitarian and/or decorative. Bestsellers: $57.50-585. Retail price set by joint agreement. Requires exclusive area representation. Reports in 1 week. Dealer pays return shipping and insurance for exhibited work.
Profile: "The stained glass objects are displayed within sight of the working distance and area of stained glass windows being assembled. Hanging display is used in studio area."

STONE MOUNTAIN CRAFTS, INC., Star Rt., Box 15, Traphill NC 28685. (919)957-8948. Contact: Ruth W. Holbrook. Craft shop. Estab. 1970. Represents 50 low income Wilkes County

craftworkers. Price range: 66¢-$100; bestsellers: 66¢-$10. 25% commission. Shop sets retail price. Reporting time varies. Best selling time: spring and fall.
Acceptable Work: Considers clothing; dollmaking; needlecrafts; quilting; woodcrafting; corn shuck items; denim items; and knitted and crocheted Christmas tree decorations. One-of-a-kind pieces only; utilitarian and/or decorative.

VILLAGE CRAFTSMEN, Box 248, Howard St., Ocracoke Island NC 27960. (919)928-5541. Contact: Philip or Julia Howard. Craft shop. Estab. 1970. Represents 100 craftworkers. Price range: $1-250; bestsellers: $1-50. Buys outright. Shop sets retail price. Prefers exclusive area representation. Reports as soon as possible. "Do not send unsolicited samples unless you do not need to have them returned." Work may be shipped or hand-delivered. Dealer pays shipping to shop on merchandise ordered and in-transit insurance on same.
Acceptable Work: Considers batik; candlemaking; clothing; glass art; jewelry; leatherworking; metalsmithing; needlecrafts; pottery; quilting; wall hangings; weavings; woodcrafting; wrought iron; soap; baskets; and beads. Primitive handmade production-line items; utilitarian and/or decorative.
Profile: "We are located on a turn-of-the-century picturesque sandy lane on an island off the coast of North Carolina. Although our customers are generally tourists, we stock quality-made American crafts which we display with creativity." Heaviest wholesale buying time: spring and summer; best selling time: late spring, summer and early fall.

WA YAH' STI INDIAN TRADITIONS, Box 130, Hollister NC 27844. (919)586-4519. Contact: Arnold or Pat Richardson. Mail order shop. Estab. 1975. Represents 2 craftworkers in American Indian arts and crafts. Considers leatherworking, pottery, stone sculpture and Indian arts; traditional and contemporary. Primitive one-of-a-kind pieces. Price range: $1.50-800. Buys outright. Retail price set by joint agreement. Work may be shipped or hand-delivered. Dealer pays shipping to shop and insurance for exhibited work. Heaviest wholesale buying time: winter and spring; best selling time: summer and fall.

WOHALI TRADERS, Box 45A, Rt. 1, Cherokee NC 28719. (704)497-9649. Contact: Lois J. deVries. Estab. 1973. Represents 25 craftworkers. Considers candlemaking; jewelry; leatherworking; metalsmithing; needlecrafts; pottery; quilting; wall hangings; weavings; woodcrafting; and any authentic Indian handicrafts. Especially needs non-silver crafts made by Indian tribes from outside North Carolina. Finished one-of-a-kind and handmade production-line items; utilitarian and/or decorative. Price range: 50¢-$1,000; bestsellers: $1-75. Buys outright or on consignment; 40% commission. Retail price set by joint agreement. Requires exclusive area representation. Query with transparencies or photos, or inquire at shop.
Profile: Each item is labeled with the craftsman's name. Heaviest wholesale buying time: spring and early summer; best selling time: summer and early fall.

YANCEY COUNTY COUNTRY STORE, Box 8, Town Square, Burnsville NC 28714. (704)682-3779. Contact: Mrs. G.A. Downing or Mrs. Jay Nichols. Craft and gift shop. Estab. 1967. Represents 100 mountain craftworkers. Price range: $1-350. Works on consignment; 25-33⅓%commission. Retail price set by joint agreement. Work may be shipped or hand-delivered. Dealer pays insurance for exhibited work.
Acceptable Work: Considers candlemaking; ceramics; clothing; decoupage; dollmaking; glass art; jewelry; leatherworking; pottery; quilting; wall hangings; weavings; and woodcrafting. Primitive and fine handmade production-line items; utilitarian and/or decorative.
Profile: "Our shop is like a museum, with many old things not for sale, etc. Customers are from all states and 24 foreign countries." Best selling and heaviest wholesale buying time: summer.

North Dakota

ARACHNE, 620 Main, Fargo ND 58102. (701)232-0354. Contact: Suzanne Smemo. Craft and supply shop. Estab. 1975. Represents 8 craftworkers. Considers clothing; wall hangings; and weavings. "Special need for hand spinners and knitters." One-of-a-kind pieces; utilitarian and/or decorative. Price range: $4-350; bestsellers: $4-125. Works on consignment; 30% commission. Retail price set by joint agreement. Reports in 4 weeks. Dealer pays insurance for exhibited work.
Profile: "The shop is a mixture of studio; gallery; supply shop; and a meeting place for craftspeople." Best selling time: Christmas.

THE COLLAGE, 23 N. 3rd St., Grand Forks ND 58201. (701)772-7900. Contact: Barb Lander. Craft shop/gallery/gift shop. Estab. 1974. Represents 100 craftworkers. Price range: $2.50-150; bestsellers: $5-45. Works on consignment and buys outrights; 33⅓%commission. Retail price set by joint agreement. Rental gallery fee: $3, 1 time only. Reports in 1 week. Work may be shipped or hand-delivered. Dealer pays insurance. Displays work 90 days.

Acceptable Work: Considers batik; candlemaking; clothing; dollmaking; glass art; leatherworking; metalsmithing; needlecrafts; pottery; quilting; soft sculpture; tole painting; wall hangings; weavings; woodcrafting; patchwork; wooden toys; and sandcasting. Fine one-of-a-kind and handmade production-line items; utilitarian and/or decorative.

Profile: "Customers are students and faculty, air base personnel and the general public of all ages." Heaviest wholesale buying time: August-November; best selling time: September-December.

MINOT ART GALLERY, Box 325, Minot ND 58701. (701)838-4445. Director: Galen R. Willert. Gallery/gift shop. Estab. 1970. Price range: $1-300; bestsellers: $1-100. Works on consignment; 30% commission. Craftworker sets retail price. Reports in 4 weeks. Work may be shipped or hand-delivered. Displays work 3 months in shop; 1 month in gallery.

Acceptable Work: Considers all crafts except ceramics. Especially needs glassware. Fine one-of-a-kind pieces; utilitarian and/or decorative.

Profile: Customers are high school students through senior citizens; farmers, middle class people, air force base personnel and college students." Best selling time: September-May.

UNIVERSITY OF NORTH DAKOTA ART GALLERIES, Box 8136, University Station, Grand Forks ND 58202. (701)777-4195. Director: Laurel J. Reuter. Gallery. Estab. 1971. Gallery is for exhibition, but work may be for sale. Work may be shipped or hand-delivered. Dealer pays shipping and insurance. Exhibitions are 3-6 weeks.

Acceptable Work: Considers batik; ceramics; clothing; glass art; jewelry; metalsmithing; quilting; soft sculpture; wall hangings; weavings; and clay. Fine one-of-a-kind pieces; decorative only.

Ohio

ASHTABULA ARTS CENTER, 2928 W. 13th St., Ashtabula OH 44004. (216)964-3396. Contact: Jo Weigand, Elaine Schafer, Penny Sockman or Caron Van Gilder. Gallery/gift shop/arts center. Estab. 1953. Represents 15-20 craftworkers. Price range: $1-5,000; bestsellers: $7-500. Works on consignment; 20-30% commission. Works through committee approval for exhibition in gallery. Retail price set by joint agreement. In exhibit gallery craftworker sets retail price. Reports in 4 weeks. Work may be shipped or hand-delivered at craftworker's expense. Dealer pays insurance for exhibited work.

Acceptable Work: Considers batik; ceramics; clothing; dollmaking; glass art; jewelry; pottery; soft sculpture; wall hangings; and weavings. All styles; utilitarian and/or decorative.

Profile: "Work is displayed in glass cases or hung on exhibit walls. There is excellent exposure as we conduct classes all year; we average 1,200 people through the center each week. Customers are 25-45; female; culturally oriented with above average income." Best selling time: pre-Christmas.

CAMPUS MARTIUS MUSEUM, 601 2nd St., Marietta OH 45750. (614)373-3750. Museum gift shop. Prefers local craftworkers but no real restrictions. Price range: 25c-$20; bestsellers: 25c-$5. Buys outright. Retail price set by joint agreement. Prefers exclusive area representation. Work may be shipped or hand-delivered.

Acceptable Work: Considers Ohio and West Virginia crafted candlemaking; dollmaking; jewelry; metalsmithing; pottery; and woodcrafting. Especially needs low price items of quality for school children. Utilitarian and/or decorative.

Profile: "Craft items for sale are displayed in glass cases, on shelves, or on a wall." Heaviest wholesale buying time: early spring; best selling time: May-October.

CEDAR POINT, INC. Merchandise Department, Sandusky OH 44870. (419)626-0830. Crafts Manager: Jeff Savage. Craft shop. Estab. 1971. Represents 10-20 craftworkers per week. Considers all crafts except glass art. All styles; utilitarian and/or decorative. Price range: $1-50; bestsellers: $1-10. Craftworkers set up and sell on a percentage of their gross sales. Craftworker sets retail price. Reports as soon as possible between January 1-mid-August. Samples may be shipped or hand-delivered. Dealer pays return shipping for samples only and insurance for exhibited work.

Profile: "We are a Visiting Crafts Center and do not handle the items. The craftsmen set up a display and sell themselves. We get customers of all ages and incomes since we are located in an amusement park." Best selling time: mid-May — mid-September.

THE CRAFTY FOX, 3240 E. Market, Warren OH 44484. Contact: Lynne Boling. Gift shop. Estab. 1973. Represents 300 craftworkers. Price range: $1-100; bestsellers: $1-10. Works on consignment and buys outright; 35% commission. Retail price set by joint agreement. Rental gallery fee: $3/year. Requires exclusive area representation. Reports in 1-4 weeks. Work may be shipped or hand-delivered. Displays work 4 months maximum. Customers are upper middle class housewives. Heaviest wholesale buying time: summer; best selling time: September-December.
Acceptable Work: Considers all crafts except ceramics; leatherworking; and soft sculpture. Fine handmade items; utilitarian and/or decorative.

CREATION ART AND CRAFT CENTER, 717 Chillicothe St., Portsmouth OH 45662. (614)353-8838. Contact: Fred Tindall or Ann Arthur. Craft shop/gallery. Estab. 1976. Represents 12 craftworkers. Price range: 4c-$1,800. Buys outright. Gallery sets retail price. Reports in 4 weeks. Work may be shipped or hand-delivered. Dealer pays shipping and insurance. Displays work 6-12 months. Customers are middle class and have incomes of approximately $15,000 per year. Best selling and heaviest wholesale buying time: winter.
Acceptable Work: Considers batik; candlemaking; ceramics; decoupage; glass art; jewelry; leatherworking; pottery; tole painting; wall hangings; weavings; and woodcrafting. Especially needs weavings. All styles; utilitarian and/or decorative.

CREATIVE CLUTTER BY VERGENE, 22 S. Market St., Troy OH 45373. Contact: Vergene Wetz. Gift shop. Estab. 1970. Represents 5-10 craftworkers. Price range: $1.95-100; bestsellers: $2.50-20. Works on consignment: 25-33⅓% commission. Retail price set by joint agreement. Requires exclusive area representation. Reports immediately. SASE. Pays monthly in person for work sold. Hand-delivered work only.
Acceptable Work: Considers batik; dollmaking; glass art; needlecrafts; Shaker style furniture; children's barnwood plaques; doll furniture; ceramics; floral arrangements; and door ornaments. All styles; utilitarian and/or decorative.
Profile: "Work is displayed in windows and grouped on walls. We are a home accessory shop mostly; we carry some fabric for upholstery and draperies." Best selling time: Christmas and Mother's Day.

DOLLHOUSE WORLD, 20391 Miller Ave., Euclid OH 44119. (216)486-6664. Contact: Jean Schroeder. Dollhouse and miniature shop. Estab. 1973. Represents 15 craftworkers. Considers dollhouses; miniature furniture and accessories; all 1"-1' scale. Fine one-of-a-kind and handmade production-line items; utilitarian and/or decorative. Price range: $1-500; bestsellers: $2-200. Works on consignment and buys outright; 30-40% commission. Retail price set by joint agreement. Sometimes requires exclusive area representation. Reports in 2 weeks. Work may be shipped or hand-delivered. Dealer pays return shipping and insurance for exhibited work.
Special Needs: "Exquisite oriental pieces; moderately priced Victorian pieces; English Tudor style furniture. I would also like to develop a line of bed coverings, crewel type, etc."
Profile: "We usually have more expensive furniture in locked glass cases; held for a period of 6 months-1 year; other items are on racks and shelves, open and closed. I want to use a few good craftsmen who will follow my ideas and still be creative and have ideas of their own that we can discuss. For new people I want to work on a consignment basis to start and if all goes well would buy outright on an exclusive basis." Best selling and heaviest wholesale buying time: Christmas.

DON DRUMM STUDIOS AND GALLERY, 437 Crouse St., Akron OH 44311. (216)434-4452. Contact: Don or Lisa Drumm. Rental gallery. Estab. 1960. Represents 100 craftworkers. Price range: $10-1,000; bestsellers: $25-250. Buys outright and works on consignment for shows; 40-60% commission. Retail price set by joint agreement. Requires exclusive area representation. Reports in 2 weeks. Work may be shipped or hand-delivered; prefers UPS. Dealer pays shipping to shop (will not accept COD) and insurance for exhibited work.
Acceptable Work: Considers ceramics; dollmaking; glass art; jewelry; leatherworking; metalsmithing; pottery; soft sculpture; wall hangings; and weavings. Especially needs gifts in the $10-25 price range. Fine one-of-a-kind and handmade production-line items; utilitarian and/or decorative.
Profile: "Our gallery consists of different rooms of display; items are changed and moved around featuring things in special changing displays. A large number of items are functional crafts." Best selling time: winter and Christmas sales.

ARTHUR L. FELDMAN FINE ARTS, 53 The Arcade, Cleveland OH 44114. (216)861-3580. Contact: A.L. Feldman. Considers ceramics. Specializes in internationally known artists. Price range: $100-10,000, prints/ceramics; bestsellers: $200-500. Buys outright. Gallery sets retail price. Query. Gallery pays shipping to gallery.

FRONTIERSMEN GIFT SHOP, 67 S. Main St., Centerville OH 45459. (614)433-8691. President: Anna Mae Lockard. Estab. 1972. Represents 70 craftworkers; 85% from Appalachia. Considers glass art; metalsmithing; pottery; quilting; soft sculpture; woodcrafting; doll houses; miniatures; pewter; and wooden toys. Finished one-of-a-kind and handmade production-line items OK; utilitarian and/or decorative. Price range: 50c-$150; bestsellers: $4.50-10. Buys outright. Shops sets retail price. Requires exclusive representation within 5 miles. Write. Reports in 2 weeks. Shipping to shop paid by Lockard.
Profile: Presents items in front windows and on display tables in center of shop. Best selling time: July-August, November-December; heaviest wholesale buying time: April and October. "Customers with high incomes, average age 35, and interested in the unusual."

THE GALLERY, Box 293, Put-in-Bay OH 43456. (419)285-3611. Contact: Thomas S. Houser or Sandra Littman. Craft shop/gallery. Estab. 1969. Represents 40 craftworkers. All styles; utilitarian and/or decorative. Price range: $2-200; bestsellers: $2-35. Works on consignment and buys outright; 30% commission. Craftworker sets retail price. Shipping to shop negotiable; dealer pays return shipping, transit insurance and insurance for exhibited work.
Acceptable Work: Considers batik; candlemaking; ceramics; clothing; decoupage; dollmaking; glass art; jewelry; leatherworking; metalsmithing; needlecrafts; pottery; quilting; tole painting; wall hangings; weavings; and woodcrafting.
Profile: "We are a seasonal shop, summer only, located on South Bass Island. Customers are tourists, boaters and cottage people."

THE GALLERY ON MAIN STREET, 114½ W. Main St., Circleville OH 43113. (614)474-2078. Contact: Buyer. Craft shop/gallery/gift shop. Estab. 1973. Represents 80 craftworkers. Considers all crafts. "Pumpkin motif is popular because of 'Pumpkin Show' held annually in October." All styles; utilitarian and/or decorative. Price range: $1-85; bestsellers: $2-25. Works on consignment; 25% commission. Retail price set by joint agreement; requires exclusive area representation. 3 months minimum exposure. Best selling time: Christmas.

GEAUGA COUNTY HISTORICAL SOCIETY, CROSSROADS COUNTRY STORE, Box 153, Burton OH 44021. (216)834-4012. Secretary: Ruth Ann Head. Country store. Estab. 1962. Represents several craftworkers whose work is representative of 19th century America. Price range: $200 maximum; bestsellers: $15 maximum. Buys outright. Gallery sets retail price. Reports in 2 weeks. Work may be shipped or hand-delivered. Dealer pays shipping and insurance for exhibited work.
Acceptable Work: Considers candlemaking; metalsmithing; needlecrafts; pottery; quilting; tole painting; woodcrafting; and miniatures. Primitive one-of-a-kind and handmade production-line items; utilitarian and/or decorative.
Profile: "Our store is a combination of 2 buildings both circa 1850 and the atmosphere is that of a typical country store of that period. The setting for the store is a restored 19th century village with 3 old homes furnished with antiques, dress shop, church, etc." Best selling and heaviest wholesale buying time: March-October.

GOLDEN HOBBY SHOP, 906 E. Broad St., Columbus OH 43205. (614)222-8329. Director: Carol Seitz. Operated by the Columbus Recreation and Parks Department. Craft shop. Estab. 1971. Represents 1,400 Franklin County craftworkers over 60 years of age. Price range: 10c-$220. Works on consignment; 10% commission. Retail price set by joint agreement. Reports immediately. Work may be shipped or hand-delivered. Dealer pays insurance for exhibited work. Displays work 1 year. Best selling time: Easter and August through December.
Acceptable Work: Considers all crafts except soft sculpture. Primitive and fine one-of-a-kind pieces; utilitarian and/or decorative.

THE HAMLET, 3687 Ira Rd., Bath OH 44210. (216)666-8883. Contact: Joyce Vyhnalek. Craft shop/gift shop. Estab. 1970. Represents 220 craftworkers. Price range: 35c-$150; bestsellers: 35c-$40. Works on consignment; 30% commission. Craftworker sets retail price. Requires exclusive area representation. Work may be shipped or hand-delivered. Dealer pays insurance for exhibited work.
Acceptable Work: Considers batik; ceramics; clothing; decoupage; dollmaking; glass art; jewelry; leatherworking; metalsmithing; needlecrafts; pottery; quilting; soft sculpture; tole painting; and woodcrafting. All styles; utilitarian and/or decorative.
Profile: "We are located in a building that is over 120 years old and set among tall pines out in

the country. We get a large percentage of tourists. Most of our customers are upper middle class and professional types." Best selling time: September-December.

THE HOLDEN ARBORETUM, 9500 Sperry Rd., Mentor OH 44060. (216)946-4400. Contact: Tree House Manager. Museum gift shop. Estab. 1977. Represents 5 craftworkers. Price range: $1-200; bestsellers: $5-50. Works on consignment; commission is negotiable. Retail price set by joint agreement. Reports in 3 weeks. Work may be shipped or hand-delivered. Displays work 1-3 months.
Acceptable Work: Considers batik; glass art; jewelry; pottery; quilting; wall hangings; weavings; and woodcrafting. Especially needs crafts dealing with birds, wildflowers or wildlife. All styles; utilitarian and/or decorative.
Profile: "The Holden Arboretum is a 2,700 acre museum of woody plants. The gift shop is surrounded by a beautiful expanse of land. It is a comfortable building with fireplaces and picture windows. Customers enjoy the out-of-doors." Best selling time: holidays.

IMAGES GALLERY, 4324 W. Central Ave., Toldeo OH 43616. (419)537-1400. Director: Frederick D. Cohn. Considers glass art and sculpture. Buys outright and works on consignment. Gallery sets retail price. Prefers exclusive area representation. Send slides or call for interview. SASE.

MARGE'S BACK PORCH, Box 123, 38 N. Main St., Waynesville OH 45068. (513)897-4746. Contact: Marge Schenk. Craft shop/gift shop/antique and miniature shop. Estab. 1976. Represents 40 craftworkers. Price range: $1.50-75; bestsellers: $2-25. Works on consignment and buys outright; 30% commission. Retail price set by joint agreement. Requires exclusive area representation. Reports in 2 weeks. Work may be shipped or hand-delivered. Dealer pays insurance for exhibited work. Displays work 90 days.
Acceptable Work: Considers candlemaking; ceramics; clothing; decoupage; glass art; jewelry; metalsmithing; needlecrafts; pottery; quilting; tole painting; wall hangings; weavings; woodcrafting; china and porcelain painting; tinwork; flower arranging; pen and ink sketches; and pet paintings. All styles; utilitarian and/or decorative. Especially needs functional moderately priced wood pieces; unusual jewelry.
Profile: "Most persons coming to our area are antique enthusiasts, having 25 antique shops in the Village. Therefore, to get individuals in your shop it is imperative that some antiques be handled. The crafts should also complement the antique lovers." Heaviest wholesale buying time: spring-fall; best selling time: June-December.

THE MASSILLON MUSEUM, 212 Lincoln Way E., Massillon OH 44646. (216)833-4061. Director: Mary M. Merwin. "We are not a gallery to promote sales, but have exhibitions to promote the artists and craftsmen who wish exposure. They must be professional." Considers batik; ceramics; glass art; jewelry; metalsmithing; mobiles; pottery; sculpture; soft sculpture; wall hangings; and weavings. Maximum size: 4x9'. Price range: $10-50, crafts. 20% commission on sold work. Artist sets retail price. Send slides. SASE. Gallery pays insurance on exhibited work. "We endeavor to exhibit the work of Ohio artists and craftsmen who meet the standards."

THE MILFORD POTTERY, 235-B Main St., Milford OH 45150. (513)831-1463. Contact: Catherine A. Gatch. Craft shop. Estab. 1976. Represents 8-10 craftworkers. "Prefer Cincinnati area craftsmen, but will accept others." Considers pottery. All styles; utilitarian and/or decorative. Price range: $1-200; bestsellers: $1-30. Works on consignment and buys outright; 30-40% commission. Retail price set by joint agreement. Reports in 1-2 weeks. Work may be shipped or hand-delivered.
Profile: "We normally display items mixed with other craftsmen's work. However, in the case of a major showing of someone's work, we will set up a separate display of 1 person's work." Best selling and heaviest wholesale buying time: summer and Christmas.

MILLER GALLERY, 2722 Erie Ave., Cincinnati OH 45208. (513)871-4420. Contact: Barbara, Norman or Laura Miller. Gallery. Estab. 1962. Represents 20 craftworkers. Price range: $3-1,000; bestsellers: $10-70. Works on consignment and buys outright; 40% commission. Craftworker sets retail price. Requires exclusive area representation. Reports in 2 weeks. Work may be shipped or hand-delivered. Dealer pays insurance for exhibited work.
Acceptable Work: Considers ceramics; glass art; jewelry; pottery; soft sculpture; wall hangings; weavings. Especially needs hand blown art glass; unique fiber works; art jewelry; fine glazed porcelain; and fine glazed stoneware. Fine one-of-a-kind and handmade production-line items; utilitarian and/or decorative.
Profile: "New items get prime space the first month; regular space the next 3 months, then are

rotated between storage and display. Customers are in the upper socio-economic level; educated; income from $15,000-200,000." Heaviest wholesale buying time: pre-Christmas; best selling time: Christmas.

THE PATCHWORK FACTORY, INC., 671 Sawburg Ave., Alliance OH 44601. (216)823-6708. Contact: Betty Malone. Craft and gift shop. Estab. 1972. Represents 150-200 craftworkers. Price range: 75c-$780; bestsellers: $3-300. Works on consignment; 33⅓% commission. Retail price set by joint agreement. Work may be hand-delivered. We do not insure work. If item is damaged we pay for repairs or buy the item if damage is due to our negligence.
Acceptable Work: Considers candlemaking; ceramics; clothing; decoupage; dollmaking; glass art; jewelry; leatherworking; needlecrafts; pottery; quilting; soft sculpture; tole painting; wall hangings; weavings; and woodcrafting. Especially needs patchwork; wood items; and stained glass. Fine one-of-a-kind and handmade production-line items; utilitarian and/or decorative.
Profile: "We have some displays of a mixture of all types of crafts together; but mostly show the same types of work grouped together." Best selling and heaviest wholesale buying time: early fall to holidays.

PEOPLES AND CULTURES SHOP-IN-THE-FLATS, 1330 Old River Rd., Cleveland OH 44113. (216)621-3749. Manager: Amparo Hernandez. Estab. 1972. Represents 150 craftworkers from the Greater Cleveland area. Considers batik; ceramics; decoupage; dollmaking; jewelry; leatherworking; metalsmithing; quilting; needlecrafts; pottery; soft sculpture; wall hangings; weavings; and woodcrafting related to cultural heritage. Primitive or finished, one-of-a-kind or handmade production-line items; utilitarian and/or decorative. Price range: 90c-$500; bestsellers: $1-2.50 Christmas ornaments. Works on consignment; 30% commission. Retail price set by joint agreement. Make appointment to show work to selection jury. Reports in 2 weeks.
Profile: New crafts exhibited in feature display. Best selling time: Christmas and spring. "Customers are all ages, colors, creeds, incomes — those interested in diverse cultures of Cleveland."
Special Needs: Clothing with ethnic stitchery; new culturally-related crafts; toys; games; pillows; instruments; and cooking utensils.

POTPOURRI INC., 585 Dover Center, Bay Village OH 44140. (216)871-6500. Manager: Dorli Rosenzopf. Estab. 1968. Represents 50 craftworkers. Considers candlemaking; ceramics; glass art; jewelry; pottery; and tole painting. Especially needs woodcrafting and metal sculpture. Prefers "early American style, nothing super modern— it doesn't sell here." Finished handmade production-line items OK; utilitarian and/or decorative. Price range: $2-250; bestsellers: $5-25. Works on consignment; 40% commission. Retail price set by joint agreement. Requires exclusive area representation. Query with transparencies or photos. Reports in 3 weeks.
Profile: Items displayed 3 months minimum. Heaviest wholesale buying time: Christmas. Customers are middle-aged housewives with middle and upper incomes; they buy crafts for gifts.

SEVENTEENTH COLONY HOUSE, 18 S. High St., Box 367, Dublin OH 43017. (614)889-1204. Contact: G. Theodore. Gift shop. Estab. 1969. Represents 4-6 craftworkers. Price range: $10-1,000; bestsellers: $25-300. Works on consignment and buys outright; 40% commission. Retail price set by joint agreement. Requires exclusive area representation. Reports in 4 weeks. Work may be shipped or hand-delivered. Dealer pays shipping to shop. Displays work 2 weeks maximum. Customers are 25-55; couples with both people working; income of $30,000 and up. Heaviest wholesale buying time: fall; best selling time: fall and winter.
Acceptable Work: Considers glass art; jewelry; metalsmithing; pottery; and woodcrafting. Especially needs pewter; glass paper weights; lamps; figurines and jewelry; bronze figurines; and wood. All styles; utilitarian and/or decorative.

STORY BOOK CRAFTS, 6021 Dayton Rd., Springfield OH 45502. (513)864-7781. Contact: Elmo or Betty Spriggs. Craft shop/gallery/gift shop/glassblowing studio. Estab. 1955. Represents 332 "Master Craftsmen." Price range: $1.50-5,000; bestsellers: $8.50-425. Works on consignment and buys outright; 33⅓% commission. Retail price set by joint agreement. Requires exclusive area representation. Reports as soon as possible. Work may be shipped or hand-delivered. Dealer pays shipping and insurance for exhibited work. Displays work 30 days.
Acceptable Work: Considers batik; candlemaking; ceramics; glass art; jewelry; leatherworking; metalsmithing; pottery; soft sculpture; wall hangings; weavings; woodcrafting; bronze sculptures; copper and silver enamels; crystalline porcelains; lithophanes; and grandfather clocks. Limited one-of-a-kind items; utilitarian and/or decorative.
Profile: "We have excellent spot lighting and backgrounds to best suit the art objects; lighted all

glass cases for protection of items such as jewelry. Our customers range from 20-late 60's; interested in fine art; many are collectors; income ranges from $15,000 to many who are in the millionaire bracket. Many commission special work."

SYNERGY, 314 W. 4th St., Cincinnati OH 45506. (513)323-6470. Contact: G. Steinberg. Gallery of wearables. Estab. 1977. Represents 5 craftworkers. Price range: $1-1,500; bestsellers: $15-50. Works on consignment and buys outright; 30% commission. Gallery sets retail price. Requires exclusive area representation. Reports in 3 weeks. Work may be shipped. Dealer pays insurance for exhibited work. Displays work 1 month.
Acceptable Work: Considers clothing; jewelry; and personal accessories. All styles; utilitarian and/or decorative.
Profile: "We publicize individual shows to a mailing list of 5,000. Customers are looking for unique and beautiful items; are in late 20's through 60's." Heaviest wholesale buying time: fall; best selling time: fall and winter.
To Break In: "Would like to see a complete presentation of slides, photos, etc., with prices, colors, sizes and fabric; also description of unusual craft processes in use and list of shows craftperson has participated in."

ROSS WIDEN GALLERY, 5120 Mayfield Rd., Lyndhurst OH 44124. (216)461-3430. Contact: Mrs. Widen. Gallery. Estab. 1947. Represents 10-12 craftworkers. Price range: $5-1,500; bestsellers: $100 maximum. Works on consignment; 33⅓% commission. Retail price set by joint agreement. Requires exclusive area representation. Reports in 2 weeks. Work may be shipped or hand-delivered. Dealer pays insurance for exhibited work.
Acceptable Work: Considers batik; ceramics; glass art, jewelry; pottery; soft sculpture; wall hangings; weavings; and woodcrafting. All styles; utilitarian and/or decorative.
Profile: "We don't usually exhibit local persons very often as they are seen in other local galleries. Our customers are middle-aged; intelligent; and are in upper income brackets." Best selling time: fall and winter.

Oklahoma

ADA GIFTS AND CRAFTS, 715 E. Main, Ada OK 74820. (405)332-5540. Contact: Jimmie Nell Blum. Craft and gift shop. Estab. 1976. Represents 20-30 craftworkers. Price range: $1.50-45; bestsellers: $2-15. Works on consignment and buys outright; 40% commission. Retail price set by joint agreement. Reports in 2 weeks. Work may be shipped or hand-delivered. Dealer pays return shipping.
Acceptable Work: Considers batik; candlemaking; ceramics; decoupage; glass art; jewelry; pottery; wall hangings; weavings; and woodcrafting. Primitive and fine one-of-a-kind pieces; utilitarian and/or decorative. Especially needs pillow making and new designs for planters and plant hangers.
Profile: "We are located in an old residence with a relaxed atmosphere and an emphasis on people and service. Customers are university students; women aged 18-50; and Indians with an interest in jewelry and weaving." Best selling time: winter.

THE APPLE BASKET, 1015 8th, Woodward OK 73801. (405)256-6813. Contact: Frankie Herzer. Gift shop. Estab. 1972. Represents 100 craftworkers. Price range: $1-150; bestsellers: $5-50. Works on consignment; 40% commission. Retail price set by joint agreement. Requires exclusive area representation. Reports in 1 week. Work may be shipped or hand-delivered. Dealer pays insurance for exhibited work.
Acceptable Work: Considers batik; candlemaking; ceramics; decoupage; dollmaking; glass art; jewelry; leatherworking; metalsmithing; needlecrafts; pottery; quilting; soft sculpture; tole painting; wall hangings; weavings; and woodcrafting. Especially needs slogan plaques and Western and country-styled crafts. Primitive and fine one-of-a-kind pieces; utilitarian and/or decorative.
Profile: "Customers are 25-50 years old; art oriented; high income." Displays work 3-12 months. Heaviest wholesale buying time: 1st and 3rd quarters; best selling time: 2nd and 4th quarters.

CARAVAN GALLERY, LTD., 6029 S. Sheridan, Tulsa OK 74145. (918)627-7575. Contact: Mrs. William W. Haugh. Considers traditional and abstract sculpture and jewelry. "We request a broad representation of work — 6 to 20 pieces, depending on the medium. Lately, we've been handling more contemporary, exclusively American artists. Our clientele tends to be young businessmen and middle-aged persons of upper-middle class income." Price range: $5-2,000; bestsellers: $200-500. 40% commission. Exclusive representation in the Tulsa area required, plus commission on art sold 60 days after show. Send photos or brochures of work. Sponsors openings. Exhibited art insured.

CHICKASAW COUNCIL HOUSE MUSEUM, Rt. 1, Box 14, Tishomingo OK 73460. (405)371-3351. Contact: Beverly J. Wyatt. Museum gift shop. Estab. 1971. Represents 20 Chickasaw Indian craftworkers. Price range: 75c-$50; bestsellers: $1-22.50. Works on consignment; 30% commission. Retail price set by joint agreement. Reports in 1 week. Work may be shipped or hand-delivered. Dealer splits cost of shipping. Heaviest wholesale buying time: spring-summer; best selling time: summer.
Acceptable Work: Considers ceramics; jewelry; leatherworking; metalsmithing; pottery; wall hangings; and weavings. All styles; utilitarian and/or decorative.

THE GAZEBO, LTD., 4972 S. 79th East Ave., Tulsa OK 74145. (918)664-7094. President: Norma Caylor. Gift shop. Estab. 1967. Represents 25-35 craftworkers. Price range: 50c-$325; bestsellers: $3-150. Buys outright. Gallery sets retail price. Requires exclusive area representation. Reports in 2 weeks. Work may be shipped or hand-delivered. Dealer pays insurance for exhibited work. Displays work 3 months maximum.
Acceptable Work: Considers ceramics; dollmaking; glass art; jewelry; metalsmithing; needlecrafts; pottery; wall hangings; weavings; miniatures; rocks and minerals; and woodcrafting. Especially needs anything new in the miniature field. Finished, one-of-a-kind and hand-made production-line items; decorative.
Profile: "My shop is interested mostly in miniatures, dollhouses, 1"-1' scale; any and every kind of miniature." Displays work 3 months maximum. Heaviest wholesale buying time: August; best selling time: Christmas.

GILCREASE MUSEUM GIFT SHOP, 2500 W. Newton, Rt. 6, Tulsa OK 74127. (918)581-5313. Manager: Shirley Massongill. Gift shop. Estab. 1964. Represents 70 craftworkers. Price range: 10c-$600; bestsellers: 10c-$100. Buys outright. Keystone sets retail price. Work may be shipped or hand-delivered. Dealer pays shipping and insurance.
Acceptable Work: Considers jewelry; metalsmithing; needlecrafts; pottery; woodcrafting; and beadwork. Fine one-of-a-kind and handmade production-line items; utilitarian and/or decorative.
Profile: "We handle mostly reproductions from the Museum collection and top quality Indian crafts. Customers are interested in the arts; 25-60 years old; middle to high income." Heaviest wholesale buying time: spring and fall; best selling time: April-December.

GREEN COUNTRY ART CENTER, 1825 E. 15th, Tulsa OK 74104. (918)932-4259. Director: R.L. Schellstede. Gallery. Estab. 1967. Represents 25 craftworkers. Considers paintings and sculpture. Fine one-of-a-kind pieces; decorative only. Especially needs woodcarvings and metal sculptures. Price range: $10-several thousands; bestsellers: $25-500. Buys outright. Retail price set by joint agreement. Requires exclusive area representation. Reports in 1-2 weeks. Work may be shipped or hand-delivered.
Profile: "A special showing might be only a few days, special opening and advertising. Ordinary consignment to be in gallery 4-6 weeks. Customers are young married couples who buy gifts and work for decorating apartments; collectors who are usually older businessmen." Heaviest wholesale buying time: early summer; best selling time: late summer-fall.

LEA'S HALLMARK SHOP, 201 W. 6th St., Okmulgee OK 74447. Contact: W.D. Barnes. Gift shop. Estab. 1976. Represents 1 craftworker. Considers needlecrafts; wall hangings; and weavings. Handmade production-line items; utilitarian and/or decorative. Price range: $1-15; bestsellers: $3-10. Works on consignment; 25-35% commission. Reports in 2 weeks. Work may be shipped or hand-delivered. Dealer pays insurance for exhibited work.
Profile: "Approximate income of customers: $10,000-12,000; young married to elderly." Displays work 30 days. Heaviest wholesale buying time: July and September; best selling time: November-December.

THE MABEE-GERRER MUSEUM, 1900 W. MacArthur Dr., Shawnee OK 74801. (405)273-9870. Director: Robert G. Dodson. Estab. 1918. Price range: $5-150. Works on consignment; 40% commission. Retail price set by joint agreement. Requires exclusive area representation. Reports in 4 weeks. Work may be shipped or hand-delivered. Dealer pays insurance.
Acceptable Work: Considers batik; candlemaking; ceramics; glass art; jewelry; leatherworking; metalsmithing; pottery; soft sculpture; wall hangings; weavings; and woodcrafting. Primitive and fine one-of-a-kind pieces; utilitarian and/or decorative.
Profile: "We have a combination of over 400 oil paintings; 300 prints and 6,000 artifacts from all civilizations of ancient history and some primitive cultures of today. Customers are middle class of typical age range with emphasis on youth."

NANCY'S CORNER, 1 Williams Center, 2nd St. Level, Tulsa OK 74103. Contact: Nancy Patton. Craft shop/gift shop. Estab. 1973. Represents 10-20 craftworkers. Price range: $5-750; bestsellers: $5-125. Works on consignment or buys outright; 30% commission. Retail price set by joint agreement. Requires exclusive Tulsa area representation. Work may be shipped or hand-delivered by prior consent. Dealer pays shipping to shop and insurance for exhibited work only if ordered.
Acceptable Work: Considers silver jewelry; needlecrafts; pottery; quilting; baskets; soft sculpture; wall hangings; weavings; and woodcarving. Fine one-of-a-kind and handmade production-line items; utilitarian and/or decorative.
Profile: "Our store is furnished with Shaker reproductions and primitive antique pieces, a good background for handmade things. The college educated young married people seem to be our steadiest customers." Heaviest wholesale buying time: summer; best selling time: Christmas.

OKLAHOMA INDIAN ARTS AND CRAFTS CO-OPERATIVE, Box 966, Anadarko OK 73005. Manager: Netti Standing. Estab. 1955. Represents 60 craftworkers. Considers Indian art; beadwork; metalwork; featherwork; sewing; and dollmaking. Finished handmade production-line items. Price range: 85c-$800; bestsellers: 85c-$40. Buys outright. Gallery sets retail price. Requires exclusive area representation. Reports in 4 weeks. Work may be hand-delivered. Dealer pays shipping to shop and in-transit insurance. Best selling and heaviest wholesale buying time: summer.

PASEO DESIGN CENTER, 2927 Paseo, Oklahoma City OK 73103. Contact: Marion Stewart. Craft shop/gallery/gift shop. Estab. 1972. Represents 12-15 craftworkers. Price range: $3.50-300; bestsellers: $3.50-25. Works on consignment; 33⅓% commission. Retail price set by joint agreement. Reports in 2 weeks. Hand-delivered work only. Displays work 30-60 days.
Acceptable Work: Considers batik; candlemaking; ceramics; clothing; dollmaking; glass art; jewelry; leatherworking; metalsmithing; pottery; quilting; soft sculpture; wall hangings; and weavings. Fine one-of-a-kind and handmade production-line items; utilitarian and/or decorative.
Profile: "Displays work in glass cases and on walls. Customers are in the $15,000-30,000 per year income bracket; young to upper middle age." Best selling time: fall-winter.

THE PERSIMMON SEED, 1436 S. Carson, Tulsa OK 74119. (918)587-7973. Contact: Inez Running-rabbit. Gallery. Estab. 1962. Represents 4 craftworkers. Price range: $40-1,000; bestsellers: $40-100. Works on consignment; 40% commission. Gallery sets retail price. Rental gallery fee: 25%. Reports in 2 weeks. Work may be hand-delivered.
Acceptable Work: Considers dollmaking; jewelry; leatherworking; metalsmithing; needlecrafts; pottery; and quilting. Primitive and fine one-of-a-kind pieces; utilitarian and/or decorative.
Profile: Customers are educated in the arts. Heaviest wholesale buying time: spring and fall; best selling time: fall.

SHAWNEE ARTS AND CRAFTS CENTER, 429 W. Midland, Shawnee OK 74801. (405)273-5335. Contact: Maxine Jones. Craft and gift shop. Estab. 1975. Represents 3 craftworkers. Works on consignment and buys outright; 20% commission. Retail price is set by shops in area. Reports in 1 week. Hand delivered work only.
Acceptable Work: Considers batik; ceramics; decoupage; dollmaking; glass art; jewelry; pottery; soft sculpture; tole painting; wall hangings; weavings; macrame; and handcrafted stoneware. "We are going into more soft goods, such as tote bags; aprons; and decorative items for kitchen and bathrooms."
Profile: "We teach 10 classes in our shop every week. I have free workshops for churches, schools, etc. I've taught art for 6 years in public school and have a masters degree in North American Indian Art. The area is approaching a renaissance in appreciating and creating art." Best selling time: November-January 1.

STEPHENS COUNTY HISTORICAL MUSEUM, Box 1294, Fuqua Park, Duncan OK 73533. (405)252-0717. Director: Charlotte L. Jenkins. Museum gift shop. Estab. 1977. Represents 3-4 craftworkers. Price range: 10c-$10; bestsellers: 10c-$3. Buys at wholesale price; 10% commission. Retail price set by joint agreement. Reports in 4 weeks. Work may be shipped or hand-delivered.
Acceptable Work: Considers decoupage; dollmaking; glass art; jewelry; metalsmithing; needlecrafts; pottery; quilting; tole painting; and woodcrafting. Especially needs "souvenir type gifts depicting Southwestern themes: oil field or Indian artifacts. Would like to develop a line of

ashtrays (ceramic or inexpensive metal) with museum logo." Finished crafts; utilitarian and/or decorative.
Profile: "Work is displayed in glass cases that can be locked. Some have mirrors and fluorescent lights." Heaviest wholesale buying time: spring; best selling time: summer and pre-Christmas.

TALISMAN GALLERY, 115 E. 12th, Bartlesville OK 74003. Contact: Jody Kirberger. Craft shop/gallery. Estab. 1964. Represents 25-30 craftworkers. Works on consignment; 33⅓% commission. Craftworker sets retail price. Work may be shipped or hand-delivered. Dealer pays return shipping.
Acceptable Work: Considers batik; ceramics; clothing; glass art; jewelry; metalsmithing; pottery; soft sculpture; wall hangings; weavings; and woodcrafting. Finished and handmade production-line items; utilitarian and/or decorative.
Profile: "Bartlesville is an educated town with money. All ages and all incomes." Best selling and heaviest wholesale buying time: Christmas.

26 EAST ART CENTER, INC. 26 E. 18th St., Tulsa OK 74119. (918)582-3382. President: Nelson P. Kifer. Craft shop/gallery. Estab. 1972. Represents 60-80 craftworkers. Price range: $5-2,000; bestsellers: $4-600. Works on consignment; 40% commission. Craftworker sets retail price. Reports in 1 week. Work may be shipped or hand-delivered. Dealer pays return shipping. "We direct our merchandise to the 35-50 year olds." Best selling time: fall and spring.
Acceptable Work: Considers batik; ceramics; glass art; jewelry; pottery; and soft sculpture. Finished and one-of-a-kind pieces; utilitarian and/or decorative.

WEWOKA TRADING POST, 524 S. Wewoka, Wewoka OK 74884. (405)257-5580. Contact: Idabel Bishop. Estab. 1974. Represents 25 local craftworkers. Considers dollmaking; jewelry; Seminole patchwork; wall hangings; and weavings. Especially needs Seminole beadwork and sculpture. Finished one-of-a-kind items only; utilitarian and/or decorative. Price range: 25c-$250. Buys outright or on consignment; 25% commission. Retail price set by gallery or joint agreement. Write.

Oregon

THE ART MERCHANT, Box 443, Sisters OR 97759. (503)549-4571. Contact: Vallerie Robinson. Gallery/gift shop/rental gallery. Estab. 1976. Represents 50 craftworkers. Price range: $2-11,500; bestsellers: $10-500. Buys outright. Retail price set by joint agreement. Requires exclusive area representation. Reports in 4 weeks. Work may be shipped or hand-delivered. Dealer pays return shipping and insurance.
Acceptable Work: Considers batik; dollmaking; jewelry; metalsmithing; pottery; soft sculpture; wall hangings; weavings; and woodcrafting. All styles; utilitarian and/or decorative.
Profile: "Artist must be approved by panel; after acceptance work is shown continuously." Displays work 1-3 months. Best selling time: summer.

BURGETT'S MYRTLEWOOD SHOPS, Box 1067, Bandon OR 97411. (503)347-2248. Contact: Jim or Joan Burgett. Craft and gift shop. Estab. 1936. Represents 40 craftworkers. Price range: 50c-$2,600; bestsellers: $5.95-22. Buys outright. Retail price set by joint agreement. Requires exclusive area representation. Reports immediately. Work may be shipped or hand-delivered. Dealer pays insurance for exhibited work.
Acceptable Work: Considers candlemaking; jewelry; tole painting; and woodcrafting. Especially needs $5-10 items in hardwoods. All styles; utilitarian and/or decorative.
Profile: "We are located in a scenic area on the Oregon coast; customers are tourists from western US and Canada." Best selling time: summer.

CASA DEL SOL, 82 N. Main St., Ashland OR 97520. (503)482-5443. Contact: John Connors. Craft shop/gallery. Estab. 1971. Represents 10 craftworkers. Price range: $3-5,000; bestsellers: $3-30. Works on consignment; 34% commission. Retail price set by joint agreement. Requires exclusive area representation. Reports in 2 weeks. Hand-delivered work only. Displays work 1 month in shows. "Customers are in their 20's on up; well-educated and of moderate to good income." Heaviest wholesale buying time: spring; best selling time: summer.
Acceptable Work: Considers batik; candlemaking; ceramics; dollmaking; glass art; pottery; soft sculpture; and woodcrafting. Fine one-of-a-kind and handmade production-line items; utilitarian and/or decorative.

COLUMBIA ART GALLERY, 514 State, Hood River OR 97051. Director: Mary Ann Meyer. Gallery/gift shop. Estab. 1973. Represents 8-10 craftworkers. Price range: 75c-$2,000; bestsellers: $1-500. Works on consignment; 25% commission. Retail price set by joint agreement. Reports in 1 month. Work may be shipped or hand-delivered. Dealer pays return shipping

and insurance for exhibited work. Displays work 6 weeks.
Acceptable Work: Considers batik; ceramics; handmade clothing; glass art; jewelry; leatherworking; metalsmithing; pottery; quilting; soft sculpture; wall hangings; weavings; and woodcrafting. Especially needs silver work small sculptural things; batik; window screens; and blown glass goblets. Fine pieces only; utilitarian and/or decorative.
Profile: "We are located in an old mansion on the Columbia River bank and have a highly sophisticated clientele." Best selling and heaviest wholesale buying time: Christmas and spring.

CONTEMPORARY CRAFTS ASSOCIATION, 3934 SW Corbett Ave., Portland OR 97201. (503)223-2654. Contact: Elyse Hallahan. Craft shop/gallery. Estab. 1938. Represents 800 craftworkers. Price range: $3-5,000. Works on consignment; 25% commission. Craftworker sets retail price. Reports in 2 weeks. Work may be shipped or hand-delivered with prior agreement. Dealer pays insurance for exhibited work.
Acceptable Work: Considers batik; ceramics; glass art; jewelry; leatherworking; metalsmithing; needlecrafts; pottery; quilting; soft sculpture; wall hangings; weavings; and woodcrafting. Fine one-of-a-kind contemporary pieces; utilitarian and/or decorative.
Profile: "If our space allows, most pieces are exhibited in our consignment and sales gallery (shelves, stands, wall space)." Best selling time: Christmas.

COOS ART MUSEUM, 515 Market Ave., Coos Bay OR 97420. (503)267-3901. Director: Maggie Karl. Museum gallery/museum gift shop/rental gallery. Estab. 1965. Represents over 100 craftworkers. Price range: 25c-$200; bestsellers: $10 minimum. Works on consignment; 25-30% commission. Craftworker sets retail price. Requires exclusive area representation. Reports immediately. Hand-delivered work only. Dealer pays insurance for exhibited work. Best selling time: Christmas.
Acceptable Work: Considers all crafts except clothing; decoupage; and tole painting. Especially needs jewelry. Primitive and fine one-of-a-kind pieces; utilitarian and/or decorative.

FAVELL MUSEUM OF WESTERN ART & INDIAN ARTIFACTS, Box 165, Klamath Falls OR 97601. (503)882-9996. Contact: Gene Favell. Considers glass art; jewelry; metalsmithing; pottery; sculpture; and woodcrafting. Specializes in Western and Indian art. Sculpture must have pedestals. Price range: $5-200, Indian crafts. Buys outright or on consignment; 35% commission. Retail price set by joint agreement or craftworker. Sometimes requires exclusive area representation. Query with samples or call for interview. SASE. 1 month minimum exposure.

HORNER MUSEUM GIFT AREA, Oregon State University, Gil Coliseum, Corvallis OR 97331. Field Representative: Karen S. Piepmeier. Museum gift shop. Estab. 1976. Price range: 25c-$25; bestsellers: 25c-$10. Works on consignment; 50% commission. Gallery sets retail price. Reports as soon as possible. Work may be hand-delivered. Displays work 1 year.
Acceptable Work: Considers only crafts that reflect the exhibits in the museum. Exhibits in the museum deal with history, natural history, and anthropology. Fine pieces only; utilitarian and/or decorative.
Profile: "When an item is accepted in the gift area, it is priced and displayed on a shelf or in a case with its price. Customers are primarily museum visitors." Heaviest wholesale buying time: summer; best selling time: fall, winter and spring.

MAUDE J. KERNS ART CENTER, 1910 E. 15th Ave., Eugene OR 97403. (503)345-1126. Contact: Director. Craft shop, gallery and rental gallery. Estab. 1955. Represents 145 craftworkers in the craft shop, 100 in rental sales. Price range: $1.50-150; bestsellers; $1.50-35. Works on consignment; 30% commission. Retail price set by craftworker. All work is juried before acceptance. Reports in 4 weeks. Work may be shipped or hand-delivered; dealer pays insurance on exhibited work.
Acceptable Work: Considers batik; candlemaking; dollmaking; toys; glass art; jewelry; leatherworking; metalsmithing; pottery; quilting; soft sculpture; wall hangings; weavings; and woodworking. Fine one-of-a-kind and handmade production-line items; utilitarian and/or decorative. "All work must be of original design and made from natural materials — no assembled work accepted."
Profile: "We represent quality crafts displayed in a clean way. We jury all work submitted, so as to have a cohesive presentation. The work of each artist is grouped together for special displays. Consignment periods are 6 months, after which time items are reevaluated." Best selling time: May, September and December.

LAWRENCE GALLERY, Box 187, Sheridan OR 97396. (503)843-3633. Contact: Gary Lawrence. Fine arts and crafts gallery. Estab. 1977. Represents 135 craftworkers. Price range:

$5-5,000; bestsellers; $10-400. Works on consignment; 30-35% commission. Retail price set by gallery. "We have jury composed of 5 artists who view all work. Once an artist is accepted, all of his work is generally allowed, unless it's of noticeably low quality. The jury strives for high quality. Out-of-area artists who want to be juried should send slides and a resume." Reports in 4 weeks. "We pay the artist often within 1 week, 4 weeks at most." Work should be hand-delivered; "must contact us before shipping."
Acceptable Work: Considers batik; ceramics; glass art; jewelry; pottery; paintings; and sculpture. Fine one-of-a-kind pieces, except for pottery, which can be handmade production-line items; utilitarian and/or decorative.
Profile: Gallery has 2,000 square feet of display space and track lighting. Shows last 3-5 weeks. "Because of our large gallery, we prefer to keep pieces 3 months and exhibit them even when they're not in a specific show." Best selling time: summer. "Most customers are middle-aged, upper-middle to upper class, beginning buyers and collectors."

MOSSY CREEK POTTERY AND GALLERY, Box 368, Gleneden Beach OR 97388. Owner: Bob Richardson. Craft shop and gallery. Estab. 1973. Represents Oregon craftworkers. Considers fine weavings and woodcarvings. One-of-a-kind and production-line items; utilitarian and/or decorative. Price range: $3-300. Works on consignment; 30% commission. Retail price set by joint agreement. Requires exclusive area representation. Reports in 4 weeks. Work should be hand-delivered, if a prior agreement has been made.
Profile: "We handle limited amounts of crafts during our season on a full-time basis. Some or all of each artist's work is always on display, with displays changing constantly as sales occur." Best selling time: summer. "Our customers are very knowledgeable, and are looking for the best. Most are tourists visiting the Oregon coast."

NIKNAK GALLERY INC./DBA SOPHISTICAT, 917 SW Alder St., Portland OR 97205. (503)228-1511. Owners: Sherry and Helen Seward. Gift shop and boutique. Estab. 1975. Represents 6 craftworkers. Price range: $5-200; bestseller: $80-100. Works on consignment and buys outright; 35% commission. Retail price set by gallery or craftworker. Requires exclusive area representation. Reports in 2 weeks. Work may be shipped or hand-delivered.
Acceptable Work: Considers ceramics; clothing; jewelry; pottery; quilting; soft sculpture; wall hangings; and weavings. Needs "funky, advanced soft sculpturing." Fine one-of-a-kind and handmade production-line items; utilitarian and/or decorative.
Profile: "We're unique because the clothes we sell are advanced for Portland, and because of the personal treatment we give our customers." Work shown in window and on wall displays. Promoted through newspaper ads. Best selling time: Christmas. Customers are looking for the unusual; "we have young working gals, tourists and $50,000 a year matrons."

THE RED COCK CRAFTSMEN'S OUTLET, 1423 NW Hwy. 101, Lincoln City OR 97367. (503)994-2518. Contact: Laurel Soeby. Craft and gift shop. Estab. 1972. Represents 30 Oregon and Northwest craftworkers. Price range: $1-125; bestsellers: $2-20. Works on consignment and buys outright; 30% commission. Retail price set by craftworker. Requires exclusive area representation. Reports in 3 weeks. Work may be shipped or hand-delivered, if a prior agreement has been made.
Acceptable Work: Considers batik; jewelry; needlecrafts; pottery; wall hangings; weavings; woodcrafting; prints; photography; and fiber arts. "I'd like to also get more children's things and some metalwork." Primitive one-of-a-kind and handmade production-line items; utilitarian and/or decorative.
Profile: "Works are displayed so they can be touched, in settings similar to how they might be displayed in the home (with the exception of small items such as jewelry). Displays are revamped constantly." Heaviest wholesale buying time: spring-summer; best selling time: summer. "Customers are age 20-50, $10,000-50,000 annual income; they generally tend to be a young thinking, upwardly mobile group interested in all kinds of arts and crafts."

RIVER GALLERY, Rt. 1, Box 193, Nehalem OR 97131. (503)368-5711. Owner: Carey Tate. Gallery. Estab. 1974. Represents 15 craftworkers. Price range: $5-300; bestsellers: $5-100. Works on consignment; 34% commission. Retail price set by gallery. Requires exclusive area representation. Reports in 1 week. Work may be shipped or hand-delivered.
Acceptable Work: Considers batik; ceramics; glass art; jewelry; metalsmithing; pottery; soft sculpture; wall hangings; weavings; woodcrafting; and sculpture. "We are seeking weavers, potters and metal sculptors." Primitive and fine one-of-a-kind pieces; utilitarian and/or decorative.
Profile: "The gallery is located in a 1900 building in the rustic atmosphere of the Oregon coast.

Items are given prime showing for 1 month, then up to 3 months in available space." Heaviest wholesale buying time: spring and summer; best selling time: summer and Christmas. Customers are upper income bracket, tourists and vacationing property owners.

SCHOOL OF THE ARTS AND CRAFTS SOCIETY-BOOKSTORE/SALES GALLERY, 616 NW 18th Ave., Portland OR 97209. (503)228-4741. Bookstore/Sales Gallery Manager: Sharon Morales. Gift shop. Estab. 1975. Represents 35-40 craftworkers. Price range: 50c-$100; bestsellers: 50c-$35. Works on consignment; 25% commission. Retail price set by craftworker. Reports in 2 weeks. Work may be shipped but prefers hand-delivered. Dealer pays return shipping and insurance on exhibited work.
Acceptable Work: Considers batik; ceramics; dollmaking; glass art; jewelry; metalsmithing; pottery; wall hangings; weavings; woodcrafting; and notecards in various media, e.g. silkscreen, calligraphed, watercolor. One-of-a-kind and handmade production line items; utilitarian only.
Profile: "We're part of an established craft school, which also has an exhibition gallery. Because there are frequently special events taking place at the school, we have a diverse and interested clientele." Work displayed on shelves, pedestals, glass cases and walls for 2-2½ months. Heaviest wholesale buying and best selling time: fall and pre-Christmas

SUNBOW GALLERY, 206 SW Stark St., Portland OR 97204. (503)221-0258. Co-owners: Janice Butler, Toni Tollen, Sandi Clark and Lyn Toney. Craft shop and gallery. Estab. 1976. Represents 100 craftworkers. Price range: 50c-$17,000; bestsellers: 50c-$90. Works on consignment; 33⅓% commission. Retail price set by joint agreement. Fee charged for exhibit gallery space; craftworker pays flyer expenses for show. Reports in 3 weeks. Slides of work may be mailed; hand-delivered work only.
Acceptable Work: Considers batik; clothing; glass art; jewelry; leatherworking; pottery; soft sculpture; wall hangings; weavings; woodcrafting; toys; handbound books; and dried flowers. Fine one-of-a-kind and handmade production-line items; utilitarian and/or decorative.
Profile: Work is displayed for 90 days. Monthly shows feature a certain artist or group. Best selling time: August-December. "Our customers are downtown business and working people and gallery followers."

WHITE BIRD GALLERY, Box 502, Cannon Beach OR 97110. (503)436-2681. Contact: Evelyn Georges. Fine art and crafts gallery. Estab. 1971. Represents 50+ craftworkers. Considers batik; ceramics; clothing; glass art; jewelry; pottery; quilting; soft sculpture; wall hangings; weavings; and woodcrafting. "We have a special need for large platters." Fine one-of-a-kind and some handmade production-line items; utilitarian and/or decorative. Price range: $5-500; bestsellers: $25-150. Works on consignment and buys outright; 33⅓% commission. Retail price set by joint agreement. Requires exclusive area representation. Reports in 3-4 weeks. Shipping is negotiable; dealer pays insurance for exhibited work.
Profile: "After 7 years in the same location we feel we have earned our excellent reputation for quality crafts. We are a beach town so we draw many tourists as well as our own following." Best selling time: summer.

Pennsylvania
ANDROGYNY CRAFTS GALLERY, 507 S. 4th St., Philadelphia PA 19147. (215)925-6427. Contact: Marcia Serepy. Craft shop/gallery. Estab. 1977. Represents 40 American craftworkers. Price range: $10-450; bestsellers: $16-60. Works on consignment and buys outright; 40% commission. Retail price set by joint agreement. Reports in 3 weeks. Work may be shipped or hand-delivered. Dealer pays shipping to shop and insurance for exhibited work.
Acceptable Work: Considers ceramics; decoupage; glass art; jewelry; leatherworking; pottery; soft sculpture; wall hangings; weavings; and woodcrafting. All styles; decorative only. Especially needs any kind of pieces well done in a sexual motif.
Profile: Shop has "interesting and imaginative displays, spiral staircase, original beams and woodwork. Customers are professionals; 25-50 years old; $25,000 income." Heaviest wholesale buying time: winter-spring; best selling time: winter.

ARTESANS GALLERY, Box 411 AA, Oakdale PA. (412)923-1177. Contact: Kathleen Zimbicki. Craft shop. Estab. 1976. Represents 45 craftworkers. Price range: $2-200. Works on consignment and buys outright; 30% commission. Retail price set by joint agreement. Best selling time: Christmas.
Acceptable Work: Considers batik; glass art; jewelry; leatherworking; metalsmithing; pottery tole painting; wall hangings; weavings; and woodcrafting. Utilitarian and/or decorative.

ARTISAN'S COOPERATIVE, Box 221, Chadds Ford PA 19317. Executive Director: Deirdre Bonifaz. Craft shop. Estab. 1973 in support of rural artisans. Price range: 80c-$500; bestsellers: $2.75-350. Buys outright. Artisan's Cooperative pays shipping to shop and insurance for exhibited work.
Acceptable Work: Considers batik; candlemaking; ceramics; clothing; dollmaking; glass art; jewelry; leatherworking; metalsmithing; pottery; quilting; soft sculpture; wall hangings; handwoven clothing; woodcrafting; folk toys; broomcraft; basketry; and cornhusk flowers and dolls. All styles; utilitarian and/or decorative.
Profile: Shop has "high quality authentic crafts throughout; vivid colors in displays and a feeling of fantasy." Customers are in middle to high income bracket; professionals; all ages. Best selling time: last quarter; and heaviest wholesale buying time: third quarter. "Member groups are grassroots community organizations independently striving to serve their members, mostly women, who live in rural, isolated areas of US (Appalachia, deep South, New England). We purchase small percentage of crafts from individuals who complement but do not compete with work from members groups."

ARTISAN'S COOPERATIVE, New Market, Philadelphia PA. See above.

BARE WALL GALLERY, 712 Green St., Harrisburg PA 17102. (717)236-8504. Contact: Ronn Fink. Estab. 1972. Represents 50 craftworkers. Considers batik; candlemaking; jewelry; metalsmithing; needlecrafts; pottery; wall hangings; weavings; woodcrafting; and wooden toys. Primitive and finished one-of-a-kind and handmade production-line items; utilitarian items only. Price range: $3-100; bestsellers; $3-30. Buys outright. Craftworker sets retail price. Requires exclusive area representation. Write. Reports in 1 week. Dealer pays shipping to shop. Best wholesale buying time: June; best selling time: December.
To Break In: "Craftsmen striving to be professional need help in developing their lines and in setting up merchandising practice. The most frequent problems craftsmen seem to have are limited selection of items, fluctuating prices and little respect for order dates. When I place an order with a craftsman and he fails to produce, I'm hurt, and what is more is that another craftsman is also hurt because if I had known the items on order were never to be delivered, I would have ordered from another craftsman."

BIRD IN THE HAND, INC., 427 Broad St., Sewickley PA 15143. (412)741-8286. Contact: Katharine N. Amsler. Estab. 1969. Represents 50 craftworkers. Considers ceramics; glass art; jewelry; leatherworking; pottery; wall hangings; weavings; and woodcrafting. Finished, one-of-a-kind items OK; utilitarian and/or decorative. Price range: $5-1,000. Buys outright or on consignment; 40% commission. Retail price set by joint agreement. Requires exclusive area representation. Write or query with transparencies or photos. Reports in 2 weeks. Dealer pays shipping from shop and insurance for exhibited work.
Profile: Gallery has 2 floors, each with separate shows. One-man show on lower level runs about 1 month; upper level displays work on walls, boxes and cases for 6 months maximum. Heaviest wholesale buying time: Christmas season. Customers buy crafts for artistic value and usefulness.

THE BLUE SKY GALLERY, 3861 Old William Penn Hwy., Murrysville PA 15668. (412)325-2713. Director: Mimsie Stuhldreher. Gallery. Estab. 1972. Represents 100 craftworkers. Price range: $3-400; bestsellers: $3-50. Works on consignment and buys outright; 33⅓% commission. Retail price set by joint agreement. Requires exclusive area representation. Reports in 3 weeks. Work may be shipped or hand-delivered by previous arrangement. Dealer pays shipping and insurance. Shows are 3 weeks; consignment work is shown for 3 months.
Acceptable Work: Considers candlemaking; ceramics; glass art; leatherworking; metalsmithing; pottery; quilting; soft sculpture; wall hangings; weavings; and woodcrafting. Fine one-of-a-kind and handmade production-line items; utilitarian and/or decorative. Especially needs small, finished wood items: functional Shaker-type stools, boxes, etc.
Profile: "Crafts are displayed in the old kitchen, for the most part. Framed and matted items in another room. The shows are held in the Inn parlor. We are housed in a handsome, red brick, 160 year old building. Customers are young to middle aged with middle income." Heaviest wholesale buying time: late summer and early fall; best selling time: November and December.

CANDLEWIC COMPANY, 2101 Black Horse Dr., Warrington PA 18976. (215)343-6359. Vice President: Elizabeth Binder. Craft shop/wholesale candle supplier. Estab. 1964. Represents 6 craftworkers who manufacture candleholders. Considers candlemaking; glass art; woodcrafting; and "any item for candles." One-of-a-kind and handmade production-line items; utilitarian and/or decorative. Price range: $1.25-75; bestsellers: $5.50-15. Works on consignment; buys out-

right; 50% commission. Shop sets retail price. Reports in 1 week.
Profile: "All candle items purchased in bulk, 1 dozen-2 dozen per item. We also manufacture candles at shop." Tourist area. Best selling time: September-December.

CENTER OF THE HISTORY OF AMERICAN NEEDLEWORK, Box 8162, Pittsburgh PA 15217. (412)422-8749. Director: R. Maines. Study center. Estab. 1974. Represents 1-10 needle and textile arts craftworkers who are Center members. Price range: 50c-$400; bestsellers: $5-15. Displays work; 25% commission. Craftworker sets retail price. Reports in 2 weeks. Work may be shipped or hand-delivered. Dealer pays insurance for exhibited work. Displays work 6 weeks.
Acceptable Work: Considers batik; clothing; dollmaking; jewelry; needlecrafts; quilting; soft sculpture; wall hangings; and weavings. All sytles; utilitarian and/or decorative.
Profile: "We are entirely non-exclusive with regard to form and style; we do not as yet have an exhibit fee, nor do we charge admission; our goal is to further interest and research in the needle and textile arts." Open only November-December.

CHMIELEWSKI GALLERY, 1131 Hamilton St., Allentown PA 18101. (215)439-0900. Contact: Ron or Linda Chmielewski. Gallery. Estab. 1976. Represents 10 craftworkers. Price range: $2-125; bestsellers: $8-25. Works on consignment and buys outright; 40% commission. Retail price set by joint agreement. Requires exclusive area representation. Reports in 2 weeks. Work may be hand-delivered. Displays work 30 days minimum.
Acceptable Work: Considers batik; ceramics; pottery; soft sculpture; wall hangings; and weavings. Especially needs flat ceramic wall pieces and fiber wall hangings. Primitive and finished one-of-a-kind pieces; utilitarian and/or decorative.
Profile: "Work is displayed on tables, pedestals or hanging. Average client is middle-aged, middle to upper income and a professional." Heaviest wholesale buying time: fall; best selling time: fall and early winter.

THE CLAY PLACE GALLERY, 5600 Walnut St., Pittsburgh PA 15232. (412)441-3799. Director: Elvira L. Peake. Gallery/craft shop/supply shop. Estab. 1973. Considers pottery and sculpture clay works and occasionally glass and enamels. Price range: $4-250; bestsellers: $4-150. Works on consignment; 33% commission. Buys outright; 50% commission. Craftworker sets retail price. Requires exclusive area representation during show. Query with slides and photos. SASE. Reports in 4 weeks. Dealer pays insurance for exhibited work.
Profile: "We hold 11 one-person shows and 1 group show each year. We sponsor the openings and provide promotion. Craftworker installs exhibit."

THE COLLABORATIVE, 107 S. Main St., New Hope PA 18938. (215)862-9103. President: Beatricia Sagar. Craft shop. Estab. 1971. Represents 75 craftworkers. Price range: $10-1,000; bestsellers: $25-250. Works on consignment; 45% commission. Retail price set by joint agreement. Requires exclusive area representation. Reporting time varies. Work may be shipped or hand-delivered. Dealer pays return shipping and insurance for exhibited work. Work is displayed for 2 months.
Acceptable Work: Considers ceramics; clothing; glass art; jewelry; leatherworking; metalsmithing; needlecrafts; pottery; quilting; soft sculpture; wall hangings; weavings; and woodcrafting. Especially needs jewelry and stained glass. Fine, one-of-a-kind and handmade production-line items; utilitarian and/or decorative.
Profile: "Most work is kept together. The name of the craftperson is important. Our displays are housed in a beautiful new building." Heaviest wholesale buying time: spring and fall; best selling time: summer and Christmas.

THE COLLECTION, 5424 Walnut St., Pittsburgh PA 15232. (412)683-6668. Jewelry shop. Estab. 1977. Represents 10-12 craftworkers. Considers wedding bands and engagement rings. Fine, one-of-a-kind and handmade production-line items. Price range: $32-2,500; bestsellers: $32-300. Works on consignment and buys outright; 50% commission. Craftworker sets retail price. Requires exclusive area representation. Reports in 2 weeks. Work may be shipped or hand-delivered. Dealer pays shipping and insurance.
Profile: "Each goldsmith has his own tray or tray with nameplate; velvet and cork and felt display materials and recessed lighting in cases."

COLONIAL CHARTER, 510 Laurel Dr., Monroeville PA 15146. (412)372-1760. Contact: Barbara Day. Gift shop. Estab. 1975. Represents 75 craftworkers. Price range: $1.75-400; bestsellers: $5-250. Works on consignment; 33⅓% commission. Retail price set by joint agreement. Reports in 3 weeks. Work may be shipped or hand-delivered. Dealer pays shipping and in-

surance for exhibited work. Work displayed 3 months minimum. Works a great deal in custom work. Heaviest wholesale buying time: fall and spring; best selling time: fall.
Acceptable Work: Considers ceramics; clothing; dollmaking; glass art; needlecrafts; pottery; quilting; tole painting; wall hangings; weavings; and woodcrafting. Especially needs woodworking in miniatures. All styles; utilitarian and/or decorative.

COOK FOREST SAWMILL CRAFT SHOP, Box 6, Cooksburg PA 16217. (814)927-6634 summer; 744-9940, fall-spring. Contact: John Rose. Craft shop. Estab. 1975. Represents 60 craftworkers who work from original designs with basic materials. Price range: 25c-$150; bestsellers: $2-10. Works on consignment and buys outright; 30% commission. Retail price set by joint agreement. Reports in 2 weeks. Work may be hand-delivered. Dealer pays insurance for exhibited work.
Acceptable Work: Considers batik; candlemaking; ceramics; dollmaking; glass art; jewelry; leatherworking; metalsmithing; needlecrafts; pottery; quilting; soft sculpture; tole painting; wall hangings; weavings; and woodcrafting. Primitive, one-of-a-kind and handmade production-line items; utilitarian and/or decorative. "We follow the quality standards of the Pennsylvania Guild of Craftsmen with special consideration for traditional designs."
Profile: "The items are displayed on shelves or hanging as appropriate with limited handling by the public. We have glass cases for small items. The Sawmill Craft Shop is located inside Cook Forest State Park which recieves more than 1,000,000 visitors per year." Best selling time: summer and late spring and early fall weekends.

THE CRAFT CONNECTION, LTD., 122 Old York Rd., Jenkintown PA 19046. (215)885-7111. President: Rosamond Isenberg. Craft shop/gallery. Estab. 1975. Represents 50 craftworkers. Price range: $2-400; bestsellers: $15-50. Works on consignment and buys outright; 50% commission. Retail price set by joint agreement. Requires exclusive area representation. Reports in 4 weeks. Work may be shipped or hand-delivered. Dealer pays return shipping and insurance for exhibited work. Work is usually shown for 2 months. Heaviest wholesale buying time: summer; best selling time: Christmas, May and June.
Acceptable Work: Considers ceramics; glass art; jewelry; leatherworking; pottery; soft sculpture; wall hangings; weavings; and woodcrafting.

CRAFT STORE, 39 Maplewood Mall, Philadelphia PA 19119. (215)842-3620. Partners: Rose Malley, Dori Flood, John Graham and Helen Highley. Craft shop. Estab. 1971. Represents 100 craftworkers. Price range: $4-150; bestsellers: $7.50-20. Works on consignment and buys outright; 33⅓% commission. Retail price set by joint agreement. Reports in 4 weeks. Hand-delivered work only. Work is displayed on a 30-day trial basis.
Acceptable Work: Considers batik; ceramics; clothing; glass art; jewelry; leatherworking; metalsmithing; pottery; soft sculpture; wall hangings; weavings; woodcrafting; and puppets. Fine one-of-a-kind and handmade production-line items; utilitarian and/or decorative.
Profile: "All 5 partners are craftspeople. We feel we do craftspeople a service by displaying and selling their wares in an interesting environment. The partners do not receive a salary. Customers are 20-30 years old; professionals and homemakers." Heaviest wholesale buying time: fall; best selling time: Christmas and June.

CREATIVE HANDS, Peddlers Village, Lahaska PA 18931. (215)706-7012. Partners: Friedl Allen and Florence Kummer. Gift shop. Estab. 1963. Represents 10 craftworkers. Price range: $5-50; bestsellers: $5-25. Works on consignment and buys outright; 30% commission. Gallery sets retail price. Reports in 2 weeks. Work may be shipped or hand-delivered. Dealer pays shipping and insurance for exhibited work. Best selling and heaviest wholesale buying time: fall.
Acceptable Work: Considers batik; candlemaking; ceramics; decoupage; jewelry; pottery; wall hangings; weavings; and woodcrafting.

DANDELION 2, 1700 Locust St., Philadelphia PA 19103. (215)546-7655. Contact: Beth Fluke. Craft and jewelry shop. Estab. 1969. Represents 60 craftworkers. Price range: $1.25-100; bestsellers: $5-35. Buys outright. Retail price set by joint agreement. Reports in 2 weeks. Work may be shipped or hand-delivered by prior arrangement. Customers are 20-40 years old; center city professionals and students. Heaviest wholesale buying time: spring-summer; best selling time: Christmas.
Acceptable work: Considers batik; candlemaking; ceramics; glass art; jewelry; pottery; and soft sculpture.

DEEPWOOD CRAFTS GALLERY, 137 E. Pitt St., Bedford PA 15522. (814)623-9175. Contact: Penny Henry. Craft shop/gallery. Estab. 1971. Represents 50-75 craftworkers. Considers wall hangings; pottery; jewelry; toys; and Christmas tree ornaments. Utilitarian and/or decorative. Price range: $1.50-300; bestsellers: $10 and up. Buys outright. Gallery sets retail price. Requires exclusive area representation. Work may be shipped. Dealer pays shipping to shop and insurance for exhibited work.

Special Needs: Especially needs Christmas tree ornaments and items for young men and boys. "Hope to have a year-round Christmas tree corner — fiber, metal, clay and other."

Profile: "Each item is treated as something special. I use a lot of driftwood, barn boards, etc. I move things after a period of time so it doesn't look 'old hat.' Customers are young marrieds and tourists." Heaviest wholesale buying time: summer; best selling time: fall.

Sales Tip: "I like 30 day terms. It's a big help for a buyer. Also, cards or tags with some personal information is always of interest and helps sell. I do appreciate a small *first* order sometimes until I know how well a piece is going to move."

HELEN DRUTT GALLERY, 1625 Spruce St., Philadelphia PA 19103. (215)735-1625. Director: Helen Drutt. Gallery. Estab. 1974. Represents 35 craftworkers. Works on consignment; 40% commission. Retail price set by joint agreement. Requires exclusive area representation. Reports in 3 months. Dealer pays return shipping and insurance for exhibited work.

Acceptable Work: Considers ceramics; clothing; glass art; and jewelry. Fine one-of-a-kind pieces; utilitarian and/or decorative.

Profile: "The gallery is committed to an exhibition schedule of 8 shows per year in addition to representing the work of the artists continually. It makes an effort to educate the community and to make critical definitions in the field."

ELDER CRAFTSMEN OF PHILADELPHIA, 1628 Walnut St., Philadelphia PA 19120. (215)545-7888. Director: Evelyn Samuel. Nonprofit craft shop. Estab. 1960. Represents 500 craftworkers age 60 or older. Price range: $1-400. Works on consignment; 25% commission. Retail price set by joint agreement. Crafts may be shipped or hand-delivered. Work is displayed in windows and inside displays. Best selling time: Christmas.

Acceptable Work: Considers ceramics; clothing; decoupage; needlecrafts; pottery; quilting; and woodcrafting. One-of-a-kind handmade items; utilitarian and/or decorative.

The Elder Craftsmen, a nonprofit shop in New York City, represents over 500 craftworkers age 60 and over. Handling work from elderly persons in more than 30 states, the shop also serves as a model for similar shops throughout the country, including one listed here in Philadelphia.

WESLEY EMMONS, 258 S. 16th St., Philadelphia PA 19102. (215)546-4245. Contact: Wesley Emmons. Custom jewelry shop. Estab. 1952. Represents 6 craftworkers. Price range: $25-10,000. Works on consignment and buys outright; 40% commission. Retail price set by joint agreement. Requires exclusive area representation. Reports in 3 weeks. Work may be shipped or

hand-delivered. Dealer pays return shipping and insurance for exhibited work.
Acceptable Work: Considers jewelry and metalsmithing. Especially needs gold and silver jewelry. No base metals. Fine one-of-a-kind pieces; utilitarian and/or decorative.
Profile: "Work is displayed in locked glass cases with alarm security. Cases are custom made. Customers are all ages, interests and income." Heaviest wholesale buying time: fall; best selling time: Christmas.

THE EMPORIUM, Rt. 7, Box 381, Johnstown PA 15905. (814)288-2843. Contact: Jack Roseman. Gallery/bookstore. Estab. 1974. Represents 100 craftworkers. Price range: $2-350; bestsellers: $5-100. Works on consignment and buys outright; 25% commission. Retail price set by joint agreement. Requires exclusive area representation. Reports in 2 weeks.
Acceptable Work: Considers batik; candlemaking; ceramics (not molded); clothing; glass art; jewelry; leatherworking; metalsmithing; pottery; quilting; soft sculpture; wall hangings; weavings; woodcraftings; and handmade furniture. Fine, one-of-a-kind and handmade production-line items; utilitarian and/or decorative.
Special Needs: Men's gifts; furniture; graphics; fantasy subjects (dragons, unicorns, wizards); frogs; and horses in any medium.
Profile: "We are located in a 100-year-old remodeled church in a scenic suburb; original wood ceilings 21' high; walls are wormy chestnut and cedar shingles." Heaviest wholesale buying time: summer and fall; best selling time: August and December. Many college students and professional customers.

EVERHART MUSEUM SALES SHOP, Nay Aug Park, Scranton PA 18510. Contact: Mrs. W.R. Julius Jr. Museum gift shop. Estab. 1968. Represents 20-25 craftworkers. Price range: $2.50-50; bestsellers: $2.50-25. Buys outright. Gallery sets retail price. Reports in 3-4 weeks. Work may be shipped or hand-delivered. Dealer pays shipping to shop. Best selling time: April-December.
Acceptable Work: Considers ceramics; dollmaking; glass art; jewelry; pottery; and woodcrafting. All styles; utilitarian and/or decorative.

EVERYDAY PEOPLE, 6th and Reed Ave., Monessen PA 15062. (412)684-3450. Director: Carol E. Burrows. Craft shop/school. Estab. 1974. Represents 50 low income, elderly and handicapped craftworkers. Price range: 50c-$35; bestsellers: $1-5. Works on consignment; 20% commission. Craftworker sets retail price. Work may be hand-delivered. Stop by shop for interview.
Acceptable Work: Considers candlemaking; ceramics; clothing; dollmaking; jewelry; needlecrafts; pottery; quilting; wall hangings; and weavings. Primitive and one-of-a-kind pieces; utilitarian and/or decorative.
Profile: "There is a rotating arrangement; prices are reduced 10% after 2 months; another 10% after another 2 months; returned after 6 months. Our purpose is to supplement the income of elderly and low income as well as handicapped people. Customers are middle income school students and housewives." Best selling time: Christmas and late summer.

FONTANA GALLERY, 307 Iona Ave., Narberth PA 19072. Director: Joy Kushner. Considers jewelry; mobiles; and sculpture. Maximum size: 50" square. Works on consignment; 40% commission. Retail price set by joint agreement. Requires exclusive area representation. Send slides or photos of work. SASE.

FRIENDS OF THE FREE LIBRARY GIFT SHOP, Logan Square, Philadelphia PA 19103. (215)567-4562. Contact: Manager. Gift shop. Estab. 1975. Represents local craftworkers. Price range: 50c-$75; bestsellers: $2-10. Works on consignment; negotiable commission. Retail price set by joint agreement. Reports in 1 week. Work may be shipped or hand-delivered. Dealer pays insurance for exhibited work. Work displayed under glass is shown for 2 months; work on walls displayed 1 month.
Acceptable Work: Considers ceramics; glass art; jewelry; soft sculpture; and woodcrafting. Fine, one-of-a-kind and handmade production-line items; utilitarian and/or decorative.
Profile: "We are located in the Free Library of Philadelphia and support the library through our sales. Customers are library employees, city employees and library users." Heaviest wholesale buying time: late summer-fall; best selling time: winter holidays.

GALLERY 500, 500 Germantown Pike, Lafayette Hill PA 19444. (215)825-3222. Contact: Rita Greenfield. Craft shop/gallery. Estab. 1968. Represents 50 craftworkers. Price range: $6-1,000; bestsellers: $10-200. Works on consignment and buys outright; 40% commission. Retail price set by joint agreement. Requires exclusive area representation. Reports in 4 weeks. Work may be

shipped or hand-delivered. Dealer pays shipping and insurance. Displays work about 1 month. Customers are between 20 and 45; middle socio-economic level.
Acceptable Work: Considers batik; ceramics; glass art; jewelry; leatherworking; pottery; soft sculpture; wall hangings; weavings; and woodcrafting. Fine, one-of-a-kind and handmade production-line items; utilitarian and/or decorative.

GOLDEN DOOR GALLERY, Parry Barn, 52 S. Main St., New Hope PA 18938. (215)862-5529. Director: Mary Gardner. Considers sculpture. Specializes in representational art, "although we do carry a few abstracts." Works on consignment; 40% commission. Price range: $30-1,200. Retail price set by joint agreement. Usually requires exclusive area representation. Send photos of work. SASE. Gallery pays insurance on exhibited work. Displays work 2-6 months.

THE GOLDSMITH SHOP, 5600 Walnut St., Pittsburgh PA 15232. Contact: Ronald E. McNeish. Considers jewelry; metalsmithing; and handmade pipes. Price range: $10-20,000. Buys outright. Retail price set by joint agreement. Requires exclusive area representation. Prefers to see samples. Items displayed 2 weeks minimum. Openings sponsored.

GOUNDIE HOUSE MUSEUM SHOP, 501 Main St., Bethlehem PA 18018. Manager: Sharon H. Baker. Museum gift shop. Estab. 1967. Represents 40 craftworkers who live in Pennsylvania and work in craft or materials relating to the period from 1741-1850. Price range: 30c-$980; bestsellers: $1-25. Works on consignment and buys outright; 50% commission. Craftworker is required to set his price; retail price is determined from that. Reports in 1-2 weeks. Work may be hand-delivered. Dealer pays insurance for exhibited work.
Acceptable Work: Considers candlemaking; dollmaking; glass art; leatherworking; metalsmithing; needlecrafts; pottery; hand quilting; tole painting; woodcrafting; paper craft; and miniatures. Especially needs basketry. All styles; utilitarian and/or decorative.
Profile: "The shop is located in an 1810 restored Federal home; 2 rooms are museum rooms. Because of the structure, there are no contemporary display units used, but all items are shown in antique and suitable furnishings." Best selling and heaviest wholesale buying time: Christmas.

THE HAHN GALLERY, 8439 Germantown Ave., Philadelphia PA 19118. (215)247-8439. Director: Maurice or Roslyn Hahn. Gallery. Estab. 1975. Represents 15-25 craftworkers. Price range: $10-1,000; bestsellers: $5-50. Works on consignment and buys outright; 40% commission. Retail price set by joint agreement. Requires exclusive area representation. Reports in 1 month. Work may be shipped or hand-delivered. Dealer pays shipping and insurance.
Acceptable Work: Considers ceramics; glass art; jewelry; metalsmithing; pottery; quilting; soft sculpture; wall hangings; weavings; and woodcrafting. Fine, one-of-a-kind and handmade production-line items; utilitarian and/or decorative.
Profile: "We tend to maintain continuous small displays of each craftperson's work; occasionally we feature some with larger displays and works in windows. We are a complete art gallery which represents artists. We have 3 week changing shows, group shows and we give our artists publicity and exposure as artists." Heaviest wholesale buying time: summer; best selling time: Christmas.

HERITAGE HOUSE, 314 E. 8th Ave., Homestead PA 15120. (412)462-9620. Manager: Cheryl Panfil or Linda Sells. Gift shop. Estab. 1975. Represents 75-100 craftworkers. Price range: $1-100; bestsellers: $1-35. Works on consignment; 40% commission. Retail price set by joint agreement. Reports in 2 weeks. Work may be shipped or hand-delivered. Dealer pays return shipping and insurance for exhibited work. Crafts are displayed for 90 days.
Acceptable Work: Considers clothing; decoupage; dollmaking; jewelry; leatherworking; needlecrafts; quilting; tole painting; wall hangings; weavings; and woodcrafting. Especially needs leather, metal and wood crafts and items made as men's gifts. Primitive handmade production-line items; utilitarian and/or decorative.
Profile: "New items are prominently featured and often listed as new items in the store in general advertising. Customers are all ages with low to moderate income." Heaviest wholesale buying time: late summer and early fall; best selling time: Christmas.

THE HOLE IN THE WALL GALLERY, 3099 Leechburg Rd., Lower Burrell PA 15608. (412)335-8888. Contact: Ron or Sidney Raymond. Gallery/gift shop. Estab. 1971. Represents 25-35 craftworkers. Price range: $5-200; bestsellers: $5-20. Buys outright. Reports in 2 weeks. Work may be shipped or hand-delivered. Dealer pays insurance for exhibited work. Customers are female; 15-45 years old. Best selling and heaviest wholesale buying time: Christmas, May and June.

Acceptable Work: Considers batik; candlemaking; ceramics; glass art; jewelry; leatherworking; metalsmithing; needlecrafts; pottery; quilting; soft sculpture; wall hangings; weavings; and woodcrafting. Fine, one-of-a-kind and handmade production-line items; utilitarian and/or decorative.

I AND WE, 5320 Germantown Ave., Philadelphia PA 19144. (215)438-5757. Contact: Stan Levin. Gift shop. Estab. 1973. Represents 22-30 craftworkers. Maximum price: $35; bestsellers: $10-15. Works on consignment and buys outright; 30% commission. Retail price set by joint agreement. Reports immediately. Work may be shipped or hand-delivered. Dealer pays return shipping and insurance for exhibited work. Heaviest wholesale buying time: June; best selling time: November-April.
Acceptable Work: Considers batik; candlemaking; ceramics; decoupage; glass art; jewelry; leatherworking; pottery; and soft sculpture. Handmade production-line items and primitive pieces; utilitarian and/or decorative.

INTERNATIONAL ART GALLERY, 212 Valley Brook Rd., McMurray PA 15317. (412)833-3788. Contact: Margaret Woolf. Craft shop/gallery. Estab. 1960. Represents 50-75 craftworkers. Price range: $5-200; bestsellers: $10-40. Works on consignment and buys outright; 33⅓% commission. Retail price set by joint agreement. Requires exclusive area representation within a 10-mile radius. Reports in 4-8 weeks. Work may be shipped or hand-delivered. Dealer pays shipping to shop and insurance for exhibited work.
Acceptable Work: Considers ceramics; glass art; jewelry; metalsmithing; pottery; quilting; tole painting; wall hangings; and weavings. Especially needs enameling (small utilitary pieces) and metal sculpture (wall and standing pieces). Fine, one-of-a-kind and handmade production-line items; utilitarian and/or decorative.
Profile: "We have craftsmen from Maine to California. Customers are young and middle aged; middle to high income." Heaviest wholesale buying time: summer; best selling time: November-December.

RICHARD KAGAN STUDIO AND GALLERY, 326 South St., Philadelphia PA 19147. (215)925-2370. Contact: Richard Kagan. Gallery. Estab. 1973. Represents 15 woodworkers. Finished, one-of-a-kind and handmade limited production wood items. Utilitarian and/or decorative. Price range: $50-5,000; bestsellers: $400-1,500. Works on consignment and buys outright; 30% commission. Craftworker sets retail price. Requires exclusive area representation. Reports in 2 weeks. Work may be shipped or hand-delivered. Dealer pays return shipping and insurance for exhibited work. Work is displayed 6-12 months.
Profile: "We exhibit wood furniture and objects exclusively. Woodwork represented is of museum quality and status. Customers are 25-60 years old; income is $10,000-100,000." Displays work 6-12 months. Best selling time: spring and fall.

KINGPITCHER GALLERY, 5219 5th Ave., Pittsburgh PA 15232. (412)687-4343. Director: Ms. Philo A. Pitcher. Considers sculpture and soft sculpture. Maximum size: 9x6. Specializes in contemporary work. Works on consignment; 40% commission. Retail price set by joint agreement. Requires exclusive area representation. Send slides or photos of work. SASE. Gallery pays shipping from gallery and insurance on exhibited work. Work is displayed 3 weeks maximum.

KIPP GALLERY, Indiana University of Pennsylvania, Indiana PA 15701. Director: Ned O. Wert. Gallery. Estab. 1963. Represents craftworkers who are professionals, not"church bazaar artists."
Acceptable Work: Considers batik; ceramics; glass art; jewelry; pottery; sculpture; soft sculpture; and weaving.
Profile: "We are a professional nonsales gallery well publicized in Pennsylvania and we appeal to craftworkers who are seeking shows (group and one-man). Work may be offered for sale. A professional staff reviews applicants and schedules a complete gallery program 1 year in advance. We are funded by Student Coop and NEA to promote the arts to a 5 county area as well as the university community of 12,000."

LANGMAN GALLERY, 218 Old York Rd., Jenkintown PA 19046. Director: Richard Langman. Gallery. Estab. 1972. Represents 10-30 craftworkers. Price range: $25-5,000. Works on consignment; 40% commission. Retail price set by joint agreement. Requires exclusive area representation. Reports in 2 weeks. Dealer pays return shipping and insurance for exhibited work.
Acceptable Work: Considers batik; ceramics; clothing; glass art; jewelry; metalsmithing;

quilting; soft sculpture; wall hangings; weavings; and woodcrafting. Fine, one-of-a-kind decorative pieces only.

Profile: "Our craft art show is one of the largest privately sponsored national exhibits in the country. All inquiries should include color slides or photos with prices and SASE." Displays work 6 weeks. Heaviest wholesale buying time: fall and winter; best selling time: November-December.

LEBANON COUNTY HISTORICAL SOCIETY MUSEUM STORE, 924 Cumberland St., Lebanon PA 17042. (717)272-1473. Manager: Patricia L. Attwood. Museum gift shop. Estab. 1976. Represents 15-25 Pennsylvania folk art craftworkers. Price range: $3-100; bestsellers: $3-50. Buys outright. Gallery sets retail price. Rental gallery fee: $1 per adult. Reports in 2 weeks. Work may be shipped or hand-delivered. Dealer pays shipping to shop.

Acceptable Work: Considers candlemaking; dollmaking; glass art; jewelry; metalsmithing; needlecrafts; pottery; quilting; tole painting; wall hangings; weavings; and woodcrafting. Primitive and fine one-of-a-kind pieces; utilitarian and/or decorative.

Profile: "We display work in showcases, wall hangings and in antique color cupboards, etc. Customers are 20-60 years old with $10,000 and up income." Best selling time: fall and Christmas.

MAIN LINE CENTER OF THE ARTS, Old Buck Rd. and Lancaster Ave., Haverford PA 19041. (215)525-0272. Administrative Director: Eleanor Daitzman. Art center. Estab. 1937. Represents 25-40 craftworkers. Price range: $5-250; bestsellers: $5-150. Works on consignment. Craftworker sets retail price. All inquiries should be made by late spring for show in October. Work may be shipped or hand-delivered.

Acceptable Work: Considers all crafts. All styles; utilitarian and/or decorative.

Profile: "We have 3 new galleries with attractive cloth covered walls, excellent professional lighting and large jewelry case." Best selling time: fall.

MAPLESHADE POTTERY, Box 7, Rt. 4, Indiana PA 15701. (412)463-3005. Partner: W. Stump. Craft shop. Estab. 1976. Represents 10-20 craftworkers. Price range: 25c-$500; bestsellers: $10-20. Works on consignment and buys outright; 40% commission. Craftworker sets retail price. Reports in 4 weeks. Work may be shipped or hand-delivered. Dealer pays insurance for exhibited work. Heaviest wholesale buying time: fall and late spring; best selling time: Christmas and summer.

Acceptable Work: Considers batik; candlemaking; glass art; jewelry; leatherworking; metalsmithing; pottery; wall hangings; weavings; and woodcrafting. Especially needs leather, wood, and glass. All styles; utilitarian and/or decorative.

MERCER MUSEUM SHOP, Pine and Ashland Sts., Doylestown PA 18901. (215)345-0210. Manager: Constance R. Shook. Museum gift shop. Estab. 1967. Represents 40-50 craftworkers whose work relates to the museum's theme: "The Tools of the Nation Maker": implements and crafts employed by the men and women who built our nation, particularly in eastern Pennsylvania. Price range: 35c-$150; bestsellers: $5-30. Works on consignment and buys outright; commission negotiable. Requires exclusive area representation. Reporting time varies with time of year. Hand-delivered work only. Dealer pays insurance for exhibited work. Heaviest wholesale buying time: February through November.

Acceptable Work: Considers candlemaking; dollmaking; jewelry; metalsmithing; needlecrafts; pottery; quilting; tole painting; and woodcrafting. Primitive, one-of-a-kind and handmade production-line items; utilitarian and/or decorative.

MUSEUM SHOP, PHILADELPHIA MUSEUM OF ART, Box 7646, Philadelphia PA 19101. (215)763-8100. Contact: Shelley Hodupp. Museum shop. Estab. 1928. Represents 20 craftworkers. Price range: $1.50-300; bestsellers: $1.50-150. Works on consignment and buys outright; commission varies. Shop sets retail price. Reports in 2 weeks. Work may be shipped or hand-delivered. Dealer pays shipping to shop and insurance for exhibited work.

Acceptable Work: Considers ceramics; glass art; jewelry; metalsmithing; pottery; soft sculpture; and woodcrafting. Especially needs good glass and inexpensive items for children. All styles; utilitarian and/or decorative.

Profile: "We have a very large shop with well lit display cases. We feature an artist with a grouping of pieces and a sign with the name and place of the studio." Heaviest wholesale buying time: early spring and summer; best selling time: September-Christmas.

OLD BEDFORD VILLAGE, Box 1976, Bedford PA 15522. (814)623-1156. Manager: Marian Miller. Craft shop. Estab. 1976. Represents 45 craftworkers. "In the craft shop, preference is given to Bedford County craftspeople, then to Pennsylvania craftspeople, then to craftspeople from other areas." Price range: $1-400; bestsellers: $1-12. Buys outright. Retail price set by joint agreement. Reporting time varies. Work may be shipped or hand-delivered. Dealer pays shipping to shop.

Acceptable Work: Considers batik; candlemaking; clothing; dollmaking; jewelry; leatherworking; metalsmithing; pottery; quilting; wall hangings; weavings; and woodcrafting. Primitive and fine handmade production-line items; decorative only.

Profile: "Old Bedford Village is a park comprised of log buildings moved from various locations to the Old Bedford Village site. The Village represents the historical period from 1750-1850. The houses are furnished in period pieces; in several of the buildings craftsmen demonstrate how crafts were done in this period. The craft shop is open 7 days a week April-October. The Village is closed through the winter with the exception of the Christmas celebration the week before Christmas. Items are displayed on shelf space and in 2 glass cases. There are also items displayed on the wall. Stock is rotated periodically. Our shop offers only juried handcrafted items." Best selling and heaviest wholesale buying time: summer tourist season.

THE OPEN DOOR ART SHOP, 319 Market St., Lewisburg PA 17837. Contact: Irene Mahon. Craft shop/gallery. Estab. 1970. Represents 150 craftworkers. Price range: 25c-$365; bestsellers: $3-30. Buys outright. Craftworker sets retail price. Requires exclusive area representation. Reporting time varies. Work may be shipped or hand-delivered with consent. Dealer pays shipping and insurance for exhibited work. Work is displayed for 1 month.

Acceptable Work: Considers batik; ceramics; clothing; dollmaking; glass art; jewelry; leatherworking; metalsmithing; needlecrafts; pottery; quilting; wall hangings; weavings; woodcrafting; limited edition prints; books of poetry; papercraft; and soft toys. Especially needs silver jewelry. Fine, one-of-a-kind and handmade production-line items; utilitarian and/or decorative.

Profile: "Customers are all ages; middle income." Heaviest wholesale buying time: summer; best selling time: winter and spring.

OVERLY-RAKER VILLAGE, R.D. 1, McConnellsburg PA 17233. (717)485-4705. Contact: Helen Overly. Estab. 1972. Represents 20-25 craftworkers. Considers candlemaking; dollmaking; glass art; jewelry; leatherworking; metalsmithing; pottery; quilting; and woodcrafting. Finished, one-of-a-kind and handmade production-line items only; utilitarian and/or decorative. Price range: $5-100; bestsellers: $15-40. Buys outright. Retail price set by joint agreement. Write. Reports in 2 weeks.

Profile: Items displayed 1 month on antique furniture and trees. Heaviest wholesale buying time: July; best selling time: October-December.

THE PEASANT SHOP, 845 Lancaster Ave., Bryn Mawr PA 19010. (215)525-6548. Contact: Elliott Herman or Laird Goulding. Craft and gift shop. Estab. late 1920's. Represents 50-60 craftworkers. Price range: $5-500; bestsellers: $5-50. Buys outright. Gallery sets retail price. Requires exclusive area representation. Reports in 1 week. Work may be shipped or hand-delivered. Dealer pays shipping to shop and insurance for exhibited work.

Acceptable Work: Considers batik; candlemaking; ceramics; clothing; glass art; jewelry; leatherworking; metalsmithing; pottery; wall hangings; weavings; and woodcrafting. Primitive and finished handmade production-line items; utilitarian only.

Profile: "We have a full time visual display person who will display a line in a professional setting. Window treatments usually change bi-weekly; in-store displays rotate weekly. Customers are upper middle to upper class; very design conscious and extremely quality oriented." Heaviest wholesale buying time: pre-Christmas; best selling time: Christmas.

WILLIAM PENN MUSEUM SHOP, Box 1026, Harrisburg PA 17120. (717)787-2678. Manager: Miss O'Brien. Museum gift shop. Estab. 1972. Represents 25-30 Pennsylvania craftworkers. Price range: 50c-$100; bestsellers: 50c-$5. Works on consignment and buys outright; 30% commission. Retail price set by joint agreement. Requires exclusive area representation. Reports in 4 weeks. Work may be shipped or hand-delivered. Dealer pays shipping.

Acceptable Work: Considers candlemaking; ceramics; clothing; dollmaking; glass art; jewelry; metalsmithing; needlecrafts; pottery; quilting; tole painting; wall hangings; weavings; woodcrafting; papercrafts; and quilling. Especially needs tinware. All styles; utilitarian and/or decorative.

Profile: "Display locations are changed every 3-4 weeks. We relate items to Pennsylvania history and the exhibits in our museum. Customers: 75% are children between 7 and 12 with up to $5 to spend; 25% are adults that spend from $1-10." Work displayed 3 months. Heaviest wholesale buying time: December-February; best selling time: March-July.

PENNSYLVANIA HANDICRAFTS, 905 3rd Ave., New Brighton PA 15066. (412)843-6621. Contact: James B. Watkins. Craft shop. Estab. 1970. Represents 40+ craftworkers. Price range: 15c-$2,000; bestsellers: 15c-$45. Works on consignment and buys outright; 33⅓%commission. Craftworker sets retail price. Requires exclusive area representation within 15 mile radius. Work may be shipped or hand-delivered. Dealer pays return shipping and insurance for exhibited work. Work is displayed for 90 days.
Acceptable Work: Considers cast plaster; wooden jewelry; and woodcrafting. Needs early American line of woodcrafting. Especially needs early American line of woodcrafting. All styles; utilitarian and/or decorative.
Profile: "We will hand carve anything; we will custom any wood work. All work is treated like it belongs to me. We will hand cut glass from a good 5x7 photo to the finest detail. Customers are 95% working people." Best selling time: October-December.

THE PHILADELPHIA ART ALLIANCE, 251 S. 18th St., Philadelphia PA 19103. (215)545-4302. Considers all crafts. Price range: $10-1,500. Works on consignment; 30% commission. Craftworker sets retail price. Query or write for interview. Gallery pays insurance on exhibited work. Work is exhibited for 6 weeks.

THE QUILTERY, Benfield Rd., Rt. 4, Boyertown PA 19512. Contact: Marjorie P. Cannon. Mail order shop. Estab. 1971. Represents 25 craftworkers. Price range: $75-750; bestsellers: $250. Buys outright. Price set by joint agreement. Reports in 1 week. Work may be shipped. Dealer pays shipping and insurance.
Acceptable Work: Considers quilting. All styles; utilitarian and/or decorative. "I provide all quilt fabrics according to customers' specifications. Do not like to have any 'foreign' fabrics introduced by the quilters."
Profile: "Work receives national exposure in publications such as *House and Garden, Early American* and *Yankee*. Customers are interested in the finest quality, handmade, traditional home furnishings. Nearly all are women, all ages. Money is no object to them." Best selling and heaviest buying time: all months except December.

WILLIAM RIS GALLERIES, 2208 Market St., Camp Hill PA 17011. (717)2737-8818. Contact: Barbara Schreckengaust. Craft shop/gallery. Estab. 1966. Represents 125 craftworkers. Considers ceramics; glass art; jewelry; pottery; sculpture; wall hangings; weavings; woodcrafting; and enameled plates and plaques with birds, animals, and flowers. Fine one-of-a-kind and handmade production-line items; utilitarian and/or decorative. Price range: $5-500; bestsellers: $5-150. Works occasionally on consignment and buys outright; 40%commission. Retail price set by gallery or joint agreement. Requires exclusive area representation. Reports in 2 weeks. Dealer pays shipping.
Profile: "We feature monthly exhibitions of craftsmen's work." Customers age 20-55 with middle and upper incomes.

WILLIAM RIS GALLERIES, 251 W. Chocolate Ave., Hershey PA 17033. See above.

BETTY SEIDEL SHOPS, Cherryville Inn, Cherryville PA 18035. (215)767-2403. Contact: Betty Seidel. Museum gift shop. Estab. 1937. Represents 40 craftworkers. Price range: $2-500; bestsellers: $20-500. Buys outright. Craftworker sets retail price. Requires exclusive area representation. Work may be shipped or hand-delivered. Dealer pays shipping to shop.
Acceptable Work: Considers ceramics; clothing; decoupage; dollmaking; glass art; jewelry; needlecrafts; soft sculpture; decorated eggs; and porcelain bread dough. Fine one-of-a-kind pieces; utilitarian and/or decorative.
Special Needs: Especially needs elegant boxes (Victorian style); mirrors; memorabilia boxes; elegant lamps; wall hangings; decoupage; dolls; and soft sculptured pillows.
Profile: "We are famous for our ultra displays. Each and every piece of merchandise is put in a very special setting so that it is shown off to the best advantage. Customers are business and professional types; retired upper class." Best selling time: Easter-spring and July-December.

CHARLES E. SHOOP, 5539 Walnut St., Pittsburgh PA 15232. (412)621-9666. Contact: Charles E. Shoop or Charles Wojton. Gift shop. Estab. 1960. Represents 35-40 craftworkers. Price range: $1-2,000; bestsellers: $10-50. Buys outright. Craftworker sets retail price. Requires exclusive area representation. Reports in 2 weeks. Work may be shipped or hand-delivered. Dealer pays shipping to shop and insurance for exhibited work. Displays work until sold. "Customers are all ages, interests and incomes; we are in an area surrounded by colleges and private schools." Heaviest wholesale buying time: spring and fall; best selling time: fall.

Acceptable Work: Considers ceramics; dollmaking; glass art; jewelry; metalsmithing; pottery; soft sculpture; tole painting; and woodcrafting. Fine, one-of-a-kind and handmade production-line items; utilitarian and/or decorative.

C. LESLIE SMITH SILVERSMITH SHOP, 921 Hamilton Mall, Allentown PA 18101. (215)432-4504. Contact: C. Leslie Smith. Craft shop/gift shop. Estab. 1952. Represents 10-12 craftworkers. Price range: $1.50-1,000; bestsellers: $10-50. Buys outright. Craftworker sets retail price. Requires exclusive area representation. Reports in 2 weeks. Work may be shipped or hand-delivered. Dealer pays insurance for exhibited work. Heaviest wholesale buying time: fall; best selling time: Christmas.
Acceptable Work: Considers candlemaking; ceramics; glass art; jewelry; leatherworking; metalsmithing; pottery; wall hangings; weavings; and woodcrafting. Fine, one-of-a-kind and handmade production-line items; utilitarian and/or decorative.

THE SOURCE GALLERY, 121 S. Penna Ave., Greensburg PA 15601. (412)836-1190. Manager: Carol Pollock. Estab. 1972. Represents 100 western Pennsylvania craftworkers. Considers batik; jewelry; metalsmithing; pottery; and prints. Especially needs fiberwork. Finished one-of-a-kind and handmade production-line items; utilitarian and/or decorative. Price range: $10-300; bestsellers: $10-75. Works on consignment; 33⅓% commission. Retail price set by joint agreement. Requires exclusive area representation. Write. Reports in 2 weeks.
Profile: Items displayed 3 months with new items featured. Gallery holds 4 shows annually. Heaviest wholesale buying time: winter and spring. Accepts work only from western Pennsylvania craftworkers. Customers are young working professionals, college students and collectors.

SPIRIT OF THE EARTH, 105 S. Main St., New Hope PA 18938. President: Beatricia Sagar. Muscum gallery. See The Collaborative, New Hope, Pennsylvania.

THE STORE, 719 Allegheny River Blvd., Verona PA 15147. (412)828-6121. Director: Elizabeth Raphael. Craft shop/gallery. Estab. 1972. Represents 400 craftworkers. Price range: $1-3,000; bestsellers: $5-200. Buys outright. Gallery sets retail price. Reports in 1 week. Work may be shipped or hand-delivered. Dealer pays shipping to shop and insurance. Work is displayed 6 weeks minimum. Call or write. If you write, send slides or photos.
Acceptable Work: Considers batik; ceramics; clothing; dollmaking; glass art; jewelry; leatherworking; metalsmithing; needlecrafts; pottery; quilting; soft sculpture; wall hangings; weavings; and woodcrafting. "Only American designer handcrafts." Finished, one-of-a-kind and handmade production-line items; utilitarian and/or decorative.
Profile: "I believe we have the largest inventory of designer handcrafts in the country. We use our front room as a gallery (to introduce all new work every other month) but always have a full selection of crafts in the larger space that is the 'regular' store." Heaviest wholesale buying time: June and January; best selling time: November-December.

THE SUN SHOP, 491 Lancaster Ave., Frazer PA 19355. (215)647-0374. Contact: Bob Frantz. Estab. 1972. Represents 15 craftworkers. Considers ceramics; glass art; jewelry; pottery; and woodcrafting. Especially needs planters. Finished one-of-a-kind and handmade production-line items; utilitarian and/or decorative. Price range: $2-100; bestsellers: $8-25. Buys outright or on consignment (for very expensive items); 40% commission. Retail price set by joint agreement. Call for interview. Reports in 3 weeks. Dealer pays insurance; negotiates shipping cost.
Profile: Each craftworker's work displayed by itself. Purchased crafts are permanently displayed; consigned crafts by agreement. Heaviest wholesale buying time: fall and early spring; best selling time: fall. "We limit the types of crafts and offer a large variety of those particular types." Customers ages 25-40 with $25,000 incomes and fairly conservative tastes.

TEASEL CRAFTS, 63 E. State St., Doylestown PA 18901. (215)345-9288. Contact: Charlotte Miller or Sue Thomas. Craft shop. Estab. 1975. Represents 75-100 craftworkers. Price range: 50c-$75; bestsellers: $2-40. Works on consignment; 33⅓% commission. Retail price set by joint agreement. Reports in 2 weeks. Work may be shipped or hand-delivered. Dealer pays insurance for exhibited work.
Acceptable Work: Considers batik; candlemaking; ceramics; dollmaking; glass art; jewelry; leatherworking; needlecrafts; pottery; quilting; soft sculpture; tole painting; woodcrafting; macrame; and baby clothing. All sytles; utilitarian and/or decorative.
Profile: "Items are shown to best advantage and displays are rearranged often. We are a good mix of local, non-professional craftspeople and professionals." Work displayed 3 months minimum. Heaviest wholesale buying time: June-December; best selling time: pre-Christmas.

TRIAL BALLOON, 726 Scalp Ave., Johnstown PA 15904. Contact: Dolly C. Reeder. Gift shop. Estab. 1972. Represents 20 craftworkers. Price range: $5-500; bestsellers: $5-25. Buys outright. Retail price set by joint agreement. Requires exclusive area representation. Reports in 3 weeks. Work may be shipped at artisan's cost with prior consent only.

Acceptable Work: Considers ceramics; clothing; glass art; jewelry; leatherworking; metalsmithing; needlecrafts; weavings; woodcrafting; wind bells; chimes; desk sculpture; and Christmas ornaments. All styles, utilitarian and/or decorative.

Special Needs: Especially needs ribbon candles; summer handbags; porcelain and earthenware electric lamps; silver and 14K stick pins; and sculpture.

Profile: "We group works by one artisan, with front windows a must for handblown glass. Handmade brick walls as background and custom cabinets as handsome foil for our displays." Heaviest wholesale buying time: fall and May-June; best selling time: Christmas.

WINFIELD HOUSE, Rt. 15, Winfield PA 17889. (717)524-7006. Manager: Tripat Singh. Craft shop. Estab. 1972. Represents 75 craftworkers. Price range: $1-350; bestsellers: $1-10. Works on consignment and buys outright; 33% commission. Craftworker sets retail price. Requires exclusive area representation. Reports in 1 week. Work may be shipped or hand-delivered. Dealer pays shipping and insurance. Best selling and heaviest wholesale buying time: fall.

Acceptable Work: Considers batik; candlemaking; ceramics; clothing; glass art; jewelry; leatherworking; metalsmithing; pottery; tole painting; wall hangings; weavings; and woodcrafting. All styles; utilitarian and/or decorative.

WOODMERE MUSEUM SHOP, 9201 Germantown Ave., Philadelphia PA 19118. (215)247-0476. Secretary: Mrs. Puchek. Museum gift shop. Estab. 1977. Represents 25-30 craftworkers. Price range: $3-500; bestsellers: $3-150. Works on consignment; 20% commission. Craftworker sets retail price. Reports in 3 weeks. Work may be shipped or hand-delivered with consent. Dealer pays insurance for exhibited work. Displays work for 2 months.

Acceptable Work: Considers batik; ceramics; clothing; dollmaking; jewelry; needlecrafts; pottery; soft sculpture; wall hangings; weavings; woodcrafting; and small antiques. Finished and one-of-a-kind pieces; utilitarian and/or decorative.

Profile: "All items must first be approved by the Museum Shop committee. Correspondence and photos are acceptable. Work for consideration by committee must be hand-delivered." Heaviest wholesale buying time: early fall; best selling time: November-December.

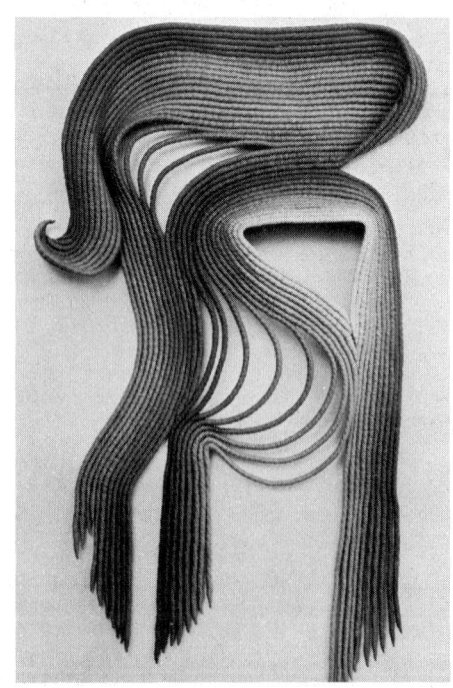

The Works Craft Gallery, Philadelphia, Pennsylvania, is divided into three sections — one for general display and two for exhibition display. Lillian Ball's fiber sculpture "Winter Wave" was recently exhibited at the gallery. "We will view work personally only if an appointment is made first," said Ruth Snyderman, director.

THE WORKS CRAFT GALLERY, 319 South St., Philadelphia PA 19147. (215)922-7775. Contact: Ruth or Rick Snyderman. Estab. 1965. Represents 230 craftworkers. Consider batik; ceramics; glass art; jewelry; metalsmithing; pottery; quilting; soft sculpture; wall hangings; weavings; and woodcrafting. One-of-a-kind and handmade production-line items only; utilitarian and/or decorative. Price range: $3.50-1,800; bestsellers: $5-40. Buys outright or on consignment; 40% commission. Craftworker sets retail price. Requires exclusive center city representation. Send transparencies or photos and arrange interview. Reports in 2 weeks. Gallery pays shipping and insurance for exhibited work.
Profile: Craftworker's item(s) displayed as a unit and marked with name and medium. Items rotated weekly in gallery. Heaviest wholesale buying time: October-December.

Rhode Island

COOPER AND FRENCH, LTD., 130 Thames St., Newport RI 02840. (401)849-6512. Director: Marve H. Cooper. Estab. 1974. Represents over 150 craftworkers. Considers ceramics; glass art; jewelry; leatherworking; metalsmithing; pottery; quilting; soft sculpture; wall hangings; weavings; and woodcrafting. Especially needs sea subjects. Finished handmade production-line items; utilitarian and/or decorative. Price range: $2-3,000; bestsellers: $5-20. Buys outright or on consignment for exhibitions. 40% commission. Craftworker sets retail price. Query with transparencies or photos, or arrange interview. Reports in 1 week. Dealer pays shipping to shop and insurance on exhibited work. Heaviest wholesale buying time: spring and fall; best selling time: summer and Christmas.

FAYERWEATHER CRAFT CENTER, Box 206, W. Kingston RI 02892. (401)789-9072. Director: Eleanor H. Sickler. Craft and gift shop. Estab. 1966. Represents 40 craftworkers. Price range: $1-100; bestsellers: $1-20. Works on consignment; 33⅓% commission. Retail price set by joint agreement. Work may be shipped or hand-delivered. Dealer pays insurance on exhibited work, but we are not responsible for shoplifting.
Acceptable Work: Considers batik; candlemaking; ceramics; clothing; decoupage; jewelry; leatherworking; metalsmithing; needlecrafts; quilting; tole painting; wall hangings; weavings; and woodcrafting. All styles; utilitarian only.
Profile: A nonprofit organization offering classes, workshops and demonstrations. Season runs May 1-December 23. Located in a historic home built in 1820. Work is displayed on tables. Best selling time: summer and Christmas. Most customers are connected with the University of Rhode Island, which adjoins Kingston.

LENORE GRAY GALLERY, INC., 15 Meeting St., Providence RI 02903. Director: Lenore Gray. Considers sculpture; soft sculpture; wall hangings; and weavings. Specializes in contemporary art. Sculpture must have stand. Works on consignment; negotiates commission. Retail price set by joint agreement. Requires exclusive area representation. Send slides. SASE. Gallery pays insurance on exhibited work.

SLATER MILL MUSEUM SHOP, Slater Mill Historic Site, Roosevelt Ave., Pawtucket RI 02862. (401)725-8638. Shop Manager: Letitia Carter. Museum gift shop. Estab. 1967. Represents 20-25 craftworkers from the Rhode Island Association of Craftsmen. Price range: $1-40; bestsellers: $1.50-30. Works on consignment; 25-30% commission. Retail price set by joint agreement. Hand-delivered work only.
Acceptable Work: Considers ceramics; clothing; dollmaking; glass art; jewelry; leatherworking; needlecrafts; pottery; quilting; wall hangings; weavings; and woodcrafting. All styles; utilitarian and/or decorative.
Profile: Exclusively handles work of the Rhode Island Association of Craftsmen. "Consignment items are inventoried and displayed, with a check written to the artist for a sale. Craftsmen are encouraged not to leave items on display past 1 year." Best selling time: late spring, summer and Christmas. Many customers are tourists.

THE SPECTRUM OF AMERICAN ARTISTS AND CRAFTSMEN, INC., Bannister's Wharf, Newport RI 02840. See The Spectrum of American Artists and Craftsmen, Inc., Brewster, Massachusetts.

WELCOME ROOD STUDIO, S. Killingly Rd., Foster RI 02825. (401)397-3045. Contact: Elizabeth Zimmerman. Estab. 1970. Represents 6 local craftworkers. Considers primarily stoneware pottery; also glass art, metalsmithing, quilting, soft sculpture, wall hangings, weavings and woodcrafting. Finished, one-of-a-kind and production-line items only; utilitarian and/or decorative. Price range: $3.50-100; bestsellers: $3.50-25. Works on consignment; 25% commission. Retail price set by joint agreement. Arrange interview. Reports in 4 weeks.

Profile: Crafts remain in shop until sold. All items, except wall hangings, are rearranged monthly. Best selling time: fall-Christmas. "It is primarily a salesroom for the stoneware pottery produced on the premises. Other work is an addition to this, but does not receive the same volume turnover." Customers are primarily young married couples; they buy crafts for usefulness.

ZERO WAMPUM, Rte. 7, Wampum Rd., Narragansett RI 02882. (401)789-7172. Contact: Amy Klingensmith. Gift shop. Estab. 1971. Represents 6 craftworkers. Price range: 50c-$100; bestsellers: $1.50-30. Buys outright. Retail price set by joint agreement. Reports in 2 weeks. Work may be shipped or hand-delivered; dealer pays insurance on exhibited work. Heaviest wholesale buying time: spring and fall; best selling time: summer and winter.
Acceptable Work: Considers candlemaking; jewelry; leatherworking; pottery; soft sculpture; wall hangings; and weavings. Needs belts; wallets; pottery candlesticks; oil lamps; and hand-dipped candles. Fine handmade production-line items; utilitarian and/or decorative.

South Carolina

ANDERSON COUNTY ARTS COUNCIL, 405 N. Main St., Anderson SC 29621. (803)224-8811. Executive Director: Sue A. Parks. Gallery and gift shop. Estab. 1976. Represents 20-25 craftworkers. Price range: 15c-$300; bestsellers: $1-20. Works on consignment; 33⅓% commission for nonmembers; 20%, members. Retail price set by craftworker. Requires a one-time $5 entry fee. Reports in 4 weeks on sales; inquiries in 1 week. Work may be shipped or hand-delivered; dealer pays insurance on exhibited work.
Acceptable Work: Considers batik; candlemaking; clothing; dollmaking; glass art; jewelry; leatherworking; metalsmithing; needlecrafts; pottery; quilting; soft sculpture; wall hangings; weavings and woodcrafting. All styles; utilitarian and/or decorative.
Profile: "When received, items are inventoried and then displayed in cases or on the walls. There's no time limit on displays." Best selling time: Christmas. Customers are generally members of the Arts Council, middle to upper income bracket.

THE BUTTERFLY, 1902 Ebenezer Rd., Rock Hill SC 29730. (803)366-7914. Owner: Peggy Tuthill. Gift shop. Estab. 1975. Represents 300 craftworkers. Price range: 79c-$600. Works on consignment and buys outright; 35% commission. Retail price set by joint agreement. Requires exclusive area representation. Send pictures, description, and price list. Reports in 4 weeks. Work may be shipped or hand-delivered.
Acceptable Work: Considers batik; candlemaking; ceramics; Christmas decorations; dollmaking; glass art; jewelry; leatherworking; metalsmithing; needlecrafts; pottery; quilting; soft sculpture; tole painting; wall hangings; weavings; and woodcrafting. Needs quilts and "always looking for original new types of crafts." All styles; utilitarian and/or decorative.
Profile: Located in 19th century house with 8 rooms of crafts. Work displayed on antiques and handcrafted furniture throughout the house. Heaviest wholesale buying time: late summer; best selling time: fall-winter. "Customers are from the upper socio-economic strata, college students, and young marrieds."

THE CARGO HOLD, INC., 342 King St., Charleston SC 29401. (803)722-1377. Contact: Tom Young. Estab. 1973. Represents 5 craftworkers. Considers blown glass and finely finished silver jewelry. Finished one-of-a-kind items only; utilitarian and/or decorative. Price range: 50c-$95; bestsellers: $3-30. Buys outright, also "occasionally on consignment to locals"; 33⅓% commission. Retail price set by joint agreement. Write. Reports in 3 weeks. Dealer pays insurance for exhibited work and shipping to shop if bought outright. "Can supply cabochons to jewelers; will consider trading materials for finished pieces."
Profile: "Prominently displayed according to method of purchase." Heaviest wholesale buying time: fall and spring. "Customers, ages 20-35, have great appreciation for quality art but not enough funds to pursue their tastes."

FINE ARTS CENTER OF KERSHAW COUNTY, INC., Box 845, Camden SC 29020. (803)432-0473. Executive Director: Lise Swensson. Arts center/gallery. Estab. 1975. Price range: $10-50. Works on consignment; 20% commission. Craftworker sets retail price. Reporting time varies. Work may be hand-delivered. Displays work 1 month.
Acceptable Work: Considers batik; needlecrafts; pottery; quilting; wall hangings; and weavings. Primitive and fine and one-of-a-kind pieces; utilitarian and/or decorative.
Profile: "Crafts are displayed on walls, pedestals and in showcases. Customers are middle to upper-class adults; middle-aged to elderly." Best selling time: late fall.

THE GALLERY, 385 S. Spring St., Spartanburg SC 29301. (803)582-7616. Gallery. Estab.

1969. Represents 20 craftworkers. Considers all crafts. Primitive and fine one-of-a-kind pieces; utilitarian and/or decorative. Price range: $2-1,000; bestsellers: $10-300. Works on consignment; 33⅓% commission. Retail price set by joint agreement. Reports in 1-4 weeks. Work may be shipped or hand-delivered. Dealer pays insurance for exhibited work.
Profile: "The Gallery schedules 9 changing exhibits per year. Crafts are displayed in the rear gallery at all times on lighted shelves, some with locking glass covers, except during the middle of November to the middle of December at which time we schedule our 'Annual Crafts Show' and craftwork fills the entire gallery." Initial contact should be made with slides or photos that can be returned to the craftsperson. Heaviest wholesale buying time: fall; best selling time: Christmas.

HARBOUR TOWN CRAFTS, Harbor House #7, Box 3065, Hilton Head Island SC 29928. (803)671-3643. Owner: Mrs. C. Alden Baker. Craft shop. Estab. 1971. Represents 250-300 craftworkers. Price range: $1.50-500; bestsellers: $8.50-90. Buys outright. Retail price set by joint agreement. Requires exclusive area representation. Send slides of work for consideration. Hand-delivered work only; dealer pays insurance on exhibited work. "We're located in a plush resort, so we strive to have unusual, top grade crafts."
Acceptable Work: Considers dollmaking; jewelry; metalsmithing; pottery; wall hangings; weavings; and woodcrafting. Fine one-of-a-kind and handmade production-line items; utilitarian and/or decorative.

HOFFMAN'S THIS 'N THAT SHOPPE, 3268 India Hook Rd., Rock Hill SC 29730. (803)366-4832. Contact: Mrs. Cordelle R. Hoffman. Gift shop. Estab. 1975. Represents 6-10 craftworkers. Price range: 75c-$100; bestsellers: $5-25. Works on consignment; 30% commission. Retail price set by joint agreement. Requires exclusive area representation. Reports in 4 weeks. Work may be shipped or hand-delivered.
Acceptable Work: Considers ceramics; decoupage; dollmaking; needlecrafts; pottery; quilting; tole painting; wall hangings; weavings; and woodcrafting. Especially needs any type craft suitable for home use and toys. Fine one-of-a-kind and handmade production-line items; utilitarian and/or decorative.
Profile: "We are a unique shop, handling merchandise from ribbon to some very fine crystal and collector's items." Heaviest wholesale buying time: fall; best selling time: fall-winter.

OLD SLAVE MART MUSEUM AND GALLERY, 6 Chalmers St., Charleston SC 29401. (803)722-0079. Director: Louise A. Graves. Museum of black heritage. Estab. 1937. Represents 100-200 black craftworkers. Considers batik; candlemaking; ceramics; decoupage; dollmaking; glass art; jewelry; leatherworking; metalsmithing; needlecrafts; pottery; quilting; soft sculpture; tole painting; wall hangings; weavings; and woodcrafting. Primitive and finished, one-of-a-kind and handmade production-line items; utilitarian and/or decorative. Price range: 25c-$75; bestsellers: $2-10. Buys outright or on consignment; 25% commission. Retail price set by joint agreement. Query with transparencies or photos, or arrange interview. Reports in 2-3 weeks. Dealer pays shipping from shop and insurance for exhibited work.
Profile: Items arranged in glass cases in relation to other crafts and art. Items displayed approximately 6 weeks. Heaviest wholesale buying time; fall and spring; best selling time: spring and summer. Only shop in Charleston featuring work of black artists/craftworkers. Over 35,000 visitors annually. Customers buy for artistic value and gifts.

South Dakota

AGRICULTURAL HERITAGE MUSEUM, South Dakota State University, Brookings SD 57007. (605)688-6226. Director: John C. Awald. Museum gift shop. Estab. 1967. Price range: give aways — $100; bestsellers: $1-10. Buys outright. Gallery sets retail price. Reports in 2 weeks.
Acceptable Work: Considers candlemaking; ceramics; clothing; dollmaking; metalsmithing; pottery; quilting; wall hangings; weavings; and woodcrafting. Primitive one-of-a-kind and handmade production-line items; utilitarian and/or decorative.
Profile: "Ours is a theme museum. We emphasize the development of agriculture in the state of South Dakota from a humanistic approach. The materials we sell are directly related towards our role as educators in this area." Heaviest wholesale buying time: spring and fall; best selling time: Christmas.

THE COUNTRY STORE, W. Hwy. 18, Winner SD 57580. (605)842-0573. Contact: Donna or Wayne Nelson. Gift shop. Estab. 1975. Represents 10-20 craftworkers. Considers candlemaking; clothing; decoupage; glass art; jewelry; quilting; wall hangings; weavings; and woodcrafting. All styles; utilitarian and/or decorative. Price range: $5-100; bestsellers: $5-20. Works on consignment and buys outright; 30-40% commission. Retail price set by joint agreement. Requires exclusive area reprsentation. Reports in 2 weeks, longer April-September. Return shipping negotiable: dealer pays insurance for exhibited work.

Profile: "Shop is situated in a grain elevator complex; only 1 of type in area. Customers are farmers, ages 25-45. Business depends on farm economy; they will spend in good years but absolutely won't in bad. Also some lawyers, doctors and government workers." Best selling time: pre-Christmas.

DEADWOOD GULCH ART GALLERY, 665½ Historic Main St., Deadwood SD 57732. (605)578-3636. Gallery/gift shop. Estab. 1967. Represents 3-4 craftworkers. Considers ceramics; pottery; wall hangings; weavings; and woodcrafting. Finished utilitarian pieces only. Works on consignment; 30-40% commission. Retail price set by joint agreement. Requires exclusive area representation. Work may be hand-delivered. Heaviest wholesale buying time: spring; best selling time: summer.

FRIENDS OF THE MIDDLE BORDER MUSEUM, Box 1071, 1311 S. Duff St., Mitchell SD 57301. (605)996-2122. Director: William W. Anderson. Museum gift shop. Estab. 1952. Represents 15-20 craftworkers. Price range: $1-125; bestsellers: $2-25. Works on consignment and buys outright; 20% commission. Retail price set by joint agreement. Reports in 1 week. Work may be shipped or hand-delivered. Dealer pays return shipping and insurance.

Acceptable Work: Considers dollmaking; glass art; jewelry; leatherworking; metalsmithing; needlecrafts; pottery; quilting; soft sculpture; tole painting; wall hangings; weavings; and woodcrafting. Primitive one-of-a-kind and handmade production-line items; utilitarian and/or decorative.

Profile: "Most items are marked and put on display behind glass if necessary or in the open, but always in view. We have heavy traffic 5 months of the year (May through September). We are open by appointment other times of the year." Heaviest wholesale buying time: April and May; best selling time: summer.

THE GARRET, 119 W. 3rd St., Mitchell SD 57301. (605)996-4111. Chairman: Jennell Henderson. Gallery/gift shop. Estab. 1971. Represents 25-30 South Dakota, North Dakota, Minnesota, Iowa and Wisconsin craftworkers. Price range: $2-2,500; bestsellers: $10-150. Works on consignment and buys outright; 20% commission. Retail price set by joint agreement. Reports in 1 week. Work may be shipped or hand-delivered. Dealer pays insurance for exhibited work.

Acceptable Work: Considers batik; glass art; jewelry; metalsmithing; needlecrafts; pottery; wall hangings; weavings; woodcrafting; rosemaling; Indian beadwork; assemblages; and signed lithographs. Fine one-of-a-kind pieces; utilitarian and/or decorative.

Profile: "Work is displayed in a small but comfortable sales room. Some items are suspended, some placed in shelving, some hung on walls." Heaviest wholesale buying time: spring and fall; best selling time: summer and Christmas.

THE PIERRE NATIONAL BANK, 420 S. Pierre St., Box 998, Pierre SD 57501. (605)224-7391. Marketing Officer: Jim Larson. Bank. Estab. 1889. Represents 1 craftworker. Price range open. Only displays work. Craftworker sets retail price. Requires exclusive area representation. Reports in 2 weeks. Work may be shipped or hand-delivered. Displays work 2 weeks. "We have easels and some floor space available. We will do our best to display work to the best advantage or follow specific directions."

Acceptable Work: Considers ceramics; decoupage; glass art; jewelry; and soft sculpture.

PRAIRIE PEOPLES HANDICRAFT MARKET, INC., Armour SD 57313. (605)928-3937. Chairman of the Board: Judy Winter. Gift shop. Estab. 1971. Represents 350 craftworkers. Price range: 25c-$125; bestsellers: $25-50. Works on consignment: 35% commission. Craftworker sets retail price. Reports in 4 weeks. Work may be shipped or hand-delivered. Dealer pays insurance for exhibited work.

Acceptable Work: Considers batik; candlemaking; ceramics; clothing; decoupage; jewelry; leatherworking; needlecrafts; pottery; quilting; wall hangings; weavings; and woodcrafting. Primitive handmade production-line items only; utilitarian and/or decorative.

Profile: "We have customers of all ages since our prices vary so much. We are in a rural area, but most of our customers are middle class; middle to low income." Displays work for period decided by craftworker. Best selling time: summer and Christmas.

ROSSER'S ARTS AND CRAFTS CENTER, 617 Spencer Ave., Gregory SD 57533. (605)835-8864. Contact: Carol Rosser. Craft shop. Estab. 1974. Represents 12 craftworkers. Price range: $1-75. Works on consignment; 20% commission. Retail price set by joint agreement. Requires

exclusive area representation. Reports "immediately." Work may be shipped or hand-delivered. **Acceptable Work:** Considers decoupage; dollmaking; jewelry; leatherworking; needlecrafts; pottery; wall hangings; and weavings. Handmade production-line items only; utilitarian and/or decorative.
Profile: "We take great care in displaying items; usually use a protective covering of clear plastic. We arrange for eye appeal. Customers are moneyed ranch people and students interested in crafts." Heaviest wholesale buying time: spring and fall; best selling time: all months except January, February and July.

SOUTH DAKOTA MEMORIAL ART CENTER SHOP, Medary Avenue at Harvey Dunn Street, Brookings SD 57007. (605)688-5423. Contact: Rex Gulbranson. Museum gift shop. Estab. 1970. Represents 20 craftworkers. Price range: $3-50; bestsellers: $5-15. Works on consignment and buys outright; 30% commission. Craftworker sets retail price. Reports in 3 weeks. Work may be shipped or hand-delivered. Dealer pays shipping and insurance.
Acceptable Work: Considers ceramics; glass art; jewelry; leatherworking; metalsmithing; needlecrafts; pottery; quilting; soft sculpture; wall hangings; weavings; and woodcrafting. Especially needs jewelry. Fine one-of-a-kind and handmade production-line items; utilitarian and/or decorative.
Profile: "The shop is located in the South Dakota Memorial Art Center on the campus of South Dakota State University. The center offers a series of changing monthly temporary exhibitions." Heaviest wholesale buying time: spring and fall; best selling time: summer and winter.

WESTERN WOODCARVINGS, Box 747, Custer SD 57730. (605)673-4404. Contact: Dale Schaffer. Museum gallery/gift shop. Estab. 1972. Represents 30+ Western-style craftworkers. Considers woodcrafting. Fine one-of-a-kind and handmade production-line item; decorative only. Price range: 5c-$1,500; bestsellers: $10-100. Buys outright. Shop sets retail price. Requires exclusive area representation. Reports in 2 weeks. Dealer pays return shipping.
Profile: "We have a large collection of animated woodcarvings." Customers are almost exclusively tourists of varied income levels. Best selling time: summer.

Tennessee

ARROWCRAFT SHOP AND GALLERY, Box 567, Gatlinburg TN 37738. (615)436-4604. Contact: Faye Cook, shop; or Bette Raymond, gallery. Craft shop/gallery. Estab. 1926. Represents 30-40 craftworkers. Shop has traditional and contemporary production items; gallery has one-of-a-kind innovative pieces. Price range: $2-50 in shop; $50-600 in gallery. Gallery works on consignment and shop buys outright; 40% commission. Retail price set by joint agreement. Reports in 3 weeks. Work may be shipped or hand-delivered. Shop pays insurance for exhibited work.
Acceptable Work: Considers batik; ceramics; glass art; jewelry; metalsmithing; pottery; quilting; soft sculpture; wall hangings; weavings; and woodcrafting. "Seeks excellence in craftmenship and design." Fine one-of-a-kind and handmade production-line items; utilitarian and/or decorative.
Profile: "The shop has its roots deep in the heritage of east Tennessee and the Appalachians. Hand weaving is its specialty with work done by some 70 local weavers under direction of Arrowcraft weaving designer." Heaviest wholesale buying time: late spring-early fall; best selling time: summer-fall.

BOUTZ FAMILY GLASSBLOWERS, Box 74, Lookout Mountain TN 37350. (615)266-5019. Contact: Donavon Boutz. Craft shop. Estab. 1968. Represents 20 craftworkers. Price range: $2.50-500; bestsellers: $2.50-25. Buys outright. Gallery sets retail price. Requires exclusive area representation. Reports in 2-4 weeks. Work may be shipped or hand-delivered. Dealer pays shipping to shop and insurance for exhibited work.
Acceptable Work: Considers ceramics; glass art; jewelry; pottery; and woodcrafting. All styles; utilitarian and/or decorative.
Profile: "Our shop has a very wide selection in an attractive setting with good customer traffic." Heaviest wholesale buying time: spring-summer; best selling time: summer and Christmas.

THE COMPLEX, 711 W. 17th St., Knoxville TN 37916. Buyer: Mr. Chappell. Craft shop/gallery/gift shop. Estab. 1973. Represents 45-50 craftworkers. Price range: $20-300; bestsellers: $20-50. Buys outright. Retail price set by joint agreement. Requires exclusive area representation. Reports in 3 weeks.
Acceptable Work: Considers ceramics; glass art; jewelry; metalsmithing; and pottery. All styles; utilitarian and/or decorative.
Profile: "We deal with name craftsmen and promising craftsmen on a national scale (18 states),

giving us a broad variety of approaches and styles." Heaviest wholesale buying time: fall-winter; best selling time: fall and spring.

THE CRAFT CRANNY, 2216 Bandywood Dr., Nashville TN 37215. (615)298-4691. Contact: Nancy Saturn. Craft shop. Estab. 1970. Represents 100 craftworkers. Price range: $2-250; bestsellers: $2-50. Buys outright. Craftworker sets retail price. Requires exclusive area representation. Slides of work may be sent. Dealer pays shipping to shop and insurance for exhibited work.
Acceptable Work: Considers all crafts except needlecrafts, decoupage and tole painting. All styles; utilitarian and/or decorative.
Profile: "All work is shown until it is sold. Displays are moved around weekly seeking fresh background to enhance each piece."Customers are 20-45 years old with average to upper incomes. Heaviest wholesale buying time: fall; best selling time: Christmas and June. "Shop puts on an annual Crafts Fair (in June) at which 100 craftspeople are invited to exhibit."

THE CRAFTSMAN'S HAND, 712B Signal Mountain Blvd., Signal Mountain TN 37377. (615)886-3542. Contact: Pat Hoyes. Craft shop. Estab. 1977. Represents 10 craftworkers. Price range: 75c-$300; bestsellers: 75c-$20. Works on consignment; 30% commission. Retail price set by joint agreement. Reporting time varies. Work may be shipped or hand-delivered. Dealer pays insurance for exhibited work.
Acceptable Work: Considers candlemaking; ceramics; clothing; dollmaking; needlecrafts; soft sculpture; wall hangings; weavings; and woodcrafting. Primitive one-of-a-kind and handmade production-line items; utilitarian and/or decorative.
Special Needs: Woodcarving; unusual toys (marionettes, miniatures and doll houses); baby quilts and children's decorator crafts; natural material flowers; and mountain crafts and furniture.
Profile: "We are developing a reputation for child-oriented toys and baby gifts. Customers' income ranges from middle to high upper bracket." Heaviest wholesale buying time: October-Christmas.

EAST TENNESSEE CRAFTS INC., Village Green Craft Shop, Box 653. Norris TN 37828. Craft Clerk Secretary: Jean Hunt. Craft shop. Estab. 1976. Represents 100 Tennessee craftworkers. Price range: 50c-$175; bestsellers: $2.50 minimum. Works on consignment and buys outright; 25% commission. Craftworker sets retail price. Requires exclusive area representation. Reports in 3 days. Work may be shipped or hand-delivered. Dealer pays return shipping.
Acceptable Work: Considers clothing; dollmaking; glass art; jewelry; leatherworking; needlecrafts; pottery; quilting; wall hangings; weavings; woodcrafting; nature hangings; macrame; barnboard picture frames; and wood clocks and lamps. Primitive one-of-a-kind and handmade production-line items; utilitarian and/or decorative.
Profile: "Everything in our shop has been handcrafted by a Tennessee craftsperson. We blend traditional and contemporary feeling, that one complements the other. Our customers are tourists in the summer; all ages, interest and incomes; and locals from surrounding towns who are repeat customers." Best selling time: May 30-September 10.

GALLERY III, 122 Stadium Dr., Hendersonville TN 37075. (615)824-7675. Contact: Pat Beaver. Craft shop/gallery. Estab. 1968. Represents 50 craftworkers. Price range: $2-150; bestsellers: $10-40. Buys outright. Retail price set by joint agreement. Reports in 3 weeks. Work may be shipped or hand-delivered. Dealer pays shipping to shop.
Acceptable Work: Considers glass art; jewelry; metalsmithing; pottery; quilting; wall hangings; weavings; and woodcrafting. All styles; utilitarian and/or decorative.
Profile: "Our customers know that they are buying the best when they buy from us and we stand behind everything and expect our craftsmen to do the same. Customers are upper middle income, educated, aged 25-45." Heaviest wholesale buying time: fall; best selling time: fall and winter.

LADY BUG GALLERY, 208 E. Main St., Johnson City TN 37601. Contact: Sandy Joy. Considers ceramics; sculpture; jewelry; metalsmithing; needlecrafts; rugs; tapestries; glass; leather; tie dye; batik; and woodcrafts. Price range: $1-500. Buys outright or on consignment; 30% commission. Retail price set by joint agreement. Requires exclusive area representation. Send transparencies or photos. Shipping costs shared. Items displayed 4 weeks minimum.

OATES GALLERY, 97 N. Tillman, Memphis TN 38111. (901)323-5659. Director: Rena Dewey. Considers sculpture. Buys outright and works on consignment; 45% commission. Retail price set by joint agreement. Requires exclusive area representation. Send photos; if gallery is in-

terested, will arrange interview. SASE. Gallery pays insurance on exhibited work and may pay shipping and in-transit insurance.
Profile: Work is displayed 2-4 weeks. Some work may be displayed that is not for sale during an exhibition.

THE ORANGE PEEL, 223 Lindell St., Martin TN 38237. (901)587-9316. Contact: Carolyn Stone, Anne Rob, Carolyn James, Barbara Trentham. Gift shop. Estab. 1976. Represents 70 craftworkers, preferably within a 100-150 mile radius. Price range: 50c-$100; bestsellers: $1-25. Works on consignment; commission varies. Reports in 4 weeks. Work may be shipped or hand-delivered. Dealer pays return shipping if work is solicited. Best selling time: fall.
Acceptable Work: Considers candlemaking; dollmaking; jewelry; needlecrafts; pottery; quilting; tole painting; woodcrafting; pinecone craft and inexpensive art. Primitive handmade production-line items; utilitarian and/or decorative.

THE PLUM NELLY SHOP, 1201 Hixson Pike, Chattanooga TN 37405. (615)266-0585. Contact: Celia Marks. Estab. 1971. Represents 300 out-of-town craftworkers. Considers candlemaking; ceramics; metalsmithing; needlecrafts; pottery; wall hangings; weavings; and woodcrafting. "We use the Southern Highland Handicrafts Guild standards in judging crafts to be bought for our shop; however, we don't limit ourselves to the crafts accepted for membership in that organization." Finished, one-of-a-kind and handmade production-line items; utilitarian and/or decorative. Price range: $1-200; bestsellers: $3-35. Buys outright. Retail price set by joint agreement. Requires exclusive Chattanooga representation. "We usually spot new work at craft fairs and shows, but frequently craftsmen know us by reputation and write to set up an appointment to show their work." Reports in 2 weeks. Dealer pays shipping from shop and insurance on exhibited work. "Send work by UPS; it is then automatically insured while in-transit."
Profile: "We buy with considerable discrimination and time period between purchase and sale is not of great concern to us." Heaviest wholesale buying time: spring and summer; best selling time: Christmas. Customers are young career women and male executives in their 30's.
To Break In: "I am an ex-food editor and author of 2 cookbooks and therefore am extremely practical in my approach to functional items. Those items to be used in the kitchen come in for special scrutiny (i.e., handles large enough to grasp while holding a cloth pot holder, smooth bottoms, dishwasher-safe, etc.)."

QUILTER'S HAVEN, Box 151, Bell Buckle TN 37020. (615)275-2292. Contact: Mildred W. Locke. Quilter's supply shop. Estab. 1975. Represents 10 craftworkers. Price range: $1-500. Buys outright. Reports in 3 weeks. Work may be shipped or hand-delivered.
Acceptable Work: Considers quilting; utilitarian and/or decorative. Especially needs traditional quilts (grandmother's flower garden, Dresden plate, double wedding ring) approximate size 90x-108; preferably all cotton with fabrics washed before being made.
Profile: "My shop is in a 100-year-old house on a farm. I ship quilts all over the United States."

RIDGEWAY GALLERY, 132 Ridgeway Center, Oak Ridge TN 37830. (615)483-6690. Manager: Mirjam Koehler. Considers ceramics; sculpture; tapestries; rugs; glass; jewelry; and metalsmithing. Price range: $2-1,000. Buys outright (50% discount) or on consignment (33⅓ commission). Craftworker sets retail price. Send transparencies or photos. Gallery pays half shipping costs and insurance for exhibited work. Items displayed 6 months minimum. Sponsors openings.

SERENDIPITY GALLERIES, 516 N. University Ave., Murfreesboro TN 37130. Director: Mrs. Louis Rowland. Gallery. Estab. 1967. Represents 40-45 craftworkers. Price range: $3-50; bestsellers: $1.50-20. Works on consignment and buys outright. Retail price set by joint agreement. Reports in 3 weeks. Work on consignment may be shipped or hand-delivered by prior arrangement. Dealer pays insurance for exhibited consignment work.
Acceptable Work: Considers candlemaking; ceramic sculpture; jewelry; metalsmithing; pottery; quilting; soft sculpture; wall hangings; weavings; and woodcrafting. One-of-a-kind pieces; utilitarian only. Especially needs contemporary pottery: cups, mugs and covered casseroles.
Profile: "We are the only shop in a city of 20,000; customers have middle income to upper middle; professional people; some have art background." Displays work 4-8 weeks. Heaviest wholesale buying time: mid-spring; best selling time: fall-winter.

STOREHOUSE, INC., 4105 Hillsboro Rd., Nashville TN 37215. See Storehouse, Inc., 2737 Apple Valley Rd. NE, Atlanta, Georgia.

STUDIO S GALLERY, 1426 Avon Rd., Murfreesboro TN 37130. (615)896-0789. Contact: Lewis D. Snyder. Craft shop/gallery/studio. Estab. 1970. Represents 6 craftworkers. Considers needlecrafts; pottery; wall hangings; weavings; and woodcrafting. Fine one-of-a-kind and hand-made production-line items; utilitarian and/or decorative. Price range: $2.50-500; bestsellers: $5-100. Buys outright. Retail price set by joint agreement. 30% commission on gallery shows. Hand-delivered work only.
Profile: "We operate a production shop and gallery." Customers are college to middle age; middle income and up. Best selling time: summer-fall.

VILLAGE CRAFTS, 5204 Homberg Dr., Knoxville TN 37919. (615)584-2562. Contact: Alex Woodcox. Craft shop. Estab. 1975. Represents 30-40 Tennessee craftworkers. Price range: 50c-$249; bestsellers: $1.25-39.98. Works on consignment and buys outright; 30% commission. Craftworker sets retail price. Work may be hand-delivered. Dealer pays shipping to shop if work is purchased and in-transit insurance.
Acceptable Work: Considers batik; ceramics; leaded and stained glass; jewelry; metalsmithing; pottery; tole painting; wall hangings; weavings; and woodcrafting. Primitive and fine one-of-a-kind pieces; utilitarian and/or decorative.
Profile: "Customers are 20-70, intellectual and from students to people with upper bracket incomes." Displays work 60 days. Best selling and heaviest wholesale buying time: pre-Christmas.

Texas

ALABAMA-COUSHATTA INDIAN ARTS & CRAFTS, Rt. 3, Box 640, Livingston TX 77351. (713)563-4391. Superintendent: Emmett Battise. Estab. 1967. Represents 6 craftworkers. Considers jewelry; pottery; Indian beadwork; and basketmaking. Primitive and finished, one-of-a-kind and handmade production-line items OK; utilitarian and/or decorative. Price range: $1-750; bestsellers: $1-35. Buys outright. Gallery sets retail price. Write. Reports in 3 weeks. Dealer pays shipping from shop and insurance for exhibited work. Best selling time: summer; heaviest wholesale buying time: spring.

THE ART CENTER, Box 5396, 1300 College Dr., Waco TX 76708. (817)752-4371. Director: Paul Rogers Harris. Museum gift shop. Estab. 1972. Price range: $1-50; bestsellers: $1-20. Works on consignment and buys outright. Retail price set by joint agreement. Requires exclusive city representation. Reports in 3 weeks. Dealer pays insurance for exhibited work.
Acceptable Work: Considers batik; candlemaking; ceramics; glass art; jewelry; leatherworking; metalsmithing; pottery; quilting; soft sculpture; wall hangings; weavings; and woodcrafting. All styles; utilitarian and/or decorative.
Profile: "Items are attractively displayed and regularly rotated for maximum exposure. The unique selection of craft items sets our shop apart from other retail stores in the area." Customers are upper income of all ages. Heaviest wholesale buying and best selling time: fall.

ART-DESIGN-CRAFT CENTER, 1131 E. Yandell Dr., El Paso TX 79902. Managing Director: Edgar L. Schnadig. Estab. 1962. Represents 5 craftworkers. Price range: $5-750. Works on consignment and buys outright; 40-50% commission. Retail price set by joint agreement. Reporting time varies. Work may be shipped or hand-delivered. Dealer pays return shipping if work was requested.
Acceptable Work: Considers wall batik; unusual ceramics; glass art; metalsmithing; unusual pottery; soft sculpture; wall hangings; weavings; and woodcrafting. All styles; utilitarian and/or decorative.

BELLFORT FRAME AND ART CENTER, 7732 E. Bellfort, Houston TX 77061. (713)649-5855. Gallery/frame shop. Estab. 1968. Represents 3 craftworkers. Price range: $20-500. Works on consignment and buys outright; 30% commission. Retail price set by joint agreement. Reports in 1 week. Work may be shipped or hand-delivered. Dealer pays return shipping.
Acceptable Work: Considers needlecrafts; pottery; tole painting; wall hangings; weavings; and woodcrafting. Primitive and fine one-of-a-kind pieces; utilitarian and/or decorative.

BIG THICKET MUSEUM, Box 198, Saratogo TX 77585. (713)274-2971. Director: Eddie C. Rowland. Museum gift shop. Estab. 1970. Represents craftworkers whose work deals with pioneer or rustic crafts. Price range: $1-100; bestsellers: $1-50. Works on consignment and buys outright; 30-50% commission. Gallery sets retail price. Reports in 2 weeks. Work may be shipped or hand-delivered.
Acceptable Work: Considers all crafts except soft sculpture. All styles; utilitarian and/or decorative.
Profile: "We are the only museum within a 40-mile radius. We are limited to Big Thicket natural

or cultural history items. Local people shop us heavily at Christmas." Best selling and heaviest wholesale buying time: spring-summer.

BLACK'S ART GLASS STUDIO, 3225 N. Flores, San Antonio TX 78212. (512)736-5201. Contact: G. Vernon Black. Glass studio. Estab. 1942. Represents 7 craftworkers. Considers glass art. Fine one-of-a-kind pieces only. Minimum price: $50.

CERAMIC HUT, 260 Walnut, Colorado City TX 79512. (915)728-3942. Contact: Johnnie Hammond. Estab. 1971. Represents 2 craftworkers. Considers ceramics; decoupage; tole painting; wall hangings; and weavings. Especially needs vases, 9-10" high. Finished handmade production-line items only; utilitarian and/or decorative. Price range: $75-250; bestsellers: $30-250. Buys outright. Shop sets retail price. Requires exclusive area representation. Write first. Reports in 3 weeks.
Profile: Displays items 2 weeks. Heaviest wholesale buying season: November-December. Only shop in a 40-mile area. Customers ages 25-65; income of age 25 about $500 per month. They buy crafts for originality.

CHAPARRAL, 2505 River Oaks Blvd., Houston TX 77019. (713)522-2501. President: Dawsie Crain. Embroidery center. Estab. 1962. Represents 10 craftworkers. Price range: 25c-$1,000; bestsellers $7.50-50. Works on consignment and buys outright; 40% commission. Retail price set by joint agreement on consigned items. Reports in 1 week. Work may be hand-delivered or shipped.
Acceptable Work: Considers clothing; needlecrafts; quilting; and soft sculpture. One-of-a-kind and handmade production-line items; utilitarian and/or decorative.

CONTEMPORARY GALLERY, 2425 Cedar Springs, Dallas TX 75201. (214)747-0141. Contact: R.H. Kahn. Gallery. Estab. 1964. Represents 10 craftworkers. Price range: $10-5,000. Works on consignment and buys outright; 40% commission. Retail price set by joint agreement. Requires exclusive area representation. Reports in 2 weeks. Work may be shipped or hand-delivered. Dealer pays insurance for exhibited work.
Acceptable Work: Considers ceramics; glass art; jewelry; pottery; soft sculpture; wall hangings; weavings; and woodcrafting. One-of-a-kind designer pieces; utilitarian and/or decorative.
Profile: "One-man exhibits are for 6 weeks; general display has no time limitation."

CRAFT INDUSTRIES, 78 Woodlake Sq., Houston TX 77063. (713)789-8170. Contact: Linda Lee or Mary Frances Bailey. Craft shop/gallery. Estab. 1970. Represents 30 North American craftworkers. Price range: $1.50-3,000; bestsellers: $3-350. Works on consignment; 40% commission. Retail price set by joint agreement. Requires exclusive area representation. Reports in 2 weeks. Work may be shipped or hand-delivered.
Acceptable Work: Considers batik; ceramics; metalsmithing; needlecrafts; pottery; quilting; soft sculpture; wall hangings; weavings; woodcrafting; and handblown glass. All styles; utilitarian and/or decorative.
Profile: "Our shop is within a complex which houses a total system of education for the public including classes, supplies, and workshops in clay and weaving as well as finished crafts and we find that by illustrating the process within the shop, we sell more than simply by being a gallery situation." Best selling and heaviest wholesale buying time: fall and spring.

THE DOOR KNOB, INC., 3022 Sandage, Ft. Worth TX 76109. (817)923-6661. President: Betty Mellina. Gift shop. Estab. 1970. Represents 8-12 craftworkers. Price range: $4-250; bestsellers: $4-50. Works on consignment and buys outright;33⅓% commission. Retail price set by joint agreement. Reports in 3 weeks. Work may be shipped or hand-delivered. Dealer pays insurance for exhibited work.
Acceptable Work: Considers ceramics; jewelry; needlecrafts; pottery; quilting; soft sculpture; and woodcrafting. Especially needs dolls, animals and woodcarvings. Primitive and fine handmade production-line items; utilitarian and/or decorative.
Profile: "Customers are college-age, young married couples and middle-age people." Heaviest wholesale buying time: spring and fall; best selling time: winter-spring.

EL PASO MUSEUM OF ART GIFT SHOP, 1211 Montana, El Paso TX 79902. (915)543-3800. Contact: Mrs. Robert W. Hanson or Mrs. Milton Leech. Museum gift shop. Estab. 1961. Represents 15-20 craftworkers. Price range: 10c-$400; bestsellers: $5-25. Works on consignment and buys outright; 15% commission. Craftworker sets retail price. Reports immediately. Work may be shipped or hand-delivered.
Acceptable Work: Considers ceramics; jewelry; metalsmithing; needlecrafts; pottery; wall

hangings; weavings; woodcrafting; and stained glass. All styles; utilitarian and/or decorative.
Special Needs: "There does not appear to be local craftsmen in the field of glass; we would like to know sources for fine paper, stationery, Shaker boxes or other crafts that are indigenous to definite areas of the nation."
To Break In: "Make written inquiry first addressed to the gift shop chairman. We prefer a full price range indication on items; we would be pleased to received slides which can be returned if desired. Definitely do not send items which have not been ordered by purchase order." Best selling time: fall.

ESTUDIOS RIO, GALLERY OF CONTEMPORARY ARTS AND CRAFTS, 518 Doherty St., Box 632, Mission TX 78572. Contact: Xavier Gorena. Considers ceramics; sculpture; glass; jewelry; metalsmithing; batik; prints; and mixed media. Price range: $5-1,000. Works on consignment; 40% commission. Craftworker sets retail price. Requires exclusive area representation. Charges commission on crafts sold in area after showing. "We require resume and/or bio with transparencies or photos." Items displayed 8 weeks minimum.

GALLERIE OF FINE ARTS, 342 W. Main St., Fredericksburg TX 78624. (512)997-7495. Contact: Karl B. or Joyce Guiney. Gallery/gift shop. Estab. 1975. Represents 35 craftworkers. Price range: $5-1,500; bestsellers: $15-300. Works on consignment and buys outright; 35% commission. Retail price set by joint agreement. Requires exclusive area representation. Reports in 1 week. Hand-delivered work only.
Acceptable Work: Considers batik; candlemaking; dollmaking; glass art; jewelry; pottery; quilting; wall hangings; weavings; and woodcrafting. Especially needs pottery, raku and stained glass. One-of-a-kind designer pieces; utilitarian and/or decorative.
Profile: "Our building is 3,600 square feet; we have many ample methods of display. Our customers are approximately 45 years old and are principally interested in fine works by Texas artists and craftsmen." Displays work 90 days minimum.

THE GALLERY AT THE SOUTHWEST CRAFT CENTER, 300 Augusta, San Antonio TX 78209. (512)224-1848. Director: Jamie Killian. Gallery. Estab. 1975. Represents 75 craftworkers. Price range: 75c-$4,000; bestsellers: $5-35. Works on consignment; 60% commission. Retail price set by joint agreement. Reports in 1 week. Work may be shipped or hand-delivered. Dealer pays insurance for exhibited work. Displays work 6 months. Best selling time: Christmas.
Acceptable Work: Considers batik; candlemaking; ceramics; clothing; dollmaking; glass art; jewelry; leatherworking; metalsmithing; needlecrafts; pottery; quilting; soft sculpture; wall hangings; weavings; and woodcrafting. Especially needs glass and wood. Fine one-of-a-kind and handmade production-line items; utilitarian and/or decorative.

HANDWEAVERS OF HOUSTON, INC., 2902 Ferndale, Houston TX 77098. (713)529-7126. Contact: Barbara Metyko. Craft shop. Estab. 1974. Price range: $20-500; bestsellers: $40-175. Works on consignment; 60% commission. Retail price set by joint agreement. Reports in 1 week. Hand-deliver work. Dealer pays insurance for exhibited work.
Acceptable Work: Considers dollmaking; needlecrafts; soft sculpture; wall hangings; and weavings. One-of-a-kind designer pieces; utilitarian and/or decorative.
Profile: "Customers are 20-30 years old, middle income, buy for beauty of handmade articles; 30-45 years old, upper middle income, can afford luxury items; and 45 and older, upper middle income." Best selling time: fall and spring.

HELEN JOHNSON GALLERY, Box 1159, San Antonio TX 78294. (512)224-7865. Contact: Helen Johnson. Gallery. Estab. 1971. Represents 25 craftworkers. Price range: 35c-$2,000; bestsellers: 35c-$300. Works on consignment and buys outright; 60% commission. Retail price set by joint agreement. Requires exclusive area representation. Reports in 4 weeks or longer. Work may be shipped or hand-delivered with prior approval.
Acceptable Work: Considers ceramics; jewelry; metalsmithing; pottery; and woodcrafting. Especially needs pottery that sells for a reasonable price. Fine one-of-a-kind and handmade production-line items; utilitarian and/or decorative.
Profile: "We are next to the convention center; our customers are all age groups, all income brackets and from all over the world." Heaviest wholesale buying time: spring and early fall; best selling time: March-November.

LAGUNA GLORIA ART MUSEUM, Box 5568, Austin TX 78763. (512)458-8191. Manager: Susan Stone. Museum gift shop. Represents 12 craftworkers. Price range: 50c-$100; bestsellers: 50c-$15. Works on consignment; 30% commission. Craftworker sets retail price. Reports in 4

weeks. Work may be shipped or hand-delivered. Dealer pays return shipping.
Acceptable Work: Considers ceramics; glass art; jewelry; pottery; wall hangings; and weavings. Fine one-of-a-kind and handmade production-line items; utilitarian and/or decorative.
Profile: "Items are displayed on wooden shelves. The majority of our crafts are from Texas artists and we also stock commerical museum shop items." Displays work 3 months. Best selling time: October-December.

LEADER ART GALLERY, 409 N. Park, Uvalde TX 78801. (512)278-7883. Contact: Ann Alejandro. Gallery. Estab. 1970. Represents 30 craftworkers. Price range: $7.50-6,500; bestsellers: $7.50-30. Works on consignment; 30% commission. Retail price set by joint agreement. Reports within 3 weeks. Work may be hand-delivered. Dealer pays return shipping.
Acceptable Work: Considers ceramics; jewelry; pottery; quilting; soft sculpture; and woodcrafting. All styles; utilitarian and/or decorative. Especially needs Christmas decorations, handmade tree skirts, ornaments, wreaths and carved animals (especially jewelry-sized birds, etc.).
Profile: "We display on walls, shelves, hearth, mantel, furniture. We are located in a beautiful, old, historic home." Heaviest wholesale buying time: spring and Christmas; best selling time: summer and Christmas.

MOONSHELL GALLERIES, 409 Old S. Austin St., Rockport TX 78382. (512)729-7155. Contact: Hugh or Jane Goodrich or Dub Farley. Gallery/gift shop. Estab. 1971. Represents 12 craftworkers. Price range: $1.50-1,500; bestsellers: $5-1,500. Works on consignment and buys outright; 40% commission. Retail price set by joint agreement. Requires exclusive area representation. Reports in 2 weeks. Work may be shipped or hand-delivered. Dealer pays return shipping. Heaviest wholesale buying time: spring, best selling time: summer.
Acceptable Work: Considers batik; candlemaking; ceramics; glass art; jewelry; pottery; and quilting. Especially needs birds and light and colorful things. Fine one-of-a-kind and handmade production-line items; utilitarian and/or decorative.

THE MUSEUM SHOP, West Texas Museum Association, Box 4499, 4th St., and Indiana Ave., Lubbock TX 79409. (806)742-2436. Supervisor: Sue Putteet. Museum gift shop. Estab. 1971. Represents 100-125 craftworkers. Price range: 20c-$500; bestsellers: $15-250. Works on consignment and buys outright; 40% commission. Requires exclusive area representation. Reporting time varies. Work may be shipped or hand-delivered with prior permission. Dealer pays insurance for exhibited work.
Acceptable Work: Considers batik; ceramics; clothing; decoupage; dollmaking; glass art; jewelry; leatherworking; metalsmithing; needlecrafts; pottery; soft sculpture; wall hangings; weavings; woodcrafting; basketry; and fabrics. All styles; utilitarian and/or decorative.
Profile: "Work is displayed in locked cases; some things on shelves. We want work to relate to museum exhibits and/or collection." Heaviest wholesale buying time: spring and fall; best selling time: winter.

NARANJO'S AMERICAN INDIAN ARTS, 10001 Westheimer #20A, Houston TX 77042. (713)783-0833. Contact: Al or Stella Naranjo. Craft shop/art gallery/metalsmithing school. Estab. 1975. Represents 200+ American Indian craftworkers. Price range: $1-5,500; bestsellers: $5-200. Works on consignment and buys outright; 33⅓% commission. Retail price set by joint agreement. Reports in 1 week. Work may be shipped or hand-delivered. Dealer pays return shipping and insurance.
Acceptable Work: Considers clothing; jewelry; leatherworking; metalsmithing; needlecrafts; pottery; wall hangings; weavings; and woodcrafting. Primitive and fine one-of-a-kind pieces; utilitarian and/or decorative. Especially needs Indian baskets, beadwork, contemporary jewelry and weavings.
Profile: "We are the only Indian Art Gallery in Houston. Customers are teenagers to elderly people with middle to high income; single and young marrieds; professional people; and some art collectors." Heaviest wholesale buying time: September-November; best selling time: October-December.

THE PARLOUR, 2124 The Strand, Galveston TX 77550. (713)762-4006. Contact: Judith Copeland. Estab. 1975. Represents 200 craftworkers. Considers candlemaking; dollmaking; glass art; jewelry; leatherworking; metalsmithing; needlecrafts; pottery; quilting; wall hangings; weavings; and woodcrafting. Finished, one-of-a-kind and handmade production-line items OK; utilitarian and/or decorative. Price range: $1.50-200; bestsellers: $5-30. Buys outright or on consignment; 33⅓% commission. Retail price set by joint agreement. Requires exclusive area representation. Write. Reports in 2 weeks. Dealer pays shipping from shop and insurance for exhibited work.

Profile: Items displayed 3 months maximum; marked down after 45 days. Best selling time: summer-Christmas, Customers are tourists, local residents and medical students; they buy crafts for gifts. "This area is restored Victorian on the order of a small New Orleans."

PLASTER UNLIMITED, 506 West Ave., Levellant TX 79336. Contact: Mr. or Mrs. Douglas Hill. Plaster art shop. Estab. 1975. Considers plaster and white ware. Price range: 25c-$50; bestsellers: $10. Buys outright. Gallery sets retail price. Work may be shipped or hand-delivered. Heaviest wholesale buying time: January-September; best selling time: October-December.

SANDIE'S SHOWCASE, 2511 State Line, Texarkana TX 75501. (214)792-3071. Contact: Sandie Walker. Gallery/gift shop. Estab. 1971. Represents 8 craftworkers. Price range: $2.50-500; bestsellers: $15-150. Buys outright. Retail price set by joint agreement. Requires exclusive area representation. Reports in 4 weeks. Work may be shipped or hand-delivered with permission. Dealer pays return shipping.
Acceptable Work: Considers batik; ceramics; jewelry; needlecrafts; pottery; quilting; soft sculpture; wall hangings; weavings; and woodcrafting. All styles; utilitarian and/or decorative.
Profile: "We carry a wide range, primitive to finer pieces, of unusual items and have a wide appeal in price range, age groups and tastes. Personalized service is our biggest asset."

THE SHED, 1649 Blalock, Houston TX 77080. President: Gwen Murphy. Gallery/fibers studio. Estab. 1975. Represents 45-50 craftworkers. Price range: 75c-$2,400, bestsellers: $15-300. Works on consignment and buys outright; 40% commission. Retail price set by joint agreement. Reports as soon as possible. Work may be shipped or hand-delivered with prior permission. Dealer pays return shipping and insurance for exhibited work.
Acceptable Work: Considers batik; clothing; dollmaking; glass art; jewelry; leatherworking; needlecrafts; pottery; quilting; soft sculpture; wall hangings; weavings; and woodcrafting. Especially needs rugs, handwoven clothing and utilitarian crafts. All styles, utilitarian and/or decorative.
Profile: "Items should be ready for hanging or display. We change displays frequently and keep things well card for. Customers are young professional people; craftsmen and artists; average income about $20,000." Displays work 6 months. Heaviest wholesale buying time: spring and fall; best selling time: Christmas.

THE SHED, INC., 9851 Warwana, Houston TX 77080. (713)461-3870. President: Gwen Murphy. Estab. 1975. Represents 1-50 craftworkers. Price range: 50c-$1,800; bestsellers: $2. Works on consignment; 40% commission. Retail price set by joint agreement. Work may be shipped or hand-delivered after prior approval. Dealer pays return shipping and insurance for exhibited work.
Acceptable Work: Considers batik; ceramics; clothing; dollmaking; glass art; jewelry; leatherworking; metalsmithing; needlecrafts; pottery; quilting; soft sculpture; wall hangings; weavings; woodcrafting; and basketry. Especially needs refined well-designed fibers not "so wild and wooly." All styles; utilitarian and/or decorative.
Profile: "Items are given good care at all times; we are craftsmen ourselves. Displays are rotated often. Customers are mostly 25-45; young professionals." Best selling and heaviest wholesale buying time: spring and pre-Christmas.

THE SKETCH BOX, 1011, W. 5th Ave., Corsicana TX 75110. (214)874-8845. Contact: Betty Graham or Peggy Drain. Considers batik; glass art; jewelry; mobiles; pottery; sculpture; tole paintings; weavings; and woodcrafting. Maximum size: 5x4. Specializes in Southwestern landscapes, and Indian and Western art. Works on consignment: 30% commission. Price range: $10-95, tole paintings. Retail price set by joint agreement. Requires exclusive area representation. Query with slides or photos. SASE. Work is displayed 3-6 weeks.

SOL DEL RIO, 1020 Townsend, San Antonio TX 78209. (512)828-5555. Director: Dorothy Katz. Gallery. Estab. 1970. Represents 15 craftworkers. Price range: $2-1,000; bestsellers: $2-150. Works on consignment and buys outright; 40% commission. Retail price set by joint agreement. Requires exclusive area representation. Reporting time varies. Work may be shipped or hand-delivered. Dealer pays return shipping and insurance for exhibited work. Heaviest wholesale buying time: fall; best selling time: fall and spring.
Acceptable Work: Considers batik; ceramics; glass art; jewelry; pottery; quilting; soft sculpture; wall hangings; weavings; and woodcrafting. Primitive and fine one-of-a-kind pieces; utilitarian and/or decorative.

SOPHIENBURG MUSEUM SHOP, 401 W. Coll, New Braunfels TX 78130. (512)629-1572. Contact: Linda P. Dietert. Museum gift shop. Estab. 1977. Represents 10 craftworkers. Price range: 25c-$35; bestsellers: 25c minimum. Works on consignment; 33⅓% commission. Retail price set by joint agreement. Work may be shipped or hand-delivered. Dealer pays return shipping and insurance for exhibited work. Displays work 90 days. Best selling time: June-December. **Acceptable Work:** Considers dollmaking; jewelry; metalsmithing; quilting; and woodcrafting. Primitive one-of-a-kind and handmade production-line items; utilitarian and/or decorative.

SPORTSMAN'S GALLERY, 5015 Westheimer, Houston TX 77056. Contact: Mike Mahoney. Considers Western sculpture. Openings sometimes sponsored. Exhibited art insured. 8 weeks exposure.

STOREHOUSE, INC., Highland Mall, Upper Level, Autin TX. See Storehouse, Inc., Apple Valley Road, Atlanta, Georgia.

STOREHOUSE, INC., 8415 Preston, Center Plaza, Dallas TX. See Storehouse, Inc., Apple Valley Road, Atlanta, Georgia.

STOREHOUSE, INC., 13601 Preston Rd., Carillon Plaza, Dallas TX 75240. See Storehouse, Inc., Apple Valley Road, Atlanta, Georgia.

STOREHOUSE, INC., 6547 San Pedro, San Antonio TX 78216. See Apple Valley Road, Atlanta, Georgia.

THE SYNDICATE, 1066 Valley View Center, Dallas TX 75240. (214)233-6694. See below.

THE SYNDICATE, 1072 Town East Mall, Mesquite TX 75150. (214)279-2911. Contact: Steven Dean. Gift shop/rental gallery. Estab. 1976. Represents 60-90 craftworkers. Considers all types art and crafts. All styles; utilitarian and/or decorative. Price range: 50c-$2,500; bestsellers: $3-60. Works on consignment, buys outright and rents space plus commission; 25% commission. Retail price set by joint agreement. Requires exclusive representation in mall where store is located. Reports monthly with checks. All work is juried. Dealer pays insurance for exhibited work.
Profile: "We're located in major shopping malls rather than free standing or open center stores. We have the look of an exclusive boutique but with reasonable pricing. Welfare and success of craftworker first consideration; we have very strong reputation for fairness to craftworker." Customer averages 18-49 years; middle and lower middle class; good mix of apartment and single family home dweller; and median income of $15,750. Best selling time: winter.

THE THUMB PRINT, 1007 E. Rundbero Lane #142, Austin TX 78753. Contact: Vicki Simpson. Estab. 1976. Represents 3-4 craftworkers. Considers decoupage; glass art; needlecrafts; tole painting; wall hangings; weavings; and woodcrafting. Primitive and finished, one-of-a-kind and handmade production-line items OK; utilitarian and/or decorative. Price range: 50c-$250; bestsellers: $3-10. Works on consignment; 40% commission. Retail price set by joint agreement. Write. Reports in 2 weeks. Dealer pays insurance for exhibited work. Buys and sells most crafts in fall. Shop takes special orders. Customers are ages 24-40 with upper-middle incomes.

WITTE MUSEUM SHOP, 3801 Broadway, San Antonio TX 78209. (512)826-0647. Manager: George Schriever. Museum gift shop. Estab. 1968. Represents 20 craftworkers. Price range: $1-1,200; bestsellers: $1-40. Works on consignment and buys outright; 30-40% commission. Retail price set by joint agreement. Reports in 2 weeks. Work may be shipped or hand-delivered. Heaviest wholesale buying time: fall and spring; best selling time: Christmas and summer. **Acceptable Work:** Considers candlemaking; ceramics; clothing; dollmaking; glass art; jewelry; pottery; wall hangings; weavings; and woodcrafting. Especially needs anything with armadillos on it. All styles; utilitarian and/or decorative.

YE OLD TOWN SHOPPE, 113 E. Main, Eagle Lake TX 77434. (713)234-3911. Contact: Candy McCreary. Estab. 1976. Represents 15 craftworkers. Considers batik; candlemaking; dollmaking; needlecrafts; quilting; wall hangings; weavings; and woodcrafting. Finished one-of-a-kind items only; utilitarian and/or decorative. Price range: $5-150; bestsellers: $5-10. Works on consignment; 20% commission. Craftworker sets retail price. Write or call. Reports in 10 days.
Profile: "We display crafts in front window the first week." Best selling time: fall. "Ours is the only craft shop in town; located downtown in an old building with a player piano featured."

ZJAY GALLERY, 403 E. Commerce, San Antonio TX 78205. (512)225-9311. Contact: Pat Pickett. Gallery/gift shop. Estab. 1975. Represents 15 craftworkers. Price range: $5-425; bestsellers: $15-225. Works on consignment and buys outright; 33⅓% commission. Gallery sets retail price as well as craftworker. Reports in 4 weeks. Work may be shipped or hand-delivered. Dealer pays return shipping and insurance for exhibited work.
Acceptable Work: Considers glass art; jewelry; pottery; soft sculpture. Especially needs jewelry made in silver with smooth elegant lines with and without stones; and earth tone pottery. Fine handmade production-line items; utilitarian and/or decorative.
Profile: "We specialize in items created by black Americans. Customers are young adults." Displays work 3 months. Heaviest wholesale buying time: early spring; best selling time: summer.

Utah

BRIGHAM CITY MUSEUM-GALLERY, Box 583, Brigham City UT 84302. (801)723-6769. Director: Frederick M. Huchel. Museum gallery. Estab. 1970. Represents 5 craftworkers. Price range: $5-300; bestsellers: $5-20. Works on consignment; 20% commission. Craftworker sets retail price. Requires exclusive area representation. Reports in 2 weeks. Hand-delivered work only. Displays work 3½ weeks.
Acceptable Work: Considers ceramics; clothing; dollmaking; glass art; jewelry; leatherworking; needlecrafts; pottery; quilting; and woodcrafting. All styles; utilitarian and/or decorative.
Profile: "We have a greater variety of displays than most, including a historical museum, an art gallery, and a wildlife/natural resources museum. We serve all the citizens of our local and extended community area and we are a major stopping place for tourists through this area." Heaviest wholesale buying time: spring and fall; best selling time: summer.

THE GALLERY SHOP, Salt Lake Art Center, 54 Finch Lane, Salt Lake City UT 84102. (801)328-2762. Contact: Manager. Museum gift shop. Estab. 1974. Represents 50 Western craftworkers. Price range: $3.25-200; bestsellers: $5-50. Works on consignment and buys outright; 25% commission. Craftworker sets retail price. Reports in 2 weeks. Work may be shipped or hand-delivered. Dealer pays return shipping and insurance for exhibited work.
Acceptable Work: Considers ceramics; clothing; glass art; jewelry; metalsmithing; needlecrafts; pottery; quilting; soft sculpture; wall hangings; weavings; and woodcrafting. Primitive and fine one-of-a-kind pieces; utilitarian and/or decorative.
Profile: "A piece is usually displayed 3-6 months, depending on the time it was brought in. If a grouping is brought in, we try to display it in a prominent spot where it will receive the most attention. The group is then featured for a month and then rotated to another position. Our shop customers are generally members of our Art Center, with a strong sense of supporting the local artists." Heaviest wholesale buying time: fall; best selling time: Christmas.

TAYLOR-LONDON'S OLD CURIOUSITY SHOP, c/o 2460 E. 7600 S., Salt Lake City UT 84121. Contact: John Taylor or Rosanne Southwick. Gallery/antiques/framing. Estab. 1977. Represents 8-12 craftworkers. Price range: $10-15,000; bestsellers: $15-500. Works on consignment; 40% commission. Retail price set by joint agreement. Reports in 2 weeks. Work may be shipped or hand-delivered. Dealer pays return shipping and insurance for exhibited work.
Acceptable Work: Considers ceramics; glass art; needlecrafts; pottery; soft sculpture; and woodcrafting. Especially needs needlepoint. Primitive and fine one-of-a-kind pieces; utilitarian and/or decorative.
Profile: "Items are displayed with proper lighting and in or out of display cabinets, depending on the item and size. Customers are 30+ and have an income range of $25,000 and up." Heaviest wholesale buying time: fall and spring; best selling time: Christmas and fall.

Vermont

BECKERHOFF IN STOWE, LTD., Box 62, Stowe VT 05672. (802)253-7668. Contact: Helen Beckerhoff. Jewelry shop. Estab. 1977. Represents 10 craftworkers. Considers jewelry. Fine one-of-a-kind and handmade production-line items; utilitarian and/or decorative. Price range: $3.50-1,500; bestsellers: $5-500. Buys outright. Retail price set by joint agreement. Reports in 1 week. Work may be shipped or hand-delivered. Dealer pays return shipping and insurance.
Profile: "Purchased work is displayed with other jewelry; exhibits are advertised and displayed separately. Customers are 15-60, sports oriented and have incomes of $10,000 and up." Displays work 2-6 weeks. Heaviest wholesale buying time: spring; best selling time: summer and fall.

A CANDLE IN THE NIGHT, 64 Main St., Brattleboro VT 05301. (802)257-0471. Manager: Larry Simons. Craft shop. Estab. 1973. Represents 10 craftworkers. Price range: $2-500. Works on consignment and buys outright; 25% commission. Craftworker sets retail price. Requires ex-

clusive area representation. Reports immediately when interested. Hand-delivered work only.
Acceptable Work: Considers batik; candlemaking; ceramics; clothing; jewelry; quilting; wall
hangings; weavings; and woodcrafting. Especially needs wooden boxes, handmade clothing and
an occasional weaving or rug. All styles; utilitarian and/or decorative.
Profile: "All small items are kept in showcases. Space is a problem and small items must be able
to fit in existing cases. Our ceiling is 18½ feet high making it easy to display rugs and hangings."
Heaviest wholesale buying time: pre-Christmas and pre-summer; best selling time: summer and
Christmas.

COLONIAL VERMONT, INC., Rt. 7, Shelburne VT 05482. (802)985-2742. Contact: R.
Gazley. Estab. 1965. Represents several craftsmen. Considers metalsmithing, furniture, woodcrafting and pottery. Finished, one-of-a-kind utilitarian items OK. All prices. Buys on consignment; 40% commission. Retail price set by joint agreement. Requires exclusive area representation. Write. Reports in 2 weeks. Dealer pays insurance for exhibited work.

CORNWALL CRAFTS, Rt. 2, Middlebury VT 05753. (802)462-2438. Contact: Nancy Means
Wright. Craft and furniture shop. Estab. 1958. Represents 40-50 Vermont craftworkers. Price
range: $1-700; bestsellers: $1-50. Works on consignment and buys outright; 30-40% commission.
Showroom sets retail price. Requires exclusive area representation. Reports in 1 week. Work
may be shipped or hand-delivered with prior permission. Dealer pays insurance for exhibited
work.
Acceptable Work: Considers batik; candlemaking; ceramics; decoupage; glass art; leatherworking; metalsmithing; some needlecrafts; pottery; some quilting; soft sculpture; wall hangings;
weavings; and woodcrafting. Fine one-of-a-kind and handmade production-line items; utilitarian
and/or decorative.
Profile: "We are located in an old barn. We have quality handcrafted furniture and crafts, low-
keyed atmosphere and are family-run. We have moderate prices and price down, not up. We give
very personal service." Heaviest wholesale buying time: June-October; best selling time: July-
December.

COTTAGE CRAFTS OF VERMONT, Box 214, Weston VT 05161. (802)824-6015. Contact:
Clancy or Hank Parker. Craft shop. Estab. 1975. Represents 200 craftworkers. Price range: $1-
400; bestsellers: $10-75. Buys outright. Gallery sets retail price. Requires exclusive area
representation. Reports in 2 weeks. Work may be shipped or hand-delivered. Dealer pays return
shipping and insurance for exhibited work.
Acceptable Work: Considers batik; ceramics; dollmaking; glass art; jewelry; leatherworking;
metalsmithing; pottery; quilting; soft sculpture; wall hangings; and weavings. Especially needs
medium-priced leather goods; glass (not stained glass pieces); jewelry (bone, for example) and
items that can be personalized by the craftworker for the customer. All styles; utilitarian and/or
decorative.
Profile: "We are one of the few craft shops offering good quality crafts nationwide via mail order
catalogs; we also feature Indian crafts. Work is displayed by general category. Shop customers
range from blue collar workers on vacation to extremely high income families. Our mail order
customer is above average in taste and income, usually a collector who spends $30-200 by mail."
Displays work from Memorial Day through Columbus Day. Heaviest wholesale buying time:
February-April and July-August; best selling time: July-August and October-November.

DAKIN FARM, Ferrisburg VT 05456. (802)877-2936. Contact: Sam Cutting. Craft and gift
shop. Estab. 1955. Represents 20 craftworkers. Price range: 50c-$50; bestsellers: $1-10. Buys
outright. Gallery sets retail price. Reports in 10 days. Work may be shipped or hand-delivered.
Dealer pays return shipping. Heaviest wholesale buying time: spring; best selling time: summer
and Christmas.
Acceptable Work: Considers candlemaking; ceramics; clothing; and woodcrafting. Primitive
handmade production-line items; utilitarian only.

EBENEZER ALLEN COUNTRY STORE & GIFT SHOP, Burlington Square Mall,
Burlington VT 05401. (802)863-4215. Contact: John Luck. Estab. 1972. Represents 60
craftworkers. Considers candlemaking; ceramics; dollmaking; glass art; jewelry; leatherworking;
metalsmithing; pottery; quilting; and woodcrafting. Finished handmade production-line items;
utilitarian and/or decorative. Price range: $1-400; bestsellers: $1.65-30. Buys outright or occasionally on consignment; 33⅓% commission. Shop sets retail price. Requires exclusive area
representation. Query with transparencies or photos. Reports in 3 weeks. Dealer pays shipping to
shop and insurance for exhibited work. Heaviest wholesale buying time: Christmas and summer.

EBENEZER ALLEN COUNTRY STORE & GIFT SHOP, Rt. 2 and 314, South Hero VT 05486. (802)372-4619. Contact: John Luck. Estab. 1972. Represents 30 craftworkers. Considers candlemaking; ceramics; dollmaking; glass art; jewelry; leatherworking; metalsmithing; pottery; quilting; and woodcrafting (furniture). Finished handmade production-line items; utilitarian and/or decorative. Price range: $1-800; bestsellers: $1.65-80. Buys outright or occasionally on consignment; 33⅓% commission. Shop sets retail price. Requires exclusive area representation. Query with transparencies or photos. Reports in 3 weeks. Dealer pays shipping to shop and insurance for exhibited work. Heaviest wholesale buying time: Christmas and summer.

THE ENCHANTED DOLL HOUSE, Manchester Center VT 05255. (802)362-1327. President: Jean Schramm. Vice President: Barbara Haviland. Craft and toy shop. Estab. 1963. Represents 20 craftworkers. Price range: $1.25-1,000; bestsellers: $65. Buys outright. Shop sets retail price. Requires exclusive area representation. Reports in 2 weeks. Work may be shipped or hand-delivered. Dealer pays shipping.
Acceptable Work: Considers dollmaking; soft sculpture; miniatures; and doll houses. Especially needs toys and collector's items (dolls, dollhouses, miniatures and stuffed animals). Handmade production-line items only.
Profile: "We are housed in an 1850 house; we have 10 rooms of toys, dolls, crafts, dollhouses and books." Best selling time: summer and fall.

ETHAN ALLEN GIFT SHOPPE, Rt. 1, Pownal VT 05261. (413)458-3497. Contact: Charles Gray. Craft shop. Estab. 1958. Represents 1 craftworker. Considers all crafts. Handmade production-line items; utilitarian and/or decorative. Price range: $1-5. Works on consignment; 35% commission. Reports within 2 weeks. Work may be shipped or hand-delivered. Dealer pays insurance for exhibited work. Displays work 30-60 days. Heaviest wholesale buying time: spring; best selling time: summer and fall.

THE FEDERAL ESTABLISHMENT, 1 Federal St., St. Albans VT 05478. (802)524-2735. Contact: Roger King-Hall. Estab. 1974. Represents 20 craftworkers. Considers batik; candlemaking; glass art; jewelry; leatherworking; metalsmithing; pottery; quilting; soft sculpture; wall hangings; weavings; and woodcrafting. Finished handmade porduction-line items; utilitarian and/or purely decorative. Price range: $1-50; bestsellers: $1-18. Buys outright; 34% commission. Retail price set by joint agreement. Write. Reports in 1 month.

GOOD STUFF GIFTS, Box F, Main St., Stowe VT 05672. (802)253-4526. Contact: Amy E. Good. Craft and gift shop. Estab. 1977. Represents 30-40 craftworkers. Price range: $1-150; bestsellers; $4-8. Works on consignment and buys outright; 30% commission. Gallery sets retail price. Requires exclusive area representation. Reports in 2 weeks. Work may be shipped or hand-delivered. Shop pays shipping to shop and insurance.
Acceptable Work: Considers candlemaking; ceramics; dollmaking; glass art; leatherworking; pottery; soft sculpture; and woodcrafting. Fine one-of-a-kind and handmade production-line items; utilitarian and/or decorative. Especially needs handmade miniature animals out of wood or other material and enamel work.
Profile: "Most things are displayed on natural wood tables, some things are hung on walls. I handle mostly crafts that no one else in the area carries and a large selection of inexpensive, useful items." Customers range from tourists of all ages with middle to upper income, to winter skiers." Displays work 1 year. Heaviest wholesale buying time: summer; best selling time: summer and fall.

GREEN MOUNTAIN SUGAR HOUSE, Rt. 1, Ludlow VT 05149. Contact: Ann Harlow Rose or David S. Harlow. Gift shop. Estab. 1967. Represents 20-25 Vermont or New England craftworkers. Price range: $1-75. Works on consignment and buys outright. Gallery sets retail price. Requires exclusive area representation. Reports in 2 weeks. Work may be shipped or hand-delivered. Dealer pays return shipping and insurance for exhibited work.
Acceptable Work: Considers candlemaking; ceramics; glass art; jewelry; leatherworking; wall hangings; weavings; and woodcrafting. All styles; utilitarian and/or decorative.
Profile: "Our customers are 95% tourists and skiers." Best selling and heaviest wholesale buying time: summer-fall.

THE HANDCRAFTS SHOP, Weston VT 05161. Contact: Steve or Gail Wiggett Bezore. Craft shop/studio. Estab. 1970. Represents 15-20 craftworkers. All styles; utilitarian and/or decorative. Price range: $2-100; bestsellers: $2-25. Works on consignment and buys outright; 33⅓% commission. Craftworker sets retail price. "Sometimes we help beginning craftworkers to establish prices if they wish us to." Requires exclusive representation in town. Reports in 3 weeks. Dealer pays shipping to shop if outright purchase; in-transit insurance negotiable; and dealer pays insurance for exhibited work.

Acceptable Work: Considers candlemaking; ceramics; decoupage; glass art; jewelry; leatherworking; metalsmithing; pottery; wall hangings; weaving; and woodcrafting. "Modernistic styles and media will be considered, although most of our material is more traditional. We welcome inquiries from any craftworker whose items are in the $5-40 range. We rarely buy more expensive items, but we will consider them. We are only open summers; craftworker should write to us during the winter." All styles; utilitarian and/or decorative.

Profile: "We are located in a 180 year old farmhouse in a small, picturesque town known for its shops and summer theatre." Customers are usually tourists and summer residents who are appreciative of crafts. Displays work for indefinite period. Best selling time: late summer and early fall.

JENKS JEWELRY, 23 Elm St., Woodstock VT 05091. (802)457-3574. Contact: Bill Jenks. Craft shop/metalwork studio. Estab. 1972. Represents 4 craftworkers. Price range: $5-600; bestsellers: $10-40. Works on consignment; 30% commission. Retail price set by joint agreement. Bring work in person. Reports in 4 weeks. Work may be hand-delivered. Dealer pays insurance for exhibited work.

Acceptable Work: Considers jewelry and metalsmithing. Fine one-of-a-kind and handmade production-line items; utilitarian and/or decorative.

Profile: Heaviest wholesale buying time: summer; best selling time: summer and fall.

THE MILLER'S THUMB, Greensboro VT 05841. (802)533-2960. Contact: Gertrude W. Corwin. Craft shop/gift shop. Estab. 1966. Represents 60 Vermont craftworkers. Price range: 50c-$250; bestsellers: $1-50. Works on consignment and buys outright; 33⅓% commission. Retail price set by joint agreement. Reporting time varies. Work may be shipped or hand-delivered with prior permission. Dealer pays shipping to shop and insurance for exhibited work.

Acceptable Work: Considers all crafts except dollmaking; soft sculpture; and tole painting. Especially needs leather crafts and handweaving. Quality stressed. Fine one-of-a-kind and handmade production-line items; utilitarian and/or decorative.

Profile: "Our building is a remodeled grist mill with stream running underneath; we have an uncommercial atmosphere and give personal attention. Customers have interests from farming to high-level business and professional people." Heaviest wholesale buying time: spring. Shop open late June-September.

THE POMFRET SHOP, Old Barnard Stage Rd., South Pomfret VT 05067. (802)457-2464. Contact: Mr. or Mrs. D. Cleveland. Estab. 1972. Represents 12 craftworkers. Considers ceramics; glass art; metalsmithing; needlecrafts; pottery; quilting; wall hangings; weavings; and woodcrafting. Especially needs garden sculpture; plant containers; fountains; bird baths; houses; feeders; and Christmas decorations. Primitive and finished, one-of-a-kind and handmade production-line items OK; utilitarian and/or decorative. Price range: $5-350; bestsellers: $5-20. Buys outright or on consignment; 33⅓% commission. retail price set by joint agreement. Requires exclusive area representation. Query with color transparencies or b&w prints. Reports in 2 weeks. Dealer pays shipping to shop.

Profile: "Our shop is small, but uncluttered. When we take a craft in, it is tagged with the maker's name and price and given prime location." Best selling time: summer and fall; heaviest wholesale buying time: winter and spring. "We go out of our way to handle things that others do not have; plant displays use artificial lighting; outdoor deck features container gardening."

QUAIGH DESIGN CENTRE, INC., Box 114, Wilmington VT 05363. (802)464-2780. Contact: Lilias MacBean Hart. Craft shop. Estab. 1968. Represents 75 northern New England craftworkers. Price range: $1-250; bestsellers: $2.50-35. Buys outright. Gallery sets retail price. Requires exclusive area representation. Only replies if interested. Work may be shipped or hand-delivered. Dealer pays shipping to shop.

Acceptable Work: Considers batik; candlemaking; ceramics; glass art; jewelry; leatherworking; metalsmithing; needlecrafts; pottery; wall hangings; weavings; and woodcrafting. Fine handmade production-line items; utilitarian and/or decorative.

Profile: "Each craftperson's work is usually displayed in one place. We always buy items which are useful, a good price, well designed and professionally presented. Our customers range from the local resort worker to the odd millionaire." Heaviest wholesale buying time: spring-summer; best selling time: summer-fall.

SAMARA, Box 1115, Stowe VT 05672. (802)253-8318. Contact: Lynn W. Miles. Craft shop. Estab. 1972. Represents 100 craftworkers. Price range: 25c-$150; bestsellers: $5-50. Works on consignment and buys outright; 33⅓% commission. Craftworker sets retail price on consignment items. Reports in 1 week. Work may be shipped or hand-delivered. Dealer pays insurance for exhibited work.

Acceptable Work: Considers batik; candlemaking; dollmaking; glass art; jewelry; leatherworking; metalsmithing; pottery; quilting; soft sculpture; wall hangings; weavings; and woodcrafting. Fine one-of-a-kind and handmade production-line items; utilitarian and/or decorative.

Profile: "Every item in the shop is handcrafted by primarily local craftsmen with special attention given to display. Custom work is available in most mediums. We have many tourists from urban centers such as Boston, New York and Montreal— mostly skiers in winter, all ages, all incomes." Heaviest wholesale buying time: early spring and pre-Christmas; best selling time: summer.

L. J. SERKIN CO., 51 Elliot St., Brattleboro VT 05301. (802)257-7044. Contact: John or Lucy Serkin. Craft shop. Estab. 1973. Represents 80 craftworkers. Price range: $5-200; bestsellers: $10-40. Buys outright. Retail price set by joint agreement. Requires exclusive area representation. Reports in 1 week. Work may be shipped or hand-delivered. Dealer pays shipping and insurance for exhibited work.

Acceptable Work: Considers batik; candlemaking; dollmaking; glass art; jewelry; leatherworking; metalsmithing; pottery; soft sculpture; and functional handweaving. Fine handmade production-line items; utilitarian.

Profile: "Most work is displayed by craftsman, i.e. each person's work is displayed as a whole. Customers are early 20's to late 70's; middle class and up." Heaviest wholesale buying time: May-June and November; best selling time: July-August and December.

THE SOFT TOUCH, LTD., 161 Main St., Burlington VT 05401. (802)862-8506. President: E. Michael Goldblatt. Craft shop/gallery/gift shop. Estab. 1976. Represents 10-15 craftworkers. Price range: $1-1,500; bestsellers: $1-50. Works on consignment and buys outright; 25% commission. Craftworker sets retail price. Reports in 4 weeks. Work may be shipped or hand-delivered. Dealer pays insurance for exhibited work.

Acceptable Work: Considers candlemaking; ceramics; clothing; glass art; jewelry; leatherworking; metalsmithing; pottery; quilting; soft sculpture; wall hangings; weavings; and woodcrafting. Primitive and fine one-of-a-kind pieces; utilitarian and/or decorative. Especially needs quilts for waterbeds; blown glass; and unusual stone or wood carvings.

Profile: "Art should be framed, or matted at the very least. Work is wall displayed, lighted; an attempt is made to draw attention to each piece or a special showing is given to a specific artist. Free area advertising to displaying exhibitor." Best selling and heaviest wholesale buying time: fall-winter.

STONE SOLDIER POTTERY, Jacksonville VT 05342. (802)368-7077. Contact: Connie Burnell. Craft shop. Estab. 1968. Represents 35-40 craftworkers. Price range: $2-500; bestsellers: $2.50-100. Buys outright. Craftworker sets retail price. Requires exclusive area representation. Reports in 2 weeks. Work may be shipped or hand-delivered. Dealer pays shipping to shop and insurance.

Acceptable Work: Considers glass art; jewelry; leatherworking; metalsmithing; pottery; soft sculpture; wall hangings; weavings; woodcrafting; and blown and stained glass. Fine one-of-a-kind and handmade production-line items; utilitarian and/or decorative. Especially needs stained glass; candles; and jewelry.

Profile: "We make pottery on the premises; our customers are young and middle aged, mostly college-educated with an appreciation for crafts." Heaviest wholesale buying time: spring and fall; best selling time: summer-fall and Christmas.

STOWE ART BARN, Rt. 1, Mountain Rd., Stowe VT 05672. Contact: Vera Beckerhoff. Craft shop/gallery. Estab. 1973. Represents 50 craftworkers. Price range: $3-150; bestsellers: $5-20. Works on consignment and buys outright; 40% commission. Retail price set by joint agreement. Requires exclusive area representation. Work may be shipped or hand-delivered. Dealer pays shipping to shop and insurance for exhibited work if wholesale.

Acceptable Work: Considers candlemaking; glass art; jewelry; leatherworking; metalsmithing; pottery; quilting; soft sculpture; wall hangings; weavings; and woodcrafting. Especially needs hand printed cards and small stained glass pieces and blown glass. Handmade production-line items; utilitarian and/or decorative.

Profile: "We move items around and try to display a full selection. We are located in a barn; run by a professional craftsperson and our customers are interested in crafts and moving towards a greater appreciation in art." Best selling and heaviest wholesale buying time: summer-fall.

SUNSHINE SNOWY DAY, Box 1305, Stowe VT 05672. (802)244-7546. Contact: John Wetmore. Craft shop. Estab. 1970. Represents 24 craftworkers, "prefer New England craftworkers but not strictly limited." Considers candlemaking; ceramics; clothing; glass art; jewelry; leatherworking; metalsmithing; pottery; soft sculpture; wall hangings; weavings; and woodcrafting. All styles; utilitarian and/or decorative. Price range: $1.50-250; bestsellers: $8.75-40. Buys outright. Retail price set by joint agreement. Reports in 2 weeks. Dealer pays shipping to shop and all insurance. Best selling time: fall.

VERDE-MONT GIFTS, 50 Main St., Middlebury VT 05753. (802)388-6504. Contact: Bernice W. Fucile. Estab. 1967. Considers candlemaking; glass art; metalsmithing; pottery; soft sculpture; woodcrafting; and nonsilver jewelry (Fucile is silversmith). All styles; utilitarian and/or decorative. Price range: $1-25; bestsellers: $2.50-20. Buys outright or on consignment; 40% commission. Craftworker sets retail price. Requires exclusive area representation. Query with color transparencies or b&w prints. Reports in 2 weeks. Dealer pays shipping from shop and insurance for exhibited work.
Profile: Items displayed on shelves or behind glass. Consigned work held 2 months. Heaviest wholesale buying time: summer and pre-Christmas. Middlebury is a college town. "Customers are all ages; they buy crafts for their usefulness and individuality."

VERMONT CRAFTS MARKET, INC., Main St., Box 17, Putney VT 05346. (802)387-5981. President: Kenneth Brown. Mail order shop. Estab. 1975. Represents 120 craftworkers. Price range: $4-800; bestsellers: $16.95-300. Buys outright. Shop sets retail price. Reports in 3 weeks. Dealer pays shipping if work was solicited.
Acceptable Work: Considers all crafts. Finished and handmade production-line items; utilitarian and/or decorative.
Profile: "Generally, we prefer to order samples for catalog consideration after we have seen slides, photos or a letter. Volume production capability a must. Keep wholesale cost as absolutely low as can be and still make a decent profit. High catalog production costs can often make our high mark-up result in unrealistic retail prices." Heaviest wholesale buying time: August-November, January-April; best selling time: September-November.

VERMONT HISTORICAL SOCIETY, Pavilion Office Bldg., Montpelier VT 05602. (802)828-2291. Contact: Virginia McManis. Museum gift shop. Estab. 1839. Represents 10-15 Vermont craftworkers. Price range: 25c-$15; best sellers: 25c-$5. Works on consignment and buys outright; 30% commission. Gallery sets retail price. Reports in 3 weeks. Work may be shipped or hand-delivered. Dealer pays shipping.
Acceptable Work: Considers candlemaking; ceramics; dollmaking; glass art; jewelry; leatherworking; metalsmithing; pottery; and woodcrafting. Handmade production-line items; utilitarian and/or decorative.
Profile: "We only carry Vermont crafted items and try to keep inexpensive items in stock. Our customers are school age, mainly elementary school groups and tourists of all ages and backgrounds." Displays work 3 months. Heaviest wholesale buying time: summer-fall; best selling time: summer-fall and Christmas.

VERMONT LUMBER SPECIALITIES, Groton VT 05046. Contact: B.D. Rowell. Craft shop/gift shop. Estab. 1945. Represents 5 craftworkers who use only Vermont materials. Considers ceramics; dollmaking; leatherworking; metalsmithing; pottery; and woodcrafting. "Special need for wooden colonial kitchen utensils." Primitive one-of-a-kind and handmade production-line items; utilitarian only. Price range: $1-500; bestsellers: $1-250. Buys outright. Craftworker sets retail price. Reports in 2 weeks. Shipping payments are shared. Best selling time: August and October-December.

VERMONT STATE CRAFT CENTER AT WINDSOR HOUSE, Box 110, Windsor VT 05089. (802)674-6729. Contact: Cornelis Pieterse. Craft shop/gallery/gift shop/educational center. Estab. 1975. Represents 200 Vermont craftworkers. Price range: 30c-$500; bestsellers: 30c-$20. Works on consignment and buys outright; 30% commission. Retail price set by joint agreement. Exhibitor's work may be shipped or hand-delivered. Dealer pays shipping to shop and insurance.
Acceptable Work: Considers most crafts; utilitarian and/or decorative. No kits, imports, etc.
Profile: "We have a large showroom which we rearrange every 60 days. We are located in an historic building, and works are accepted by a jury system." Heaviest wholesale buying time: summer-fall; best selling time: summer, fall and holidays.

WEAVER'S WEB, 39 Barre St., Montpelier VT 05602. (802)223-8889. Contact: Christine Abrams. Craft shop/weaving studio. Estab. 1975. Represents 4-10 craftworkers. Price range: $3-

300. Works on consignment and buys outright; 34% commission. Retail price set by joint agreement. Work may be shipped or hand-delivered. Dealer pays insurance for exhibited work. Heaviest wholesale buying time: fall; best selling time: Christmas.
Acceptable Work: Considers clothing; glass art; pottery; wall hangings; and weavings. Fine one-of-a-kind and handmade production-line items; utilitarian and/or decorative.

Virginia

ALEXANDRIA BICENTENNIAL MUSEUM SHOP, 201 S. Washington, Alexandria VA 22314. (703)548-1812. Director: Ms. Dene Garbow. Museum gift shop. Estab. 1974. Represents 4-6 craftworkers. Price range: $1-50; bestsellers: $1-30. Works on consignment and buys outright; 40-50% commission. Retail price set by joint agreement. Reports in 3 weeks. Work may be shipped or hand-delivered. Dealer pays insurance for exhibited work.
Acceptable Work: Considers ceramics; decoupage; dollmaking; glass art; jewelry; needlecrafts; pottery; quilting; and woodcrafting. One-of-a-kind and handmade production-line items; utilitarian and/or decorative.
Profile: "A new item is put on display in a prominent place; often a sign is made explaining the new item. We only want American crafts — reproductions of colonial crafts." Best selling and heaviest wholesale buying time: Christmas.

ANDERSON GALLERY, Virginia Commonwealth University, 907½ W. Franklin St., Richmond VA 23220. Director: Harriet Dubowski. University gallery. Estab. 1970. Represents 2-3 craftworkers. Takes work for exhibit only, with sales as a service with 25% commission. Craftworker sets retail price. Reports in 4-8 weeks. Work may be shipped or hand-delivered. Gallery pays insurance for exhibited work.
Acceptable Work: Considers ceramics; glass art; jewelry; metalsmithing; pottery; soft sculpture; wall hangings; weavings; and woodcrafting. Fine one-of-a-kind pieces; utilitarian and/or decorative.
Profile: "Exhibits change monthly; crafts are displayed in a manner appropriate to the work. Customers are from the University and surrounding Richmond communities." Best selling and heaviest wholesale buying time: Christmas.

BAYLY MUSEUM SHOP, UNIVERSITY OF VIRGINIA, Rugby Rd., Charlottesville VA 22906. Manager: Beverley W. Hereford. Museum gift shop. Estab. 1977. Represents 10 craftworkers. Price range: under $1-1,000; bestsellers: $1-100. Works on consignment; 25% commission. Craftworker sets retail price. Work may be shipped or hand-delivered. Museum pays insurance for exhibited work.
Acceptable Work: Considers batik; ceramics; glass art; jewelry; metalsmithing; needlecrafts; pottery, soft sculpture; and woodcrafting. All styles; utilitarian and/or decorative.
Profile: "Size is a handicap; items need to be relatively small. Customers are students, faculty wives and the general public." Best selling and heaviest wholesale buying time: Christmas.

THE CAVE HOUSE, 279 E. Main., Abingdon VA 24210. (703)628-7721. Manager: Tina Blanton. Craft shop operated by Holston Mountain Arts & Crafts Co-op. Estab. 1971. Represents 200 craftworkers who live within a 40 mile radius of the shop. Price range: 75c-$400; bestsellers: $2-15. Works on consignment; 40% commission. Craftworker sets retail price. Reports in 1 week. Work may be shipped or hand-delivered. Shop pays insurance for exhibited work.
Acceptable Work: Considers batik; ceramics, dollmaking; glass art; jewelry; leatherworking; metalsmithing; needlecrafts; pottery; quilting; tole painting; wall hangings; weavings; woodcrafting; baskets; crocheting; knitting. Especially needs baskets, brooms and quilts. Primitive, and fine handmade production-line items; utilitarian and/or decorative.
Profile: "We are located in a big, old house in historical district of Abingdon. Many wealthy people come to Abingdon to see a play, take part in the Virginia Highlands Festival or to visit the Martha Washington Inn." Displays work 6 months. Best selling time: Christmas and summer.

CRAFTERS' GALLERY, Rt. 2, Box 215, Charlottesville VA 22901. (804)295-7006. Contact: Bob Leiby or Don Nelson. Craft shop/gallery. Estab. 1974. Represents 100 craftworkers. Price range: $1-1,600; bestsellers: $20-70. Works on consignment and buys outright; 40% commission. Craftworker sets retail price. Requires exclusive area representation. Reports in 2 weeks. Work may be shipped or hand-delivered, if requested. Shipping costs are shared; dealer pays insurance for exhibited work.
Acceptable Work: Considers batik; ceramics; glass art; jewelry; leatherworking; metalsmithing; pottery; quilting; soft sculpture; wall hangings; weavings; and woodcrafting. One-of-a-kind and handmade production-line items; utilitarian only.
Profile: "We are noted for fine display; our building is an old barn with several rooms.

Customers are professional, moneyed and sophisticated." Best selling time: November-December, May and summer.

CRAFTWORKS, 104C S. Alfred St., Alexandria VA 22314. (703)836-7298. Contact: Rebecca Koladis. Gallery. Considers all crafts. Especially needs quilts and soft sculpture. Works on consignment and buys outright. Sponsors rotating shows.

DAWNTREADER, 11 Elliewood Ave., Charlottesville VA 22903. (804)977-3200. Contact: Wilhem F. Golluh. Craft shop. Estab. 1976. Represents 6 craftworkers. Price range: 25c-$250; bestsellers: 25c-$20. Buys outright; 33⅓% commission. Retail price set by joint agreement. Requires exclusive area representation. Reports in 2 weeks. Hand-delivered work OK. Dealer pays return shipping and insurance for exhibited work.
Acceptable Work: Considers jewelry and metalsmithing. Fine one-of-a-kind and handmade production-line items; decorative only. Especially needs sterling inlay pendants (small).
Profile: "Work is put in center display for a few weeks, and if it does not sell, it is moved to a side display. Customers are college students and middle-aged housewives." Heaviest wholesale buying time: September-December; best selling time: October-December.

EVANS FARM COUNTRY STORE, 1696 Chain Bridge Rd., McLean VA 22101. Buyer: Caroline Van Wagoner. Craft gift and antiques shop. Estab. 1962. Represents 25 craftworkers. Price range: $2.50-500; bestsellers: $2.50-60. Works on consignment and buys outright; 40% commission. Retail price set by joint agreement. Reports in 2 weeks. Work may be hand-delivered. Displays work 3 months. Heaviest wholesale buying time: spring and fall; best selling time: summer and Christmas.
Acceptable Work: Considers ceramics; clothing; decoupage; glass art; jewelry; needlecrafts; wall hangings; weavings; and woodcrafting. Especially needs weaving and rug braiding. Handmade production-line items; utilitarian and/or decorative.

FERRUM CRAFT SHOP, Rt. 1, Box 242, Ferrum VA 24088. (703)365-7256. Director: Lois Scott. Craft shop. Estab. 1969. Considers all crafts. Price range: $1-650. Works on consignment; 25% commission. Craftworker sets retail price.
Profile: "The shop is a project of Franklin County Community Action. Its original purpose was to help supplement low income people by selling their crafts. We now accept crafts from anyone, anywhere. This gives us an excellent variety of crafts. There is a craft and price for everyone."

FIRST IMPRESSIONS, 13809 Lee Hwy., Centreville VA 22020. (703)631-9019. Contact: Barbara Sanders. Estab. 1972. Represents 300 craftworkers (mostly local). Considers all crafts; especially needs traditional styles. Fine one-of-a-kind and handmade production-line items; utilitarian and/or decorative. Price range: 75c-$50; bestsellers: $1.50-22. Works on consignment; 35% commission. Retail price set by joint agreement. Write. Reports in 2 weeks. Dealer pays "break-in" insurance for exhibited work.
Profile: Items displayed 3 months maximum among antiques. Best selling time: fall and spring; heaviest wholesale buying time: late summer and fall.

FREDERICKSBURG GALLERY OF ART, 813 Sophia St., Fredericksburg VA 22401. (703)373-5646. Director: Marcia Chaves. Gallery. Estab. 1962. Represents 20 craftworkers. Price range: $1.50-200; bestsellers: $2-30. Works on consignment; 34% commission. Craftworker sets retail price. Reports in 3 weeks. Work may be shipped or hand-delivered. Dealer pays return shipping and insurance for exhibited work.
Acceptable Work: Considers batik; glass art; jewelry; metalsmithing; pottery; weavings; and woodcrafting. Fine one-of-a-kind items; utilitarian and/or decorative.
Profile: "Items are handled with great care and display is changed often. We are in an old historic building and are on the historic tour guide of Fredericksburg." Best selling and heaviest wholesale buying time: fall.

GREEN SPRING FARM GALLERY, 4601 Green Spring Rd., Alexandria VA 22312. (703)941-6066. Director: Peggy Amsterdam. County arts council. Estab. 1964. Represents craftworkers from Fairfax County and surrounding area. Price range: $2-150; bestsellers: $2-50. Works on consignment; 25% commission. Craftworker sets retail price. Rental gallery fee: $1-2 per show. Reports immediately. Work may be hand-delivered.
Acceptable Work: Considers batik; ceramics; glass art; jewelry; needlecrafts; pottery; wall hangings; weavings; and woodcrafting. Finished, one-of-a-kind and handmade production-line items; utilitarian and/or decorative.

Profile: "Shop is located in an historic house (circa 1764) restored and open to the public. Customers are all ages and middle income." Displays work 2 months. Best selling time: spring-summer and winter holidays.

HAMPTON ARTS AND HUMANITIES, 22 Wine St., Hampton VA 23669. (804)723-1776. Craft Programmer: John W. Robinson. City Culture Center. Estab. 1955. Represents 15 craftworkers. Exhibits work only; no sales. Requires exclusive area representation. Reports in 1 week. Hand-delivered work only.
Acceptable Work: Considers candlemaking; ceramics; decoupage; glass art; jewelry; leatherworking; metalsmithing; needlecrafts; pottery; quilting; soft sculpture; tole painting; wall hangings; weaving; and woodcrafting; Fine one-of-a-kind and handmade production-line items; utilitarian and/or decorative.

HAND WORK SHOP, INC., 316 N. 24th St., Richmond VA 23223. (804)649-0674. Executive Director: Ruth T. Summers. Craft shop/gallery. Estab. 1963. Represents 150-200 craftworkers. Price range: 75c-$600; bestsellers: $5-45. Works on consignment and buys outright 33⅓% commission. Retail price set by joint agreement. Requires exclusive area representation. Reports in 2 weeks. Work may be shipped or hand-delivered. Dealer pays shipping to shop and insurance for exhibited work. Displays work 3 months.
Acceptable Work: Considers batik; candlemaking; ceramics; jewelry; leatherworking; metalsmithing; pottery; quilting; wall hangings; weavings; woodcrafting; blown glass; and forged iron. Fine one-of-a-kind and handmade production-line items; utilitarian and/or decorative.
Profile: "We are a tax exempt nonprofit organization dedicated to the appreciation of fine designer craft work. We sponsor gallery shows plus a large retail craft fair annually in November. Customers have an income of $15,000-30,000; are in the 25-55 year range." Displays work 3 months. Heaviest wholesale buying time: January-February; best selling time: September-December.

THE KNOTTY PINE, 113 King St., Alexandria VA 22314. (203)836-7475. Contact: Lynn Murphy. Handcrafted furniture and gifts. Estab. 1975. Represents 20 craftworkers. Price range: $8-50; bestsellers: $8-30. Works on consignment. Gallery sets retail price. Requires exclusive area representation. Reporting time varies. Work may be shipped or hand-delivered. Dealer pays shipping and insurance for exhibited work.
Acceptable Work: Considers ceramics; leatherworking; pottery; quilting; wall hangings; weavings; and woodcrafting. Primitive one-of-a-kind and handmade production-line items; utilitarian and/or decorative.
Profile: "Our customers are 25-35 years old; married couples." Displays work 3 months. Heaviest wholesale buying time: fall; best selling time: Christmas and summer.

THE PEANUT PATCH, Box 183, Main St., Courtland VA 23837. (804)653-2028. Contact: Judy S. Riddick or Gayuelle E. Riddick. Craft shop. Estab. 1973. Represents 200 craftworkers. Price range: 50c-$330; bestsellers: $2.50-15. Works on consignment and buys outrght; 40-50% commission. Retail price set by joint agreement. Reports in 2 weeks. Work may be shipped or hand-delivered if previously arranged. Dealer pays shipping to shop if bought outright.
Acceptable Work: Considers ceramics; clothing; decoupage; dollmaking; glass art; jewelry; metalsmithing; needlecrafts; pottery; quilting; tole painting; and woodcrafting. Fine one-of-a-kind and handmade production-line items; utilitarian and/or decorative.
Special Needs: "We always hunt for peanut and pig items, since this is pig and peanut country. We like fine quilts and nice patchwork items."
Profile: "We display our crafts to fit in with the decor of the shop. Customers are adults; middle and upper income; many tourists." Displays work 6 months or longer. Heaviest wholesale buying time: fall; best selling time: fall-winter.

STRASBURG MUSEUM, Strasburg VA 22657. (703)465-3175. Manager: Evelyn Fraser. Estab. 1972. Represents 8-10 craftworkers. Price range: $1-30. Buys outright. Gallery sets retail price. Reports in 4 weeks. Work may be hand-delivered. Dealer pays insurance for exhibited work.
Acceptable Work: Considers ceramics; clothing; dollmaking; leatherworking; needlecrafts; pottery; quilting; and woodcrafting. Primitive and fine one-of-a-kind pieces; utilitarian and/or decorative. Especially needs items in the low price range; items that might appeal to school children as souvenirs.
Profile: "We have local crafts and artwork on sale; we also give pottery classes and take special orders." Displays work 5 months. Heaviest wholesale buying time: April-August; best selling time: summer.

UNIQUE SHOP, 213 King St., Alexandria VA 22314. (703)836-6686. Contact: Ethel Beun. Craft and gift shop. Estab. 1969. Represents 50 craftworkers. Price range: $1-75; bestsellers: $2-15. Works on consignment and buys outright; 33⅓% commission. Craftworker sets retail price. Work may be shipped or hand-delivered. Dealer pays return shipping and insurance for exhibited work. Heaviest wholesale buying time: late summer; best selling time: Christmas.
Acceptable Work: Considers ceramics; decoupage; glass art; jewelry; metalsmithing; needlecrafts; pottery; quilting; soft sculpture; tole painting; wall hangings; weavings; and wood-crafting. Primitive and fine handmade production-line items; utilitarian and/or decorative.

VIRGINIA HANDCRAFTS, INC., 2008 Langhorne Rd., Lynchburg VA 24501. (804)846-7029. Manager: Jan Spinelli. Craft shop/gallery. Estab. 1965. Represents 200 craftworkers. Price range: $1-750; bestsellers: $15-300. Works on consignment and buys outright; 40% commission. Gallery sets retail price. Requires exclusive area representation. Reports in 2 weeks. Work may be shipped or hand-delivered. Dealer pays shipping and insurance for exhibited work.
Acceptable Work: Considers batik; candlemaking; glass art; jewelry; leatherworking; metalsmithing; soft sculpture; wall hangings; weavings; pottery; and woodcrafting. Fine one-of-a-kind and handmade production-line items; utilitarian and/or decorative.
Profile: "We work hard on effective display; try to change as frequently as possible. Our customers are all ages and income brackets, but we do have Lynchburg's most affluent citizens making up a large percentage of our clientele." Heaviest wholesale buying time; August-September; best selling time: October-December.

VIRGINIA MUSEUM, Boulevard & Grove Ave., Richmond VA 23221. (804)786-6386. Contact: Curatorial Department. Estab. 1936. Sponsors biennial painting, sculpture, crafts, photography, graphic design and printmaking shows in Virginia. Open to Virginia residents, those born in the state or having minimum 3-year residency. Charges entry fee; 20% sales commission. Write for more information.

VIRGINIA POLYTECHNIC INSTITUTE & STATE UNIVERSITY ART GALLERY, Department of Art, Virginia Polytechnic Institute and State University, Blacksburg VA 24061. (703)951-5547. Contact: Dean Carter. University art gallery. Considers all crafts. All styles; utilitarian and/or decorative. Bestsellers: $5-200. Retail price set by joint agreement. Reports in 4 weeks. Work may be shipped or hand-delivered.
Profile: "Small items are shown in closed glass cases. When unlocked, area is always supervised. Customers are students, faculty and townspeople." Displays work 1 month. Best selling time: Christmas.

YARN BAZAAR, 421 S. Washington St., Alexandria VA 22314. (703)548-0408. Contact: Patricia Baehler. Craft, gift and craft supplies shop. Estab. 1968. Price range: $2-30; bestsellers: $2-15. Works on consignment and buys outright; 50% commission. Retail price set by joint agreement. Requires exclusive area representation. Work may be shipped or hand-delivered. Dealer pays shipping to shop and insurance for exhibited work.
Acceptable Work: Considers decoupage; needlecrafts; and Christmas ornaments. Fine one-of-a-kind pieces; utilitarian and/or decorative.
Profile: "We are in an old townhouse divided into 3 rooms. The first is a boutique with window display on main road to Mt. Vernon. The second room is for needlepoint and crewel displays and the third room is devoted to knitting and crocheting. Customers tend to be more conservative; middle to upper income." Heaviest wholesale buying time: summer; best selling time: fall-summer.

Washington

ALPHA DOUBLE PLUS, Box 98457, Des Moines WA 98457. (206)246-1570. Contact: Morton Silverbow. Estab. 1973. Represents 40 gay craftworkers. Considers batik; ceramics; glass art; jewelry; metalsmithing; needlecrafts; pottery; soft sculpture; wall hangings; weavings; and wood-crafting. Especially needs figurative works. All styles; utilitarian and/or decorative. Price range: $5-35; bestsellers: $5-175. Buys outright or on consignment; 50% commission. Gallery sets retail price. Query with transparencies or photos. Reports in 3 weeks. Dealer pays shipping from shop and insurance. Heaviest wholesale buying time: spring and fall. Affluent customers.

BONNEVILLE GALLERY, 3102 Harborview Dr., Box 32, Gig Harbor WA 98335. (206)858-9890. President: M.V. Bonneville. Craft shop/gallery. Estab. 1969. Represents 50 craftworkers. Price range: $3.50-1,000. Works on consignment and buys outright; 35% commission. Retail price set by joint agreement. Reports in 2 weeks. Work may be shipped or hand-delivered. Dealer pays return shipping and insurance for exhibited work. Heaviest wholesale buying time:

spring and fall; best selling time: summer and fall.
Acceptable Work: Considers batik; ceramics; clothing; jewelry; soft sculpture; wall hangings; and weavings.

BURIEN ARTS GALLERY, Box 66574, 421 SW 146th, Seattle WA 98166. (206)244-7808. Director: Mrs. Robert Monroe. Gallery. Estab. 1969. Represents 80 craftworkers. Price range: 35c-$1,000; bestsellers: $5-18. Works on consignment. Craftworker sets retail price. Reports in 4 weeks. Work may be hand-delivered. Displays work 1-2 months. Best selling time: September-December.
Acceptable Work: Considers batik; ceramics; clothing; decoupage; glass art; jewelry; leatherworking; metalsmithing; needlecrafts; pottery; quilting; soft sculpture; tole painting; wall hangings; weavings; and woodcrafting. Primitive and fine one-of-a-kind pieces; utilitarian and/or decorative.

CANNON SHOP, Fort Lewis Military Museum, Fort Lewis WA 98433. (206)967-4523. Manager: Peggy Hamilton. Museum gift shop. Estab. 1973. Considers jewelry; metalsmithing; and pottery. Primitive handmade production-line items; utilitarian and/or decorative. Price range: 15c-$20. Works on consignment and buys outright. Retail price set by gift shop manager. Dealer pays insurance for exhibited work.
Profile: "Largest military museum west of Rockies and only military museum in Pacific Northwest. Customers are retired military (some on active duty) and many civilians." Best selling time: May-September.

GAIL CHASE GALLERY, 22 103rd NE, Bellevue WA 98004. (206)454-1250. Contact: Gail Chase. Craft shop/gallery. Estab. 1969. Represents 80 craftworkers. Price range: $3.50-200; bestsellers: $20-100. Buys outright and works on consignment. 40% commission. Craftworker sets retail price. Requires exclusive area representation. Send slides and price list. Reports in 2 weeks. Work may be shipped or hand-delivered. Dealer pays return shipping and insurance for exhibited work.
Acceptable Work: Considers batik; ceramics; clothing; glass art; jewelry; pottery; soft sculpture; wall hangings; and weavings. Especially needs servicable, reasonably-priced stoneware. All styles; utilitarian and/or decorative.
Profile: "Customers are age 25-45, with incomes of $20,000-40,000." Heaviest wholesale buying time: fall; best selling time: winter.

THE COUNTRY CRAFTSMEN, Rt. 1, Box 529, Long Beach WA 98631. (206)642-2644. Contact: Bonny Lowry. Estab. 1975. Represents 50 craftworkers. Considers all media — toys; clothing; cards and gift wrap with a country-type look. Finished, one-of-a-kind and production-line, handmade items OK; utilitarian and/or decorative. Price range: 10c-$200; bestsellers: 15c-$15. Works on consignment; 33⅓% commission. Craftworker sets retail price. Write or submit work in person. Reports in 2 weeks. Dealer pays shipping from shop and insurance for exhibited work.
Profile: Craftworkers are notified before the 10th of each month as to whether they have made sales. Best selling time: summer; heaviest wholesale buying time: February and August. Shop, located in retirement and family tourist area, looks like a cottage. "We are strictly country-casual in a countrified setting." Customers ages 30+ with average incomes.

CREATIVE CRAFTS, 2103 S. Seator Mall, Fed Way WA 98003. (213)839-1530. Manager: Robert Martin. Rental gallery. Estab. 1977. Represents 70 craftworkers. Price range: $1-1,600; bestsellers: $5-50. Handles crafts on rental and commission basis. Craftworker sets retail price. Reports in 3 weeks. Work may be shipped or hand-delivered. Dealer pays insurance for exhibited work.
Acceptable Work: Considers batik; candlemaking; ceramics; decoupage; dollmaking; glass art; jewelry; leatherworking; metalsmithing; needlecrafts; pottery; quilting; soft sculpture; tole painting; wall hangings; weavings; and woodcrafting. Fine handmade production-line items; utilitarian and/or decorative.
Profile: "Each craftsman has his own display designed and built by him, according to the theme of the store." Best selling time: Christmas.

FIFTH AVENUE GALLERY, 1312 5th Ave., Seattle WA 98101. (206)624-3233. Contact: Carl Brecht. Craft shop/gallery/gift shop/vacuum mounting press. Represents 24-30 craftworkers. Considers batik; decoupage; quilting; wall hangings; weavings; and woodcrafting. All styles; purely decorative. Price range: $25-18,000; bestsellers: $10-800. Works on consignment and buys outright. Gallery sets retail price. Requires exclusive area representation. Reports in 2 weeks.

Dealer pays return shipping; shipping insurance; and insurance for exhibited work. Best selling time: May and December.

THE LEGACY, LTD., 71 Marion Viaduct, Seattle WA 98104. (206)624-6350. Contact: Mardonna McKillop. Considers metalsmithing; pottery; sculpture; and woodcrafting. Maximum size: 3x6'. Specializes in Indian and Eskimo art based on traditional themes and produced by native artists. Price range: $60-1,200, sculpture; $200-3,000, woodcarvings. Bestsellers: $20-300. Buys outright or on consignment; 30-40% commission. Retail price set by joint agreemet. Requires exclusive area representation. Send slides of work. SASE. Dealer pays shipping from shop and insurance for exhibited work. Items displayed 3-6 weeks.

MIZPAH ART GALLERY, 625 Commerce, Tacoma WA 98402. (206)627-1707. Contact: Beverly Shipton. Gallery. Estab. 1974. Represents 3 craftworkers. Price range: $2.50-300; bestsellers: $10-200. Works on consignment; 40% commission. Craftworker sets retail price. Reports in 4 weeks. Work may be shipped. Dealer pays return shipping.
Acceptable Work: Considers glass art; metalsmithing; and pottery. Fine one-of-a-kind pieces; utilitarian and/or decorative.
Profile: "Our gallery is run with Christian principles and love, integrity being the most important commodity. I have a beautiful relationship with my artists and craftspeople and I want it to remain so." Displays work 3 months. Best selling time: Christmas and summer.

THE MUSHROOM GALLERY, 714 Sprague Ave. W., Spokane WA 99201. (509)747-6427. Contact: Joy Arsenault. Craft shop/gallery/gift shop. Estab. 1975. Represents 75-100 craftworkers. Price range: $20-500; bestsellers: $5-300. Works on consignment and buys outright; 40% commission. Retail price set by joint agreement. Reports in 2 weeks. Work may be shipped or hand-delivered. Dealer pays insurance for exhibited work.
Acceptable Work: Considers batik; ceramics; dollmaking; glass art; jewelry; soft sculpture; wall hangings; and weavings. Fine one-of-a-kind and handmade production-line items; utilitarian only.
Profile: Work is "displayed in groupings with antiques or simple sculpture stands, combined with other crafts. The gallery and gifts are rearranged every 3 months. Customers are local people interested in the arts, sports and civic affairs; moderate to high income." Best selling time: pre-Christmas and summer.

NORTHWEST CRAFT CENTER, Seattle Center, Seattle WA 98109. (206)624-7563. Manager: Ruth Nomura. Craft shop/gallery. Estab. 1963. Represents 200 Northwest resident craftworkers. Price range: $2-500; bestsellers: $5-50. Works on consignment; 40% commission. Craftworker sets retail price. Reports in 4 weeks. Work may be shipped or hand-delivered. Best selling time: summer and Christmas.
Acceptable Work: Considers batik; ceramics; jewelry; metalsmithing; and pottery. All styles; utilitarian only.

PACIFIC CENTER OF THE ARTS AND CRAFTS, Box 448, Grayland WA 98547. (206)267-1351. Contact: Ed or Sovia Pratt. Craft shop/gallery/gift shop. Estab. 1970. Represents 200 craftworkers. Price range: 50c-$1,500; bestsellers: under $10-under 300. Works on consignment; 33⅓% commission. When an artist is demonstrating, shop takes only 25% commission. Retail price set by joint agreement. Requires exclusive area representation. Reports in 1 week. Work may be shipped or hand-delivered.
Acceptable Work: Considers candlemaking; ceramics; decoupage; dollmaking; glass art; jewelry; metalsmithing; needlecrafts; pottery; tole painting; watt hangings; weavings; and woodcrafting. Fine one-of-a-kind and handmade production-line items; utilitarian and/or decorative.
Profile: "We have a large variety of handcrafts and art, paintings and art supplies all under one management in an unusual setting: an old school house." Heaviest wholesale buying time: spring-early fall; best selling time: February-October.

PATTY'S PLACE, 515 5th Ave. S., Edmonds WA 98020. (206)774-6446. Contact: Patty Price. Craft, gift and quilt shop. Estab. 1972. Represents 100-150 craftworkers. Price range: 50c-$375; bestsellers: $5-125. Works on consignment and buys outright; 35% commission; 20% on quilts. Retail price set by joint agreement. Reports in 1 week. Work may be hand-delivered only by request. Dealer pays return shipping.
Acceptable Work: Considers clothing; decoupage; jewelry; leatherworking; metalsmithing; needlecrafts; pottery; quilting; soft sculpture; tole painting; wall hangings; weavings; and woodcrafting. Fine one-of-a-kind and handmade production-line items; utilitarian and/or decorative.

Profile: "We try to group items so they complement each other. We are located in an old house built in 1894 and have carefully selected items in all price ranges. Customers are mostly married women, ages 20-80. Heaviest wholesale buying time: fall; best selling time: fall-winter.

POKO, INC., 317 1st Ave. S., Seattle WA 98104. Secretary: L. Porlier. Gallery/gift shop. Estab. 1974. Represents 3 craftworkers. Minimum price: $1.49. Works on consignment; 50% commission. Retail price set by joint agreement. Requires exclusive area representation. Reporting time varies. Work may be shipped or hand-delivered. Dealer pays insurance for exhibited work. Best selling and heaviest wholesale buying time: summer and Christmas.
Acceptable Work: Considers batik; ceramics; pottery; soft sculpture; wall hangings; and weavings. Fine one-of-a-kind and handmade production-line items; utilitarian and/or decorative.

POTTERY NORTHWEST, 226 1st Ave. N., Seattle WA 98109. (206)285-4421. Director: Sid Morton. Gallery/studio workshop. Estab. 1966. Represents 55 craftworkers. Considers ceramics and pottery. Fine one-of-a-kind and handmade production-line items; utilitarian and/or decorative. Price range: $10-575; bestsellers: $10-40. Retail price set by joint agreement. Reports in 4 weeks. Dealer pays insurance for exhibited work.
Profile: "We are 1 of the few galleries that handles only ceramics." Customers are 20-50 years and of middle to high middle income. Best selling time: October-January.

PRINCESS ANGELINE GALLERY, 214 1st Ave. S., Seattle WA 98104. (206)682-3105. Manager: Janice Hype. Gallery. Estab. 1976. Represents 50 craftworkers. Price range: 35c-$300. Works on consignment; 40% commission. Craftworker sets retail price. Reports in 4 weeks. Work may be shipped or hand-delivered. Dealer pays insurance for exhibited work.
Acceptable Work: Considers batik; jewelry; pottery; wall hangings; weavings; woodcrafting; and enamel. Finished and one-of-a-kind pieces; utilitarian and/or decorative.
Special Needs: Large decorative, one-of-a-kind woven hangings of original design.
Profile: "All work submitted is screened by a gallery board once a month. Customers are adults with previous exposure to fine crafts." Displays work 90 days. Heaviest wholesale buying time: fall; best selling time: July-August and November-December.

SKYLIGHT GALLERY, 115 N. Laurel, Port Angeles WA 98362. (206)457-0009. Proprietor: Kay Myers. Gallery. Estab. 1971. Represents 100 craftworkers. Price range: $1-500; bestsellers: $3.50-50. Works on consignment; 40% commission. Retail price set by joint agreement. Requires exclusive area representation. Reports in 1 week. Work may be shipped or hand-delivered. Displays work 6 months maximum.
Acceptable Work: Considers batik; ceramics; dollmaking; glass art; jewelry; metalsmithing; pottery; soft sculpture; wall hangings; and weavings. Especially needs wood, metal and leather. Designer pieces; utilitarian and/or decorative.
Profile: "Customers are all ages; teenagers to senior citizens. Most are interested in pottery and jewelry." Best selling time: Christmas and summer.

SPENCER POTTERY, 5021 S. 144, Seattle WA 98168. (206)242-2372. Contact: Lorene Spencer. Craft shop. Estab. 1952. Represents 2-3 craftworkers. Price range: $3-200; bestsellers: $4-30. Buys outright. Requires exclusive area representation. "Phone or write a letter before you come." Reports in 1 week. Best selling and heaviest wholesale buying time: summer and fall.
Acceptable Work: Considers candlemaking; glass art; and pottery. Especially needs candles and soaps. Fine one-of-a-kind and handmade production-line items; utilitarian only.

VALLEY ART CENTER, INC., 842 6th St., Clarkston WA 99403. (509)758-8331. Contact: Janice Trusty. Gallery/gift shop. Estab. 1967. Represents 100+ craftworkers. Price range: $5-75; bestsellers: $5-25. Works on consignment; 25% commission. Craftworker sets retail price. Requires exclusive area representation. Reports in 2 weeks. Work may be shipped or hand-delivered. Dealer pays insurance for exhibited work. Displays work 3 months.
Acceptable Work: Considers batik; ceramics; decoupage; dollmaking; glass art; metalsmithing; needlecrafts; pottery; quilting; tole painting; wall hangings; weavings; and woodcrafting. Fine one-of-a-kind pieces; utilitarian and/or decorative.
Profile: "Displays are rotated weekly so that by the end of the 3 months, the items have received the widest possible exposure." Best selling time: early summer and Christmas.

THE WEED LADY AND OTHER WONDROUS WARES AND GINGHAM GALLERY, 832 102nd NE, Bellevue WA 98004. (206)455-3056. Manager: Charmel Huffman. Craft shop/gallery/gift shop. Represents 20 craftworkers. Price range: $1-500; bestsellers: $1.50-50.

Works on consignment and buys outright; 30% commission. Retail price set by joint agreement. Requires exclusive area representation. Work may be shipped or hand-delivered.

Acceptable Work: Considers batik; decoupage; dollmaking; stained glass art; ceramic jewelry; needlecrafts; pottery; quilting; wall hangings; weavings; soft sculpture; woodcrafting; ornaments; pressed flower pictures; and clothespin dolls. One-of-a-kind and handmade production-line items; utilitarian and/or decorative.

Profile: "We are the only shop with such a variety of special services: preserving and drying; offering classes, etc." Best selling and heaviest wholesale buying time: prior to all holidays.

THE WEED LADY AND OTHER WONDROUS WARES AND GINGHAM GALLERY, 408 Main St., Edmonds WA 98020. (206)775-3800. See above.

Believing "the quality of work has improved and craftworkers have become more professional" Art and Mark Adair consider batik, ceramics, clothing, glass art, jewelry, pottery, quilting, soft sculpture, wall hangings, weavings, and woodcrafting for their Clay and Fiber Gallery, Taos, New Mexico, and Clay and Fiber II, Taos Ski Valley.

THE WOOD SHOP, 402 Occidental St., Seattle WA 98104. (206)624-1763. Contact: Marcia or Will Norwood. Estab. 1972. Represents 50 craftworkers. Considers batik; dollmaking; jewelry; pottery; and woodcrafting. Finished one-of-a-kind and handmade production-line items; utilitarian and/or decorative. Price range: up to $100; bestsellers: up to $50. Works on consignment; 33⅓% commission. Retail price set by joint agreement. Prefers exclusive area representation. Write or stop in. Reports immediately. Dealer pays insurance for exhibited work.

Profile: "We make wooden toys and dulcimers in the store." Heaviest wholesale buying time: summer and Christmas. Primarily works with young customers with middle to upper incomes; they buy crafts for gifts.

WOOD'S GALLERY, 114 4th N., Edmonds WA 98020. (206)774-6314. Contact: Rick Wood. Gallery/gift shop/rental gallery/antiques. Estab. 1977. Represents 20-40 craftworkers. Price range: $2-3,000; bestsellers: $15-350. Works on consignment; 33⅓% commission. Retail price set by joint agreement. Reports in 2 weeks. Work may be shipped or hand-delivered. Displays work 1 month.

Acceptable Work: Considers batik; candlemaking; clothing; decoupage; dollmaking; glass art;

leatherworking; metalsmithing; needlecrafts; pottery; soft sculpture; tole painting; wall hangings; weavings; and woodcrafting. Especially needs ceramics; jewelry; woodcarvings; and metal sculpture from $35-several hundred dollars. Fine one-of-a-kind and handmade production-line items; utilitarian and/or decorative.

Profile: "The gallery has a unique atmosphere; good wall space, gallery lighting and extensive fixtures; furnishings of museum quality. Customers are from middle class to extremely wealthy. Send photos first; I prefer to meet artists personally and grow from there." Best selling time: summer and winter.

Washington D.C.

BENCSIK GALLERY, 5029 Connecticut Ave. NW, Washington DC 20008. Director: R. Kornemann. Gallery. Estab. 1960. Represents 5 craftworkers. Considers batik; ceramics; decoupage; glass art; jewelry; metalsmithing; needlecrafts; pottery; quilting; soft sculpture; tole painting; wall hangings; weavings; and woodcrafting. All styles; utilitarian and/or decorative. Price range: $5-10,000; bestsellers: $20-100. Works on consignment; 50% commission. Retail price set by joint agreement. Requires exclusive area representation. Reports in 4 weeks. Minimum 1 month display.

Profile: Very well-educated, cultured, sophisticated customers of high income. Many diplomats, congressmen, and socialites. Good age mix.

To Break In: "We accept any media, any artist — complete unknowns. We're willing to work hard to back and establish the reputations of a few really fine artists and craftsmen. We *must* have biographies; clippings; show notices; slides; or actual samples submitted to us by mail first. *Must* include SASE or package for anything to be returned. Will consider allowing craftspeople to work and demonstrate in our gallery; good exposure."

THE CORCORAN SHOP, The Corcoran Gallery of Art, 17th St., and New York Ave. NW, Washington DC 20006. (202)638-3211. Adminstrator: Ellen Wright. Museum gift shop. Represents 1-2 craftworkers. Price range: 80c-$125; bestsellers: 80c-$20. Buys outright. Retail price set by joint agreement. Reports in 1 week. Work may be shipped or hand-delivered. Dealer pays return shipping and insurance for exhibited work.

Acceptable Work: Considers jewelry; soft sculpture; and hand-printed notecards. Fine one-of-a-kind and handmade production-line items; decorative only.

Profile: "Our gift items are contemporary and well-designed; we have a total absence of folk crafts or ethnic art. Customers are age 30 or older and interested in art; middle-class or above." Best selling time: Christmas.

CRAFTSMEN OF CHELSEA COURT, 1311 Connecticut Ave. NW, Washington DC 20036. Director: Maxine Brown. Craft shop. Estab. 1970. Represents 750 craftworkers. Price range: $10-2,500; bestsellers: under $35-150. Buys outright; 40% commission. Gallery sets retail price. Requires exclusive area representation. Reports in 2 weeks. Work may be shipped or hand-delivered. Dealer pays shipping to shop and insurance.

Acceptable Work: Considers ceramics; glass art; jewelry; metalsmithing; soft sculpture; wall hangings; weavings; and woodcrafting. Especially needs well designed and executed silver and gold jewelry; art glass; and unusual ceramics. Fine one-of-a-kind and handmade production-line items; utilitarian and/or decorative.

Profile: "Customers are 25-55; medium to upper income. We are in an area near art galleries and theaters and cater to residents of the metropolitan area." Heaviest wholesale buying time: April-September; best selling time: November-December, spring and early summer.

EARTHWORKS HEADSHOP, 1724 20th St. NW, Washington DC 20009. (202)332-4323. General Manager: Larry P. Maccubbin. Headshop. Estab. 1971. Represents 20-30 craftworkers. Price range: $2-300; bestsellers: $4-50. Buys outright. Retail price set by joint agreement. Reports in 2 weeks. Work may be shipped or hand-delivered. Dealer pays shipping to shop and insurance for exhibited work.

Acceptable Work: Considers candlemaking; ceramics; glass art; jewelry; leatherworking; metalsmithing; pottery; woodcrafting; and smoking accessories. All styles; utilitarian.

Profile: "We carry only items which are useful as accessories in the use of soft drugs, e.g. marijuana or cocaine. This includes pipes, waterpipes, stash boxes, tooting straws, silver spoons and the like. Customers average age is 21-35; average income is $10,000-25,000; government workers and professional people." Heaviest wholesale buying time: September-November; best selling time: November-December.

GALLERY 10 LTD., 1519 Connecticut Ave. NW, Washington DC 20036. (202)232-3326. Considers contemporary fine art in all media. Maximum size: 6x9'. Work must be ready to install.

Price range: $50-1,000. 40% commission. Retail price set by joint agreement. Query. Send slides or photos if in Eastern region. 4 week exposure.

LAMBDA RISING, 2012 S St. NW, Washington DC 20009. (202)462-6969. Manager: Rich McGinnis. Gay book and gift shop. Considers all fine art. "We will only accept work which reflects a gay (male or lesbian) theme or has been completed by a gay artist." Minimum price: $5; bestseller range: $5-80. Works on consignment; 25% commission. Artist sets retail price. Query with samples. SASE. Shop pays insurance on exhibited work. Work held until sold.

THE MIDNIGHT SUN, 1700 Pennsylvania Ave. NW, Washington DC 20006. (202)393-4769. President: A. Kranish. Gift shop and gallery. Estab. 1965. Represents 100-150 craftworkers. Price range: $2.50-150; bestsellers: $2.50-35. Buys outright. Gallery sets retail price. Reporting time varies. Work may be shipped or hand-delivered. Best selling time: Christmas and heaviest wholesale buying time: spring-summer.
Acceptable Work: Considers candlemaking; ceramics; glass art; jewelry; and pottery. One-of-a-kind and handmade production-line items; utilitarian only.

PRESERVATION SHOPS, National Trust for Historic Preservation, 740-748 Jackson Place NW, Washington DC 20006. Museum gift shop. Represents 10-20 craftworkers. Considers ceramics; clothing; dollmaking; glass art; jewelry; needlecrafts; pottery; quilting; metalsmithing; and woodcrafting. "Limited to traditional crafts that are appropriate to our museum shops." One-of-a-kind and handmade production-line items; utilitarian and/or decorative. Price range: $2-150; bestsellers: $2-25. Buys outright; retail price set by joint agreement. Reports in 2-4 weeks. Dealer pays all shipping.
Profile: "The majority of customers are middle class to upper class tourists interested in history, antiques, and the like. We also have a lot of school tours." Best selling time: Christmas and spring. Also publishes annual gift catalog.

SMITH-MASON GALLERY MUSEUM, 1207 Rhode Island Ave. NW, Washington DC 20005. (202)462-6323. Director: Helen S. Mason. Considers batik; ceramics; glass art; jewelry; metalsmithing; pottery; and sculpture. Specializes in contemporary art. Price range: $50-5,000, paintings/sculpture/prints: $50-1,000, prints. Works on consignment; 40% commission. Artist sets retail price. Query with samples or send slides or photos of work. SASE. Gallery pays insurance on exhibited work. 6 weeks maximum exposure.

West Virginia

ARABIA'S ART GALLERY, Walton Star Route, Box 1A, Spencer WV 25276. (304)927-2200. Contact: Philip V. Arabia. Gallery. Estab. 1969. Represents 20 craftworkers. Price range: $3-500; bestsellers: $10-20. Buys outright. Gallery sets retail price. Reports in 2 weeks. Work may be shipped or hand-delivered. Dealer pays insurance for exhibited work.
Acceptable Work: Considers batik; candlemaking; ceramics; dollmaking; glass art; jewelry; metalsmithing; needlecrafts; pottery; quilting; wall hangings; weavings; and woodcrafting. Fine, one-of-a-kind and handmade production-line items; utilitarian and/or decorative.
Profile: "Signs are made to give artists credit. Our customers are as varied as the local population. We have bank presidents and farmers; MD's and back-to-the-land enthusiasts." Heaviest wholesale buying time: fall; best selling time: Christmas and summer.

THE ART PALETTE, 1231 Ohio Ave., Box 274, Dunbar WV 25064. (304)768-3814. Contact: Lillie Dawson. Craft shop/gallery/art supplies shop. Estab. 1977. Represents 12 craftworkers. Price range: $2-125; bestsellers: $2-15. Works on consignment and buys outright; 20% commission. Craftworker sets retail price. Reports in 2 weeks. Work may be shipped or hand-delivered. Dealer pays insurance for exhibited work.
Acceptable Work: Considers batik; glass art; jewelry; leatherworking; metalsmithing; pottery; quilting; soft sculpture; tole painting; wall hangings; weavings; and woodcrafting. Primitive and fine craft pieces, utilitarian and/or decorative.
Profile: "We take local artist's work to hang, who might not otherwise have somewhere to hang their work. Our customers are all ages: school children to adults; basically artistically inclined; middle income to higher. Make an appointment before coming to the shop." Heaviest wholesale buying time: pre-Christmas; best selling time: fall.

CABIN CREEK QUILTS, Box 383, Cabin Creek WV 25035. (304)595-3928. Director: Mack Miles. Craft and quilt shop. Estab. 1970. Represents 100 West Virginia, low income craftworkers. Considers clothing; needlecrafts; quilting; and wall hangings. Fine, one-of-a-kind and handmade production-line items; utilitarian only. Price range: $2.50-600; bestsellers: $2.50-

300. Works on consignment; members only. 20% commission. Reports in 3 weeks. Work may be shipped or hand-delivered. Coop pays shipping and insurance.

Profile: "Work is rotated about once a month. Customers are all ages; interested in handmade items and the arts; and have higher income." Best selling and heaviest wholesale buying time: summer and fall.

CABIN CREEK QUILTS, 200 Broad St., Charleston WV 25301. (304)342-0326. See above.

COLLECTOR'S CORNER, HUNTINGTON GALLERIES, McCoy Rd., Park Hills, Huntington WV 25701. (304)529-2701. Manager: Betsy Broh or Carole McCullah. Museum gift shop. Estab. 1972. Represents 50 craftworkers. Price range: $2-300; bestsellers; $5-50. Works on consignment and buys outright; 33⅓% commission. Retail price set by joint agreement. Reports in 1 month. Work may be shipped or hand-delivered. Dealer pays insurance for exhibited work. Heaviest wholesale buying time: fall; best selling time: Christmas.

Acceptable Work: Considers ceramics; glass art; jewelry; leatherworking; needlecrafts; pottery; wall hangings; weavings; and woodcrafting. Fine one-of-a-kind pieces; utilitarian and/or decorative.

FAITH WORKSHOP, 1418 McCorkle Ave., Charleston, WV 25304. (304)744-4677. Contact: Mitchell Balaban. Craft shop/workshop/retailer. Estab. 1977. Price range: 39c-$25. Works on consignment; 20% commission. Craftworker sets retail price. Reports in 1 week. Work may be shipped or hand-delivered. Dealer pays insurance for exhibited work. Best selling time: Christmas.

Acceptable Work: Considers batik; candlemaking; ceramics; clothing; decoupage; dollmaking; leatherworking; needlecrafts; pottery; quilting; and woodcrafting. All styles: utilitarian and/or decorative.

MOUNTAIN CRAFT SHOP, American Ridge Rd., Rt. 1, New Martinsville WV 26155. (304)455-3570. Contact: Dick Schnacke. Craft shop. Estab. 1965. Represents 60 craftworkers from West Virginia. Price range: 60c-$39; bestsellers: $1.50-6.75. Buys outright. Retail price set by joint agreement. Reports in 1 week. Work may be shipped or hand-delivered.

Acceptable Work: Considers dollmaking; folk toys; games; puzzles; and doll furniture. Primitive and handmade production-line items; utilitarian only.

Profile: "We handle solely folk toys, dolls, games, etc. Our items appeal to all ages, interests and income levels." Best selling time: summer-fall.

THE OLD MILL, Mountain Industries, Inc., Harman WV 26270. Manager: Mary Beth Lind. Craft shop. Estab. 1973. Represents 50 West Virginia traditional craftworkers. Price range: $1-200; bestsellers: $1-20. Works on consignment; 33% commission. Retail price set by joint agreement. Hand-delivered work OK.

Acceptable Work: Considers candlemaking; ceramics; dollmaking; leatherworking; needlecrafts; pottery; quilting; wall hangings; weavings; and woodcrafting. Especially needs any authentic traditional pieces: quilts, toys and handspun yarns. Primitive utilitarian pieces only.

Profile: "Our shop is an old grist mill, still operating. The first floor is the water-powered mill works and mill museum. The second floor is display and demonstration area for traditional handcrafts authentic to West Virginia 50 or more years ago. Customers are tourists and families with a wide range of incomes." Heaviest wholesale buying time: spring; best selling time: summer.

PRICKETTS FORT MEMORIAL FOUNDATION, INC., Pricketts Fort State Park, Rt. 3, Fairmont WV 26554. (304)363-3030. Curator: Ron Chrislip. Museum gift shop. Estab. 1975. Represents 15 craftworkers. Buys outright. Retail price set by joint agreement. Requires some exclusive area representation. Reports in 3 weeks. Work may be shipped or hand-delivered. Dealer pays shipping to shop.

Acceptable Work: Considers dollmaking; leatherworking; metalsmithing; pottery; quilting; and woodcrafting. High quality 18th and 19th century reproductions only. Primitive and finished pieces; utilitarian and/or decorative.

Profile: "This is not a souvenir shop. We want only approved 18th and 19th century repros." Heaviest wholesale buying time: spring and fall; best selling time: summer and winter.

THE SERENDIPITY ARTS AND CRAFTS SHOP, E. German St., Shepherdstown WV 25443. Contact: Helen Myers Seeley. Craft shop. Estab. 1971. Represents 3 craftworkers. Price range: 25c-$69.95; bestsellers: $1-5. Works on consignment and buys outright; 40% commission.

Retail price set by joint agreement. Reports in 4 weeks. Work may be hand-delivered. Dealer pays insurance for exhibited work.
Acceptable Work: Considers decoupage; dollmaking; jewelry; needlecrafts; wallhangings; weavings; macrame; and assemblage. Primitive and fine one-of-a-kind pieces; utilitarian and/or decorative. Especially needs "Ram's Head" buttons for college uniforms, etc.
Profile: "I get college students, art majors, scout leaders, tourists, county extension homemakers and just good out and out crafters." Heaviest wholesale buying time: Christmas; best selling time: Christmas, Easter, and tourist season (spring-late fall).

THE SHOP, Dept. of Culture and History, Cultural Center, Capitol Complex, Charleston WV 25305. (304)348-0220. Marketing Coordinator: Rebecca Stelling Winkles. Craft shop. Estab. 1976. Represents 100 West Virginia craftworkers. Price range: 50c-$1,500; bestsellers: 50c-$60. Buys outright. Retail price set by joint agreement. Reports in 2 weeks. Work may be shipped or hand-delivered. Dealer pays shipping and insurance.
Acceptable Work: Considers batik; candlemaking; ceramics; clothing; dollmaking; glass art; jewelry; leatherworking; metalsmithing; needlecrafts; pottery; quilting; soft sculpture; toys; wall hangings; weavings; and woodcrafting. Fine one-of-a-kind and handmade production-line items; utilitarian and/or decorative.

SUNRISE SHOPS, 755 Myrtle Rd., Charleston WV 25314. (304)344-8035. Manager: Alma M. McMillan. Museum gallery and gift shop. Estab. 1974. Represents 10 craftworkers. Price range: $2-500; bestsellers: $2-15. Works on consignment and buys outright; 33⅓% commission. Craftworker sets retail price. Requires exclusive area representation. Reports in 4 weeks. Work may be shipped or hand-delivered. Dealer pays return shipping and insurance for exhibited work.
Acceptable Work: Considers batik; ceramics; glass art; jewelry; metalsmithing; pottery; wall hangings; small sculptures; and weavings. Especially needs jewelry; glass and original design Christmas ornaments. Primitive and fine one-of-a-kind pieces; utilitarian and/or decorative.
Profile: "A copy of items received with identifying number used in inventory along with an agreement of sales and display terms is sent to the craftsman. We emphasize crafts from out of state. Customers are children as well as adults; all walks of life are represented." Heaviest wholesale buying time: July-August; best selling time: October-December and May-June.

WOOD 'N THREAD, 1418 McCorkle Ave. SE, Charleston WV 25304. (304)744-4677. Contact: Mitch Balaban. Craft shop. Estab. 1977. Represents 50 craftworkers. Price range: 50c-$325; bestsellers: $1.94-18. Works on consignment; 20% commission. Retail price set by joint agreement. Reports in 1 week. Work may be hand-delivered or shipped. Dealer pays insurance for exhibited work.
Acceptable Work: Considers all crafts except metalsmithing; soft sculpture; and tole painting. All styles; utilitarian and/or decorative.
Profile: Displays are constantly rotated. "We are operated by a workshop for retarded adults and include items produced by clients in our workshop, workshops around the state and local craftpersons." Best selling time: Christmas.

YESTERYEAR TOY COMPANY, INC., Box 4383, Charleston WV 25304. (304)744-2162. President: Terence Barron. Craft and gift shop/manufacturer. Estab. 1971. Represents 50 craftworkers. Price range: 50c-$500; bestsellers: $2-15. Works on consignment and buys outright; 50% commission. Shop sets retail price. Reports in 1 week. Work may be shipped or hand-delivered. Dealer pays return shipping and insurance for exhibited work. "Customers are mostly quite affluent." Best selling time: spring and late fall.
Acceptable Work: Considers all crafts; primarily wooden toys 1875-1900. All styles; utilitarian and/or decorative.

Wisconsin

THE ART BARN, Rt. 1, Country Lane, Waupaca WI 54981. (715)258-2082. Gallery. Estab. 1967. Represents 125 craftworkers. Price range: 35c-$200; bestsellers: $10-90. Works on consignment; 30% commission. Retail price set by joint agreement. Requires exclusive area representation. Reports in 2 weeks. Work may be shipped or hand-delivered.
Acceptable Work: Considers batik; candlemaking; ceramics; clothing; decoupage; dollmaking; glass art; jewelry; leatherworking; metalsmithing; needlecrafts; pottery; quilting; soft sculpture; tole painting; wall hangings; weavings; woodcrafting; rosemaling; tree ornaments; cone art (wreaths); dried flower arrangements; and puppets. All styles; utilitarian and/or decorative.
Profile: "Work is displayed in a rustic setting, artists and crafters grouped — a 'real barn' atmosphere." Displays work 90 days. Heaviest wholesale buying time: spring; best selling time: summer.

ART CENTER, Prospect Mall, 2233 N. Prospect Ave., Milwaukee WI 53202. (414)271-9600. Contact: Peter J. Kondos. Considers all crafts. Maximum size: standard framing. Buys outright and on consignment. Specializes in traditional art. Minimum price: $5+. Retail price set by gallery. Requires exclusive area representation. Query first with slides and/or photos. SASE.

ART CRATE, INC., 334 S. Knowles Ave., New Richmond WI 54071. (715)246-6861. Contact: Bette Buell. Gallery. Estab. 1972. Represents 230 craftworkers. Price range: $3-600; bestsellers: $50-75. Works on consignment and buys jewelry outright; 40% commission. Craftworker sets retail price. Reports in 2 weeks. Work may be shipped or hand-delivered. Dealer pays insurance for exhibited work.
Acceptable Work: Considers batik; candelmaking; ceramics; glass art; jewelry; leatherworking; metalsmithing; pottery; wall hangings; and weavings. Fine one-of-a-kind pieces; utilitarian and/or decorative.
Profile: "Work is displayed until written request is sent to have artist remove it. Jewelry is displayed as long as it is a current and desirable design." Heaviest wholesale buying time: fall; best selling time: Christmas and summer.
To Break In: "We only work with individual craftsmen, not through agents. A preference is for full-time artists and craftsmen for good quality work and salable items."

ART INDEPENDENT GALLERY, 706 Main St., Lake Geneva WI 53147. (414)248-3612. Contact: Richard or Mary Jane Herr. Craft shop/gallery. Estab. 1968. Represents 270 craftworkers. Price range: $3-3,000; bestsellers: $300 maximum. Works on consignment; 40% commission. Retail price set by joint agreement. Reports in 2 weeks. Work may be shipped or hand-delivered.
Acceptable Work: Considers batik; ceramics; clothing; glass art; jewelry; leatherworking; metalsmithing; needlecrafts; sculpture; wall hangings; weavings; and woodcrafting. Fine one-of-a-kind pieces; utilitarian and/or decorative.

ARTISTS ACCESS LIBRARY, 111 King St., Madison WI 53703. (608)257-6969. Contact: Program Coordinator. Gallery/artists' referral service. Estab. 1974. Considers batik; ceramics; glass art; jewelry; leatherworking; metalsmithing; needlecrafts; pottery; soft sculpture; tole painting; wall hangings; weavings; and woodcrafting. All styles; utilitarian and/or decorative. "The gallery space is a subsidiary portion of the referral concept of the Library. AAL gets 15% commission of pieces bought as result of show. AAL membership is $15. If artist wants to use show space it's $5/week. We prefer artist to hang own show. Usual duration of show is 2 weeks." Craftworker sets retail price.
Profile: "The Library has 24x8 wall space for actual hanging of work. There is also a slide projector for pictures of work not necessarily on exhibit. Slides and video of work are put on permanent file. Plans for exposure through use of public access TV are in near future."

ARTSPACE, LTD., 790 N. Jefferson St., Milwaukee WI 53202. (414)276-8989. Contact: Suzanne Berland. Craft shop/gallery. Estab. 1975. Represents 75 craftworkers. Price range: $2.50-500; bestsellers: $5-200. Works on consignment and buys outright; 40% commission. Craftworker sets retail price. Requires exclusive area representation. Reports in 2 weeks. Work may be shipped or hand-delivered if prearranged. Dealer pays insurance for exhibited work.
Acceptable Work: Considers batik; ceramics; dollmaking; glass art; needlecrafts; pottery; quilting; soft sculpture; wall hangings; weavings; and woodcrafting. Especially needs functional ceramics and well-designed, functional flameware. Fine, one-of-a-kind and handmade production-line items; utilitarian and/or decorative.
Profile: "Displays are reviewed every week; changed at regular intervals." Heaviest wholesale buying time: summer; best selling time: October-December.

ARTWORKS, INC., 1520 Main St., Marinette WI 54143. (715)732-0379. Director: Joyce Murphy. Gallery. Estab. 1973. Represents 50 member craftworkers. Price range: 75c-$350; bestsellers: 75c-$12. Works on consignment; 20% commission. Craftworker sets retail price. Reports in 1 week.
Acceptable Work: Considers batik; candlemaking; ceramics; clothing; dollmaking; glass art; jewelry; needlecrafts; pottery; quilting; wall hangings; weavings; and woodcrafting. One-of-a-kind pieces; utilitarian and/or decorative.

THE BERGSTROM MUSEUM SHOP, Bergstrom Art Center, 165 N. Park Ave., Neenah WI 54956. (414)722-3348. Contact: Manager. Craft shop/gallery/rental gallery. Estab. 1959. Represents 75 artists and craftworkers. Price range: $2-800; bestsellers: $7.50-150. Works on consignment and buys outright; 25% commission. Craftworker sets retail price. Reports in 2

weeks. Work may be shipped or hand-delivered. Dealer pays insurance for exhibited work.
Acceptable Work: Considers batik; ceramics; glass art; jewelry; metalsmithing; pottery; soft sculpture; wall hangings; weavings; and woodcrafting. Especially needs glass inventory and high quality Christmas items. Fine one-of-a-kind pieces; utilitarian and/or decorative.
Profile: "Since the Bergstrom has one of the foremost collections of paperweights (and Germanic glass), we stress glass items; also Wisconsin artists." Displays work 6 months. Heaviest wholesale buying time: prior to December holidays and summer.

CABIN CRAFT SHOPPES, On the Bay, Ephraim WI 54211. (414)854-2916. Contact: June or Marty Matoushek. Craft and gift shop. Estab. 1933. Price range: $2.50-1,000; bestsellers: $2.50-50. Buys outright. Gallery sets retail price. Requires exclusive area representation. Work may be shipped or hand-delivered. Dealer pays shipping to shop and insurance for exhibited work.
Acceptable Work: Considers ceramics; clothing; jewelry; leatherworking; metalsmithing; pottery; wall hangings; weavings; and woodcrafting. Fine, one-of-a-kind and handmade production-line items; utilitarian and/or decorative.
Profile: "We intermingle craftwork with production/manufactured merchandise." Heaviest wholesale buying time: spring; best selling time: summer-fall.

THE CHANGING SCENE, 418 E. Silver Spring Dr., Milwaukee WI 53217. (414)964-8877. President: Betty Burns. Craft shop/gallery/gift shop. Estab. 1968. Represents 300 craftworkers. Price range: $1-200; bestsellers: $5-50. Works on consignment and buys outright; 50-60% commission. Retail price set by joint agreement. Prefers exclusive area representation. Reports in 2 weeks. Dealer pays all shipping and insurance for exhibited work.
Acceptable Work: Considers candlemaking; ceramics; clothing; decoupage; dollmaking; glass art; jewelry; leatherworking; metalsmithing; needlecrafts; pottery; quilting; soft sculpture; tole painting; wall hangings; weavings; and woodcrafting. All styles; utilitarian and/or decorative.
Profile: "We are a well established business in a good location. Our crafts show imagination and creativity." Heaviest wholesale buying time: August-December; best selling time: Thanksgiving-Christmas.

COMMUNITY CRAFT AND ART CO-OP, INC., 118 N. Carroll, Madison WI 53701. Manager: Sharon Friedland. Craft shop. Estab. 1971. Represents 30 member craftworkers. Price range: 75c-$275; bestsellers: $5-30. Works on consignment; 25% commission. Craftworker sets retail price. Reports in 1-2 weeks. Hand-delivered work OK.
Acceptable Work: Considers batik; candlemaking; jewelry; leatherworking; pottery; wall hangings; weavings; and woodcrafting. Fine one-of-a-kind pieces; utilitarian and/or decorative.
Profile: Craftworker "must be member of coop; must work in store 8 hours per month. Membership fee is $10. All profits returned to member exhibitors." Displays work 12 months. Best selling and heaviest wholesale buying time: Christmas.

COUNTRY CRAFTS, Rt. 2, Plymouth WI 53073. (414)893-8095. Partner: Rebecca Summers. Gift shop/tea room. Estab. 1973. Represents 300 craftworkers. Price range: 50c-$500; bestsellers: 50c-$75. Works on consignment and buys outright; 25% commission. Retail price set ·by joint agreement. Requires exclusive area representation. Reports in 1 week. Work may be shipped or hand-delivered. Dealer pays return shipping.
Acceptable Work: Considers all crafts except clothing. Primitive and fine one-of-a-kind pieces; utilitarian and/or decorative. Especially needs hand-blown glass.
Profile: "Some artists' work is displayed as a group; others are arranged with other works to enhance interest and use of item. We are located in a large barn in the country. Customers are all ages; 50% are women over 50; average to upper income bracket." Heaviest wholesale buying time: January-May; best selling time: May 1-October 24.

CREATIVE ART STUDIO, 104 Main St., Weyauwega WI 54983. (414)867-3557. Artist in residence: Barbara Danthine Radtke. Craft shop/studio. Estab. 1969. Represents 10 craftworkers. Price range: $1-500. Works on consignment and buys outright; 20% commission. Retail price set by joint agreement. Requires exclusive area representation. Reports in 2 weeks. Work may be shipped or hand-delivered. Dealer pays insurance for exhibited work.
Acceptable Work: Considers batik; candlemaking; ceramics; dollmaking; glass art; jewelry; leatherworking; pottery; wall hangings; and weavings. Fine, one-of-a-kind and handmade production-line items; utilitarian and/or decorative.
Profile: "We have 4 display rooms along with 2 large display windows; our displays change constantly. We have our studio with the shop so visitors can see what we are making and we have lots of tour groups visit us." Best selling and heaviest wholesale buying time: spring-fall.

ELVEHJEM ART CENTER, Museum Shop, 800 University Ave., Madison WI 53706 (608)263-2246. Manager: Kathy Parks. Museum gift shop. Estab. 1970. Represents 20 craftworkers. Considers batik; ceramics; and jewelry. All styles; utilitarian and/or decorative. Price range: $5-75; bestsellers: $5-15. Buys outright. Retail price set by joint agreement. Reports in 2 weeks. Work may be hand-delivered. Dealer pays shipping and insurance for exhibited work. **Profile:** "We are located on the University of Wisconsin campus and near the center of downtown. Customers are primarily UW students and staff." Best selling and heaviest wholesale buying time: fall.

FIRST NATIONAL BANK, Box 30, Monroe WI 53566. President: C.E. Blue. Bank. Estab. 1856. Represents 4 craftworkers. Considers decoupage; wall hangings; and weavings. Primitive and fine pieces; utilitarian and/or decorative. Price range: $10-500; bestsellers: $10-100. Displays work only. No commission. Craftworker sets retail price. Reports in 2 weeks. Work may be hand-delivered. "Schedule an interview at the displayer's best time so as not to disrupt the daily routine." Best selling time: spring and summer. Displays work 30-90 days.

THE HAYLOFT, 760 S. Lakeshore Dr., Lake Geneva WI 53147. (414)248-8952. Manager: Laura Braden. Craft, gift and antiques shop. Estab. 1976. Represents 80 craftworkers. Price range: $1-800; bestsellers: $2-75. Works on consignment and buys outright; 33⅓% commission. Retail price set by joint agreement. Reports in 4 weeks. Work may be shipped or hand-delivered. Dealer pays insurance for exhibited work.
Acceptable Work: Considers batik; ceramics; dollmaking; jewelry; leatherworking; metalsmithing; needlecrafts; pottery; quilting; soft sculpture; tole painting; wall hangings; weavings; and woodcrafting. Especially needs glass blowing. Fine one-of-a-kind pieces; utilitarian and/or decorative.
Profile: "All consignors have been pleased with the way their work is displayed. If they are not, we take suggestions and are happy to make changes. The building is an old stable and carriage house. It was built in 1900. Each horse stall is set up as an individual room with antiques. Crafts are displayed in the carriage room. Most customers have a high income." Best selling time: summer.

JOHN MICHAEL KOHLER ARTS CENTER, 608 New York Ave., Sheboygan WI 53081. (414)458-6144. Director: Ruth Kohler. Museum sales gallery. Estab. 1967. Represents 60-85 craftworkers. Price range: $3-500; bestsellers: $5-100. Works on consignment and buys outright; 33⅓% commission. Retail price set by joint agreement. Requires exclusive area representation. Reports in 4 weeks. Work may be shipped or hand-delivered. Dealer pays shipping and insurance.
Acceptable Work: Considers ceramics; glass art; jewelry; metalsmithing; pottery; soft sculpture; wall hangings; weavings; and wood. Especially needs glass; pillows and other fiber work; jewelry; and ceramics and functional pottery. Fine, one-of-a-kind and handmade production-line items; utilitarian and/or decorative.
Profile: "Each work is displayed as an individual art object in an elegant gallery." Heaviest wholesale buying time: February and June-October; best selling time: October-December.

PETER J. KONDOS ART GALLERIES, 700 N. Water, Milwaukee WI 53202. (414)271-8000. Contact: Peter Kondos. Considers sculpture. Maximum height: 6'. Art must be offered for sale. Buys outright or on consignment; negotiates commission. Price range: $5-2,000; bestsellers: $5-250. Gallery sets retail price. Requires exclusive area representation. Displays work 2 weeks-1 month. Query with slides or photos of work. SASE.

THE LOOMS, Far End, Shake Rag St., Mineral Point WI 53566. (608)987-2277. Contact: Ken Colwell. Craft shop/textile museum. Estab. 1970. Represents 2-3 craftworkers. Considers wall hangings and weavings. Primitive and fine one-of-a-kind pieces; utilitarian and/or decorative. Price range: 50c-$250; bestsellers: $2.50-100. Works on consignment; 20% commission. Buys locally only; no mailing or shipping. Craftworker sets retail price. Reports in 1-2 weeks.

MADISON ART CENTER, INC., 720 E. Gorham St., Madison WI 53703. (608)257-0158. Contact: Jane Liska. Write with slides or photos. Photos must be fully insured and representative of artist's work. Biographical information also helpful. Works on 10% commission. Insurance and all transportation handled by gallery.

MARATHON COUNTY HISTORICAL SOCIETY, 403 McIndoe St., Wausau WI 54401. (715)848-6143. Director: Edward T. Schoenberger. Museum gallery. Estab. 1952. Considers batik; ceramics; jewelry; metalsmithing; soft sculpture; wall hangings; and weavings. Primitive and fine pieces. Exhibitions only. Craftworker sets retail price. Reports in 2 weeks. Work may be shipped or hand-delivered. Museum pays insurance.

Profile: "All possible care is given to items on display; small items are displayed in cases that are locked. The gallery of the museum is located in the home of a former lumber baron of Wausau."

The Kiva: Artisan's Gallery, Scarsdale, New York, is looking for innovative, museum-quality crafts in any media, such as this ceramic "Magical Cart" by Elisa D'Arrigo. Bestsellers at the gallery range in price from $80-300.

MATHIS GALLERY, 735 Center, Racine WI 53403. (414)637-1111. Contact: Emile Mathis. Gallery. Estab. 1972. Represents craftworkers whose work relates to ethnic origins. Price range: $20-100. Works on consignment and buys outright; 40% commission. Retail price set by joint agreement. Rental gallery fee: cost of installation and opening, if any, plus percentage of sales. Reports in 4 weeks. Work may be shipped or hand-delivered. Dealer pays insurance for exhibited work.

Acceptable Work: Considers glass art; quilting; wall hangings; and weavings. Primitive and fine one-of-a-kind pieces; utilitarian and/or decorative.

Profile: "Customers are 25 and up; interested in house decorating; with incomes of $30,000 and up." Displays work 4-8 weeks. Heaviest wholesale buying time: spring and late summer; best selling time: late spring and pre-Christmas.

MILWAUKEE ART CENTER WISCONSIN GALLERY, 750 N. Lincoln Memorial Dr., Milwaukee WI 53202. (414)271-9508. Contact: Manager. Considers experimental art and sculpture. Maximum size: 4x4'. 30% commission. Artist sets price. Prices from $50-1,000. Open to Wisconsin artists. Call for appointments. 3,000 members notified of spring and fall collections and special openings.

MINI GALLERY, Wustum Museum of Fine Arts, Racine WI 53404. (414)636-9177. Contact: Director. Gift shop/rental gallery. Estab. 1971. Represents 8-15 craftworkers. Size of flat work limited to 3x4'; 3D work to 12x24x12". Price range: 50c-$30; bestsellers: $1-10. Works on consignment; 30% commission. Craftworker sets retail price. Reports in 2 weeks. Work may be shipped or hand-delivered. Dealer pays insurance. Best selling time: summer.

Acceptabe Work: Considers ceramics; glass art; jewelry; needlecrafts; pottery; soft sculpture; wall hangings; weavings; and woodcrafting. All styles; utilitarian and/or decorative.

NEW VISIONS GALLERY, INC., 1000 N. Oak Ave., Marshfield WI 54449. (715)387-5562. Director: Renee K. River. Gallery. Estab. 1975. Represents 1-6 craftworkers. Considers all crafts except candlemaking; decoupage; and tole painting. All styles; utilitarian and/or decorative. Price range: $5-800; bestsellers: under $35. Works on consignment; 20% commission. Retail price set by joint agreement. Reports in 2 weeks. Work may be shipped or hand-delivered. Dealer pays return shipping and insurance for exhibited work.
Profile: "The item is unpacked, checked for damage, a report is made. It is stored until displayed, either in a case or out, dependent on the size. Some pieces require additional security such as either wiring down or tape on the bottom to deter movement. We are located in the main entrance of the fifth largest clinic in the United States." Displays work 4-6 weeks.

THE OPEN DOOR, LTD., 118 W. Verona, Verona WI 53593. (608)845-6662. Contact: Hans or Diane Hofmann. Gallery. Estab. 1976. Represents 64 craftworkers. Considers all crafts. Fine one-of-a-kind pieces; utilitarian and/or decorative. Price range: $2-800. Works on consignment; 35-40% commission. Retail price set by joint agreement. Requires exclusive area representation. Reports in 2-4 weeks. Work may be shipped or hand-delivered. Dealer pays return shipping and insurance for exhibited work.
Profile: "Most of my artists attend art fairs. Between us, we decide if an item has sat too long, then it goes to the fairs." Best selling time: summer and Christmas.

THE PIK PLACE, 710 Beech St., West Bend WI 53095. (414)338-2444. Contact: Bette Fehring. Craft shop. Estab. 1976. Represents 100 craftworkers. Price range: $1.25-45; bestsellers: $2.25-10. Works on consignment; 30% commission. Retail price set by joint agreement. Requires exclusive area representation. Reports in 4 weeks. Work may be shipped or hand-delivered with prior approval. Dealer pays insurance for exhibited work.
Acceptable Work: Considers ceramics; decoupage; glass art; tole painting; wall hangings; weavings; macrame; patchwork; and rosemaling. Utilitarian and/or decorative. Especially needs some new ideas from a different part of the country.
Profile: "We have an old house and display items as they would appear in a home. We get customers from grade school to middle age on up. I would judge most of our customers to be in the $10,000-15,000 income bracket." Displays work 4-6 weeks. Best selling time: September-December.

RONBACH SHOP, Box 312, Boulder Junction WI 54512. (715)385-2205. Contact: Ellen Christgau. Gift shop. Estab. 1975. Represents 35 craftworkers. Price range: 50c-$60; bestsellers: $2-30. Buys outright. Requires exclusive area representation. Reports in 2 weeks. Work may be shipped or hand-delivered. Dealer pays return shipping and insurance for submitted work.
Acceptable Work: Considers glass art; jewelry; leatherworking; metalsmithing; tole painting; woodcrafting; Christmas ornaments. Especially needs original, moderately-priced, shippable articles made of natural materials. Primitive and handmade production-line items; utilitarian and/or decorative.
Profile: "All items are very visible. We use a background of barnwood walls and display units. We cannot handle very large items. We feature crafts made of natural materials. Our customers are tourists; the majority are women." Heaviest wholesale buying time: January-May; best selling time: May 15-October 15.

THE STATE HISTORICAL SOCIETY OF WISCONSIN, 816 State St., Madison WI 53706. (608)262-3271. Contact: Beth E. Witz. Museum gift shop. Estab. 1955. Represents 5-6 craftworkers. Price range: $1.25-50; bestsellers: 50c-$35. Works on consignment and buys outright; commission varies. Retail price set by joint agreement. Reports in 3 weeks. Work may be shipped or hand-delivered. Dealer pays shipping and insurance for exhibited work.
Acceptable Work: Considers candlemaking; ceramics; glass art; jewelry; metalsmithing; needlecrafts; pottery; woodcrafting; and plant portraits. Fine, one-of-a-kind and handmade production-line items; utilitarian and/or decorative.
Profile: "Our display area is limited; we try to remain as historical and within Wisconsin or at least mid-West in scope as possible. Displays work 60 days. Heaviest wholesale buying time: spring and Christmas; best selling time: spring.

TWELMEYER GALLERIES, 6415 W. North Ave., Wauwatosa WI 53213. (414)771-4114. Director: Linda A. Twelmeyer. Gallery. Estab. 1976. Represents 1 craftworker "but would like to increase." Price range: $10-1,000; bestsellers: $10-200. Works on consignment; 40% commission. Retail price set by joint agreement. Reports in 1 week. Work may be shipped or hand-delivered. Dealer pays return shipping (if work was solicited).

Acceptable Work: Considers glass art; quilting; and woodcrafting. Especially needs fine glass in all price ranges: blown glass, not stained glass. Needs paper weights, vases and bibelot. Primitive and fine one-of-a-kind pieces; utilitarian and/or decorative.

Profile: "Work is shown in display cases (glassed) or on table tops (depending on fragility) or on wall. We usually show work at least 1 month in main gallery, then rotate on/off prime area display. Our customers range from young single and married adults just starting to collect on a low budget, to established wealthy and serious collectors."

WEE LITTLES SHOPPE, W64 N713 Washington Ave., Cedarburg WI 53012. (414)377-6170. Contact: Doris Casey. Miniatures and dolls. Estab. 1972. Represents 30 craftworkers. All styles; decorative only. Price range: 10c-$900; bestsellers: 50c-$200. Works on consignment and buys outright; 30% commission. Shop sets retail price. Requires exclusive area representation. Reports up to 4 weeks. Dealer pays insurance for exhibited work.

Acceptable Work: Considers all crafts in miniature. "Special need for hand-crafted miniature furniture scaled 1"-1', especially Victorian and other period furniture. Regular size dolls; dollhouse dolls; and clothing for dollhouse dolls are in demand."

Profile: "This is a hobby for all ages but we cater to the adult collector in the middle to upper income bracket."

THE WHIFFERDILL, Rt. 1, Trempealeau WI 54661. (608)534-6271. Contact: Jeanette Sasgen. Craft and gift shop. Estab. 1975. Represents 50-75 craftworkers. Price range: $1.50-600; bestsellers: $5-150. Works on consignment; 25% commission. Craftworker sets retail price. Requires exclusive area representation. Reports in 1 week. Work may be shipped or hand-delivered. Dealer pays insurance for exhibited work.

Acceptable Work: Considers batik; candlemaking; ceramics; decoupage; dollmaking; glass art; jewelry; leatherworking; metalsmithing; pottery; tole painting; wall hangings; weavings; and woodcrafting. Primitive and fine one-of-a-kind pieces; utilitarian and/or decorative.

Profile: "We are in a rural location near a well-known supper club and at the entrance to a state park. Our customers are generally more affluent; 30-50 years old, who appreciate handcrafted items. Displays work 4-6 months. Best selling time: April-December.

Wyoming

THE BLUE DUCK, 119 Ivinson, Laramie WY 82070. Contact: Bill or Joleen Arthur. Gallery. Estab. 1977. Represents 40 craftworkers. Price range: $1.50-250; bestsellers: $3-20. Works on consignment and buys outright; 40% commission. Reports in 2 weeks. Work may be shipped or hand-delivered. Dealer pays return shipping and insurance for exhibited work. Best selling and heaviest wholesale buying time: fall.

Acceptable Work: Considers batik; dollmaking; glass art; jewelry; pottery; quilting; soft sculpture; wall hangings; weavings; and woodcrafting. Especially needs soft sculpture and toys. Fine one-of-a-kind and handmade production-line items; utilitarian and/or decorative.

THE CEDAR CHEST, 1401 W. Spruce, Rawlins WY 82301. (307)324-7737. Contact: Della M. Vivian. Estab. 1976. Represents 6 craftworkers. Price range: $5-300; bestsellers: $5-50. Works on consignment and buys outright; 25% commission. Retail price set by joint agreement. Requires exclusive area representation. Reports in 4 weeks. Work may be hand-delivered. Dealer pays insurance for exhibited work.

Acceptable Work: Considers batik; ceramics; dollmaking; jewelry; pottery; soft sculpture; and woodcrafting. Fine one-of-a-kind and handmade production-line items; utilitarian and/or decorative.

Profile: "Pictures are displayed on easels and gallery wall; batiks on wall dowels or over furniture as merchandising drape; dolls, etc. on ladder." Best selling and heaviest wholesale buying time: summer and Christmas season.

GALLERY THREE TWENTY THREE, INC., 323 S. David, Casper WY 82601. (307)234-8158. Contact: Linda Marion. Estab. 1972. Represents 60 craftworkers. Considers ceramics; leatherworking; pottery; wall hangings; weavings; and woodcrafting. Especially needs jewelry, fiber arts; baskets; stained glass; and handcrafted furniture. Finished one-of-a-kind and handmade production-line items; utilitarian and/or decorative. Price range: $1.50-1,000; bestsellers: $5-100. Will buy outright but prefers consignment; 33⅓% commission. Craftworker sets retail price. Write or query with transparencies or photos. Reports in 2 weeks. Dealer pays shipping from shop and insurance for exhibited work.

Profile: Items displayed 6 months. Heaviest wholesale buying time: November-December. Customers are young singles and marrieds with moderate incomes and older couples with large incomes.

GRAND TETON LODGE CO., Box 250, Moran WY 83013. (307)543-2811. Merchandise Manager: David M. Ware. Craft shop/gallery/gift shop. Estab. 1955. Represents 50 craftworkers. Price range: $2-200; bestsellers: $3-25. Buys outright. Requires exclusive area representation. Reports in 4 weeks. Work may be shipped or hand-delivered. Dealer pays shipping to shop. Heaviest wholesale buying time: late winter and spring; best selling time: summer.
Acceptable Work: Considers candlemaking; ceramics; clothing; jewelry; leatherworking; metalsmithing; pottery; soft sculpture; wall hangings; weavings; and woodcrafting. Fine handmade production-line items; utilitarian and/or decorative.

HAPPY PEASANT GALLERY, Box 1116, Jackson Hole WY 83001. (307)733-3792. Contact: Keith Fay. Gallery/gift shop. Estab. 1964. Represents 12 craftworkers. Price range: $5-500; bestsellers: $5-25. Gallery sets retail price. Requires exclusive area representation. Reports in 2 weeks. Work may be shipped or hand-delivered. Dealer pays return shipping and insurance for exhibited work. "Customers have medium to better than average income." Best selling time: summer.
Acceptable Work: Considers glass art; jewelry; pottery; wall hangings; weavings; and woodcrafting. Primitive and fine one-of-a-kind pieces; utilitarian and/or decorative.

LIBERTY GIFTS, 1005 Dewar Dr., Rock Springs WY 82901. (307)382-9829. Contact: Miss Bruna. Gift shop. Estab. 1974. Represents 1 craftworker. Price range: open. Works on consignment; 20% commission. Craftworker sets retail price. Requires exclusive area representation. Reports in 4 weeks. Work may be shipped or hand-delivered. Displays work 3 months. Best selling time: Christmas.
Acceptable Work: Considers batik; decoupage; jewelry; pottery; tole painting; wall hangings; and weavings. Primitive and fine one-of-a-kind items; decorative only.

PINK CORRAL GIFT SHOP, 49 W. Broadway, Box 962, Jackson WY 83001. (307)733-4667. Contact: Rollie W. Pettit. Craft shop/gallery/gift shop. Estab. 1971. Represents 12-15 craftworkers. Price range: $50-1,000; bestsellers: $50-400. Buys outright. Retail price set by joint agreement. Requires exclusive area representation. Reports immediately. Work may be shipped or hand-delivered. Dealer pays insurance for exhibited work. Heaviest wholesale buying time: March; best selling time: June-August.
Acceptable Work: Considers candlemaking; ceramics; glass art; jewelry; pottery; and woodcrafting. Fine one-of-a-kind and handmade production-line items; utilitarian only.

A TOUCH OF GLASS, STAINED GLASS STUDIO, Art Museum Bldg., 104 Rancho Rd., Casper WY 82601. (307)234-4758. Contact: Barbara Harris. Craft shop/ gallery. Estab. 1974. Represents 2 craftworkers. Considers glass art and wall hangings. Fine one-of-a-kind and handmade production-line items; utilitarian and/or decorative. Price range: $25-5,000. Works on consignment; 33% commission. Gallery sets retail price. Work may be hand-delivered. Heaviest wholesale buying time: summer-fall; best selling time: winter. "Some ready-made items on hand for resale."

Canada

ART SALES AND RENTAL SOCIETY, Box 3142, S. Postal Station, Halifax, Nova Scotia Canada B3J 3G6. President: Irma M. Teichert. Museum gift shop/rental gallery. Estab. 1976. Represents 12-15 Canadian craftworkers mostly from Nova Scotia. Considers batik; ceramics; decoupage; jewelry; metalsmithing; pottery; wall hangings; weaving; woodcrafting; toys; and dried flower arrangements. "Special need for small handwoven items and fine stoneware or porcelain pieces." Fine one-of-a-kind pieces mostly but some handmade production-line items; decorative only. Price range: $1.50-300; bestsellers: $1.50-30 small crafts; $45-85 hangings. Works mostly on consignment, buys outright occasionally; 25% commission. Craftworker sets retail price. Prefers exclusive area representation. Reports in 2 weeks. Hand delivered work only. Dealer pays insurance. Customers are knowledgeable clientele plus tourists. Best selling time: late spring-early fall.

ARTISAN'S STUDIO, 400 Front St., Nanaimo, British Columbia Canada. President: Lois Kemp. Craft shop. Estab. 1975. Represents 15-18 craftworkers from Nanaimo and surrounding area. Considers batik; clothing; dollmaking; jewelry; needlecrafts; pottery; quilting; wall hangings; weavings; woodcrafting; baskets; and macrame. Fine one-of-a-kind and handmade production-line pottery; utilitarian and/or decorative. Price range: $1-200; bestsellers: $5-70. Members: 10% commission plus membership and 2 days work in shop. Craftworker sets retail price. Customers of all ages. Best selling time: Christmas and summer.

THE BANFF CENTRE, Box 1020, Banff, Alberta Canada T0L 0C0. (408)762-3391, ext. 375. Curator: Barry Morrison. Gallery. Estab. 1977. Represents 1-15 contemporary craftworkers. Considers batik; ceramics; glass art; jewelry; pottery; sculpture; soft sculpture; and weaving. Works on consignment; 25% commission. Craftworker sets retail price. Invitational exhibitions throughout year.

BRITISH COLUMBIA FOREST MUSEUM Rt. 4, Duncan, British Columbia Canada V9L 3W8. (604)748-9389. Curator: Bob Griffin. Museum gift shop. Estab. 1964. Represents 4 craftworkers. Considers woodcrafting and any craft dealing with wood or forestry. All styles; utilitarian and/or decorative. Bestsellers: under $5. Works on consignment and buys outright occasionally; 40% commission, negotiable. Retail price set by joint agreement. Reports as soon as possible. Dealer pays shipping depending on cost.
Profile: "We are a logging forestry museum with an operating steam railroad. We are especially interested in wood, lumbering and rail items. Our aim is to illustrate man's inter-relationship with the forest environment. At present our shop is quite small but plans are in process for increasing it." Customers are usually tourists. Best selling time: summer.

CABLE COOKHOUSE, Sayward, British Columbia Canada V0P 1R0. (604)282-3444, 282-5545. Contact: Mr. or Mrs. Glen Duncan. Craft shop. Estab. 1966. Represents 9 craftworkers. Considers ceramics; jewelry; leatherworking; pottery; wall hangings; weavings; woodcrafting; woodcarving; soapstone carving; ivory; scrimshaw; carved horn bone; and dolls that children can play with. Fine one-of-a-kind and handmade production-line items; utilitarian and/or decorative. Price range: $2-250; bestsellers: $2-45. Works on consignment and buys outright; 40% commission. "If new craftworker, start on consignment to see how well articles sell." Retail price set by joint agreement. Requires exclusive area representation.
Profile: "Shop is open only 6 months of the year. Most crafts depict Vancouver Island, especially wood and bone articles. We find most handmade articles only interest well travelled and above average income persons. Pottery sells to all incomes but young marrieds in particular." Customers are both local and tourists of all ages.

CAMPBELL RIVER AND DISTRICT MUSEUM, 1235 Island Hwy., Campbell River, British Columbia Canada V9W 2C7. (604)287-3103. Curator/Administrator: Jay S. Stewart. Museum gift shop. Estab. 1964. Represents 25-30 Kwagiutl, West Coast, and Salish craftworkers. Considers batiked petroglyph rubbings; jewelry; silver and gold metalsmithing; woodcrafting (masks, plaques, poles, and rattles); Salish and West Coast basketry. "Traditional and contemporary art of the Northwest Coast Indians." One-of-a-kind and handmade production-line items; utilitarian and/or decorative. Price range: $11-1,000; bestsellers: $40-150. Buys outright. Retail price set by joint agreement. Accepts work by prior arrangement. Most customers during the summer are tourists; at Christmas local people shop at the Museum. Best selling time: summer and Christmas.

CARLSON'S ART ROOM, 518A 4th Ave. SE, Medicine Hat, Alberta Canada T1A 2N6. (403)526-5881. Contact Earl or Joyce Carlson. Gallery. Estab. 1973. Represents 6-10 craftworkers. Considers ceramics; glass art; metalsmithing; pottery; soft sculpture; wall hangings; and weavings. Fine one-of-a-kind and handmade production-line items; utilitarian and/or decorative. Price range: $5-1,000; bestsellers: $5-250. Works on consignment and buys outright. Retail price set by joint agreement. Prefers exclusive area representation. All shipping and shipping insurance costs are by joint agreement; dealer pays insurance for exhibited work. Best selling time: fall and winter.

CHAPMAN GALLERIES LTD., 12 Sutton Close, Red Deer, Alberta Canada T4N 3S8. (403)346-7170. Manager: L. Joan Chapman. Gallery. Considers batik; jewelry; pottery; wall hangings; and weaving. Fine designer crafts only. Price range: $2.50-5,600; bestsellers: $15-40. Works on consignment; 50% commission. Retail price set by joint agreement. Hand-delivered work; or mailing or shipping only by prior arrangement. Shipping costs by joint agreement; dealer pays insurance for exhibited work. "Gallery is in an old 2-story house and is the only fine art gallery in Red Deer." Best selling time: pre-Christmas.

CLOTH AND CLAY, INC., 8 Notre Dame Rd. S., St. Agatha, Ontario Canada N0B 2L0. (519)886-7400. Contact: Nancy Martin. Craft shop/gallery. Estab. 1973. Represents 20-25 craftworkers usually from a 50-mile radius. Considers batik; clothing; dollmaking; glass art; jewelry; leatherworking; needlecrafts; pottery; quilting; soft sculpture; wall hangings; weavings; and woodcrafting. "Try to establish a Waterloo County heritage because of the strong Mennonite background here." Fine one-of-a-kind pieces; utilitarian and/or decorative. Price range: $2-1,500; bestsellers: $4-50. Works on consignment; 34% commission. Retail price set by joint agreement. Prefers exclusive area representation. Reports in 1 week. Hand delivered work only. Dealer pays for all insurance.

Profile: "We are in a unique building 144 years old with a country atmosphere. There is no craft gallery near this area. The 5 owners are all practicing craftspeople who are helping to make known other craftspeople." Reports on sales the end of each month. Customers are mostly middle age, middle income. Best selling time: fall and spring.

COLLAGE BOUTIQUE, 1162 Cedar Ave., Trail, British Columbia Canada (604)364-2614. Co-managers: Phyllis Matteucci and Janet Crema. Gift shop. Estab. 1971. Represents 50-100 craftworkers. Considers batik; candlemaking; clothing; dollmaking; glass art; jewelry; leatherworking; metalsmithing; pottery; quilting; wall angings; weavings; and woodcrafting. All styles; utilitarian and/or decorative. Price range: 25c-$80; bestsellers $1-28. Works on consignment and buys outright;33⅓% commission. Craftworker sets retail price. "We are one of the few local shops who touch anything homemade." Customers are of all ages and all interests.

Custom order one-of-a-kind hooked and knotted rugs are the speciality of B. Rugged, New York City. Customers' own designs for rugs come from original drawings, children's art, and from the masters. This hooked rug is based on a cut out from Matisse's "Parakeet and Mermaid." — Photo by Gayle Gleason.

COOPERATIVE ARTISANALE DE CHETICAMP LTEE., Box 98, Cheticamp, Nova Scotia Canada B0E 1H0. Secretary/Treasurer: Luce Marie Boudrean. Craft shop/museum. Represents 400 craftworkers. Considers hand hooked rugs and doilies. Fine handmade production-line items; utiliarian and/or decorative. Works on consignment and buys outright; 15% commission. Shops sets retail price. Hand-delivered work only. Dealer pays all insurance. Customers are mostly middle aged and low income. Best selling time: summer.

THE CRAFT GALLERY OF THE ONTARIO CRAFTS COUNCIL, 346 Dundas Street W., Toronto, Ontario Canada M5T 1G5. (416)366-3551. Executive Director: Paul Bennett. Gallery. Estab. 1976. Considers all professional crafts. Price range: $10-1,000; bestsellers: $10-100.

Works on consignment; 33⅓% commission. Retail price set by joint agreement. "Write explaining work and background (for exhibition); further information will be sent." Reports in 1 week. OCC pays return shipping and insurance for exhibited work. Work exhibited for 1 month.
Profile: "We provide regular 1-man shows and group shows. We will pay for opening (minus costs of refreshments); standard promotion; and 300 invitations.

EARTH MUSE, Box 1775, Jasper, Alberta Canada T0E 1E0. (403)852-4773. Contact: Jean Nixon. Craft shop. Estab. 1975. Represents 20 craftworkers, preferably Canadian but have no restrictions. Considers batik; candlemaking; ceramics; decoupage; glass art; jewelry; leatherworking; metalsmithing; needlecrafts; pottery; quilting; soft sculpture; wall hangings; weavings; woodcrafting; and unique knit products. All styles; utilitarian and/or decorative. Price range: 4c-$400; bestsellers: 4c-$100. Buys outright. Retail price set by joint agreement. Requires exclusive area representation. Dealer pays return shipping and insurance for exhibited work. Best selling time: summer.

FANSHAWE PIONEER VILLAGE, Box 6278, Station D, London, Ontario Canada. Contact: C. Cruickshank. General store gift shop in pioneer village. Estab. 1954. Represents 12-20 craftworkers, preferably local. Considers candlemaking; clothing; dollmaking; jewelry; leatherworking; needlecrafts; pottery; quilting; woodcrafting; and any pioneer type crafts, especially toys. Primitive one-of-a-kind and handmade production-line items; utilitarian and/or decorative. Price range: 25c-$20; bestsellers: 25c-$5. Works on consignment; 20% commission. Retail price set by joint agreement. Hand-delivered work only.
Profile: "This is a general store in a pioneer village setting unique in the London area. Only pioneer-type crafts are sold. Many school groups who want small souvenirs visit the shop. We also have many middle income customers from out of the country who want Canadian pioneer crafts." Best selling time: summer.

FORT EDMONTON PARK, 10th Flr., CN Towers, c/o City Parks and Recreation, Edmonton, Alberta Canada T5J 0K1. (403)436-5565. Director: Ken Kobylka. Museum gallery/gift shop. Estab. 1972. Represents 50 university students with historical and/or crafts background. Considers candlemaking; leatherworking; needlecrafts; quilting; walll hangings; weavings; woodcrafting; basket weaving; and nature crafts. Handmade production-line items; utilitarian and/or decorative. Price range: $2-30; bestsellers: $3-5. Buys outright. Shops sets retail price. Reports in 3 weeks. Dealer pays shipping to shop. "Shop sells items in line with time period of Park." Customers are mostly tourists. Best selling time: summer.

FORTRESS OF LOUISBOURG REPRODUCTIONS, Louisbourg, Nova Scotia Canada B0A 1M0. (903)733-2208. Director: Terry MacLellan. Museum gift shop. Estab. 1976. Represents 10-15 craftworkers in Cape Breton Island area. Considers leatherworking; metalsmithing; needlecrafts; pottery; woodcrafting; and weaving. "Especially need all types of ceramics; glassware; bottles; and brass and pewter casting." Only reproductions of 18th century furnishings appropriate to the fortress; utilitarian and/or decorative. Price range: 35c-$1,200; bestsellers: $2-20. Buys outright. Shop sets retail price. Requires exclusive area representation. Reports in 2 weeks. Shipping to shop payment is negotiable; dealers pays insurance for exhibited work.
Profile: "We are sole distributor of licensed reproductions based on antiques and artifacts in the collection of the Fortress of Louisbourg. Crafts are displayed in furnished rooms in historic buildings." Annually 135,000 tourists from Canada and the US visit the fortress. Best selling time: May 15-October 15.

GALLERY GIFT SHOP, Confederation Centre of the Arts, Charlottetown, Prince Edward Island Canada C1A 7L9. (902)892-2464, ext. 149. Manager/Buyer: Antoinette Sutherland. Gift shop. Estab. 1965. Represents 50-75 Canadian craftworkers. Considers batik; candles; ceramics; clothing; decoupage; dolls; glass art; jewelry; leathercraft; metalsmithing; pottery; wall hangings; weavings; and woodcrafting. Fine one-of-a-kind and handmade production-line items; utilitarian and/or decorative. Buys outright. Retail price set by joint agreement. Prefers exclusive area representation. "We sell no souvenirs, strictly work of noted Canadian craftsmen." Best selling time: summer.

GALLERY HOUSE SOL, 45 Charles St., Georgetown, Ontario Canada L7G 2Z4. (416)877-6460. Contact: John and Gisela Sommer. Craft shop/gallery. Estab. 1962. Represents 10 Canadian craftworkers. Considers batik; ceramics; glass art; jewelry; needlecrafts; pottery; wall hangings; and weaving. Fine one-of-a-kind pieces; utilitarian and/or decorative. Price range:

$10-600; bestsellers: $10-35. Works on consignment and buys outright; 33⅓% commission. Craftworker sets retail price. Charges fee for exhibit space; exhibitors share expense of invitations and postage. Reports in 3 weeks. Hand delivered work only. Dealer pays return shipping and insurance for exhibited work.

Profile: "The gallery is set up as a private home. Art and craft works are changed every 3 weeks and arranged to mutual advantage. It is the house of an older couple with great interest and knowledge in fine arts and crafts. We ask our visitors to enjoy with us the best we can find." Customers are mostly younger to middle-aged. Best selling time: late fall and late spring.

GIBSON HOUSE MUSEUM, 5172 Yonge St., Willowdale, Wello, Ontario Canada M2M 5P6. (807)225-0146. Contact: Mrs. I. C. Cairns. Gallery/museum gift shop. Estab. 1971. Represents 10 craftworkers. Considers candlemaking; ceramics; decoupage; jewelry; needlecrafts; pottery; quilting; tole painting; wall hangings; and weavings. Works on consignment and buys outright; 40% commission. Retail price set by joint agreement. Charges 20% or more of sales for exhibit space. Requires exclusive area representation. Reports in 4 weeks. Best selling time: fall.

HERITAGE GALLERIES LTD., 905 Heritage Dr. SW, Calgary, Alberta Canada T2V 2W8. Considers sculpture; no abstracts. Buys outright or on consignment; 33⅓% commission. Craftworker sets retail price. Write for interview.

LAURENTIAN UNIVERSITY MUSEUM AND ARTS CENTRE, Department of Cultural Affairs, Laurentian University, Sudbury, Ontario Canada P3E 2C6. (705)675-1151, ext. 400. Director: Pamela Krueger. Museum gallery/gift shop. Estab. 1967. Considers batik; ceramics; dollmaking; glass art; jewelry; leatherworking; metalsmithing; needlecrafts; pottery; quilting; soft sculpture; wall hangings; weavings; and woodcrafting. Fine and primitive one-of-a-kind pieces; utilitarian and/or decorative. Price range: $1-1,000. Works on consignment; 25% commission. Retail price set by joint agreement. Reports in 2 weeks. Dealer pays return shipping and insurance for exhibited work. The newly organized shop is connected to the art gallery. Best selling time: summer and Christmas.

THE LOON'S NEST, Station Mall, Sault Ste. Marie, Ontario Canada. (705)254-3700. Contact: Helen Gillespie. Craft shop. Estab. 1972. Represents 150 Canadian craftworkers. All styles; utilitarian and/or decorative. Price range: 25c-$850; bestsellers: $6-50. Works on consignment and buys outright; 33% commission. Retail price set by joint agreement. Requires exclusive area representation. Reports in 2 weeks. "We provide a critique of the craft when requested." Dealer pays shipping to shop and insurance for exhibited work.

Acceptable Work: Considers batik; candlemaking; clothing; glass art; jewelry; leatherworking; needlecrafts; pottery; quilting; soft sculpture; wall hangings; weavings; woodcrafting; unusual dolls; and crafts with Northern or outdoor theme. Customers are art and craft oriented professionals with income of $15,000 and up; 20-40 years of age. Best selling time: August and December.

MATSQUI-SUMAS-ABBOTSFORD MUSEUM, 33660 S. Fraser Way, Abbotsford, British Columbia Canada V2S 2B9. (604)853-0313. Curator: O. Diane Kelly. Museum gallery/gift shop. Estab. 1969. Represents 10 local craftworkers. Considers candlemaking; jewelry; metalsmithing; needlecrafts; pottery; wall hangings; and weavings. All styles; utilitarian and/or decorative. Price range: 50c-$50; bestsellers: 50c-$5. Works on consignment, buys outright and accepts donated crafts; 25% commission. Craftworker sets retail price. Reports in 4 weeks. Hand-delivered work only.

Profile: "The single most unique feature of our shop is the quality and nature of the work we carry by local craftworkers. The money we make from these projects goes to support a nonprofit organization. Our customers form a very general cross-section of the public at large, therefore our shop does not specialize in 1 particular craft or art style." Best selling time: summer.

THE MONTREAL MILITARY AND MARITIME MUSEUM, Box 1024, Station A, Montreal, Quebec Canada H3C 2W9. (514)861-6738. Manager: B. D. Bolton. Museum gift shop. Estab. 1955. Represents 3 craftworkers. Considers candlemaking; ceramics; decoupage; dollmaking; glass art; jewelry; leatherworking; metalsmithing; pottery; quilting; and woodcraftings. "Prefer historic Canadian; military; and maritime themes." Primitive handmade production-line items; utilitarian and/or decorative. Price range: $1-500; bestsellers: $1-25. Works on consignment and buys outright; commission varies. Retail price set by joint agreement. Dealer pays return shipping. Best selling time: May-October.

MUSEUM OF NORTHERN BRITISH COLUMBIA, MUSEUM ART GALLERY, Box 669, Prince Rupert, British Columbia Canada V8J 3S1. (604)624-5637. Contact: Curator or Art Gallery Committee. Museum gallery. Estab. 1971. Preference given to local residents. Considers work in all media, including school classes and "not for sale." "The Museum Art Gallery exists primarily for display, and sales are a minor part of its life. Museum art gallery allows local exhibitors to sell; 10% commission." Retail price set by craftworker. Reporting time varies. City of Prince Rupert pays insurance for exhibited work.
Profile: "Gallery is part of museum complex but run by volunteer committee. It is covered by the security and insurance arrangements of the Museum of Northern British Columbia. About 90,-000 visitors, primarily tourists, pass through the Gallery annually."

NATIONAL POSTAL MUSEUM, Confederation Heights, Ottawa, Ontario Canada K1A 0B1. (613)998-8570. Manager: J.E. Kraemer. Pioneer post office sales counters. Considers craft items related to the post office service. Buys outright after committee approval, and occasionally commissions work. Manager recommends retail price. Reports in 6 weeks. Museum pays for return shipping; shipping insurance; and insurance for exhibited work.

NOR'WESTER AND LOYALIST MUSEUM, Box 69, Williamstown, Ontario Canada K0C 2J0. (613)347-3547. Curator: M. Light. Museum gift shop. Estab. 1967. Represents 3 craftworkers. "We try to keep in stock only those products of local interest; we restrict the craft not the type of craftworker." Considers batik; candlemaking; decoupage; jewelry; needlecrafts; pottery; quilting; tole painting; wall hangings; weavings; and woodcrafting. One-of-a-kind designer pieces; utilitarian and/or decorative. Price range: 25c-$60; bestsellers: $2-10. Works on consignment; commission negotiable. Craftworker sets retail price. Reports in 4 weeks. Hand-delivered work only.
Sales Tip: "Items of local interest (Scottish items and reproductions of NWC trading goods) sell best. Customers are of all ages and low-moderate income." Best selling time: July-October.

THE OLD BRONTE POST OFFICE GALLERY, 86 Bronte Rd., Oakville, Ontario Canada L6L 3B8. (416)827-7214. Secretary: Dorothy Keene. Craft shop/gallery. Estab. 1975. Represents 40 Canadian craftworkers. Considers batik; ceramics; glass art; jewelry; pottery; wall hangings; weavings; woodcrafting; and sculpture + all of original design. Fine one-of-a-kind pieces; utilitarian and/or decorative. Price range: $2-200. Works on consignment; 33⅓% commission. Retail price set by joint agreement. "For one-man shows we take ⅓ of sold item; artist pays for invitations and stamps." Reports in 1 week. Dealer pays limited return shipping and limited exhibition insurance.
Profile: "We have a pleasant, relaxed atmosphere and a wide variety of shows and work." Customers are young marrieds with 2 incomes looking for furnishing and collectibles; and shoppers of wedding and shower gifts. Pottery sells well. Best selling time: fall and at one-man shows.

OLEARY LIBRARY AND MUSEUM ASSOCIATION, Oleary, Prince Edward Island Canada C0B 1V0. President: L. G. Dewar. Museum gallery/gift shop. Estab. 1973. Considers clothing and woodcrafting. Primitive pieces only; utilitarian and/or decorative. Shop sets retail price. Best selling time: summer.

ONTARIO CRAFTS COUNCIL, 346 Dundas St. W., Toronto, Ontario Canada M5T 1G5. (416)366-3551. Executive Director: Paul Bennett. Craft shop/gallery. Estab. 1976. Represents 100 Canadian craftworkers. Considers batik; ceramics; clothing; dollmaking; glass art; jewelry; leatherworking; metalsmithing; needlecrafts; pottery; quilting; soft sculpture; wall hangings; weavings; and woodcrafting. Fine one-of-a-kind and handmade production-line items; utilitarian and/or decorative. Price range: $5-4,000; bestsellers: $9-35. Works on consignment and buys outright in gallery, store varies; 33⅓% commission. Craftworker sets retail price. Reports in 2 weeks. Dealer pays return shipping and insurance for exhibited work.
Profile: "The gallery is in a renovated Victorian house and occupies all the first floor. We are the main craft gallery in Toronto and directly opposite the Art Gallery of Ontario." Customers are middle income, middle class. Best selling time: fall.

OTHER DELIGHTS, 491 Bloor St. W., Toronto, Ontario Canada. (416)961-5226. Manager: Gwen Brooks. Craft and gift shop. Estab. 1974. Represents 50 craftworkers. Price range: $3.50-35; bestsellers: $4-15. Works on consignment; 40% commission. Retail price set by joint agreement. Reports in 1 week. Hand-delivered work only. Dealer pays insurance for exhibited work. Items are displayed in the window as well as on the floor for periods up to 1 year. Customers are

mostly students, ages 18-25. Heaviest wholesale buying and best selling time: Christmas.
Acceptable Work: Considers batik; candlemaking; dollmaking; ceramics; glass art; jewelry; leatherworking; needlecrafts; pottery; quilting; wall hangings; weavings; and woodcrafting. Fine one-of-a-kind and handmade production-line items; utilitarian and/or decorative.

PLACE DES ARTS, 166 King Edward, Coquitlam, British Columbis Canada V3K 4T2. (604)526-2891. Director: Leonore Peytons. Gallery/art center. Estab. 1972. Represents 10 craftworkers. Considers batik; ceramics; glass art; jewelry; leatherworking; needlecrafts; pottery; quilting; wall hangings; weavings; and woodcrafting. Fine one-of-a-kind pieces; utilitarian and/or decorative. Price range: $3-500; bestsellers: up to $350. Works on consignment; 15% commission. Retail price set by joint agreement. $15/exhibit space for 2 weeks in gallery. Requires exclusive area representation. Reports in 8 weeks. Dealer pays insurance for exhibited work.
Profile: "The nonprofit gallery is part of a teaching center for 600 students." Customers are middle income. Best selling time: September-July.

SHAW-RIMMINGTON GALLERY, 20 Birch Ave., Toronto, Ontario Canada M4V 1C8. (416)923-3484. Director: Marie Shaw-Rimmington. Gallery. Estab. 1966. Represents 5 craftworkers. Considers contemporary dollmaking; glass art; jewelry; soft sculpture; wall hangings; and weavings. Fine one-of-a-kind pieces; decorative only. Works on consignment; 40% commission. Retail price set by joint agreement. Requires exclusive area representation. Customers middle income and middle age.

SHETANI GALLERY, 589 Markham St., Toronto, Ontario Canada M6G 2L7. (416)534-4734. Director: Rhoda Lipton. Craft shop/gallery. Estab. 1976. Represents 20+ craftworkers. All styles; utilitarian and/or decorative. Price range: $5-500; bestsellers: $15-50. Works on consignment and buys outright; 34% commission. Retail price set by joint agreement. "Craftspeople share cost of one-man show opening." Dealer pays return shipping on ordered items and insurance for exhibited work.
Acceptable Work: Considers batik; ceramics; clothing; dollmaking; glass art; jewelry; leatherworking; metalsmithing; needlecrafts; pottery; quilting; and woodcrafting. "These are crafts that have been shown to date; this may change."
Profile: "We handle international as well as Canadian crafts." Customers are mostly upwardly mobile, well-educated women with broad interests; ages 25-45. Best selling time: Christmas and summer tourist season.

SUNBURY SHORES ARTS AND NATURE CENTRE, Box 100, St. Andrews, New Brunswick Canada E0G 2X0. (500)529-3386. Director: H. Kreiberg. Gallery. Estab. 1964. Represents 10-12 craftworkers; "emphasis on Canadian and maritime craftworkers but not restrictive." Considers batik; needlecrafts; quilting; wall hangings; and weaving. Fine one-of-a-kind and handmade production-line items; utilitarian and/or decorative. Price range: 50c-$900. Exhibits work only; 30% commission. Will act as occasional sales agent. Retail price set by joint agreement. Reports in 2 weeks. Dealer pays return shipping and insurance for exhibited work.
Profile: "We primarily exhibit and do not stand in the way of craftworkers who wish to sell some of the pieces in the show. Profit to us is incidental. The gallery has neutral backgrounds; controlled lighting; burglar and fire alarms; and a 2-4 week exhibit period. St. Andrews is a summer seaside resort with tourists from Europe and North America of all ages and incomes."

YE WISE OWL SHOPPE LTD., 237 City Centre, Kitimat, British Columbia Canada. (604)632-5544. President: Joanne Monaghan. Craft shop/gift shop. Estab. 1974. Represents 200+ craftworkers. Considers batik; candlemaking; ceramics; clothing; decoupage; dollmaking; glass art; jewelry; leatherworking; metalsmithing; needlecrafts; pottery; quilting; wall hangings; weavings; and woodcrafting. All styles; utilitarian and/or decorative. Price range: 60c-$1,300. Works on consignment and buys outright; 33⅓% commission. Retail price set by joint agreement. Dealer pays limited insurance for displayed work. "We have items from almost every country in the world; we try to have something for everyone."

Shows & Fairs

In June 1977, 500 craftworkers at the Northeast Craft Fair at Rhinebeck, New York, earned more than $2 million in sales.

What's the point? If you're not already exhibiting your crafts at shows and fairs, you're probably missing out on one of the most valuable markets available.

The listings in this section include a wide variety of shows and fairs, but one thing they all have in common is their ability to help you gain income— and exposure— for your work.

One of the nicest features of shows and fairs is they benefit both the beginner and veteran craftworker. In a recent *Craftworker's Market* survey, 500 professional craftworkers said shows are the beginner's best chance of breaking into the field — to gain sales, exposure, a knowledge of public response to your work, and recognition through awards.* The same professionals believe shows provide them with these same benefits.

In addition to tracking down individual shows, artists and craftworkers interested in exhibiting their work should write the show sponsors listed in the Professional Show Promoters section of this book. Often times the art and craft events held in malls and at shopping centers are the result of a professional show sponsor's efforts.

Almost all shows permit participants to sell their work — and often encourage sales. And, the buyers attracted by shows are no means restricted to the day-to-day consumer, but frequently gallery and shop owners attend shows looking for new work. One Atlanta shop owner was recently overheard explaining to a craftworker that she buys nothing from craftpersons who visit her shop. All her merchandise is ordered from craftworkers showing at fairs.

In addition to making sales at the show itself, craftpersons and artists who make their cards available, frequently continue to receive orders from individuals after the show.

Exhibiting actually provides you a means of meeting your customer face to face, and witnessing his/her reaction to your work. This feedback can help you develop better-selling lines.

And what is the competition doing? The show helps you answer this question. A few moments taken to browse the various booths gives the artist or craftperson an excellent perspective on what is happening in his/her field.

If awards are offered, the show gives you an even greater chance for recognition. Whether your ultimate goal is to continue exhibiting at shows, or to become a gallery exhibitor, it's helpful to have a few awards under your belt. Many of the better galleries and shows will watch for this type of recognition on your resume.

And award money isn't to be shunned either. The Gum Tree Festival of Tupelo, Mississippi, attracts approximately 12,000 people each year, and gives awards totalling $5,400. When all is considered— the sales potential, the exposure, and the possibility of winning award money — it's hard to understand why anyone would pass up the opportunity to exhibit in a show like this.

Once you have developed an adequate inventory, a complementary display and business cards, you'll only need to find the right show for you. There are certain things to keep in mind as you start entering the shows and fairs listed in this book. First of all, show dates and fees are often determined in the late planning stages, so remember entry fees can change, and show dates are given according to the month or season held. (You'll have to write for an entry form, anyway, in order to participate in a show.) Also, pay attention to the figures given for attendance at shows, and whether or not the entries are prejudged (screened) prior to acceptance.

As you're hunting shows for your crafts, consider entering some outside your locale. Often the cost of travel, lodging, meals, shipping and packing are offset by the sales and exposure you get — particularly at wholesale shows such as the Northeast Craft Fair, Rocky Mountain Craft Fair, Pacific Coast Fair, Winter Market of American Crafts, and Professional Arts, Crafts & Indoor Plants Show.

* Those listings preceded by an asterisk present awards for prize-winning crafts.

Alabama

*ART ON THE ROCKS, Box 973, Gadsden AL 35902. Sponsor: Gadsden Art Association. Annual outdoor show held the first Sunday in May. Entries accepted until 1 week before show. No entry fee. Awards $25 1st and $15 2nd prize. Prejudging. Work may be offered for sale; 15% commission. Craftworker must attend show.
Acceptable Work: Considers batik; candlemaking; dollmaking; glass art; jewelry; leatherworking; metalsmithing; needlecrafts; pottery; soft sculpture; tole painting; weavings; wall hangings; and woodcrafting. Work must be framed or matted when applicable.

*ART-ON-THE-LAKE SHOW, Box 192, Guntersville AL 35976. (205)582-3833. Show Chairman: Mrs. James McCain. Sponsor: Twentieth Century Club. Purpose: to support the club's charity projects. Estab. 1961. Annual show held in April on the lawn and in the hallways and classrooms of Carlisle Park School. Average paid attendance: 1,500. Entries accepted until show date. Entry fee: $5 per artist; no restrictions on size of display area within reason. Work may be offered for sale; no commission. "Public seems to show more interest in traditional work than in the abstract." Craftworker or representative must attend show; demonstrations encouraged. Considers all crafts, "but chairman reserves right to reject unsuitable artwork." Awards 3 ribbons in craft category.
Promotion: Announcements of show appear in art and craft magazines; newspapers; and on local radio stations. "Photos suitable for newspaper articles and information concerning the entrant are desirable; however, we cannot guarantee they will be used."

THE BROOK HIGH SCHOOL ARTS & CRAFTS FESTIVAL, Rt. 1, Brooks Acres, Killen AL 35645. (205)757-2115. Director: William R. Dean. Sponsor: Honors History Club. "To promote interest in arts and crafts in local area and to offer outlet for artists and craftsmen to sell their handiwork." Estab. 1973. Annual indoor show (with some outside space) held 3 days in April. Average attendance: 15,000-18,000. Entries accepted until show date. Entry fee: $20 per display area with 12' lateral front footage. Work may be offered for sale; no commission. Craftworker must attend show; demonstrations encouraged. Sponsor provides electricity for demonstrations and 24-hour security protection. Considers all crafts. No nails may be placed in walls or floors; no frames may obstruct the view of other craftworkers. Show promoted through radio, newspaper, TV, billboards and posters.
Sales Tip: "Have an attractive display, be talkative with visitors, offer to demonstrate how your craft is done."

CALICO FORT ARTS & CRAFTS FAIR, Box 15, Fort Deposit AL 36032. (204)227-8731. Contact: Registration Chairman. Purpose: "to expose our area to the best quality arts and crafts available." Estab. 1972. Annual outdoor show held 2 days in April. Average attendance: 20,000. Invitational. Entry fee: $25/12x12 display area. Prejudging by slides or photos plus resume; entry fee due after prejudging. Work may be offered for sale; no commission. Prefers craftworker attends show; demonstrations OK. Registration limit: 250. Sponsor provides display panels for $2 rental fee; and electricity for demonstrations. Considers all original crafts.
Promotion: Show is advertised by TV in 3 states; national magazines; local radio; and newspapers. Craftworker should provide 8x10 b&w glossy of he/she working with craft.

*CHALAKA ARTS AND CRAFTS FESTIVAL, Box 1245 Sylacauga AL 35150. Chairman: Shirley Cardwell. Sponsor: Sylacauga Parks & Recreation Department. Estab. 1968. Annual outdoor show held 2 days in June. Average attendance 100-150. Entries accepted until 1 week before show. Entry fee: $15/entry. Prejudging; entry fee refunded for refused work. Work may be offered for sale. Craftworker must attend show. Considers all crafts. Presents $1,500 in cash prizes and ribbons.

*CHRISTMAS CRAFTS FAIR, c/o Mrs. John T. Williamson, 919 Manor Dr. NE, Cullman AL 35055. (205)734-7939. Sponsor: Second Century League. Purpose: "To provide a purchasing opportunity, and cultural and educational experience for area families." Estab. 1974. Annual indoor show held 2 days the first weekend in December. Average attendance: 4,000. Entries accepted until show date, but "in the past, show has been filled by early October." Entry fee: $20/8x8 display space, "payable in advance and accompanied by entry form. Confirmation of space(s) and additional exhibitor information will be mailed immediately upon receipt of fee and entry form." Prejudging of new entrants by slide or photo showing complete display; entry fee refunded for refused work. Work may be offered for sale; no commission. Craftworker must attend show; demonstrations encouraged. Registration limit: 66. Sponsor provides chairs; limited electricity for demonstrations; tables; and area is patrolled by police after closing time on Friday. Categories: 2-dimensional; 3-dimensional. Awards yet to be decided.

Accepted Work: Considers batik, candlemaking, ceramics, dollmaking, jewlery, glass art, macrame, leatherworking, pottery, metalsmithing, sculpture, weaving, woodcrafting, basketry, scrimshaw, and soft sculpture. No work done from kits, patterns or commercial molds; dried flower arrangements; terrariums; or items made from skins, bones or feathers of endangered species.

Promotion: Show is advertised by radio, TV, banners, billboards, posters, handbills, area newspapers, art and craft publications, and local calendar of events. "5x7 b&w photos are appreciated for publicity purposes, but are not required."

FALL CRAFT SHOW, Box U-1028, University of South Alabama, Mobile AL 36688. Contact: Registration Chairman. Sponsor: The Port City Craftsmen, and The Recreation Club of the University of South Alabama. "We are craftsmen organized for the main purpose of providing an outlet for handcrafted items. We also work as a teaching aid to the Leisure Services Department at the University of South Alabama, and the students who will be our park directors, and recreation directors of the future get on the job training for putting on major craft shows." Estab. 1974. Annual indoor show held 2 days the weekend before Thanksgiving at the University gymnasium. Attendance: 15,000-20,000. Entries accepted until mid-October. Entry fee: $20/10x10 display area. Work may be offered for sale; no commission. Craftworker must attend show ("exceptions can be made with prior arrangements in writing"); demonstrations OK. Registration limit: 160. Sponsor provides chairs; some electricity for demonstrations; coffee; unloading assistance; overnight parking for self-contained campers; table rental; 24-hour security; and a change booth for emergency change making. Show is advertised by radio; TV; posters; flyers; and direct mail. "Our advertising covers a 4-state area."

Acceptable Work: Considers most crafts. "We do not allow kits, assemblies (simply putting together manufactured items such as necklaces when you place a manufactured item on a chain and attach a clasp) or imported items. All items should be crafted by the exhibitor. Indian jewelry only if you are the Indian."

Sales Tip: "We suggest that rapid turn-over profit-makers be included. Mobile is not inclined to collect a lot of expensive work." 1977 exhibitor sales estimated at $50,000+ ("from partial statistics turned in by exhibitors").

FALLFEST, DeSoto Caverns, Rt. 1, Box 50-A, Childersburg AL 35044. (205)378-7252. Festival Coordinator: Caryl Lynn Mathis. Estab. 1975. Annual outdoor show held 2 days in fall. Average attendance: 10,000. Entries accepted until 4 weeks before show. Entry fee: $12. Display area: 12x12. Prejudging by slides and photos; entry fee refunded for refused work. Work may be offered for sale; no commission. Craftworker must attend show; demonstrations encouraged. Registration limit: 100. Sponsor provides electricity for demonstrations and 24-hour security. Show is advertised by radio; TV; magazines; newspapers; and signs and posters throughout the Southeast. Submit promotional material 2 months before show. Considers all crafts.

FESTIVAL IN THE PARK, 1010 Forest Ave., Montgomery AL 36106. (205)265-8593. Festival Chairman: Martha Fitzpatrick. Program Coordinator: Edith Upchurch. Sponsor: Montgomery Parks & Recreation and the Festivals in the Park Committee. Purpose: "nonprofit, to encourage community participation." Estab. 1973. Annual outdoor show held 1 day in September at Oak Park. Average attendance: 20,000. Entries accepted until 4 weeks before show. Entry fee: $10 per 10x10 display area. Work may be offered for sale; no commission. Craftworker must attend show; demonstrations OK. Registration limit: 250. Sponsor provides electricity for demonstrations. Considers all handmade crafts. Show promoted through TV; radio spots; newspapers throughout the state; and TV and radio talk shows.

*FIRST MONDAY'S ART SUNDAY, 601 Scott St., Scottsboro AL 35768. (205)259-5848. Chairman: Ann Chamblis. Sponsor: 3-Arts Club and Jackson County Arts Council. Estab. 1972. Annual outdoor show held Sunday of Labor Day weekend. Average attendance: 1,000. Entries accepted until 1 week before show. Entry fee: $5/entry. Work may be offered for sale; no

commission. Craftworker must attend show; demonstrations encouraged.
Acceptable Work: Considers batik; ceramics; leatherworking; needlecrafts; pottery; tole painting; weavings; wall hangings; and woodcrafting.
Awards: Presents $650 in cash prizes. Judge for each category is from an area college or museum.

Festival in the Park, Montgomery, Alabama, has grown in attendance from 5,000 in 1973 to 10,000 in 1977 and has become a major event in the area. There is space for 300 craftworkers working in any handmade craft discipline. Photo by J.A. Pinkerton.

*HALEYVILLE MERCHANTS ASSOCIATION ARTS & CRAFTS SHOW, 2401 15th Ave., Haleyville AL 35565. Show Coordinator: Mrs. Edwin Burleson. Purpose: "to provide the opportunity for artists and craftsmen to display and sell, and get viewers to visit the mall." Estab. 1975. Annual show held 1 day in the fall. Average attendance: 4,000. Entries accepted until 2 weeks before show. Entry fee: $15 per artist. Work may be offered for sale; no commission. Craftworker must attend show; demonstrations OK. Registration limit: 50-60 craftworkers; equal number of artists. Sponsor provides 6x12 display area and electricity for demonstrations. Categories: watercolor and acrylic; oil; drawing; and crafts. Considers all original crafts. Awards $700+ in cash prizes. Show advertised by radio, TV and magazines.
Sales Tip: "Crafts sell especially well — especially those used by interior decorators and the housewife. During the 1977 show, 75% of the 100 exhibitors reported on a comment sheet that they had good to excellent sales."

INDIAN CRAFTS FESTIVAL & PIONEER FAIR, c/o DeSoto Caverns, Rt. 1, Box 50-A, Childersburg AL 35044. (205)378-7272. Sponsor: Desoto Caverns. Estab. 1975. Annual outdoor show held 2 days in April. Average attendance: 10,000. Entries accepted until 4 weeks before show. Entry fee: $12 per 12' square display area. Prejudging by 2 slides or photos; entry fee refunded for refused work. Work may be offered for sale; no commission. Craftworker must attend show; demonstrations encouraged. Registration limit: 100 craftworkers. Sponsor provides electricity for demonstration and 24-hour security. Considers all crafts.
Promotion: Show promoted by radio, TV, magazines, newspapers, signs and posters throughout the Southeast. "Any promotional material is appreciated, but must be supplied 2 months prior to show dates," said Caryl Lynn Mathis, festival coordinator.

*KENTUCK ARTS AND CRAFTS FESTIVAL, Box 127, Northport AL 35476. Executive Director: Georgine Clarke. Sponsor: Kentuck of Northport, Inc. Purpose: to promote quality art and crafts. Estab. 1973. Annual outdoor show held 2 days in October. Average attendance: 15,000. Entries accepted until early summer; some categories remain open until 1 month before show. Entry fee: $15/15x15 display area. Prejudging by slides; entry fee refunded for refused work. Work may be offered for sale; no commission. Craftworkers must attend show; demonstrations OK. Registration limit: 200-225. Sponsor provides electricity for demonstrations and 24-hour security. Show is advertised by TV; radio; newspaper; billboards;

posters; magazines; and bumper stickers. Submit slides for TV spots; b&w shots for newspaper; and resume for articles. Presents cash awards of $400 and purchase awards of $400.

KUDZU KUNTRY BLUEGRASS CELEBRATION, Lurleen B. Wallace SJC., Box 1418, Andalusia AL 36420. (205)222-6591. Secretary, LBW CAC: Alice Smith. Sponsor: LBW Community Arts Council. "This show is held in conjunction with our annual bluegrass festival." Estab. 1976. Annual outdoor show held 1 day in the fall. Average attendance: 800. Entries accepted until 1 week before show. Entry fee: $5/10x10 display space. Work may be offered for sale; no commission. Craftworker must attend show; demonstrations OK. Registration limit: 50 craftworkers. Sponsor provides chairs, electricity for demonstrations and table. Considers all crafts, but "we prefer handmade crafts."
Sales Tip: "As a general rule, we find that items priced under $25 sell best. An attractive booth draws potential buyers."
Promotion: Show promoted by radio; TV (public service announcements); area newspapers; brochures; flyers; and posters.

MUCKLE'S RIDGE FESTIVAL, Rt. 1, Box 180, Browns AL 36724. Chairperson: Margaret Wheeler. Sponsor: Club 15. Purpose: "To bring artisans, craftsmen, their wares, and new people into the community." Estab. 1973. Annual outdoor show held the first Sunday in May. Average attendance: 3,000. Entries accepted until 1 week before show. Entry fee: $15/10x7 display area. Work may be offered for sale; no commission. Craftworker needn't attend show; demonstrations OK. Sponsor provides electricity for demonstrations, "but please specify with entry forms." Considers all arts, crafts and hobbies.
Sales Tip: "Mother's Day is the day after, or the weekend after, the festival, therefore items suitable for gifts might increase sales."

*OPELIKA ARTS FESTIVAL, Box 2095, Opelika AL 36801. (205)749-0965. Chairman: Dee Porter. Sponsor: Opelika Arts Association. Purpose: held "as a service to the public and to make money." Estab. 1968. Annual outdoor show held 1 day in April. Average attendance: 5,000. Entries accepted until 3 weeks before show. Entry fee: $10/artist. Display area: 6-10 linear feet. Work may be offered for sale; no commission. Craftworker must attend show; demonstrations OK. Registration limit: 150. Sponsor provides display panels and fencing.
Acceptable Work: Considers decoupage; dollmaking; glass art; jewelry; leatherworking; macrame; needlecrafts; pottery; sculpture; tole painting; and woodcrafting. "Bring own tables; S hooks; plastic sheet in case of rain; and chairs."
Awards: Presents $1,000 in cash; 1st, 2nd and 3rd place ribbons; and 8 merit awards of $50 each in painting, crafts and sculpture.

PATCHWORK DERBY, Box 1481, Andalusia AL 36420. (205)222-7441. Contact: Angie Metcalf. Sponsor: Junior League. "We are using this money to sponsor a Girl Scout Hut in our community." Estab. 1977. Annual outdoor show (with stable as covering) held 2 days in April. Average attendance: 150. Entries accepted until 2 weeks before show. Entry fee: $15/6x3 display area. Work may be offered for sale; no commission. Craftworker must attend show; demonstrations OK. Sponsor provides electricity for demonstrations, and 24-hour security. Show is advertised by local radio; TV; newspaper ads; and notices to craft magazines and art councils. Considers all crafts.

RIVERFRONT MARKET DAY, Box 586, Selma AL 36701. (205)872-8265. Coordinator: Sam H. O'Hara. Sponsor: Selma and Dallas County Historical Preservation Society. Estab. 1971. Annual outdoor show held 1 day in the fall. Average attendance: 20,000-30,000. Entries accepted until 1 week before show. Entry fee: $15/uncovered or $25/covered display area. Work may be offered for sale; no commission. Craftworkers must attend show. Registration limit: 250. Sponsor provides electrical outlets. Considers all crafts.

RUMBLING WATERS ARTS & CRAFTS SHOW & SALE, Box 456, Wetumpka AL 36092. Exhibitor Chairperson: Gail Bass. Sponsor: Rumbling Waters Arts Club. Purposes: "We as an arts club are interested in all arts, and especially crafts. We use the money made on the show for civic projects in Wetumpka, and to improve our show area." Estab. 1970. Annual outdoor show (with approximately 32 spaces inside Community House) held 1 day in October. Average attendance: 2,500. Entries accepted until show date. Entry fee: $7.50/12x12 display area outside, or 10x4 display area inside. Work may be offered for sale; no commission. Craftworker must attend show; demonstrations OK. Registration limit: 200. Sponsor provides electricity for demonstrations. Considers all orginal crafts.

Sales Tip: "We have many Air Force people in this area, and they are very receptive to most crafts if displayed attractively. Unique work and those crafts really handcrafted sell well."
Promotion: Show is advertised by TV, newspapers and posters. "Our advertising has been very extensive and very good for the last several years. Pictures and articles for newspaper promotions are helpful."

*SPRING CELEBRATION OF THE ARTS, 809 Andrew Jackson Way, Huntsville AL 35801. (205)534-2511. Contact: Registrar. Sponsor: Huntsville Art League & Museum Association. Purpose: to "present original work by artists and craftsmen— most of them from this area or the Southwest — to the public in the tri-cities area. It also provides the Art League with its major source of revenue with which to present this show and its annual jury show." Estab. 1963. Annual outdoor show (indoors in bad weather) held 2 days in May. Attendance: "thousands." Entries accepted until 2 weeks before show. Entry fee: $15/10x10 display area. Work must be offered for sale; no commission. Craftworker or member of his/her family must attend show; demonstrations OK. Registration limit: 200.
AcceptableWork: Considers batik; ceramics (no molds); glass art; leatherworking; macrame; metalsmithing; mobiles; sculpture; soft sculpture; weaving; woodcrafting and other original crafts. No candles or decoupage.
Awards: Presents $1,000+ in cash awards and ribbons. "The Huntsville Museum of Art will have a show of the prize-winning works. Originality and degree of execution is important."

SPRING CRAFT SHOW, Box U-1028, University of South Alabama, Mobile AL 36688. Contact: Registration Chairman. Sponsor: The Port City Craftsmen, and The Recreation Club of the University of South Alabama. "We are craftsmen organized for the main purpose of providing an outlet for handcrafted items. We also work as a teaching aid to the Leisure Service Department at the University of South Alabama; and the students who will be our park directors and recreation directors of the future get on the job training for putting on major craft shows." Estab. 1974. Annual indoor show held 2 days the last weekend of April in the University gymnasium. Attendance: 15,000-20,000. Entries accepted until about 1 month before show. Entry fee: $20/10x10 display area. Work may be offered for sale; no commission. Craftworker must attend show ("exceptions can be made with prior arrangements in writing"); some demonstrations OK. Registration limit: 160 spaces. Sponsor provides chairs; electricity for demonstrations; 24-hour security; coffee; unloading assistance; overnight parking for self-contained campers; and rental of tables. Show is advertised by radio; TV; flyers; posters; and direct mail. "Our advertising covers a 4-state area."
Acceptable Work: Considers all handmade crafts. "We do not allow kits, assemblies (simply putting together manufactured items such as necklaces when you place a manufactured item on a chain and attach a clasp) or imported items. All items should be crafted by the exhibitor. Indian jewelry only [accepted] if you are the Indian. Your application must contain everything you intend to sell. We also assign booths to give the public as varied a show as possible."

*TALLADEGA SQUARE ARTS & CRAFT SHOW & SALE, Box 263, Talladega AL 35160. Chairman: Mrs. Larry Barksdale. Sponsor: Talladega Arts Council. Purpose: "to educate our community to the arts (visual and crafts) that are available in our country." Estab. 1974. Annual outdoor show held 2 days in September. Average attendance: 1,500-2,000 for 2 days. Entries accepted until show date. Entry fee: $15/artist. Display area: 9x12. Work must be offered for sale; no commission. Craftworker must attend show; demonstrations OK. Sponsor provides electricity for demonstrations and fencing if desired. Show is advertised by newspapers; TV; flyers; magazines; and radio.
Acceptable Work: Considers batik; ceramics; dollmaking; glass art; jewelry; leatherworking; macrame; metalsmithing; needlecrafts; pottery; soft sculpture; tole painting; sculpture; weaving; and woodcrafting. Presents $500, best in show; $150, 1st place; and 7 merit awards.
Sales Tip: "Items that are not priced high [sell best]. Public is mostly of moderate income, thus can't afford works that have large price tags."

*WEST MOBILE ARTS & CRAFTS SHOW, Box 16243, Mobile AL 36616. (205)344-3750. Contact: Raymond McCoy. Sponsor: Mobile Federal Savings and Loan Association. Estab. 1973. Annual outdoor show held 2 days in May. Entries accepted until 1 week before show. Entry fee: $15/10x10 display area. Awards $1,650 in cash prizes; $250 in purchase prizes; and ribbons. Work may be offered for sale; no commission. Craftworker must attend show; demonstrations OK.
Acceptable Work: Considers batik; candlemaking; ceramics; glass art; jewelry; leatherworking; metalsmithing; pottery; soft sculpture; tole painting; and woodcrafting. "All craftsmen must send photo of work before they will be accepted."

Alaska

HOONAH ARTS FAIR, Box 157, Hoonah AK 99829. (907)945-3212. President: Bob Hutton. Sponsor: Hoonah Arts & Crafts. Purpose: "to raise money for Hoonah Arts & Crafts." Estab. 1969. Annual indoor show held 1 day in December. Average attendance: 400. Entries accepted until 1 week before show. No entry fee. 10x10 display area. Work may be offered for sale; 10% commission. Craftworker needn't attend; demonstrations permitted. Sponsor provides chairs, electricity for demonstrations and table.

Acceptable Work: Considers batik; candlemaking; ceramics; dollmaking; glass art; jewelry; leatherworking; macrame; metalsmithing; mobiles; needlecrafts; pottery; sculpture; soft sculpture; tole painting; weaving; woodcrafting; and other crafts that are "100% handmade."

TANANA VALLEY FAIR MOSQUITO MARKET, Box 188, Fairbanks AK 99707. (907)452-3750. Director: Jennifer B. Johnston. Purpose: "to use the space available on the fairgrounds and to supply a market for people otherwise unable to have one." Indoor show held 2 days in May, June and July. Average attendance: 500. Entries accepted until show date. Entry fee: $7.50/8x8 display area. Work may be offered for sale; no commission. Craftworker must attend show; demonstrations OK. Sponsor provides electricity for demonstrations; table; and 24-hour security protection. Show is promoted by radio, posters and local newspapers. Considers all crafts. To improve sales "be an active seller. Converse with the customers."

TANANA VALLEY STATE FAIR CRAFT MARKET, Box 188, Fairbanks AK 99707. (907)452-3750. Secretary: Mary Brazo. Commercial space: Carl Romick. Sponsor: Tanana Valley State Fair Association. Purpose: "to give craftsmen a place to sell their products at a time and place when a good audience is available." Estab. 1971. Annual outdoor show (with some tent space) held 5 days in August. Average attendance: 76,000. Entries accepted until show. Entry fee: $45/10x15 outside display area; $50/8x8 tent space. Work may be offered for sale; no commission. Craftworker must attend; demonstrations required whenever possible. Sponsor provides limited electricity for demonstrations and 24-hour security. Considers "all crafts which have been made by the person marketing them." Show promoted by radio, newsletters, newspapers, and some magazine advertising.

Sales Tip: "Fairbanks is very craft-minded, and most items which show quality workmanship sell. Cleanliness and attractiveness of display probably do most to increase sales."

Arizona

*ARCOSANTI FESTIVAL, 6433 Doubletree Rd., Scottsdale AZ 85253. (602)948-6145. Director: Bruce Joseph. Sponsor: Cosanti Foundation. "This is a major arts festival held at Paolo Soleri's experimental town, Arcosanti. A conference is also held at the site during the festival. It is intended to bring the arts to the entire region, encourage contemporary visual and performing arts and help establish Arcosanti as a cultural center." Estab. 1975. Annual outdoor show held 2 days in fall at Arcosanti, Arizona. Average attendance: 10,000. Entries accepted until 3 weeks before show. Entry fee: $50/5x10 display area. Prejudging by slides or photos; entry fee refunded for refused work. Work may be offered for sale; 10% commission. Craftworker must attend show; demonstrations OK. Sponsor provides electricity for demonstrations and 24-hour security protection. Exhibit area has tents and some materials for use by exhibitors. Presents 3 cash awards.

Acceptable Work: Considers ceramics; glass art; jewelry; metalsmithing; sculpture; soft sculpture; weaving; and woodcrafting.

Promotion: Show is advertised by local and national media; PSA; paid advertising posters, and handbills. "Photographs of the artist working may be helpful."

*FESTIVAL ARTS & CRAFTS FAIR, 8 W. Paseo Redondo, Tucson AZ 85705. (602)622-6911. Coordinator: Hap Engle. Sponsor: Tucson Festival Society, Inc. Purpose: "The show is one event of the month-long Tucson Festival, whose purpose is to promote and celebrate the cultural heritage of the Southwest." Average attendance: 50,000. Entries accepted through January. Entry fee: $65/artist. Display area: 8x8. Prejudging by slides, photos or work itself; entry fee refunded for refused work. Work may be offered for sale; no commission. Craftworker must attend show; demonstrations OK. Registration limit: 100. "We provide, if requested, an open framework booth. We supply electricity to all booths. Armed guards are on duty from show closing to reopening." Show is promoted by newspaper, radio, TV, and brochures. Categories: pottery; jewelry; fabric arts; painting; prints and photos; woodcraft; and sculpture.

Acceptable Work: Considers batik; candlemaking; ceramics; dollmaking; glass art; jewelry; leatherworking; macrame; metalsmithing; mobiles; needlecrafts; pottery; sculpture; soft sculpture; tole painting; weavings; and woodcrafting.

Awards: Presents $100, $75, and $50 prizes for best booth decorations. "Because of the nature of the awards, the only advice I have is— good design, originality and include decorative qualities."

*FOUNTAIN FESTIVAL, Box 18318, Fountain Hills AZ 85268. (602)837-1466. Chairman: Mary Read. Sponsor: Chamber of Commerce. Estab. 1975. Annual outdoor show held 3 days in November. Average attendance: 10,000. Entries accepted until 2 weeks before show. Entry fee: $25/6x10 display area; $60/10x10 tent. Awards $1,000+ in (guaranteed) prizes. Prejudging of jewelry by slides and/or photos; no entry fees refunded for refused work. Work may be offered for sale; no commission. Craftworker must attend show; demonstrations encouraged. Registration limit: 130 booths. Considers all crafts.

HARVEST ARTS AND CRAFTS FAIR, 1204 W. Silverlake Rd., Tucson AZ 85713. Recreational Program Supervisor: Carolyn L. Lenz. Sponsor: Pima County Parks & Recreation. Purpose: "to give the artist an opportunity to sell his work. This is primarily a selling show and not an exhibition show." Estab. 1972. Annual outdoor show held 1 day in October. Attendance: 750-1,000. Entries accepted until show date. Entry fee: $2/artist. Display area: 8x8. Work may be offered for sale; no commission. Craftworker must attend show; demonstrations OK. Sponsor provides electricity for demonstrations. Show is advertised by posters; newspapers; radio, and TV. Considers all crafts made by the exhibitor only.

IDES OF MARCH ARTS & CRAFTS FAIR, 1204 W. Silverlake Rd., Tucson AZ 85713. Recreation Program Supervisor: Carolyn Lenz. Sponsor: Pima County Parks & Recreation. Purpose: "to give the artist the opportunity to sell his work. This is a selling show, not an exhibit show." Estab. 1972. Annual outdoor show held 1 day in March. Attendance: 750-1,000. Entries accepted until show date. Entry fee: $2/artist. Display area: 8x8. Work must be offered for sale; no commission. Craftworker must attend show; demonstrations OK. Sponsor provides electricity for demonstrations. Show is advertised by radio; posters; newspapers; and TV. Considers all crafts made by the exhibitor. "Artist must provide all of his own presentation equipment, supplies and materials. Work ranging up to $100 sells best."

INDIAN ARTISTS AND CRAFTSMEN OF NORTH AMERICA, 22 E. Monte Vista, Phoenix AZ 85004. Contact: Arts & Crafts Chairman. Sponsor: Heard Museum Guild. Annual show. November 1 closing date. No entry fee. Considers sculpture, crafts and jewelry. Art must relate to North American Indian heritage. Ship items prepaid to museum or hand deliver.

*SCOTTSDALE ARTS FESTIVAL, Scottsdale Center for the Arts, 7383 Scottsdale Mall, Scottsdale AZ 85251. (602)994-2301. Visual Arts Manager: John Armstrong. Purpose: "Total celebration of the arts. To give craftspeople a quality festival to display/sell through." Estab. 1969. Annual outdoor show held 2 days the first weekend of March. Average attendance: 45,000. Entries accepted until 4 weeks before show. Entry fee: $10/artist, and $50 booth rental fee after acceptance in show. Maximum 10 entries/craftworker. Prejudged by slides; no $10 fees refunded for refused work (booth rental due after prejudging). Work may be offered for sale; no commission. Craftworker must attend show. Registration limit: approximately 50. Sponsor provides chairs; display panels; and 24-hour security. Considers all crafts. Amount of cash awards varies depending upon the income from entry fees. Also grants some booth rental fee waivers.

TWO FLAGS FESTIVAL OUTDOOR SHOW, Box 256, Douglas AZ 85607. (602)364-5974. Contact: Chairman. Estab. 1971. Annual outdoor show held 1 day in May. Entries accepted until 2 weeks before show. "No booth fee charge." Work may be offered for sale; 20% commission. Craftworker must attend show; demonstrations OK. Sponsor provides limited electricity. Registration limit: 40-65. Considers all handicrafts. "Would like a resume and photo from each craftsman for publicity purposes."
Sales Tip: "We would rather see a number of inexpensive items offered to sell. Higher prices do not go over well. Average customer is retired and on Social Security, plus, being a border city, we have a numerous amount of the lower income Mexican families from Mexico."

Arkansas
ARKANSAS RIVER VALLEY ARTS & CRAFTS FAIR & SALE, Box 1122, Russellville AR 72801. (501)968-1552. Contact: Lois Griffin. Estab. 1970. Annual indoor show held 3 days in November. Average attendance: 20,000. Entries accepted until spaces filled; space granted in order of application. Entry fee: $20/6x8 display area. Work must be offered for sale; no commission. Craftworker must attend show; demonstrations encouraged. Registration limit; 167. Considers handmade crafts.

ARTS AND CRAFTS FAIR, c/o Mrs. John McDaniel, Rt. 2, Forrest City AR 72335. Sponsor: Forrest City Junior Auxiliary. Estab. 1976. Annual indoor show held 2 days in September. Average attendance: 1,300. Entries accepted 2 weeks before show. Entry fee: $15/8x10 display area. Prejudging by slides; photos; recommendations; and, if possible, personal examination. Entry fee refunded for refused work. Work may be offered for sale; no commission. Craftworker must attend show; demonstrations OK. Registration limit: 76. Sponsor provides chairs; electricity for demonstration; and table for $1 fee. Considers all crafts.
Promotion: Show is advertised by radio; TV; and mail circulars. "Craftworker may be asked to furnish information and background material for publicity purposes."

BELLA VISTA ARTS & CRAFTS FESTIVAL, Kingsdale Recreation Center, Bella Vista AR 72712. (501)855-3061. Recreation Director: Pam Collins. Sponsor: Village Art Club. Purpose: "to provide a marketplace for artists and craftsmen." Estab. 1968. Annual outdoor show (with some tents) held 3 days in the fall. Average attendance: 70,000. Entries accepted until 4 weeks before show. Entry fee: $15/6x8 display area inside tent, or $15/12x12 display area outside tent. Prejudging by photos or slides; entry fee refunded for refused work. Work may be offered for sale; 10% commission. Craftworker must attend show; demonstrations OK. Sponsor provides electricity for demonstrations; fencing in tents; and 24-hour security. Considers all crafts "made by the exhibitor himself." Awards given for most attractive booth space. 1977 exhibitor sales totaled $40,000.
Promotion: Show is advertised in newspapers, magazines, radio and TV. "Send photo of yourself doing your craft, and a story about yourself and your craft [to the above address]."

*DELTA ART EXHIBITION, MacArthur Park, Box 2137, Little Rock AR 72203. (501)372-4000. Director: Townsend Wolfe. Sponsor: The Arkansas Arts Center. Estab. 1958. Annual indoor show held 4 weeks in the fall. Average attendance: 13,000. Entries accepted until 3 weeks before show. Entry fee: $5/artist. Display area: 300 running feet. Maximum 2 entries per artist. Prejudging by slides. Work may be offered for sale; 10% commission. Craftworker needn't attend show; no demonstrations. Registration limit: 60-80. Sponsor provides insurance on exhibited work; shipping costs to artist from show and 24-hour security. Categories: paintings and sculpture. Considers sculpture and soft sculpture. Maximum size: 500 lbs. Presents a $1,000 Grand Award, and an additional $3,000 for purchase awards.

FUN FESTIVAL, Box 1500, Hot Springs AR 71901. (501)321-1700. Director of Special Events: Ike Isenhower. Sponsor: Hot Springs Chamber of Commerce. Purpose: "to promote Hot Springs." Estab. 1971. Annual outdoor show (with large tents provided with electricity) held 10 days in June. Average attendance: 50,000. Entries accepted until show. Entry fee: $100/artist. Display area: 12x6. Prejudging by slide or photo. Work may be offered for sale; no commission. Craftworker must attend show; demonstrations required. Registration limit: 40. Sponsor provides chairs; electricity for demonstrations; fencing; tables; and a "security guard from closing time till opening time." Show is advertised by "radio, TV, nationwide advertising, 100,000 books mailed throughout the year, and about 100,000 flyers." Considers all crafts.

GRAND PRAIRIE FESTIVAL OF ARTS, Box 65, Stuttgart AR 72160. Annual show usually held in September. Categories include art, crafts, hobbies, music, prose and poetry.

NEWTON COUNTY ARTS AND CRAFTS SHOW, Box 58, Jasper AR 72641. (501)428-5298. Secretary: Esther Curtis. Semiannual indoor show held 3 days in May and 3 days in October. Entries accepted until 1 week before show. Entry fee: $10/6x8 display area. Work may be offered for sale; no commission. Craftworkers must attend show; demonstrations OK. Sponsor provides electricity for demonstrations and 24-hour security. Considers all crafts.

OKTOBERFEST, Box 1500, Hot Springs AR 71901. (501)321-1700. Director of Special Events: Ike Isenhower. Sponsor: Hot Springs Chamber of Commerce. Purpose: "so that tourists and home people alike would have something to do." Estab. 1975. Annual indoor show held 4 days in October. Average attendance: 27,000. Entries accepted until show date. Entry fee: $75/display area. Prejudging by slides or photos; entry fee refunded for refused work. Work must be offered for sale; no commission. Craftworker must attend show; demonstrations OK. Registration limit: 40. Sponsor provides chairs; tables; and "guard on duty on off hours." Show is advertised on radio, TV, by nationwide advertising, 100,000 books mailed throughout the year, and about 100,000 flyers. Considers all crafts.
Sales Tip: "The better types of crafts sell here. For instance, the person who does ceramics for the Fun Festival [see above] will generally bring their porcelain to this show."

OUACHITA COUNTY ARTS & CRAFTS FAIR, Box 576, Camden AR 71701. (501)836-6858. CEA Staff Chairman: Mrs. Gladys Lindsey. Sponsor: Ouachita County Extension Homemaker's Council & City of Camden. Purpose: "to make the public aware of good quality arts and crafts, and to help craftpersons find an outlet for the sale of their crafts." Estab. 1970. Annual indoor show held 2 days in October. Average attendance: 5,000. Entries accepted until 2 weeks before show. Entry fee: $5/5x10 display area. Work may be offered for sale; 10% commission. Craftworker must attend show; demonstrations encouraged. Registration limit: approximately 100. Sponsor provides chairs; display panels; electricity for demonstrations; and 24-hour security. Show is advertised by newspaper; radio; TV; posters; and direct mail. Considers "all handmade arts and crafts."

OZARKS ARTS & CRAFTS FAIR, Rt. 1, Hindsville AR 72738. Executive Director: Blanche H. Elliott. Purpose: "to bring recognition to Ozark artists and craftsmen who work with their hands in preserving the cultural heritage of the Ozark regions." Estab. 1954. Annual indoor show (with some 60x180' tents) held at War Eagle, Arkansas, 3 days in October. Average attendance: 100,000. Entries accepted until show date. Entry fee: $10/6x8 display area; $20/12x8 display area. Prejudging by slides, photos and actual samples; entry fee due after prejudging. SASE. Work may be offered for sale; 10% commission. Craftworker must attend show; no demonstrations. Registration limit: 300. Ozark residents of the 4-state Ozark region (Arkansas, Missouri, Kansas, Oklahoma). Sponsor provides tables and 24-hour security. Considers all crafts native to the Ozarks; no plastics or supplies of any kind. Presents award plaques for 10 most attractively displayed booths.

OZARK FOOTHILLS CRAFT GUILD SPRING SHOW & SALE, Box 140, Mountain View AR 72560. (501)269-3896. Director: James Sanders. Sponsor: Ozark Foothills Craft Guild. Purpose: held during the Mountain View Folk Festival. "Chance to expose the public at large to the finest examples of crafts produced in the Ozarks region. All income (net) is used to promote the objective of the Guild (a nonprofit organization)." Estab. 1962. Annual indoor show (with collapsible booths) held 3 days the third weekend of April. Average attendance: 12,000. Entries accepted until 2 weeks before show. Entry fee: $10/Guild member; $15/non-member. Display area: 6x10. Prejudging by "slides, and upon acceptance— once booth is set up— standards committee reviews all work relative to slides sent for prejudging. Work must maintain same standards as in slides." Entry fee refunded for refused work. Work may be offered for sale; 10% commission. Craftworker must attend show; demonstrations encouraged. Registration limit: 100. Sponsor provides some coverings; electricity for demonstrations; fencing above grounds; tables; 24-hour protection; sales tax charts; discounted coffee; and some bags and tissue for wrapping work. Considers all crafts except ceramics, any synthetic materials or plastic. Maximum size: 11x8.
Sales Tip: "Demonstrations assist sales and overall 19th century atmosphere. Items under $10 retail sell fastest, but good sales in all media. Total exhibitor sales average $30,000."
Promotion: Show is advertised by "TV in 4 states; radio; news releases in every news publication in the 5-state area; several nationally-distributed magazines; and craft publications. Photographs for use with news releases are welcomed. Interviews with craftspersons are at times arranged."

OZARK FRONTIER TRAIL FESTIVAL AND CRAFT SHOW, Box 140, Mountain View AR 72560. (501)269-3896. Director: James Sanders. Sponsor: Ozark Foothills Craft Guild. Purpose: "Chance to expose the public at large to the finest examples of crafts produced in the Ozarks region. All income (net) is used to promote the objectives of the Guild (a nonprofit organization)." Estab. 1962. Annual indoor show (with 3 buildings, collapsible booths, and tent) held for 3 days the second full weekend in October at Heber Spings, Arkansas. Average attendance: 15,000. Entries accepted until 2 weeks before show. Entry fee: $10/Guild member; $15/non-member. Display area: 6x10. Prejudging by "slides, and upon acceptance— once booth is set up — standards committee reviews all work relative to slides sent for prejudging. Work must maintain same standards as in slides." Entry fee refunded for refused work. Work may be offered for sale; 10% commission. Craftworker must attend show; demonstrations encouraged. Registration limit: 100. Sponsor provides some coverings; electricity for demonstrations; fencing around grounds; tables; 24-hour protection; sales tax charts; discounted coffee; and some bags and tissue for wrapping work. Considers all crafts except ceramics, any synthetic materials or plastic. Maximum size: 11x8.
Sales Tip: "Demonstrations assist sales and overall 19th century atmosphere. Items under $10 retail sell fastest, but good sales in all media." Total exhibitor sales average $50,000.
Promotion: Show is advertised by "TV in 4 states; radio; news releases in every news publication in the 5-state area; several nationally-distributed magazines; and craft publications. Photographs for use with news releases are welcomed. Interviews with craftspersons are at times arranged."

PIONEER CRAFT FESTIVAL, Box 426, Rison AR 71665. (501)325-6536. Chairman: James L. Moore Jr. Sponsor: Cleveland County Historical Society. Purpose: "to endow our museum and Pioneer Village Restoration Fund." Estab. 1971. Annual indoor show held 2 days the third weekend in March. Average attendance: 13,000. Entries accepted until 4 weeks before show ("waiting list exhibitors will be called if there is a last-minute cancellation"). Entry fee: $5/5x6 single booth; $10/5x12 double booth; $15/8x20 triple booth. Prejudging of new exhibitors by photos or samples of work. Work may be offered for sale; 10% commission. Craftworker must attend show; demonstrations OK. Registration limit: 90-100. Sponsor provides electricity for demonstrations; tables; 24-hour security; and "2 locked steel buildings plus a third building semi-enclosed and guarded."

Acceptable Work: Considers all crafts "handmade from natural materials (no plastics, etc.). Purse kits are the only kits allowed."

Sales Tip: "The pioneer crafts are selling best today — baskets, dolls, wood, anything unusual and different. Ceramics and macrame seem to be on the decline. Lapidary is also declining in our area. Handpainted china items sell well."

Promotion: Show is advertised by the Arkansas State Parks & Tourism Department in state papers, the *Ozark Mountaineer*, by posters in local cities, and in the calendar of events in national publications.

*PRINTS, DRAWINGS & CRAFTS EXHIBITION, MacArthur Park, Box 2137, Little Rock AR 72203. (501)372-4000. Director: Townsend Wolfe. Sponsor: The Arkansas Arts Center. Estab. 1968. Annual indoor show held for 4 weeks in the spring. Average attendnace: 12,000. Entries accepted until 3 weeks before show. Entry fee: $5 handling fee/artist. Display area: approximately 300 running feet. Maximum 2 entries/artist. Work may be offered for sale; 10% commission. Craftworker needn't attend show; no demonstrations. Registration limit: 100. Sponsor provides insurance on exhibited work; shipping costs to craftworker from show; and 24-hour security. Categories: prints (in all media); photography (in color and/or monochrome); crafts (metal, clay, textile, glass, wood, plastics and combined media). 1977 exhibitor sales totaled approximately $200.

Acceptable Work: Considers batik; candlemaking; ceramics; dollmaking; glass art; jewelry; lapidary; leatherworking; macrame; metalsmithing; mobiles; needlecrafts; pottery; soft sculpture; weaving; and woodcrafting.

Awards: Presents $200 awards in crafts, textiles, jewelry, ceramics, prints, drawings and photography categories. In addition, up to $2,000 in purchase awards is given.

*SUGGIN FOLKLIFE ART SHOW, c/o Mildred Gregory, 324 Walnut St., Newport AR 72112. (501)523-6250. Sponsor: Suggin Folklife Society. Estab. 1972. Annual indoor show held 2 weeks in the spring. Average attendance: 500. Entries accepted until show date. Entry fee: $1-5/item being displayed. Maximum 2 entries/category; 6 total. Work may be offered for sale; no commission. Artist needn't attend show; no demonstrations. Show is advertised by newspaper and radio. Categories: youth; adult. Considers small sculpture.

Awards: Presents purchase prizes of $50 and up; and 1st, 2nd and 3rd honorable mention ribbons. "Pick out best work and enter. Study works of the winners for future reference."

*TOYS DESIGNED BY ARTISTS EXHIBITION, MacArthur Park, Box 2137, Little Rock AR 72203. Director: Townsend Wolfe. Sponsor: The Arkansas Arts Center. Purpose: "This unique exhibition, open to all artists in the United States, gives the artists a chance to bring together creative and original ideas, and the materials used to give form to those ideas. Childlike innovation and imagination is joined with a sophisticated treatment of color, shape, texture and line to create toys." Estab. 1973. Annual indoor show held 4-8 weeks in the winter. Average attendance: 15,000-25,000. Entries accepted until 3 weeks before show. Entry fee: $5 handling fee/artist. Display area: about 200 running feet. Maximum 3 entries/artist. Work may be offered for sale; 10% commission. Craftworker needn't attend show; no demonstrations. Registration limit: approximately 60. Sponsor provides display panels; insurance on exhibited work; shipping costs to artists from show and 24-hour security.

Acceptable Work: Considers all crafts. "Entries must be original and completed one year prior to the show. Entries are the artists' conception of a toy — not necessarily a functional toy for children to play with. Directions or diagrams on use of the toy must accompany entry where necessary."

Awards: Presents purchase awards to 5 or more entries. "The purchase award is the price of the object less 10%. All purchase awards become the property of the AAC for its permanent collection."

Sales: "Sales are handled by the Exhibitions Department of The Arkansas Arts Center. The

AAC is a nonprofit organization and no sales taxes are charged. Sales from the 1977 show amounted to about $1,600."

Promotion: "The Toys Designed by Artists Exhibition is sponsored by the Arkansas Arts Center, who is solely responsible for publicity to national, regional and local publications."

California

*ALAMEDA COUNTY FAIR, Box 579, Pleasanton CA 94566. (415)846-2881. Manager: Lee R. Hall. Assistant Manager: Peter Bailey. Estab. 1907. Annual outdoor show (with some indoor space) held 15 days in the summer. Average attendance: 400,000. Entries accepted until 3 weeks before show. Entry fee: $2/item being displayed in competition; prejudging of actual work; no entry fees refunded for refused work. Work may be offered for sale; 10% commission. Craftworker needn't attend; demonstrations OK. Registration limit: 100. Sponsor provides electricity for demonstrations and 24-hour security. Categories: art; painting; sculpture; and photography. Considers sculpture. Maximum size: 52x52". Awards $55-100 for 1st-3rd places.

AMERICAN FOLK ARTS FESTIVAL, 832 Bancroft Way, Berkeley CA 94810. (415)548-5440. Contact: Steve Kyle or Warren Cook. Sponsor: General Expositions Company. Trade show. Purpose: "to introduce American crafts and craftspeople to the continent historically famous for handcrafts." First year show is to be held in Europe in 1978. Annual indoor show held 3 days during the spring at Amsterdam, Holland. Expected 1978 attendance: 20,000. Entries accepted until 4 weeks before show. Entry fee: $275/10x10 display area, although "we are searching for grants and other ways to cut down on expenses." Prejudging by slides, photos, or item brought to office; entry fees refunded for refused work. Work may be offered for sale; no commission. Craftworker must attend show; demonstrations OK. Registration limit: 140. Sponsor provides electricity; general lighting and cleaning; and 24-hour security. "We will also handle as much of the freight and customs formalities as possible." Considers all crafts, although the number of booths in each category is limited. "All exhibitors are required to be in 19th century American costume during the hours of the fair, and are required to build a booth that fits into the image of the fair."

Promotion: ". . . we will be placing a series of ads in Holland's major newspapers and in the *International Herald-Tribune*, plus distributing a huge number of posters and handbills. There will also be a coordinated publicity campaign to the radio and television stations and newspapers. To further immediate and continuing sales we will be inviting importers and gallery buyers from all over Europe to attend the fair."

*AN ANCIENT ART UPDATED, Box 721, La Jolla CA 92037. (714)755-7125 or 454-0595. Chairman of Show: Correen Kaufman. Sponsor: Enamel Guild West. Purpose is to "give enameling and the enameler a chance to show." Biannual indoor show held 4 weeks in San Diego at the Jewish Center Gallery and 2 weeks in Los Angeles at the El Camino College gallery from February-April. Entries accepted until 4 weeks before show. No entry fee; but exhibitor must be a member of the Guild. Maximum 3 entries/artist. Prejudging of actual work. Work may be offered for sale; 25% commission. Craftworker needn't attend show; no demonstrations. Sponsor handles sales; provides a free catalog; holds a reception; and insures exhibited work. "No work may be withdrawn from the exhibition before its conclusion."

Acceptable Work: Considers all enameling that is suitably prepared for display. "Because the show is to travel it is imperative that all pieces submitted be packed in easily repackable containers. All work arriving by mail must have return postage enclosed and, if more than one piece is sent, provision must be made for returning rejected pieces to the artist while accepted pieces go on to the show. Special arrangements must be made for works over 100 pounds or over 4' in any dimension."

Awards: Presents cash awards of $75, $50 and $20. Juror is Larry Urrutia, gallery director of the San Diego State University.

ART FOR FUN(D)'S SAKE CRAFT FAIR, 5504 W. Crestridge, Rancho Palos Verdes CA 90274. (213)541-2479. Contact: Chairman. Sponsor: Palos Verdes Community Arts Association. Purpose: to provide "financial support of the Palos Verdes community arts association — a nonprofit gallery, classrooms, etc." Estab. 1962. Annual outdoor show held 2 days in October or November. Average attendance: 5,000. Entries accepted until 6 weeks before show. Entry fee: $50/10x10 display area. Prejudging by photos to be submitted with application. Entry fee due after prejudging. Work may be offered for sale; no commission. Craftworker must attend show; demonstrations OK. Registration limit: 85-100. Sponsor provides some electricity for demonstrations and 24-hour security. Considers all crafts except lapidary. Craftworker required to provide an interesting and attractive booth.

Promotion: Show is advertised through mailers to residents; sign boards; and newspaper coverage. Craftworkers will be contacted for photos if necessary.

*ART IN ALL MEDIA, Southern California Exposition, Fairgrounds, Del Mar CA 92014. (714)755-1161 or 297-0338. Contact: Entry Department. Sponsor: 22nd District Agricultural Association. "Southern California Expo will present to the public, the very finest exhibition of paintings, graphics, sculpture and crafts available from southern California artists and craftsmen." Estab. 1882. Annual indoor show held 2 weeks in the summer. Average attendance: 650,000. Entries accepted until 4 weeks before show. Entry fee: $3/item being displayed. Prejudging by actual work; no entry fees refunded for refused work. Work may be offered for sale; 25% commission. Craftworker needn't attend show; no demonstrations. Sponsor provides the necessary display unit; 24-hour security; and handles sales. Show is advertised in newspapers throughout southern California; TV; radio; direct mail; and lectures to various clubs, schools, etc. Categories: ceramics, metal, enamel jewelry; fibers, textiles, macrame; and other craft media. 1977 exhibitor sales totalled $10,000 +.
Acceptable Work: Considers batik; ceramics; glass art; jewelry; enamel; macrame; metalsmithing; mobiles; pottery; sculpture; soft sculpture; tole painting; weaving; and woodcrafting. "No crafts made with instructor's assistance. They must be in good taste and suitable for family viewing."

ARTS 'N CRAFTS BY THE SEA, Box 404, Hermosa Beach CA 90254. (213)376-0951. Executive Manager: Charles A. Pinney. Sponsor: Hermosa Beach Chamber of Commerce. Estab. 1969. Annual outdoor show held 2 days during Labor Day weekend. Average attendance: 100,-000. Entries accepted until 2 weeks before show. Entry fee: $40 or $60/10x10 display area, depending upon location. Prejudging "by 3 photos, slides or submissions of actual samples of item (if small)." Entry fee refunded for refused work. Work may be offered for sale; no commission. Craftworker must attend show; demonstrations encouraged. Registration limit: 250. Sponsor provides electricity for demonstrations and water.
Acceptable Work: Considers all crafts. No "manufactured or machine-crafted [items] — except such manufactured items needed to complement craft (i.e., gnarled wood clocks, buckles for tooled leather belts, or stamped leather belts for handcrafted belt buckles). Desire 50% or better to be handcrafted."
Sales Tip: "Demonstrate; have a friendly, positive attitude; exhibit quality products and craftsmanship; provide uniqueness or unusual crafts; and price fairly." Recommend conspicuous display of artist's name and mailing address for follow-up work on order."
Promotion: Show is advertised by advanced mailings of applications; newspapers; *Holiday Magazine*; *West Arts Magazine*; and flyers distributed at other shows. Promotional materials may be provided at the craftworker's discretion.

*BEVERLY HILLS AFFAIRE IN THE GARDENS ART SHOW, 450 N. Crescent Dr., Beverly Hills CA 90210. (213)550-4864. Recreation Services Manager: Michelle Merrill. Sponsor: City of Beverly Hills Recreation Department. Estab. 1976. Annual outdoor show held 2 days in the spring. Average attendance: 7,000-9,000. Entries accepted until 4 weeks before show. Entry fee: $40/9x12 display area, 7' height limitation. Prejudging by pamphlets; slides; photos; and previous awards. Entry fee refunded for refused work. Work may be offered for sale; no commission. Craftworker must attend show; demonstrations OK. Registration limit: 200. Categories: oil/acrylic; photography; sculpture; watercolor; jewelry; drawing; prints; graphics; ceramics; and other. Considers all crafts except clothing and furniture.
Awards: Presents ribbons for each category. "An artist who is able to demonstrate his/her talent (displays, portfolio, awards) is at an advantage when being judged."
Promotion: Show is advertised by papers; TV; radio; flyers; posters; etc. "Each artist is requested to submit 1-4 b&w 8x10 or 5x7 glossies and a brief resume. These will be used for promotion in the various media. They prefer action shots of the artist at work or artistically photographed pieces of the work. These can be sent in with the application."

BROCKMAN GALLERY CHRISTMAS CRAFTS SHOW, 4334 Degnam Blvd., Los Angeles CA 90008. (213)294-3766. Program Coordinator: Pat Johnson. Sponsor: Brockman Gallery Productions. Estab. 1968. Annual indoor/outdoor show held 3 weeks in December. Average attendance: 700-800. Entries accepted until 2 weeks before show. Prejudging. Work may be offered for sale; 40% commission. Registration limit: 100. Sponsor provides inside display equipment and pays insurance on exhibited work.
Acceptable Work: Considers batik; ceramics; dollmaking; glass art; jewelry; leatherworking; metalsmithing; pottery; soft sculpture; weavings; wall hangings; and woodcrafting.

CALICO ART FESTIVAL, 8813 Excelsior Ave., Hanford CA 93230. (209)584-5884. Show Chairman and Co-ordinator: Willie Camara. Sponsor: Kings River Parent-Teachers Club. "Held as a fund-raising for our country school." Estab. 1975. Annual outdoor show held 1 day in October. Average attendance: 2,000. Entries accepted until 1 week before show (although some later applications accepted). Entry fee: $5 plus 1 donation ($5 value)/10x10 or 10x12 display area. "We don't judge as an art show, but I do require photos or slides — as we keep a small show and limit the amount of each category." Entry fee refunded for refused work. Work may be offered for sale; no commission prior to 1978 show. Craftworker must attend show; demonstrations OK. Registration limit: 55. Sponsor provides electricity for demonstrations. "We will accept any good craft. We are striving for a top show — with our craftspeople going away with a profit — we want people who do top work and don't mind day outdoor shows. Some of our locations are sunny — artists are responsible for their own set ups and umbrellas if needed."
Promotion: "We really promote this show and our theme is always Calico Art Festival. We are a well-known group in our area. We put ads in local papers [and] we get much free publicity since we are a nonprofit school organization — on radio and local TV stations. Lots of posters! If we get local extra newspaper coverage, we enjoy featuring an artist or 2; and therefore would need to have some good, interesting glossy b&w photos that could be used in a newspaper article."
Profile: "Our show is held out in the country — away from the bustle of town — pleasant and relaxing day. Many people from throughout the area are doing their Christmas shopping at this show. Also we try to make our artists and craftspeople at home with a free meal plus coffee at set-up time. We make our profit largely from the barbeque and Bingo games."

CALIFORNIA CRAFTS, E.B. Crocker Art Gallery, 216 O St., Sacramento CA 95814. (916)446-4677. Sponsor: Creative Arts League of Sacramento. Biennial crafts exhibition.

*****THE CALIFORNIA CRAFTSMAN**, 559 Pacific St., Monterey CA 93940. Director: June Braucht. Sponsor: Monterey Peninsula Museum of Art. Purpose: "it's our way of having a high quality crafts exhibition for the area." Estab. 1976. Biennial indoor show held the month of October during even-numbered years. Average attendance: 2,500. Entry fee: $5/craftworker. Maximum 3 entries/craftworker. Prejudging by slides in August; no entry fees refunded. Work may be offered for sale; 20% commission. Craftworker needn't attend show; no demonstrations. Sponsor provides insurance on exhibited work; handles all sales; and the exhibition is installed by the museum. Awards "to be determined by the entry fees received. Judging will be done for creativity and craftsmanship."
Acceptable Work: Considers ceramics; glass art; jewelry; leatherworking; macrame; metalsmithing; pottery; textile arts; and woodcrafting. Works "must be easily manageable by 2 people."
Promotion: Show is advertised in *Craft Horizons, Artweek, Westart*, and by direct mail. "If work is accepted he [the craftworker] should provide an 8x10 glossy photograph for possible use in the catalog."

*****CALIFORNIA 3-DIMENSIONAL REGIONAL EXHIBIT AND COMPETITION**, 482 S. 2nd St., San Jose CA 95113. (408)294-4545. Business Director: Dr. Delmar Kolb. Exhibit Director: Kathleen Barrett. Sponsor: San Jose Art League. Purpose: "a recognition of the validity of the artist's creativity and acquired skills." Estab. 1970. Annual indoor show held 1 month late November-early December. Average attendance: 500/month. Entries accepted in 2-3 weeks before show. Entry fee: $3/item. Display area: 1,200 square feet. Prejudging by actual work; entry fee not refunded. Work may be offered for sale; 25% commission. Craftworker needn't attend show; no demonstrations. Sponsor provides display panels and 24-hour security. Show is advertised by *Artweek, Westart*, major California newspapers; *Ceramics Monthly*; and mailings. Presents cash awards totaling $1,000. Considers ceramics; glass art; jewelry; macrame; metalsmithing; mobiles; pottery; sculpture; soft sculpture; weaving; and woodcrafting.

*****CAPTIAL WOODCARVERS ASSOCIATON SHOW**, 3037 Great Falls Way, Sacramento CA 95826. (916)383-5606. Vice President: Roland Rosenberger. Purpose: "to promote woodcarvers club and art of woodcraft." Estab. 1972. Annual indoor show held the first weekend in November. Attendance: 8,000-10,000. Entries accepted until show date. Entry fee: $5/artist. Display area: 4x8. Maximum 1 entry/category. Work may be offered for sale; 10% commission. Craftworker must attend show; demonstrations OK. Registration limit: 60. Chairs and tables can be rented if sponsor is given 2 weeks notice. Categories: woodcrafting; painted work; carving in the round; decorative carving; whittling; and ornamental and special. Presents $250 in cash prizes, and ribbons to all participants and class winners.

Promotion: Show is advertised on local TV; in 2 daily newspapers; and in regional shopping news publication. Craftworker should supply b&w photos, "plus business cards are optional."

*CATALINA FESTIVAL OF ART, Box 161, Avalon CA 90704. Contact: Festival Committee Chairman. Annual show held in September. Sponsor: Catalina Art Association. "Work must be brought to Avalon by the artists or they must arrange for someone they may know here to handle it." The festival consists of 3 categories: the Invitational Exhibit; the Street Show, which includes a nonjuried painting section, preregistered photography division and young artists section; and a preregistered craft show. "Some artists do not realize the exhibit area is family oriented (open free to the public) and so they include occasional works not suitable for a general audience, i.e., graphic nudes, which must be pulled. Also that it is a 'traditionalist' show and is judged accordingly. Abstract, pop, surrealist, etc. rarely are in the award winning list."

*CELEBRATION OF THE ARTS, 20600 Roscoe Blvd., Canoga Park CA 91306. (213)341-6434. Contact: Chairman. Sponsor: St. John's in the Valley United Methodist Church. Estab. 1970. Annual indoor/outdoor show held 2 days in May. Average attendance: 2,000. Entries accepted until 1 week before show. Entry fee: $10/10x12 display area. Awards $50 best of show in youth and adult divisions; and 1st, 2nd and 3rd place ribbons. Work may be offered for sale; 10% commission. Craftworker must attend show; demonstrations encouraged. Registration limit: 120. Considers all crafts. Needlework must be framed.

CHRISTMAS ART & CRAFT SALE, 1221 4th St., Davis CA 95616. (916)756-4100. Director: Marian Hamilton. Sponsor: Davis Art Center. Purpose: "fund raiser for art center." Estab. 1965. Annual indoor show held 3 weeks in December. Average attendance: 1,500. Entries accepted until 4 weeks before show. No entry fee. Prejudging by slides or actual work. Work must be offered for sale; 25% commission. Craftworker needn't attend show; no demonstrations. Registration limit: 100. Sponsor provides setup and sales personnel. Show is advertised by newspapers; radio; and flyers. Considers all crafts except decoupage and tole painting. "All work must be ready for display." 1977 show sales totaled $17,500.

*CONTRA COSTA COUNTY FAIR, 10th and L Sts., Antioch CA 94509. (415)757-4400. Secretary-Manager: C. Larry Gately. Sponsor: 23rd District Agricultural Association. Estab. 1975. Annual indoor show held 5 days in August. Average attendance: 75,000. Entries for judging accepted until 4 weeks before show. Entry fee: $30/10x10 display booth; 50c/each item entered for judging. Work may be offered for sale; no commission in booths. Craftworker must attend show in order to purchase booth display area; demonstrations OK. Sponsor provides some display panels; electricity for demonstrations and 24-hour security. Show is advertised in newspapers, and on radio and TV. Presents $30 best of show cash prize and ribbons.
Acceptable Work: Considers ceramics; decorative painting; dolls; draped dolls; fabric dolls; wood carving; decoupage including paper tole; 3-dimensional and Repousse; ecology crafts — dried flowers and pods; ecology boxes; handmade jewelry; macrame; models — cars, planes, ships; pottery — thrown or hand-built; stained glass; hydrocal painting (including gold leaf); and most other crafts.

*DESIGNER/CRAFTSMAN, Civic Center Plaza, Richmond CA 94804. (415)234-2397. Curator: J.T. Soult. Sponsor: Richmond Art Center. Purpose: to "support and present finely designed and crafted ware in the same light as 'fine art.' Also to encourage new craftspeople to exhibit their work." Estab. 1951. Annual indoor show held 4 weeks, October-November. Average attendance: 2,000. Entry fee: $5/piece; set counts as 1 piece. Maximum 3 pieces per artist. Work may be offered for sale; 30% commission. Craftworker needn't attend show; no demonstrations. Sponsor provides insurance on exhibited work. Show is advertised by press releases to news media; radio and TV spot announcements; art magazines and art press; and show announcements. 1977 cash awards totalled $1,275; purchase awards, $250; $100 merit award; and $50 memorial award. 1977 show sales totalled $250. Considers all crafts. Write for prospectus.

DOWN TOWN FULTON SHOW, Art Enterprise, Box 231, Rackerby CA 95972. Contact: M.P. Schiedeck. Estab. 1973. Biennial outdoor show held 4 days in May and 5 days in September at Fresno, California. Entries accepted until show date. Entry fee: $25/artist. Prejudging by slides or photos; entry fee refunded for refused work. Work may be offered for sale; 10% commission. Craftworker must attend show; demonstrations OK. Registration limit: 200. Sponsor provides electricity for demonstrations. Show is advertised by TV, radio and newspapers. Considers all crafts.

Glass art, batik, ceramics, dollmaking, jewelry, leatherworking, macrame, metalsmithing, pottery, soft sculpture, weaving, and woodcrafting are considered for the Guildford Handcrafts Exposition, Guildford, Connecticut. The 3-day July show is sponsored by the Guildford Handcraft Center.

DOWN TOWN NOVATO CENTER, Art Enterprise, Box 231, Rackerby CA 95972. Contact: M.P. Schiedeck. Estab. 1973. Quarterly outdoor show (with some overhangs) held 4 days in January, April, August and November at Novato, California. Entries accepted until show date. Entry fee: $20/artist. Prejudging by slides or photos; entry fee refunded for refused work. Work may be offered for sale; 10% commission. Craftworker must attend show; demonstrations OK. Show is advertised by newspapers. Considers all crafts except clothing.

*EHRMAN MANSION ART SHOW & FAIR, Box 126, Carnelian Bay CA 95711. (916)583-6208 or 587-6446. Chairman: Joanna Gillis. Sponsors: North Tahoe Art Guild, North Lake Tahoe Federated Women's Club, Lake Tahoe State Park Advisory Committee and Chamber of Commerce. Estab. 1967. Annual indoor show held the second week in August. Average attendance: 5,000-6,000. Entries accepted until show date. Entry fee: $5/entry. Maximum 3 entries per exhibitor. Prejudging; entry fee refunded for refused work. Work may be offered for sale; 10% commission. Considers all media. Presents cash prizes. Judges are professional artists experienced in the various media.

*FESTIVAL OF ARTS & CRAFTS, 11740 E. Telegraph Rd., Santa Fe Springs CA 90670. (213)864-7511. Assistant Supervisor of Recreation: Jamie Herbon. Sponsor: City of Santa Fe Springs Parks & Recreation Department. Purpose is "to give local artists and residents an opportunity to view, buy and sell artwork." Estab. 1959. Annual indoor/outdoor show held 2 days in July. Average attendance: 800. Entries accepted until first week in July for juried art; beginning of June through the first week in July for art and craft sales application. No entry fee. Display area: for sales approximately 6x6. Maximum 3 juried entries/category; only 1 category may be entered. Prejudging ("arts and crafts amateurs and professionals are judged the morning before the show opens"). Work may be offered for sale; no commission. Juried craftworkers needn't attend show. Sponsor provides chairs; table; and 24-hour security. Categories: amateur and professional arts crafts and general crafts divisions. Presents best of show plaque.

Acceptable Work: In crafts division considers batik; ceramics; glass art; jewelry; lapidary; leatherworking; macrame; metalsmithing; needlecrafts; pottery; weaving; and woodcrafting. In general crafts division considers candlemaking; decoupage; and dollmaking. In arts division considers sculpture; soft sculpture; and tole painting. "Entries may not exceed weight that can be lifted by one man. Entries that are wet, unfinished, damaged, poorly framed, or not matted are unacceptable. Entries not in one piece, requiring special handling, lighting or installation are subject to committee approval." Maximum size: 5x5.

Sales Tip: "Have some lower-priced items." Ceramics, jewelry, novelties and paintings sell well.

Promotion: Show is advertised by press releases; brochures to local schools, arts and crafts suppliers and display shops; signs and posters; and announcements on the radio and in magazines.

FESTIVAL OF THE ARTS, Sacramento Regional Arts Council, 562A Downtown Plaza, Sacramento CA 95814. Chairman: Albert Hellenthal. Annual open-air mall show held 2 days the last weekend in September. Entry fee: $10/5x10 display area. No commission. Craftworker or representative must be present at exhibit at all times. Considers original work only. No size limit.

*FIBER SHOW, 158 E. Blithedale Ave., Mill Valley CA 94941. (415)383-3630. Chairman: Giselle Kappus. Sponsor: Mill Valley Arts Guild. Purpose: "to give the artist a chance and place to exhibit his original work (also to sell and/or rent), but no high pressure salesmanship. Mill Valley Arts Guild is nonprofit." Estab. 1976. Annual indoor show held 3 weeks in June. Attendance: 500-700. Entries accepted until 1 week before show. Entry fee: $6/artist. Maximum 3 entries/artist. Prejudging of original work by 3-person jury (artists-teachers); no entry fees refunded for refused work. Work may be offered for sale; 30% commission. Craftworker needn't attend show; no demonstrations. Sponsor provides coverings; display panels; insurance on exhibited work; tables; and 24-hour security. Show is advertised by newspaper releases; mailed and hand-delivered invitations and flyers; posters; and paid ads. Categories include weavings; clothing; and fiber. Considers all crafts except tole painting; candlemaking; decoupage; dollmaking; and glass art. Presents $200 in cash prizes; $200 in purchase prizes; and merit award ribbons.

FIESTA DEL ARTES, Box 404, Hermosa Beach CA 90254. (213)376-0951. Executive Manager: Charles A. Pinney. Sponsor: Hermosa Beach Chamber of Commerce. Estab. 1969. Annual outdoor show held 2 days during Memorial Day weekend. Average attendance: 100,000. Entries accepted until 2 weeks before show. Entry fee: $40 or $60, depending upon location. Display area: 10x10. Prejudging by 3 photos, slides, or submission of actual sample (if small). Entry fee refunded for refused work. Work may be offered for sale; no commission. Craftworker must attend show; demonstrations encouraged. Registration limit: 250. Sponsor provides electricity for demonstrations and water.

Acceptable Work: Considers all crafts. No "manufactured or machine-crafted [items] — except such manufactured items needed to complement craft (i.e., gnarled wood clocks, buckles for tooled leather belts, or stamped leather belts for handcrafted belt buckles). Desire 50% or better to be handcrafted."

Sales Tip: "Demonstrate; have a friendly, positive attitude; exhibit quality products and craftsmanship; provide uniqueness or unusual crafts; and price fairly." Recommend conspicuous display of artist's name and mailing address for follow-up work on order."

Promotion: Show is advertised by advanced mailings of applications; newspapers; *Holiday Magazine; West Arts Magazine*; and flyers distributed at other shows. Promotional materials may be provided at the craftworker's discretion.

FIRST SUNDAY IN THE PARK, Box 967, Ventura CA 93001. (805)644-7421. Recreation Supervisor: Laurel Leavy. Sponsor: Ventura City Parks & Recreation Department. Purpose: "To provide a location and opportunity for craftsmen and artists to display and sell their craftwork." Estab. 1973. Outdoor show held 1 Sunday during the months of February, March, April, May, June, August, September, November and December. Attendance: 1,500-3,100. Entries due the Wednesday before the Sunday of the show. Entry fee: $5/8x10 display area. "New entries are screened by a clear photo or by bringing the work into the recreation office. Judged on craftsmanship quality." Entry fee due after prejudging. Work may be offered for sale; no commission. Craftworker must attend show; demonstrations OK. Sponsor provides electricity for demonstrations. Considers all crafts.

Promotion: Show is advertised by newspaper releases; radio announcements; newspaper display ads; announcements in publications; and posters.

GIFT FESTIVAL, Box 848, Lodi CA 95240. (209)369-2771. Secretary/Manager: De Von C. Lee. Sponsor: Lodi Grape Festival & National Wine Show. Purpose: "to create interim use of the festival grounds, and provide the public with a fun and unique shopping atmosphere." Estab. 1977. Annual indoor show held 2 days in early December. Average attendance: 5,000. Contracts for booth space are on a first come, first serve basis. Entry fee: "average of $40 per 100 square feet." Work may be offered for sale; no commission. Craftworker must attend show; demonstrations OK. Registration limit: 80. Sponsor provides display panels; electricity for demonstrations; wooden booths; some table spaces; and 24-hour security. Show is advertised by radio and newspaper. Considers all handcrafted items. Awards $100 for Christmas tree decorating contest; and prizes to best decorated booth and exhibitor. "The public is looking for Christmas gifts that are unique and reasonably-priced. Sales can be improved by well-displayed merchandise."

*HALF MOON BAY ART & PUMPKIN FESTIVAL, Box 274, Half Moon Bay CA 94019. (415)762-5202. Arts Chairman: Mary Bettencourt. Purpose is "to raise funds to beautify and improve this small coastal 'turn of the century' town. Proceeds purchased 16 old-fashioned street lights, Victorian benches, street trees and flowers." Estab. 1971. Annual outdoor show held 2 days in October. Average attendance: 150,000. Entries accepted until beginning of September. Entry fee: $75/10x10 display area. Prejudging by slides or photos sent with application (these will be returned). Entries also reviewed during the show. "Previous entrants with quality merchandise get preferential placement." Entry fee refunded for refused work. Work may be offered for sale; no commission. Craftworker must attend show; demonstrations OK. Limited to 200 booths/festival. Sponsor provides limited electricity for demonstrations. Considers all crafts. Presents ribbons, and prize for best pumpkin decorated in spirit of craft.
Promotion: Publicity office: (415)346-4446. Show is "heavily promoted by posters, radio, TV, newspaper publicity. Can sometimes use photos."

*HANCOCK PARK FESTIVAL OF ART, 155 W. Washington Blvd., Los Angeles CA 90015. (213)749-6941, ext. 215. Contact: Cultural Arts Section. Sponsor: County of Los Angeles Department of Parks & Recreation. Purpose is to give area artists a chance to display and sell their work; and provide Los Angeles with a variety of activities to view and participate in. Estab. 1977. Annual outdoor show held weekends during the summer (June-September). Average attendance: 3,000. Entries accepted until 1 week before show. Entry fee to be determined. Display area: 10x15. Prejudging by slides and/or photos accompanying entry form. Entry fee due after prejudging. Work may be offered for sale; commission to be determined. Craftworker must attend show; demonstrations OK. Registration limit: 25-30. "Some weekends will be specifically designated for a particular art medium (e.g., photography show, painting and sculpture, etc.)" Awards, ribbons and cash prizes will be given at some shows."
Sales Tip: "Displays are very important to the overall effect of the artwork. Most artists that put time and effort into their displays not only win the awards, but also sell more. The public will usually buy items that are ready to display in their home or can be given as a gift. Each individual artist must have a sales permit issued by the city."

HILLCREST PARK LIVELY ARTS FESTIVAL, 303 W. Commonwealth Ave., Fullerton CA 92632. (714)525-7171, ext. 251. Supervisor: Ron Brocklehurst. Coordinator: Donna Noblitt. Sponsor: Fullerton Park & Recreation Department. "Hillcrest Park Lively Arts Festival is planned to be an exciting celebration bringing together 'all' age groups and art forms. In doing so, we hope to provide the community with a rich resource showcase and an enriching experience both for the performer and the observer." Estab. 1974. Annual outdoor show held 2 days in the fall. Average attendance: 12,000. Entries accepted until show date. Entry fee: $20/artist. Display area: 10x10. Prejudging by slides or photos ("to make sure they are handcrafted"); entry fee due after prejudging. Work may be offered for sale; no commission. Craftworker needn't attend show; demonstrations OK. Registration limit: 100. Sponsor provides electricity for demonstrations and 24-hour security. Considers all crafts.
Promotion: Show is advertised in local, county and statewide newspapers; in *Westart Magazine*; by flyers and posters; and large mailings.

HOLIDAY FAIRE, 1201 W. Malvern, Fullerton CA 92633. (714)879-6860. Program Coordinator: Martha L. Bartholomew. Sponsor: Muckenthaler Cultural Center. Purpose: "to provide an opportunity for artists/craftspeople to show their creations and to give the community a special presentation of craft objects for Christmas or holiday gift giving." Estab. 1969. Annual indoor show held 2 weeks in December. Average attendance: 5,000. Entries accepted until 6 weeks before show. "Individual artist's work dispersed throughout exhibition area." Maximum

100 pieces per artist. Prejudging by resume; slides; or photos. Work may be offered for sale; 25% commission. Craftworker needn't attend show; no demonstrations. Registration limit: 50. Sponsor provides installation in the gallery space and staff management. Show is advertised by printed announcements and the news media. Considers all crafts except candlemaking; decoupage; and lapidary. Maximum size of works 30x40. Needlework must be framed.

*INK & CLAY, c/o Art Department, California State Polytechnic University, 3801 Temple Ave., Pomona CA 91768. (714)598-4567. Chairman: Diane Divelbess. Estab. 1972. Annual indoor show held the month of January. Average attendance: 100/day. Entries accepted until 3 weeks before show. Entry fee: $4/item being displayed. Display area: 1,500 square feet. Prejudging. No entry fees refunded for refused work. Work may be offered for sale; 20% commission. Craftworker needn't attend show; no demonstrations. Sponsor provides insurance on exhibited work and on work shipped to artist; and 24-hour security. Categories: printmaking; ceramics. Considers ceramics weighing 300 pounds or less. Awards $1,000 in purchase prizes.

*INTERNATIONAL FINE ARTS EXHIBIT, 801 Main St., El Centro CA 92243. (714)352-8230. Exhibit Chairman: Marian F. Wheeler. Sponsor: Pilot Club of Golden Sands. "Our purpose is to promote art, provide an opportunity for the local community to see what is current in art, and provide funds for scholarships and other community services projects." Estab. 1976. Annual indoor show held 1 week in the fall. Deadline for slides for prejudging: August. Deadline for receipt of entry form and fee: September. Deadline for receipt of work: 1 week before show. Jury fee: $1/1-5 slides. Entry fee: $5/item being displayed. Maximum 5 entries/artist. Work may be offered for sale; 20% commission. Craftworker needn't attend show; no demonstrations. Registration limit: 180. Considers sculpture weighing 40 pounds or less. "Crated works accepted provided they are shipped in reusable container, and return postage included."
Awards: Presents $50 sweepstakes prize; several purchase awards; 1st, 2nd, 3rd and honorable mention ribbons; Guy C. Archer Memorial Award for outstanding artist; Judge's Award; Juror's Award; and Popularity Award. "The show is half modern and half traditional. Both schools have an equal chance for awards."
Sales Tip: Items under $500 sell best. "The Pilot Club of Golden Sands handles all sales and sales taxes."
Promotion: Show is advertised by magazine articles; newspaper and radio advertising; and invitations to known collectors for a champagne showing. Brochures on the artist and his work will be given out, if provided by the artist."

JOHNNY APPLESEED DAY, Box 658, Paradise CA 95969. (916)877-9356. Contact: Executive Vice President. Sponsor: Chamber of Commerce. Renewed in 1977. Annual show held the first Saturday in October (commercial craftworkers, indoor; artists and hobbyist craftworkers, outdoors). Average attendace: 12,000. Entries accepted until 2 weeks before show. Entry fee: $20/8x8 display area for hobbyist craftworkers, $35/8x8 display area for commercial craftworkers. Work may be offered for sale; no commission. Artists charged a $5 hanging fee plus commission on sales. Demonstrations OK. Categories: artists (hangings only); craft items (non-commercial); and craft items (commercial). "Commercial or noncommerical determined by retail license held with State of California." Considers all crafts. Show is advertised by magazine; newspapers; radio; TV; posters; etc.

LAKE TAHOE ART AND CRAFT FAIR, Box 7112, South Lake Tahoe CA 95731. (916)544-4696. Director: Wayne Denney. Sponsor: Artists' Co-op. Purpose: "to promote artists." Estab. 1976. Annual outdoor show held 3 days during tourist season (May-September). Booths are covered top and back. Entries accepted until show date. Entry fee: $25/10x10 display area. Prejudging by slides and photos; entry fee refunded for refused work. Work may be offered for sale; 10% commission. Craftworker must attend show; demonstrations OK. Registration limit: 60. Sponsor provides coverings; electricity for demonstrations; and fencing. Show is advertised by radio; newspaper; posters; 30' road banner; and highway marquee.

MAMA'S FOLK ART FESTIVAL, Los Arboles Artisans Coop, 5200 Mowry Ave., Suite L, Fremont CA 94538. (415)791-9691. Manager: Mollie Howard. Purpose: "to promote our coop here in this shopping center and to make money to cover expenses of show." Estab. 1972. Annual outdoor show (with overhang about 18' wide) held 2 days in May. Average attendance: 1,000 +. Entries accepted until show date. Entry fee: $15/10x5 display area. Prejudging by slides, photos, "or in person on a given day to be noted on entry form"; entry fee refunded for refused work. Work may be offered for sale; 10% commission. Craftworker must attend show "unless by arrangement with us"; demonstrations OK. Registration limit: 50. Sponsor provides security protection from 6 p.m.-12 p.m.; refreshments; and indoor plumbing. Show is advertised by flyers; mailings to past customers; and ¼-page ads in 2 local papers. Considers all crafts. "Display to be in theme of show — no card tables with something thrown on. Like old wood — anything that looks professional." Total exhibitor sales average "$1,000-1,500 per day."

Sales Tip: "Well-presented items sell much better. By getting involved with the people [the craftworker will make the most sales] — not just sitting with arms folded or reading a book. Selling is an art — those who work at it, sell the most."

*MILL VALLEY ARTS GUILD WINTER FESTIVAL, 158 E. Blithedale Ave., Mill Valley CA 94941. (415)383-3630. Coordinator: Martha Hannon. Sponsor: Mill Valley Arts Guild (non-profit artist's cooperative). Purpose: "to raise money to run our artists/craftsmen cooperative so all Bay Area (San Francisco) will have a place to exhibit and sell and rent their art. We are non-profit — but funds go for maintenance, prizes, and annual scholarships for high school artists." Estab. 1976. Annual indoor show held the month of December in 3 large rooms in the Mill Valley Arts Guild Gallery. Attendance: 400-500. Entries accepted the last 2 days of November. Entry fee: $2/artist. Maximum 20 small pieces; 5 large pieces/artist. Prejudging by Mill Valley Arts Guild members (artists and craftworkers); no entry fees refunded for refused work. Work may be offered for sale; 30% commission. Craftworker needn't attend show; no demonstrations. Sponsor provides chairs; display panels; insurance on exhibited work; tables; and 24-hour security.

Acceptable Work: Considers "all Christmas gift items — toys, ornaments, pottery, paintings, sculpture, handmade clothing, fiberworks, furniture, baked Christmas foods, weaving and jewelry. All entries must be original — no copies, prints, etc." All work must be ready for presentation. Maximum size: 20x22.

Awards: Presents cash prizes; ribbons; and merit awards. "Enter only top original work. Jurors are expert in their media."

Sales Tip: Viewing public buys "top quality items for gift-giving at reasonable prices. Most artists/craftsmen lower their prices for this Christmas show to help the Mill Valley Arts Guild." Coordinator handles sales and sales tax. $1,000 profit was made in 1977.

Promotion: "Extensive publicity is conducted through the use of newspapers; TV; radio; flyers; and invitations."

MONTEREY COUNTY FAIR, Art Enterprise, Box 231, Rackerby CA 95972. Contact: M.P. Schiedeck. Estab. 1973. Annual outdoor show held 6 days in September at Monterey, California. Average attendance: 145,000. Entries accepted until 1 week before show. Entry fee: $65/exhibitor. Display area: 10x10. Prejudging by slides or photos; entry fee refunded for refused work. Work may be offered for sale; 10% commission. Craftworker must attend show; demonstrations OK. Registraton limit: 60. Sponsor provides electricity for demonstrations. Considers all crafts.

*MOORPARK COLLEGE FESTIVAL OF THE ARTS, 7075 Campus Rd., Moorpark CA 93021. (805)529-2321. Contact: Betty Sullivan. Sponsor: Community Services. Estab. 1972. Annual indoor show held the month of May (also sponsors a 1-day unjuried show at this time). Average attendance: 1,000, first day; 5,000 during the month. Entries accepted until show. Entry fee: $4/entry for those submitted 1 week prior to show; $3 when entry forms are submitted before that time. "Our gallery is small and can only hold 20-30 works." Work may be offered for sale; no commission. Sponsor provides display equipment and insurance on exhibited work. Considers sculpture.

Awards: Presents $100 1st prize and possibly cash awards for 2nd and 3rd places and $500 purchase prize. Judges are "outstanding southern California artists, applying current artistic standards of judgement."

*MOTHER LODE ART SHOW, Box 905, Placerville CA 95667. Sponsor: Placerville Arts Association. Estab. 1966. Annual indoor show held 2 weeks in August. Average attendance: 500. Entries accepted on entry days 1 week before show. Entry fee: $4/item. Prejudging by actual work; entry fee not refunded for refused work. Work may be offered for sale; 10% commission. Craftworker needn't attend show; no demonstrations. The artist is responsible only for bringing and picking up his work. The Arts Association hangs and staffs the show. Show is advertised by magazine notices; newspaper articles; and notices. Presents cash awards of $60, $30, $20; purchase awards of $1,200; and ribbons for best of show, 1st, 2nd, 3rd, and honorable mention in each category. 1977 show sales totalled $1,500. Considers batik; ceramics; macrame; pottery; sculpture; and weaving.

MOUNTAIN AIRE, Box 4698, Modesto CA 95352. (209)521-6310. Sponsor: Rock 'N Chair Productions. Estab. 1974. Annual outdoor show held in conjunction with Music Festival 2 days in June. Average attendance: 10,000/day. Entries accepted until 1 week before show. Write for entry fee. Prejudging; entry fee refunded for refused work. Work may be offered for sale; no commission. Demonstrations OK. Registration limit: 75. Considers all handmade crafts. "Wares directed toward ages 15-35 sell best."

OCTOBERFEST ART CRAFT AND ANTIQUE SHOW & SALE, Box 207, Clovis Chamber of Commerce, Clovis CA 93613. (209)299-7273. Secretary: Lori Phipps. Purpose: "to promote the city of Clovis." Estab. 1972. Annual outdoor show held 1 day in October. Average attendance: 1,500. Entries accepted until 2 weeks before show. Entry fee: $12.50/10x10 display area; $17.50/10x15 display area; $22.50/10x20 display area. Work may be offered for sale; no commission. Craftworker must attend show; demonstrations OK. Registration limit: 80. Considers all crafts.

OJAI CRAFTS FESTIVAL, Box 331, Ojai CA 93023. (805)646-0117. Director: Martin Isaacson. Sponsor: Ojai Valley Art Center. Purpose: "fund-raising for on-going programs at the center." Estab. 1974. Annual indoor/outdoor show held 2 days in the fall. Average attendance: 25,000. Entries accepted until 6 weeks before show. Entry fee: $15/6x10 display area. Prejudging by slides; $5 retained for refused work. Work may be offered for sale; 10% commission. Craftworker must attend show; demonstrations OK. Registration limit: 60. Sponsor provides electricity for demonstrations. Considers all crafts.
Sales Tip: "Items suitable and priced for Christmas gifts sell best. Craftspeople are responsible for handling their own sales and sales taxes." 1977 exhibitor sales totalled approximately $20,-000.
Promotion: Show is advertised by radio; TV; newspaper; direct mail; and posters. "Send 8x10 b&w glossies of artist involved with his craftwork, along with a brief paragraph on background. Also send address of major paper in artist's community."

OUTDOOR ARTS AND CRAFTS FAIR, 801 Main St., El Centro CA 92243. (714)352-8230. Exhibit Chairwoman: Marion F. Wheeler. Sponsor: Pilot Club of Golden Sands. Estab. 1976. Annual outdoor show held 2 days in November. Entries accepted until 2 weeks before show. Entry fee: $25/artist. Display area: 12x12. Work may be offered for sale; no commission. Artist or agent must attend show; demonstrations OK ("special space consideration is given to those demonstrating"). Registration limit: 25. Considers all crafts. "Show is on grass. No plastic ground covers; no dowels over ¼". Nothing obscene or pornographic allowed. Items under $50 sell best."
Promotion: Show is advertised by newspapers; magazines; radio; and advertisements. "Photographs of artist at work, etc., suitable for newspaper use, will be used if accepted by the newspapers."

PACIFIC STATES CRAFTS FAIR, Box 31298, San Francisco CA 94131. (415)567-4999. Director: Marcia Chamberlain. Sponsor: American Craft Enterprises, Inc. Estab. 1976. Annual indoor show held 4 days (2 trade, 2 public) in August at San Francisco's Ft. Mason facilities. Average attendance: 20,000. Entries accepted until March 1. Entry fee determined by size of display area. Prejudging by 5 color slides "to be reviewed by a selection committee." Entry fee due after prejudging. Work may be offered for sale; no commission. Craftworker must attend show; demonstrations OK. Sponsor provides coverings; electricity for demonstrations; 24-hour security ("however ACE will not be liable for loss or damage"). 1977 exhibitor sales totalled "almost half a million dollars." Show is advertised in craft publications; trade papers/publications; newspapers and multimedia. Professionals from the 13-states of the Pacific Region only.
Acceptable Work: Considers batik; candlemaking; ceramics; dollmaking; glass art; jewelry; handmade musical instruments; leatherworking; macrame; metalsmithing; mobiles; needlecrafts; pottery; sculpture; soft sculpture; weavings; and woodcrafting. "Kits designed to produce an object, even though inspired and produced by a craftperson, should not be submitted. Categories not generally acceptable are the following: painting; photography; graphics; dried flowers; seed and pod decorations; cut bottles; and embellished objects such as painted boxes, weathered boards, stones, shells, buttons and decorated furniture. We ask that craftspeople make their display as creative as their work."

PEACH TREE MALL, 3608 Cinnabar Ave., Carson City NV 89701. (702)883-0968. Director: Bea Griffin. Sponsor: Creative Artists Group. Estab. 1973. Annual indoor show held 4 days in July at Marysville, California. Entries accepted until show date. Entry fee: $20/display area.

Work may be offered for sale; 10% commission. Craftworker must attend show; demonstrations OK. Registration limit: 100. Sponsor provides electricity for demonstrations and 24-hour security. Considers all crafts. Show is advertised by newspaper and radio. "Send me pictures."

PROFESSIONAL ARTS, CRAFTS AND INDOOR PLANTS SHOW, 10992 Ashton Ave., Los Angeles CA 90024. (213)479-7055. Producer/Director: Glen Beckman. Sponsor: Industry Productions of California, Inc. "This show is held for American artists and craftspeople that wish to make wholesale sales and contacts with buyers for department stores, gift shops, plant shops, boutiques, etc." Estab. 1976. Semiannual indoor show held 1 week in January and 1 week in July at the Pacific Design Center in Los Angeles. Average attendance: 10,000. Entries accepted until 2 weeks before show. Entry fee: $225-250/8x10 or 10x10 display area. Work may be offered for sale; no commission. Craftworker must attend show; demonstrations OK. Registration limit: 150-200. Sponsor provides 24-hour security. Considers all crafts. Presents awards for the best exhibit and best direct mail promotion.

Sales Tip: "The first 4 days are for wholesale buyers only, and the exhibitor should have a good supply of business cards, catalog sheets and price lists. The final 2 days are for direct retail sales to the general public. As of the January 1977 show, we have over 50 exhibitors that have qualified for the "$5,000 and Up Club" (established for exhibitors who write $5,000 and up in wholesale orders during and/or 30 days following any single event").

Promotion: Show is advertised with "over 50,000 special invitations mailed to wholesale buyers with heavy newspaper advertising for retail days. We provide any reasonable quantity of wholesale invitations (at no cost) to the exhibitor for mailing to his/her own wholesale customer and/or prospect list."

*QUILT FAIRE, Box 2494, Castro Valley CA 94546. (415)537-2688. Contact: Maud Maslin. Sponsor: Gail Moore Quilters and The Hayward First Committee. Purpose: "to share the beautiful quilts of the past and present; to encourage people to try the techniques. We have many fine demonstrations so guests can learn new and different things. To help carry on the knowledge and know how to future generations." Estab. 1974. Annual indoor show held 2 days in October at Hayward, California. Average attendance: 4,000-5,000. Entries accepted until 3 weeks before show. Work may not be offered for sale. Craftworker needn't attend show; demonstrations OK. Sponsor provides electricity for demonstrations and 24-hour security. Show is advertised by many national magazines; radio; TV; and 144 newspapers. Presents ribbon awards. Considers all crafts in the quilting area.

*RIVERSIDE COUNTY SUMMER OUTDOOR ART SHOW, Riverside County Art and Culture Center, Cherry Valley CA 92223. (714)845-2626. Annual outdoor show held in mid-June. Considers ceramics; creative crafts; and sculpture. Entry fee: $5. Craftworker must attend show. Work may be offered for sale; no commission. Presents cash awards. California artists only.

RIVERSIDE DOWNTOWN SATURDAY MARKET, 3900 Main St., 4th Flr., Riverside CA 92522. (714)787-7584. Manager: Stephen Schultz. Estab. 1976. Show held Friday and Saturday of every week. Entry fee: $15/craftworker. Work may be offered for sale; no commission. Craftworker must attend show; demonstrations OK. Considers all crafts. Send for brochure.

SACRAMENTO HARVEST FESTIVAL, 832 Bancroft Way, Berkeley CA 94710. (415)548-5440. Contact: Steve Kyle, Warren Cook, or Ellen Schwartz. Sponsor: General Expositions Corporation. Estab. 1974. Annual indoor show held 3 days in October in Sacramento, California. Entries accepted until full; "booths are rented according to seniority." Entry fee: $135/10x10 display area. Prejudging by 6 photos or slides or actual work. Work may be offered for sale; no commission. Craftworker must attend show; demonstrations OK. Sponsor provides electricity for demonstrations; backdrop drapery; side rails; 24-hour security; cleaning; motel or hotel accommodations at group rate; inexpensive trucking of booth setup and stock round-trip between other Harvest Festival shows. Presents awards for best costumes; best designed booths; and best demonstrating booths. Show is advertised by newspaper; radio; TV; billboard; direct mailing; poster; discount coupon; news releases; and TV guest appearances. Considers all crafts.

Profile: "The Harvest Festivals are patterned after the famous country autumn fairs of 19th century America. These fairs were held to give thanksgiving for bountiful crops and as a last celebration before the hard winter set in. Craftworkers are required to be in 19th century costume."

*SALZ TANNERY ANNUAL LEATHER AS ART CONTEST, 1040 River St., Santa Cruz CA 95060. (408)423-1480. Manager: Judy Rumford. Purpose: "to encourage fine artistry, and promote the use of leather as an art medium." Estab. 1975. Annual indoor/outdoor show held 2 days in the summer. Average attendance: 8,000. Entries accepted until 4 weeks before show. No entry fee. Maximum 3 entries/artist. Prejudging by slides. Work may be offered for sale; no commission. Craftworker needn't attend show; no demonstrations. Sponsor provides display panels; insurance on exhibited work and on work shipped to artist; shipping cost to artist from show; and 24-hour security. Show is advertised in art publications; newspapers; on radio; and through mailing lists. Categories: decorative and functional. Leatherworking only. Presents cash prizes and ribbons.

SAN DIEGO HARVEST FESTIVAL, 832 Bancroft Way, Berkeley CA 94710. (415)548-5440. Contact: Steve Kyle, Warren Cook, or Ellen Schwartz. Sponsor: General Expositions Corporation. Estab. 1975. Annual indoor show held 3 days in November in San Diego, California. Entries accepted until full; "booths are rented according to seniority." Entry fee: $135/10x10 display area. Prejudging by 6 photos or slides or actual work. Work may be offered for sale; no commission. Craftworker must attend show; demonstrations OK. Sponsor provides electricity for demonstrations; backdrop drapery; side rails; 24-hour security; cleaning; motel or hotel accommodations at group rate; inexpensive trucking of booth setup and stock round-trip between other Harvest Festival shows. Presents awards for best costumes; best designed booths; and best demonstrating booths. Show is advertised by newspaper; radio; TV; billboard; direct mailing; poster; discount coupon; news releases; and TV guest appearances. Considers all crafts.
Profile: "The Harvest Festivals are patterned after the famous country autumn fairs of 19th century America. These fairs were held to give thanksgiving for bountiful crops and as a last celebration before the hard winter set in. Craftworkers are required to be in 19th century costume."

*SAN FRANCISCO ANNUAL ARTS FESTIVAL, 165 Grove St., San Francisco CA 94102. (415)558-3465. Director: Elio Benvenuto. Sponsor: City of San Francisco. Purpose: "promotion for the arts in general; and a cultural happening for the public." Estab. 1946. Annual outdoor show (with some awning covering provided) held 5 days "the last part of September." Average attendance: 375,000. Entries accepted until 4 weeks before show. No entry fee. Display area: 8x8x5. Prejudging by 5 works. Work may be offered for sale; no commission. Craftworker must attend show; demonstrations OK. Registration limit: "approximately 120 artists residing within 9 Bay Area counties." Presents prizes up to $5,000 and ribbons.
Acceptable Work: Considers batik; ceramics; glass art; jewelry; soft sculpture; metalsmithing; weaving; and woodcrafting.

SAN FRANCISCO HARVEST FESTIVAL, 832 Bancroft Way, Berkeley CA 94710. (415)548-5440. Contact: Steve Kyle, Warren Cook, or Ellen Schwartz. Sponsor: General Expositions Corporation. Estab. 1972. Annual indoor show held 2 3-day weekends in December at San Francisco, California. Entries accepted until full; "booths are rented according to seniority." Entry fee: $270/10x10 display area for 2 weekends. Prejudging by 6 photos or slides or actual work. Work may be offered for sale; no commission. Craftworker must attend show; demonstrations OK. Sponsor provides electricity for demonstrations; backdrop drapery; side rails; 24-hour security; cleaning; motel or hotel accommodations at group rate; inexpensive trucking of booth setup and stock round-trip between other Harvest Festival shows. Presents awards for best costumes; best designed booths; and best demonstrating booths. Show is advertised by newspaper; radio; TV; billboard; direct mailing; posters; discount coupons; news releases; and TV guest appearances. Considers all crafts.
Profile: "The Harvest Festivals are patterned after the famous country autumn fairs of 19th century America. These fairs were held to give thanksgiving for bountiful crops and as a last celebration before the hard winter set in. Craftworkers are required to be in 19th century costume."

SAN JOSE HARVEST FESTIVAL, 832 Bancroft Way, Berkeley CA 94710. (415)548-5440. Contact: Steve Kyle, Warren Cook, or Ellen Schwartz. Sponsor: General Expositions Corporation. Estab. 1978. Annual indoor show held 3 days in October in San Jose, California. Entries accepted until full; "booths are rented according to seniority." Entry fee: $135/8x10 display area. Prejudging by 6 photos or slides or actual work. Work may be offered for sale; no commission. Craftworker must attend show; demonstrations OK. Sponsor provides electricity for demonstrations; backdrop drapery; side rails; 24-hour security; cleaning; motel or hotel accommodations at group rate; inexpensive trucking of booth setup and stock round-trip between other Harvest Festival shows. Presents awards for best costumes; best designed booths; and best demonstrating booths. Show is advertised by newspaper; radio; TV; billboard; direct mailing;

poster; discount coupon; news releases; and TV guest appearances. Considers all crafts.
Profile: "The Harvest Festivals are patterned after the famous country autumn fairs of 19th century America. These fairs were held to give thanksgiving for bountiful crops and as a last celebration before the hard winter set in. Craftworkers are required to be in 19th century costume."

*SAN MATEO COUNTY FAIR CRAFTS EXHIBITION, Box 1027, San Mateo CA 94403. (415)345-3541. Contact: Lois Kelley. Sponsor: San Mateo County Fair Arts Committee, Inc. Annual indoor show held 13 days in August. Entries accepted until 2 weeks before show. Entry fee: $5/entry. Prejudging; no entry fees refunded for refused work. Work may be offered for sale; no commission. Sponsor provides display panels and equipment. Presents $11,000 in cash scholarships, cash and merchandise or services.
Acceptable Work: Considers original batik; ceramics; glass art; jewelry; metalsmithing; pottery; soft sculpture; weavings; and woodcrafting.

SANTA CRUZ COUNTY FAIR, Box 231, Rackerby CA 95972. Contact: M.P. Schiedeck. Sponsor: Art Enterprise. Estab. 1973. Annual outdoor show held 4 days in September at Watsonville, California. Average attendance: 125,000. Entries accepted until show date. Entry fee: $35/artist. Display area: 10x10 or 10x12. Prejudging by slides or photos; entry fee refunded for refused work. Work may be offered for sale; 10% commission. Craftworker must attend show; demonstrations OK. Sponsor provides electricity for demonstrations. Considers all crafts.

SANTA'S CHRISTMAS GIFT SHOW, 1225 Vienna Dr. #322, Sunnyvale CA 94086. (408)734-3238. Producer: Ron Roupe. Purpose: "to give the small business person an opportunity to sell, make money, and increase his business and business contacts." Estab. 1976. Annual indoor show held 5 days in November (Thanksgiving week) at the Santa Clara County Fairgrounds in San Jose. Average attendance: 25,000. Entries accepted up until 2 weeks before show. Entry fee: $300/10x10 display area; $400 for corners. Prejudging by photos; entry fee refunded for refused work. Work may be offered for sale; no commission. Craftworker must attend show; demonstrations OK. Registration limit: 150-200. Sponsor provides electricity for demonstrations; drapery backdrops; and 24-hour protection. Considers all crafts.
Sales Tip: "Be interested in the public — customer attention [talking and answering questions] is very important. Everything for Christmas presents [sells well]."
Promotion: Show is advertised by TV; radio; newspaper flyers; and word of mouth. Craftworkers should supply "whatever they feel would help them — brochures, cards, mailing lists, etc."

SAWDUST FESTIVAL, Box 1234, Laguna Beach CA 92652. (714)494-3030. Secretary: Tracey Moscaritolo. Purpose: to exhibit and sell arts and crafts of Laguna Beach area artisans and artists. Estab. 1966. Annual outdoor show held 6 weeks, July-August. Average attendance: 250,000. Entries from local residents only accepted until 6 months before show. Entry fee: $150/6 weeks of show. Work may be offered for sale; no commission. Craftworker or representative must attend show; demonstrations OK. Registration limit: 160. Sponsor provides electricity for demonstration; fencing; and 24-hour security. Show is advertised by a publicity and advertising budget — TV; radio; brochures; and magazines. "Each participant is asked to complete a publicity questionnaire." Considers all crafts.

SONOMA COUNTY FAIR, c/o Art Enterprise, Box 231, Rackerby CA 95972. Contact: M.P. Schiedeck. Estab. 1976. Annual outdoor show held 2 weeks in July at Santa Rosa, California. Average attendance: 600,000. Entries accepted until 1 week before show. Entry fee: $100-150/exhibitor. Display area: 10x10. Prejudging by slides or photos; entry fee refunded for refused work. Work may be offered for sale; 10% commission. Craftworker must attend show; demonstrations OK. Sponsor provides electricity for demonstrations. Considers all crafts.

SONORA CHRISTMAS FAIR, Box 1135, Twain Harte CA 95383. Contact: Richard Burleigh. Sponsor: Fire on the Mountain Glass Shop. Estab. 1975. Annual indoor show held 2 days during Thanksgiving weekend at Sonora, California. Attendance: 7,500-8,000. Entries accepted until mid-October. Write for entry fee. Display area: 8x10. Prejudging; entry fee refunded for refused work. Work must be offered for sale; no commission. Craftworker must attend show; demonstrations OK. Registration limit: 65-70. Sponsor provides chairs and electricity for demonstrations. Considers all crafts.

*SOUTH LAKE FESTIVAL OF THE ARTS, 492 South Lake Ave., Pasadena CA 91101. (213)792-4417. Director: Ray Leier. Sponsor: South Lake Business Association. Purpose: "to create a place where artists may present their work to the buying public, as well as a fundraiser for the South Lake Association." Estab. 1974. Semiannual outdoor show held 3 days in the fall and spring. Attendance: 2,000-6,000. Entries accepted until 2 weeks before show; "some entries may be accepted if particular media is not filled." Entry fee: $35/artist. Display area: 4x12 "unless otherwise requested." Prejudging by "photos of work to be exhibited, plus description of display booth (no card tables allowed);" entry fee refunded for refused work. Work may be offered for sale; no commission. Craftworker must attend show; demonstration OK. Registration limit: 150. Awards ribbons. 1977 fall show grossed $60,000 +.

Acceptable Work: Considers batik; candlemaking; ceramics; dollmaking; glass art; jewelry; leatherworking; macrame; metalsmithing; mobiles; needlecrafts; pottery; sculpture; soft sculpture; weaving; woodcrafting; and "most fine crafts. Artists must provide a professional presentation of their work."

SOUTH TAHOE ART FESTIVAL, Box 711, South Lake Tahoe CA 95705. Director: Peter Darvas. Sponsor: Lampson Plaza Merchants Association. Estab. 1974. Annual outdoor show held 4 days in August. Average attendance: 80,000-100,000. Entries accepted until 4 weeks before show. Entry fee: $20/10x20 display area; $5/jury fee. Prejudging by 3 slides or 3 color photos; 1 of display urged. Entry fee refunded for refused work. Work may be offered for sale; 10% commission. Craftworker must attend show; demonstrations OK. Registration limit: 80. Sponsor provides electricity for demonstrations if requested in advance; and 24-hour security. Considers all crafts except candlemaking; decoupage; dollmaking; soft sculpture; and tole painting.

*SOUTHERN CALIFORNIA EXPOSITION, Del Mar Fairgrounds, Del Mar CA 92014. (714)755-1161. Exhibit/Supervisor: Lolly Stuckenschneider. Sponsor: 22nd District Agricultural Association. Estab. 1880. Annual indoor show held 2 weeks in the summer. Average attendance: 650,000. Entries accepted until 3 weeks before show. Entry fee varies according to item being displayed. Craftworker needn't attend show; demonstrations OK. Sponsor provides display panels; electricity for demonstrations; and 24-hour security.

Acceptable Work: Considers batik; ceramics; decoupage; dollmaking; glass art; lapidary; macrame; metalsmithing; needlecrafts; sculpture; weaving; and woodcrafting.

Awards: Presents various cash awards and ribbons. "Entries that are different and unusual, not too abstract, appeal most [to the judges]."

SOUTHERN CALIFORNIA POWWOW, Box 112, Baldwin Park CA 91706. (213)442-8441 or 337-5300. Directors: Jill Tilander and Cecilia Fischer. Sponsor: F&T Associates. Purpose: "to spread the gem and mineral hobby mainly. But realizing that 'variety is the spice of life,' we are open to all crafts and hobbies that a person might do on a small scale, in a small shop at home. The 'little' person can't afford booths at large shows, so we hope this can be an outlet for him to spread his hobby a little." Estab. 1977. Annual show with 184 covered spaces and 115 uncovered spaces held outdoors 3 days in July at the Los Angeles County Fairgrounds in Pomona, California. Average attendance: 3,000. Entries accepted until show date. Entry fee: $50, covered; $60, covered corners; $40, noncovered; $50, noncovered corners/12x25 display area. Work may be offered for sale; no commission. "Booth must be attended during hours open to public; demonstrations highly encouraged." Sponsor provides electricity for demonstrations; and offers tables, chairs, and coverings for rent. Considers all crafts.

Promotion: Show is advertised in *Gem & Minerals, Lapidary Journal* and *Rock and Gem*; by radio (including a live 4-hour broadcast on Saturday); in local newspapers; information sent to over 200 gem and mineral clubs in the West; and by ads in *Desert* magazine, *Westart, The Goodfellow Review of Crafts*, and *Sunshine Artists, U.S.A.* "We would appreciate any copy on special things that would draw the public."

*SOUTHLAND ART SHOW, Box 115, Twenty-nine Palms CA 92277. (714)367-9633. President: Lee Lukes Pickering. Sponsor: Twenty-nine Palms Artists Guild. Estab. 1963. Annual indoor show held 3 weeks during November. Average attendance: 500. Entries accepted until 3 days before show. Entry fee: $2/item being displayed. Maximum 1 entry/category; 3 entries total. Prejudging of work presented at show. Work may be offered for sale; 33⅓% commission. "Works are handled on consignment with our staff handling all sales." Craftworker needn't attend show; demonstrations OK. Sponsor provides chairs; display panels; and electricity for demonstrations. Show is advertised by radio; newspapers; direct mail; and annual exhibit brochure. Awards ribbons.

Acceptable Work: Considers batik; ceramics; decoupage; macrame; mobiles; pottery; sculpture; and soft sculpture. Maximum size: 20 inches in any direction. "Works must be wired and framed, or mounted [when applicable]."

*SUMMER OUTDOOR ART SHOW, 9401 Oak Glen Rd., Cherry Valley CA 92223. (714)845-2626. Director: Mary Jo O'Neill. Sponsor: Edward-Dean Museum of Decorative Arts. Annual outdoor show held 1 day in June. Average attendance: 100. Entries accepted until 1 week before show. Entry fee: $5/category entered. Maximum 10 entries/category. Work may be offered for sale; no commission. Craftworker or representative must attend show; demonstrations OK. Considers all crafts. Presents cash prizes.

*SUTTER STREET ART FESTIVAL, 7107 Carriage Dr., Citrus Heights CA 95610. Director: Joanne Burkett. Sponsor: Sutter Street Merchants Association. "Our profits are used for further restoration and upkeep of the historic area, and we like to promote the arts since there are many art and crafts shops here." Estab. "in the 1960s." Annual outdoor show (with some covered spaces) held 2 days in June at Folsom, California. Average attendance: 20,000. Entries accepted until 1 week before show. Entry fee: $20/artist. Display area: 6x8 or 8x8. Prejudging by slides or photos and description of work; entry fee refunded for refused work. Work may be offered for sale; no commission. "We can handle tax for those with no resale number." Craftworker must attend show; demonstrations OK. Registration limit: 300. Sponsor provides electricity for demonstrations; and security during show hours. Show is advertised by TV; radio; newspapers; and magazines. Considers all crafts. "Exhibitors must provide own props and display supplies." **Awards:** Presents $200 in cash awards and ribbons. "Our preference is for winners fitting the theme of our town. It is a gold rush mother lode setting, and we like good realism."

TEHACHAPI MOUNTAIN FESTIVAL ART FAIRE, Box 165, Tehachapi CA 93561. (805)822-5158. Sponsor: Tehachapi Valley Arts Association. Purpose: "promotion of the arts and joint venture with Tehachapi Mountain Festival which is held annually, and brings many visitors to the town." Estab. "approximately 1967." Annual outdoor show (with trees and parachutes for shade) held 2 days in August at the Tehachapi city park. Entries accepted until 3 weeks before show. Entry fee: $15/10x10 (or larger) display area. Prejudging by slides or photos; entry fee refunded for refused work. Work may be offered for sale; no commission. Craftworker must attend show; demonstrations permitted. Sponsor provides coverings; display panels; and electricity for demonstrations. Show is promoted by "publicity in local and regional newspapers (Kern County); *LA Times; Westart* magazine; local radio and TV; and posters. **Acceptable Work:** Considers all crafts. "We encourage individuals and originality. We try to avoid duplications of too similar a craft at show." If hooks are needed, craftworker must provide. **Sales Tip:** "Public buying mood is quite flexible, but tends to go for original and good works from less than a dollar to $100-200 price range."

TRUCKEE OUTDOOR ARTS AND CRAFTS FAIR, Box 1239, Truckee CA 95734. (916)587-2025. Contact: Kris Benett and Ken Lipsitz. Sponsor: Truckee Art Guild. Purpose: "to enhance the cultural arts in Truckee and to provide a distribution point for local artisans." Estab. 1972. Annual outdoor show held 4 days in August. Average attendance: "thousands." Entries accepted until 3 weeks before show. Entry fee: $30/craftworker. Display area: 10x10. Work may be offered for sale; no commission. Craftworker must attend show; demonstrations OK. Registration limit: 80. Considers all crafts.

UFM-MONTEREY'S FREE UNIVERSITY ARTS & CRAFTS SHOW, 980 Fremont Ave., Monterey CA 93940. (408)649-1150, ext. 283. Coordinator: Sherry Pastor. Estab. 1974. Annual outdoor show held 3 days in late November or early December. Average attendance: 20,000. Entries accepted "until we are full." Entry fee: $10 for students; $15 for local craftworkers; and $20 for out-of-town craftworkers. Display area: 8x8. Prejudging by photos or slides; entry fee refunded for refused work. Work may be offered for sale; 10% commission. Craftworker must attend show; no demonstrations. Registration limit: 75. Sponsor provides electricity for demonstrations. Show is advertised by radio; TV; newspapers; and posters. Considers most crafts. 1977 exhibitor sales totalled $15,000.

UNION STREET SPRING FESTIVAL & CRAFTS FAIR, Union Street Association, 2149 Union St., San Francisco CA 94123. (415)567-3055 or 346-4446. Coordinator: Terry Pimsleur. Purpose: "to raise funds for the association to promote and improve historic Cow Hollow area of San Francisco." Estab. 1976. Annual outdoor show held 2 days in June on 5 blocks of Union Street. Attendance: 40,000-50,000/day. Entries accepted until 4 weeks before show. Entry fee: $100/10x8 display area. Prejudging by slides or photos; entry fee refunded for refused work. Work may be offered for sale; no commission. Craftworker must attend show; demonstrations OK. Registration limit: 200-250 (merchants on Union Street have preference as to space). Sponsor provides some electricity for demonstrations; and special patrol for security ("but not

responsible for loss"). Considers all crafts. "Tables must be draped and must not protrude into street beyond 10 feet from curb."
Promotion: Show is advertised in newspapers; radio; TV; posters; and radio remote broadcast. "Can sometimes use pictures."

UNIVERSITY OF SOUTHERN CALIFORNIA CRAFT CENTER, YWCA University Park, Los Angeles CA 90007. (213)741-6208. Contact: Jo Ann Fried. Estab. 1970. Semiannual show held 3 days in May and December. Entry fee: $40. Work may be offered for sale; no commission. Craftworker must attend show; demonstrations OK. Registration limit: 100. Considers all crafts.
Sales Tip: "Gold jewelry; ceramics; stained glass; and fabric arts do well. There is more likelihood of selling expensive, fine works as people have come to appreciate handcrafted items. Bestsellers are $.50-100."

VALLEY BETH SHALOM TEMPLE'S ANNUAL COMMUNITY ARTS & CRAFTS FAIRE, 4401 Trancas Place, Tarzana CA 91356. (213)342-7664. Chairpeople: Elaine Granof, Clark Weissman. Purpose: "to create funds for our education department." Estab. 1976. Annual outdoor show held the Sunday before Thanksgiving at Encino, California. Average attendance: 6,000. Entries accepted until 3 weeks before show. Entry fee: $25-35/10x16 display area. Prejudging by slides, photos or brochures; entry fee refunded for refused work. Work may be offered for sale; no commission. Craftworker must attend show; demonstrations OK. Registration limit: 100. Sponsor provides electricity for demonstrations. Considers all "handcrafted items."
Promotion: Show is advertised by newspapers; flyers; radio and TV spots; posters; and mailers to 1,200 members of the Temple. "Submit a brief paragraph on your background."

VALLEY CRAFT GUILD CHRISTMAS SHOW, 7798 Ironwood Dr., Dublin CA 94566. (415)828-2607. Director: Donna Franks. Estab. 1971. Annual indoor show held 2 days in November. Average attendance: 2,000. Entries accepted until August. Entry fee: $25/4x5 display area; $50/8x5 display area. Maximum 1 entry/category per artist. Prejudging of actual work; entry fee refunded for refused work. Work may be offered for sale; no commission. Craftworker must attend show; demonstrations OK. Registration limit: 41. Sponsor provides chairs and electricity for demonstrations. Show is advertised by newspapers; flyers; posters; and mailers. Considers all crafts. Items in the $2-10 range tend to sell best.

***WESTWOOD CERAMIC SUPPLY COMPANY GALLERY SHOWS**, 14400 E. Lomitas Ave., City of Industry CA 91744. (213)330-0631. Director: Adrienne Dykman. Sponsors semiannual theme shows. Prejudging by slides. Work may be offered for sale; 20% commission. Cash awards. Write for prospectus.

Colorado

***ARTISTS ALPINE HOLIDAY**, Box 149, Ouray CO 81427. (303)325-4766. Secretary: Ramona Radcliff. Sponsor: Ouray County Arts Association. Purpose: "to provide and promote culture in a remote and culturally-deprived area." Estab. 1961. Annual indoor show held 1 week in August. Average attendance: 3,000. Entries accepted until 2 days before show. Entry fee: $4/item being displayed. Display area: 75x100. Maximum 3 entries per category. Work may be offered for sale; 15% commission. Craftworker needn't attend show; a few demonstrations permitted if requested. Sponsor provides display panels. Show is advertised by newspapers; local TV; and radio. Considers sculpture. Awards $105 in each medium; $500 in purchase prizes; and ribbons. 1977 exhibitor sales totalled $5,000 +.

CARBONDALE MOUNTAIN FAIR, Box 174, Carbondale CO 81623. (303)963-2798. Director: Laurie Loeb. Sponsor: Carbondale Council on Arts and Humanities. Purpose: to give exposure to the arts. Estab. 1972. Annual outdoor show held 2 days in July. Average attendance: 4,000. Entries accepted until 6 weeks before show. Entry fee: $15/10x10 display area. Prejudging by slides; entry fee refunded for refused work. Work may be offered for sale; 10% commission. Craftworker must attend show; demonstrations OK. Registration limit: approximately 100. Sponsor provides electricity for demonstration. Show is advertised by radio; TV; newspapers; and posters. Considers all crafts. 1977 exhibitor sale totalled approximately $27,000.

CHERRY CREEK FESTIVAL OF THE ARTS, 1400 Josephine, Denver CO 80206. (303)322-1688. Contact: Chairman. Sponsor: Cherry Creek Merchants' Association and Assistance League of Denver. Purpose: fundraiser. Estab. 1975. Annual outdoor show (with some tents) held 2 weekends in June. Entries accepted until 2 weeks before show. Entry fee: $45/8x8 display area. Prejudging by slides and photos for new participants; entry fee refunded for refused work.

Work may be offered for sale; 20% commission. Craftworker must attend show; demonstrations OK if confined within space allotted. Registration limit: 138. Sponsor provides pegboard. Show is advertised by newspaper; radio; TV; art and craft publications; and posters. Submit slides, photos or press releases from previous shows to be used for local advertising. Considers all crafts.

EL DIEZ Y SEIS DE SEPTIEMBRE, 501 E. Chester, Lafayette CO 80026. (303)665-3310. Contact: Dan Escalante or Cece Garcia. Purpose: "cultural enrichment and education." Estab. 1973. Annual outdoor show held 1-2 days "September 16 or thereabouts." Average attendance: 500. Entries accepted until 3 weeks before show. Entry fee: $10/10x10 display area. Prejudging; "our only requirement is that they be oriented towards an ethnic group — Indian, Mexican, etc." Entry fee due after prejudging. Work may be offered for sale; no commission. Craftworker or representative must attend show; demonstration OK. Sponsor provides electricity for demonstrations and 24-hour security. Considers all crafts except those that are highly flammable.
Promotion: Show is advertised in newspapers; on radio; and by posters. "Send photos or samples for preshow display at local businesses."

*JEFFERSON UNITARIAN CHURCH ANNUAL JURIED ART SHOW, 14350 W. 32nd Ave., Golden CO 80401. Chairperson: Carley Whitley. Purpose: "public education in the arts — Unitarians are big on public education in all fields." Estab. 1961. Annual indoor show held the month of October. Average attendance: "1,000 plus churchgoers." Entries accepted until 1 week before show. Entry fee: $4/category. Maximum 6 crafts per category/artist. Prejudging by actual work; no entry fees refunded for refused work. Work may be offered for sale; 20% commission. Craftworker needn't attend show; no demonstrations. Sponsor provides insurance on exhibited work, and 24-hour security. Categories: crafts; painting; graphics; and sculpture. Considers "all crafts not made with kits or under teacher's supervision."
Awards: Presents $600 in cash prizes, and special recognition ribbons. "Contemporary art seems to be preferred by most jurors."
Sales Tip: "Viewers tend to buy more traditional art and functional crafts. No sales tax. Church members handle sales."
Promotion: "Show has good reputation locally as being one of 2-3 best juried shows. Press releases are sent to major Colorado newspapers and to several national art publications. The 2 Denver papers and 1 weekly paper usually cover the show with full-page review and photos."

LOVELAND'S ANNUAL ARTS & CRAFTS FESTIVAL, c/o Joyce C. Musslewhite, #4 Enchanted Way, Rt.4, 480A Pole Hill, Loveland CO 80537. Sponsor: Loveland Art League. Purpose: "to make people aware of what the artists are producing and to give the artists a chance to display and sell their products." Estab. 1965. Annual outdoor show held 1 day in August. Attendance: 3,000-4,000. Entries accepted until 2 weeks before show. Entry fee: $3.50/artist for pre-registration; $5/artist for walk-in entries. Display area: 10x12. Work may be offered for sale; no commission. Craftworker must attend show; demonstrations OK. Registration limit: 200. Considers all crafts.
Promotion: Show is advertised by radio; newspapers; and TV. "When sending in the registration fee he [the craftworker] might include a brochure on himself and products. We use the information in our news releases."

OWN YOUR OWN ART SHOW, University of Southern Colorado Art Department, Pueblo CO 81001. (303)549-2552. Art Professors: Ed Sasbel and Bob Wands. Sponsor: USC Art Department and Pueblo Junior League. "Own Your Own Art Show is organized to stimulate sales by artists from Colorado, New Mexico, Wyoming, Montana, Idaho, Utah, Nevada and Arizona." Estab. 1961. Annual indoor show held 2 days in November. Attendance: 5,000-10,000. Entries accepted until 1 week before show. Entry fee: $5/artist. Prejudging; no entry fees refunded for refused work. Work may be offered for sale; 25% commission "for USC art scholarships." Craftworker needn't attend show; no demonstrations. Registration limit: 300-500. Sponsor provides insurance on exhibited work (although limited); 24-hour security; and "the Pueblo Junior League handles all sales and sends check to artist within 2 weeks after show." Show is advertised in national magazines; Colorado newspapers; and TV. Categories: ceramics; sculptures; textiles; jewelry; watercolors; oils and acrylics; mixed media (2-D or 3-D); photographs; and prints. Considers ceramics; jewelry; metalsmithing; pottery; sculpture; soft sculpture; weaving; and woodcrafting.

RENAISSANCE ARTS FAIRE, 1395 S. Humboldt, Denver CO 80210. (303)778-6190. Director: Rae Ann McMurtry. Sponsor: Pastimes Alive. Purpose: "a celebration of Renaissance life and spirit creating a living history involving visual and performing arts." Estab. 1975. Annual outdoor show held 5 days (2 weekends) in September, west of Denver. Average attendance: 15,000+. Entries accepted until 2 weeks before show. Entry fee: $50 before June 1; $55 June 1-August 15; $75 late fee. "This fee is for 1 artist; 2 may share by adding 20%." Display area: 12x-12. Prejudging by slides; SASE; entry fee due after prejudging. Work may be offered for sale; no commission. Craftworker must attend show; demonstrations encouraged. "If demonstrations or presentations can fit into our educational or entertainment guidelines, fees may be partially or totally excused." Registration limit: under 100. Sponsor provides electricity for demonstrations and night security. Show is advertised by local TV; radio; magazines; newspapers; and club newsletters. Considers all crafts that directly relate to the Renaissance period in theme or process.

ROCKY MOUNTAIN CRAFT FAIR, National Crafts Ltd., Gapland MD 21736. (301)432-8438. Director: Noel Clark. Estab. 1977. Annual indoor show held in August at the Merchandise Mart in Denver. Average attendance: 10,000. Prejudging by 5-10 35mm color slides. Work may be offered for sale; no commission. Craftworker must attend show; demonstrations OK. Registration limit: 150. Sponsor provides electricity for demonstrations and 24-hour security. Considers all crafts. Show is advertised by radio; newspaper and magazine ads; posters; flyers; and mailings to National Wholesale Buyer List.

*SPRING ART GALA, c/o P.J. Robinson, Box 16, Craig CO 81625. Sponsor: Moffat County Council for the Arts and Humanities. Purpose: "to improve the quality of regional work, and to educate the public in modern techniques and appreciation of them." Estab. 1974. Annual indoor show held 5 days in the spring. Average attendance: 2,500. Entries accepted until 2 weeks before show. Maximum 2 entries/craftworker. Work may be offered for sale; 10% commission. Craftworker needn't attend show; no demonstrations. Sponsor provides chairs; display panels; table; and 24-hour security. Show is advertised by newspapers; radio; and direct mail.
Acceptable Work: Considers batik; jewelry; macrame; pottery; sculpture; weaving; and soft sculpture. Maximum size: "not to exceed 70 pounds or 100" in length and girth combined. Work must have been completed within the last 2 years. All entry information must be attached to the work. If for sale, must be clearly marked."
Awards: Presents $500 in cash; $75 in purchase prizes; and honorable mention certificates. "Neat presentation and originality are stressed."

*THREADS UNLIMITED, 809 15th St., Golden CO 80401. (303)279-3922. Executive Director: Marian Metsopoulos. Sponsor: Foothills Art Center. Purpose: "to further the fiber arts and help promote their acceptance by the public." Estab. 1975. Annual indoor regional show held the month of June. Average attendance: 2,000. "The competition is open to artists living in Colorado, Kansas, Wyoming, Nebraska, Oklahoma, New Mexico and Utah." Entries accepted until 2 months before show date. Entry fee: $3/item being displayed. Maximum 3 entries/craftworker. Prejudging by slides ("maximum of 3 slides per piece of work — 1 must be detail of work"); no entry fees refunded for refused work. Work may be offered for sale; 25% commission. Craftworker needn't attend show; no demonstrations. Limited to approximately 70 pieces of work/show. Sponsor provides $50 deductible theft insurance on exhibited work; 24-hour security; hangs show; and handles all sales and collects and pays sales tax. Considers macrame; needlecrafts; soft sculpture; weaving; and other "work where fiber is the predominant material." Maximum size: 8x8. Cash awards are to be determined. Judges look for "expert craftsmanship, finishing, and above all, excellent design and use of color."
Promotion: Show is advertised in newspapers; magazines; radio; and TV. Requests resumes to give buyers of work. "Buyers want to know about the artist."

Connecticut

ARTS & CRAFTS FAIR, c/o Mrs. Donald Perry. 11 Robin Lane, Milford CT 06460. (203)878-8101. Contact: Mrs. Donald Perry. Sponsor: Wepawang Chapter of Hadassah. Purpose: "to raise money for the Hadassah medical organization which goes to hospitals and medical centers in Israel who continually do research and training." Estab. 1972. Annual outdoor show held 1 day in the spring at the Milford Green. Entries accepted until show date. Entry fee: $15/display area. Work may be offered for sale; no commission. Craftworker needn't attend show; demonstrations OK. Sponsor provides electricity for demonstration. Show is advertised by radio and the local media. Craftworkers are urged to supply promotional materials about themselves and their work. Considers all crafts.

ARTS & CRAFTS FESTIVAL, Box 764, Middletown CT 06457. Sponsor: Junior Woman's Club of Middletown. Purpose: "to raise money for community projects. We profit from artists'

fees and canteen setup at site." Estab. 1968. Annual outdoor show held 1 day in the spring. Entries accepted until 3 months before show. Entry fee: $15/craftworker. Display area: 10x12. Prejudging by slides, photos, descriptions — "whatever accompanies applications." Entry fee refunded for refused work. Work may be offered for sale; no commission. Craftworker must attend show; "demonstrations left up to the discretion of our committee." Registration limit: 100. Sponsor provides chairs; limited electricity for demonstrations; fencing; coffee; lunch; and table. Considers all crafts.
Promotion: Show is advertised by local newspapers; TV; radio; posters; and in craft magazines. "When sending in application, include photos, description, or any material available."

BLACK EXPO & BAZAAR, 140 Goffe St., New Haven CT 06511. (203)777-3661. Contact: Sylvin Nisbet. Sponsor: Black Coalition of Greater New Haven, Inc. "Black Expo & Bazaar is a showcase and appraisal of the cultural and socio-economic standing of the Afro-American communities, providing an overview of 'Grass Roots' vitality." Estab. 1972. Annual indoor show held 4 days in October. Average attendance: 25,000. Entries accepted until 2 weeks before show. Entry fee: $250/8x10 display area; $60/4x5 display area. Work may be offered for sale; no commission. Craftworker must attend show; demonstrations OK. Registration limit: 154. 8x10 display area includes electricity; table; 3-side fencing; and 24-hour security. 4x5 display area includes electricity and 24-hour security. Considers all crafts.
Sales Tip: Bestsellers include jewelry; ceramics; macrame; needlecrafts; pastel portraits; novelty items (e.g., item buttons with photos of individuals, etc.); and woodcrafts.

*BRISTOL MUM FESTIVAL ART SHOW, Chamber of Commerce c/o Bristol Art League, Bristol CT 06010. Contact: Co-chairman. "Held in conjunction with 2-week long festival promoted by the city of Bristol, the Chrysanthemum city of the world." Annual indoor show held 1 week in the fall. Attendance: 1,500-2,000. Entries accepted until 3 weeks before show (work must be delivered 1 week before show). Entry fee: $5/item being displayed. Maximum 5 entries/category. Prejudging: "a judge from the area is chosen each year by the Committee. The judge views the entries 2 or 3 days before the show opens in person. The opening night of the show is awards night, and prizes are presented then." No entry fees refunded for refused work. Work may be offered for sale; 10-15% commission. Craftworker needn't attend show; demonstrations OK. Registration limit: 200+. Sponsor provides display panels; electricity for demonstrations; 24-hour security; and Bristol Art League handles sales. Categories: oil; watercolor; mixed media; graphic; sculpture; objective and nonobjective. Awards $25-200 in cash; and ribbons.
Acceptable Work: Considers framed batik and sculpture. "Entries must have been completed within the past 2 years. Artists must be over 18 years of age. No uncrating. Entries must not have been in the art show previously."

BRISTOL WOMEN'S COLLEGE CLUB CRAFT FAIR, 283 Divinity St., Bristol CT 06010. President: K. Acocella. Purpose: "fundraiser for our scholarship fund." Annual indoor show held 2 days in October. Average attendance: 4,000. "Request application in summer." Entry fee: $20/6' table. Work may be offered for sale; no commission. Craftworker must attend show; demonstrations OK. Registration limit: 50. Sponsor provides electricity for demonstrations and table. Show is advertised on local and regional TV; radio; and posters. "With application craftsmen can send in information on themselves [for publicity purposes]." Considers all crafts.

CHRISTMAS ARTS FESTIVAL, Silvermine Guild of Artists, 1037 Silvermine Rd., New Canaan CT 06840. (203)966-5617. Gallery Director: Dee Robinson. "This exhibition includes all artist members of Silvermine Guild. It is not open to any craftsperson who is not a member of the Guild. Membership is through jurying— work is submitted to be juried by the artist members of the Board of Trustees of the Silvermine Guild of Artists." Estab. 1935. Annual indoor show held from Thanksgiving until Christmas. Average attendance: 2,000. Show is advertised by publicity releases and ads that appear in local media and in the *New York Times.*

CHRISTMAS STOCKING CRAFT SHOW, Sterling House Community Center, 2283 Main St., Stratford CT 06497. (203)378-2606. Executive Director: Mary R. Hardy. Estab. 1971. Annual indoor show held 2 days in late November. Average attendance: 3,600. Application with photos or slides for prejudging due 6 weeks before show. Entry fee: $18/6x6 plus $3 for each additional running foot of space requested up to 12. Maximum 1 category/craftworker. Work may be offered for sale; no commission. Craftworker must attend show; no demonstrations. Registration limit: 40. Sponsor provides chairs; electricity; table; and overnight security. Considers all crafts.

Promotion: Show is advertised by news stories; radio announcements; flyers; posters; and the promotion committee. Some information is requested by Committee for newspaper purposes.

CRAFT FAIR, 87 William St., Portland CT 06480. (203)342-2641. Chairman: Sari Rosenbaum. Sponsor: Middletown Chapter of Hadassah. Estab. 1971. Annual outdoor show held 1 day in September at Middletown, Connecticut. Average attendance: 10,000. Entries accepted until show date or until filled. Entry fee: $15/10x16 display area. Maximum 1 booth per craftworker. Work may be offered for sale; no commission. Craftworker or representative must attend show. Registration limit: 184. Considers all crafts.

CREATIVE CRAFTS FAIR, 1 Heather Lane, East Granby CT 06026. Contact: Susan J. Eaton. Sponsor: East Granby YWCA. Women's Club. "The purpose for this show is to raise money for the Women's Club, which donates a good portion to the East Granby schools for the purchase of extra items otherwise not possible." Estab. 1977. Annual indoor show held 2 days in the spring. Average attendance: 1,200. Entries accepted until 4 weeks before show. Entry fee: $7.50 for 1 day; $10 for both days. Prejudging by photos or slides; entry fee due after prejudging. Work may be offered for sale; 10% commission. Craftworker or representative must attend show; demonstrations OK. Registration limit: 40-50. Sponsor provides chairs; electricity for demonstrations; and a table for a fee. Show is advertised in newspapers; posters; radio; and craft publications. Considers all crafts. 1977 exhibitor sales totalled approximately $1,300.

CYSTIC FIBROSIS ARTS AND CRAFTS FAIR, 772 Whipperwill Lane, Stratford CT 06497. (203)377-3921. Contact: Dorothy Jevarjian. Purpose: fundraiser. Estab. 1973. Annual outdoor show held in spring at Boothe Memorial Park. Entries accepted up until show. Entry fee: $15/display area. Work may be offered for sale; no commission. Craftworker needn't attend show; demonstrations OK. Registration limit: 100. Show is advertised by radio and local media. Submit promotional material about self and work. Considers all crafts.

*DANBURY AMATEUR ART SHOW, Greater Danbury Chamber of Commerce, 20 West St., Danbury CT 06810. (203)743-5565. Executive Assistant: William McGee. Annual indoor show held 4 days in October-November. Entry fee: $2/entry. Maximum 3 entries per craftworker. Work must be offered for sale; 20% commission goes toward art scholarship for 2 high school seniors. Considers sculpture. Presents best of show and 1st, 2nd and 3rd place ribbons.

FARMINGTON CRAFTS EXPO, Box 370, Farmington CT 06032. (203)224-8388. Contact: Director. Sponsor: American Crafts Expositions. Estab. 1972. Annual outdoor show held 3 days in summer (tent space available). Average attendance: 20,000+. Entries accepted until 4 weeks before show. Prejudging; entry fee refunded for refused work. Work may be offered for sale; no commission. Craftworker must attend show; demonstrations OK. Registration limit: 200. Considers all crafts.

*FESTIVAL OF ARTS, Box 486, Fairfield CT 06430. Contact: Chairman. Sponsor: Fairfield Jaycees and Jaycee Women. "This show is held for the purpose of supporting the ongoing projects of the Fairfield Jaycees, and a selected local charity or organization chosen annually by the Jaycee Women." Estab. 1969. Annual outdoor show held 1 day in September. Average attendance: 5,000. Entries accepted until show date as space is available. Entry fee to be announced. Prejudging by slides or photos. "Only the highest quality handmade items are accepted." Entry fee refunded for refused work. Work may be offered for sale; no commission. Craftworker needn't attend show; demonstrations OK. Registration limit: "crafts limited to 2 per category and may not exceed 40 participants." Sponsor provides a limited number of display panels. Presents cash for best in show; and 1st, 2nd and 3rd place ribbons.

Acceptable Work: Considers batik; ceramics; dollmaking; glass art; jewelry; lapidary; leatherworking; macrame; metalsmithing; pottery; sculpture; scrimshaw; nail art; bread dough; and dried flower arranging.

Promotion: Show is advertised by publicity in directories; newspapers in New York, New Jersey and all of New England; radio announcements; posters; and banners used locally. "Often we will contact individuals for [publicity materials] as we see fit."

*GOLDENBELLS FESTIVAL ART & CRAFT MARKET, 161 Wayland St., Hamden CT 06518. (203)288-0436. Chairman: Dorothy Pomarico. Sponsor: town of Hamden. Purpose: "it is a festival to welcome spring by the townspeople. The market is just 1 of several events that occur during the 2-week festival. Hamden is a very art-oriented town with a wide variety of tastes." Estab. 1973. Annual indoor show held 2 days in the spring. Average attendance: 2,000. Entries accepted until 2 weeks before show. Entry fee: $12/6x10 display area. Work may be offered for sale; no commission. Craftworker must attend show; demonstrations encouraged. Registration limit: 60 craftworkers; 20-40 artists. Sponsor provides chairs; electricity for demonstrations; table; and 24-hour security. Presents cash awards ("amount determined yearly by town business contributions"); and gift certificates.

Acceptable Work: Considers batik; candlemaking; ceramics; dollmaking; glass art; jewelry; lapidary; leatherworking; macrame; metalsmithing; mobiles; needlecrafts; pottery; sculpture; soft sculpture; tole painting; weaving; and woodcrafting. "If you're proud of your work bring it. If you're just hoping someone will take it off your hands because you can't stand it, leave it home."

Promotion: Show is advertised by radio ads and interviews; posters; handbills; TV interviews and notices; newspaper and magazine ads; billboards; and feature stories on the festival. "Personal publicity info regarding self and product will be used for newspaper articles which run every week for 2 months prior to show."

Charged purchases (BankAmericard/Visa, Mastercharge, and American Express) averaged $30-58 in the sales handled by the central office of the 1978 Farmington Crafts Expo, Farmington, Connecticut. The 3-day June show was the most successful in its 7-year history with increased sales, attendance, and exhibiting craftworkers.

*GREATER HARTFORD CIVIC AND ARTS FESTIVAL, 250 Constitution Plaza, Hartford Ct 06103. (203)278-3378. Director: Evelyn R. Warner. Sponsor: Greater Hartford Arts Council, Downtown Council, and Greater Hartford Chamber of Commerce. Purpose: to promote the arts. Estab. 1971. Annual outdoor show (partial covering) held 9 days in June. Average attendance: 100,000+. Entries accepted until 5 weeks before show. Prejudging by actual work. Work may be offered for sale; 10% donation. Craftworker needn't attend show. Sponsor provides insurance on exhibited work. Show is advertised by radio; TV; newspapers; flyers; and mailings. Presents cash and purchase awards and ribbons. Eligible media include materials such as clay; fiber; glass; metal; and wood.

GREENWICH HANDCRAFT SHOW AND SALE, 12 E. Putnam Ave., Greenwich CT 06830. (203)869-0934. Executive Director: Mrs. Zinn. Sponsor: Central Junior High PTA. Purpose: "to bring high quality crafts to town and to promote the American artist-craftsmen. Also to educate the general public and as a fundraiser." Estab. 1972. Annual indoor show held 2 days in November. Entry fee: $15/craftworker. Display area: 8x8-8x12. Prejudging by slides; $2 jurying fee. Entry fee due after prejudging. Work may be offered for sale; 15% commission. Craftworker must attend show; demonstrations encouraged. Registration limit: 60. Sponsor provides chairs; electricity for demonstrations; and 24-hour security. Show is advertised by direct mailing; posters; radio; newspapers; and magazines. Write for screening application. Considers most crafts.

GUILFORD HANDCRAFTS EXPOSITION, Guilford Handcraft Center, Box 221, Guilford CT 06437. (203)453-5947. Exposition Chairman: Ali Kubler. "The purpose of the Exposition is to support the Guilford Handcraft Center, a nonprofit school, gallery and shop dedicated to the furtherance of interest and participation in crafts, and to expose the general public to crafts as an art form." Estab. 1956. Annual outdoor show (under tents on the Guilford Green) held 3 days in July. Average attendance: 40,000. "Applications available in December and due in February." Display area: 10x12. Prejudging by 5 slides due with application and $5 prejudging fee. Work may be offered for sale; 25% commission. Craftworker must attend show; demonstrations encouraged. Registration limit: 100. Sponsor provides chairs; coverings; electricity for demonstrations; table; and 24-hour security. Presents cash awards for best display.
Acceptable Work: Considers batik; ceramics; dollmaking; glass art; jewelry; leatherworking; macrame; metalsmithing; pottery; soft sculpture; weaving; and woodcrafting. No crafts "taken basically from nature— each piece must clearly show the impact of the artist on his materials."
Promotion: Show is advertised by newspaper and radio publicity. "A brochure is distributed and available to exhibitors, as well as display posters. Newspaper releases will be made available to individual craftsmen for use in their local papers."

*THE HUDSON VALLEY ART ASSOCIATION, INC., c/o Rayma Spaulding, 15 Minivale Rd., Stamford CT 06907. Annual show held first Sunday in May at White Plains. Entries accepted until 8 days before show. Membership includes exhibition fee for 1 exhibit. Fee for non-members is $10. Maximum 1 entry per artist. Considers sculpture not previously exhibited in County Center. Only works done in realistic manner. Work may be offered for sale; 10% commission. Exhibitors outside the area may have work handled by transfer agent who will submit work for $30 fee.
Awards: Presents Hudson Valley Art Association Gold Medal of Honor for oil, watercolor, sculpture and graphics; over $2,400 in cash awards; and honorable mention in all classes.

INTERNATIONAL CHRISTMAS EXHIBITION FROM AROUND THE WORLD, 1814 Newfield Ave., Stamford CT 06903. Associate Director: Darrel Couturier. Sponsor: Couturier Galerie. Estab. 1963. Annual indoor show held the month of December. Average attendance: 2,000. Entries accepted until 6-8 months preceding show. No entry fee. Prejudging by slides or photos. Work may be offered for sale; 40% commission. Craftworker needn't attend show; demonstrations OK. Registration limit: 10-25. Sponsor provides electricity for demonstrations; table; and normal gallery situation.
Acceptable Work: Considers ceramics; decoupage; glass art; jewelry; macrame; needlecrafts; pottery; sculpture; and weaving. All work "must be of original design, non-duplicated, and signed where applicable. Work will be selected as to suitability to the gallery."
Promotion: Show is advertised by invitations (announcements); radio; and newspaper ads. Exhibitor should supply biographical data and glossy b&w photos of work and/or color slides.

INTERNATIONAL GUEST EXHIBITION OF PAINTING, SCULPTURE & GRAPHICS, 1814 Newfield Ave., Stamford CT 06903. Associate Director: Darrel Couturier. Sponsor: Couturier Galerie. Estab. 1962. Annual indoor show held 4-6 weeks in the spring. Attendance: 1,000-1,500. Entries accepted until 6 months before show. No entry fee. Maximum 2-5 entries/category. Prejudging by slides or color photos. Work may be offered for sale; 40% commission. Craftworker needn't attend show; no demonstrations. Registration limit: 10-12. "Normal gallery situation." Categories: paintings; sculpture; and graphics. Considers mobiles and sculpture.
Promotion: Show is advertised by invitations; newspaper ads; and radio. "Biography and photo of artist with a work is helpful for publicity when the work is accepted. Photos must be glossy b&w 5x7 or 8x10."

MARLBOROUGH CREATIVE ARTS FESTIVAL, Box 42, Marlborough CT 06447. (203)295-9389. President: Mrs. Sandy Paquette. Sponsor: Marlborough Community Arts, Inc. Estab. 1974. Annual outdoor show held 2 days in mid-September; large tent and covered pavilion available. Average attendance: 6,000. Entries accepted until 4 weeks before show. Entry fee: $15/craftworker. Prejudging by photos; entry fee due after prejudging. Work may be offered for sale; no commission. Craftworker needn't attend show; demonstrations OK. Registration limit: 60. Sponsor provides coverings (tent); display panels; pegboard; electricity for demonstrations; table; and chicken wire art screens. "If craftsmen wish to use pegboard booth backings, they must supply their own S-hooks." Show is advertised by newspaper ads; posters; radio; and magazines. Considers all crafts.

MEET THE ARTISTS, 41 Green St., Milford CT 06460. (203)874-5672. Director: Denise Curt. Purpose: "for artists and artisans to take pride in their work and talent by being materialistically successful." Annual indoor show held 4 days in October at Meriden Square, Connecticut. Average attendance: "thousands." Entries accepted until 1 week before show. Entry fee: $35/4x-10 display area. Prejudging by slides; photos; brochure; and recommendations. SASE. Entry fee refunded for refused work. Work may be offered for sale; no commission. Craftworker must attend show; demonstrations OK. Registration limit: 100. Sponsor provides electricity for demonstrations and 24-hour security. Show is advertised by TV; radio; newspapers; magazines; preshow mall posters; mailers; photo stories; Commission on the Arts Calendar; and Chamber of Commerce State Visitors Events. Submit 5x7 b&w glossy photos and resume for promotion. **Acceptable Work:** Considers batik; dollmaking; large glass art; macrame; metalsmithing; mobiles; needlecrafts; some pottery; sculpture; soft sculpture; tole painting; weaving; and woodcrafting. Bestsellers: $5-400.

*MYSTIC OUTDOOR ART FESTIVAL, Box 300, Mystic CT 06355. (203)536-8559. Director: John Lazarek. Sponsor: Chamber of Commerce. Estab. 1958. Annual show held 2 days in August. Average attendance: 75,000. Application requests due May 1; applications due May 21. Entry fee: $20/entry. Prejudging; entry fee refunded for refused work. Work may be offered for sale; no commission. Craftworker must attend show; pastel and charcoal artists may demonstrate. Registration limit: 430. Considers sculpture. Presents $300, best in show; and other cash prizes and medals.

*NCAA JURIED SHOW, c/o NCCC, Park Place, Winsted CT 06098. (203)379-8543. Contact: Elaine Reeve. Sponsor: Northwestern Connecticut Art Association. Estab. 1971. Annual indoor show held 2 weeks in June-July. Average attendance: 500+. Entries accepted until 1 week before show. Entry fee: $6-7/entry. Maximum 2 entries per craftworker. Prejudging; no entry fees refunded for refused work. Work may be offered for sale; no commission. Open to craftworkers living in the New York City area or New England. Registration limit: approximately 125 works. Presents $700 in cash prizes and $500 in purchase awards.

*NEW ENGLAND PAINTING AND SCULPTURE EXHIBITION, 1037 Silvermine Rd., New Canaan CT 06840. (203)966-5617. Gallery Director: Dee Robinson. Sponsor: Silvermine Guild of Artists. Annual indoor/outdoor show held 1 month in June. Attendance: 5,000-6,000. Entries accepted until 1 month before show. Entry fee: $10/artist. Maximum 2 entries/artist. Work may be offered for sale; 33⅓% commission. Craftworker needn't attend show; no demonstrations. Sponsor provides display panels. Considers soft and other sculpture. Presents cash awards.

*ON THE GREEN, Box 304, Glastonbury CT 06033. Vice President: Ann Asmuth. Sponsor: Glastonbury Art Guild. Estab. 1970. Annual outdoor show held 2 days in September. Average attendance: 15,000. Entries accepted until 4 weeks before show. Entry fee: $25/member; $35/nonmember. Display area: 10x10. Work may be offered for sale; commission to be determined. Craftworker must attend show; demonstrations OK. Registration limit: 100. Sponsor provides fencing. Categories: judged oils, watercolors, mixed media and sculpture graphics; nonjuried in the same media; and crafts. Considers all crafts. Presents 3 $50 1st prizes.

*PUTNAM AREA CHAMBER OF COMMERCE SIDEWALK ART EXHIBIT, Box 489, Putnam CT 06260. (203)928-3407. Art Exhibit Chairman: Gregory King. Purpose: to bring the arts to the people of northeastern Connecticut, Massachusetts, and Rhode Island. Estab. 1964. Annual outdoor show held 1 day in May. Average attendance: 2,000-5,000. Entries accepted until 2 weeks before show. Entry fee: $12/adult craftworker; $1/student 18 and under. Work may be offered for sale; no commission. Craftworker must attend show; demonstrations OK.

Registration limit: 25-50. Sponsor provides electricity for demonstrations. Show is advertised by free publicity. Presents cash awards of $50 for 1st, $25 for 2nd, $15 for 3rd; student awards of $25 for 1st, $15 for 2nd, $10 for 3rd; and ribbons for 1st, 2nd, and 3rd in each category. Considers all crafts. Bestsellers: pottery; jewelry; and leather products.

ST. JOSEPH COLLEGE ARTS & CRAFTS FAIR, c/o Mrs. Thomas Horan, 1083 Hopmeadow St., Simsbury CT 06070. (203)658-2488. Sponsor: St. Joseph College Alumnae Association. Purpose: to raise money for scholarship fund. Estab. 1967. Annual indoor show held 2 days in March. Average attendance: 2,000. Entries accepted until 2 months before show. Entry fee: $20/display area. Prejudging by slides and/or photos; entry fee refunded for refused work. Craftworker must attend show; demonstrations OK. Registration limit: 50-60. Sponsor provides chairs and tables. Considers all crafts.

*SLATER MEMORIAL MUSEUM, 108 Crescent St., Norwich CT 06360. (203)887-2505, ext. 218. Museum Director: Joseph P. Gualtieri. Annual show held in April. Entry fee: $4/item; Friends of the Museum may submit 1 piece free. Maximum 2 entries per craftworker. Work may be offered for sale; 20% commission. Entries must be hand-delivered. Considers sculpture. Maximum 200 pounds. Open to Connecticut residents only. Presents cash awards of $250, $100, $75 and $50.

SPRING MARKET, Connecticut Craft Professionals, Inc., Box 5463, Hamden CT 06518. Directors: Eva Orsini and Bill Richards. Purpose: to provide a wholesale and retail outlet for professional craftworkers. Estab. 1977. Annual indoor show held 1 day wholesale, 2 days retail in March at New Haven, Connecticut. Average attendance: 10,000. Entries accepted until announced deadline. Entry fee: $90/8x10 display area plus $5 application fee. Prejudging by slides; entry fee refunded for refused work. Work must be offered for sale; no commission. Craftworker must attend show; demonstrations OK. Registration limit: 200. Sponsor provides electricity and 24-hour security. Show is advertised by mailing lists; newspapers; TV; and radio. Submit b&w glossies for publicity. 1978 show sales totalled $50,000+. Considers all crafts except kits; imports; agents; embellishments; and assemblages.

SUMMER CRAFT SHOW & BAZAAR, First Church of Christ, Town St., East Haddam CT 06423. Chairman: Karl P. Stofko. Purpose: church fundraiser. Estab. 1968. Annual outdoor show held 1 day in July. Attendance: 800-1,000. Entries accepted until show date. Entry fee: $3/artist. Display area: approximately 10'. Work may be offered for sale; 10% commission. Craftworker must attend show; demonstrations OK. Registration limit: 25-30. Sponsor provides chairs. Considers all crafts.

WEST HARTFORD SPRING ARTS & CRAFTS FAIR, c/o Sheila Accortt, 21 Michael Rd., Simsbury CT 06070. (203)658-1762. Sponsor: Connecticut River Valley Region Women's American O.R.T. Purpose: fundraiser for Women's American O.R.T., "which supports a network of 700 vocational schools in 23 countries throughout the world." Estab. 1974. Annual outdoor show held 1 day in May. Average attendance: 8,000. Entries accepted until show date. Entry fee: $15/display area measuring 2 parking stalls. Maximum 8 craftworkers/craft category. Work may be offered for sale; no commission. Craftworker must attend show; demonstrations OK (no electricity available). Registration limit: 150. Considers all crafts. **Promotion:** Show is advertised by newspapers; TV; radio; and posters. Exhibitors should provide b&w photos.

WESTPORT CREATIVE ARTS FESTIVAL, 44 Imperial Ave., Westport CT 06880. (203)227-4240. Sponsor: Westport Young Woman's League. Estab. 1976. Annual indoor invitational show held 2 days in November. Average attendance: 3,600+. Entries accepted until show is full. Entry fee: $15/8x10 display area. Prejudging by slides, photos and other shows; entry fee due after invitation is issued. Work must be offered for sale; 15% commission. Craftworker must attend show; no demonstrations. Registration limit: 66-70. Sponsor provides chairs; tables on first come basis; 24-hour security protection; program; handling of Visa and Master Charge; unloading assistance; Saturday dinner and booth-sitting. Considers all crafts. **Promotion:** Show is advertised by newspaper articles; paid advertising; regional publications; postcards; posters; radio spots; and directional signs and banners. Craftworker should provide as much information as possible for press releases, including glossies.

WESTPORT HANDCRAFTS FAIR, 552 Hoydens Hill Rd., Fairfield CT 06430. Co-chairman: Bobbie Schneider. Sponsor: Westport-Weston Cooperative Nursery School. Estab. 1966. Annual outdoor show held 2 days in May. Entries accepted until 3 months before show. Entry fee:

$15/10x10 display area. Prejudging; "good cross section of items may be delivered by craftsman (at his expense) to place of jurying, or approximately 7 slides of photos are acceptable." Entry fee due after prejudging. Work may be offered for sale; 15% commission. Craftworker must attend show; demonstrations encouraged. Registration limit: 90. Sponsor provides electricity for demonstrations.

Acceptable Work: Considers batik; candlemaking; ceramics; decoupage; dollmaking; glass art; jewelry; lapidary; leatherworking; macrame; metalsmithing; needlecrafts; pottery; soft sculpture; weaving; and woodcrafting. Work must be that of attending craftworker.

Promotion: "Good write-ups with photos [appear] in all area papers, Connecticut magazines, *Yankee* magazine; *New York Times Connecticut Weekly*; and local papers of craftsmen." Also promoted by radio. Exhibitor should supply 5x7 or 8x10 b&w glossies.

*YAAF EXHIBITION OF FINE ART, Box 362, Fairfield CT 06430. Contact: Jack Farkas or Paul Strauss. Sponsor: Young Artist Association of Fairfield. Annual show. Entry fee: $7.50. Work may be offered for sale; 25% commission. Sponsor provides display equipment, but sculptures must be equipped with stands. Considers fine sculpture. Presents cash and purchase awards.

Delaware

BRANDYWINE ARTS FESTIVAL, 1307 Orange St., Wilmington DE 19801. (302)651-8364. Contact: George Sargisson. Purpose: "to stimulate interest in the arts; to develop appreciation of the performing arts; to create the opportunity for the public to discover the countless hours of enjoyment and pleasure derived from the arts; to provide cultural expression for people of all tastes; and to present a show window for the working artists emphasizing the natural beauties of the historic Brandywine area and to encourage all artists to share their talents with thousands of people who will be afforded an opportunity to view and purchase the art displayed." Estab. 1966. Annual outdoor show held 2 days in September. Average attendance: 12,000-15,000. Entries accepted until 4 weeks before show. Entry fee: $40/10x10 display area. Work offered for sale; 20% commission. Craftworker or representative must attend show; demonstrations recommended. Show is advertised by brochures; billboards; posters; and flyers. Submit promotional material. Considers all crafts.

CAPE HENLOPEN CRAFT FAIR & FOLK LIFE FESTIVAL, 119 W. 3rd St., Lewes DE 19958. (302)645-7640. Contact: Assistant Curator. Sponsor: Lewes Historical Society. Purpose: "to raise money for Lewes Historical Society educational programs." Estab. 1972. Annual outdoor show held 1 day in July. Average attendance: 1,000. Entries accepted until 1 week before show. Entry fee: $10/artist. Prejudging by slides, photos or samples (if feasible); entry fee refunded for refused work. Work may be offered for sale; no commission. Craftworker must attend show; demonstrations required. Registration limit: 60. Sponsor provides electricity for demonstrations.

Acceptable Work: Considers batik; candlemaking; ceramics; decoupage; dollmaking; jewelry; leatherworking; metalsmithing; needlecrafts; pottery; sculpture; soft sculpture; tole painting; weaving; and woodcrafting. "Special interest in marine and historical crafts; furniture-making, for example."

Sales Tip: "Public buys items that are good quality solid craftsmanship. Not interested in items that are gaudy or that [the customers] might easily make themselves— such as shell animals or bead jewelry."

Promotion: Show is advertised by posters; radio; newspapers; and flyers. "Glossy photos help in promotion articles."

*CRAFTS EXHIBITION, 2301 Kentmere Pkwy., Wilmington DE 19806. (302)571-9594. Director of Education: Marion Johnson. Sponsor: Delaware Art Museum. Purpose: "to present examples of the finest contemporary craftmanship." Estab. 1956. Annual indoor show held 6 weeks beginning in November. Average attendance: 4,000. Entries accepted until 5 weeks before show. Entry fee: $8/artist. Maximum 3 entries/category; 3, total. Prejudging by slides; no entry fees refunded for refused work. Work must be offered for sale; 20% commission. Craftworker needn't attend show; no demonstrations. Registration limit: 150. Sponsor provides insurance on exhibited work and 24-hour security. Show is advertised in local papers and *Craft Horizons*. Presents 3 $100 cash awards and purchase prizes. Utilitarian objects sell the best. "Pottery was our largest selling item."

Acceptable Work: Considers textiles; ceramics; glass; jewelry; leatherworking; metalsmithing; needlecrafts; sculpture; soft sculpture; weaving; and woodcrafting. "Work received must be conceived, designed and executed by the exhibitor."

CRAFTSMEN'S FAIR AT DELAWARE ART MUSEUM, 2301 Kentmere Pkwy., Wilmington DE 19806. (302)571-9594. Education Director: Marion Johnson. Estab. 1972. Annual outdoor show held 1 day in June. Average attendance: approximately 2,000. Entries accepted until filled. Entry fee: $15/artist. Prejudging. Work must be offered for sale; no commission. Craftworker must attend show; demonstrations encouraged. Considers jewelry; enamels; leatherworking; glass art; textiles; metalsmithing; needlecrafts; pottery; weaving and woodcrafting.

Florida

ALTAMONTE MALL, 2918 Martel Dr., Dayton OH 45420. (513)254-2900. Director: Clarence Freeland. Annual indoor show held in Altamonte, Florida, 1 week in January. Closing date for entry: 1 week before show. Entry fee: $75. Prejudging. Work may be offered for sale; no commission. Craftworker must attend show; demonstrations OK. Sponsor provides 10x10' display area. Considers all crafts.

THE ART FESTIVAL IN THE VILLAGE, Box 35, Lake Buena Vista FL 32830. Contact: Chairman. Sponsor: Walt Disney World Shopping Village. Purpose: "to provide a showcase for original art and crafts; to make the public aware of current and coming trends in creative works; and build good will for our village." Estab. 1975. Annual outdoor show held 3 days in November at Walt Disney World Village. Average attendance: 80,000. Entries accepted until August. Entry fee: approximately $40/12x10 display area. Prejudging by 3 35mm slides of work, and 1 slide of booth or display; entry fee refunded for refused work. Work should be offered for sale; no commission. Craftworker must attend show; demonstrations OK by arrangement. Registration limit: 50-60. Sponsor provides electricity for demonstrations; 24-hour security; coffee and donuts; assistance in setting up; display sitters for lunch and breaks; discount on accommodations; complimentary admission to Walt Disney World theme park; and free T-shirt. Show is advertised by radio, magazines; newspapers; TV; postcards; calendar of events; and in-flight magazines. Categories: oils and acrylics; watercolors; graphics; photography; sculpture; ceramics; and creative crafts.
Acceptable Work: Considers batik; ceramics; glass art; jewelry; leatherworking; macrame; mobiles; pottery; sculpture; soft sculpture; weaving; and woodcrafting. No bread sculpture; mass-produced buckles and leather; or clothing.
Awards: Presents $8,500 in cash; $2,000-5,000 in purchase awards; and 51 ribbons. To win awards "maximize the potential of the media (professionally); push the media to perfection and beyond accepted limits."
Sales: "Several artists, photographers, ceramicists sold out. Some reported $9,000 in sales. Others showed low to medium sales."

*****ARTS & CRAFTS FESTIVAL**, St. Augustine Arts & Crafts Council, Box 547, St. Augustine FL 32084. (904)829-8175. Director: Frederick White. Estab. 1964. Annual outdoor show held days during Palm Sunday weekend. Average attendance: 100,000. Entries accepted until 4 weeks before show. Entry fee: $50/12x12 display area. Prejudging by 3 slides of work and 1 slide of display; entry fee refunded for refused work. Work may be offered for sale; no commission. Craftworker must attend show; demonstrations OK. Registration limit: 144. Sponsor provides electricity for demonstrations; insurance on exhibited work; and 24-hour security. Categories: painting; glass; textiles; leather; sculpture; graphics; ceramics; mixed media; metalwork; and photography. Considers all crafts. Presents $7,200 in cash; $1,000+ in purchase prizes; and ribbons.
Promotion: Show is advertised by TV; radio; and newspapers. "Exhibitors should supply biography and b&w photographs for publicity."

*****ARTS FESTIVAL**, Box 1453, Cape Coral FL 33904. (904)334-4977. President: Norman Jones. Sponsor: Lee County Alliance of the Arts. Estab. 1976. Annual outdoor show (with some locations under store marquees) held 1 week in November at Fort Myers, Florida. Entries accepted until November. Entry fee: $5/10x12 display area. Prejudging; no entry fees refunded for refused work. Work may be offered for sale; no commission (donations accepted). Craftworker must attend show; demonstrations OK. Categories: visual arts and crafts. Considers all crafts except soft sculpture. Awards cash prizes and 3 honorable mention ribbons in each category.

*****ARTS POTPOURRI IN THE PARK**, 344 S. Beach St., Daytona Beach FL 32074. (904)252-4769. Chairman: Carol Ann Moritz. Financial Director: Barbara Stevens. Sponsor: YWCA. Purpose: "to help the YWCA in our community services." Estab. 1974. Semiannual outdoor show held 2 days in March and in November. Attendance: 10,000-15,000. Entries accepted until show date. Entry fee: $15/10x20 display area. Work may be offered for sale; no commission. Craftworker must attend show; demonstrations OK. Registration limit: 200. Sponsor provides limited electricity for demonstrations. Show is advertised by local newspapers; magazine listings; radio; and TV. Considers all crafts. Awards 1st, 2nd and 3rd place ribbons.

BEAUX ARTS FESTIVAL OF ART, c/o Lowe Art Museum, 1301 Miller Dr., Coral Gables FL 33146. Contact: Mrs. William Mooney. Entry fee: $42/10x12 display area. Work may be offered for sale; no commission. Considers ceramics; sculpture; and crafts.

*BOYNTON BEACH ANNUAL FESTIVAL OF THE ARTS, 128 E. Ocean Ave., Boynton Beach FL 33435. (305)732-2636. Recreation Supervisor: Laura Mudryk. Sponsor: recreation department; chamber of commerce; and the community school. Purpose: "to offer a cultural event for the surrounding areas and the citizens." Estab. 1974. Annual outdoor show held 2 days in March. Attendance: 15,000-20,000. Entries accepted until 2 weeks before show. Entry fee: $15 for professionals, $12 for amateurs/8x12 display area. Maximum 3 entries/category for judging, unlimited for nonjuried areas. Prejudging by 3 slides and photos. Work may be offered for sale; no commission. Craftworker must attend show; demonstrations OK. Registration limit: 200. Sponsor provides electricity for demonstrations. Categories: paintings; watercolors; sculpture; graphics; jewelry; ceramics; and mixed media. Considers batik; ceramics; jewelry; leatherworking; macrame; pottery; sculpture; weaving; and woodcrafting. Presents $1,000 in cash; and 1st, 2nd and 3rd place ribbons.

BREVARD MALL FESTIVAL OF ARTS & CRAFTS, 615 S. "H" St., Lake Worth FL 33460. (305)582-6133. Director: J.J. Readey. Annual indoor show held 3 days in February. Average attendance: 3,000. Entries accepted until 1 week before show. Entry fee: $20/12x5 display area. Prejudging by 3 slides or color photos; entry fee refunded for refused work. Work may be offered for sale; no commission. Craftworker or representative must attend show; demonstrations OK. Registration limit: 40. Sponsor provides electricity for demonstrations "if requested in advance." Considers all crafts. "Prefers batiks and needlework framed."
Promotion: Show is advertised by newspapers and radio. Exhibitor should supply 8x10 b&w glossy photos and resume for newspaper releases.

*CITRUS COUNTY FESTIVAL OF THE ARTS, Citrus County Art League, Box 131, Lecanto FL 32661. Sponsor: Art League and Chamber of Commerce. Purpose: fundraiser. Estab. 1970. Annual outdoor show held 1 day in November at Inverness, Florida. Entries accepted up until show. Entry fee: $12/pre-registration; $15/10x10 display area. Work may be offered for sale; no commission. Craftworker needn't attend show; demonstrations OK. Show is advertised by local papers and *Sunshine Artist*. Presents cash awards for 1st, 2nd, and 3rd; ribbon for honorable mention.

COASTLAND CENTER INVITATIONAL WINTER FESTIVAL OF ART, 615 South "H" St., Lake Worth FL 33460. (305)582-6133. Director: Jim Readey. Sponsor: Coastland Center and J.J. Readey. Estab. 1978. Annual indoor show held 3 days in February at Naples, Florida. Attendance: 12,000. Entries accepted until 1 week before show. Entry fee: $35-40/12x8 display area. Prejudging by 5 slides that are representative of work; entry fee refunded for refused work. Work may be offered for sale; no commission. Craftworker or representative must attend show; demonstrations OK. Registration limit: 50. Sponsor provides 24-hour security and electricity for demonstrations if requested in advance. Considers framed batiks; and stone metal and wood sculpture. "Most work must be framed. Portfolio may be used."
Promotion: Show is advertised by newspapers, radio and TV. Send "8x10 b&w glossy for newspaper release — also resume."

COCO PLUM WOMAN'S CLUB JEWELED EGG SHOW Coco Plum, 1375 Sunset Dr., Coral Gables FL 33143. (305)279-2241. Chairman: Mrs. G.I. Drury. Purpose: "Showing our art plus making money for mental health." Estab. 1970. Annual indoor show held 3 days in February. Average attendance: 1,500. Entries accepted until 4 weeks before show. Entry fee: $30/8' table, plus $25 or 1 jeweled egg to be raffled for mental health. Maximum 6 eggs. Work may be offered for sale; no commission. Craftworker must attend show; demonstrations OK. Registration limit: 60. Sponsor provides chairs; coverings; electricity for demonstrations; table; and 24-hour security. Considers decoupage; dollmaking; tole painting; and other types of egg shell art.

COLLEGE PORT SIDEWALK ART FESTIVAL, 2501 Edgewater Dr., Orlando FL 32804. (305)843-4084. Coordinator: Rita Diamond. Sponsor: College Park Merchants Association. Estab. 1967. Annual outdoor show held 2 days in April. Attendance: 50,000-75,000. Entries accepted until 4 weeks before show. Entry fee: $25/artist. Display area: 12x10. Work may be offered for sale; no commission. Craftworker must attend show; demonstrations OK. Registration limit: 200-250. Sponsor provides 24-hour security. Show is advertised by newspapers; TV; posters; and postcards. Considers all crafts. "Merchant Association handles sales tax, collected at end of day from all artists."

*CONTEMPORARY CRAFTS EXPO, Prema Productions, Box 3848, Indialandic FL 32903. (305)773-3148. President: Michael Picow. Purpose: "to enhance the community of quality crafts and to serve the family of craftspeople and the patrons of the arts." Estab. 1978. Annual indoor show held 3 days in the spring at Ft. Meyers, Florida. Attendance: 8,000-10,000. Entries accepted until 4 weeks before show. Entry fee: $75, $110, or $135/8x10, 8x15, or 8x20 display area. Prejudging by 3 slides or photos or work and 1 of display; entry fee refunded for refused work. Work may be offered for sale; no commission. Craftworker must attend show; demonstrations OK. Registration limit: 60. Sponsor provides electricity for demonstrations and 24-hour security. Considers all crafts. Presents $850 in cash, and ribbons.
Promotion: A professional ad agency advertises the show on radio; by newspapers; billboard coverage; and possibly TV ("depending upon finances"). "A b&w photo would be fine to use as promotional means for newspapers and literature."

*CORAL GABLES MIRACLE MILE SIDEWALK ART SHOW, Coral Gables Chamber of Commerce, 50 Aragon Ave., Coral Gables FL 33134. (305)446-1657. Executive Director: Tom E. Chegin. Sponsor: Chamber of Commerce and Miami Palette Club. Purpose: "to bring both culture and potential business to Coral Gables shopping area." Estab. 1964. Annual outdoor show held 3 days during the last weekend of January. Average attendance: 10,000+. Entries accepted until show date; "checks accepted only until a week before the show, after that time, only money orders or certified checks will be accepted." Entry fee: $45/artist. Display area is "approximately 25' wide; artists may use no more than 50% of the sidewalk width, or approximately 7'. Description of media is required on the application." Work may be offered for sale; no commission. Artist must attend show; demonstrations OK. Considers sculpture. Presents $750 in cash; $500 in purchase prizes; and honorable mention ribbons.
Promotion: "The show is promoted year-round in artists' publications and is widely promoted locally by newspaper, TV and radio coverage — through public service, advertising and news releases during October-January."

*DELAND OUTDOOR ART FESTIVAL, Rt. 2, Box 674F, Deland FL 32720. (305)734-1562. Co-chairman: Joyce N. Campbell. Purpose: "we love arts locally, and we want to share with others." Estab. 1965. Annual outdoor show held 2 days in March. Entries accepted until show date. Entry fee: $10/artist. Display area: 12' parking space. Work may be offered for sale; no commission. Craftworker must attend show; demonstrations OK. Categories: oils; acrylics and mixed media; watercolor; sculpture; graphics and photography; and creative crafts. Considers all crafts. Presents $1,295 in cash awards; merit awards; best display award; and ribbons and cash prizes.
Sales Tip: You "should have name cards and literature. Many ask [about the work] on Saturday and come back Sunday to buy. Have attractive display racks and stands."

FALL ARTS & CRAFTS SHOW, Box 883, Panama City FL 32401. Contact: Show Chairman. Sponsor: Panama Art Association. Purpose: "to raise money for scholarship fund and building fund." Estab. 1976. Annual indoor show held 2 days in the fall. Entries accepted until 2 weeks before show. Entry fee: $20/artist. Work may be offered for sale; no commission. Craftworker must attend show; demonstrations OK. Registration limit: 65-70. Sponsor provides electricity for demonstrations. Considers all crafts.
Sales Tip: "Small gift-type items sell best. State of Florida has collector present for state sales tax and Panama Art Association collects the city tax from the artist. 1977 show sales totalled $8,500."

*FALL FOR ART, 228BB, Rt. 1, Sanford FL 32771. Vice President: Carol Gentry. Sponsor: Sanford-Seminole Art Association. Estab. 1959. Annual outdoor show held 2 days in October. Average attendance: 10,000. Entries accepted until 2 weeks before show. Entry fee: $15/8x14 display area. Work may be offered for sale; no commission. Craftworker must attend show; demonstrations OK. Categories; oils and acrylics; watercolor and pastels; graphics and

photography; sculpture; and creative crafts. Presents $1,300+ in cash, and ribbons.
Acceptable Work Considers batik; ceramics; jewelry; lapidary; leatherworking; macrame; metalsmithing; mobiles; needlecrafts; pottery; sculpture; soft sculpture; weaving; and woodcrafting. "No sewing as in clothes, quilts or doll clothes; junk jewelry; decoupage; or commercial furniture. All work must be framed or hung (as in wall hangings and batiks). May have other works in portfolio."
Sales Tip: "To improve sales, provide a friendly personality, be willing to talk to people without 'pressure tactics,' and have a good attitude with show people (sometimes your best buyers and traders)." Forms will be provided for sales tax.
Promotion: Show is advertised by newspaper; radio; TV; art magazines; posters; flyers; bumper stickers; and T-shirts. "The artist should tell [us] what his craft is— describe if unusual— and for publicity, name some awards and shows he/she has entered."

*FESTIVAL OF THE ARTS, City of Miami Beach, Bin O, Miami Beach FL 33139. (305)673-7733. Chairperson: Pearl Kipnis. Sponsor: Fine Arts Board. Purpose: "to increase interest in the creative and performing arts." Estab. 1971. Annual outdoor show held 2 days in February. Average attendance: 200,000. Entries accepted until 2 months before show. Entry fee: $5 prejudging fee, and $45/10x10 display area. Prejudging by 3 slides from each category entered; no $5 entry fees refunded for refused work. Work may be offered for sale; no commission. Craftworker must attend show; demonstrations OK. Sponsor provides 24-hour security. Categories: painting, graphics and drawings; sculpture; crafts; and photography. Considers all crafts.
Awards: Presents $500 1st prize; $150 2nd prize; $1,000 purchase prize; and $100 best display award. Awards total $4,350.

FLORIDA FOLK FESTIVAL, Box 265, White Springs FL 32096. (904)397-2192. Director: John Robertson. Program Coordinator: Barbara Beauchamp. Sponsor: Stephen Foster Center. Purpose: "to showcase Florida folk arts." Estab. 1953. Annual outdoor show held 4 days in May. Average attendance: 30,000. Entries accepted until 4 weeks before show. No entry fee. Display area: 6x12 or 12x12. Prejudging. Work may be offered for sale; 15% commission. Craftworker must attend show; demonstrations OK. Registration limit: 25-50. Sponsor provides coverings and 24-hour security.
Acceptable Work: Considers candlemaking; dollmaking; jewelry; lapidary; leatherworking; metalsmithing; needlecrafts; pottery; tole painting; weaving; woodcrafting; quilting; spinning; natural dyeing; and other folk crafts.
Promotion: Show is advertised by news releases to all TV; radio; and newspapers in Florida and southern Georgia. Exhibitor should supply "background information on themselves as well as 8x10 b&w glossy photo showing their involvement in their craftwork."

FLORIDA FOREST FESTIVAL ARTS & CRAFTS SHOW & SALE, Box 892, Perry FL 32347. (904)584-5366. Chairman: Nadine O. Loughridge. Sponsor: Perry-Taylor County Chamber of Commerce. Purpose: "to add interest to Festival; promote local artists; and give the county's rural population a chance to see and buy arts and crafts." Estab. 1971. Annual outdoor show (with 30 canopies for rent) held 1 day in October. Average attendance: 31,000. Entries accepted until 1 week before show. Entry fee: $3/9x9 display area. Work may be offered for sale; 10% commission. Craftworker must attend show; demonstrations OK. Registration limit: 55. Sponsor provides electricity for demonstrations, and carries liability insurance. Considers all crafts. "B&w photos showing artist with work are appreciated." 1977 exhibitor sales totalled $3,708.70.

FOURTH OF JULY CELEBRATION & OPEN AIR CRAFTS FAIR, Box 265, White Springs, FL 32096. (904)397-2192. Program Director: Barbara Beauchamp. Sponsor: Stephen Foster Center. Purpose: "to showcase the folk artist in Florida and their works." Estab. 1976. Annual outdoor show held 3 days July 4th weekend. Attendance: 5,000-8,000. Entries accepted until 3 weeks before show. Entry fee: $10. Display area: 6x12 or 12x12. Prejudging by slides or photos; entry fee refunded for refused work. Work may be offered for sale; 15% commission. Craftworker must attend show; demonstrations OK. Registration limit: 25-100. Sponsor provides coverings and 24-hour security.
Acceptable Work: Considers candlemaking; dollmaking; jewelry; lapidary; leatherworking; metalsmithing; needlecrafts; pottery; soft sculpture; tole painting; weaving; woodcrafting; quilting; quilling; spinning; natural dyeing; pine needle crafts; palmetto; dried natural flowers of Florida; cabinetmaking; and whip braiding.
Promotion: Show is advertised by "news releases to all newspapers, TV and radio stations in

south Georgia and Florida. Exhibitors should supply biographical information on themselves and glossy 5x7 b&w photo of themselves showing their involvement in craft."

*GASPARILLA SIDEWALK ART FESTIVAL Box 10591, Tampa FL 33679. Estab. 1970. Annual outdoor show held 2 days in March. Entries accepted until 3 months before show. Entry fee: $30/artist. Display area: 8x12. Prejudging by 3 slides of work; refunds $25 of entry fee for refused work. Work may be offered for sale; no commission. Craftworker must attend show; demonstrations OK. Registration limit: 300. Sponsor provides electricity for demonstrations. Presents $8,700 in cash prizes with a $2,500 best of show award.
Acceptable Work: Considers ceramics; jewelry; pottery; sculpture; and weaving. "Crocheting; knitting; millinery; picture frames; velvet paintings; manufactured or kit jewelry; ceramics cast from commercial molds; art supplies; commercial displays; decoupage; candles or wearing apparel are not eligible to be exhibited."

*GREAT GULFCOAST FESTIVAL, Rt. 7, Box 403T, Pensacola FL 32506. Contact: Art Chairman. Sponsor: Pensacola Arts Council. Estab. 1972. Annual outdoor show held 2 days in November. Average attendance: 30,000. Entries accepted until 4 weeks before show. Entry fee: $30/artist. Prejudging by 3 2x2 slides/category entered; entry fee refunded for refused work. Work may be offered for sale; no commission. Craftworker must attend show; demonstrations encouraged. Sponsor provides "overnight security guard for both nights of the show." Show is advertised by magazines; TV; radio; billboards; newspapers; and through local businesses. Each artist handles his own sales and collects sales tax. "The tax collector will be present on the final day of the show."
Acceptable Work: Considers sculpture (dimensional forms in wood, metal, plastic and clay); pottery (stoneware, raku and porcelain); fiber (batik, macrame and weaving); and crafts (jewelry, stained glass, leather, etc.). "No decorated eggs; crocheting; knitting; shellcraft; millinery; velvet painting; art supplies; picture frames; coin jewelry; manufactured belts or handbags; or mass-produced jewelry."
Awards: Presents $4,000 in cash; $1,000, best of show; $150 1st prize, $100, 2nd prize, and $50 3rd prize in each category. "Work in portfolios will not be judged."
Profile: "The Great Gulfcoast Festival is an all volunteer effort to bring top quality arts and crafts to the people of Pensacola and surrounding towns. There are performing arts — ballet, music, drama— all free to the public. Children's art show and puppet shows and movies are also free."

GROUP SHOWING OF AMERICAN ARTISTS, 9476 Harding Ave., Surfside FL 33154. (305)864-8725. Contact: Iris G. Klein. Sponsor: House of Fine Art, Inc. Purpose: "to promote loccal and out-of-state American craftsmen." Estab. 1962. Annual indoor show held for 1 year. Display area: 4x8. Maximum 5-7 pieces per craftworker. Prejudging by slides; photos; and other shows. Entry fee refunded for refused work. Work may be offered for sale; 40% commission. Craftworker needn't attend show; no demonstrations. Registration limit: 6-8 at a time. Sponsor provides coverings; display panels; and electricity. Show is advertised by invitations. Submit b&w photo and resume. Considers batik; candlemaking; ceramics; decoupage; dollmaking; pottery; sculpture; and soft sculpture.

HALLANDALE CIVIC CENTER FUND ARTS, CRAFTS & PLANTS FESTIVAL, City Hall, 308 S. Dixie Hwy., Hallandale FL 33009. (305)454-9890. Coordinator: Seymour Sorin. Purpose: "to promote the development of a Cultural Arts Complex on the premises of the Arts, Crafts & Plants Show." Estab. 1978. Annual outdoor show held 1 day in January. Attendance: 6,000-7,000. Entries accepted until 1 week before show. Entry fee: $20/12x8 display area. Work may be offered for sale; no commission. Craftworker must attend show; demonstrations OK. Considers all crafts.

*HALLANDALE FALL ART FESTIVAL, c/o Chamber of Commerce, Box 249, Hallandale FL 33009. Chairman: Joseph H. Hanff Jr. Annual outdoor show held Thanksgiving weekend at Gulfstream Race Track. Entry fee: $35-40. Provide display sturdy enough to withstand weather and crowds. Work may be offered for sale; no commission. Presents cash awards and ribbons.

*IMAGES — A FESTIVAL OF THE ARTS, Box 2051, New Smyrna Beach FL 32069. (904)427-6975. Chairman: Holly Bivins. Estab. 1977. Annual outdoor show held 2 days in February. Average attendance: 70,000. Entries accepted until 3 months before show. Entry fee: $5 prejudging fee, and $20/12x12 display area. Prejudging by 3-35mm slides/category;$20 display area. Fee refunded for refused work. Work may be offered for sale; no commission. Craftworker must attend show; demonstrations OK. Registration limit: 200-210. Sponsor provides electricity for demonstrations and 24-hour security.

Acceptable Work: Considers batik; ceramics; glass art; jewelry; leatherworking; macrame; metalsmithing; mobiles; needlecrafts; pottery; sculpture; soft sculpture; weaving; woodcrafting; broom-making; basketry; and bookbinding.

Awards: Presents $6,500 in cash prizes; $1,000 in purchase awards; and ribbons. "Judges [are] looking for excellence, identity of design, creativity, and master craftsmanship."

Promotion: Show is advertised by radio, TV and newspapers. "Special 16-page festival section will go in 85,000 newspapers the day before the festival. [Submit] color slides for TV and newspaper purposes, also b&w glossies for newpapers."

Originally having started as a Bicentennial celebration, the Haines Township Dutch Fall Festival met with such success that it is now an annual event with a variety of activities such as hog butchering, bread baking, quilting, chair caning, tatting and other colonial crafts such as the candle-dipping pictures here. A large exhibit space on Main Street is provided for each craftworker participating in the 2-day October festival.

*INDIALANTIC SEASIDE ART SHOW, Box 3157, Indialantic FL 32903. (305)723-6387. Registration Chairman: Bernice T. Smith. Sponsor: Indialantic Improvement Association. Estab. 1967. Annual outdoor show held 2 days in April. Average attendance: 35,000. Entries accepted until 3 weeks before show. Entry fee: $22/display space. Prejudging by slides; entry fee refunded for refused work. Work may be offered for sale; no commission. Craftworker must attend show; demonstrations OK. Registration limit: 300. Categories: painting (oils, acrylic, mixed media); watercolors; graphics, drawings, pastels; sculpture; photography; and creative crafts. Presents $3,600 in cash prizes and $1,000 in purchase awards.

Acceptable Work: Considers batik; ceramics; glass art; jewelry; leatherworking; macrame; metalsmithing; pottery; sculpture; and weaving. Maximum size: 12'.

*KEY BISCAYNE ART FESTIVAL, 150 W. McIntyre, Key Biscayne FL 33149. (305)361-5418. Director: Frank DeLaurier. Sponsor: Key Biscayne Community School PTA. Purpose: "to provide the community with exposure to various artists and craftsmen and their work." Estab. 1964. Annual outdoor show held 3 days in January. Average attendance: 5,000. Entries accepted until show date. Entry fee: $40/12x12 display area by December 1; after that date $50. Prejudging by slides and photos; "entries not accepted are assigned to award-exempt section." Work may be offered for sale; no commission. Craftworker must attend show; demonstrations OK. Considers all crafts. Presents $1,000+ in cash awards.

*LAKE WALES SIDEWALK ART SHOW 922 Pembrook Place, Lake Wales FL 33853. (813)676-2003. Registrar: Gwenn Burr. Sponsor: Lake Wales Arts Council. Estab. 1970. Annual outdoor show held 1 day in the spring. Average attendance: 1,000. Entries accepted until show date. Entry fee: $10/12' display area. Work may be offered for sale; no commission. Craftworker must attend show; demonstrations OK. Sponsor provides sitter so craftworker can take a lunch break. Categories: watercolors; mixed media; graphics; drawings; photography; and crafts and sculpture. Present $3,000 in prizes: $100 1st prize in each category; purchase awards; and ribbons.
Acceptable Work: Considers candlemaking; ceramics; dollmaking; glass art; jewelry; lapidary; leatherworking; macrame; metalsmithing; mobiles; pottery; sculpture; soft sculpture; weaving; and woodcrafting. No clothing.

LEE SIDEWALK ARTS & CRAFTS SHOW, Box 711, Fort Myers FL 33902. (813)334-1171. Vice President: B. Bloodworth. Sponsor: Lee County Bank. Purpose: "to provide an outlet for talented craftsmen who are in the area." Estab. 1974. Annual outdoor show held 1 day in January. Average attendance: 20,000. Entries accepted until 5 weeks before show. Entry fee: $10/10x10 display area. Work must be offered for sale; no commission. Craftworker must attend show; demonstrations OK. Registration limit: 325. Sponsor provides electricity for demonstrations. Show is advertised by newspapers; posters; radio and TV. Considers all crafts. "The exhibitor handles all sales and sales tax. The sponsor collects the sales tax at the end of the day, and sends it to the State Department of Revenue. 1977 sales tax totalled $670."

MERRITT SQUARE FESTIVAL OF ARTS & CRAFTS, 615 S. "H" St., Lake Worth FL 33400. (305)582-6133. Director: J.J. Readey. Estab. 1970. Annual indoor show held 3 days in January at Merritt Island, Florida. Average attendance: 8,000. Entries accepted until 1 week before show (usually full about 3 weeks before show). Entry fee: $35/12x7 display area. Prejudging by 3 slides or color photos. Work may be offered for sale; no commission. Craftworker or representative must attend show; demonstrations OK. Registration limit: 70. Sponsor provides electricity for demonstrations if requested in advance, and 24-hour security. Supply 8x10 b&w glossy photo for newspaper release.
Acceptable Work: Considers framed batik: decoupage; dollmaking; glass art; metalsmithing; mobiles; needlecrafts; pottery; sculpture; tole painting; woodcrafting; egg craft; and shell craft.

*MIAMI BEACH FESTIVAL OF THE ARTS, Bin "O", Miami Beach FL 33139. Contact: Pearl Kipnis. Annual outdoor show held in February at Miami Beach Convention Center. Sponsor: Fine Arts Board of the City of Miami Beach. Entry fee: $5 application fee, $45/category entered. Art may be offered for sale; no commission. Presents cash awards over $4,000. Categories include painting; graphics; drawings; sculpture; and crafts.

MICANOPY FALL HARVEST FESTIVAL, Box 74, Micanopy FL 32667. Booth Chairwoman: Claire Thibeau. Purpose: "to encourage persons within northern Florida, and of course the Micanopy community, to participate either as exhibitors or visitors to an event such as this; and to raise funds for civic projects in Micanopy." Estab. 1975. Annual outdoor show held 1 day in the fall. Average attendance: 6,000. Entries accepted until 2 weeks before show. Entry fee: $10/artist. Display area: 6x12. Work may be offered for sale; no commission. Craftworker must attend show; demonstrations OK. Registration limit: 100. Sponsor provides limited electricity for demonstrations. Show is advertised by local radio; TV; posters; newspapers; and calendars. Considers all crafts.

*MOUNT DORA ART FESTIVAL, Box 231, Mount Dora FL 32757. Chairman: Harlow C. Middleton. Estab. 1975. Annual outdoor show held 2 days in February. Attendance: 25,000-50,000. Entries accepted until 5 weeks before show. Entry fee: $5 prejudging fee plus $15 if accepted. Display area: 8x14. Prejudging by slides; no prejudging fees refunded for refused work. Work may be offered for sale; no commission. Craftworker must attend show; demonstrations OK. Registration limit: 250. Sponsor provides electricity for demonstrations. Categories: painting; graphics; photography; sculpture; watercolors; and crafts. Considers all crafts. Presents $4,300+ in cash awards, and $800 best of show purchase award.

Promotion: Show is advertised "in local papers; trade magazines; TV and radio; by visiting other shows and handing out brochures; and sending brochures to all Florida colleges and universities."

OCEAN EAST MALL FESTIVAL OF ARTS & CRAFTS, 615 S. "H" St., Lake Worth FL 33460. (305)582-6133. Director: J.J. Readey. Estab. 1974. Semiannual indoor show held 2 days in the late summer and winter at Stuart, Florida. Average attendance: 2,000, summer show; 4,000, winter show. Entries accepted until 2 weeks before show. Entry fee: $30/12x5 display area. Prejudging by 3 slides or color photos; entry fee refunded for refused work. Work may be offered for sale; no commission. Craftworker or representative must attend show; demonstrations OK. Registration limit: 60. Sponsor provides electricity for demonstrations if requested in advance. Submit 8x10 b&w glossy photo and resume for newspaper release.
Acceptable Work: Considers batik; candlemaking; decoupage; dollmaking; glass art; jewelry; leatherworking; macrame; metalsmithing; mobiles; needlecrafts; pottery; sculpture; soft sculpture; tole painting; weaving; and woodcrafting. "No puka, heshi, turquoise, liquid silver, coral or Indian-style jewelry. Prefer batiks and needlework framed."

ORANGE PARK MALL FESTIVAL OF ART, 615 S. "H" St., Lake Worth FL 33460. (305)582-6133. Director: J.J. Readey. Estab. 1976. Semiannual indoor show held 4 days in the spring and fall at Jacksonville, Florida. Average attendance: 12,000/show. Entries accepted until show date. Entry fee: $40/12x7 display area. Prejudging by 3 slides or color photos; entry fee refunded for refused work. Work may be offered for sale; no commission. Craftworker or representative must attend show; demonstrations OK. Sponsor provides electricity for demonstrations if requested in advance. Considers framed batik; and stone, wood and metal sculpture.

ORANGE PARK MALL OLDE TYME ARTS & CRAFTS FAIRE, 615 S. "H" St., Lake Worth FL 33460. (305)582-6133. Director: J.J. Readey. Estab. 1976. Annual indoor show held 4 days "around July 4th each year" at Jacksonville, Florida. Attendance: 12,000-15,000. Entries accepted until 1 week before show (but show usually fills earlier). Entry fee: $40/12x7 display area. Prejudging by 3 slides or photos; entry fee refunded for refused work. Work may be offered for sale; no commission. Craftworker or representative must attend show; demonstrations OK. Registration limit: 70. Sponsor provides electricity for demonstrations if requested. Submit 8x10 b&w glossy photo and resume for newspaper release. Considers all crafts.

ORANGE PARK MALL WINTER CRAFT SHOW, 615 S. "H" St., Lake Worth, FL 33460. (305)582-6133. Director: J.J. Readey. Estab. 1976. Annual indoor show held 4 days in January at Jacksonville, Florida. Attendance: 12,000-15,000. Entries accepted until 1 week before show (usually fills 5 weeks in advance). Entry fee: $45/12x7 display area. Prejudging by 3 slides or color photos; entry fee refunded for refused work. Work may be offered for sale; no commission. Craftworker or representative must attend show; demonstrations OK. Registration limit: 70. Sponsor provides electricity for demonstrations if requested in advance and 24-hour security. Supply 8x10 b&w photo and resume for newspaper release. Considers all crafts except clothing and lapidary. "Like most hangings to be framed."

*OSCEOLA ART FESTIVAL, Box 776, Kissimmee FL 32741. (305)847-3174. Publicity Director: Rosetta Land. Jaycee President: Pete Edwards. Estab. 1965. Annual outdoor show held 2 days the third weekend in October. Average attendance: 15,000. Entries accepted until show date. Entry fee: $20/artist. Display area: 12'. Work may be offered for sale; no commission. Craftworker must attend show; no demonstrations. Categories: acrylic; creative crafts; graphics; mixed media; oil; sculpture; and watercolor.
Acceptable Work: Considers all crafts. "Objects produced from commercial molds or kits will be ineligible for judging. The review committee reserves the right to remove any exhibit or work of art."
Awards: Presents $2,800 in cash awards; $3,500 in purchase prizes; and 1st, 2nd and 3rd place ribbons.

*OUTDOOR CRAFTS FESTIVAL, Ringling Museum's Annual Crafts Festival, Box 1838. Sarasota FL 33578. (813)355-5101. Contact: Members Council Secretary. Sponsor: Members Council, Ringling Museums. Estab. 1972. Annual outdoor show held 2 days in November. Average attendance: 5,000. Entries accepted until 10 weeks before show. "Must be Florida craftworker." Entry fee: $5 application fee plus $25/accepted craftworker. Display area: 10x12. Prejudging by "3 35mm slides of 3 different objects created within the past year in each category entered"; application fee not refunded. Work may be offered for sale; no commission. Craftworker must attend show; demonstrations OK. Registration limit: approximately 60. Sponsor provides electricity for demonstrations and 24-hour security.

Acceptable Work: Considers ceramics; enameling; glass; jewelry; leather; metal; mixed media; sculpture; textiles; and wood. "Decision of acceptance by 3-person jury. Only highly professional work accepted."

Awards: Presents best in show $500; 4 merit awards $200 each; 2 honorable mentions $100 each; best presentation $50; and purchase awards.

PARK SHORE PLAZA FESTIVAL OF ARTS & CRAFTS, 615 S. "H" St., Lake Worth FL 33460. (305)582-6133. Director. J.J. Readey. Estab. 1974. Annual outdoor show (with some spaces covered with an overhang from building) held 3 days in January at Naples, Florida. Average attendance: 8,000. Entries accepted until 1 week before show; "however it usually fills up about 6 weeks in advance, and jewelry fills about 3 months before show." Entry fee: $40/12x4 display area. Work may be offered for sale; no commission. Craftworker or representative must attend show; demonstrations OK. Registration limit: 100. Submit 8x10 x&w photo and resume for newspaper release. Considers all crafts. "In this mall inexpensive items are the fast movers."

*PATRIOTS ART FESTIVAL, Box 1205, Largo FL 33540. (813)584-2119. Chairman/President: Ramon G. Florez. Sponsor: Patriotic Krewe of Largo, Inc. Estab. 1977. Annual outdoor show held 3 days in February. Average attendance: 25,000+. Entries accepted until show date. Entry fee: $20/display area. Work may be offered for sale; no commission. Craftworker must attend show; demonstrations OK. Registration limit: 300. Sponsor provides electricity for demonstrations. Categories: oil painting; watercolor; pottery; photography; crafts; and sculpture. Considers all crafts. Presents $600 best of show award; $75, $50, $25 and $15 prizes; and 1st, 2nd, 3rd and 4th place ribbons.

PROMENADES SHOPPING CENTER FESTIVAL OF ARTS & CRAFTS, 615 S. "H" St., Lake Worth FL 33460. (305)582-6133. Director: J.J. Readey. Estab. 1976. Annual outdoor show (with some spaces covered with overhang) held 2 days in February at Port Charlotte, Florida. Average attendance: 5,000. Entries accepted until 1 week before show. Entry fee: $30/12x8 display area. Prejudging by 3 slides or color photos; entry fee refunded for refused work. Work may be offered for sale; no commission. Craftworker or representative must attend show; demonstrations OK. Registration limit: 100. Considers all crafts.

RENAISSANCE CELEBRATION, Box 20374, Tallahassee FL 32344. Director: Candi Paparone. Estab. 1974. Annual outdoor show held 2 days in the fall. Attendance: 5,000-15,000. Entries accepted until show date. Entry fee: $25/12x12 display area. Prejudging by slides; entry fee refunded for refused work. Work may be offered for sale; no commission. Craftworker must attend show; demonstrations OK. Registration limit: 75. Sponsor provides limited electricity for demonstrations. Considers all crafts "if design and execution is superior. No smoking [permitted] in park; no nails in trees; pick up trash."

Promotion: Show is advertised by radio; TV; newspapers; magazines; posters; and T-shirts. "Any photos or information will be used."

*SABAL CHASE OUTDOOR ART AND ARTISANS FAIR, c/o Woody Kepner Associates, Box 450548, Miami FL 33145. (305)854-4765. Account Representative: Linda Elfman. Sponsor: Arvida Corp., Primary Housing Division (developers of the community of Sabal Chase). "The show was originally designed as a traffic builder for the residential community under development. Now Sabal Chase is nearly sold out — Arvida is community minded, and found such acceptance by residents and the general public, they decided to continue the show." Estab. 1976. Annual outdoor show held 2 days in the fall. Average attendance: 3,000. Entries accepted until 2 weeks before show. No entry fee ("but this may change in the future"). Display area: approximately 10x10. Work may be offered for sale; no commission. Craftworker must attend show; demonstrations encouraged. Registration limit: 200. Sponsor provides electricity for demonstrations if requested in advance. Considers all crafts.

Awards: Presents $1,000 in purchase prizes accompanied by ribbons; $300 1st prize; $150 2nd prize; and $50 for 3rd. "Awards were made in 1977 by a committee of Arvida staff. Most effective in any case is a clean, orderly style of presentation. Only one type of work — prints and paintings, sculpture, ceramics, etc. — may be shown per artist or artisan."

Sales Tip: "The public at these shows comes to take advantage of original pieces available in time for Christmas. Reasonable prices naturally are necessary; but some expensive sales were reported both years. Our visitors are very impressed with demonstrations and personable artists. This is a young, high-income demographic area. Entry form requires a tax number. IRS watches this one for some reason."

Promotion: Show is advertised by local papers; radio; public service advertising; posters in neighborhood stores; shopping centers; and gas stations. "Exhibitors can provide nonreturnable 8x10 b&w glossy photo of artist with work for promotional consideration. May submit color nonreturnable slides."

*ST. CLOUD ANNUAL ART FESTIVAL, Box 5, 923 New York Ave., St. Cloud FL 32769. (304)892-3671. Contact: Director. Estab. 1966. Annual outdoor show held 2 days the first weekend in March. Average attendance: 1,000+/day. Entries accepted until show date. Entry fee: $15/12x12 display area. Work may be offered for sale; no commission. Craftworker must attend show; demonstrations OK. Sponsor provides limited electricity for demonstration and 24-hour security. Categories: objective (oil, acrylic, mixed media); nonobjective (oil, acrylic, mixed media); other media (watercolor, pastel, charcoal and ink); sculpture; ceramics; and crafts. Considers all crafts.
Awards: Presents $1,300+ in cash prizes; some purchase awards; and 1st, 2nd, 3rd and 4th place ribbons.

*SANIBEL SHELL FAIR, Box 90, Sanibel FL 33957. (813)472-2155. Chairman: Joseph G. Winterrowd. Sponsor: Sanibel Community Association. "Sanibel has long been known for its shelling beaches. This fair emphasizes knowledge and classification of, and appreciation for shells." Estab. 1937. Annual indoor/outdoor show held 5 days (1 day judging, 4 days open to public) in March. Entries accepted until noon on the Saturday preceding the show; exhibits due Wednesday noon preceding show. Display area: 2x20. Maximum 1 entry/category. Work may be offered for sale; no commission. Craftworker needn't attend show; no demonstrations. Sponsor provides table and 24-hour security. Categories: self-collected division; student division; scientific division; anomalies division; commercial (professional) division; and artistic division. Shell crafts only. Presents ribbons and trophies.

*SEAS NATIONAL, Municipal Auditorium, Panama City FL 32401. (904)763-4696. Auditorium Manager: Cecil Koon. Purpose: "to create the finest exhibit in the country, affording all artists an oportunity to compete at their own level. Hopefully we will bring the finest art to Panama City." Estab. 1964. Annual indoor show held 1 month May-June. Entries accepted until 2 weeks before show. Entry fee: $12/entry; 3 items to entry. Maximum 2 pieces per artist per category; 6 total. Work may be offered for sale; 20% commission. Craftworker needn't attend show; no demonstrations. Show is advertised by radio; TV; and magazines. Submit social security number for bond purchases. Presents cash awards. Considers mobiles; pottery; sculpture; and woodcrafting.

7 LIVELY ARTS FESTIVAL, INCORPORATED, ART SHOW, c/o Hollywood Recreation Division, 2030 Polk St., Hollywood FL 33020. (305)921-3399. Performing Arts Coordinator: Monnie Levin. Purpose: "to culturally enrich the community." Estab. 1969. Annual outdoor show held 2-3 days in April. Attendance: 50,000-70,000. Entries accepted until 2 weeks before show. Entry fee: $35/6x15 display area. Prejudging by slides; entry fee refunded for refused work. Work may be offered for sale; no commission. Craftworker must attend show; demonstrations OK. Sponsor provides electricity for demonstrations. Show is advertised by radio; local newspapers; and *Sunshine Artists U.S.A.*
Acceptable Work: Considers batik; dollmaking; glass art; jewelry; lapidary; leatherworking; macrame; metalsmithing; mobiles; pottery; sculpture; soft sculpture; weaving; and woodcrafting to Country Fair portion of show.

*SOCIETY OF THE ARTS' ANNUAL FESTIVAL OF THE ARTS "ARTI GRAS", Box 831, North Miami FL 33161. (305)891-7466. Chairman: Pat Bourquin. Estab. 1968. Annual outdoor show held 2 days in the spring (performing arts events are held 4 days). Attendance: 20,000-35,000. Entries accepted until 2 weeks before show. Entry fee: $25/12x6 display area, plus $5 judging fee. Work must be offered for sale; no commission. Craftworker must attend show; demonstrations OK. Registration limit: about 40. Sponsor provides electricity for demonstrations; fencing; and 24-hour security. Professional public relations firm handles promotion. Categories: paintings (oils, acrylics, watercolor); photography; sculpture and metalworking; fabrics and fibers (no awards for macrame); and graphics. Presents $3,000+ in cash and ribbons for best in category; award of merit; and honorable mention. Gift items sell best.
Acceptable Work: Considers batik; candlemaking; hand-thrown ceramics; jewelry; lapidary; macrame; metalsmithing; mobiles; pottery; sculpture; soft sculpture; weaving; tole painting; and woodcrafting.

SOUTH FLORIDA FAIRS & EXPOSITIONS, INC., Box 15915, West Palm Beach FL 33406. (305)793-0333. "The South Florida Fair began as an agricultural fair. It has grown to include many facets of educational, entertaining, cultural and exciting events, displays and activities." Estab. 1912. Annual indoor/outdoor show (with some tents) held 10 days in the winter. Average attendance: 430,000. Work may be offered for sale. Considers ceramics; pottery; crochet; decoupage; repousse; dollmaking; embroidery; knitting; macrame; needlework; china painting; quilting; rugs; weaving; jewelry; leatherworking; and woodworking. Florida craftworkers only. Write for brochure.

SOUTH FLORIDA SPRING ARTS & CRAFTS FESTIVAL, Fantasma Productions, 1675 Palm Beach Lakes Blvd. #902, West Palm Beach FL 33401. (305)686-6397. Contact: Debi Cooper. Purpose: "to provide area residents and tourists with a 'fun' outing — browsing and shopping and live entertainment. As we do charge admission to the public, a financially successful event is, of course, what we hope for." Estab. 1975. Annual indoor show held 1 day in the spring. Average attendance: 4,000 paid. Entries accepted until 1 week before show. Entry fee: $30/8x3 table. Work may be offered for sale; no commission. Craftworker needn't attend show; demonstrations OK. Registration limit: 100. Sponsor provides chairs; electricity for demonstrations; and table. Considers all crafts. "If display exceeds prescribed area, 2 booth spaces may be taken."
Sales Tip: "Attractive display is a must! 'Working' craftsmen often attract many customers. Artist advised to have crafts in all price ranges, if possible. We publicize our shows for 'browsing and shopping.' Our spring show falls at a peak 'tourist' time in Florida. Artists advised to gear sales towards those markets."
Promotion: "As promotion is our business, we totally saturate the media. 'Print' advertising begins 6 weeks prior to the show; radio and TV, 4 weeks prior. We appreciate photos along with some background material."

SOUTH FLORIDA WINTER ARTS & CRAFTS FESTIVAL, Fantasma Productions, 1675 Palm Beach Lakes Blvd. #902, West Palm Beach FL 33401. (305)686-6397. Contact: Debi Cooper. Purpose: "to provide area residents and tourists with a 'fun' outing — browsing and shopping and live entertainment. As we do charge admission to the public, a financially successful event is, of course, what we hope for." Estab. 1975. Annual indoor show held 1 day in the winter at Riviera Beach, Florida. Average attendance: 4,000 paid. Entries accepted until 1 week before show. Entry fee: $30/8x3 table. Work may be offered for sale; no commission. Craftworker needn't attend show; demonstrations OK. Registration limit: 80. Sponsor provides chairs; electricity for demonstrations; and table. Considers all crafts. "If display exceeds prescribed area, 2 booth spaces may be taken."
Sales Tip: "Attractive display is a must! 'Working' craftsmen often attract many customers. Artist advised to have crafts in all price ranges, if possible. We publicize our show for 'browsing and shopping.' Our winter show appeals to the Christmas shopper. Artists advised to gear sales towards those markets."
Promotion: "As promotion is our business, we totally saturate the media. 'Print' advertising begins 6 weeks prior to the show; radio and TV, 4 weeks prior. We appreciate photos along with some background material."

*SPRING ARTS FESTIVAL, Box 1530, 3000 NW 83rd St., Gainesville FL 32602. (904)377-5161, ext. 383. Director: Karen Beach. Sponsor: Santa Fe Community College, Chamber of Commerce and City of Gainesville. Purpose: "to expose the north central Florida area residents to fine arts and crafts. This also gives area artists a chance to display their art and craftwork to a large audience." Estab. 1970. Annual outdoor show held 2 days during the first weekend in April. Average attendance: 70,000. Entries accepted until 2 months before show. Entry fee: $20/10x12 display area plus $5 application fee. Prejudging by slides; entry fee, but not application fee, refunded for refused work. Work may be offered for sale; no commission. Craftworker must attend show; demonstrations OK. Show is advertised by newspaper; radio; and magazines. Registration limit: 250. Categories: painting (oil, acrylic, mixed-media); painting (watercolor); sculpture; pottery; jewelry; fiber arts; leatherwork; graphics; photography; and open crafts.
Acceptable Work: Considers batik; ceramics; glass art; jewelry; stained glass; leatherworking; macrame; metalsmithing; pottery; sculpture; soft sculpture; weaving; and woodcrafting. "No pattern or mass-produced macrame or cloth items; crocheting or knitting; novelty items; antiques; string beads; clothing; feather or shell crafts; fork, spoon or coin jewelry; or embellished items. Artwork must be in good taste and appropriate for family viewing."
Awards: Presents $6,000 in cash and $4,000 in purchase prizes. "Display work so that judges have easy access to it. Make display as attractive as possible."

*SPRING ARTS POTPOURRI IN THE PARK, 344 S. Beach St., Daytona Beach FL 32014. (904)252-4769. Chairman: Carol Ann Moritz. Sponsor: YWCA. Purpose: fundraiser. Estab. 1975. Semiannual outdoor show held 2 days in March and November. Average attendance: 10,-000. Entries accepted until show. Entry fee: $15/10x20 display area. Work may be offered for sale; no commission. Craftworker must attend show; demonstrations OK. Sponsor provides some electricity for demonstrations. Show is advertised by magazines; newspapers; radio; flyers; posters; and TV. Considers all crafts. Presents 1st, 2nd, 3rd, honorable mention and merit ribbons.

SUWANNEE RIVER CRAFTS SHOW-SALE, Box 265, White Springs FL 32096. (904)397-2192. Director: John Robertson. Sponsor: Stephen Foster Center (a rural folk arts center). Purpose: "to promote crafts learned by craftsmen in the Suwannee Valley area of Florida, using Florida materials (foliage) and the old-timey crafts such as quilting, spinning, weaving, needlework, pine needle crafts, palmetto crafts, wood carving, wooden toys, etc." Estab. 1975. Annual indoor show held 1 month in the late spring. Average attendance: about 13,000. Entries accepted until 1 week before show. No entry fee. Prejudging by slides, photos or actual work. Work may be offered for sale; 15% commission. Craftworker needn't attend show; demonstrations OK. Registration limit: 25-50. Sponsor provides coverings; electricity for demonstrations; and 24-hour security. "People who attend most of our special events are looking for the unique folk craft that they normally do not find in shops."
Acceptable Work: Considers candlemaking; dollmaking; jewelry; lapidary; leatherworking; metalsmithing; needlecrafts; pottery; weaving; woodcrafting; quilting; spinning; and natural dyeing.
Promotion: Show is advertised "by news releases (usually 4 before show) to southern Georgia and all Florida radio, TV and daily and weekly newspapers." Submit 8x10 b&w glossy photo showing involvement with craft.

*TARPON SPRINGS ARTS AND CRAFTS SHOW, 112 S. Pinellas Ave., Tarpon Springs FL 33589. (813)937-6109. Director: John Tarapani. Sponsor: Tarpon Springs Chamber of Commerce. Estab. 1974. Annual outdoor show held 2 days in the spring. Average attendance: "thousands." Entries accepted until 1 month before show. Entry fee: $30/15x10 display area. Prejudging ($5 nonreturnable fee) by slides, photos or personal demonstrations; entry fee refunded for refused work. Work may be offered for sale; no commission. Craftworker must attend show; demonstrations OK. Show is advertised by artist publications and radio. Categories: watercolor; oils and mixed media; sculpture; graphics; crafts; and photography. Presents $6,000+ in cash, and $1,000+ in purchase awards.
Acceptable Work: Considers candlemaking; dollmaking; glass art; jewelry; macrame; metalsmithing; mobiles; pottery; sculpture; woodcrafting; and soft sculpture. "No tile, beads or shell work; velvet painting; knitting; crocheting; or plants."

*TITUSVILLE ART LEAGUE ANNUAL SHOW, Box 6133, Titusville FL 32780. Contact: Chairman. Estab. 1964. Annual indoor show held 1 week in the spring. Entries accepted until show date. Entry fee: $3/entry. Display area: 4x6. Prejudging: no entry fees refunded for refused work. Work may be offered for sale; no commission. Demonstrations on approval. Sponsor provides display panels. Craftworker provides display stand for unusual-size work.
Acceptable Work: Considers batik; ceramics; glass art; jewelry; leatherworking; metalsmithing; pottery; soft sculpture; weavings; wall hangings; and woodcrafting.
Awards: Present $300, best in show; 5 $100 1st places; 10 $50 merit awards; $1,200 in purchase awards; and 38 ribbons. Judges are professional artists.

UNIVERSITY MALL WINTER CRAFT SHOW, 615 S. "H" St., Lake Worth FL 33460. (305)582-6133. Director: J.J. Readey. Estab. 1976. Annual indoor show held 4 days in the fall at Pensacola, Florida. Average attendance: 18,000. Entries accepted until 1 week before show. Entry fee: $35/12x7 display area. Prejudging by 3 slides or color photos; entry fee refunded for refused work. Work may be offered for sale; no commission. Craftworker or representative must attend show; demonstrations OK. Registration limit: 70. Sponsor provides electricity for demonstrations if requested in advance. Show is advertised by TV; radio; and newspapers. "Submit b&w 8x10 glossy photos and a resume for use in promotion." Considers all crafts.

*VERO BEACH ART CLUB WINTER ART SHOW, 3136 Atlantic Blvd., Vero Beach FL 32960. Purpose: "to give the artist and craftsman an opportunity to show and sell his work; and to support our Vero Art Club Gallery— a nonprofit gallery." Estab. 1950. Annual outdoor show held 2 days in January. Entries accepted until 2 weeks before show or until filled. Entry fee:

$25/12x8 display area. Work may be offered for sale; no commission. Craftworker must attend show; demonstrations OK. Registration limit: 200. Categories: oil; acrylic and mixed media; watercolor; photography; drawings; pastels; graphics; sculpture; and creative crafts. Presents $1,500 in cash; purchase prizes; and 1st, 2nd and 3rd ribbons.

Acceptable Work: Considers batik; candlemaking; glass art; leatherworking; macrame; metalsmithing; pottery; sculpture; tole painting; weaving; woodcrafting; and jewelry by invitation. No velvet paintings; crocheting; fork spoon jewelry; decorated eggs; knitting; novelty shell crafts; clothing; coin jewelry; or mass-produced jewelry.

Promotion: Show is advertised by special newspaper supplement listing all artists and space numbers; TV; and radio. "B&w glossy photos might be used by our local newspaper."

*WINTER PARK MALL CRAFT SHOW, 560 N. Orlando Ave., Winter Park FL 32789. (305)644-4476. Director of Marketing: Sonja Unger. "Art shows and crafts shows are held in the Mall to bring in traffic as well as to introduce a little culture to the masses." Estab. 1970. Annual show held 3 days in the spring. Entries accepted until show is filled. Entry fee: $20/6x12 display area. Prejudging by 3 slides or photos of work and exhibit; entry fee refunded for refused work. Work may be offered for sale; no commission. Craftworker must attend show; demonstrations encouraged. Registration limit: 100. Sponsor provides electricity for demonstrations. Presents $200, best of show; 5 $75 awards of merit; and ribbons.

Acceptable Work: Considers batik; candlemaking; ceramics; dollmaking; glass art; leatherworking; macrame; metalsmithing; pottery; sculpture; and woodcrafting.

Promotion: Show is advertised in newspaper ads; radio; and by news releases to the media. "Anytime we have promotional information about unusual or extremely talented artists this is usually picked up by the press."

*WINTER PARK SIDEWALK ART FESTIVAL, Box 597, Winter Park FL 32790. Chairman: James G. Shepp. Purpose: "to provide the community with the best possible arts and crafts available today." Estab. 1959. Annual outdoor show held 3 days in March. Average attendance: 200,000. Deadlines for entries on application. Entry fee: $35/craftworker plus $5 jury fee. Display area: 9x12. Prejudging by 3 slides per category; entry fee refunded for refused work. Work may be offered for sale; no commission. Craftworker must attend show; demonstrations OK. Registration limit: 90. Sponsor provides electricity for demonstrations. Show is advertised by local radio spots and national articles such as in *Southern Living*. Presents cash awards totaling $10,000; best of show purchase award of $1,000; and ribbons. Considers batik; ceramics; dollmaking; glass art; jewelry; lapidary; leatherworking; macrame; metalsmithing; mobiles; pottery; sculpture; soft sculpture; weaving; and woodcrafting.

*YBOR SQUARE CHRISTMAS CRAFTS CARNIVAL, Box 2350, Tampa FL 33601. (813)247-5411. Manager: Byron B. Crowder. Sponsor: Ybor Square/Trend Publications, Inc. Estab. 1975. Annual indoor/outdoor show held 2 days in December. Entries accepted until 1 week before show. Entry fee: $20/10x10 outside display area; $30/10x10 inside display area. Prejudging by slides or photos of work; entry fee refunded for refused work. Work may be offered for sale; no commission. Craftworker must attend show; demonstrations OK. Registration limit: 80-100. Sponsor provides electricity for demonstrations; tables for rent; and 24-hour security. Show is advertised by newspapers; radio; TV; and art and crafts magazines.

Acceptable Work: Considers batik; candlemaking; ceramics; dollmaking; glass art; jewelry; lapidary; leatherworking; macrame; metalsmithing; mobiles; pottery; sculpture; tole painting; soft sculpture; weaving; and woodcrafting. "No crocheting; knitting; millinery; picture frames; manufactured or kit jewelry; ceramics cast from commercial molds; commercial displays; or wearing apparel.

Awards: Presents $200, 1st place, 4 $50 2nd places; 4 $25 3rd places; and ribbons for above winners and honorable mentions. "Our shows are judged by an outside juror."

*YBOR SQUARE FALL ARTS & CRAFTS FIESTA, Box 2350, Tampa FL 33601. (813)247-5411. Manager: Byron B. Crowder. Sponsor: Ybor Square/Trend Publications, Inc. Estab. 1975. Annual indoor/outdoor show held 2 days in October. Entries accepted until 1 week before show. Entry fee: $20/10x10 outside display area; $30/10x10 inside area. Prejudging by slides or photos; entry fee refunded for refused work. Work may be offered for sale; no commission. Craftworker must attend show; demonstrations OK. Registration limit: 80-100. Sponsor provides electricity for demonstrations; tables for rental; and 24-hour security. Show is advertised by newspapers; radio; TV; and art and crafts magazines.

Acceptable Work: Considers batik; candlemaking; ceramics; dollmaking; glass art; jewelry; lapidary; leatherworking; macrame; metalsmithing; mobiles; pottery; sculpture; tole painting;

soft sculpture; weaving; and woodcrafting. "All works must be original and done by exhibitor. Crocheting; knitting; millinery; picture frames; manufactured or kit jewelry; ceramics cast from comercial molds; art supplies; commercial displays; or wearing apparel not accepted.
Awards: Presents $300, best of show; 10 awards of merit at $100 each; 10 honorable mentions at $25 each; and ribbons. "Our shows are judged by an outside juror."
Profile: "Ybor Square is the second tourist attraction in Tampa, a restored cigar factory in the old Latin quarter of the city. When Trend Publications purchased and restored Ybor Square, the atmosphere was naturally appealing to artists and craftsmen, and many of our permanent tenants themselves (antique dealers, craftsmen, specialty store owners) are heavily involved in shows throughout Florida."

*YBOR SQUARE SPRING ARTS & CRAFTS FIESTA, Box 2350, Tampa FL 33601. (813)247-5411. Manager: Byron B. Crowder. Sponsor: Ybor Square/Trend Publications, Inc. Estab. 1975. Annual indoor/outdoor show held 2 days in April. Entries accepted until 1 week before show. Entry fee: $20/10x10 outside display area; $30/10x10 inside area. Prejudging by slides or photos; entry fee refunded for refused work. Work may be offered for sale; no commission. Craftworker must attend show; demonstrations OK. Registration limit: 80-100. Sponsor provides electricity for demonstrations; tables for rent; and 24-hour security. Show is advertised by newspapers; radio; TV; and art and crafts magazines.
Acceptable Work: Considers batik; candlemaking; ceramics; dollmaking; glass art; jewelry; lapidary; leatherworking; macrame; metalsmithing; mobiles; pottery; soft sculpture; tole painting; weaving; sculpture; and woodcrafting. No crocheting; knitting; millinery; manufactured or kit jewelry; ceramics from molds; commercial displays; or wearable apparel.
Awards: Presents $300, best of show; 10 $100 awards of merit; 10 $25 honorable mentions; and ribbons. "Our shows are judged by an outside juror."

*YBOR SQUARE SUMMER CRAFTS CARNIVAL, Box 2350, Tampa FL 33601. (813)247-5411. Manager: Byron B. Crowder. Sponsor: Ybor Square/Trend Publications, Inc. Estab. 1975. Annual indoor/outdoor show held 2 days in July. Entries accepted until 1 week before show. Entry fee: $20/10x10 display area outside; $30/10x10 display area inside. Prejudging by slides or photos; entry fee refunded for refused work. Work may be offered for sale; no commission. Craftworker must attend show; demonstrations OK. Registration limit: 80-100. Sponsor provides electricity for demonstrations; tables for rent; and 24-hour security. Show is advertised by radio; TV; newspapers; and art and crafts magazines. Presents $200, 1st place; 4 $50 2nd places; 4 $25 3rd places; and ribbons for 1st, 2nd, 3rd and honorable mentions.
Acceptable Work: Considers batik; candlemaking; ceramics not made from commercial molds; dollmaking; glass art; jewelry; lapidary; leatherworking; macrame; metalsmithing; mobiles; pottery; sculpture; soft sculpture; tole painting; weaving; and woodcrafting. No comercial displays; wearables; knitting; millinery; or crocheting.

Georgia

*ALBANY ARTS FESTIVAL, Box 571, Albany GA 31707. Contact: Registration Chairman. Sponsor: Southwest Georgia Art Association. Purpose: "foremost is the opportunity to expose a variety of original work to the public. Secondly, the Southwest Georgia Art Assocation welcomes this opportunity to support and encourage the working artist." Estab. 1967. Annual indoor/outdoor show (booths available) held 2 days in April. Average attendance: 10,000. Entries accepted until 4 weeks before show. Entry fee: $25/display area. Prejudging by 3 slides or photos; entry fee refunded for refused work. Work may be offered for sale; no commission. Craftworker must attend show; demonstrations OK. Sponsor provides display panels; electricity for demonstrations; and 24-hour security. Considers all crafts completed no earlier than 4 years prior to the show. "All work must be suitably mounted, framed, or matted." Awards $900 in cash; and $1,300 in purchase prizes.
Promotion: "Our show is promoted extensively in southwest Georgia, north Florida, and southeast Alabama in newspapers and on radio and TV. Artists are encouraged to include photos and information when applications are submitted."

*ARTS FESTIVAL OF ATLANTA, Suite 610, 33 North Ave., Atlanta GA 30308. (404)885-1125. Director: Pat Gann. Purpose: "to bring the artists and the public into contact, and make the arts, the creative free expression of man, an integral part of the community." Estab. 1954. Annual indoor/outdoor show held 9 days in May. Average attendance: 500,000. Entries accepted until 2 months before show. Entry fee: $60, first 4 days; $40 last 4 days; $5 prejudging fee. Display area: 10x10. Prejudging by slides; entry fee (not prejudging fee) refunded for refused work. Work may be offered for sale first 4 days of show; no commission. Craftworker must attend show; demonstrations OK. Registration limit: 150 each of the 4 days. Sponsor provides electricity for demonstrations and 24-hour security. Show is advertised by radio; TV; and the print media. Considers all crafts except candlemaking; decoupage; painted rocks; plastic, paper or feather flowers; shellcraft; T-shirts; and beads. Presents $5,000 in cash, and $1,000 in purchase prizes.

THE BERRY PATCH ARTS AND CRAFT FESTIVAL, Berry Academy, Mt. Berry GA 30149. (404)234-9446, ext. 265. Director: Phil Johns. Estab. 1972. Annual outdoor show held 2 days in April. Average attendance: 3,000-6,000. Entries accepted until 4 weeks before show. Entry fee: $15/15x15 display area. Entries prejudged by photo or slide; entry fee refunded for refused work. Work may be offered for sale; no commission. Craftworker must attend show; demonstrations OK. Registration limit: 100. Sponsor provides some chairs; electricity for demontrations; 24-hour security; and attempts to meet individual needs. Considers all crafts including musical instruments; bobbin lace; and baskets.
Sales Tips: "Our public buys for the most part things that serve a purpose or can be used around the house. Many gifts are purchased also."
Promotion: Show is advertised by TV spots plus interviews in Atanta, Chattanooga and Huntsville; radio spots plus interviews in multi-state area; national and regional magazine ads and articles; newspapers in Georgia, Alabama, North Carolina, South Carolina, Florida, Tennessee and other states; and posters sent upon request to all entries. Submit photos and printed articles.

*COUNTRY ROADS, Union St., Vienna GA 31092. (912)268-4056. Director: Luanne Sewell. Sponsor: Junior Woman's Club. Purpose: "to foster the development of arts and crafts." Estab. 1972. Annual indoor show held 2 days in March. Average attendance: 2,000. Entries accepted until 2 weeks before show. Entry fee: $20/8x12 display area. Maximum 2 entries/category. Prejudging by slides, photos and brochures; checks are not cashed for rejected work. Work may be offered for sale; no commission. Craftworker must attend show; demonstrations OK. Registration limit: 20. Sponsor provides electricity for demonstrations and 24-hour security. Amount of cash awards varies, "depending on our club's finances."
Acceptable Work: Considers batik; candlemaking; dollmaking; glass art; jewelry; leatherworking; macrame; metalsmithing; mobiles; needlecrafts; pottery; sculpture; soft sculpture; tole painting; weaving; and woodcrafting.
Promotion: Show is advertised by radio; TV; and newspapers — no paid advertising. "We run 13 features in our local newspaper to prepare the consumer. Each feature runs about ¼ to ½ a page. We like photos, biographical sketches, awards list and a description of technique [from craftworker]."

DECATUR CIVIC CHORUS ANNUAL ARTS & CRRAFTS FAIR, Box 1361, Decatur GA 30031. (404)634-1382. Director: Mary Anne Sharp. Sponsor: Decatur Civic Chorus. "The Decatur Civic Chorus is a nonprofit organization. This fair enables us to travel; buy music; and covers operational expenses of our free public concerts." Estab. 1972. Annual indoor show held 3 days in the fall. Average attendance: 45,000. Entries accepted until 2 weeks before show. Entry fee: $40/8x10 display area. Work may be offered for sale; no commission. Craftworker must attend show; demonstrations OK. Registration limit: 62. Sponsor provides coverings; display panels; electricity for demonstrations; and tables for rent. Considers all crafts. Maximum size: 8x10. "All display tables must be draped uniformly. The chorus has free draping for those craftsmen lacking their own. An action display attracts the most attention."

*FIREHOUSE ARTS AND CRAFTS FESTIVAL, Box 375, Dalton GA 30720. (404)278-0168. Sponsor: Creative Arts Guild, Inc. Estab. 1963. Annual indoor/outdoor show held 2 days in September. Entries accepted until 2 weeks before show. Entry fee: $15/artist. Display area: 10x-15. Maximum 4 entries per craftworker indoors. No prejudging, but prefer new exhibitor send pictures or slides of work. Work may be offered for sale; 10% commission. Craftworker must attend show if entered for outdoor spaces; demonstrations OK. Registration limit: 100 for outdoor spaces. Categories: painting; drawing; graphics; sculpture; pottery; ceramic sculpture; handwork; creative photography; and crafts. Presents cash awards of $1,000; purchase awards vary (1977-$3,600). 1977 show sales totaled $22,700.
Acceptable Work: Considers batik; candlemaking; ceramics; jewelry; lapidary; leatherworking; macrame; metalsmithing; pottery; sculpture; soft sculpture; weaving; and woodcrafting.
Promotion: Show is advertised by newspaper and radio public service announcements; and interview shows. Craftworker provides b&w glossy photos; background information; and resume.

*GEORGIA JUBILEE, 195 Holt Ave., Macon GA 31201. (912)743-1380. Chairman: Ken Pipkin. Purpose: fundraiser. Estab. 1974. Annual indoor/outdoor show held 2 days (preview party Friday night) in May. Average attendance: 7,000-8,000. Entries accepted until 4 weeks before show. Entry fee: $30/juried entry; $20/crafts. Prejudging by 3 slides; entry fee refunded for refused work. Work may be offered for sale; no commission. Craftworker must attend show; demonstrations OK. Sponsor provides limited electricity for demonstrations and some security. Show is advertised by radio; TV; newspapers; and magazines. Presents cash awards of $1,150 and ribbons. Considers all crafts.

*GEORGIA MOUNTAIN FAIR, Box 444, Hiawassee GA 30546. (404)896-2256. President: Robert L. Anderson. Sponsor: Towns County Lions Club. Estab. 1950. Annual indoor/outdoor show (with tents and exhibit buildings) held 9 days in August. Average attendance: 150,000. Entries accepted until show is filled. Work may be offered for sale; 5-10% commission. Craftworker must attend show and "all exhibitors must have an educational exhibit, demonstrating what they sell." Registration limit: 100. Sponsor provides chairs; coverings; display panels; electricity for demonstrations; insurance on exhibited work; table; and 24-hour security.
Acceptable Work: Considers candlemaking; ceramics; decoupage; dollmaking; glass art; jewelry; leatherworking; macrame; metalsmithing; needlecrafts; pottery; sculpture; soft sculpture; tole painting; weaving; and woodcrafting.

HOLIDAY HAPPENING, Chattahoochee Art Association, 715 Chattanooga Ave., Dalton GA 30720. (404)278-0217. Treasurer: Polly Boggess. Estab. 1976. Annual indoor show held 2 days in November. Entries accepted until 1 week before show. Entry fee: $10/nonmember; $5/member. Display area: 8x10. Work may be offered for sale; no commission. Craftworker must attend show; demonstrations OK. Registration limit: 50-60. Sponsor provides electricity for demonstrations and 24-hour security. Considers all crafts.
Sales Tips: "This show is slanted toward Christmas presents, decorations, etc." Show is advertised by newspaper; radio; and national magazines. Craftworkers will be asked for publicity release if needed.

MILLION PINES ARTS AND CRAFTS FESTIVAL, Box 238, Soperton GA 30457. (912)529-4414. Chairman: Jack Pournelle. Sponsor: City of Soperton. Estab. 1973. Annual outdoor show held 2 days in November. Average attendance: 10,000. Entries accepted until Oct. 1. Entry fee: $25/12x12 display area. Entries prejudged by slides or photos. Entry fee refunded for refused work. Work may be offered for sale; no commission. Craftworker must attend show; demonstrations OK. Registration limit: 125. Sponsor provides electricity for demonstrations and 24-hour security. Categories: artists and craftsmen. All crafts considered. Show is advertised by newspapers; magazines; TV; and radio. Submit b&w photo and brief paragraph on exhibition.

NEW SALEM MOUNTAIN FESTIVAL, Rt. 2, Rising Fawn GA 30783. (404)675-4444. Director: Charles Counts. Sponsor: New Salem Community Improvement Club. Estab. 1974. Annual outdoor show held 2 days in October on top of Lookout Mountain. Entry fee: $20/approximately 18x20 display area. Entries prejudged by slides, photos or personal examination. Work may be offered for sale; no commission. Craftworker must attend show; demonstrations OK. Registration limit: 50. Sponsor provides electricity for demonstrations and 24-hour security. Show is advertised by TV; radio; newspapers; mailing; and brochures. Submit 8x10 glossy b&w self-photo and biographical material.
Acceptable Work: Considers batik; candlemaking; ceramics; decoupage; dollmaking; glass art; jewelry; leatherworking; macrame; metalsmithing; needlecrafts; pottery; sculpture weaving; woodcrafting; and basketry.

OAK GROVE COUNTRY FAIR, Box 439, Pine Mountain GA 31822. (404)663-2425 or 663-4577. Chairman: Larry Thompson. Business Manager: Carolyn Thompson. Sponsor: Oak Grove Congregational Christian Church. Estab. 1972. Annual outdoor show held 2 days in August at Oak Grove Community, 5 miles north of Pine Mountain, Georgia. Average attendance: 10,000. Entries accepted until 2 weeks before show. Entry fee: $15/15x15 display area. Work may be offered for sale; no commission. Craftworker must attend show; demonstrations OK. Registration limit: 250. Sponsor provides electricity for demonstrations and 24-hour security. Show is advertised by radio; TV; direct mail; and handbills. Submit photos for promotion. Considers all crafts.

OKEFENOKEE FESTIVAL ARTS AND CRAFT SHOW, Box 335, Folkston GA 31537. (912)496-7129. Chairman: Donna A. Nance. Sponsor: Charlton County Chamber of Commerce. Estab. 1969. Annual outdoor show held 2 days in October. Average attendance: 3,000-5,000. Entries accepted up until show date. Entry fee: $10/display area. Work may be offered for sale; no commission. Craftworker must attend show; demonstrations OK. Sponsor provides electricity for demonstrations. Show is advertised by TV; radio; magazines; newspapers; and mailing brochures. Considers all crafts.

*POWERS' CROSSROADS COUNTRY FAIR AND ART FESTIVAL, Box 899, Newnan GA 30263. (404)253-2011. Director: Harriet Alexander. Sponsor: Coweta Festivals, Inc. Estab. 1971. Annual outdoor show held 3 days in September. Average attendance: 25,000-30,000. Entries accepted until 19 weeks before show. Entry fee: $65/16' display area; $40/10'. Prejudging by slides; entry fee refunded for refused work. Work may be offered for sale; no commission. Craftworker must attend show; demonstrations OK. Registration limit: 280. Sponsor provides 24-hour security. Show is advertised by TV; newspapers; magazines; and radio. Submit b&w glossy and publicity information. Considers all crafts. Presents $2,500+ in cash and purchase prizes.

PRATER'S MILL COUNTRY FAIR, 101 Timberland Dr., Dalton GA 30720. President: July Alderman. Vice President: Jane Harrell. Estab. 1971. Semiannual outdoor show held 2 days in May and October. Average attendance: 20,000 per show. Entries accepted until 3 months before show. Entry fee: $20/15x15 display area. "All new exhibitors need to submit slides or photos of their work." Entry fee due after prejudging. Work may be offered for sale; no commission. Craftworker must attend show; demonstrations OK. Registraton limit: 145. Sponsor provides electricity for demonstrations and 24-hour security. Considers all crafts.
Promotion: Submit b&w glossy photo; copies of press releases; previously published articles; background information; training information; other shows attended; and interesting public relations for promotional purposes.

VALDOSTA JUNIOR SERVICE LEAGUE ARTS AND CRAFTS SHOW, Box 2043, Valdosta GA 31601. Contact: Registration Chairman. Purpose: fundraiser. Estab. 1975. Annual indoor show held 2 days in December. Average attendance: 5,000. Entries accepted until 2 weeks before show. Entry fee: $35/12x12 display area. Work may be offered for sale; no commission. Craftworker must attend show; demonstrations OK. Sponsor provides chairs; fencing; table; and 24-hour security. Show is advertised by TV; radio; newspapers; billboards; League Members flyers; and brochures. Submit photographs; newspaper clippings; and articles. Considers all handworked crafts.

YELLOW DAISY FESTIVAL, Stone Mountain Park, Box 778, Stone Mountain GA 30086. (404)469-9831. Director, Special Events: Barbara Hamilton. Estab. 1969. Annual outdoor show held 3 days in September. Average attendance: 90,000. Entries accepted until 2 weeks before show. Entry fee: $50/craftworker. Display area: 10x10 enclosed horse stall. Prejudging by 3 slides or photos and short resume; entry fee refunded for refused work. Work may be offered for sale; demonstrations OK. Registration limit: 200. Sponsor provides electricity for demonstrations and 24-hour security. Show is advertised by radio; TV; and city-wide promotions. Considers all crafts.

Idaho

*"ART ON THE GREEN," Box 901, Coeur d'Alene ID 83814. (208)664-9052. Contact: Opal Brooten. Sponsor: Citizens Council for the Arts. Estab. 1969. Annual outdoor show (with booths) held 3 days in August. Average attendance: 6,000. Entries accepted until 1 week before show; booth applications must be in 6 weeks before show. Entry fee: $3/entry; $15/8x8' display area. Maximum 2 entries per category per craftworker; maximum 2 craftworkers per booth. Prejudging; no entry fees refunded for refused work. Work may be offered for sale; 20% commission. Craftworker must attend show; demonstrating craftspeople given preference.
Acceptable Work: Considers all crafts except decoupage created within the last 2 years. Maximum weight: 150 pounds. No fragile items such as unfired ceramics or plaster. Entries not equipped for exhibiting will be disqualified.
Awards: Presents $2,500 in cash prizes, and ribbons. Judging panel consists of 3 professional artists or art teachers.

*CHRISTMAS SHOW, Box 333, Eagle ID 83616. (208)939-6426. President: Doug Fitzgerald. Sponsor: Spectra Productions. Estab. 1972. Annual indoor show held 4 days in December at Boise, Idaho. Average attendance: 26,500. Entries accepted until 1 week before show. Entry fee: $135/10x10 booth; $35/3x8 table. Work may be offered for sale; no commission. Craftworker or representative must attend show; demonstrations OK. Registration limit: 300. Sponsor provides: display panels; electricity for demonstrations; fencing; and 24-hour security. Show is advertised by posters; TV; radio; and newspaper. Cash awards. Considers candlemaking; ceramics;

decoupage; dollmaking; jewelry (no turquoise); leatherworking; macrame; metalsmithing; pottery; sculpture; tole painting; weaving; and woodcrafting. 1977 show sales totalled $350,000.

Illinois

*ALBANY PARK ARTS AND CRAFTS FAIR, Albany Park Chamber of Commerce, 3440 W. Lawrence, Chicago IL 60625. (312)463-5420. Chairman: Dave Cheesman. Estab. 1976. Annual outdoor show held 2 days in June. Entries accepted until 3 weeks before show; "Entries will be accepted past deadline but late entries may not be printed in free programs." Entry fee: $12/8' display area. Work may be offered for sale; no commission. Craftworker must attend show; demonstrations OK. Show is advertised by Albany Park Chamber of Commerce through newspaper; radio; and TV community news. Presents gold, silver, and bronze medals with ribbons and printed award certificates. Considers all crafts. "Jewelry; lapidary; batik; pottery; and leather craftspeople must submit photos or prove their work is original and not kits."

ALUMNAE ARTS AND CRAFTS SHOW OF ROSARY HIGH SCHOOL, 901 N. Edgelawn Ave., Aurora IL 60506. (312)896-0831. Alumnae Association Moderator: Sister Mary Gretchen, O.P. Estab. 1976. Annual indoor show held 2 days in the fall. Entries accepted until 1 week before show; if space is available late entries are welcome if their exhibit is unusual. Entry fee: $10/6x8 display area. Work may be offered for sale; no commission. Craftworker must attend show; demonstrations by invitation only. Registration limit: 60-70. Sponsor provides chairs; electricity for demonstrations; table; doughnuts and coffee in the morning; and lunch is served all day. Considers all crafts.
Promotion: Show is advertised by letters to parents of students and alumnae; radio; newspapers; church bulletins; posters; school papers; and flyers. Submit b&w photos for news releases. Appreciates materials of exhibits to put in area and Diocesan newspaper.

AMERICAN ARTISTS AND ARTISANS, American Society of Artists, Inc., 700 N. Michigan Ave., Chicago IL 60611. (312)751-2500. Estab. 1978. Annual outdoor show held 2 days in June in Naperville, Illinois. Entries accepted until 6 weeks before show. Entry fee: $18/nonmember. Display area: 5x10. Prejudging by 5 slides or photos. Entry fee refunded for refused work. Work may be offered for sale; no commission. Craftworker must attend show; demonstrations OK. Sponsor provides electricity for demonstration; badges; programs; and exhibit cards. Show is advertised by ads; posters; and flyers. Submit b&w glossy photos of self with work for publicity. Considers all crafts except decoupage; dollmaking; lapidary; and needlecrafts.

*ANDERSONVILLE FESTIVAL ART FAIR, Andersonville Chamber of Commerce; 5344 N. Clark St., Chicago IL 60640. Estab. 1965. Annual outdoor show held 2 days in June. Average attendance: 10,000-15,000. Entries accepted until 4 weeks before show. Entry fee: $15/8' display area. Prejudging by photos or slides; entry fee refunded for refused work. Work must be offered for sale; no commission. Craftworker must attend show; demonstrations OK. Presents medal; ribbon; and certificate awards. Considers all crafts.

ARTISTS & ARTISANS AT WORK, American Society of Artists, 700 N. Michigan, Chicago IL 60611. (312)751-2500. Contact: Director. Estab. 1978. Annual outdoor show held 2 days in May at Downers Grove, Illinois. Entries accepted until 6 weeks before show. Entry fee: $18/nonmember. Display area: 5x10. Prejudging by slides or photos; entry fee refunded for refused work. Work may be offered for sale; no commission. Craftworker must attend show; demonstrations encouraged. Sponsor provides electricity for demonstrations. Considers batik; candlemaking; ceramics; glass art; jewelry; leatherworking; macrame; metalsmithing; mobiles; pottery; sculpture; soft sculpture; tole painting; weaving; and woodcrafting.
Promotion: Show is advertised by posters; flyers; paid advertising; and free publicity. "Submit b&w glossy photos of self with work."

ARTS AND CRAFTS BAZAAR, 1413 Cora St., Des Plaines IL 60018. (312)827-7870. Ways and Means Chairman: Lisa Anderson. Sponsor: Central School PTA. Estab. 1977. Annual indoor show held 1 day in October. Entries accepted until show date if there are openings. Entry fee: $10/5x10 display area. Work may be offered for sale; no commission. Craftworker needn't attend show; demonstrations OK. Sponsor provides limited electricity for demonstrations. Considers all crafts.
Promotion: Show is advertised by "weekly press releases to all local papers starting 2½ months before show. Over 25 releases to radio, TV, and newspapers; paid ads in papers covering over 15 neighboring towns; by posters and flyers; and listings in community event forums. Craftworker should send release with photo of work to his local paper and same to our local papers."

ARTS AND CRAFTE IN ACTION, American Society of Artists, 700 N. Michigan, Chicago IL 60611. (312)751-2500. Estab. 1978. Annual indoor show held 2 days in September at Hoffman Estates, Illinois. Entries accepted until 6 weeks before show. Entry fee: $18/nonmembers. Display area: 5x10. Prejudging by 5 slides and photos. Entry fee refunded for refused work. Work may be offered for sale; no commission. Craftworker must attend show; demonstrations OK. Sponsor provides electricity for demonstrations; badges; programs; exhibit cards; posters; and flyers. Show is advertised by ads; publicity; posters; and flyers. Submit b&w glossy photos of self with work for publicity. Considers all crafts except decoupage; dollmaking; lapidary; and needlecrafts.

ARTS FESTIVAL AT THE LAUNDRY, American Society of Artists, Inc.,, 700 N. Michigan Ave., Chicago IL 60611. (312)751-2500. Estab. 1977. Annual outdoor show held 1 day in the fall at Winnetka, Illinois. Entries accepted until 6 weeks before show or until all spaces filled. Display area: 5x10. Prejudging by slides and photos. Entry fee refunded for refused work. Work may be offered for sale; no commission. Craftworker must attend show; demonstrations OK. Sponsor provides electricity for demonstrations; badges; exhibit cards; and programs. Show is advertised by posters; flyers; and general advertising and publicity. Submit b&w glossy photos if available and additional info on self and work for publicity. Considers batik; pottery; sculpture; and wood carvings.

BLOWN GLASS II, 1521 Sherman Ave., Evanston IL 60201. (312)864-2660. R. Isaacson. Sponsor: Mindscape Gallery & Studio. Estab. 1975. Annual indoor show held the month of April. Average attendance: 2,000. Entires accepted until mid-January. Entry fee: $5/entry. Prejudging by slides; no entry fees refunded for refused work. Work must be offered for sale; 33⅛% commission. Demonstrations pre-arranged. Registration limit: 24-30. Sponsor provides insurance on exhibited work.

BRENTWOOD COMMONS ART AND CRAFT FESTIVAL, American Society of Artists, 700 N. Michigan Ave., Chicago IL 60611. (312)751-2500. Estab. 1974. Annual outdoor show with (overhang over majority of exhibits) held 2 days in August at Bensenville, Illinois. Entries accepted until 6 weeks before show. Entry fee: $18/nonmembers. Display area: 5x10. Prejudging by slides and photos; entry fee refunded for refused work. Work may be offered for sale; no commission. Craftworker must attend show; demonstrations OK. Sponsor provides electricity for demonstrations; badges; programs; and exhibit cards. Show is advertised by posters; flyers; and general publicity. Submit b&w photos if available of self and work plus any additional information for publicity. Considers all crafts except ceramics; decoupage; lapidary; needlecrafts; and tole paintings.

CHILLICOTHE ART AND CRAFT SHOW, Box 61, Rome IL 61562. (309)274-3001. Coordinator: Judy Kelley. Estab. 1977. Annual outdoor show held 1 day in September at Chillicothe, Illinois. Average attendance: 5,000. Entries accepted until 2 weeks before show. Entry fee: $15/craftworker. Display area: 6x12. Prejudging by slides and photos. SASE. Entry fee due after prejudging. Work may be offered for sale; no commission. Craftworker must attend show; demonstrations OK. Registration limit: 50. Sponsor provides electricity for demonstrations. Show is advertised by radio; newspapers; and posters. Submit b&w glossies for publicity. Considers candlemaking; jewelry; leatherworking; macrame; pottery; sculpture; weaving; and woodcrafting.

COUNTRY FAIR AND AUCTION, 826 W. Green St., Bensenville IL 60106. (312)766-3632. Arts and Crafts Chairperson: Guyla Hunt. Sponsor: Bensenville Community Church. Estab. 1977. Annual indoor/outdoor show held 1 day in October. Average attendance: 400-500. Entries accepted up until show date. Entry fee: $10/8x10 display area. Work may be offered for sale; no commission. Craftworker must attend show; demonstrations OK. Registration limit: 75. Sponsor provides electricity for demonstrations. Show is advertised by radio, newspapers and posters. Considers all crafts.

COUNTRYSIDE MALL STARVING "AMERICAN" ARTS AND CRAFTS, Rt. 4, 146 Park Drive, F.R.V.G., Barrington IL 60010. (312)639-5665. Show Director: Irene "Rae" Partridge. Sponsor: Merchants Association. Estab. 1973. Semiannual show held 2 days indoors in January and 2 days indoors and outdoors in June at Palatine, Illinois. Entries accepted until 1 week before show or until all spaces taken. Entry fee: $30/10' frontage, depth varies. Prejudging by 5 slides or photos; resume; and SASE. Entry fee refunded for refused work. Work may be offered for sale; no commission. Craftworker must attend show; demonstrations OK. Registration limit: 75-78. Sponsor provides electricity for demonstrations and 24-hour security. Considers all crafts.

Promotion: Show is advertised by display ads; articles; radio; TV; flyers/stuffers; posters; and mall signs and banners. Submit b&w nonreturnable glossy photos; resume; and name and address of local papers for blanket coverage.

*CRAFT GALLERY, 18W118 73rd Place, Westmont IL 60559. (312)964-9062. Directors: Irene Spaetzel and Sue Rockouski. Sponsor: Orland Square Mall. Estab. 1977. Annual indoor show held 4 days in January at Orland Park, Illinois. Average attendance: 60,000-80,000. Entries accepted until 2 weeks before show. Entry fee: $60/6x12 display area. Prejudging by 5 slides or photos and SASE; entry fee refunded for refused work. Work may be offered for sale; no commission. Craftworker must attend show; demonstrations OK. Registration limit: 150. Sponsor provides chairs; coverings; display panels; electricity for demonstrations; and 24-hour security. Considers all crafts. Presents cash award of $1,000 and ribbons.
Promotion: Show is advertised by area newspapers and radio. "Provide 8x10 b&w glossies of you involved with your work along with a brief resume on your background to be considered for promotional purposes."

CRAFT SHOP CRAFTS FAIR, Craft Shop, Box 67, Southern Illinois University, Edwardsville IL 62026. (618)692-2178. Estab. 1975. Semiannual show held 2 days outdoors in May and 3 days indoors in December. Average attendance: 12,000. Entries accepted until 1 week before show. Display area: 3x12. Prejudging by slides; photos; or examples of work. Entry fee due after prejudging. Work may be offered for sale; 15% commission. Craftworker must attend show; demonstrations OK. Registration limit: 20, May; 40, December. Sponsor provides chairs; electricity for demonstrations; table; and overnight storage. Show is advertised by school paper articles and ads; community articles; school calendars; flyers; and sometimes radio. Considers all crafts including basketry and quilts.

CRITTERS AND COHORTS, 1521 Sherman Ave., Evanston IL 60201. (312)864-2660. Show Coordinator: Deborah Isaacson. Sponsor: Mindscape Gallery and Studio. Purpose: "to offer a theme to give artists a change of pace from normal style; to have a fun show; and to expose public to fine quality designer crafts." Estab. 1977. Annual indoor show (in gallery) held 1 month in fall/winter. Average attendance: 3,000. Entries due June 1. Entry fee: $5/artist. Prejudging by maximum of 5 slides indicating size, media, whole/retail price with "front", "top" put on slide. Sample of work may be requested by jury. "Jury reserves right to refuse work if not up to quality of description and slides." Entry fee not refunded for refused work. Work may be offered for sale; 40% commission. Craftworker needn't attend show; no demonstrations. Registration limit: 24. Sponsor provides display panels; electricity; insurance on exhibited work; 24-hour security; all props; and display services. Categories: anything creative and one of a kind with animal or related animal themes.
Acceptable Work: Considers batik; ceramics; glass art; leatherworking; metalsmithing; pottery; sculpture; soft sculpture; weaving; and woodcrafting.
Promotion: Show is advertised by advance publicity; newspapers; trade magazines; mailing lists. Submit b&w glossy for articles; statement of purpose and media description; and brief biography. "Only artists submitting proper materials will receive publicity coverage."

CROSS COUNTY MALL ART AND CRAFT SHOW, Rome IL 61562. (309)274-3001. Coordinator: Judy Kelley. Estab. 1976. Annual indoor show held 3 days in March. Entries accepted until 2 weeks before show. Entry fee: $30/artist. Display area: 6x12. Prejudging by slides and photos. SASE. Entry fee refunded for refused work. Work may be offered for sale; no commission. Craftworker must attend show; demonstrations OK. Registration limit: 50. Sponsor provides electricity for demonstrations. Show is advertised by newspaper.
Acceptable Work: Considers candlemaking; jewelry; leatherworking; macrame; pottery; sculpture; tole painting; and woodcrafting.

A DAY IN THE COUNTRY, Pecatonica Junior Woman's Club, Pecatonica IL 61063. (815)239-1113. Co-chairperson: Sue Tipton. Estab. 1971. Annual indoor show held 1 day in October. Average attendance: 6,500. Entries accepted until 2 weeks before show. Entry fee: $15/10x10 display area. Prejudging by slides or photos. Entry fee refunded for refused work. Work may be offered for sale; no commission. Craftworker needn't attend show; demonstrations OK. Registration limit: 110. Sponsor provides electricity for demonstrations and 24-hour security. Show is advertised by radio; TV; craft magazines; area newspapers; billboards; flyers; and posters. Considers all crafts.

DEERFIELD COMMONS ARTS AND SELECTED CRAFTS FAIR, Rt. 4, 146 Park Dr., F.R.V.G., Barrington IL 60010. (312)639-5665. Show director: Irene "Rae" Partridge. Sponsor:

Merchants Association. Estab. 1971. Semiannual show held outdoors with overhead canopy 1 day in June and 1 day in September at Deerfield, Illinois. Entries accepted until 1 week before show or until all spaces taken. Entry fee: $18/5x10 display area. Prejudging by 5 slides or photos; and resume. SASE. Entry fee refunded for refused work. Work may be offered for sale; no commission. Craftworker must attend show; demonstrations OK. Registration limit: 75-78. Considers all crafts.
Promotion: Show is advertised by newspaper; radio; TV; flyers/stuffers; and mall window posters. Submit nonreturnable b&w glossy; resume; and name and address of local papers for blanket coverage.

"DISCOVER RAVINIA DAY", Highland Park Chamber of Commerce, 1811 St. Johns Ave., Highland Park IL 60035. (312)432-0284. Executive Director: Carol Abern. Estab. 1975. Annual outdoor show held 1 day in September. Average attendance: 500. Entries accepted until 2 weeks before show. Entry fee: $10/artist. Display area varies. Work may be offered for sale; no commission. Suggest craftworker attends show; demonstrations OK. Registration limit: 75. Show is advertised in local and Chicago newspapers; radio; TV; and posters. Considers all crafts.

EDENS PLAZA ARTS & CRAFT FAIR, 9476 Harding Ave., Surfside FL 33154. Contact: Iris G. Klein. Sponsor: Edens Plaza Merchants Association. Estab. 1956. Annual outdoor show held 2 days in June at Wilmette, Illinois. Average attendance: 10,000-15,000. Entry fee: $20/8x8 display area. Maximum 2 entries per craftworker. Prejudging by slides or photos (send resume and SASE). Crafts may be offered for sale; no commission. Craftworker must attend show; demonstrations OK. Considers all crafts. Submit b&w glossies and resume for newspaper publicity.

*ELMHURST OUTDOOR ART FAIR, c/o Elmhurst Artists' Guild, Box 283, Elmhurst IL 60126. Estab. 1960. Annual outdoor show held 2 days in July. Average attendance: 5,000+. "We invite entrants first then new entrants juried up to 2 weeks before show." Entry fee: $20. Display area: 10-12x5. Prejudging of new entrants by 5 slides or photos. SASE. Entry fee refunded for refused work. Work may be offered for sale; no commission. Craftworker or representative must attend show; demonstrations OK. Registration limit: 225-250. Considers all crafts except candlemaking; decoupage; dollmaking; lapidary; mobiles; and needlecrafts.
Awards: Presents 10 cash awards of $50 and ribbon for 1st place; 20 ribbons for 2nd place; and merchants' purchase awards.
Promotion: Show is advertised by radio; TV (Chicago Stations); newspapers and special editions; and special paper articles on select artists. "We are very well-known and are the largest fair in Du Page County. Craftworker may give out brochures, cards; anything but hang previous won awards/ribbons on display."

FALL FESTIVAL OF ARTS, American Society of Artists, Inc., 700 N. Michigan Ave. # 205, Chicago IL 60611. (312)751-2500. Estab. 1973. Annual indoor show held 2 days in October at Crystal Lake, Illinois. Entries accepted until 6 weeks before show or until filled. Entry fee: $20/5x10 display area. Prejudging by slides and photos. Entry fee refunded for refused work. Work may be offered for sale; no commission. Craftworker must attend show; demonstrations OK. Sponsor provides electricity for demonstrations; badges; programs; and exhibit cards.
Promotion: Show is advertised by posters; flyers; and general publicity. Submit b&w photos if available (of self and work is best) plus additional information on artist and work.

*FELICIAN COLLEGE ARTS & CRAFTS FAIR, 9476 E. Bay Harbor Dr., Bay Harbor Island FL 33154. (305)864-8725. Art Director: Iris G. Klein. Sponsor: Felician College. Estab. 1972. Annual outdoor show held 1 day in July at Chicago, Illinois. Average attendance: 4,000-5,000. Entries accepted until 4 weeks before show. Entry fee: $15/10' display area. Prejudging by slides and/or photos; entry fee due after prejudging. Work may be offered for sale; no commission. Craftworker must attend show; demonstrations OK. Sponsor provides fencing and assistance in carrying display boards. Considers all crafts. Presents $500 in purchase prizes and ribbons.
Promotion: Show is advertised by newspapers; flyers; radio (spots); and display ads. "Send b&w glossy prints and resume."

FESTIVAL, Art Department, Eastern Illinois University, Charleston IL 61920. (217)581-3410. Director, Art Fair: Bill Heyduck. Sponsor: School of Fine Arts. "This is a 3 day fine arts festival containing music, theater and art in the open air. It is a place for artists to be seen and heard as well as sell. All fees are used to support and advertise the festival." Estab. 1977. Annual outdoor show held 2 days in April. Entries accepted until 2 weeks before show. Entry fee: $10/artist;

$25/group display. Display area: 8x10. Work may be offered for sale; no commission. Craftworker must attend show; demonstrations OK. Registration limit: 100. Sponsor provides chairs and table. Show is advertised by radio; TV; and newspapers. Categories: painting; drawing; prints; sculpture; and crafts. Considers all crafts except decoupage; lapidary; and tole painting.

FESTIVAL OF THE ELMS-CRAFT FAIR, c/o Elmhurst Chamber of Commerce, 111 S. York St., Elmhurst IL 60126. (312)834-6060. Sponsor: Festival of the Elms Commission. Estab. 1976. Annual outdoor show held 2 days in June. Entries accepted until 1 week before show. Entry fee: $15/8x10 display area. Work may be offered for sale; no commission. Craftworker must attend show; demonstrations OK. Show is advertised locally by newspaper; radio; TV; and national craft magazines. Considers all crafts.

*57th STREET ART FAIR, c/o Goldhamer, 5555 S. Everett, Chicago IL 60637. Secretary: Susan Freehling. Estab. 1947. Annual outdoor show held 2 days in June. Entries accepted until about 2 months before show. Entry fee: $14/craftworker plus $2 screening fee. Prejudging by slides. Entry fee (not screening fee) refunded for refused work. Work must be offered for sale; no commission. Craftworker must attend show; no demonstrations. Registration limit: 305. Sponsor provides fencing. Show is advertised by radio; TV; posters; and editorial comments in newspapers and magazines. Categories: painting and drawing; sculpture; prints; and crafts. Considers all crafts. Presents 3 cash awards of $100.

FOX RIVER GROVE LIONS ARTS AND CRAFTS, 9612 Witchie Dr. W., Fox River Grove IL 60021. (312)639-3327. Co-chairman: Frank A. Tuman. Estab. 1977. Annual outdoor show held 1 day in August. Entries accepted until 1 week before show. Entry fee: $10/10x10 display area. Work may be offered for sale; no commission. Craftworker must attend show; demonstrations OK. Registration limit: 110. Show is advertised by newspaper; radio; and TV. Considers all crafts.

FRANCIS PARK ART AND CRAFT SHOW, Rome IL 61562. (309)274-3001. Coordinator: Judy Kelley. Estab. 1977. Annual outdoor show held 1 day in July at Kewanee, Illinois. Average attendance: 5,000. Entries accepted until 2 weeks before show. Entry fee: $15/artist. Display area: 6x12. Prejudging by slides and photos. SASE. Entry fee refunded for refused work. Work may be offered for sale; no commission. Craftworker must attend show; demonstrations OK. Registration limit: 100. Sponsor provides electricity for demonstrations. Show is advertised by newspaper. Considers candlemaking; jewelry; leatherworking; macrame; pottery; sculpture; tole painting; and woodcrafting.

*GLENVIEW ART FAIR, 2122 Dewes St., Glenview IL 60025. Sponsor: Glenview Art League. Annual invitational outdoor show. Average attendance: 10,000. Submit 5 slides for jurying by July 1. Display area: 10'. Considers sculpture. Presents $900 in cash and $600 in purchase awards. No commission.

GOLD COAST ART FAIR, 26 E. Huron St., Chicago IL 60611. Sponsors: Gold Coast Association and *Near North News*. Estab. 1958. Annual outdoor show held 3 days in August. Average attendance: 600,000. Entry fee: $25/display area. Work may be offered for sale; no commission. Craftworker must attend show; demonstrations OK. Sponsor pays insurance for exhibited work. Considers sculpture.

HILLSIDE SELECTED CRAFTS FESTIVAL, Rt. 4, 146 Park Dr., F.R.V.G., Barrington IL 60010. (312)639-5665. Show Director: Irene "Rae" Partridge. Sponsor: Merchants Association. Purpose: to promote "American" hand crafts. Estab. 1966. Annual indoor show held 2 days in May at Hillside, Illinois. Entries accepted until 1 week before show or all spaces taken. Entry fee: $30/10' frontage, depth varies. Prejudging by 5 slides or photos and resume. SASE. Entry fee refunded for refused work. Work may be offered for sale; no commission. Craftworker must attend show; demonstrations OK. Registration limit: 125. Sponsor provides electricity for demonstrations and 24-hour security. Considers all crafts.
Promotion: Show is advertised by newspaper display ads; articles; radio; TV; flyers/stuffers; posters; and electronic mall billboard sign on the expressway. Submit b&w glossy (not to be returned); resume; and name and address of local papers for blanket coverage.

HILLSIDE STARVING "AMERICAN" ARTS AND CRAFTS, Rt. 4, 146 Park Dr., F.R.V.G., Barrington IL 60010. (312)639-5665. Show Director: Irene "Rae" Partridge. Sponsor: Merchants Association. Estab. 1966. Semiannual indoor show held 2 days in February and 2 days in October at Hillside, Illinois. Entries accepted until 1 week before show or until filled. Entry fee: $30/10' frontage, depth varies. Prejudging by 5 slides or photos and resume. SASE. Entry fee refunded for refused work. Work may be offered for sale; no commission. Craftworker must attend show; demonstrations OK. Registration limit: 125. Sponsor provides electricity for demonstrations and 24-hour security. Considers all crafts.

Promotion: Show is advertised by newspaper display ads; articles; radio; TV; flyers; stuffers; posters; and electronic mall sign on expressway. Provide nonreturnable b&w glossy; resume; and name and address of local papers for blanket coverage.

HOLIDAY FESTIVAL OF ARTS AND CRAFTS, American Society of Artists, Inc., 700 N. Michigan Ave., Chicago IL 60611. (312)751-2500. Estab. 1975. Annual indoor show held 2 days in November. Entries accepted until 6 weeks before show or until all spaces filled. Entry fee: $18/nonmembers. Display area: 5x10. Prejudging by slides and photos. Entry fee refunded for refused work. Work may be offered for sale; no commission. Craftworker must attend show; demonstrations encouraged. Sponsor provides limited amount of electricity for demonstrations; badges; programs; and exhibit cards. Show is advertised by posters; flyers; and general publicity. Submit b&w photos if available (of self and work is best) plus any additional information on artist and work. Considers batik; jewelry; macrame; metalsmithing; pottery; sculpture; soft sculpture; weaving and woodcrafting.

HOUBY FESTIVAL ARTS AND CRAFT FAIR, 2130 S. 61st Ct., Cicero IL 60650. (312)863-2104. Executive Director: Norm Scaman. Sponsor: Cermak Road Business Association. Estab. 1969. Annual outdoor show held 2 days in October at Berwyn, Illinois. Average attendance: 15,-000. Entries accepted until 2 weeks before show. Entry fee: $15/6x10 display area. Work may be offered for sale; no commission. Craftworker or representative must attend show; demonstrations OK. Registration limit: 200. Show is advertised by posters and local newspapers. Considers all crafts.

HOWARD-WESTERN CRAFT & SCULPTURE FAIR, 9476 Harding Ave., Surfside FL 33154. Art Director: Iris G. Klein. Sponsor: Howard-Western Merchants Association. Estab. 1970. Annual outdoor show held 2 days in September at Chicago. Average attendance: 2,000-3,000. Entries accepted until 4 weeks before show. Entry fee: $15. Maximum 2 entries per craftworker. Work may be offered for sale; no commission. Craftworker must attend show; demonstrations by caricaturists only. Registration limit: 75. Considers original crafts.

ICE HOUSE ARTS FESTIVAL, American Society of Artists, Inc., 700 N. Michigan Ave., Chicago IL 60611. (312)751-2500. Estab. 1977. Annual indoor show held 2 days in November at Barrington, Illinois. Entries accepted until 6 weeks before show or until spaces filled. Entry fee: $25. Display area: 5x10. Prejudging by slides and photos. Entry fee refunded for refused work. Work may be offered for sale; no commission. Craftworker must attend show; demonstrations encouraged. Sponsor provides limited amount of electricity for demonstrations; badges; programs; and exhibit cards. Show is advertised by posters; flyers; and general publicity. Submit b&w photos for publicity if available (of self and work is best) plus any additional information.

Acceptable Work: Considers batik wall hangings; macrame wall hangings; sculpture; soft sculpture; and woven wall hangings.

JANESVILLE MALL ART AND CRAFT SHOW, Box 61, Rome IL 61562. (309)274-3001. Coordinator: Judy Kelley. Estab. 1974. Quarterly indoor show held 3 days in March, June, August, and November. Average attendance: 15,000-20,000. Entry fee: $35/artist. Display area: 6x12. Prejudging by slides and photos; entry fee refunded for refused work. Work may be offered for sale; no commission. Craftworker must attend show; demonstrations OK. Registration limit: 55. Sponsor provides electricity for demonstrations and 24-hour security protection. Show is advertised by newspaper and radio. Considers candlemaking; ceramics; glass art; jewelry; leatherworking; macrame; metalsmithing; pottery; sculpture; tole painting; weaving; and woodcrafting.

***LOCKPORT OLD CANAL DAYS FOLK ART AND CRAFT SHOW**, 1109 Garfield St., Lockport IL 60441. (815)838-7316. Chairman Folk Art Show: John Lamb. Purpose: "This show is designed to encourage the folk artists and craftsmen, those people who produce original work but have had little formal training. It is designed to encourage the folk art tradition in Lockport and northern Illinois where it was strong in the past but has deteriorated due to industrialization." Estab. 1973. Annual outdoor show held 2 days in June. Entries accepted until 4 weeks before show. Entry fee: $10/4x8. Prejudging. Work may be offered for sale; no commission. Craftworker must attend show; demonstrations encouraged. Registration limit: 200. Show is advertised by sending notices around the country to possible contact points like craft centers and folk art museums. Considers all crafts. Presents cash awards of $150.

MACHA MARKET — CHICAGO CRAFT-HOBBY INDUSTRY SHOW, 1100 Brandywine Blvd., Box 2188, Zanesville OH 43701. (614)452-4541. Executive Director: Walter E. Offinger Jr. Sponsor: Mid-America Craft-Hobby Association, Inc. Purpose: "to bring the buyers, distributors, representatives, manufacturers, teacher consultants and others involved in the industry together for a better industry. This is a show for the trade only, not a public show." Estab. 1977. Annual indoor show held 3 days in July at Chicago. Average attendance: 6,600. Entries accepted until 1 month before show. Entry fee: $4.75-5.25/square foot. Display area: minimum 10x10. Work may be offered for sale; no commission. Craftworker or representative must attend show. Registration limit: 400. Sponsor provides 2 chairs; 2 tables; 24-hour security; 8' high back wall drape and 3' sides with drape; waste basket; ashtrays; booth sign; 600 pounds drayage/100 square feet of exhibit space; and 1 full-page ad in directory. Show is advertised by direct mail to 10,000 buyers; advertising in all trade publications; and news releases to all trade publications. Considers all crafts.

*MARIGOLD FESTIVAL'S "ART IN THE PARK," 912 State St., Pekin IL 61554. (309)346-1994. Chairman: Marcia Burdick. Sponsor: Pekin Chamber of Commerce. Estab. 1976. Annual outdoor show held 2 days in September. Average attendance: 10,000. Entries accepted until 2 weeks before show. Entry fee: $20/8x10 display area. Prejudging by photos or slides; entry fee refunded for refused work. Work may be offered for sale; no commission. Craftworker must attend show; demonstrations OK. Sponsor provides 50 pegboard units. Show is advertised by radio; TV; and newspaper. Presents purchase awards of $1,000; award equals price of each winning piece. Considers all crafts but ceramics; dollmaking; needlecrafts; and soft sculpture.

*METRO ART & CRAFT FESTIVAL, c/o Constance E. Morrow and Grant R. Hartsock, 2006 N. North St., Peoria IL 61604. Annual outdoor show (spaces available on sidewalk under canopy) held 3 days at Metro Centre. Entry fee: $40/7x10 display area. Limit 1 craftworker per space. Work must be offered for sale; no commission. Cash awards given on basis of public vote.

MID-SUMMER FESTIVAL OF ARTS AND CRAFTS, American Society of Artists, Inc., 700 N. Michigan, Chicago IL 60611. (312)751-2500. Director, American Artisan Division: Judy Edborg. Estab. 1978. Annual outdoor show held 2 days in July at Carol Stream, Illinois. Entries accepted until 6 weeks before show. Entry fee: $18/nonmember. Display area: 5x10. Prejudging by 5 slides or photos; entry fee refunded for refused work. Work may be offered for sale; no commission. Craftworker must attend show; demonstrations encouraged. Sponsor provides electricity for demonstrations; badges; programs; and exhibit cards. Show is advertised by posters; flyers; and general publicity. Submit b&w glossy photos of self and work for publicity. Considers all crafts but decoupage; dollmaking; lapidary; and needlecrafts.

*MIDWEST CRAFT FESTIVAL, 620 Lincoln Ave., Winnetka IL 60093. (312)446-2870. Director: Helen Roberson. Sponsor: North Shore Art League. Estab. 1972. Annual indoor show held 2 days in May at Northbrook, Illinois. Average attendance: 100,000. Entries accepted until 3 months before show. $5 prejudging fee. Prejudging by 5 slides; 4 slides of single pieces and 1 may be detailed shot. No entry fees refunded for refused work. Work must be offered for sale; 15% commission. Craftworker must attend show; no demonstrations. Registration limit: 90-110. Sponsor provides chairs; coverings; display panels; and table. Show is advertised by newspaper ads; posters; radio; feature articles; and TV. Presents cash awards of $1,800; purchase awards of $500; and ribbons.
Acceptable Work: Considers batik; ceramics; glass art; jewelry; leatherworking; macrame; metalsmithing; needlecrafts; pottery; soft sculpture (fibers); weaving; and woodcrafting.

*MORTON GROVE ART GUILD FAIR, Box 391, Morton Grove IL 60053. (312)966-4264. Application Chairman: Opal Schrader. Sponsor: Morton Grove Art Guild. Estab. 1965. Annual outdoor show held 1 day in June. Entries accepted until 4 weeks before show. Entry fee: $7/Guild member; $12/nonmember. Display area: 10x10. May award purchase prizes. Work may be offered for sale; no commission. Craftworker must attend show; demonstrations OK. Registration limit: 100. Considers hand-wrought jewelry; metalsmithing; pottery; and some woodcrafting.

MT. PROSPECT PLAZA FALL ART AND CRAFT FAIR, 1058 Mt. Prospect Plaza, Mt. Prospect IL 60056. (312)255-0644. Executive Director: Adele Jeschke. Sponsor: Mt. Prospect Plaza Merchants Association Inc. Estab. 1962. Annual outdoor show held 2 days in September.

Entry fee: $15. Prejudging by photos or slides "if did not show with us in 1978". Work may be offered for sale; no commission. Craftworker must attend show; demonstrations OK. Considers pottery; ceramics; woodcraft; leather; and blown glass.

MT. PROSPECT PLAZA SUMMER ART AND CRAFT FAIR, 1058 Mt. Prospect Plaza, Mt. Prospect IL 60056. (312)255-0644. Executive Director: Adele Jeschke. Sponsor: Mt. Prospect Plaza Merchants Association Inc. Estab. 1962. Annual outdoor show held 2 days in June. Entry fee: $15. Prejudging by photos or slides "if did not show with us in 1978". Work may be offered for sale; no commission. Craftworker must attend show; demonstrations OK. Considers pottery; ceramics; woodcraft; leather; and blown glass.

*NATIONAL INVITATIONAL FIBERS AND FABRIC AND CERAMIC EXHIBITION, Springfield Art Association, 700 N. 4th St., Springfield IL 62702. (217)523-2631. Executive Director: William Bealmer. Purpose: "to bring together a quality exhibition representing the best in fibers and ceramics." Estab. 1974. Annual indoor show held 6 weeks, November-December. Entries accepted until April 1. Prejudging by 3 slides submitted prior to March 1. Work may be offered for sale; 25% commission. Craftworker needn't attend show; no demonstrations. Registration limit: 30-40. Show is advertised by newspaper; radio; and TV. Presents merit awards. Categories: fiber and fabric-weaving; non-loom weaving; batik; and combination.
Acceptable Work: Considers batik; macrame; pottery; soft sculpture; and weaving. "All fibers and fabrics must be ready for hanging."

NORTHPOINT ARTS AND SELECTED CRAFTS FESTIVAL, Rt. 4, 146 Park Dr., F.R.V.G., Barrington IL 60010. (312)639-5665. Show Director: Irene "Rae" Partridge. Sponsor: Merchants Association. Purpose: "to promote 'American' artists and craftspersons and their work." Estab. 1971. Semiannual outdoor show (with overhang and open planter areas) held 1 day in July and 1 day in September at Arlington Heights, Illinois. Entries accepted until 1 week before show or until filled. Entry fee: $18/10' frontage, depth varies. Prejudging by 5 slides or photos and resume. SASE. Entry fee refunded for refused work. Work may be offered for sale; no commission. Craftworker must attend show; demonstrations OK. Registration limit: 125-150. Show is advertised by newspaper display ads; articles; photos; posters; radio; and TV. Provide nonreturnable b&w glossy; resume; and name and address of local papers for blanket coverage.

NORTHWOODS ANNUAL CRAFT SHOW, Northwoods Merchants' Association, 4501 War Memorial Drive, Peoria IL 61613. (309)688-0445, weekdays 9-5 only. Promotion Director: Donna Kennemer. Secretary: Becky Stutzman. Estab. 1975. Annual indoor show held 2 days in March. Average attendance: 25,000-30,000. Entries accepted until 4 weeks before show. Entry fee: $30/single space. Prejudging by slides and photos; entry fee refunded for refused work. Work may be offered for sale; no commission. Craftworker must attend show; demonstrations encouraged. Registration limit: 150. Sponsor provides limited electricity for demonstrations and 24-hour security. Show is advertised by all media and mall signs. Considers all crafts.

OAK PARK VILLAGE MALL ART AND CRAFT FESTIVAL, American Society of Artists, Inc., 700 N. Michigan Ave., Chicago IL 60611. (312)751-2500. Estab. 1976. Annual outdoor show held 2 days in July at Oak Park, Illinois. Entries accepted until 6 weeks before show or until filled. Entry fee: $20/nonmember. Display area: 5x10. Prejudging by slides and photos; entry fee refunded for refused work. Work may be offered for sale; no commission. Craftworker must attend show; demonstrations encouraged. Sponsor provides electricity for demonstrations. Considers all crafts but decoupage; dollmaking; lapidary; leatherworking; and needlecrafts.
Promotion: Show is advertised by posters; flyers; radio; TV; newspapers; and magazines. Submit b&w nonreturnable glossy photos plus any additional information on self and work.

*OAKBROOK INVITATIONAL CRAFTS EXHIBITION, Oakbrook Center Associates, 100 Oakbrook Center, Oakbrook IL 60115. Executive Secretary: Joan Quackenbush. Estab. 1968. Annual outdoor show held 2 days in July. Average attendance: 100,000. Entries due February 15. Entry fee: $15. Size of display area determined by size of artist's display. Prejudging by 35mm slides; request slide entry form. Entry fee due after prejudging. Work may be offered for sale; no commission. Craftworker must attend show; no demonstrations. Registration limit: 100. Sponsor provides chairs; display panels; table; and 24-hour security. Show is advertised by radio; TV; and newspapers. Categories: fiber; clay; metal; enamel; glass; and wood. Presents 6 cash awards of $100 each for excellence and 6 ribbons for honorable mention.
Acceptable Work: Considers batik; ceramics; glass art; jewelry; leatherworking; macrame;

metalsmithing; soft sculpture; weaving; woodcrafting; and enameling.

Sales Tip: "Work sold ranges from small purchases of $5-100 to works for corporate offices in the area which may range from $200-2,000. Many artists receive commissions from individual collectors, decorators and architects from this exhibition."

OLD TOWN ART FAIR, 1818 N. Wells St., Chicago IL 60614. (312)787-6545. General Chairman: Elizabeth Barnhill. Sponsor: Old Town Triangle Association. Estab. 1950. Annual outdoor show held 2 days in June at Chicago. Average attendance: 30,000. Entries accepted until 3 months before show. Entry fee: $3 nonrefundable application fee plus donation of 1 piece of work. Display area: 20x15. Prejudging by slides. Work may be offered for sale; no commission. Craftworker must attend show; no demonstrations. Registration limit: 180. Considers batik; ceramics; glass art; jewelry; macrame; metalsmithing; pottery; sculpture; and weaving.
Promotion: Show is advertised by posters; newspapers, TV features; and artists' magazines. "We use some of the auction donations for publicity purposes so new artists benefit from quality work donated. Artists are contacted for specific stories or features to be done."

*OLNEY FALL FESTIVAL OF ARTS AND CRAFTS, 13 Willow Drive, Olney IL 62450. (618)392-3481. Chairman: Dr. Baird Smith. Sponsor: Olney Arts Council. Estab. 1975. Annual outdoor show (covering available in case of rain) held the 1st Saturday in October. Average attendance: 3,000-5,000. Entries accepted until 2 weeks before show. Entry fee: $5/20x15 display area; up to 3 items accepted from each craftworker for Arts Council booth. Work may be offered for sale; no commission for booth crafts; 10% for Arts Council booth. Craftworker must attend show; demonstrations OK. Registration limit: 40. Sponsor provides chairs; electricity for demonstrations; and table. Show is advertised by newspaper; TV; and radio. Submit b&w photos of self or work for newspaper. Presents 2 purchase awards of $100 each and 1st, 2nd, and 3rd place ribbons. Considers all crafts.

*PLAZA ART FAIR, Highland Area Arts Council, Freeport Art Museum, 511 S. Liberty, Freeport IL 61032. (815)235-9755. Director: Vincent Tolpo. Estab. 1970. Annual outdoor show (with covering for bad weather) held 1 day in September. Average attendance: 5,000. Entries accepted until 2 weeks before show. Entry fee: $10/15x15 display area. Prejudging by slides, photo or in person. Entry fee due after prejudging. Work may be offered for sale; no commission. Craftworker needn't attend show; demonstrations OK. Sponsor provides electricity for demonstrations. Show is advertised by all news media and mass mailings. Submit resume for publicity. Presents cash awards of $300 for 1st; $150 for 2nd; and $50 for 3rd places. Considers all crafts.

RANDHURST AUTUMN ART FESTIVAL, 9476 Harding Ave., Surfside FL 33154. Director: Iris Klein. Sponsor: Randhurst Corp. Estab. 1962. Annual indoor show held 3 days in October at Mt. Prospect, Illinois. Average attendance: 20,000-25,000. Entries accepted until September. Entry fee: $30/4x16 display area. Maximum 1 entry per craftworker. Prejudging; entry fee refunded for refused work. Work may be offered for sale; no commission. Craftworker must attend show; portrait sketching demonstrations OK. Registration limit: 140. Sponsor furnishes display panels. Considers batik and metal sculpture.

*RIDGE ART ASSOCIATION'S EXHIBIT AND FAIR AT EVERGREEN PLAZA, 2325 W. 113th Place, Chicago IL 60643. (312)733-1998. Fair Coordinator: Charles Taylor. Annual indoor show held 2 days in February at Evergreen Park, Illinois. Entries accepted until 1 week before show; prejudging date, mid-January. Entry fee: $15/8x10 display area. Prejudging by 5 slides. Entry fee refunded for refused work. Work may be offered for sale; no commission. Craftworker must attend show; demonstrations OK. Sponsor provides electricity for demonstrations and 24-hour security. Show is advertised by TV; radio; and newspapers. Presents cash awards and ribbons. Categories: oil; watercolor; mixed media; sculpture; and selected crafts. Considers batik; macrame; metalsmithing; pottery; and sculpture.

SANDBURG MALL ART AND CRAFT SHOW, Box 61, Rome IL 61562. (309)274-3001. Coordinator: Judy Kelley. Sponsor: Sandburg Mall Merchants Association. Estab. 1975. Semiannual indoor show held 3 days in February; 3 days in November at Galesburg, Illinois. Average attendance: 10,000-20,000. Entries accepted until 2 weeks before show. Entry fee: $35/12x6 display area. Prejudging by 2 slides or photos. SASE. Entry fee refunded for refused work. Work may be offered for sale; no commission. Craftworker must attend show; demonstrations OK. Registration limit: 80-90. Sponsor provides electricity for demonstrations. Show is advertised by radio; newspapers; posters; and marquee. Submit b&w glossies for publicity. Considers candlemaking; glass art; jewelry; leatherworking; metalsmithing; pottery; sculpture; tole painting; weaving; and woodcrafting.

SHERIDAN VILLAGE SHOPPING CENTER, c/o Constance E. Morrow and Grant R. Hartsock, 2006 N. North St., Peoria IL 61604. Annual sidewalk show (under canopy) held 3 days in June. Entry fee: $40/7x10 display area. Work must be offered for sale; no commission. Small crafts will be limited and edited.

*SPRING ARTS AND CRAFT FAIR, 2130 S. 61st Ct., Cicero IL 60650. (312)863-2104. Executive Director: Norm Scaman. Sponsor: Cermak Road Business Association. Estab. 1973. Annual outdoor show held 2 days in Spring. Average attendance: 2,000. Entries accepted until 1 week before show. Entry fee: $10/6x10 display area. Work may be offered for sale; no commission. Craftworker or representative must attend show; demonstrations OK. Show is advertised by local newspapers and posters. Presents ribbon awards. Considers all crafts.

SPRING ARTS FESTIVAL, American Society of Artists, Inc., 700 N. Michigan 205, Chicago IL 60611. (312)751-2500. Estab. 1977. Annual indoor show held 2 days in April at Crystal Lake, Illinois. Entries accepted until 6 weeks before show. Entry fee: $20/nonmembers. Display area: 5x10. Prejudging by slides and photos; entry fee refunded for refused work. Work may be offered for sale; no commission. Craftworker must attend show; demonstrations encouraged. Sponsor provides programs; badges; and exhibit cards. Show is advertised by flyers; posters; and general publicity. Submit, if possible, b&w glossy photo of self and work for publicity. Considers framed batik; woven wall hangings; sculpture; soft sculpture; and wood carvings.

SPRING FEST OF ARTS AND CRAFTS, American Society of Artists, Inc., 700 N. Michigan, Chicago IL 60611. (312)751-2500. Estab. 1978. Annual outdoor show held 2 days in May at Des Plaines, Illinois. Entries accepted until 6 weeks before show. Entry fee: $18/nonmember. Display area: 5x10. Prejudging by 5 slides or photos; entry fee refunded for refused work. Work may be offered for sale; no commission. Craftworker must attend show; demonstrations encouraged. Sponsor provides electricity for demonstrations; badges; programs; and exhibit cards. Show is advertised by general publicity; posters; and flyers. Submit b&w glossy photos of self with work for publicity. Considers all crafts but decoupage; dollmaking; lapidary; and needlecrafts.

*STARVING ARTISTS ARTS & CRAFTS FAIR, Oakton Community College, 7900 Nagle, Morton Grove IL 60201. (312)967-5120. Director: Jay Wollin. Estab. 1970. Annual outdoor show held 2 days during Memorial Day weekend. Average attendance: 18,000. Entries accepted until 6 weeks before show. Entry fee: $25/display area with 10' minimum frontage. Prejudging by 3 slides. Work may be sold for under $35; no commission. Craftworker or representative must attend show; electricity and equipment provided for demonstrations. Registration limit: 125-150. College has liability insurance and provides security guards. Committee of non-college jurors awards 5-6 purchase prizes to use as door prizes.
Acceptable Work: Considers batik; candlemaking; ceramics; decoupage; glass art; jewelry; leatherworking; metalsmithing; pottery; soft sculpture; weavings; wall hangings; and woodcrafting.

SUMMER FEST OF ARTS AND CRAFTS, American Society of Artists, Inc., 700 N. Michigan, Chicago IL 60611. (312)751-2500. Estab. 1978. Annual outdoor show held 2 days in August at Naperville, Illinois. Entries accepted until 6 weeks before show. Entry fee: $18/nonmembers. Display area: 5x10. Prejudging by 5 slides or photos; entry fee refunded for refused work. Work may be offered for sale; no commission. Craftworker must attend show; demonstrations encouraged. Sponsor provides electricity for demonstrations; badges; programs; and exhibit cards. Show is advertised by ads; posters; flyers; and general publicity. Submit b&w glossy photos. Considers all crafts but decoupage; dollmaking; lapidary; and needlecrafts.

TIMES SQUARE MALL ARTS AND CRAFTS SHOW, Rome IL 61562. (309)274-3001. Coordinator: Judy Kelley. Annual indoor show held 3 days in April at Mt. Vernon, Illinois. Accepts entries until 2 weeks before show. Entry fee: $35/craftworker. Display area: 6x12. Prejudging by slides or photos. SASE. Entry fee refunded for refused work. Work may be offered for sale; no commission. Craftworker must attend show; demonstrations OK. Registration limit: 50. Sponsor provides electricity for demonstrations. Show is advertised by newspapers. Considers candlemaking; jewelry; leatherworking; macrame; pottery; sculpture; tole painting; and woodcrafting.

TOY SHOW, Olde Town Gallery, Main St., Mahomet IL 61853. (217)586-3211. Owner-Manager: Charlotte Williamson. Estab. 1977. Annual indoor show held 1 day in December. Average attendance: 500. Entries accepted until 1 week before show. Display area: 8'. Work may be offered for sale; 33⅓% commission. Craftworker needn't attend show; demonstrations OK. Sponsor provides chairs; electricity for demonstrations; and table. Show is advertised by newspaper and mailing lists. Categories: antique and new handcrafts. Considers dollmaking; needlecrafts; soft sculpture; and woodcrafting.

*VILLAGE ART FAIR, Box 483, Oak Park IL 60302. President: Mrs. E. Howard Harvey. Purpose: to promote interest and education in art. Estab. 1954. Annual outdoor show held 1 day in September. Average attendance: 15,000. Entries accepted until 11 weeks before show. Entry fee: $20/6x12 display area. Prejudging by 6 slides; entry fee refunded for refused work. Work may be offered for sale; no commission. Craftworker must attend show; demonstrations OK. Show is advertised by all available media. Presents cash awards of $50, $100, $150, and $100 to best new artist; purchase awards totaling $1,000; and 1st, 2nd and 3rd place ribbons. Considers batik; glass art; jewelry; macrame; metalsmithing; pottery; sculpture; soft sculpture; and weaving.

VILLAGE MALL ART AND CRAFT SHOW, Box 61, Rome IL 61562. (309)274-3001. Coordinator: Judy Kelley. Estab. 1975. Semiannual indoor show held 3 days in March and 3 days in October at Danville, Illinois. Average attendance: 10,000. Entries accepted until 2 weeks before show. Entry fee: $30/craftworker. Display area: 6x12. Prejudging by slides or photos; entry fee refunded for refused work. Work may be offered for sale; no commission. Craftworker must attend show; demonstrations OK. Registration limit: 50. Sponsor provides electricity for demonstrations. Show is advertised by TV; newspapers; and radio. Submit 8x10 glossies for publicity. Considers candlemaking; ceramics; jewelry; leatherworking; macrame; metalsmithing; pottery; sculpture; tole painting; and woodcrafting.

WATER TOWER ART AND CRAFT FESTIVAL, American Society of Artists, Inc., 700 N. Michigan Ave., Suite 205, Chicago IL 60611. (312)751-2500. Estab. 1973. Annual outdoor show held 3 days in June. Entries accepted until 6 weeks before show. Entry fee: $20/nonmember. Display area: 5x10. Prejudging by 5 slides or photos and resume; entry fee refunded for refused work. Work may be offered for sale; no commission. Craftworker must attend show; demonstrations encouraged. Registration limit: 300. Sponsor provides programs; badges; and exhibit cards. Categories: paintings; sculpture; hand-wrought jewelry; pottery; fiber; and mixed-media. Considers all crafts but decoupage; dollmaking; lapidary; and needlecrafts.
Promotion: Show is advertised by radio; TV; newspaper publicity; flyers; posters; newspaper ads; and magazines. Submit glossy b&w photos and additional information on self as an artist. Photos should be of craftsperson and his/her work.

*WONDERFUL WORLD OF CRAFTS, 18W118 73rd Pl., Westmont IL 60559 (312)964-9062. Directors: Irene Spaetzel and Sue Rockouski. Sponsor: Fox Valley Center. Estab. 1976. Annual indoor show held 4 days in October at Aurora, Illinois. Average attendance: 60,000-80,000. Entries accepted until 2 weeks before show. Entry fee: $60/6x12 display area. Prejudging by 5 slides or photos and SASE; entry fee refunded for refused work. Work may be offered for sale; no commission. Craftworker must attend show; demonstrations OK. Registration limit: 150. Sponsor provides chairs; coverings; display panels; electricity for demonstrations; and 24-hour security. Considers all crafts. Presents cash awards of $1,000 and ribbons.
Promotion: Show is advertised by area newspapers and radio. "Provide 8x10 b&w glossies of you involved with your work along with a brief resume of your background to be considered for promotional purposes."

YOUR ADVENTURE IN ART, American Society of Artists, 700 N. Michigan Ave., Chicago IL 60611. (312)751-2500. Estab. 1978. Annual outdoor show held 2 days in October at Oak Park, Illinois. Entries accepted until 6 weeks before show. Entry fee: $21/nonmembers. Display area: 5x10. Prejudging by 5 slides or photos; entry fee refunded for refused work. Work may be offered for sale; no commission. Craftworker must attend show; demonstrations encouraged. Sponsor provides electricity for demonstrations; badges; programs; and exhibit cards. Show is advertised by posters; flyers; and general publicity. Submit b&w photos of self and work. Considers all crafts but ceramics; decoupage; dollmaking; lapidary; and needlecrafts.

Indiana

AN AMERICAN CELEBRATION, Box 35, La Porte IN 46350. (219)324-8425. Chairman: James L. Jessup. Sponsor: La Porte Jaycees. Purpose: "to add to our 4th of July celebration by bringing visitors to our community." Estab. 1973. Annual outdoor show held 1 day near July 4.

Average attendance: 1,500. Entries accepted until 2 months before show. Entry fee: $10/8x10 display area. Work may be offered for sale; no commission. Craftworker must attend show. Show is advertised by radio; newspapers; and TV. Considers all crafts. "We are featuring original arts and crafts for under $50."

ART & CRAFTS IN THE PARK, 211 Oakery Ave., Lawrenceburg IN 47025. (812)537-0676. Chairman: Margaret Huebner. Sponsor: Community Activities, Inc. Purpose: "to encourage and expose people to arts and crafts as a hobby to better fulfill their lives; and to offer an opportunity to sell their items. Also it offers some culture to the people of the community and surrounding area." Estab. 1970. Annual outdoor show (in shaded park) held the first Sunday after Labor Day weekend. Average attendance: 8,000. Entries accepted until show date. Entry fee: $8/10x10 display area. Work may be offered for sale; no commission. Craftworker must attend show; demonstrations OK. Registration limit: approximately 125. Sponsor provides electricity for demonstrations.
Acceptable Work: Considers batik; candlemaking; ceramics; decoupage; dollmaking; glass art; jewelry; lapidary; leatherworking; metalsmithing; needlecrafts; pottery; sculpture; soft sculpture; tole painting; weaving; and woodcrafting.
Promotion: Show is advertised by radio; TV; newspaper; direct mail; and *National Calendar of Indoor-Outdoor Fairs.* Promotion is done quite extensively for this show at nearby Cincinnati, Ohio. "If the craftworker has an unusual craft, a b&w glossy and a brief paragraph on his background will be considered for use in newspapers."

ASSOCIATION OF ARTIST & CRAFTSMEN OF PORTER COUNTY, Box 783, Chesterton IN 46304. Contact: Barbara or Robert Funke. Annual show held the first Saturday and Sunday in August. Entry fee: $20. Submit slides of work according to letter of instruction available on request. No sales commission. Considers fabrics; woven pieces; batik; silkscreen; pottery; glass; leather; jewelry; woodcarving; and metal sculpture.

*CHATAUQUA OF THE ARTS, 1119 W. Main St., Madison IN 47250. Chairman: Dixie McDonough. Sponsor: Madison Chautauqua of the Arts. "This is the only art and craft show held in this area. It is held to increase an interest in the arts and crafts." Estab. 1970. Annual outdoor show held the last weekend in September. Average attendance: 5,000-10,000. Entries accepted until 2 weeks before show. Entry fee: $20/craftworker. Prejudging by 5 slides (4 of individual pieces and 1 of the display); entry fee refunded for refused work. Work may be offered for sale; no commission. Craftworker must attend show; demonstrations recommended. Registration limit: 50. Sponsor provides electricity for demonstrations. Considers all crafts except candlemaking and ceramics. No kits; machine leather; or crafts made from molds. "Traditional items seem to sell the best."
Awards: Presents $850 in cash; $150 in purchase prizes plus ribbons for 1st, 2nd and 3rd places. Also gives an award for the best booth display. "Awards will be given on only finished pieces and on pieces completed within a year of the show date."
Promotion: Show is advertised by the local chamber of commerce; state tourism department; and by AAA motor magazines and clubs. "A biographic sketch listing the shows and awards the craftsperson has been in, and a b&w photo of the craftsperson which can be used in the newspaper would be helpful."

CHRISTMAS GIFT & HOBBY SHOW, Box 20189, Indianapolis IN 46220. (317)255-4151. Exhibit Sales Director: Thelma B. Schoenberger. Purpose: "to alert the public to the thousands of art and craft items that make great Christmas gifts." Estab. 1950. Annual indoor show held 9 days in the fall. Average attendance: 100,000. "Show is always full 2 months prior to opening." Entry fee: "approximately $1.50/square foot." Work may be offered for sale; no commission. Craftworker must attend show; demonstrations OK. Sponsor provides electricity for demonstrations and 24-hour security. Show is advertised by newspaper; radio; TV; and posters. Considers all crafts.

*CRAFT FAIR AT RIVERFRONT, 16½ SE 2nd St., Evansville IN 47711. (812)422-2111. Executive Director: Jane Moore. Sponsor: Evansville Arts & Education Council. Estab. 1975. Annual outdoor show held 2 days the last weekend in April. Average attendance: 10,000. Entries accepted until 4 weeks before show. Entry fee: $20/15x20 display area. "Slides are juried by a committee of artists. Entrant must mail 3 slides or photos representing their work and entry form. Each slide must be labeled clearly with artist's name and medium and must have indication of which side is up." Entry fee refunded for refused work. Work may be offered for sale; 10% commission. Craftworker must attend show; demonstrations encouraged. Registration limit: 50. Sponsor provides electricity for demonstrations and 24-hour security.

Acceptable Work: Considers ceramics; jewelry; metalsmithing; mobiles; pottery; sculpture; weaving; soft sculpture; and woodcrafting. "Work is selected for showing on basis of creativity and professional art form. No articles following step-by-step instructions, or under direct supervision will be considered."

Awards: Presents 1 $200, 1 $100, and 4 $50 cash awards; and ribbons. "Awards are based on excellence. Award pieces will be exhibited together. They may be sold, but must remain through the fair before being moved."

Sales Tip: "Pottery, weaving and jewelry were the most popular items, but were also the most plentiful. We need to have greater variety of media and want to encourage glassblowers, woodworkers, sculptors and furniture makers."

Promotion: Show is advertised by national crafts magazines; direct mail to 1,000+ artists; 1,000+ notices; and local media coverage. Artists will be contacted individually for promotional materials, if needed. "Promotional materials are usually collected locally."

Profile: "Crafts Fair at Riverfront emphasizes quality crafts and gives local professional craftspersons an opportunity to sell. The demonstrations which are scheduled throughout both days serve as a means of educating viewers as to the process of creating various crafts. This is a show for the serious craftsperson and quality is heavily emphasized."

*DAVIESS MARTIN COUNTY ART FESTIVAL, Box 245, Loogootee IN 47553. (812)295-3421. Public Information Director: Dean A. Dorrell. Park Superintendent: David L. Watson. Sponsor: West Boggs Park. Estab. 1975. Annual show held 2 days in August in 12x12 tents. Average attendance: 6,000. Entries accepted until show date. Entry fee: $10 ($5 refunded on craftworker's arrival). Work may be offered for sale; no commission. Craftworker must attend show. "We recommend that craftsmen demonstrate their talents as it helps promote sales." First 30 entries are given a 12x12 tent; table; and 2 chairs. Considers all original crafts. Presents awards first day of festival.

*EAGLE CREEK ARTS AND FOLK MUSIC FESTIVAL, 5901 DeLong Rd., Indianapolis IN 46254. (317)293-4827. Arts Fair Coordinator: Bill Taylor. Sponsor: Indianapolis Department of Parks. Purpose: "to present to the public a grouping of top quality professional arts/crafts on exhibit and folk musicians in concert." Estab. 1974. Annual outdoor show held the last Saturday and Sunday in July. Average attendance: 12,000-14,000. Entries accepted until 4 weeks before show. Entry fee: $15/10x10 display area. Prejudging by slides and/or photos; entry fee refunded for refused work. Work may be offered for sale; no commission. Craftworker must attend show; demosntrations OK. Registration limit: 75. Sponsor provides electricity for demonstrations and 24-hour security. Show is advertised by local and state media as well as national publications. Presents 3 cash awards of $50 for outstanding exhibit. Considers batik; candlemaking; ceramics; jewelry; lapidary; leatherworking; macrame; metalsmithing; mobiles; pottery; sculpture; weaving; and woodcrafting.

*FAIR ON THE SQUARE, Columbus Arts Guild Inc., Box 14, Columbus IN 47201. (812)372-8565. Director: Donna McCullough. "Fair on the Square is a spring celebration for our local artists. It is a well-established show which the community looks forward to attending." Estab. 1964. Annual outdoor show held on Mother's Day in the Columbus library square. Average attendance: 800-1,000, depending upon weather. Entries accepted until show. Entry fee: $8/10 square feet in open area or 10 linear feet on fence. Work may be offered for sale; no commission. Craftworker must attend show; demonstrations OK. Registration limit: 120. Sponsor provides electricity for demonstrations and fencing. Considers all crafts. Presents $500 in cash and ribbons. "Pottery sells well if small and reasonably priced."

Promotion: "Arts division of the Guild sends newsletter to artists who have exhibited before. The show is also listed in the activity columns of the surrounding big city newspapers." Show is also advertised by local newspapers; posters; and TV.

FEAST OF THE HUNTERS' MOON, 909 South St., Lafayette IN 47901. (317)742-8411. Feast Secretary: Fern Martin. Assistance Director: Carol Waddell. Sponsor: Tippecanoe County Historical Association. Estab. 1968. Annual outdoor show held 2 days in the fall at Fort Ouiatenon Historical Park at Lafayette. "Rustic brush shelters (with covered plastic tops) are constructed prior to the Feast for all booths." Average attendance: 45,000. Entries accepted until approximately 10 weeks prior to show. Entry fee $20/6x8 booth. Prejudging; "slides and written descriptions are submitted with application for juried selection for accepting the craftsman. He/she may bring any number of pieces of the accepted-type work." Entry fee refunded for refused work. Work may be offered for sale; no commission. Craftworker must attend show; demonstrations encouraged. Registration limit: 15. Sponsor provides chairs; brush shelter booth; and table.

Acceptable Work: Considers candlemaking; dollmaking; glass art; jewelry; leatherworking; metalsmithing; needlcrafts; pottery; sculpture; weaving; and woodcrafting. "All items must be made from natural materials (i.e., wood, stone, clay, etc.) which would have been available in the 18th century." No contemporary crafts.

Promotion: Show is advertised in local media and metropolitan Chicago, Indianapolis and St. Louis by radio; TV; and newspapers. "Also listed in tour and festival promotion publications throughout the Midwest. We occasionally request b&w glossies for newspaper releases."

Profile: "The Feast is primarily an educational festival, recreating life as it would have been lived at an 18th century French trading post. Our emphasis is on 18th century re-creation and demonstrations under primitive conditions of the traditional crafts. All participants are required to dress in 18th century costume. Colonial crafts are featured, and crafts are only a portion of the overall picture at the Feast of the Hunters' Moon. It is also a fundraising event for the Tippecanoe County Historical Association to continue archaeological exploration of the original site of Ft. Ouiatenon."

*FIESTA, 101 S. 9th St., Lafayette IN 47901. (317)742-1128. Director: Sharon A. Theobald. Sponsors: Lafayette Art League and Lafayette Art Association. Estab. 1974. Annual outdoor show held the Saturday before Labor Day. Entries accepted until 4 weeks before show. Entry fee: $20/10x10 display area. Prejudging; entry fee refunded for refused work. Work may be offered for sale; no commission. Craftworker must attend show; demonstrations encouraged. Registration limit: 60-100. Considers batik; ceramics; jewelry; leatherworking; metalsmithing; pottery; soft sculpture; weavings; wall hangings; and woodcrafting. Presents cash prizes.

FOLK ARTS & MUSIC FESTIVAL, Huntington North High School, 450 McGahn, Huntington IN 46750. (219)356-4218. Chairman: Jean Gernand. Sponsor: Huntington Community School Corp. "Our main purpose is to increase awareness and appreciation of all types of art, with special attention to folk arts, crafts and music." Estab. 1976. Annual indoor/outdoor show held 1 day in the fall "in our new high school and on school grounds." Attendance: 2,000-3,000; "more than quadrupled in its second year." Entries accepted until show date. Entry fee: $5/5x12 display area or 10% of sales. Work may be offered for sale. Craftworker must attend show; demonstrations encouraged. Sponsor provides chairs; electricity for demonstrations; and table. Show is advertised by newspapers; radio; TV; posters and flyers. Considers all crafts. Bestsellers: stained glass; leathercrafts; and jewelry.

GRABILL COUNTRY FAIR, c/o Freeman Byler, Grabill IN 46741. (219)627-3691. Sponsor: Grabill Chamber of Commerce. "Started as a farmers' country market and grew." Estab. 1972. Annual outdoor show held 3 days in September. Average attendance: 50,000. Entries accepted until show date. Entry fee: $25/open spaces; $35/covered space. Work must be offered for sale. Craftworker must attend show; demonstrations encouraged. Registration limit: 60. Sponsor provides electricity for demonstrations and 24-hour security. Show is advertised by TV; radio; magazines; and newspapers. Considers all crafts that "fit the conservative, religious atmosphere of the community."

HISTORIC HOOSIER HILLS GUILD FESTIVAL, 2242 Cragmont, Madison IN 47250. (812)273-1697. Chairman: Helen Gourley. Purpose: "to bring together the serious antique collector and craftsman making items of the type that were made with pride which can be used in homes and as personal items. Also held to promote interest in the Guild Shoppe." Estab. 1967. Semiannual outdoor show held 4 days during Memorial Day weekend and 3 days in the fall. Average attendance: 10,000-20,000. Entries accepted until show date. Entry fee: $6/artist. Work may be offered for sale; no commission. Craftworker must attend show; demonstrations OK. Show is advertised by radio; newspapers; magazines; and brochures. Considers "all original well-made crafts. We have a type of show which attracts only serious antique dealers and craftsmen. People who buy only purchase the better arts and crafts."

*INDIANA CRAFTS, 1200 W. 38th St., Indianapolis IN 46208. Sponsor: Indianapolis Museum of Art. Entry fee: $5. Maximum 2 entries per craftworker. Indiana exhibitors or former residents eligible. Awards $1,000+ in cash prizes.

JEFFERSONVILLE ARTS & CRAFTS FESTIVAL, 907 Poppy Place, Jeffersonville IN 47130. (812)283-7842. Show Director: Robert Mode. Sponsor: Jump Committee. "We hold the show as a part of [the celebration of the] steamboat on the bank of the Ohio River across from Louisville, Kentucky." Annual outdoor show held 2 days the second weekend in September. Average attendance: 85,000. Entries accepted until show date. Entry fee: $10/10x10 display area. Work may be offered for sale; no commission. Craftworker must attend show;

demonstrations OK. Registration limit: 150. Sponsor provides electricity for demonstrations. Show is advertised by radio; TV; newspapers; and state department of tourism. Considers all crafts.

KAMM'S BREWERY ARTS AND CRAFTS FESTIVAL, Box 806, Michawaka IN 46544. (219)259-7861. Public Relations Director: Sherrie Martin. Sponsor: 100 Center Development Company. Estab. 1971. Annual outdoor show held 2 days in July. Average attendance: 40,000. Entries accepted until 3 weeks before show. Entry fee: $25/10x10 display area. Prejudging by category; entry fee refunded for refused work. Work may be offered for sale; no commission. Craftworker needn't attend show; demonstrations encouraged. Registration limit: 150. Sponsor provides 24-hour security. Show is advertised by radio; TV; trade papers; and print. Considers all crafts except ceramics.

KOUTS ANNUAL ARTS & CRAFTS SHOW, Kouts Chamber of Commerce, Kouts IN 46347. (219)766-3766. President: Willard Paarlberg. Estab. 1976. Annual outdoor show held 1 day in July. Average attendance: 1,000. Entries accepted until show date. Entry fee: "donation." Display area: 10x10. Work may be offered for sale; no commission. Craftworker must attend show; demonstrations OK. Show is advertised by newspaper and radio. Considers all crafts.

LA PORTE JAYCEES ART SHOW, 3666 W. Schultz Rd., La Porte IN 46350. Contact: Jim Jessup. Sponsor: La Porte Jaycees. Annual show held in July. Entry fee: $10/craftworker (non-refundable). Write for application blank. Enter early as spaces are limited. Prejudging as to variety. Work may be offered for sale; no commission. Craftworker must attend show; demonstrations encouraged. Considers jewelry; pottery; sculpture; and other crafts. Show publicized extensively along with the annual Jaycees July 4 week-long celebration through area radio, TV and newspapers.

LOWELL'S ANNUAL ARTS AND CRAFTS FESTIVAL, 333 Woodland Ct., Lowell IN 46356. (219)696-7036. Director: B.E. Wheeler. Sponsor: Friends of the Library. Purpose: "to promote the arts in South Lake County. It is also a major fundraiser for our art-lending library." Estab. 1972. Annual outdoor show held 1 day in the summer. Entries accepted until 3 weeks before show. Entry fee: $10/10x8 display area. "We reserve the right to ask an artist to leave if his work should prove to be other than stated on application (an example would be if kits are presented as original work)." Work may be offered for sale; no commission. Craftworker must attend show; demonstrations encouraged. Sponsor provides electricity for demonstrations and help with setup if needed. Considers all crafts. Presents $300+ in cash prizes; award for best demonstration; and ribbons. "Limit exhibit to 1 or 2 types of art."
Promotion: "Show is advertised in 5 trade publications; state calendar; 240 newspapers in Indiana, plus major papers out of state; 3 radio stations; and at least 1 Chicago-based TV station. Business cards are essential to have at the Festival for future business as many people scout the fairs for future purchases. If the artist/craftsman also teaches his art, he could promote his classes through literature at the show."

*MADISON CHAUTAUQUA OF THE ARTS, Green Hills Pottery, 1119 W. Main St., Madison IN 47250. Contact: Dixie McDonough. Annual outdoor show held the last weekend in September. Entry fee: $20/craftworker. Prejudging by 5 slides (4 slides of individual work and 1 slide of display); "send SASE for return of slides or slides will not be returned." Craftworker must attend show. Work may be offered for sale; no commission. Considers all crafts. Presents cash prizes.

*MID-STATES CRAFT EXHIBITION, 411 SE Riverside Dr., Evansville IN 47713. (812)425-2406. Contact: Craft Committee. Sponsor: Evansville Museum of Arts and Science. Purpose: "to promote craftsmanship, provide an opportunity for craftsmen to display their work and visitors to enjoy it and buy it, and to augment the Museum's collection of contemporary crafts." Estab. 1961. Annual indoor show held 4 weeks in the winter. Average attendance: 10,000. Entries accepted 1 month before show. Handling fee: $5 for 1-3 items (limit 3); "sets may count as 1 entry." Prejudging by actual work; no refunds for refused work. Work may be offered for sale; 20% commission. Craftworker needn't attend show; no demonstrations. Sponsor provides 24-hour security, and museum staff handles display of all exhibits. Categories: ceramics; textiles; metalwork; and miscellaneous (wood, enamels, glass and other handcrafted materials). "Most sales are for home use or decoration. Under $50 items sell best."
Acceptable Work: Considers batik; candlemaking; ceramics; dollmaking; glass art; jewelry; lapidary; leatherworking; macrame; metalsmithing; mobiles; needlecrafts; pottery; soft sculpture; tole painting only if artist makes tray, etc. also; weaving; and woodcrafting. "Craftworkers

must live within 200 miles of Evansville or anywhere else in Indiana. All work must be original, made in the last 3 years, and not previously exhibited in a Mid-States Craft Exhibition. Some machine use is acceptable — potters' wheels, electric buffers and grinders for example."
Awards: Presents $500, $400, $275 and $100 purchase awards; and $100, $50, and 6 $75 merit awards. "Excellence of craftsmanship is most important [to jurors]. Creativity counts more with some jurors, while others appreciate a fine rendition of a traditional shape bowl or jar. Inflated prices do not influence jurors. They do not know what the prices are until after the judging."
Promotion: Show is advertised by direct mail brochures; press releases to news media; catalogs; and museum bulletin. "Award winners are asked to provide biographical data — this is displayed alongside work and given to news media."

NEW CARLISLE HISTORICAL DAYS, c/o Clark Hensell, Box O, New Carlisle IN 46552. (219)654-8311. Chairman: Mrs. Derm Meyer. Sponsor: Hill and Dale Men's Service Club, Inc. Estab. 1973. Annual outdoor show held 3 days in summer. Average attendance: 15,000. Entries accepted until 4 weeks before show. Entry fee: $15/12x12 display area. Work may be offered for sale; no commission. Craftworker must attend show; demonstrations OK. Show is advertised by newspapers; TV; radio; and billboards. Categories: flea market, and arts and crafts. Considers all crafts.

NILES ART GUILD ART FAIR, 7007 Fargo Ave., Niles IN 60648. Fair Chairman: Marilyn A. Brown. Purpose: "to promote local art." Estab. 1963. Annual indoor show held 2 days in April at Oak Mill Mall, Niles. Entries accepted until 2 weeks before show. Entry fee: $15, nonmember; or $10, member/10 linear feet of display space. Work may be offered for sale; no commission. Craftworker must attend show; demonstrations OK. Registration limit: 75-100. Sponsor provides 24-hour security. Show is advertised by newspapers; art magazines; and TV. Submit photos and name and address of local paper. Categories: oils and acrylics; watercolors; mixed media; sculpture; and crafts. Awards 1st, 2nd and 3rd place cash awards in each category but crafts.
Acceptable Work: Considers candlemaking; ceramics; jewelry; macrame; metalsmithing; pottery; sculpture; and woodcrafting.

OUTDOOR FINE ARTS GALLERY & ALL CRAFTS FAIR, Porter County Arts Commission, 15 Franklin St., Valparaiso IN 46383. (219)464-4080. Coordinator: Marjory Crawford. Purpose: "to make money — PAC is a nonprofit service organization and we charge admission in order to raise money for projects to help the arts in Porter County." Estab. 1971. Annual outdoor show held 2 days in the summer at Lakewood Park, Valparaiso. Attendance: 5,000-10,000. Entries accepted until 3 weeks before show. Entry fee: $20/craftworker. Prejudging by slides or photos; entry fee refunded for refused work. Work may be offered for sale; no commission. Craftworker needn't attend show (but is responsible for sales); demonstrations OK. Registration limit: 130-140. Sponsor provides electricity for demonstrations. Considers all crafts.
Promotion: Show is advertised by radio, posters and other news media within a 50-mile radius. "Good b&w photos for newspaper coverage would be helpful [for publicity purposes]."

*PLETCHER VILLAGE ART FESTIVAL, 1600 W. Market, Nappanee IN 46550. (219)773-4188. Contact: Richard Pletcher. Estab. 1963. Annual outdoor show held 4 days in August. Average attendance: 40,000. Entries accepted until about 3 months before show. Entry fee: $10/artist (this money will go toward the 15% sales commission). Display area: 12x15. Prejudging by slides or photos; entry fee refunded for refused work. Work may be offered for sale; 15% commission. Craftworker must attend show; demonstrations OK. Registration limit: 156. Sponsor provides electricity for demonstrations; fencing; and 24-hour security. Considers all crafts. Awards $1,850 in cash and $1,000 in purchase prizes.

TALBOT STREET ART FAIR, 2823 W. 52nd St., Indianapolis IN 46208. (317)297-1632. Chairman: Joe Lehman. Sponsor: Indiana Artist-Craftsmen, Inc. Purpose: "to promote public understanding of arts and crafts, and to provide a place for the craftsmen to meet the public." Estab. 1955. Annual outdoor show held 2 days in the summer. Attendance: 20,000-30,000. Entries accepted until about 2 months before show. Entry fee: $12/member; $24/nonmember. Prejudging by slides and photos of representative work. "Committee reserves the right to remove pieces if they're not up to the standard of the samples sent." Entry fee refunded for refused work. Work may be offered for sale; no commission. Craftworker must attend show; demonstrations encouraged. Registration limit: 200. Show is advertised by newspapers; radio; and TV. Submit biographical sketch and photos. Considers all crafts except decoupage. "Must be designed and made by the craftsman selling and exhibiting it." Presents ribbon for best display.

THREE RIVERS FESTIVAL ARTS AND CRAFT SHOW, 1707 Kensington Blvd., Fort Wayne IN 46805. (219)422-6949. Chairman: Betty L. Newton. Estab. 1974. Annual outdoor show held 2 days in July. Average attendance: 100,000. Entries accepted until 4 weeks before show. Entry fee: $15/10x10 display area. Work may be offered for sale; no commission. Craftworker must attend show; demonstrations OK. Registration limit: 100. Show is advertised by newspapers; magazines; house publications; and programs. Considers all crafts.

*TIPPECANOE REGIONAL PAINTING, PRINT AND SCULPTURE BIENNIAL EXHIBITION, Director: Sharon A. Theobald. Sponsor: Lafayette Art Association. Estab. 1959. Biennial show held odd-numbered years in May. Average attendance: 3,000-5,000. Entry fee: $10. Maximum 2 works/exhibitor. Works may be offered for sale; 25% commission. Sponsor provides insurance on exhibited work. Considers sculpture by Indiana artists. Presents cash and purchase prizes totalling $1,000.

*WABASH VALLEY EXHIBITION, 25 S. 7th St., Terre Haute IN 47807. (812)238-1676. Contact: Director. Sponsor: Sheldon Swope Art Gallery. Estab. 1943. Annual indoor show held 1 month in the early spring. Average attendance: 3,000. Entries accepted until early February. Entry fee: $5/first entry; $4/second, and $3/third entries. Maximum 3 entries per craftworker. Prejudging; no entry fees refunded for refused work. Work may be offered for sale; 20% commission. Open to craftworkers living within 160-mile radius of Terre Haute. Sponsor provides display equipment. Presents $6,000 in prizes.
Acceptable Work: Considers all media. Maximum size: 60" in any direction. Work must be framed or suitable for hanging.

WALKWAY FESTIVAL, 16½ SE 2nd St., Evansville IN 47708. (812)422-2111. Executive Director: Jane E. Moore. Sponsor: Evansville Arts and Education Council. Estab. 1969. Annual outdoor show held 1 day in the spring. Average attendance: 50,000. Entries accepted until 2 months before show. Entry fee: $15/artist. Display area: 10-15 square feet. "Entry to show is by invitation; those interested may submit detailed descriptions of their work in advance of deadline." Work may be offered for sale; commission to be determined. Craftworker must attend show; demonstrations encouraged. Registration limit: 100 or less. Sponsor provides electricity for demonstrations; security during 8 hours of festival; and liability insurance. Show is advertised by craft publications, and local and regional media. Categories: exhibits/sales; demonstrations/exhibits/sales; and entertainment. Considers all crafts. "There is presently an effort at upgrading the quality of work exhibited and sold."
Profile: "The Walkway Festival is a 1-day event of the Ohio River Arts Festival, encompassing 16 days of arts-related activities. The Walkway Festival gives artists and craftspeople an opportunity to display and sell, while providing the community at large a fun-filled day in which to become acquainted with various arts and crafts. Our community responds marvelously to this event. The viewing and buying public range in age from children to senior citizens with all socioeconomic levels represented."

WEST BOGGS ART FESTIVAL, Box 245, Loogootee IN 47553. (812)295-3421. Park Superintendent: David L. Watson. Sponsor: Boggs Park. Purpose: "to bring more people into this area; and to offer them the benefits of artists which has never been done in this area before." Estab. 1975. Annual outdoor show (with some tents) held 2 days in the summer. Average attendance: 10,000. Entries accepted until show date. Entry fee: $10, with $5 refunded upon arrival. Display area: "12x12 tents for the first few participants, after that they will have to furnish their own accommodations." Work may be offered for sale; no commission. Craftworker must attend show; demonstrations OK. Sponsor provides chairs; electricity for demonstrations; and table. Show is advertised by radio; TV; and newspapers. Considers all crafts. Work priced from $2-5 sells best.

*WICKER PARK ART FAIR, 5448 Hohman Ave., Hammond IN 46320. (219)931-0018. Program Chairman: Sandy Starrett. Sponsor: Northern Indiana Arts Association. Purpose: "to raise funds for the Art Center." Estab. 1970. Annual outdoor show held 2 days in May at Highland, Indiana. Average attendance: 7,000. Entries accepted until 4 weeks before show. Entry fee: $20/craftworker. Display area: 12x12. Prejudging by 3 slides of media entered; or 6 slides (3 slides of 2 works) of sculpture pieces. $15 refunded for refused work. Work may be offered for sale; no commission. Craftworker must attend show; demonstrations OK. Registration limit: 100. Sponsor provides fencing and 24-hour security. Show is advertised by newspapers; radio; TV; and local merchants. Considers batik; jewelry; lapidary; leatherworking; metalsmithing; pottery; sculpture; soft sculpture; weaving; and woodcrafting. Presents $50 1st, $30 2nd and $20 3rd prizes; and 1st, 2nd and 3rd place ribbons.

Iowa

ART IN THE PARK, c/o Norma Thomsen, 1104 N. 17th, Clarinda IA 51632. (712)542-4744. Sponsor: Clarinda Fine Arts Council. Purpose: "to provide a market for area artists particularly, as well as for anyone from further away who wants to enter; and to educate the public on the quality and quantity of art available in our area." Estab. 1973. Annual outdoor show held 1 day usually the second or third Saturday in May. Entries accepted until show date. Entry fee: $2.50/artist. Work may be offered for sale; no commission. Craftworker must attend show; demonstrations OK. "Could easily accommodate up to 100 [craftworkers]." Sponsor provides chairs; display panels; electricity for demonstrations; and table if requested at least 1 week before show. Considers all crafts. "This show is usually close to Mother's Day, so appropriate gift items sell especially well."

Promotion: "Show is advertised by radio; articles and pictures in local and statewide papers; posters; and direct mail. "If artists' names and explanations of work are received several weeks before the show, they will be included in newspaper and radio releases."

ART IN THE PARK, Box 132, Clinton IA 52732. (315)242-9635. President: Harry Petheran. Sponsor: Clinton Art Association. Estab. 1970. Annual outdoor show held 2 days the weekend after Mother's Day. Average attendance: 4,000. Entries accepted until 1 week before show. Entry fee: $10/artist. Prejudging by slides or photos; entry fee refunded for refused work. Work may be offered for sale; no commission. Craftworker or representative must attend show; demonstrations OK. Show is advertised by newspapers; radio; posters; and magazine ads.

Acceptable Work: Considers batik; candlemaking; glass art; jewelry; leatherworking; macrame; metalsmithing; pottery; sculpture; weaving; and woodcrafting.

*ARTS AND CRAFTS SHOW, Lake City Commerce, 101 E. Main St., Lake City IA 51449. Secretary: Neola M. Mack. Entries accepted up until show date. Maximum 1 piece/category; total of 3. Work may he offered for sale; no commission. Craftworker must attend show; demonstrations OK. Categories: ceramics; oil color; acrylic; water paints; macrame; mixed media; metal or woodcraft; and original handcrafts.

Acceptable Work: Considers batik; ceramics; decoupage; dollmaking; glass art; jewelry; leatherworking; macrame; metalsmithing; needlecrafts; pottery; sculpture; tole painting; weaving; woodcrafting. Cash award of $15 1st prize; $9 2nd prize for adults; and $5 and $3 for youth. Artist must provide own promotional material, tables, etc. to display work.

BELLE OF THE BEND, Artists in Action, 204 W. 2nd St., Muscatine IA 57761. Fair Director: Cheryl Weaver. "Our fair is a marketplace for artists/craftsmen wishing to promote themselves through sales of their work." Estab. 1975. Annual 1 day outdoor show held in late summer. Average attendance: 5,000-10,000. Entries accepted until 4 weeks before show. Entry fee: $10/10x10 display area; no more than 2 artists/booth. Entries prejudged by slides of work. Entry fee refunded for refused work. Work may be offered for sale; no commission. Craftworker must attend show; demonstrations OK. Registration limit: 65. Sponsor provides electricity for demonstrations. Categories: fine art and craft. "We would consider most crafts with a few limitations."

Sales Tip: "All work must display a price tag and booth must display a sign that all work is for sale. Most purchases are in the low-medium price range; cash that a person would carry rather than investment range work."

Promotion: Show is advertised by radio; TV; newspaper; Iowa Arts Council Calendar; craft magazines; posters; and newsletter. Craftworker should provide a brief resume and photos for newspaper releases.

*CARROLL SIDEWALK ART SHOW, 223 West 5th St., Carroll IA 51401. (712)792-4383. Executive Vice President: M.J. Mike Arts. Sponsor: Carroll Chamber of Commerce. Estab. 1969. Annual 1 day indoor/outdoor show (with covered canopy) held in late April. Entries accepted up until show date. Work may be offered for sale; no commission. Craftworker must attend show; demonstrations OK. Categories: oils; acrylics; fabric art; watercolors; pottery; 3-dimensional; sketches and drawings; prints; woodcuts and photography. Show is advertised by newspaper and radio.

Acceptable Work: Considers batik; decoupage; macrame; metalsmithing; mobiles; pottery; sculpture; soft sculpture; tole painting; and woodcrafting.

Awards: Presents $50 in cash to best of show; $50 purchase; and 1st, 2nd and best of show ribbons. Only 1 item per category will be judged.

MIDWEST OLD SETTLERS AND THRESHERS ASSOCIATION, INC., Rt. 1, Mt. Pleasant IA 52641. (319)385-8937. Administrator: Jerry W. Shafer. "We are an annual reunion for educational purposes relating a bit of our agricultural past for today." Estab. 1950. Annual indoor/outdoor show held for 5 days late in August and continuing into early September. Average attendance: 250,000. All entries must be approved by craft chairman by June-July. Display area: average 8x15. Work may be offered for sale; 10% commission. Craftworker must attend show; demonstrations required. Registration limit: 75. Sponsor provides electricity for demonstrations. Show is promoted by annual membership mailing of 60,000. Categories: authentic crafts must be actual craft of 1880-1920 time period and hobby crafts (but *very* limited space for these) home or personal hobby.

Acceptable Work: Considers batik; candlemaking; ceramics; decoupage; dollmaking; glass art; jewelry; lapidary; leatherworking; macrame; metalsmithing; needlecrafts; pottery; sculpture; soft sculpture; tole painting; weaving and woodcrafting. Exhibitor is limited to one type of craft.

*NATIONAL ROSEMALING EXHIBITION, 502 W. Water St., Decorah IA 52101. (319)382-3856. Contact: Betty Seegmiller. Sponsor: Norwegian-American Museum. Estab. 1967. Annual indoor show held 3 days in July. Average attendance: 15,000. Entries accepted until 1 week before show. Entry fee: $2/entry. Maximum 2 entries per craftworker. Prejudging; entry fee refunded for refused work. Work may be offered for sale; 20% commission. Sponsor furnishes display equipment and pays insurance and shipping to artist. Presents $125-150 in cash prizes and ribbons; and Medal of Honor.

Acceptable Work: Considers rosemaling on wood. "Works must measure at least 8" in one direction and contain enough decoration to reveal artist's technical skill and design ability. It is not necessary for the artist to make the article; only the painting must be original."

*NEEDLEWORK, Des Moines Symphony Guild, Employers Mutual Bldg., Des Moines IA 50309. (515)244-0189. Co-chairman: Mrs. J.C. Brenton. "This is an artistically valid exhibition of needlework that is the only such aesthetic effort regularly held in this community." Estab. 1975. Biennial indoor show held for 2 weeks in April. Average attendance: 10,000. Entries due 2 weeks before show. Entry fee: $5/item being displayed. Maximum 2 pieces/craftworker. Craftworker needn't attend show; no demonstrations. Sponsor provides display panels; table; and 24-hour security protection. Show is advertised by TV; national craft publications; and newspapers. Categories: forms of embroidery-canvas work (needlepoint); crewel; creative stitchery; counted threads; and metal threads. Design classifications: original (designed by exhibitor); adapted (designed from picture, fabric, etc. by exhibitor); custom (designed by someone other than exhibitor); and kit or copies (purchased kit, charted design or design copies from publication).

Acceptable Work: Considers needlcrafts. "Rya rugs, quilts, applique, etc., which do not incorporate embroidery as a major portion of the work are not acceptable."

Awards: Ribbons are awarded for 1st, 2nd and 3rd place in each classification and awards for best of show and most popular. "All work must be clearly marked, finished and ready for hanging or display. Indentification label (obtainable from Needlework, Employers Mutual Bldg., Des Moines IA 50309) must be sewn to back of entry if possible or otherwise securely attached."

Profile: "Needlework is a festival including 3 workshops each presented 3 times and a lecture on London's Royal School of Needlework being presented twice. Out-of-town visitors are made welcome when their attendance is made known. A preview party is scheduled for opening eve revealing winners."

*THE OCTAGON ART CENTER'S CLAY AND FIBER SHOW, The Octagon Art Center, 232½ Main St., Ames IA 50010. (515)232-5331. Director: Martha Benson. Biennial indoor juried exhibit on display 4-6 weeks January-March of even-numbered years. Average attendance: 2,000-3,000. Entries due early in January. Entry fee: $10/artist. Maximum 3 pieces/craftworker. Prejudging by actual work; no entry fee refunded for refused work. Work may be offered for sale; 25% commission. Craftworker needn't attend show; no demonstrations. Categories: ceramics and fiber. Considers ceramics; macrame; soft sculpture; and weaving. Presents $200, best-in-show; $100, ceramic award; and $100, fiber. Competition is open to all craftworkers over 18 years of age living within 500 miles of Ames.

Promotion: Show is advertised by radio; newspaper; flyer; posters and craft publications (*Ceramics Monthly, Craft Horizons*).

*OTTUMWA HEIGHTS FAMILY ART FESTIVAL, Ottumwa Heights College, Ottumwa IA 51501. (515)682-4551. President: Sister Bernadine Pieper. Sponsor: Ottumwa Heights Art Board. Estab. 1973. Annual outdoor show held the first Sunday in August. Average attendance: 3,000-5,000. Entries accepted until 2 weeks before show. Entry fee: $15/artist. Display area: 15 linear feet. Work may be offered for sale; no commission. Craftsworker must be present; demonstrations OK. Sponsor provides chairs; display panels; limited electricity for demonstrations; fencing; and table. "Displays must be set up in the morning and dismantled after 5 p.m., eliminating need for security but 'booth sitters' available." Show is advertised by poster; newspapers; radio; and TV. 1977 exhibit sales totalled $10,000-12,000.

Acceptable Work: Considers batik; ceramics; decoupage; glass art; jewelry; leatherworking; macrame; metalsmithing; mobiles; pottery; sculpture; soft sculpture; tole painting; weaving and woodcrafting. $1,000 purchase award plus ribbon awards.

PRE-CHRISTMAS POTTERY SHOW, 513 Nebraska St., Sioux City IA 51101. Sponsor: Sioux City Art Center. Estab. 1965. Annual indoor show held 2 days in December. Average attendance: 1,500. Entries accepted until 2 weeks before show. Prejudging. Work may be offered for sale; 30% commission. Craftworker needn't attend show; demonstrations OK. Registration limit: 50. Sponsor provides insurance on exhibited work; insurance on work shipped to artist; shipping costs to artists from show; table; and 24-hour security protection. Show is advertised by TV; radio; newspapers and art associations. Considers ceramics; glass art; and pottery.

*SNAKE ALLEY ART FAIR, Box 5, Burlington IA 52601. Chairmen: Jerry and Lois Rigdon. Sponsor: Art Guild Burlington, Inc. Estab. 1967. Show is an annual 1 day outdoor event held in June. Average attendance: 8,000-10,000. Entries accepted up until show date. Entry fee: $10/5x10 display area. Prejudging; entry fee refunded for refused work. Work may be offered for sale; no commission. Craftworker must attend show; demonstrations OK. Sponsor provides fencing. "There are physical problems with the Snake Alley Site. It is an inclined grade/switchback type. Leveling devices are needed. Also a need to provide own shade." Presents $25 in cash awards.

Acceptable Work: Considers batik; dollmaking; glass art; jewelry; lapidary; leatherworking; macrame; metalsmithing; pottery; sculpture; soft sculpture; weaving; and woodcrafting.

Promotion: Show is advertised by Guild mailing; area newspapers; radio; Chamber of Commerce brochure; and *Des Moines Register*.

Kansas

ART IN THE PARK, Box 198, Independence KS 67301. (316)331-0108. Chairman: Ray Rothgeb. Sponsor: Independence Arts Council. Purpose: "to provide an outlet for local and area craftsmen and artists and to make available to the community art and crafts for viewing and/or purchase." Estab. 1975. Annual indoor/outdoor (covered pavilion) show held 2 days in July. Average attendance: 4,000. Entries accepted until 2 weeks before show. Entry fee: $10-15/8x10 display area. Work may be offered for sale; no commission. Craftworker needn't attend show; demonstrations OK. Registration limit: 80. Sponsor provides electricity for demonstrations if requested in advance. Considers all original crafts.

Promotion: Show is advertised by area TV; radio and newspapers; national listings; State Arts Council newsletters; and mailing to area artists. Supply material regarding awards, qualifications, etc. to chairman 4-6 weeks in advance with request for demonstration or special showing for possible use as a press release.

ARTS AND CRAFTS FAIR, Courthouse, Box 100, Cottonwood Falls KS 66845. (316)273-6491. County Extension Home Economist: Connie Moss. Sponsor: Home Economics Advisory Council. Estab. 1976. Annual indoor show held 1 day in July. Average attendance: 300. Entries accepted until 2 days before show. Entry fee: $2/folding table, not card table. Work may be offered for sale; no commission. Demonstrations OK. Sponsor provides chairs and table. Show is advertised by newspaper; posters; magazines; flyers; and newsletters. Considers all crafts.

CHRISTMAS ARTS AND CRAFTS, c/o June DeWeese, Rt. 4, Abilene KS 67410. (913)263-3474. Estab. 1976. Annual indoor show held 2 days in December. Entries accepted until filled. Entry fee: $15/8x6 display area. Prejudging by slides and photos. Entry fee refunded for refused work. Work may be offered for sale; demonstrations OK. Registration limit: 100. Sponsor provides chairs; electricity for demonstrations; table; and 24-hour security protection. Accepts all crafts.

Promotion: Show is advertised on 3 TV networks; 7 radio stations; and 176 papers.

CHRISTMAS ARTS AND CRAFTS, c/o June DeWeese, Rt. 4, Abilene KS 67410. (913)263-3474. Estab. 1976. Annual indoor show held 2 days in November at Topeka, Kansas. Entries accepted until filled. Entry fee: $20/8x6 display area. Entries prejudged by slides or photos; entry fee refunded for refused work. Work may be offered for sale; no commission. Craftworker must attend show; demonstrations OK. Registration limit: 130. Sponsor provides chairs; electricity for demonstrations; table; and 24-hour security. Show is advertised by 3 TV networks; 7 radio stations; and 176 papers. Considers all crafts.

CHRISTMAS ARTS AND CRAFTS, c/o June DeWeese, Rt. 4. Abilene KS 67410. (913)263-3474. Estab. 1976. Annual indoor show held 2 days in November at Wichita, Kansas. Entries accepted until filled. Entry fee: $30/8x6 display area. Entries prejudged by slides or photos; entry fee refunded for refused work. Work may be offered for sale; no commission. Craftworker must attend show; demonstrations OK. Registration limit: 130. Sponsor provides chairs; electricity for demonstrations; table; and 24-hour security. Show is advertised by 3 TV networks; 7 radio stations; and 176 papers. Considers all crafts.

*JUNCTION CITY ART IN THE PARK, Box 403, Junction City KS 66441. (913)238-8698. Director: Dianne Schwartz. Sponsor: Junction City Arts Council. "Art in the Park affords our community with exposure to both the visual and the performing arts in a casual and festive atmosphere. It also makes a market available to local and out-of-town artists." Estab. 1973. Annual outdoor show (with tents and parachutes) held 1 day in September. Average attendance: 3,000. Entries accepted until 4 weeks before show. Entry fee: $10/8x8 display area. Work may be offered for sale; no commission. Craftworker must attend show; demonstration OK. Sponsor provides display panels and electricity for demonstrations. Show is advertised by wide mailing in state/out-of-state; radio; TV; and newspaper media. Presents cash awards of $100, $75, and $50. Considers all original crafts.

NEW BEGINNINGS FESTIVAL ARTS AND CRAFTS, Box 816, Coffeyville KS 67337. (316)251-2467 or (316)251-5772. Chairman Arts and Crafts Committee: Shirley Miller. Sponsor: Chamber of Commerce. Estab. 1974. Annual outdoor show (with permanent concrete canopies) held 2 days in April. Average attendance: 2,000-5,000. Entries accepted until 2 weeks before show. Entry fee: $5/8x10 (without canopy); $10/8x20. Prejudging by slides. Work must be offered for sale; no commission. Craftworker must attend show; demonstrations OK. Registration limit: 150. Sponsor provides display panels; electricity for demonstrations; and 24-hour security. Show is advertised by news releases; radio; TV; interviews; and ads.
Acceptable Work: Considers batik; glass art; jewelry; lapidary; leatherworking; metalsmithing; mobiles; pottery; sculpture; weaving; and woodcrafting.

*NORTHWEST KANSAS AREA ART SHOW & SALE, c/o Mrs. Duane Aase, 606 S. Broadway, Oberlin KS 67749. Sponsor: Sappa Valley Arts Club. Estab. 1970. Annual indoor show held 4 days in late September. Average attendance: 2,000. Entries accepted until show. Entry fee: $1/entry. Maximum 3 entries per craftworker. Awards cash prizes to first 3 winners in 6 divisions and ribbons. Work may be offered for sale; 10% commission. Demonstrations encouraged. Considers batik. Address shipped items to Decatur County Extension Office, Court House, Oberlin, Kansas 67749. No returns shipped; must be picked up.

*OLATHE AREA CHAMBER OF COMMERCE ANNUAL OLATHE ART FAIR AND CRAFTS SHOW, 201 E. Santa Fe, Box 189, Olathe KS 66061. (913)764-1050. Assistant Manager: David Palmer. Estab. 1970. Annual indoor/outdoor (covered) show held 3 days in June. Average attendance: 10,000+. Entries accepted until 1 week before show; "if there are cancellations we fill them in up until show time." Entry fee: $10/table space. Work may be offered for sale; no commission. Craftworker or representative must attend show; demonstrations OK. Sponsor provides coverings for some areas; display panels for fee; and electricity for demonstrations. Considers all crafts. Presents ribbons; plaque for best of show; and certificates for top in categories.
Promotion: Show is advertised by posters; newspapers; and mailings. "Craftworker may submit pictures, write-ups, etc., which may be used in the advertising. So far each year, all artists have been written up in the newspaper before the show so we would need list of their awards, shows they have participated in, etc."

*PARSONS OUTDOORS ARTS AND CRAFTS, Box 995, Parsons KS 67357. President: Patricia Winscott. Sponsor: Independent Art Council. Estab. 1962. Annual outdoor show (with covering) held 2 days in July. Entries accepted until full. Entry fee: $10/4x8. Work may be offered for sale; no commission. Demonstrations OK. Registration limit: 200. Sponsor provides display panels and table. Show is advertised by newspaper ads; TV; radio; and registration invitation. Categories: fine arts; fine arts and crafts; hobby crafts; and photography. Considers all crafts except ceramics. Presents cash awards; purchase awards; and ribbons.

*WALNUT VALLEY NATIONAL FLAT-PICKING CHAMPIONSHIP AND FOLK ARTS AND CRAFTS FESTIVAL, Box 245, Winfield KS 67156. (316)221-3250. Co-directors: Troy and Phyllis Boucher. Sponsor: Walnut Valley Association, Inc. Estab. 1972. Annual indoor/outdoor (covered veranda and pavilion) show held 3 days in September. Average attendance:

10,000. Entries accepted until 2 weeks before show. Entry fee: $25/8x8 outside space; $40/8x8 inside space. Entries prejudged by slides or photos; entry fee refunded for refused work. Work may be offered for sale; no commission. Craftworker must attend show; demonstrations OK. Registration limit: 120 (75 inside, 45 outside). Sponsor provides chairs upon prior request; electricity for demonstrations; table; and 24-hour security. Show is advertised by bluegrass publications; area newspapers; radio; and TV. Considers all crafts including musical instruments and folk art. Presents cash awards of $60, $50 and $40. 1977 exhibitor sales totalled $60,244.

Kentucky

*ARTS & CRAFTS FESTIVAL, Land Between the Lakes, Golden Pond KY 42231. (502)924-5602. Conservationist: Ann W. Wright. Sponsor: Murray Art Guild and TVA's Land Between the Lakes. Estab. 1969. Annual outdoor show held the last weekend in June. Average attendance: 15,000. Entries accepted until 2 weeks before show. Entry fee: $8 general exhibit fee plus additional fee for juried section. Maximum 2 entries/category; unrestricted in general show and sell portion of show. Work may be offered for sale; no commission. Craftworker must attend show; demonstrations encouraged. Registration limit: 250. Sponsor provides limited electricity for demonstrations. Considers all crafts except ceramics; decoupage; and lapidary. Juried entries are eligible for cash awards. "The majority of the show's visitors are tourists, and small and less expensive items sell more rapidly."
Promotion: Show is advertised by radio; TV; news releases; posters; flyers; magazine listing; and special mailing. Submit a description of work and resume.

SUE BENNETT FOLK FESTIVAL, Sue Bennett College, London KY 40741. (606)864-9714. Chairman: Madge Chesnut. Purpose: "to achieve a cultural affirmation of those who live in this area. To appreciate what we are, what we do, and what others do. We also have workshops, lectures, entertainment, etc." Annual indoor show held 4 days in late March or early April. Average attendance: 2,000. Entries accepted until 2 weeks before show ("if unusual craft, or one we don't have any of, sometimes can be accepted later"). No entry fee. Display area: "space for long table, about 6-7 feet." Prejudging by slides or small sample. Work may be offered for sale; no commission. Craftworker must attend show; demonstrations OK. Registration limit: about 50. Sponsor provides chairs; electricity for demonstrations; table; and 24-hour security. Considers all crafts except greenware.
Sales Tip: "Adults will buy almost anything if well-made, good design and color. We have many school children who come and a lot of them bring several dollars for inexpensive items (50c-$4)."
Promotion: Show is advertised by letters of invitation to area clubs; radio; newspapers; some TV; and posters. Submit "good b&w photographs for newspaper releases; also some interesting things about themselves and their work."

*CAPITAL EXPO, Box 496, Frankfort KY 40601. (502)875-2310. Adminstrative Manager: Trudy Laing. Purpose: "to call attention to Kentucky's contribution to the national heritage." Estab. 1974. Annual outdoor show (with some tents) held 2 days in June. Average attendance: 30,000. Entries accepted until 4 weeks before show. Entry fee: $10/8x10 display area. Prejudging by slides; entry fee refunded for refused work. Work may be offered for sale; no commission. Craftworker must attend show; demonstrations OK. Registration limit: 80. Kentucky residents. Sponsor provides chairs: electricity for demonstrations; table; and 24-hour security protection. Presents $100, $75 and $50 purchase awards.
Acceptable Work: Considers batik; candlemaking; ceramics; dollmaking; glass art; jewelry; lapidary; macrame; metalsmithing; mobiles; needlecrafts; pottery; sculpture; soft sculpture; weaving; and woodcrafting. "No plastic articles and no jewelry which hasn't been made from scratch."
Sales Tip: "Be cordial to the public, by doing this the artist can realize more sales. Talk is 95% of sales. Best sales are often realized by potters who use glazes which are colorful. Toys (wooden) are popular. Suggest individuals price their work in a range which would make sales more likely; suggest artists be aware of sales tax information; and suggest artists make areas as attractive as possible."
Promotion: Show is advertised by brochures; TV; radio; and newspapers. "If accepted, a b&w photograph of the artist at work is needed for promotion purposes. It will not be returned."

8-STATE ANNUAL, J.B. Speed Art Museum, Box 8345, Louisville KY 40208. (502)636-2893. Director: A.F. Page. Estab. 1973. Annual indoor show held the month of September. Average attendance: 6,000. Entries accepted until 5 weeks before show. No entry fee. Maximum 2 entries per artist. Prejudging. Work may be offered for sale; no commission. Craftworkers from Kentucky, Indiana, Illinois, Ohio, Virginia, West Virginia, Tennessee and Missouri only.

*GREENUP OLD FASHIONED DAYS ARTS & CRAFTS SHOW, 203 Harrison St., Greenup KY 41144. Art Show Chairman: Dorothy K. Griffith. Sponsor: Greenup Woman's Club and Greenup Merchants Association. Annual outdoor show held first Saturday in October. Entries accepted until show date. No entry fee. "Sales encouraged. Exhibitors responsible for own display and setup materials." Categories: drawings; oils; watercolors; photography; and crafts. Considers all crafts. Presents 12 "best" ribbons in crafts; and $40 cash award and rosette to grand prize winners in each category. Local craftworkers only.

*KENTUCKY GUILD OF ARTISTS AND CRAFTSMEN'S FAIR, Box 291, 213 Chestnut St., Berea KY 40403. (606)986-3192 or 986-4704. Estab. 1966. Annual outdoor show held 4 days in May. Prejudging. Work may be offered for sale. Craftworker must attend show; demonstrations OK. Registration limit: 100+ Kentucky Guild members. Presents Visitors' Choice Award. Considers all crafts.

KINGDOM COME SWAPPIN' MEETIN', College Rd., Cumberland KY 40823. (606)589-2608. Coordinator: W. Bruce Ayers. Sponsor: City of Cumberland, Tri-City Chamber of Commerce, and Southeast Community College. Purpose: "to help perpetuate folkways and methods of the Appalachian area." Estab. 1964. Annual indoor show held the second Saturday in October. Average attendance: 1,500. Entries accepted until 1 week before show. Entry fee: $5/5x8 display area. Work may be offered for sale; no commission. Craftworker must attend show; demonstrations OK. Sponsor provides chairs; coverings; and table. Show is promoted by newspaper; radio; TV; handbills; and posters. "Primarily interested in mountain crafts. Public is primarily interested [in buying] crafts which are indigenous to Appalachia."

PAPER & FELT REDEFINED, c/o Louisville School of Art, 100 Park Rd., Anchorage KY 40223. (502)245-8836. Associate Director: Diana Arcadipone. Purpose: "to provide exposure for students, and to bring the community together." Annual indoor show held 3 weeks in the winter. Attendance: 500-1,000. Entries accepted by invitation only. No entry fee. Maximum 5 entries/artist. Prejudging by slides. Work may be offered for sale; no commission. Craftworker needn't attend show; no demonstrations. Registration limit: 27. Sponsor provides insurance on exhibited work; insurance on work shipped to artist; pays shipping costs to artist from show; handles sales; and 24-hour security. Considers handmade paper; handmade felt; soft sculpture; and weaving. Free catalogs available.
Promotion: Show is advertised by national and local listings; gallery calendars; public service announcements; radio; and local newspapers. Submit resume.

WHITE HALL STATE SHRINE'S ANNUAL LABOR DAY SHOOT, Box 517, Richmond KY 40475. (606)623-9178. Contact: Vicki Smith. Sponsor: 9th Kentucky Calvary. "Our show is for those wanting to display and sell their crafts to people from various areas around the state." Estab. 1972. Annual outdoor show held 4 days during Labor Day weekend. Attendance: 3,000-5,000. Entries accepted throughout the event. Entry fee: $6/day. Display area: 20x20. Work may be offered for sale; no commission. Craftworker or representative must attend show; demonstrations OK. Sponsor provides 24-hour security and camping area. Show is advertised by TV shows; radio spots; and newspaper ads. Considers all crafts.
Profile: "Every year teams from the eastern part of the state come dressed in Civil War uniforms to compete for medals and prizes. With this we have live entertainment provided; along with an arts and crafts fair. The house, White Hall, is also open for tours. We do have a big turnout for this weekend. The area of types of people attending is very broad."

Louisiana

BOGALUSA CHAMBER OF COMMERCE ARTS, CRAFTS & ANTIQUE MART, 608 Willis Ave., Bogalusa LA 70427. (504)735-5731. Executive Director: Duane Blackwell. Purpose: fundraiser. Estab. 1975. Semiannual outdoor show (in automobile dealer's lot) held 2 days in May and October. Entries accepted until show date. Entry fee: $10/10x10 display area. Work may be offered for sale; no commission. Craftworker needn't attend show; demonstrations encouraged. Registration limit: 120. Sponsor provides chairs and table at nominal charge; coverings; electricity for demonstrations; and 24-hour security. Considers all crafts and antiques.
Promotion: Show is advertised by newspaper; radio; TV; and is usually held along with some other event that is usually tied in with the Mart. "For example, an antique auto show or free open-air concert. A photo of the artist at work stands a good chance of ending up on the front page of the *Bogalusa Daily News*."

LOUISIANA FUR & WILDLIFE FESTIVAL, c/o Bill Morris, Box 609, Cameron LA 70631. (318)775-5518. "It [the craft show] is held in conjunction with the annual Louisiana Fur &

Wildlife Festival. There are many different activities— art show, skinning, trap setting, retriever dog, trap shooting, etc." Estab. 1975. Annual indoor show held 1 day in January. Average attendance: 5,000. Entries accepted until 1 week before show or until filled. Entry fee: $15/8x10 display area (more if space is needed and is available). Work may be offered for sale; no commission. Prefers craftworker attend show; demonstrations OK. Sponsor provides chairs; electricity for demonstrations; and 24-hour security. Show is advertised by national periodicals; local newspapers; radio; and TV. Considers all crafts.

LOUISIANA NATIVE CRAFTS FESTIVAL, 637 Girard Park Dr., Layfayette LA 70503. (318)233-6611, ext. 250. Director: Beverly D. Latimer. Sponsor: Lafayette Natural History Museum Association. Purpose: "to make the people of Louisiana and tourists aware of our cultural heritage." Estab. 1972. Annual indoor/outdoor show (tents and canopies are used) held 2 days in September. Average attendance: 5,000. Entries accepted until 1 week before show (by invitation only to Louisiana craftworkers). Entry fee: $25 patron fee for any craftworker selling crafts. Prejudging by slides, photos or actual crafts; entry fee due after prejudging. Work may be offered for sale; no commission. Craftworker must attend show; demonstrations required. Registration limit: 50. Sponsor provides chairs; coverings; electricity for demonstrations; table; and 24-hour security. Show is advertised by radio; TV; and magazines in a 5-state area.
Acceptable Work: Considers candlemaking; dollmaking; jewelry; basketmaking; leatherworking; metalsmithing; needlecrafts; pottery; weaving; and woodcrafting. Criteria for entry: "the craft must have been practiced in this region prior to 1900; the product should be of Louisiana materials; or the craft must have been pertinent to the livelihood of the individual or the area."

*LOUISIANA STATE ART EXHIBITION FOR NON-PROFESSIONALS AND/OR ART STUDENTS, Jay R. Broussard Memorial Galleries, Old State Capitol, Baton Rouge LA 70801. Exhibits Director: Charles Ford. Sponsor: Louisiana Division of the Arts. Annual show held in the spring. No entry fee. Maximum 2 entries per craftworker. Work may be offered for sale; no commission. Considers all media. Open to Louisiana residents only. Presents top 10 artists with a group show.

*LOUISIANA STATE ART EXHIBITION FOR PROFESSIONAL ARTISTS, Old State Capitol, Baton Rouge LA 70801. Exhibits Director: Charles Ford. Sponsor: Louisiana Division of the Arts. Annual show held in the fall. Open to professional artists residing in Louisiana. No entry fee. Maximum 2 entries per artist. All media accepted. No sales commission. Presents purchase awards.

NEW ORLEANS JAZZ & HERITAGE FESTIVAL CRAFTS FAIR, Box 2530, New Orleans LA 70176. (504)522-4786. Crafts Coordinator: Vitrice McMurry. Sponsor: New Orleans Jazz & Heritage Foundation. Purpose: "to give the best local and national craftsmen a festive spring throng to sell to, and to give these visitors a great time in the Crescent City." Estab. 1969. Annual outdoor show (on a grassy racetrack field under many small tents) held 3 days during 2 weekends of April. Average attendance: 150,000. Entries accepted until 2 months before show. Entry fee: $100/10x10 display area. Prejudging by 3 35mm slides; entry fee refunded for refused work. Work may be offered for sale; no commission. Craftworker must attend show; demonstrations OK. Registration limit: 120. Sponsor provides coverings; electricity for demonstrations ($25 extra); table; and 24-hour security. Show is advertised by newspapers; TV; and radio. "Provide as much bio as possible for our [publicity] articles."
Acceptable Work: Considers batik; candlemaking; ceramics; dollmaking; glass art; jewelry; lapidary; leatherworking; macrame; metalsmithing; mobiles; needlecrafts; pottery; sculpture; soft sculpture; weaving; and woodcrafting.
Sales Tip: "Quality work of all prices sell here. As usual, pottery and jewelry sell best with toys and woodwork doing next best."

NEW ORLEANS MUSEUM OF ART, ARTISTS BIENNIAL, Box 19123, City Park, New Orleans LA 70179. Contact: William A. Fagaly. Biennial show. No entry fee. Write for entry deadlines and show dates. Maximum 3 entries per craftworker. Prejudging of 2-dimensional work by 1 2x2 slide of each item; of 3-dimensional works by 3 2x2 slides of each work, or 3 8x10 b&w photos of each work; and only paper documentation, typewritten proposals and/or 8x10 b&w photos of each work for conceptual pieces. Museum reserves the right to retain any or all slides for archives of regional contemporary artists. Juror recommends artists for one man exhibitions the next year. Work may be offered for sale; 10% purchase discount is required for purchases by Museum members. Considers sculpture; ceramics; fiber; and conceptual works. Open to craftworkers living and working in Kentucky, Tennessee, West Virginia, Virginia,

North and South Carolina, Georgia, Florida, Alabama, Mississippi, Arkansas, Louisiana and Texas.

RED RIVER REVEL, A CELEBRATION OF THE ARTS, 700 Clyde Fant Pkwy., Shreveport LA 71106. (318)221-1776. Sponsor: Junior League of Shreveport, Inc. Estab. 1976. Annual outdoor show (with individual booths) held 1 week (artists can opt for ½ week) in September. Average attendance: 240,000. Entries accepted until 3 months before show. Entry fee: $40/week; $20/½ week; and $5 prejudging fee. Display area: 8x10. Prejudging by 3 35mm slides. Entry fee refunded for refused work; $5 prejudging fee applied to booth rental on accepted work. Work may be offered for sale; 20% commission. Craftworker must attend show; demonstrations OK. Registration limit: about 50. Sponsor provides booth; electricity for demonstrations; 24-hour security; lighting; relief volunteers; and credit cards through central sales. Considers all original crafts.
Sales Tip: "Highest sale in 1977 was a $650 painting; lowest sales item was a $2.50 stuffed toy. 1977 artisans' sales average per artist was $792.10."
Promotion: "Festival received front page newspaper coverage week of show. TV did even the weather reports from the Revel. Radios did remotes from festival. After confirmation of acceptance is received, artists will be requested to supply glossies and biographies if possible."

*SHREVEPORT ART GUILD NATIONAL, 2911 Centenary Blvd., Shreveport LA 71104. (318)869-5169. Chairman: Jeanie Hamel. Estab. 1921. Annual indoor show held 1 month in fall. Average attendance: 2,000. Entries accepted until July 30. Prejudging by slides; no entry fees refunded for refused work. Work may be offered for sale; 10% commission. Craftworker needn't attend show; no demonstrations. Registration limit: 70. Show is advertised by local and state newspapers; local TV; and radio. Presents cash awards of $3,000 and purchase awards of $1,200. Considers ceramics and sculpture.

*SHRIMP & PETROLEUM CRAFT SHOW, 510 Duke St., Morgan City LA 70380. Publicity Manager: Madge Comeaux. Sponsor: Atchafalaya Crafters. Purpose: "to give the craftsman a chance to show his best works, and to create an awareness in the public of handcrafted items." Annual indoor show held 2 days during Labor Day weekend. Entries accepted until the day before the show. Entry fee: $2/item being displayed; half price for members of Atchafalaya. Display area: 3x3. "This is strictly a judged show for individual items. Items will be judged in separate categories by 2-3 out-of-town judges." Work may be offered for sale; 10% commission. Craftworker needn't attend show; demonstrations OK. Sponsor provides display panels; table; and 24-hour security. Show is advertised by radio; newspapers; and at schools and colleges. Considers all crafts.
Awards: Presents $25 in cash; grand award plus trophy; and 1st, 2nd, 3rd and honorable mention ribbons. "Points will be given in the following categories: neatness; originality; creativity; balance of work; and difficulty."

SPRING ARTS & CRAFTS FESTIVAL, c/o Woman's Service League, Box 299, Ferriday LA 71334. Contact: Mrs. Ed Godbold. Purpose: "to bring art appreciation to the people of the area; inspire students of art; and promote community involvement in schools of the area." Estab. 1977. Annual indoor show held 1 day in April. Average attendance: 200. Entries accepted until 2 weeks before show. No entry fee. Prejudging by teachers in regard to students' art; adult art is not prejudged. Work may be offered for sale; no commission. Craftworker must attend show; demonstrations OK. Registration limit: 53. Sponsor provides electricity for demonstrations; table; and 24-hour security. Considers all crafts. Presents $10 for best display or booth; and 1st, 2nd, 3rd and honorable mention ribbons.
Promotion: Show is advertised by local newspapers; radio; and direct correspondence. "Submit complete description of art/craftwork and address so that I may contact the artist for further questions."

*SUMMER ARTS FESTIVAL, c/o Art & Humanities Council, Box 3893, Baton Rouge LA 70821. (504)343-2997. Publications Director: Phyllis Ellard Covington. "Crafts part of Festival is only about 1/3 of the event — also performing arts and visual arts." Estab. 1974. Annual indoor/outdoor show held 3 days in the summer. Average attendance: 50,000-60,000. Entries accepted until 2 weeks before show. Entry fee: $10, nonprofessionals; $25, professionals. Display area: 10x10. Work may be offered for sale; no commission. Craftworker must attend show; demonstrations encouraged. Sponsor provides electricty for demonstrations and accident insurance. Considers all crafts. Presents cash awards. 1977 exhibitor sales totalled $75,000.
Promotion: Show is advertised by TV; radio; posters; and newspapers. "If he/she wants publicity, pictures and bio are encouraged — b&w only."

Maine

*ARTHRITIS ART COMMITTEE, Box 333, Bath ME 04530. 1-2 shows sponsored annually by the Maine Chapter, Arthritis Foundation. Entries accepted until 15 days before show. Entry fee: $10, first work; $6, each additional work. Maximum 5 entries per artist. Work may be offered for sale; 25% commission. Considers framable crafts. Awards 5 $10 first prizes, ribbons and certificates.

*BRIDGTON ART SHOW, Box 236, Bridgton ME 04009. (207)647-3472. Secretary: Sandra Libby. Sponsor: Bridgton Chamber of Commerce. Estab. 1971. Annual indoor show held Columbus Day weekend. Average attendance: 2,000-3,000. Entries accepted until 1 week before show. Entry fee: $20/2 entries. Entries prejudged by actual work. Work may be offered for sale; 20% commission. Craftworker needn't attend show; no demonstrations. Sponsor provides display panels; electricity; insurance on exhibited work; and 24-hour security. Considers all crafts.
Awards: Presents $1,000, 1st; $500, 2nd; $350, honorable mention; and $250, popular prize, chosen by shows' viewers. Show sales average $1,500.
Promotion: Show is advertised by posters and media advertising. "Printed materials relative to artist always welcome. They are displayed and offered for distribution to viewers."

CARIBOU SIDEWALK ARTS AND CRAFTS FESTIVAL, Box 357, 111 High St., Caribou ME 04736. (207)492-5231. Coordinators: Ann Chung and Bill Johnson. Sponsor: Caribou Chamber of Commerce. Estab. 1973. Annual outdoor show held 1 day in July. Average attendance: 3,000-5,000. Entries accepted up until show date. Entry fee: $5/8 foot display area. Work may be offered for sale; no commission. Craftworker must attend show; demonstrations OK. Registration limit: 100. Sponsor provides display panel at $4/rack. Show is advertised by radio; TV; newspaper; listings in arts and craft magazines; pamphlets; and posters. Considers all crafts.

THE CHRISTMAS CRAFT FAIR, Kennebee Valley YMCA, Augusta ME 04330. Chairman: Marty Thornton. Purpose: "to give the town a quality crafts fair and to provide exhibitors a place to sell." Estab. 1973. Annual indoor show held 2 days in December. Entries accepted until 4 weeks before show. Entry fee: $30/8x8 display area. Prejudging by slides or past shows; entry fee refunded for refused work. Work may be offered for sale; no commission. Craftworker must attend show; demonstrations OK. Registration limit: 70. Sponsor provides chairs; electricity for demonstrations; table, if reserved at registration time; and 24-hour security. Show is advertised by newspapers; radio; posters; and trade papers. 1977 show sales totalled $24,000. Considers all crafts except ceramics and decoupage.

H.O.M.E. FAIR, Box 408, Orland ME 04472. Chairperson: Pat Lundgren. Sponsor: Homeworkers Organized for More Employment. Estab. 1973. Annual outdoor show held 2 days in mid-August. Average attendance: 2,000+. Entry fee: $5/H.O.M.E. member; $15/nonmember; $2 additional for shade. Size of display area as needed. Work may be offered for sale; no commission. Craftworker needn't attend show; demonstrations OK. Registration limit: 80-100. Sponsor provides 24-hour security. Considers all crafts.
Promotion: Show is advertised by radio; TV; newspapers; and posters. "Greater emphasis will be placed on road signs to attract impulse tourist buying." Submit slides for TV promotion and glossies for newspaper press releases.

*KITTERY ART ASSOCIATION SIDEWALK SALE, 317 State Rd., Eliot ME 03903. Chairman: Carol Moreland. Purpose: to promote the arts. Annual outdoor show held 1 day in August. Entries accepted until 2 months before show; late entries accepted if room is available. Entry fee: $5/15x4 display area. Maximum 1 piece per artist for awards judging. Work may be offered for sale; no commission. Craftworker or representative must attend show; demonstrations OK. Registration limit: 60. Sponsor provides fencing. Show is advertised by newspapers; magazines; radio; TV; posters; and craftworker's organizations. Submit photo and promotional information. Presents cash and ribbon awards. Considers all crafts. Number paintings are not acceptable.

KITTERY ART ASSOCIATION'S WEEKEND EXHIBITS, c/o Jack Henson, 408 Ocean Ave., Portsmouth NH 03801. Annual exhibits held weekends from the first weekend of June to the last weekend of August at the Firehouse Gallery at Kittery Point, Maine. Work may be offered for sale. Considers all crafts by local craftworkers.

ROTARY CRAFTS FESTIVAL, Rotary Club of Portland, Maine, 157 High St., Portland ME 04101. (207)773-7157. Estab. 1975. Annual outdoor show held 1 day in July. Average attendance: 20,000+. Entries accepted until 4 weeks before show. Entry fee: $20/10' wide display area. Work may be offered for sale; no commission. Craftworker must attend show; demonstration OK. Registration limit: 225+. Sponsor provides table; 24-hour security; and liability insurance. Show is advertised by TV, Maine newspapers and craft magazines. Considers all crafts.

SEACOAST CRAFTS FAIR, Box 25, York ME 03909. (207)363-2397. Director: Rachel B. Grieg. Estab. 1967. Annual indoor show held 4 days in August. Average attendance: 3,000. Entries accepted until June 1. Entry fee: $20/8'x30" table space (table $4 extra). Prejudging by slides; photos; or actual work. Entry fee due after prejudging. Work may be offered for sale; no commission. Craftworker must attend show; demonstrations OK. Registration limit: 60-70. Sponsor provides chairs; coverings; electricity for demonstrations; and insurance on exhibited work. Show is advertised by TV; radio; newspapers; and posters. Considers all crafts made by New England craftworkers.

Maryland

*ACADEMY OF THE ARTS, South and Harrison Sts. (Box 605), Easton MD 21601. Contact: Curator. Annual show. Entries accepted until 1 week before show. No entry fee. Artists born in Maryland, residents of the state and Maryland students may participate. Work may be offered for sale; 20% sales commission. Awards $1,000 in prizes.
Acceptable Work: Considers multimedia; collage; ceramics; and metal and wood sculpture. Sculpture may not be impermanent material. Work must have been completed in last 2 years. No title may be changed after submission of entry card. Size limit: 62x62", 2-dimensional; 14' in total dimension; 150 lbs. Material must be shipped in crates so it can be returned.

ANNAPOLIS ARTS FESTIVAL, Box 228, Annapolis MD 21404. (301)267-7922. Executive Secretary: Kathy Greentree. Sponsor: Annapolis Fine Arts Foundation. Estab. 1962. Annual out-door show held 3 days in June. Average attendance: 25,000. Entries accepted until 3 months before show. Entry fee: "no fixed amount set at this time. Contact executive secretary to confirm. Full payment of fee due 1 month prior to show." Display area: 8x10 in tent. Prejudging by slides and photos. Entry fee due after prejudging. Work may be offered for sale; no commission. Craftworker must attend show; demonstrations OK. Registration limit: 54 craftworkers; 60 fence artists. Sponsor provides tent; electricity for demonstrations; and 24-hour security.
Acceptable Work: Considers batik; candlemaking; jewelry; leatherworking; macrame; metalsmithing; mobiles; pottery; sculpture; weaving; and woodcrafting.
Promotion: Show is advertised by radio; TV; newspapers; brochures; placemats; calendars; magazines; and books.

BIRD, ANIMAL, WILD FLOWERS AND DECOY SHOW, 475 Blackshire Rd., Severna Park MD 21146. (301)987-5052. President: Eunice Swann. Sponsor: Arts Show Association, Inc. Show is held in connection with National Audubon Society. Estab. 1977. Annual indoor show held 5 days in October. Average attendance: 100,000. Entries accepted until 2 weeks before show. Entry fee: $45/artist. Entries prejudged by slides and photos; entry fee refunded for refused work. Work may be offered for sale; no commission. Craftworker must attend show; demonstrations OK. Registration limit: 150. Sponsor provides electricity for demonstrations and 24-hour security. Show is advertised by newspaper ads; TV; and the National Audubon Society. Categories: paintings, all media; woodcarving; photography; etchings, scratchboard, pen and ink; ceramics and pottery; dimensionals; sculpture; and dried wildflowers, seeds and insects. Considers bird ceramics; needlecrafts; bird sculpture; and woodcrafting.

COLUMBIA MALL PROFESSIONAL ARTS FESTIVAL, Rt. 1, Box 153J, Auburn NH 03032. (603)483-2742. President: Jinx Harris. Estab. 1972. Semiannual indoor show held 4 days in January and August at Columbia, Maryland. Average attendance: 25,000+. Entries accepted until 1 week before show or until filled. Entry fee: $35/8x4 display area. Prejudging by slides or photos. "This is a limited craft show—careful selection of craft work." Work may be offered for sale; no commission. Craftworker must attend show; demonstrations OK. Registration limit: 30. Sponsor provides electricity for demonstrations and 24-hour security. Show is advertised by radio; TV; marquee; and post cards. Considers all crafts except ceramics; decoupage; lapidary; needlecrafts; and strung bead jewelry.

*COURTHOUSE ARTS FESTIVAL, 301 Washington Ave., Towson MD 21204. (301)494-3871. Recreation Program Coordinator: Martha F. Dearman. Sponsor: Baltimore County Department of Recreation and Parks. Purpose: "to give artists of all types a place to exhibit, compete for awards and sell their works of art in a pleasant, cultural atmosphere. And, to give people the opportunity to experience an enjoyable day with friends and to purchase original creative art works." Estab. 1951. Annual outdoor show held 1 day in June. Average attendance:

15,000-20,000. Entries accepted until 3 weeks before show. Entry fee: $12-15/10 feet wide display area. Work may be offered for sale; no commission. Craftworker must attend show; demonstration OK. Sponsor provides electricity for demonstrations. Categories: art; crafts; sculpture; photography; youth; and performing arts. All categories divided into professional and amateur. Considers all crafts. Presents 3 place ribbons plus $50, 1st prize; $25, 2nd prize; and $15, 3rd prize in the professional and amateur class.

Promotion: Show is advertised by radio; TV; all newspapers; listing in events calendars and monthly magazines; posters; letters of invitation; sponsorships of awards categories; and exhibits of artists and craftworkers and photographs in government headquarters. "Craftworker should supply resume; photo of artist at work and/or photos of works. Local artists may be requested to make personal appearance on radio or TV."

*CUMBERLAND VALLEY EXHIBITION, Box 423, Hagerstown MD 21740. (301)739-5727. Director: H. Paul Kotun. Sponsor: Washington County Museum of Fine Arts. Estab. 1932. Annual indoor show held during June. Average attendance: 5,200. Entries accepted until 2-3 weeks before show. Entry fee: $10/craftworker. Maximum 2 entries per craftworker. Work may be offered for sale; 20% commission. Open to residents and former residents of the Cumberland Valley region. Considers all art. Maximum size: 2-dimensional, 72x72". Two-dimensional work must be framed.

Awards: Presents $800 in cash prizes and $600 in purchase awards, 2-dimensional art; $200 in cash prizes and $100 in purchase awards, 3-dimensional art.

*FELL'S POINT FUN FESTIVAL, 804 S. Broadway, Baltimore MD 21231. (301)675-6756. Festival Chairman: Mary T. Geeson. Sponsor: Society for the Preservation of Federal Hill and Fell's Point. Estab. 1967. Annual outdoor show held 2 days in the fall. Average attendance: 170,-000. Entries accepted until 2 weeks before show. Entry fee: $20/10 ft. display area. "There is also a large flea market at $25/20'." Work may be offered for sale; no commission. Craftworker or representative must attend show; demonstrations OK. Registration limit: 200. Sponsor provides electricity for 20 exhibitors. Categories: art; arts and crafts; photography; flea market; and neighborhood collectibles. Considers all crafts except sculpture. Presents ribbons and certificates of award in all categories.

Sales Tips: "Traditional works sell best. In craft, work quality and originality are a must. This show usually is very trendy and, since it is the last outdoor one of the season, followers of these shows come and purchase hoping that the artist has lowered prices."

Promotion: Show is advertised by newspapers; TV; interviews; listing in *Maryland Happenings;* radio; and tourist information brochure.

FREDERICK CRAFT FAIR, National Crafts Ltd., Gapland MD 21736. (301)432-8438. Director: Noel Clark. Estab. 1975. Annual indoor/outdoor show held 1 day wholesale and 3 days retail at Frederick, Maryland, in June. Average attendance: 30,000. Entries accepted until the second week in March. Booth fee: $85-125/display area; $3 non-refundable application fee. Entries prejudged by 5-10 35mm color slides. Work may be offered for sale; no commission. Craftworker must attend show; demonstrations OK. Registration limit: 500. Sponsor provides electricity for demonstrations and 24-hour security. Considers all crafts.

Promotion: Show is advertised by newspapers; magazines; radio; TV; posters; brochures; and mailings to wholesale buyers.

GERMAN AMERICAN DAY, 1215 Hillside Rd., Pasadena MD 21122. (301)437-2068. General Chairman: Kurt P. Kuenzel Sr. Sponsor: German-American Citizen Union of Maryland. Purpose: "to keep the German ethnic groups together and show the American public what we can do. Also to create interest in our heritage." Estab. 1900. Annual outdoor show (stands will have small cover or roof) held 2 days in August. Average attendance: 140,000. Entries accepted until 4 weeks before show. Display area: 8x8 or multiples by 8' front; accepts 3 craftworkers/8' table. Work may be offered for sale; 15% commission. Craftworker must attend show; demonstration OK. Sponsor provides chairs; covering; electricity for demonstrations; fencing; table; and 24-hour security. Show is advertised by radio; TV; newspapers; flyers and state of Maryland.

Acceptable Work: Considers candlemaking; ceramics; leatherworking; needlecrafts; sculpture; soft sculpture; weaving; and woodcrafting.

JONATHAN HAGER FRONTIER CRAFT DAY, Court House Annex, Washington County Tourism, Hagerstown MD 21740. (301)791-3130. Director: Betty Jane Bupp. Estab. 1972. Annual outdoor show held 1 day in summer. Average attendance: 2,500-3,000. Entries accepted 6 months in advance. Work may be offered for sale; no commission. Craftworker must attend show; demonstrations OK. Registration limit: 25-30. Sponsor provides picnic size table.

Acceptable Work: Considers candlemaking; dollmaking; leatherworking; needlecrafts; pottery; weaving; and woodcrafting. Must be colonial or pioneer type.

Sales Tip: "Since this show is pioneer and colonial in concept we advise all participants to keep in mind that items for sale and merchandising of them is in the same way— loose and simple."

Promotion: Show is advertised by more than 250 newspapers; radio; TV; news releases; interviews; special features; and tourist publications. Submit b&w photo of action demonstrations, exhibits or specific details; if artist is unique, a detailed history of art and background; and for special interviews and programs some visuals will be required.

Wholesale craft markets, such as the Frederick Craft Fair, Frederick, Maryland, are excellent means of meeting craft shop and gallery owners, as well as getting wholesale and retail orders. The Frederick show, held 1 wholesale and 3 retail days in early June, averaged $2,500 sales per booth in 1977. Approximately 30,000 persons annually view the 500 booths.

"HANDS OF MAN" SHOW & SALE, Rt. 1, Box 153J, Auburn NH 03032. (603)483-2742. President: Jinx Harris. Estab. 1978. Annual indoor show held 3 days in December at Baltimore. Average attendance: 75,000+. Entries accepted until 1 week before show or until filled. Entry fee: $35/8x4 display area. Prejudging by slides or photos if not in a previous show. Work may be offered for sale; no commission. Craftworker must attend show; demonstrations OK. Registration limit: 170. Sponsor provides electricity for demonstrations and 24-hour security. Show is advertised by radio; TV; and newspapers. Considers all crafts except ceramics; decoupage under $5; lapidary; and strung bead jewelry.

JEWISH COMMUNITY CENTER'S CRAFT SALE, 5700 Park Heights Ave., Baltimore MD 21215. (301)542-4900. Director of Fine Arts: Freda Friedman. Estab. 1973. Annual indoor show held 2 days in October. Average attendance: 4,000. Entries accepted until 3 weeks before show. Entry fee: $50/12x6 display area. Prejudging for new craftworkers by photos, slides; entry fee refunded for refused work. Work may be offered for sale; no commission. Craftworker must attend show; demonstrations OK. Sponsor provides chairs; display panels; electricity for demonstrations; table; and 24-hour security. Show is advertised by 12,000 mailed announcements; large banners; billboards; and advertisements. Considers all crafts except decoupage and dollmaking.

MARYLAND CRAFT FESTIVAL, Sugarloaf Mountain Works, Inc., Box 319, Poolesville MD 20837. (301)279-7551. Director: Deann Verdier. Purpose: "to provide the ideal marketplace for the public to purchase unique, original arts and crafts directly from their creators and to provide the independent professional art and crafts people with a means to sell their goods." Estab. 1977. Annual indoor show held 3 days in mid-October at the Maryland State Fairgrounds near Baltimore. Approximate attendance: 10,000 paid. Entries accepted until 10 weeks before show date. Entry fee: $85/8x10 display area. Prejudging by 4 slides representative of work to be displayed; entry fee refunded for refused work. Work must be offered for sale; no commission. Craftworker must attend show; demonstrations encouraged. Registration limit: 175. Sponsor provides chairs at $1 each; electricity for demonstrations and lighting at $5/300 watts; tables at $3 each; and 24-hour security. "Maryland sales tax people will be present at the show to provide temporary sales tax licenses (free) to all who need them."
Acceptable Work: Considers batik; candlemaking; ceramics (none made from commercial molds); dollmaking ("only the very best"); glass art; jewelry; leatherworking; macrame; metalsmithing; mobiles; pottery; sculpture; soft sculpture; weaving; and woodcrafting. "All work must be completely finished."
Promotion: "We purchase advertising throughout the Baltimore metropolitan area in printed and broadcast media. The paid advertising is supplemented with a direct mail campaign to known art and craft buyers in the area plus much public relations work. B&w photos of artists' work and studio are helpful. Resumes are also helpful for public relations."

MARYLAND OKTOBERFEST INC., 1215 Hillside Rd., Pasadena MD 21122. (301)437-2068. General Chairman: Kurt P. Kuenzel Sr. Purpose: "to keep the German ethnic groups together and show the American public what we can do. Also to create interest in our hertiage." Estab. 1969. Annual indoor show held 3 days in October. Average attendance: 15,000. Entries accepted until 4 weeks before show. Display area: 8x8 or multiples by 8' front; accepts 3 craftworkers/8' table. Work may be offered for sale; 15% commission. Craftworker must attend show; demonstrations OK. Sponsor provides chairs; coverings; electricity for demonstrations; table; and 24-hour security.
Acceptable Work: Considers candlemaking; ceramics; leatherworking; needlecrafts; sculpture; soft sculpture; weaving; and woodcrafting.
Promotion: Show is advertised by radio; TV; newspapers; and flyers. Photos can be used for advance promotion.

*MILLION DOLLAR MILE ART SHOW, Box 174, Havre de Grace MD 21078. (301)939-2329. Chairman: Marge Thompson. Sponsor: Soroptimist International Club. Estab. 1963. Annual outdoor show held 2 days in August. Average attendance: 25,000-30,000. Entries accepted until 3 weeks before show. Entry fee: $25/12-14 feet. Work may be offered for sale; no commission. Craftworker must attend show; demonstrations OK. Registration limit: 400. Sponsor provides chairs; fencing; table; and 24-hour security. Presents cash awards of $2,000; ribbons for 1st; 2nd; 3rd; 4th; and honorary. Submit anything that can be used to publicize the show.
Acceptable Work: Considers batik; candlemaking; ceramics; glass art; jewelry; leatherworking; macrame; metalsmithing; pottery; scultpure; weaving; and woodcrafting.

NATIONAL CRAFT FAIR, National Crafts Ltd., Gapland MD 21736. (301)432-8438. Director: Noel Clark. Estab. 1976. Annual indoor/outdoor show is held in October in Gaithersburg, Maryland. Average attendance: 15,000. Entries are prejudged by 5 35mm color slides. Work may be offered for sale; no commission. Craftworker must attend show; demonstrations OK. Registration limit: 400. Sponsor provides electricity for demonstrations in some booths. Considers all crafts.
Promotion: Show is advertised by newspapers; magazines; radio; posters; brochures; TV; and mailing to National Wholesale Buyer List.

PARK ARTS FESTIVAL, Box 1294, Hagerstown MD 21740. (301)791-4235. President: Mrs. Cynthia L. Staggers. Sponsor: Washington County Arts Council, Inc. Estab. 1968. Annual outdoor show is held 2 days in June. Average attendance: 10,000-15,000. Entries accepted until 3 weeks before show. Entry fee: $15/artist. Display area: space provided as necessary. Entries prejudged by slides; color photos; and personal observation whenever possible. Entry fee refunded for refused work. Work may be offered for sale; no commission. Craftworker must attend show; demonstrations OK. Registration limit: 50. Sponsor provides electricity for demonstrations; fencing; table; and 24-hour security protection. Show is advertised by newspapers; radio; TV; and brochures. Considers all crafts.

*PREAKNESS FESTIVAL, c/o Art & Craft Education Inc., 475 Blackshire Rd., Severna Park MD 21146. Contact: Eunice Swann. Annual show held at Hopkins Hospital. Entry fee: $25. Craftworkers must attend and wear colonial costumes. Registration limit: 200. Considers all crafts. Presents awards and ribbons. No commission.

REVOLUTIONARY WAR DAYS, Tri-County Council for Southern Maryland, Box 301, Waldorf MD 20601. (301)645-2693. Tourism Planner: Clara L. Wooddy. Purpose: "to attract visitors into southern Maryland; to promote in general the history of southern Maryland and in particular the role that General William Smallwood played in the Revolutionary War and traditional craftsmen and their art." Estab. 1967. Annual outdoor show (with tents and pavilions) held 2 days at Smallwood State Park, Rison, Maryland the 1st weekend in May. Average attendance: 12,000. Entries accepted until 4 weeks before show. Display area: 8x10 encasements. Prejudging by minimum of 3 35mm slides and resume. Work may be offered for sale; no commission. Craftworker must attend show; demonstrations required. Registration limit: 100. Sponsor provides chairs; electricity for demonstrations; fencing; table; 24-hour security; breakfast reception; and group hotel rates.
Acceptable Work: Considers batik; candlemaking; decoupage; dollmaking; glass art; jewelry; lapidary; leatherworking; metalsmithing; needlecrafts; pottery; tole painting; weaving; woodcrafting; and any other traditional 18th century craft. "Craftsmen must demonstrate some facet of work and dress in costume. Craftsmen must provide all display material, i.e, pegboard, shelving."
Sales Tip: "Over the years we have established a reputation for producing a craft show which features traditional, hand-made crafts. Buyers come prepared to make major purchases. However, it is wise to have a selection of items for the modest buyers, i.e., under $10."
Promotion: Show is advertised by paid advertising (print only); public service announcements; press releases; feature stories; and Maryland Center for Public Broadcasting. If available craftworker should provide 35mm slides and b&w 8x10 glossies of craftworker *at work*.

SPRING ARTS & CRAFTS FAIR, Sugarloaf Mountain Works, Inc., Box 319, Poolesville MD 20837. (301)279-7551. Director: Deann Verdier. "Show is held to provide the public an opportunity to purchase original arts and crafts directly from their creators and to provide the independent artist or craftsperson an ideal marketplace for his/her products." Estab. 1976. Annual indoor show held 3 days in April at Gaithersburg, Maryland. Entries accepted until 10 weeks before show. Entry fee: $85/8x10 display area. Prejudging by 4 slides to be submitted with application; entry fee refunded for refused work. Work must be offered for sale; no commission. Craftworker must attend show; demonstrations encouraged. Registration limit: about 200. Sponsor provides chairs for $1 each; electricity for demonstrations and lighting for $5/300 watts; table for $3; and 24-hour security. "Maryland sales tax agents will provide temporary sales tax licenses free to all who need them at the show."
Acceptable Work: Considers batik; candlemaking; ceramics (none made by commerical molds); dollmaking ("only the very best"); glass art; jewelry; leatherworking; macrame; metalsmithing; mobiles; pottery; sculpture; soft sculpture; weaving; woodcrafting; and other unique crafts.
Promotion: "The show is promoted widely throughout the Washington DC metropolitan area media. Paid advertising is supplemented with an extensive direct mail campaign to thousands of area craft and fine arts fanciers. Resumes and b&w photos are very helpful. Photos of craftspeople in studios are also helpful."

SPRING CRAFT FESTIVAL, Sugarloaf Mountain Works, Inc., Box 319, Poolesville MD 20837. (301)279-7551. Director: Deann Verdier. Purpose: "to provide the ideal marketplace for the public to purchase unique, original arts and crafts directly from their creators and to provide the independent professional art and crafts people with a means to sell their goods." Estab. 1978. Annual indoor/outdoor show held 4 days during Memorial Day weekend at Baltimore. Approximate attendance: 10,000 paid. Entries accepted until 10 weeks before show. Entry fee: $75/9x12 display area. Prejudging by 4 slides representative of work to be displayed; entry fee refunded for refused work. Work must be offered for sale; no commission. Craftworker must attend show; demonstrations encouraged. Registration limit: 200. Sponsor provides chairs at $1 each; electricity for demonstrations and lighting at $5/300 watts; tables at $3 each; and 24-hour security. "Maryland sales tax people will be present at the show to provide temporary sales tax licenses (free) to all who need them."
Acceptable Work: Considers batik; candlemaking; ceramics (none made from commercial molds); dollmaking ("only the very best"); glass art; jewelry; leatherworking; macrame;

metalsmithing; mobiles; pottery; sculpture; soft sculpture; weaving; and woodcrafting. "All work must be completely finished."

Promotion: "We purchase advertising throughout the Baltimore metropolitan area in printed and broadcast media. The paid advertising is supplemented with a direct mail campaign to known art and craft buyers in the area plus much public relations work. B&w photos of artists' work and studio are helpful. Resumes are also helpful for public relations."

WINTER MARKET OF AMERICAN CRAFTS, Box 10, New Paltz NY 12561. (914)255-0039. Sponsor: American Craft Enterprises, Inc. Purpose: "(1) to provide professional craftsperson living East of the Mississippi River an exposition of high quality, (2) to provide buyers who purchase handmade objects for resale purposes a market place scheduled at a time of year which will accommodate summer and fall buying schedules, (3) to encourage professional craftsperson from diverse geographic areas and various craft traditions to come together in 1 place to stimulate the interchange of ideas and enthusiasm, and (4) to offer the general public an opportunity to see crafts, and to give all visitors a better understanding of the American craft movement." Estab. 1977. Annual indoor show held 5 days (2 trade days; 3 public days) in February at Baltimore, Maryland. Average attendance: 25,000. Entries accepted up until October 1 of previous year. Entry fee: first floor $160/8x8; $240/8x12; $320/8x16; $480/8x24. Second floor $96/8x8; $144/8x12; $192/8x16; $288/8x24. Entries prejudged by 5 2x2 color slides; $5 nonrefundable prejudging fee. Entry fee due after prejudging. Work must be offered for sale; no commission. Craftworker must attend show; no demonstration. Registration limit: 340. Sponsor provides electricity and 24-hour security; not responsible for damage, theft, or loss of an individual's work. Considers all crafts, including handmade musical instruments. No tole painting and decoupage. 1977 exhibitor sales totalled approximately $1,000,000. Show is advertised by multimedia press releases and advertising in local and major publications.

Massachusetts

*ALL ARTS FESTIVAL, Quinebaug Valley Cultural Center, Box 503, Southbridge MA 01550. (617)764-3341. General Chairman: Christine O'Brien. Sponsor: Quinebaug Valley Council for the Arts and Humanities. Purpose: to promote cultural endeavors. Estab. 1978. Annual indoor/outdoor show (juried show is indoors) held 3 days in May. Entries accepted until 2 weeks before show for reserved registration; entries accepted up until show, space permitting. Entry fee: $10/QVCAH member; $12/nonmember. Display area: 10'. Prejudging for juried show. Work may be offered for sale; no commission. Craftworker or representative must attend show; demonstrations encouraged. Sponsor provides fencing on reserved basis only. Show is advertised by all media. Submit resumes and any promotional information with application. Presents cash awards and ribbons. Considers all crafts. No dealers.

THE BERKSHIRE CRAFTS FAIR, Stockbridge MA 01262. Director: Paul J. Gibbons. Estab. 1973. Annual indoor show held 3 days in August at Great Barrington, Massachusetts. Average attendance: 3,000-5,000/day. Entries accepted until 4 months before show. Entry fee: $60/8x10 display area. Prejudging by 5 2x2 slides; $3 application fee. No entry fees refunded for refused work. Work may be offered for sale; no commission. Craftworker or representative must attend show; demonstrations OK. Registration limit: 96. Sponsor provides chairs; display panels; electricity for demonstrations; insurance on exhibited work; table; and 24-hour security. Show is advertised in all media. Considers all crafts including paper making, but decoupage; shell or button jewelry; silkscreening; lapidary and tole painting. 1977 show sales totalled $100,000+.

BURLINGTON MALL CHILDREN'S HOUR SHOW, Rt. 1, Box 153J, Auburn NH 03032. (603)483-2742. President: Jinx Harris. Estab. 1976. Annual indoor show held 5 days in August at Burlington, Massachusetts. Average attendance: 75,000+. Entries accepted until 1 week before show or until filled. Entry fee: $35/8x4 display area. Prejudging by slides or photos. Work may be offered for sale; no commission. Craftworker must attend show; demonstrations OK. Registration limit: 75-80. Sponsor provides electricity for demonstrations and 24-hour security. Show is promoted by radio; TV; and newspaper. Considers all child-oriented crafts except ceramics; decoupage under $5; lapidary; and strung bead jewelry.

BURLINGTON MALL PROFESSIONAL CRAFT AND SCULPTURE SHOW, Rt. 1, Box 153J, Auburn NH 03032. (603)483-2742. President: Jinx E. Harris. Estab. 1974. Annual indoor show held 4 days in January at Burlington, Massachusetts. Average attendance: 65,000+. Entries accepted until 1 week before show. Entry fee: $35/8x4 display area. Prejudging by slides or photos. Work may be offered for sale; no commission. Craftworker must attend show; demonstrations OK. Registration limit: 120+. Sponsor provides electricity for demonstrations and 24-hour security. Show is advertised by radio; TV; and newspaper. Considers all crafts except ceramics; decoupage; lapidary; needlecrafts; or strung bead jewelry.

*CHATHAM FESTIVAL OF THE ARTS, Box 368, Chatham MA 02633. Sponsor: Creative Arts Center. Estab. 1971. Annual show held outdoors 3 days in August. Average attendance: 10,000. Entries juried in April. Entry fee: $45/100 square feet. Prejudging by slides; if local, by samples. Entry fee refunded for refused work. Work may be offered for sale; no commission. Craftworker must attend show; demonstrations OK. Registration limit: 100. Sponsor provides fencing; 24-hour security; catering service; and volunteers as aides. Show is advertised by newspaper; flyers; radio; and TV. Presents 6 cash awards of $50. Considers all crafts except candlemaking; decoupage; and tole painting.

THE CHRISTMAS FAIR AT PROJECT, Project, Inc., 141 Huron Ave., Cambridge MA 02138. (617)491-0187. Executive Director: Sandy Schafer. Estab. 1969. Annual show held indoors 2 weeks in December. Average attendance: 1,000. Entries accepted until show date. No entry fee. Prejudging by slides; photos; or actual work. Work may be offered for sale; 30% commission. Craftworker needn't attend show; demonstration OK. Show is advertised by mailing lists; public relations lists; and paid advertising. Considers all crafts but decoupage; needlecrafts; and tole painting. 1977 show sales totalled $7,000.

*CRAFT ADVENTURE, 1305 Memorial Ave., West Springfield MA 01089. (413)732-2361. Director: Helen H. Bardwell. Sponsor: Eastern States Exposition. Purpose: "to carry on the tradition of creative handicrafts in America, to stimulate interest in good design and well-executed workmanship and encourage creative and original work." Estab. early 1950's. Annual indoor show held 1 day in September; "all winning entries displayed duration of 12-day Fair." Average attendance: 800. Entries accepted until 3 weeks before show. Maximum 2 pieces/craftworker. Craftworker needn't attend show. Sponsor provides insurance on exhibited work and 24-hour security. Show is advertised by brochures; TV; press; local ads; and posters. Considers macrame; needlecrafts; woodcrafting; rugs; needlepoint; crewel; and weaving.
Awards: Presents $10 1st prize and ribbon; $7 2nd prize and ribbon; $5 third prize and ribbon; and honorable mention ribbon. Also presents The Judges Choice Trophy; Best of Show Exposition Rosette; and special awards given by craft designers and supplier.

CRAFT FAIR, 36 Hammond St., Acton MA 01720. (617)263-7243. Show Director: William N. Clark. Estab. 1977. Annual indoor show held 2 days in November at Andover, Massachusetts. Entries accepted up until show date. Entry fee: $50-100/display area. Prejudging by slides and photos. Work may be offered for sale; no commission. Craftworker or representative must attend show; demonstrations OK. Registration limit: 50. Sponsor provides electricity for demonstrations; table; and 24-hour security. Considers all crafts.
Promotion: Show is advertised by newspaper; radio; and news releases. Submit b&w glossy; if accepted for general advertising, a negative and short biography will be requested.

CRAFT FAIR, 36 Hammond St., Acton MA 01720. (617)263-7243. Show Director: William N. Clark. Estab. 1977. Annual indoor show held 2 days in November at Boxborough, Massachusetts. Entries accepted up until show date. Entry fee: $50-100/display area. Prejudging by slides and photos. Work may be offered for sale; no commission. Craftworker or representative must attend show; demonstrations OK. Registration limit: 100. Sponsor provides electricity for demonstrations; table; and 24-hour security. Considers all crafts.
Promotion: Show is advertised by newspaper; radio; and news releases. Submit b&w glossy; if accepted for general advertising, a negative and short biography will be requested.

EASTFIELD MALL ARTS FESTIVAL, Rt. 1, Box 153J, Auburn NH 03032. (603)483-2742. President: Jinx Harris. Estab. 1968. Annual indoor show held 4 days in February at Springfield, Massachusetts. Average attendance: 40,000+. Entries accepted until 1 week before show or until filled. Entry fee: $35/8x4 display area. Prejudging by slides or photos if not in a previous show. Work may be offered for sale; no commission. Craftworker must attend show; demonstrations OK. Registration limit: 30. Sponsor provides electricity for demonstrations and 24-hour security. Show is advertised by radio; TV; and newspaper. Considers all crafts except ceramics; decoupage under $5; lapidary; and strung bead jewelry.

FALL ARTS AND CRAFTS MARKET, 361 Washington St., Brookline MA 02146. (717)734-0100. President: Susan Radonsky. Secretary: Judy Jackson. Sponsor: Brookline Art Society. Estab. 1950. Annual outdoor show held 1 day in September at Chestnut Hill, Massachusetts. Average attendance: 1,000-2,000. Entries accepted until 2 weeks before show. Entry fee:

$15/10x6 display area. Work may be offered for sale; no commission. Craftworker must attend show; demonstrations encouraged. Registration limit: 60. Sponsor provides security. Show is advertised by newspapers; flyers; posters; radio; and *Boston* magazine. Considers all crafts.

LIBERTY TREE MALL CHILDREN'S HOUR SHOW, Rt. 1, Box 153J, Auburn NH 03032. (603)483-2742. President: Jinx Harris. Estab. 1977. Annual indoor show held 4 days in June at Danvers, Massachusetts. Average attendance: 50,000+. Entries accepted until 1 week before show or until filled. Entry fee: $35/8x4 display area. Prejudging by slides or photos if not in a previous show. Work may be offered for sale; no commission. Craftworker must attend show; demonstrations OK. Registration limit: 60. Sponsor provides electricity for demonstrations and 24-hour security. Show is advertised by radio; TV; and newspaper. Considers all child-oriented crafts except ceramics, decoupage under $5; lapidary; and strung bead jewelry.

LONDONDERRY FAIRE, Rt. 1, Box 153J, Auburn NH 03032. (603)483-2742. President: Jinx Harris. Estab. 1974. Annual indoor show held 3 days in November at Boston, Massachusetts. Average attendance: 75,000+. Entries accepted until 1 week before show or until filled. Entry fee: $35/8x4 display area. Prejudging by slides or photos if not in a previous show. Work may be offered for sale; no commission. Craftworker must attend show; demonstrations OK. Registration limit: 170. Sponsor provides electricity for demonstrations and 24-hour security. Show is advertised by radio; TV; and newspapers. Considers all crafts except ceramics; decoupage under $5; lapidary; and strung bead jewelry.

MARBLEHEAD CHAMBER OF COMMERCE CRAFT SHOW, Box 76, 62 Pleasant St., Marblehead MA 01945. Executive Director: Dorthy Richardson. Purpose: to "provide opportunity for serious craftpersons to develop a market for their products that might lead to resale contact or local store outlet." Estab. 1976. Annual outdoor show held 1 day in summer. Average attendance. 4,000. Entries accepted until 4 weeks before show. Display area: 15x20. Prejudging by description and reputation; entry fee refunded for refused work. Work may be offered for sale; no commission. Craftworker needn't attend show; demonstrations OK. Show is advertised by local newspaper ads; professional PR and flyers; and local posters. Considers all crafts.

MARTHA'S VINEYARD CRAFTSMEN FAIR, c/o Ayn Chase, Box 1207, Wesley House Hotel, Oak Bluffs MA 02557. (617)693-0134. Manager: Ayn Chase. Purpose: "The show is designed mainly for Martha's Vineyard Island craftsmen. It is kept small and 1 or more crafts is represented by each craftsman. Many crafts are displayed and sold." Estab. 1968. Annual indoor show held 3 days in July. Average attendance: 3,000-5,000. Entry fee: $16.50/3x5 display area; $26.50/3x10 display area. SASE with inquiry. Work may be offered for sale; no commission. Craftworker must attend show; demonstrations OK. Registration limit: 12-15. Sponsor provides chairs; display panels; electricity for demonstrations; insurance on exhibited work; table; and 24-hour security. Show is advertised by newspapers; radio; Cape Cod advertising; posters; and flyers. Considers all crafts. 1977 show sales totalled $8,000.

***MATTOON ARTS FESTIVAL**, Box 3274, Springfield MA 01105. (413)737-0645. Co-Chairman: Sue Webster. Sponsor: Mattoon Street Preservation Association. Estab. 1975. Annual outdoor show held 2 days in September. Average attendance: 15,000. Entries accepted until June 1. Entry fee: $25/10x10 display area. Prejudging by slides; entry fee refunded for refused work. Work may be offered for sale; no commission. Craftworker must attend show; demonstrations OK. Registration limit: 90. Sponsor provides fencing if needed; insurance on exhibited work; and security protection. Show is advertised by local and regional media. Submit promotional materials at request of Committee. Categories: fine arts and crafts. Considers all crafts.

MOUNT HOLYOKE COLLEGE PEDDLER'S FAIR, c/o Show Chairman, South Hadley MA 01075. Sponsor: Mount Holyoke Sophomore Class. Purpose: "originally designed as part of Sophomore Arts Weekend, the show has now become a college tradition." Estab. 1970. Annual indoor show held 1 day in December. Average attendance: 1,500+. Entry applications sent to craftworkers by May; deadline, early September. Entry fee: $20. Display area: 3x8 table, larger upon request. Prejudging by application; slides; and/or past participation. SASE. Entry fee due after prejudging. Work may be offered for sale; no commission. Craftworker or representative must attend show; demonstrations encouraged. Registration limit: 70. Sponsor provides chairs; electricity for demonstrations; table; security during show; student help; and snack bar. Show is advertised by posters; college news; local newspapers; and radio. Show participants given news release to submit to their area media. "Any promotional work done by artist on his own is greatly appreciated." Considers all crafts.

NATICK MALL CHILDREN'S HOUR SHOW, Rt. 1, Box 153J, Auburn NH 03032. (603)483-2742. President: Jinx Harris. Estab. 1977. Annual indoor show held 4 days in April at Natick, Massachusetts. Average attendance: 50,000+. Entries accepted until 1 week before show or until filled. Entry fee: $35/8x4 display area. Prejudging by slides or photos if not in a previous show. Work may be offered for sale; no commission. Craftworker must attend show; demonstrations OK. Registration limit: 50. Sponsor provides electricity for demonstrations and 24-hour security. Show is advertised by radio; TV; and newspapers. Considers all child-oriented crafts but ceramics; decoupage under $5; lapidary; and strung bead jewelry.

NATICK MALL CRAFT AND SCULPTURE SHOW, Rt. 1, Box 153J, Auburn NH 03032. (603)483-2742. President: Jinx Harris. Estab. 1975. Annual indoor show held 4 days in July at Natick, Massachusetts. Average attendance: 60,000+. Entries accepted until 1 week before show or until filled. Entry fee: $35/8x4 display area. Prejudging by slides or photos if not in a previous show. Work may be offered for sale; no commission. Craftworker must attend show; demonstrations OK. Registration limit: 100. Sponsor provides electricity for demonstrations and 24-hour security. Show is advertised by radio; TV; and newspapers. Considers all crafts except ceramics; decoupage under $5; lapidary; and strung bead jewelry.

NEW ENGLAND BUYERS' MARKET PLACE, 205 N. Main St., Concord NH 03301. (603)224-3375. Coordinator: Peter M. Solomon. Purpose: "to provide professional craftpersons in the New England area an event of high quality in which to participate and sell their work. This show will be a wholesale only show." Estab. 1977. Annual indoor show held 3 days in April at Boston. Average attendance: 500-1,000. Entries accepted until October. Entry fee: approximately $100/10x10 display area. Prejudging by 5 slides, application form and $5 prejudging fee; entry fee due after prejudging. Work may be offered for sale; no commission. Craftworker must attend show; no demonstrations. Registration limit: 275-300. Show is advertised by craft publications; press releases; and direct mail campaign to 5,000+ buyers across the country. Considers all crafts produced by craftworkers from Maine, Massachusetts, Vermont and New Hampshire. 1977 exhibit sales exceeded $500,000.

NORTHSHORE PLAZA ARTS FESTIVAL, Rt. 1, Box 153J, Auburn NH 03032. (603)483-2742. President: Jinx Harris. Estab. 1977. Annual indoor show held 4 days in May at Peabody, Massachusetts. Average attendance: 60,000+. Entries accepted until 1 week before show or until filled. Entry fee: $35/8x4 display area. Prejudging by slides or photos if not in a previous show. Work may be offered for sale; no commission. Craftworker must attend show; demonstrations OK. Registration limit: 40. Sponsor provides electricity for demonstrations and 24-hour security. Show is advertised by radio; TV; and newspapers. Considers all crafts except ceramics; decoupage under $5; lapidary; and strung bead jewelry.

NORTHSHORE PLAZA CHILDREN'S HOUR SHOW, Rt. 1, Box 153J, Auburn NH 03032. (603)483-2742. President: Jinx Harris. Estab. 1978. Annual indoor show held 4 days in February at Peabody, Massachusetts. Entries accepted until 1 week before show or until filled. Entry fee: $35/8x4 display area. Prejudging by slides or photos if not in a previous show. Work may be offered for sale; no commission. Demonstrations OK. Registration limit: 60. Sponsor provides electricity for demonstration and 24-hour security. Show is advertised by radio; TV; and newspapers. Considers all child-oriented crafts except ceramics; decoupage under $5; lapidary; and strung bead jewelry.

OLD DEERFIELD CRAFT FAIR, c/o Memorial Hall Museum, Deerfield MA 01342. (413)773-8929. Contact: Tim Neumann. Estab. 1976. Semiannual outdoor show held 2 days in July and 2 days in October. Average attendance: 10,000. Entries accepted up until show date. Entry fee: $25/10x10 display area. Prejudging by 3 slides or photos; entry fee refunded for refused work. Work may be offered for sale; no commission. Craftworker must attend show; demonstrations OK. Registration limit: 80. Show is advertised by radio and newspapers. Considers all crafts.

*PEMBROKE ARTS FESTIVAL, 48 Congress St., Pembroke MA 02359. Contact: Ann Wilcox. Entry fee: $3/entry. Considers sculpture. Open to New England artists only. Work may be offered for sale; 30% commission. Presents $150, $100 and $50 cash prizes; $100 in purchase prizes; and a $50 popular prize.

PRUDENTIAL CENTER CHILDREN'S HOUR SHOW, Rt. 1, Box 153J, Auburn NH 03032. (603)483-2742. President: Jinx Harris. Estab. 1976. Annual indoor show held 4 days in June at Boston, Massachusetts. Average attendance: 60,000+. Entries accepted until 1 week before show or until filled. Entry fee: $35/8x4 display area. Prejudging by slides or photos if not in a previous show. Work may be offered for sale; no commission. Craftworker must attend show; demonstrations OK. Registration limit: 100. Sponsor provides electricity for demonstrations and 24-hour security. Show is advertised by radio; TV; and newspapers. Considers all child-oriented crafts except ceramics; decoupage under $5; lapidary; and strung bead jewelry.

PRUDENTIAL CENTER CRAFT AND SCULPTURE SHOW, Rt. 1, Box 153J, Auburn NH 03032. (603)483-2742. President: Jinx Harris. Estab. 1974. Annual indoor show held 4 days in September at Boston, Massachusetts. Average attendance: 80,000+. Entries accepted until 1 week before show or until filled. Entry fee: $35/8x4 display area. Prejudging by slides or photos if not in a previous show. Work may be offered for sale; no commission. Craftworker must attend show; demonstrations OK. Registration limit: 100. Sponsor provides electricity for demonstrations and 24-hour security. Show is advertised by radio; TV; and newspapers. Considers all crafts except ceramics; decoupage under $5; lapidary; and strung bead jewelry.

SOUTH SHORE PLAZA CHILDREN'S HOUR SHOW, Rt. 1, Box 153J, Auburn NH 03032. (603)483-2742. President: Jinx Harris. Estab. 1977. Annual indoor show held 4 days in November at Braintree, Massachusetts. Average attendance: 60,000+. Entries accepted until 1 week before show or until filled. Entry fee: $35/8x4 display area. Prejudging by slides or photos if not in a previous show. Work may be offered for sale; no commission. Craftworker must attend show; demonstrations OK. Registration limit: 70+. Sponsor provides electricity for demonstrations and 24-hour security. Show is advertised by radio; TV; and newspapers. Considers all child-oriented crafts except ceramics; decoupage under $5; lapidary; and strung bead jewelry.

SOUTH SHORE PLAZA FIBER FAIR, Rt. 1, Box 153J, Auburn NH 03032. (603)483-2742. President: Jinx Harris. Estab. 1978. Annual indoor show held 4 days in August at Braintree, Massachusetts. Average attendance: 70,000+. Entries accepted until 1 week before show or until filled. Entry fee: $35/8x4 display area. Prejudging by slides or photos if not in a previous show. Work may be offered for sale; no commission. Craftworker must attend show; demonstrations OK. Registration limit: 50. Sponsor provides electricity for demonstrations and 24-hour security. Show is advertised by radio; TV; and newspaper. Considers batik; dollmaking; macrame; mobiles; needlecrafts; soft sculpture; weaving; and all crafts of fiber or combined with fibers.

SOUTH SHORE PLAZA WOODEN WAY SHOW, Rt. 1, Box 153J, Auburn NH 03032. (603)483-2742. President: Jinx Harris. Estab. 1978. Annual indoor show held 4 days in June at Braintree, Massachusetts. Average attendance: 60,000+. Entries accepted until 1 week before show or until filled. Entry fee: $35/8x4 display area. Prejudging by slides or photos if not in a previous show. Work may be offered for sale; no commission. Craftworker must attend show; demonstrations OK. Registration limit: 100. Sponsor provides electricity for demonstrations and 24-hour security protection. Show is advertised by radio; TV; and newspaper. Considers wood crafts only.

Michigan

ALGONAC ART FAIR, Box 422, Algonac MI 48001. (313)794-5296, after 6. Artist Chairman: Vonnie Breck. Sponsor: Algonac Sponsors of the Arts. Purpose: "to stimulate the cultural climate of our community and give good artists of the surrounding areas an outlet for their art." Estab. 1973. Annual outdoor show (with parachutes for cover, color, and attention) held 2 days Labor Day weekend. Average attendance: 5,000. Entries accepted until 2 weeks before show. Entry fee: $15/10x10 display area. Prejudging by slides; photos; recommendation by known artist; and/or personal knowledge by committee. Entry fee due after prejudging. Work may be offered for sale; no commission. Craftworker must attend show; demonstrations encouraged. Registration limit: 75+. Sponsor provides electricity for demonstrations; fencing; and 24-hour security. Show is advertised by posters; flyers; newspaper; radio; and postcards. Categories: marine art; wood; weaving; oils; acrylics; watercolors; pen and ink; photography; jewelry; glass; sculpture; pottery; metal art; leather; musical instruments; and Indian art. Considers all crafts but candlemaking; decoupage; dollmaking; and lapidary.

ALL CRAFTS FAIR, 535 Quaker St., South Haven MI 49090. (616)637-1450. Executive Vice President: A.W. Roberts. Sponsor: Greater South Haven Area Chamber of Commerce. Estab. 1977. Annual outdoor show (indoor alternate for rain) held the Sunday of Labor Day weekend. Average attendance: 5,000. Entries accepted until 1 week before show. Entry fee: $10/10x10 display area. Work may be offered for sale; no commission. Craftworker must attend show; demonstrations OK. Show is advertised by handouts; radio; newspaper; and TV. Considers all crafts.

THE ANN ARBOR STREET ART FAIR, Box 1352, Ann Arbor MI 48106. Purpose: "The Fair was organized to bring a showing of high quality arts and crafts to the community." Estab. 1959. Annual outdoor show (booths have plastic clerestory roof) held 4 days in July. Mailing list for application closed February 1; other deadlines listed in material sent to applicants. Entry fee: $4/jury fee; $40/artist. Display area: 10x10 for 2 artists. Prejudging by 5 slides in up to 3 media. No entry fees refunded. Work may be offered for sale; 3% commission. Craftworker must attend show; demonstrations by invitation.
Acceptable Work: Considers batik; ceramics; glass art; jewelry; metalsmithing; pottery; sculpture; soft sculpture; weaving; and woodcrafting.

ANN ARBOR WINTER ART FAIR, 1725 Weldon, Ann Arbor MI 48103. Show Director: Audree Levy. Estab. 1974. Annual indoor show held 3 days in November. Average attendance: 30,000-40,000. Entries accepted until 3 months before show. Entry fee: $110/10x12 display area. Prejudging by 3 slides or photos and resume. SASE. Entry fee due after prejudging. Work may be offered for sale; no commission. Craftworker must attend show; some demonstrations OK. Sponsor provides 24-hour security. Show is advertised by TV; radio; and newspapers. Submit promotional materials only after being accepted. 1977 show sales totalled $400,000. Considers all crafts except decoupage; lapidary; needlecrafts; and tole painting.

ART AND FLOWER FESTIVAL, 1 Washington St., Grand Haven MI 49417. (616)842-4910. Sponsor: North West Ottawa Chamber of Commerce. Estab. 1955. Annual outdoor show held 2 days in July. Average attendance: 10,000.

BROOKLYN ARTISTS ANNUAL ROSE FESTIVAL, FINE ARTS AND CRAFTS SHOW AND SALE, 6250 N. Lake Rd., Clark Lake MI 49234. (517)529-9144. Secretary: Grace E. McCourtie. Estab. 1973. Annual outdoor show held 1 day in June at Jackson, Michigan. Average attendance: 5,000. Entries accepted until 3 weeks before show; $5 late entry fee. Entry fee: $10/artist. Display area: 15x15. Prejudging by slides or photos; entry fee refunded for refused work. Work may be offered for sale; no commission. Craftworker must attend show; demonstrations OK. Registration limit: 100. Show is advertised by TV; radio; and newspapers.
Acceptable Work: Considers batik; candlemaking; ceramics; glass art; jewelry; lapidary; leatherworking; macrame; metalsmithing; pottery; sculpture; soft sculpture; weaving; and woodcrafting.

CHRISTMAS CRAFT AND HOBBY SHOW, Grand Haven Community Center, Grand Haven MI 49417. (616)842-2550. Director: Jo Ennenga. Purpose: "to further the arts in our community." Estab. 1970. Annual indoor show held 2 days the first weekend in December. Average attendance: 2,500. Entries accepted until 3 weeks before show. Entry fee: $1/foot. Display area: single, 6'; double, 12'. Work may be offered for sale; no commission. Craftworker must attend show; demonstrations OK. Sponsor provides chairs; table; and 24-hour security protection. Show is advertised by radio; newspaper; and direct mail. Considers all crafts.

COAST GUARD FESTIVAL CRAFTS FAIR, 1 Washington St., Grand Haven MI 49417. (616)842-4910. Contact: Manager. Sponsor: Chamber of Commerce. Purpose: "to promote the arts in this area and to offer a very desirable summer activity for visitors and area residents." Estab. 1972. Annual outdoor show held 2 days in August. Entries accepted until 1 week before show. Display area: 15x15. Prejudging by slides and photos. Work may be offered for sale; no commission. Craftworker must attend show. Registration limit: 150. Considers all crafts.

CRAFT, ART, AND HOBBY SHOW, 470 W. Western Ave., Muskegon MI 49940. (616)726-4941. Arena Manager: Gilbert P. Buckley. Sponsor: L.C. Walker Sports Arena. Estab. 1973. Annual indoor show held 3 days in September. Average attendance: 5,000. Entries accepted up until show or until full. Entry fee: $10/10x10 display area. Work may be offered for sale; no commission. Craftworker needn't attend; demonstrations OK. Sponsor provides chairs; electricity for demonstrations; booth curtains; 24-hour security; and table for $1. Show is advertised by newspaper; radio; and mailing list. Considers all crafts.

***DANISH FESTIVAL ARTS AND CRAFTS SHOW**, Danish Festival, Inc., 302 S. Lafayette St., Greenville MI 48838. (616)754-6369. Managing Director: Mrs. Bart Fries. Estab. 1969. Annual outdoor show held 2 days in August. Average attendance: 50,000/day. Entries accepted until 3 weeks before show. Entry fee: $15/1 day; $25/2 days. Display area: 10x10. Prejudging by description of articles to be displayed; photos helpful but not necessary. Entry fee refunded for refused work. Work may be offered for sale; no commission. Craftworker must attend show; demonstrations encouraged. Registration limit: 130. Sponsor provides 24-hour security.

Categories: artists/craftworker section and handcrafters section. Considers all crafts. Presents placques and ribbons.

Promotion: Show is advertised by listings in numerous art magazines; and extensive coverage in state-wide radio, TV, and newspapers. "We also print a beautiful brochure which is sent to approximately 20,000 potential visitors." Uses some photos of work for publicity.

Sales Tip: If craftworker doesn't have sales tax license may use Show's for $1 which is collected with the application and entry fee.

DOWNTOWN BAY CITY SIDEWALK DAYS, 409 Bay City Bank Bldg., Bay City MI 48706. (517)893-3573. Administrative Assistant: Tillie Zimmerman. Sponsor: Downtown Bay City, Inc. Estab. 1963. Annual outdoor show held 3 days in July. Average attendance: 150,000. Entries accepted until 1 week before show. Entry fee: $5/day. Display area: approximately 6x9. Work may be offered for sale; no commission. Craftworker must attend show; no demonstrations. Registration limit: 30-40. Show is advertised by newspapers; radio; and TV. Considers all crafts.

*DUNDEE ARTS AND CRAFTS CLUB OUTDOOR EXHIBIT, 520 Oak St., Dundee MI 48131. Secretary: Mrs. Roger LaVoy. Estab. 1962. Annual outdoor show held 1 day in July. Average attendance: 2,000. Entries accepted until 1 week before show. Entry fee: $10/4x8 display area. Work may be offered for sale; no commission. Craftworker must attend show; demonstrations OK. Show is advertised by all media. Presents ribbons. Considers all crafts.

*FLINT ART FAIR, 1120 E. Kearsley St., Flint MI 48503. Art Fair Chairman: Deborah Chema. Sponsor: Friends of Modern Art, Flint Institute of Arts. Estab. 1967. Annual outdoor show held the second weekend in June. Average attendance: 15,000. Slides for jurying due 4 months before fair. Entry fee: $5 jurying fee plus $30/14x5 display area. Prejudging by 6 2x2 35mm slides with name and medium on each slide. "Write to Flint Institute of Arts for official entry form; entries not accepted without it." Entry fee due after prejudging. Work may be offered for sale; no commission. Craftworker must attend show; demonstrations OK. Registration limit: 125. Sponsor provides electricity for demonstrations; fencing; insurance on premises; 24-hour security; dinner Saturday night; and plastic sheeting to purchase in case of rain. Show is advertised by TV; radio; newspaper; magazines; posters; and bumper stickers. Presents 10 cash awards of $100 each. Considers all crafts except decoupage; mobiles; needlecrafts; and tole painting. 1977 show sales totalled about $80,000.

FRANKENMUTH BAVARIAN FESTIVAL, 635 S. Main St., Frankenmuth MI 48734. (517)652-6106. Contact: Chamber of Commerce. Sponsor: Frankenmuth Civic Events Council. Estab. 1959. Annual outdoor show held the second week in June. Average attendance: 250,000-300,000. Closing date for entry: March 1. Entry fee: $75/12x10 display area. Maximum 1 display area per craftworker. Prejudging by slides or photos; entry fee refunded for refused work. Work may be offered for sale; no commission. Demonstration OK. Registration limit: 50. Considers all crafts.

To Break In: "Demonstration is the key to selection. We like prices that are fair for work done. List basic price list on application. Apply before March; you'll be contacted in April."

*FROM TRASH TO TREASURES, Holland Civic Center, 150 W. 8th St., Holland MI 49423. President: Priscilla King. Sponsor: Louis Padnor Iron & Metal Co., Holland Friends of Art and the Holland Recreation Department. Annual indoor show held in May in conjunction with the Holland Fine Arts Show. Average attendance: 2,000-4,000. Entries accepted until approximately 1 month before show. Entry fee: $5. Craftworker must attend show. Sponsor provides heavy burlap-covered walls and 4x8 pegboard panels for display. Considers 3 dimensional work of recycled post-consumer or post-industrial metal products. Presents $100 in cash prizes and honorable mentions.

HOLIDAY GIFT SHOW, Ann Arbor Art Association, 117 W. Liberty, Ann Arbor MI 48104. (313)994-8004. Special Events Chairman: I.B. Remsen. Estab. 1976. Annual indoor show held the month of December. Entries accepted until 2 months before show. Entry fee: $50/artist. Display area: "mixed gallery." Prejudging by slides; entry fee refunded for refused work. Work may be offered for sale; 20% commission. Craftworker needn't attend show but "craftworker can volunteer time for sales to promote own work and commission rate is reduced by 5% for pieces sold by craftworker during that time." No demonstrations. Registration limit: 12-15. Sponsor provides 24-hour security. Considers all crafts but candlemaking; decoupage; dollmaking; needlecrafts; and tole painting.

Promotion: Show is advertised by newspapers; radio; and all public service forms of promotion. Artist is provided with mailing cards and flyers. Submit resume and b&w glossy of work for press releases.

HOLLAND FINE ARTS SHOW, Holland Civic Center, 150 W. 8th St., Holland MI 49423. President: Priscilla King. Sponsor: Holland Friends of Art and Holland Recreation Department. Estab. 1963. Annual indoor show held in May. Average attendance: 2,000-4,000. Entries accepted until approximately 1 month before show. Entry fee: $5-12/6x8x10 display area. Craftworker must attend show. Sponsor provides heavy burlap-covered walls and 4x8 pegboard panels for display. Considers sculpture.

INVITATIONAL ANN ARBOR SPRING ART FAIR, 1725 Weldon, Ann Arbor MI 48103. Show Director: Audree Levy. Estab. 1978. Annual indoor show held 3 days in March. Entries accepted until 3 months before show. Entry fee: $110/10x12 display area. Prejudging by 3 slides; resume; and SASE. Entry fee due after prejudging. Work may be offered for sale; no commission. Craftworker must attend show; some demonstrations. Registration limit: 100. Sponsor provides 24 hour security. Show is advertised by TV; radio; and newspapers. Submit b&w photo and resume. Considers all crafts but decoupage; dollmaking; needlecrafts; and tole painting.

INVITATIONAL ANN ARBOR WINTER ART FAIR, 1725 Weldon, Ann Arbor MI 48103. Show Director: Audree Levy. Estab. 1974. Annual indoor show held 3 days in November. Average attendance: 40,000. Entries accepted until 4 months before show. Entry fee: $110/10x12 display area. Prejudging by 3 slides and resume. SASE. Entry fee due after prejudging. Work may be offered for sale; no commission. Craftworker must attend show; some demonstrations. Registration limit: 100. Sponsor provides 24 hour security. Show is advertised by TV; radio; and newspapers. Submit b&w photo and resume. Categories: fine arts and crafts. Considers all crafts but decoupage; dollmaking; needlecrafts; and tole painting.

KALKASKA ARTS AND CRAFTS FESTIVAL, Rt. 4, Box 191, Kalkaska MI 49646. (616)258-9103. Director: Ann Brignac. Sponsor: Kalkaska County Chamber of Commerce. Estab. 1973. Annual indoor show held 1 day in October. Average attendance: 1,000. No entry fee. Work may be offered for sale; 10% commission. Demonstrations welcome.

LIVONIA ARTS AND CRAFTS FESTIVAL, 33001 5 Mile Rd., c/o LOVE, Livonia MI 48154. (313)421-2000, ext. 353. Festival Chairman: Marie Tuthill. Sponsor: Livonia Arts Commission. Estab. 1977. Annual show. Entry fee: $7 plus $2/electricity, if needed. Work may be offered for sale; no commission. Craftworker must attend show; demonstrations OK. Registration limit: 120. Considers ceramics; decoupage; glass art; jewelry; leatherworking; needlecrafts; weavings; macrame; and pottery.

LUDINGTON ARTS & CRAFTS FAIR, 1499 Betty Ave., C8, Ludington MI 49431. (616)843-3522. Director: Mildred Pirtle. Sponsor: West Shore Art League. Annual outdoor show held 2 days in July. Average attendance: 5,000+. Prejudging; entry fee refunded for refused work. Work may be offered for sale; no commission. Craftworker must attend show; demonstrations welcome. Registration limit: 300.
Acceptable Work: Considers batik; dollmaking; glass art; limited jewelry; limited leatherwork; metalsmithing; pottery; soft sculpture; weavings; wall hangings; and woodcrafting. "If we have seen a work before and know the quality, it needn't be prejudged again."

***MIDWEST ARTS AND CRAFTS SHOW,** 814 Bluff St., Kingsford MI 49801. (906)774-6756. Chairperson: Annette Santoni. Sponsor: Dickinson County Council for the Arts. Estab. 1967. Annual indoor/outdoor show held 2 days in June. Average attendance: 3,500+. Entries accepted until 2 weeks before show. Entry fee: $10/4x8 display area. Work may be offered for sale; no commission. Craftworker must attend show; demonstrations OK. Sponsor provides chairs; display panels; electricity for demonstrations; table; 24-hour security; hostesses; lunchroom; and miscellaneous supplies (tape, glue, scissors, pencils, etc.). Categories: media on canvas or board; media on paper; and craft. Considers all crafts. 1977 show sales totalled $10,000+. Presents cash awards totalling $250, and ribbons.
Promotion: Show is advertised by newspapers; radio; TV; and arts and craft brochures. The publicity committee contacts artists for information and photos.

***MILAN ART FAIR,** Milan Arts and Crafts Club, Milan MI 48160. Purpose: "to bring good quality art and crafts to the community of Milan and surrounding area." Estab. 1969. Annual outdoor show (indoors if raining) held 1 day in June. Average attendance: 1,500. Entries

accepted until 2 weeks before show. Entry fee: $8/4x8 table or A-frame display area. "Admittance to the Fair is screened on the basis of originality." Work may be offered for sale; no commission. Craftworker must attend show; demonstrations encouraged. Registration limit: 75. Sponsor provides display panels if requested; and electricity for demonstrations. Presents ribbon awards for best of show; 1st, 2nd, and 3rd prizes in each category; and honorable mention. Categories: fine arts (2 dimensional) and crafts (3 dimensional). Considers all crafts. Hooks for hangings must be provided by craftworker and name must be displayed on exhibit.
Promotion: Show is advertised by local paper; Ann Arbor, Michigan; radio and newspaper coverage and ads; some ads in Detroit area papers; and posters in Michigan and Toledo, Ohio, area. Provide background and any publicity information. No guarantee return on photos.

OUTDOOR AIR FAIR, Recreation and Public Service Department, Royal Oak MI 48068. (313)546-0900. Superintendent of Recreation: Susan Wedley. Purpose: "to provide a quality show for Royal Oak residents where they may purchase or browse through exhibits of various art media." Estab. 1971. Annual outdoor show held the last weekend in July. Average attendance: 5,000+. Entries accepted until about 3 months before show. Entry fee: $25/craftworker. Display area: 15x15. Prejudging by slides; entry fee refunded for refused work. Work may be offered for sale; no commission. Craftworker must attend show; demonstrations OK. Registration limit: 35. Show is advertised by posters; flyers; radio; and newspaper. "We will send news releases to craftworker's local newspaper if they will provide us with information." Considers ceramics; glass art; jewelry; leatherworking; metalsmithing; pottery; sculpture; weaving; and woodcrafting.

*PONTIAC ANNUAL ART FAIR-HERITAGE FESTIVAL, 47 Williams St., Pontiac MI 48053. (313)333-7849. Contact: Ian Lyons. Sponsor: Widetrack Festival Committee. Estab. 1975. Annual outdoor show (with some tent space) held 3 days in June. Average attendance: 2,-000. Entries accepted until 1 week before show. Entry fee: $10/entry. Prejudging by slides (send before second week in June); entry fee refunded for refused work. Work may be offered for sale; 15% commission. Craftworker must attend show; demonstrations OK. Sponsor provides display panels. Considers all original crafts.
Awards: Presents $100 1st prizes and 5 $50 honorable mentions. Judging panel consists of the Detroit Institute of Arts curator, Pontiac Arts Center director and 1 artist.

*REGIONAL, Hackley Art Museum, 296 W. Webster, Muskegon MI 49440. (616)722-6954. Assistant to the Director: Ann Archambault. Purpose: "to have an annual exhibition of the best artwork being done in western Michigan." Estab. 1927. Annual indoor show held 1 month in February. Average attendance: 3,000. Entries accepted until 2 weeks before show. Entry fee: $1/item being displayed. Display area: 4,000 square feet. Maximum 2 pieces per craftworker. "This is a museum exhibition with emphasis on artistic quality. Final exhibition is a juried show." Work may be offered for sale but emphasis not on sales; no commission. Craftworker needn't attend show; no demonstrations. Sponsor provides insurance on exhibited work and 24-hour security. Show is advertised by newspaper and brochures. Presents cash awards totalling $800. Considers all crafts but candlemaking; decoupage; dollmaking; lapidary; leatherworking; tole painting; and woodcrafting.

ROYAL OAK OUTDOOR ART FAIR, 211 Williams, Royal Oak MI 48068. (313)546-0900. Coordinator: Susan Wedley. Sponsor: Parks and Recreation Department. Estab. 1971. Annual outdoor show held in the summer. Average attendance: 3,000. Entries accepted until April. Entry fee: $25/craftworker. Prejudging; entry fee refunded for refused work. Work may be offered for sale; no commission. Craftworker must attend show; demonstrations OK. Registration limit: 85 spaces.
Acceptable Work: Considers batik; ceramics; glass art; jewelry; leatherworking; metalsmithing; pottery; weavings; and woodcrafting.

ST. CLAIR ART FAIR, Box 222, St. Clair MI 48079. (313)329-2803. Chairman: Mary Ann Garman. Sponsor: St. Clair Art Association. Estab. 1971. Annual outdoor (in covered mall) show held 3 days in late June. Average attendance: 5,000-6,000. Entries accepted until mid-March. Entry fee: $15/8x8 or 8x10 display area. Prejudging. Work must be offered for sale; 10% commission. Craftworker must attend show; demonstrations OK. Registration limit: 65.
Acceptable Work: Considers batik; ceramics; glass art; jewelry; some leatherworking; metalsmithing; pottery; soft sculpture; weavings; wall hangings; and some woodcrafting.

ST. JOSEPH ART ASSOCIATION'S OUTDOOR ART FAIR, 600 State St., St. Joseph MI 49085. (616)983-0271. Contact: St. Joseph Art Center. Estab. 1962. Annual outdoor show held 1 day in July. Average attendance: 35,000-40,000. Entries accepted until 8 weeks before show. En-

try fee: $25/20x20 display area. Prejudging; entry fee refunded for refused work. Work may be offered for sale; no commission. Craftworker must attend show; demonstrations OK. Registration limit: 150.
Acceptable Work: Considers batik; ceramics; glass art; jewelry; leatherworking; metalsmithing; pottery; soft sculpture; weavings; wall hangings; and woodcrafting. No sand sculpture.

*SOMERSET INVITATIONAL, 2801 Somerset Mall, Troy MI 48084. (313)643-6360. Director: Peg DuBois. Estab. 1970. Annual indoor show held 3 days in May. Entries accepted December-February. Entry fee: $50/display unit furnished by Mall. Prejudging by slides and resume; entry fee due after prejudging. Work must be offered for sale; no commission. Craftworker must attend show; no demonstrations. Registration limit: 40. Sponsor provides chairs; display panels; electricity; and 24-hour security. Show is advertised by radio; all local newspapers; and house newspapers. Announcement cards furnished for craftworker's clientele. Presents 5 $100 cash awards.
Acceptable Work: Considers batik; ceramics; jewelry; macrame; pottery; sculpture; soft sculpture; weaving; and woodcrafting.
Sales Tip: "This is a fine art show, not a craft show. Sales are realized in fine jewelry; ceramics; furniture; glass; fiber; and sculpture."

STURGIS NEWCOMERS CLUB ARTS AND CRAFTS FAIR, 1430 E. Rishel Rd., Sturgis MI 49091. (616)651-2816. Chairpersons: Mary Peoples and Cindy Monro. Estab. 1975. Annual indoor show held 1 day in November. Average attendance: 1,000. Entries accepted until show. Entry fee: $15/3x8 display area. Work may be offered for sale; no commission. Craftworker needn't attend show but is responsible for set-up. Demonstrations OK. Registration limit: 55. Sponsor provides chairs; some electricity for demonstrations; and table. Show is advertised by radio; TV; newspapers; posters; and flashing signs. Considers all crafts.

*TAWAS BAY WATERFRONT ART FAIR, 1115 Bay Dr., Tawas City MI 48763. (517)362-3198. Art Director: Paula Peterson. Sponsor: Tawas Bay Arts Council. Estab. 1960. Annual indoor/outdoor show held the first weekend in August. Average attendance: 5,000. Entry fee: $12/craftworker. Applications and photos due for prejudging July 1. Entry fee refunded for refused work. Work may be offered for sale; no commission. Craftworker must attend show; demonstrations OK. Registration limit: 225. Presents ribbons and cash prizes.
Acceptable Work: Considers batik; candlemaking; ceramics; glass art; jewelry; leatherworking; metalsmithing; pottery; weavings; and woodcrafting. No prefab jewelry; artificial flowers; candles from molds; knitting; crocheting; decals on wood; paper tole; ecology boxes; or dough art.

TRAVERSE BAY OUTDOOR ART FAIR, Northwestern Mid College, 1701 E. Front St., Traverse City MI 49684. (616)946-7990. Chairman: Rose L. Blodgett. Sponsor: Northwestern Michigan Artists and Craftsmen. Estab. 1957. Annual show held outdoors 1 day in July. Average attendance: 10,000. Entries accepted until May 1. Entry fee: $15/1 artist in 12x15 booth; $20/2 artists in 12x15 booth. Prejudging by slides; entry fee refunded for refused work. Work may be offered for sale; no commission. Craftworker must attend show; demonstrations encouraged. Registration limit: 150. Considers all crafts including furniture.
Sales Tips: "Items under $50 sell the fastest. Also small items such as jewelry, wood products, and wooden toys." If craftworker doesn't have sales tax license allowed to use Fair's.
Promotion: Show is advertised by radio; TV; newspapers; magazines; and posters. "If glossies are sent with registration we might use this and background information for promotion. If we find exceptional work we like to show them on a TV show promoting our Fair."

UNIVERSITY OF MICHIGAN ARTISTS AND CRAFTSMEN GUILD CHRISTMAS ART FAIR, UM Artists and Craftsmen Guild, 2nd Flr., Michigan Union, Ann Arbor MI 48104. Director: Celeste Melis. Purpose: "to educate the public in quality craftsmanship; to provide a good market for craftspeople, and to provide a festival to celebrate the making of objects." Estab. 1973. Annual indoor show held 2 days in December. Average attendance: 6,000. Only Guild members may apply; 3 year waiting list of 700 names. Display area: 8x10. Work may be offered for sale; no commission. Craftworker must attend show; demonstrations encouraged. Registration limit: 160. Sponsor provides some electricity for demonstrations and 24-hour security. Show is advertised by newspapers; radio; public service announcements; press releases; and mailings. Submit b&w photos for publicity. Considers all crafts within craft guild rules.
Sales Tip: "Don't display too much quantity. Use professional approach, business cards and literature. We aim for a public which is aware of good quality craftsmanship. Gift items and lower-priced items sell well at this Christmas fair."

UNIVERSITY OF MICHIGAN ARTISTS AND CRAFTSMEN GUILD FALL ART FAIR,
UM Artists and Craftsmen Guild, 2nd Flr., Michigan Union, Ann Arbor MI 48104. Director:
Celeste Melis. Purpose: "to educate the public in quality craftsmanship; to provide a good
market for craftspeople, and to provide a festival to celebrate the making of objects." Estab.
1973. Annual outdoor show held 2 days in fall. Average attendance: 4,000. Only Guild members
may apply; 3 year waiting list of 700 names. Display area; 8x8 or 8x10. Work may be offered for
sale; no commission. Craftworker must attend show; demonstrations encouraged. Registration
limit: 100. Sponsor provides some electricity for demonstrations. Show is advertised by
newspapers; radio; public service announcements; press releases; and mailings. Submit b&w
photos for publicity. Considers all crafts. Guild rules identify limitations of crafts.
Sales Tip: "Don't display too much quantity. Use professional approach, business cards and
literature. Our public is aware of good quality craftsmanship and expects you to be present to sell
your work."

**UNIVERSITY OF MICHIGAN ARTISTS AND CRAFTSMEN GUILD FARMINGTON
COUNTY ART FAIR,** UM Artists and Craftsmen Guild, 2nd Flr., Michigan Union, Ann Arbor
MI 48104. Director: Celeste Melis. Purpose: "to educate the public in quality craftsmanship; to
provide a good market for craftspeople, and to provide a festival to celebrate the making of objects." Estab. 1976. Annual outdoor show held 2 days in May in Farmington, Michigan. Average
attendance: 4,000. Only Guild members may apply; 3 year waiting list of 700 names. Display
area: 8x10. Prejudging. Work may be offered for sale; no commission. Craftworker must attend
show; demonstrations encouraged (especially folk arts). Registration limit: 100. Sponsor
provides some electricity for demonstrations; and 24-hour security. Show is advertised by
newspapers; radio; public service announcements; press releases; and mailings. Submit b&w
photos for promotion. Considers all crafts within Guild rules. "Wear country dress for this
theme show."
Sales Tip: "Don't display too much quantity. Use professional approach, business cards and
literature. We aim for a public which is aware of good quality craftsmanship."

**UNIVERSITY OF MICHIGAN ARTISTS AND CRAFTSMEN GUILD SUMMER ARTS
FESTIVAL,** UM Artists and Craftsmen Guild, 2nd Flr., Michigan Union, Ann Arbor MI
48104. Director: Celeste Melis. Purpose: "to educate the public in quality craftsmanship; to
provide a good market for craftspeople, and to provide a festival to celebrate the making of objects." Estab. 1971. Annual outdoor show held 4 days in July. Average attendance: 100,000.
Only Guild members may apply; 3 year waiting list of 700 names. Display area: 8x8 or 8x10.
Work may be offered for sale; no commission. Craftworker must attend show; demonstrations
encouraged. Registration limit: 500. Sponsor provides some electricity for demonstrations and
24-hour security. Show is advertised by newspapers; radio; public service announcements; press
releases; and mailings. Submit b&w photos. Considers all crafts. Guild rules identify craft standards.
Sales Tip: "Don't display too much quantity. Use professional approach, business cards and
literature. You must be present with your work. The public is interested in your philosophies of
craftsmanship and quality artwork."

UP IN CENTRAL PARK CRAFT FAIR, 1 Washington St., Grand Haven MI 49417. (616)842-
4910. Contact: Manager. Sponsor: Chamber of Commerce. Purpose: "to promote the arts in this
area and to offer a very desirable summer activity for visitors and area residents." Estab. 1955.
Annual outdoor show held 2 days in July. Average attendance: 11,000. Entries accepted until 1
week before show. Display area: 15x15. Prejudging by slide; photo; or sample of work. Work
may be offered for sale; no commission. Craftworker must attend show. Registration limit: 150.
Considers all crafts.

WARREN FESTIVAL OF ARTS, 29500 Van Dyke, Warren MI 48093. (313)573-9500.
Secretary: Jan Pierce. Sponsor: Warren Cultural Commission. Estab. 1977. Annual show held 2
days at the GM Technical Center. Entry fee: $25. Prejudging by slides. Work may be offered for
sale. Considers all crafts.

*WATERFRONT ART FAIR, 700 First Ave. S., Escanaba MI 49829. President: Mary Ellen
Quinn. Sponsor: Bay Area Art Association. Estab. 1971. Annual outdoor show held 1 Saturday
in August. Average attendance: 2,000. Entries accepted up until show. Entry fee:
$5/craftworker. Work may be offered for sale; no commission. Prefers craftworker attends
show; demonstrations OK. Registration limit: 80. Show is advertised by radio; posters; and
newspapers of Central Upper Peninsula's major towns. Submit b&w photos of works or self.
Presents purchase awards totalling $350. Considers all crafts.

ZEELAND ARTS FESTIVAL, 320 E. Main St., Zeeland Community Education, Zeeland MI 49464. (616)772-6236. Coordinator: Sue Eppert. Estab. 1975. Annual outdoor show (indoors if raining) held 2 days in June. Average attendance: 2,000. Entries accepted until show. Entry fee: $5/artist. Unlimited display area. Work may be offered for sale; no commission. Craftworker needn't attend show; demonstrations OK. Sponsor provides some chairs, tables and display panels; electricity for demonstrations; and 24-hour security. Show is advertised by posters; radio; newspapers; and flyers. Considers all crafts.

Minnesota

ARTS & CRAFTS FESTIVAL, Hutchinson Area Chamber of Commerce, 218 Main N., Hutchinson MN 55350. (612)896-5795. Executive Vice President: Clarice A. Coston. Estab. 1974. Annual outdoor show (indoors if inclement weather) held 2 days in the fall. Average attendance: 1,000. Entries accepted until 1 week before show. Entry fee: $10/display area. Work may be offered for sale; no commission. Craftworker needn't attend show; demonstrations OK. Sponsor provides electricity for demonstrations and tables for $1 rental fee. Considers all crafts.

FALL ARTS FAIR, Northfield Arts Guild, Box 21, Northfield MN 55057. Contact: Arts Fair Chairperson. "The Fall Arts Fair is a celebration for support and exposure of local artists." Estab. 1961. Annual outdoor show held 1 day in September. Attendance: 6,000-8,000. Entries accepted until 3 weeks before show. Entry fee: $15/artist. Prejudging by photos; entry fee due with application. Work may be offered for sale; no commission. Craftworker must attend show; demonstrations OK. Sponsor provides display panels. Show is advertised in local papers; radio; and by some mention in Twin City papers.
Acceptable Work: Considers batik; ceramics; dollmaking; glass art; jewelry; lapidary; leatherworking; macrame; metalsmithing; needlecrafts; pottery; sculpture; soft sculpture; weaving; and woodcrafting. "This is primarily a fine arts fair, though."

MIDWEST ART SHOW & SALE, Reiter Promotions, Inc., Box 321, Chanhassen MN 55317. (612)445-1998. Manager: Arthur Reiter. Sponsor: Miller Hill Mall Merchants' Association. Estab. 1974. Annual indoor show held 2 days in November at Duluth, Minnesota. Average attendance: 15,000. Entries accepted until 1 week before show. Entry fee: $25/12x6 display area. Prejudging: entry fee refunded for refused work. Work may be offered for sale; no commission. Craftworker must attend show; demonstrations OK. Registration limit: 70. Considers sculpture.

*MIDWEST ARTISTS' GUILD FESTIVAL OF THE ARTS, 6316 Eden Prairie Rd., Eden Prairie MN 55344. Contact: Mary Ellen Kundzins. Annual outdoor show held 2 days in August at St. Paul, Minnesota. Entries accepted until 3 months before show. Prejudging by 3 slides, including 1 slide showing detail, for each medium to be exhibited. Jury fee: $5. Work may be offered for sale; no commission. Craftworker must attend show; demonstrations OK. Open to craftworkers living in Minnesota; Wisconsin; North Dakota; South Dakota; Iowa; Illinois; and Kansas. Presents $3,000 in cash prizes and purchase awards. Considers all crafts.

*NORTH SHORE ART FAIR, Box 57, Lutsen MN 55612. (218)663-7533. Chairman: Joan H. Maw. Sponsor: North Shore Arts Association. Purpose: "to educate the public and promote artists from our area." Estab. 1968. Annual indoor/outdoor show held the second weekend in July. Average attendance: 2,000. Entries accepted until show date. Entry fee: $1/item plus $10 outside booth space. Maximum 3 pieces per category per craftworker entering the judged show. Work may be offered for sale; 15% commission. Craftworker needn't attend show; demonstrations OK. Show is advertised by brochures; newspapers; TV; and radio. Considers work "in 12 media classes (children's art also accepted at no charge). Presents cash for best of show, and ribbons in all categories.

NORTH STAR ARTS & CRAFTS FESTIVAL, Rt. 2, Park Rapids MN 56470. (218)732-3263 or 732-5250. Coordinators: Vangie Cookson or Bev Knutson. Purpose: "to give the artist and craftpeople a chance to be seen and known and sell items." Estab. 1972. Annual indoor show held 3 days in August. Entries accepted until filled. Entry fee: $25/8' space; $37/12' space; and $50/16' space. Prejudging by photos or sample of work; entry fee due after prejudging. Work may be offered for sale; no commission. Craftworker must attend show; demonstrations OK. Registration limit: 100+. Sponsor provides chairs; display panels; electricity for demonstrations; table; and 24-hour security. Show is advertised by TV; radio; newspapers; and flyers. Considers all crafts made by the exhibitor.
Sales Tip: "The biggest factors in good sales are fine workmanship; good sales personality (don't sit in booths reading books); and be interested in the viewing public — talk to people."

NORTHBROOK ARTS & CRAFTS SHOW & SALE, Reiter Promotions, Inc., Box 321, Chanhassen MN 55317. (612)445-1998. Show Manager: Arthur Reiter. Sponsor: Northbrook Shopping Center Businessmen's Association. Estab. 1974. Annual outdoor show on covered walks held 2 days in August, rain or shine. Entries accepted until 1 week before show. Entry fee: $25/10x6 display area. Entries must meet entry form requirements; entry fee refunded for refused work. Work may be offered for sale; no commission. Craftworker must attend show; demonstrations OK. Considers all original crafts.

*RED RIVER ANNUAL, Box 37, Moorhead MN 56560. (218)236-7171. Director: James O'Rourke. Sponsor: Friends of the Plains Art Museum. Estab. 1959. Annual indoor show held 7 weeks in the spring. Average attendance: 1,500. Entries accepted until 4 weeks before show. No entry fee. Maximum 1 entry/artist. Prejudging. Work may be offered for sale; 40% commission. Craftworker must attend show; no demonstrations. Sponsor provides 24-hour security; gallery talks; concerts; awards dinner; and luncheon with juror. Considers batik; ceramics; glass art; macrame; mobiles; pottery; sculpture; weaving; and soft sculpture.

SIDEWALK ARTS AND CRAFTS FAIR, 310 NE 1st St., Little Falls MN 56345. (612)632-5155. Manager: Glen Kraywinkle. Sponsor: Chamber of Commerce. Estab. 1973. Annual outdoor show held the 1st Saturday after Labor Day. Entry fee: $2.50. Work may be offered for sale; no commission. Craftworker must attend show; demonstrations OK. Show is advertised by news releases. Considers all original crafts.

UPTOWN ART FAIR, 7201 Shannon Dr., Edina MN 55435. Administrative Director: E.A. Nieland. Sponsor: Uptown Commerical Club. Purpose: "to attract people to the area and promote broader public interest in original arts and crafts, as well as give the public an opportunity to meet artists." Estab. 1964. Annual outdoor show (on sidewalks and grassy mall) held 3 days the second weekend in August at Minneapolis, Minnesota. Attendance: 125,000-150,000. Entries accepted until mid-May. Entry fee: $25/artist. Prejudging by photos or slides to be submitted with application by new exhibitors; entry fee refunded for refused work. Work may be offered for sale; no commission. Craftworker must attend show; demonstrations OK. Registration limit: 550-575. Considers all crafts except dollmaking; needlecrafts; soft sculpture; or handcrafts (stitchery, crochet, clothing, pillows, etc.). Must have Minnesota state sales tax permit.
Sales Tip: Work sells best when presented on "well-designed display fixtures; and prices are clearly marked. Framed art recommended as it sells better than unframed work. Also, be sure to bring a generous supply of work (we don't want artists to 'sell out' in 1 or 2 days)."

VICTORIAN CRAFT FESTIVAL, 265 S. Exchange St., St. Paul MN 55102. (612)222-5717. Contact: Edna Reasoner. Sponsor: Minnesota Historical Society. Estab. 1971. Annual outdoor show held in July. Average attendance: 1,000-2,000. Entries accepted until show date. No entry fee. Work may be offered for sale; no commission. Craftworker must attend show; demonstrations OK. Considers all Victorian period crafts.

WEAVERS GUILD FIBER FAIR, 427½ Cedar Ave., Minneapolis MN 55454. (712)332-7521. Contact: Fiber Fair Committee. Sponsor: Weavers Guild of Minnesota, Inc. Purpose: fundraiser. Estab. 1974. Annual indoor show held 2 days in November. Average attendance: 1,600. Entries received 2 days before show. Entry fee: $15/membership in Weavers Guild of Minnesota plus $3/Fiber Fair fee. Prejudging by actual work at time submitted; fees not refunded for refused work. Work may be offered for sale; 15% commission. Craftworker must attend show; demonstrations OK. "All participating craftsmen are asked to help during the show as salesmen, demonstrators, displayers, check-out, jury, etc." Sponsor provides chairs; display panels; insurance on exhibited work; and 24-hour security. Show is advertised by newspaper; radio; flyers; and posters.
Acceptable Work: Considers crafts as they relate to fiber arts including weaving; hand-spun wool; dollmaking; macrame; mobiles; needlecrafts; soft sculpture; tatting; lace; natural dyestuff; dyed handspun wool; crochet; and knitting. Bestsellers: scarves; shawls; mittens; small hangings; toys; some afghans; and throw pillows.

Mississippi

*ART IN THE PARK, Box 790, Meridian MS 39301. (601)693-1306. Executive Vice President: W.J. Johnson, Jr. Sponsor: Lively Arts Festival. Estab. 1977. Annual outdoor show (indoors if rain) held 1 day in April. Average attendance: 3,500. Entries accepted until 2 weeks before show. Entry fee: $25/artist for competition; $15/artist for noncompetitive. Display area: 10x10. Work may be offered for sale; no commission. Craftworker must attend show; demonstrations OK. Registration limit: 100 spaces. Show is advertised by trade publications and through other publicity of the weekly Lively Arts Festival. Presents $950 in cash, and $750 in purchase prizes. **Acceptable Work:** Considers batik; candlemaking; decoupage; dollmaking; glass art; jewelry; leatherworking; macrame; metalsmithing; mobiles; needlecrafts; pottery; sculpture; soft sculpture; tole painting; weaving; and woodcrafting.

BARTER DAY, Chamber of Commerce, Drawer S, Morton MS 39117. (601)732-6135. Director: Gilbert W. Renfrow. Purpose: "gives the people in central Mississippi an opportunity to view and purchase arts and crafts that cannot be bought otherwise." Estab. 1969. Annual outdoor show held the third weekend in June. Attendance: 5,000-10,000. Entries accepted until show date. No entry fee. Display area: "varies, but usually 10x15." Work may be offered for sale; no commission. Craftworker needn't attend show; demonstrations OK. Sponsor provides coverings and electricity for demonstrations. Considers all crafts. Novel and practical items sell best. Craftworker handles sales.
Promotion: Show is advertised by radio; newspapers; posters; and leaflets. "If an artist has a unique exhibit or demonstration, he should send information 4 weeks prior to the show."

*BATESVILLE ANNUAL ART MART, Box 528, Batesville MS 38606. (601)563-3126. Secretary: Mary M. Evans. Purpose: "to promote appreciation of art, and provide an outlet for special crafts." Estab. 1966. Annual outdoor show (in pecan grove under shady trees) held 1 day in June. Average attendance: 3,000. Entries accepted until show date. Entry fee: $5/display area. Work may be offered for sale; no commission. Craftworker must attend show; demonstrations OK. Sponsor provides electricity for demonstrations. Categories: paintings, watercolor and mixed media; graphics and drawings; sculpture; crafts; and pottery. Considers all crafts. "Each year we provide purchase prizes of different amounts."

*CALICO FAIR, c/o Art Association of Columbus, Box 2251, East End Station, Columbus MS 39701. Contact: Chairman. "This annual event enables the Art Association to make money to have workshops and field trips. We also have given some scholarships; and are saving towards a building." Estab. 1968. Annual outdoor show (with a pavilion with tables) held 1 day in the fall. Average attendance: 3,000-6,000. Entries accepted until 2 weeks before show. Entry fee: $10/artist, with an additional $5 fee for admission into the awards portion of the show. Prejudging by slides or photos; entry fee refunded for refused work. Work may be offered for sale; no commission. Craftworker must attend show; demonstrations OK. Sponsor provides limited covering; electricity for demonstrations; fencing; and some tables. Considers all crafts.
Awards: Presents purchase prizes; honorable mention, 1st, 2nd and 3rd place ribbons; and cash awards of merit and $200 best in show award. "Most judges do look at the total look (display) in picking individual prize winners. They also seem to pick someone who has a lot of items on hand — not just a few."
Sales Tip: "Crafts are good sellers. In this area people start their Christmas buying at this time — Christmas decorations, stocking stuffers — this type of thing is good."
Promotion: Show is advertised in magazines; newspapers; and TV. "Materials for promotional purposes would be helpful. If anyone would like to have advance publicity we will do what we can. Pictures should be b&w glossy and include name on the back. Resumes are also helpful. Photos will not be returned by mail, but will be held and may be picked up at the Calico Fair."

THE CANTON FLEA MARKET ARTS & CRAFTS SHOW, Box 202, Canton MS 39046. (601)859-1606. Secretary: Ginny Ray. Sponsor: Madison County Chamber of Commerce. Purpose: "to promote Canton and Madison County." Estab. 1964. Semiannual outdoor show held the second Thursday in May and October. Average attendance: 20,000. "New applications are cut off about 6 weeks before the show because the invitations go out then [to persons selected by jurying.]" Entry fee: $12. Display area: 12x12. Prejudging; "invitation recipients are selected by the information on their application and the photos that they send in." Entry fee due after prejudging. Work must be offered for sale; no commission. Show is advertised by newspaper articles and craft magazines. Considers all crafts "except unfinished crafts (left for the buyer to finish); dried arrangements; and exhibits with dried components."
Profile: "The main exhibit is located on the grounds of the Courthouse Square. Other exhibits are located on the grounds of the Old Jail Museum (i.e., dried arrangements, antiques, etc.). A live potted plant show and sale and additional arts and crafts will be held on the grounds of the Grace Episcopal Church."

THE GREAT RIVER ROADS CRAFT FAIR, Box 1785, Natchez MS 39120. (601)442-6221. Chairman: Bill Dixon Jr. Sponsor: Jaycees. Purpose: "to promote an appreciation for the well made, hand produced article; to provide a professional atmosphere for the sale of contemporary and heritage crafts. To develop for our community a craft event which attracts tourists and to provide educational opportunities for individuals interested in artistic expressions in the craft field." Estab. 1973. Annual indoor show held 3 days in October. Average attendance: 5,000+. Entries accepted until 3 months before show. Entry fee: $50. Display area: 10x10. Prejudging by 2-5 slides. Work may be offered for sale; no commission. Craftworker must attend show; demonstrations OK. Registration limit: 65. Sponsor provides electricity for demonstrations; tables; chairs; 24-hour security; free coffee; catered supper; and free parking areas. Considers all crafts.

Promotion: SHow is advertised by statewide public service announcements; newspaper ads throughout wide radius, sponsors appearance on area TV; distribution; distribution of thousands of flyers; posters; placemats in local restaurants; post cards to club members of stamping store mailing; telephone company's Bell Notes, notice in all craft publications which run craft columns; and radio. Submit b&w glossies of you and your work for publicity.

*MERIDIAN MUSEUM OF ART BI-STATE SHOW, Box 5773, Meridian MS 39301. (601)693-1501. Director: William M. Watkins, III. Sponsor: Meridian Art Association, Inc. and the Museum. Purpose: "to promote the best in visual arts throughout the states of Mississippi and Alabama, and to offer the viewing public the opportunity to take part in this promotion." Estab. 1974. Annual indoor show held the month of February. Average attendance: 800+. Entries accepted until 1 week before show. Entry fee: $7 for 2 works. Maximum 2 works/artist. Prejudging by actual work. No entry fees refunded for refused work. Work may be offered for sale; 20% commission. Craftworker needn't attend show; no demonstrations. Sponsor provides insurance on exhibited work and 24-hour security. Show is advertised by newspaper; TV; direct mail; radio; and billboards. Considers all crafts; work must be ready for presentation. Maximum size: 50" in either direction, or 30 pounds. "Outrageous prices are discouraged." Museum staff handles sales.

Awards: Presents $1,200 in cash prizes. This includes $500 best in show award; 4 $100 juror awards; and 6 $50 awards of merit. "Enter dynamic show pieces and not pieces that would sell to the general public."

Missouri

ANTIQUE SHOW AND COLLECTORS FLEA MARKET, 524 W. Martin Ave., Campbell MO 63933. (314)264-2936, evenings. Contact: Nevah Clubb. Sponsor: NEAMM Enterprises. Estab. 1977. Indoor show held the first Sunday each month at the community building. Entry fee: $6.50/8' table. Work may be offered for sale; no commission. Craftworker must attend show; demonstrations OK. Considers candlemaking; ceramics; decoupage; dollmaking; glass art; jewelry; needlecrafts; pottery; and quilting.

*"AROUND THE TABLE," 6640 Delmar St., St. Louis MO 63130. (314)725-1151. Chairperson: Ruth Hyman. Sponsor: Craft Alliance Gallery (with funding from Missouri Arts Council). Purpose: "to provide a showcase for artists/craftsmen who are not regular members of the gallery. High quality is the essence of this show. Only those living in Missouri and a 170-mile radius in Illinois are eligible." Estab. 1976. Annual indoor show held 3 weeks in August. Entries must be hand-delivered about 6 weeks before show. Entry fee: $10. Maximum 3 works/craftworker. All work will be juried in July. Work may be offered for sale; 33-1/3% commission. Craftworker needn't attend show; no demonstrations required, but workshops will be held for those who wish to participate." Sponsor provides insurance on exhibited work; 24-hour security; gallery space; and staff to handle sales. Presents "at least a $200 1st prize, plus others to be announced."

Acceptable Work: "All work should be that which is used 'Around the Table,' such as plates, cups, glasses, furniture, candlesticks, decorative work, woven cloths, aprons, hostess gowns, utensils, mugs, hangings, lamps, etc." Considers batik; ceramics; glass art; jewelry; macrame; metalsmithing; mobiles; pottery; sculpture; soft sculpture; weaving; woodcrafting; and any combination of the above.

Sales Tip: "Most sales are of functional work. It's difficult to anticipate what may appeal on an artistic level. We do not consider this a sales-oriented show, however; even though some definitely are consummated."

Promotion: Show is advertised by mail; newspapers; TV; radio; and magazines. "Give some educational and professional background (space will be provided on entry forms)."

ARTS & CRAFTS FALL FESTIVAL SHOW & SALE, Union Merchants Association, Box 168, Union MO 63084. (314)583-8979. Secretary: Linda Ballou. Purpose: "to attract shoppers to Union; and for public enjoyment and availability of craft items to citizens and visitors in the area." Estab. 1975. Annual outdoor show held 1 day in September. Average attendance: "a few thousand." Entries accepted until show date. Entry fee: $2/1 parking space, or approximately

18' of space. Work may be offered for sale; no commission. Craftworker or representative must attend show; demonstrations OK. Sponsor provides fencing. Considers all crafts.
Promotion: Show is advertised by newspaper and radio advertising in the Union, Washington, St. Clair, Pacific, and Beaufort areas. Supply cards with name, address and phone number.

BENNETT SPRING HILLBILLY DAYS, c/o Lebanon Chamber of Commerce, Inc., Lebanon MO 65536. Estab. 1973. Annual outdoor show held 3 days in the summer. Entries accepted until about 2 weeks before show. Entry fee: $25/8' display area; $20/15' area outside main tent; $20/15' display area outside main tent plus additional footage at $1.50/foot. "Work not handcrafted will be refunded." Work may be offered for sale; no commission. Craftworker must attend show; demonstrations "strongly encouraged." Sponsor provides 24-hour security, but "the Bennett Spring Hillbilly Days committee and the Lebanon Chamber of Commerce will not be responsible for any loss, theft or damage." Considers all Ozarkian handcrafts.

BUSHWACKER ARTS & CRAFTS FESTIVAL, c/o Paula McIntosh, 330 N. Webster, Nevada MO 64772. (417)667-7744. Sponsor: Eta Theta chapter of Beta Sigma Phi. Purpose: "to raise funds for charitable purposes in the community. Our income is the fee charged for display area only." Estab. 1972. Annual outdoor show held 1 day in June. Entries accepted until show date. Entry fee: $7.50/6x9 display area. "All work is expected to be for sale unless craftsman specifies otherwise"; no commission. Craftworker must attend show; demonstrations OK. Registration limit: about 50. "Electricity for demonstrations can be arranged if asked for in advance." Show is advertised by direct mail, radio and newspapers. Considers all crafts.

CASS COUNTY LOG CABIN FESTIVAL, 400 E. Mechanic, Harrisonville MO 64701. (816)884-5352. Secretary-Treasurer: Irene Webster. Sponsor: Chamber of Commerce and Cass County Historical Society, Inc. Purpose: "to promote demonstrations and crafts based on pioneer life. A log cabin built in 1835 is the focal point for the festival activities." Annual indoor/outdoor show (with some tents) held 3 days during the first weekend in October. Average attendance: 6,000. Entries accepted until 1 week before show. Entry fee: $10/5x7 display area inside tent, or 7x10 area outside tent. Work may be offered for sale; 10% commission. Craftworker must attend show; demonstrations OK. Registration limit: 40. Sponsor provides electricity for demonstrations; fencing; and 24-hour security. Show is advertised by magazines; direct mail; posters and pamphlets; and billboards. Submit descriptions of work for promotion. Considers all crafts; handmade crafts preferred. Bestsellers: work priced under $10. 1977 exhibitor sales totalled about $14,000.

CHRISTMAS CRAFT BAZAAR, Box 901, Cape Girardeau MO 63701. (314)334-9233. Contact: Director. Sponsor: Southeast Missouri Council on the Arts, Inc. Purpose: "to allow craftpersons the opportunity to show and sell their goods. To promote interest in crafts as an art form." Estab. 1971. Annual indoor show held 2 days in November at the Arena Building, Cape Girardeau. Average attendance: 2,500-3,000. Entries accepted until 2 weeks before show. Entry fee: $15/8'x30" table. Work may be offered for sale; no commission. Craftworker must attend show; demonstrations recommended. Registration limit: 125-130. Sponsor provides chairs; electricity for demonstrations and table. Show is advertised in 45+ local papers; by radio spots; and public service announcements. Considers all craft.
Sales Tip: "This Bazaar is held around Christmas time to give the public an opportunity to buy early gifts. Items of this nature sell big. I wouldn't advise bringing too many items with large costs."

DUCKS UNLIMITED MIDWEST WILDLIFE ART SHOW, 1900 Swift Ave., North Kansas City MO 64116. (816)471-3414. Chairman: David Wells. Estab. 1972. Annual indoor benefit show held 1½ days in March. Average attendance: 3,000. Closing date for entry: December. Entry fee: 1 original donated work. Maximum 15 entries per artist. Prejudging: donation refunded for refused work. Work may be offered for sale; no commission. Craftworker must attend show; demonstrations OK. Registration limit: 90. Considers wood and decoy carving. Emphasis placed on realism.

*****FINE ARTS SHOW**, Battlefield Mall, Springfield MO 65804. (417)883-8444. Promotion Director: Nancy Dillard. Sponsor: Merchant Association. Purpose: "so the artist can have a good outlet for his art in the Ozarks, and to promote better art in Springfield." Estab. 1975. Annual indoor show held 3 days in the fall. Average attendance: 125,000. Entries accepted until 2 weeks before show. Entry fee: $50/10x20 display area. Prejudging by slides and photos; entry fee refunded for refused work. Work may be offered for sale; no commission. Craftworker must attend show; demonstrations OK. Registration limit: 40. Sponsor provides electricity for demonstrations and insurance on exhibited work. Show is advertised by 2 TV stations; 2 radio stations; and the *Ozark Mountaineer* newspaper. Categories: painting; drawing; jewelry; pottery; photography; sculpture; special art; and fibers. Considers jewelry; pottery; sculpture; and fiber arts. Presents $100 for the best of show; judged by the artists in the show.

FOLK MUSIC & CRAFTS FESTIVAL, Box 339, West Plains MO 65775. (417)256-8573. Chairman of the Board: Linda T. Shortridge. Sponsor: West Plains Council on the Arts. "This crafts show is set up as a learning experience, and all craftsmen are required to demonstrate." Estab. 1975. Annual indoor show held 1-2 days during first full weekend after Labor Day. Average attendance: 1,500. Entries accepted until show date. No entry fee for artist; but each person entering grounds pays $1 admission. Display area: 10x10. Work may be offered for sale; no commission. Craftworker must attend show. Sponsor provides electricity for demonstrations. Show is advertised by local coverage in all media and direct mail. "All participants are required to fill out an index card questionnaire [for publicity purposes] upon registration." Considers all crafts.

INVITATIONAL CRAFT FAIR, 111 E. Brookside Dr., Springfield MO 65807. (417)866-2716. Curator of Education: Dudley Murphy. Sponsor: Springfield Art Museum. "Our purpose is to bring the public and craftspeople together for sales and educational enrichment. The public needs a place to see high quality crafts and it has been our opportunity to provide this meeting place." Estab. 1974. Annual outdoor show held 2 days in the spring. Average attendance: 6,000-8,000. Entries accepted until 2 weeks before show. Entry fee: $15/15x15 display area. Prejudging by 6 slides or photos; entry fee due after prejudging. Work may be offered for sale; no commission. Craftworker must attend show; demonstrations welcomed. Registration limit: 40-50. Sponsor provides electricity for demonstrations. Considers batik; fine glass art; jewelry; leatherworking; metalsmithing; pottery; sculpture; soft sculpture; weaving; and woodcrafting. "No handicrafts— 'fine art' quality crafts only." Bestsellers: work priced under $25.
Promotion: Show is advertised by newspaper ads; TV public service time; posters; and news releases to radio, TV and newspapers. "A resume and b&w photo of the artist and his/her work would be helpful."

"A variety of pieces should be available [at the Invitational Craft Fair, Springfield, Missouri] since the majority of sales are in the 'under $25 category,'" explains Dudley Murphy, curator of education for the Springfield Art Museum. Murphy would like to receive a resume and b&w photo of exhibiting craftworkers for use in promotion.

LAKE OF OZARKS ARTS & CRAFTS SHOW & SALE, 224 Oklahoma St., Rt. 2, Camdenton MO 65020. (314)346-5962. Director: Christene Burner. Estab. 1971. Annual indoor/outdoor show held 3 days during the third weekend in September. Average attendance: 20,000. Entries accepted until 2 weeks before show ("but usually sold out in July"). Entry fee: $15/8x10. Work may be offered for sale; no commission. Craftworker must attend show; demonstrations OK. Registration limit: 131. Sponsor provides electricity for demonstrations; and 24-hour security. Considers all handmade crafts.

MID-AMERICAN METALCRAFTS, 1005 Indiana St., Lawrence KS 66044. (913)842-3550. Director: John Scott, Jr. Sponsor: Mid-American Crafts Exhibits, Inc. Estab. 1975. Annual indoor show held 6 weeks (November-December) in Kansas City, Missouri at the public library. Average attendance: 35,000. Slides for prejudging accepted until July 15; works accepted until September 15. "This exhibition is limited to craftspeople who live and work in Kansas or Missouri. Slides are reviewed and artwork selected for relevance to educational program of the exhibition. Works selected are photographed for an exhibition catalog." Work may not be offered for sale; "this is a nonprofit educational exhibit of art." No demonstrations. Registration limit: 25-35. Library provides insurance on exhibited work; insurance on work shipped to artist; 24-hour security and library display cases. Considers jewelry; metalsmithing; small metal sculpture; and vitreous enamels.
Promotion: Show is advertised by radio announcements; newspaper notices; posters; mailings; an invitational private opening; and the illustrated exhibition catalog. Craftworker should provide personal data; may add comments on works and crafts in general; and b&w glossies of work, of self, and of personal workshop areas.

NATIONAL CRAFTS FESTIVAL, Silver Dollar City MO 65616. (417)338-8212. Special Events Manager: Ken Bell. Sponsor: Silver Dollar City, Inc. Estab. 1962. Annual outdoor show (with some tents and portable shelters) held 3 weeks (with the exception of Mondays and Tuesdays) in the fall. Average attendance: 180,000. "Entries accepted when there is an available space." No entry fee. Prejudging by slides or photos with application, or personal interview preferred. Work may be offered for sale; 20% commission. Craftworker must attend show. "Demonstrations required 80% of the time. (Demonstration can be a blend of talking about your craft and actually making an item.) No power tools are allowed. Any modern materials which would not have existed in the late 1800s must be disguised (Elmer's Glue can be put in a mason jar.)" Registration limit: about 50. Sponsor provides chairs; coverings; electricity for demonstrations; table; and 24-hour security. Show is advertised by TV; radio; and newspapers. "All crafts must be fitting with the 1800s theme of Silver Dollar City."

*****OZARK CRAFT FESTIVAL**, Battlefield Mall, Springfield MO 65804. (417)883-8444. Promotion Director: Nancy Dillard. Sponsor: Merchant Association. Annual show held 3 days in the summer. Entry fee: $20/10x9 display area. Prejudging by slides or photos of work. "Mall will spend $1,500 to advertise work." Awards cash.

RENAISSANCE FESTIVAL, Kansas City Art Institute, 4415 Warwick Blvd., Kansas City MO 6411. (816)561-4852. Assistant to President, Development: Susan Hubbard. Estab. 1977. Annual outdoor show held 4 weekends (8 days) in October. Average attendance: 10,000+. Entry fee. Prejudging by slides. Work may be offered for sale; no commission. Craftworker must attend show; demonstrations OK. Considers baskets; candlemaking; carvings and sculpture; ceramics; calligraphy; children's toys; dolls; glass art; leather accessories; jewelry; lapidary; metalsmithing; mobiles; needlecrafts; pillows; pottery; wall hangings; and weavings. Craftworkers must be clothed in Renaissance period dress.

JOSEPH RUBIDOUX ARTS & CRAFTS FAIR, c/o Karen Organ, 2905 Jule, St. Joseph MO 64501. (816)232-1323. Sponsor: St. Joseph Historical Society. Purpose: "money goes to restoration of Rubidoux Row." Estab. 1970. Annual indoor show held 3 days the first full weekend in October. Attendance: 20,000-25,000. Entries accepted until 3 weeks before show. Entry fee: $15/10x6 display area. Work may be offered for sale; no commission. Craftworker must attend show; demonstrations OK. Registration limit: 100. Sponsor provides electricity for demonstrations and 24-hour security. Show is advertised by newspaper; craft magazines; and brochures. Considers all crafts.

SANTA-CALI-GON DAYS, Box 147, Independence MO 64051. (816)252-2880. Public Relations Director: Elizabeth Hill McClure. Sponsor: Chamber of Commerce. Purpose: "to provide the community with a means of entertainment for the holiday weekend; to provide a source of fund-raising for local organization; and to promote the city to tourists." Estab. 1974.

Annual outdoor show (with 3 big tents) held 4 days during Labor Day weekend. Average attendance: 250,000. Entries accepted until show date. Entry fee: $30/8x8 display area. Work may be offered for sale; no commission. Craftworker must attend show; demonstrations OK. Registration limit: 165-170. Sponsor provides some electricity for demonstrations and 24-hour security in the form of a roving policeman. Considers all crafts.

Promotion: "If work is of an unusual nature, a b&w photo and description might be included with registration." Advertising handled by Chamber of Commerce.

SPRING NATIONAL CRAFTS FESTIVAL, Silver Dollar City MO 65616. (417)338-8212. Special Events Manager: Ken Bell. Sponsor: Silver Dollar City, Inc. Estab. 1977. Annual outdoor show (with some tents and portable shelters) held 2 weeks (with the exception of Mondays and Tuesdays) in the spring. Average attendance: 95,000. "Entries accepted when there is an available space." No entry fee. Prejudging by slides or photos with application, or personal interview preferred. Work may be offered for sale; 15% commission. Craftworker must attend show. "Demonstrations required 80% of the time. (Demonstration can be a blend of talking about your craft and actually making an item.) No power tools are allowed. Any modern materials which would not have existed in the late 1800s must be disguised (Elmer's Glue can be put in a mason jar.)" Registration limit: about 50. Sponsor provides chairs; coverings; electricity for demonstrations; table; and 24-hour security. Show is advertised by TV; radio; and newspapers. "All crafts must be fitting with the 1800s theme of Silver Dollar City."

Montana

*ELECTRUM FESTIVAL OF THE ARTS, Box 1231, Helena MT 59601. President: Sally Starnes. Sponsor: Helena Arts Council. Purpose: "to provide a quality show for the Northwest area, and to enable artists and craftsmen, whose works are not generally eligible for fine arts shows, to show." Estab. 1970. Annual indoor show held 2 days in the fall. Average attendance: 5,000-10,000. Entries accepted until 1 week before show. Entry fee: $2/item being displayed, plus $25/8x4 display area. Maximum 2 entries per craftworker per category. Work may be offered for sale; 20% commission. Craftworker needn't show; demonstrations OK if pre-arranged. Registration limit: 50. Sponsor provides chairs; electricity for demonstrations; shipping costs to winning craftworkers from show; and table. Considers all crafts. Presents cash awards and ribbons. Helena Arts Council handles sales; "Montana has no sales tax."

FLATHEAD VALLEY ART FESTIVAL, 2nd Ave. & 3rd St., Box 83, Kalispell MT 59901. (406)755-5268. Director: John R. Brice. Sponsor: Hockaday Center for the Arts and The Flathead Valley Art Association. Purpose: "to encourage interested persons to develop arts and crafts; to interest the town and others in functions at the Hockaday Center; and to bring artisans together to share ideas." Annual outdoor show held 3 days in August. Write for entry deadline. Entry fee: $15/12x12 display area. Work may be offered for sale; no commission. Craftworker must attend show; demonstrations OK. Registration limit: 65+. Sponsor provides electricity for demonstrations. Considers all crafts.

Sales Tip: "Kalispell is somewhat of a tourist town. Anything goes. Local people lean toward western [themes]."

Promotion: Show is advertised by radio; TV; and newspapers. Exhibitor should list type of craftwork done so list may be compiled for media.

*J.K. RALSTON MUSEUM & ART CENTER JURIED EXHIBIT, Box 50, Sidney MT 59270. (406)482-3500. Director: Linda K. Mann. Sponsor: Mon-Dak Historical & Arts Society. Estab. 1975. Annual indoor show held the month of October. Average attendance: 200. Entries accepted until 1 week before show. Entry fee: $3/craftworker. Maximum 2 entries per craftworker. Prejudging; entry fee refunded for refused work. Work may be offered for sale; 25% commission. No demonstrations. Work must have been done within 2 years prior to show. Sponsor provides display equipment. Crafts should be shipped prepaid; will be returned COD. Considers ceramics; metalsmithing; and soft sculpture. Maximum size: 6x4' depth; ½x1' or 5 lbs. Presents cash awards and ribbons for best of show; honorable mention; and most popular work.

Nebraska

COUNTRYSIDE VILLAGE ART FAIR, 8715 Countryside Plaza, Omaha NE 68114. (402)391-2200. Contact: Jim Chase. Sponsor: Countryside Village Merchants Association. Estab. 1970. Annual outdoor show held the first weekend in June. Average attendance: 20,000. Entries accepted until 4 weeks before show. Entry fee: $30/8x14 display area. Prejudging; entry fee due after prejudging. Work may be offered for sale; no commission. Craftworker must attend show; demonstrations OK. Registration limit: 160.

Acceptable Work: Considers batik; pottery; wood; glass; metal; clay and stone sculpture; and silver/gold jewelry.

KFOR ARTS AND CRAFTS, 8110 A St., Lincoln NE 68510. Co-directors: Jo Rall and Esther Pitney. Sponsor: Rall and Associates and KFOR Radio. Purpose: to provide a place where artists can sell. Estab. 1972. Annual indoor show held 2 days in November. Average attendance: 15,000 a day. Entries accepted until full. Entry fee: $25/craftworker. Display area: 12x15. Prejudging by actual work; entry fee due after prejudging. Work may be offered for sale; no commission. Craftworker must attend show; demonstrations OK. Registration limit: 70-100. Sponsor provides chairs; electricity for demonstrations; table; 24-hour security; hospitality bag; and free breakfast first day. Show is advertised by 2,000 personal handwritten letters; flyers; posters; ads; newspapers; and extensive radio coverage. Submit name cards for future reference. Presents cash award of $50 for best all-around exhibit. Considers all crafts except ceramics and soft sculpture.

OMAHA SUMMER ARTS FESTIVAL (ARTS FESTIVAL ON THE MALL), 1615 Howard #1, Omaha NE 68102. (402)345-5401. Director: Vic Gutman. Sponsor: Summer Arts Festival, Inc. Purpose: a community event, a showcase for the arts in Omaha. Estab. 1975. Annual outdoor show held 3 days in June. Average attendance: 100,000. Entries accepted until 4 weeks before show. Entry fee: $30/craftworker. Display area: 10x10. Prejudging by 3 slides per medium; entry fee refunded for refused work. Work may be offered for sale; no commission. Craftworker must attend show; demonstrations encouraged. Registration limit: 200. Sponsor provides 24-hour security; rental of display items; free coffee and donuts; relief help; lounge; convenient parking; and reduction in hotel costs. Show is advertised by all media and 24-page supplement in newspaper. Inform your own customers of show. Considers all crafts.

Nevada

*GOLD HILL ART FESTIVAL, Box 510, Virginia City NV 89440. (702)847-0737. Director: Diane Gordon. Sponsor: Gold Hill Pottery and Art Gallery. Purpose: "to provide a setting for a successful festival for individual craftsmen; and to educate the public in terms of fine craftsmanship." Estab. 1974. Annual outdoor show held 3 days during Memorial Day weekend at Gold Hill, Nevada. Average attendance: 10,000-20,000. Entries accepted until March 30; prejudging done by April 15; notification of craftperson by April 30. Entry fee: $20/exhibitor. Display area: 6x12 (larger areas available for increased fee). Jury of 9 craftworkers prejudge work by slides and photos. Entry fee due after acceptance. Work may be offered for sale; no commission. Craftworker must attend show; demonstrations encouraged. Registration limit: 40. Sponsor provides 24-hour security. Show is advertised by radio; TV; local newspapers; posters; handbills; and banners. Considers batik; ceramics; candlemaking; jewelry; lapidary; leatherworking; macrame; metalsmithing; pottery; sculpture; soft sculpture; weaving; and woodcrafting. No hobby crafts. Presents $100 minimum in purchase prizes.

*MARYSVILLE MALL ART & CRAFT SHOW, 3608 Cinnabar Ave., Carson City NV 89701. (702)883-0968. Director: Bea Griffin. Sponsor: Creative Artists Group. Estab. 1962. Annual indoor show held 4 days in the summer at Marysville, California. Average attendance: 50,000. Entries accepted until show date. Entry fee: $25/10x10 display area. Work may be offered for sale; 10% commission. Craftworker must attend show; demonstrations OK. Sponsor pays insurance on exhibited work. Awards cash prizes.
Acceptable Work: Considers batik; candlemaking; ceramics; decoupage; dollmaking; glass art; leatherworking; metalsmithing; needlecrafts; pottery; soft sculpture; tole painting; weavings; wall hangings; woodcrafting; and all sculpture.

New Hampshire

CANAAN CRAFTSMEN'S CHRISTMAS FAIR, Canaan Community Center, Rt. 4, Canaan NH 03741. Annual indoor show held 1 day the Saturday following Thanksgiving. Entry fee: $1. Registration limit: 30 local craftworkers. Considers all crafts. "I call craftsmen living in Canaan only."

CRAFTSMEN'S FAIR, 205 N. Main St., Concord NH 03301. (603)224-3375. Director: Merle D. Walker. Sponsor: League of New Hampshire Craftsmen. Annual outdoor show held 6 days in August. Average attendance: 30,000. Considers all crafts. "Participants must meet residency requirements."

LOON MOUNTAIN ARTS & CRAFTS SHOW, c/o Loon Mountain Recreation Corp., Lincoln NH 03251. (603)745-8111. Marketing Assistant: Rita M. Rand. Purpose: "to lend proper atmosphere to a well-designed, well-cared-for area which tries to offer something for everyone, and to promote arts and crafts of quality." Estab. 1967. Semiannual indoor/outdoor show held 3 days in August and in October. Average attendance: 2,000/day. Entries accepted until 1 week before show. Entry fee: "to be determined." Display area: 8x10 inside; or larger space outside if desired. Work may be offered for sale; no commission. Craftworker must attend show; demonstrations "preferred, if possible." Registration limit: about 35. Sponsor provides 24-hour security; tables; and chairs for a fee. Show is advertised by radio; newspapers; and flyers. Considers batik; candlemaking; ceramics; decoupage; jewelry; lapidary; leatherworking; macrame; metalsmithing; pottery; tole painting; weaving; and woodcrafting.

Craftworkers who meet residency requirements may participate in the Craftsmen's Fair, Concord, New Hampshire. Said to be the oldest continuing craft fair in the country, it is sponsored for six days in August by the League of New Hampshire Craftsmen.

MALL OF NEW HAMPSHIRE PROFESSIONAL CRAFT AND SCULPTURE SHOW, Rt. 1, Box 153J, Auburn NH 03032. (603)483-2742. President: Jinx Harris. Estab. 1978. Annual indoor show held 5 days in January at Manchester, New Hampshire. Average attendance: 70,000+. Entries accepted until 1 week before show. Entry fee: $35/8x4 display area. Prejudging by slides and photos. Work may be offered for sale; no commission. Craftworker must attend show; demonstrations OK. Sponsor provides electricity for demonstrations and 24-hour security. Show is advertised by radio; TV; and newspapers. Considers all crafts except ceramics; lapidary; and strung bead jewelry.

NEW HAMPSHIRE ARTS FESTIVAL, Rt. 1, Box 153J, Auburn NH 03032. (603)483-2742. President: Jinx Harris. Estab. 1978. Annual indoor show held 5 days in April at Manchester, New Hampshire. Average attendance: 50,000+. Entries accepted until 1 week before show or until filled. Entry fee: $35/8x4 display area. Prejudging by slides or photos if not in a previous show. Work may be offered for sale; no commission. Craftworker must attend show; demonstrations OK. Registration limit: 40. Sponsor provides electricity for demonstrations and 24-hour security. Show is advertised by radio; TV; and newspapers. Considers all crafts except ceramics; decoupage under $5; lapidary; and strung bead jewelry.

OLD HOME DAY, 32 Windham Rd., Pelham NH 03076. (603)635-2023. Chairman: Charles T. Newton. Sponsor: First Congregational Church. Purpose: "to raise money for church and community." Estab. 1906. Annual outdoor show held 1 day in September. Average attendance: 8,000. Entries accepted until show is filled. Entry fee: $20-25/table. Work may be offered for sale; no commission. Craftworker needn't attend show; demonstrations OK. Registration limit: 25. Sponsor provides electricity for demonstrations and table. Considers all crafts; "we try to keep duplication to a minimum." Bestsellers: "items $10 and under seem to move very well." 1977 total exhibitor sales estimated at $20,000.

REGIONAL CRAFTSMEN'S FAIR, The Common, Rts. 4 and 118, Canaan NH 03741. Estab. 1970. Annual outdoor show (bring own canopies) held 3 days the last weekend in July. Entries accepted until 4 weeks before show, if show is not filled (jewelry seems to be swamped). Entry fee: $1 each day per craftworker. Work may be offered for sale; no commission. Craftworker must attend show; demonstrations encouraged. Registration limit: 90. Considers all crafts. "Encourage the craftsmen to have items $4 and under — but not everything [should be priced that low]."

THEATRE BY THE SEA STREET FAIR, 91 Market St., Portsmouth NH 03801. (603)431-5846. Publicist: Sandi Bianco. Sponsor: Board of Trustees of Theatre by the Sea. "The Street Fair is one of the Theatre's major fund-raising activities as a nonprofit arts organization." Annual outdoor show held 1 day in the summer. Average attendance: 8,000. Entries accepted until 1 week before show. Entry fee: $15/6' frontage. Work should be offered for sale; no commission. Craftworker or representative must attend show; demonstrations encouraged. Registration limit: 150. Sponsor provides electricity for demonstrations. Protection from sun recommended. Considers all crafts.

Sales Tip: "Because many Fair attendees are summer tourists, smaller transportable items are recommended. Moderately-priced items seem to move faster."

Promotion: Show is advertised by multiple press releases; arts magazines; TV; radio; public service announcements; and posters. "B&w studio photos can be used; feature articles can be adapted; name of participant's home town newspaper will be used for exclusive release."

THE YULETIDE FAIR, 148 Concord St., Manchester NH 03104. (603)623-0313. Gallery Coordinator: Richard Frantz. Sponsor: Manchester Institute of Arts & Sciences. Purpose: "fundraiser for our educational fund; and to promote quality crafts and craftsmen in the New England area." Annual indoor show held 3 days in late November or early December. Average attendance: 2,000. Write for information on entry deadline. No entry fee. Prejudging by slides and in-person viewing. Work must be offered for sale; 30% commission. Craftworker needn't attend show but must deliver and pick up work. Registration limit: 50-60. Gallery provides complete display; insurance; handles sales; and 24-hour security. Considers all crafts. Bestsellers: "small items, suitable for Christmas gifts. Most under $30."

Promotion: Show is advertised by newspapers; radio announcements; invitations to members; and news releases. Submit business cards, pamphlets or explanatory material on the craft."

New Jersey

*THE ART CENTRE OF NEW JERSEY, Annual Regional Exhibition and Sale, 16 Washington St., East Orange NJ 07017. Annual indoor show held in the spring. Maximum 2 entries per artist. Open to residents of New Jersey, New York, Connecticut and Pennsylvania. 25% commission. Considers sculpture. Size limit: sculptures, 24x24, 50 lbs. Work must be recent and original. Work sent by express or mail not accepted. Awards, including both cash and purchase prizes, total about $2,000.

*CAPE MAY COUNTY ART LEAGUE BOARDWALK ART SHOW, 1050 Washington St., Cape May NJ 08204. Contact: Helen Dilday. Entry fee to be announced. Display area: 10'. No sales commission. Considers handcrafts. Presents awards.

CHERRY HILL MALL ARTS FESTIVAL, Rt. 1, Box 153J, Auburn NH 03032. (603)483-2742. President: Jinx Harris. Estab. 1970. Annual indoor show held 4 days in July at Cherry Hill, New Jersey. Average attendance: 65,000+. Entries accepted until 1 week before show or until filled. Entry fee: $35/8x4 display area. Prejudging by slides or photos if not in a previous show. Work may be offered for sale; no commission. Craftworker must attend show; demonstrations OK. Registration limit: 50. Sponsor provides electricity for demonstrations and 24-hour security. Show is advertised by radio; TV; and newspaper. Considers all crafts except ceramics; lapidary; decoupage under $5; and strung bead jewelry.

CHERRY HILL MALL CRAFT AND SCULPTURE SHOW, Rt. 1, Box 153J, Auburn NH 03032. (603)483-2742. President: Jinx Harris. Estab. 1972. Annual indoor show held 4 days in April at Cherry Hill, New Jersey. Average attendance: 60,000+. Entries accepted until 1 week before show or until filled. Entry fee: $35/8x4 display area. Prejudging by slides or photos if not in a previous show. Work may be offered for sale; no commission. Craftworker must attend show; demonstrations OK. Registration limit: 120. Sponsor provides electricity for demonstrations and 24-hour security. Show is advertised by radio; TV and newspaper. Considers all crafts except ceramics; lapidary; decoupage under $5; and strung bead jewelry.

CHERRY HILL MALL PROFESSIONAL CRAFT AND SCULPTURE SHOW, Rt. 1, Box 153J, Auburn NH 03032. (603)483-2742. President: Jinx Harris. Estab. 1972. Annual indoor show held 4 days in October at Cherry Hill, New Jersey. Average attendance: 80,000+. Entries accepted until 1 week before show or until filled. Entry fee: $35/8x4 display area. Prejudging by slides or photos if not in a previous show. Work may be offered for sale; no commission. Craftworker must attend show; demonstrations OK. Registration limit: 120. Sponsor provides electricity for demonstrations and 24-hour security. Show is advertised by radio; TV; and newspaper. Considers all crafts except ceramics; decoupage under $5; lapidary; and strung bead jewelry.

CRAFT DAY IN THE PARK, Box 5005, Clinton NJ 08809. (201)735-4101. Director: Gloria Lazor. Sponsor: Clinton Historical Museum Village. Purpose: "to relate colonial crafts to the total museum experience. We are an 18th and 19th century Museum which displays, through our exhibits, life in these 2 periods." Estab. 1975. Annual outdoor show held 1 day in mid-July. Average attendance: 1,000. Entries accepted until 1 week before show. Work may be offered for sale; no commission. Craftworker must attend show; demonstrations OK. Registration limit: 40. Sponsor provides electricity for demonstrations.

Acceptable Work: Considers batik; candlemaking; ceramics; decoupage, dollmaking; glass art; jewelry; lapidary; leatherworking; macrame; metalsmithing; needlecrafts; pottery; tole painting; weaving; and woodcrafting.

Promotion: Show is advertised by newspaper features; radio announcements; posters; listing in calendars of events in tri-state area; membership mailing; and newsletter.

CRAFTS, 409 Wesley Ave., Ocean City NJ 08226. (609)399-7628. Chairman: Shirley A. Waldron. Sponsor: Ocean City Cultural Arts Center. Estab. 1972. The show is an annual 2 day event held in September at the Ocean City Boardwalk Music Pier. "Each craftsman is given the option of exhibiting his work within closed quarters or outdoors in a connecting pavilion." Average attendance: 3,000-4,000. Entries accepted until mid-August. Entry fee: $20/8x10 table; 2 craftsmen may share a table for $35; more than 1 table may be reserved for $10 extra. Prejudging by slides or photos; entry fee refunded for refused work. Work may be offered for sale. Craftworker must attend show; demonstrations OK. Registration limit: 60. Sponsor provides chairs; electricity for demonstrations; table; and 24-hour security protection. Show is advertised by radio; TV; direct mail; and news stories.

Acceptable Work: Considers batik; glass art; jewelry; leatherworking; macrame; metalsmithing; mobiles; pottery; soft sculpture; weaving; and woodcrafting.

Sales Tips: "The artist should do well in his sales if his work is displayed attractively. However, the craftsman demonstrating his skill does do better."

CREATIVE CRAFTS, 756 E. Broad St., Westfield NJ 07090. Co-chairwomen: Liz Shapiro, Lee Schoenfeld. Sponsor: Sisterhood — Temple Emanu-El. Estab. 1966. Annual indoor show held 5 days early in November. Average attendance: 3,500. Entries are screened up to 4 weeks prior to show. Entry fee: $10. "On site screening preferred" but prejudging is done occasionally by slides or photos. Entry fee due after prejudging. Work may be offered for sale; 25% commission. Registration limit: 150. Sponsor provides display panels; insurance on exhibited work; insurance on work shipped to artist; shipping costs to artists from show; 24-hour security protection.

Acceptable Work: Considers batik; ceramics; decoupage; glass art; jewelry; leatherworking; macrame; metalsmithing; mobiles; pottery; sculpture; soft sculpture; weaving; and woodcrafting.

Promotion: Show is advertised by magazine; newspaper, radio; publicity and ads. Artist should provide b&w photos and biographies.

CUMBERLAND COUNTY FAIR, 104 West Ave., Bridgeton NJ 08302. (609)451-2998. General Manager: Robert P. Wheaton. Sponsor: Cumberland County Cooperative Fair Association. Purpose: "we have promoted an agricultural fair since 1823 — [and believe] a fair should encompass all areas of interest, something for everybody, to be a well-rounded fair." Estab. 1968. Annual outdoor show (with some tents) held 6 days in July at Cumberland County Fairgrounds, Millville, New Jersey. Average attendance: 80,000. Entries accepted until 2 weeks before show. Entry fee: $100/10x10 display area. Work may be offered for sale; no commission. Craftworker must attend show; demonstrations OK. Sponsor provides electricity for demonstrations and 24-hour security. Considers all crafts.

Promotion: Fair is advertised by a professional advertising and public relations agency through newspapers; radio; TV; billboards; posters; and brochures. Submit photos or background information.

*DEPTFORD MALL PATRIOTS ART BRIGADE, 131 Paradise Dr., Berlin NJ 08009. (609)767-3228. Director: Barbara Reeder and Dory Mann. Estab. 1968. Indoor show held 4 days in April and September. Average attendance: 10,000. Entries accepted until 2 weeks before show. Entry fee: $40/12x4 display area. Work may be offered for sale; no commission. Demonstrations OK. Registration limit: 100.

Acceptable Work: Considers batik; candlemaking; dollmaking; glass art; metalsmithing; needlecrafts; pottery; soft sculpture; tole painting; weavings; wall hangings; woodcrafting; ceramics; jewelry; leather by invitation only; and handmade miniature toys. No poured ceramics.

Awards: Presents ribbons. Judging by a panel of 3 college professors, professional artists and craftworkers.

INDOOR HANDCRAFT SHOW, 155 Kline Blvd., Berkeley Heights NJ 07922. (201)464-3785, 9-10 p.m. only. Chairman: Susan Fishman. Sponsor: Women's American O.R.T. — Summit Chapter. Purpose: fundraiser. Estab. 1973. Annual indoor show held 2 days in May in various New Jersey locations. Average attendance: 1,500. Entries accepted until 3 weeks before show. Entry fee: $25/8' display area. Prejudging by samples of craft if possible; slides or photos are acceptable. Entry fee refunded for refused work. Work may be offered for sale; no commission. Craftworker must attend show; demonstrations OK. Registration limit: 50. Sponsor provides chairs; electricity for demonstrations; and 24-hour security. Show is advertised by newspapers; craft magazines; radio; and direct mail. Considers all crafts except dried flowers. Maximum size of works: table top area or to fit on hanging racks. Requirements: all tables must be draped to the floor on all 4 sides; no cartons visible.

*INDIAN SUMMER ART SHOW, 205 Montpelier Ave., Atlantic City NJ 08401. (609)345-5491. Director: Florence Miller. Sponsor: Atlantic City Art Center and City of Atlantic City. Purpose: "for the advancement of art; recognition of artists; and art education for public." Estab. 1963. Annual outdoor show held 2 days in September. Average attendance: "thousands— it is the weekend of the Miss America crowning." Entries accepted until 1 week before show. Entry fee: $25/artist. Display area: 15' along boardwalk rail. Work may be offered for sale; no commission. Craftworker must attend show; demonstrations OK if arranged prior to show. "Displays are completely up to the exhibiting artists. They must provide backdrops — windbreakers and protection — in case of inclement weather." Categories: fine arts and crafts. Presents $3,000 in cash; purchase prizes; and ribbons.

INTERNATIONAL FOLK FESTIVAL, 841 Georges Rd., Brunswick NJ 08902. (201)246-5788. Executive Administrator: Jacqueline E. Rubel. Sponsor: Middlesex County Cultural & Heritage Commission. Purpose: "to encourage a greater awareness of the diverse cultures." Estab. 1974. Annual indoor show held 1 day in June at Middlesex County College, Edison, New Jersey. Average attendance: 15,000. Entries accepted until 4 weeks before show. No entry fee. Prejudging by slides; photos; or portfolio. Work may not be offered for sale. Craftworker must attend show; demonstrations encouraged. Sponsor provides chairs; electricity for demonstrations; insurance on exhibited work; table; and 24-hour security. Show is advertised by radio; printed media; and TV. Submit photos and resume for promotion. Considers batik; ceramics; decoupage; dollmaking; glass art; jewelry; quilting; leatherworking; macrame; metalsmithing; needlecrafts; pottery; soft sculpture; tole painting; weaving; and woodcrafting.

MOORESTOWN MALL ARTS FESTIVAL, Rt. 1, Box 153J, Auburn NH 03032. (603)483-2742. President: Jinx Harris. Estab. 1964. Annual indoor show held 4 days in November at Moorestown, New Jersey. Average attendance: 60,000+. Entries accepted until 1 week before show or until filled. Entry fee: $35/8x4 display area. Prejudging by slides or photos if not in a previous show. Work may be offered for sale; no commission. Craftworker must attend show; demonstrations OK. Registration limit: 50. Sponsor provides electricity for demonstrations and 24-hour security. Show is advertised by radio; TV; and newspapers. Considers all crafts except ceramics; decoupage under $5; lapidary; and strung bead jewelry.

MOORESTOWN MALL CHILDREN'S HOUR SHOW, Rt. 1, Box 153J, Auburn NH 03032. (603)483-2742. President: Jinx Harris. Estab. 1976. Annual indoor show held 4 days in June at Moorestown, New Jersey. Average attendance: 45,000+. Entries accepted until 1 week before show or until filled. Entry fee: $35/8x4 display area. Prejudging by slides or photos if not in a previous show. Work may be offered for sale; no commission. Craftworker must attend show; demonstrations OK. Registration limit: 100. Sponsor provides electricity for demonstrations and 24-hour security. Show is advertised by radio; TV; and newspapers. Considers all child-oriented crafts except ceramics; decoupage under $5; lapidary; and strung bead jewelry.

MOORESTOWN MALL CRAFT AND SCULPTURE SHOW, Rt. 1, Box 153J, Auburn NH 03032. (603)483-2742. President: Jinx Harris. Estab. 1975. Annual indoor show held 4 days in August at Moorestown, New Jersey. Average attendance: 60,000+. Entries accepted until 1 week before show or until filled. Entry fee: $35/8x4 display area. Prejudging by slides or photos if not in a previous show. Work may be offered for sale; no commission. Craftworker must attend show; demonstrations OK. Registration limit: 110. Sponsor provides electricity for demonstrations and 24-hour security. Show is advertised by radio; TV; and newspapers. Considers all crafts except ceramics; decoupage under $5; lapidary; and strung bead jewelry.

MORRISTOWN CRAFTMARKET, Box 2305-R, Morristown NJ 07960. Technical Director: Michael F. Feno. Sponsor: New Jersey Designer-Craftsmen/Kiwanis Club of Randolph

Township. Estab. 1977. Annual indoor show held 2 days in October. Attendance: 13,000, first year. Entries accepted until 6 months before show. Entry fee: $5/craftworker. Display area: 10x-10'. Prejudging by 5 slides; no entry fees refunded for refused work. Work may be offered for sale; no commission. Craftworker must attend show; demonstrations OK. Registration limit: 135. Sponsor provides electricity for demonstrations and 24-hour security. Show is advertised by a paid publicist. 1977 show sales for craftworkers totalled $90,000.

Acceptable Work: Considers batik; candlemaking; ceramics; dollmaking; glass art; jewelry; leather working; macrame; metalsmithing; pottery; soft sculpture; weaving; and woodcrafting.

*NATIONAL RAKU EXHIBITION, Peters Valley Craftsmen, Layton NJ 07851. (201)948-5202. Contact: Molly Mechem. Purpose: "to exhibit exceptional pieces of raku ceramics for the enjoyment and education of the public. This is an 'art'-oriented public." Annual indoor show held 6 weeks in the spring at the Peters Valley Craftsmen Gallery. Average attendance: 1,200. Entries accepted until approximately 2 months before show. Entry fee: $4/item being displayed. Maximum 3 entries/craftworker. Prejudging by slides; no entry fees refunded for refused work. Work may be offered for sale; approximately 33⅛% commission. Craftworker needn't attend show; no demonstrations. Registration limit: about 20. Sponsor provides display panels; electricity for demonstrations; insurance on exhibited work; and handles sales. Show is advertised by press releases and magazines. Submit 8x10 b&w glossies for publicity. Considers raku ceramics. Presents purchase prizes.

*PATRIOTS ART BRIGADE, 131 Paradise Dr., Berlin NJ 08009. (609)767-3228 or 767-1874. Directors: Barbara Reeder and Dory Mann. "I feel there is much talent in our own back yard, and it is a wonderful proving ground for the experienced and inexperienced artist or craftsman." Estab. 1969. Semiannual indoor show held 4 days (Thursday-Sunday) in April and in September at Deptford, New Jersey. Average attendance: 100,000. Entries accepted until 3 weeks before show. Entry fee: $40/12' space. Prejudging by slides, personal interview, or photos; entry fee refunded for refused work. Work may be offered for sale; no commission. Craftworker must attend show; demonstrations OK. Registration limit: 60-100. Sponsor provides electricity for demonstrations; 24-hour security; and insurance on accidents. Considers all crafts (but ceramics; jewelry; and leatherworking by invitation only).

Awards: Presents ribbons. "Work must be of professional quality. We employ different judges— at least 2 for art and 2 for crafts. Crafts are very hard to judge. We try to have them judged on quality of workmanship — idea of presentation. Neatness counts as it is a mall situation."

Sales Tip: "An artist or craftsman should have 2 types of work with him — low cost items and higher priced things. We've had decorators for department stores give exclusive contracts to craftsmen which can be a permanent job for them. A Hilton Hotel manager passing through took fancy to a woodcarver and ordered several birds carved to be made into lamps for the hotel. Your best work is the surest way to sales."

Promotion: Show is advertised in local papers; *Philadelphia Enquirer* weekend magazine; *Courrier Post;* radio; and posters. "Sometimes we can get a photographer from the newspaper to take pictures of the show and interview prize winners. Sometimes we feature a really unusual craft in our preshow publicity."

PETERS VALLEY CRAFT FAIR, Peters Valley Craftsmen, Layton NJ 07851. Contact: Jeanne E. Patterson. Estab. 1969. Annual outdoor show held 2 days in the summer. Entries accepted until about 4 months before show. Entry fee: $7/artist. Prejudging by slides. Considers all crafts.

QUAKER BRIDGE MALL ARTS FESTIVAL, Rt. 1, Box 153J, Auburn NH 03032. (703)483-2742. President: Jinx Harris. Estab. 1976. Annual indoor show held 4 days in June at Princeton, New Jersey. Average attendance: 60,000+. Entries accepted until 1 week before show or until filled. Entry fee: $35/8x4 display area. Prejudging by slides or photos if not in a previous show. Work may be offered for sale; no commission. Craftworker must attend show; demonstrations OK. Registration limit: 50. Sponsor provides electricity for demonstrations and 24-hour security. Show is advertised by radio; TV; and newspapers. Considers all crafts except ceramics; decoupage under $5; lapidary; and strung bead jewelry.

QUAKER BRIDGE MALL CHILDREN'S HOUR SHOW, Rt. 1, Box 153J, Auburn NH 03032. (603)483-2742. President: Jinx Harris. Estab. 1977. Annual indoor show held 4 days in January at Princeton, New Jersey. Average attendance: 25,000+. Entries accepted until 1 week before show. Entry fee: $25/8x4 display area. Prejudging by slides or photos. Work may be offered for sale; no commission. Craftworker must attend show; demonstrations OK. Registra-

tion limit: 75. Sponsor provides electricity for demonstrations and 24-hour security. Show is advertised by radio; TV; and newspapers.
Acceptable Work: Considers batik; candlemaking; decoupage; dollmaking; glass art; jewelry; leatherworking; animal macrame; metalsmithing; mobiles; pottery; sculpture; and soft sculpture. "This show is for child-oriented items only."

SEAVIEW SQUARE MALL CRAFT AND SCULPTURE SHOW, Rt. 1, Box 153J, Auburn NH 03032. (603)483-2742. President: Jinx Harris. Estab. 1978. Annual indoor show held 4 days in April at Ocean, New Jersey. Average attendance: 50,000+. Entries accepted until 1 week before show or until filled. Entry fee: $35/8x4 display area. Prejudging by slides or photos if not in a previous show. Work may be offered for sale; no commission. Craftworker must attend show; demonstrations OK. Registration limit: 120. Sponsor provides electricity for demonstrations and 24-hour security. Show is advertised by radio; TV; and newspapers. Considers all crafts except ceramics; decoupage under $5; lapidary; and strung bead jewelry.

*WEST HUDSON COMMUNITY ARTS FESTIVAL, 66 Dukes St., Kearny NJ 07032. (201)998-1067. Chairman: Phyllis Adams. Sponsor: The Halfpenny Playhouse. Purpose: to "display the artistry of New Jersey but not to the exclusion of artists in other states. To promote the goodwill of the town of Kearny and the county of Hudson to both the general public and the artistic community. To assist in improving the quality of life in the community and the encouragement of budding talent by including juniors and non-professionals who receive the same cash awards as the professionals. We deliberately inter-mix pros, non-pros, and juniors to provide the artists and public with a variety of quality and artists." Estab. 1969. Annual outdoor show held 1 day in June. Average attendance: 15,000. Entries accepted up until show date. Entry fee: $5/10' on snow or anchor-fencing; $3/senior citizen over 63; and no fee/juniors. Work may be offered for sale; no commission. Craftworker or representative must attend show; demonstrations encouraged. Sponsor provides fencing.
Awards: Presents cash awards of at least $3,000 and ribbons to best in show, 1st, 2nd, 3rd and honorable mentions in all categories. "Only honorable mentions do not receive cash awards." Average show sales totalled $50,000+. Considers all crafts.
Promotion: Show is advertised by "major feature stories with pictures starting 2 weeks prior to event in all major papers including *New York Times, New York News* and New Jersey dailies and weeklies. Listed on all community bulletin boards of all New York and New Jersey AM and FM radios. Heavy poster coverage of nearby affluent areas in northern New Jersey. Listed in newsletters of multiple state and private arts agencies. Listed in all events calendars of all New York and New Jersey newspapers. Ads in selected arts magazines. The minimum the artist should have available is a calling card. We find many sales are made within 3 months after events. Suggest, where financially feasible, that artists provide public with a free flyer or brochure with samples of his work included in photographs and information on his training; awards; and showing."
Sales Tip: "Our public comes from Pennsylvania, New Jersey, New York, and Connecticut. They are looking for bargains not normally available at the larger New York outdoor events. Our entrants come from as far away as Florida and Wyoming because of the heavy selling traffic. Decorative items such as flowers, rag dolls, jewelry, wall hangings and glass items are heavy sellers. Public likes to buy, where possible, those items created on the spot."

WILLOWBROOK MALL ART SHOW, Rt. 1, Box 153J, Auburn NH 03032. (603)483-2742. President: Jinx Harris. Estab. 1969. Annual indoor show held 4 days in February at Wayne, New Jersey. Average attendance: 100,000. Entries accepted until 1 week before show or until filled. Entry fee: $35/8x4 display area. Prejudging by slides or photos if not in a previous show. Work may be offered for sale; no commission. Craftworker must attend show; demonstrations OK. Registration limit: 30. Sponsor provides electricity for demonstrations and 24-hour security. Show is advertised by radio; TV; and newspapers. Considers all crafts except ceramics; decoupage under $5; lapidary; and strung bead jewelry.

WILLOWBROOK MALL WOODEN WAY SHOW, Rt. 1, Box 153J, Auburn NH 03032. (603)483-2742. President: Jinx Harris. Estab. 1977. Annual indoor show held 4 days in May at Wayne, New Jersey. Average attendance: 75,000+. Entries accepted until 1 week before show or until filled. Entry fee: $35/8x4 display area. Prejudging by slides or photos if not in a previous show. Work may be offered for sale; no commission. Craftworker must attend show; demonstrations OK. Registration limit: 50. Sponsor provides electricity for demonstrations and 24-hour security. Show is advertised by radio; TV; and newspapers. Considers only crafts of wood.

WOODBRIDGE CENTER CRAFT AND SCULPTURE SHOW, Rt. 1, Box 153J, Auburn NH 03032. (603)483-2742. President; Jinx Harris. Estab. 1975. Annual indoor show held 4 days in February at Woodbridge, New Jersey. Average attendance: 85,000+. Entries accepted until 1 week before show or until filled. Entry fee: $35/8x4 display area. Prejudging by slides or photos if not in a previous show. Work may be offered for sale; no commission. Craftworker must attend show; demonstrations OK. Registration limit: 130. Sponsor provides electricity for demonstrations and 24-hour security. Show is advertised by radio; TV; and newspapers. Considers all crafts except ceramics; lapidary; decoupage under $5; and strung bead jewelry.

New Mexico

ARTS & CRAFTS FAIR OF THE SOUTHWEST, Box 122, Roswell NM 88201. Contact: Exhibitors' Chairman. Sponsor: Roswell Jaycees. Estab. 1973. Annual indoor show held first weekend in May. Average attendance: 4,000. Entries accepted until March 1. Entry fee: $40/booth with 8x8' pegboard; $20/additional craftworker. Prejudging; entry fee refunded for refused work. Work must be offered for sale; no commission. Open to craftworkers ages 18+. Craftworker must attend show; demonstrations encouraged. Registration limit: 100 booths.
Acceptable Work: Considers batik; candlemaking; ceramics; dollmaking; glass art; jewelry; leatherworking; metalsmithing; needlecrafts; pottery; soft sculpture; tole painting; weavings; wall hangings; woodcrafting; and mosaics. Only safety catches on jewelry are accepted as manufactured.

DE VARGAS SUMMER ARTS AND CRAFTS SHOW, Box 205, Santa Fe NM 87501. (505)988-1110. President: Jane Dunn. Sponsor: Southwest Arts, Inc. Purpose: fundraiser. Estab. 1975. Annual indoor show held 3 days in July. Entries accepted until 3 weeks before show. Entry fee: $50/craftworker; $50/8x4 display area. Prejudging, first year only, by slides and photos; entry fee refunded for refused work. Work may be offered for sale; no commission. Craftworker must attend show; demonstrations OK. Registration limit: 80-100. Sponsor provides electricity for demonstrations and 24-hour security. Show is advertised by radio; newspaper; posters; and direct mail. Considers all crafts.

*NEW MEXICO ARTS & CRAFTS FAIR, Box 30044, Albuquerque NM 87190. (505)265-3171. Manager: Ann Anthony. Estab. 1962. Annual outdoor show (with some booths) held the last Friday, Saturday and Sunday in June. Average attendance: 100,000. Closing date for entry: February. Entry fee: $60/booth plus $7.50 jury fee. Samples due for prejudging in February; no prejudging fees refunded for refused work. Work must be offered for sale; no commission. Open to New Mexico residents, ages 18+. Craftworker must attend show and use booths; demonstrations required. Sponsor provides lighting. Considers all crafts. Presents $1,000 in purchase prizes and $50 awards of excellence.

*NEW MEXICO CRAFTS BIENNIAL, Box 2087, Santa Fe NM 87501. (505)827-2544. Curator: Judith Cohen. Sponsor: Museum of International Folk Art, a division of the Museum of New Mexico. Estab. 1953. Biennial indoor show suspended until 1981.

PEANUT VALLEY FESTIVAL, Campus Union, Eastern New Mexico University, Portales NM 88130. (505)562-2631. Director of Student Activities: Bill Martin. Estab. 1974. Annual indoor show held 3 days in October. Average attendance: 4,000. Entries accepted until 1 week before show. Entry fee: $15/display area. Work may be offered for sale; no commission. Craftworker must attend show; demonstrations OK. Sponsor provides display panels and electricty for demonstrations. Show is advertised by newspaper; radio; and *New Mexico Magazine*. Considers all crafts.

PLAZA ARTS AND CRAFTS SHOW, Girls' Club, 301 Hillside, Santa Fe NM 87501. (505)982-2042. Director of Girls' Club: Helen Brown. Sponsor: Santa Fe Girls' Club Auxiliary. Purpose: fundraiser. Estab. 1972. Annual outdoor show held 1 day in August. Average attendance: 2,000. Entries accepted until 2 weeks before show. Entry fee: $25-30/craftworker. Display area: 10x10. Prejudging preferred by photos; accepts slides. Entry fee refunded for refused work. Work may be offered for sale; no commission. Craftworker must attend show; demonstrations OK if space permits. Registration limit: 200. Sponsor provides trash bags; parking areas; and relief people. Show is advertised by newspapers; magazines; TV; and radio. Considers all crafts.

SANTA FE FESTIVAL OF THE ARTS, Box 1928, Santa Fe NM 87501. (505)983-7317. Executive Director: Sara Sheldon. Sponsor: Santa Fe Foundation. "Goals are to promote Santa Fe as a national art center and to bring national exposure to artists and craftsmen who show here." Estab. 1978. Annual indoor show held 10 days in October. Average attendance: 5,000. Entries accepted until 4 weeks before show. Prejudging by slides; no entry fees refunded for refused work. Work may be offered for sale; 20% commission. Craftworker needn't attend show; demonstrations OK. Sponsor provides display panels; electricity for demonstrations; and 24-hour security. Show is advertised by national magazine ads; national newspaper press releases; direct mail; TV; and radio. Submit photos and resumes for catalog.

Acceptable Work: Considers batik; ceramics; glass art; jewelry; leatherworking; macrame; metalsmithing; needlecrafts; pottery; soft sculpture; weaving; and woodcrafting. "This is a tri-cultural show with Indian, Hispanic, and other crafts. Everything is displayed as fine arts— on pedestal, in a case, or on a wall. Display up to discretion of committee."

SOUTHWEST CRAFTS BIENNIAL, Box 2087, Santa Fe NM 87501. (501)827-2544. Curator: Judith Cohen. Sponsor: Museum of International Folk Art, a division of the Museum of New Mexico. Estab. 1953. Biennial indoor show suspended until 1981.

*SWAIA INDIAN MARKET, Box 1964, Santa Fe NM 87501. (505)983-5220. Executive Secretary: Sally M. Kandarian. Sponsor: Southwestern Association on Indian Affairs. Purpose: "to promote quality Indian handmade arts and crafts and to provide a setting where craftworker and buyer can confront each other to the benefit of both." Estab. 1922. Annual outdoor invitational show held 2 days in August. Average attendance: 30,000+. Entries accepted until 1 month before show. Entry fee: $50/6x8 display area. Maximum 3 pieces per category per artist for awards. Prejudging by slides; entry fee due after prejudging. Work may be offered for sale; no commission. Craftworker must attend show; demonstrations OK. Registration limit: 326. Sponsor provides coverings and display panels. Show is advertised by mailings and all media. Presents cash awards and ribbons. Considers all handcrafted Southwestern Indian arts.

*TAOS FESTIVAL OF THE ARTS, Drawer I, Taos NM 87571. (505)758-3873. Manager: Betty Armantrout. Sponsor: Taos County Chamber of Commerce. Estab. 1975. Annual indoor/outdoor show held 1 week in October. Average attendance: 2,000. Entries accepted until 4 weeks before show. Entry fee: $25/8x10 display area. Prejudging by slides; $5 of entry fee not refunded for refused work. Work may be offered for sale; no commission. Craftworker must attend show; demonstrations encouraged. Registration limit: 40. Sponsor provides 12-hour security protection. Show is advertised by national magazines; newspapers; TV; and radio. Presents 8 cash awards of $50. Considers all crafts except decoupage; mobiles; and tole painting.

New York

ADVENTURES IN CRAFTS DECOUPAGE SALE AND EXHIBIT, 218 E. 81st St., New York NY 10028. (212)628-8081. Contact: Dee Davis. Sponsor: Multiple Sclerosis. Purpose: "to acquaint the public with decoupage and all its variations; to interest them in the craft; to help the craftspersons sell their decoupage." Estab. 1975. Annual indoor show held 2 weeks in March. Entries accepted up until show. Entry fee: $5/artist. Display area: 400 square feet. Maximum 12 pieces per craftworker. Prejudging ("usually I have seen the craftsman's work at my studio"); entry fee due after prejudging. Work may be offered for sale; 25% commission. Craftworker must serve a 2-hour shift as a salesperson; demonstrations OK. Registration limit: 35+. Sponsor provides tables and 24-hour security. Considers quality decoupage.

Sales Tip: Offer variety — boxes; purses; plates; lamps; pictures; and plaques. 1977 show sales totalled $1,200.

Promotion: Show is advertised by posters; and press releases to newspapers and radio. Invitations sent by Adventures in Crafts and participants receive invitations to send.

ALBANY WINTER CARNIVAL, INVITATION CRAFTS SHOW, Albany City Arts Office, 75 New Scotland Ave., Albany NY 12208. (518)472-7580 or 472-7513. Administrative Assistant: Carol Clas. Sponsor: Albany League of Arts. Annual indoor show held 1 day in January. Average attendance: 15,000. Entries accepted until 1 week before show. Prejudging by slides and/or photos; invitational show. Work may be offered for sale; no commission. Craftworker must attend show; demonstrations possible, "depends on the needs of the craftsperson." Sponsor provides chairs; tables; and easels. Show is advertised by newspapers; TV; and radio. Considers all crafts.

*ALLENTOWN OUTDOOR ART FESTIVAL, Box 66, Market Station, Buffalo NY 14203. Contact: Chairman of Entries. Sponsor: Allentown Village Society. Estab. 1958. Annual outdoor show held 2 days in June. Estimated attendance: 250,000. Application forms available in February. Entries accepted until 8 weeks before show. Display area: 15' street frontage. Prejudging by slides; entry fee refunded for refused work. Work may be offered for sale; no commission. Craftworker must attend show; demonstrations OK. Registration limit: about 150 in crafts (470 total). Show is advertised by newspapers; radio; TV; trade magazines; and posters. Presents cash awards and ribbons for 1st, 2nd, 3rd and honorable mention. Considers all crafts except decoupage and needlecrafts.

*ALLIED ARTISTS OF AMERICA EXHIBITION, 1083 5th Ave., New York NY 10028. (203)355-1013. Public Relations Chairman: Catherine Ballantyne. Estab. 1913. Annual indoor show held 2 weeks during October-November. Average attendance: 2,000. Entries accepted until 2 weeks before show. Entry fee: $8/artist. Maximum 1 entry per artist. Prejudging; no entry fees refunded for refused work. Work may be offered for sale; 20% commission. "All work must be delivered and unpacked by the artist or an agent." Out-of-town exhibitors should send their entries at an early date to agents W.S. Budworth & Son, or Berkeley Express & Moving Co. (write Ballantyne for addresses). Considers sculpture. Maximum size: 24x34x80. Presents approximately $900 in cash prizes.

*ART IN PARK, Box 641, Elmira NY 14901. (607)734-0885. Chairperson: Cameron Macdonell. Sponsor: Southern Tier Arts Association Inc. Estab. 1976. Annual outdoor show held 2 days in May. Average attendance: 15,000. Entries accepted until 3 weeks before show. Entry fee: $8/8x10 display area. Prejudging by slides and photos; entry fee refunded for refused work. Work may be offered for sale; no commission. Craftworker must attend show; demonstrations OK. Registration limit: 150. Show is advertised by radio; TV; and newspaper. Presents cash and purchase awards. Bestsellers: functional art and jewelry.
Acceptable Work: Considers batik; glass art; jewelry; lapidary; leatherworking; metalsmithing; mobiles; pottery; sculpture; soft sculpture; weaving; and woodcrafting.

*ASID INTERNATIONAL EXPOSITION OF DESIGNER SOURCES, 730 5th Ave., New York NY 10019. (212)586-7111. Coordinator: Ed Gips. Sponsor: American Society of Interior Designers. Estab. 1971. Annual indoor show held 4 days in July. Average attendance: 2,000. Entries accepted until 2 weeks before show. Charges entry fee for 8x10' display area. Prejudging; no entry fees refunded. Considers all crafts. Presents ribbons.

*AUTUMN ART FESTIVAL, 19 Bernard Ave., Norwood NY 13668. (315)353-9909. Chairperson: Jane Peacock. Sponsor: Village of Norwood. Estab. 1972. Annual show held in outdoor arena with open sides 1 day in September. Average attendance: 5,000. Entries accepted until 1 week before show. Entry fee: $2/artist. Work may be offered for sale; no commission. Craftworker must attend show; demonstrations OK. Sponsor provides easels and fencing. Show is advertised by newspapers; radio; TV; and many publications. Presents ribbons and cash awards of $20, 1st; $15, 2nd; $10, 3rd; and $5, 4th in each category. Considers all crafts except glass art; lapidary; metalsmithing; mobiles; soft sculpture; and tole painting.
Sales Tip: "If artist can send information and photos for promotion at time of entry it will be included in pre-publicity of the show. This helps the public decide ahead what is available."

CHRISTMAS ARTS AND CRAFTS SHOW, 25 Seneca St., Shortsville NY 14548. (716)289-9439. President: Ronald L. Johnson. Sponsor: Finger Lakes Craftsmen. Estab. 1975. Annual indoor show held 2 days in December at Rochester, New York. Average attendance: 10,000+. Entries accepted until show is full (sometimes early). Entry fee: $50-85/10x7 display area. Work may be offered for sale; no commission. Craftworker must attend show; demonstrations OK. Registration limit: 200. Sponsor provides 24-hour security. Show is advertised by TV; radio; and newspaper ($3,000 budget). Considers all crafts.

*COOPERSTOWN ANNUAL NATIONAL ART EXHIBITION, Cooperstown Art Association, 22 Main St., Cooperstown NY 13326. (607)547-9777. Exhibition Director: Olga Welch. Estab. 1928. Annual indoor show held 4 weeks in the summer. Entries accepted by agent until 6 weeks before show. Entry fee: $7.50. Maximum 1 piece per craftworker. Prejudging. Categories: painting; sculpture; and crafts. Considers all crafts. Presents cash awards totalling $3,000.

*CORN HILL ARTS FESTIVAL, 21 Atkinson St., Historic Corn Hill District, Rochester NY 14608. (716)546-6754. Advisor: Wayne Frank. Sponsor: Corn Hill Neighbors. Estab. 1968. Annual outdoor show held 2 days in July. Average attendance: 50,000-70,000. Entries accepted until June 30. Entry fee: $25/craftworker. Display area: 10'. Work may be offered for sale; no commission. Craftworker must attend show; demonstrations OK. Registration limit: 500. Show is advertised by newspaper; TV; radio; and Rochester's Bureau of Special Events and Tourism. Submit nonreturnable photo for publicity if you have an unusual craft. Presents $500 in cash. Considers all crafts.

Over $3,000 in cash prizes is awarded at the Cooperstown Annual National Art Exhibition in Cooperstown, New York, for paintings, sculpture, and crafts. A maximum of one piece per craftworker may be exhibited in the juried show which was established in 1928. Photo by Frank Rollins.

CRAFT DAYS, Madison County Historical Society, 435 Main St., Oneida NY 13421. (315)363-4136. Director: John H. Braunlein. Estab. 1965. Annual outdoor show under tents held 2 days in September. Average attendance: 5,500. Entries accepted until about 3 months before show. Display area: 6x8 under tent; 6x16 outside. Prejudging by personal interview. Work may be offered for sale; no commission. Craftworker must attend show; demonstrations required. Registration limit: 135. Sponsor provides electricity for demonstrations. Considers all crafts. **Promotion:** Show is advertised by radio; TV; and newspaper news releases. Posters and placemats are distributed in local and area restaurants and signs placed at major intersections. Submit photos and biographical data.

CRAFT FESTIVAL, Schenectady Museum, Nott Terrace Heights, Schenectady NY 12308. Chairman: Cheryl Gerding. Sponsor: Designer Crafts Council of Schenectady Museum. Estab. 1971. Annual indoor show held 2 days in September. Average attendance: 5,000. Entries accepted until 5 months before show. Entry fee: $5 prejudging fee plus $25 upon acceptance. Display area: 10x10. Prejudging by slides; entry fee not refunded for refused work. Work may be offered for sale; no commission. Craftworker must attend show; demonstrations OK. Registration limit: 80-100. Sponsor provides electricity for demonstrations and 24-hour security. Show is advertised by newspapers; radio; TV; and posters. Considers all crafts.

CRAFTS AND CREATIONS, Putnam Arts Council, Box 156, Mahopac NY 10541. (914)628-3664. Chairman: Louise Wood. Estab. 1971. Annual indoor show held 2 days in November during Thanksgiving weekend. Average attendance: 1,000. Entries accepted until filled. Entry fee: $20/8' display area. Prejudging by slides and photos; entry fee due after prejudging. Work may be offered for sale; no commission. Craftworker must attend show; demonstrations OK. Registration limit: 30. Sponsor provides chairs. Show is advertised by newspaper; radio; posters; and mailings. Submit publicity photos. Considers all crafts. Bestsellers: holiday gifts.

CRAFTS FAIR, First United Methodist Church, Davison St. and Atlantic Ave., Oceanside NY 11572. (516)766-9787. Committee Member: Adele Jack. Estab. 1973. Annual indoor show held 2 days in May. Average attendance: 350-400. Entries accepted until 1 week before show. Entry fee: $20/8' display area. Tables must have skirts (crepe paper). Prejudging by photos; entry fee due after prejudging. Work may be offered for sale; no commission. Craftworker must attend show; demonstrations OK. Registration limit: 30-33. Sponsor provides chairs and 24-hour security. Show is advertised by radio; magazines; and posters. Each craftworker is sent a poster to display in a prominent place. Considers all crafts.

CROTON CRAFTS FAIR, Box 277, Croton On Hudson NY 10520. (914)271-5302. Crafts Chairperson: Monya Brown. Sponsor: Croton Council on the Arts. Estab. 1975. Annual outdoor show held 2 days in the third week in September. Average attendance: 4,000-5,000. Entries accepted up until filled. Entry fee: $35/10x10 display area. Prejudging by 4-5 slides, photos or actual work (include 1 slide of display). Entry fee due after prejudging. Work must be offered for sale; no commission. Craftworker or representative must attend show; demonstrations "only if we agree to them." Registration limit: 100. Sponsor provides picnic table and security. Considers pottery; jewelry; macrame; wood; fine arts; weaving; soft cloth work; batik; leather; stained glass; blown glass; candles and other original crafts.
Sales Tip: "An attractive display is a huge help, also a varied price range. We suggest that all artists have inexpensive items, up to $10 plus higher priced things. Business cards are helpful and a pleasant, friendly manner as well."
Promotion: Show is advertised by posters; postcards; radio; newspaper listings and articles; a banner in the middle of the village; and large wooden signs in area. Submit b&w glossies of display or close-up of self with work to be sent to papers.

*CURBSTONE CRAFT FESTIVAL, 55 St. Paul St., Rochester NY 14604. (716)454-2220. Contact: Jim O'Brien. Sponsor: Downtown Promotion Council of the Rochester Area Chamber of Commerce, Inc. Estab. 1973. Annual outdoor show held 3 days in June. Entries accepted until 4 weeks before show. Entry fee: $20/10' display area. Prejudging by photos or slides; entry fee refunded for refused work. Work must be offered for sale; no commission. Craftworker or representative must attend show; demonstrations OK. Sponsor provides 8' table at $9. Presents ribbons for best of show; 1st place; 2nd; and 3rd. Considers ceramics; jewelry; leatherworking; macrame; metalsmithing; needlecrafts; pottery; sculpture; soft sculpture; weaving; and woodcrafting.

*FESTIVAL OF AMERICAN CRAFTSMANSHIP, Box 20, Hasbrouck Heights NJ 07604. (212)874-4992. Coordinator: Brenda Brigham. Sponsor: American Concern for Artistry and Craftsmanship. Purpose: "to provide a crafts festival of excellent quality, diversity, originality and high marketability; to provide the public with a rich cultural experience." Estab. 1977. Annual outdoor show held 2 weekends in July at Lincoln Center Plaza, New York City. Average attendance: 60,000. Entries accepted until 4 weeks before show. Entry fee: $50/10x8 display area (for 2 days). Prejudging by 5 color slides (SASE for return); entry fee refunded for refused work. Work may be offered for sale; no commission. Craftworker must attend show; demonstrations OK. Registration limit: 125. Sponsor provides electricity for demonstrations; 24-hour security; extensive public relations campaign; and notification of wholesale buyers. Show is advertised by radio; TV; newspapers; magazines; posters; and flyers. Presents cash, purchase and certificate awards.
Acceptable Work: Considers batik; candlemaking; ceramics; dollmaking; glass art; jewelry; leatherworking; macrame; metalsmithing; needlecrafs; pottery; sculpture; soft sculpture; weaving; woodcrafting; basketry; puppetry; bookbinding; knives; pipes; scrimshaws; and brooms.

FESTIVAL OF THE ARTS, Rm. 101A Alumni Hall, State University College at Oneonta, Oneonta NY 13820. (607)432-2070. Executive Directors: Leonard and Dorothy Ryndes. Sponsor: Upper Catskill Community Council of the Arts, Inc. Estab. 1970. Annual indoor/outdoor show held 1 day in June. Average attendance: 30,000. Entries accepted until 2 weeks before show. Display area: 10'. Prejudging by slides. Work may be offered for sale; 5% commission on all sales after $50. Craftworker must attend show; demonstrations OK. Registration limit: 450-500. Sponsor provides chairs; fencing; table; and electrical outlets. Categories: traditional and contemporary crafts and fine arts. Considers all crafts.

FLUSHING ART LEAGUE OUTDOOR EXHIBITION, c/o Anna M. Kraus, 43-24 160th St., Flushing NY 11358. (212)358-0388. Sponsor: The Flushing Art League. "We are incorporated to further the arts, aid the artist in any way we can." Estab. 1957. Annual or semiannual outdoor show held 2 weekends the first 2 weeks in May and/or September. Entries accepted until show date. Entry fee: $15/10 running feet of 6' high fence. Work may be offered for sale; no commission. Craftworker must attend show; demonstrations OK if prearranged. Sponsor provides fencing. Show is advertised by newspapers; radios; TV; flyers and posters. Categories: art and crafts. Considers all crafts except wearables. Presents cash awards and ribbons for art, but no craft awards. "Our September show sales were good [in 1977], among others 2 $300 pictures were sold, one for $375."

FULTON COUNTY STREET ARTS FESTIVAL, Fulton County Arts Council, 40 N. Main St., Gloversville NY 12078. (518)725-6248. Executive Director: Joanna Vedder. Purpose: "to bring all of the arts together under 1 banner for the benefit of all." Estab. 1977. Annual outdoor show held 1 day in June. Average attendance: 10,000. Entries accepted up until show date. Entry fee: $5/half of standard street parking place, about 9x12. Work may be offered for sale; no commission. Craftworker or representative must attend show; demonstrations encouraged. Sponsor provides electricity for demonstrations. Show is advertised by radio; newspaper articles and ads throughout central New York state; and posters in tourist areas. Submit any information of special interest about your craft. Considers all crafts.
Sales Tip: "People geneally do not come with large amounts of cash. Items of over $50 probably will not sell that day. Some exhibitors did well in special orders though."

*GALLERY IN THE PARK, Upper Shad Rd., Pound Ridge NY 10576. (914)764-4613. Director: Anne Cook. Sponsor: Pound Ridge Lions Club. Estab. 1970. Annual outdoor show held 2 days in May. Entries accepted until show. Entry fee: $35/12 linear feet of display area. Prejudging by nonreturnable slides and photos; entry fee refunded for refused work. Work may be offered for sale; no commission. Craftworker must attend show; demonstrations OK. Registration limit: 120. Sponsor provides electricity for demonstrations when prearranged; fencing; and insurance on exhibited work. Considers sculpture; pottery; jewelry; fiber; glass; wood and leather. Presents cash awards.

*GALLERY NORTH OUTDOOR ART SHOW, N. Country Rd., Setauket NY 11733. Contact: Sharon Cowles or Marjorie Bishop. Sponsor: Gallery North. Estab. 1965. Annual outdoor show held 2 days in July. Entry fee: $20/10' display area. Work may be offered for sale; no commission. Craftworker must attend show; demonstrations OK. Registration limit: 225. Presents $1,000 in cash prizes.
Acceptable Work: Considers batik; ceramics; glass art; jewelry; leatherworking; metalsmithing; pottery; weavings; wall hangings; woodcrafting; graphics; and sculpture.

GARRISON ART CENTER ARTS AND CRAFTS FAIR, Box 4, Garrison NY 10524. Chairman of Board: Laura S. Jones. Purpose: fundraiser. Estab. 1969. Annual outdoor show held 2 days in August. Average attendance: 10,000. Entries accepted until 8 weeks before show. Entry fee: $25/12x8 display area; only 1 artist per area. Prejudging by a minimum of 5 slides or photos and a resume. Entry fee due after prejudging. Work must be offered for sale; 10% commission. Craftworker or representative must attend show; demonstrations OK. Registration limit: 100. Sponsor provides electricity for demonstrations if notified in advance. Show is advertised by radio and newspaper in 100-mile radius, including coverage by the *New York Times.* Submit photos. 1977 show sales totalled $27,339.70. Considers all crafts except candlemaking and decoupage.

GERMAN ALPS FESTIVAL, Main St., Hunter NY 12442. (518)263-4141. President: Don Conover. Estab. 1976. Annual indoor/outdoor and under tent show held 17 days in summer. Average attendance: 240,000. Entries accepted until 3 weeks before show. Entry fee: "craftsmen who mainly demonstrate pay nothing; others are on 10% commission; and pure commercial [exhibitors] pay footage fee." Display area: 10x10. Prejudging by slides or photos. Work may be offered for sale. Craftworker must attend show; demonstrations OK. Registration limit: 50. Sponsor provides chairs; coverings; electricity for demonstrations; table; and 24-hour security. Categories: pure crafts (demonstration); ethnic crafts; semi-crafts (commercial); and pure commercial. Considers all crafts.
Promotion: Show is advertised by brochures; newspaper stories; and magazine articles. Submit past credits; biographical material; and reviews of work to be used in press releases, articles and in festival program.

GLENS FALLS FARMER'S MARKET, 9479 Gansevoort Rd., Gansevoort NY 12831. (518)793-4576. Crafts Chairman: Jeannette von Linden. Estab. 1976. Outdoor show held every Saturday morning July through October at Glens Falls, New York. Average attendance: 1,000+ each Saturday. Entries accepted up until show. Entry fee: $35/8' area for season; $25/4' area for season. Work may be offered for sale; no commission. Craftworker must attend show; demonstrations OK. Sponsor provides electricity for demonstrations. Show is advertised by

posters; newspapers; and craft-oriented national magazines and newspapers. Considers all crafts.
Profile: "The purpose of the Glens Falls Farmer's Market is to provide an economic marketplace for area producers to sell their crops and for area craftspeople to sell their handmade wares. It offers the customer a source of quality, locally grown produce, as well as a source of unique handcrafted items. Exhibitions, demonstrations, and games are planned to encourage the whole family to come and stroll through the street."

GREATER UTICA SUMMER FESTIVAL CRAFT SHOW, c/o Central New York Community Arts Council, 800 Park Ave., Utica NY 13501. (315)798-5039. Executive Director: Philippa Kennedy. Estab. 1977. Annual outdoor show held 3 days in July. Average attendance: 10,000. Entries preferred 2 weeks before show, but exceptions made until show. Entry fee: $10/craftworker. Display area: 10x10. Work may be offered for sale; no commission. Craftworker must attend show; demonstrations OK. Sponsor provides some electricity for demonstrations. Show is advertised by all of the media sources in 3 counties. Submit photos of work. Considers all crafts. No dealers allowed as exhibitors.

GUILD OF BOOK WORKERS EXHIBITION, 1059 3rd Ave., New York NY 10021. (212)752-0813. Contact: Exhibition Chairman. Estab. 1906. Indoor show held every 2-3 years and open to members of the Guild of Book Workers only. Considers hand bookbindings; calligraphy; and hand-decorated papers.

*GUILDERLAND ANNUAL FALL ARTS FESTIVAL, Guilderland League of Arts, Inc., Box 305, Guilderland Center NY 12085. President: Carol L. Zwuicklbauer. Estab. 1974. Annual outdoor show held the first Sunday after Labor Day. Average attendance: 5,000. Entries accepted until 1-2 weeks before show. Entry fee: $5/nonresident. Display area: 6x8 or larger. Work may be offered for sale; no commission. craftworker must attend show; demonstrations encouraged. Sponsor provides fencing. Show is advertised by newspapers; TV; radio; posters; and bulletins. Submit promotional materials. Awards ribbons and certificates. Categories: music; dance; photography; drama; arts and crafts; and literature. Considers all crafts.

HARVEST CRAFTS FESTIVAL, Box 1688, Westhampton Beach, NY 11978. (516)288-4263. Directors: Barbara Hope and Don Gaiti. Sponsor: Creative Faires, Ltd. Purpose: "to create professional market places for professional craftspeople in order for them to sell; make contact for future business; receive feedback from the public for their own personal advancement; gain by sharing with their peers; and being able to see how someone from another part of the country is handling a similar medium. We are craftspeople ourselves running our shows and believe very strongly in this premise." Estab. 1974. Annual indoor show held 3 days in November at Nassau Coliseum, Uniondale, New York. Average attendance: 25,000+. Entries accepted until 3 weeks before show. Entry fee: $200/10x12 full or corner booth; $155/10' pie wedge booth. Prejudging by 5 slides or representative work plus slide or photo of booth exhibit. Entry fee refunded for refused work. Work may be offered for sale; no commission. Craftworker must attend show; demonstrations encouraged. Registration limit: 185. Sponsor provides electricity for demonstrations; 24-hour security; all union costs; and decorator set up (back drop). Considers ceramics; leather; wood; glass; weaving; fiber; batik; silver/gold; metal; sculpture; wax; and lucite. "Since we run professional shows the crafts exhibited are of high quality. We cannot state emphatically enough the importance of a good display. We furnish complete suggestion sheets to aid neophytes and inspire all to create exciting environments for themselves and the public."
Sales: Central Mastercharge/Visa booth to serve craftworker and public; booked over $8,500 through this facility in 1977.
Promotion: Show is advertised by TV; radio; newspapers; magazines; posters; discount coupons; bank promotions; supermarket promotions; colleges; libraries; and bumper stickers. "We provide the craftspeople with promotional material; we request b&w photos at times for newspaper articles."

*HOLIDAY ARTS & CRAFTS FAIR, Box 201, Washington Mills NY 13479. Chairman: Gary McGuire. Sponsor: Upstate New York Craftsmen's Guild. Estab. 1977. Annual indoor show held 2 days in December at Utica, New York. Average attendance: 5,000. Entries accepted until 6 weeks before show. Entry fee: $35-50/8x5 display area. Maximum 1 entry per category; 2, total. Work may be offered for sale; no commission. Craftworker must attend show; demonstrations OK. Registration limit: 100. Sponsor provides chairs; electricity for demonstrations; table; 24-hour security; set up assistance; and food discount. Show is advertised by posters; printed media; and personal invitations. Submit resume and description of work for publicity consideration. Considers all crafts except heshi jewelry. Presents $150 in cash prizes and ribbons. "Average reported sale price: $300; price range: $10-1,000. Nationally rated."

HOLIDAY CRAFTS FAIR, WBAI-FM, 505 8th Ave., New York NY 10018. (212)279-3400. Manager: Anna Kosof. Purpose: fundraiser. Estab. 1971. Annual indoor show held 2 3-day weekends in December. Average attendance: 50,000. Entry fee: $75/weekend. Prejudging. Work may be offered for sale: 15% commission. 1977 show sales totalled $500,000+. Considers all handcrafts.

*PAULA INSEL ANNUAL EXHIBITION, 987 3rd Ave., New York NY 10022. (212)577-5740. Director: Paula Insel. Sponsor: Galerie Paula Insel. Purpose: "the show is a vehicle for artists to expose their talents." Estab. 1975. Annual indoor show held 2 weeks in the fall. Entries accepted until 1-2 months before show. Entry fee: $8/item being displayed. Maximum 3 works/category. Work may be offered for sale: 40% commission. Craftworker needn't attend show; demonstrations OK. Sponsor provides chairs; display panels; electricity for demonstrations; and shipping costs to craftworker from show. Show is advertised by newspapers; magazines; and mailing lists. Considers batik; ceramics; glass art; macrame; mobiles; needlecrafts; pottery; enamels; sculpture; tole painting; and woodcrafting. Presents ribbons and merchandise for award-winning work.

INTERNATIONAL CRAFT SHOW, 27 W. 53rd St., New York NY 10019. (212)586-0026. Executive Director: Harry Dennis. Sponsor: New York State Craftsmen Inc. Purpose: "once a year, comprehensive, craft wholesale and retail marketplace in New York City." Estab. 1973. Annual indoor show held 1 week in spring. Average attendance: 18,000. Entries accepted up until show. Entry fee: $550-600/10x10 display area. Prejudging by individual review including slides and photos; entry fee due after prejudging. Work may be offered for sale; no commission. Craftworker must attend show; demonstrations OK. Sponsor provides booth background and 24-hour security. Show is advertised by all media including radio; TV; newspapers; and magazines. Submit 8x10 b&w glossy or slides. Considers all crafts. Bestsellers: 50c bookmark to $5,000 bed.

*KENAN CRAFT FESTIVAL, (formerly 100 American Craftsmen Craft Festival), 433 Locust St., Lockport NY 14094. (716)433-2617. Arts and Education Director: John D. O'Hern. Sponsor: Kenan Center, Inc. Purpose: "to offer highest quality crafts; provide craftsmen to exchange ideas; and to show new directions in craft techniques and materials." Estab. 1970. Annual indoor show held 3 days in June. Average attendance: 12,000. Entries accepted until 4 months before show. Entry fee: $35/10x10 display area. Prejudging by slides; $3 jurying fee; entry fee due after prejudging. Work may be offered for sale; no commission. Craftworker must attend show; demonstrations OK. Registration limit: 100. Sponsor provides chairs; electricity for demonstrations; table; 24-hour security; and manages credit card booth for 3% of sales. Show is advertised by all media. Considers all crafts. Presents cash awards totalling $150 and ribbons.

LEWISTON COUNCIL ON THE ARTS CRAFT AND SALE SHOW, Box 1, Lewiston NY 14092. Chairman: Mrs. Leonard Longley. Purpose: "to further and develop understanding of the various crafts and art forms in this portion of the state." Estab. 1971. Annual outdoor show (with tents) held 2 days in June. Average attendance: 5,000-7,000. Entries accepted until 2 weeks before show or until filled. Entry fee: $15/tent; $10/outside. Prejudging by slides or photos. Work may be offered for sale; no commission. Craftworker must attend show; demonstrations preferred. Sponsor provides some arrangements for electricity. Show is advertised by posters; magazines; newspapers; handbills; and interviews on TV and radio. Considers all crafts.

*LILAC FESTIVAL DECORATED EGG SHOW, 16 Old Forge Lane; Pittsford NY 14534. (716)385-3332. Director: Ronald Guidone. Estab. 1978. Annual indoor show held 2 days in May at Rochester, New York. Entries accepted until 4 weeks before show. Entry fee: $15/artist; $40/dealer. Display area: 6x2½' tables. Work may be offered for sale; no commission. Craftworker must attend show; demonstrations OK. Registration limit: 65. Sponsor provides chairs; electricity for demonstration; table; and 24-hour security. Egg decorating seminars are held the day after the show. Show is advertised by TV; magazines; radio; and newspapers. Presents awards of ribbons and grand trophy for best of show. Considers decorated real eggs only.

LOWER ADIRONDACK REGIONAL ARTS COUNCIL ARTS AND CRAFTS FESTIVAL, Box 659, 184 Glen St., Glens Falls NY 12801. Festival Co-chairman: Christine Walton. Purpose: to "promote the artist and performing artist. It is an inexpensive avenue for local artists to become known." Estab. 1972. Annual outdoor show held 2 days in June. Average attendance: 10,000. Entries accepted until 2 weeks before show. Entry fee: $8/10x10 display area plus $2 LARAC membership fee. Work may be offered for sale; no commission. Craftworker must attend show; demonstrations OK. Registration limit: 225. Sponsor provides electricity for demonstrations and water. Show is advertised by Warren County Department of Publicity and Tourism and local newspapers. Submit promotional material. Considers all crafts.

MADISON SQUARE PARK FAIR, Tregre and Miller Associates, Inc., 261 3rd Ave., New York NY 10010. (212)674-5094. Contact: Paul Miller or Jeanne Tregre. Sponsor: 13th Precinct Community Council. Estab. 1976. Annual outdoor show held 2 days in June. Entries accepted until 2 weeks before show. Entry fee: $50/10x10 display area. Work may be offered for sale; no commission. Demonstrations OK. Show is advertised by radio; TV; newspapers; magazines; and trade publications. Considers all crafts.

*NEW YORK STATE CRAFTS, HOME ARTS AND FINE ARTS COMPETITION, New York State Fair Grounds, Syracuse NY 13209. (315)487-7741. Director, Art and Home Center: Elizabeth J. Crowley. Sponsor: New York State Fair. Estab. 1950. Annual indoor show held 10 days in late summer. Average attendance: 350,000. Entries accepted until 3 weeks before show. Entry fee: $5. Submit up to 10 crafts in each division. Maximum 2 pieces per category; 6 total. Prejudging. Entry fee not refunded for refused work. Work may be offered for sale; 25% commission. Craftworker needn't attend show; demonstrations permitted if prearranged. Presents cash awards of $1,770, crafts; $2,201 home arts, and ribbons. Categories: fine arts (paintings); graphics and sculpture; crafts (pottery); rugs; wall hangings; metal; wood; weaving; and leatherwork.
Acceptable Work: Considers batik; glass art; jewelry; leatherworking needlecrafts; pottery; sculpture; weaving; and woodcrafting. Strictly a competition; only prize winners on display.

NORTH COUNTRY ARTS & CRAFTS, Northville Chapter, Box 285, Northville NY 12134. President: Corinne Sherman. Estab. 1974. Annual outdoor show held 2 days in July. Average attendance: 5,000. Entries accepted up until show, space permitting. Entry fee: $15/12x15 display area. Work may be offered for sale; no commission. Craftworker must attend show; demonstrations OK. Registration limit: 75. Sponsor provides chairs; electricity for demonstrations; and fencing. Show is advertised by newspapers; radio; and posters. Considers all crafts.

NORTHEAST CRAFT FAIR, Box 10, New Paltz NY 12561. (914)255-0039. President: Carol Sedestrom. Sponsor: American Craft Enterprises, Inc. Purpose: "to provide craftspeople in the Northeast an exposition of high quality in which to exhibit and sell their work; to provide buyers a market place to purchase quality handmade items at a time of year to accomodate summer and fall buying schedule; to encourage craftspeople from various area and diverse traditions to come together to stimulate the interchange of ideas and enthusiasm; and to offer general public the opportunity to see crafts and give a better understanding of the American craft movement." Estab. 1965. Annual indoor/outdoor show (with 3 large tents) held 5 days (2 trade; 3 public) in June at Rhinebeck, New York. Average attendance: 40,000. Entries accepted until February 1. Entry fee: $100/inside; $75/tent, and $60/outside. Display area: 10x10. Prejudging by "color slides of the type of work planned for exhibit. Slides will be considered solely on the merits of the work pictured, not upon any other qualifications of the craftsperson who produced the work. Submit 5 slides of the type of work you plan on exhibiting at the show. Slides must be 2x2 including cardboard or plastic mount. $5 jurying fee." Entry fee due after prejudging. Work must be offered for sale; no commission. Craftworker must attend show; demonstrations OK. Registration limit: about 500. Sponsor provides electricity for demonstrations and 24-hour security. Considers all crafts including handmade musical instruments. 1977 show sales totalled "a little more than $2,000,000."

NORTHERN NEW YORK CRAFTS FESTIVAL, 101 E. Main St., Malone NY 12953. (518)483-4550. Vice Chairman: Doug Kelley. Sponsor: Greater Malone Community Council's Arts Committee and the Malone Extension Center of North Country Community College. Estab. 1976. Annual outdoor show (tents and hangar available if it rains) held the Saturday and Sunday after July 4. Average attendance: 1,500. Entries accepted up until show. Entry fee: $10/craftworker with demonstration; $15/craftworker without demonstration plus $5 additional charge for entries received 1 week prior to show or less. Display area: 10x10, larger if needed. Work may be offered for sale; no commission. Craftworker or representative must attend show; demonstrations encouraged. Sponsor provides chairs; electricity for demonstrations; and night security. Considers all crafts. 1977 show sales totalled $2,500.
Promotion: Show is advertised by news releases throughout New York state, Quebec, Ontario, and Vermont; mailings to craft shops and organizations; and posters throughout the area.

*OLD SARATOGA HISTORICAL ASSOCIATION ART SHOW, Brown's Point, RD 6 Burgoyne Rd., Saratoga Springs NY 12866. Chairperson: Kate Leone. Estab. 1967. Annual outdoor show held 1 day in August at Schuylerville, New York. Entries accepted up until show. Entry fee: $5/craftworker. Work may be offered for sale; 10% commission. Craftworker must attend show; demonstrations encouraged. Sponsor provides fencing. Show is advertised by newspapers; radio; TV; and posters. Presents cash awards and ribbons. Considers all crafts including quilting; knitting; and crotcheting.

PALMYRA CANALTOWN DAYS, Box 64, Palmyra NY 14522. Craft Chairman: Bruce Wideman. Purpose: to relive the days when the Erie Canal was an important part of upstate New York. Estab. 1966. Annual outdoor show held 2 days in September. Average attendance: 20,000-25,000. Entries accepted until 1 week before show. Entry fee: $8/10x10 display area. Work may be offered for sale; no commission. Craftworker must attend show; demonstrations encouraged. Registration limit: 100. Show is advertised by radio and newspapers. Considers all crafts.

*PARK ART FESTIVAL, c/o Harry Davis, 39 N. Church St., Cortland NY 13045. (607)756-8215. Program Director: Harry N. Davis. Sponsor: Cortland Art League. Estab. 1968. Annual outdoor show held 2 days Father's Day weekend. Average attendance: 1,000+. Entries accepted until 1 week before show. Entry fee: $7.50/10x10 display area. Work may be offered for sale; commission only on purchase award prizes. Craftworker must attend show; demonstrations OK. Sponsor provides fencing. Show is advertised by all media. Considers all crafts.

PHELPS ANNUAL SAURKRAUT FESTIVAL, c/o Judy Clingerman, Rt. 2, Phelps NY 14532. (315)548-9237. Estab. 1966. Annual indoor show held the first Saturday in August. Average attendance: 5,000. Entries accepted until early July or until filled. Entry fee: $8/15x15 display area. Work may be offered for sale; no commission. Craftworker must attend show; demonstrations OK. Registration limit: 30-35. Sponsor provides electricity for demonstrations. Show is advertised by TV; radio; newspapers; and posters. Considers all crafts.

PINKSTERFEST SUMMER 'MINIFEST', 75 New Scotland Ave., Arts Office, Albany NY 12208. Director: Sandra Seifter. Sponsor: Albany City Arts Office. Estab. 1974. Semiannual outdoor show held 1 day in May and 2 days in summer. Average attendance: 25,000. Entries accepted until 1 week before show. No entry fee. Prejudging by slides or photos. Work may be offered for sale; no commission. Craftworker must attend show; demonstrations OK. Registration limit: 200. Sponsor provides 24-hour security. Show is advertised by newspapers; TV; radio; posters; and flyers. Considers all crafts.

PLEASURE FAIRE OF THE RENAISSANCE AND SUMMER MARKETPLACE, Rt. 2, Farden Rd., Sterling NY 13156. (315)947-5782. Creators and Producers: Dennis T. and Caroline Ouellette. Estab. 1977. Annual outdoor show held all weekends in July and August and first weekend in September. Entries accepted until 4 weeks before opening day; exceptions are made for unusual circumstances. Entry fee: $25 for entire season. Exhibitors build their own permanent or semi-permanent booths in keeping with Renaissance theme. Prejudging by slides; photos; or personal visit in advance with examples of work. Entry fee due after prejudging. Work may be offered for sale; 10% commission. Craftworker or representative must attend show; demonstrations encouraged. Show is advertised by posters; newspaper ads; press releases; and local TV talk shows.
Acceptable Work: Considers batik; candlemaking; ceramics; decoupage; dollmaking; glass art; jewelry; lapidary; leatherworking; macrame; metalsmithing; mobiles; needlecrafts; pottery; sculpture; soft sculpture; weaving; woodcrafting; block printing; scrimshaw; dried flowers; and musical instruments. "Work must be representative in subject matter and medium of that produced in the Renaissance period (1450-1750). Exhibitors must provide and appear in Renaissance costume during Faire hours."
Profile: "The Renaissance Faire, a gay and colorful reproduction of the English world trade faires of the 16th century, has been created to combine history, beauty, culture, and pleasure into one important recreational activity in central New York. Comprising all the elements of old English faires— marketable fine arts and handcrafts; unusual food and drink; live theatre; music and dance; and a natural forest location— the Faire has been designed as a place where beautiful people can do beautiful things in a beautiful setting."

ROCKLAND ARTS DAY, Box 267, Spring Valley NY 10977. (914)352-5777. Executive Director: Bette Uris. Sponsor: Arts Council of Rockland. Estab. 1972. Annual indoor show held 1 day in the fall. Average attendance: 3,000. Entries accepted until 3 weeks before show. Entry fee: $15/10x10 display booth. Prejudging by 5 35mm slides of representative works; entry fee refunded for refused work. Work may be offered for sale; no commission. Craftworker or representative must attend show; no demonstrations. Registration limit: 100. Categories: crafts; fine arts; performances; children's theatre; and ethnic foods. Considers all crafts.

Promotion: Show is advertised by publicity in all media; advertising in newspapers; the art council's monthly tabloid; posters; flyers; and direct mail. "Anything useful for publicity will be appreciated."

SPRING ARTS & CRAFTS SHOW, 25 Seneca St., Shortsville NY 14548. (716)289-9439. President: Ronald L. Johnson. Sponsor: Finger Lakes Craftsmen. Estab. 1970. Annual indoor show held 2 days in the spring at Rochester, New York. Average attendance: 10,000+. Entries accepted until show is full (sometimes early). Entry fee: $50-85/10x7 display area. Work may be offered for sale; no commission. Craftworker must attend show; demonstrations OK. Registration limit: 200. Sponsor provides 24-hour security. Show is advertised by TV; radio; and newspapers ($3,000 budget). Considers all crafts.

SUMMER INDOOR ARTS & CRAFTS SHOW, 25 Seneca St., Shortsville NY 14548. (716)289-9439. President: Ronald L. Johnson. Sponsor: Finger Lakes Craftsmen. Estab. 1975. Annual indoor show held 2 days in July at Rochester, New York. Average attendance: 10,000+. Entries accepted until show is full (sometimes early). Entry fee: $50-85/10x7 display area. Work may be offered for sale; no commission. Craftworker must attend show; demonstrations OK. Registration limit: 200. Sponsor provides 24-hour security. Show is advertised by TV; radio; and newspapers ($3,000 budget). Considers all crafts.

TAMA COUNTY FAIR, Tregre and Miller Associates, Inc., 261 3rd Ave., New York NY 10003. (212)677-7774. Contact: Paul Miller or Jeanne Tregre. Sponsor: 3rd Avenue Merchants Association. Purpose: community fundraiser. Estab. 1976. Annual show held 1 day in the fall. Entries accepted until 2 weeks before show. Entry fee: $50/10x12 display area. Work may be offered for sale; no commission. Craftworker or representative must attend show; demonstrations OK. Show is advertised by TV; radio; newspapers; magazines; and trade publications. Considers all crafts.

THANKSGIVING WEEKEND CHRISTMAS ARTS & CRAFTS SHOW, 25 Seneca St., Shortsville NY 14548. (716)289-9439. President: Ronald L. Johnson. Sponsor: Finger Lakes Craftsmen. Estab. 1970. Annual indoor show held 3 days during Thanksgiving weekend at Rochester, New York. Average attendance: 15,000+. Entries accepted until show is full (sometimes early). Entry fee: $60-95. Work may be offered for sale; no commission. Craftworker must attend show; demonstrations OK. Registration limit: 200. Sponsor provides 24-hour security. Show is advertised by TV; radio; newspaper; and $3,000 paid advertising. Considers all crafts.

TREASURES OF YESTERDAY, TODAY, TOMORROW, Tregre and Miller Associates, Inc., 261 3rd Ave., New York NY 10010. (212)674-5094. Contact: Paul Miller or Jeanne Tregre. Annual indoor show held 3 days in December. Entries accepted until 4 weeks before show. Entry fee: $300/10x10 display area. Work may be offered for sale; no commission. Craftworker must attend show; demonstrations OK. Sponsor provides chairs; display panels; electricity for demonstrations; tables; and 24-hour security. Considers fine handcrafted items only. Show is advertised by TV; radio; newspapers; and trade publications.

ULSTER COUNTY COUNCIL FOR THE ARTS SHOWCASE, 96 Maiden Lane, Kingston NY 12401. (914)339-4330. Coordinator, Arts Events: Terry Graham. "The council's purpose is to promote the arts and crafts in the area through events sponsored by this nonprofit organization." Estab. 1977. Annual indoor/outdoor show held 3 days in the summer at Stone Ridge, New York. Average attendance: 5,000. Entries accepted until 4 weeks before show. Entry fee: $10/artist. Display area: 6x6 display booth. Prejudging by slides, photos and fact sheets; entry fee due after prejudging. Work may be offered for sale; no commission. Craftworker must attend show; demonstrations OK. Registration limit: 50. Sponsor provides chairs; electricity for demonstrations; table; and 24-hour security. Show is advertised by national listings; public service announcements; flyers; radio; and TV. Considers all crafts.

*VILLAGE ARTISTS' AND CRAFTSMEN'S ART AND CRAFT FAIR, Box 292, Hamilton NY 13346. Estab. 1975. Annual outdoor show held 2 days in July. Average attendance: 6,000-7,000. Entries accepted until 6 weeks before show. Entry fee: $25/VAC members; $30/nonmembers. Display area: 6x10. Prejudging by 5 slides; entry fee refunded for refused work. All work offered for sale; no commission. Craftworker must attend show. Presents cash awards. Considers all crafts.

*WATERFRONT ART FESTIVAL, 21 Hidden Creek Circle, Pittsford NY 14534. (716)381-8772, 394-4362, 624-4220. Director: Adele Elmer. Purpose: "to provide an outstanding opportunity for artists and craftspeople to sell at a top quality show and to provide to the public a cultural and educational experience including musical entertainment totally free." Estab. 1974. Annual outdoor show held 3 days in August at Canandaigua Lake, New York. Average attendance: 60,000. Entries accepted until 3 weeks before show. Entry fee: $35/10x6 display area. Prejudging by 3 slides; entry fee refunded for refused work. Work should be offered for sale; no commission. Craftworker must attend show; demonstrations encouraged. Registration limit: 150. Sponsor provides electricity for demonstrations; fencing; and 24-hour security. Show is advertised by radio; newspaper display ads; news releases; signs; and cable TV. Submit b&w glossies of self at work or of specific pieces of work. Presents 4 craft cash awards of $50 each; 1 best of show craft award of $100; ribbons; and certificates. Considers batik; ceramics; jewelry; leatherworking; macrame; metalsmithing; pottery; sculpture; soft sculpture; weaving; woodcrafting; blown glass; and blacksmithing.
Profile: "This show has become a tradition. Artists and craftsmen come from all over US to participate. Early registration is strongly urged."

*WESTBURY ANNUAL OUTDOOR ART & CRAFTS FESTIVAL, Greater Westbury Arts Council, Inc., 600 Old Country Rd., Rm. 306, Garden City NY 11530. (516)741-6760. Executive Director: Roberta Oborne. Purpose: fundraiser. Estab. 1974. Annual outdoor show held 2 days in June at Westbury, Long Island, New York. Average attendance: 1,000-2,000. Entries accepted until 4 weeks before show. Entry fee: $25/6x15 display area. Maximum 2 entries per category for prejudging. Prejudging by slides only; entry fee due after prejudging. Work may be offered for sale; no commission. Craftworker must attend show; demonstrations OK. Registration limit: 80. Sponsor provides electricity for demonstrations and fencing. Show is advertised by press releases; periodicals; radio; direct mail; posters; and flyers. Considers all crafts. Presents $100 best in show and ribbons. Bestsellers: "stained glass and pewter work seem to be becoming more popular."

WESTCHESTER HOME FURNISHINGS ART & CRAFT SHOW, Rt. 1, Box 218, Bedford NY 10506. (914)234-3704. Director: Lydia Ward. Purpose: "to provide a warm and interesting marketplace for our fine American artists and craftspeople to retail and wholesale their work, and to bring the finest quality craftsmanship and artistry to the viewing and buying public." Estab. 1977. Annual indoor show held 3 days in the spring at White Plains, New York. Average attendance: 5,000. Entries accepted until 2 weeks before show. Entry fee: $95/8x10 booth. Prejudging by 5 slides, including 1 of display; entry fee refunded for refused work. Work may be offered for sale; no commission. Craftworker must attend show; demonstrations OK. Registration limit: 110. Sponsor provides electricity for demonstration and tables and chairs for rental. Considers all crafts except jewelry and other wearables.
Sales Tip: "Westchester is an educated and sophisticated area — they appreciate beautiful things, so a good display is required. Quality of display should match the quality of the work."
Promotion: Show is advertised by New York City and Westchester radio stations; major newspapers in the tri-state area (New York, New Jersey and Connecticut); postcards; and special invitations to wholesale buyers and decorators. "Please send b&w glossy (5x7 or 8x10) with brief resume. This has helped exhibitors to 'sell out.' Often it encourages commission work— always it brings people to the show— specifically to see what they saw in the paper. Photo should be of exhibitor at work or classy shot of a single piece."

WESTFIELD ARTS & CRAFTS FESTIVAL, Box 145, Westfield NY 14787. (716)326-2614. Chairman: Linda C. Dunn. Sponsor: Chamber of Commerce. "Our show is strictly held to offer any artist or craftsman the opportunity to show and sell. We feel that if they feel proud of their works we have no right to refuse, therefore no prejudging. This also means that everyone takes their chances. If they do well, fine; if not; they haven't lost much!" Estab. 1971. Annual outdoor show held the last Friday and Saturday in July. Average attendance: 10,000+. Entries accepted until 2 weeks before show. Entry fee: $10, if paid in advance; $15, if paid the day of the show. Work may be offered for sale; no commission. Prefers craftworker attend show; demonstrations encouraged. Registration limit: 225. Sponsor provides electricity for demonstrations and 24-hour security. Show is advertised by radio; newspapers; and billboards. Submit brief resume and photo for publicity consideration. Considers all handcrafts.

North Carolina

ARTS ALIVE FESTIVAL, Box 744, Mocksville NC 27028. (704)634-3112. President: Martha Kontos. Sponsor: David County Arts Council. Estab. 1975. Annual outdoor show held 1 day in September. Average attendance: 10,000. Entries accepted up until show date. Entry fee: $5/craftworker. Work may be offered for sale; no commission. Craftworker must attend show; demonstrations OK. Considers all crafts.

Promotion: Show is advertised by newspapers; radio; brochures; and pamphlets. Submit any pamphlets or brochures available; description of craft-making methods; and information for ordering during the year to be used for publicity.

*ARTS & CRAFTS FESTIVAL OF SOUTHEASTERN NORTH CAROLINA, Rt. 2, Box 940, Elizabethtown NC 28337. (919)588-4898. Executive Director: Ann A. Hood. Sponsor: Southeastern North Carolina Arts Council. Purpose: "to present the total realm of the arts in an educational and entertaining way. Primary objective is to promote, encourage and develop the arts in southeastern North Carolina." Estab. 1966. Annual indoor/outdoor show (in gym and on campus) held 2 days in the spring at Lake Waccamaw, North Carolina. Average attendance: 10,-000. Entries accepted until 4 weeks before show. Entry fee: $5/ craftworker's year's membership to the Council. Maximum 2 entries/category. Entry to craft show by invitation only. Work may be offered for sale; 10% commission. Craftworker must attend show; demonstrations mandatory. Registration limit: 200. Sponsor provides electricity for demonstrations; 24-hour security; receipt books; name tags; complementary coffee and relief during show time; and free listing in rosters and calendars throughout US. Considers all crafts, including cornshuck crafts and pineneedle crafts. Must be work of craftworker from a southeastern North Carolina county.

Awards: Presents $75, $45 and $30 cash awards for adults; $20, $10 and $5 cash awards for students; $800 in purchase prizes; and ribbons. "Stress originality and imagination."

Sales Tip: "There is a good market here for the $5-100 range of crafts, and the $50-200 range of artwork." 1977 craft sales totalled $3,700; artworks totalled $2,500.

Promotion: Show is advertised by national, regional, state and local calendars; news releases; TV; radio; brochures; and posters. "Show chairman will contact individuals for publicity information if needed."

AUTUMN LEAVES FESTIVAL, Box 913, Mt. Airy NC 27030. (919)786-6116. Executive Vice President: Jim Grimes. Purpose: "for the entertainment of those who attend; and to increase tourism." Estab. 1967. Annual indoor/outdoor show held 3 days in October. Average attendance: 200,000. Entries accepted until 3 weeks before show. Entry fee: $25/10x12 display area. Prejudging by slides, photos, or actual art; entry fee due after prejudging. Work may be offered for sale; no commission. Craftworker must attend show; demonstrations OK. Registration limit: 60. Sponsor provides electricity for demonstrations and 24-hour security. Considers all crafts.

Promotion: Show is advertised by radio; TV; newspapers; and state and regional publications. Submit photo and resume for newspaper publicity; or craftwork for TV promotion.

CABARRUS COUNTY AGRICULTURAL FAIR ARTS & CRAFTS SHOW, Box 563, Concord NC 28025. (704)782-0621 or 786-7221. General Manager: Clyde Propst, Jr. Fair estab. 1953; craft portion estab. 1972. Annual indoor show held 1 week in September. Average attendance: 110,000. Entries accepted until filled. No entry fee (but $50 deposit required to reserve a booth; refunded at end of show). Display area: 34 8x8 booth spaces with 10' aisles. Work may be offered for sale; no commission. Craftworker must attend show; demonstration required. Sponsor provides electricity for demonstrations and 24-hour security. Considers all crafts.

CRAFTSMAN'S FAIR OF THE SOUTHERN HIGHLANDS, Box 9145, Asheville NC 28805. (704)298-7928. Coordinator: Alex Miller. Sponsor: Southern Highlands Handicraft Guild. Estab. 1948. Semiannual indoor show held 5 days in July and October. Average attendance: 25,-000. Open to Guild members. No entry fee. Prejudging. Work may be offered for sale; no commission. Craftworker must attend show. Sponsor provides display panels and equipment. Considers all crafts.

*DURHAM ART GUILD ANNUAL JURIED EXHIBIT, 810 W. Proctor St., Durham NC 27707. Contact: James C. McIntyre. Annual show held in the spring. Entry fee: $8. Maximum 2 entries per artist. Work may be offered for sale; 30% commission. Considers sculpture. No work requiring special display devices. Presents $1,700 in cash, and $1,000 in purchase prizes. Crated works must be sent prepaid express. Parcel post entries not accepted.

FESTIVAL IN THE PARK, 308 E. 5th St., Charlotte NC 28202. (704)372-8900. Director: A. Grant Whitney. The Festival is "nonprofit and absolutely free to everyone with no commercialism of any type involved. It is an opportunity for expression of mind, hand and talent by everyone, regardless of race or creed." Estab. 1964. Annual outdoor show (with brightly colored Camelot style tents) held 6 days in September. Average attendance: 1,000,000. Entries accepted until show date. No entry fee. Display area: "each tent inside exhibit space measures about 10x-10." Work may not be offered for sale, "but may take orders for delivery after festival hours"; no commission. Craftworker must attend show; demonstrations required. Registration limit: 100. Sponsor provides chairs; coverings; display panels; electricity for demonstrations; table; and 24-hour security. Show is advertised by radio; TV; and newspaper. Considers all crafts.

MT. MITCHELL CRAFTSMENS FAIR, Box 175, Burnsville NC 28714. (704)682-7413. Director: Jerry Newton. Sponsor: Yancey County Chamber of Commerce. "The promotion of mountain crafts is the major purpose in the creation of this fair." Estab. 1956. Annual outdoor show (with covered booths) held the first Friday and Saturday in August. Average attendance: 7,000. Entries accepted until 4 weeks before show. Entry fee: $10 registration/artist. Display area: 8x10. Prejudging by slides; entry fee refunded for refused work. Work may be offered for sale; 10% commission. Craftworker must attend show; demonstrations OK. Registration limit: 130. Sponsor provides coverings and electricity for demonstrations. Show is advertised by newspapers and magazines. Considers batik; candlemaking; ceramics; dollmaking; glass art; jewelry; leatherworking; macrame; metalsmithing; needlecrafts; pottery; sculpture; weaving; and woodcrafting.

*NORTH CAROLINA ARTISTS EXHIBITION, North Carolina Museum of Art, Raleigh NC 27611. Head, Collections Care and Preparation: Benjamin F. Williams. Estab. 1937. Annual indoor show held in spring. Average attendance: 10,000. Entries accepted until 2-4 weeks before show. Entry fee: $5/craftworker. Maximum 2 entries/craftworker. Prejudging by actual entries presented to a 3-man, out-of-state jury of professionals in the art field. No entry fees refunded for refused work. Work may be offered for sale; 30% commission. Craftworker needn't attend show; no demonstrations. Insurance on exhibited work; table; handles sales; and 24-hour security. Show is advertised by museum news releases; calendar; the news media; and art magazines. Considers all crafts. Maximum size: 80". Presents cash and purchase prizes; honorable mentions; and a gold medal award. "Open only to North Carolina residents, natives of the state, and to nonresidents who have lived in North Carolina for at least 5 years."

*PIEDMONT CRAFTS EXHIBITION, Box 6011, Charlotte NC 28207. (704)334-9723. Curator of Exhibitions: Jerald Melberg. Sponsor: Mint Museum of Art. Estab. 1976. Biennial indoor show held 6 weeks in the late winter/early spring. Entries accepted until 5 weeks before show. Entry fee: $7 for up to 4 entries. Maximum 2 entries per craftworker. Prejudging; no entry fees refunded for refused work. Work may be offered for sale; 30% commission. Open to residents of Alabama, Florida, Georgia, Kentucky, Louisiana, Mississippi, North and South Carolina, Tennessee, Virginia and West Virginia. Considers all crafts. Presents approximately $4,500 in cash and purchase prizes.

PLANTERS CRAFTSMEN, c/o Kathy Conner, 608 S. Howard Circle, Tarboro NC 27886. (919)823-1744. Sponsor: Planters National Bank. "Purpose is to encourage crafts as a hobby or trade possibility. We include both professionals and amateurs, and community groups such as school art clubs, nursing homes, NEED, Inc. We seek to educate the public in traditional and contemporary crafts." Annual indoor show held 2 days in December at Rocky Mount, North Carolina. Entries accepted until 2 weeks before show. Entry fee: $15/8x6 display area. Work may be offered for sale; no commission. Craftworker or representative must attend show; demonstrations OK. Sponsor provides chairs; electricity for demonstrations; and table. Considers all crafts.
Sales Tip: "Christmas items— traditional, utilitarian crafts which are colorful but well-finished sell well. Quilts, toys, woodworking and tincraft seem to be the public's favorites. Fine arts do not seem to sell well."
Promotion: Show is advertised in Raleigh, Tarboro, Rocky Mount, Greenville, and Washington, North Carolina by radio and TV. "Please provide own business cards. Many orders are placed by way of those business cards after the show."

SOUTHEASTERN-NORTHGATE ART SHOW, 1922 Hollywood St., Winston-Salem NC 27107. (919)723-8788. Director: Nancy Goslen. Sponsor: Southeastern Art Shows. Purpose: "to provide a place where artist/craftsmen can meet directly with public in an informal atmosphere and to encourage the purchase and collection of fine arts and crafts from today's artists." Estab. 1975. Annual indoor show held 3 days in January at Durham, North Carolina. Entries accepted until 6 weeks before show. Entry fee: $45-55/craftworkers. Display area: 8-16'. Prejudging by slides or photos; entry fee refunded for refused work. Work may be offered for sale; no commission. Craftworker must attend show; demonstrations OK. Registration limit: 20-25. Show is advertised by newspaper; radio; and direct mail. Submit glossy photos and resume. "Some exhibitors sold $1,000-1,200 during show."

Acceptable Work: Considers batik; ceramics; glass art; macrame; mobiles; pottery; sculpture; soft sculpture; weaving and woodcrafting.

SOUTHERN CHRISTMAS SHOW, 1945 Randolph Rd., Charlotte NC 28207. (704)376-6594. President: Robert E. Zimmerman. Sponsor: Southern Shows, Inc. "We are consumer and trade show managers. Our revenue is strictly from ticket sales and booth rental." Estab. 1967. Annual indoor show held 9 days in November at the Charlotte Merchandise Mart. Entry fee: $165/8x12 display area; $313.50/8x24 booth; $478.50/8x36; or $1,170/8x48 booth. Work may be offered for sale; no commission. "Craftworker's presence is not mandatory, but we prefer that they be present if at all possible. Booth must be manned at all times." Demonstrations encouraged. Sponsor provides chairs; prefabricated pegboard; electricity for demonstrations; table; and 24-hour security. Categories: Olde Towne ("exhibitors in Olde Towne are required to provide for visitors a special feature, visually pleasing and in Olde Towne tradition, or an educational feature, with historical significance"); Art and Crafts; Commercial (gifts, food, holiday merchandise exhibited by companies for merchandising and/or retail sales); and Bazaar (church and other nonprofit organizations qualify for space in this area. All items sold must be homemade or handmade). Considers all crafts. Bestsellers: "Christmasey items."

Promotion: Show is advertised by newspaper, radio and TV advertising— mostly local, but some regional; national trade magazines and regional publications; newspaper and TV/radio interviews; and other public relations activities handled by a full-time director. "Submit biographical/background material on you, your craft and your business, along with b&w 8x10 photos of you with your craft."

SOUTHERN LIVING SHOW, 1945 Randolph Rd., Charlotte NC 28207. (704)376-6597. President: Robert E. Zimmerman. Sponsor: Southern Living Magazine. "We are consumer and trade show managers. Our revenue is strictly from ticket sales and booth rental." Estab. 1959. Annual outdoor show held 9 days the last week of February and the first week of March at the Charlotte Merchandise Mart. Average attendance: 100,000. Entries accepted until show is filled. Entry fee: $165/8x12 display area; $313/8x24 display booth; $478/8x36 booth; or $594/8x48 area. Prejudging by slides. Work may be offered for sale; no commission. "Craftworker's presence is not mandatory, but we prefer that they be present if at all possible. Booth must be manned at all times." Demonstrations encouraged. Sponsor provides chairs; display panels; table; 24-hour security; electricity at a fee; and liability insurance. "Show is 70% horticulture and home products. Limited area devoted to crafts." Considers all crafts. Bestsellers: "the more original, unusual, the better."

Promotion: Show is advertised by newspaper; radio; and TV advertising — mostly local, but some regional; national trade magazines and regional publications; newspaper and TV/radio interviews; and other public relations activities handled by a full-time director. "Submit biographical/background material on you, your craft and your business, along with b&w 8x10 photos of you with your craft."

*SUNBONNET FESTIVAL, Rt. 3, Box 142, Yadkinville NC 27055. (919)679-2941. Executive Director: Bill Casstevens. Sponsor: Yadkin Arts Council. Estab. 1975. Annual outdoor show (with some tents, awnings and booths) held 2 days in August. Average attendance: 5,000-6,000. Entries accepted until 1 week before show. Entry fee: $5/4 entries plus $10/booth. Maximum 4 entries per category or 8 total. Prejudging "by experts in their field brought in from outside the county." No entry fees refunded for refused work. Work may be offered for sale; 20% commission on juried show only. Craftworker must attend show; demonstrations OK. Registration limit: 35 booths; 100 craftworkers. Sponsor provides electricity for demonstrations; table; and 24-hour security. Considers all crafts.

Awards: Presents $75 1st, $50 2nd, 2 $25 3rd, and 3 $5 honorable mention awards; and $150 in purchase prizes. "Our judges tend to be experts in their field. The purchase prize is awarded by collaboration of judges and the Arts Council. The show is so varied that any quality work can win."

Promotion: Show is advertised by TV; radio; newspapers; posters; and direct mail campaigns. Submit photos and biographical information for press releases.

SUNDAY ON THE SQUARE, Arts Council of Fayetteville, Box 318, Fayetteville NC 28302. (919)323-1776. Assistant Director: Sylvia Miller. Purpose: "an attempt to identify artists and introduce them to the community; also to provide art activities as a family and community event."

Estab. 1974. Annual indoor/outdoor show held 1 day in the spring. Average attendance: 15,000. Entries accepted until 1 week before show. Entry fee: $15/4x6 display area. Work may be offered for sale; no commission. Craftworker must attend show; demonstrations OK. Sponsor provides electricity for demonstrations. Show is advertised by TV; radio; newspapers; and regional and national magazines. Considers all crafts. "Area has a large ethnic and military population."

Horticulture, home decorating and craft exhibits help make the Southern Living Show in Charlotte, North Carolina, the largest indoor/outdoor show in the South with an attendance of 100,000. Carding and spinning, ancient crafts still practiced in areas of the Appalachian mountains, are demonstrated.

*TRIANGLE FESTIVAL OF CRAFTS, c/o Durham Arts Council, 810 W. Proctor St., Durham NC 27707. Executive Director: James C. McIntyre. Purpose: "to present professional designer crafts to the community and to provide a market for sale of professional crafts." Estab. 1966. Annual indoor show held 3 days in spring. Average attendance: 10,000. Entries accepted until 6 weeks before show. Entry fee: $10/craftworker. Display area: 10x4. Prejudging by 3 pieces of work; entry fee due after prejudging. Work may be offered for sale; 20% commission. Craftworker must attend show; demonstrations OK. Registration limit: 60. Sponsor provides chairs; electricity for demonstrations; fencing; table; and 24-hour security. Show is advertised by radio; TV; news media; and posters. Submit photos. Presents purchase awards totalling $300-500 and the AR Cole Award for Best Pottery, ribbon. Considers all crafts.

VILLAGE ART & CRAFT FAIR, c/o New Morning Gallery, 3½ Kitchen Place, Asheville NC 28803. (704)274-2831. Director: John Cram. Purpose: "to provide promotion for the gallery and for Biltmore Village." Estab. 1972. Annual outdoor show held 2 days in August. Average attendance: 10,000. Entries accepted until 2 weeks before show. Entry fee: $60/8x10 display area. Prejudging. "Artists and craftsmen at great distances usually submit slides or photos; regional and local participants may have their work juried at the gallery." Work must be offered for sale; no commission. Craftworker must attend show; demonstrations welcomed. Registration limit: 125. Sponsor provides limited electricity for demonstrations. Show is advertised by chamber of commerce; radio; newspapers; posters; and flyers.
Acceptable Work: Considers batik; candlemaking; ceramics; dollmaking; glass art; jewelry; lapidary; leatherworking; macrame; metalsmithing; pottery; sculpture; soft sculpture; weaving; and woodcrafting.
Sales Tip: "We recommend a broad selection of work, high and low prices; major works often attract attention, but sales will come from the lower price items as a whole."
Profile: "The Fair is held on the church grounds of All Souls Episcopal Church. It is a charming tree-covered setting for which many of the repeat craftsmen have commented as being one of the

nicest settings and atmosphere for a fair. We also provide music all day of a complementary nature. The event is held the same weekend as the Mountain Dance and Folk Festival which generates a lot of fresh and interested buyers into the Asheville market."

North Dakota

KOLACHE DAY, Lidgerwood Chamber of Commerce, Lidgerwood ND 58053. President: Gregory Palm. Estab. 1971. Annual indoor show held 1 day in the spring. Average attendance: 1,100. Entries accepted until show. Work may be offered for sale; no commission. Craftworker must attend show; demonstrations OK. Sponsor provides chairs; electricity for demonstrations; and table. Show is advertised by radio and newspaper. Submit b&w glossies for newspaper and letter for publicity purposes. Considers all crafts.

MINOT ART ASSOCIATION ART FAIR, Box 325, Minot ND 58701. (701)838-4445. Director: Galen R. Willert. Estab. 1975. Annual outdoor show held 1 day in September. Average attendance: 500+. Entries accepted until 1 week before show. Entry fee: $10. Display area: 12x-12. Work may be offered for sale; no commission. Craftworker must attend show; demonstrations OK. Registration limit: 50. Show is advertised by radio; flyers; and calendar of events. Considers all crafts except mold-type ceramics.

MINOT ART GALLERY ARTFEST, Box 325, Minot ND 58701. (701)838-4445. Director: Galen R. Willert. Estab. 1975. Annual indoor show held 3 days in March. Average attendance: 500+. Entries accepted until 1 week before show. Entry fee: $20/12x12 display area. Work may be offered for sale; no commission. Craftworker must attend show; demonstrations OK. Registration limit: 60. Show is advertised by radio; brochure; and calendar of events. Considers all crafts except candlemaking; mold-type ceramics; and dollmaking.

*NORTH DAKOTA ART EXHIBITION, Box 325, Minot Art Gallery, Minot ND 58701. (701)838-4445. Director: Galen Willert. Sponsor: Minot Art Association. Estab. 1976. Annual indoor show held the month of March. Average attendance: 1,000. Entries accepted until 1 week before show. Entry fee: $3/2 entries. Maximum 2 entries per craftworker. Prejudging; no entry fees refunded for refused work. Work may be offered for sale; 30% commission. Registration limit: 50 craftworkers from North Dakota, Minnesota, Montana, South Dakota, and members of the Art Association. Considers all original crafts. Presents cash and purchase prizes.

RED RIVER STREET FAIR, Box 962, Fargo ND 58102. (701)237-3721. Arts Coordinator: Jay Gage. Sponsor: Downtown Business Association. Estab. 1977. Annual outdoor show held 3 days in July. Average attendance: 60,000. Entries accepted until 5 weeks before show. Entry fee: $20/artist. Display area: 15x15. Prejudging by 3 35mm slides. SASE. Entry fee refunded for refused work. Work may be offered for sale; no commission. Craftworker must attend show; demonstrations OK. Sponsor provides electricity for demonstrations; and light hospitality. Categories: public sales/display-painting; drawing; sculpture; fibers; wood; metal; jewelry; leather; poetry/literature; glass; clay; plastics; and folk arts. Demonstrations OK in quilting; painting; pottery; wood-carving; jewelry; blacksmithing; dulcimer; spinning; and weaving. Considers all crafts including folk toys; musical instrument construction; and basketry. Use of good design concepts in display presentation; no clutter. Work clearly labeled and priced. Work should fulfill definition of finished status. No propping of works on non-booth display surfaces. **Sales Tip:** "Larger sales volume occurs under $80 level; buying does occur to $500 level. Viewing public purchases in all areas; does not separate crafts and fine arts categories. Utility has a strong appeal."
Promotion: Show is advertised by state-wide newspapers; shopping newspapers; tourism journals; community and public TV-radio; brochures; and posters. Artists are reached by local; state; regional; and national publications. Submit unique information or photos; local artists are recruited for TV promotions.

SHEYENNE VALLEY ARTS AND CRAFTS FESTIVAL, Ft. Ransom ND 58033. Sponsor: Sheyenne Valley Arts and Crafts Association. Purpose: "to provide an opportunity for artists and craftsmen to display their work." Emphasis is given to encouraging local persons to participate. Estab. 1966. Annual indoor/outdoor show held the last weekend in September. Average attendance: 2,000-3,000. Entries accepted until 2 weeks before show. Entry fee: $3/3x3 display area. Work may be offered for sale; no commission. Craftworker must attend show; demonstrations OK. Registration limit: 75-100. Sponsor provides chairs; coverings; fencing; and table. Show is advertised by radio; TV; and other mass media. Considers all crafts.

Ohio

APPALACHIAN FESTIVAL, 1015 Vine St., Rm. 304, Cincinnati OH 45202. Director: Carole A. Welch. Sponsor: Appalachian Community Development Association. Purpose: "to provide an Appalachian identity focus; to assist Appalachian regional craft group and individuals with sales in a metropolitan market; and to raise funds for community projects." Estab. 1971. Annual indoor show held 5 days in spring. Average attendance: 18,000-20,000. Entries accepted until 8 weeks before show. Entry fee: $35/10x12 display area. Prejudging by photos or slides. Work may be offered for sale; 10% commission. Craftworker must attend show; demonstrations OK. Registration limit: 120. Sponsor provides chairs; display panels; electricity for demonstrations; table; 24-hour security; housing; and 2 meals at show. Show is advertised by an advertising agency; focus is at both national and local level. Submit autobiographic information; photos; and, if possible, names of "prime buyers" for publicity. Considers Appalachian traditional crafts made by craftworkers working in the Appalachian region. 1977 show sales totalled $100,000.

*AREA ARTISTS ANNUAL, 524 Wick Ave., Youngstown OH 44502. (216)743-1711. Annual indoor show held 3 weeks in November. Entries accepted until 3 weeks before show. Entry fee: $1/item. Maximum 3 pieces per category; 9 total. Work may be offered for sale; 10% commission. Craftworker needn't attend show; no demonstrations. Considers all crafts. "Open to artists within a 40 mile radius of Youngstown, including former residents. Label works on back with name, address, title, medium and price, if for sale. No hooks or wires. Entries must be delivered and removed by hand. Rejects may be picked up after the show opens. There will be a storage charge of $1/week for each item not picked up by February." Presents cash and purchase awards.

ART AND CRAFT EXPO, 1446 Secor Rd., Toledo OH 43607. (419)535-0432. Director: Dennis Manos. Sponsor: DJM Productions. Estab. 1976. Annual indoor show held 2 days in November. Average attendance: 5,000. Entries accepted until 1 week before show. Entry fee: $40/10x10 display area. Entries prejudged by slides; photos; and resume. Entry fee refunded for refused work. Work may be offered for sale; no commission. Craftworker must attend show; demonstrations OK. Sponsor provides chairs; electricity for demonstrations; table; and 24-hour security. Show is advertised by posters; magazines; radio; and newspapers. Considers all crafts except ceramics and needlecrafts.

ART IN THE PARK, 142 Riverbend Dr., Dayton OH 45405. (513)225-5433. Director: Pat Shoop-Lowry. Sponsor: City of Dayton Division of Recreation and Riverbend Arts Council. Estab. 1967. Annual outdoor show held 2 days during Memorial Day weekend. Average attendance: 15,000-20,000. Closing date for entry: 3 weeks before show. Entry fee: $20/craftworker. "If an application appears questionable, artist is asked to bring work to center to be previewed." Entry fee refunded for refused work. Crafts may be offered for sale; no commission. "Out-of-state artists do exhibit in our show, but we prefer to promote area artists and we call some artists from the previous year who had interesting exhibits." Craftworker must attend show. "Demonstrating is stressed as it makes for a more interesting show. We have a yearly outdoor raku firing demonstration. There is a student and instructor show plus excellent entertainment." Registration limit: 125.
Acceptable Work: Considers batik; leatherworking; metalsmithing; pottery; weavings; wall hangings; woodcrafting; handmade jewelry; and sculpture using casting or construction methods; enameling; lapidary; macrame; stained glass; and handmade instruments such as dulcimers. "We strive for a fine arts or fine arts type craft show. One-of-a-kind items."

*ARTISAN FAIR, BOSTON MILLS, Box 173, Peninsula OH 44264. (216)657-2807. Director: Don Getz. Sponsor: Junior Women's Civic Club of Akron and the *Cleveland Plain Dealer* Charities. Purpose: to present top quality craftwork to a very art conscious group of buyers. Estab. 1976. Annual indoor/outdoor (large tents) show held 3 days Labor Day weekend. Average attendance: 10,000. Entries accepted until mid-July. Entry fee: $35-75, depending on type of display area. Display area: 10x10 lawn space; 10x14 tent spaces; and 5x15 indoor spaces. Prejudging by 5 slides; $4 screening fee. Entry fee refunded for refused work. Work may be offered for sale; no commission. Craftworker must attend show; demonstrations recommended. Registration limit: 250. Sponsor provides chairs; electricity for demonstrations; and 24-hour security. Show is advertised by newspapers; TV; radio; and posters. Considers all crafts except decoupage; dollmaking; needlecrafts; and tole painting. All works must be tagged with prices.
Awards: Presents cash awards of $250 for best of show; $100, 2nd; $50, 3rd; and certificates. En-

trants judge work; they submit a ballot for best craftsman in exhibit. All awards are based on these ballots.

Profile: The first day of this exhibit is a wholesale day, open for galleries, gift shops, and department store buyers to review the exhibitor's displays and place orders for work to be delivered at a later date. Exhibitors are not required to participate. 1977 show sales totalled $85,000.

*ARTS AND CRAFTS; FINE ARTS; HOBBY CRAFTS; COUNTRY CRAFTS, 47 N. 4th St., Zanesville OH 43701. (614)452-7571. Chairperson: Sally Bonecutter. Sponsor: Zanesville Area Chamber of Commerce. Estab. 1973. Annual outdoor show held 3 days in June. Average attendance: 200,000. Entries accepted until 10 weeks before show. Entry fee: $40/8x10 display area plus $5 prejudging fee. Work may be offered for sale; no commission. Craftworker must attend show; demonstrations OK. Registration limit: 138. Sponsor provides electricity for demonstrations and 24-hour security. Show is advertised by ads through Ohio; leaflets; and statewide coverage. Presents cash awards and ribbons. Categories: fine arts; country crafts; and hobby crafts. Considers all crafts.

*ARTSAFFAIR, 630 S. 3rd St., Columbus OH 43206. (614)244-2606. Coordinator: Jan Schmidt. Sponsor: Greater Columbus Arts Council. Purpose: "to present to the community a culturally stimulating arts festival." Estab. 1973. Annual outdoor show held 3 days in June. Average attendance: 30,000-40,000. Entries accepted until 9 weeks before show. Entry fee: $25-60/display area. Display area: 10x10; 5x10; or 8x10 ground space. Prejudging by 5 slides or photos accompanied by entry form and brief resume. Slides and photos should cover all types of work which would be offered for sale and should be marked with name, media and size of work. Work may be offered for sale; no commission. Craftworker must attend show; demonstrations OK. Registration limit: 100. Sponsor provides display panels on booths only and electricity for demonstrations. Presents purchase awards of $200. Categories: painting; sculpture; graphics; photography; fiber; clay; metal; glass; plastic; leather; and wood. Considers all crafts except candlemaking; decoupage; dollmaking; lapidary; mobiles; needlecrafts; and tole painting.

Sales Tip: "Good display is important to good sales. Our past shows show that the public buys from every media shown; ceramics are very good. Fibers do not always go well if the weather is hot."

Promotion: Show is advertised by all media; TV; radio; newspapers; posters; and billboards. Submit brief resume with slides/photos; Festival Committee retains 2 slides for publicity purposes.

*BOSTON MILLS INVITATIONAL ART FESTIVAL, Box 173, Peninsula OH 44264. (216)657-2807. Director: Don Getz. Sponsor: Akron Society of Artists and *Cleveland Plain Dealer* Charities. Purpose: "to expose the buying public to the best art and crafts available in this part of the country." Estab. 1971. Annual indoor/outdoor (small canopies and large tents) show held 4 days in July. Average attendance: 13,000. Entries accepted until 2 months before show. Entry fee: $30/4x4 table, limit 2; $45/10x10 open tent spaces, limit 2; $55/10x12 small canopy space; and $35/10x10 open lawn space, limit 2. Prejudging by 5 slides; $5 screening fee. Entry fee refunded for refused work. Work must be offered for sale; no commission. Craftworker must attend show; demonstrations OK. Registration limit: 80-100. Sponsor provides chairs; electricity for demonstrations; and 24-hour security. Show is advertised by newspapers; TV; radio; posters; and direct mail.

Acceptable Work: Considers batik; ceramics; glass art; lapidary; macrame; metalsmithing; mobiles; pottery; sculpture; and weaving. All works must be tagged with prices.

Awards: Presents cash awards of $250 for best of show; $100, 1st in crafts; $50, 2nd in crafts; certificates; and purchase awards. Entrants in exhibit are the judges; they submit a ballot for best craftsmen and artist in exhibit. All awards are based on these ballots.

Sales Tip: "This is a buying public as they pay an admission to see exhibit. They purchase well in all price ranges as they realize this has always been a quality exhibit." 1977 show sales totalled $145,000.

*CEDAR POINTS' CRAFTS SHOW, Merchandise Department, Cedar Point Inc., Sandusky OH 44870. (419)626-0830, ext. 2271. Crafts Manager: Jeff Savage. Estab. 1973. Annual outdoor show (indoor space available in case of rain) held the last week in July. Average attendance: 163,-415. Entries accepted until 4 weeks before show. No entry fee. Display area: 10x10. Prejudging by slides or photos sent with application. Work may be offered for sale; 20-30% commission. Craftworker must attend show; demonstrations OK. Registration limit: 50-100. Sponsor provides chairs; covering; electricity for demonstrations; fencing; table; 24-hour security; and night storage. Show is advertised by TV; radio; magazines; newspapers; posters; and billboards.

Considers batik; candlemaking; ceramics; decoupage; dollmaking; and jewelry. 1977 show sales totalled $27,917.

*CERAMIC, SCULPTURE AND CRAFT SHOW, 524 Wick Ave., Youngstown OH 44502. (216)743-1711. Assistant to the Directors: Beth M. Walton. Sponsor: Butler Institute of American Art. Annual indoor show held from first non-holiday Sunday in January to last Sunday in February. Entries accepted until 4 weeks before show. Entry fee: $3.50/classification. Maximum 3 pieces per artist per 4 categories. Work may be offered for sale; 10% commission. Presents cash and purchase awards totalling $1,500. Categories: ceramics; sculpture; enamel jewelry; and crafts. Considers all crafts including quilting and clothing.

COLUMBUS ART-CRAFT-HOBBY-MINIATURE FAIR, 1100 Brandywine Blvd., Box 2188, Zanesville OH 43701. (614)452-4541. Show Director: Walter E. Offinger, Jr. Annual indoor show held 2 days in October at Columbus, Ohio. Average attendance: 10,000. Entries accepted until 1 month before show. Entry fee: $75. Work may be offered for sale; no commission. Craftworker or representative must attend show; demonstrations OK. Registration limit: 250. Sponsor provides 3-6' tables and 2 chairs/10x10 space. Show is advertised by direct mail; newspapers; radio; TV; and craft publications. Considers all crafts.

COSHOCTON CANAL FESTIVAL, Box 266, Coshocton OH 43812. (614)622-5411. Coshocton Area Chamber of Commerce, Executive Manager: John O'Reilly. Estab. 1970. Annual outdoor show held 3 days in August. Average attendance: 100,000. Entries accepted until 1 week before show. Entry fee $20/10' frontal space; $10/each additional 5'. Work may be offered for sale; no commission. Craftworker needn't attend show; demonstrations OK. Registration limit: 50-60. Sponsor provides electricity for demonstrations and 24-hour security. Show is advertised by radio; newspapers; magazines; and periodicals. Considers all crafts.

*DAYTON ART INSTITUTE, Box 941, Dayton OH 45401. Biennial show. Open to Ohio residents. Work may be offered for sale; 10% commission. Exhibited work insured by the Dayton Art Institute. Contact Registrar for further details. Considers sculpture. Recent works not previously shown in the Dayton area only. Presents purchase awards.

BOB EVANS FARM FESTIVAL, 3776 S. High St., Columbus OH 43207. (614)491-2225. Festival Chairman: Robert S. Wood. Purpose: "to familiarize people with the ole time country gatherin'." Estab. 1971. Annual outdoor show held 3 days in October in Rio Grande, Ohio. Average attendance: 100,000. Entries accepted until 10 weeks before show. Display area: 10x15 in craft tent, barn or in field. Work may be offered for sale; no commission. Craftworker must attend show; demonstrations are a *must*. Registration limit: 60 for craft tents; as space allows for field demonstrations. Sponsor provides electricity for demonstrations and 24-hour security. Show is advertised by TV (1977 ABC-network); newspapers; and magazines such as *Grit*. All crafts must be in keeping with Festival theme; especially if a demonstration is possible, i.e. — broom-making; rail splitting; shake making; weaving; and basket making.

FESTIVAL OF THE FISH, 5488 Liberty Ave., Vermilion OH 44089. (216)967-4477. Chairman: Herb Feakins. Sponsor: Vermilion Chamber of Commerce. Annual outdoor show (large tent for some displays) held 4 days the third week in June. Average attendance: 100,000. Entries accepted until show. Work may be offered for sale; no commission. Craftworker must attend show; demonstrations OK. Sponsor provides electricity for demonstrations and 24-hour security. Show is advertised by Ohio Festivals and Events; Lake Erie Firelands Tourist Council; radio; and newspapers. Submit photos for publicity. Considers all crafts. "In Vermilion anything nautical usually sells well."

FUNCTIONAL CERAMICS, Art Center Museum, The College of Wooster, Wooster OH 44691. (216)264-1234, ext. 388. Show Coordinator: Phyllis Clark. Purpose: "to make people aware of the excellent functional ceramic work being done today and to give the practicing functional potters a chance to show their work in a creditable show without all the funky stuff taking precedent; and to give functional potters the recognition they deserve for the work of merit." Estab. 1974. Annual invitational indoor show held 3 weeks in the spring. Average attendance: 1,000. Maximum 10 pieces per craftworker. Prejudging by slides or photos. Work may be offered for sale; 20% commission. Craftworker needn't attend show; demonstrations at times. Registration limit: 20-40. Sponsor provides insurance on exhibited work; insurance on work shipped to artist; shipping costs to artists from show; and all of the display. Considers ceramics and pottery. Maximum size: less than 100 pounds. "Pots are to be numbered and priced and a matching identification list is required to accompany the pots."

Sales Tip: "Our public is aware of good functional work and will not buy inferior or campy products."

Promotion: "We have had excellent coverage by *Ceramic Monthly* magazine; local news media; state monthly magazines; mailers; and by the potters themselves. We need the biographical material on the artist and a photo of him to include in the exhibition after he is accepted."

Twenty to forty potters are invited each year to participate in Functional Ceramics, Wooster, Ohio. The exhibition's purpose is to show the public the excellent functional ceramic products being made today. This tea set is by Molly Cowgill. Photo by Craig Clark.

GREAT LAKES MALL, 2918 Martel Dr., Dayton OH 45420. (513)254-2900. Director: Clarence Freeland. Annual indoor show held 10 days in October-November at Mentor (near Cleveland). Closing date for entry: 1 week before show. Entry fee: $90. Prejudging. Work may be offered for sale; no commission. Craftworker must attend show; demonstrations OK. Sponsor provides 10x10 display area. Considers all crafts.

*INDIAN SUMMER ARTS AND CRAFTS FESTIVAL, 101 Rathbone Terrace, Marietta OH 45750. (614)373-8027. Director: Arthur Howard Winer. Sponsor: Indian Summer Festival, Inc. Purpose: "to provide artists and crafters with an opportunity to exhibit and sell their work and to educate the general public to quality craftsmanship. Each participant is asked to assist by demonstrating and conversing with the viewing public." Estab. 1955. Annual indoor show 3 days in September. Average attendance: 15,000. Entries accepted until 2½ months before show. Entry fee: $30/10x10 display area; $25/space; plus $5 prejudging fee. Country craftworkers *required* to demonstrate; no $25 fee. Prejudging by slides and photos; $25 space fee refunded for refused work. Work may be offered for sale; no commission. Craftworker must attend show; demonstrations encouraged. Registration limit: 125. Sponsor provides display panels; electricity for demonstrations; table (craftworker must pay $2.50 rental fee); and 24-hour security. Show is advertised by brochures; posters; press packs; press releases; radio; and TV. Submit b&w photos of self at work. Considers all crafts. Presents ribbons of craftsmanship.

INVITATIONAL COLUMBUS SPRING ART FAIR, 1725 Weldon, Ann Arbor MI 48103. Show Director: Audree Levy. Sponsor: American Cancer Society. Estab. 1977. Annual indoor show held 2 days in March at Columbus, Ohio. Average attendance: 10,000. Entries accepted until 2 months before show. Entry fee: $110/10x12 display area. Prejudging by 3 slides and resume. SASE. Entry fee due after prejudging. Work may be offered for sale; no commission. Craftworker must attend show; some demonstrations OK. Registration limit: 100. Show director provides 24-hour security. Show is advertised by TV; radio; and newspapers. Submit b&w photo and resume. Considers all crafts except decoupage; needlecrafts; and tole painting.

*MARIETTA COLLEGE CRAFTS NATIONAL, Marietta College, Art Department, Marietta OH 45750. (614)373-4643. Director: Arthur Howard Winer. Purpose: "to display and reward the creative efforts of artists and craftspersons in the USA." Estab. 1972. Annual indoor show held 30 days October-November. Average attendance: 5,000. Entries accepted until 6 weeks before show. $10 jurying fee. Prejudging by slides. Work may be offered for sale; 25% commission. Craftworker needn't attend show; no demonstrations. Sponsor provides insurance on exhibited work; 24-hour security; and exhibition set-up." Accepted artists should send hanging instructions." Show is advertised by 3,500 posters; 4,000 catalogs; 15,000 prospectuses; 12,000 news releases; radio; and TV. Accepted artists send photos of work for promotion. Considers all crafts. Presents cash awards of $3,500; purchase awards of $1,500; and $500 Following Sea Gallery awards.

*THE MARIETTA NATIONAL, Marietta College Department of Art, Marietta OH 45750. (614)373-4643. Director: Arthur Howard Winer. Purpose: "to display and reward the creative efforts of painters and sculptors in US." Estab. 1967. Annual indoor show held 6 weeks April-May. Entries accepted until 2 months before show. Entry fee: $10/artist. Maximum 3 pieces/artist. Prejudging by slides. Work may be offered for sale; 25% commission. Artist needn't attend show; no demonstrations. Registration limit: 200. Show is advertised by listings in art and craft magazines; press releases; posters; radio; and TV. Submit background information. Considers sculpture in all media. Presents $1,000 sculpture awards and $1,500 purchase awards.

THE MASSILLON MUSEUM SIDEWALK SHOW, 212 Lincoln Way E., Massillon OH 44646. (216)833-4061. Director: Mary M. Merwin. Sponsor: Woman's Board of Members of the Museum, Inc. Purpose: "to promote the artist and make his work available for purchase to the public." Estab. 1961. Annual indoor/outdoor show held 3 days in June. Average attendance: 2,-000. Entries accepted until 3 days before show. Entry fee: $3/craftworker. Maximum 25 pieces per craftworker. Work may be offered for sale; 20% commission. Craftworker needn't attend show; demonstrations OK. Sponsor provides chairs; electricity for demonstrations; insurance on exhibited work; and table. Categories: paintings; prints; drawings; photographs; and crafts. Considers all crafts.

*MAY SHOW, The Cleveland Museum of Art, Cleveland OH 44106. Associate Curator: Tom Hinson. Annual indoor show held the month of May. Entries accepted until 2 months before show. Maximum 2 pieces per craftworker. Prejudging by slides. "2 dimensional works should be represented by 2 35mm slides, 2x2 mounts; 1 an overall view, the other a detail. 3 dimensional works should be represented by 3 35mm slides, 2x2 mounts; 1 of the views should show an indication of scale. The artist's name, title, media and dimensions must be marked on each slide. On the front of each slide the top of the work should be indicated and the entry number in upper right." SASE. Work may be offered for sale; 10% commission. Sponsor will carry cost of unpacking work. "All entrants will receive a preview invitation. All accepted artists will be sent 1 complimentary catalog copy." Presents 4 $1,000 cash awards.
Acceptable Work: Considers glass art; jewelry; metalsmithing; enamels; pottery; and furniture. Will only accept work "by artists who now live, work, or were born in the following Ohio counties: Ashland; Ashtabula; Cuyahoga; Erie; Geauga; Huron; Lake; Lorain; Mahoning; Medina; Portage; Summit; or Trumbull. Artist must be 18 or older. All silver objects should indicate whether sterling silver or silver plate was used. Clay objects must be fired. Fasten 1 tag securely with tape on the upper-left corner of the back side of each object. Do not use tacks or similar means to secure tags. If your entry has more than 1 part, secure a tag to each piece, indicating on each tag the number of units the object has. On textiles: attach tag at bottom edge."

MILLCREEK MALL, 2918 Martel Dr., Dayton OH 45420. (513)254-2900. Director: Clarence Freeland. Annual indoor show held 1 week in August-September at Erie, Ohio. Closing date for entry: 1 week before show. Entry fee: $75. Display area: 10x10. Prejudging. Work may be offered for sale; no commission. Craftworker must attend show; demonstrations OK. Considers all crafts.

*MONTGOMERY KIWANIS SIDEWALK ART SHOW, 9399 Shelly Lane, Cincinnati OH 45242. (513)793-4390. Chairman: Harry Henderly. Sponsor: Montgomery Kiwanis Club. Estab. 1955. Annual outdoor show held the next to the last Sunday in September. Average attendance: 5,000-10,000. Entries accepted until show date. Entry fee: $10/adult entry; $1/youth entry. Work may be offered for sale; no commission. Craftworker must attend show; demonstrations OK. Considers all crafts.
Awards: Presents $485, cash prizes; $300, youth scholarship; $100 bicycle; 3 grand prizes and 60+ 1st, 2nd, 3rd and honorable mention ribbons. Judges are local artists and art teachers.

*OHIO ARTISTS AND CRAFTSMEN SHOW, 212 Lincoln Way E., Massillon OH 44646. (216)833-4061. Director: Mary Merwin. Sponsor: The Massillon Museum. Purpose: "to give outstanding craftsmen an opportunity to show their work and also to expose the public to the work of Ohio craftsmen." Estab. 1937. Biennial indoor show held 2 months, July-August during even-numbered years. Average attendance: 2,500. Entries accepted until 3 weeks before show. Entry fee: $3/craftworker. Maximum 4 pieces per craftworker. Prejudging; no entry fees refunded for refused work. Work may be offered for sale; 10% commission. Craftworker needn't attend show; no demonstrations. Sponsor provides insurance on exhibited work and 24-hour security. Show is advertised by radio; newspapers through Ohio; and magazines. Considers batik; ceramics; glass art; jewelry; metalsmithing; mobiles; pottery; sculpture; and soft sculpture. Presents purchase awards and prizes totalling $1,500.

OUTDOOR ARTS FESTIVAL, School of Fine Arts, 38660 Mentor Ave., Willoughby OH 44094. (216)951-7500. Exhibit Coordinator: David Kelly. Purpose: "to offer a show place for creative practicing artists and craftsmen and to promote programs, classes and facilities the School of Fine Arts offers." Estab. 1972. Annual outdoor show held 3 days in July. Average attendance: 10,000. Entries accepted until show date unless otherwise announced. Entry fee: $15.75/12x12 display area. Prejudging by slides and photos; entry fee refunded for refused work. Work may be offered for sale; no commission. Craftworker must attend show; demonstrations encouraged. Sponsor provides electricity for demonstrations and 24-hour security. Considers all crafts.
Promotion: "All television, radio stations and newspapers receive news releases regarding this event and there is a community-wide distribution of flyers. The festival is advertised statewide through the news media, Ohio Arts Council and the Ohio Artists and Craftsmen Association." Submit 8x10 b&w glossies of self involved with work; brief paragraph on background; and name of newspaper serving your area.

RICHMOND MALL, 2918 Martel Dr., Dayton OH 45420. (513)254-2900. Director: Clarence Freeland. Annual indoor show held 1 week in October at Cleveland, Ohio. Closing date for entry: 1 week before show. Entry fee: $75. Display area: 10x10. Prejudging. Work may be offered for sale; no commission. Craftworker must attend show; demonstrations OK. Considers all crafts.

*SHOW OF THE CRAFT GUILD OF GREATER CINCINNATI, 933 Avondale Ave., Cincinnati OH 45229. (513)281-8042. Newsletter Editor: Vivian Kline. Purpose: "educational, to acquaint the public with the original work being done today within a 50-mile radius of Cincinnati." Estab. 1966. Annual indoor show held 4 weeks March-April. Average attendance: 2,000. Entries accepted until 1 week before show. Maximum 3 pieces per craftworker. Prejudging by actual work. Work may be offered for sale; 20% commission. Craftworker needn't attend show; no demonstrations. Show is advertised by radio; newspapers; posters; and mailings. Considers all crafts. Awards 4 cash prizes.

SOUTHERN PARK MALL, 2918 Martel Dr., Dayton OH 45420. (513)254-2900. Director: Clarence Freeland. Indoor show held 1 week in September at Youngstown, Ohio. Closing date for entry: 1 week before show. Entry fee: $75. Prejudging. Work may be offered for sale; no commission. Craftworker must attend show; demonstrations OK. Sponsor provides 10x10 display area. Considers all crafts.

*SPRING SHOW, 129 N. Metcalf St., Lima OH 45801. Contact: Director. Annual show. Entry fee: $4, students; $5, Lima Art Association members; $6, non-members. Maximum 3 entries. No sales commission. Open to artists living within 75 miles of Lima, Ohio. Presents $100, best of show; $60, best 2-dimensional; $60, best 3-dimensional; three $30 prizes.

SQUARE FAIR, Box 1124, Lima OH 45805. (419)225-6156. Executive Director: Dean R. Gladden. Sponsor: Lima Area Arts Council. Purpose: "to allow artists a chance to display and sell works and to enhance the downtown area." Estab. 1976. Annual outdoor show held 2 days in August. Average attendance: 10,000. Entries accepted until 3 weeks before show. Entry fee: $10/display area. Work may be offered for sale; no commission. Craftworker needn't attend show; demonstrations OK. Sponsor provides electricity for demonstrations. Show is advertised by radio; TV; and news media. Considers all crafts.

SUMMERFAIR INC., Box 3277, Cincinnati, OH 45201. Contact: Director. Annual outdoor exhibit held the first weekend in June. Closing date: March. Prejudging by slides. Considers a variety of media.

SUMMIT MALL, 2918 Martel Dr., Dayton OH 45420. (513)254-2900. Director: Clarence Freeland. Annual indoor show held 1 week in October at Akron, Ohio. Closing date for entry: 1 week before show. Entry fee: $65. Prejudging. Work may be offered for sale; no commission. Craftworker must attend show; demonstrations OK. Sponsor provides 10x10 display area. Considers all crafts.

E.J. THOMAS CHRISTMAS ART AND CRAFTS SHOW, 4871 Brecksville Rd., Richfield OH 44286. (216)659-3318. Director: Carol Raab. Sponsor: R&R Promotions. Purpose: "to provide a selling outlet for professional and semi-professional and qualifying amateurs, and to bring a quality show to the public." Estab. 1977. Annual indoor show held 3 days in December at Akron, Ohio. Average attendance: 12,000-15,000. Entries accepted until 4 weeks before show. Entry fee: $80-150/10x10 display area. Prejudging by slides and photos; entry fee refunded for refused work. Work may be offered for sale; no commission. Craftworker must attend show; demonstrations OK. Registration limit: 90. Sponsor provides electricity for demonstrations and 24-hour security; tables and chairs may be rented. Show is advertised by TV; radio; newspapers; magazines; posters; flyers; promotional gimmicks; and press releases. Submit pictures and promotional description of work and self. Considers all crafts.

*TOLEDO FESTIVAL OF THE ARTS, Box 7401, Toledo OH 43615. (419)536-8365. Contact: Beverlee Anderson. Sponsor: Arts Commission of Greater Toledo; Crosby Gardens Division of Forestry; Toledo Artists Club; and Garden Club Forum. Purpose: "to provide artists with the opportunity to make the general public aware of their work and hopefully to make a living off their work; and to increase the awareness and the knowledge of the public towards the art." Estab. 1965. Annual outdoor show held 2 days in June. Average attendance: 80,000. Entries accepted until 1 week before show. Entry fee: $40/booth; $10/table; and $10/1 side of easel. Display area: booth, 10x8; table, 2½x8; and easel, 4x6. Prejudging by photos, slides and actual work. Entry fee refunded for refused work. Work may be offered for sale; no commission. Craftworker must attend show; demonstrations OK. Registration limit: 350. Sponsor provides coverings with booths; electricity for demonstrations if notified before; and 24-hour security. Show is advertised by radio; TV; newspapers; magazines; and posters. Submit resume. Presents cash awards of $25 for each 1st place winner; $500 for purchase for permanent collection; and ribbons for 1st, 2nd, 3rd, and honorable mention. "Winners are chosen for the overall quality of their work not for specific pieces." Considers all crafts except candlemaking; decoupage; dollmaking; needlecrafts; and tole painting.

*WESTERVILLE MUSICAL AND ARTS FESTIVAL, 5 W. College Ave., Westerville OH 43081. (614)882-8917. Executive Secretary: Jan Strausser. Sponsor: Westerville Area Chamber of Commerce. Purpose: "as a celebration of the arts; to continue development of all the arts throughout the area; recognizing that this development is vitally important to the growth of both the individual and the community." Estab. 1974. Annual outdoor show held 2 days in July. Average attendance: 30,000. Entries accepted until 1 week before show. Entry fee: $30. Display area: 10'. Prejudging by slides or photos; entry fee refunded for refused work. Work may be offered for sale; no commission. Craftworker must attend show; demonstrations OK. Registration limit: 100. Sponsor provides electricity for demonstrations. Show is advertised by TV; radio; newspapers; other periodicals; and flyers. Photos may be requested for publicity. Considers all crafts except needlecrafts and knitting. Presents $1,600 in cash awards and ribbons.

*WESTLAND ARTS AND CRAFTS SHOW, 4273 Westland Mall, Columbus OH 43228. Contact: Thomas Gilbride. Annual show. Sponsor: Westland Shopping Center. Entry fee: $20. Space provided each exhibitor is 2 5x7 panels of the 6 sides of an art rack. Additional space available at $20. One craftworker per space. Original work only. No commission. Awards $750 in prizes.

WONDERFUL WORLD OF OHIO MART, Stan Hywet Hall, 714 N. Portage Path, Akron OH 44303. (216)836-5533. Director of Public Relations: Louise Goodman. Sponsor: Women's Auxiliary Board, Stan Hywet Hall Foundation, Inc. Purpose: fundraiser. Estab. 1967. Annual indoor/outdoor show (with some tents) held 4 days in October. Average attendance: 20,000. Entries accepted 7 months before show. Entry fee: $80-100, depending on location. Display area: 10x10. Prejudging by work samples; entry fee due after prejudging. Work must be offered for sale; no commission. Craftworker must attend show; demonstrations requested. Registration limit: 70. Sponsor provides chairs; table; 24-hour security; and booth space is marked off. 1977 show sales totalled $70,000. Considers all crafts.
Promotion: Show is advertised by the public relations director of Stan Hywet Hall Foundation, using radio; TV; newspapers; magazines; and brochures distributed to all visitors to Stan Hywet

Hall for some 2-3 months prior to the Mart. Submit biographical material (questionnaire provided) and b&w photos suitable for newspaper reproduction.

WOODVILLE MALL, 2918 Martel Dr., Dayton OH 45420. (513)254-2900. Director: Clarence Freeland. Annual indoor show held in Toledo 1 week in October. Closing date for entry: 1 week before show. Entry fee: $55. Display area: 10x10. Prejudging. Work may be offered for sale; no commission. Craftworker must attend show; demonstrations OK. Considers all crafts.

YANKEE PEDDLER FESTIVAL, Box 07150, Cleveland OH 44107. (216)221-1801. Contact: Frank Cajka. Estab. 1973. Annual outdoor show held 3 weekends in September at Canal Fulton, Ohio. Average attendance: 38,000-40,000. Entries accepted until 2 months before show. Entry fee: $100/10x10 display area. Prejudging by photos or slides; entry fee due after prejudging. Work may be offered for sale; no commission. Craftworker must attend show; demonstrations required. Registration limit: 150. Sponsor provides 24-hour security. Show is advertised by TV; radio; newspaper; brochures; and bus tour companies. Submit photos acceptable for promotion in your vicinity. Considers all crafts of 1776-1825 period except ceramics; decoupage; mobiles; and soft sculpture.

Oklahoma

ANTIQUE, QUILT & CRAFT SHOW, c/o Mrs. J.C. Pond, Box 127, Medford OK 73759. (405)393-2888. Sponsor: Grant County Historical Society. Estab. 1974. Annual indoor show held 1½ days the second weekend in April. Average attendance: 300-400. Entries accepted until show date. No entry fee. Work may be offered for sale; no commission. Craftworker must attend show; demonstrations OK. Sponsor provides chairs; electricity for demonstrations; and 24-hour security. Considers all crafts.

FREE ART FAIR, c/o Mrs. J.C. Pond, Box 127, Medford OK 73759. (405)393-2888. Sponsor: The Medford Progress Club. Estab. 1966. Annual indoor show held the second weekend in November. Average attendance: 300-400. Entries accepted until show date. No entry fee. Work may be offered for sale; no commission. Craftworker must attend show; demonstrations OK. Sponsor provides chairs; electricity for demonstrations; and 24-hour security. Considers all crafts.

LAWTON FORT SILL ANNUAL ART SHOW, Lawton Fort Sill Art Council, 1601 NW 75th St., Lawton OK 73505. Contact: Barbara Ainsworth. Annual exhibition for all media. No commission. Hand-deliver entries.

*OKLAHOMA CITY FESTIVAL OF THE ARTS, 3014 Paseo, Oklahoma City OK 73103. (405)521-1426. Festival Coordinator: Jackie Jones. Sponsor: Arts Council of Oklahoma City. Purpose: "to bring a wide range of fine arts and crafts to the public; to celebrate the arts in all forms; to give the artist exposure to over 250,000 potential customers; and to support the other programs of the Arts Council, including an extensive arts in education program." Estab. 1967. Annual outdoor show (with panels covered by tents) held 6 days the last week in April. Entries accepted until show date for weekend craft market. Entry fee: $75/10x10 display area. Work may be offered for sale; no commission. Craftworkers encouraged to attend show; demonstrations OK. Sponsor provides electricity for demonstrations and 24-hour security. Categories: visual arts (6-day show); and crafts (2-day show). Considers all crafts. Awards $500-1,000 in purchase prizes.
Sales Tip: "Have as wide a range of sizes and prices as possible. Also, the artist's attitude to public is a major factor in sales. Crafts are extremely popular with the buyers at this show, but the competition in the crafts area is putting an emphasis on creativity and uniqueness of work as well as quality of technical expertise." 1977 2-day craft show sales totalled $50,000+.
Promotion: Show is advertised "in local newspapers; some advertising in national magazines; plus recommendations as 'thing to do' in publications such as TWA travel magazine. Public service radio and TV spots, plus broadcast of leading talk show from festival grounds [is also used]."

Oregon

ALBANY HOLIDAY MARKET, c/o Creative Arts Guild, Box 841, Albany OR 97321. (503)928-2815. Executive Director: Terri Hopkins. Purpose: "to provide an inexpensive outlet for local craftspeople; and to let the public become aware of the variety and quality of local crafts." Estab. 1976. Annual indoor show held 4 Saturdays between Thanksgiving and Christmas. Average attendance: 10,000. Entries accepted until show. Entry fee: $5/day/7x7 display area. Work may be offered for sale; no commission. Craftworker needn't attend show (but is

responsible for own sales); no demonstrations. Registration limit: 45. Considers all crafts.
Promotion: Market is advertised by public service announcements; paid advertising; posters; signs; and newspaper articles and photos.

ALBANY SPRING ARTS FESTIVAL, Box 841, Albany OR 97321. (503)928-2815. Director: Terri Hopkins. Sponsor: Creative Arts Guild. Estab. 1969. Annual indoor/outdoor show held 2 days in early May. Average attendance: 20,000. Entries accepted until 1 week before show. No entry fee. Maximum 2 entries per craftworker. Work may be offered for sale; 20% commission. Demonstrations OK. Considers all crafts by residents.

CHRISTMAS CRAFT FAIR, Rt. 2, Box 87C, Pendleton OR 97801. (503)276-4237. Chairperson: Loree Tucker-McKenna. Sponsor: Pendleton Arts Council. Estab. 1971. Annual indoor show held 2 days in November, Friday and Saturday following Thanksgiving. Average attendance: 600-1,000. Entries accepted until show filled. Entry fee: $1/booth. Display area: 10' wide but exceptions made if work larger. Work may be offered for sale; 10% commission. Craftworker or representative must attend show; demonstrations encouraged. Registration limit: 25. Sponsor provides chairs; electricity for demonstrations; table and 24-hour security. 1977 show sales totalled over $3,000. Considers all crafts including hand-made Christmas decorations.

COOS ART MUSEUM CRAFT SHOW, 515 Market Ave., Coos Bay OR 97420. (503)267-3901. Director: Maggie Karl. Purpose: "to show contemporary crafts to southwestern Oregon." Annual indoor show held 1 month in July. Entries accepted until 4 weeks before show. Entry fee: $5/craftworker. Maximum 2 entries/category. Prejudging. No entry fees refunded for refused work. Work may be offered for sale; 25% commission. Craftworker needn't attend show; demonstration OK. Sponsor provides chairs; coverings; display panels; electricity for demonstrations; insurance on exhibited work; table; museum staff handles sales; and 24-hour security. Considers all crafts; functional only. "The craftperson provides his own presentation for his/her work." 1977 exhibitor sales totalled $400.

*FRAGILE ART COMPETITION, 420 Governor Bldg., Portland OR 97204. (503)227-6700. Editor: Fred Abrams. Sponsor: *Glass* magazine. Competition. Purpose: "to further glass as an art form, and acquaint the public with the possibilities of glass. At the same time to give recognition to creative glass artists." Estab. 1977. "Entries are judged the year before the show by an international jury. Entry fee: $5 for each slide. Prejudging. "Artists must submit slides of work; finalists are decided; then jurors choose award winners. All finalists are eligible for the show; show participants are chosen for a show in New York City." Categories: decorative objects; etched/engraved glass; functional ware; lamps and lampshades; panels; sculpture; and student work (students may compete directly against professionals by entering into those categories). **Awards:** Presents $1,000 and publication of work on cover of *Glass* to winner; additional cash prizes to runners up; up to $1,000 in purchase awards; and finalists are eligible for the New York show and publication in *Glass* magazine. "Professionally shot photos or slides may help immensely. Good work with bad photography does not do well because the photo does not do justice to the glass."

NEHALEM ARTS FESTIVAL, Rt. 1, Box 193, Nehalem OR 97131. (503)368-5711. Director: Carey Tate. Sponsor: Nehalem Bay Merchants Association. Purpose: "the show is held for the artist to promote art sales." Estab. 1973. Annual outdoor show held 2 days in July. Average attendance: 2,000. Entries accepted until 2 weeks before show. No entry fee. Work may be offered for sale; no commission. Craftworker must attend show; demonstrations OK. Show is advertised by flyers; newspaper advertising; and state tour guides. Registration limit: 50. Categories: paintings; sculpture; ceramics; leather; weaving; jewelry; and miscellaneous crafts. Considers all crafts.

PORTLAND HARVEST FESTIVAL, 832 Bancroft Way, Berkeley CA 94710. (415)548-5440. Contact: Steve Kyle, Warren Cook, or Ellen Schwartz. Sponsor: General Expositions Corporation. Estab. 1978. Annual indoor show held 3 days in November in Portland, Oregon. Entries accepted until full; "booths are rented according to seniority." Entry fee: $135/8x10 display area. Prejudging by 6 photos or slides or actual work. Work may be offered for sale; no commission. Craftworker must attend show; demonstrations OK. Sponsor provides electricity for demonstrations; backdrop drapery; side rails; 24-hour security; cleaning; motel or hotel accommodations at group rate; inexpensive trucking of booth setup and stock round-trip between other Harvest Festival shows. Presents awards for best costumes; best designed booths; and best demonstrating booths. Show is advertised by newspaper; radio; TV; billboard; direct mailing;

posters; discount coupons; news releases; and TV guest appearances. Considers all crafts.
Profile: "The Harvest Festivals are patterned after the famous country autumn fairs of 19th century America. These fairs were held to give thanksgiving for bountiful crops and as a last celebration before the hard winter set in. Craftworkers are required to be in 19th century costume."

SATURDAY MARKET, Box 427, Eugene OR 97440. (503)686-8885. Contact: Manager: Sponsor: Saturday Market (a nonprofit corporation). Purpose: "to provide craftspeople with a place to sell their work, and the public with a place to view it." Estab. 1970. Outdoor show held every Saturday from April-December. Entries accepted until market day; spaces assigned by lottery. Entry fee: "$3 first time; then $3-9, depending upon income of preceeding time." Display area: 8x8. Work may be offered for sale; no commission. Craftworker must attend show; demonstrations OK. Registration limit: 220. Considers all crafts "that are gathered from natural materials, or made or grown by the vendor (or a household family member)."

Pennsylvania

APPLE HARVEST FESTIVAL, Box 38, Biglerville PA 17307. Arts and Crafts Chairman: Jeanette Taylor. Sponsor: Upper Adams Jaycees. Purpose: fundraising. Estab. 1964. Annual outdoor show (most of festival is outdoors; limited number of indoor spaces available; some buildings have open sides) held 2 weekends in October at Arendtsville, Pennsylvania. Average attendance: 40,000-80,000. Entries accepted until 4 weeks before show. Entry fee: $25/weekend. Display area: 10x10. Prejudging by photos, slides, or descriptive resumes of the items. "They are prejudged only to the extent that we do not allow junk type items into the festival; all exhibitors must deal in a true art or craft." Entry fee due after prejudging. Work may be offered for sale; no commission. Craftworker must attend show; demonstrations encouraged. Registration limit: 85, indoor; 150, outdoor. Sponsor provides electricity for demonstrations and 24-hour security. Show is advertised by brochures; news releases; radio; and TV. Submit photographs of your work for publicity. Considers all crafts.

CENTRAL PENNSYLVANIA FESTIVAL OF THE ARTS SIDEWALK SALE, Box 1023, State College PA 16801. Estab. 1964. Annual outdoor show held 4 days in July. Average attendance: 150,000-175,000. Entries accepted until 4 months before show date. Entry fee: $40/10x3, 10x4 or 10x6 display areas. Prejudging by 3 slides per each category entered; $3 nonrefundable jury fee. Entry fee refunded for refused work. Work may be offered for sale; no commission. Craftworker must attend show. Registration limit: 400. Sponsor provides fencing. Show is advertised by local radio; TV; newspapers (Philadelphia, Pittsburgh and Harrisburg); and Pennsylvania Tourist Bureau. 1977 show sales totalled $400,000. Categories: ceramics; fibers; glass; jewelry; leather; metal; paintings and graphics; photographs; wood; wax; and other. Considers all crafts except decoupage.

*CENTRE SQUARE ART FAIR, Downtown Improvement Group, Inc. and Community Art League, Easton PA 18042. (215)258-2281, 253-1487. Estab. 1965. Annual outdoor show held 1 day in September. Entries accepted until 2 weeks before show. Entry fee: $7/10' display area. Work may be offered for sale; no commission. Craftworker must attend show; demonstrations OK. Presents cash awards of $700 and ribbons for 1st, 2nd, and 3rd. Considers all original crafts.

CHERRIES JUBILEE CRAFT SHOW, Box 516, Kimberton PA 19442. (215)933-7563. Sponsor: Virginia Graham. Estab. 1976. Annual indoor show held 2 days in February (George Washington holiday weekend) at Valley Forge, Pennsylvania. Average attendance: 1,200-2,000. Entries accepted until 1 week before show. Entry fee: $30/10x6 display area. Prejudging by previous shows; entry fee refunded for refused work. Work may be offered for sale; no commission. Craftworker must attend show; demonstrations encouraged. Registration limit: 60. Sponsor provides chairs; electricity for demonstrations; tables; and individual requests within reason. Show is advertised by Montgomery County Tourist Bureau; newspaper ads; pamphlets; TV; radio; flyers; and press releases. Submit glossies and write-up to put in PR work and brochure. **Acceptable Work:** Considers candlemaking; ceramics; decoupage; dollmaking; leatherworking; macrame; metalsmithing; needlecrafts; pottery; tole painting; weaving; and woodcrafting. "We prefer traditional or colonial crafts."

*CLOTHESLINE EXHIBIT, Box 293, Waynesboro PA 17268. (717)597-4376. Vice President: Ann Brown. Sponsor: Waynesboro Studio Club. Purpose: "to bring arts and crafts to general public, also gives local artists and craftsmen a chance to compete. Each year the quality of show has improved." Estab. 1951. Annual outdoor show (indoors if rain) held 1 day in June. Average attendance: 1,200. Entries accepted until 3 weeks before show. Entry fee: $7/artist. For judging maximum 5 pieces per craftworker; no limit for display and sale. Prejudging by actual work; "no work refused unless copies or kits." Work may be offered for sale; no commission. Craftworker must attend show; demonstrations OK. Registration limit: 30-40. Sponsor provides electricity for demonstrations if inside and fencing. "Exhibit at own risk." Show is advertised by 6 newspapers; 8 radio stations; and TV. Submit with entry form any additional information you would like to include for promotional purposes. Considers all crafts.

Awards: Presents ribbons for 1st, 2nd, 3rd and honorable mention for each category. "Cash awards vary from year to year; merchants and businesses contribute."

*CRAFT EXHIBITION OF THE CENTRAL PENNSYLVANIA FESTIVAL OF THE ARTS, Box 1023, State College PA 16801. Estab. 1966. Annual indoor show held 1 week in July at University Park, Pennsylvania. Presents cash awards of $2,000.

*EGGORAMA, Egg Shell Craft, 66 E. Union Blvd., Bethlehem PA 18018. Contact: Mary Ellen Ellington or Peter Evans. Indoor exhibition. Entry fee: craftsman, $25/table; dealer, $40/table (6' table). Entries accepted until show date if not filled. No commission. Craftworker or representative must attend show. Considers all media in egg shell decoration. Presents best of show and ribbons in each category.

A FAIR IN THE PARK, Arts and Crafts Center of Pittsburgh, Pittsburgh PA 15232. (412)361-0873. Contact: Chairman. Sponsor: Craftsmen's Guild of Pittsburgh. Purpose: "to give the artist exposure to the public and to educate the public on what is good quality art. Also to give the artists the opportunity to learn from each other." Estab. 1969. Annual 3 day outdoor show held in September. Average attendance: 40,000. Entries accepted until 6 weeks before show. Entry fee: $30/artist. Display area: 10x10. Entries prejudged by slides; entry fee refunded for refused work. Work may be offered for sale; no commission. Craftworker must attend show; demonstrations recommended. Registration limit: 125. Sponsor provides electricity for demonstrations and 24-hour security. 1977 show sales totalled over $70,000. Considers all crafts except decoupage; lapidary; mobiles; and tole painting.

Promotion: Show is advertised by "a good publicity campaign in magazines; newspapers; TV; and radio spots. In 1977 we started having a live radio show broadcasted from the fair grounds and will repeat this."

*FALL CRAFT MARKET AT PARK CITY MALL, Box 5153, Lancaster PA 17601. President: R.D. Faulkner. Sponsor: Conestoga Valley Chapter, Pennsylvania Guild of Craftsmen. Purpose: fundraising. Estab. 1973. Annual indoor show held 3 days in November. Average attendance: 60,000. Entries accepted until 6 weeks before show. No entry fee. "Show open only to members of the Pennsylvania Guild of Craftsmen." Maximum 1 item per category per artist. Display area: 10x15. Prejudging by 4 slides for new craftworkers; floor jurying from past shows. Work may be offered for sale; 20% commission, $100 maximum. Craftworker must attend show; demonstrations required 20% of showtime. Registration limit: 90. Sponsor provides electricity for demonstrations and some security. Show is advertised by billboards; newspaper; posters; radio; and TV interview shows. Submit b&w photos of self at work for publicity. Presents purchase awards of $200. 1977 show sales totalled approximately $40,000. Considers all crafts except mobiles; kits and assemblage. Bestsellers: glass; leather; and pottery.

FALL FOLIAGE FESTIVAL, Bedford PA 15522. (814)847-2282. Co-chairman: Mrs. Robert Barnhart. Estab. 1964. Annual indoor/outdoor show held 2 weekends in October. Average attendance: 10,000. Entries accepted until 1 week before show. Entry fee: per weekend $10/10-12' of sidewalk. Work may be offered for sale; no commission. Craftworker needn't attend show; demonstrations OK. "Craftsmen are responsible for their own belongings. Items are displayed on town sidewalks. Must be torn down each evening." Show is advertised by radio; TV; and newspapers. Considers all crafts. Bestsellers: not more than $15 items.

FORT ARMSTRONG FOLK FESTIVAL, 325 Market St., Kittanning PA 16201. (412)548-4118. President: Dr. William E. Martin. Purpose: "to preserve the crafts of a past gone era for the benefit of our children." Estab. 1971. Annual outdoor show (some picnic shelter; may bring tents) held 5 days in August. Average attendance: 40,000-50,000. Entries accepted until 4 weeks before show; "we reserve a certain number of spaces up to show time for unusual and worthy crafts." Entry fee: $35-40/12x12 display area (includes lighting and plugs 100 volt hookups); plus $15 for special 220 volt electric hookup. Prejudging by slides; photos; promotional material; references; and other shows. Entry fee refunded for refused work. Work may be offered for sale; no commission. Craftworker must attend show; demonstrations encouraged. Registration limit: 70. Sponsor provides roping; and 24-hour security. Show is advertised by flyers; 40 newspapers;

brochures; Pittsburgh TV; local cable TV; and radio. Submit all background information for newspaper release. Considers all crafts; especially ones relating to the colonial era.

GRAND IRISH JUBILEE, 123 S. Main St., Mahanoy City PA 17948. (717)773-2284. Manager: Frank Guinan. Purpose: "to advance interest in Irish customs; music; dancing; and personality." Estab. 1975. Annual outdoor show (with closed buildings) held 4 days in September at Barnesville, Pennsylvania. Average attendance: 15,000. Entries accepted until 1 week before show. Work may be offered for sale; 10% commission. Craftworker must attend show; demonstrations OK. Registration limit: 20. Sponsor provides electricity for demonstrations. Show is advertised by brochures; newspapers; ethnic radio programs and publications; radio; and TV. Submit photos for promotion. Considers batik; candlemaking; ceramics; glass art; leatherworking; pottery; weaving; woodcrafting; Irish themes; and resulting products.

*GREATER HARRISBURG ARTS FESTIVAL, Box 770, Harrisburg PA 17108. (717)238-5184. General Chairman: Milton Adolphus. Sponsor: Greater Harrisburg Arts Council. Estab. 1967. Annual indoor/outdoor show held Memorial Day weekend through following weekend. Average attendance: 100,000. Entry fee: $5/craftworker. Maximum 3 pieces per craftworker for juried show. Work may be offered for sale; no commission. Craftworker must attend show; demonstrations OK. Registration limit: 150. Booths and utilities provided for $5/day. Considers batik; candlemaking; ceramics; decoupage; glass art; jewelry; leatherworking; metalsmithing; needlecrafts; soft sculpture; tole painting; weaving; and quilting.

HAINES TOWNSHIP DUTCH FALL FESTIVAL, c/o Jack Smith, Rt. 45, Aaronsburg PA 16820. (814)349-5280. Purpose: "this festival was held for the Bicentennial. It was so successful and worthwhile the townspeople wanted to continue it." Estab. 1976. Annual outdoor show held 2 days in October. Average attendance: 8,000. Entries accepted until 2 weeks before show. Work may be offered for sale; no commission. Craftworker must attend show; demonstrations preferred. "We provide a large exhibit space in front of each single home on Main Street and will assist in getting items that perhaps craftworker could not bring." Sponsor provides 24-hour security. Show is advertised by newspaper; radio; and TV. Submit b&w photos. Considers all crafts.

"HANDS OF MAN" SHOW & SALE, Rt. 1, Box 153J, Auburn NH 03032. (603)483-2742. President: Jinx Harris. Estab. 1978. Annual indoor show held 3 days in December at Philadelphia. Average attendance: 75,000+. Entries accepted until 1 week before show or until filled. Entry fee: $35/8x4 display area. Prejudging by slides or photos if not in a previous show. Work may be offered for sale; no commission. Craftworker must attend show; demonstrations OK. Registration limit: 170. Sponsor provides electricity for demonstrations and 24-hour security. Show is advertised by radio; TV; and newspapers. Considers all crafts except ceramics; decoupage under $5; lapidary; and strung bead jewelry.

"HANDS OF MAN" SHOW & SALE, Rt. 1, Box 153J, Auburn NH 03032. (603)483-2742. President: Jinx Harris. Estab. 1978. Annual indoor show held 3 days in December at Pittsburgh. Average attendance: 75,000+. Entries accepted until 1 week before show or until filled. Entry fee: $35/8x4 display area. Prejudging by slides or photos if not in a previous show. Work may be offered for sale; no commission. Craftworker must attend show; demonstrations OK. Registration limit: 170. Sponsor provides electricity for demonstrations and 24-hour security. Show is advertised by radio; TV; and newspapers. Considers all crafts except ceramics; decoupage under $5; lapidary; and strung bead jewelry.

THE HANNA'S TOWN FOLK FESTIVAL, Westmoreland County Historical Society, 221 N. Main St., Greensburg PA 15601. (412)836-1800. Festival Chairman: Arlene Kendra. Sponsor: Elizabeth Hanna Guild of the Westmoreland County Historical Society. Estab. 1976. Annual outdoor show (some canopies available) held 1 day in July at Hanna's Town. Average attendance: 8,000-10,000. Entries accepted until 2 weeks before show. Entry fee: $15/16x10 display area. Prejudging by slides or photos; entry fee due after prejudging. Work may be offered for sale; no commission. Craftworker must attend show; demonstrations preferred. Registration limit: 30. Considers candlemaking; dollmaking; metalsmithing; tole painting; colonial crafts; and early Americana such as pewter. Bestsellers: "Generally things that can be easily carried in hand; items around or under $5. The greatest 1 last year was wooden toys."
Promotion: "Show is advertised by 20 newspapers; news releases to 43 newspapers; radio announcements to about 27 radio stations; publicity pictures in advance in local newspapers; listing in brochures; events calendars in several local magazines; posters; and yearly events handbill."

Submit photo and resume.

Profile: "For this one day a year we attempt to recreate a modern version of life on the frontier. For those whose craft can't be sold we pay for their demonstration. We are particularly looking for a broom maker and hornsmith. This is educational and historical and in keeping with the theme of our organization."

HAZLETON CREATIVE ARTS FESTIVAL SIDEWALK SALE, c/o Greater Hazleton Chamber of Commerce, Hazleton PA 18201. (717)455-1508. Public Relations Chairman: Alice Laputka. Sponsor: Greater Hazleton Fine Arts Council. Purpose: "to encourage appreciation of original art and crafts; exposure for artists; cultural experience for local and regional residents." Estab. 1975. Annual outdoor show (indoors in case of rain) held 2 days in May. Average attendance: 8,000-10,000. Entries accepted until 3 weeks before show. Entry fee: $4/day; $7/both days. Display area: 10'. Work may be offered for sale; no commission. Craftworker must attend show; demonstrations OK. Registration limit: 100. Sponsor provides electricity for demonstrations; fencing; minimal insurance on exhibited work; and 24-hour security. Show is advertised by regional and local newspapers; regional and local radio; regional TV; posters; street banner; and leaflets. Considers all crafts.

HEAD HOUSE CRAFTS FAIR, 328 Bourse Bldg., Philadelphia PA 19106. Publicist: Mary Dolan. Sponsor: Head House Craftsmen's Association. Purpose: "to bring quality crafts to the people of Philadelphia in a pleasant, outside atmosphere for their summer weekend pleasure; to provide a marketplace for quality craftspeople to sell their wares." Estab. 1968. Annual outdoor show (arcade) held 12 consecutive weekends June-August. Entries accepted until 6 weeks before show. Entry fee: $30/weekend. Display area: 6x10. Prejudging by actual work. Work may be offered for sale; no commission. Craftworker must attend show; demonstrations encouraged. Registration limit: 50. Sponsor provides display panels; electricity for demonstrations; table; and 24-hour security. Considers all crafts. Bestsellers: "items not normally available in area stores."

Promotion: "A professional advertising and public relations firm is employed for the 3 month period each year. We use local newspapers; posters; door stuffers; personal appearances on TV by craftspeople; and public service spots on radio and TV." Submit b&w photos of work and biographical sketch by mail.

"A professional advertising and public relations firm is employed for the 3 month period [of the show] each year," says Mary Dolan, publicist for the Head House Craftsmen's Fair, Philadelphia, Pennsylvania. The outdoor show is held in a pillared arcade for 12 consecutive weekends, June-August. A 6x10 display area is $30 per weekend.

*JENKINTOWN FESTIVAL OF THE ARTS, c/o Jenkintown Library, York and Vista Rds., Jenkintown PA 19046. (215)884-0593. Chairman: Marketta Reich. Purpose: fundraiser. Annual outdoor show held the second Sunday in June. Average attendance: 25,000. Entries accepted until 4 weeks before show. Entry fee: $20/15x20 display area. Prejudging by actual work or 4 slides; entry fee refunded for refused work. Work may be offered for sale; no commission. Craftworker needn't attend show; demonstrations OK. Sponsor "rents racks for those who don't have their own display apparatus." Show is advertised by radio; TV; magazines; newspapers; and posters. Presents ribbon awards. Considers all original crafts.

*JURIED CRAFT SHOW, Box 1023, State College PA 16801. Chairman: Jinx Webster. Sponsor: Central Pennsylvania Festival of the Arts. Estab. 1966. Annual indoor show held 1 week in July. Average attendance: 100,000. Applications for entry due mid-June. Entries accepted until 1 week before show. Entry fee: $7/2 items. Maximum 2 items per exhibitor. Work may be offered for sale; no commission. Craftworker needn't attend show; no demonstrations. Sponsor provides display panels and 24-hour security. Show is advertised by mailing lists and craft publications. Presents 4 cash awards of $500. Considers batik; ceramics; macrame; metalsmithing; pottery; weaving; woodcrafting and glass.

*JURIED CRAFTS EXHIBITION OF THE CENTRAL PENNSYLVANIA FESTIVAL OF THE ARTS, Box 1023, State College PA 16801. Managing Director: Lurene Frantz. Estab. 1966. Annual indoor show held 1 week in the summer. Average attendance: 9,000. Entries accepted until 2 weeks before show. Entry fee: $7/1-2 entries. Maximum 2 entries per craftworker. Prejudging; no entry fees refunded for refused work. Work may be offered for sale. Show is hung on the campus of the Pennsylvania State University. Considers ceramics; glass; metals; fibers; and wood. Presents $3,000 in cash prizes.

LEHIGH VALLEY MALL ARTS FESTIVAL, Rt.1, Box 153J, Auburn NH 03032. (603)483-2742. President: Jinx Harris. Estab. 1977. Annual indoor show held 4 days in July at Allentown, Pennsylvania. Average attendance: 50,000. Entries accepted until 1 week before show or until filled. Entry fee: $35/8x4 display area. Prejudging by slides or photos if not in a previous show. Work may be offered for sale; no commission. Craftworker must attend show; demonstrations OK. Registration limit: 50. Sponsor provides electricity for demonstrations and 24-hour security. Show is advertised by radio; TV; and newspaper. Considers all crafts except ceramics; decoupage under $5; lapidary; and strung bead jewelry.

LEWISBURG CRAFT FAIR, Box 532, Lewisburg PA 17837. (717)524-7006. Director: David Bussard. Sponsor: Winfield House. Estab. 1973. Annual indoor show held 3 days in October. Average attendance: 7,500. Entries accepted until 3 months before show. Entry fee: $45/9x7 display area. Prejudging by slides and samples; entry fee due after prejudging. Work may be offered for sale; no commission. Craftworker must attend show; demonstrations OK. Registration limit: 75. Sponsor provides electricity for demonstrations. Show is advertised by all available media. Considers all crafts except ceramics; decoupage; and needlecrafts.

*THE MANNINGS NATIONAL JURIED SHOW, Rt. 2, East Berlin PA 17301. (717)624-2223. Director: Harry E. Manning. Sponsor: The Mannings Creative Crafts. Purpose: "to promote and encourage handweavers and fiber craftsmen; to give a market to these people who have no exposure to the buying public." Annual indoor show held 3 weeks April-May. Average attendance: 1,200. Entries accepted until 2 weeks before show. Entry fee: $5/item. Maximum 1 item per craftworker. Prejudging by actual work. Work may be offered for sale; 20% commission. Craftworker needn't attend show; no demonstrations. Registration limit: 300. Sponsor provides display panels and insurance on exhibited work. Show is advertised by *Shuttle, Spindle and Dyepot*, magazine of the Handweaver's Guild of America; mailing list; newspapers; and other weaving publications. Submit complete description of technique and material used. Presents cash awards of $2,500. 1977 show sales totalled $1,000. Considers only handweaving and macrame. Maximum size: 4x8; "exceptions to this would be coverlets; blankets; etc. which could be displayed folded."

MAXWELL HOUSE MINIATURE SHOW AND SALE, 310 Hillcrest Dr., Edinboro PA 16412. (814)734-4594. Contact: Pam Maxwell. Purpose: "to give the public in our area a chance to learn more about miniatures and to make purchases." Estab. 1976. Annual indoor show held 2 days in October. Average attendance: 2,000. Entries accepted until 1 week before show. Entry fee: $20/6' table, some wall space available. Work may be offered for sale; no commission. Craftworker must attend show; demonstrations OK. Registration limit: 25. Sponsor provides chairs; covering; electricity for demonstrations; table; and 24-hour security. Show is advertised by TV; radio; newspaper; trade magazines; mailing list; and posters. "We advertise in a 100 mile radius which includes Buffalo, Pittsburgh and Cleveland." Considers dollhouse miniatures only; "any form of dollhouses, furniture, miniature items used in or for a house." Maximum size of works: 1"-1' scale.

Sales Tip: "We have new collectors; they want inexpensive items. We have serious collectors; they want high quality original work."

MIFFLIN COUNTY GOOSE DAY CELEBRATION, 13 S. Dorcas St., Lewistown PA 17044. (717)248-6713. Executive Director: Anita Corless. Sponsor: Mifflin County Festival Association. Estab. 1973. Annual outdoor show held September 29-October 2. Average attendance: 22,-000. Work may be offered for sale; no commission. Craftworker must attend show;. demonstrations OK. Sponsor provides fencing. Show is advertised by brochures; calendar of events; travel shows; news releases; and paid ads. Submit photos and resume for publicity. Considers all crafts.

*MIFFLIN-JUNIATA ARTS FESTIVAL, 507 Lindbergh Way, Lewistown PA 17044. (717)248-0582. Chairman of Arts and Crafts Exhibit: Thiry Olbrich. Purpose: "to bring cultural arts to community." Estab. 1967. Annual outdoor show held 1 day in May. Average attendance: 10,000-20,000. Entries accepted until 10 days before show. Display area: 10x10. Work may be offered for sale; 10% commission. Craftworker must attend show; demonstration OK. Sponsor provides electricity for demonstrations; fencing; picnic table; and camping area. Show is advertised by newspaper; radio; TV community spots; brochures; and various listings. Presents ribbon awards. Considers all crafts.

MONROEVILLE MALL ARTS FESTIVAL, Rt. 1, Box 153J, Auburn NH 03032. (603)483-2742. President: Jinx Harris. Estab. 1972. Annual indoor show held 5 days in February at Monroeville, Pennsylvania. Average attendance: 65,000+. Entries accepted until 1 week before show or until filled. Entry fee: $35/8x4 display area. Prejudging by slides or photos if not in a previous show. Work may be offered for sale; no commission. Craftworker must attend show; demonstrations OK. Registration limit: 50. Sponsor provides electricity for demonstrations and 24-hour security. Show is advertised by radio; TV; and newspapers. Considers all crafts except ceramics; decoupage under $5; lapidary; and strung bead jewelry.

MONROEVILLE MALL CHILDREN'S HOUR SHOW, Rt. 1, Box 153J, Auburn NH 03032. (603)483-2742. President: Jinx Harris. Estab. 1976. Annual indoor show held 5 days in August at Pittsburgh, Pennsylvania. Average attendance: 75,000+. Entries accepted until 1 week before show or until filled. Entry fee: $35/8x4 display area. Prejudging by slides or photos if not in a previous show. Work may be offered for sale; no commission. Craftworker must attend show; demonstrations OK. Registration limit: 75. Sponsor provides electricity for demonstrations and 24-hour security. Show is advertised by radio; TV; and newspapers. Considers all child-oriented crafts except ceramics; decoupage under $5; lapidary; and strung bead jewelry.

MONTGOMERY MALL CRAFT AND SCULPTURE SHOW, Rt. 1, Box 153J, Auburn NH 03032. (603)483-2742. President: Jinx Harris. Estab. 1977. Annual indoor show held 4 days in April at Montgomeryville, Pennsylvania. Average attendance: 50,000+. Entries accepted until 1 week before show or until filled. Entry fee: $35/8x4 display area. Prejudging by slides or photos if not in a previous show. Work may be offered for sale; no commission. Craftworker must attend show; demonstrations OK. Registration limit: 110+. Sponsor provides electricity for demonstrations and 24-hour security. Show is advertised by radio; TV; and newspapers. Considers all crafts except ceramics; decoupage under $5; lapidary; and strung bead jewelry.

MOUNTAIN CRAFT DAYS, Rt. 2, Somerset PA 15501. (814)445-6077. Director: Elizabeth M. Haupt. Sponsor: Somerset Historical and Genealogical Society Inc. Purpose: "to enable visitors to see authentic representations of the early crafts as practiced by our pioneer ancestors." Estab. 1971. Annual outdoor show (with tents and wood slab shelters) held 3 days in September. Average attendance: 18,000. Entries accepted until 1 month before show. Work may be offered for sale; 10% commission. Craftworker must attend show; demonstrations required. Sponsor provides 2 chairs; 1 table; and 24-hour security. Show is advertised by radio; TV; newspaper; and brochures. Considers candlemaking; ceramics; leatherworking; metalsmithing; pottery; tole painting; weaving; woodcrafting; and crafts pertaining to the pioneer period.

NESHAMINY MALL ARTS FESTIVAL, Rt. 1, Box 153J, Auburn NH 03032. (603)483-2742. President: Jinx Harris. Estab. 1970. Annual indoor show held 4 days in April at Cornwell

Heights, Pennsylvania. Average attendance: 50,000+. Entries accepted until 1 week before show or until filled. Entry fee: $35/8x4 display area. Prejudging by slides or photos if not in a previous show. Work may be offered for sale; no commission. Craftworker must attend show; demonstrations OK. Registration limit: 50. Sponsor provides electricity for demonstrations and 24-hour security. Show is advertised by radio; TV; and newspapers. Considers all crafts except ceramics; decoupage under $5; lapidary; and strung bead jewelry.

NESHAMINY MALL PROFESSIONAL CRAFT AND SCULPTURE SHOW, Rt. 1, Box 153J, Auburn NH 03032. (603)483-2742. President: Jinx Harris. Estab. 1973. Annual indoor show held 4 days in August at Cornwells Heights, Pennsylvania. Average attendance: 55,000+. Entries accepted until 1 week before show or until filled. Entry fee: $35/8x4 display area. Prejudging by slides or photos if not in a previous show. Work may be offered for sale; no commission. Craftworker must attend show; demonstrations OK. Registration limit: 120. Sponsor provides electricity for demonstrations and 24-hour security. Show is advertised by radio; TV; and newspapers. Considers all crafts except ceramics; decoupage under $5; lapidary; and strung bead jewelry.

NORTHERN APPALACHIAN FESTIVAL, Box 1771, Bedford PA 15522. (814)623-1771. Executive Secretary: Wendy Cox. Sponsor: Bedford County Heritage Commission, Inc. Purpose: "to better inform the public on the reason for the higher prices on articles which are handcrafted; the hours of work that go into making such items; that not everyone that says, 'Oh, I can make that,' can really make it. We do this through the demonstrations." Estab. 1974. Annual outdoor show (semi-enclosed with full roofs, barns at fairgrounds) held 2 days Memorial Day weekend. Average attendance: 3,000. Entries accepted until show or until full. Entry fee: $20/10x10 display area. Work may be offered for sale; no commission. Craftworker must attend show; demonstrations a must. Sponsor provides electricity for demonstrations; water; food stands; and security during show. Considers all crafts.
Promotion: Show is advertised by 3 TV shows on 2 local stations and 1 Pittsburgh station; radio; newspapers; posters; flyers; brochures; and the Pennsylvania Festival Association. Submit b&w photos for newspaper; color photos and/or slides for TV (nonreturnable); and resume.

OXFORD VALLEY MALL CHILDREN'S HOUR SHOW, Rt. 1, Box 153J, Auburn NH 03032. (603)483-2742. President: Jinx Harris. Estab. 1977. Annual indoor show held 4 days in May at Langhorne, Pennsylvania. Average attendance: 60,000+. Entries accepted until 1 week before show or until filled. Entry fee: $35/8x4 display area. Prejudging by slides or photos if not in a previous show. Work may be offered for sale; no commission. Registration limit: 65. Sponsor provides electricity for demonstration and 24-hour security. Show is advertised by radio; TV; and newspapers. Considers all child-oriented crafts except ceramics; decoupage under $5; lapidary; and strung bead jewelry.

*PENNSYLVANIA GUILD OF CRAFTSMEN'S MARKET, 227 W. Beaver Ave., State College PA 16801. (814)234-0833. Executive Director: Lyn Jackson. Estab. 1947. Annual show held 1 day wholesale and 3 days retail in August at Lancaster, Pennsylvania. Prejudging. Registration limit: 200. Present awards. Considers all crafts.

PENNSYLVANIA MAPLE FESTIVAL, Box 222, Meyersdale PA 15552. (814)634-0213. Director: Doris B. Clapper. Estab. 1958. Annual indoor show held 9 days in March. Average attendance: 12,000-15,000. Entries accepted until 1 week before show. Entry fee: $15/10x8. Prejudging by photos; entry fee refunded for refused work. Work may be offered for sale; 15% commission. Craftworker must attend show; demonstrations encouraged. Registration limit: 50. Sponsor provides chairs; electricity for demonstrations; fencing; table; and 24-hour security. Show is advertised by radio; TV; newspaper; brochures; magazines; AAA magazines; and tours. Submit photos. Presents cash awards of $96 for quilts. 1978 show sales totalled $1,154. Considers all crafts.

PERRYOPOLIS AREA HISTORICAL SOCIETY INC. PIONEER DAYS, Box 238, Perryopolis PA 15473. (412)736-4542. President: Charles R. Lynch. Purpose: fundraiser. Estab. 1967. Annual indoor/outdoor show held 2 days in October. Average attendance: 20,000. Entries accepted until 1 week before show. Entry fee: $25/10x10 display area. Work may be offered for sale; 40% commission. Craftworker must attend show; demonstrations OK. Registration limit: 25. Sponsor provides chairs; electricity for demonstrations; table; and 24-hour security. Show is advertised by newspaper; magazines; radio; and TV. Considers all crafts including antique crafts.

*THE PHILADELPHIA CRAFT SHOW, Women's Committee, Philadelphia Museum of Art, Box 7646, Philadelphia PA 19101. (215)232-1171. Co-chairmen: Phyllys Fleming and Mary Lee Lowry. Purpose: "to advance public appreciation of craftart." Estab. 1977. Annual indoor show held 3 days in November. Average attendance: 12,000. Entries accepted until 5 months before show. Entry fee: $100/10x10 display area; $5 prejudging fee. Prejudging by 5 slides; entry fee due after prejudging. Work may be offered for sale; no commission. Craftworker must attend show. Registration limit: 100. Sponsor provides chairs; electricity; and 24-hour security. Presents cash awards. 1977 show sales totalled $102,000. Considers all crafts except candlemaking; mobiles; needlecrafts; sculpture; and tole painting.
Promotion: Show is advertised by newspapers; magazines (craft and art); TV; radio; flyers; and newsletters (craft organizations and museum). Submit slides and biographical material. Photos of local artists taken by newspapers.

PLYMOUTH MEETING MALL CRAFT AND SCULPTURE SHOW, Rt. 1, Box 153J, Auburn NH 03032. (603)483-2742. President: Jinx Harris. Estab. 1971. Annual indoor show held 4 days in September at Plymouth Meeting, Pennsylvania. Average attendance: 55,000+. Entries accepted until 1 week before show or until filled. Entry fee: $35/8x4 display area. Prejudging by slides or photos if not in a previous show. Work may be offered for sale; no commission. Craftworker must attend show; demonstrations OK. Registration limit: 120. Sponsor provides electricity for demonstrations and 24-hour security. Show is advertised by radio; TV; and newspaper. Considers all crafts except ceramics; decoupage under $5; lapidary; and strung bead jewelry.

RED CROSS CRAFT MARKET, Box 88, Allenwood PA 17810. Show Director: Fred Brown. Sponsor: Lycoming County Red Cross. Purpose: to be a marketplace for creative American handcrafts. Estab. 1977. Annual indoor show held 2 days in April at Williamsport, Pennsylvania. Average attendance: 10,000. Entries accepted until 4 weeks before show or until filled. Entry fee: $45/10x10 display area, 1 exhibitor; $65/10x10 display area, 2 exhibitors (limit 2 per space). Prejudging by 4 35mm slides; entry fee refunded for refused work. Work may be offered for sale; no commission. Craftworker must attend show; demonstrations OK. Registration limit: 100. Sponsor provides electricity for demonstrations and 24-hour security. Show is advertised by radio; newspaper; billboards; posters; and flyers. Submit b&w glossies and background information. Considers all crafts except decoupage; lapidary; mobiles; needlecrafts; and tole painting. "Gift certificates are given to the public to be used on craft purchases; we reimburse the craftworker in cash."

REGIONAL ART EXHIBITION, 438 W. Broad St., Hazleton PA 18201. (717)454-5333. Chairman: E. Ruth Howe. Sponsor: Hazleton Art League. Estab. 1954. Annual indoor show held 2 weeks in April. Average attendance: 600. Entries accepted until 2 weeks before show. Entry fee: $7/1 entry; $3/additional entry. Maximum 3 entries per craftworker. Prejudging; no entry fees refunded for refused work. Work may be offered for sale; 20% commission. Sponsor provides display panels and insurance (up to $300 per entry) on exhibited work. Deliver work in person.
Acceptable Work: Considers sculpture by artists living within 100-mile radius of Hazleton. Maximum size: 45"x6'; 50 lbs. Work must have base. "In order to create a balanced show with a variety of media, subject matter and styles, sometimes good work will be rejected."

SHIPPENSBURG FAIR CRAFTS-ARTS-ANTIQUE SHOW, c/o Rose Dillner, Blythstead, Shippensburg PA 17257. (717)532-8155. Chairman: Rose Dillner. Sponsor: Shippensburg Bi-County Fair. Purpose: "a program of demonstrating craftsmen for the fair crowd." Estab. 1969. Annual outdoor show (demonstrating craftsmen under tents) held 1 day in July. Entries accepted until 3 weeks before show. No fee for demonstrating craftsmen. Non-demonstrating craftworkers will be in open-air section $10/15' display area. Work may be offered for sale; no commission. Craftworker must attend show; show is basically demonstrating show. Registration limit: 125. Sponsor provides coverings and electricity for demonstrating craftworkers only. Show is advertised by TV; radio; national craft magazines; newspaper; and posters. Considers all crafts; especially interested in early primitive crafts. Maximum size: 10x10 unless permission is obtained.

SOUTH HILLS VILLAGE ARTS FESTIVAL, Rt. 1, Box 153J, Auburn NH 03032. (603)483-2742. President: Jinx Harris. Estab. 1972. Annual indoor show held 4 days in March at Pittsburgh, Pennsylvania. Average attendance: 75,000+. Entries accepted until 1 week before show or until filled. Entry fee: $35/8x4 display area. Prejudging by slides or photos if not in a previous show. Work may be offered for sale; no commission. Craftworker must attend show;

demonstrations OK. Registration limit: 60. Sponsor provides electricity for demonstrations and 24-hour security. Show is advertised by radio; TV; and newspapers. Considers all crafts except ceramics; decoupage under $5; lapidary; and strung bead jewelry.

SOUTH HILLS VILLAGE CHILDREN'S SHOW, Rt. 1, Box 153J, Auburn NH 03032. (603)483-2742. President: Jinx Harris. Estab. 1977. Annual indoor show held 4 days in July at Pittsburgh, Pennsylvania. Average attendance: 75,000+. Entries accepted until 1 week before show or until filled. Entry fee: $35/8x4 display area. Prejudging by slides or photos if not in a previous show. Work may be offered for sale; no commission. Craftworker must attend show; demonstrations OK. Registration limit: 75. Sponsor provides electricity for demonstrations and 24-hour security. Show is advertised by radio; TV; and newspapers. Considers all child-oriented crafts except ceramics; decoupage under $5; lapidary; and strung bead jewelry.

SOUTH HILLS VILLAGE PROFESSIONAL ARTS FESTIVAL, Rt. 1, Box 153J, Auburn NH 03032. (603)483-2742. President: Jinx Harris. Estab. 1972. Annual indoor show held 4 days in October at Pittsburgh, Pennsylvania. Average attendance: 85,000+. Entries accepted until 1 week before show or until filled. Entry fee: $35/8x4 display area. Prejudging by slides or photos if not in a previous show. Work may be offered for sale; no commission. Craftworker must attend show; demonstrations OK. Sponsor provides electricity for demonstrations and 24-hour security. Show is advertised by radio; TV; and newspapers. Considers all crafts except ceramics; decoupage under $5; lapidary; and strung bead jewelry.

SPRING ARTS FESTIVAL, Johnstown Area Arts Council, Box 402, Johnstown PA 15907. (814)536-1333. Executive Secretary: Maryanne Larison. Purpose: "a chance to exhibit and sell craft to about 25,000 people." Estab. 1963. Average attendance: 25,000. Annual indoor show held 3 days in April. Entries accepted until 4 weeks before show. Entry fee: $25/10x10 display area. Prejudging by slides; photos; or actual work. Work may be offered for sale; no commission. Craftworker must attend show; demonstrations required. Considers all crafts.

*SPRING SHOW, 338 W. 6th St., Erie PA 16507. (814)459-5477. Executive Director: John L. Vanco. Sponsor: Erie Art Center. Purpose: "annual presentation of the best regional art." Estab. 1898. Annual indoor show held 2 months April-May. Average attendance: 2,500. Entries accepted until 1 month before show. Entry fee: $3/item. Display area: 1,000 square feet. Maximum 2 pieces per craftworker. Work may be offered for sale; 25% commission. Craftworker needn't attend show; no demonstrations. Registration limit: 60-70. Sponsor provides insurance on exhibited work and 24-hour security. Show is advertised regionally through newspaper; TV; radio; and direct mail. Presents cash awards of $1,000 and purchase awards of $2,000. 1977 show sales totalled $3,000. Considers batik; ceramic sculpture; mobiles; sculpture; and soft sculpture. Maximum size: 60" and 100 pounds.

SPRINGFIELD MALL CHILDREN'S HOUR SHOW, Rt. 1, Box 153J, Auburn NH 03032. (603)483-2742. President: Jinx Harris. Estab. 1977. Annual indoor show held 4 days in February at Springfield, Pennsylvania. Average attendance: 25,000+. Entries accepted until 1 week before show or until filled. Entry fee: $35/8x4 display area. Prejudging by slides or photos if not in a previous show. Work may be offered for sale; no commission. Craftworker must attend show; demonstrations OK. Registration limit: 60. Sponsor provides electricity for demonstrations and 24-hour security. Show is advertised by radio; TV; and newspapers. Considers all child-oriented crafts except ceramics; decoupage under $5; lapidary; and strung bead jewelry.

SPRINGFIELD MALL CRAFT AND SCULPTURE SHOW, Rt. 1, Box 153J, Auburn NH 03032. (603)483-2742. President: Jinx Harris. Estab. 1975. Annual indoor show held 4 days in September at Springfield, Pennsylvania. Average attendance: 55,000. Entries accepted until 1 week before show or until filled. Entry fee: $35/8x4 display area. Prejudging by slides or photos if not in a previous show. Work may be offered for sale; no commission. Craftworker must attend show; demonstrations OK. Sponsor provides electricity for demonstrations and 24-hour security. Show is advertised by radio; TV; and newspaper. Considers all crafts except ceramics; decoupage under $5; lapidary; and strung bead jewelry.

*SPRING CRAFT MARKET AT PARK CITY MALL, Box 5153, Lancaster PA 17601. President: R.D. Faulkner. Sponsor: Conestoga Valley Chapter, Pennsylvania Guild of Craftsmen. Purpose: fundraising. Estab. 1974. Annual indoor show held 3 days in May. Average attendance: 40,000. Entries accepted until 6 weeks before show. "Show open only to members of the Pennsylvania Guild of Craftsmen." Display area: 10x15. Maximum 1 item per category per artist. Prejudging by 4 slides for new craftsmen; floor jurying from past shows. Entry fee due after prejudging. Work may be offered for sale; demonstrations required 20% of showtime. Registration limit: 90. Sponsor provides electricity for demonstrations and some security. Show is advertised by billboards; newspaper; posters; radio; and TV interview shows. Submit b&w photos of self at work. Presents cash awards of $200. 1977 show sales totalled $40,000. Considers batik; candlemaking; ceramics; glass art; jewelry; lapidary; leatherworking; macrame; metalsmithing; pottery; sculpture; soft sculpture; tole painting; weaving; and woodcrafting. Bestsellers: glass; leather; and pottery.

SPRINGS FOLK FESTIVAL, Box 134, Springs PA 15562. Chairman Crafts Committee: John Hepler. Sponsor: Springs Historical Society and Penn Alps, Inc. Purpose: "to revive and preserve the arts and crafts of the area by providing a market for craftsmen and demonstrating and teaching pioneer and contemporary arts and crafts." Estab. 1957. Annual outdoor show (with some shelters and building) held 2 days in October. Average attendance: 10,000-12,000. Entries accepted until 2 months before show; will fill cancellations. Display area: 8x8. Prejudging by slides; photos; or actual work. Work may be offered for sale; 15% commission. Craftworker must attend show; demonstrations required. Registration limit: 100. Sponsor provides display panels; electricity for demonstrations; table; 24-hour security; and roof. Show is advertised by newspaper ads; radio; travel magazines; and folders.
Acceptable Work: Considers candlemaking; dollmaking; glass art; leatherworking; metalsmithing; needlecrafts; pottery; sculpture; tole painting; weaving; woodcrafting; and other types of Early American crafts of Appalachia.

*STITCHERY '79, c/o Clare Hoffman, Registrar, 1200 Heberton St., Pittsburgh PA 15206. (412)362-2720. Sponsor: Embroiderers' Guild of Pittsburgh, Inc. Estab. 1959. Biennial indoor show held 3 weeks in the spring. Next show scheduled for April 22-May 13, 1979. Average attendance: 2,500. Slide submissions for jury date due January 17, 1979. Entry fee: $10 for maximum 3 entries per craftworker. Prejudging by 3 slides of each piece entered; no entry fees refunded for refused work. Work may be offered for sale; 30% commission. Craftworker needn't attend show; no demonstrations. Sponsor provides $100 deductible insurance on exhibited work and 24-hour security. Show is advertised by the press; educational radio and TV; publications in arts; etc. Considers soft sculpture and "work including the embellishment of a surface or area with fiber and needle." Presents 2 $100 and 1 $500 cash awards; $1,000 purchase award fund; and other prizes as available.

*THREE RIVERS ARTS FESTIVAL, 4400 Forbes Ave., Pittsburgh PA 15213. (412)687-7014. Executive Director: Barbara Widdoes. Sponsor: Carnegie Institute. Purpose: "to showcase the work of artists and performers in western Pennsylvania." Estab. 1960. Annual indoor/outdoor show held 10 days, May-June. Average attendance: 200,000. Entries accepted until 2 months before show. Entry fee: $100, first 5 days; $75, second 5 days/4x8 display area. Maximum 3 pieces per exhibit. Prejudging by slides; $6 jurying fee. Work must be offered for sale; no commission in attended space; 25% commission in exhibit space. Craftworker needn't attend unless entering attended portion of show; limited demonstrations. Registration limit: 175. Show is advertised by all media. Submit publicity card attached to entry form. Presents cash and purchase awards. 1977 show sales totalled $71,500. Considers all crafts except candlemaking; decoupage; dollmaking; lapidary; mobiles; and tole painting.

WAYNESBORO'S CRAFT DAY, 323 E. Main St., Box 512, Waynesboro PA 17268. Coordinator: Frances H. Miller. Sponsor: Chamber of Commerce. Estab. 1975. Annual outdoor show held 1 day in September. Entries accepted until show. Entry fee: $5/1 parking space, approximately 22'. Work may be offered for sale; no commission. Craftworker needn't attend show; demonstrations OK. Registration limit: 120. Show is advertised by newspaper and radio. Considers all crafts.

Rhode Island

CRAFTS MARKETPLACE, Rainbow Enterprises, 1 Rose Ct., Narragansett RI 02882. (401)789-8260. Contact: Andrea Kotula. Estab. 1973. Annual outdoor show held 3 days in July at Newport, Rhode Island. Entry fee: $45. Considers all crafts.

PAWTUXET VILLAGE ARTS & CRAFTS FESTIVAL, 30 Waco Ct., Warwick RI 02889. Chairman: Robert Quinlan. Sponsor: Gaspee Days Committee. Purpose: "primarily the love of good art, good craftwork and a good time." Held in conjunction with the regional Gaspee Day celebrations." Estab. 1968. Annual outdoor show held 2 days the first weekend in June. Average attendance: 100,000. Entries accepted until show. Entry fee: $15/15 linear feet of space on sidewalk. Prejudging by slides or photos, or sometimes by personal presentation; entry fee due after prejudging. Work may be offered for sale; no commission. Craftworker must attend show; demonstrations OK. Registration limit: 150. Sponsor provides fencing. Considers all crafts. 1977 exhibitor sales totalled approximately $75,000.

*SOUTH COUNTY ART ANNUAL, 1319 Kingston Rd., Kingston RI 02881. Contact: Helme House. Sponsor: South County Art Association. Annual indoor show held the second and third weeks in April. Entry fee: $3/item. Maximum 2 entries per artist. Work may be offered for sale; 15% commission. Work must be hand-delivered. Considers sculpture. Presents $250 in cash prizes.

THE USQUEPAUGH JOHNNY CAKE FESTIVAL, Box 221, West Kingston RI 02892. (401)783-4054. Manager: Peter W. Smith. Sponsor: Johnny Cake Festival Committee. Estab. 1974. Annual outdoor show held 2 days during late October. Average attendance: 10,000. Entries accepted until 4 weeks before show. Entry fee: $15/8x8 display area. Work may be offered for sale; no commission. Craftworker must attend show and demonstrate. Sponsor provides electricity for a $5 fee. Show is advertised by posters throughout the county and ads in Providence papers. Considers all crafts.
Sales Tip: "Our craft show is primarily a selling show. We advise craftspeople to promote their items for holiday gift giving as this is the last outdoor show in Rhode Island before the holiday season. Also, for an additional $15, the craftsperson can place an ad in the festival program which can be used like a business card to promote their Christmas mall shows."
Profile: "The Usquepaugh Johnny Cake Festival is essentially a village street fair with parades, antique auto show, petting zoo and animal rides, band concerts and various homemade foods (most especially johnny cakes which are a native Rhode Island food of the Indians). There are Indian dancing demonstrations and crafts as well as commercial crafts."

WARWICK MALL CHILDREN'S HOUR SHOW, Rt. 1, Box 153J, Auburn NH 03032. (603)483-2742. President: Jinx Harris. Estab. 1977. Annual indoor show held 4 days in April at Warwick, Rhode Island. Average attendance: 50,000+. Entries accepted until 1 week before show or until filled. Entry fee: $35/8x4 display area. Prejudging by slides or photos if not in a previous show. Work may be offered for sale; no commission. Craftworker must attend show; demonstrations OK. Registration limit: 60. Sponsor provides electricity for demonstrations and 24-hour security. Show is advertised by radio; TV; and newspaper. Considers all child-oriented crafts except ceramics; decoupage under $5; lapidary; and strung bead jewelry.

WARWICK MALL PROFESSIONAL CRAFT AND SCULPTURE SHOW, Rt. 1, Box 153J, Auburn NH 03032. (603)483-2742. President: Jinx Harris. Estab. 1971. Annual indoor show held 4 days in October at Warwick, Rhode Island. Average attendance: 60,000. Entries accepted until 1 week before show or until filled. Entry fee: $35/8x4 display area. Prejudging by slides or photos if not in a previous show. Work may be offered for sale; no commission. Craftworker must attend show; demonstrations OK. Registration limit: 100. Sponsor provides electricity for demonstrations and 24-hour security. Show is advertised by radio; TV; and newspapers. Considers all crafts except ceramics; decoupage under $5; lapidary; and strung bead jewelry.

*WESTERLY ART FESTIVAL, 159 Main St., Westerly RI 02891. Secretary: Diane B. Howard. Sponsor: Westerly-Pawcatuck Area Chamber of Commerce. Purpose: "The Westerly Art Festival is held as a community project. All funds are maintained in a separate fund and used exclusively for the Art Festival." Estab. 1967. Annual outdoor show held 2 days in July. Average attendance: "several thousand." Entries accepted until show. Entry fee: $12/fine artist; $20 for applied art; and $1 for students. Prejudging of applied art only; by slides, photos or samples of work. Entry fee refunded for refused work. Work may be offered for sale; no commission. Craftworker or representative must attend show; demonstrations OK. Registration limit: 50 for applied art; no limit on fine art exhibitors. Sponsor provides fencing for students; 24-hour security; coffee and donuts; and pages to help loading and unloading. Categories: graphic art; b&w rendering; sculpture; photography; paintings; batik; and applied art.
Acceptable Work: Considers batik hangings; ceramics (but no greenware); glass art; jewelry; lapidary; leatherworking; macrame; metalsmithing; mobiles; needlecrafts; pottery; sculpture; tole painting; weaving; woodcrafting; and decoupage if designs are done by the artist.
Awards: Presents $25, $15 and $10 awards in each category; $2,000 in purchase awards; and ribbons. "Artists select 1 piece of work in each category that they wish to have judged."

WICKFORD ART FESTIVAL, Box 321, North Kingston RI 02852. (401)295-5944. Chairman: Ella Rex. Sponsor: Wickford Art Association. Estab. 1960. Annual outdoor show held 3 days in July. Entries accepted until 4 weeks before show. Entry fee: $25 for 1-3 days. Maximum 25 entries per craftworker. Work may be offered for sale; no commission. Craftworker must attend show; demonstrations OK. Considers ceramics; leatherworking; macrame; metalsmithing; pottery; sculpture; tole painting, and woodcrafting.

South Carolina

ARTS IN THE PARK, 405 N. Main St., Anderson SC 29621. (803)224-88ll. Programs Director: Becky Michaels. Sponsor: Anderson County Arts Council. Purpose: "to promote the craftworker and his work to a community eager to support creative artists and their work." Estab. 1974. Annual outdoor show (indoors in case of rain) held 1 day in October. Average attendance: 2,500. Entries accepted until 4 weeks before show. Entry fee: $15/10' frontage space. Work may be offered for sale; no commission. Craftworker must attend show; demonstrations OK. Sponsor provides electricity for demonstrations. Considers all crafts except decoupage; lapidary; and tole painting. Bestsellers: pottery; leatherwork; weaving; and functional crafts. **Promotion:** Show is advertised by press releases; public service announcements; special feature stories on TV or in newspapers; flyers; posters; and invitations to all Art Council members. Submit resume; b&w photos; and slides.

CHRISTMAS CRAFT & ART SHOW, Box 1177, Aiken SC 29801. Contact: M. F. Facciolo. Sponsor: Aiken Recreation Department. Estab. 1970. Annual indoor show held in December. Average attendance: 10,000. Entry fee: $10. Display area: 5x8. All media OK. Work may be offered for sale; no commission. Craftworker must attend show.

COASTAL CRAFTERS EXPO, 7737 Nellview Dr., Charleston Heights SC 29405. (803)552-3973. Sponsor: City of Rock Hill Mall. Estab. 1978. Annual indoor show held 3 days in February at Rock Hill, South Carolina. Entries accepted until 2 weeks before show. Entry fee: $45/8x10 display area. Prejudging by 2 slides or photos if new to Coastal Crafters shows. Entry fee refunded for refused work. Work may be offered for sale; no commission. Craftworker must attend show; demonstrations OK. Registration limit: 80. Sponsor provides electricity for demonstrations; 24-hour security; liability and property damage insurance. Show is advertised by radio; TV; and newspapers. Considers all crafts.

EDISTO RIVER FUN FESTIVAL, 1520 Wannamaker, Box 843, Summerville SC 29483. (803)873-6840, 873-3329. Exhibitions Chairman: Charlsie Vorwerk. Sponsor: Dorchester County Arts Commission. Purpose: "to promote art in all its various forms within the county on a continuing basis." Estab. 1977. Annual outdoor show (with pavilions and lodge house) held 2 days in October at Givhans Ferry State Park, South Carolina. Average attendance: 12,000-15,000. Entries accepted up until show date. Entry fee: $10/12x12 display area. Work may be offered for sale; no commission. Craftworker must attend show; demonstrations OK. Registration limit: 50. Sponsor provides electricity for demonstrations; fencing; and table/$5 charge. Show is advertised by radio; TV; newspapers; magazines; brochures; and billboards. Submit 8x10 glossies with brief background. "All material received will be considered." Considers all crafts.

*HILL SKILLS, 627 Pelham Rd., Greenville SC 29615. (830)288-4088. Manager: Rachel Pringle McKaughan. Purpose: "Hill Skills began as a tri-centennial city function to show and sell crafts made in the area. It has grown to a national show with top craftsmen from all states exhibiting. Three-quarters of the show educates by demonstration." Estab. 1970. Annual indoor show held 5 days in October. Average attendance: 20,000+. Entries accepted until mid-February. Entry fee: $60/10x10 display area. Work may be offered for sale; no commission. Craftworker must attend show; demonstrations encouraged. Registration limit: 150. Sponsor provides curtains; electricity for demonstrations; and shopping bags. Considers all crafts. **Promotion:** Show is advertised by billboards; posters; flyers; TV; shoppers guides; placemats; newspapers; and penny postcards. "Will select craftworkers to send items for showing on TV month before show."

HISTORIC CAMDEN CRAFTS FESTIVAL, Box 605, Camden SC 29020. (803)432-4181, 432-2525. Executive Vice President: Jack L. Brantley. Sponsor: Greater Kershaw County Chamber of Commerce. Estab. 1973. Annual outdoor show (with tents) held 2 days in May. Average attendance: 5,000. Entries accepted until 4 weeks before show. Entry fee: $20. Prejudging by actual work; entry fee refunded for refused work. Work may be offered for sale; no commission. Craftworker must attend show; demonstrations OK. Registration limit: 50. Sponsor provides coverings; electricity for demonstrations; and 24-hour security. Show is advertised by radio; TV; newsletter; and newspapers. Submit photos and resume for promotion. Considers all crafts.

INVITATIONAL CRAFTS SHOW, The Gallery, 385 S. Spring St., Spartanburg SC 29301. (803)582-7616. Sponsor: Spartanburg County Art Association. Purpose: "to promote the area of crafts as a fine art form that is functional as well as artistic." Estab. 1970. Annual indoor show held 1 month November-December. Average attendance: 800. Entries accepted until 1 month before show. Work must be offered for sale; 33⅓% commission. Craftworker needn't attend show; demonstrations OK. Registration limit: 35. Sponsor provides insurance on exhibited work and 24-hour security. Show is advertised by newspaper; radio; posters; invitations; and TV public service announcements. Submit resume or biography and slides. 1977 show sales totalled $4,000.
Acceptable Work: Considers batik, candlemaking; jewelry; lapidary; leatherworking; macrame; metalsmithing; needlecrafts; pottery; weaving; and woodcrafting.
Sales Tip: "This is basically a sales show with almost all work selling. It is specifically scheduled for the Christmas shopping period and special publicity is designed to attract the holiday shopper."

*SOUTH CAROLINA ARTS COMMISSION EXHIBITION, 829 Richland St., Columbia SC 29201. (803)758-3442. Contact: Coordinator. Annual indoor show held 3-4 weeks in the spring. No entry fee. Prejudging by slides. Maximum 2 entries per craftworker. Work may be offered for sale; no commission. Presents $5,000 in purchase prizes.
Acceptable Work: Considers batik; ceramics; glass art; jewelry; needlecrafts; pottery; soft sculpture; weavings; wall hangings; and woodcrafting completed by South Carolina residents or craftworkers having lived at least 1 year in the state. "Works of professional quality are desired since those purchased will become works in the state's art collection; therefore simple hobby crafts are not acceptable."

SOUTHEASTERN HOBBY FAIR, Box 384, Jackson SC 29831. (803)471-3859. General Chairman: W. Melvane Scott. Sponsor: Town of Jackson. Purpose: "to encourage people, especially young and old, to become involved in a hobby." Estab. 1970. Annual outdoor show held 2 days in November. Average attendance: 5,000. Entries accepted up until show. Work may be offered for sale; no commission. Craftworker needn't attend show; demonstrations OK. Show is advertised by national magazines; TV; newspaper; and radio. Considers all crafts.

South Dakota

BROOKINGS SUMMER FOLK ARTS FESTIVAL, Box 555, Brookings SD 57006. Board Member: Dave Huebner. Sponsor: Estab. 1972. Annual outdoor show held 2 days in July. Average attendance: 20,000. Entries accepted until 1 week before show. Entry fee: $15 prior to July; $20 after July. Display area: 8x12. Work may be offered for sale; no commission. Craftworker must attend show; demonstrations OK. Registration limit: 250. Sponsor provides electricity for demonstrations and 24-hour security. Show is advertised by radio; TV; billboards; newspapers; posters; and brochures. Considers all crafts made by the exhibitor. Presents awards for best pioneer costume worn by exhibitor and booth awards. "A state tax representative should be on hand to collect sales tax."

CREATIVE CRAFT SHOW N SELL, Box 430, Madison SD 57042. (605)256-4114. Co-chairmen: Esther Brandes or Sylvia Tonsager. Sponsor: Creative Crafts. Purpose: "to give local and area people who do not maintain a shop, but do crafts, an opportunity to sell these items." Estab. 1973. Annual indoor show held 1 day in November. Average attendance: 1,800. Entries accepted until show date. Entry fee: $8 before November; $10 after. Display area: 8x6. Work may be offered for sale; no commission. Craftworker must attend show; demonstrations OK. Registration limit: 80. Sponsor provides electricity for demonstrations. Show is advertised by local radio and newspaper ads and public service announcements and flyers put in business windows. Considers all crafts.

LEMMON CHAMBER OF COMMERCE CHRISTMAS FAIR, 500 A Main Ave., Lemmon SD 57638. (605)374-5716. Executive Secretary and Manager: Yvonne Seifert. Purpose: "to promote Lemmon during the holiday season." Estab. 1972. Annual indoor show held 1 day in November or December. Average attendance: 700. Entries accepted until 1 week before show (may be on a list in case there is an opening after the 1 week deadline). Entry fee: $5/6x8 display area. Work may be offered for sale; no commission. Craftworker must attend show; demonstrations OK. Registration limit: about 60. Sponsor provides electricity for demonstrations. Show is advertised by newspapers; circulars; radio; and direct mail. Considers all crafts. "Most of the crafts sold at this Fair are for Christmas gifts or personal use. So, generally gear the crafts for Christmastime."

*NORTHWESTERN CRAFTSMEN, South Dakota Memorial Art Center, Harvey Dunn St. at Medary Ave., Brookings SD 57007. (605)688-5423. Assistant to the Director: Rex Gulbranson. Purpose: "to promote and show craftsmen from Iowa, Minnesota, Nebraska, North Dakota and South Dakota." Estab. 1974. Biennial indoor show held 1 month-6 weeks February-March during odd-numbered years. Entry by invitation only. No entry fee. Maximum 3 entries per craftworker. Prejudging by slides or photos. Work may be offered for sale; 20% commission. Craftworker needn't attend show; no demonstrations. Registration limit: 30-40. Sponsor provides insurance on exhibited work and on work shipped to artist from show; shipping costs to artist from show; 24-hour security; publishes a show catalog; and sales are handled by the South Dakota Memorial Art Center Shop. Show is advertised by newspaper publicity; radio; and South Dakota State University's entertainment calendar. Submit resume for publicity. Presents purchase awards. Bestsellers: items under $200.
Acceptable Work: Considers batik; ceramics; glass art; jewelry; macrame; metalsmithing; mobiles pottery; sculpture; soft sculpture; and weaving.

*RED CLOUD INDIAN ART SHOW, Red Cloud Indian School, Pine Ridge SD 57770. (605)867-5491. Director: Brother C.M. Simon, S.J. Purpose: "to better acquaint people with Indian heritage and Indian art." Estab. 1968. Annual indoor show held from mid-June to mid-August. Average attendance: 4,000+. Entries accepted until 3 weeks before show. No entry fee. Maximum 3 crafts/craftworker. "If entries exceed exhibit space, they are prejudged at show, and extras are put in the gift shop." All work must be offered for sale; no commission. Craftworker needn't attend show; demonstrations OK. Registration limit: 80+. Sponsor provides insurance on exhibited work and on work shipped to craftworker; 24-hour security; and handles sales. Categories: oil paintings; watercolors; graphics; mixed media; and 3-dimensional. Considers sculpture. "Indian theme not necessary, but preferred." Presents $1,150 in cash prizes and $1,500 in purchase awards. Bestsellers: "good quality work, with Indian themes in the less than $200 price range."

SHORT GRASS ARTS FESTIVAL, Box 55, Pierre SD 57501. (605)224-7402. President: Polly Nelson. Sponsor: Short Grass Arts Council. Purpose: "to promote the arts in this area. Also to provide a way for artisans to display and sell their work." Estab. 1973. Annual outdoor show held 2 days in the summer at Steamboat Park. Average attendance: 500-1,000. Entries accepted until 3 weeks before show. Entry fee: $8/10x10 display area. Work may be offered for sale; no commission. Craftworker must attend show; demonstrations encouraged. Sponsor provides electricity for demonstrations and fencing; assumes no liability. Considers all crafts.
Sales Tip: "Pottery seems to sell well. Knitted items, especially for babies, and Western art also sell quite well. A well-designed booth seems to attract people, as well as a well thought out demonstration. Be prepared for all sorts of questions."
Promotion: Show is advertised by radio; TV; newspapers; and posters. "Send 8x10 b&w glossies of you involved with your work with information on background for promotional consideration. Feature articles in the newspaper with pictures of the artist seem to go over well."

Tennessee

ARTS & CRAFTS MART, Standards Committee, Box 3361, Kingsport TN 37664. Sponsor: Metropolitan Sertoma Club. Annual indoor show held in the spring. Average attendance: 3,500. Entries accepted until 2 months before show for previous entries. Write for entry blank and closing date information for new entries. Entry fee: $50 and $100 per craftworker for 8x8' and 8x16' display units. Send 3-5 slides, resume and price list. Craftworker must attend show; no commission. Registration limit: 44. Sponsor provides display panels and equipment (pegboard 8x2'x6" table; electricity if required). Considers all crafts.

ARTS & CRAFT SHOW & SALE, Box 141, Murfreesboro TN 37130. (615)893-1646 or 893-6537. Chairman: W. Harold Duncan. Sponsor: Noon Lions Club. Purpose: fundraiser. Semi-annual indoor show held 2 days in the spring and 2 days in the fall. Average attendance: 5,000/-day. Applications for entry sent out to potential exhibitors 90 days prior to show. Entry fee: $10/8x10 (or larger) display area. "Prejudging by slides, unless work has been seen by a member of the committee at another show and invitation was issued"; entry fee due after prejudging. Work may be offered for sale; 10% commission. Craftworker must attend show; demonstrations OK. Registration limit: 80. Sponsor provides insurance on exhibited work; handles Visa and MasterCharge; and 24-hour security. Show is advertised by radio; newspaper; and TV. Considers all crafts except batik. 1977 exhibitor sales totalled approximately $30,000.

*ARTS & CRAFTS SHOW, Box 611, Lawrenceburg TN 38464. President: Alice Dixon. Sponsor: Lawrence County Arts Commission. Estab. 1971. Annual indoor/outdoor show held 2 days in August. Average attendance: 20,000. Entries accepted until show date. Entry fee: $10, outdoors; $15, indoors/12x12 display area. Work may be offered for sale; no commission. Craftworker must attend show; demonstrations OK. Sponsor provides electricity for demonstrations and 24-hour security. Show is advertised by radio; magazines; billboards; and posters. Considers all crafts. Presents $10, 1st prize; and 2nd and 3rd place ribbons.

BENTON COUNTY ARTS & CRAFTS SHOW, Box 428, Camden TN 38320. (901)584-4601. Extension Agent: Wileva Mullins. Sponsor: Home Demonstration Council. Estab. 1970. Annual indoor show held 3 days in November. Attendance: 2,000-3,000/day. Entries accepted until 2 weeks before show. Entry fee: $5/10x10 display area. Work may be offered for sale; 1% commission. Craftworker must attend show; demonstrations OK. Sponsor provides electricity for demonstrations. Show is advertised by radio; newspapers; signs; direct mail; and posters. Submit photos and information to be used in newspaper publicity. Considers all crafts. 1977 exhibitor sales totalled approximately $7,000.

*DAVID CROCKETT ARTS AND CRAFTS FESTIVAL, Lawrrence County Arts Commission, Box 611, Lawrenceburg TN 38464. Contact: Ardythe Craig. Annual show held in August. Entries accepted until show date. Entry fee: $10, outside; $10-15, inside. Work may be offered for sale; no commission. Considers sculpture; ceramics; leathercraft; needlecraft; metalcraft; jewelry; and lapidary. Presents cash purchase prizes and ribbons.

*DOGWOOD ARTS FESTIVAL STATE CRAFTS FAIR, Box 2506, Knoxville TN 37901. (615)523-2151, ext. 204. Director: Art Keeble. Sponsor: The Arts Council, West Town Mall and Dogwood Arts Festival. Purpose: "to provide a market for craftsmen of Tennessee; to educate the public as to the strength of Tennessee crafts; and to augment the Dogwood Arts Festival." Entries accepted until 8 weeks before show. Entry fee: $5/10x15 display area. Prejudging by 5 slides submitted with application; no entry fees refunded for refused work. Work may be offered for sale; 10% commission. Craftworker must attend show; demonstrations OK. Registration limit: 75. Sponsor provides chairs; electricity for demonstrations; table; 24-hour security; name cards; assistance maps; unloading assistance; booth assistance; MasterCharge and Visa facilities; and show officials collect sales tax at the end of the show. Presents $500 in cash awards; $100, best of show; and 8 $50 merit awards. Bestsellers of 1977: glass, pottery and wood. 1977 exhibitor sales totalled $27,000.
Acceptable Work: Considers batik; dollmaking; stained and blown glass; jewelry; leatherworking; macrame; metalsmithing; possibly mobiles; needlecrafts; pottery; sculpture; soft sculpture; weaving; and woodcrafting. "No dried flower arrangements; pressed flowers; seed pod decorations; decorated or painted boxes; decoupage; or objects made of commercially-produced parts or paintings."

FOOTHILLS CRAFT GUILD SHOW & SALE, Box 99, Oak Ridge TN 37830. Co-director: Jude Martin. Sponsor: The Guild and Oak Ridge City Department of Recreation. Purpose: "to educate the public; to give Tennessee craftsmen a reliable outlet; to provide cash for scholarships, the guild library, monthly newsletter, poster contest and high school craft show competitions." Estab. 1968. Annual indoor show held 3 days always the first weekend in November. Average attendance: 12,000. No entry fee; but $5 membership fee. Display area: 8x8-8x16. "Write for application. Craftsman must submit 3 pieces of work; if they pass standards set by 2 standards judges, then they are voted on by board of directors; if that passes, then the work is voted on by the membership." Work may be offered for sale; 20% commission. Craftworker must attend show; demonstrations encouraged. Registration limit: 80-95. Sponsor provides chairs; electricity for demonstrations; table; volunteer relief; and 24-hour security. Presents "Chucky," an original sculpture by Chuck Caldwell, for the best-looking booth.
Acceptable Work: Considers batik; candlemaking; ceramics; dollmaking; glass art; jewelry; lapidary; leatherworking; macrame; metalsmithing; needlecrafts (stitchery); pottery; sculpture; soft sculpture; weaving; woodcrafting; basketry; brooms; wrought iron; bread dough; quilting; needlepoint; counted thread embroidery; and pipes. No decoupage or fine arts.
Promotion: Show is advertised by newspaper articles and ads; listings in national craft magazines; posters and postcards; and TV coverage. "On sending in booth contracts they [the craftworker] should send photos, list name and address of their local newspapers, and answer all questions concerning publicity."

GRINDERS SWITCH ARTS & CRAFTS FAIR, 107 Huddleston St., Centerville TN 37033. (615)729-3054. Chairman: Martha Chessor. Sponsor: Hickman County Art Guild. Estab. 1974. Annual outdoor show held 2 days in June. Average attendance: 8,000. Entries accepted until show date. Entry fee: $10/12x30 display area. Work must be offered for sale; no commission.

Craftworker must attend show; demonstrations encouraged. Considers all crafts.

Profile: "Displays are set up in wooded camping sites and vehicles may be kept at exhibitor's site without distraction. Overnight camping, a bath house and showers are available at $3/night."

LIONS CLUB SPRING ARTS & CRAFT SHOW, Box 141, Murfreesboro TN 37130. (615)893-1646. Co-chairman: W.H. Duncan. Semiannual indoor/outdoor show held 2 days in April and November. Average attendance: 10,000. Closing date for entry: about 30 days before show. Entry fee: $10/8x10 display area. Prejudging; display area fee refunded for refused work. Work must be offered for sale; 10% commission. Craftworker must attend show. Registration limit: 58 booths, fall; 88 booths, spring. Sponsor provides insurance during exhibit period and MasterCharge and Visa at no discount to exhibitor. Considers all crafts.

MEMPHIS MUSIC HERITAGE FESTIVAL, 722 S. Highland St., Memphis TN 38111. (901)458-8753. Crafts Coordinator: Richard Wert. Sponsor: Joseph Schlitz Brewing Co. Estab. 1977. Annual outdoor show held 2 days Labor Day weekend. Average attendance: 75,000. Entry deadline open. Entry fee: $40/8x10 display area. Work may be offered for sale; no commission. Craftworker needn't attend show; demonstrations OK. Registration limit: 60. Sponsor provides coverings and electricity for demonstrations. Considers all crafts.

*MIDLAND CENTER ARTS AND CRAFTS FESTIVAL, Drawer H, Maryville TN 37801. Festival Director: Robert Long. Sponsor: Blount County Arts & Crafts Guild and Midland Merchants. "The Blount County Arts & Crafts Guild is obligated by its by-laws to provide shows annually for display and sale of art. $1 of each registration goes to scholarship (art) fund of the Blount County Arts & Crafts Guild. Remainder pays for expenses and publicity." Estab. 1977. Annual outdoor show (under covered mall) held 2 days in June at Alcoa, Tennessee. Average attendance: 30,000. Entries accepted until 2 weeks before show. Entry fee: $20/5x12 display area. Prejudging of new exhibitors by 3 slides or photos; entry fee due after prejudging. Work must be offered for sale. Craftworker must attend show; demonstrations OK if approved prior to show. Registration limit: 200. Sponsor provides electricity for demonstrations and MasterCharge and Visa facilities for a 5% charge. Presents $1,000 in purchase awards and ribbons.

Acceptable Work: Considers batik; dollmaking; jewelry; lapidary; leatherworking; macrame; metalsmithing; needlecrafts; pottery; sculpture; tole painting; weaving; and woodcrafting. No crackle art; commercial jewelry; crochet; decoupage; dip flowers; knitting; marble figures; plaster art; paper tole; or ceramics from commercial molds.

Promotion: Show is advertised by TV (48 paid spots on 3 Knoxville channels, plus 18 public service spots); radio (85 paid spots and 120 public service spots in 28 cities); newspaper (48 inches in *Knoxville News Sentinel* and *Journal* run in 3 editions, and 48 inches in the *Maryville Daily Times*; 500 posters; 2,000 leaflets; and 2,000 enclosures. Submit b&w photo of self with work for newspaper use. Resumes for articles are also welcome.

MID-SOUTH ARTS AND CRAFTS SHOW/SALE, 5618 Fox Meadows Cove, Memphis TN (901)363-4178. Sponsor: Virginia and Bill Miller. Estab. 1971. Annual indoor show held 3 days in November at Cook Convention Center in Memphis. Average attendance: 20,000. Entries accepted until approximately 3 months before show. Entry fee: $60/10x10 display area. Prejudging by 8x10 glossy prints or minimum 3 slides; entry fee refunded for refused work. Work may be offered for sale; no commission. Craftworker must attend show; demonstrations OK. Registration limit: 300. Sponsor provides chairs; table; and 24-hour security. Considers all crafts.

Promotion: Show is advertised in area newspapers; TV; and by radio. "Submit 8x10 glossies of exhibitor with his work and brief description of craft and individual's background."

MID-SOUTH CRAFTS FAIR, Memphis Pink Palace Museum, 3050 Central Ave., Memphis TN 38111. (901)755-1040. Chairman: Mary J. Custer. Estab. 1973. Annual outdoor show held 4 days in October. Entry fee: $7.50/display area. Work may be offered for sale; 20-25% commission for craftsmen in educational section. Craftworker must attend show; demonstrations encouraged. Registraton limit: 100. Considers batik; candlemaking; dollmaking; glass art; jewelry; leatherworking; metalsmithing; needlecrafts; pottery; quilting; wall hangings; weavings; woodcrafting; furniture; and musical instruments.

MISSISSIPPI RIVER CRAFT SHOW, Brooks Memorial Art Gallery, Overton Park, Memphis TN 38112. Biennial show held during odd-numbered years. Open to craftworkers residing in a state bordering on the Mississippi River.

NASHVILLE HOBBY & CRAFT CHRISTMAS MARKET, c/o Fred and Ruth Hicks, Rt. 1, Box 155-D, Fairview TN 37062. (615)799-0084. "We produce a variety of attractions each year — flea markets, fairs, auctions, fundraising events and 1 craft show in the Tennessee area." Estab. 1974. Annual indoor show held 2 days the first weekend in December. Average attendance: 20,000-25,000. Entries accepted until show date or until filled. Entry fee: $35/10x10 display area. Work may be offered for sale; no commission. Craftworker must attend show; demonstrations OK. Sponsor provides chairs; electricity for demonstrations; tables (extras at $3 each); and 24-hour security. "State tax is collected on all sales and turned in to the tax man at the closing of the show." Considers all crafts. "Corner space is provided for craftspeople who demonstrate their work as long as available. These always have the best sales."
Promotion: Show is advertised by newspaper; radio; 3 TV stations; shoppers' papers; and local magazines. Submit slides for TV publicity and b&w photos for newspaper releases.

NATIONAL CRAFTS FESTIVAL, Silver Dollar City, Pigeon Forge TN 37863. (417)338-8212. Special Events Manager: Ken Bell. Estab. 1977. Annual outdoor show held 1 week in October. Average attendance: 25,000. "Entries accepted when there is an available space." No entry fee. Prejudging by slides or photos with application, or personal interview preferred. Work may be offered for sale; 15% commission. Craftworker must attend show; "demonstrations required 80% of the time." Registration limit: about 50. Sponsor provides chairs; coverings; electricity; for demonstrations; table; and 24-hour security. Show is advertised by TV; radio; and newspapers.
Acceptable Work: Considers dollmaking; glass art; lapidary; leatherworking; macrame; metalsmithing; needlecrafts; sculpture; tole painting; and woodcrafting. "All crafts must be fitting with the 1800s theme of Silver Dollar City."
Profile: "Demonstration can be a blend of talking about your craft and actually making an item. No power tools are allowed. Any modern materials which would not have existed in the late 1800s must be disguised (Elmer's Glue can be put in a Mason jar)."

PIKEVILLE ARTS & CRAFTS SHOW, Rt. 1, Box 314A, Pikeville TN 37367. (615)447-6280. Chairperson: Mary E. Smith. Sponsor: Black Fox Festival. Estab. 1975. Semiannual outdoor show (indoors if rain) held 2 days in May and 2 days in September. Average attendance: about 20,000. Entries accepted until 2 weeks before show. Entry fee: $5/craftworker. Display area: 10x10. Prejudging by photo; entry fee refunded for refused work. Work may be offered for sale; 10% commission. Craftworker or representative must attend show; demonstrations OK. Registration limit: 50 (no more than 2/category). Show is advertised by TV; radio; newspapers; and trade magazines. "Submit b&w Polaroid or glossies for publicity purposes."
Acceptable Work: Considers batik; candlemaking; glass art; decoupage; lapidary; needlecrafts; mobiles; pottery; sculpture; soft sculpture; tole painting; weaving; woodcrafting; and basketry.

RIVERGATE MALL SUMMER FESTIVAL OF ARTS & CRAFTS, 615 S. "H" St., Lake Worth FL 33460. (305)582-6133. Director: J.J. Readey. Estab. 1976. Annual indoor show held 1 week in June at Nashville, Tennessee. Attendance: 12,000-15,000. Entries accepted until 1 week before show. Entry fee: $50/10x10 display area. Prejudging by 3 slides or color photos; entry fee refunded for refused work. Work may be offered for sale; no commission. Craftworker or representative must attend show; demonstrations OK. Registration limit: 60. Sponsor provides electricity for demonstrations if requested in advance. Submit 8x10 b&w glossy photo and resume for newspaper release.
Acceptable Work: Considers batik; decoupage; dollmaking; glass art; mobiles; needlecrafts; sculpture; soft sculpture; tole painting; woodcrafting; egg craft; and china painting.

SIGNAL MOUNTAIN FALL FESTIVAL OF ARTS & CRAFTS, Rt. 1, Walker Rd., Signal Mountain TN 37377. (615)886-3584. Contact: Jake Hinds. Estab. 1972. Annual outdoor show held the first weekend in October. Average attendance: 8,000-10,000. Closing date for entry: 2 weeks before show. Entry fee: $12.50/entry. Crafts may be offered for sale; no commission. Craftsman must attend show; demonstrations OK. Considers all crafts.

TUCKALEECHEE COVE ARTS, CRAFTS & MUSIC FESTIVAL, Box 176, Townsend TN 37882. (615)448-6461. Chairman: Jean Pullon. Sponsor: Townsend Chamber of Commerce. Purpose: "to create an awareness of crafts, especially mountain crafts, as we are in a tourist area. Townsend is the western entrance to the Great Smoky Mountain Park." Estab. 1974. Annual outdoor show (with spaces under a large circus tent) held 3 days the last weekend in September. Average attendance: 8,000-10,000. Entry fee: $35/space under circus tent; $25 if you bring your own canopy. Display area: 10x10 or 12x12. Prejudging by 3 photos or slides; entry fee refunded for refused work. Work may be offered for sale; no commission. Craftworker must attend show; demonstrations OK. Sponsor provides electricity for demonstrations and night security. Show is advertised by radio and TV. Considers all crafts except decoupage; soft sculpture; crackle art; dip flowers; marble figures; plaster art; or paper tole.

*WEBB SCHOOL ART & CRAFT FESTIVAL, The Webb School, Bell Buckle TN 37020. (615)275-3641. Chairman: Carol Norton. Estab. 1977. Annual outdoor show held 2 days in the fall. Average attendance: 4,000. Entries accepted until September 1. Entry fee: $15 ($5 refunded to demonstrators). Display area: 15x15. Prejudging by 5 slides or photos; entry fee due after prejudging. Work may be offered for sale; no commission. Craftworker must attend show; demonstrations encouraged. Registration limit: 100. Sponsor provides electricity for demonstrations. Categories: graphics; painting; sculpture; jewelry; pottery; fibers; and traditional crafts. Considers all original crafts except ceramics and decoupage.
Awards: Presents $1,000+ total awards; $500+, purchase; 1st, 2nd and 3rd place ribbons in each category; and 2 best of show awards (1 in art division; 1 in craft division).
Promotion: Show is advertised by newspapers; radio; TV; posters; and postcards. "Submit b&w photo of self and work, or, preferably, self working at craft."

*THE WISHING WELL ARTS & CRAFTS FESTIVAL, c/o The Wishing Well, 7501 E. Brainerd Rd., Chattanooga TN 37421. (615)899-9496. Contact: Susanne or Bob Johnson. Estab. 1976. Annual outdoor show held 2 days in September. Entries by invitation only. Will accept photos of work for consideration. Work may be offered for sale; no commission. Considers all crafts. Presents awards.

Texas

AMERICANA DAY CELEBRATION, Box 424, Baytown TX 77520. (713)427-7477. Recreation Supervisor: Laurie Kelley. Sponsor: City of Baytown Park and Recreation Department. Estab. 1973. Annual outdoor show held 4th of July. Average attendance: 20,000. Entries accepted until about 2 weeks before show. Entry fee: $10/8x10 display area. Work may be offered for sale; no commission. Craftworker must attend show; demonstrations OK. Registration limit: 80. Show is advertised by radio; newspapers; and posters. Considers all crafts.

APRIL ARTS AND CRAFTS FAIR, 1938 Heights Blvd., Houston TX 77008. (713)862-4880. Contact: Herman G. Miller. Sponsor: The Center of Things. Estab. 1977. Annual indoor/outdoor show held 1-2 days in April. Entries accepted until 2 weeks before show. Entry fee: $30/outside; $40/inside. Display area: 12x12. Prejudging by slides; photos; or description. Entry fee refunded for refused work. Work may be offered for sale; no commission Craftworker needn't attend show; demonstrations OK. Registration limit: 100. Sponsor provides, only if necessary, chairs and table. Show is advertised by newspaper; posters; and handbills. Considers all crafts.

ART JAMBOREE, 4906 Eider, Corpus Christi TX 78413. (512)992-4537, 855-4805. Artists' Chairman: Yvonne Hipp. Sponsor: The Auxiliary to the Art Museum of South Texas and Delta Delta Delta Alumnae. Purpose: fundraiser. Estab. 1963. Annual outdoor show held 1 day in April. Average attendance: 5,000. Entries accepted until about 3 weeks before show. Entry fee: $40/craftworker. Display area: $35/10x10 shared booth; $75/retail business. Work may be offered for sale; no commission. Craftworker must attend show; demonstrations OK. Registration limit: 200. Show is advertised by "as much advertising as we can acquire from donations; been very good in the past." Considers all crafts.

ARTS AND CRAFTS FAIR, 401 N. Carancahua, Corpus Christi TX 78412. (512)882-4351. Executive Director: Jean Keas. Sponsor: YWCA and City Park and Recreation. Purpose: "This show has a long history of providing a service to the community in bringing good craftsmanship and art work to the public." Estab. 1950. Annual indoor show held 2 days in November. Entries accepted until 3 months before show. "Applicants must get on our mailing list by May or no later than June to meet the entry deadline." Entry fee: $45 plus table costs/8x12 display area. Prejudging by slides or photos; entry fee refunded for refused work. Work may be offered for sale; no commission. Craftworker must attend show; demonstrations OK if feasible. Registration limit: 200. Sponsor provides chairs; display panels; limited electricity for demonstrations; 24-hour security; and Bank Americard/MasterCharge service. Show is advertised by newspaper; radio; TV; and poster campaign. Categories: art; craft; and bazaar. Considers all crafts.

*ARTS AND CRAFTS FESTIVAL, Box 75, Killeen TX 76541. (817)634-2168. Arts and Crafts Chairman: John E. Carter. Sponsor: Greater Killeen Chamber of Commerce, Killeen Art Guild, and Arts and Crafts Teachers in the Killeen Independent School District. Purpose: "to stimulate an interest in original artistic endeavors both in the artist and the observer regardless of age." Estab. 1964. Annual indoor show held 3 days in April. Average attendance: 8,000. Entries accepted until 1 day before show; "exhibitors must reside within 75 miles of Killeen." Maximum 2 pieces per craftworker per category. Work may be offered for sale; 20% commission. Craftworker must attend show; no demonstrations. Sponsor provides display panels and table. Show is advertised by local and area media. Presents cash awards totalling $200; "judged on 60% originality, 40% workmanship." Considers all crafts.

*ARTS IN ACTION, Amarillo Chamber of Commerce, Amarillo Bldg., Amarillo TX 79101. (806)374-5238. Assistant Manager: F. LeRoy Tillery. Purpose: a showcase for artists and craftsmen. Estab. 1972. Annual indoor show held 2 days in November. Average attendance: 5,000. Entries accepted until 3 weeks before show; late entries accepted until full. Entry fee: $40/8x10 display area. For awards, maximum 1 piece per craftworker. Prejudging by slides or photos; entry fee refunded for refused work. Work may be offered for sale; no commission. Craftworker must attend show; demonstrations OK. Registration limit: 150. Sponsor provides chairs; display panels for extra fee; electricity for demonstrations; table; and 24-hour security. Show is advertised by local and statewide media; "we are one of 4 regional state shows." Submit publicity photo and promotional information. Presents ribbon awards for 1st; 2nd; 3rd; and honorable mention in 11 categories. Considers all crafts.

BLACK EYED PEA JAMBOREE ARTS AND CRAFTS SHOW, Box 608, Athens TX 75751. (214)675-5181. Adminstrative Assistant: Mary Lou Williams. Sponsor: Athens Chamber of Commerce. Purpose: "to promote Athens, the Black Eyed Pea capitol of the world. The arts and craft show is a major portion of the 3 day event." Estab. 1971. Annual outdoor show held 3 days in July. Average attendance: 10,000. Entries accepted until 1 week before show. Entry fee: $15/display area. Work may be offered for sale; no commssion. Craftworker must attend show; no demonstrations. Registration limit: 125-150. Sponsor provides fencing for $5, and 24-hour security. Show is advertised by news media and trade magazines. Submit promotional material. Considers all crafts.

BOND'S ALLEY ART AND CRAFT FAIR, Hillsboro City Library, Hillsboro TX 76645. Chairman: Scotty Cason. Purpose: fundraiser. Estab. 1964. Annual indoor/outdoor show (with tents and parachute awnings) held 2 days in June. Average attendance: 4,000-5,000. Entries accepted until filled. Entry fee: $15-45/6x6 display area. Work may be offered for sale; no commission. Craftworker must attend show; demonstrations OK. Registration limit: 120. Sponsor provides coverings and display panels. Show is advertised by brochures; mailings; newspapers; TV; magazines; radio; and posters. Considers all crafts.

BORGER FINE ARTS FESTIVAL, Box 911, Borger TX 79007. (806)274-2211. Secretary: Evelyn French. Sponsor: Women's Division of the Borger Chamber of Commerce. Purpose: "to promote the arts and crafts and to project the hospitable attitude of our town." Estab. 1968. Annual indoor show held 3 days in October. Average attendance: 6,000. Entries accepted until 2 weeks before show. Entry fee: $5/6x10 display area. Work may be offered for sale; no commission. Craftworker or representative must attend show; demonstrations OK. Sponsor provides electricity for demonstrations; table for $5; and 24-hour security. Show is advertised by newspaper; radio; news media; and personal invitation. Submit publicity materials. Considers all crafts.

BOSQUE COUNTY RUN, Box 645, Meridian TX 76665. Vice President: Sid Terry. Sponsor: Bosque Valley Arts and Crafts Fiesta Committee. Estab. 1972. Annual outdoor show held 1 day in June. Average attendance: 3,000. Entries accepted up until show date. Entry fee: $5/10x12 display area. Work may be offered for sale; no commission. Craftworker must attend show; demonstrations OK. Sponsor provides electricity for demonstrations and 24-hour security. Show is advertised by newspaper ads; direct mail; and letters to other Chambers of Commerce. Submit photos and background information. Considers all crafts.

BUFFALO GAP ART FESTIVAL, Box 1858, Abilene TX 79604. (915)673-4587. Contact: Chairman. Sponsor: Abilene Fine Arts Museum. Estab. 1977. Annual outdoor show held 2 days in May at Buffalo Gap, Texas. Average attendance: 10,000. Entries accepted until 4 weeks before show. Entry fee: $35-60/display area. Prejudging. Entry fee refunded for refused work. Work may be offered for sale; no commission. Craftworker or representative must attend show; demonstrations OK. Registration limit: 100. Show is advertised by newspapers; radio; TV; newsletter; and art and crafts directories. "Any PR by the craftworker will be considered in the general promotion." Considers all crafts.

CENTRAL TEXAS ARTS AND CRAFTS SALE, Box 75, Killeen TX 76541. (817)634-2168. Arts and Crafts Chairman: Frank Norvell. Sponsor: Greater Killeen Chamber of Commerce and Killeen Art Guild. Estab. 1976. Annual indoor show held the first Sunday in May. Average attendance: 5,000. Entries accepted until 3 days before show. Entry fee: $35/10x10 display area. "There is no prejudging but new exhibitors are asked to send slides or pictures of items to be sold at the time of their registration." Work may be offered for sale; no commission. Craftworker must attend show; no demonstrations. Registration limit: 75. Show is advertised by local and area media and invitations. Considers all crafts. Bestsellers: craft items indigenous to area.

CRAFTS VILLAGE AT KERRVILLE MUSIC FESTIVALS, Box 1466, Kerrville TX 78028. (512)896-3800. President: Rod Kennedy. Sponsor: Kerrville Festivals Inc. Purpose: "to complete the festival atmosphere and provide creative people with an outlet for their work." Estab. 1973. Outdoor show (with 50 permanent craft booths) held 4 times a year for 3 days during Memorial Day weekend; 4th of July weekend; last weekend in July; and Labor Day weekend. Average attendance: 4,000. Entries accepted until 1 week before show. Entry fee: $25/8x8 display area. Work may be offered for sale; no commission. Craftworker must attend show; demonstrations OK. Registration limit: 50. Sponsor provides electricity for demonstrations and 24-hour security. Show is advertised by 50,000 brochures; 1,000 posters; radio advertising; and heavy publicity campaigns for each weekend. Considers all crafts. Bestsellers: for 4th of July weekend work oriented toward Western motif; for last weekend in July work oriented toward Christian themes.

FIESTA, 4215 University Ave., Lubbock TX 79413. (806)762-6411, ext. 363. Supervisor: Georgia Booker. Sponsor: Lubbock Garden Arts Center, Inc. Purpose: "to provide sales space for artists, craftsmen, and nonprofit organizations." Estab. 1970. Annual outdoor show held 1 day in September. Average attendance: 5,000-6,000. Entries accepted until 4 weeks before show. Entry fee: $35/5½x8½ display area. Work may be offered for sale; no commission. Craftworker must attend show; demonstrations OK. Sponsor provides coverings. Show is advertised by Center newsletter; local news media; and handbills. Considers all crafts.

*THE GREATER WOODLANDS ARTISAN FAIR, 10911 Fawnlily, The Woodlands TX 77380. (713)367-3176. President-Treasurer: Maggie Cates. Sponsor: Correlated Arts Team, Inc. Purpose: to provide "an outlet for artists to show and establish themselves locally and statewide. To have a traditional show that people will come to and shop for Christmas gifts. To emphasize the handcrafted gifts at the holiday gift-giving time and to educate the public to the value of handcrafter art." Estab. 1977. Annual indoor show held 3 days the weekend following Thanksgiving. Average attendance: 3,000. Entries accepted up until show as long as space is available. Entry fee: $40/10x10 display area; $25/5x10 display area; and $5/booth sharing. Prejudging; entry fee due after prejudging. Work may be offered for sale; no commission. Craftworker must attend show; demonstrations OK. Registration limit: 100. Sponsor provides chairs; coverings; electricity for demonstrations; table; 24-hour security; coffee and tea during show; Saturday night open house; and smocks to identify craftworker. Presents cash awards of $25; $15; and $10. Considers all crafts.
Promotion: Show is advertised by newspapers; magazines; TV; radio; posters; and mailout to art groups and area residents. Submit resume; b&w photos; brief description of artworks and crafts to be sold; and slides if available.

KALEIDOSCOPE, Beaumont Art Museum, 1111 9th St., Beaumont TX 77702. (713)832-3432. Director: Betty W. Hirsch. Estab. 1974. Annual outdoor show held 2 days in May. Average attendance: 22,000. Entries accepted until 5 months before show. Entry fee: $100/individual 8x10 display area; $60/shared 8x10 display area. Prejudging by slides; entry fee refunded for refused work. Work may be offered for sale; no commission. Craftworker must attend show; demonstrations OK. Considers all crafts except decoupage and tole painting.

KERMEZAAR, El Paso Museum of Art, 1211 Montana Ave., El Paso TX 79902. (915)543-3800. Chairman: Tallmade Brown. Sponsor: Members Guild, El Paso Museum of Art Association. Purpose: fundraiser. Estab. 1970. Annual indoor show held 3 days in October. Average attendance: 10,000. Entries accepted until about 3 months before show. Entry fee: $100/8x8x11 display area. Prejudging by 3 slides; entry fee refunded for refused work. Work may be offered for sale; no commission. Craftworker must attend show; demonstrations OK. Registration limit: 130. Sponsor provides display panels and 24-hour security. "Chairs; table; electricity; and other supplies may be rented at our cost by craftworkers." Show is advertised by local and regional newspapers; magazines; billboards; flyers; radio; and TV. Submit basic biographical details.

LUBBOCK GARDEN & ARTS CENTER "FIESTA," 4215 University Ave., Lubbock TX 79413. (806)762-6411. Contact: Georgia Booker. Estab. 1967. Annual outdoor show held the second Saturday in September. Average attendance: 5,000-6,000. Entry fee: $35/8x8x6 booth. Craftworker must attend show; demonstrations encouraged. Registration limit: 100 booths. Considers all crafts.

*MAYFEST, 3505 W. Lancaster, Fort Worth TX 76107. (817)738-9181. Chairman: Sharon Lemond. Sponsor: Junior League of Fort Worth; Park and Recreation Department, City of Fort Worth; Streams and Valleys Committee of Fort Worth; and Tarrant County Water Control and Improvement District 1. Estab. 1973. Annual outdoor show (substantial wooden frame booths with canvas coverings) held 4 days in May. Average attendance: 100,000-125,000. Entries accepted until 3 months before show. Entry fee: $75/gallery booth, 252 square feet covered area; $50/full booth, 84 square feet covered area; $25/half booth, 42 square feet. Prejudging by 5 slides; entry fee refunded for refused work. Work may be offered for sale; no commission. Craftworker must attend show; demonstrations encouraged. Registration limit: 50 full booths; 10 gallery booths. Sponsor provides chairs; coverings; display panels; electricity for demonstrations; table; and 24-hour security. Show is advertised by local news media and listing services. Presents cash awards of $400 and purchase awards of $2,600. Considers all crafts.

MINEOLA ARTS AND CRAFTS FAIR, 1009 N. Pacific St., Mineola TX 75773. 569-5082. President: Cliff Wilson. Sponsor: Mineola Art League. Estab. 1976. Annual indoor show held 2 days in December. Average attendance: 2,500. Entries accepted until 1 week before show. Entry fee: $20/10' table or 10' space. Work may be offered for sale; no commission. Craftworker must attend show; demonstrations OK. Registration limit: 60. Sponsor provides chairs; electricity for demonstrations; and table. Show is advertised by TV; radio; newspapers; magazines; and letters. Submit any promotional material. Considers all crafts.

*NATIONAL DRAWING AND SMALL SCULPTURE SHOW, Del Mar College, Ayers at Baldwin, Corpus Christi TX 87404. (512)882-6231, ext. 216. Chairman: Joseph A. Cain. Estab. 1967. Annual indoor show held in the spring. Entry fee: $5/item plus $5 for return postage and handling. Prejudging of sculpture only by slides; entry fee not refunded. Sponsor provides 24-hour security. Show is advertised by art magazines. Presents cash awards of $3,000 and purchase awards of $2,000. Considers sculpture and soft sculpture. "Small sculpture not to exceed 48" in any dimension or 150 pounds." One-man shows offered to award winners in sculpture and drawing.

*PARIS ART FAIR, 308 S. Main, Paris TX 75460. (214)785-5221. Executive Director: Linda Clark. Sponsor: Young Women's Christian Association. Purpose: "to promote art and artists in an area without a museum." Annual outdoor show held 2 days in April. Average attendance: 5,000. Entries accepted until 3 weeks before show. Entry fee: $2/item for prize money, and $25/10x10 display area. Work may be offered for sale; 20% commission from competition; no commission for booth sales. Craftworker must attend show; demonstrations OK. Sponsor provides electricity for demonstrations and 24-hour security. Show is advertised by newspapers; magazines; and TV. Presents cash awards of $100 and 16 ribbons. Considers all crafts except decoupage; lapidary; and tole painting.

PEARSALL FALL ARTS AND CRAFTS FESTIVAL, 309 E. San Marcos St., Pearsall TX 78061. (512)334-2242. Manager: Dale Martin. Sponsor: Pearsall Chamber of Commerce. Estab. 1972. Annual indoor/outdoor show (with brick veranda with roof) held 1 day in October. Average attendance: 500. Entries accepted until show is filled. Entry fee: $20/craftworker. Display area: 10x10. Work may be offered for sale; no commission. Craftworker or representative must attend show; demonstrations OK. Registration limit: 50. Sponsor provides electricity for demonstrations. Show is advertised by ads in local artist magazines and crafts publications; radio; and newspapers. Considers all crafts.

RIVER ARTS FESTIVAL, 308 E. Hopkins St., San Marcos TX 78666. (512)392-5666. Arts/Craft Show Chairman: Mrs. Willard Cox. Sponsor: Heritage Association of San Marcos, Inc. and Southwest Texas State University. Estab. 1973. Annual outdoor show held 1 day in April. Average attendance: 5,000. Entries accepted until 2 weeks before show. Entry fee: $15/craftworker. Display area: 10x10. Work may be offered for sale; no commission. Craftworker must attend show; demonstrations encouraged. Registration limit: 90. Sponsor provides electricity for demonstrations. Considers all crafts.
Promotion: Show is advertised by Texas Travel Agency; Texas Tourist Development; TV; *Southern Living*; local and nearby newspapers; and University News Service. Submit brochures

or cards on background and work.

Profile: "The Festival takes advantage of the beauty of our river, establishes rapport between the performers, mostly from the University's music department, and the people of San Marcos and the Central Texas area. It provides a show case for the artists and craftsmen in our area. We hope to build up a festival that will be a unique experience for this part of the country. It is altogether a family festival; you might say old-fashioned in the full meaning of the word."

RUNNING WATER DRAW ARTS AND CRAFTS FESTIVAL, Wayland College, Plainview TX 79072. (806)296-5521. Director: Robert Strong. Sponsor: Rotary Club of Plainview. Purpose: fundraiser. Estab. 1975. Annual indoor show held 3 days in October. Average attendance: 6,000. Entries accepted until show. Entry fee: $15/8x12 display area. Prejudging by 3 slides representative of the type of work planned to be sold; 2x2 color horizontal slides preferred. Entry fee refunded for refused work. Work may be offered for sale; 15% commission on first $600 sold; 10% commission on next $2,000 sold. Craftworker must attend show; demonstrations recommended. Registration limit: 125. Sponsor provides chairs; display panels; electricity for demonstrations; insurance on exhibited work; 24-hour security; water; and booth assistance. 1977 show sales exceeded $50,000. Considers all crafts.

Promotion: Show is advertised by radio; TV; newspapers; magazines; civic club programs; and city billboard signs. Submit 2x2 color horizontal slides of the types of work to be exhibited.

Profile: "The Festival is the only 1 of its kind in this large geographic area outside of 2 large regional cities so it is well attended by surrounding towns and counties. Exhibitors at this festival must at this time reside in Texas, New Mexico or Oklahoma."

*SALADO ART FAIR, Box 444, Salado TX 76571. Chairman: Gretchen Jackson. Sponsor: Chamber of Commerce. Estab. 1967. Annual outdoor show held the first full weekend in September along the banks of Salado Creek. Average attendance: 10,000. Entries accepted until June 1. Entry fee: $35/craftworker for a 10x10 display area; $50 if shared. Prejudging. Work must be offered for sale; no commission. Craftworker must attend show; demonstrations OK. Registration limit: 150-175. Sponsor provides 6x8 rack. Considers all crafts. Presents $3,000 in purchase prizes and ribbons.

*SAN ANTONIO ARTISTS' EXHIBITION, 310 W. Ashby, San Antonio TX 78212. (512)732-6048. Chairman: Amy Freeman Lee. Sponsor: San Antonio Art League. Purpose: "to encourage the young artists in the area by allowing them to enter a competition judged by a nationally or internationally known juror and compete with their peers for awards and purchase prizes." Estab. 1929. Annual indoor show held 2 weeks in April. Average attendance: 2,000. Entries accepted until 2 weeks before show. Entry fee: $5/entry unless Art League member. "Only artists with established current residence within 60 mile radius of San Antonio are eligible." Maximum 2 pieces per craftworker. Prejudging by actual work; entry fee not refunded for refused work. Work may be offered for sale; 30% commission. Craftworker needn't attend show; no demonstrations. Registration limit: 100. Sponsor provides 24-hour security and hangs or displays all work. Show is advertised by newspaper and radio. Presents cash awards and purchase prizes approximating $4,000. Considers all crafts except candlemaking and dollmaking.

SAN GABRIEL ARTS AND CRAFTS SHOW, Box 346, Georgetown TX 78626. (512)863-3351. Manager: Vivian Wood. Sponsor: Greater Georgetown Area Chamber of Commerce. Estab. 1971. Annual indoor show held 2 days in November. Average attendance: 3,000. Entries accepted until 1 week before show or until full. Entry fee: $10/6x6 display area; $12.50/10x10 display area. Work may be offered for sale; no commission. Craftworker must attend show; demonstrations OK. Registration limit: 50-60. Sponsor provides chairs; electricity for demonstrations; table; and 24-hour security. Show is advertised by radio; TV; and newspapers. Considers all crafts.

SANTA'S TREASURE HOUSE ARTS AND CRAFTS BAZAAR, Box 764, Raymondville TX 78580. (512)689-3171. Manager: Jo Via. Sponsor: Raymondville Chamber of Commerce. Estab. 1971. Annual indoor show held 1 day in December. Average attendance: 500. Entries accepted up until show. Entry fee: $10/8x8 display area. Work may be offered for sale; no commission. Craftworker needn't attend show; demonstrations OK. Registration limit: 50. Sponsor provides chairs; electricity for demonstrations; and table. Show is advertised by newspaper; public service announcements on TV and radio; and posters. Considers all crafts. Bestsellers: gift items.

SOUTHWESTERN CRAFT AND HOBBY SHOW, 1100 Brandywine Blvd., Box 2188. Zanesville OH 43701. (614)452-4541. Trade Show Director: Walter E. Offinger, Jr. Sponsor: Southwestern Craft & Hobby Association. Purpose: "to bring the industry together. Open to trade buyers only." Estab. 1974. Annual indoor show held 3 days in the summer at Dallas. Average attendance: 4,500. Entries accepted until 1 month before show. Entry fee: $275/100 square feet. Display area: 10x10 minimum; no subletting. Work may be offered for sale; no commission. Craftworker or representative must attend show; demonstrations OK. Registration limit: 300. Sponsor provides chair; table; 24-hour security; waste basket; 3' high side rails draped; 8' draped backwall; and booth sign. Show is advertised by direct mail sent to 8,000 buyers; advertising in most trade publications; and news releases to all trade publications. Considers all crafts.

*SPRING ART AND CRAFTS SHOW AND SALE, 4200 Ansley Lane, Denison TX 75020. (214)465-5647. Booth Reservation Chairperson: Mrs. John R. Summers. Sponsor: Grayson County Frontier Village, Inc. Purpose: fundraiser. Estab. 1975. Semiannual indoor show held 3 days in May, 3 days in December. Average attendance: 9,000-10,000. Display area: 7x9. Work may be offered for sale; no commission. Craftworker must attend show; demonstrations OK. Registration limit: 70. Sponsor provides 24-hour security. Show is advertised by TV; radio; news media; posters; and flyers. Presents 1st, 2nd, and 3rd place ribbon awards for most attractive booth. Considers all crafts including soft goods such as crochet; embroidery; aprons; bonnets; and pot holders.

*SPRING FLING, 2 Eureka Circle, Witchita Falls TX 76308. (817)692-0923. Director: Larry Francell. Sponsor: Wichita Falls Museum Guild. Purpose: "to bring quality arts and crafts to the Wichita Falls area." Estab. 1971. Annual outdoor show (with covered booths) held 2 days in April. Average attendance: 15,000. Entries accepted until 2 months before show. Entry fee: $50/craftworker. Display area: 8x8x8. Prejudging by slides; entry fee refunded for refused work. Work may be offered for sale; no commission. Craftworker must attend show; demonstrations OK. Registration limit: 75-80. Sponsor provides coverings; display panels; table; and 24-hour security. Show is advertised by all media and various promotional materials. Submit any promotional materials for publicity. Presents cash awards of $100 in each category; purchase awards of artist's price on top entry; and ribbons. Categories: 2 dimensional pottery; fiber; toys; musical instruments; and jewelry. Considers all crafts.

STARVING ARTIST ART SHOW, 508 Paseo de La Villita, San Antonio TX 78205. (512)226-3593. Chairperson: Cleo Edmunds. Sponsor: The Historic Little Church of La Villita. Purpose: "to help beginning artists get established and as a fundraiser." Estab. 1963. Annual outdoor show held 1 day in April. Average attendance: 50,000. Entries must be postmarked by February 1. Display area: 10' long. Work may be offered for sale; 10% commission. Craftworker must attend show; demonstrations encouraged. Registration limit: 1,000. Sponsor provides electricity for demonstrations if prearranged. Show is advertised by newspapers. Considers all crafts.

STARVING ARTIST'S SALE, GKCC, Box 75, Killeen TX 76541. (817)634-3268. Chairman: John E. Carter. Sponsor: Greater Killeen Chamber of Commerce and KIOOD Art Guild. Purpose: "to provide funds for community art projects and to stimulate the interest of artists and craftsmen." Estab. 1967. Annual outdoor show held 1 day in October. Entries accepted until 3 days before show. Entry fee: $25/12x12 display area. Work may be offered for sale; no commission. Craftworker or representative must attend show; no demonstrations. Registration limit: 110. Show is advertised by letters; radio; TV; and newspaper. 1977 show sales totalled $10,000. Considers all crafts.

*TEXAS AREA ARTISTS AT VALLEY VIEW CENTER, 2040 Valley View Center, Dallas TX 75240. (214)661-2424. Marketing Director: Carol Kirchhoff. Sponsor: Texas Area Artists. Estab. 1974. Annual indoor show held 1 week in May. Average attendance: 250,000. Entries accepted until 6 weeks before show. Display area: 10x15. Work may be offered for sale; 10% commission. Craftworker must attend show; demonstrations OK. Registration limit: 50. Sponsor provides electricity for demonstrations and 24-hour security. Show is advertised by newspaper and radio. Submit explanation about craft and resume for publicity. Presents ribbon awards. Considers sculpture. "Pegboard not acceptable. Themed booths only."

TEXAS FOLKLIFE FESTIVAL, Box 1226, San Antonio TX 78294. (512)226-7651. Festival Manager: Claudia Ball. Sponsor: The Institute of Texan Cultures. Estab. 1972. Annual outdoor show held 4 days in August. Average attendance: 90,000+. Entries accepted until "several months before show. Entrance is by invitation only and it is limited to Texas artists and craftspeople." Display area: multiples of 8'. Work may be offered for sale; 15% commission; artist paid a per diem in event of no sales. Craftworker must attend show; demonstrations required.

Sponsor provides electricity for demonstrations; fencing; table; and 24-hour security. Show is advertised by news releases; radio and TV public service announcements; magazines; brochures; posters; and slide shows. Submit b&w photos of self at work. Considers candlemaking; dollmaking; lapidary; leatherworking; macrame; needlecrafts; pottery; weaving; woodcrafting; and folk arts.

Profile: "The Festival is an extension of the main floor exhibit of the Institute of Texan Cultures. It shows living folkways and history of Texans who are the descendents of more than 26 ethnic and cultural groups. These ethnic demonstrations (arts, entertainment, foods) stand alongside folkcrafts, folksongs and storytellers and give the visitor a true and full taste of life in Texas."

*TEXAS STATE ARTS AND CRAFTS FAIR, Box 1527, Kerrville TX 78028. (512)896-5711. Executive Director: Audie Hamilton. Sponsor: Texas Arts and Crafts Foundation. Purpose: "to showcase the vast array of handcrafted arts and crafts made by native Texans. No out of state artists are allowed to enter." Estab 1972. Annual outdoor show (with huge tents) held 3 days in May. Average attendance: 33,500. Entries accepted until 5 months before show. Entry fee: $85/8x10 covered or 16x20 outdoors display area; $100/display area with electricity. Entry limited to 2 categories. Prejudging by 3 color slides per category; entry fee due after prejudging. Work must be offered for sale; no commission. Craftworker must attend show; demonstrations encouraged. Registration limit: 200. Sponsor provides coverings; display panels; fencing; and 24-hour security. Young artist competition. Considers all crafts except decoupage and tole painting.

Promotion: Show is advertised by full-color brochures; promotional tours; TV; and radio. "We get excellent editorial coverage because we are the official Texas art event." After acceptance submit resume and b&w photo for personal news release to home paper.

THE WESTHEIMER COLONY ART FESTIVAL, 908 Westheimer, Houston TX 77006. (713)521-0133. Contact: Chairperson. Estab. 1973. Semiannual outdoor show held 2 days in April and 2 days in October. Average attendance: 400,000-500,000. Entries accepted until 4 weeks before show. Entry fee: $75/10x10 display area. Prejudging by slides or photos; entry fee refunded for refused work. Work may be offered for sale; no commission. Craftworker must attend show; demonstrations OK. Sponsor provides liability insurance and police guards during show. Show is advertised by magazines; newspapers; TV; and radio. Considers all crafts.

WIMBERLEY COUNTRY ARTS AND CRAFTS FAIR, Box 2182, Austin TX 78768. (512)474-6981. Executive Director: Kathryn A. Fuhrhop. Sponsor: March of Dimes, Capital Area Chapter. Purpose: fundraiser. Estab. 1974. Annual outdoor show held 2 days in May. Average attendance: 10,000. Entries accepted until 3 weeks before show. Entry fee: $35/12x12 display area; $45 with electricity (110 volts). Prejudging by 3 color slides; entry fee refunded for refused work. Work may be offered for sale; donation of 1 item for auction — 10% of bid proceeds kept by exhibitor. Craftworker must attend show; demonstrations OK. Registration limit: 150. Sponsor provides 24-hour security; free babysitting; and limited number of campsite accommodations. Show is advertised by radio; TV; periodicals; billboards; flyers; and posters. Submit 8x10 b&w glossies of media and self and resume. Considers all crafts.

Utah

FAR COUNTRY CRAFT FAIR, Box 785, Moab UT 84532. (801)259-5360. Contact: Dottie Swasey. Sponsor: Southeastern Utah Fine Arts Guild. Estab. 1973. Annual outdoor show held 2 days during Memorial Day weekend. Average attendance: 3,000-5,000. Entries accepted until show date. Entry fee: $20/10x10 display area. Work may be offered for sale; no commission. Craftworker must attend show; demonstrations OK. MasterCharge and Visa system available. Show is advertised by radio; newspapers; and flyers. Considers all crafts. Bestsellers: "lower cost items, say under $50. But sales are good in pottery, jewelry, tie dye and batik."

GREAT WEST FAIR, c/o Festival of the American West, Utah State University, UMC 14, Logan UT 84322. (801)752-4100, ext. 7569. Director: Steve Black. Sponsor: Utah State University. Purpose: "to preserve pioneer, Indian, Spanish, and other ethnic arts of the early West near the turn of the century; to demonstrate and exhibit handmade articles; and to provide an opportunity for the public to participate." Estab. 1971. Annual outdoor show (with canopy tents and tepees) held 8 days in the summer. Average attendance: 60,000. Entries accepted until 2 weeks before show. No entry fee; "we pay honorariums of $25/day to each participant." Display area: 10x10. Prejudging by "physical inspection if possible, 5 slides if not." Craftworker must attend show and demonstrate. Registration limit: 100. Sponsor provides chairs; display panels; fencing; table; 24-hour security; and "sales are handled in a special Craftworker's Store so craftsmen can concentrate on demonstrating and interesting the public in their craft."

Acceptable Work: Considers folk art such as candlemaking; dollmaking; leatherworking;

metalsmithing; needlecrafts; pottery; weaving; pewter; woodcrafting; calligraphy; and blacksmithing. No modern crafts — should be turn of the century arts.

Promotion: Show is advertised by radio; TV; newspapers; magazines; and other means. "Submit photos of self working at craft. B&w glossy is optional."

Demonstrating craft-workers earn a $25 per day honorarium at the Great West Fair, Logan, Utah. Sales of Indian, Spanish, and early West crafts are handled in the "Craftworker's Store" so craftspeople are free to demonstrate and discuss their work with the public.

*NATIONAL APRIL ART EXHIBIT, 126 E. 400 South, Springville UT 84663. (801)489-7305. Director: T.G. Rose. Sponsor: Springville Museum of Art. Estab. 1903. Annual indoor show held during April. Average attendance: 10,000. Entry fee: $2/work. Optional prejudging by slides; no entry fees refunded for refused work. Work may be offered for sale; 20% commission. Sponsor pays insurance for exhibited work. Considers 2-dimensional crafts. Presents up to $3,-000 in cash and purchase prizes.

PARK CITY ART FESTIVAL, Box 758, Park City UT 84060. (801)649-8899. Sponsor: Chamber of Commerce. Annual outdoor show held in mid-August. Closing date for entry: 8-10 weeks before show. Entry fee: $15; "display fee of approximately $50-75." Crafts may be offered for sale. Craftworker must attend show. Sponsor provides display equipment. Show criteria for crafts varies each year. Information brochure available.

*SPRINGVILLE QUILT AND FIBER SHOW, 126 E. 400 South, Springville UT 84663. (801)489-9434. Assistant Curator: Dusty Collings. Sponsor: Springville Museum of Art. Purpose: "to stimulate better quality quilting and fiber arts in western US." Estab. 1975. Annual indoor show held the month of June. Average attendance: 7,000. Entries accepted until 2 weeks before show. Entry fee: $4/item. Maximum 2 pieces per craftworker. Prejudging by actual work; no entry fees refunded for refused work. Work may be offered for sale; 20% commission. Craftworker needn't attend show; demonstrations might be arranged. Registration limit: 70.

Sponsor provides 24-hour protection. Show is advertised by radio, news, newsletter, and mailers. Presents cash awards of about $1,000 and about 15 ribbons. Considers only quilts. "Submit work with excellent craftsmanship and original, creative design. Tabs for stapling must be sewn on top, back of quilts 24" apart and 2" down from top edge."

Vermont

ANTIQUES AND UNIQUES FESTIVAL, c/o Vermont Children's Aid Society, 72 Hungerford Terrace, Burlington VT 05401. (802)864-9883. Business Manager: Kennedy Snow. Purpose: fundraiser. Estab. 1971. Annual outdoor show held 1 Saturday in July (but never 4th of July weekend) at Craftsbury Common, Vermont. Average attendance: 2,000-3,000. Entries accepted until 1 week before show. Entry fee: $20/24x16 display area. "Screening of new entrants is done by photo, brochure or description with application; firm no refund policy after acceptance of application." Work may be offered for sale; no commission. Craftworker must attend show; demonstrations OK. Registration limit: 100. Categories: crafts and antiques. Considers all crafts; "antique dealer booths comprise about 35% of the show."
Promotion: "Publicity releases go to newspapers, TV stations and magazines in Vermont, New York, New Hampshire, Massachusetts, Maine and Quebec. Submit pictures and description of work for newspaper articles."

THE BENNINGTON CHRISTMAS CRAFT SHOW, Box 92, Readsboro VT 05350. Director: Riki Moss. Sponsor: Craftproducers Inc. Estab. 1968. Annual indoor show held 3 days in November at Bennington College. Entries accepted until mid-April. Entry fee: $75. Prejudging by 5 slides; entry fee due after prejudging. Work may be offered for sale; no commission. Craftworker must attend show; demonstrations OK. Registration limit: 60. Sponsor provides chairs; electricity for demonstrations; table; and 24-hour security. Show is advertised by flyers; posters; newspaper; and radio. Considers all crafts.

THE CRAFT FAIR AT BROMEY MOUNTAIN, Box 92, Readsboro VT 05350. Director: Riki Moss. Sponsor: Craftproducers Inc. Estab. 1977. Annual indoor show held 2 days in the fall at Peru, Vermont, north of Manchester. Entries accepted until June. Entry fee: $60/artist. Display area: 8x10. Prejudging by 5 slides; entry fee due after prejudging. Work may be offered for sale; no commission. Craftworker must attend show; demonstrations OK. Registration limit: 40. Sponsor provides chairs; electricity; table; and 24-hour security. Show is advertised by newspapers; flyers; posters; and radio. Considers all crafts except decoupage.

CRAFTPRODUCERS CRAFT FAIR AT MOUNT SNOW, Box 92, Readsboro VT 05350. Directors: Riki Moss and Charley Dooley. Sponsor: Craftproducers Inc. Estab. 1974. Annual indoor show held 3 days in July at West Dover, Vermont (at the base lodge of Mount Snow ski area). Average attendance: 5,000. Entries accepted until mid-April. Entry fee: $70/artist. Display area: about 8x10. "We prejudge by 5 slides. Craftsperson must submit slides of work he intends to exhibit (not the exact pieces, but work in this category)"; entry fee due after prejudging. Work may be offered for sale; no commission. Craftworker must attend show; demonstrations OK. Registration limit: 70. Sponsor provides chairs; electricity; table; 24-hour security; free camping; a party; and swimming pool. Show is advertised by radio; posters; ads; and flyers. Considers all crafts except decoupage and tole painting. 1977 exhibitor sales totalled approximately $50,000.

THE MOUNT SNOW CRAFT FAIR, Craftproducers Inc., Box 92, Readsboro VT 05350. Contact: Charles Dooley or Riki Moss. Estab. 1974. Semiannual indoor show held 3 days in August and October. Average attendance: 4,000 in August; 6,000 in October. Write for prospectus and closing deadlines. Entry fee: $70, August; $75, October. Display area: 8x10 or smaller. Prejudging by slides. Work may be offered for sale; no commission. Craftworker must attend show; demonstrations OK if arranged in advance. Registration limit: 70. Sponsor provides chair; table; 24-hour security; and electricity. Show is advertised by radio; newspapers; flyers; and posters. Considers all crafts. 1977 August exhibitor sales totalled $40,000; October sales totalled $56,000.

*OLD WORLD CRAFT SHOW, c/o Michael Holland, Star Route at Pico, Rutland VT 05701. (802)775-1939. Sponsor: Killington/Pico Rotary Club. Estab. 1972. Annual indoor show held 2 days in the summer. Entries accepted until 4 weeks before show. Entry fee: $40/artist. Display area: 8x10. Prejudging by 5 slides or photos; entry fee due after prejudging. Work may be offered for sale; no commission. Craftworker must attend show; demonstrations OK. Registration limit: 60. Sponsor provides chairs; electricity; tables; and moving help. Show is advertised by central Vermont radio stations; posters; flyers; and newspapers. Submit any descriptions for publicity consideration. Awards plaque. Bestsellers: work under $100.

Acceptable Work: Considers all crafts. "We try to have no more than 3 of any 1 craft. This past show had craftsmen from Connecticut, Massachusetts, New Hampshire and Maine; but 80% are Vermonters."

THE SOUTHERN VERMONT CRAFT FAIR, Box 92, Readsboro VT 05350. Director: Riki Moss. Sponsor: Craftproducers Inc. Estab. 1977. Annual outdoor show held 3 days in August at Bennington, Vermont, at Bennington College. Average attendance: 7,000. Entries accepted until mid-April. Entry fee: $75/artist. Display area: 8x10 or 10x10. Prejudging by 5 slides; entry fee due after prejudging. Work may be offered for sale; no commission. Craftworker must attend show; demonstrations OK. Registration limit: 100. Sponsor provides chairs; electricity; free camping; and a party. Show is advertised by radio; newspapers; flyers; and posters. Considers all crafts except decoupage and tole painting. Bestsellers: $5-30. 1977 exhibitor sales totalled approximately $60,000.

STRATTON ARTS FESTIVAL, Stratton Mountain VT 05155. Sponsor: Vermont Council of the Arts. Annual indoor show usually held from mid-September to mid-October. No entry fee. Work must be offered for sale; 30% commission. Sponsor provides plywood display panels and $200 deductible insurance minus commission. Ship entries UPS or deliver in person by appointment. Considers all crafts by Vermont craftworkers.

VERMONT MAPLE ART & CRAFT SHOW, Rt. 3, St. Albans VT 05478. Chairperson: Lucille Mae Callum. Purpose: "to promote the Vermont Maple Festival and the maple syrup industry." Estab. 1969. Annual indoor show held 3 days in April. Average attendance: 5,000. Write for entry specifics. Display area: 6' table. Work may be offered for sale; no commission. Craftworker must attend show; demonstrations OK. Registration limit: 60. Sponsor provides some chairs; table; and 24-hour security. Considers all crafts except lapidary; metalsmithing; mobiles; sculpture; and soft sculpture."

Virginia

*APPLE HARVEST ARTS & CRAFTS FESTIVAL, Drawer E., Middletown VA 22601. (703)869-1120. Chairman: Dr. William H. McCoy. Sponsor: Winchester Rotary Club. Purpose: "service to the community and to the participating artists and craftsmen. Earnings are used for upgrading the festival; and for the Rotary-sponsored charitable purposes." Estab. 1975. Annual outdoor show held 2 days in September. Average attendance: 10,000. Entries accepted until 3 weeks before show. Entry fee: $30/20' of running space. Prejudging by slides or photos; entry fee refunded for refused work. Work may be offered for sale; demonstrations encouraged. Registration limit: 120-150. Sponsor provides 24-hour security. Considers all crafts. Presents ribbons. **Promotion:** Show is advertised by news releases in 5 states; 125 newspapers and periodicals; radio ads in Virginia, West Virginia and DC; posters; flyers and through the Virginia travel bureau." Submit b&w glossy photos of self engaged in craft."

ARTS IN THE PARK, 1112 Sunset Ave., Richmond VA 23221. (804)353-8198. Chairman: Mrs. R. S. Lovelace III. Sponsor: Carillon Civic Association. Purpose: to promote the arts in Richmond and as a community project. Estab. 1971. Annual indoor/outdoor show held 2 days in May. Average attendance: 120,000+. Entries accepted until 2 weeks before show. Entry fee: $20/8x10 display area. Work may be offered for sale; no commission. Craftworker must attend show; demonstrations OK. Show is advertised by TV; radio; newspapers; and posters. Considers all crafts except ceramics; decoupage; mobiles; and soft sculpture.

BLACKSTONE CHAMBER OF COMMERCE ANNUAL ARTS & CRAFTS FESTIVAL, Box 295, Blackstone VA 23824. (804)292-4624. Chairperson: Mrs. J. L. Tramel. Purpose: "to further promote interest in arts and crafts in our rural locality; and to expose local artists and craftpersons to a wider range of arts and crafts." Estab. 1970. Annual indoor show held 2 days during the first weekend in October preceded by a Thursday. Average attendance: 4,000. Entries accepted until 4 weeks before show; "thereafter to fill a cancellation." Entry fee: $10 for craftworkers with sales tax numbers; other pay 5% commission of $200 of sales following show. Display area: 8x10. Prejudging "for crafters new to our show. Please send either nonreturnable color slides or photos"; application fee refunded for refused work. Work should be offered for sale. Craftworkers must attend show; demonstrations encouraged. Registration limit: 80-90. Sponsor provides chairs; electricity; table; and overnight security. Considers all crafts. **Sales Tip:** "Be friendly, courteous and prompt. Prices under $50 are rapid sales items; prices $100 and upward move well." 1977 exhibitor sales totalled $17,700.

*BOARDWALK ART AND CRAFT SHOW, 2 Boundary St., Colonial Beach VA 22443.

(804)224-3555. Secretary: James D. Karn. Sponsor: Colonial Beach Chamber of Commerce. Purpose: "We are in a historic part of Virginia (10 miles from Washington's birthplace) and this show is held to promote the area." Estab. 1967. Annual outdoor show held 2 days in August. Average attendance: 25,000. Entries accepted until 2 weeks before show. Entry fee: $12/craftworker. Display area: 10'. Work may be offered for sale; no commission. Craftworker must attend show; demonstrations OK. Registration limit: 100. Show is advertised by radio; newspaper; and direct mail. Presents cash awards of $400, best in show; $200, 1st; $100, 2nd; $50, 3rd; purchase awards and ribbons. Considers all crafts.

*BUCKROE BEACH ART SHOW, 38 Hampton Roads Ave., Hampton VA 23661. (804)723-6162. Board Member: Herbert Goldstein. Sponsor: Peninsula Exchange Club. Purpose: fundraiser for student scholarships. Estab. 1965. Annual outdoor show held 3 days in August. Average attendance: 25,000+. Entries accepted until show. Entry fee: $20/8' display area. Work may be offered for sale; no commission. Craftworker must attend show; demonstrations OK. Sponsor provides fencing. Show is advertised by newspapers; posters; and radio. Considers all crafts. Presents about $1,000 in cash prizes in all categories, and ribbons for 1st, 2nd and 3rd places.

*ENAMELS, c/o Chairman Gwen Anderson, 6520 Ivy Hill, McLean VA 22101. (703)356-7936. Sponsor: National Enamelists' Guild. Purpose: "to expose the public to the beautiful enameling done by craftsmen of today. Many people are unaware of the strides made in the last 20 years." Estab. 1974. Biennial national indoor show held 1 month from May to June at the Torpedo Art Center, 20 minutes from Washington DC. Entries accepted until 5 days before show. Entry fee: $7/1-3 entries; $2 additional for each entry over 3. Maximum 6 enamels/craftworker. Prejudging by actual piece of work; no entry fee refunded for refused work. Work may be offered for sale; 20% commission. Craftworker needn't attend show (may ship work); no demonstrations. Registration limit: approximately 100-150. Sponsor provides display panels; theft insurance on exhibited work; and 24-hour security. Show is advertised by newspaper; magazines; newsletters; and radio. Categories: vitrious enamel on metal; vitrious enamel on clay; and vitrious enamel on glass. Presents cash awards. "Last show our sales ranged from $60-600, with only a few pieces in show under $100."
Acceptable Work: "Only enamels with original design. Student work done under or with teacher supervision is not acceptable. Work must not have won award in any national competition. Maximum size: 3x5 or 50 pounds."

*FESTIVAL IN THE PARK, Box 3300, Danville VA 24541. (804)799-5200. Director: Tish McCune. Estab. 1975. Annual outdoor show (with parachutes for art area) held 3 days in May at Ballou Park in Danville. Average attendance: 70,000. Entries accepted until 2 months before show for crafts. Entry fee: $10/15x20 display area. Prejudging by slides; entry fee refunded for refused work. Work may be offered for sale; no commission. Craftworker must attend show; demonstrations encouraged. Sponsor provides electricity for demonstrations. Show is advertised by radio; TV; newspapers; and magazines. Considers all crafts. Presents $2,000 in cash and 1st, 2nd and 3rd place ribbons.

FESTIVAL OF LEAVES, Box 1836, Front Royal VA 22630. (703)635-8663. Co-chairpersons: Mary Helen Loftin and Ruth Monnington. Sponsor: Warren Heritage Society. Estab. 1970. Annual show held 2 days in October. Average attendance: 5,000. Closing date for entry: 3 weeks before show. No entry fee. Prejudging. Work may be offered for sale; 15% commission. Craftworker must attend show. Registration limit: 50. Sponsor provides display equipment and pays insurance on exhibited work. Considers all crafts.

FOURTH OF JULY CARNIVAL, Box 162, Fredericksburg VA 22401. (703)371-4504. Executive Director: Ronald Shibley. Director: Historic Frdericksburg Foundation Inc. Purpose: fundraiser. Estab. 1975. Annual outdoor show (with canopies) held 1 day during July 4 weekend. Average attendance: 4,500-10,000. Entries accepted until 2 weeks before show. No entry fee. Work must be offered for sale; 25% commission. Prefers craftworker attends show; demonstrations encouraged. Sponsor provides electricity for demonstrations. Show is advertised by press releases to New England and mid-Atlantic newspapers. Bestsellers: items under $20. "Best mix is several low cost pieces if higher priced items are also being offered."

GREENWOOD ARTS AND CRAFTS FAIR, Box 281, Greenwood VA 22943. Sponsor: Greenwood Community Center. Purpose: to benefit Greenwood Community Center. Estab. 1968. Annual indoor/outdoor show held 2 days in September. Average attendance: 8,000. Entries accepted until July 1. Entry fee: $25-50/10x6 display area. Prejudging by slides or photos;

entry fee refunded for refused work. Work may be offered for sale; no commission. Craftworker must attend show; demonstrations OK. Registration limit: 100. Sponsor provides chairs; electricity for demonstrations; table; and 24-hour security. Show is advertised by radio; newspapers; posters; and flyers. Submit photos of self at work for promotion. In 1977 show "several craftworkers sold over $1,000; some over $2,000." Considers all crafts except ceramics and soft sculpture.

MARKET SQUARE FAIR, Box 162, Fredericksburg VA 22401. (703)371-4504. Executive Director: Ronald E. Shibley. Sponsor: Historic Fredericksburg Foundation, Inc. Purpose: fundraiser. Estab. 1737. Annual outdoor show held second Saturday in May. Average attendance: 5,000. Entries accepted until 2 weeks before show. No entry fee. Work may be offered for sale; 25% commission. Craftworker must attend show; demonstrations encouraged. Sponsor provides electricity for demonstrations. Show is advertised by newspaper releases, radio ads, and posters. Considers all crafts. Bestsellers: items under $20.

NEW MARKET ARTS & CRAFTS SHOW, Box 506, New Market VA 22844. (703)740-3212. Contact: William H. Garber. Sponsor: New Market Arts & Crafts Club. Purpose: "to get artisans' work before the public and assist them with sales." Estab. 1961. Annual indoor/outdoor show held the last Saturday and Sunday in September. Average attendance: 2,000-5,000. Entries accepted until show date. Entry fee: 25c/item being displayed. Work may be offered for sale; 15% commission. Craftworker needn't attend show; demonstrations OK. Sponsor provides chairs; display panels; electricity for demonstrations; and 24-hour security. Show is advertised by radio; newspapers; posters; literature in motel rooms; and signs. Considers all crafts.

NEWMARKET NORTH ARTS & CRAFTS SHOW, 1219 Elmart Lane, Richmond VA 23235. (804)745-1085. Coordinator: Mary Lehner. Sponsor: Newmarket North Merchants Association. Estab. 1976. Annual indoor show held 4 days in July at Hampton, Virginia. Average attendance: 50,000-60,000. Entries accepted until 2 weeks before show (only accepts money order or certified check within 3 weeks of show). Entry fee: $40/10x10 display area. Prejudging by "at least 2 slides or photos of representative work. Also like overall picture of display with exhibitor in background, or exhibitor at work." Entry fee refunded for refused work. Work may be offered for sale; no commission. Craftworker must exhibit during store hours; demonstrations encouraged. Registration limit: 90 (usual number, about 65). Sponsor provides some A-frame panels; electricity for demonstrations; and 24-hour security.
Acceptable Work: Considers batik; candlemaking; decoupage; dollmaking; glass art; jewelry; leatherworking; macrame; metalsmithing; mobiles; needlecrafts; wheel thrown or hand-built pottery; sculpture; soft sculpture; tole painting; weaving; and woodcrafting. "A person must specialize in 1 category and list items in category to be exhibited. There is a quota on each category. A person who does some of everything upsets the quota."
Profile: Show is advertised in daily newspaper; radio spots; and in-house advertising. "Many artists keep names and addresses of former customers and send a card to arrive on first day of show to let them know they are in the show. This seems to help them very much. Exhibitors should have a name plate on their exhibit and some printed material for the patrons to pick up."

*AN OCCASION FOR THE ARTS, Box 1491, Williamsburg VA 23185. Estab. 1969. Annual outdoor show held 1 day in October. Average attendance: several thousand. Entries accepted until 4 months before show; $1 mailing and handling fee. Entry fee: $20. Display area: 3x6. Prejudging by 3 slides (2x2 35mm) with craftworker's name and arrow marking top. SASE. Work must be offered for sale; prices must be displayed on all work; each craftworker is responsible for making a poster to announce his work. Registration limit: 85. Presents 5 cash awards of $100 each and purchase awards totalling $1,725. Considers all crafts.

*PORTSMOUTH NATIONAL SEAWALL ART SHOW, c/o Parks and Recreation Dept., 430 High St., Portsmouth VA 23704. (804)393-8481. Director: Donna Morris. Sponsor: Parks and Recreation Department and Chamber of Commerce. Estab. 1970. Annual outdoor show held Memorial Day weekend. Average attendance: 20,000. Entries accepted until 4 weeks before show. Entry fee: $13/6x8 display area; $17 with wire fencing. Maximum 3 spaces per craftworker. Work may be offered for sale; no commission. Craftworker or representative must attend show; demonstrations encouraged. Registration limit: 700. No crafts accepted in advance. Considers all original crafts.
Awards: Presents $2,500, cash prizes; $2,000+, purchase awards; 35 ribbons. Judging done by 3 well-known East Coast artists or art educators.

POWHATAN ARTS AND CRAFT SHOW AND SALE, Box 187, Powhatan VA 23139. Chairman: Mrs. Robert C. Baltimore. Sponsor: Powhatan Junior Woman's Club. Purpose: fundraiser. Estab. 1976. Annual indoor dshow held 2 days in fall. Entries accepted up until show. Entry fee: $15/10x10 display area. Work may be offered for sale; no commission. Craftworker must attend show; select demonstrations. Registration limit: 50. Sponsor provides chairs; display panels (bulletin boards); electricity for demonstrations; table; overnight security; and name banners. Show is advertised by newspaper ads; community service radio and TV announcements; illuminated billboards; flyers; and posters. Considers all crafts. Bestsellers: "Christmas decorations and gifts. Children's items draw interest as well as handmade furniture. Ceramics have not proved to be a big seller."

*RICHMOND CRAFT FAIR, 316 N. 24th St., Richmond VA 23223. (804)649-0674. Director: Ruth T. Summers. Sponsor: Hand Work Shop, Inc. Purpose: fundraiser. Estab. 1976. Annual indoor show held 3 days in November. Average attendance: 12,000-15,000. Entries accepted until about 5 months before show. Entry fee: $3/slide fee plus $30/8x10 display area. Prejudging by 5 color slides, standard size mount. Booth fee due after prejudging. Work must be offered for sale; 15% commission. Craftworker must attend show; demonstrations OK. Registration limit: 125-135. Sponsor provides chairs; electricity for demonstrations; table; 24-hour security; and exhibitor curtains. Show is advertised by TV public service announcements and talk shows; flyers; posters; and press releases. Submit photo and resume. 1976 show sales totalled $90,000. Presents cash awards of $1,125 and purchase awards of $1,650. Categories: folk and designer crafts.
Acceptable Work: Considers designer crafts and all crafts except decoupage; dollmaking; mobiles; needlecrafts; tole painting; dried flowers; seed and pod decorations; cut bottles; embellished objects such as painted waxes, weathered woods, stones, shells, buttons, and furniture; raw materials; unfinished objects; and Christmas decorations. Bestsellers: functional plus decorative, $25-40 range.

THE ROANOKE CRAFT FESTIVAL, Box 8161, Roanoke VA 24014. Coordinator: Anne Ferguson. Sponsor: Docent Guild of the Roanoke Fine Arts Center. Purpose: fundraiser. Estab. 1971. Annual indoor show held 3 days in November. Average attendance: 11,000. Entry fees accepted until 6 months before show. Entry fee: $55-200/display area. Prejudging by slides; photos; or actual work. Work may be offered for sale; no commission. Craftworker must attend show; demonstrations OK. Registration limit: 84. Sponsor provides chairs; coverings; display panels; 24-hour security; some free housing; lounge; coffee; tea; and relief workers. Show is advertised by numerous magazines; radio; TV; posters; and newspapers. Submit promotional material only if requested. 1977 show sales totalled $89,000. Considers all crafts.

VIRGINIA BEACH FOLK ARTS FESTIVAL, 4700 Recreation Dr., Virginia Beach VA 23451. (804)467-4884. Festival Coordinators: Elaine Philps and Bea Arline. Sponsor: Virginia Beach Department of Parks and Recreation. Annual outdoor show (with tent space for fiber crafts) held 2 days in May. Average attendance: 25,000-30,000. Entries accepted until 4 weeks before show. Entry fee: $5/craftworker. Prejudging by 4 35mm slides or color photos; entry fee due after prejudging. Work may be offered for sale; no commission. Craftworker or representative must attend show; demonstrations OK. Registration limit: 115. Sponsor provides electricity for demonstrations; table; relief personnel; water for demonstrations; and tent space if needed. Presents 1st, 2nd and 3rd place plaques for best display.
Acceptable Work: Considers batik; candlemaking; old traditional decoupage and dollmaking; glass art; jewelry; lapidary; leatherworking; macrame; needlecrafts; pottery; sculpture; soft sculpture; tole painting; weaving; woodcrafting; old world crafts; and skills handed down through the generations.
Promotion: Show is advertised by national publications; newspaper; posters; flyers; statewide craft show listings; area magazines; TV; and radio. Submit resume and 8x10 b&w glossy demonstrating craft or with display (nonreturnable).
Profile: "The Festival is a celebration of our rural cultural heritage with sales and demonstrations of Old World crafts and skills. We try to provide a family weekend of fun with live entertainment and an opportunity to view and purchase fine handcrafted items not available on the average market. We hope to help preserve the skills and crafts of the past that are in danger of dying out."

VIRGINIA CRAFTS COUNCIL CRAFT FAIR, 717 Rugby Rd., Charlottesville VA 22903. (804)295-6360. Executive Director: Mary Maher. Purpose: "to provide member craftspeople with a good spring outlet for both wholesale and retail sales. To educate the buying public as to the nature, variety and quality of contemporary and traditional crafts." Estab. 1972. Annual indoor show held 3 days in April. Average attendance: 5,000-6,000. "Open to Virginia Crafts Council members only. However, Virginia Crafts Council membership is open to all; must be a member by November 15 of preceding year to enter next year's show; not limited to Virginia residents." Entry fee: $25/10x10 display area. Prejudging by sides if not of exhibiting member status; by actual work for those of exhibiting member status. Entry fee refunded on refused work. Work may be offered for sale; 15% commission on total sales over $200 and under $1,000; 10% on total sales above $1,000. Craftworker must attend show; demonstrations encouraged and paid for. Registration limit: 80-100. Sponsor provides chairs; electricity for demonstrations; table; 24-hour security; free housing with area hosts; and relief personnel. 1977 show sales totalled $42,000. Considers all crafts except painted rocks, decoupage boxes; dried flower arrangement; seed and pod decorations; cut bottles; and embellished objects.

Promotion: Show is advertised by private mailing of brochures; radio; TV; newspapers; magazines; posters across the State of Virginia and Washington DC. Submit photos and resume. "Craftsperson may supply his or her personal mailing list. Brochures will be addressed and sent to those people."

Washington

ALLIED ARTS STREET FAIR, Box 573, Wenatchee WA 98801 (509)662-1213. Coordinator: Judy Mills. Sponsor: Allied Arts Council of North Central Washington. Purpose: fundraiser and to provide a place for quality craftsmen to exhibit. Estab. 1973. Annual outdoor show held 3 days in September. Average attendance: 5,000-10,000. Entries accepted until 1 week before show. Entry fee: $20/2 blocks. Prejudging by sides; photos; and descriptions. Entry fee refunded for refused work. Work may be offered for sale; no commission. Craftworker must attend show; demonstrations OK. Registration limit: 100. Sponsor provides electricity for demonstrations. Show is advertised by all media. Considers all crafts.

*ANACORTES ARTS AND CRAFTS FESTIVAL, Box 6, Anacortes WA 98221. Chairman: Ron Smith. Purpose: "to expand the cultural environment of our city and to provide exposure for the Northwest's many fine artists and craftspeople." Estab. 1960. Annual outdoor show held 2 days in August. Average attendance: 20,000+. Entries for booth space accepted until about mid-May. Entries for juried show accepted until 2 weeks before show. Entry fee: $3/category in juried show; $30/10x12 display area. Maximum 2 pieces per artist per category; total 20. Prejudging by actual work; entry fee due after prejudging. Work may be offered for sale; 20% commission on sales over $125. Craftworker must attend show; demonstrations OK. Registration limit: 90. Sponsor provides electricity for demonstrations; table; 24-hour security; and some festival booths. Show is advertised by newspaper; direct mailin; posters; TV; and radio. Presents cash awards of $3,500 and purchase awards of $300-1,000, not necessarily awarded each year. 1977 show sales totalled $40,000. Considers all crafts.

ANGELES ARTS IN ACTION, Box 176, Port Angeles WA 98362. (206)457-3004. Fair Manager: Virginia DelGuzzi. Estab. 1968. Annual outdoor show held 2 days in July. Entries accepted until 4 months before show. Prejudging by slides; photos; or actual work. "Northwest artists given preference." Work may be offered for sale. Registration limit: 90. Considers jewelry, leather, candles, and macrame.

APPLE BLOSSOM FESTIVAL ARTS AND CRAFTS FAIR, Box 850, Wenatchee WA 98801. (509)662-2118. Manager: Dianne Gamel. Sponsor: Washington State Apple Blossom Festival Association. Purpose: "to give the spectators of our festival an opportunity to purchase artistic items; to keep our festival attractive and with family appeal." Estab. 1975. Annual outdoor show held 3 days in May. Average attendance: 100,000. Entries accepted until 2 weeks before show. Entry fee: $25/10x10 display area. Prejudging by photos and descriptions; entry fee refunded for refused work. Work may be offered for sale; no commission. Craftworker must attend show; demonstrations OK. Registration limit: 120. Sponsor provides electricity for demonstrations and 24-hour limited security. Show is advertised by brochures; magazines; radio; and newspaper. Considers all crafts. Bestsellers: "items that enhance their homes — pottery; jewelry; and woods."

*CLARK COUNTRY FAIR, 17402 NE Delfel Rd., Ridgefield WA 98642. (206)573-1921. Manager: David A. Pittman. Purpose: "agriculture fair, geared to youth in the community, 4-H, FFA, etc." Estab. 1868. Annual show held 6 days in August at Vancouver. Average attendance: 162,000. Display area: 10x10 and up. Prejudging; no entry fees refunded for refused work. Work may be offered for sale in commercial area only; no commission. Craftworker needn't attend show; demonstrations OK. Registration limit: 100. Sponsor provides electricity for demonstrations; table; and 24-hour security. Show is advertised by news media; radio; TV; billboards; and posters. Presents cash awards and ribbons. Categories: open class; 4-H and FFA; premium awards; and commercial exhibitors. Considers all crafts.

*EDMONDS ART FESTIVAL, Box 212, Edmonds WA 98020. (206)776-6381. President: Jim Hamlin. Estab. 1957. Annual indoor/outdoor show held 3 days in June. Average attendance: 50,000. Entries accepted until 1 week before show. Entry fee: $3/2 entries. Maximum 2 entries per category per craftworker. Work must be offered for sale; 25% commission. Sponsor provides display equipment and insurance. Deliver and pick up work in person.
Acceptable Work: Considers batik; ceramics; dollmaking; glass art; jewelry; leatherworking; mosaics; mobiles; macrame; metalsmithing; needlecrafts; pottery; soft sculpture; weavings; wall hangings; and woodcrafting.
Awards: Presents a total of $4,750 in cash prizes for all categories. Craft portion is awarded $1,000.

*EVERETT WATERFRONT SHOW, Box 2937, Everett WA 98203. (206)252-4580. Show Chairman: Robyn Wicklund. Sponsor: Creative Arts Association. Purpose: fundraiser. Estab. 1967. Annual outdoor show (tents) held 3 days in June. Average attendance: 125,000-126,00. Entries accepted until 2 weeks before show. Entry fee: $3/category; $1/children; $50 plus 15% commission/booth free. Display area: 10x10. Maximum 2 pieces per artist per category. Prejudging by actual work. Work may be offered for sale; 25% commission. Craftworker must attend show; demonstrations OK. Sponsor provides coverings; electricity for demonstrations; insurance on exhibited work; 24-hour security; and tent, optional. Show is advertised by newspaper articles; reader boards; and local TV. Presents cash awards of $1,500-2,000; 3 purchase awards of $100 and 1 of $150; and ribbons.
Acceptable Work: Considers batik; candlemaking; ceramics; glass art; jewelry; lapidary; leatherworking; macrame; metalsmithing; needlecrafts; pottery; sculpture; soft sculpture; weaving; and woodcrafting. Maximum size of works: 48".

FREE AIR ARTS FAIR, Box 1995, Vancouver WA 96886. (206)696-8171. Supervisor: Margaret Bostwick. Sponsor: City of Vancouver. Annual outdoor show held the 4th of July. Average attendance: 40,000-60,000. Entries accepted until 1 week before show. Entry fee: $2/display area size as needed. Work may be offered for sale; no commission. Craftworker must attend show; demonstration OK. Registration limit: 100. Show is advertised by newspapers and TV. Individual craftworker averaged $200 in 1977 show. Considers all crafts.
Profile: "The Fair is a part of a day long community celebration that features the largest fireworks display outside of Washington DC. The artists are invited to bring families and participate in games and races; enjoy entertainment; and join with us in celebrating the 4th of July."

*NORTHWEST CRAFTS EXHIBITION, Henry Art Gallery, University of Washington, Seattle WA 98195. (206)543-2280. Director: Richard Grove. Purpose: "biennial survey of crafts in the Northwest" (Washington; Oregon; Idaho; Montana; Wyoming; and Alaska). Estab. 1952. Biennial 1-month show held during odd-numbered years. Entries accepted until 6 weeks before show. No entry fee. Maximum 3 pieces per artist. Prejudging by slides. Work may be offered for sale; 25% commission. Craftworker needn't attend show; no demonstrations. Registration limit: about 147. Sponsor provides insurance on exhibited work and 24-hour security. "This is a museum exhibition with staff installation." Show is advertised by mailing and public media. Presents cash, purchase, and solo-exhibition awards. Considers all crafts.

*PACIFIC NORTHWEST ARTS AND CRAFTS FAIR, 10310 NE 4th, Bellevue WA 98004. Contact: Fair Chairman. Purpose: to provide a market place for arts and crafts of the highest quality. Estab. 1947. Annual outdoor show (with canopies and awnings) held 3 days in July. Average attendance: 100,000. Entries accepted until 4 months before show. Entry fee: $1.50/item. Maximum 2 pieces per artist per category. Prejudging by actual work; entry fee not refunded for refused work. Work may be offered for sale; 20% commission. If booth, craftworker must attend show; if work on exhibit only, craftworker needn't attend show; demonstrations OK. Registration limit: 160 in booths; 150 in exhibition. Sponsor provides electricity for demonstration and 24-hour security. Show is advertised by newspapers, mailings, radio, and TV. Presents cash awards of $10,000 for all categories. 1977 show sales totalled $375,-000. Considers all crafts except candlemaking; decoupage; lapidary; mobiles; and tole painting.

SEATTLE HARVEST FESTIVAL, 832 Bancroft Way, Berkeley CA 94710. (415)548-5440. Contact: Steve Kyle, Warren Cook, or Ellen Schwartz. Sponsor: General Expositions Corporation. Estab. 1977. Annual indoor show held 3 days in November at Seattle, Washington. Entries accepted until full; "booths are rented according to seniority." Entry fee: $135/8x10 display area. Prejudging by 6 photos or slides or actual work. Work may be offered for sale; no commission. Craftworker must attend show; demonstrations OK. Sponsor provides electricity for demonstrations; backdrop drapery; side rails; 24-hour security; cleaning; motel or hotel accom-

modations at group rate; inexpensive trucking of booth setup and stock round-trip between other Harvest Festival Shows. Presents awards for best costumes; best designed booths; and best demonstrating booths. Show is advertised by newspaper; radio; TV; billboard; direct mailings; posters; discount coupons; news releases; and TV guest appearances. Considers all crafts.
Profile: "The Harvest Festivals are patterned after the famous country autumn fairs of the 19th century America. These fairs were held to give thanksgiving for bountiful crops and as a last celebration before the hard winter set in. Craftworkers are required to be in 19th century costume."

SIDEWALK SHOW, 89 Lee Blvd., Richland WA 99352. (509)943-9815. Chairman: Jack Hess. Sponsor: Allied Arts Association. Estab. 1950. Annual outdoor show held 2 days in July. Average attendance: 10,000-15,000. Closing (postmark) date for entry: 6 weeks before show. Entry fee: $15/craftworkers. Display area: 15x15. Work must be offered for sale; 15% commission. "Items $200 or less sell very well." Craftworker must attend show; demonstrations encouraged. Registration limit: 225. Sponsor provides some electricity (if pre-requested) and security. Presents $50 for best display. Considers all crafts except decoupage. Write for prospectus in mid-March.

SILVERDALE'S WHALING DAYS, Box 1218, Silverdale WA 98383. Contact: Central Kitsap Chamber of Commerce. Show held in July. Average attendance: 20,000. Closing date for entry: 2 weeks before show. Entry fee: $25. Craftworker must attend show. Considers a variety of media.

*WESTERN WASHINGTON FAIR ART SHOW, Box 430, Puyallup WA 98371. Curator: Marcia Jartun. Annual show. Entry fee: $3. Limit 2 entries. Work may be offered for sale; 25% commission. Presents $750 in prizes.
Acceptable Work: Original work completed within the past 2 years, not previously shown in the area OK. Open to Washington artists ages 18+. All media except sculpture. Size limit: maximum, 6x7; minimum, 8x12".

WHISTLIN' JACK ARTS AND CRAFTS, 4210 Terrace Heights Rd., Yakima WA 98901. (509)453-3379. Sponsor: Whistlin' Jack Lodge. Purpose: "this area is very popular as a tourist attraction; tourists are looking for gifts from this area." Estab. 1974. Indoor/outdoor show (depending on weather) held 3 days in July; 3 days in September; and 3 days Memorial Day weekend at Cliffdale, Washington. Average attendance: 3,000-5,000. Entries accepted until 2 weeks before show. Entry fee: $25/10x10 display area. Prejudging by photos; entry fee due after prejudging. Work may be offered for sale; 10% commission. Craftworker must attend show; demonstrations encouraged. Registration limit: 30. Sponsor provides chairs; electricity for demonstrations; and free camping area. Show is advertised by all media. Submit b&w photos. Considers all crafts.

*YAKIMA MALL CHRISTMAS SHOW, c/o Ruth Wyman Reese, 4210 Terrace Heights Rd., Yakima WA 98901. (509)453-3379. Annual indoor show held 5 days in November. Entries accepted until filled. Entry fee: $25. Work may be offered for sale; no commission. Craftworker must attend show. Registration limit: 40. Sponsor provides some security. Show is advertised by all media. Presents awards. Considers all crafts. Bestseller: Christmas items.

West Virginia

ALDERSON-BROADDUS COLLEGE ARTS & CRAFTS FAIR, Box 1397, A-B College, Philippi WV 26416. (304)457-1700, ext. 235. Director of Student Activities: Carl Hatfield. Estab. 1974. Annual indoor show held 1 day in October. Average attendance: 2,000. Closing date for entry: 2 weeks before show. No entry fee. Maximum 1 entry per craftworker. Work may be offered for sale; no commission. Considers primarily West Virginia craftworkers. Craftworker must attend show; demonstrations OK. Registration limit: 40. Sponsor provides tables. Considers all crafts

APPALACHIAN ARTS AND CRAFTS FESTIVAL, Box 1798, Beckley WV 25801. (304)252-7328. Executive Director: Robert L. McKeands. Sponsor: Beckley-Raleigh County Chamber of Commerce. Purpose: to preserve Appalachian heritage. Annual indoor/outdoor show held 3 days in August. Work may be offered for sale; 15% commission. Craftworker must attend show; demonstrations OK. Sponsor provides chairs; display panels and electricity for demonstrations. Show is advertised by paid public relations company. Submit photographs for promotion. 1977 show sales totalled $60,000. Considers all crafts; "Appalachian heritage is our objective."

*BRAXTON COUNTY ARTS AND CRAFTS SHOW, 940 Riverside Dr., Gassaway WV 26624. (304)364-2340. Chairman, Art Committee: Mrs. George Hoylman. Sponsor: Woman's Club of Gassaway. Purpose: "to encourage arts and crafts among citizens of Braxton County; to offer them and others a chance to sell products; to promote appreciation for the arts." Estab. 1964. Annual indoor show held 2 days in April. Average attendance: 1,000. Entries accepted until 2 weeks before show for out of county craftworkers; entries accepted up until show for county residents. Entry fee: $10/display area. Work may be offered for sale; no commission. Craftworker or representative must attend show; prearranged demonstrations OK. Sponsor provides chairs; electricity for demonstrations; security; and tables. Show is advertised by newspapers; radio; and local TV. Presents ribbon awards for local work and best of show. Considers all crafts.

CAPITAL CITY ART AND CRAFT SHOW, Box 4373, Charleston WV 25304. (304)356-3427. Co-chairman: W. F. Lany Sr. Sponsor: Kanawha City Lions Club. Purpose: fundraiser. Estab. 1973. Annual indoor show held 3 days in November. Average attendance: 12,000. Entries accepted until "maximum number of booths are filled." Entry fee: $17.50/10x10 display area. Prejudging by slides or photos; entry fee due after prejudging. Work may be offered for sale; 15% commission. Craftworker must attend show; demonstrations OK. Registration limit: 130. Sponsor provides chairs; display panels; electricity for demonstrations; fencing; table; and 24-hour security. Show is advertised by radio; TV; direct mail; talk shows; banners; posters; leaflets; and newspapers. Submit resume and photos of work. 1976 show sales totalled $46,000+. Considers all crafts.

*CHRISTMAS IN SEPTEMBER FESTIVAL, c/o The Serendipity, Shepherdstown WV 25443. Contact: Helen Myers Seeley. Purpose: "to promote the newer crafts in this, the oldest town in West Virginia which is steeped in the traditional crafts." Estab. 1977. Annual indoor show held 2 days in September. Average attendance: 1,000. Entries accepted until 1 week before show. Entry fee: $2/8' table. Work must be offered for sale; no commission. Craftworker must attend show; demonstrations "practically mandatory." Registration limit: 30. Sponsor provides chairs; electricity for demonstrations; table; 24-hour security; and poster for each display table. Show is advertised by newspaper; radio; and newsletter. Submit photo. Presents cash awards of $25, $10 and $5. Considers all crafts. "Table must be draped; where possible, work should be plastic wrapped." Most sales are less than $10.

*EXHIBITION 280, Huntington Galleries, Park Hills, Huntington WV 25701. (304)529-2701. Contact: Program Coordinator. Estab. 1952. Annual indoor show held 6 weeks in the fall. Average attendance: 6,000. Entries accepted until October 2. Entry fee: $10/craftworker. Maximum 3 entries per craftworker. Prejudging of slides due August 11; no entry fees refunded for refused work. Work may be offered for sale; no commission. Considers all crafts completed by residents within a 280-mile radius of Huntington. Write for prospectus in summer. Presents $1,500 in cash and $2,500 in purchase prizes.

GRAND CENTRAL MALL ARTS FESTIVAL, Rt. 1, Box 153J, Auburn NH 03032. (603)483-2742. President: Jinx Harris. Estab. 1977. Annual indoor show held 4 days in March in Parkersburg, West Virginia. Average attendance: 35,000+ Entries accepted until 1 week before show; or until filled. Entry fee: $35/8x4 display area. Prejudging by slides or photos if not in a previous show. Work may be offered for sale; no commission. Craftworker must attend show; demonstrations OK. Registration limit: 30. Sponsor provides electricity for demonstrations and 24-hour security. Show is advertised by radio; TV; and newspaper. Considers all crafts except ceramics; decoupage under $5; lapidary; and strung bead jewelry.

JOHN HENRY FOLK FESTIVAL, Box 135, Princeton WV 24740. (304)487-1148. Director: Edward J. Cabbell. Sponsor: John Henry Memorial Foundation, Inc. Estab. 1973. Annual outdoor show with tents held Labor Day weekend. Closing date for entry: 2 months before show. No entry fee. Prejudging by photos or slides (send resume) conducted by panel of Appalachian artists/craftworkers. Work may be offered for sale; 10% commission. Exhibitor must be from an Appalachian state or region and must attend show; demonstrations OK. Considers all traditional Appalachian crafts (at least 1 work should be related to John Henry folk legend).

HERITAGE DAYS, Parkersburg Community College, Parkersburg WV 26101. (304)422-8525. Chairman: Nancy Pansing. Purpose: "to promote heritage skills and the craftsmen; to promote an appreciation of the skills." Estab. 1974. Annual indoor show held 3 days in May. Average attendance: 9,000. Entries accepted until 3 weeks before show. Entry fee: $10/display area. Prejudging by slides, photos and samples; entry fee refended for refused work. Work may be offered for sale; no commission. Craftworker must attend show; demonstrations a must. Registration limit: 50. Sponsor provides chairs; electricity for demonstrations; table; 24-hour security; dinner; and lodging. Show is advertised by newspapers; radio; TV; brochures; and local and national show listings. Submit upon acceptance a photo and resume for publicity.

Acceptable Work: Considers batik; candlemaking; ceramics; dollmaking; glass art; jewelry; leatherworking; macrame; metalsmithing; needlecrafts; pottery; sculpture; tole painting; weaving; woodcrafting; quilting; apple dolls; and spinning. "Emphasis on heritage crafts with modern design."

HUNTINGTON DOGWOOD ARTS AND CRAFTS FESTIVAL, Box 2767, Huntington WV 25727. (304)696-5940. Contact: Promotion Supervisor. Sponsor: City of Huntington and Huntington Civic Center. Purpose: to promote quality arts and crafts in the Huntington community. Annual indoor show held 5 days in May. Average attendance: 70,000. Entries accepted until 10 weeks before show. Entry fee: $25/10x10 display area. Prejudging by 3 slides or photos; entry fee refunded for refused work. Work must be offered for sale; demonstrations required. Sponsor provides chairs; electricity for demonstrations; table; and 24-hour security. Show is advertised by billboards; newspapers; professional entertainment; and general publicity. Considers all crafts.

MOUNTAIN HERITAGE ARTS AND CRAFTS FESTIVAL, Box 430, Charles Town WV 25414. (304)725-5514. Manager: George E. Vickers. Sponsor: Jefferson County Chamber of Commerce, Inc. Purpose: for the promotion of the arts and crafts. Estab. 1972. Semiannual invitational outdoor show (with tents) held 3 days in June, and 3 days in September near Harpers Ferry, West Virginia. Average attendance; 32,000 paid. Entry fee: $25/8x16 display area; $50/16x16 display area. Work may be offered for sale; 15% commission. Craftworker must attend show; demonstrations mandatory. Registration limit: 130. Sponsor provides electricity for demonstrations; 24-hour security; apple boxes and plywood for table tops and enclosure of booth; and pegboard background. Show is advertised by press releases; ads in newspapers, magazines and radio; billboards; brochures; and TV. Notice of prejudging and instructions upon request.

*MOUNTAIN STATE ART AND CRAFT FAIR, Cedar Lakes, Ripley WV 25271. (304)372-6263. Sponsor: West Virginia Artists and Craftsmens Guild; West Virginia Department of Agriculture; Governor's Office of Economic and Community Development; Bureau of Vocational and Technical Education; West Virginia University Extension Service; and West Virginia Department of Natural Resources. Purpose: "to promote, develop and perpetuate the friendly exchange of information and sale of arts and crafts of West Virginia. In so doing we hope to acquaint the general public and visitors to the State of West Virginia with various cultural aspects of arts and crafts in our state." Estab. 1963. Annual indoor/outdoor show (exhibits are in building or under tents) held 5 days in June/July. Average attendance: 50,000. Applications accepted until 7 months before show. Display area: 6x8, 6x12, 6x16, 10x20 and 20x-20 in tents; 6x8 and 6x16 in building. Prejudging by at least 5 pieces of actual work in each category. Work may be offered for sale; 15% commission. Craftworker must attend show; demonstrations required. Registration limit: 100 regular; 30 special exhibits. Sponsor provides display panels; electricity for demonstrations; table; and 24-hour security. Presents 5 awards of excellence each $100 and plaque; and letters of commendation to 5 additional craftworkers. 1977 show sales totalled $257,707.47. Considers all crafts except ceramics; decoupage; and any craft made outside of West Virginia. "This is a show for West Virginia craftsmen and artists only."

Promotion: "The Fair Board of Trustees utilizes the services of West Virginia University journalism students. Each year the school's public relations graduate assistant serves as PR director to supervise senior PR students. Promotional vehicles include a general brochure and accommodations director; several specialized brochures; news releases; magazine articles; public service radio spots; and personal appearances of craftsmen before groups and on TV. Craftworkers receive promotional materials for personal distribution."

OGLEBAY INSTITUTE CRAFT FESTIVAL, Oglebay Park, Wheeling WV 26003. (304)242-7700. Director, Creative Arts: Mary E. Fish. Purpose: "to promote crafts that reflect the highest standards of craftmanship by offering a specific time and place for demonstration, display and sale of work in order that the artist and viewer may reach a better mutual understanding and appreciation." Estab. 1950. Annual indoor show held 2 days in June. Average attendance: 2,700. Entries accepted until 1 week before show. Entry fee: $20/8' table and/or pegboard display area. Work may be offered for sale; no commission. Craftworker or representative must attend show; demonstrations encouraged. Registration limit: 70. Sponsor provides chairs; display panels; electricity for demonstrations; table; and 24-hour security. 1977 show sales totalled $3,012. Considers all crafts including musical instruments.

Promotion: Show is advertised by newspaper ads; hobby magazines; public service radio and TV; mail; posters placed in craft shops and interstate tourists stops within 30 miles; and state of West Virginia brochure that is distributed nationally. Submit photos and stories.

*OGLEBAY INSTITUTE UPPER OHIO VALLEY ART SHOW, Oglebay Institute, Oglebay Park, Wheeling WV 26003. (304)242-7700. Art Specialist: Ken Morgan. Estab. 1964. Annual indoor show held 1 month in the fall. Average attendance: 1,000. Entries accepted until 1 week before show. Entry fee: $4, Institute member entry; $5, nonmember entry. Maximum 2 entries per exhibit. Work may be offered for sale; 20% commission. Open to West Virginia artists and those living within 75-mile radius of Wheeling. For insurance purposes, work must be delivered by the craftworker or an agent.
Acceptable Work: Considers batik; glass art; leatherworking; metalsmithing; pottery; soft sculpture; weavings; wall hangings; and woodcrafting.
Awards: Presents $1,000 in cash; and 12 merit and some honorable mention ribbons. Judging panel consists of college art instructors or professional artists.

PIONEER DAY OF POCOHANTAS COUNTY, 8th St., Marlinton WV 24954. (304)799-4993. Director: Douglas Dunbrack. Purpose: "for local people to show their wares and encourage others to do the same, and to bring other craftsmen to our area." Estab. 1967. Annual indoor/outdoor show held 3 days in July. Average attendance: 10,000. Entries accepted until show. Entry fee: $1/pioneer badge. Work may be offered for sale; 10% commission. Craftworker must attend show; demonstrations OK. Sponsor provides chairs; display panels; electricity for demonstrations; table; 24-hour security; and some booths and dividers. Show is advertised by newspapers; leaflets; posters; TV; and radio. Considers all crafts.

*RHODODENDRON STATE OUTDOOR ART AND CRAFT FESTIVAL, 3804 Noyes Ave. SE, Charleston WV 25304. (304)925-3364. President: Eleanor Chandler. Purpose: "to help artists; craftsmen; and photographers." Estab. 1967. Annual outdoor show held 1 day in June. Average attendance: 10,000. Entries accepted until show. Entry fee: $5/craftworker. Display area: 7x10. Work may be offered for sale; no commission. Craftworker must attend show; demonstrations OK. Presents cash awards of approximately $3,000 and several purchase awards, but varies each year. Considers all crafts.

SHOW AND SELL, Moundsville Area Chamber of Commerce, Box 186, Moundsville WV 26041. (304)845-2773. Assistant Secretary: Jean Barger. Estab. 1976. Annual outdoor show (with some roofed areas) held 2 days in August. Average attendance: 20,000. Entries accepted until 2 weeks before show. Entry fee: $5/display area equal to 1 car's parking space. Work may be offered for sale; no commission. Craftworker or representative must attend show; demonstrations encouraged. Sponsor provides electricity for demonstrations if requested in advance. Show is advertised by continuous newspaper releases; radio, TV, and newspaper ads; and bulletins. Submit photos for publicity. Considers all crafts. "This is not a luxury-buying market."

SOUTH PARKERSBURG BAND BOOSTERS CHRISTMAS ARTS AND CRAFT SHOW, Rt. 1, Box 226, Washington WV 26181. (304)863-5654. President: Janet Nicola. Purpose: fundraiser. Estab. 1972. Annual indoor show held 2 days in November. Average attendance: 2,000+. Entries accepted until 4 weeks before show. Entry fee: $20/8' display area; $22.50/8' display area with table. Work may be offered for sale; no commission. Craftworker must attend show; demonstrations OK. Registration limit: 56-75. Sponsor provides chairs; electricity for demonstrations; insurance on exhibited work; and 24-hour security. Show is advertised by TV; newspapers; *West Virginia Craft Events*; flyers; and posters (covered in Pennsylvania also). Submit nonreturnable photos and a brief description of work for publicity. Considers all crafts except ceramics; decoupage; soft sculpture; and weaving.

STONEWALL JACKSON JUBILEE, Box 956, Weston WV 26452. (304)269-4660. Contact: Beth Alderman. Sponsor: Jubilee, Inc. Purpose: "to promote the culture and arts of the central West Virginia and Appalachian region." Estab. 1974. Annual indoor show held 3 days in Septmber. Average attendance: 10,000. Entries accepted until 3 weeks before show. Display area: 5x8 minimum. Prejudging of 1 item in each category. Work must be offered for sale; 15% commission. Craftworker must attend show; demonstrations required. Registration limit: 80-100. Sponsor provides chairs; electricity for demonstrations; fencing; limited insurance on exhibited work; table; 24-hour security; and coffee in lounge. Show is advertised by brochures; listing; radio; TV; and newspaper ads. Submit photographs for publicity. 1977 shows sales totalled $33,342. Considers all crafts except mobiles. "Crafts must be representative both in style and method of creation of the Appalachian region." Bestsellers: "$5-500, should have full price range."

WEST VIRGINIA OIL AND GAS FESTIVAL, Box 25, Sistersville WV 26175. Craft Sales Chairman: Susan L. Boyles. "Sistersville is an oil boom historical town; the festival is built around this history. Crafts are part of this." Estab. 1969. Annual outdoor show (with tents and shelters) held 4 days in September. Average attendance: 25,000-30,000. Entries accepted until 1 week before show. Display area: 10x10. Work may be offered for sale; 15% commission. Craftworker must attend show; demonstrations OK. Sponsor provides coverings; electricity for demonstrations; fencing; table; and 24-hour security. Show is advertised by general publicity; news releases; and travel shows. Considers all crafts. Bestsellers: $2-5 items.

Wisconsin

APPLE BLOSSOM ART & CRAFTS FAIR, Rt. 2, Gay Mills WI 54631. Contact: Beverly Gainor. Annual indoor show. Entry fee: $10. Display area: 10x10. Craftworker must attend show.

*****ARTARAMA**, Rt. 1, Eagle River WI 54521. (715)479-8947. Chairman: Donna Schwarts. Sponsor: Chamber of Commerce. Estab. 1971. Annual outdoor show held 1 day in July. Average attendance: 2,000. Entries accepted until 1 week before show. Entry fee: $8/10' display area. Work may be offered for sale; no commission. Craftworker must attend show; demonstrations OK. Registration limit: 150. Sponsor provides electricity for demonstrations. Show is advertised by radio; newspaper; posters; and mailings. 1977 show sales totalled $20,000. Presents 6 $50 cash awards of excellence; purchase awards of $500; ribbons for honorable mention and junior awards. Categories: artwork; graphics; craft; handicraft; photography; sculpture; fiber; oils and acrylic; watercolor; pottery; and jewelry.

ART FAIR, Box 29, New Holstein WI 53061. Contact: Lee Tikalsky. Sponsor: Kiwanis Club. Annual show. Entry fee: $5/approximately 15' display area. Work may be offered for sale; no commission. All media acceptable unless objection expressed at registration. Write for more information.

ART FAIR USA, 1655 S. 68th St., West Allis WI 53214. (414)774-1636. Director: Dennis R. Hill. Estab. 1975. Semiannual show held indoors 2 days in March; outdoors 2 days in July. Average attendance: 15,000. Entries accepted until 8 weeks before show. Entry fee: $30/10x10 display area. Prejudging for new exhibitors by resume and 5 slides with name; media; size of work printed on back of each. SASE. Entry fee refunded for refused work. Work may be offered for sale; no commission. Craftworker must attend show; demonstrations OK. Considers sculpture; ceramics; jewelry; textiles; glass; enamelware; leather work; and work in wood and metal.

ARTS & CRAFTS BY THE HANDICAPPED, c/o Mr. and Mrs. Robert Hoss, Box 1422, Waukesha WI 53187. Annual indoor show held 3 days in October at Brookfield, Wisconsin. Open only to "the handicapped and disabled from the state of Wisconsin. New exhibitors must send chairman statement from their doctor before registration." No entry fee. Work must be offered for sale; no commission.

*****ARTS & CRAFTS FAIR**, Forest Mall, 835 W. Johnson St., Fond du Lac WI 54935. Contact: Lois Frank. Sponsor: Forest Mall Merchants Association. Estab. 1974. Annual indoor show held 3 days in October. Average attendance: 6,000-10,000. Closing date for entry: 2-3 weeks before show. Entry fee: $15/10x10 tent display area. Prejudging; entry fee refunded for refused work. Work may be offered for sale; 10% commission donated to charity. Craftworker must attend show. Registration limit: 70-75. Considers all crafts. Presents best of show and 1st, 2nd and 3rd place ribbons.

ARTS AND CRAFTS MARKET, GSR Box 6, Medford WI 54451. President: Anita Dittrich. Sponsor: Taylor County Arts Council and University of Wisconsin, Medford. Purpose: "to give all persons a chance to show and sell whatever kind of art or craft they do." Estab. 1972. Annual indoor show held 2 days in June. Average attendance: 1,000. Entries accepted until 2 weeks before show. Entry fee: $6/5x10 display area. Work may be offered for sale; no commission. Craftworker must attend show; demonstrations OK. Registration limit: 75. Sponsor provides electricity for demonstrations and 24-hour security. Show is advertised by TV; radio; newspaper; posters; and signs. Submit description of craft. Considers all crafts.

*BELOIT & VICINITY EXHIBITION, Wright Art Center, Beloit College, Beloit WI 53511. (608)365-3391. Director: Marylou S. Williams. Sponsor: Wright Art Center and Beloit Art League. Estab. 1957. Annual indoor show held 4 weeks in May-June. Average attendance: 800-1,000. Entries accepted until 3 weeks before show. Entry fee: $7/entry. Maximum 1 entry per craftworker. Prejudging; no entry fees refunded for refused work. Work may be offered for sale; 15% commission. Sponsor provides display equipment. Deliver crafts in person. Presents $2,000 in cash and $250 in purchase prizes.
Acceptable Work: Considers batik; ceramics; glass art; soft sculpture; weavings; and wall hangings by craftworkers within driving distance of Beloit. No student work. Crafts must be ready for installation. No brackets.

BLACKHAWK INDIAN VALLEY ARTS AND CRAFTS SHOW, Box 61, Rome IL 61562. (309)274-3001. Coordinator: Judy Kelley. Sponsor: Janesville Mall Merchants Association. Semiannual indoor show held 3 days in March and in June at Janesville, Wisconsin. Average attendance: 10,000-20,000. Entries accepted until 2 weeks before show. Entry fee: $35-40/12x6 display area. Prejudging by 2 slides or photos. SASE. Entry fee refunded for refused work. Work may be offered for sale; no commission. Craftworker must attend show; demonstrations OK. Registration limit: 55. Sponsor provides electricity for demonstrations. Show is advertised by radio and newspapers. Submit b&w glossies.
Acceptable Work: Considers glass art; jewelry; metalsmithing; pottery; sculpture; tole painting; weaving; and woodcrafting.

*CEDAR CREEK FESTIVAL OF ARTS AND CRAFTS, Box 205, Cedarburg WI 53012. Festival Director: Lynn Titus. Sponsor: Cedarburg Junior Woman's Club. Purpose: "to promote art in our community and let the public see good art from Midwest artists." Estab. 1975. Annual indoor show held 1 day in fall. Average attendance: 1,000. Entries accepted until "midsummer". Entry fee: $15/12x10 display area. Prejudging by 5 slides and resume; entry fee refunded for refused work. Work must be offered for sale; no commission. Craftworker or representative must attend show; demonstrations OK. Registration limit: 50. Sponsor provides chairs; electricity for demonstrations where possible; table; lunch; lounge; and set-up help. Show is advertised by TV; radio; publicity articles in local newspapers and *Milwaukee Journal* and *Milwaukee Sentinal;* and news releases to college art departments. Presents cash awards and ribbons. Considers batik; ceramics; glass art; jewelry; leatherworking; macrame; metalsmithing; needlecrafts; pottery; sculpture; weaving; and woodcrafting.

DANE COUNTY HUMANE SOCIETY ANIMAL ART FAIR, 2250 Pennsylvania Ave., Madison WI 53704. (608)249-6656. Manager: Karla Joy Baumgartner. Purpose: fundraiser. Estab. 1977. Annual outdoor show held 1 day in September. Average attendance: 6,000-8,000. Entries accepted until 6 weeks before show. Display area: 15x10. Prejudging by slides or photos. Work may be offered for sale; 10% commission. Craftworker must attend show; demonstrations OK. Registration limit: 150. Sponsor provides electricity for demonstration; security during show; and sales receipt book. Show is advertised by public service announcements; newspaper; and local magazine. Submit photo of craft to be displayed. Considers all crafts that relate to animals, wild or domestic subject matter. Bestsellers: average price $15.

A DETAILED LOOK, NATIONAL METALSMITHING AND JEWELRY INVITATIONAL, Art Department, University of Wisconsin, 800 W. Main St., Whitewater WI 53190. Contact: Kelley Morris. Purpose: "to provide a 'detailed look' at current metalsmithing and jewelry concepts for local; regional; and national visitors; faculty; and students." Estab. 1978. Annual indoor show held 2-3 weeks in fall. "This is an invitation only show. Not competitive, and no call for work."

FOLK ART FAIR, 95 N. Moorland Rd., Brookfield Square WI 53005. Show Coordinator: Rosemary Roth. Sponsor: Brookfield Square Merchants' Association. Purpose: to revive an interest in the old crafts. Estab. 1978. Annual indoor show held 3 days in August. Entries accepted until 4 weeks before show. Entry fee: $25/display area. Prejudging by photo or slide of several pieces of craft and 1 photo of entire display. Entry fee due after prejudging. Work may be offered for sale; no commission. Craftworker must attend show; demonstrations encouraged. Registration limit: 75-100. Sponsor provides electricity for demonstrations and 24-hour security. Show is advertised by newspaper and radio. Submit 8x10 glossy of self involved in work and resume. Considers candlemaking; dollmaking; leatherworking; macrame; metalsmithing; needlecrafts; pottery; sculpture; soft sculpture; tole painting; weaving; woodcrafting; and all folk art.

*FOND DU LAC ARTISTS ASSOCIATION ANNUAL ARTS AND CRAFTS FAIR, Rt. 3, Box 444, Fond du Lac WI 54935. (414)921-1209. President: John Delfeld. Purpose: to bring good art and craftsmanship to the community. Estab. 1967. Annual indoor/outdoor show held 2 days in June. Average attendance: 2,000. Entries accepted until 4 weeks before show. Entry fee: $12/10x10; $25/20x10. Work may be offered for sale; no commission. Craftworker or representative must attend show; demonstrations OK. Sponsor provides limited amount of chairs; display booths; electricity for demonstrations; out of doors fencing; limited amount of tables; and 24-hour security. Show is advertised by local and area radio spots and talk shows; TV; newspapers; and posters. Presents purchase awards of over $1,200 and ribbons. Considers all crafts except soft sculpture.

FOREST MALL ARTS & CRAFTS FAIR, 835 W. Johnson St., Fond du Lac WI 54935. Contact: Lois Frank and/or Sarah Navis. Sponsor: Forest Mall Merchants Association. Estab. 1974. Annual indoor show held 3 days in April. Average attendance: 6,000-10,000. Closing date for entry: 2-3 weeks before show. Entry fee: $12-15/10x10 tent display area. Prejudging; entry fee refunded for refused work. Work may be offered for sale; 10% commission donated to charity. Craftworker must attend show. Registration limit: 70-75.
Acceptable Work: Considers batik; candlemaking; ceramics; glass art (no glass blowing); leatherworking; metal sculpture; creative stitchery; pottery; weavings; wall hangings; and woodcrafting.

*FOREST MALL'S ARTS AND CRAFTS FAIR/SALE, 835 W. Johnson St., Fond du Lac WI 54935. (414)922-6724. Contact: Sarah Navis or Lois Frank. Estab. 1974. Annual indoor show held 3 days in October. Average attendance: 6,000. Entries accepted until 2 weeks before show. Entry fee: $15/10x10 display area. Prejudging by slides; photos; or actual work. Entry fee refunded for refused work. Work may be offered for sale; 10% commission. Craftworker must attend show; demonstrations OK. Registration limit: 70-75. Sponsor provides electricity for demonstrations. Show is advertised by publicity clips in 20 newspapers and by 5 radio stations. Presents ribbon awards. Considers batik; candlemaking; ceramics; glass art; leatherworking; macrame; metalsmithing (not including jewelry); pottery; sculpture; soft sculpture; tole painting; and woodcrafting. All tables used must be draped to the floor; cannot use brown butcher paper.

GAYS MILLS PACE CLUB ARTS & CRAFTS FAIR, Pace Club, Gays Mills WI 54631. Contact: Mrs. Richard Gainor. Semiannual indoor/outdoor show held 1 day in May and September. Average attendance: 1,000+. Entries accepted until filled. Entry fee: $10/10x5 display area. Work may be offered for sale; no commission. Craftworker must attend show; demonstrations encouraged. Registration limit: 75-100. Considers all crafts.

*GREAT RIVER FESTIVAL OF TRADITIONAL MUSIC AND CRAFTS, 1409 State St., LaCrosse WI 54601. Co-chairwoman, Crafts: Barbara Starner. Purpose: "to enrich the area's experience and education in traditional music and crafts. We emphasize demonstrations." Estab. 1976. Annual outdoor show (inside in case of rain) held 2 days in September. Average attendance: 5,000. Entries accepted until 2 weeks before show. Entry fee: $15/display area as large as needed. Prejudging by 3 slides; no entry fees refunded for refused work. Work may be offered for sale; no commission. Craftworker must attend show; demonstrations OK. Registration limit: 75. Sponsor provides chairs; electricity for demonstrations; fencing; table; and 24-hour security. Presents cash awards of $800-1,000; "all table-area fees are turned into prizes for crafts."
Acceptable Work: Considers batik; candlemaking; ceramics; decoupage; dollmaking; glass arts; jewelry; leatherworking; macrame; metalsmithing; mobiles; needlecrafts; pottery; sculpture; tole painting; weaving; woodcrafting; folk instruments; puppets and marionettes; dollhouses; eggs; lacemaking; wrought iron; and quilting. Bestsellers: crafts for children and folk instruments.
Promotion: Show is advertised by posters; ads in 40 area newspapers; series of feature articles in local newspapers; TV; radio; and articles in area magazines. Submit b&w glossy of self at work and any feature article material.

GREATER MILWAUKEE CRAFT FAIR, 1655 S. 68th St., West Allis WI 53214. (414)774-1639. Director: Dennis R. Hill. Estab. 1972. Annual indoor show held 3 days in November. Average attendance: 15,000. Entries accepted until 3 weeks before show. Entry fee: $50/10x10 display area. Prejudging by resume and 5 slides with name; media; and size of work on back. SASE. Entry fee refunded for refused work. Work may be offered for sale; no commission. Craftworker must attend show; demonstrations OK. Registration limit: 165. Sponsor provides display panels on request and 24-hour security.
Acceptable Work: Considers batik; candlemaking; ceramics; glass art; jewelry; lapidary;

leatherworking; weaving; woodcrafting; wooden toys; leaded glass; Christmas ornaments; enameling; sand-casted candles; wall hangings; corn husk crafts; painted eggs; stitchery; and stained glass.

*HOLLAND DAY ART FAIR "ON THE GREEN," Cedar Grove WI 53013. Contact: Mrs. Robert Klein or Mrs. Carl Winkelhorst. Annual outdoor show held the last Saturday in July. Average attendance: 10,000. Entries accepted until July 23. Entry fee: $8/10x10 display area. Craftworker must attend show. Work may be offered for sale; no commission. Considers all crafts. Presents trophies and ribbons.

HOLLY DAY FAIR, N101W15273 Starlite Dr., Germantown WI 53022. (414)251-5477. Co-chairman: Margaret Ramstack. Sponsor: Germantown Jr. Woman's Club. Purpose: fundraiser. Estab. 1977. Annual indoor show held 1 day in November. Average attendance: 1,000+. Entries accepted until 10 weeks before show. Entry fee: $10/10x6 display area. Work may be offered for sale; no commission. Craftworkers must attend show; demonstrations OK. Registration limit: 90. Sponsor provides electricity for demonstrations if requested. Show is advertised by newspaper articles; posters; flyers; signs; and newspaper ads. Considers all crafts.

INDIAN HEAD ART FAIR, Wisconsin Indian Head Country, Inc., 3015 E. Clairemont Ave., Eau Claire WI 54701. Show Director: Jean Johnson. Annual show held in March. Entry fee: $15/12x5 display area; limit 2 spaces/exhibitor. Entries accepted until January for previous exhibitors; February for new exhibitors. Prejudging of new exhibitors by representation of work and current resume. Work may be offered for sale; 10% commission charged on total gross sales exceeding $100. Demonstrations OK. Considers woodcuts; jewelry (gold, silver, copper, semi-precious stones); wood carving and turning; batik; leather; pottery; and wood, metal and clay sculpture.

INDOOR ART AND CRAFT FAIR — COUNTY FAIRE, 18127 William St., Lancing IL 60438. (312)895-3710. Coordinator: Sylvia Krugowski. Sponsor: County Faire Merchants Association. Estab. 1977. Semiannual indoor show held 3 days in spring and in fall at Grafton, Wisconsin. Entries accepted up until show. Entry fee: $16/craftworker. Display area: 8x8. Prejudging by slides or photos; entry fee refunded for refused work. Work may be offered for sale; no commission. Craftworker must attend show; demonstrations OK. Sponsor provides electricity for demonstrations. Show is advertised by all crafts publications, *Sunshine Artists*, newspaper releases; and shopping center paid advertising. Submit advance notices to your customers in area. Considers all crafts except Indian jewelry and macrame.

*KENOSHA ART FAIR, Kenosha Public Museum, 5608 10th Ave., Kenosha WI 53140. Annual show. Sponsor: Friends of the Kenosha Public Museum. Entry fee: $10/12' fencing. Work must be offered for sale; no commission. Considers all crafts.
Awards: Presents $500 in cash prizes; "Kady Faulkner Honorary Awards"; $150 museum purchase prize; purchase pledges; and pledger's choice award.

KETTLE MORAINE ART AND CRAFTS, 2831 S. 10th St., Sheboygan WI 53081. (414)458-6561. Chairman: Karen Lewandoske. Purpose: to provide an outlet for the work of craftsmen and artists. Estab. 1973. Annual indoor show held 1 day in April at West Bend, Wisconsin. Average attendance: 5,000. Entries accepted until 1 week before show; "show usually filled 1 month before show." Entry fee: $5.50/8x5 display area. Work may be offered for sale; no commission. Craftworker must attend show; demonstrations OK. Registration limit: 85. Sponsor provides chairs and electricity for demonstrations. Show is advertised by radio and newspapers. Considers all crafts.

KETTLE MORAINE CHRISTMAS FAIR, 2831 S. 10th St., Sheboygan WI 53081. (414)458-6561. Chairman: Karen Lewandoske. Purpose: to provide an outlet for the work of craftsmen and artist. Estab. 1973. Annual indoor show held 1 day in November at West Bend, Wisconsin. Average attendance: 5,000. Entries accepted until 1 week before show; "show usually filled 1 month before show." Entry fee: $5.50/8x5 display area. Work may be offered for sale; no commission. Craftworker must attend show; demonstrations OK. Registration limit: 85. Sponsor provides chairs; and electricity for demonstrations. Show is advertised by radio and newspapers. Considers all crafts.

KING RICHARD'S FAIRE — A RETURN TO THE RENAISSANCE, Box 432, Lake Forest IL 60045. (312)689-2800. General Manager: Robert F. Rogers. Sponsor: Greathall of Illinois, Limited. Purpose: "to provide the most unusual and exciting art and craft marketplace in the

Midwest." Estab. 1973. Outdoor show held 13 days on July and August weekends at Bristol, Wisconsin. Entries accepted until 3 weeks before show. Entry fee: $150/before January 15th; $175/by April 15th; $200/after April 15th. Display area: 20' frontage, unlimited depth. Prejudging by prints; slides; or actual work. Entry fee refunded for refused work. Work may be offered for sale; no commission. Craftworker must attend show; demonstrations OK. Registration limit: 175. Sponsor provides electricity for demonstrations; fencing; and 24-hour security. Presents cash awards for best demonstration; best shop; and best costume. Considers any craft practiced during the Renaissance Period. "All craftsmen must be costumed in attire of the period."
Promotion: Show is advertised by 12 month campaign provided by PR firm featuring paid TV spots in Milwaukee and Chicago markets; complete radio and newspaper blitz in Chicago, Milwaukee and outlying areas.

*MONUMENT SQUARE ART FAIR, 223 6th St., Racine WI 53403. (414)633-5332 or 633-3215. Secretary-Treasurer: Mrs. John R. Hackl. Sponsor: AAUW Racine Branch; Downtown Association of Racine; Junior Woman's Club; Racine Art Association; Racine Art Guild; Racine Department of Park and Recreation; and Woman's Club of Racine. Purpose: "to bring the best in art to Racine." Estab. 1963. Annual invitational indoor/outdoor show held 2 days in June. Average attendance: 10,000. Entries accepted until 2 months before show. Entry fee: $25/12x5 display area. Prejudging by 10 slides or 3 pieces of work in January; slides marked as to size, media, and craftworker's name. SASE. Work may be offered for sale; no commission. Craftworker needn't attend show; demonstrations encouraged. Sponsor provides limited number of chairs; snow fencing outside and inside; limited electricity for demonstrations; and 24-hour security. Show is advertised by newspapers; radio; TV; and public announcement and talk programs. Presents cash awards of $1,000 and ribbons. 1977 show sales totalled $56,500+. "Gift certificates for sale all during the year and program of purchase pledges." Considers batik; ceramics; glass; jewelry; leatherworking; macrame; metalsmithing; needlecrafts; pottery; sculpture; soft sculpture; weaving; and woodcrafting.

*MUSCODA ARTS AND CRAFTS FAIR, Box 246, Muscoda WI 53573. (708)739-3679. Chairman: Rita Storms. Sponsor: Art Fair Committee. Estab. 1972. Annual indoor/outdoor show held 2 days in August. Average attendance: 2,000. Entries accepted until 1 week before show; $6 late entry fee. Entry fee: $5/10' display area. Work may be offered for sale; no commission. Craftworker or representative must attend show; demonstrations OK. Sponsor provides chairs; electricity for demonstrations; and 24-hour security. Presents ribbon awards. 1977 show sales totalled $4,800. Considers all crafts.

NEW HOLSTEIN KIWANIS ARTS AND CRAFTS FAIR, Box 29, New Holstein WI 53061. (414)898-5766 business, 898-5232 home. Chairman: Lee J. Tikalsky. Purpose: fundraiser and to bring arts and crafts to the community. Estab. 1973. Annual outdoor show (with shelter and pavilion available in case of rain) held 1 day in September. Entries accepted until 1 week before show. Entry fee: $5/10x15 display area. Work may be offered for sale; no commission. Craftworker must attend show; demonstrations encouraged. Sponsor provides electricity for demonstrations and fencing. Show is advertised by radio; TV; listings in area newspapers and advertisers (100 mile radius); and listings with arts and crafts associations. Considers all crafts.

*NORTHEASTERN WISCONSIN ART ANNUAL, 129 S. Jefferson St., Green Bay WI 54301. Curator of Art, Neville Public Museum: James W. Kreiter. Annual show usually held in the late fall. Entry fee: $2/entry. Maximum 5 entries per artist. Open to residents (ages 18+) of the following Wisconsin counties: Brown, Calumet, Door, Fond du Lac, Kewaunee, Manitowoc, Marinette, Oconto, Outagamie, Shawano, Sheboygan, Waupaca and Winnebago. Work must be offered for sale, under $400. No commission. Work must be hand-delivered. Sponsor insures exhibited items for ⅔ of the sale price. No 2-dimensional work over 5x5; no 3-dimensional work over 150 lbs. Considers all work. Presents 3 $200 purchase prizes; ribbons; and entrance into a 4-person exhibition.

*OUTDOOR ARTS FESTIVAL, Box 204, Watertown WI 53094. Corresponding Secretary: Sandra Pirkel. Estab. 1965. Annual outdoor show held 1 day in August. Entries accepted until show date. Entry fee: $5/display area. Work may be offered for sale; 10% commission. Craftworker must attend show; demonstrations encouraged. Considers all original, fine crafts. Presents $600+ in purchase prizes and ribbons.

RACINE CHRISTMAS GIFT MARKET, 420 Main St., Racine WI 53402. (414)637-4471. Director: Daniel Thekan. Purpose: to bring artists and their patrons together before Christmas.

Estab. 1971. Annual indoor show held 1 day in December. Average attendance: 1,500. Entries accepted up until show date or until filled. Entry fee: $15/80 square feet of display area. Prejudging by slides; entry fee due after prejudging. Work may be offered for sale; no commission. Craftworker needn't attend show; demonstrations OK. Registration limit: 145. Sponsor provides chairs; electricity for demonstrations; and table. Show is advertised by radio and newspapers. Considers all crafts. Bestsellers: items that will make good Christmas gifts.

SANTAVILLE ARTS AND CRAFTS FAIR, Waukesha County Technical Institute, 800 Main St., Pewaukee WI 53072. (414)691-3200, ext. 313. Contact: Janet Birch or Barbara Ollhoff. Sponsor: Fashion Unlimited Club. Purpose: fundraiser. Estab. 1973. Annual indoor show held 2 days the weekend prior to Thanksgiving. Average attendance: 4,000. Entries accepted until 3 months before show. Entry fee: $25/9x6 display area. Prejudging by photos; entry fee refunded for refused work. Work may be offered for sale; no commission. Must donate 1 item for door prize. Craftworker must attend show; demonstrations OK. Registration limit: 115. Sponsor provides chairs; limited electricity for demonstrations; and table. Show is advertised by newspapers; radio; TV; and posters. Considers all crafts and Christmas decorations. Bestsellers: smaller items for Christmas gifts and decorations.

*SAUK COUNTY ART FESTIVAL, Box 222, Baraboo WI 53913. (608)356-5013. President: Robert Griffith. Sponsor: Sauk County Art Association. Purpose: to promote art and as a fundraiser. Estab. 1964. Annual outdoor show held 2 days in August. Average attendance: 5,000. Entries accepted until 1 week before show. Entry fee: $12/10' display area. Work may be offered for sale; no commission. Craftworker or representative must attend show; no demonstrations. Registration limit: 175. Show is advertised by TV; radio; and newspapers. 1977 show sales totalled $21,000+. Presents purchase awards. Considers candlemaking; dollmaking; glass art; jewelry; lapidary; leatherworking; macrame; metalsmithing; pottery; tole painting; weaving; and woodcrafting.

*SHAWANO ARTS AND CRAFTS FAIR, Shawano County Art Council, Box 213, Shawano, Gresbam WI 54166. Chairman: Ruth A. Gehr. Purpose: "to promote and develop public interest in fine art and crafts; and to enable the exhibitor to market his product." Estab. 1969. Annual outdoor show held 1 day in July at Shawano, Wisconsin. Average attendance: 3,000-4,000. Entries accepted until 2 weeks before show or until spaces are filled. Entry fee: $15/12' display area. Work may be offered for sale; no commission. Craftworker must attend show; demonstrations OK. Registration limit: 120. Sponsor provides fencing. Show is advertised by various arts and crafts listings; area and local newspapers, including Milwaukee paper. Presents cash awards; purchase awards; and ribbons. Considers all crafts.

*SPRING ARTS/CRAFTS SHOW, 835 W. Johnson, Fond du Lac WI 54935. (414)922-5730. Contact: Marketing Director. Sponsor: Forest Mall Shopping Center. Estab. 1974. Annual indoor show held 3 days in April. Entries accepted until 2 weeks before show. Entry fee: $15/10x10 display area. Prejudging by slides; photos; or samples; entry fee refunded for refused work. Work may be offered for sale; 10% commission. Craftworker must attend show; demonstrations OK with certain restricting rules. Registration limit: 70. Sponsor provides electricity for demonstrations. Show is advertised by radio and publicity releases. Presents ribbon awards for best of show, 1st, 2nd, 3rd, and honorable mention. 1977 show sales totalled $8,000.
Acceptable Work: Considers batik; candlemaking; ceramics; dollmaking; glass art; leatherworking; macrame; metalsmithing (but no jewelry); pottery; sculpture; soft sculpture; tole painting; and woodcrafting.

*SPRING CRAFT FAIR, Box 234, Park Plaza Shopping Center, Oshkosh WI 54902. (414)233-5051, ext. 344. Promotion Assistants: Dorothy Schroeder and Joey Jenks. Semiannual indoor show held 3 days in spring and fall. Average attendance: 25,000. Entries accepted up until show. Entry fee: $25/6x15 display area. Prejudging for new entrants by slides or photos; entry fee refunded for refused work. Work may be offered for sale; no commission. Craftworker must attend show; demonstrations encouraged. Registration limit: 70. Sponsor provides electricity for demonstrations ($5 fee). Show is advertised by radio and newspaper. Submit information on your craft. Presents awards based on working demonstrations. Considers all crafts except decoupage; jewelry; and lapidary.

SUMMERFEST, 120 N. Harbor Dr., Milwaukee WI 53202. Contact: Don Montgomery. Estab. 1968. Annual outdoor show held 12 days in July. Average attendance: 600,000. Closing date for entry: January 1. Entry fee: $1,000. Work may be offered for sale; no commission. Registration limit: 24. Considers all crafts.

*VOLKSFEST OF THE ARTS, 303 Grant St., Waunakee WI 53597. (608)849-5534. President: Colette Koltes. Sponsor: Waunakee Art Council. Purpose: fundraiser. Estab. 1975. Annual outdoor show held 2 days in July. Average attendance: 7,000+. Entries accepted until 2 weeks before show. Entry fee: $12/12x12 display area. Work may be offered for sale; no commission. Craftworker must attend show; demonstrations OK. Registration limit: 75. Show is advertised by state and local newspapers; local TV; and radio. Presents cash awards; purchase prizes; and ribbons. Considers all crafts.
Profile: "This affair honors Waunakee's German background. It is the only German festival of arts in Wisconsin and as far as we know the only in surrounding states. Other events of the day include folk entertainment; German beer garden; kinder parade; and German foods."

*WISCONSIN FESTIVAL OF ARTS, 1655 S. 65th St., West Allis WI 53214. (414)774-1639. Director: Dennis R. Hill. Biennial show held indoors 2 days in November, 2 days in May at Milwaukee, Wisconsin. Average attendance: 15,000. Entries accepted until 4 weeks before show or until filled. Entry fee: $50/10x10 display area. Prejudging by resume; and 5 slides with artist's name, media, and size of work printed on back of each. SASE. Entry fee refunded for refused work. Work may be offered for sale; no commission. Craftworker must attend show; demonstrations OK. Registration limit: 165. Sponsor provides display panels on request. Presents by category 2 par excellence cash awards of $250 and 12 excellence cash awards of $150. Considers ceramics; glass art; jewelry; leatherworking; metalsmithing; sculpture; woodcrafting; textiles; and enamelware.

*WO-ZHA-WA DAYS ART FAIR, Box 183, Wisconsin Dells WI 53965. (608)254-8594. President: Cheryl Wenker. Sponsor: Wisconsin Dells Art Association. Purpose: to promote art in the community and a fundraiser. Estab. 1973. Annual outdoor show (tents) held 2 days in September. Average attendance: 2,000-3,000. Entries accepted up until show. Entry fee: $15/10x10 display area. Work may be offered for sale; no commission. Craftworker must attend show; demonstrations OK. Show is advertised by various craft and art show listings; local and state newspapers; radio; and TV interviews. Presents cash awards of $365; purchase awards of $1,000, and ribbons for 1st and 2nd place in each category. Considers all crafts except ceramics.

Wyoming

*ALL AMERICAN INDIAN DAYS ARTS AND CRAFTS SHOW, Box 451, Sheridan WY 82801. Contact: Mrs. Brad Spear. Purpose: "to promote interest in Indian arts and crafts; to promote good relationships between Indian and non-Indian." Estab. 1953. Annual indoor show held 3 days in July. Average attendance: 1,000-3,000. Entries accepted up until show. Entry fee: $5/reservation; $25/tables with display boards behind. "AAID will pay $25 to Indian wishing to display, not sell." Work may be offered for sale; 20% commission. Craftworker needn't attend show; demonstrations OK. Sposor provides chairs; display panels; electricity for demonstrations; insurance on exhibited work; insurance on work shipped to artist; prepaid shipping costs to artists from show; table; and 24-hour security. Show is advertised by all media. Presents cash awards, ribbons and plaques. Considers all crafts which are authentic native Indian work. Bestsellers: beadwork; baskets; and jewelry.

*WIND RIVER VALLEY NATIONAL SHOW, Box 26, Dubois WY 82513. Estab. 1948. Annual indoor show held the first week of August. Average attendance: 1,500. Entries accepted until 3 weeks before show. Entry fee: $5 for first entry; $2.50 each for second and third. "Price your work if you wish to sell it." Considers sculpture.
Awards: Presents $2,000, cash prizes; $500, purchase awards; $250 library award; sweepstakes; and 1st, 2nd, 3rd and honorable mention ribbons.

Canada

*THE CANADIAN CRAFT SHOW LTD., 458 St. Clements Ave., Toronto, Ontario Canada M5N 1M1. (416)489-9711. Contact: Martin Rumack. Purpose: "to provide an all-Canadian Christmas season craft and art show, gathering fine artisans from across Canada to sell (retail) their own works." Estab. 1975. Annual indoor show held 1 week in late November or early December. Average attendance: 42,000. Entry payment deadline is 2½ months before show. Entry fee; $350/10x10 display area. Prejudging by slides, photos, samples and/or personal interviews; entry fee refunded for refused work. Work may be offered for sale; no commission. Craftworker must attend show; demonstrations encouraged. Registration limit: 270. Sponsor provides display panels; electricity for demonstrations; 24-hour security; plastic shopping bags; and Chargex and MasterCharge facilities. Show is advertised by flyers; posters; listings; interviews on radio, TV, and in magazines; back of city buses; printed shopping bags; and paid ads on radio, newspapers and magazines. Considers all crafts handmade in Canada. Awards 4 $50 cash prizes.

CHRISTMAS CRAFT MARKET, Box 3355, Halifax, Nova Scotia Canada B3J 3J1. Sponsor: Nova Scotia Designer Craftsmen. Purpose: "to promote the appreciation and sale of fine craftwork." Annual indoor show held 3 days in November. Average attendance: 10,000+. Entries accepted until approximately 2 months before show. Entry fee: $75/10x10 display area. Prejudging by slides, photos or actual work; entry fee refunded for refused work. Work may be offered for sale; no commission. Craftworker must attend show; demonstrations OK. Registration limit: 100 local craftworkers only. Sponsor provides chairs; lounge area with coffee and tea; information booth; table; and 24-hour security. Show is advertised by posters; radio; TV; newspapers; and word of mouth. Presents $50 for best booth.
Acceptable Work: Considers batik; candlemaking; dollmaking; glass art; jewelry; leatherworking; macrame; metalsmithing; mobiles; needlecrafts; pottery; tole painting; weaving; and woodcrafting. "Skill with materials must be exhibited."

*FAIR NOVEMBER, c/o University Centre Programming Office, University of Guelph, Guelph, Ontario Canada N1G 2W1. (519)824-4120, ext. 3902. Assistant Programming Officer: Diana McClure. Purpose: "Fair November is an expose and sale of Canadian crafts. Artists are chosen from across Canada but primarily from Ontario. The purpose of the show is to educate the public and provide a broader base for understanding and appreciating crafts." Estab. 1974. Annual indoor show held 2 days in November. Average attendance: 15,000. Entries needed for jury show 3 months prior to show. Entry fee: $10/artist. Display area: 12 running feet. Prejudging by slides; photos; and references from reputable people in crafts; entry fee due after prejudging. Work may be offered for sale; 10% commission. Craftsman must attend show; demonstrations OK. Registration limit: 70. Sponsor provides chairs; display panels whenever possible; electricity for demonstrations; insurance on exhibited work; table; and 24-hour security protection. Categories: fiber; metal; clay; wood; and miscellaneous.
Acceptable Work: Considers all crafts except decoupage; mobiles; sculpture; soft sculpture; and tole painting.
Awards: Presents $250, cash; ribbons; and "if a piece is considered excellent, it is purchased by the University." Categories for jurying: craftsmanship; use of media; design; originality; and execution. Show sales for Fair November 1977 were around $31,000.
Promotion: Show is advertised by posters; flyers; newspaper; and radio ads. "Six weeks prior to the show we attempt to arrange short stories in the local newspaper and interviews on the radio to discuss some of the upcoming exhibitions. We ask that many of our artisans send us any pertinent information they have such as reviews and critiques of their work."

FESTIVAL OF THE ARTS MARKET, Box 3355, Halifax, Nova Scotia Canada B3J 3J1. Sponsor: Nova Scotia Designer Craftsmen. Purpose: "to promote the appreciation and sale of fine craftwork." Annual indoor show held 3 days in August. Average attendance: 10,000+. Entries accepted until approximately 2 months before show. Entry fee: $50/4x6 display area. Prejudging by slides, photos or actual work; entry fee refunded for refused work. Work may be offered for sale; no commission. Craftworker must attend show; no demonstrations. Registration limit: 70 Nova Scotia craftworkers only. Sponsor provides chairs; information booth; table; and 24-hour security. Show is advertised by posters; radio; TV; newspapers; and word of mouth. Presents $50 for best booth.
Acceptable Work: Considers batik, candlemaking; dollmaking; glass art; jewelry; leatherworking; macrame; metalsmithing; mobiles; needlecrafts; pottery; tole painting; weaving; and woodcrafting. "No beaded wire jewelry. Skill with materials must be exhibited."

*OTTAWA CHRISTMAS CRAFT SALE, Box 5709, Station F, Ottawa, Ontario Canada. 820-2684. Directors: Dan and Barbara Gamble. Sponsor: Gamble Craft Productions Ltd. Purpose: "to help Canadian craftspeople make a full-time living at crafts by providing them with a secure annual market where they know they will do well." Canadian craftworkers only. Estab. 1975. Annual indoor show held 1 week in early December. Average attendance: 40,000. Entries accepted until mid-June. Entry fee: $300/100 square feet. Prejudging by slides and photos (minimum of 5, maximum of 10); and resume; entry fee due after prejudging. Work may be offered for sale; no commission. Craftworker must attend show; demonstrations OK. Registration limit: 167 booths. Sponsor provides chairs; display curtains; electricity for demonstration; table; 24-hour security; advertising; exhibitor's lounge; floor plans; and booth identification.

Considers all crafts except commercially molded ceramics. Awards 3 cash awards of $300.
Promotion: $12,000 advertising campaign for 1977 show; and b&w photos are appreciated for publicity.

ROCKHOUND ROUND-UP, Box 297, Parrsboro, Nova Scotia Canada B0M 1S0. Chairperson: Marilyn Smith. Sponsor: Chamber of Commerce. Purpose: "to bring people to our area; to promote the lapidary and craftsmen; to teach local people how to do new arts." Estab. 1966. Annual indoor show held 3 days in August. Attendance: 2,500-3,000. Entries accepted until 4 weeks before show. Entry fee: $30/7'3"x3' table; or 10% of sales up to cost of space for demonstrators. Prejudging by slides and photos plus written description of work; entry fee refunded for refused work. Work may be offered for sale; 10% commission. Craftworker must attend show; demonstrations OK. Registration limit: 10-15. Sponsor provides chairs; coverings on tables; display panels; electricity for demonstrations; night watchman; water; canteen facilities; and table. Categories: mineral and gem (rough and finished); and crafts. Considers all crafts. "Macrame must be exhibited demonstrating the purpose it is used for." Presents plaques for best displays.
Sales Tip: "Reasonably-priced items sell best. I have found when work is demonstrated there is more interest. Dealer handles sales — we collect taxes from them."
Promotion: Show is advertised in newspapers in Halifax, Amherst, Parrsboro, and Springhill; on radio; rock magazines; and flyers. "If [craftworkers] have any speciality they should tell use so we can promote. If they will demonstrate we should know also."

WINNIPEG FOLK FESTIVAL, 171 Lilac St., Winnipeg, Manitoba Canada R3M 1S1. (204)284-9840. Office Manager: Lorna Hiebert. "The arts and crafts area is part of a folk music festival, which also has a dance area. The purpose of the festival is two-fold — we wish to help maintain the health of folk traditions and, at the same time, many people are being reintroduced to their roots." Estab. 1974. Annual outdoor show (with some tents) held 3 days in July at Birds Hill Provincial Park. Average attendance: 25,000. Entries accepted until 4 weeks before show. Entry fee: $45/10x20 display area. Work may be offered for sale; no commission. Craftworker must attend show; demonstrations essential. Registration limit: 32. Sponsor provides 2 chairs; coverings; electricity for demonstrations; insurance on exhibited work; table; and 24-hour security.
Acceptable Work: Considers all crafts. "The arts and crafts area at the Festival is called the Handmade Area. All crafts are to be handmade, or original in design. We tend to stay away from commercial ventures — we prefer to lend support to those artists and craftsmen who have few commercial outlets. We require that the artist/craftsmen take a large amount of pride in their work. We appreciate the craftsman having a piece of work in various stages of completion in order that the consumer will have a chance to see the different steps involved. Only 1 craftsperson is allowed per craft. That is we will only have 1 potter, 1 leatherworker, etc. The artist is responsible for an attractive display suitable for promotion of his particular craft."
Promotion: "The festival is promoted by posters in 19 cities in North America; also by a brochure going out to a mailing list of 3,000 people; as well as local TV, radio and billboard ads. Newspaper ads are placed in Manitoban papers as well as folk music magazines such as *Folkscene* and *Come For to Sing*."

Puerto Rico

*PAULA INSEL ANNUAL EXHIBITION, 39 Los Meros, Ponce, Puerto Rico 00731. (809)844-8478. Director: Paula Insel. Sponsor: Galerie Paula Insel. Purpose: "the show is a vehicle for artists to expose their talents." Estab. 1956. Annual indoor show held 2 weeks in the spring. Entries accepted until 1-2 months before show. Entry fee: $8/item being displayed. Maximum 3 works/category. Work may be offered for sale; 40% commission. Craftworker needn't attend show; demonstrations OK. Sponsor provides chairs; display panels; electricity for demonstrations; and shipping costs to craftworker from show. Show is advertised by newspapers; magazines; and mailing lists. Considers batik; ceramics; glass art; macrame; mobiles; needlecrafts; pottery; enamels; sculpture; tole painting; and woodcrafting. Presents ribbons and merchandise for award-winning work.

Writing Outlets

If you're a producing craftworker, there is someone who would like to hear from you—someone who would like you to try your hand at writing.

"Although we buy a fair number of articles every year, most of them come from cabinetmakers, not freelance writers," said John Kelsey, editor of *Fine Woodworking*. "We've found that writers who aren't also amateur woodworkers can't produce the type of material we want. They don't know what questions to ask, let alone how to explain the answers."

It's the familiarity with the craft discipline that counts—if you know your media, you can write about it.

Read "The Craft of Writing Craft Articles," then study these writing outlets. They can provide a whole new market for your craft abilities.

ARTS & ACTIVITIES, 591 Camino de la Reina, Suite 200, San Diego CA 92108. (714)297-5350. Editor: Leven C. Leatherbury. Estab. 1937. Circ. 32,000. Monthly (except July and August) magazine. For art teachers and classroom teachers in grades K-12. "We hope to serve art instructors by providing them with articles describing specific lessons and projects for use in the classroom." Buys approximately 5 how-to craft articles/issue. Pays $35-125/500 word ms. Photos and/or illustrations should accompany ms; no additional payment. "Any holiday-related material must be submitted at least 3 months before publication." Free sample copy and writer's guidelines.

ARTWEEK, 1305 Franklin St., Oakland CA 94612. (415)736-0422. Editor: Cecile N. McCann. Estab. 1970. Circ. 13,000. Tabloid published weekly September-May (biweekly June-September). For "the broadest possible art community. We function as a trade publication covering art activity on the West Coast and Texas, including all areas of fine arts; crafts and photography as art; video and performance; legislation; and other news important to our community." Buys 44-132 mss related to exhibits in the West per year. Buys all rights. Pays $5 minimum/500-1,000 word ms. Object photos required. No additional payment for photos. Sample copy 75c; free writer's guidelines.

CANADA CRAFTS MAGAZINE, 380 Wellington St. W., Toronto, Ontario Canada M5V 1E3. Editor: Gwen P. Dempsey. Circ. 10,000. Bimonthly craft marketing, technique, and education publication. "A periodical of interest to craftspeople, craft educators, craft collectors and those who just like crafts. We produce a quality magazine with profile of Canadian artists and their works and new processes in any media. We welcome any opinions succinctly expressed that would be of interest to our readers." Buys first rights but may reassign rights after publication. Considers craft marketing tips, how-to's, and features on successful craftworkers. Length: 1,000-2,000 words. Pays $15 up to 500 words with photos. Buys approximately 6 articles per issue. "All material submitted must be received before the 10th of the month previous to publication. *Canada Crafts* published the first of every other month of February; April; June; August; October; and December. SASE. Sample copy $2; free writer's guidelines.

CANADA QUILTS, 360 Stewart Dr., Subdury, Ontario Canada P3E 2R8. (705)522-9211. Editor: Mary M. Conroy. Estab. 1973. Circ. 2,500. Newsletter published 5 times annually (February; April; June; September; and November). "Readers are mostly women who quilt as a hobby, teach quilting, or make quilts and quilted items for sale. Offset printed with photos, it is designed to provide a forum for exchange of information of ideas for quilters in Canada; US; UK; New Zealand; Australia; and West Germany. 2/3 of readership is Canadian." Buys first rights, but may reassign rights after publication. Considers articles on quilting marketing tips; how-to's; features on successful craftworkers and stitchery items in some categories. Length: 200-1,500 words. Pays $4-25; 2c/word. Also interested in photos and illustrations accompanying ms. Pays $1-3. Buys quilting and stitchery patterns. Pays $1-5. Buys approximately 15-20 articles/year. Buys approximately 15-20 patterns/year. "Christmas novelty items; gift items; decorations; etc. in quilting; patchwork; applique; needlepoint; crewel work; and related areas are needed by October." SASE. Sample copy $1.

CERAMIC INDUSTRY, 5 S. Wabash Ave., Chicago IL 60603. (312)372-6880. Editor: J.J. Svec. Estab. 1923. Circ. 7,000. Monthly ceramic manufacturing publication. Readers are ceramic manufacturers in glass; whitewares; porcelain; enamel; and electronic ceramics. "We publish know-how on production." Publication is copyrighted. Buys articles by assignment only. Pays $35/page. Sample copy $1.25.

CERAMIC SCOPE, Box 48643, Los Angeles CA 90048. (213)939-4821. Editor: Mel Fiske. Editor of Ceramic Articles: Victoria Crenson. Estab. 1964. Circ. 6,300. Monthly ceramic hobby marketing; technique; business; and education publication. Readers are ceramic hobby dealers (retailers); teachers; distributors; and manufacturers. Information in *Ceramic Scope* keeps them abreast of current marketing trends; legislative efforts; and economic developments. Buys all rights or first rights, but may reassign rights after publication. Considers articles on ceramic marketing tips; how-to's; and features on successful ceramic studios. Length: 1,000-2,500 words. Pays $100-200. Also interested in photos and illustrations accompanying ms. Buys approximately 1 article per issue. "Need material on Christmas merchandising by March 15 for special May Christmas selling issue." SASE. Free sample copy.

CERAMICS MONTHLY, Box 12448, Columbus OH 43212. (614)488-8236. Editor: Spencer L. Davis. Editor of Craft Articles: William C. Hunt. Estab. 1953. Circ. 45,000. Monthly (except July and August) craft marketing; technique; education; and hobby publication. Buys all rights. Considers articles on craft marketing tips; how-to's; and features on successful craftworkers. Length: 500-2,000 words. Pays $400 maximum. Also interested in photos and illustrations accompanying ms. Pays $7-14. Buys approximately 40-50 articles per year. SASE.

COBBLESTONE, Box 1128, Los Alamitos CA 90720. (213)438-3424. Editor: Janet Valentine. Editor of Craft Articles: Greg Evans. Estab. 1975. Circ. 5,000. Quarterly general art publication. Readers are "artists and we are here to provide information about all the arts." Buys first rights. Considers features on successful craftworkers. Length: 500-1,000 words. Pays $5-50. Also interested in photos and illustrations accompanying ms. Pays $5-50. Buys approximately 4 articles per year. SASE. Free sample copy and writer's guidelines.

CRAFT CONNECTION, Box 1182, Minneapolis MN 55440. Editor: Janet Koplos. Editor of Craft Articles: Jennifer A. Hamlin. Estab. 1975. Circ. 2,500+. Bimonthly communication organ sponsored by the Minnesota Crafts Council. Majority of readers are "full time professional craftspeople. The remainder are hobbyists and collectors plus many libraries and teachers. We are nontechnical, all media, and focus solely on the 12 Midwestern states. Issues address pre-selected themes. Recent topics have included jurying; marketing; crafts education; traditional crafts; and production of one-of-a-kind crafts. We publish interviews; calendar; art fair lists; and show announcements." Buys reprint rights. "We use the copyright symbol but are concerned only with credit on reprinting." Considers craft marketing tips; features on successful craftworkers; and investigative and analytical articles related to publication's theme. Length: 750-2,500 words. Pays $15-30; at present we do not pay for reviews. Also interested in b&w 5x7 or 8x10 photos accompanying ms. Pays $10 base fee plus $3/photo used. Buys approximately 3-4 articles per issue including freelance assignments. Most are commissioned with known freelancers or written by the editors. "We are particularly interested in locating people outside of Minnesota who will freelance on a regular basis." SASE. Free sample copy.

CRAFT HORIZONS of the American Crafts Council, 44 W. 53rd St., New York NY 10010. (212)977-8983. Editor: Rose Slivka. Estab. 1941. Circ. 40,000. Bimonthly craft technique and education publication. Readers are professional and amateur craftspeople, artists, teachers, architects, designers, decorators, collectors, connoisseurs and the general public. Covers all crafts and discusses the technology, the materials, and the ideas of the artists who do the work wherever it is being done throughout the world. Buys first rights, but may reassign rights after publication. Considers craft how-to's and features on successful craftworkers. Length: approximately 1,000 words. Pays $75-150. Also interested in photos accompanying ms. Pays $7.50 maximum. "Most articles are assigned and average about 9 features per issue." SASE. Free sample copies. "Prospective authors should familiarize themselves with past issues of the magazine and then submit queries."

CRAFT PUBLICATIONS, INC., 6553 Warren Dr., Norcross GA 30093. (404)449-8200. Product Manager: Cathy Bonds. Publisher craft instruction books. "We are interested in receiving material on any craft projects which might be applicable to a 'how-to' book. The payment for these projects varies with subject matter, degree of difficulty, and the number of projects required." Commissions ms. and buys ms. outright. Submit resume. SASE for ms. Reports in 4-8 weeks.

CRAFTNEWS, 346 Dundas St. W., Toronto, Ontario Canada M5T 1G5. (416)366-3551. Editor: Elizabeth Dingman. Estab. 1976. Circ. 3,000. Bimonthly craft marketing and educational newsletter. Readers are professional and amateur craftworkers. Considers craft marketing tips; features on successful craftworkers; services and commodities important to advancement of work; teaching, selling, and exhibiting opportunities open; and an exchange of information on those aspects of life and philosophy of benefit to craftworkers. Length: 200-500 words. Also interested in photos and illustrations accompanying ms.Payment varies. SASE. Sample copy $1. Published by Ontario Crafts Council.

THE CRAFTS REPORT, 1312 3rd Ave W., Seattle WA 98119. Editor: Michael Scott. Estab. 1975. Circulation: 3,800+. Monthly craft marketing publication. "Readers are professional craftspeople, educators, administrators, etc. We furnish news and information related to marketing, management and money matters as they affect craftspeople who produce to sell." Buys all rights or first rights, but may reassign rights after publication. Considers articles on craft marketing tips or features on successful craftworkers. Length: 100-1,000 words. Pays $10-100. Also interested in photos accompanying ms. Buys approximately 2-3 articles/issue. SASE. Free sample copy and writer's guidelines.

CRAFTSMAN, 346 Dundas St. W., Toronto, Ontario Canada M5T 1G5. (416)366-3551. Editor: Elizabeth Dingman. Estab. 1976. Circ. 3,000. Bimonthly craft marketing and educational publication. Readers are professional and amateur craftworkers. Considers craft marketing tips; features on successful craftworkers; services and commodities important to advancement of work; teaching, selling, and exhibiting opportunities open; and information on those aspects of life and philosophy of benefit to craftworkers. Length: 200-500 words. Payment varies. Also interested in photos and illustrations accompanying ms. SASE. Sample copy $1. Published by Ontario Crafts Council.

CREATIVE CRAFTS, Box 700, Newton NJ 07860. (201)383-3355. Editor: Sybil C. Harp. Estab. 1967. Circ. 65,000. Bimonthly hobby (some marketing) publication. Publishes 1 annual, *The Miniature Magazine*. Readers are serious adult hobbyists. "Our projects are not sophisticated in design but often challenging from a technical aspect. We are almost entirely how-to. Our readers are mostly women over 35. We want to give them new, appealing ideas and detailed, step by step instructions for executing them." Buys all rights. Considers craft how-to's. Length: 1,500 words average. Pays $50/page. Also interested in photos and illustrations accompanying ms. Pays $35 minimum. Buys 50-60 articles/year. "I am in need of articles on miniatures, especially fine miniature craftsmanship in the scale of 1"-1'. We feature a special miniature section in each issue." SASE. Sample copy $1; free writer's guidelines.

DECORATING AND CRAFT IDEAS, Box 2522, Birmingham AL 35201. Editor: Evelyn L. Brannon. Editor of Craft Articles: Jane Ford Mentzfus. Estab. 1970. Circ. 750,000+. Craft technique publication published 10 times annually. Readers are "intelligent, creative people who enjoy working with their hands to beautify their environment." Buys all rights. Considers craft how-to's. Pays $25-150. Occasionally interested in photos accompanying ms. Pays $25-100. "Virtually all our articles involve the use of a pattern and when we buy a story we buy the patterns." Buys 120+ articles per year. "Send submissions for Christmas in June or July." SASE. Free sample copy and writer's guidelines.

DENOVO, Box 12758. New Brighton MN 55112. Editor: Jill Hanna. Estab. 1977. Quarterly craft marketing, technique, education and visual arts publication. Readers are anyone interested in the visual arts from either a customer or patron aspect to those working in different medias; teaching; and running supply outlets, galleries, studios, and museums. Buys first rights, but may reassign rights after publication. Considers craft marketing tips and features on successful craftworkers. Length: 1,000 words. Pays $10. Also interested in photos and illustrations accompanying ms. Buys minimum of 15 articles per year. SASE. Sample copy $1.50; free writer's guidelines.

EARLY AMERICAN LIFE, Box 1831, Harrisburg PA 17105. (717)234-2674. Editor: Robert G. Miner. Estab. 1970. Circ. 275,000. Bimonthly publication. Buys all rights. Considers craft how-to's. Length: 1,500-3,000 words. Pays $75-300. Also interested in photos and illustrations accompanying ms. Payment depends on quality. Occasionally buys craft patterns. SASE.

PAT DEPKE INC., 20 W. Conron, Danville IL 61832. President: Patricia Depke. Publisher craft instruction books. "Books are soft back; generally 24-128 pages. All crafts welcomed. Books published under contract. Payment on royalty basis." Submit resume. SASE for ms. Reports in 4 weeks.

FIBERARTS, 3717 4th NW, Albuquerque NM 87107. (505)345-2530. Editor: Rob Pulleyn. Editor of Craft Articles: Linda Vozar. Estab. 1975. Circ. 15,000. Bimonthly craft information and technique publication. Readers are "women, well educated (92% college educated) professionals and semiprofessionals. Average income from fiber $1,323. 21% work in fiber full time; 42% part time; 88% classify themselves as 'fiber artist'; and 46% teach. For the person who is seriously involved in fiber (weaving, dyeing, soft sculpture, stitchery, clothing, basketry, etc.). We try to give our readers a feeling for what others are doing; how to get more out of their own work; and give them ideas and information." Buys all rights and reprint rights. Considers craft marketing tips; features on successful and/or good craftworkers; and techniques and various artists who use them. Length: 500-2,500 words. Pays $25 minimum. Also interested in photos and illustrations accompanying ms. Pays cost+. Buys 50-60 articles per year. "We publish 3 special issues a year covering particular topics. Contact us for specifics." SASE. Free sample copy and writer's guidelines.

FINE WOODWORKING, Box 355, 52 Church Hill Rd., Newtown CT 06470. (203)426-8171. Editor: John Kelsey. Estab. 1975. Circ. 100,000. Professional journal for small shop cabinetmakers published bimonthly. Readers are "serious amateur woodworkers and professional woodworkers who work alone or in small shops. We cover all aspects of high quality work, emphasizing design, technique, and making a living." Publication is copyrighted. Considers craft how-to's and features on successful craftworkers. Length: 600-5,000 words. Pays $25-800; $100/magazine page, prorated. Also interested in photos accompanying ms. Pays $10-200. Buys 100 articles per year. "Most of our articles come from cabinetmakers, not freelance writers." SASE. Free writer's guidelines.

THE GOODFELLOW REVIEW OF CRAFTS, Box 4520, Berkeley CA 94704. (415)845-7645. Editor: Christopher Weills. Editor of Craft Articles: Bette London and Susan Clark. Estab. 1973. Circ. 10,000. Bimonthly craft marketing, technique, and education publication. Readers are "composed of active craftspeople, both professional and part time, as well as members of the general public appreciative of American crafts." Buys first rights, but may reassign rights after publication; first North American serial rights; and reprint rights. "We encourage writers to market their stories in many different markets, even if similar material." Considers craft marketing tips; how-to's; features on successful craftworkers; and all facets of the crafts world, with emphasis on individuals. Length: 600-2,500 words. Pays $10-40. Also interested in photos and illustrations accompanying ms. Pay $5-10. Buys 10-12 articles per year. SASE. Free sample copy and writer's guidelines.

HUNTER PUBLISHING CO., Box 9533, Phoenix AZ 85068. (602)944-1022. Manager: Les Thomas. Craft book publisher. "To date we have published books on silk flowers and fiber arts. We are interested in reviewing ms dealing with craft subjects complete with original ideas; pictures; layout; etc." Books range from 24-52 pages. Submit resume and ms for review; write for personal interview. SASE. Reports in 2 weeks.

INTERWEAVE, 2938 N. County Rd. 13, Loveland CO 60537. (303)667-7936. Editor: Linda C. Ligon. Estab. 1975. Circ. 5,000. Quarterly marketing and technique publication. *Interweave* is a general interest magazine for people in weaving and related fiber crafts. We try to strike a balance between features on individuals doing interesting work and informational articles on technique, history and marketing. Articles for all levels of expertise." Buys first rights, but may reassign rights after publication. Considers craft marketing tips; how-to's; and features on successful craftworkers. Length: 2,500 words average. Pays $25; $5 for book reviews and other minor items. Also interested in photos and illustrations accompanying ms. Pays $5. Buys 4-6 articles/issue. SASE. Sample copy $2; free writer's guidelines.

LEISURE TIME PUBLISHING, 1615 E. Catalina, Phoenix AZ 85016. President: Robert Auffret. Publisher of craft instruction books. Buys 450 craft designs for publication annually. Pays minimum of $75. Send Polaroids and 1 set of sample instructions. Reports in 2 weeks.

MAKE IT WITH LEATHER, Box 1386, Fort Worth TX 76101. (214)335-8500. Editor: Earl Warren. Estab. 1965. Craft technique publication. "Readers are a cross-section of all levels of education, income, and skills. 60% men, 40% women. Large number of young people below 17 years of age. Average subscriber is above average in dollar amount spent for craft supplies." Buys all rights. Considers how-to's. Length: 2,000 words maximum. Pays $50-300 depending on patterns, photos, instructions, and quality of leather item. Also interested in photos and illustrations accompanying ms. Buys color transparencies for front cover. Buys patterns. SASE. Free sample copy and writer's guidelines.

NATIONAL NEEDLEWORK NEWS, 171 Guadalupe Dr., Sonoma CA 95476. Publisher and Editor: Sherry Baker. Estab. 1975. Circ. 10,865. Quarterly craft technique and education trade paper. Readers are "needlework shop owners and buyers; department managers and buyers for major chains; fabric store owners; yarn and craft shop owners; and a few consumers. Provides how-to's for running successful needlework store and new techniques for needlework." Buys first rights. Considers new needlework techniques only, oriental would be of special interest now. Length: 1-2 pages, double spaced. Pays $15-25. Also interested in photos and illustrations accompanying ms. Pays $5-10. Buys 15+ articles/year. SASE.

OCULAR, 1549 Platte St., Denver CO 80202. (303)458-6064. Editor: Eric Schwartz. Estab. 1976. Circ. 2,000. Quarterly directory of information for artists. Provides information and opportunities for the visual artist. Buys all rights. Considers features on successful craftworkers and is open to other possibilities. Length: 2,000-3,000 words. Pays $90-125 (rare). Also interested in photos and illustrations accompanying ms. Payment varies. "Buys very few articles now, but looking." SASE.

THE ORIGINAL ART REPORT, Box 1641, Chicago IL 60690. Editor: F. Salantrie. Estab. 1967. Monthly publication. Readers are art critics; museum trustees; collectors; artists; and gallery owners. Considers craftsmanship in the marketplace and in the art condition. Length: 1,000 words. Pays $5. SASE. Free sample copy and writer's guidelines.

THE RUG HOOKER, NEWS AND VIEWS, North St., Kennebunkport ME 04046. (207)967-3711. Editor: Joan Leith Moshimer. Estab. 1972. Circ. 5,000. Bimonthly rug-hooking craft technique, education, hobby, and woman's publication. "Our readers want help with all aspects of rug hooking, traditional as opposed to punch and latchet. Amusing stories; how-to designs; help on composition; and hooking fruit, flower, and pictorial designs. Dye formulas. Free designs to trace out of the magazines with tips for color planning." Buys all rights. Considers craft how-to's and features on successful craftworkers. Length: 500-3,000 words. Pays $5-30. Also interested in photos and illustrations accompanying ms. Pays $2-10. Buys craft patterns, occasionally. Pays $5-10. Buys 20 articles per year. Needs Christmas material by July 1 of previous year. SASE. Free sample copy.

SCHOOL ARTS, 50 Portland St., Worcester MA 01608. Editor: David Baker. Estab. 1901. Circ. 30,000. Monthly (except July and August) education publication. Buys all rights. Considers craft how-to's and features on successful craftworkers. Length: 500-1,500 words. Pays $25-100. Also interested in photos and illustrations accompanying ms. SASE. Free sample copy.

WEAVER'S NEWSLETTER, Box 259, Homer NY 13077. Co-editors: Cyril and Ora Koch. Estab. 1976. Circ. 5,300. Published monthly September-May. Readers are weavers; spinners; and fiber artists. "Provides news of trends in the field; notices of exhibits and competitions; major commissions; guild events; marketing information; legislation and government activities; research; equipment and book reviews." Buys all rights. Considers features on successful fiber craftworkers; academic programs in weaving; unusual collections; travel of interest to the weaver; health and safety tips for the weaver, spinner, and dyer. Length: 800-1,000 and 1,600-1,800 words. Pays $50-100. Buys 20 articles per year. SASE. Free sample copy.

WESTART, Box 1396, Auburn CA 95603. (916)885-3242, 885-0969. Editor: Jean L. Couzens. Estab. 1962. Circ. 7,700+. Semimonthly publication. Readers are artists, craftworkers, teachers, students and patrons of the arts. "We provide an overview of the West Coast art scene — current art news; information on competitions; and some features." Buys first North American serial rights. Considers general articles on crafts and trends. Length: 800 words. Pays 30c/column inch. Also interested in photos and illustrations accompanying ms. Buys 3-4 articles per year. SASE. Sample copies 50c.

THE WORKING CRAFTSMAN, 1290 Shermer, Box 42, Northbrook IL 60062. (312)498-0073. Editor: Marilyn Heise. Estab. 1971. Circ. 10,000. Quarterly (plus 1 special issue) craft marketing publication. Readers are professional and part time craftspeople; art teachers; craft shop owners; and hobbyists. Buys first rights, but may reassign rights after publication. Considers craft marketing tips and features on successful craftworkers. Pays $35. Also interested in photos and illustrations accompanying ms. Pays $5. "Inquire as to theme of special issue." SASE. Sample copy $2.25; free writer's guidelines.

Agents

Selling not only takes time away from producing your work but for some craftworkers it is also an unpleasant and difficult experience— pounding the pavements, endless phone calls, a sales "pitch." If this is your situation, the alternative is to find somebody who already has the connections and the sales experience— an agent.

But getting an agent is easier said than done. Since part of the agent's income depends on how much of your work he/she can sell, he/she will accept only the best work available. The agent will also expect reliability and production capacity in filling the orders he/she has sold. In effect, you don't hire an agent; he/she employs you.

Agent services are not free; an agent takes from 15-33% commission on the selling price. However, keep in mind that an agent taking 33%, but who is providing greater sales volume, is probably worth more to you than the agent claiming 15% but selling less of your work.

If you do decide to get an agent to represent you, get all agreements in writing. You'll want to include the following in a contract: What is the precise commission the representative will receive? Will it vary according to assignment? If the agent lands you one job with an agency or firm, will a commission be paid to him for future assignments from that account? Will the agent get a fee for every project you do regardless of who obtained the assignment? Leave nothing undiscussed, and don't sign anything you're not completely satisfied with.

Check out the agent; he'll be doing the same. Try to learn who his clients are, then contact them. Ask them how well he has sold their work. Look for a representative who has been with the same clients for several years, not one who has hopscotched from craftworker to craftworker.

Before you seriously start thinking about getting an agent, try to build up your sales and reputation on your own. The best way to do that is by making the most of the markets in this book. Chances are the agent you'll be working with tomorrow is using *Craftworkers Market* to find potential customers.

THE ARTESIAN WELL, 120 Franklin St., Cedar Grove NJ 07009. Contact: Judy or Bob Asdal. Craft representatives. Estab. 1976. Represents 30 craftworkers. Price range: $2-500; bestsellers: $10-50. Works on consignment and buys outright; commission is individually arranged. Retail price set by joint agreement. Reports in 3 weeks. Work may be shipped or hand-delivered. Heaviest wholesale buying time: summer and fall.
Acceptable Work: Considers batik; ceramics; glass art; leatherworking; metalsmithing; pottery; quilting; wall hangings; weavings; and woodcrafting. Finished and handmade production-line items; utilitarian and/or decorative.

FIRST ADDITIONS, 2920 N. Commonwealth, 4B, Chicago IL 60657. (312)248-1999. Contact: Sue Nechin. Representative. Estab. 1975. Bestsellers: $12-60 (wholesale). "I show samples to buyers. Craftworkers are paid for what is actually purchased by shops. I don't work on consignment." Craftworker sets his/her price; 20% commission is added; shop sets retail price. Requires exclusive area representation. Reports as soon as possible. Work may be shipped or hand-delivered. Dealer pays return shipping.
Acceptable Work: Considers batik; clothing; jewelry; leatherworking; needlecrafts; quilting; soft sculpture; and anything wearable, especially accessories. One-of-a-kind and handmade production-line wearable items; utilitarian and/or decorative.
Profile: "To my knowledge, no one else in the Chicago area is representing craftspeople in order to put high-fashion, one-of-a-kind handmade wearables into exclusive shops and boutiques, not craft galleries. Customers are young working women and up; no age limit. They are interested in being first with the latest and price is rarely an obstacle if something is exciting enough."
To Break In: "Makers of wearables should read *Women's Wear Daily*, especially on Fridays (accessories day) to keep up with the latest seasonal trends, shapes and colors. Accessories have to work with the clothing that is in the shops." Heaviest wholesale buying time: summer, fall and winter.

MOUNTAIN LAUREL, 82A Lemon Lane, Rhinebeck NY 12572. (914)876-7438. Contact: Laurel Burnstine Shelmandine. Represents 15-20 craftworkers. Sells work throughout the East Coast. "Basically I am looking for very high quality, well executed work that fits in the fine craft market. I also offer consultation services on bookkeeping methods, etc. for the craftworker and a referral service for galleries, specialty shops and some department stores."

ONE ART SERVICE, 790 Madison Ave., New York NY 10021. (212)249-4561. Director: Richard K. Larcada. Contact: Bill De Bar. Keeps information on artists (slides and photos) to convey to clients. 20-40% negotiable commission.

PEMA BROWNE LTD., 185 E. 85th St., New York City NY 10028. (212)369-1925. Contact: Pema or Perry Browne. Estab. 1966. Represents approximately 11 local craftworkers, working in a variety of media, to national and regional freelance markets. Works on 25-30% commission. Send photos or slides of work; "need a portfolio of at least 10-20 pieces representative of his or her work." SASE.

RITASUE SIEGEL AGENCY, 60 W. 55th St., New York NY 10019. (212)586-4750. Contact: Ritasue Siegel. Estab. 1969. Represents 400+ manufacturers from the US and Europe. Interested in hearing from craftworkers specializing in candlemaking, ceramics and jewelry. Employer pays agency fees. Send 20 nonreturnable 35mm slides mounted on cardboard. SASE.
Special Needs: Work should be of a "very high level of finish; realistic and traditional, as opposed to abstract; intricate and ornamental (cutesy too); and pertain to giftware, silverware, china and porcelain — mass markets."
To Break In: "Find out what sells best. Reproduce it. Gain acceptance as a source. Then introduce innovation. Always deliver what and when you promise. Keep careful records. Be businesslike. Take excellent photographs. Keep samples neat and clean."

WESTERN NORTH CAROLINA CRAFT FEDERATION, 131 S. Balsam St., Hazelwood NC 28738. (704)456-8079. Manager: Barbara Wood. Federation serving as a marketing agent. Estab. 1975. Represents 200 low income, elderly western North Carolina craftworkers. Price range: $1.75-260. Craftworker sets retail price. Reports as soon as possible. Work may be shipped or hand-delivered. Heaviest wholesale buying time: summer; best selling time: fall.
Acceptable Work: Considers clothing; dollmaking; leatherworking; needlecrafts; pottery;

quilting; wall hangings; weavings; and woodcrafting. Authentic handmade pieces; utilitarian and/or decorative.

WHAT'S NEW, 1900 S. Broadway, Los Angeles Mart #316, Los Angeles CA 90009. (213)479-5453. Contact: Steve Askin. Estab. 1970. Represents approximately 20 craftworkers, working in a variety of media, to shops and galleries in the US and Canada. Works on 20% commission—paid when artist is paid. Write with photos or slides of work to arrange interview. SASE.

Apprenticeships

If you find yourself wanting to begin a career in the crafts field, but not knowing which way to turn, you may want to consider working on a one-to-one basis with an experienced craftworker. The individuals and groups in this section are willing to work with interested beginners to teach them the creative and marketing skills that help talented individuals become professional craftworkers.

STEVE ALBAIR, 425 N. McArthur St., Macomb IL 61455. Works 30-45 hours a week in metalwork (jewelry). Consigns at shops/galleries. Will work with apprentices "strictly on an individual basis because my work is more on the order of an art form and has a limited marketability. I accept 1 apprentice at a time for 3 month periods."

ALETTA, Leonard Rd., Shutesbury MA 01072. (413)256-0174. Works 35-45 hours a week in ceramics: stoneware and flameware. Sells from own studio; sells at shows; consigns work at shops/galleries; sells work outright to shops. Will work with 1 apprentice on a 3 month trial period, stay for 1 year total. Applicaions should be *written* in a letter of application. Work for approximately 20 hours per week. Studio space available.

FARIS ABDULLAH ASHKAR, Box 274, Swannonoa NC 28778. (704)686-5353. Works 15-20 hours a week in wood (Arabic calligraphy, chandeliers, cabinetmaking, model building); macrame materials (plant hangers, sculpture, wall hangings); cloth (clothing design and execution); and design concepts for a variety of media. Sells from own studio; sells at shows; consigns work at shops/galleries; sells work outright to shops; and sells at craft fairs. "Will negotiate with prospective apprentice concerning what he wants to learn."

KEN AND KATHLEEN DALTON, Box 95, Coker Creek TN 37314. (715)261-2157. Works 40-60 hours a week in white oak, bark, vine, and handspun wood basketry and wood carving. Sells from own studio; sells at shows; and sells work outright to shops. Interested in hearing from craftworkers looking for apprenticeships.

WILLIAM R. DERREVERE, 1347 E. 19th St., Tulsa OK 74120. (918)749-6032. Works 30-40 hours a week in jewelry and metalsmithing. Sells from own studio; sells at shows; and consigns work at shops/galleries. "If an individual enjoys the way I work (being concerned with form, surfaces, and manipulating of materials) then I would be interested in working with such an individual. The length of time would depend upon the individual and what they want to learn and how fast they pick up new ideas. Fees and payments would depend upon the person's situation. The main concern would be learning and sharing information, not capital gains."

LYNN EARNEST, Star Rt. 1, Box 128, Griffithsville WV 25521. (304)524-7578. Works 10-16 hours a day in batik. Sells from own studio; sells at shows (exhibits one-man or more); and sells some work outright to shops. Will accept apprentice for 6-9 months. MFA instruction. Can obtain college credit. Must pay for room and board and hours of instruction. Studio use.

BABETTE S. FARIAN, 34-48 81st St., Jackson Heights NY 11372. (212)424-0208. Works 24-32 hours a week in ink; watercolors; acrylics; and textile design. Sells from own studio; sells at shows; consigns work through galleries; works in textile and greeting card studios; and freelances. "I have never had an apprentice but I have had students. If they come to me it would have to be 1 at a time; $5/hour, 3 hour limit. If I would go to a student it would be $30/3 hours. I can teach painting; drawing; or textile design and give lectures and demonstrations."

JUDITH FIRMEE, 4033 Glenbrook Dr., Arlington TX 76015. (817)265-1906. Works 40+ hours a week in spinning; weaving; and fiber arts. Sells from own studio; sells at shows; sells work outright to shops/galleries; sells work to interior design firms; and does special commission work. "My students pay a fee of $5/2 hour sessions. An apprentice may provide work instead of money being exchanged. A letter of application should be sent with name, address, phone, and prior experience with the media involved. An apprentice may work as long as desired over a 2 month period, about 1 day per week or 2-3 half days. My space is limited but I could accommodate up to 4 aides, 1 at a time."

KEN FRIEDMAN, 6361 Elmhurst Dr., San Diego CA 92120. (714)583-7935. Work schedule varies according to other commitments (also lectures and writes). "I make objects which are in essence shrines and icons, also ritual tools and implements for use in performance activities. I am an artist who is also a critic and sociologist." Sells from own studio; sells at shows; consigns work at galleries; and is commissioned for special projects. "Each apprentice works with me individually for as long as the apprentice and I determine. In terms of specific programs, the question is what the apprentice needs and wants. A few days learning about how I make my shrines and rituals is very different from serious study in the sociology of developing a career or research into cross-cultural ritual object making. Payment is by negotiation. I suggest that a potential apprentice initially read some writings, study my biography and career in various reference books, and be prepared to work hard. I stress both actual art making and discourse and thinking about art. I am not interested in apprentices who are only interested in their own work or medium. My apprentices also have the option to earn college degrees by studying with me through International College, either for BA, MA in studio or Ph.D. in comparative arts and sociology of art. To enroll in the degree program all college entrance requirements must be met and tuition paid."

JOEL GODSTON, 87 Meadowgate, Wethersfield CT 06109. (203)563-4335. Works up to 15 hours a week in metal (welding); mosiac (glass); and wood. Sells at shows; consigns work at shops/galleries; and sells work outright at shops. "I've never conducted an apprentice program but feel it could be a summer project of 2-3 months, 1-2 times a week for 2-4 hours on a 1 to 1 basis with welding."

GRETE BODOGAARD HEIKES, Rt. 1, Box 20, Vermillion SD 57079. (605)624-3056. Works 30 hours a week in fiber. Sells from own studio; sells at shows; works by commission; and sells through coop gallery. "So far I had a girl from Finland for 1 year and a girl from Norway for 1 year. They both were weavers. I pay tuition at USD for drawing classes and the apprentice lives with us on the farm. They work 25 hours a week on my work and have time for their own work. I spent 4 years in an apprentice program in Denmark and felt that was a good number of years. 1 apprentice per year for my studio, maybe later 2."

DAVID HOFFMAN, 1601 Trumansburg Rd., Ithaca NY 14850. Works 60 hours a week in wood. Sells from own studio and at shows; consigns work and sells outright to shops/galleries; and designs custom furniture and interiors. Will work with up to 3 apprentices for 1-6 month periods. "Payment negotiated on basis of experience. Make application by letter."

DENNIS L. JENKINS, 505 W. Mifflin St., Madison WI 53703. (608)255-2875. Works 60 hours a week in printmaking; etching; silkscreen; and painting. Sells from own studio; sells at shows; consigns work at shops/galleries; sells work outright to shops; and sells work to interior design firms. Will work with apprentice for 1 year. 1 person accepted. Apply by letter or in person with resume and portfolio. No fees or payments.

PHYLLIS JOHNS, Rt. 1, Box 33, Grayslake IL 60030. Works 20-30 hours a week in stoneware pottery. Sells from own studio; sells at shows; wholesales work at shops/galleries; and sells at home parties. Will work with 1 apprentice. Application must be in writing. Small payment or in exchange for board and room. "I'm moving to Connecticut and studio will be there. Mail will be forwarded."

MEADOW-JEROME JOHNSON, 2390 Mix Canyon Rd., Vacaville CA 95688. (707)446-3896. Directors of Mix Canyon Foundation for the Unusual Arts. Jerome fabricates in aluminum, wood and non ferrous metal; builds large outdoor sculptures; paints in acrylics; and produces collage. Meadow works in silver and Plexiglas; colored pencil; fiberglas; clay; and soft sculpture. Wholesales ceramics and soft sculpture to shops; interior design firms; and national retail outlets. Student apprenticeship program is being developed through the Foundation as a supplement to existing teaching programs in the San Francisco Bay Area and Northern Valley. The program will be directed toward students with a minimum of 3 years of art training or its equivalent and will be chosen on their media interests and technical experience. A modest tuition from students participating in the 4-6 week program will cover food and lodging. Write for more information.

CHRISTOPHER M. JUPP, 407 N. Race, Urbana IL 61801. Works 50 hours a week in various metals — gold, silver, brass, copper and pewter. Sells from own studio and at shows, and consigns work at shops/galleries. "I have no particular [apprenticeship] program, but I would be open to suggestions and offers."

JOHN H. KILLMASTER, 2723 N. 36th St., Boise ID 83703. (208)342-5935. Teaches enameling 6-8 hours a week to college level students and works 15-20 hours a week in porcelain enamels fired on steel or copper. Usually large scale, i.e. murals; panels; shaped forms; and sculptural and fountain forms. "Most of my work has been commissions or the result of competitive awards outside this area. I could arrange in the summer a 4-5 week session for at least 5 apprentices working on steel, developing murals, or 3-D forms for exterior applications. Interested persons should contact me. Costs would involve supplies and $5/hour working in the studio with my equipment and under my supervision. Apprentices could campout in summer on my land. They would have to bring their own tent, etc. and board out. There would be ample opportunity to enjoy Idaho's mountains, water, and sun."

FRANK ANDREW KIRBUS, 6256 Highland Rd., Highland Heights OH 44143. (216)442-3211. Works in metal. Sells from own studio; consigns work at shops/galleries; lectures and conducts workshops in mobiles and metal sculpture; and sells work outright to shops. Will work with apprentice. Write for more information.

KAREL MIKOLAS, Rt. 1, Studio 131, Slatington PA 18080. Works 40-50 hours a week in glass in combination with other materials (sculpture). Formerly worked in wood and bronze. Sells from own studio; consigns work at shops/galleries; and works on commission. Will work with apprentice on individually-arranged basis.

GARY W. MILLER-GOLDSMITH, 6 Watrous Lane, Milford CT 06460. (203)878-1112. Works 55 hours a week in gold; silver; and precious stones. Sells from own studio; consigns work at shops/galleries; and sells work outright to shops. Will work with apprentice "ages 14-25 on a 7 year program, 4 year program, 8 hour day, 5 day week, $4,000/year payable quarterly in advance with job placement. There are 2 openings for 1979."

JAMES C. MYFORD, 327 State St., Grove City PA 16127. (412)458-9672. Works 20-25 hours a week in aluminum sculpture. Sells some from own studio; sells at shows; consigns work at shops/galleries; and does large outdoor commissions. Will work with apprentice "probably 9 months or 1 year program. 1 at a time. Most likely worked out through grant or something similar."

NORTH CAROLINA DEPARTMENT OF CULTURAL RESOURCES, Summer Intern Program, North Carolina Arts Council, Raleigh NC 27611. Offers 3 summer internships in arts administration. Must have 4 year college degree, strong administrative and business abilities, and wide knowledge and appreciation of the arts. Preference will be given to North Carolina residents or those with close ties to the state. Also desirable is the ability to accept employment in September if positions should be available. Write for applicaton; application deadline is March 1.

NORTHERN KINGDOM PRINTWORKS, 44 Central St., Bangor ME 04401. (207)942-7245. Works 50-70 hours a week in silk screen printing; art prints; cards; and artistic T-shirts. Sells at shows; consigns work at galleries; and sells work outright to shops. Will work with apprentice on unstructured basis. Studio is small. Pay or fee is negotiable.

ALBERT PALEY, 335 Aberdeen St., Rochester NY 14619. (716)328-7533, 654-8244 (studio). Works 40 hours a week in jewelry (gold, silver, stones) and blacksmithing (architectural metal work and sculpture). Sells from own studio; sells at shows; sells work outright to shops; and sells work to interior design firms. "In the past I have had 3 NEA Master-Apprenticeship Grants in my blacksmithing studio. All worked extremely well for me and apprentices. Please contact."

WILLIAM REYNOLDS, 711 Front St., Marietta OH 45750. (614)373-3750. Works 20-40 hours a week in wood and metal plus research time in historical aspects of the Pennsylvania rifle. Sells from own studio and sells at shows. Will work with aapprentice "1 month in studio work; apprentice will receive 20 hours per week instruction; 30-40 hours per week on his own work. 1 apprentice at a time. Fees arranged on experience; living quarters can be reasonably arranged."

PAUL H. SALES, 7 Howland St., Plymouth MA 02360. Works full-time in wood. Sells from own studio; at shows; consigns work at shops/galleries; and sells work to interior design firms. "Length of apprenticeships vary, depending on what the apprentice is looking for. Application should be made directly to the studio. Fees and payments can be worked out with application."

ANNA SALIBELLO, Jockey Hollow Rd., Bernardsville NJ 07924. (201)766-3577. Works 20-40 hours a week in salt glazed ceramics. Sells from own studio; sells at shows; consigns work at shops/galleries; and sells work outright to shops. Will work with 1 apprentice for 6 months minimum time. "No money to be exchanged; payment is made by agreed upon exchange of work time for free use of studio; clay; kiln; glazes; and lessons. Application by mail preferred but phone acceptable as a preliminary."

C. R. SCHIEFER, Rt. 3, Box 417, Martinsville IN 46151. (317)342-6211. Works full time in stone sculpture, limestone and marble. Sells from own studio; sells at shows; sells work outright to shops; and sells some work to interior design firms. "I have no formal apprentice program but I have allowed some men to live with me for a week or so for work provided and let them work alongside me to learn the use of an air hammer with limestone and to learn sanding; cutting; and finishing work."

CHARLES C. SCOTT, Box 213, 934 Mineral Rd., Glenville WV 26351. (304)462-7186. Works 30 hours a week in pottery (stoneware and porcelain); painting; and photography. Sells from own studio; sells at shows; sells work outright to shops; and displays at competitive art exhibitions and one-man shows. Will work with pottery apprentice. "The apprentice should have the basic skills of throwing functional pottery and the desire to further his skills and to learn the operation of a pottery shop; to market; and to exhibit and demonstrate his craft at fairs. He would be required to assist in summer pottery workshops at my studio. The studio has 1,250+ square feet which includes living accommodations for 2 people. The shop has 3 potter's wheels, 2 Gilmore looms; some machinery; and a blacksmith shop in another building. I would accept 1 apprentice, a young married couple, or 2 persons who are of high moral character. Living accommodations would be provided in exchange for work. Length of stay would be commensurate with the desire of learning. There would be a profit sharing of all wares made and sold by the apprentice. Applicants should send letter; slides; and resume for screening. Applicants considered must have personal interview."

STANLEY SPRECHER, 477 Abbottsford, Philadelphia PA 19144. (215)438-6390. Works 24-40 hours a week in metal craft. Sells from own studio; sells at shows; consigns work at shops/galleries; and works in craft with mentally disturbed people. Will work with 10 apprentices (teenager and up and handicapped people) at 1 time if in Philadelphia area. Fees would depend on what medium, hours, and equipment.

KAREN L. STONER, Box 1447, Orient WA 99160. Works 45-60 hours a week (depending upon season and fair schedules) in ceramics (functional pottery). Sells from own studio and shows; consigns work and sells outright at shops/galleries; and sponsors private pot selling parties. Will work with 1 apprentice at any given time for "any span of time from 1 month to a year or more, mostly depending upon the needs of the apprentice. Some experience necessary; at least 1 or 2 college courses or equivalent experience, and must have basic throwing skills." No payment, so apprentice must be able to support self. Free housing available. Write, explaining background and reasons for wanting to be an apprentice.
Profile: "I have been making a living by producing and selling crafts for the past 8 years— even put myself through a private university graduate school selling pots."

STUDIOS WEST — ENCINITAS, 167 Saxony Rd., Encinitas CA 92024. (714)753-8186. Director: Ralph Ritchie. Gallery Manager: Tanya Vint. Studio/gallery/sculpture garden. Estab. 1969. "Now and then we invite a trained, young, promising person to work with us for about a year to learn the details and survival aspects of working as an independent creative craftworker. We are not a school in the sense that we have students and classes, but everyone here contributes and benefits from the learning process. We rarely respond [to inquiries] unless in person visit or SASE."

Associations & Organizations

You're absolutely certain the piece of jewelry manufactured by a large costume jewelry company infringes upon the design you've had copyrighted, but with no funds of your own how can you fight a company that size?

A project for outdoor metal sculpture has been growing in your mind, and you're positive it would not only contribute to your career but would also enhance your community. Unfortunately, you don't know where to turn to make your dream a reality.

As a craftworker you enjoy the independence of working on your own, but there are times when you need the company and support of others who share your professional interests.

Where do you turn for help in situations like these?

We offer you the Associations & Organizations section of this book with more than 200 listings of groups that can help you find the answers to these and other problems and needs that you face daily as a craftworker. Some are designed specifically to give craftworkers assistance, while others are simply organizations where craftspeople can get together to discuss and act upon common goals.

Alabama

ALABAMA ASSEMBLY OF COMMUNITY ARTS COUNCILS, 500 East Blvd., Suite 119, Montgomery AL 36109. (205)272-5175. Executive Director: Marlo Bussman. Estab. 1974. Members: 45 community arts councils. Open to any member of a local art council in Alabama. Board meets quarterly; total membership meets annually. Organization's purpose is to "serve community arts councils; provide assistance; coordinate activities; assist statewide arts organizations; and to be a clearinghouse. Membership not open to craftspersons; craftspersons benefit from our services through local arts councils."
Activities: Publishes monthly newsletter; holds statewide conferences and joint conferences with statewide arts organizations and community councils; and sponsors an annual regional conference.

ALABAMA STATE COUNCIL ON THE ARTS, 449 S. McDonough, Montgomery AL 36130. (205)832-6758. Programs Coordinator: Cherie E. Kelly. Sponsors Artists-in-Schools Programs and grants to individuals and craft organizations working in any craft discipline. Offers residencies with salary of $1,080 per month and grants of $2,500-5,000. Available to craftworkers with arts degree and good exhibition record. To apply send resume and 10 slides of work. Deadline for application: March 1.

ATMORE COUNCIL OF FINE ARTS, 617 S. Carney St., Atmore AL 36502. (205)368-5933. Treasurer: Rev. Thomas Powell. Estab. 1975. Members: 100. Open to any citizen of Atmore and vicinity. Meets monthly to promote artistic awareness and cultural education. Sponsors musical presentations; theater; and arts and craft exhibits. Write for membership.

COFFEE COUNTY ARTS ALLIANCE, Box 848, Enterprise AL 36330. Membership Secretary: Mark Holt. Estab. 1974. Members: 75. Open to all. Meets monthly from September-May to promote the arts in the area. Write for membership information if residing near Enterprise.
Activities: "We put on a music and drama series each year and sponsor an arts festival in May, where artists of all types, for a fee, may display their work and offer it for sale."

DECATUR ART GUILD, Box 662, Decatur AL 35602. President: F.A. France. Estab. 1967. Members: 140. Open to all. Meets monthly to educate and promote arts and crafts in the area. Publishes newsletter; sponsors annual "Art in the Park," a bimonthly arts and crafts show; and holds monthly art or craft program. Write for membership; $5 annual dues.

GREATER BIRMINGHAM ARTS ALLIANCE, Box 2152, Birmingham AL 35201. (205)251-1228. Director: Jack Horlacher. Estab. 1971. Members: 300 individuals, 65 organizations. Open to any cultural organization in the area; individual members are actually financial contributors. Meets monthly to "serve as a clearing house and information center for cultural activities; to assist groups and individuals in getting grants; to promote the visual arts through our gallery and juried exhibition; and to assist member organizations with publicity and promotion."

Activities: Sponsors 3 annual juried exhibitions, mini-concerts, seminars, workshops, classes, and monthly gallery exhibitions of work by artists (not necessarily local); and publishes quarterly newsletter and monthly calendar. "We maintain an artists' file and mailing list for artists and craftspeople in the Southeastern region. Artists and craftsmen may submit their names and addresses and information about their media."

NORTHEAST ALABAMA CRAFTSMEN'S ASSOCIATION, Box 1113, West Station, Huntsville AL 35807. (205)881-6186. Membership Chairman: Ann Morton. Estab. 1973. Members: 200+. Open to all "interested in the advancement; preservation; and promotion of crafts. Each person must have a legitimate craft (by our definition) and all active members must reside within a 100 mile radius of Huntsville, Alabama." Meets monthly to promote the study; appreciation; preservation; and enjoyment of handicrafts. Publishes monthly newsletter; sponsors 2 annual craft shows, workshops, monthly instructional programs at meetings, and craft demonstrations in local schools. Write for membership.

PORT CITY CRAFTSMEN, INC., Box U-1028, Mobile AL 36688. President: Melaine Mastin. Sponsors scholarship for individual working in any craft discipline. Offers $125 scholarship quarterly to University of Southern Alabama student majoring or minoring in recreation and leisure studies. To apply contact University of South Alabama, Department of HPER.

Alaska

KETCHIKAN ARTS AND CRAFTS GUILD, c/o Louise Kern, Western Arts and Crafts Guild, Box 6572, Ketchikan AK 99901. (907)225-4810. Estab. 1965. Members: 20-30. Open to all. Meets monthly. Sponsors annual art show. Attend any meeting for membership.

OOMINGMAK, Musk Ox Producers Co-operative, 604 H St., Anchorage AK 99501. (907)272-9225. Director: John Teal Jr. Estab. 1969. Members: 130. Open to worker or producer in connection with the breeding and raising of musk ox, the production or manufacture of textile products from the underwool of the musk ox, or in the research and development of designs and uses for the underwool of the musk ox. A member must be elected by vote of the majority of the board of directors. Meets yearly and as needed "to cultivate the musk ox for his underwool and to produce products from the wool." Sponsors workshops and publishes newsletter.

Arizona

ARIZONA COMMISSION ON THE ARTS AND HUMANITIES, 6330 N. 7th St., Phoenix AZ 85014. (608)271-5882. Visual Arts Coordinator: Deborah Whitehurst. Sponsors Artists-in-Schools programs; grants; and technical assistance grants for individuals and craft organizations working in any craft discipline. Offers grants for specific projects to nonprofit state organizations, that have cash or in-kind match. "Currently 2 out of 4 Artists-in-Schools are craftspeople — 1 potter; 1 weaver." To apply write letter with brief description of project and/or organization and brief budget. Deadline for application: June 1. Publishes monthly bulletin.

ARTS COMMUNITY ASSOCIATION OF ARIZONA, Box 41600, Tucson AZ 85717. (602)327-2787. Director: John Zeeb. Estab. 1977. Members: 200. Open membership. Meets bimonthly to "share information; promote tourism by developing arts attraction in the state; to promote development in the state by making it attractive via the arts." Publishes a monthly newsletter, *The Arts in Arizona*, carrying news of interest to artists and audiences (i.e. news of classes, auditions, competitions and art show registrations, calendars of events, etc.)." Mail check for $5 for 1 year membership; $8 for 2 year membership. A form will be sent in the newsletter."

THE NATIONAL STANDARDS COUNCIL OF AMERICAN EMBROIDERERS, 8601 E. MacKensie, Scottsdale AZ 85251. Public Relations Chairman: Mrs. Richard Bessom. Conducts a correspondence school and sponsors seminars for individuals working in needlecrafts and soft sculpture. Sponsors a biennial exhibit for embroiderers 18 or older. Publishes *The Flying Needle.*

PIMA COUNTY PARKS AND RECREATION DEPARTMENT, 1204 W. Silverlake Rd., Tucson AZ 85713. (602)792-8815. Arts Director: John Zeeb. Crafts Director: Carolyn Lenz. Sponsors Artists-in-Schools programs and employment for individuals working in any craft discipline. Offers hourly wages of $3-5.70. Available to craftworkers "with skill in craft that's needed at the time. Most employees are college graduates; many have had graduate work. Must be personable and willing to do a certain amount of record keeping." To apply request a "Parks and Recreation application from Pima County Personnel Department, 151 W. Congress, Tucson AZ 85701. Fill out 2 copies and send 1 to Personnel and 1 to Carolyn Lenz, Crafts Supervisor. At position applied for, write Rec. Spec I."

WOMANKRAFT, Box 4694, Tucson AZ 85719. Treasurer: Ann Bannard. Estab. 1974. Members: 20. Membership as artist-craftswoman is open to any woman who is interested in the purposes of Womankraft and who can, in the judgment of the existing membership, make a positive contribution to the organization. Supporting membership open to all. Meets biweekly to "educate the public to the quality art of local women and to aid artist — craftwomen in becoming professionals by sharing technical knowledge and the creative enthusiasm of its members." Sponsors workshops; demonstrations; performances; and gallery shows. Write for memberhip; $15, Artist-Craftswoman fee; $10, Supporting.

Arkansas

ARKANSAS STATE ARTS AND HUMANITIES, Continental Building, Suite 500, Markham and Main, Little Rock AR 72201. (501)371-2539. Director of Education: Carol Gaddy. Sponsors Artists-in-Schools programs and grants to individuals and craft organizations working in batik; candlemaking; ceramics; glass art; jewelry; leatherworking; macrame; metalsmithing; needlecrafts; pottery; soft sculpture; weavings; and woodcrafting. Available to craftworker of high quality to work. To appy contact office. Deadline for application: March.

OZARK FOOTHILLS ARTS AND CRAFTS ASSOCIATION, Box 140, Mountain View AR 72560. (501)269-3896. Director: James H. Sanders III. Nonprofit tax exempt organization. Sponsors workshops and provides marketing information for individuals working in all materials. Offers fibers workshop; has compiled a Regional Crafts Documentary; and holds a wood workshop. Participants must be producing craftspeople in the state of Arkansas who pass standards set by the review committee; present 5 pieces of work; and pay $5 in dues annually. To apply work with/through the Association in its program development. Publishes bimonthly Guild Newsletter.

California

ADVOCATES FOR THE ARTS, UCLA School of Law, 405 N. Hilgard, Los Angeles CA 90049. (213)825-3309. Adminstrator: Audrey Greenberg. Estab. 1974. Members: 60+. Open to lawyers. Organization's purpose is to "provide free legal assistance to visual and performing artists and art organizations who otherwise would be unable to afford counsel." Sponsors legal semiars; research into funding sources for community art; and research in arts-related topics and historic preservation, copyright, contracts, libel, etc. For assistance write with statement of problem; statement of financial need in order to qualify for free legal help; and name and contact phone number.

ANTELOPE VALLEY ARTS COUNCIL, Box 2811, Lancaster CA 93534. (805)942-0100. Membership Chairperson: Beryl Amspoker. Estab. 1974. Members: 10 organizations, 55 individuals. "Members must be artists or arts patrons with an interest in promoting the cultural development of Antelope Valley." Meets monthly "to promote the creative human spirit in the people of Antelope Valley." Write for membership.
Activities: Publishes monthly newsletter and cultural calendar; distributes art directory; sponsors annual juried art show and informational workshops; maintains a library of art publications; and serves as a political spokesman for the arts.

ARTS COUNCIL OF BAKERSFIELD, Box 1244, Bakersfield CA 93302. (805)324-9000. President: Gretchen Reinecke. Estab. 1977. Members: 50 organizations, 50 individuals. Meets monthly to promote the arts in the Bakersfield area. For membership send $5 to above address if individual; $10 for arts related nonprofit organizations.
Activities: Publishes monthly newsletter and calendar of events; sponsors arts symposiums, informational workshops; and sends *State of the Arts*, publication of Information and Services Division of the California Arts Council, to members monthly.

CENTER FOR THE VISUAL ARTS, 1333 Broadway, Oakland CA 94612. (415)451-6300. Resource Aide: Rita Gardner. Estab. 1973. Members: 600. Open to established or emerging artists. The organization is a nonprofit arts service whose main focus is a Slide Registry with

10,000+ slides, together with a data bank. Sponsors shows; workshops; newsletters; biographical file; photography services; studio listings; and legal service. Write for application and information.

COUNCIL OF ARTS, Greater San Jose Area, 123 S. 3rd St., San Jose CA 95113. (408)279-1131. Contact: Membership Chairman. Estab. 1969. Members: 80+ organizations, many individuals. Open to all. Meets monthly "to promote appreciation; understanding; and support for the arts in a large metropolitan area. To improve communications between audience and artist." Sponsors seminars, workshops, and photo competition; publishes art magazines and calendar of cultural events. Call or write for membership application; $15 annual dues, organizations; $10 annual dues, individuals.

DIABLO ALLIANCE FOR THE ARTS, 321 Gold Club Rd., Pleasant Hill CA 94523. (415)685-1230. Director: John T. Miller. Estab. 1976. Members: 120 groups, 50 individuals. Open to any nonprofit arts organization in Central Contea Costs County and to any individual. Meets as needed to disseminate information regarding the arts and to promote local arts groups. Publishes monthly newsletter and calendar of events and organizes arts festival. Write with $5 for individual membership.

ENAMEL GUILD: WEST, Box 721, La Jolla CA 92037. (714)454-0595. President: Kay Whitcomb. Sponsors juried exhibitions; workshops; special programs; and prizes for individuals and organizations working in enameling. Offers 2 scholarships per workshop to work as aid for maestro-teacher. Available to all with interest in medium. To apply send 2 references to prove need. Deadline for application: April. Publishes newsletter with latest information for exhibitions; group purchases; program data; and board meeting decisions.

THE OAKLAND MUSEUM ART DEPARTMENT, 1000 Oak St., Oakland CA 94607. (415)273-3005. Contact: Hazel Bray. Museum gallery/archives of California art. Estab. 1916. Represents 200 California and California-related craftworkers. Considers all crafts. All styles; utilitarian and/or decorative. Collects art, doesn't sell it. Buys outright and receives extended loans and gifts/donations. Work may be shipped or hand-delivered. Dealer usually pays insurance for exhibited work.
Profile: "Every single artifact receives museum standard handling and packing, installation and respect. We serve the nation and the world on behalf of California artists and art."

OTIS ART ISTITUTE OF LOS ANGELES COUNTY, 2401 Wilshire Blvd., Los Angeles CA 90057. (213)387-5288. Financial Aid Officer: Judith Lymburner. Sponsors grants; scholarships; and work-study program to individuals working in ceramics and pottery. Awards are based on financial need; minority scholarships are based on academic achievement. Available to craftworkers who have completed 60 semester units at an accredited college or university, including 24 semester units in general studies; 6 semester units in history or survey of art; and a minimum of 30 semester units in studio art. "After applying for admission to the Institute financial aid applications can be filled out; all necessary forms are available at the financial aid office." Deadline for application: February 1.

ROHNERT PARK CULTURAL ARTS CORPORATION, 6750 Commerce Blvd., Rohnert Park CA 94928. Contact: President. Estab. 1965. Members: 15. Open to all with an "interest in the arts; in the community cultural growth; and a willingness to give service to the community to allow expansion for its citizens." Meets monthly to "expand the cultural and aesthetic awareness in the city; to support groups willing to build on that premise; and to advise city council on aesthetic principles." Sponsors art shows, school programs, and annual festival; publishes quarterly newsletter. "Membership is open to Rohnert Park citizens and they may obtain membership by paying $3 to the corporation."

SANTA CRUZ ASSOCIATION OF ARTISTS AND CRAFTSPEOPLE, 1001 Center St., Santa Cruz CA 95060. (408)425-0648. Provides marketing information sales and display space; and slide index artists registry to individuals working in any discipline. Available to all living in Santa Cruz County. Write for information.

Colorado

CARBONDALE COUNCIL ON ARTS & HUMANITIES, Box 174, Carbondale CO 81623. (303)963-2798. Director: Laurie Loeb. Estab. 1972. Members: 86. Open to all. Meets monthly "to promote and encourage the arts and integrate them into the total life of the community." Write for brochure.

Activities: Publishes quarterly newsletter of community functions, available sources of funding and other activities; and sponsors annual craft fair, concerts, dance programs, films, lectures and workshops.

NATIONAL CARVERS MUSEUM FOUNDATION, Woodcarver Rd., Monument CO 80132. (303)481-2656. President: Harry Meech. Provides marketing information and instruction to individuals and organizations working in woodcrafting and woodcarving. Available to all. Write for application.

Connecticut

CONNECTICUT COMMISSION ON THE ARTS, 340 Capitol Ave., Hartford CT 06106. (203)566-4770. Contact: Grants or Artists-in-Schools Program. Sponsors Artists-in-Schools programs and grants for individuals and organizations working in any craft discipline. "Send letter of intent, or call the Commission, and discuss your needs. You will then be instructed how to make formal application."

CONNECTICUT GUILD OF CRAFTSMEN, INC., Box 209, Manchester CT 06040. (203)646-8577. Executive Director: Kate Hull. Provides marketing information to individuals and organizations working in any craft discipline. Write. Publishes newsletter and CGC Special Edition.

EAST HARTFORD FINE ARTS COMMISSION, c/o Town Hall, Main St. E., East Hartford CT 06108. Members: 15. Membership by mayor's appointment. "We are a town commission." Meets monthly to further fine arts.

GREENWICH ARTS COUNCIL, 101 W. Putnam Ave., Greenwich CT 06830. (203)622-7932. Director of Adminstration: Nancy Landon. Estab. 1973. Members: 700. Open to all with interest in the arts. Board of directors meets monthly to "promote; develop; and coordinate all arts in Greenwich. We are an information and resource bureau for the arts from New York to Boston. For membership send $5. We maintain a 'Talent Bank' of available artists. If you wish to be listed, please ask for a 'Talent Bank Form.'"

HANDWEAVERS GUILD OF AMERICA, Box 7-374, 65 La Salle Rd., West Hartford CT 06107. (203)233-5124. Liaison Director: Sue Brander. Sponsors scholarships for craftworker working in weaving. Offered in 1977 18 $1,000 scholarships; amounts vary from year to year. Available to students enrolled in an accredited school in the US; money may be used only for furthering education in fiber arts. To apply request scholarship form. Deadline for application: March 1.

NEW ENGLAND ARTISTS AND CRAFTSMEN'S GUILD INC., Box 142, Enfield CT 06082. Executive Director: Mr. McGibbon. Estab. 1976. Members: 1,600. Open to all interested in arts and crafts. Meets annually to "bring together artists and craftsmen as well as people in the community to create and foster an interest in all phases of artistic expression and endeavors." Publishes a newsletter; offers classes and seminars; and provides legal referrals and marketing assistance to members.
Application for Membership: "Send name, address, and resume of art or craft involvement with $12. Make check payable to NEACG Inc."

WESTPORT-WESTON ARTS COUNCIL, Box 5033, Westport CT 06880. (203)226-1806. President: Barbara Wick. Estab. 1968. Members: 350. Open to all. Meets to encourage and support the arts. Sponsors shows; classes; and newsletter. Write for membership; $10 individual fee.

Delaware

DELAWARE ART MUSEUM, Education Dept., 2301 Kentmere Pkwy., Wilmington DE 19806. (302)571-9594. Education Director: Marion F.T. Johnson. Sponsors fall, spring and summer classes for individuals and organizations working in batik; ceramics; jewelry; needlecrafts; pottery; soft sculpture; and weavings. Offers purchase prizes and other cash awards in exhibitions; sponsors film, lectures, and workshops. "We do have Artist-Craftsmen in-Residence sponsored by the National Endowment For the Arts." As part of the in-residence program Ted Hallman (weaver-designer) conducted a workshop in creative drafting which focused on developing a strong working concept of the technology of drafting for weaving on floor looms." Apply by written request. Deadline for application: June.

Florida

DEPARTMENT OF CRAFTS DESIGN, Florida State University, Tallahassee FL 32305.

(904)644-5474. Leader, Craft Program: Professor Robert Bocz. Sponsors fellowships and teaching assistantships for craftworkers in batik; ceramics; jewelry; metalsmithing; pottery; soft sculpture; weavings; woodcrafting; and synthetics. Offers $2,000 per year salaries for teaching assistantships. Available to craftworker with bachelor's degree in crafts design; clearcut goal to become professional; good design sense; skill in at least 1 craft media; willingness to work hard; and modest record of entering state and local craft shows. To apply request form; submit slides. Interview advisable. Deadline for application: February.

GAINESVILLE CULTURAL COMMISSION, Box 490, Gainesville FL 32602. (904)374-2199. Cultural Coordinator: Eleanor R. Kaufman. Estab. 1973. Members: 12 commissioners. Commissioners chosen by City Commission; volunteers must be interested in encouraging all the arts in the community. Monthly meetings held the third Wednesday each month at 7:30 p.m. Purpose is to promote the arts and cultural events in the community. "The Cultural Commission acts as a clearinghouse for organizations, artists, and the public." Submit resume for consideration as a Cultural Commissioner; all volunteer workers accepted.
Activities: "The Cultural Commission sponsors art events; seminars; workshops; and awards for individuals and groups who enhance the life of the community through the arts. In addition, a monthly newsletter/calendar of culturally-related activities is published. Information on grants and public relations is provided through workshops and individual help."

Georgia

CROCHET ASSOCIATION INTERNATIONAL, Box 131, Dallas GA 30132. (404)445-7137. Executive Director: William E. Elmore. Estab. 1976. Members: goal of 10,000 by 1979. Open to anyone pledged to create articles of pleasure for others. Meets annually to educate and advance crochet. Sponsors annual national show and workshops at request of members and publishes a bimonthly newsletter. Write for membership application.

DEKALB COUNCIL FOR THE ARTS, INC., Box 875, Decatur GA 30031. (404)876-3686. Director: Shirley Peavy. Estab. 1972. Members: 500. Open to general public. Board of Directors meets monthly; annual general membership meeting in May. Organization's purpose is "to promote and sustain the arts within the community and to sponsor and encourage involvement in all of the arts by all citizens in the area through cultural and educational activities in DeKalb County and its surrounding areas."
Activities: "Publishes quarterly newsletter and arts calendar. Annually publishes *Arts in Education Resource Guide*, listing artists who have expressed interest in working with school children and have a program developed for presentation in the schools. This Resource Guide is distributed to the Cultural Arts Chairman and media centers of all elementary and secondary schools in area."
Application for Membership: "If a craftperson is interested in joining the Arts Council or being listed in the Resource Guide, he should contact the Council office listed above for application form."

GEORGIA COUNCIL FOR THE ARTS AND HUMANITIES, 225 Peachtree St. NE, Suite 1600, Atlanta GA 30303. (404)656-3967. Director: John Bitterman. Grants made to local sponsors on matching-funds basis and are used to aid painters, sculptors, graphic designers and muralists. Also co-sponsors workshops, exhibits and competitions.

GEORGIA DESIGNER CRAFTSMEN, INC., 135 W. Wieuca Rd. NW, Atlanta GA 30342. Secretary: Polly Harrison. Members: 200. Members must have "an active interest in Georgia crafts." Meets quarterly. "Represents craftsmen in Georgia through the promotion of creative thinking, the sharing of ideas, and the elevation of standards of all crafts by developing and maintaining quality and integrity in individual works and group exhibitions." Sponsors annual workshops in various media; quarterly newsletters; and exhibitions. Write for membership information. Membership dues: $10/year.

GEORGIA MOUNTAIN ARTS ASSOCIATION, Box 67, Tallulah Falls GA 30573. (404)965-6561. Coop Manager: Lassie Bradshaw. Estab. 1967. Members: about 75. Members must produce "a quality, salable craft that is in keeping with the tradition of our Appalachian area." Meets every 3 months. Submit "a quality craft and pay a $3 membership fee annually for membership."
Activities: "We exhibit at the Georgia Mountain Fair, Hiawasse, Georgia; at the Appalachian Festival, Cincinnati, Ohio; and at the Stay and See Georgia Craft Show, Atlanta. These are annual events." Also maintains coop craft store.

GEORGIA VOLUNTEER LAWYERS FOR THE ARTS, 100 Colony Sq., Suite 1910, Atlanta GA 30361. (404)892-8246. President: Robert C. Lower. Provides legal counseling to individuals and organizations working in any craft discipline. Available to individuals who meet financial eligibility requirements; groups must be nonprofit and tax exempt. Call to apply.

Idaho

IDAHO COMMISSION ON THE ARTS AND HUMANITIES, c/o Statehouse, 304 W. State St., Boise ID 83720. (208)384-2119. Artists-in-Schools Coordinator: Bitsy Bidwell. Sponsors Artists-in-Schools programs and grants to individuals and craft organizations working in any craft discipline.
Individuals: Provides short residencies at $1,300 monthly salary and long residencies at $1,000 monthly salary. Available to professional craftworker, usually residents of Idaho or near-by states. "Recently placed a metal sculptor/blacksmith in a junior high school for 1 month to share skills and artistic viewpoint with crafts students." To apply send resume; 3 recommendations; 5-10 examples of work (slides are nonreturnable); and a statement of philosophy (i.e. "if you got this job in the schools, what would be your goals and/or objectives with students, teachers, community?"). Deadline for application: March 15.
Organizations: Offers general grants up to $15,000, average usually $5,000. Available to non-profit, tax-exempt organizations. "Although theoretically possible, no crafts group outside of the state has ever applied for general funds." To apply request official application form (15 copies). Deadline for application: February 15 and August 1.

Illinois

AMERICAN SOCIETY OF ARTISTS, INC., 700 N. Michigan Ave., Suite 205, Chicago IL 60611. (312)751-2500. Membership Chairman: Helen Del Valle. Estab. 1972. Members: 500+. Membership depends upon quality of work. Write for membership application and describe media. SASE.
Activities: "Publishes a quarterly bulletin listing art and craft shows across the nation plus other helpful information. Publishes an *Art Lovers' Bulletin* for the public which lists art and craft shows in Illinois. Has a lecture and demonstration service — participants give lectures; demonstrations; and workshops for various groups.
Assistance: Provides assistance to registered ($10 annually) handicapped artists in all media who live in US. Write giving brief description of problems encountered in art/craft world and ask for registration form.

COLLEGE OF FINE AND APPLIED ARTS, University of Illinois, 110 Architecture Bldg., Urbana IL 61801. (217)333-1661. Dean: Jack H. McKenzie. Sponsors fellowship to individual craftworker. Offers Kate Neal Kinley Memorial Fellowship, 1 award of $2,500 for 1 academic year. Available to "graduates of the College of Fine and Applied Arts of the University of Illinois at Urbana-Champaign or graduates of a similar institution of equal educational standing whose principal studies have been in architecture design or history; all branches of art; or all branches of music. Preference given to applicants under 25. This is a competition. Every candidate must present something tangible for the committee to judge. 1977-78 winner is in Italy completing a Ph.D. dissertation in Art History. Runner-up is planning a career as concert violinist." To apply write for application blank and brochure. Deadline for application: April 15.

HIGHLAND AREA ARTS COUNCIL, Freeport Art Museum, 511 S. Liberty, Freeport IL 61032. (815)235-9755. Director: Vincent Tolpo. Estab. 1975. Members: 400. Open to all. Meets monthly to promote arts and fine crafts. Publishes monthly newsletter; operates Freeport Art Museum; and sponsors 3 annual art fairs. Write for membership.

LAWYERS FOR THE CREATIVE ARTS, Suite 720, 111 N. Wabash, Chicago IL 60602. (312)263-6984. Director: Thomas R. Leavens. Estab. 1972. 130 attorney members. Provides legal counseling for individuals and organizations working in any craft discipline. Offers legal counsel for art/craft related legal problem. Available to those unable to affort legal counsel. Request application. Publications: "Have forms; pamphlets; *Law and the Arts* ($3); and booklets available for assistance also." Also conducts seminars.

THE QUINCY SOCIETY OF FINE ARTS, 1624 Maine, Quincy IL 62301. (217)222-3432. Executive Director: Sam W. Grabarski. Estab. 1948. "The Society is a community arts council that serves as an administrative office for 12 arts organizations. We do from time to time hold exhibitions; workshops; demonstrations; and Artist-in-Residence programs sponsored through the IAC and the National Endowment for the Arts."

Indiana

EVANSVILLE ARTS & EDUCATION COUNCIL, 16½ SE 2nd St., Evansville IN 47708. (812)422-2111. Executive Director: Jane E. Moore. Estab. 1970. Members: 42 member organizations and numerous individual artists/craftworkers. "Members should have an interest in the cultural arts and education." Bimonthly meetings "to promote the quality of life through the enhancement of art, education and culture. Individuals may become members by submitting a $5 membership fee."
Activities: "The EAEC's largest annual event is the Ohio River Arts Festival. In addition to festival events, member organizations hold plays, music events, dance performances, etc. every day and night of the Festival.

INDIANA ARTS COMMISSION, 155 E. Market St., Indianapolis IN 46204. (317)633-5649. Grants Officer: Bobbie Garver. Sponsors Artists-in-Schools programs and grants to craft organizations working in any craft discipline. Available to nonprofit organizations who use the services of Indiana craftworkers. Write to apply; 4 application deadlines each year.

LA FONTAINE ARTS COUNCIL, 44 E. Park Dr., Huntington IN 46750. (219)356-0824. Estab. 1978. Members: 40. Meets to further arts in Huntington County.
Activities: Plans underway to publish newsletter. "We are a new organization and would like to get on some mailing lists so we can begin to get information to our community."

NORTHERN INDIANA ART ASSOCIATION, 5448 Hohman Ave., Hammond IN 46320. (219)931-0018. Project Director: Sandy Starrett. Estab. 1942. Members: 1,200. Open to all. The Association promotes the arts in the Calumet Region. Sponsors monthly art exhibits, classes, art programs in schools, poetry readings, concerts, and theatrical productions; organizes cultural activities; and publishes a monthly newsletter. Write or call for membership. "Send check or money order if not applying in person; $15 fee."

POTTERY GUILD, Lafayette Art Center, 101 S. 9th, Lafayette IN 47901. (317)742-1128. Pottery Instructor: Audrey Rossmann. Members: 15. Open to all with 3 semesters of pottery instruction and 4 pots for evaluation. Meets monthly for exchange of ideas and group criticism. Offers the opportunity to use the studio at the Art Center. Write for membership.

Iowa

CLARKE AREA ARTS COUNCIL, 630 W. McLane, Osceola IA 50213. (515)342-4272. President: Mary Ellen Kimball. Estab. 1972. Members: 200. Open to all. Meets bimonthly (or when necessary) to "increase awareness in the arts; promote education in the arts; support artists; and provide artistic and creative activities for the community." Membership is by payment of dues; students, $1; individual, $2; and $5, family.
Activities: Sponsors traveling exhibits; workshops; Artists-in-the Schools program; arranges programs in the arts; and publishes a newsletter and an art calendar.

IOWA DESIGNER CRAFTSMEN, 513 Nebraska St., Sioux City IA 51101. President: Bruce Bienemann. Provides aid for shows and workshops for individuals and organizations working in any craft discipline. Available to Iowa residents. Write for information.

SURFACE DESIGN ASSOCIATION, Iowa State University, Ames IA 50010. Membership: Sara Edmiston. Estab. 1971. Members: 450. Open to all interested in creation; production; and promotion of all phases of surface design. Meets to improve communication among artists; designers; industry; and teachers working in surface design on textiles and related media. Sponsors biennial national conference; national and regional exhibitions; development of visual materials; and a newsletter. Write for membership.

Kansas

ASSOCIATION OF COMMUNITY ARTS COUNCILS OF KANSAS, 509-A Kansas Ave., Topeka KS 66603. (913)296-4092. Projects Coordinator: Amanda Livingston. "We employ 1-2 artists a year to do workshops and/or residencies." Available to craftworker representing a media we are currently interested in providing; prefer Midwestern craftworker largely because of cost factors. Write for more information.

LAWRENCE ARTS CENTER, 9th and Vermont, Lawrence KS 66044. (913)843-9444. Director: Ann P. Evans. Estab. 1975. Members: 300. Open to all. Organization provides a "community arts facility that creates a stimulating environment; encourages artistic endeavors; offers creative experiences; and is responsible and responsive to the community in further developing the quality of cultural life." Sponsors monthly gallery exhibits; workshops; and regularly scheduled classes. Write for membership.

Kentucky

APPALSHOP INC., Box 743, 118 Main St., Whitesburg KY 41858. (606)633-5708. Contact: Bob Cooper. Offers assistance in programming or in curriculum development of Appalachian history, culture, and contemporary social issues; library of films available for rental purchase or review; mountain music records; a regional drama and story telling company; quarterly magazine of area literature and art; and a program of still photography. Write for more information.

ART CENTER ASSOCIATION, 1622 Story Ave., Louisville KY 40206. (502)583-6300. Director: Lynn Landis. Provides complete up to date listings of art fairs in Kentucky and southern Indiana. Available to individuals and organizations working in any craft discipline. Write or call. **Publications:** "We publish a monthly newsletter which provides a great deal of information for local artists. Probably most widely of interest is a list of exhibition opportunities which is updated monthly."

KENTUCKY ARTS COMMISSION, 100 W. Main St., Frankfort KY 40601. (502)564-3757. Artists-in-Schools Coordinator: Nancy Carpenter. Crafts Coordinator: Anne Ogden. Sponsors Artists-in-Schools programs; grants to organizations; and marketing information to individuals and craft organizations working in any craft discipline.
Individuals: "Will accept applications for Artists-in-Schools program from artists and craftsmen in any medium; placement depends on needs of the schools." To apply send request for information and program guidelines. Deadline for application: April 1.
Organizations: Offers funding up to half the cost of a project for community residencies; workshops; technical assistance; salary assistance; exhibition events; and special projects. To apply submit application form available from Kentucky Arts Commission offices. Deadline for application: May 1.
Publications: Kentucky Arts Commission Quarterly, free upon request, articles and announcements of arts and crafts events in Kentucky; and directory of Kentucky exhibition spaces.

LOUISVILLE SCHOOL OF ART, 100 Park Rd., Louisville KY 40203. (502)245-8836. Director of Student Financial Aid; Carolyn Stephenson. Sponsors grants; scholarships. BEOG; SEOG and NDSL's to craftworkers in ceramics; metalsmithing; and soft sculpture. Offers merit scholarships and Departmental Assistantships of $200 per semester. Available to full-time students at the Louisville School of Art. To apply contact Director of Financial Aid.

SOUTHERN KENTUCKY GUILD OF ARTISTS AND CRAFTSMEN, INC., Box 1874, Bowling Green KY 42101. President: Judith Grumbacher. Provides marketing information and scholarships to individuals working in any craft discipline; offers $300 art scholarships, art supplies, and materials; and sponsors 3 shows and sales annually. Works with craftworkers living in the area. "We are interested in helping those who plan a career in art; who show a high level of skill; and who need financial assistance." To apply contact the Guild.

Louisiana

ACADIANA ARTS COUNCIL, Box 53762, Lafayette LA 70505. (318)233-7060. Executive Director: Tom Boozer. Estab. 1972. Members: 500. Open to any supporter of the arts. Meets annually. "A nonprofit organization whose principal purpose is the development, promotion, and coordination of educational, cultural and artistic activities of the city and the area of Arcadiana." Publishes seasonal newsletter; holds children's workshops; and supports concerts, art shows and fairs. "Write to us and include $10 membership fee."

LAFAYETTE NATURAL HISTORY MUSEUM ASSOCIATION, 637 Girard Park Dr., Lafayette LA 70503. (318)233-6611, ext. 250. Membership Chairmen: Mary Lib Guercio and Bill Hollingsworth. Estab. 1969. Members: 900. Open to all. Meets quarterly "to strive to keep the community aware of their cultural heritage and regional history. Benefits of the Museum Association member: 1)Museum's monthly bulletin, 2)use of Museum's library of books and periodicals, stored collections and resource files, 3)advance notice of regional craft workshops and 10% discount, 4)invitations to special events and preview openings of exhibits, 5)museum store, 10% discount, 6)free admission to the Louisiana Native Crafts Festival. A craftsman, after meeting the criteria of participating in the Louisiana Native Crafts Festival, is asked to become a Patron of the Museum Association. This is a $25 a year membership."

LOUISIANA CRAFTS COUNCIL, 139 Broadway, New Orleans LA 70118. (504)861-8267. Manager: Lynne Higbee. Estab. 1961. Members: 1,200. Open to all interested in crafts. Board meets monthly; members meet yearly to "train creative handcraftsmen and educate public to appreciate handcrafts." Write for membership.
Activities: Presents monthly exhibitions; annual workshops; craft fair; year-round craft classes; craft sales shop for Louisiana craftsmen members; and publishes monthly newsletter.

ST. TAMMANY ART ASSOCIATION, 129 N. New Hampshire St., Covington LA 70433. (504)892-8650. President: Caroline Wood. Provides marketing information; teaching opportunities; sales opportunities; and juried shows for individuals working in any craft discipline. Available to members. Write for information.

Maine

ACADIAN CRAFTS ASSOCIATION, 29 Catherine St., Madawaska ME 04756. (207)728-3295. Manager: Theresa Violette. Estab. 1970. Members: 75. "Members have to produce and know how to knit or crochet. They have a year to qualify as a member." Meets bimonthly to "help supplement the family income by working in their own homes and selling handmade articles through the coop." Publishes annual newsletter; sponsors adult evening classes and workshops.

MAINE STATE COMMISSION ON THE ARTS AND THE HUMANITIES, State House, Augusta ME 04333. (207)289-2724. Community Arts Development Associate: Betty S. Smith. Sponsors programs and grants to craft organizations working in any craft discipline. Available to any legally established State of Maine nonprofit corporation with tax-exempt status. "All grants awarded on a matching basis with a 1-1 or better match required." To apply write or call for a copy of grants guidelines. Publishes a bimonthly newsletter and calendar.

Maryland

CRAFTPEOPLE'S GUILD OF FREDERICK COUNTY, c/o Nancy Bodmer, Box 163, Buckeystown MD 21717. (301)874-5782. Membership Chairperson: Nancy Bodmer. Estab. 1972. Members: 32. Individuals must have a "professional attitude towards art and crafts and an interest in selling. Only original work." Monthly meetings "to promote art and crafts in the community and inform members of shows, wholesale stores and outlets for work. Sponsors 2 craft shows annually at Christmas and during the spring. For membership "get in touch with me by phone or letter. Work is then juried by a committee of Guild members. Dues are $15/year."

GLEN ECHO PARK, The National Park Service, Glen Echo MD 20768. (301)492-6282. Director, Chautauqua Programs: Bev Chapman. Sponsors Craftsmen-in-Residence programs providing free studio space, a sales outlet and an opportunity to teach. To apply write for prospectus. Submit resume and cover letter.

Massachusetts

BOSTON AREA SPINNERS AND DYERS, c/o Einstein, 11 Oak Ave., Belmont MA 02178. President: Sylvia Einstein. Estab. 1970. Members: 150-200. Open to anyone with interest in spinning and dyeing. Meets monthly (except summer) to exchange information on spinning and dyeing and related activities. Sponsors workshops; and publishes newsletter and a journal. Write for membership.

COOPERATIVE EXTENSION SERVICE, Division of Continuing Education, Draper Annex, University of Massachusetts, Amherst MA 01003. (413)545-2013. Crafts Specialist: Rick Feldman. Provides assistance in grant applications; legal counseling; marketing information; consulting; individualized assistance; referral service; newsletter; and organizing for individuals and craft organizations working in any craft discipline. Available to craftworkers from western Massachusetts, "involved on a professional or desiring to approach a professional level in both quality and livelihood, that is earning at least half their income from crafts design and creation, or wanting to achieve that." Recently "an elderly man was helped to develop a pricing and marketing scheme for his woodwork. He has entered the crafts profession only within the last year following retirement." Write or call for assistance. Publishes monthly newsletter.

LAWYERS FOR THE ARTS, Massachusetts Arts and Humanities Foundation, 100 Boylston St., Boston MA 02116. (617)482-8100. Coordinator: Linda McKinney. Provides marketing and legal information through attorneys for individuals and organizations working in any craft discipline. Available to all with art-related legal problem. To apply write "by letter explaining their craft and why they would like to speak with an attorney. If financially unable to pay full fees, include that as well."

MASSACHUSETTS ARTS AND HUMANITIES FOUNDATION, INC., 100 Boylston St., Boston MA 02116. (617)482-8100. Executive Director: Richard S. Linzer. Provides Artists Fellowship, Artists-in-Residence and Lawyers for the Arts programs. Offers 55 $3,000 Artists Fellowships programs to painters, printmakers, sculptors and other creative artists. Available to Massachusetts residents, ages 18+, who are not students.

NORTH END-WATERFRONT ARTS COUNCIL, 20 Parmenter St., Boston MA 02113. (717)227-2927. Arts Coordinator: Karen Wakefield. Estab. 1975. Members: 200. Open to any craftsperson from the North End-Waterfront area of Boston. Meets monthly to "weave the arts into the fabric of the community." Sponsors a variety of visual art exhibits for local artists in the community, theatre productions, arts and crafts programs with senior citizens; and has a video-tape component with youth. Write for membership.

PETERSHAM CRAFT CENTER, Petersham Craft Shop, Rt. 32, Petersham MA 01366. (617)724-3415. Estab. 1954. Members: 350. Open to all. The Center attempts to meet the artistic needs of surrounding communities. Sponsors 1 day workshops and classes in various arts and crafts; holds exhibits and classes; and operates a shop "where artists/craftsmen can sell on consignment." Write for additional information.

THE SOCIETY OF NORTH AMERICAN GOLDSMITHS, 591 Washington St., Wellesley MA 02181. (717)235-8266. Secretary-Treasurer: Joel Bagnal. "Society's purpose is to promote, encourage, and represent the educational and professional activities and standards of the goldsmithing profession in North America. Associate membership, open to public, includes subscription to *Goldsmiths' Journal.*
Activities: Publishes a bimonthly *Goldsmiths' Journal*; sponsors annual conference, exhibitions and workshops; has a book ordering department (30% discount to members); and slide rental department maintained. Also serves as a resource to museums and art centers.

Michigan

ALGONAC SPONSORS OF THE ARTS, Box 422, Algonac MI 48001. Director: Vonnie Breck. Estab. 1968. Members: 60. Open to any interested individual. Meets monthly to "promote education of the arts in our area; exchange ideas; and to make contact with people in the arts." Promotes opera; workshops; annual outdoor art fair; and publishes a newsletter.
Application for Membership: "Send name and address to above address and $5 membership fee stating what phase of the arts your interest holds and what jobs you would be willing to do on a volunteer basis. What services can you supply?"

EASTERN UPPER PENINSULA CRAFTSMEN, c/o Pat Wilson, Rt. 1, Box 246A, Sault Ste. Marie MI 49783. (906)632-8103. Estab. 1964. Members: 40. Open to all wanting to work for same goals. Meets monthly to "stimulate production; upgrade quality; and allow those of craft orientation to interact." Write for membership.
Activities: "We are 1 of the major support groups for the Upper Peninsula Crafts Council which hosts yearly conference. We stock a cooperative workshop; sales area; and demonstration site. We encourage and support on a 1-1 basis craftsmen of the area. We sponsor displays; demonstrations; and assist the Sault area arts council's summer arts festival."

GLASS ART SOCIETY, 20300 N. Greenway, Southfield MI 48075. Treasurer: Sylvia Vigiletti. Estab. 1971. Members: 300. Open to all interested in glass as an art medium. "The Glass Art Society is a nonprofit organization formed to further the educational aims of individuals working with glass, and the public. The Society, interested in communication, tries to bridge the gap between arts, science, education and the public by holding annual conferences and publishing a newsletter where information helps stimulate, promote and improve the glass arts. Write to the above address for membership information. Send information for newsletter to Marvin Lipotsky, editor, California College of Arts and Crafts, Oakland CA 94618.

MICHIGAN COUNCIL FOR THE ARTS, 1200 6th Ave., Detroit MI 48226. (800)572-1160. Contact: Tom Rudd. Works through professional, nonprofit organizations and institutions, which offer employment to artists for programming, commissions, fellowships and scholarships. Program is currently being developed to include artists working independently of established institutions. Open to Michigan artists. Send name and address to: Support to Individual Artists Program. It is anticipated that this program will include 1) direct grants; 2)an exposure component — which will develop new audiences and marketplaces for individual artists; 3) a service component — which may include legal assistance, equipment pools, or an 'ombudsman' to help solve artists' problems.

NATIONAL GUILD OF DECOUPEURS, 807 Rivard Blvd., Grosse Pointe MI 48230. (313)882-0682. Executive Director: Ann Standish. Sponsors decoupage instruction through membership in chapter activity and national conventions. "Members earn certificates as they advance from Layman to Journeyman to Mastercraftsman by being juried for various Guild techniques. To join Guild individual must execute a box which is then judged for cutting; coloring of print; composition; finish; and lining. The Guild continually helps decoupeurs throughout the country. Currently chapters are administering hand coloring programs to anyone interested to learn that technique. Exhibitions are held throughout the country, sponsored by chapters or individuals, and a national exhibition is held annually." Write Guild Headquarters. Publishes monthly newsletter, distributed to members only.

SQUIRES STREET SQUARE ASSOCIATION, Box 520, Rockford MI 49341. (616)866-2000. Secretary: Barb Stein. Estab. 1970. Members: 35. Open to owners of retail shops in area. Meets monthly to advertise and promote. Sponsors annual festival.

TRAVERSE CITY ARTS COUNCIL INC., Box 681, Traverse City MI 49684. (616)947-7120. Membership Chairperson: Mrs. Richard Cain. Estab. 1968. Open to all. Meets monthly to promote cultural activities in the Grand Traverse Area. Sponsors Old Town Art Center exhibits; art in schools program; film series; workshops; Michigan Opera Theatre; and a monthly arts calendar and newsletter.
Application for Membership: Write to Mrs. Richard Cain, 2236 E. Timberlane Dr., Traverse City MI 49684. Fee: $6, individual; $10, family.

TRENTON CULTURAL ARTS COMMISSION, 2800 3rd, Trenton MI 48183. Chairman: David M. Ward. Estab. 1970. Members: 9. Members are appointed by mayor. Meets monthly to promote the cultural arts in the city. Activities: publishes newsletters and submits newspaper releases. Write for more information.

UPPER PENINSULA CRAFTS COUNCIL, 606 Pine St., Marquette MI 49855. (906)226-8807. Director: Anita E. Meyland. Provides marketing information; workshops; and demonstrations to individuals and organizations working in any craft discipline. Offers assistance in starting craft shops and boutiques. Available to all. To apply write Council. Publishes newsletters.

Minnesota

ART INSTITUTE AT THE DEPOT, 506 W. Michigan St., Duluth MN 55802. (218)727-8013. Director: Robert A. DeArmond. Estab. 1906. Members: 150. Open to anybody interested in arts and crafts. Purpose of the institute is "educational; to promote creativity; and to be a service to artists in the area." Sponsors art shows; craft shows; visiting artist workshops; and classes. Write for complete information on membership.

BUSH FOUNDATION FELLOWSHIP FOR ARTISTS, E-900 First National Bank, St. Paul MN 55101. (612)227-0891. Provides up to $10,000 for 12-18 month period for painters, sculptors or graphic artists to complete projects or to advance careers. Offers 8 awards. Applicants must be at least 25 years old, and have resided in Minnesota at least 1 year prior to filing application. Must also present evidence of professional accomplishment through publication, exhibition and examples of recent work.

MINNESOTA CRAFTS COUNCIL, Box 1182, Minneapolis MN 55440. President: Claudia Brown. "Education and service organization for professional craftspeople. Sponsors juried exhibitions and major juried art fair. Publishes *Craft Connection* as a communication network among Midwestern craftspeople and as a means of examining important issues. Gallery and resource center planned."

MINNESOTA STATE ARTS BOARD, 314 Clifton Ave., Minneapolis MN 55402. (612)874-1335. Assistance to Individual Artist Coordinator: Peder A. Sulerud. Estab. 1966. Meets monthly. A state agency that supports all of the arts in Minnesota. Provides newsletter on request and sponsors periodic workshops.

SOUTHWEST MINNESOTA ARTS AND HUMANITIES COUNCIL, Box 583, Marshall MN 56258. (507)537-1471. Executive Director: Mary K. Martin. Estab. 1974. Members: 1,200. Open to any interested individual or organization. Board of directors meets monthly; members annually to "encourage the growth, development and enjoyment of the arts and humanities in southwest Minnesota by providing a variety of services and programs to individuals, schools and community groups." Write for membership enclosing $10 annual base rate for individuals; $20 organizations.

Activities: "Provides a monthly syndicated regional arts column; a quarterly arts magazine; an annual listing of available arts programs; a resource directory of local artists and organizations; and an information and referral service for arts and humanities questions. Develops various programs including cooperative residencies by individual artists and touring groups; as well as a regional workshop. Provides funding for area residents through a grant program provided by the Minnesota State Arts Board and through the Cultural Bank, an 'insurance fund', available to organizational members."

UP NORTH HANDCRAFTS/LADY SLIPPER DESIGNS, 314 Houston Ave., Crookston MN 56716. (218)281-3720. Resource Coordinator: Lisa Schumacher. Provides marketing information; design; consultation; and marketing assistance to individuals and organizations working in any craft discipline. Available to residents of rural Minnesota who are seriously interested in earning a full time or supplementary income from their craft work. "We work mostly with production craftspeople who are willing to fill orders on a regular basis for extended periods of time. We are best able to help craftspeople get their first taste of the business world and try to accomodate the individual's needs at the same time. We have worked most successfully with craftspeople open to design and marketing suggestions. We are an active marketing venture doing volume wholesale business with retail stores around the country. One of a kind and art works are handled at our retail outlet." To apply call or write describing craft; may also apply to demonstrate craft at Itasca State Park for daily honorarium or for a show in the park's gallery. Deadline for application: May 1 for Itasca project; no deadline for other parts of project.

WEAVERS GUILD OF MINNESOTA, INC., 427½ Cedar Ave., Minneapolis MN 55454. (612)332-7521. Administrative Assistant: Katherine Frank. Office Manager: Margaret Pidde. Provides library; workshops; classes; demonstrations; and exhibits to individuals and organizations working in all fiber crafts: weaving; spinning; dyeing; lace-making; crochet; knitting; macrame; and needlecrafts. Available to craftworkers with interest in fiber arts. Publishes the *Minnesota Weaver*, a monthly newsletter with articles about weaving; spinning; dyeing; book reviews; show reviews; and information about the Guild and Twin Cities exhibits.

Mississippi

HATTIESBURG CIVIC ARTS COUNCIL, Box 693, Hattiesburg MS 39401. President: Michelle Heidelberg. Estab. 1970. Members: 750. Open to all with an interest in the arts. Board meets monthly to foster interest in the arts and provide local shows in various facets of the visual and performing arts. Sponsors monthly gallery shows. Write for membership enclosing check: $2, student; $5, individual; $10, couple; $25, donor; $50, sponsor; $100, patron; $250, benefactor; and $250, corporate.

MISSISSIPPI GULF COAST CRAFTSMEN'S BUILD, INC., Box 58, Gulfport MS 39501. (601)863-7833. Membership Chairman: Karl E. Koberger. Estab. 1974. Members: 153. Board of Directors meets monthly; general membership at specially called meetings. Organization's purpose is "to encourage the activities of handcraftsmen of the Mississippi Gulf Coast in pursuit of their craft." Sponsors newsletter; 2+ annual shows; other special shows through the year; and co-sponsored shows. Application for Membership: Exhibiting members must submit minimum of 3 craft items for pre-judging. $6/single membership; $4/each additional family member at same address. Write for more information.

MISSISSIPPI UNIVERSITY FOR WOMEN, Art Department, Box W-70 M.U.W., Columbus MS 39701. (601)328-4881. Chairman, Art Department: Charles E. Ambrose. Sponsors scholarships for craftworkers in batik; ceramics; glass art; jewelry; macrame; metalsmithing; needlecrafts; pottery; soft sculpture; and weavings. Offers the Paula B. Robertson Art Scholarship of $250; other scholarships available through Financial Aid Office. Available to craftworkers who pass university admission requirements; scholarships are competitive. To apply submit a transcript of credits and work portfolio. Deadline for application: "No deadline, but application should be submitted as soon after the first of the year as possible."

Missouri

MISSOURI ARTS COUNCIL, Raeder Place, 727 N. 1st St., St. Louis MO 63102. (314)241-7900. AIS Coordinator: Norma Thurman. Sponsors Artists-in-Schools programs and financial assistance to individuals and organizations working in ceramics; pottery; soft sculpture; and woodcrafting.

Individuals: Offers 9 month stipend of $10,800 for Artists-in-Schools Programs. Available to craftworkers with in-school residency experience; desire to work with students and teachers; desire to share his/her art; ability to communicate verbally; and high quality of work. To apply contact in writing. Deadline for application: August.

Organizations: Provides dollar for dollar matching funds for nonprofit, incorporated organizations.

OZARKS WHITTLERS & WOODCARVERS, 1625 S. Broadway, Springfield MO 65807. (417)865-7705. President: Ruth Sheeley. Estab. 1970. Members: 100. Open to all with an interest in wood and/or woodcarving. Meets monthly to "promote and perpetuate carving; to foster mutual admiration and respect for woodcarving." Publishes a newsletter and sponsors a carving display at Ozark Empire Fair. Write for application, stating reason for desiring membership.

SILVER DOLLAR CITY CRAFT GUILD, Silver Dollar City, Branson MO 65616. (417)338-2611. Coordinator of Craft Guild: Judy Miller. Estab. 1977. Members: 200. Open to craftworkers whose work meets Craft Guild Committee standards. Meets semiannually to "preserve our native handcraft heritage; to insure that the tradition of the independent craftsman continues; and to supply unique, distinctive items, at a fair price, to the American public." Publishes quarterly newsletter and offers ID cards for members and family's admission to Silver Dollar City; seasonal purchases of products by Silver Dollar City; exposure of member's products to over 1,000,000 people per year; and affiliation with the center for craft sales in a 7-state area. Write for membership and, if possible, mail a sample of the craft item or arrange for an interview.

Montana

MONTANA ARTS COUNCIL, 235 E. Pine St., Missoula MT 59801. (406)243-4883 or 543-8286. Contact: Patricia K. Simmons. Participates in the Artists-in-Schools program for painters, sculptors and graphic designers. All grants made on matching funds basis. Application deadline: April 1. Query with resume, awards and published samples.

Nebraska

NEBRASKA ARTS COUNCIL, 8448 W. Center Rd., Omaha NE 68124. (402)544-2122. Director of Arts Education: Eleanor B. Jones. Sponsors Artists-in-Schools programs; grants; Artists-in-Communities programs; arts touring program; and Artists Resource Directory to individuals and organizations working in any craft discipline.

Individuals: Offers $500 per 5-day residency; sponsoring organizations may apply for up to 50% of fee. "All artists working in the residency programs are screened by a professional panel that reviews both the quality of work and artist's ability to relate to communities and schools in a residency situation." To apply, contact Nebraska Arts Council for application forms and Artists-in-Schools Program requirements. Deadline for application: February 1.

Organizations: Offers major grants up to $20,000; mini grants up to $500 to Nebraska organizations. To apply, contact Nebraska Arts Council for application forms. Deadline for application: major grants, March 15; mini grants, 4 weeks prior to project.

Nevada

CITY OF LAS VEGAS CULTURAL AND COMMUNITY AFFAIRS, Branch of the Dept. of Recreation and Leisure Activities, 749 Casino Center Blvd. N., Las Vegas NV 89101. (702)386-6511. Supervisor, Fine Arts Division: Patricia Marchese. Estab. 1976. The organization is "a governmental agency of the City of Las Vegas. The CCA provides cultural services to the community including facilities; programs; classes; outreach and touring activities; and pilot programs and special events in the visual and performing arts. Support services; technical assistance; and resource info is also made available."

Activities: Publishes quarterly class and program schedules; brochures on major programs and special events. Sponsors an annual community-wide 3-day arts festival in the fall. Write for information on the festival.

NEVADA STATE COUNCIL ON THE ARTS, 4600 Kietzke Lane, Bldg. D, Number 134, Reno NV 89502. (702)784-6231. Executive Director: J.D. Deere. Sponsors Artists-in-Schools programs; fellowships; and grants to individuals and organizations working in any medium. Offers $2,5000 annual fellowship. Available to Nevada resident with quality proposal; high level of art; and, in some cases, matching funds. To apply, contact council office. Deadline for application: April 1 and September 1.

New Hampshire

LEAGUE OF NEW HAMPSHIRE CRAFTSMEN, 205 N. Main St., Concord NH 03301.

(603)224-3375. Director: Merle D. Walker. Estab. 1932. Members: 3,500. Open to anyone interested in the League's purposes. Chartered to educate and promote New Hampshire craftsmen and to educate the public to the value of crafts in their lives. Write for membership. Sponsors seminars, annual fairs, and classes; provides a library, resource center, scholarship aid, cooperative buying programs, and marketing assistance; and publishes a newsletter.

NEW HAMPSHIRE COMMISSION ON THE ARTS, 40 N. Main St., Phenix Hall, Concord NH 03301. (603)271-2789. Executive Director: John Coe. Sponsors Artists-in-Schools programs and grants to organizations working in any craft discipline. Offers approximately 50-70 grants per year from $100-12,000. Available to New Hampshire organizations. To apply contact Commission. Deadline for application: April 15.

New Jersey

BURLINGTON COUNTY CULTURAL AND HERITAGE COMMISSION, c/o 49 Rancocas Rd., Mt. Holly NJ 08060. (609)267-3300, ext. 228 or 381. Executive Administrator: Keith W. Betten. Estab. 1970. Commissioners: 9. "Commissioners are appointed to 5-year terms by the County Board of Chosen Freeholders, the elected administrators of counties in New Jersey." Meets monthly to "initiate, develop, and execute programs of interest to the county's cultural and historical community; to assist, support, and promote the programs and activities of all county arts and historical institutions and organizations; and to develop the county owned Smithville Mansion Complex as a regional center for the arts and humanities. Publishes bimonthly newsletter; sponsors festivals, workshops, and gallery space; and provides Grantmanship Assistance and National Nomination Assistance.

HUDSON COUNTY DIVISION OF CULTURAL AND HERITAGE AFFAIRS, Department of Health and Social Services, County Administration Bldg., Jersey City NJ 07306. (201)659-5062. Division Director: Charles K. Robinson. Provides Artists-in-Schools programs; application assistance for fellowships and grants; legal referral; marketing information; and general counseling to individuals and craft organizations working in any craft discipline. Available to craftworkers living or working in Hudson County. "Recently assisted craftworker in developing a resume sent to major arts and crafts organizations in the state. Craftworker is currently employed through this effort." Call for appointment. Publishes *Artists/Craftworkers Directory*.

MIDDLESEX COUNTY CULTURAL AND HERITAGE COMMISSION, 841 Georges Rd., North Brunswick NJ 08902. (201)246-5788. Executive Administrator: Jacqueline E. Rubel. Estab. 1970. Members: 9 commissioners. "Commissioners are appointed by the County Board of Chosen Freeholders. Individuals interested in working in areas of cultural or historic importance may serve as members of the Advisory Committee." Meets monthly to "promote the establishment of New Brunswick as the cultural center for New Jersey." Sponsors workshops; festivals; Artists in the Schools; and newsletter. Write or call if you are a central New Jersey resident interested in Advisory Committee.

MONTCLAIR STATE COLLEGE, Fine Arts Department, Upper Montclair NJ 07034. (201)893-4307. Department Chairman: Dr. Charles Martens. Provides graduate assistantship for craftworker in batik; ceramics; jewelry; leatherworking; metalsmithing; pottery; soft sculpture; and weavings. Offers 1 graduate assistantship leading toward MA in ceramics; fibers; fabrics; and jewelry. Provides full tution for 2 years and salary during 1st year. Write to apply.

NEW JERSEY STATE COUNCIL ON THE ARTS, 109 W. State St., Trenton NJ 08608. (609)292-6130. Acting Executive Director: Eileen Lawton. Sponsors Artists-in-Schools programs; fellowships; and grants to individuals and organizations working in any craft discipline. Offers matching grants varying in amount, maximum $10,000; fellowships, maximum $3,000. "Grant awards based on quality of the submitted proposal." To apply, contact office in the fall of each year for grant application. Deadline for application: grants, February 1; fellowships, March 1.

PETERS VALLEY CRAFTSMEN, Layton NJ 07851. (201)948-5200. Executive Directors: Judy and Dennis McCarthy. Incorporated 1970. Open to all interested in crafts. Members: 1,000+. Provides intern and residency programs for individuals working in ceramics, jewelry, blacksmithing, weaving, woodworking, and photography; has spring, summer and fall workshop program; provides marketing information; maintains a store and gallery; publishes a newsletter; and produces an annual craft fair. Write for information.

New Mexico

FOUR CORNERS NAVAJO ARTS & CRAFTS COOPERATIVE, Box 1356, Shiprock NM 87420. (505)368-5103. Manager: Eleanor M. Light. Estab. 1974. Members: 150. Members "must be at least a quarter Navajo Indian and must produce Navajo arts and crafts." Monthly meetings. Purpose: "to get more than just wholesale price for the craftperson, as opposed to dealing with traders who pay half cash and half groceries for items at wholesale prices; to improve marketing systems; and to have an outlet for buyers to avoid the middleman. We are a nonprofit organization and we travel across the country setting up our own shows which are strictly Navajo or done by Navajo Indians."
Application for Membership: Accepts arts or crafts brought in as a sample of work, or to be entered in a show. Membership card is given upon the second use of the show sale, and is signed and approved by the board president and manager. Using the cooperative frequently is expected."

SANTE FE WORKSHOPS OF CONTEMPORARY ART, Box 1344, Santa Fe NM 87501. (505)983-5573. Advisory Director: Geraldine Price. Offers half tuition scholarships to painters, photographers, sculptors, printmakers and weavers. Application deadline: May 30 for 8-week summer session.

New York

ALBANY LEAGUE OF ARTS INC., 135 Washington Ave., Albany NY 12210. (518)449-5380. Executive Director: Carol Bullard. Estab. 1946. Members: 800. Open to people interested in the arts. Meets annually with several other get-togethers a year "not to create art but to help those who do. Service is the word."
Activities: Sponsors an annual Arts Sampler Fair held at Empire State Plaza in Albany, featuring performances; crafts booths; arts exhibits; and displays. Cosponsors Albany's Winter Carnival and Pinksterfest.
Application for Membership: "Individual/family membership is $15 a year. Membership begins at receipt of membership fee."

ALLEGANY INDIAN ARTS AND CRAFTS CO-OP, Haley Community Center, Salamanca NY 14779. (716)945-1790, ext. 39. Chairman: Delores Oldshield. Estab. 1971. Members: 53. Open to Senecas of all ages on the Allegany Indian Reservation. Meets weekly to preserve the Seneca culture. Membership is $1 a year.
Activities: Seneca craftsmen teach beadwork; basketry; huskcrafts; and leather work. Contemporary items such as bookmarks; key chains; rings; and small dolls are also made. Materials are supplied at cost to members and the coop maintains quality control and standardizes selling price for the crafts. Coop attends many shows for sales and display purposes.

AMERICAN COUNCIL FOR THE ARTS, 570 7th Ave., New York NY 10018. (212)354-6655. Development Coordinator: Kathy Hoblitzelle. Estab. 1961. Members: 950. Open to all. Meets annually. Organization is a "private, nonprofit membership organization serving all the arts nationally. It specializes in information services, management training and advocacy at the federal level for all the arts."
Activities: Publishes *Word From Washington,* a newsletter issued to members 10 times a year to report on developments at the federal level affecting artists, craftspersons; and nonprofit arts organizations. Publishes *ACA Reports,* a "newspacket" issued to members 10 times a year; discusses trends from across the country in programming, fundraising, financial management, audience development, arts education, and public relations.
Application for Membership: "A craftsperson can join ACA as an individual member ($30 per year) by writing to ACA and asking to join. He/she can also join as a member of Advocates for the Arts, the citizens' action program of ACA, for $15 a year, entitling him/her to receive *Word From Washington.*"

AMERICAN CRAFTS COUNCIL, 44 W. 53rd St., New York NY 10019. Estab. 1943. "The Council is a national, nonprofit organization. Its program of communication, education, and service to craftsmen and the public includes publication of *Craft Horizons;* the Museum of Contemporary Crafts; research and education; and a regional and international program of workshops, seminars, conferences, and tours." Membership is open to all. Write for application.

AMERICAN SCANDINAVIAN FOUNDATION, 127 E. 73rd St., New York NY 10021. (212)879-9779. Contact: Exchange Division. Sponsors awards for outstanding young American men and women for advanced study in the Scandinavian countries in their field of specialization.

Offers range from $500 (short-term) to $5,000 for 1 academic year. Available to applicants who have completed undergraduate education at time of overseas project and have acquired working language knowledge. Application should be typewritten with accompanying slides or portfolio; and $10 check, nonrefundable service fee. Deadline for application: November 1.

ART INFORMATION CENTER, INC., 189 Lexington Ave., New York NY 10016. (212)725-0335. Director: Betty Chamberlain. Provides information on craft courses in the New York area and art galleries in New York City that handle crafts as art. Available to individuals and craft organizations working in batik; ceramics; glass art; jewelry; metalsmithing; pottery; soft sculpture; weaving; tapestries; and wall hangings. Write requesting appointment. SASE.

ARTS DEVELOPMENT SERVICES, INC., 237 Main St., Buffalo NY 14203. (716)856-7520. Only nonprofit associations or organizations can become ADS associates or affiliates. The agency's purpose is to encourage the arts in Erie County. Sponsors a variety of workshops; publishes a bimonthly newspaper and cultural directories.

CHEMUNG VALLEY ARTS COUNCIL, 171 Cedar St., Corning NY 14830. (607)962-5871. Secretary: Evelyn Einfeldt. Estab. 1972. The organization is "a public nonprofit tax exempt agency designed to serve broad cultural interests of the total community. It exists in direct response to an expressed community need for a central agency to plan; coordinate; initiate; expand; complement; and strengthen arts programs with the firm objective of enhancing and broadening cultural life in the Chemung Valley." Write or call for information on membership. **Activities:** Publishes a monthly cultural events calendar/newsletter. Has sponsored Summer Dance Workshops; Artists Showcase for area educators; children's summer theatre workshop; public relations workshop; The Art of Collecting Workshop, designed to enhance marketing skills of area artists; a 3-day residency of the Acting Company; Syracuse Ballet Theatre performance; and lecture-demos in the school.

CINTAS FELLOWSHIP PROGRAM, Institute of International Education, 809 United Nations Plaza, New York NY 10017. Secretary: Robert F. Morris. Provides fellowships to professional artists. Offers 6 $4,000 fellowships to architects, painters, sculptors, and printmakers. Available to artists with Cuban citizenship or lineage. Receives applications from January 1-March 1.

CREATIVE ARTISTS PUBLIC SERVICE PROGRAM, (CAPS), 250 W. 57th St., New York NY 10019. (212)247-6303. Contact: Larry Hulse. Provides assistance to graphic/mixed media artists, painters and sculptors. Available to "artists who are not matriculated students as of June and are state residents." Submit samples.

EAST END ARTS AND HUMANITIES COUNCIL, 133 E. Main St., Riverhead NY 11901. (516)727-0900. Executive Director: Mardythe DiPirro. Estab. 1972. Members: 600. Must be resident of east end of Suffolk. Meets monthly to sponsor events and to service the artists in the area. Prints monthly calendar newsletter and sponsors workshop and an ongoing art gallery. Write or call for membership.

THE EMBROIDERERS' GUILD OF AMERICA, INC., 6 E. 45th St., Rm. 1501, New York NY 10017. (212)986-0460. Estab. 1958. Members: 16,000. "Membership open to anyone who has an interest in embroidery." Meets monthly; nonprofit educational organization. "Write to Guild requesting membership application."
Activities: Guild offers correspondence courses; program for teachers certification; classes; master craftsman programs in various techniques; lecturers and field trips; national seminars and biennial national exhibits; functions as parent body of chapters; and serves as an informational source for individual needleworkers throughout the US. Guild also maintains a reference library at its main office and publishes *Needle Arts*, a quarterly magazine.

FINE ARTS SOCIETY OF THE CAYUGA MUSEUM OF HISTORY AND ART, 203 Genesee St., Auburn NY 13021. (315)253-8051. Director: Professor Walter K. Long. Estab. about 1880. Members: 50. Members must have deep interest, acceptable work, and controlled creativity. Meets monthly to foster good work in area. Sponsors 1 large show and 2 workshops annually. Write for membership, $10 annual fee for Cayuga Museum of History and Art membership; $3 for Fine Arts Society.

FREEPORT COMMUNITY ARTS COUNCIL, Box 97, Freeport NY 11520. (516)223-2522. Coordinator: Lila Diringer. Estab. 1974. Nonmembership organization. "We have 'Friends' [cost is from $5/individual to $50/artists, students, teachers and others interested in the arts]. Send a check payable to the FAC to be listed as a 'Friend.' " Brochures will be sent to all who request them.

Activities: Presents programs, workshops and exhibits for the benefit of artists and the community. "We have workshops in dance, music, writing and the arts (silver, jewelry, design, etching, calligraphy, life drawing and watercolors). Brochures are seasonally sent."

FULTON COUNTY ARTS COUNCIL, INC., 40 N. Main St., Gloversville NY 12078. (518)725-6248. Executive Director: Joanna Vedder. Estab. 1974. Members: 500. Open to all. Annual meetings of the board of directors and committees. Purpose: "to sponsor, foster and encourage the arts and cultural activities in Fulton County, New York. Write or call Council office for application and information."

Activities: Publishes a monthly arts newsletter and calendar of cultural activities; sponsors an annual festival; and provides a resident artist program.

THE GENESSEE GUILD, 73 Wilmarth Rd. N., Pittsford NY 14534. (716) 381-0090. Director: Yvonne Goh. Estab. 1974. Members: 50. Members must have "an interest in handspinning craft, tools or technique." Monthly meetings "to promote and preserve the craft of handspinning and related arts." Publishes a quarterly newsletter. Write to above address for membership information. Membership fee: $2.

GRANTS FOR GRADUATE STUDY ABROAD, Institute of International Education, 809 United Nations Plaza, New York NY 10017. (212)883-8278. Provides fellowships and scholarships to craftworkers "based on the cost of living in countries."

THE GREATER WESTBURY ARTS COUNCIL, INC., 600 Old Country Rd., Rm. 306, Garden City NY 11530. (516)741-6760. Executive Director: Roberta Oborne. Estab. 1974. Members: 150 plus 30 board members. Open to all with an interest in the arts and a willingness to support. Meets quarterly to "foster; support; initiate the arts in our area; and to service those already existing art organizations and individual artists and craftspeople." Publishes monthly newsletter and sponsors an annual art and craft festival. Write for membership, $5 annual dues.

GREENWICH HOUSE POTTERY, 16 Jones St., New York NY 10014. (212)242-4106. Director: Jane Hartsook. Provides scholarships to potters. Offers 5 $100 Madeline Sadin Scholarships per semester; $100 Madeline Sadin Award; $200 Frances Simches Scholarship. Available to students. Send resume and letter stating need. Application deadline: September 1.

LAKE COUNTRY CRAFTSMAN, INC., Box 1477, Rochester NY 14603. Membership Chairman: Dan Neuberger. Estab. 1969. Members: 90. Membership is open to all persons who are interested in promoting quality craftsmanship. Meets first Monday of the month to "encourage and promote quality craftsmanship." Sponsors workshops, annual spring show for members, and annual fall sale for members; and publishes monthly newsletter. Request application form from Membership Chairman.

LAMB TO LOOM WEAVERS' GUILD, 45 Hawthorne Rd., Binghamton NY 13903. (607)722-3590. Contact: Lavinia Adler. Estab. 1971. Members: 15. Members must have "an interest in handweaving— traditional or contemporary." Monthly meetings September-June "to share information about handweaving and related interest areas— spinning, dyeing, etc. The Guild sponsors 1 special workshop a year, usually in the early spring, with a well-known weaver as instructor. Phone the above number for time and place of meeting, and then join us at a meeting. Upon payment of dues (minimal) the person becomes a member."

LONG ISLAND CRAFTSMEN'S GUILD, Hofstra University, Hempstead NY 11550, (516)560-3313. Membership Chairperson: Steven Shapiro. Estab. 1957. Members: 400. Open to amateur and professional craftworkers and those with an interest in crafts. Meets bimonthly to "develop the crafts movement by reinforcing the efforts of those interested in the crafts through the exchange of information and experiences that will benefit both artisan and community." Write for membership form.

Activities: Sponsors several invitational and juried shows annually; individual media group meetings for the purpose of exchanging information; workshops; and classes in cooperation with Hofstra; and publishes monthly newsletter.

LOWER ADIRONDACK REGIONAL ARTS COUNCIL, 184 Glen St., Box 659, Glens Falls NY 12801. (518)798-1144. Vice President of Membership: Lois Cayzer. Estab. 1972. Members:

400. Open to all. Meets monthly to promote and provide arts for the Adirondack area. Write for membership; $2, individual fee; $10, organizational fee.
Activities: Publishes newsletter; sponsors workshops, school program, continuing education program, summer arts and crafts festival, and concerts.

NEW YORK STATE CRAFTSMEN, INC., 27 W. 53rd St., New York NY 10019. (212)586-0026. Administrative Assistant: Jeannette Visek. Estab. 1954. 1,200 members. Membership open to craftworkers and craft-oriented individuals, organizations, corporations and residents of all states.

NORTHERN ADIRONDACK CRAFT GUILD, THE CRAFTS BARN, 61 Market St., Potsdam NY 13676. (315)265-9806. Manager: Jean Boismenu. Estab. 1970. Members: 200. For membership work must be juried. "Provides a retail outlet and visibility for the craftsmen in our area of northern New York." Sponsors 2 annual shows. Write for membership.

ROME PRIZE FELLOWSHIP, American Academy in Rome, 41 E. 65th St., New York NY 10021. Executive Secretary: Ruth D. Green. Provides fellowships to individuals. Offers 1-year residency at Academy in Rome, $300 monthly stipend and $1,300 travel allowance to sculptors and painters. Write for application. Application deadline: November 15.

STAINED GLASS CLUB, Box 244, Norwood NY 07648. (201)768-7055. Executive Secretary: Nancy Truman. Estab. 1967. Members: 3,000. Open to anybody working in stained glass, either as an apprentice or an experienced craftsperson or with an interest in stained glass, either as an aesthetic or a functional art form. Meets through the mail "to disseminate information about stained glass as well as selling tools and supplies." Write for membership information; $18 annual dues.

STUDIO WORKSHOP, 3 W. 18th St., New York NY 10011. (212)243-0219. President: Richard Rapport. Estab. 1967. Members: 700. Open to all. Meets weekly to teach the various arts. Sponsors workshops in all the arts. Write or call for membership.

THISTLEDOWN HANDSPINNERS GUILD, Box 648, Norwich NY 13815. Contact: Membership Chairman. Estab. 1973. Members: 92. "Our active members must have workable knowledge of spinning; work on at least 1 demonstration per year; make at least 1 item of own handspun yarn to be shown membership on completion; and attend at least 6 from a total of 16 meetings per year." There are also student and inactive memberships. Holds 4 special events annually and meets monthly "to preserve and perpetuate the art of handspinning; to promote interest in spinning by educating the public through demonstrations, lectures, displays, and news media; to provide instruction and social life in spinning for its members." Write for membership.
Activities: Sponsors workshops and seminars and publishes a monthly newsletter.

TOMPKINS COUNTY QUILTERS' GUILD, Women's Community Bldg., 100 W. Seneca St., Ithaca NY 14850. (607)272-1247. President: Barbara Dimock. Estab. 1974. Members: 20. Open to all with an interest in the art and craft of quilting. Meets biweekly to "promote; encourage; support; and stimulate quilting. Also to provide education and fellowship for members." Sponsors shows; quilting bees; workshops; and plans to establish a museum. Call for time and date of meeting; attend if interested in membership.

UPPER CATSKILL COMMUNITY COUNCIL OF THE ARTS, INC., Rm. 101A, Alumni Hall, State University College, Oweonta, NY 13820. (607)432-2070. Executive Directors: Leonard and Dorothy Rywdes. Estab. 1970. Members: 25. Open to artists, craftspeople; anyone with a profound interest in the arts or with business ability. Meets monthly to "promote arts; crafts; and historical societies to insure a higher quality of life. To provide the public with free exposure to all art forms." Sponsors an annual festival of the arts. Membership is by invitation.

VILLAGE ARTISTS AND CRAFTSMEN, Box 292, Hamilton NY 13346. (315)824-1343. Corresponding Secretary: Janice Moreland. Estab. 1975. Members: 80. Open to all. Board of directors meets monthly to "stimulate interest in the fine arts and crafts; to hold art exhibits to provide opportunities for purchase and sales; to provide educational opportunities for adults and children; and to fund a scholarship for students interested in art or the crafts." Sponsors monthly newsletter; and annual art and craft fair.

VOLUNTEER LAWYERS FOR THE ARTS, 36 W. 44th St., New York NY 10036. (212)575-1150. Provides legal counseling to individuals and organizations working in any craft discipline.

Available to individuals who have current art-related legal problems and whose income is less than $6,000 per year; available to nonprofit organizations with budgets less than $100,000 per year. To apply, write details of artistic activity; specific legal assistance requested; and validation of income. Also publishes books and pamphlets relating to law and the arts.

North Carolina

THE ARTS ASSOCIATION OF ALAMANCE COUNTY, 135 W. Elm St., Graham NC 27253. (919)226-4495. Craft Shop Director: Linda Votta Sullivan. Arts association estab. 1957; craft shop estab. 1971. Members: 500. Open to all. "Educational nonprofit organization to promote and foster cultural development in the community." Write for membership information.
Activities: Sponsors 2 visual arts galleries and craft shop; courses in conjunction with the technical institute; and publishes a quarterly newsletter which is sent to members and is used by the local newspaper (circ. 26,000) as an insert.

ARTS COUNCIL OF FAYETTEVILLE, INC., Box 318, 822 Arsenal Ave., Fayetteville NC 28302. (919)323-1776. Executive Director: Carolyn Carlson. Estab. 1973. Members: 37 organizations. "We do not have individual members; member organizations are eligible for membership in the Arts Council if they are an art organization or support the arts. Groups must be located within Cumberland County." Meets bimonthly to "support its member organizations through administrative assistance; audience development; programs; publicity; and financial aid. It serves as the central informational and coordinating center, a financial resource service, and advocate for the arts. It organizes special cultural projects."
Activities: Publishes *SPECTRA*, a bimonthly newspaper that is art related; provides 2 annual workshops; writes a weekly newspaper column; and sponsors social programs.

BURKE ARTS COUNCIL, 115 E. Meeting St., Morganton NC 28655. (704)433-7282. Executive Director: June J. Hollingsworth. Estab. 1975. Members: 500. Open to all interested in the arts. Promotes arts in the county. Write for membership. Publishes monthly newsletter; sponsors monthly exhibits, sales gallery and annual festival; and holds classes and workshops.

NORTH CAROLINA ARTS COUNCIL, Department of Cultural Resources, Raleigh NC 27611. (919)733-7897. Administrative Assistant: Stella Lehrer. Sponsors Visiting Artist program; Artists-in-Schools programs; and grants to nonprofit arts organizations working in any craft discipline. Grants available only to nonprofit organizations. Offers minimum salary of $10,000 for 9 month period in the Visiting Artist program. Available to craftworker with Master's degree or equivalent training. "Applications are encouraged from members of racial minorities." To apply, contact Department of Cultural Resources. Deadline for application: "different grant categories have different deadlines;" visiting Artist program, March 1.

PIEDMONT CRAFTSMEN, INC., 300 S. Main St., Winston-Salem NC 27101 (919)725-1516. Director: Lida Lowrey. Estab. 1964. Members: 225. Open to residents of one of the following states: Virginia; Maryland; North Carolina; South Carolina; Georgia; Florida; Alabama; or Tennessee. All major craft media are eligible. Meets annually for the development and appreciation of fine craftwork.
Activities: Sponsors workshops, lectures, special programs, exhibitions, a library and consulting services; publishes a bimonthly publication; maintains a craft shop; and provides its members and the public with a meeting place and forum for the exchange of ideas.
Application for Membership: Write for information and jury forms. 5 pieces of work in 1 category must be submitted for jurying.

SOUTHEASTERN NORTH CAROLINA ARTS COUNCIL, Rt. 2, Box 940, Elizabethtown NC 28337. (919)588-4898. Executive Director: Ann A. Hood. Estab. 1966. Members: 200. Open to individuals, families, and businesses in 8 southeastern North Carolina counties (Bladen; Columbus; Cumberland; Duplin; New Hanover; Robeson; Brunswick; and Pender) who have a desire to further the arts. Meets monthly to promote; encourage; and develop the arts. Sponsors annual arts and crafts festival the last weekend in April; classes; exhibits; workshops; and demonstrations. Write for membership. $5, individual fee; $10, family; $100, business; $50, patron; $25, associate; and $10, SENC Craftsmen's Guild.

SOUTHERN HIGHLAND HANDICRAFT GUILD, Box 9545, Asheville NC 28805. (704)298-7928. Secretary: Carol R. Smith. Estab. 1930. Members: 621. Open to eligible craftworkers living in the southern Appalachian mountain region whose work (5 examples in a media) meets approval. Meets annually to "seek cooperation among all agencies and individuals interested in conserving and developing crafts; to encourage a wider appreciation of mountain crafts; to raise and maintain standards of design and craftsmanship and encourage individual expression; to study costs of production, marketing, and other problems; to give information and instruction on methods, sources of supply, and management of individual or group production." Sponsors 2 major workshops annually and 2 annual craft fairs. Write or call for membership.

Ohio

BRECKSVILLE FINE ARTS COUNCIL, Box 53, Brecksville OH 44141. Estab. 1970. Members: 100. Council "sponsors and publicizes fine arts programs by every club in the city. We suggest programs and subsidize all organization." Sponsors annual Civic Art Show.

CLEVELAND AREA ARTS COUNCIL, 108 The Arcade, Cleveland OH 44114. (216)781-0045. Contact: Nina Gibans. Provides grants outright or through matching funds from the State Council. Recently presented $1,000 grant for sculptural design.

THE CRAFT GUILD OF GREATER CINCINNATI, 933 Avondale Ave., Cincinnati OH 45229. (513)281-8042. Newsletter Editor: Vivian Kline. Estab. 1966. Members: 430. "Members must live in a 50-mile radius of Cincinnati. Our members must be interested in crafts, or work in any craft medium." Meets monthly to educate its members. Publishes newsletter 10 times annually and holds 2 shows a year. Write for brochure.

FINE ARTS COUNCIL OF TRUMBULL COUNTY (FACT), Box 48, 303 Mahoning Ave., NW, Warren OH 44482. (216)399-1212. Administrative Coordinator: Mary Ann Marton. Estab. 1972. Members: 12 organizations. Members are organizations directly representing the arts to the community and business representatives. Monthly meetings. "FACT is a nonprofit, incorporated, tax-exempt organization founded to encourage the arts in Trumbull County through the community arts group, schools, and other groups such as AAUW (children's concerts sponsors) and Junior Women's League (pilot artist in classroom program)." Craftworkers may apply for membership on an individual basis.
Activities: "Have sponsored Great Lakes Shakespeare Festival performance as a fundraiser; Summer Program for children in outlying school districts in cooperation with Trumbull County Board of Education; publishes calendar of arts activities in county; gives workshops; and provides grant writing assistance."

GUILD OF OHIO DOLLMAKERS, c/o Janet Masteller, 1590 Bean Oller Rd., Delaware OH 43015. (714)369-5081. Membership Chairman: Ruth M. Hopple, 934 Broadmoor Dr., Dayton OH 45415. Estab. 1975. Members: 25. Open to all 18 or older actively making dolls of wood; cloth; wax; ceramic; composite material (i.e. plastic, compo, papier mache, metal, not found material). Active members must attend 2 of the 4 general meetings each year. Meets 4 times yearly to "share; study; and educate through workshops and seminars in all phases of dollmaking and related subjects, and to promote awareness of our achievements thorugh exhibits and publicity." Sponsors annual convention.
Application for Membership: "You must be sponsored by 2 members of the Guild and must attend 1 meeting as a guest at which time you must present 2 or more samples of your work and fill out an application form in duplicate. Membership is open to original doll artists only, outside the state of Ohio. Makers of repro dolls who live and work in Ohio may join, however. Initiation fee is $10 yearly, dues are $5."

OHIO ARTS COUNCIL, 50 W. Broad St., Suite 3600, Columbus OH 43227. (614)466-2613. Individual Artists Coordinator: Barbara B. Clark. Sponsors Artists-in-Schools Programs; fellowships; and grants for individuals and craft organizations working in any craft discipline. Offers fellowship support of $5,000; project support up to $2,500; and minigrants up to $500. "Applicants for fellowship support must be creative artists established in their careers who have made significant contributions over a number of years. The artist is required to have a body of work and have established a professional reputation. Project support applicants who show extraordinary potential can be in the earlier stages of their careers." Request Aid to Individual Artist application. Requires resume and 10 slides (2x2 35mm) "they should be of high quality, if the craftsperson is not a photographer, he should get a professional to take the slides. Be sure that all 10 slides are consistent in quality." Deadline for application: February 1; minigrant deadline: February 1 and August 1.

RIVERBEND ARTS COUNCIL, 142 Riverbend Dr., Dayton OH 45405. (513)225-5479, 225-5433. Chairman: Raymond Bittner. Estab. 1968. Open to all. Board meets monthly to aid in the development and promotion of cultural art activities in the Dayton area." Sponsors classes and workshops and co-sponsors an annual art fair. Write for membership.

WEAVERS GUILD OF GREATER CINCINNATI, Peach Mountain Studio, 6117 Ridge Ave., Cincinnati OH 45213. (513)631-7520. President: Millie Stratton. Estab. 1949. Members: 275. Open to all interested in weaving. Meets monthly to further interest in weaving and fibers. Sponsors conferences; shows; workshops; newsletter; and sales and demonstrations at schools, fairs, and community groups. Write for membership.

Oklahoma

ARTS COUNCIL OF OKLAHOMA CITY, 3014 Paseo, Oklahoma City OK 73103. (405)521-1426. Estab. 1967. Members: 49 organizations. Members are nonprofit art-oriented clubs, organizations and agencies. Meets 4 times each year to support and promote arts in the Oklahoma City area. Sponsors Festival of the Arts in April and small crafts show in the fall. "Any craftsman who wants to be added to mailing list for prospectus for our 2 shows should write to Jackie Jones at the Arts Council."

OKLAHOMA ARTS AND HUMANITIES COUNCIL, 640 Jim Thorpe Bldg., Oklahoma City OK 73105. (405)521-2931. Community Services Coordinator: Cheryl Alters. Sponsors Artists-in-Residence programs and grants for nonprofit craft organizations. Grants do no generally exceed $5,000 and approximately $1,000 monthly salary is paid to Artists-in-Residence. Available to professional craftworkers with exhibition and workshop experience. Craftworkers interested in Artists-in-Residence should send resume with 3 references and a minimum of 5 slides of their work. Write or call for financial assistance application. Deadline for application: financial assistance — March 1, June 1, September 1, and December 1; Artists-in-Residence — April 30.

OKLAHOMA DESIGNER-CRAFTSMEN, 716 E. Eufaula, Norman OK 73071. (405)360-2779. President: John Atlee. Provides marketing information and sponsors exhibitions, workshops, and touring exhibits for individuals and organizations working in any craft discipline. Offers $1,200 cash awards annually in juried exhibitions. Available to residents or former residents of Oklahoma; must have exhibited in an Oklahoma Designer-Craftsmen exhibition and must be current member. Write letter of inquiry to Executive Director. Deadline for application: September 1. Publishes *ODC Newsletter* (subscription $10 per year, $7.50 renewal); and ODC catalogs for single medium exhibitions and annual state-wide exhibition ($1 plus $.50 postage and handling).

Oregon

MAUDE I. KERNS ART CENTER, 1910 E. 15th Ave., Eugene OR 97403. (503)345-1126. Contact: Membership Committee or Director. Estab. 1955. Members: 950. Open to all persons interested in furthering art activities. Meets yearly "to encourage and promote quality art education and creative efforts." Write for membership.
Activities: "We operate a school, gallery, rental sales and gift shop. We have monthly gallery exhibitions and quarterly classes in crafts and fine arts. We publish a newsletter."

McMINNVILLE ASSOCIATION OF THE ARTS, 417 N. Adams, McMinnville OR 97128. (503)472-8810. Coordinator: Lesli Grina. Estab. 1973. Members: 250+. Open to all. Meets monthly to "enjoy the process of active participation in the creative arts. This participation reflects the needs and interests of school children and senior citizens as well as other members of the community."
Activities: Sponsors monthly exhibits; workshops; arts and crafts fair; art auction; and a monthly newletter.
Application for Membership: Write including a check for desired membership. $4/student; $7.50/individual; $10-24/family; $25-49/contributing member; $50-99/sustaining; $100-999/patron; and $1,000 for life.

OREGON ARTS COMMISSION, 835 Summer St. NE, Salem OR 97301. (503)378-3625. Community Coordinator: Angus Randolph. Sponsors Artists-in-Schools programs; fellowships; grants; legal counseling; and marketing information for individuals and organizations working in batik; candlemaking; ceramics; decoupage; dollmaking; glass art; jewelry; leatherworking; metalsmithing; needlecrafts; pottery; and soft sculpture. Offers 10 annual $1,000 fellowships. Available to Oregon professionals. Recently "aided potter with travel project to South America to work with native tribes who are doing low fire pots. Potter is developing new techniques." To apply contact Commission. Deadline for application: October. Publishes newsletter and bulletin.

SALEM ART ASSOCIATION, 600 Mission St., Salem OR 97301. (503)581-2228. Contact: Lorraine Dye. Estab. 1943. Members: 1,300. Open to all interested in the arts. Meets annually to "further the arts in Salem and the Willamette Valley and to give an opportunity for artists to sell and exhibit their work in an inviting and informal setting." Sponsors gallery exhibits; classes; sales-rental; special events; an annual summer art festival; and a newsletter. Write or call for membership. Annual dues: $15, family, and $10, individual.

Pennsylvania

ARMSTRONG COUNTY LEAGUE OF ARTS, 105 Appleby Park, Ford City PA 16226. (412)762-9913. Secretary: Carroll G. Klingensmith. Estab. 1974. Members: 132. Open to any family, person or student interested in the objects and purposes of ACLOA. Meets monthly to "unify the activities related to the arts and provide a center for all arts and related activities in Armstrong County, Pennsylvania, and surrounding communities." Write for membership details.
Activities: Sponsors an annual art and craft show; sends out monthly newletters to members; and holds classes which are open to the public.

BUCKS COUNTY GUILD OF CRAFTSMEN, 111 Chapel Rd., New Hope PA 18938. (215)862-2374. Public Relations: Emil W. Peters. Estab. 1946. Members: 150. "Membership in the Guild is not restricted to working craftsmen, but is open to all persons residing within the Bucks County and immediate surrounding areas, who have an interest in the craft movement and can bring business acumen or managerial skill to the aid of the organization." Meets monthly except July and August "to promote and protect the interests of the workers in the handcrafts; to encourage the study and promotion of the handcrafts; to cooperate with all agencies and individuals in furthering a broader participation in, and appreciation of those crafts; to raise and maintain standards of design and craftsmanship by means of group meetings, publications, and exhibitions; to assist in the establishment and maintenance of sales outlets for quality handcrafts; and to help secure for handcraft workers information on sources of materials, craft education, and market requirements." Holds 2 annual fairs.
Application for Membership: "All meetings are open to public attendance. We encourage poten-

The juried works of 175 craftworkers attracted 200,000 viewers at the 10-day Three Rivers Arts Festival, Pittsburgh, Pennsylvania. Sales totalled $71,500 in 1977. Stage performances, strolling players, demonstrators, and children's events add to the festivities. Photo by Susan Lewis.

tial members to visit possibly 3 or more meetings to determine feasibility of membership. Particularly as members, participation beyond the fairs activities must be expected to perpetuate the existence and fulfillment of the aims and purposes of the Guild."

COMMONWEALTH OF PENNSYLVANIA, Council of the Arts, 2001 N. Front St., Harrisburg PA 17111. (717)787-6833. Crafts Program Director: Alice Eakin. Sponsors Artists-in-Schools program and grants to craft organizations working in any craft discipline. Artists-in-Schools guidelines and grants program guidelines available upon request — nonprofit organizations only. Write or call for application package.

LEHIGH VALLEY CRAFTS ASSOCIATION, 346 N. 8th St., Allentown PA 18102. (215)432-5792. Membership Chairman: Peggy Hobbs. Estab. 1977. Members: 70. Open to all interested in the crafts and to active craftspeople. Board meets monthly; general meetings vary. Purposes are "to stimulate interest in the work of local craftspeople; to provide the public with an opportunity to see and learn about quality crafts; to encourage education in crafts among both members and the public; and to encourage the interchange of ideas." Write for application.
Activities: Sponsors juried and nonjuried exhibits; workshops; and bus trips. Publishes a newsletter.

PENNSLVANIA COUNCIL ON THE ARTS, #3 Shore Drive Office Center, 2001 N. Front St., Harrisburg PA 17102. (717)787-6883. Coordinator: Alice Eakin. Operates Artists-in-Schools programs and provides grants to nonprofit Pennsylvania arts/crafts organizations. Write or call for application and more information.

THE PENNSYLVANIA GUILD OF CRAFTSMEN, INC. AND CRAFT ARTISTS OF PENNSYLVANIA, INC., 227 W. Beaver Ave., State College PA 16801. (814)234-0833. Provides marketing information and services; educational information; cultural exchange; and juried exhibit awards of recognition to individuals and organizations working in any craft discipline. Write for information.

SOCIETY OF CRAFT DESIGNERS, 2017 Walnut St., Philadelphia PA 19103. Executive Director: Ruth P. Livesey. Estab. 1975. Members: 150. Open to those interested in promoting good designs for the consumer craft market or in writing for that market. Meets annually and holds educational seminars "to provide a meeting place for those in the profession and to maximize their educational opportunities as professionals." Publishes internal newsletters and sponsors occasional exhibits of members' work. Request membership folder with application form.

Rhode Island

RHODE ISLAND STATE COUNCIL ON THE ARTS, 334 Westminster Mall, Providence RI 02903. (401)277-3880. Estab. 1967. Council board meets monthly to encourage and promote the arts for the benefit of Rhode Island citizens. Sponsors grants; Artists-in-Schools programs; community arts programs; and grants in aid to individual artists. Write for guidelines if Rhode Island resident or Rhode Island nonprofit tax exempt incorporation.

South Carolina

ANDERSON COUNTY ARTS COUNCIL, 405 N. Main St., Anderson SC 29621. (803)224-8811. Executive Director: Sue A. Parks. Estab. 1972. Members: 300. Meets yearly to "stimulate the practice and appreciation of the arts; to develop cooperative programs that allow groups and individuals to work together toward a common end of greater arts understanding among people; and to elevate the style and quality of life for the community."
Activities: Sponsors classes; performances; festivals; exhibits; conferences; workshops; and sales shop. Provides central information resource center; calendar of events; clerical assistance; dark room facilities; and information on nationwide college art courses. Assists member groups with publicity and promotion; subscription and membership; publications; exhibits; coordinating events; and administrative problems.
Application for Membership: "We have individual; couple; family; business; and organization memberships. Write for application."

ARTS COUNCIL OF SPARTANBURG COUNTY, INC., 385 S. Spring St. , Spartanburg SC 29301. (803)583-2776. Assistant Director: Ava B. Jennings. Estab. 1968. Members: 46 organizations. Membership information will be given upon request. The organization "coordinates the activities of 46 member organizations and channels inquiries and applications to the proper person. Also operates the Spartanburg Arts Center which houses these organizations and has changing exhibits, etc." Sponosors art and craft shows.

GREENWOOD HANDWEAVERS' GUILD, Rt. 1, Box 168-A, Hodges SC 29653. (803)374-7880. President: Larry P. Howell. Estab. 1977. Members: 12. Open to all wishing to learn more about weaving and fabric design. Meets monthly to "advance handweaving and fabric design; to share ideas and knowledge; and to demonstrate to the community the validity of these media as fine art." Sponsors annual show; biennial slide lecture; annual workshop; and an annual special project done as a group for benefit of the community. Write for membership; $5 annual dues; checks payable to Greenwood Handweavers' Guild.

SOUTH CAROLINA ARTS COMMISSION, 829 Richland St., Columbia SC 29201. (803)758-3442. Grants Coordinator: Penelope Knight. Sponsors Artists-in-Schools programs; fellowships; and marketing information to individual craftworkers working in batik; ceramics; jewelry; metalsmithing; pottery; soft sculpture; weavings; woodcrafting; and folk crafts. Offers 1 $2,500 Individual Artist Fellowship in crafts. Available to professional craftworker of exceptional promise or proven professional ability who is a resident of South Carolina. "The Commission is dedicated to support craftsmen showing the greatest potential for professional accomplishment and with greatest financial need." To apply write for application form. Deadline for application: April 15.

SOUTH CAROLINA ARTS COMMISSION, Crafts Development Program, 16 Charlotte St., Charleston SC 29403. (803)722-2759. Coordinator: William W. Robinson. Provides marketing and other technical assicstance to individual craftspeople and groups working in any craft discipline in South Carolina. Produces promotional and informational materials (brochures, directories, etc.) concerning state-produced handcrafts. Publishes *SC Crafts,* a bimonthly newsletter. Write for additional information.

South Dakota

HOT SPRINGS ART COUNCIL, Rt. 1, Box 30B, Hot Springs SD 57747. (605)745-6696. President: Marjorie Briggs. Estab. 1975. Members: 100. Meets monthly to help all persons in arts and crafts. Sponsors gallery shows and an arts and crafts festival. Write for membership.

SOUTH DAKOTA ARTS COUNCIL, 108 W. 11th St., Sioux Falls SD 57102. (605)339-6646. Program Director: Dennis Holub. Sponsors Artists-in-Schools programs; fellowships; and grants to individuals and organizations working in any craft discipline. Offers fellowships usually up to $1,000; offers mini grants of $500 or less; and assistance over $500. Grants available to South Dakota nonprofit craft organizations; grants and fellowships available to craftworkers who are residents of South Dakota for at least 2 years. "There is no resident requirement for Artists-in-Schools but must be willing to travel and communicate craft area to all age levels plus be able to work in school environment. Recently granted fellowship to potter to develop clays from a specific area of South Dakota and to a weaver to pursue new tapestry technique. A grant was given to blacksmith to video master smith in rural South Dakota town." To apply request forms from Council. Deadline for application: fellowships, March 15; Artists-in-Schools, March 15; grants, January 15, April 15, June 15, and September 15.

Tennessee

ARTIST AND CRAFTSMEN'S GUILD OF JACKSON, General Delivery, Spring Creek TN 38378. (801)424-9675. Membership Chairman and Treasurer: Floyed Dyer. Estab. 1974. Members: 100. Open to people interested in promoting crafts in the area and willing to work toward this goal. All artists and craftspeople are welcome in western Tennessee, especially Madison County. Meets the last Tuesday of each month to "promote art and crafts in the area; and to find outlets for our members to sell their art and crafts." Publishes monthly newsletter; holds shows in spring, summer, and fall and smaller weekend shows.
Application for Membership: If resident of western Tennessee apply to Joyce Todd at above address. Resident of Madison County, $5 a year; $10, nonresident. "We welcome patron members from anywhere in USA, $25 a year."

CUMBERLAND MOUNTAIN CRAFT ASSOCIATION, Holiday Hills, Rt. 9, Crossville TN 38555. (615)484-4577. Executive Director: Betty Kington. Estab. 1967. Members: 145. Must be Tennessee resident and work must meet standards. Board of Directors meets monthly. Organization's purpose is to promote and sell crafts. Sponsors annual craft show. Write for membership form; submit with 3-5 pieces of work.

OAK RIDGE COMMUNITY ART CENTER, Box 105, Badger Rd., Oak Ridge TN 37830. (615)482-1182. Acting Director: Jewel Stallions. Provides grants and scholarships to craftworkers in batik; candlemaking; ceramics; jewelry; leatherworking; macrame;

metalsmithing; needlecrafts; pottery; soft sculpture; tole painting; weavings; and woodcrafting. Available for students taking Art Center classes. To apply contact Director.

TENNESSEE CRAFTS ENTERPRISES, INC., 222 Capitol Hill Bldg., Nashville TN 37219. (615)741-1701. Crafts Marketing Coordinator: Bill Powell. Offers marketing information and marketing outlets for individuals and organizations working in any craft discipline. Tennessee Arts Commission (same address), Roy Overcast, Director of Crafts, offers Artists-in-Schools programs and grant assistance. Both programs available to resident Tennessee craftworkers. To apply request forms.

Texas

CORPUS CHRISTI ARTS COUNCIL, Box 6683, Corpus Christi TX 78411. (512)855-3861. Director: Denise Schulz. Estab. 1960. Members: 120. Types of membership: "Members at Large, persons who have an interest in the cultural development of our community; Organization Membership, organizations with an arts-related background and/or organizations who have an interest in the cultural development of our community; Associated Organization Membership, associate organizations with an arts-related background and/or organizations (associate) who have interest in the cultural development of our community." Monthly meetings "to foster, encourage, and promote increased participation in, and public support of, fine arts and cultural activities; to encourage, initiate and coordinate cooperative and joint programs and activities among organizations engaged in artistic and cultural activities; and generally to work for the development and improvement of the artistic and cultural resources of the community. Apply with credentials either by phone or mail."
Activities: "The Corpus Christi Arts Council co-sponsors Bayfest, a free family festival located on the bayfront and held in the fall. The Council is responsible for the weekly newspaper calendar, functioning as a publicity clearinghouse for local arts groups, and other services for the community."

HOUSTON DESIGNER CRAFTSMEN, 1408 Michigan, Houston TX 77006. (713)527-8862. Membership Chairperson: Christi Bean. Estab. 1960. Members: 250. Open to all with interest. Meets monthly "to promote fine crafts through juried shows; fairs; programs; etc." Write for membership; $10 fee.
Activities: Sponsors annual craft show; bimonthly workshops; and publishes monthly newsletter.

TEXAS COMMISSION ON THE ARTS AND HUMANITIES, Box 13406, Capitol Station Austin TX 78711. (512)475-6593. Estab. 1965. The Commission is a state agency governed by 18 members appointed by the Governor for 6-year terms. Purpose is "to foster the development of a receptive climate for the arts and humanities that will culturally enrich and benefit Texans in their daily lives."
Activities: Provides staff consultations and sponsors Artists-in-Schools program; special arts projects; dance touring programs; and grants program.

Vermont

ARTS COUNCIL OF WINDHAM COUNTY, 67 Main St., Brattleboro VT 05301. (802)254-5511. Executive Director: Karen Meyer Rappaport. Estab. 1974. Members: 1,000. Organizational members must be nonprofit arts organizations; individual members join by paying a membership fee. Meets annually (trustees monthly) to "provide support services (promotion, publicity, consultations) and act as a clearinghouse for the arts in southern Vermont." A membership form will be sent upon request.
Activities: Directs a school arts program; sponsors workshops; publishes a monthly newspaper and an annual Directory of Artists, Artisans and Arts Resources.

CRAFT PROFESSIONALS OF VERMONT, Rt. 1, West Burke VT 05871. Executive Secretary: Jean Kennedy. Estab. 1974. Members: 150. Open to "Vermont resident craftsmen who pass screening of work for individualism; inventiveness; and craftmanship can become active members. People or groups interested in furthering CPV goals may become sponsoring members no matter where they live." Meets annually; Board meets every 6 weeks to promote professional standards; holds workshops and seminars for all state craftsmen; and explore marketing opportunities for members."
Activities: Sponsors seminars; workshops; retail fairs for members only; and publishes a newsletter.
Application for Membership: "Write for information to executive secretary. Procedure includes slides of work; fee; resume; application, viewing of actual work; vote by screening committee elected from board of directors and from membership at large who are guided in voting on work by set of established principles of CPV."

VERMONT ARTISANS, INC., Box 44, Strafford VT 05072. (802)765-9861. Administrator: Dorothy Swayze. Estab. 1972. Members: 90. Open to all. Meets monthly to "stimulate arts and crafts through the operation of a store, gallery, workshops and a meeting place." Sponsors workshops; gallery shows; monthly dances; classes; craft fairs; pottery studio; store; and monthly newsletter. Write for membership; $10 annual dues.

VERMONT COUNCIL ON THE ARTS, INC., 136 State St., Montpelier VT 05602. (802)828-3291. Sponsors Artists-in-Schools programs and grants to individuals and organizations working in any craft discipline. Offers individual grants from $500-1,000; organizational grants from $1,500-3,500. Available to Vermont residents and organizations. "Recently provided grant to craftworker producing a series of large batiks." To apply write for handbook containing application form and instructions. Deadline for application: May 1.

VERMONT STATE CENTER AT FROG HOLLOW, Frog Hollow Rd., Middlebury VT 05753. Director: Tricia Nolan. Estab. 1971. Members: 250 exhibiting craftspeople, 300 supporting members. Open to Vermont residents producing high quality crafts which are juried monthly for technical excellence; mark of individuality; and creative use of the medium. Meets monthly to "provide educational; informational; and marketing opportunities for residents of Vermont." Write for membership.
Activities: Supports school programs; workshops; information services; resource directories; career training programs; and publishes bimonthly bulletin.

Virginia

COMMISSION OF ARTS AND HUMANITIES, 400 E. Grace St., 1st Flr., Richmond VA 23219. (804)786-4492. Executive Director: J. Haynie. Provides Artists-in-Schools programs and grants to craftsworkers and organizations. Offers $10,800 9-month stipends for Artists-in-Schools and $100-5,000 in arts expansion/public service projects grants. Available to professional craftworkers and nonprofit tax-exempt organizations. To apply for AIS, send resume, slides and brief letter describing your method of operation in working with school children. Write or call for interview.

McGUFFEY ARTS ASSOCIATION, INC., 201 2nd St. NW, Charlottesville VA 22901. Executive Secretary: Fay Kayhoe. Estab. 1975. Members: 43 renting members, 33 associate members. Renting membership based on quality of work, ability to work within a cooperative and to meet city lease requirement for keeping studio open to the public. Associate membership based on quality of work. Meets monthly. Purpose is to "provide studio space for artists and craftsmen; to provide a retail outlet for their work; to provide the city of Charlottesville with an art center; and to provide art, crafts, and dance lessons to the public." Sponsors gallery shows, workshops, and sales.
Application for Membership: "Write for or pick up an application form. Meetings are held 4 times a year to review forms and evaluate work of artist applying. Actual work, not slides, must be brought."

NORTHERN VIRGINIA WOODCARVER ASSOCIATION, 4400 Olley Lane, Fairfax VA 22032. (703)323-5865. Secretary-Treasurer: William Cronenberg. Estab. 1973. Members: 130. Open to all at least 10 years old and interested in wood and woodcarving; senior citizens and disabled persons particularly welcome. Meets monthly for regular meeting; 2 Sundays per month for teaching. Association's purpose is to promote woodcarving; to provide fellowship with persons of same interest; and to exchange ideas, tools, wood, and expertise. Sponsors 2 annual shows, 1 annual "Artistry in Wood" show featuring craftsmen east of the Mississippi; and participates in about 30 craft shows, school and church bazaars. Write William Cronenberg, 7931 Shreve Rd., Falls Church VA 22043 for application blank and brochure. $5 annual fee.

VIRGINIA CRAFTS COUNCIL, 717 Rugby Rd., Charlottesville VA 22903. (804)295-6360. Executive Director: Mary Maher. Estab. 1967. Members: 400. General membership open to all; exhibiting status membership given to members for the life time of their membership following jurying by 5 pieces of work. Meets annually; regional councils meet at different times during the year "to encourage craftsmanship, design and technique, and to widen the public understanding of creative crafts." Write for membership.
Activities: Sponsors annual craft fair, workshops, and exhibitions and publishes monthly newsletter.

VIRGINIA MOUNTAIN CRAFTS GUILD, 777 Paragon Ave., Salem VA 24153. Director: Dorothy Mahoney. Estab. 1975. Members: 1,000+. Open to mountain craftpeople in southwestern Virgina. Meets quarterly to "improve and maintain the quality of their crafts; to work toward a wider exhibition and sale of their crafts; and to encourage a widespread appreciation of Virginia's mountain crafts heritage." Sponsors workshops; traveling exhibit; and newsletter. Write for membership; work must be juried to show or sell with the Guild.

VIRGINIA MUSEUM, Education in the Arts Committee, Boulevard and Grove Ave., Richmond VA 23221. Sponsors fellowships for individuals working in any craft discipline. Offers $1,500 student fellowship; $3,600 graduate fellowship; and $2,400 professional fellowship. Available to native-born or 5-year resident Virginians who seek financial aid for additional education or experience in the arts. To apply write for application form. Deadline for application: April 1. "Craftspeople compete for fellowships with applicants in all the arts."

Washington

ARTS COUNCIL OF THE MID-COLUMBIA REGION, Box 735, Richland WA 99352. (509)943-0524. President: George Gurwell. Members: 250. Open to people interested in the arts. Meets monthly to support and promote the arts. Publishes monthly newsletter and calendar; sponsors professional touring events, workshops, films, and exhibits; provides sponsor support to Artist-in-Schools Program; and makes available arts information, resources, and consulting services.
Application for Membership: Send dues to above address: patron, $25+; family, $10; individual, $5; and student, $3.

CENTRALIA COMMUNITY COLLEGE, Box 639, Centralia WA 98531. (206)736-9391. Financial Aid Director: Joseph Beaulieu. Provides grants and scholarships to artists. Offers $250,000 in Basic Educational Opportunity Grants to potters, painters and other artists. Application deadline: April 1.

COOPERATIVE ARTS COUNCIL OF CLARK COUNTY, Box 1995, Vancouver WA 98663. (206)969-8171. President: Donald G. Senecal. Estab. 1974. Members: 25 organizations. Open to all. Meets monthly to promote the arts. Sponsors visitations by professional artists, scholarships and awards. Send $5 for individual membership; $10/organization.

THE CREATIVE ARTS LEAGUE, 620 Market St., Kirkland WA 98033. Director: Nancy Silvernale. Estab. 1960. Members: 250. Open to anyone interested in the visual arts. Meets monthly to "further the interests of members; to offer classes or workshops in those subjects in which there is an interest." Sponsors annual art fair; publishes monthly newsletter; and holds free workshops. Write for memberships.

INTERNATIONAL GUILD OF CRAFT JOURNALISTS, AUTHORS, AND PHOTOGRAPHERS, 1312 3rd Ave.W., Seattle WA 98119. (206)282-0311. President: Michael Scott. Estab. 1976. Members: 160. Members must be involved in the communications aspects of the crafts field as editors, staff writers, freelancers, photographers, authors, publishers, etc. Meets biennially. Purpose "to exchange information and promote better writing in the crafts field; encourage recognition of the professionalism of craft writers; improve relations between writers and editors." Sponsors newsletter and workshops; every member receives a press card. Write for membership.

KING COUNTY ARTS COMMISSION, 300 King County Administration Bldg., Seattle WA 98104. (206)344-7580. Visual Arts Coordinator: Jerry Allen. Estab. 1966. Commissioners appointed by County Executive. Meets monthly to promote and encourage the visual, performing, and literary arts through King County. Publishes newsletter; and sponsors workshops, demonstrations and occasional programming.

Washington D.C.

AMERICAN FOLKLIFE CENTER, Library of Congress, Washington DC 20540. (202)426-6590. Director: Alan Jabbour. Deputy Director: Ray Dockstader. Estab. 1976. A Federal agency under the guidance of a Board of Trustees. Meets to "present and preserve American folklife."
Activities: "The Center has authority to exhibit; conduct conferences; field studies; workshops; and basic research. We publish a quarterly newsletter, *Folklife Center News*, available on request."
Membership: "We do not maintain a membership list but attempt to respond to individual inquiries, above and beyond the newsletter mailing list."

ARMY ARTS AND CRAFTS PROGRAM, HQDA (DAAG-MSA), Washington DC 20314. (202)693-7778, 693-7779. Arts and Crafts Director: Elizabeth E. Reed. Estab. 1942. "Facilities

are open to military personnel; their families; and some civilians provided authorization is obtained in advance." Facilities are open daily, weekends and holidays at most locations. Program's purpose is cultural; educational; and recreational. This largely depends on the individual's needs and interest." Contact Program for geographical locations.
Activities: Sponsors annual Army Arts and Crafts Week; Designer-Craftsman Contest open to military personnel; classes; workshops; shows; and festivals.

ARTISTS EQUITY ASSOCIATION, 3726 Albemarle St. NW, Washington DC 20016. Estab. 1947 "by a group of professional artists who conceived it as a means of speaking collectively for artists' rights. Nonprofit aesthetically nonpartisan organization for the visual artist." Provides legal referral services; group insurance; model contracts; group travel; Action Kits (complete series; publications on a variety of topics of concern to visual arts); and publishes the *Artists Equity Association News*. Members are entitled to discounts on various craft publications.

INDIAN ARTS AND CRAFTS DEVELOPMENT PROGRAM, Indian Arts and Crafts Board, US Department of the Interior; Washington DC 20240. (202)343-2773. General Manager: Robert G. Hart. Provides advice; counseling; and promotion exhibitions to individuals and craft organizations working in any craft discipline. Available to "Native Americans (Indian, Eskimo, Aleut). Requests submitted by non-Native sources must be accompanied by evidence of direct support by Indian, Eskimo, or Aleut groups. Recently assisted the Houma Tribe of Louisiana to organize a 2 week woodcarving workshop for local craftsmen". To apply "a letter is sufficient including a description of the project and its objectives; evidence of the interest of Native American artists and craftsmen, and the extent of their expected participation; an estimate of the funds being sought for the projects; and a brief resume of the organizations already contacted for funding or other assistance with the project."
Publications: *Source Directory* (native American owned and operated arts and crafts businesses); *Bibliography* (native American arts and crafts of the US); and *Fact Sheet: General Information* (about the activities of the IACB).

NATIONAL ENAMELISTS GUILD, 5120 Fulton St. NW, Washington DC 20016. Treasurer: Ann Nichelson. Estab. 1973. Members: 100+. Open to all interested in enameling. Meets bimonthly "to promote good craftsmanship through study of the techniques and problems involved in enameling; to inform general public about enameling as an art craft; and to cooperate with other enameling or other craft organizations with similar educational interests or objectives." Write for membership; $7.50 annual dues.
Activities: Sponsors workshops; exhibitions of either a regional or national nature; and bimonthly newsletter. "We also buy supplies in quantity to take advantage of price reduction and to make overseas purchase of enamels easier for members."

POTOMAC CRAFTSMEN, INC., c/o Metropolitan Memorial Methodist Church, Nebraska and New Mexico Aves. NW, Washington DC 20016. Contact: Membership Chairman. Estab. 1944. Members: 500. Open to all interested in fiber arts. Meets monthly "to widen our knowledge of weaving and increase the number of techniques known; to investigate and study fabrics made throughout the world; to improve our manual weaving methods; to gain inspiration from one another by sharing our weaving; and to promote the use of handwoven articles of quality." Sponsors workshops and an annual show and publishes a newsletter. Write for membership.

West Virginia
CABIN CREEK QUILTS COOPERATIVE, Box 383, Cabin Creek WV 25035. (304)595-3928. Director: Mack Miles. Estab. 1970. Members: 100. "Members must be a resident of West Virginia and of low income according to the CSA poverty guidelines. Needlework is our main field of interest." Board of Directors meets monthly; entire membership meets once a year. Goal is to provide a market for items made by members. Sponsors a limited number of private shows around the country along with workshops and demonstrations; also wholesales and retails through coop-owned shops. "Contact our office if you believe you qualify. We then need to see a sample of your work and will proceed from there."

MORGANTOWN ART ASSOCIATION, 540 Martin Ave., Morgantown WV 26505. (304)599-3795. President: Mrs. Willis H. Hertig. Estab. 1958. Members: 85-100. Open to all interested in art education, self improvement, and with a concern for arts in the community. Meets 4 times a year to "encourage and promote a public interest in and an understanding of all schools of visual arts; to create and develop a closer relationship between art and the community; and to disseminate art information." Sponsors exhibition of visual arts; all member show; street sales; Christmas art mart; and 4 annual organized programs. Write for membership.

WEST VIRGINIA DEPARTMENT OF CULTURE AND HISTORY, Arts and Humanities Division, Science and Culture Center, Capitol Complex, Charleston WV 25305. (304)348-0240. Contact: Executive Director. Awards 9-month Artists-in-Residence grants to sculptors, painters and craftworkers. Grants made on matching funds basis. Submit resume and awards won. Resumes forwarded to communities applying for artist residencies.

Wisconsin

COMMUNITY CRAFTS & ART COOP, 118 N. Carroll St., Madison WI 53705. (608)257-4790. Manager: Sharon Friedland. Estab. 1971. Members: 33. "Original designs and quality craftsmanship a must. Members must work in coop store 8 hours a month. Meets annually. Cooperative retail outlet for members' products on a nonprofit basis. "Submit samples of work for acceptance by quality control committee." Membership fee: $10.

GREATER MILWAUKEE COUNCIL OF ARTS FOR CHILDREN, 647 W. Virginia St., Milwaukee WI 53204. (414)276-3550. Council Director: Joyce Broan. Estab. 1973. Members: 275. Open to all interested in the work of the Council. Organization promotes, develops and coordinates activities in the arts for children. Sponsors an art festival for the handicapped and publishes a monthly newsletter and a children's arts calendar. Write for membership.

WISCONSIN ARTS BOARD, 123 W. Washington Ave., Madison WI 53702. (608)266-0190. Grants Officer: Lea Ward-James. Sponsors Artists-in-Schools Programs; fellowships; individual project grants; and legal counseling to individuals and craft organizations. Offers 5 $2,000 fellowships each fiscal year. Available to craftworkers who have been Wisconsin residents for at least 12 months prior to application. Degree credit students not eligible. Write for Arts Board application form. Deadline for fellowship application: September 1. Deadlines for project grants vary; request guidelines from Arts Board.

WISCONSIN RURAL ARTIST ASSOCIATION, INC., 9096 Liberty School Rd., Omro WI 54963. (414)685-5472. Correspondence Secretary: Patti Smerling. Estab. 1954. Members: 430-450. Active membership open to Wisconsin residents and amateurs; associate or patron membership open to anyone interested in arts and crafts. Meets annually and by correspondence to "promote arts and crafts in Wisconsin; to provide Wisconsin residents with aids to continuing education; to promote amateur visual arts and crafts." Write for membership.
Activities: Aids programs for amateur artists and craftspeople; publishes quarterly magazine style newsletter; sponsors touring art show, special projects, and traveling slide show; and presents awards to regional art and craft show winners.

Canada

THE CANADA COUNCIL, Box 1047, Ottawa, Ontario Canada K1P 5V8. (613)237-3400. Chief, Information Services: Mario Lavoie. Provides Artists-in-Residence programs and grants to sculptors, painters, architects, graphic artists, administrators, illustrators and organizations. Available to Canadian citizens or landed immigrants. Write, outlining field of interest and assistance required.

ONTARIO POTTERS ASSOCIATION, c/o Hamilton and Region Arts Council, Hamilton Place, Box 2080, Hamilton, Ontario Canada L8N 3Y7 (416)529-9485. Executive Assistant: Claudette Marko. Estab. 1975. Members: 635. Open to any person interested in the development of ceramic art. Meets annually to "further the ceramic arts and to bring about public participation in and appreciation for handcrafted pottery and glass." Write for membership; $15 annual fee.
Activities: Publishes 4 newsletters annually and 2 semiannual magazines; sponsors a biennial exhibition; and operates a nonprofit shop in Toronto where work is sold and one-man or group shows are held.

Virgin Islands

VIRGIN ISLANDS COUNCIL ON THE ARTS, Caravelle Arcade, Christiansted VI 00820. (809)773-3075. Executive Director: Stephen J. Bostic. Provides Artists-in-Schools programs, grants and scholarships to artists/craftworkers and organizations. Application deadline: 2 months before project would begin. "Potential applicants should discuss proposal with Council staff before submitting formal request."

Courses

Find yourself in a creative impasse? Wish you could turn your craft knowledge into a college degree? Want to broaden your skills into other craft areas?

If you've answered yes to any of the above, perhaps it's time for you to enroll in a course where you can find inspiration from a qualified instructor — or perhaps even from fellow students.

The workshops and courses listed here range from beginning to advanced. Many are offered for credit. Write to those that interest you and ask for a school bulletin or brochure which will give you up-to-date changes in fees and courses.

Alabama

AUBURN UNIVERSITY DEPARTMENT OF CONSUMER AFFAIRS, School of Home Economics, Auburn AL 36830. (205)826-4084. Ceramics offered to 25 students during fall, winter and spring semesters; weaving offered to 5-15 students in fall, winter, spring and summer; surface design offered to 15 students during fall and spring semesters. Semester equals 10 weeks of instruction. Credit available; offers degree in textile design.
Application: Apply to Registrar at above address. School of Home Economics will request slides or actual work from graduate level applicants.

JACKSONVILLE STATE UNIVERSITY, Jacksonville AL 36265. (205)435-9820. Head, Department of Art: Dr. Emile E. Burn. Ceramics held 2 semesters annually; Craft Media, 1 semester; Jewelry, 1 mini-semester. Credit available. Instructors have MFA degrees and 5+ years teaching experience. Emphasizes technical skills and knowledge. Apply to University Admissions Office at above address.

THE MUSEUM ART EDUCATION COUNCIL, 2000 8th Ave. N., Birmingham AL 35203. (205)254-2571. Coordinator: Alis Eaton Bennett. Offers pottery 4 times annually for 80 potters for 8 weeks; Inkle Loom 4 times annually for 4 weeks (unlimited registration); Intermediate Weaving 4 times annually for 10 weavers for 4 weeks; and Frame Loom, Drop Spinning, Quilting As Art; enameling, batik, and macrame 4 times annually for 8 weeks (unlimited registration). Fee: $25-45/course, includes registration and materials. Credit available; "It is up to the particular institution to decide whether or not to give various units of credit for work done at the Museum Art Education Council." Write for application information.
Purpose: "Beginning, intermediate, or advanced instruction in desired media and in a wonderfully friendly and casual atmosphere as well as being housed in the Birmingham Museum of Art."

TROY STATE UNIVERSITY, Department of Art, Troy AL 36081. (205)566-3000, ext. 278. Chairman, Department of Art: Dr. R. C. Paxson. Offers pottery and sculpture every quarter for 20 students; metal design and crafts in recreation 2 quarters for 20 students. Quarter equals 10 weeks. Fee: tuition fee plus $15, includes registration and materials. Credit available.
Application: Request admission requirements/mail to Chairman, Department of Art. Slides and photos of work should be presented. SASE.

UNIVERSITY OF NORTH ALABAMA, Florence AL 35630. (205)766-4100. Offers Ceramics 1-4 and General Crafts 1-2 (includes batik, candlemaking, needlecrafts and weavings). "All courses meet 18 weeks during the fall and spring semesters and will meet 8 weeks during the summer." Registration limit: 18, Ceramics 1-2; Ceramics 3-4, independent study. Fee: $90/course includes $30/credit hour, $15 entrance fee and $15 materials cost (includes clays, glazes, firing, etc.). Credit available.
Purpose: Ceramics course will help student "develop building/throwing skills, glazing (if interested, glaze formulating), and gas and electric firing. Many of our graduates have built large gas kilns and other equipment and are professional potters."
Application: Write J. Hollie Allen, Director of Admissions, at the above address. "If desired, request information on cost of meals and lodging."

Alaska

DEPARTMENT OF CONFERENCES AND INSTITUTES, Artists and Dealers Survival Conference, 117 Eielson Bldg., Fairbanks AK 99701. (907)479-7800. Program Development Specialist: Nancy Brimhall. Estab. 1977. All levels of workshops in marketing; technique; artist/dealer relationships; copyright protection; taxes; museum policies; insurance; loan agreements; art legislation; current publications; contract negotiations; and pricing. "How to Workshops" include: hang a show; prepare a portfolio; photograph for exhibits; ship and frame; write proposals; and keep records. Offered annually to a maximum of 150 students usually 2-3 days in the spring. Emphasizes all areas of crafts. Fee: $45, includes registration and materials. Write for application.
Purpose: "Skills necessary to deal with the business world in a forum for discussing practical matters and issues facing artists today. Specifically designed for Alaskan artists although the conference covers a wide range of issues pertinent to all types of artists. We usually have a participants show."

UNIVERSITY OF ALASKA, College of Arts & Sciences, 3221 Providence Dr., Anchorage AK 99504. Courses offered in ceramics; jewelry; and metalsmithing. "We offer a full 4-year program (BA, BFA and teacher educational certification). Work on semester system." Credit available.
Admissions: Write to Admissions & Records at the above address for catalog listing fees and entrance requirements.

Arizona

ARCOSANTI, c/o Richard Johnson, The Rolling Arcosanti Hot Mud Review, Arcosanti AZ 86333 or c/o Tim Dalton, Winter Wood, Arcosanti AZ 86333. Ceramics offered to 3 students 4 times annually for 5-week sessions; Wood Interior Finishing and Wood Furniture-making offered to 20-30 students once annually each for 4-5-week sessions; and construction offered to up to 100 students 9 times annually for 5 week sessions. Entry fee: $450, ceramics; $400, woodworking; $435, construction. Fee covers registration, materials, lodging and meals. If student is already enrolled in another school, credit can sometimes be earned for course. Instructors are resident craftworkers and resident builders of Arcosanti. Write.
Purpose: School aims to teach care and maintenance of tools and studio; crafting techniques; responsibilities of a craftworker; and self-fulfillment.

CENTRE FOR ANTI GRAVITY, The Rolling Arcosanti Hot Mud Review, Arcosanti AZ 86333. Contact: Richard Johnson. Estab. 1978. Basic and artisan workshops in technique offered 4 times annually to 1-3 students for 5-20 weeks. Emphasizes ceramics. Fee: $450/workshop. Includes registration; some materials; lodging and meals; and insurance. Write for application; state interests and intent. Workshops provide insight into new age values and techniques.

MOHAVE COMMUNITY COLLEGE, 1971 Jagerson, Kingman AZ 86401. Art Division Chairperson: Paul Kessel. Ceramics 1-4; Stained Glass; Jewelry 1-2; Metalsmithing 1-2; Metal Casting 1-2; and Fiber Crafts each offered to 20 students 2 times annually for 17 weeks. Fee: $15 for 2 semester courses (includes registration and some materials). Credit available. Purpose: "to teach sound basic knowledge of craft fundamentals." Has classes in 3 locations: Kingman, Bull Head City, and Lake Havasu City, Arizona. Write to above address for application.

NORTHERN ARIZONA UNIVERSITY, College of Creative Arts, Flagstaff AZ 86001. Chairman, Art Department: Dr. R. Piotrowski. Offers advanced intermediate and beginning courses in ceramics; jewelry; weaving and glass art 2 times annually for 16-week sessions. Registration limit: 20-25 students. Fee: $22/credit plus $10 application fee; material fee varies. Write Registrar at above address for application.

PENDLETON FABRIC CRAFT SCHOOL, 407 Jordan Rd., Box 233, Sedona AZ 86336. (603)282-3671. Contact: Mary Pendleton. Basic and advanced workshops in "How To" offered spring, summer, and fall for 10-12 students per instructor for 4-5 days. "Intermediate and advanced students must advise us of what weaving they have done in the past." Emphasizes weaving and spinning. Fee: $70/workshop includes registration and use of equipment. Materials fee: varies. Write for application. Purpose: a complete knowledge of weaving in the areas covered in the class.

UNIVERSITY OF ARIZONA, Department of Art, Tucson AZ 85721. (602)884-3016. Professor: Maurice Grossman. Offers beginning and advanced ceramics for 20 students during summer, fall, and spring; beginning, intermediate, and advanced metalwork and jewelry for 20 students during fall and spring; and beginning, intermediate, and advanced fibers for 20 students during summer, fall, and spring. Course length is 15 weeks; summer program is 5 weeks. Credit available; offers BFA or MFA. Write Admissions Office for application and catalog. $10 application fee for out-of-state residents.

Arkansas

THE ARKANSAS ARTS CENTER, Box 2137, Little Rock AR 72203. (501)372-4000. Education Registrar: Thom Hall. Offers ceramics; glass art; jewelry; glassblowing; stained glass; enameling; woodworking; and design for 12 weeks during the fall and spring semesters and 8 weeks during the summer semester. Fee: about $50 for registration, insurance and tuition. No credit available. Instructors are practicing artists. "Class schedules and registration forms are mailed upon request, and are available in person at the center."

California

ART IN ARCHITECTURE, 1434 S. Spaulding Ave., Los Angeles CA 90019. (213)933-1194. Director of Design: Dr. Joseph Young. Estab. 1955. Advanced workshop in marketing and technique offered annually for 1 week to 5-10 art school graduates interested in making their career in the architectural arts. Empahsizes mosaics; stained glass; and cast concrete. "We are involved with all permanent media pertaining to improving the architectural environment." Fee: $200/workshop includes registration and materials. Write for appplication. "Give background of interest in architectural arts plus at least 2 references and 5 35mm slides." SASE.
Purpose: "An introduction into the professional standards and intensive information on contracts; fundings; location of clients; public relations; etc."

BAULINES CRAFTSMAN'S GUILD, Box 305, Bolinas CA 94924. Treasurer: A. E. Carpenter. Offers ceramics; glass art; leatherworking; weaving and wood working for 3 month sessions for 10-20 students. Fee: $200-450/month, includes registration. Credit can be arranged through Antioch West and College of Arts and Crafts, Oakland. Write for brochure.

THE BINDERY, 7513 Melrose Ave., Los Angeles CA 90069. (213)653-0071. President: Frank Buxton. Offers bookbinding throughout year for 10 students and bookcrafts as requested for 10 students in 1-2 day workshops. Fee: $10/lesson for bookbinding classes, includes registration and materials in workshops. Materials fee: $3/book completed. Apply in person, call or write.
Purpose: "A student will learn basic bookbinding skills as well as learn the fundamentals of design for modern book covers. We stress practical application of the methods taught and urge students to work at home or elsewhere outside of class sessions to increase their skills. We expect students to do new skills in each class. Students can expect to complete their 1st book, either rebind or new blank book, within 4 class sessions. Our students complete 1 or more books each class thereafter. Students may join the classes at any time, 1st of month preferred, and can study with us as long as they desire. We have advanced, intermediate, and beginner students in each class. Workshops are limited to 1 specific skill only, blank books; note-pad cover; protective boxes; or the like, and are announced as enough requests are given. Generally the workshops are held in the summer and fall."

CALIFORNIA LUTHERAN COLLEGE, Art Department, 60 W. Olsen Rd., Thousand Oaks CA 91360. (805)492-2411. Department Chairman: B. M. A. Weber. Offers pottery 2 semesters to 10 students. Fee: cost of 3 credits ($87/credit), includes registration and materials. Credit available.
Purpose: "He/she can expect to gain the best instruction available in the field of pottery and special individual attention and concern by one of the finest artists in the field. There is also the possibility of an exchange program where he/she may live in the Netherlands."
Application: Write the Art Department. Application to the college is $15. "Only requirement is teacher's approval of student's desire and interest to work as a potter."

CALIFORNIA POLYTECHNIC STATE UNIVERSITY, Art Department, San Luis Obispo CA 93407. (805)546-2324. Department Head: T. V. Johnston. Offers woods; metals; and ceramics 4 quarters annually for 24 students. Quarter length is 10 weeks. Fee: $66/quarter registered students, includes registration. Materials fee: $10. Credit available; offers BS in Applied Art and Design.
Application: Apply to Admissions Office. $20 application fee. Submit portfolio. SASE.

CALIFORNIA STATE/SAN BERNARDINO, 5500 State College Pkwy., San Bernardino CA 92407. (714)887-7459. Chairman: Leo Doyle. Offers ceramics; jewelry; woodworking; glass blowing; and weaving every quarter for 24 students for 10 weeks; stained glass is offered as an extension class for 24 students for 10 weeks. Fee: $49/5 units. Lab fee: $10. Credit available; offers BA in all areas mentioned above. Apply to Office of Admissions.

CALIFORNIA STATE UNIVERSITY, Art Department, Sacramento CA 95816. (916)454-6166. Contact: Ellen Van Fleet. Estab. 1971. Basic and advanced workshops in technique offered annually to 15 University registered students for 1 semester. Empahsizes cloisonne. Fee: $100/workshop; includes registration, some materials and tools. Write for catalogue. Purpose: "medieval enameling and related silversmithing. Students will complete at least 4 jewels and settings. Will help revive an art form that was lost for 400 years."

CANDLELITE HOUSE, 8449 San Juan Ave., South Gate CA 90280. Contact: Margaret Finley. Offers candlemaking 12 times annually for 4 weeks for 10 students; Intermediate Candlemaking 6 times annually for 8 weeks for 10 students; Advanced Candlemaking 6 times annually for 8 weeks for 10 students; mold making 3 times annually for 5 advanced students; and wax formulation 3 times annually for 12 weeks for 5 advanced students. Fee: $25-250/course, includes registration. Students supply own materials. Write for application.

CORONADO SCHOOL OF FINE ARTS, 176 C Ave., Box 156, Coronado CA 92118. (714)435-8541. Director: M. Lewis. Offers batik twice annually for 8 weeks. Fee: $260/course, includes registration. Separate materials fee. Write for application; $10 fee.

CREATIVE ARTS GROUP, 108 N. Baldwin, Sierra Madre CA 91024. (213)355-8350. Director: Shirley Lukesh. Offers ceramics 4 times annually for 10 students; patchwork 3 times annually for 18 students; batik and fabric printing 3 times annually for 10 students; spinning and dyeing 3 times annually for 5 students; and stained and leaded glass 4 times annually for 18 students. Course length is 8 weeks. Fee: $28/class, includes registration. Materials fee: $6-8.50. Call or write for free brochure.
Purpose: "Introduction to new techniques; experience of working with a professional artist who is making his/her living in field; and input from fellow students."

CUSTOM HANDWEAVERS, Allied Arts Guild, Arbor Rd. and Creek Dr., Menlo Park CA 94025. (415)325-0626. Contact: Kathy Davis. Various levels of workshops in technique offered to 4-5 students for 3 weeks, 3 times a week. Emphasizes weaving. Write or call for application. Purpose: greater comfort with the loom and various techniques. Instruction: Kathy Davis, production weaver for 6 years, and Enid Wood, weaver with 30 years experience.

DE ANZA COLLEGE, 21250 Stevens Creek Blvd., Cupertino CA 95014. (408)996-4567. Fine Arts Division Chairman: William Cleveland. Offers jewelry; metalsmithing; needlecrafts; quilting; soft sculpture; weaving; and furniture making. Students supply own materials. Credit available. Write for application. "Must live in district to qualify for free community college."

THE DE YOUNG MUSEUM ART SCHOOL, Golden Gate Park, San Francisco CA 94118. (415)558-3109. Registrar: Sasha Ferrer. Offers batik; ceramics; jewelry; metalsmithing; soft sculpture; sculpture; basketry; quilting; textiles; stained glass; enameling; and cloisonne. Fee: $22-60/class.
Application: Write with $1 for brochure containing registration form. You will be put on mailing list for 1 year. $5 registration fee if class is dropped after first week. Samples of work required only for advanced programs. SASE.

DESIGN AND CONCEPTS IN STAINED GLASS IN CHARTRES, FRANCE, 1204 San Fernando Rd., Los Angeles CA 90065. (213)221-6442. Contact: Roger Darricarrere. Estab. 1968. Annual summer workshop in design offered to 8 students for 3 weeks. Emphasizes glass art. Fee: $400/workshop; includes registration, materials and transportation in France. Write for more information.
Purpose: "Making of a watercolor sketch; the making of a cartoon in color; the preparation of a working drawing and template. We will also work on contracts; specifications; and installations of leaded and faceted glass. We will explore different techniques of leaded glass; faceted glass embedded in epoxy; 3-dimensional faceted glass embedded in concrete; and the designing and making of a sculpture of glass and metal. Samples of the work will be executed. We will have about 11 days of field trips."

EARTH, AIR, FIRE, WATER, Box 128, Nevada City CA 95959. (916)265-4845. Contact: Douglas Tweed. Offers ceramics once annually 4 weeks for 35 people. Fee: $425/course includes registration; materials; lodging; and meals. Write for application. Credit can be arranged through California State University, Sacramento Extension Service; 4 semester units upper or lower division credit.

Purpose: "Our program focuses on the production of pottery with limited use of modern technological aides. Students mine and process raw clay and glaze material and spend much of their time in our outdoor studio producing pots to fill a huge, 6 chamber climbing kiln. We do lots of wood firing, both stoneware and saltware."

EVOLUTION ART INSTITUTE, 6030 Roblar Rd., Petaluma CA 94952. (707)795-5096. Secretary: Sue Raney. Offers 2-3 day workshops in ceramics; woodworking; and blacksmithing monthly or bimonthly for 8-10 students. Fee: $50-75/workshop, includes registration and materials. Materials fee occasionally. "We are not accredited, but some schools will give you credit for courses, i.e. Sonoma State College." Write for application.

FRESNO CITY PARKS AND RECREATION DEPARTMENT, Cultural Arts for You Program, Fresno Memorial Auditorium, 2425 Fresno St., Rm. 102, Fresno CA 93721. (209)488-1181. Cultural Arts Supervisor: Christopher F. Curcio. Estab. 1975. Basic sessions in technique offered 4 times annually to a maximum of 20 students per class for 8 weeks, class meets once weekly. Emphasizes ceramics; decoupage; glass art; needlecraft; quilting; weaving; clay sculpture; decorative crafts; and macrame. Fee: $2.50-10/session, includes registration. Students supply own materials. "Registration forms are available throughout the city at various public locations and can be obtained by calling the Cultural Arts office."
Purpose: "Beginning level instruction in a specific craft with the completion of a number of projects. Intermediate instruction is anticipated in the more popular subject areas in the future."

GAVILAN COLLEGE, 5055 Santa Therese Blvd., Gilroy CA 95020. (408)847-1400. Humanities Division Director: Kent Child. Offers ceramics 3 quarters and summer school for 60 students; jewelry 3 quarters for 25 students; stained glass 3 quarters for 20 students (noncredit); and crafts design (batik, ceramics, glass art, jewelry, leatherworking, and metalsmithing) spring quarter for 30 students. Quarter is 12 weeks; summer school is 6 weeks. Fee: $6/class district residents; $81/class nondistrict students, includes registration. Students provide most materials. Credit available. Apply to Registrar.

ROBIN GREY'S THE BATIK ART PLACE, 530 A Miller Ave., Mill Valley CA 94941. (415)383-3848. Offers batik and fabric handpainting. Fee: $20-100. Materials fee: varies. Credit available, "usually through student's school." Write for application. No sample of work required unless for apprenticeship.

HALLIE'S ALLEY JEWELRY SCHOOL, 13045 Ventura Blvd., Studio City CA 91604. (213)986-1975. Contact: Hallie or Stan Katz. Estab. 1970. Basic and advanced workshops in technique; design inspiration; and motivation offered annually for a total of 100 students accomodated in 12 different workshops offered during 1 week. Emphasizes jewelry and metalsmithing. Fee: $8.50-15/each class; includes registration, printed matter, and some supplies. Write for application.

IDYLLWILD SCHOOL OF MUSIC AND THE ARTS, University of Southern California, Idyllwild Campus, Box 38, Idyllwild CA 92349. (714)659-2171. Offers 1 week courses throughout the summer in Tewa Pottery; Hopi Silversmithing; Navajo Two Grey Hills Weaving; Navajo Sandpainting; basketweaving; and ceramics. Fee: $100-165/course, includes registration. Materials fee varies. Credit available. Write or call for application; $10 fee. "A learning vacation for the entire family in the beautiful San Jacinto Mountains."

LAGUNA BEACH SCHOOL OF ART, 2222 Laguna Canyon Rd., Laguna Beach CA 92651. (714)494-1520. Director: Ruth Salyer. Offers ceramics for 12 students; jewelry and metalsmithing for 15 students. All courses are offered 4 times annually; quarter length is 9 weeks, 6 hours per week. Fee: $70/quarter. Materials fee varies. Credit available. "Most colleges accept credit from our school but since our quarters are only 9 weeks, the credit would be less than full credit." Write for brochure.

THE LIGHT THROUGH YONDER WINDOW, 4209 Lankershim Blvd., North Hollywood CA 91602. (213)985-4637. Contact: Kristin Newton or Walt Hurlburt. Offers stained glass every 6 weeks for 12 beginning students for 6 week sessions; stained glass 4 times annually for 20 advanced students daily for 1 week; and 2-hour slide lectures 4-6 times annually for 50 people. Fee: $24/beginners; $65-85/advanced; $1/slide show, includes registration, some materials, and use of equipment. Materials fee varies. Call or write for application.

MENDOCINO ART CENTER, Box 36, Mendocino CA 95460. (707)937-0228. Director, Textiles: Lolli Jacobsen. Estab. 1976. All levels of workshops in marketing and technique. 3 year program offered annually. Emphasizes batik; weaving; textile printing and dyeing; and all aspects of woven and printed textiles. Fee: $1,800/annually, includes registration; some materials; and special classes.
Application: Write for application. "Slides, photos or actual work may be sent or accompany the person for the day in the studio mutual interview." SASE.

PACIFIC BASIN SCHOOL OF TEXTILE ARTS, Box 7033, Berkeley CA 94707. (415)526-9836. Codirectors: Pat McGraw and Inger Jensen. Offers quilting; soft sculpture; weaving; chemical and natural dyes; design; and basketry. Fee: $19-110/class, includes registration and some materials. "Credit can be arranged but this is up to the student to pursue with their college. We have had people earn credit at Antioch." Write for application.

PASADENA CITY COLLEGE, 1570 E. Colorado Blvd., Pasadena CA 91106. (213)578-7238. Department Chairman: Walter Girdner. Offers 4 sections of crafts; 7 sections of ceramics; jewelry; and 2 sections of fiber crafts. All classes are offered twice annually for 18 weeks for 24 students; and crafts, ceramics, and fiber crafts are offered for 6 weeks in summer. Fee: no charge for district resident; write Dean of Admissions for nonresident fee. Materials fee: $10-20. Credit available. Write Dean of Registration or Dean of Admissions.

THE POT FARM, 2909 Santa Monica Blvd., Santa Monica CA 90404. (213)828-7071. Contact: Dori Marler. All levels of workshops in technique offered throughout the year. No registration limit. Emphasizes ceramics. Write for brochure. Purpose: open workshop among various artists and variety of throwing and firing techniques.

POTTERY CLASSES WORKSHOP, 1950 Parkside Dr., Concord CA 94519. (415)671-3059 Director: Mel Simpson. Sponsor: City of Concord. Estab. 1969. Quarterly advanced and basic workshops in technique held at 3031 Willow Pass Road. Emphasizes wheel-thrown ceramics. Limited to 20 craftworkers. Session length: 8 weeks. Fee of $26 covers registration; materials fee based on amount of clay used. Write for brochure. No samples required. Course offers "knowledge of, and experience in, pottery techniques (throwing, etc.)." Instructor Mel Simpson earned M.F.A. in ceramics from Washington State University.

SAN DIEGO POTTERS' GUILD, Studio 29, Spanish Village, Balboa Park, San Diego CA 92101. (714)239-0507. Offers pottery wheel courses throughout the year, 7 week sessions of 3 hours each for 7 students. Fee: $45/session, includes registration and materials. Admission on space available basis. Call or write.

SAN DIEGO STATE UNIVERSITY, Art Department, San Diego CA 92103. (714)286-6511. Contact: Arline M. Fisch. Offers ceramics; jewelry; metalsmithing; weaving; furniture design; enameling; and surface design (fiber). "Full schedule of courses offered in spring and fall semesters (15 weeks). Beginning, advanced, and graduate level courses in metal; wood; fiber; clay; enamel; and general crafts." Fee: $35/unit through College of Extended Studies, includes registration. Materials fee: $5-15. Credit available; offers AB in Applied Arts and Sciences, MA in Art.
Application: Contact Art Department Graduate Coordinator for graduate level; Admissions Office for matriculation; and College of Extended Studies for course work only. Application fee varies with program. Graduate level requires portfolio review of 10-20 slides. SASE.

SAN FRANCISCO MUSEUM OF MODERN ART SCHOOL, Van Ness Ave. at McAllister St., San Francisco CA 94102. (415)863-8800. Supervisor: Dennis O'Leary. Offers ceramics; jewelry; and metalsmithing. Fee: $50/museum members; $60/nonmembers; includes registration and materials. Credit can be arranged through San Francisco State University. Write for application.

SHASTA COLLEGE, General Crafts, Old Oregon Trail at 299 E., Redding CA 96001. (916)241-3523. Contact: Dan Ralston. Offers 6 sections of ceramics; 5 sections of jewelry; 1 section of crafts (batik, candlemaking, glass art, and weaving); and 1 section of glass design. All classes are offered twice annually for 25 students for 18 weeks. Fee: $15/class, includes lab fee. Credit available. Write letter of inquiry to Art Department or Director of Admissions.

SOME PLACE TEXTILE STUDIO, 2990 Adeline St., Berkeley CA 94703. (415)843-7178. Director: Kaethe Knot. Estab. 1966. Basic and advanced workshops in technique offered monthly to 15 students. Emphasizes lace. Materials fee: $45. Write for more information. Purpose: understanding of lace from a historical and contemporary perspective. Instruction: Kaethe Knot, lace artist; appraiser; and teacher since 1965.

SPECIAL STUDIES IN WOOD WORK (FURNITURE), Box 40442, Santa Barbara CA 93103. (805)966-0035. Contact: Robin Stewart-Metze. Offers independent studies in wood work for 3 students. Fee: $100/month, includes registration and some tools. Write for information. Submit slides or photos of work. SASE.

UNIVERSITY OF CALIFORNIA, DAVIS, Design Office, Applied Behavioral Sciences Department, Davis CA 95616. (916)752-1165. Master Adviser: Helge Olsen. "Each student in design plans an individualized program in consultation with a faculty adviser. The program can concentrate on a speciality in costume, textiles, environments, or general design." University fee: $228.50/California resident; $863.50 for nonresident. Students provide own materials in studio classes; costs range from $10-30. Credit available; degree offered. Write to Admissions Office for college catalog and application. $20 nonrefundable application fee.

UNIVERSITY OF CALIFORNIA, SAN DIEGO, Crafts Center, B-023, La Jolla CA 92093. (714)452-2021. Operations Manager: Ron Carlson. Offers ceramics 4 times annually for 175 students; woodcarving and glass art 4 times annually for 25 students. Course length is 9 weeks. Fee: $25/students, $50/others, includes registration and some materials. Write for application.

WATTS TOWERS ARTS CENTER, 1727 E. 107th St., Los Angeles CA 90002. (213)569-8181. Director: John Outterbridge. Estab. 1976. Basic and advanced workshops in technique offered 4 times annually to 10 students for 6-10 weeks. Emphasizes ceramics and leatherworking. "This is a community facility free to the public." Call at the beginning of a session to register.
Purpose: "The craftsman will have an opportunity to deal with clay hand building techniques; the use of the potter's wheel; firing; glazing; and other related matters."

WOMAN'S WORKSHOP, 17042 Devonshire St. 215, Northridge CA 91325. (213)363-1112. Director: Gloria Abramson. Offers quilting, weaving, and stained glass for 12 students; ceramics for 10 students; and jewelry for 8 students. All courses offered 4 times annually for 8 weeks. Fee: $30-38/course, includes registration. Write for application.
Purpose: "Our courses are basically for beginners who wish to 'just try a course.' Instructors are all qualified, most have taught at Workshop several years and have other experience. We hope to encourage people with leisure time to try various classes for enjoyment."

WOODSHOP, Box 40442, Santa Barbara CA 93103. (805)966-0035. Contact: Robin Metze. Estab. 1978. Basic, advanced, and helper workshops in marketing and technique offered semimonthly and by special arrangement to 5-10 students for 1 weekend. Emphasizes woodwork and wood carving sculpture. Fee: $5/workshop, includes registration and materials. Write for application. Submit slides or photos for advanced workshop. SASE.

Colorado

COLORADO MOUNTAIN COLLEGE, Summervail Workshop, Box 1114, Vail CO 81657. (303)476-4040. Director: Randy Milhoan. Estab. 1971. Basic and advanced workshops in marketing; technique; and interrelationships of fine arts, carfts, business, and critical thought offered annually to 100 students for sessions ranging from 2 days to 8 weeks. Year round classes also offered. Emphasizes batik; ceramics; glass art; jewelry; leatherworking; metalsmithing; quilting; weaving; and sculpture. Fee: $13/hour Colorado residents; $45/hour out of state residents, includes tuition. Materials fee: $10-20. Write Director for application. "Teachers must submit 10 slides; 3 letters of recommendation; and a current resume." SASE. Students are admitted on an open door policy.

COLORADO STATE UNIVERSITY, University Two, Lory Student Center, Fort Collins CO 80523. (303)491-6626. Director: Ruth Burnham. Offers batik; ceramics; jewelry; leatherworking; needlecrafts; weaving; blockprinting; calligraphy; macrame; and stained glass 2-4 times annually for 6-8 weeks for 10-12 beginners. Fee: $8-15/course includes registration and some materials. Write for application.
Purpose: "Opportunity to teach newcomers or exposure to the crafts of others. This is not a strict, formalized program. Free university structure."

COLORADO WOMEN'S COLLEGE, Art Department, Montview and Quebec, Denver CO 80220. (303)394-6921. Chairman: Maynard Whitney. Offers ceramics and printmaking twice annually for 6 weeks for 20 students; Primitive Pottery and jewelry once annually for 3 weeks for 15 students; and sculpture once annually for 6 weeks for 20 students. Fee: $100/credit hour, includes some materials. Some materials are purchased by student. Credit available. Write to Office of Admissions. $15 application fee.

COMMUNITY FREE SCHOOL, Box 1724, Boulder CO 80306. (303)447-8733. Bookkeeper: Andria Bronsten. Basic and advanced workshops in technique offered every 7 weeks to 5-15 students once a week for 7 weeks. Emphasizes batik; glass art; jewelry; metalsmithing; needlecrafts; quilting; and weavings. Fee: $20-60, includes registration and some materials. Write or call for application.

DUNCONOR DESIGN WORKSHOPS, Box 2000, Crested Butte CO 81224. (303)349-5252. Director: Harold O'Connor. Estab. 1975. Advanced (graduate level) workshops in technique offered annually from mid-May-September and by special arrangement to 8 professional craftworkers for 2 weeks. Emphasizes jewelry and metalsmithing. Fee: $280/workshop, includes registration and tuition. Write for application. Submit 5 slides or b&w photos; short resume of experiences; and statement of intent of study. SASE.
Purpose: "Practical approach to metalwork in workshop atmosphere; stresses learning by doing. Learn methods to increase proficiency in design and production of jewelry with a high level of craftsmanship/design and professional attitudes for making a living from the craft."

MESA COLLEGE, North Ave. at 12th St., Box 2647, Grand Junction CO 81501. (303)248-1510. Contact: L.D. Runner. Offers ceramics/handbuild and ceramics/wheel 4 quarters annually for 15 students; jewelry/metalsmithing 3 quarters annually for 15 students; fiber arts 2 quarters annually for 15 students; and general crafts 4 quarters annually for 25 students. Course length is 12 weeks. Fee: $15/credit hour. Lab fee: $5. Credit available. Write for application.

METROPOLITAN STATE COLLEGE, 1006 W. 11th St., Lakewood CO 80215. (303)629-3090. Chairman: Robert Mangold. Offers Ceramics 1,2,3, and 4 each level twice annually; Metalwork and Jewelry 1,2,3, and 4 twice annually; and Design in Wood 1,2,3, and 4 twice annually. Fee: $61.50/3 credits resident; $141/3 credits nonresident, includes registration. Students provide own materials. Credit available; offers BA.
Application: "We are primarily a degree granting program. All classes have prerequisites. Advanced placements can be made at the instructor's discretion based on samples of student work. Slides are usually satisfactory. Samples not returned if unsolicited." Write to Admissions Office.

UNIVERSITY OF NORTHERN COLORADO, Department of Fine Arts, Greeley CO 80639. (303)351-2143. Chairman: Dr. Robert B. Turner. Offers Introduction to Pottery once annually; Advanced Pottery, Weaving, and Crafts Studio 4 times annually; and Glaze Form twice annually. All classes are offered for 10 weeks for 20 students. Materials fee: $5-15. Credit available. Write for application. Submit slides of work. SASE.

UNIVERSITY OF SOUTHERN COLORADO, Belmont Campus, 2200 Bonforte Ave., Pueblo CO 81001. (303)549-2552. Contact: Ed Sajbel or Lewis Tilley. Offers Ceramics 1,2; Metalsmithing 1, 2; jewelry, enameling; and Woods 1,2 once each semester. Kiln Construction; glazing; and Ceramic History once annually. All courses are 15 weeks for 20 students. Materials fee: $20 approximately. Credit available; offers 2 year certificate, BA or BS. Write Admissions Office or Art Department. $10 application fee.

WESTERN STATE COLLEGE OF COLORADO, Gunnison CO 81230. (303)943-0120. Head, Art Department: Dr. August Grosland. Offers 5 sections of Basic Crafts 1 semester and 4 weeks summer school; 1 section of Advanced Crafts 1 semester; 2 sections of Leather Crafts and Plastics 1 semester and 2-4 weeks summer school; and 3-4 sections of Ceramics 1 semester and 2-4 weeks summer school. All classes are for 24 students. Semester length is 17 weeks. Fee: $13/semester hour resident; $53/semester hour nonresident, includes registration. Materials fee: $10. Credit available; offers degree program.
Purpose: "Opportunities for basic, intermediate, advanced craft and/or art courses. Also independent study. Most classes permit ample individual and class instruction in comfortable facilities in a Rocky Mountain atmosphere, comfortable, relaxing, and casual."
Application: Contact Office of Admissions; Office of Publication for catalogs, program brochures, etc.; or Office of Summer Term. $10 application fee.

Connecticut

THE BINDERY, 17 Broadway, New Haven CT 06511. (203)776-5841. Contact: Connie Mortensen. Offers 4 classes of hand book binding 4-5 times annually for 8 weeks for 7 students in each class. Individual private lessons in advanced book restoration can be arranged. Fee: $70/hand book binding, includes registration and materials, leather cost not included. Credit occasionally can be arranged for advanced students.

Purpose: "A basic understanding of the structure of a book; page repair techniques; an idea of whether advanced work is possible or indicated. Instruction is on an individual basis in group classes with many skill levels in any 1 class. At least 5 students in past 3 years are now working in professional restoration situations."
Application: Write the Bindery. Slides/photos and actual work must be seen before final acceptance for advanced book restoration. SASE.

BROOKFIELD CRAFT CENTER, INC., Box 122, Brookfield CT 06804. (203)775-4526. Registrar: Betty McCaffrey. Estab. 1954. Basic and advanced workshops in technique offered throughout the year to 12 interested students for 1-10 day sessions. Emphasizes batik; ceramics; glass art; jewelry; leatherworking; metalsmithing; needlecrafts; quilting; soft sculpture; and weavings.

CARRIE WEAVES STUDIO, 20 Dyer Ave., Collinsville CT 06022. (203)693-0073. Contact: Carrie Sinish. Estab. 1973. Basic and advanced workshops in technique offered throughout the year to 10 students with genuine interest in weaving for 2 hour lessons. Emphasizes weaving. Fee: $20/4-2 hour lessons, includes registration. Students supply own materials. Write or call for application.
Purpose: Knowledge of weaving; the use of 4 harness loom; drafting; and design.

FARMINGTON VALLEY ARTS CENTER, Avon CT 06001. (203)678-1867. Adminstrative Assistant: Beth Barrett. Estab. 1972. Basic and advanced workshops in technique offered monthly to 5-10 students on weekly basis. Emphasizes ceramics; jewelry; leatherworking; needlecrafts; weaving; calligraphy; pottery; and bronze. Fee: $35-45/workshop, includes registration and some materials. Materials fee: $5. Write for application; submit slides. SASE. Or call and talk to Director.

GUILFORD HANDCRAFT CENTER, Box 221, Guilford CT 06437. (203)453-5947. Director: Beth Parrott. Estab. 1968. Basic and advanced workshops in marketing; business; and technique offered to 300-350 students for sessions of varying lengths. Emphasizes batik; pottery; glass art; jewelry; metalsmithing; quilting; soft sculpture; and weavings. Write for application. "Instructors are prominent regional/national craftworkers with teaching/workshop experience and recognized creative ability."

HARTFORD ART SCHOOL OF THE UNIVERSITY OF HARTFORD, 200 Bloomfield, West Hartford CT 96117. (203)243-4396. Assistant to the Dean: S. H. Keller. Offers Pueblo Pottery; Primitive Pottery; Natural Dyeing; American Indian Basketmaking; Traditional Native Crafts; and Seminole Applique and Patchwork 3 weeks in summer for 20 students per class Fee: $150/class (average), includes registration. Credit available. Write Traditional Native Crafts, Hartford Art School.

Purpose: "An insight into traditional native techniques particularly North American, but some African techniques. The attempt in the courses is to impart a sense of the culture and society which developed particular craft techniques. Adaptation of these techniques to contemporary forms."

SOUTHERN CONNECTICUT STATE COLLEGE, 501 Crescent St., New Haven CT 06515. Offers Pottery 1-2 twice annually for 16 students; Ceramics 1 twice annually for 18 students; Raku and Ceramics 2 once annually for 18 students; kiln construction and glazing and decoration once annually for 16 students. Course length is 15 weeks. Pottery 1-2 and Ceramics 1 are offered for 5 weeks in summer. Fee: $5-50/credit hour, includes registration. Materials fee: $25. Credit available. Write to Registrar.

THENDARA STUDIO, 590 Oxford Rd., Oxford CT 06483. (203)888-0755. Offers stained glass throughout the year for 10 students and glass painting as needed for 6 students for 10 weeks. Fee: $6/2 hours stained glass; $150/glass painting, includes registration. Students provide own materials. Apply in person. "Perfect or professional work. It is not a hit and miss method or learned by trial. We are only interested in persons who are interested."

WOODCARVER'S WEEKEND, New England Artist & Craftsmens' Guild Inc., Box 142, Enfield CT 06082. President: Ron Seagrave. Estab. 1975. Basic and advanced workshops in technique offered to 2-3 students for 1 weekend, held 4 times annually. Emphasizes woodcarving. Fee: $50 includes registration and materials. Write for application. Slides of work must be submitted prior to acceptance. SASE.

Delaware

THE ART STUDIOS, Absalom Jones Community Center, Wilmington DE 19804. (302)571-7730. Studio Manager: Kathy Harker. All levels of workshops in technique offered annually for 8-15 students for 1 weekend and 8 week sessions. Emphasizes batik; ceramics; jewelry; quilting; soft sculpture; and weaving. Fee: $20-50, includes registration and some materials. Call for application.

Purpose: "This is a center for adult education concentrating on 8 week workshops for beginning and intermediate students and intensive weekend workshops for a more in-depth experience in technique."

DELAWARE ART MUSEUM, 2301 Kentmere Pkwy., Wilmington DE 19806. (302)571-9594. Contact: Registrar, Education Department. Offers ceramics and weaving 3 times annually for 12 students; jewelry 3 times annually for 10 students. Course length is 13 weeks. Some credit available. Call or write Registrar.

UNIVERSITY OF DELAWARE, Department of Art, Newark DE 19711. (302)738-2244. Chairman: Daniel K. Teis. Offers ceramics; jewelry; metalsmithing; quilting; soft sculpture; weaving; and fibers on beginning through advanced levels for 18-20 students per class. Fall and spring semesters are 15 weeks; winter, 5 weeks; and summer sessions, 2-6 weeks. Fee: $102/3 credit hours resident; $243/3 credit hours nonresident, includes registration. Materials fee: $10-20. Write Admissions Office.

Florida

CERAMIC LEAGUE OF MIAMI SCHOOL, 8873 SW 129th St., Miami FL 33176. (305)235-9732. Contact: School Committee. Offers Beginning Pottery Techniques; Wheel; Handbuilding; Glaze Formulation; Glaze Application; and Sculpture 5 times annually at beginning, intermediate, and advanced levels. Course length is 6 weeks. Fee: $35/course; includes registration and materials. Write or call for application.

ECKERD COLLEGE, St. Petersburg FL 33733. (813)867-1166. Contact: John Eckert. Offers Ceramics 1 once or twice annually for 16 beginning students and throwing once annually for 16 intermediate students. Course length is 7 weeks. Fee: $390, includes registration. Materials fee: $5-10. Credit available. Write Admissions Office. $15 application fee.

FLORIDA STATE UNIVERSITY, Center for Participant Education, Pot Shop, 215 University Union, Tallahassee FL 32306. Arts and Craft Director: Grant Gelhardt. Offers pottery 4 times annually for 10 weeks for 30 students. Fee: $15/course, includes materials. Write Pot Shop for application.

FLORIDA STATE UNIVERSITY, Craft Design Program, EDU 123, Tallahassee FL 32306. (904)644-5474. Chair, Department Art Education/Craft Design: Dr. V.M. Brouch. Offers Ceramics 1 five times annually for 20 students; Advanced Ceramics and enamels twice annually for 20 students; Wheel Throw 5 times annually for 15 students; Fibers 1 and woods 3 times annually for 20 students; Advanced Fibers and metals 4 times annually for 20 students; and synthetics once annually for 20 students. Course length is 10 weeks. Credit available; offers MA. Write Graduate Admissions Office. $25 application fee. Submit slides/photo portfolio. SASE.

GROVE HOUSE SCHOOL OF ARTS AND CRAFTS, 3496 Main Hwy., Coconut Grove FL 33133. (305)445-5633. School Director: Ellie Schneiderman. Offers batik/ceramics; glass art; jewelry; metalsmithing; soft sculpture; and weaving throughout the year. Course length is 4-8 weeks. Fee: $25-50/course, includes registration. Write for application.

JACKSONVILLE UNIVERSITY, University Station, Jacksonville FL 32211. (904)744-3950, ext. 246. Art Chairman: Dr. Barre Barrett. Offers hand pottery 5 times annually for 18 students; wheel throwing 5 times annually for 14 students; blown glass 3 times annually for 20 students; and jewelry once annually for 12 students. Course lengths are 18 weeks; spring or summer sessions are 8 weeks. Fee: $15/ceramics; $35/glass, includes fuel and glazes. Materials fee in jewelry depends on price of material. Credit available. To apply write Registrar. Submit slides and photos.

LAFAYETTE ARTS AND CRAFTS CENTER, 912 Myers Park Dr., Tallahassee FL 32301. (904)224-7220. Director: Marsha Patterson. Offers pottery 4 quarters annually, 3 classes per quarter, for 10 weeks for 12 students; 4-Harness Weaving 4 quarters a year for 8 weeks for 8 students; chair caning 4 quarters a year for 4 weeks for 12 students; and quilting 4 quarters a year for 4 weeks for 12 students. Fee: $10-20, includes registration and materials. Students furnish own materials sometimes. Write for application.

MIAMI DADE COMMUNITY COLLEGE, 11011 SW 104 St., Miami FL 33176. (305)596-1281. Chairman South: Margaret Pelton. Chairman North: Patrick Delong. Offers ceramics 4 times annually for 20 students; jewelry 3 times annually for 20 students; and fabric once annually for 20 students. Semester courses are 14 weeks; week term courses are 6 weeks. Fee: $175/course. Materials fee: $8-10. Credit available. "All courses may be repeated for credit for advanced work. Students can advance as far as they like." Write for application.

OKALOOSA-WALTON JUNIOR COLLEGE, Niceville FL 32578. Chairman, Fine and Performing Arts: Dr. Richard Warren. Offers pottery 3 times annually for 40 students; jewelry, fiber and textile design, and sculpture once annually for 20 students; and China Painting as needed for 15 students for 8 weeks. All other courses are 15 weeks. Fee: $36/course; $11/semester hour for credit courses, includes registration. Materials fee: $25 average. Credit available; offers AA and work can be applied toward BA. Write Registrar. $5 application fee. "There is some degree of freedom in setting up special programs to fit the needs of the individual craftworker. Valuable courses in design; drawing; painting; art history; and photography can also be taken."

UNIVERSITY OF MIAMI, Box 248106, Coral Gables FL 33124. (305)284-2542. Chairman: Gerald Winter. Offers 6 ceramics classes per semester plus summer school for 15 students per class and 3 weaving/fibers classes per semester plus summer school for 20 students per class. Class length is 15 weeks. Fee: $5-25/course, includes registration. Materials fee: $15-20. Credit available. Write to Admissions Office.

THE UNIVERSITY OF WEST FLORIDA, Pensacola FL 32504. (904)476-9500, ext. 440 or 481. Chairman, Art Philosophy, and Religious Studies: Robert L. Armstrong. Offers ceramics 4 times annually for 120 beginning and advanced students and jewelry 3 times annually for 90 beginning and advanced students. Course length is 10 weeks, 5 quarter hours. Fee: $16.50/quarter hour, includes registration and some supplies. Credit available. Write to Admissions Office. $15 application fee.

Georgia

BERRY COLLEGE, Art Department, Box 580, Mt. Berry GA 30149. (404)232-5374. Contact: Jere Lykins. Offers Ceramics 1,2 and Weaving once annually for 15 students; and Ceramics 3 three times annually for 15 students. Course length is 10 weeks. Fee: $180 tuition, includes registration. Credit available. Write College Admissions. $10 application fee.

CHASTAIN ARTS AND CRAFTS CENTER, City of Atlanta, Bureau of Parks and Recreation, 135 W. Wieuca Rd. NW, Atlanta GA 30342. (404)252-2927. Arts and Crafts Supervisor: Madelyn Summers. Workshops at all levels in technique offered to 8-10 students per class for 1 month sessions held annually in May. Emphasizes batik; ceramics; jewelry; soft sculpture; weavings; fibers; woodcarving; framemaking; rug hooking; calligraphy; basketry; enameling; stained glass; chair caning; and color theory. Fee: 75c/hour for Atlanta residents, $1/hour for nonresidents; separate materials fee. "Registration is made in person at Chastain, beginning April 3, with workshops filled on a first come, first serve basis."

COLUMBUS COLLEGE, Art Department, Columbus GA 31907. (404)568-2047. Contact: Zoe Allison. Offers Textile Design/Batik and Weaving once annually for 18 students; Jewelry twice annually for 18 students; weaving once annually for 18 students; and Creative Use of Fibers/Needlecrafts biannually for 18 students. Course length is 10 weeks. Fee: $16/credit hour, includes registration. Credit available. Program stresses "a view of many techniques and its application to fine arts." Write Art Department. Submit slides or portfolio or work. SASE.

CRAFT CAREER CENTER, Box 1368, 127 Main St., Lilburn GA 30247. (404)921-2153. Director: Ella Wilkerson. Estab. 1961. Basic and advanced workshops in technique offered monthly to 15 students with teacher/shop association for sessions lasting 3 days-1 week. Fee: $30/day includes registration, lunch and some materials. Write for craft calendar. "Workshops teach students unusual techniques that enable them to sell their finished work, and intructors how to teach this craft."

LAKE LANIER STONEWARE POTTERS, Agnes Scott College, Decatur GA 30030. (404)373-2571 or 373-0914. Director: Robert Westervelt. Basic, intermediate and advanced workshops in technique offered to a maximum of 8 students for sessions lasting 1-4 weeks, held each summer. Emphasizes pottery design and production; and kiln building. Fee: $85/week, includes registration and materials; lodging and meals arranged individually. Write for application. 4 slides of work may be submitted but not required. SASE.

Hawaii

BERNICE P. BISHOP MUSEUM, Box 6037, Honolulu HI 96818. (808)847-3511, ext. 103. Education Coordinator: Marilyn L. Nicholson. Estab. 1969. Basic and advanced workshops in technique offered monthly to 12 students per class for sessions lasting 6-10 weeks. Emphasizes batik; needlecrafts; quilting; soft sculpture; weaving; drawing; painting; and Hawaiian crafts, both traditional and contemporary. Fee: varies. Materials fee: $12. Write for brochure.
Purpose: "Workshops provide a basic knowledge of the subject area covered and usually 3-4 finished pieces depending on media, in addition to samples of various techniques."

HONOLULU ACADEMY OF ARTS, Art Center, 900 S. Beretania St., Honolulu HI 96816. (808)538-3693. Curator, Art Center: Violet A. Scott. Offers ceramics and collage twice annually for 20 beginning students; and weaving and jewelry twice annually for 16 beginning students. Course length is 14 weeks. Fee: $65/course, includes registration and tuition. Lab fee: $10-15. Credit can be arranged through Hawaii Pacific College. Write, call, or visit for application.

Idaho

SUN VALLEY CENTER FOR ARTS AND HUMANITIES, Box 656, Sun Valley ID 83353. (208)622-3539. Director/Ceramics Department: Jim Romberg. Estab. 1974. Intermediate and advanced workshops in theory and technique offered to 25 students for 8-10 week sessions, held 4 times annually. Emphasizes ceramics: firing, kiln building, glaze theory, aesthetics, and clay bodies. Fee: $350-400 includes registration, instruction and studio use. Materials fee: 7c/lb. wet clay. Write for application. Slides of work must be submitted prior to acceptance. SASE. "Our classes offer total exposure to all phases of ceramics, as well as the experience of working with master craftsmen."

Illinois

BELLEVILLE AREA COLLEGE, Art Dept., Belleville IL 62221. (618)235-2700. Chairman, Art Department: Wayne Shaw. Offers ceramics 3 times annually for 18 students; jewelry twice annually for 25 students; and sculpture 3 times annually for 18 students. Course length is 18 weeks. Fee: $50/course, includes registration and materials. Credit available. Write for application. $5 application fee. Submit slides and photos. SASE.

BLACK HAWK COLLEGE, 6600 34th Ave., Moline IL 61265. (309)796-1311. Art Department Chairman: Joseph Ramsauer. Offers ceramics twice annually for 36 students; and jewelry twice annually for 20 students. Course length is 16 weeks. Fee: $58/course, includes registration. Materials fee: $7. Credit available. "Requires a good basic 2 year art foundation." Write to Registrar.

BRADLEY UNIVERSITY, School of Art, Peoria IL 61625. (309)676-7611. Acting Director: James A. Hansen. Offers Ceramics and Jewelry/Art Metal twice annually, plus summer school on an irregular basis, for 20 advanced and 20 beginning students; and sculpture twice annually for 18 advanced and 18 beginning students. Course length is 16 weeks; summer school is 4 weeks. Fee: $225/3 credits (tuition) and $18/3 credits (class fee), includes registration. Materials fee: $18. Credit available. Write Admissions Office. $15 application fee. Sample of work required for graduate student. SASE.

COLLEGE OF DUPAGE, Lambert Rd. at 22nd St., Glen Ellyn IL 60137. (312)858-2800. Contact: Bill Smith or John Wantz. Offers Ceramics 1, 2, 3 and Jewelry 1, 2, 3 three times annually for 25 students. Course length is 11 weeks. Fee: $33/class, includes registration. Credit available. "Program offers varying degrees of mastery in design and execution in the medium involved." Write for application. $5 1st registration fee.

EASTERN ILLINOIS UNIVERSITY, Lincoln at 6th St., Charleston IL 61920. (217)581-2318. Contact: Robert B. Sonderman. Offers jewelry once annually for 26 students; and 3 sections of general crafts 3 times annually for 30 students. Course length is 15 weeks. Materials fee: $1.50-50. Credit available. Write for application.

EASTERN ILLINOIS UNIVERSITY, Art Department, Charleston IL 61920. (217)581-3410. Contact: Suzan G. Braun. Offers Ceramics 1-5, Weaving 1-4, and Jewelry 1-3 three times annually for 20 students; and textiles twice annually for 20 students. Course length is 1 semester. Fee: University tuition and fees, includes registration. Materials fee: $7.50-12. Credit available; offers BA and MA. Write to Admissions Office.

ILLINOIS STATE UNIVERSITY, Art Department, Normal IL 61761. (309)438-5621. Crafts Area Chairman: Ed Niemi. Offers ceramics, jewelry-metals, and weaving-textiles each semester and summer for 20 students; and glass blowing each semester and summer for 14 students. Fee: $30/credit. Materials fee: varies by level and work done. Credit available; offers BS, BFA, MS, MFA, and Doctorate. "Specialized 2-4 week courses are offered in several of the areas during each summer session. Taught by visiting faculty, credit by Illinois State University."
Application: Write to the Art Department or to the specialized area of interest. Portfolio required for work toward graduate credit. Not required on undergraduate or person interest level. SASE.

LOOMS AND LESSONS, 6014 Osage Ave., Downers Grove IL 60515. (312)964-1211. Contact: Ruth Nordquist Myers. Offers continuous classes of weaving for 6 students for 6 weeks. Fee: varies, includes materials and use of studio equipment. Call for information. "Classes designed for local residents and nearby commuters only."

THE LOOM ROOM, 451 Duane St., Glen Ellyn IL 60137. (312)858-8057. Contact: Gary Babbitt. Estab. 1978. Beginning and basic workshops in technique offered monthly to 6 interested students for 6 week sessions. Emphasizes fibers and weaving. Fee varies for personal instruction and use of looms; separate materials fee. Call or write for information.
Purpose: "The purpose of this workshop is the basic understanding of handweaving as well as the capabilities of weavings themselves. This is not just a workshop, but rather an ongoing class in weaving with occasional demonstrations on the other textile arts."

MUNDELEIN COLLEGE, 6363 Sheridan Rd., Chicago IL 60660. (312)262-8100. Contact: Betty Matula. Offers Fibers 1, 2, and advanced once annually for 24 students (2 advanced) and Art of Adornment once annually for 20 students. Course length is 10 weeks. Fee: $230/course, includes registration. Credit available. Write to Admissions Office.
Purpose: Fibers 1 (dye process) includes tie-dye; batik; silk screen; block print; and direct painting on cloth. Fibers 2 (thread process) includes frame loom and 4 harness weaving plus some optional processes, i.e. sprang macrame. Art of Adornment is an introduction to jewelry; leathercraft; and enameling approaches.

NORTHEASTERN ILLINOIS UNIVERSITY, Bryn Mawr and St. Louis Ave., Chicago IL 60625. (312)583-4050. Contact: Art Department Chairman. Offers Ceramics 1-3; Advanced Ceramics; and Independent Study in Ceramics 3 times annually. Fee: $10/course, includes some clay; glaze; and firing cost. Credit available. Write Registrar.

NORTHERN ILLINOIS UNIVERSITY, Visual Arts Building, DeKalb IL 60115. (815)753-1473 or 753-1474. Chairman, Art Department: Dr. Robert Even. Offers ceramics 3 times annually for 120 beginning and advanced students; jewelry/metals 3 times annually for 100 beginning and advanced students; weaving 3 times annually for 80 beginning and advanced students; and textile design and Off Loom Weaving 3 times annually for 24 students. Courses are offered in fall, spring, and summer. Fee: $39.50/semester class in-state, $66.50/out of state; $28.75/summer class in-state, $65.75/out of state, includes registration and University fees. Materials fee: $10-20. Credit available; offers BFA, MA, and MFA.
Application: Write Office of Admissions for undergraduate level; Graduate Coordinator for graduate level. Slides and/or actual work required for graduate level. SASE.

OLDE FOREN GALLERY, Main St., Mahomet IL 61853. (217)586-3211. Coordinator: Charlotte Williamson. Estab. 1974. Basic workshops in technique offered to 12 students for 1 day sessions twice annually. Emphasizes weaving. Fee: $20, includes registration and materials. Write for application. "We offer basic weaving techniques from a professional fulltime weaver."

QUINCY COLLEGE, 1831 College, Quincy IL 62301. (217)222-8020. Chairperson: Fr. Tom Brown. Offers Introduction Ceramics twice annually for 50 students; Advanced Ceramics twice annually for 24 students; Introduction Weaving once annually for 30 students; and Introduction Jewelry once annually for 25 students. Course length is 15-16 weeks. Fee: $50/hour, 3 credit hours, includes registration. Materials fee: $25. Credit available; college credit can also be earned through John Wood Community College at state college system tuition rates through Quincy College. "Program provides breadth as well as depth conceptually and technically." Ideally we should see a little of the applicant's work as well as slides and photos." SASE.

ROSARY COLLEGE ART DEPARTMENT, 7900 Division St., River Forest IL 60305. (312)366-2490. Chairman: Sister Milla Derby. Basic and advanced workshops in technique and creative work offered to 7 creative students per class for 1 semester annually. Emphasizes batik; ceramics; jewelry; metalsmithing; needlecrafts; quilting; and soft sculpture. Write registrar for application. Samples of work must be submitted prior to acceptance. SASE.

SOUTHERN ILLINOIS UNIVERSITY/EDWARDSVILLE, Craft Shop, Box 67, Edwardsville IL 62026. (618)692-2178. Contact: Director, Craft Shop. Offers batik; candlemaking; ceramics; decoupage; glass art; jewelry; leatherworking; metalsmithing; needlecrafts; quilting; soft sculpture; tole painting; weaving; knitting; crochet; flower arranging; and kid's workshop 3 times annually for 10 students. Course length is 6 weeks. Fee: $4-15, includes registration and some materials. To apply call for personal interview. Bring work samples at time of interview.
Purpose: "General knowledge of methods and applications, and the satisfaction of having spent a little free time constructively."

TRADITIONAL GLASSWORKS STUDIO, 206 S. First St., Champaign IL 61820. (217)359-8820. Estab. 1975. Basic and advanced workshops in design and craftsmanship offered to 12 students for 8 week sessions, held every 10-12 weeks. Emphasizes stained glass art. Fee: $60. Materials fee: $30 minimum. Call or write for information. "Workshop teaches the step by step construction of a stained glass window, including elements of design, glass cutting, leading, soldering and cementing. Will also touch on the copper foil method of construction."

UNIVERSITY OF ILLINOIS, Art Department, Crafts Option, 142 FAB, Champaign IL 61820. Contact: D.E. Frith. Offers all levels of ceramics; metal; and glass all semesters. Course length is 16 weeks. Fee: tuition, includes registration. Materials fee: $10-50. Credit available; offers BFA and MFA. Apply to Registrar.

Indiana

EARLHAM COLLEGE, Richmond IN 47374. (317)962-6561. Contact: Garrett Boone. Offers Ceramics 3 times annually for 15 students; Advanced Ceramics once annually for 12 students; and Crafts once annually. Course length is 10 weeks. Fee: $310/course, includes registration and use of facilities. Materials fee: $15-20. Credit available. Contact Art Department.

INDIANA UNIVERSITY SOUTH EAST, 4201 Grant Line Rd., New Albany IN 47150. (812)945-2731. Contact: John R. Guenther. Offers 3 sections of ceramics twice annually for 4-15 students; and 2 sections of textiles twice annually for 4-12 students. Course length is 16 weeks. Fee: $15/course, includes materials. Credit available. Contact Admissions Office. "Provides a workable knowledge and skills and in ceramic art and textile arts."

NEW HARMONY GALLERY OF CONTEMPORARY ART, Owen Block, Main St., New Harmony IN 47631. (812)682-3156. Director: John Begley. Estab. 1975. "Our programs are growing and changing constantly; for updated information, please contact us."

UNIVERSITY OF EVANSVILLE ART WORKSHOPS, c/o Art Department, Evansville IN 47702. (812)479-2043. Head of Art Department: Les Miley. Estab. 1965. Basic and advanced workshops in ideas and materials offered to 40 students for 2-4 week summer sessions annually. Emphasizes ceramics; weaving; and lithography. Fee: $156 includes registration and tuition; separate materials fee. Write for application. Slides or photographs of work must be submitted prior to acceptance. SASE. Workshops are held in New Harmony, Indiana.

UNIVERSITY OF NOTRE DAME, Department of Art, Notre Dame IN 46556. (219)283-7602. Chairman: Rev. James Flanigan. Offers 3 sections of Ceramics 1 twice annually for 20 students per section; Ceramics 2 twice annually for 20 advanced students; Soft Sculpture and Traditional Fibre twice annually for 20 students; and Ceramics Workshop summer session of 2 weeks (80 hours) for 40 students. Course length is 15 weeks. Fee: $70/credit plus $15 for summer session, includes materials and registration. Credit available. Write Graduate School; Director of Summer Session; or Director of Admissions for undergraduates.

Purpose: "Thorough practical experience in all aspects of the craft. An opportunity in summer to work intensively with 3-4 nationally known craftworkers."

Iowa

COE COLLEGE, 1221 1st Ave., NE, Cedar Rapids IA 52401. (319)398-1600. Offers ceramics; raku; and textiles once annually for 13 weeks for 20 students. Fee: $175/course, includes registration. Materials fee: $20. Credit available. Write to Admissions.

DES MOINES ART CENTER, Greenwood Park, Des Moines IA 50312. (515)277-4405. Director of Education: Georgeann Kudron. Offers pottery/ceramics; batik; fibers; weaving; and jewelry twice annually and once in summer. Course length is 16 weeks; summer session is 6 weeks. Fee: $30/semester, includes tuition. Materials fee: $3-15. Credit can be arranged through Grandview College; Simpson College; and Des Moines Area Community College. Write Education Department.

ELLSWORTH COMMUNITY COLLEGE, 1100 College Ave., Iowa Falls IA 50126. (515)648-4611. Director of Admissions: Phil Rusley. Offers Pottery 1 once annually for 12 beginning potters; Pottery 2 once annually for 12 advanced potters; Special Problems in Pottery twice annually for 4 advanced potters; and Creative Crafts once annually for 15 beginning students. Course length is 19 weeks. Fee: $36.90/course for Iowa residents; $73.80/course for nonresident (if taking less than 12 semesters hours); includes registration. Materials fee: $5-10. Credit available. Write or call Director of Admissions. $10 application fee.

I.M.U. CRAFT CENTER, University of Iowa, Iowa City IA 52242. (319)353-3119. Supervisor: Wanda Matthess. Estab. 1967. Basic Workshops in technique offered to 12-20 interested students for sessions lasting 2-20 weeks, held 3 times annually. Emphasizes batik; ceramics; jewelry; leatherworking; metalsmithing; needlecrafts; quilting; weavings; bookbinding; picture framing; calligraphy; and woodcarving. Fee: $5-40, depending on workshop, includes registration and materials. Call or write for information. "We also have workshop areas available and individual instruction. These are non-academic workshops."

MORNINGSIDE COLLEGE, Morningside Ave., Sioux City IA 51106. (712)277-5212. Chairman, Department of Art: Frank Breneisen. Offers Ceramics 1,2 twice annually for 30 students; jewelry and general crafts once annually for 15 students; and general crafts once annually for 10 students. Course length is 15 weeks. Fee: $90/course, includes registration; materials; and continuing education units. Credits available. Write Admissions Office.

SOUTH BEAR SCHOOL, Rt. 5, Decorah IA 52101. (319)382-5221. Director: Dean Schwarz. Estab. 1970. Basic and advanced workshops in technique offered annually to 18 students per class for sessions ranging from 4-9 weeks. Emphasizes ceramics; weaving; spinning; and dyeing. Fee: $200-880, includes lodging and meals. Materials fee: $6. Write for application. "Students must be high school age or above and either submit a portfolio, have a personal interview or show proof of serious interest. Final student selection will be at the staff's discretion. Instruction is directed towards each student's individual development with regard to work discipline, philosophy of art, creativity and craftsmanship. A close student/faculty relationship is stressed, with critiques and demonstrations as the principle teaching tools."

Kansas

COFFEYVILLE COMMUNITY JUNIOR COLLEGE, 11th & Willow, Coffeyville KS 67337. (316)251-7700, ext. 47. Offers ceramics twice annually for 25 students; and crafts once annually for 25 students. Course length is 16 weeks. Fee: $24/class, includes registration and materials. Materials fee: $6. Credit available. Write Director of Admissions.

LAWRENCE ARTS CENTER, 9th & Vermont, Lawrence KS 66044. (913)843-9444. Director: Ann P. Evans. Estab. 1975. Basic and advanced workshops in technique offered to 12-20 students for weekend sessions held twice annually. Emphasizes batik; ceramics; jewelry; metalsmithing; needlecrafts; quilting; and weaving. Fee: $15-25. Materials fee $5-20. Write for application.

UNIVERSITY OF KANSAS, Department of Design, Visual Arts Building, Lawrence KS 66045. Contact: Gary Nemchock. Offers ceramics; jewelry; weaving; glass blowing; and silversmithing throughout the year. Course length is 18 weeks; summer school is 8 weeks. Fee: $28.85/credit hour for resident. Credit available. Write to Design Department. Requires samples of work prior to acceptance. SASE.

Kentucky

ASBURY COLLEGE, Lexington Ave., Wilmore KY 40390. (606)858-3511. Art Department Head: Rudy Medlock. Offers pottery 3 times annually for 14 beginning potters; crafts and weaving 3 times annually for 18 beginning students; and stained glass once annually for 15 beginning students. Course length is 10 weeks. Fee: $100/course, includes registration. Students supply own materials. Credit available. Write Director of Admissions.

LOUISVILLE SCHOOL OF ART, 100 Park Rd., Anchorage KY 40223. (502)245-8836. Associate Director: Diana Arcadipone. Offers ceramics, printmaking, and textile design 3 times annually and fiber construction once annually. Fee: $70/credit part time, includes materials; tuition; and lab fee. Credit available.
Application: Write to Admissions Office for catalog, brochure, and application. $15 application fee. "For full time (12 credits) admissions a portfolio of 10 pieces is required along with application form and fee; 3 letters of recommendation; and transcripts. Slides are acceptable or personal presentation." SASE.

MOREHEAD STATE UNIVERSITY, Art Department, Morehead KY 40351. Professor: Dr. B.J. Bryant. Estab. 1977. Basic workshops in the building and playing of dulcimers offered to 20 students for a 1 week session held annually in June. Emphasizes wood istrument construction. Fee varies, includes registration, lodging and meals. Materials fee: $15. Write for information. "During the workshop, each student will construct a complete dulcimer of his design. Dr. Bryant himself has made over 100 dulcimers, and has received research grants on the subject."

MURRAY STATE UNIVERSITY, Art Department, Murray KY 42071. (502)762-3784. Chairman: Robert W. Head. Offers pottery to 32 advanced potters; pottery to 15 beginners and 5 advanced; weaving to 18 beginners and advanced; textiles to 10 beginners and advanced; and metals to 14 beginners and 6 advanced. All courses held twice annually; course length is 16 weeks. Fee: $20/hour, includes registration; $6 materials fee. Credit available; offers degree in weaving and textiles, metalsmithing, or ceramics. Write Art Department. Center for continuing education offers basic and advanced workshops in technique to 12-15 students for 10 week sessions twice annually. Emphasizes gunsmithing, "as it pertains to building muzzle loading firearms." Fee: $25, includes registration; separate materials fee. Write Joe Keelsar, Rt. 1, Box 252, Almo KY 42020, for information, or the Center for Continuing Education.

WESTERN KENTUCKY UNIVERSITY, Department of Industrial Education and Technology, Bowling Green KY 42101. (502)745-3251. Department Head: Dr. Franklin Conley. Offers Recreational Crafts 1 twice annually for 80 students and Recreational Crafts 2 twice annually for 20 students. Course length is 18 weeks. Fee: $60/class, resident; $93/class, nonresident, includes registration. Materials fee: $10. Credit available; offers degree in industrial arts and industrial technology. Contact Office of Admissions.

Louisiana

BLANCHET SCHOOL, Rt. 4, Box 397, Abbeville LA 70510. (318)893-3301. Contact: Catherine Blanchet. Basic and advanced workshops in technique offered to 8-10 students for sessions ranging from 1 week to 5-10 Saturdays. Emphasizes tapestry (high warp) weaving. Write for application. Purpose: basic tapestry techniques (traditional) based on the techniques used and taught by Ronald Cruickshank.

THE CRAFT ALLIANCE, 1075 Dalzell, Shreveport LA 71104. (318)222-1780. Director: Roger Runge. Estab. 1972. Basic and advanced workshops in technique and artistic communication offered to 25-30 students semiannually for 1 weekend. Emphasizes ceramics. Fee: $20-25/workshop; includes registration, lodging, and meals. Write asking to be put on workshop mailing list.
Purpose: "A deeper understanding of the creative process through communication with artists of proven, outstanding merit and thorough observation of the particular artist's work in process. Most workshops are observation type."

LOOM ROOM, INC., 623 Royal St., 5 Patio, New Orleans LA 70130. (504)522-7101. President: Glenna Geisert. Estab. 1977. Basic workshop in technique offered to 3-4 students at monthly sessions ranging from 1 day to 4 weeks. Emphasizes weaving. Fee: $45/workshop includes registration and some materials. Write for application. Purpose: basic weaving techniques.
Special Workshops: "We will arrange special workshops for beginning or advanced weaver for those interested who can come to New Orleans. We do need to schedule these at least 1 month in

advance. In the past these have lasted 1-3 days. These workshops are set up for the specific interests of the participants. Cost has been determined by time and number of people interested."

NORTHEAST LOUSIANA UNIVERSITY, Department of Art, Monroe LA 71209. (318)342-3110. Head, Department of Art: Dr. Edward E. Schutz. Offers ceramics 3 times annually for 16 students; jewelry, leather, and metal once annually for 20 students; and weaving twice annually for 16 students. Course length is 18 weeks. Fee: $80/3 hours; $110/6 hours; $206/9 or more hours, includes registration. Students supply own materials. Credit available. Write to Registrar. $1 application fee.
Purpose: "The development of skills that will enable him to become an accomplished performer in whichever area he selects to do work in."

TULANE UNIVERSITY, Newcomb Art School, Tulane University Art Department, New Orleans LA 70118. (504)815-4631. Head of Ceramics and Glass Blowing: Gene H. Koss. Offers Ceramics 1-3 throughout the year for 15-24 students for 1 semester; Graduate Ceramics throughout the year for 4 students for 2 years; and glass blowing throughout the year for 18 students for 1 year. Fee: $20/clay; $35/glass, includes materials. Credit available. "Stresses new experiences with ideas and techniques." Write to Tulane Administration. Slides of work should be presented. SASE.

Maine

BRUNSWICK CRAFT LEAGUE, 3 Cedar St., Brunswick ME 04011. (207)729-0327. Director: Kenn Guimond. Offers stained glass; weaving; spinning; silversmithing; and pottery 4 times annually for 10 weeks. "A full range of workshops are offered throughout the summer." Fee: $65/course (average), includes registration. "State of Maine grants recertification credit for Maine teacher certification." Write for application.

BUSYHAUS/PAPERMAKING WORKSHOPS, Box 422, N. Andover ME 01845. (617)688-2619. Co-director: Robert Hauser. Offers papermaking 12 times annually for 10-200 students. Course length is 1 day-1 week. Fee: $30-500, includes registration and materials. Credit can be arranged with participating institution.

HINCKLEY SCHOOL OF CRAFTS, Hinckley ME 04944. (207)453-9991. Director: Susan Steele. Offers pottery 4 times annually for 120 students; weaving 4 times annually for 20 students; textile design and jewelry 4 times annually for 80 students. Course length is 10 weeks. Fee: $50/course, includes registration. Materials fee: $10-18. Write for application.
Purpose: "We are a community oriented program. Our goal is to provide professional craft instruction to beginners and intermediate craftspeople. Our facilities are very well equipped and our emphasis is on technique and creativity. We also run special Jan-Plan programs for college students and teacher workshops."

LEVERETT CRAFTSMEN AND ARTISTS, Business for Craftspeople Workshop Series, Leverett ME 01054. (413)549-6871. Craft Business Coordinator: Dick Wolfe. Offers workshops in marketing and business skills for craftworkers. Write or call for application.

Maryland

CREATIVE EDUCATION PROGRAM, Glen Echo Park, Glen Echo MD 20768. (301)492-6282. Registrar: Diane Kellogg. Offers pottery 8 times annually for 120 students of all levels for 6 weeks; and batik, glass art, jewelry, metalsmithing, needlecrafts, quilting, soft sculpture, weaving, woodworking, and enameling 4 times annually for 15 students for 10 weeks. Fee: up to $2.50/hour of instruction, includes registration. Credit available. "Many students have gotten credit through various universities in which they are already enrolled. This is worked out between the individual student and the university." Write or call for a brochure which includes registration form. For advanced courses actual work is presented at personal interview.
Purpose: "Technical skills as well as cultivation of sensitivity to design and composition and expression at whatever level the student has achieved."

EAGLE CERAMICS INC., Making it in Clay, 12266 Wilkins Ave., Rockville MD 20852. (301)881-2253. President: Lee Eagle. Estab. 1977. Advanced and some basic workshops in marketing and "Earning a Living in Clay" offered to 25 students in workshop and 140 students in lecture at weekend sessions held monthly. Emphasizes ceramics. Fee: $164/8 weekends, includes registration. Write for application. Purpose: wide knowledge of clay.

THE MARYLAND INSTITUTE COLLEGE OF ART, 1300 Mt. Royal Ave., Baltimore MD 21217. (301)669-9200. Chairman Craft Department: Richard Wagner. Offers ceramics; jewelry;

metalsmithing; soft sculpture; weaving; wood; puppetry; and fabric design (dyeing techniques, stitchery, and applique). Fee: $60/credit and up, includes tuition. Credit available. Send for catalog. Work samples required if applying for a degree program. SASE.

MONTGOMERY COLLEGE, 51 Mannakee St., Rockville MD 20850. (301)762-7400. Crafts Coordinator: Janet F. Maddox. Offers ceramics, jewelry/metalsmithing; and crafts 3 semesters annually; weaving 2 semesters annually; and cloisonne 3 times annually for 8 weeks. Other course lengths are 16 weeks; summer course is 10 weeks. Fee: $22/credit hour for Montgomery County residents, includes registration. Most materials are supplied by student. Credit available; offers AA degree. For application call or write Montgomery College.

MORGAN STATE UNIVERSITY, Crafts Workshop, Department of Art, Baltimore MD 21239. (301)444-3020. Chairman: Oliver P. Scott. Estab. 1977. Basic workshops in technique and materials offered annually to 30-45 students enrolled in undergraduate crafts courses. Session runs from January-May. Fee: $78/workshop, includes registration and college credit. Write for application.

TOWSON STATE UNIVERSITY, Art Department, Baltimore MD 21204. (301)321-2800. Contact: John or Dorothy Fix. Offers Beginning Ceramics, Advanced Ceramics, Beginning Jewelry, and Advanced Jewelry each semester for 25 students; metalsmithing and enameling once annually for 25 students; Fabric Design/Dyeing, weaving, and wood twice annually for 25 students; and Fabric Design/Printing once annually for 25 students. Course length is 14 weeks. Fee: $28/undergraduate credit; $45/graduate credit. Credit available; offers BA with a specialization in crafts.
Application: Part-time students write Office of Continuing Studies; full time students write Office of Admissions. "Students must take Fundamentals of Design and 3-Dimension Design as prerequisites."

UNIVERSITY OF MARYLAND, Department of Design, College Park MD 20742. (301)454-2135. Crafts Coordinator: Hal McWhinnie. Offers batik; ceramics; jewelry; metalsmithing; needlecrafts; soft sculpture; and weaving. Credit available. $10 application fee.

THE WEAVER'S PLACE, 4900 Wetheredsville Rd., Baltimore MD 21207. (301)448-2428. Contact: Lee or Keith Smith. Offers Beginning Weaving 4 times annually for 20 students for 9 weeks; Intermediate Weaving twice annually for 10 students for 9 weeks; Spinning 3 times annually for 8 students for 3 weeks; and 5-8 special workshops annually. Fee: varies with the course, average $3/hour; includes registration, materials, and use of equipment. Write for application.

Massachusetts

THE ART INSTITUTE OF BOSTON, 700 Beacon St., Boston MA 02215. (617)262-1223. Registrar: Carol Pine-Thiessen. Offers Beginning Clay; Intermediate Clay; and Advanced Clay 3 times annually for 14 students. Course length is 16 weeks. Fee: $165/course, includes registration, firings, and tools. Materials fee: $50. Credit available.

BOSTON CENTER FOR ADULT EDUCATION, 5 Comm Ave., Boston MA 02116. (617)267-4430. Contact: Registration Office. Estab. 1977. Basic and advanced workshops in "Selling Your Crafts" to 15 students for 5 week sessions, held 4 times annually. Emphasizes various marketing methods. Fee: $25. Call or write for application.

BOSTON UNIVERSITY, Program in Artisanry, 620 Commonwealth Ave., Boston MA 02215. (617)353-2022. Assistant to the Director: Dr. Elmer Taylor. Offers ceramics and metals 3 times annually for 35 students; textiles 3 times annually for 50 students; and wood 3 times annually for 25 students. Course length is 16 weeks. Fee: $3,850/year, includes registration. Credit available. Write Office of Admission. Submit 15-20 color slides of work. SASE. $20 application fee.

BRADFORD COLLEGE, S. Main St., Bradford MA 01830. (617)372-7161. Chairman, Art Department: Richard Newman. Offers ceramics, jewelry, and weaving twice annually for 12 students of mixed levels; full year of 2-D Design for 25-30 students, and 3-D Design once annually. Course length is 15 weeks. Fee: $60/credit hour, includes registration. Materials fee: $15-20. Credit available. Write Admissions or Registrar's Office.

BROOKLINE ARTS CENTER, 86 Monmouth St., Brookline MA 02146. (617)566-5715. Director: Marilyn Berliner. Estab. 1964. Basic and teaching workshops in technique offered to a maximum of 12 students for sessions ranging from 1 day to once a week for 4-9 weeks. Emphasizes ceramics; glass art; jewelry; metalsmithing; needlecrafts; quilting; calligraphy; teaching crafts; Ukraine egg making; hand paper making; and puppetry. Fee $2-3/hour includes registration and materials (with certain exceptions). Separate materials fee depending on quantities of materials used. Write or call for application.

CRAFT CENTER, 25 Sagamore Rd., Worcester MA 01605. (617)753-8183. Executive Director: Angelo Randazzo. Offers wood; metal; clay; and fiber throughout the year. Professional workshop offered throughout the year. Special 2 year and portfolio program for full time students. Write Educational Coordinator for information.

ENDICOTT COLLEGE, Hale St., Beverly MA 01915. (617)927-0585. Chairman, Art Department: J. David Broudo. Offers Ceramics 1-2 three times annually for 25 students; Metal 1-2 three times annually for 15 students; and Fiber 1-2 three times annually for 12 students. Course length is 9 weeks. Fee: $4,100; includes registration, lodging, meals, and full degree program. Credit available. Write Director of Admissions.

THE GLASS EYE, Box 642, Eastham Village Green, North Eastham MA 02651. (617)255-5044. Contact: John Knight. Estab. 1971. Basic and advanced workshops in technique offered to 5 students for 6 week sessions held in winter. Demonstrations held in July-August; no registration limit. Emphasizes basic knowledge of stained glass work, both lead and copper. Fee: $45/workshop includes registration. Materials fee: depends on project. Write or call for application.

HABITAT INSTITUTE FOR THE ENVIRONMENT, Box 136, 10 Juniper Rd., Belmont MA 02178. (617)489-3850. Program Director: Ann LeRoyer. Estab. 1971. Basic workshops in technique offered for sessions ranging 1 day to 8 weeks, held 4 times annually. Emphasizes spinning; plant dyeing; papermaking; and weaving. Fee: $10-40, includes registration and materials. Write for application.

HARCOURT BINDERY, 9 Harcourt St., Boston MA 02116. (617)536-5755. Contact: Sam and Emily Ellenport. Estab. 1974. Basic and advanced workshops in technique offered to 5-10 students for sessions ranging 1-3 days, held monthly. Emphasizes bookbinding; papermaking; and marbling. Fee: $25-100, includes registration and materials. "Write us for a schedule."

H.O.M.E. LEARNING CENTER, Box 408, Orland MA 04472. (207)469-2026. Co-director: Andrew Seager. Offers ceramics twice annually for 25 students for 15 weeks; knitting twice annually for 12 students for 10 weeks; leather twice annually for 30 students for 12 weeks; pottery twice annually for 12 students for 7 weeks; and spinning/dye twice annually for 12 students for 6 weeks. No fee for courses. Materials fee: $7.50/clay. "We offer a diploma from the Bucksport High School when the student earns 17 credits." Write, call, or visit H.O.M.E. Learning Center. $5 application fee.

THE HOOSUCK INSTITUTE, 121 Union St., North Adams MA 01247. (413)664-6382. Associate Director: Cynthia Nystrom. Estab. 1975. Basic and advanced workshops in marketing; technique; and design and business administration offered to 10-12 interested students for sessions ranging from 2-week programs to full-time. Emphasizes ceramics; glass art; jewelry; metalsmithing; needlecrafts; quilting; weaving; stringed instruments building; sculpture; graphic design; stained glass; blown glass; and woodworking. Limited fee: $160-1,800 for registration and tuition; separate materials fee. Write for application. "Workshops are offered by master artisans who run their own successful craft businesses in this facility. Licensed by the Commonwealth of Massachusetts."

MASSACHUSETTS COLLEGE OF ART, Department of 3-D Fine Arts, 364 Brookline Ave., Boston MA 02215. (617)731-2340. Department Head: Dan Dailey. Offers ceramics; glass art; jewelry; metalsmithing; soft sculpture; weaving; and sculpture. Request college catalog and bulletin for specific course information and fees. Credit available. Write to Admissions Office. Submit slide portfolio. SASE. $10 application fee.

NANTUCKET SCHOOL OF NEEDLERY, 121 Union St., North Adams MA 01247. (413)664-9893. Director: Mary Ann Bienecky. Offers a home study course in needlecraft. Fee: $20/lesson, includes registration, materials, and critiques. "Send for a brochure. The brochure gives thorough description of the home study course in needlecraft and contains registration form and index of lessons."

PETERSHAM CRAFT CENTER, Rt. 32, Petersham MA 01366. (617)724-3415. Offers ceramics; jewelry; needlecrafts; stained glass; quilting; tole painting; and weaving. "We try to hold classes as requested by members in the community." Fee: $1.50/hour, includes registration. Write for application. "Most of our students are beginners anxious to try a new craft. In many cases they will continue to take a course until they become proficient. Some then continue to work at home or perhaps advance to an accredited school."

POTTERY WORKSHOP, 44 McClellan St., Amherst MA 01002. (413)253-9360. Contact: Fred Englander. Offers Elementary Pottery 4 times annually for 8 students for 10 weeks. Fee: $80/course, includes registration. Materials fee: $5.

PROJECT, INC., 141 Huron Ave., Cambridge MA 02138. (617)491-0187. Executive Director: Sandy Schafer. Estab. 1962. Weekly workshops offered to 8-12 students for 10 week sessions. Emphasizes batik; ceramics; glass art; jewelry; and quilting. Write for application.

REGIS COLLEGE, 235 Wellesley St., Weston MA 02193. (617)893-1820. Chairman, Art Department: Sister Louisella Walters. Offers ceramics twice annually for 15 students for 1 semester and general crafts twice annually for 20 students for 1 semester. Fee: $180/4 credits, includes tuiton. Materials fee: $15/semester. Credit available. Write Admissions. $10 application fee.

SPRINGFIELD COLLEGE, Art Department, 263 Alden St., Springfield MA 01109. (413)787-2332. Chairman, Art Department: William Blizard. Offers ceramics 4 times annually for 20 students and Advanced Ceramics 3 times annually for 15 students. Course length is 10 weeks. Fee: $75/noncredit course; $158/credit course, includes registration. Materials fee: $20. Credit available.

TRURO CENTER FOR THE ARTS AT CASTLE HILL INC., Box 756, Truro MA 02666. (617)349-3714. Director: Joyce Johnson. Offers work study program; exchange of tuition for work around the Center. No board and room provided. Emphasizes ceramics; jewelry; pottery; weaving; and woodcrafting. Write for application. Must have background in specific craft. "Our greatest advantage is to young people who are thinking of a career in the arts and crafts. They are able to take advantage of a variety of workshops in exchange for working around the Center at sometimes menial tasks. It is not recommended for students over 20 years of age."

Michigan

ALBION COLLEGE, Albion MI 49224. (517)629-5511. Contact: Richard Leach. Offers Ceramics 1-3 four to five times annually for 40-60 students for 15 weeks; Ceramics Workshop 1-3 twice annually, 1 held at Petosky, Michigan, for 20 students for 4 weeks, 5 days a week. Fee: $135/semester credit hour; $250/summer school. Materials fee: $30. Credit available. Write Registrar or Dean, Summer School. $58 matriculation fee; $10 summer school fee.

CENTRAL MICHIGAN UNIVERSITY, Dept. of Industrial Education and Technology, 204 Wightman Hall, Mt. Pleasant MI 48859. (517)774-3033. Contact: Dr. Franklyn C. Ingram. Offers arts and crafts (2 credits) each semester and summer school for 30 students per section. Semester length is 16 weeks; summer school is 6 weeks. Fee: $24/credit, Michigan residents; $62/credit, nonresident. Excess materials fee: $2.50 plus materials used. Graduate or undergraduate credit available. Write Admissions Office. Regular admissions fee.
Purpose: "Beginning or advanced experiences in the required areas indicated. Advanced work possible particularly in leatherworking and the plastic areas. Opportunities to take additional course work in related fields in the University."

EASTERN MICHIGAN UNIVERSITY, Ypsilanti MI 48197. (313)487-1268. Head, Art Department: Kingsley Calkins. Offers advanced ceramics, ceramics, jewelry and metal, and 3D Design 4 times annually for 15 students; and textiles 3 times annually for 15 students. Fall and winter terms are 15 weeks; spring and summer terms are 5-7 weeks. Fee: tuition based on a scale. Credit available. Write to Office of Admission or Graduate Admissions. "Normal enrollment and admission procedures."

FOLK ARTS, 1506 Lynn Ave., Marquette MI 49855. (906)226-3931. Contact: Pat Virch. Offers Norwegian Rosemaling twice annually for 8 students; and Early American Decorative Painting once annually for 8 students. Course length is 5 days. Fee: $75/class, includes registration. Materials fee: $3/Early American class. Write or call for application. SASE.

Purpose: "Intensive instruction and history concerning the folk arts. Projects are finished at your own speed. Techniques are developed in depth."

GRAND VALLEY STATE COLLEGE, 147 CFA College Landing, Allendale MI 49401. (616)895-6611, ext. 486. Chairperson, Art Department: Beverly J. Berger. Offers Introduction to Ceramics and Introduction to Metal 4 times annually for 16 students; Intermediate Ceramics and Advanced Ceramics 3 times annually for 15 students; and Intermediate Metal and Advanced Metal 3 times annually for 16 students. Course length is 10 weeks. Fee: $75/class, includes materials. Materials fee: $10-30. Credit available. Write for application. $10 application fee.

Purpose: "Technical competence and aesthetic growth in the area in which they enrolled. The courses are oriented to present technique yet give room for individual expression with the encouragement of critical examination."

ROBERT L. KIDD ASSOCIATES, 107 Townsend St., Birmingham MI 48011 (313)642-3838. Manager: Anthony Scarano. Offers Beginning Weaving and Intermediate Weaving 5 times annually for 12 students for 6 weeks; knitting and needlepoint 4 times annually for 10 students for 4 weeks; and basketry 4 times annually for 10 students for 3 weeks. Fee: $12-65, includes registration and tuition. "Students receive 10% discount if supplies are purchased from R.L. Kidd Associates. Write for current schedule, Department CCS. SASE.

MICHIGAN STATE UNIVERSITY, Department of Human Environment and Design, College of Human Ecology, Human Ecology Building, East Lansing MI 48824. (514)355-7715. Assistant to the Chairperson for Student Affairs: Dr. Gertrude Nygren. Offers weaving and textile design 4 times annually for 20 students; crafts with materials 3 times annually for 20 students. Course length is 10 weeks; 3 credits. Fee: $23/credit, resident; $47.50/credit, nonresident. Includes registration. Students supply own materials.

Purpose: "Person may expect to gain a sound technique basis to which they should be able to apply their own previous experience from other design courses. The courses are generally only taken by the majors within the department and offer a situation to apply knowledge learned in other courses."

Application: Write to the Office of Admissions, Room 150, Administration Building for an undergraduate application. "Must be accepted by the University as student and must have junior class standing to be eligible for all 3 courses."

C.S. MOTT COMMUNITY COLLEGE, Fine Arts Division, 1401 E. Court St., Flint MI 48503. (313)762-0443. Chairman: S.E. Morello. Offers ceramics and metalsmithing/jewelry twice annually for 16 students. Course length is 16 weeks. Fee: $48/class in-district; $81/class out-of-district; $117/class out-of-state, includes registration and materials. "Student provides costly materials such as precious metals or stones." Credit available. "Strong prerequisites or substantial experience in field required for enrollment." Write for application. $25 1st tuition fee.

Purpose: "Intense experience at basic and/or advanced levels. Excellent facilities and equipment. Strong committment to quality concept as well as product."

NORTHERN MICHIGAN UNIVERSITY, Art and Design Department, Marquette MI 49855. Contact: William C. Leete. Offers ceramics; jewelry; metalsmithing; weaving; wood working; and furniture design for 4 credit hours every semester for 10-30 students. Semester length is 16 weeks. Fee: $25/credit, includes registration. Materials fee: $25, wood is not covered by fee. Credit available. Write to Admissions.

Purpose: Knowledge of physical; psychological; and social concerns as related to the visual arts through experience in a particular medium.

SIENA HEIGHTS COLLEGE, 1247 Siena Heights Dr., Adrian MI 49221. (517)263-0751. Chairperson: Jeannine Klemm. Offers ceramics; metal arts; and Wood, Stone, and Metal Sculpture twice annually for 30 beginning and 30 advanced students. Length of semester course is 2 semesters or 14 weeks. $57.50/semester hour, includes registration and some materials. Materials fee: $10-30. Credit available. Write to Admissions Office. "For art major in Master's program slides are required. No more than 10 slides of quality pieces." SASE.

UNIVERSITY OF MICHIGAN, School of Art, 2000 Bonisteel Blvd., Ann Arbor MI 48109. (313)764-0397. Offers weaving; jewelry; metalsmithing; and ceramics 2-3 times annually. Registration limit and length of course depends on semester. Course fee and materials fee depend on time and class. Credit available; offers BFA.

Application: Application to the School of Art is obtained through the Admissions Office, University of Michigan, 1220 Student Activities Building, Ann Arbor, Michigan 48109. $15 application fee. "If applying for a regular semester, application is by portfolio, 15-20 color slides of the student's work. If freshman, would be mostly drawing and design work. If transfer student, would contain any work done— drawing; painting; ceramics; weaving; etc." SASE; 1 slide is kept when applicant applies for regular semester.

Minnesota

BLACK DIAMOND WOODWORKS, Rt. 1, Morristown MN 55052. Director: Glen Miller. Estab. 1975. Basic workshops in technique offered to 5 knowledgeable woodworking students for 4-6 day sessions held annually. Emphasizes wood inlay and marquetry. Fee: $15, includes materials. Write for application prior to June 1.

CIR-KIT CONCEPTS, INC., 612 N. Broadway, Rochester MN 55901. (507)288-8237. Vice President: Dana Sokol. Offers electrical workshops. "Workshops are sponsored primarily by miniature stores with us as workshop leaders. We teach the wiring of dollhouses using a tape wiring system." Write for catalog.

MOORHEAD STATE UNIVERSITY, Moorhead MN 56560. (218)236-2104. Contact: Dr. Albert G. Mudgett. Offers Recreational Crafts and Leather Craft twice annually for 25 students; Metal Activities and Creative Metals once annually for 20 students; and Lapidary biannually for 16 students. Course length is 10 weeks; summer school is 5 weeks. Fee: $9.25/credit, undergraduate resident; $18.50/nonresident, includes registration and materials for processing. Credit available. Apply to Admissions and Records or attend first class, evening session. $10 application fee.

ST. CLOUD STATE UNIVERSITY, Art Department, St. Cloud MN 56301. (612)255-4283. Chairman: Dr. James Roy. Offers ceramics and jewelry 3 times per quarter for 20 students; glassworking 3 times per quarter for 10 students; metalsmithing once per quarter for 20 students; and weaving twice per quarter for 20 students. Course length is 11 weeks. Fee: $30/courses, includes registration. Materials fee: $20-40. Credit available. Contact Admissions and Records Office.

UNIVERSITY OF MINNESOTA, Summer Arts Study Center, 1128 La Salle Ave., Minneapolis MN 55403. (612)373-1925. Assistant Director: Mark Swanson. Offers pottery once each summer for 2 weeks for 30 potters, all levels; stained glass, color, fabric design, fiber/off loom, and quiltmaking once each summer for 1 week for 25 students, all levels; and pewter casting and holloware once each summer for 20 students. Fee: $70-90/course, includes registration. Material fee: up to $25. Undergraduate or graduate credit available. Write for application.
Purpose: "Skill at any level. Our courses are taught at a northern Minnesota resort and comprehensive, all day, away from other distractions and peopled by highly motivated persons."

THE WOOD CARVING SCHOOL, 3056 Excelsior Blvd., Minneapolis MN 55416. (612)927-7491. Contact: Chris Effrem. Estab. 1955. Basic and advanced workshops in technique offered to 10-12 students for 7 day sessions. Emphasizes woodcarving. Fee: $95/week. Materials fee: minimum of $100. Write for application. "During the workshop, students should learn types of carvings, how to sharpen tools, how to use tools, how to carve and the different types of carving woods."

Mississippi

DELTA STATE UNIVERSITY, Cleveland MS 38732. (601)843-2151. Head of Art Department: Malcolm Norwood. Offers Ceramics 4 times annually for 20 students for two 5 month semesters and 2 summer sessions of 5 weeks each; Fiber (Embellishment) once annually for 20 students for 5 month semester; Fiber (Weaving) once annually for 15 students for 5 month semester; and Foundry Procedures twice annually for 15 students for 2 semesters of 5 months each. Fee: $24/semester hour part-time student; $250/University fees full-time instate student, includes registration. Fiber students supply own materials. Credit available; offers degrees in Fine Arts, Art Education, and Commercial Art. Write Registrar.
Purpose: "Courses are taught by practicing artists in a total art and education environment. Small university offers opportunity for personalized instruction and contacts."

MERIDIAN JUNIOR COLLEGE, 5500 Hwy. 19 N., Meridian MS 39301. Contact: Randy Shoutts. Offers Pottery 1-2 three times annually for 20 students for 18 weeks. Fee: $40/course, includes registration and materials. Credit available. Program includes "handbuilding; wheel throwing; glaze calculation; and firing." Write for application.

MISSISSIPPI STATE UNIVERSITY, Industrial Education Dept., Drawer N. U., Mississippi State MS 39762. (601)325-5932. Crafts Coordinator: Dr. R. D. Brook. Offers General Crafts (ceramics, art metal, and leather) 3 times annually for 25 students for 18 weeks. Fee: $93/course, includes registration. Credit available. Write or call Industrial Education Department.

MISSISSIPPI UNIVERSITY FOR WOMEN, Box W-70 MUW, Columbus MS 39701. (601)328-4881. Chairman, Art Department: Charles E. Ambrose. Offers pottery and textile design twice annually for 25 students; weaving and glassblowing once annually for 15 students; and metal crafts/jewelry once annually for 25 students. Course length is 3 months. Fee: $25/semester hour, includes registration and materials. Lab fee: $3. Credit available; offers BFA in 3-Dimensional Design with a concentration in crafts. Write Admissions Office.

Missouri

BIG ANVIL FORGE SCHOOL OF BLACKSMITHING, General Delivery, Moody MO 65777. (417)284-3992. Contact: Bob Patrick. Offers blacksmithing 9 times annually for 20 students for 1-6 weeks. Fee: $100/week, includes registration and materials. $25/week room and board; extra fee for materials for unassigned projects. Write for brochure and schedule list.
Purpose: "The instruction is designed to give the student or blacksmith skill in either general blacksmithing or in a specialized skill chosen by special arrangement with the instructor."

CENTRAL MISSOURI STATE UNIVERSITY, Warrensburg MO 64093. (816)429-4030. Assistant Dean, Applied Sciences and Technology: Dr. Robert Goetz. Offers crafts (ceramics, leather, and plastics) 3 times annually for 30 students; metal crafts/lapidary (jewelry and lapidary) 3 times annually for 20 students; and ceramics twice annually for 20 students. Course length is 10½ weeks. Fee: $60/course, includes registration. Materials fee: $15-50. Credit available. Write to Admissions Office.

CULVER-STOCKTON COLLEGE, Canton MO 63435. (314)288-5221. Contact: G.F. Kenner. Offers pottery twice annually for 16 beginning students for 15 weeks; jewelry once annually for 16 beginning students for 15 weeks; glass blowing once annually for 8 beginning or advanced students for 3 weeks; and Advanced Crafts twice annually for 32 students for 15 weeks. Fee: $252/course, includes tuition. Materials fee: $15-24. Credit available; offers BA or BFA with emphasis on 1 or more crafts. Write to Admissions Office. "Student must be admitted to the College." $10 application fee.

DRURY COLLEGE, Springfield MO 65803. (417)865-8731, ext. 263. Head of Art Department: John Simmonds. Offers Pottery 1 twice annually and evening class for 18 students; Pottery 2 twice annually for 10 students; jewelry evening class for 10 students; and Weaving 1-2 twice annually for 15 students. Credit available; offers BA. Write to Admissions.

MISSOURI SOUTHERN STATE COLLEGE, Newman and Duquesne Rds., Joplin MO 64801. (417)624-8100, ext. 263. Director: Darral A. Dishman. Offers Beginning and Advanced Ceramics twice annually for 20 students; Beginning and Advanced Jewelry twice annually for 16 students; and Arts and Crafts Education (batik, leatherworking, and weavings) twice annually for 24 students. Course length is 16 weeks. Fee: $10/class, includes materials. Credit available; offers BA and BS in Art Education. Advanced craft/studio studies available. Write for application. Must be college enrolled art student. $500 MSC tuition.

NORTHWEST MISSOURI STATE UNIVERSITY, Maryville MO 64468. (816)582-7141, ext. 178, 273, 279. Chairman, Department of Art: Robert Sunkel. Offers Introductory Ceramics; Advanced Ceramics; Wheel Throwing; Advanced Problems in Ceramics; Introductory Jewelry; Advanced Jewelry; Metalsmithing; Advanced Metalsmithing; Advanced Problems in Metalsmithing; and Design with Fibers twice annually for 10-17 students. Course length is 16 weeks. "In addition we offer gradute-level 2-week short courses during the summer; each short course focuses on a particular aspect of the area." Fee: $22/hour, 8 hours or less, Missouri resident and $44/hour nonresident; $190/hour, 9 or more hours, Missouri resident and $385/hour nonresident. Includes registration and tuition. Summer session fees: $22/hour, 5 hours or less, Missouri resident and $44/hour, nonresident; $130/hour, 6 or more hours, Missouri resident; $260/hour, nonresident. Credit available; offers BA, BFA, and BSE. Write Director of Admissions.

THE SCHOOL OF THE OZARKS, Point Lookout MO 65726. (417)334-6411. Chairman, Department of Art: Ken Burchett. Offers pottery 3 times annually for 12 students for 10-16 weeks; stained glass and weaving twice annually for 12 students for 16 weeks. Fee: $100.05/course. "We are a work-study institution. Students work on campus to pay registration; tuition; lodging; and meals. Credit available. Write Registrar. Provides introductory undergraduate instruction.

SOUTHEAST MISSOURI STATE UNIVERSITY, 900 Normal St., Cape Girardeau MO 63701. (314)651-2143. Contact: Dr. Edwin L. Smith. Offers batik 2 courses per semester for 25 students per class; ceramics 4 courses per semester for 20 students each class; jewelry 3 courses per semester for 20 students each class; metal and sculpture 2 courses of each for 15 students per class; and weaving 1 course per semester for 20 students. Course length is 16 weeks. Fee: $15-20/hour, includes registration. Credit available. Write to Head of Art Department. Submit slides of work. SASE.

Montana

COLLEGE OF GREAT FALLS, Department of Art, Great Falls MT 59405. Contact: Dan Price. Offers pottery twice annually for 10 beginning students; Raku Pottery once at summer session for 10 beginning and advanced students; batik once at summer session for 10 beginning students; and jewelry once annually for 10 beginning students. Course length is 18 weeks; summer session is 5 weeks. Fee: $10-20/course, includes materials, maintenance, and miscellaneous. Credit available. Write Registrar. $10 application fee.
Purpose: "Each of these classes is structured to give the student an in-depth experience in the materials and techniques of each area."

EASTERN MONTANA COLLEGE, 150 H 30th St., Billings MT 59101. Head, Art Department: Ben C. Steele. Offers ceramics 4 times annually for 20 students; metal/jewelry and fiber arts once annually for 20 students; weaving once annually for 10 students; and general crafts 3 times annually for 25 students. Course length is 12 weeks. Fee: $483/year in-state; $1,455/year out of state, includes registration. Credit available. Write Admissions Director. $10 application fee.

MILES COMMUNITY COLLEGE, 2715 Dickinson St., Miles City MT 59301. Contact: Sydney Sonneborn. Offers pottery 3 times annually; jewelry and crafts once annually for 10 students; and stained glass 2 times annually for 10 students. Course length is 10 weeks. Fee: $30, includes registration. Credit available. Write Registrar.
Purpose: "This is a community college and is restricted by state law to teach lower division courses. Program provides basic knowledge of materials and techniques as well as concepts in design."

MONTANA STATE UNIVERSITY, School of Art, Bozeman MT 59715. (406)994-2952. Contact: Richard Helzer. Offers ceramics; metalsmithing; and jewelry 3 times annually for 30 students. Course length is 10 weeks. Fee: regular University tuition, includes registration. Credit available. Write to Office of Admissions. $10 application fee.

ROCKY MOUNTAIN COLLEGE, Crafts Methods, Poly Dr., Billings MT 59102. Contact: Patricia Cherewick. Offers stitchery applique 4 times annually, no student limit; crafts methods 1-2 times annually, no student limit; and leaded glass 2-4 times annually for 10-15 students. Course length is 6-8 weeks. Fee: $10-25/course, includes registration. Credit available; "some are adult education courses others are college courses." Write.

Nebraska

CHARDON STATE COLLEGE, Fine Arts Department, Chadron NE 69337. (308)432-4451, ext. 326. Contact: Richard Bird. Offers Crafts 1 (batik and weaving) 3 times annually for 20 students; Crafts 2 (jewelry) once annually for 20 students; glassblowing once annually for 15 students; Ceramics 1 three times annually for 20 students; and Ceramics 2 once annually for 20 students. Course length is 18 weeks. Fee: $15.50/credit hour in-state; $27.50/credit hour out-of-state, includes registration and most materials. Credit available. Write Office of Admissions.
Purpose: "Chadron State College has a unique campus in which numbers are small. There are excellently equipped studios with no overcrowded studios and space to work within."

KEARNEY STATE COLLEGE, Department of Industrial Education, Kearney NE 68847. (308)236-4353. Contact: Dr. Everett A. Sheffield. Offers jewelry and lapidary once annually for 24 students; leathercraft once annually for 24 students; and general crafts twice annually for 24 students. Course length is 17 weeks. Fee: $45/course, includes registration. Credit available. Write Admissions Office. $10 application fee.

NEBRASKA WESLEYAN UNIVERSITY, Lincoln NE 68504. (402)466-2371. Head, Department of Art: Betty Wallace. Offers Ceramics 1 twice annually for 24 students; Ceramics 2 twice annually for 12 students; jewelry, fiber and stained glass once annually for 12 students. Course length is 16 weeks. Fee: regular University tuition, includes registration and materials. Credit available. Offers "thorough training in craft and design by instructors with MFA's." Write Admissions Office.

PERU STATE COLLEGE, Peru NE 68421. (402)872-3815. Chairman of Applied Arts: Dr. Lester Russell. Offers handcrafts 3 times annually for 24 students; Industrial Crafts 1 once annually for 24 students. Course length is 1 semester. Fee: $15.50/semester hour resident tuition plus fees; $27.50/semester hour nonresident tuition plus fees. Credit available. Provides "basic skills and knowlege of various craft areas." Write Admissions Office.

PLATTE TECHNICAL COMMUNITY COLLEGE, Columbus NE 68601. Contact: Richard Abraham. Offers beginning and advanced pottery and beginning and advanced arts and crafts twice annually for 18 weeks. Fee $13.75/course, includes registration and materials. Credit available. Write or call college for application.

Nevada
NORTHERN NEVADA COMMUNITY COLLEGE, 901 Elm, Elko NV 89801. (702)738-8493. Chairperson, Art Department: Sarah Campsey. Offers crafts (composite) twice annually for 15 students for 15 weeks; stained glass once annually for 15 students for 10 weeks; ceramics once annually for 15 students for 15 weeks; weaving once annually for 6 students for 12 weeks; and Pioneer Crafts once annually for 10 students for 8-15 weeks. Fee: $1/instruction hour, includes registration. Fee: varies. Credit available; "Some classes are credited by University of Nevada system and transferable to most universities." Write Chairperson, Art Department.

TUSCARORA POTTERY SCHOOL, Tuscarora NV 89834. Contact: Dennis Parks. Offers pottery twice annually to 8 students for 4 months and a 1 month summer pottery course for 16 students. Fee: $565/month, includes registration; materials; lodging; meals; and firing. Credit available; prior arrangement should be made with the chairman of your art department. Colleges that have granted credit are The Claremont Colleges; St. John's University; and Franconia College. To apply write above address; $15 application fee. Submit slides of work. SASE.

Purpose: To learn prospecting and processing local materials; kiln and wheel construction/clay aesthetics; single-fire glazing; raku, salt and high temperature firing; firing with oil (drain oil and diesel); and what to do with what you make (exhibiting and selling).

New Hampshire
THE BROTMAN FORGE, Box 157, Lyme NH 03768. (603)795-4545. Director: Harvey Brotman. Estab. 1976. Basic workshops in technique offered to 6 students for sessions ranging 4-6 weeks, held 8 times annually. Emphasizes blacksmithing and metalsmithing. Fee: $400/4 weeks, $575/6 weeks for registration and materials. Students purchase materials beyond those supplied for basic projects. Write for application. "The course is designed to teach the student the technical skill of the blacksmith's craft."

KEENE STATE COLLEGE, School of Continuing Education, Joslin House, Keene NH 03431. (603)352-1909, ext. 370. Contact: Leslie Voiers. Estab. 1979. Advanced workshops in the methodology of teaching weaving offered annually to 25 students for 3 week sessions, 2 consecutive summers. "Students must prove their competence and level as a weaver through a slide portfolio and application." Fee: current College tuition. Write for application. "Instructors are professional weavers, who, in turn, want to help their students attain greater craft professionalism, and growth as an instructor."

PHOENIX WORKSHOPS, Rt. 1, Goffstown NH 03045. (603)774-3582. Codirector: Gerry Williams. Offers kiln building 1 week for 15 advanced students; beginning pottery; advanced pottery, and weaving 2 weeks for 15 students; and Master's Class (pottery) 2 weeks for 6 students. Fee: $75/course. Write for application. $15 application fee. Submit portfolio for Master's Class.

SHARON ARTS CENTER, Rt. 2, Box 361, Peterborough NH 03458. (603)924-7256. Classes Coordinator: Deborah Porter. Estab. 1947. Workshops at all levels in technique offered in 10 week sessions 4 times annually. Emphasizes ceramics; jewelry; quilting; tole painting; and weaving. Fee: $40, includes registration; separate materials fee. Call or write for application.

New Jersey

ARTS WORKSHOP AT THE NEWARK MUSEUM, 43-49 Washington St., Newark NJ 07100. (201)733-6635. Supervisor: Jean West. Offers ceramics and Ceramic Glaze Chemistry 3 times annually for 24 students; Hand Built Ceramics and Frame Loom Weaving 3 times annually for 12 students; and 4 Harness Weaving 3 times annually for 36 students. Fee: $38/course, Museum members, senior citizens and students; $50/nonmembers, includes registration. Materials fee: $8-15. Credit available. "Students have received credit under an independent study program at the college they are attending." Write for application.

Purpose: "Our courses are basically for students from the beginning to intermediate levels of study. Our program aims to educate our students in the fundamental techniques and materials used in their area of study. We offer 1-3 day workshops for the advanced students and professional craftworkers who are interested in specific concentrated topics."

BOIN ARTS AND CRAFTS COMPANY, 87 Morris St., Morristown NJ 07960. (201)539-0600. Contact: Warren E. Boin. Estab. 1936. Basic and advanced workshops in technique. Offered monthly to 20 students for 3-4 hours. Emphasizes batik; candlemaking; decoupage; glass art; jewelry; leatherworking; quilting; and new crafts as they come along. No fee. Write for application. Workshops provide basic information.

CANDLES CREATED BY MARTIN, 680 Leigh Terrace, Westwood NJ 07675. (201)666-2259. Contact: Rose Martin. Estab. 1970. Basic workshop in technique offered quarterly to 10 students 1 night a week for 6 weeks. Emphasizes candlemaking. Fee: $40/workshop, includes registration and materials. Call for more information.

EARTH AND FIRE CERAMIC STUDIO AND GALLERY, Box 5, 20 Morris St., Morristown NJ 07960. (201)455-9368. Contact: Sy Shames and Michael Feno. Estab. 1969. Basic and advanced workshops in technique offered every 10 weeks to 10 students, 1 class weekly for 10 weeks; 5 weeks in summer. Fee: $80/workshop, includes materials. Firing charge: 1c/cubic inch. Write for application.

MIDDLESEX COUNTY COLLEGE, Woodbridge Ave., Edison NJ 08817. (201)548-6000, ext. 380. Contact: Lore Lindenfeld or Marion Weiss. Offers 8 sections of ceramics 3 times annually, 140 openings; 5 sections of weaving 3 times annually, 80 openings. Course length is 15 weeks. Fee: $17/contact hour (courses are 3 contact hours), includes registration and materials. Material fee: $10. $3 parking fee. Write Admissions Office.

MONTCLAIR STATE COLLEGE, Upper Montclair NJ 07043. (201)893-4167. Contact: Deborah Healy. Estab. 1976. Basic workshops in technique offered quarterly for 1 week to 20 students interested in recreational crafts. Emphasizes batik; candlemaking; decoupage; glass art; jewelry; leatherworking; tole painting; and stained glass. Fee: about $120/workshop; includes registration; materials; and credit. Write for college catalog.

OLDEBROOKE SPINNERY INC., Mountain Rd., Lebanon NJ 08833. (201)534-2360. Contact: Betty Oldenburg. Offers throughout the year spinning once a week for 4 weeks for 10 students; weaving once a week for 4 weeks for 6 students; and natural dyeing 1 day for 10 students. Fee: $45/spinning; $40/weaving; $15/natural dyeing, includes registration and materials. "Students have received credit by doing independent studies outside of their school with me." Write.

PAULA'S PLACE, 1 W. Main St., Marlton NJ 08053. (609)983-6880. Contact: Paula Vallen. Offers pottery 6 times annually for 24 students for 6 weeks; weaving 6 times annually for 36 students for 6 weeks; and macrame 8-10 times annually for 4 weeks. Fee: $2.50/hour, depending on length of course. Write for brochure.

Purpose: "Fundamentals of the crafts, the basics mostly. Good for hobbyist. Many students have gone on to college for more in-depth study."

PETERS VALLEY CRAFTSMEN, INC., Layton NJ 07851. (201)948-5200. Executive Director: Judy and Dennis McCarthy. Estab. 1968. All levels of workshops in marketing and technique offered 3 times annually to approximately 12 students in each craft area for 1 day-2 weeks. Emphasizes batik; ceramics; jewelry; metalsmithing; needlecrafts; quilting; soft sculpture; weaving; blacksmithing; and wood. Write or call for fee information and application.

THE SALEM CRAFTSMEN'S GUILD, 3 Alvin Place, Upper Montclair NJ 07043. (201)764-8828. President: S.D. Gerlando. Estab. 1968. Basic and advanced workshops in technique offered quarterly to 50 students for 10 weeks. Emphasizes ceramics; pottery; and ceramic sculpture. Fee: $65, includes materials and bisque firing. Materials fee: $1/pound for glaze firing. Write or call for application. Workshops provide knowledge in advanced and/or basic skills in pottery making.

STUDIO FOR THE LAPIDARY ARTS, 145 Summit Ave., Berkeley Heights NJ 07922. (201)464-3757. Director: G.H. Collings. Estab. 1968. All levels of workshops in technique offered throughout September-June to 25 students for 10 weeks. Emphasizes jewelry; metalsmithing; lapidary; and cutting faceted gems. Fee: $42/workshop, includes registration and all tools and equipment. Write or call for application.

WEISS STUDIO AND CRAFT WORKSHOPS, 161 Culberson Rd., Basking Ridge NJ 07920. (201)766-5228. Contact: Nadine H. Weiss. Offers ceramics; weaving; stitchery; clay sculpture; and rug hooking throughout the year in sessions of eight 3 hour lessons for 12 students. Also conducts craft tours in the US and abroad. Itineraries available. Fee: $54/session, includes most materials. Write for application; $10 application fee which is applied to fee.

New Mexico

CARRIZO ART AND CRAFT COURSES, Drawer A, Ruidoso NM 88345. (505)257-2375. Director: Hilma G. Collier. Estab. 1956. Basic and advanced workshops in technique and design offered annually to 20 students for 2 weeks, 5-6 hours per day. Emphasizes glass art; and jewelry. Fee: $90-200. Meals and lodging are available on the premises. Write for brochures and application. Instructors are nationally known craftworkers. Workshop's purpose is technical expertise and design.

COLLEGE OF SANTA FE, St. Michael's Dr., Santa Fe NM 87501. (505)982-6201. Contact: Brother Ronald C. Berger. Offers ceramics and jewelry twice annually, no student limit; and weaving once annually for 15 students. Course length is 16 weeks. Fee: $57/credit, includes registration and tuition. Materials fee: $25. Credit available. Write Art Department. "Acceptance into our program takes place after the student has been exposed to the basic, introductory courses and program in the first year."

MARY LOU COOK WORKSHOP, 321 Calle Loma N., Santa Fe NM 87501. (505)983-2894. Director: Mary Lou Cook. Estab. 1960. Basic and advanced workshops in technique, philosophy, motivation, and inspiration offered on request for any number of students for 1 day-1 week. Emphasizes needlecrafts; calligraphy, basketmaking; cross-stitch; and pastecraft. Call for application.

EASTERN NEW MEXICO UNIVERSITY, Portales NM 88130. (505)562-2652. Chairman, Department of Art: Chris Gikas. Offers ceramics and jewelry 3 times annually with unlimited registration; and metalsmithing annually with unlimited registration. Course length is 16 weeks. Weaving is offered 2 weeks in the summer for 15 students. Students furnish materials. Credit available; offers degree.
Application: Write Director of Admission at above address. Slides and photos will be accepted for craftworker applying for scholarship. SASE.

NEW MEXICO STATE UNIVERSITY, Box 3572, Las Cruces NM 88003. (505)646-3329. Contact: Dr. Lee Richards. Offers jewelry twice annually for beginning, intermediate, and advanced students; weaving once annually for 10 beginners; and ceramics twice annually for 10 beginners. Fee: regular University registration. Credit available; offers majors in jewelry and ceramics. Write Registrar.

TEXTILE WORKSHOPS INC., 320 Artist Rd., Santa Fe NM 87501. (505)982-5204. Director: Mary W. Davis. Estab. 1972. Advanced workshops in technique offered annually to 15 students (professional standards only) for 30 hours. Emphasizes ceramics; quilting; weavings; dyeing; and embroidery. Fee: $90/workshop, includes registration and materials. Write for application.

New York

ABBEY SCHOOL OF JEWELRY AND DESIGN, 305 7th Ave., New York NY 10001. (212)691-1080. Director: John R. Sharpe. Estab. 1973. Basic and advanced workshops in technique offered in 3 10-week sessions. Emphasizes jewelry. Write for fees and application.

ADAMY'S PLASTICS AND MOLD-MAKING, 19 Elkan Rd., Larchmont NY 10538. (914)834-6276. Director: George E. Adamy. Estab. 1968. Basic and advanced workshops in technique offered throughout the year for up to 25 students in daily or weekly sessions. Emphasizes plastics and mold-making. Fee: $25/day and up, includes registration. Materials fee. Call for application. Instructor has teaching experience and is the developer of first plastics and mold-making credit courses at the university level for art majors. Workshop provides basics to professional know-how.

ADIRONDACK LAKES CENTER FOR THE ARTS, Blue Mountain Lake NY 12812. (518)352-7715. All levels of workshops in technique offered during the summer to 10 students. Emphasizes pottery; jewelry; woodcarving; batik; weaving; quilting; basketry; natural dyeing; and leatherworking. Students supply own materials. Write for more information.

ADVENTURES IN CRAFTS, 218 E. 81st St., New York NY 10028. (212)628-8081. President: Dee Davis. Estab. 1970. Basic and advanced workshops in technique offered to 6 students for 5 weeks. Emphasizes decoupage. Fee: $25-65. Write or call for application.

ARC EN CIEL, 1885 Palmer Ave., Larchmont NY 10538. (914)834-2616. Contact: Doris Goldfischer or Richard Cronk. Offers stained glass 6 times annually for 8 beginning students for 8 weeks and intermediate and advanced stained glass 5 times annually for 4-6 students for 10 weeks. Fee: $90/beginning class; $80/intermediate-advanced, includes registration and materials. Advanced students supply own materials. Write, call, or visit for application. Samples of work required for intermediate students who learned basic skills elsewhere. SASE. Credit available; independent study.
Purpose: "Excellent foundation of basic skills in stained glass (copper foil technique); can proceed to professional competency."

ARTIST-CRAFTSMEN SCHOOL AND GALLERY, 5622 Mosholu Ave., Riverdale, Bronx NY 10471. (212)549-9570. Contact: L. Navarro. Offers Beginning-Advanced Handbuilding and Beginning-Advanced Wheel 10 times annually for 5 students. Course length varies. Fee: $4/hour includes registration and materials. Write or call for application.

NANCY BRIGGS SILVERSMITHING AND JEWELRY, 5 Stillwoods Rd., Brookhaven NY 11719. (516)286-9253. Contact: Nancy Briggs. Offers jewelry through the year for 8 students. "Students attend for any length of time they choose." Fee: $8/class session; includes registration. "Credit can be earned as an independent study through several colleges but arrangements must be made by the individual student." Call for application.

B. RUGGED, 51 Spring St., New York NY 10012. (212)226-8230. Contact: Susanna Cuyler. Estab. 1976. Basic and advanced workshops in technique offered privately or to a group for 1 hour lesson. Emphasizes hooked rugmaking. Fee: $5/1 hour lesson. Write, call, or visit. Instructor is author, experienced rug maker and teacher.
Purpose: "Learn how to use a variety of speed hooking tools; techniques; rug design; transfer methods; and material amounts. Also can rent frames and hooks which reduces price."

THE BOOKLYN MUSEUM ART SCHOOL, 188 Eastern Pkwy., Brooklyn NY 11238. (212)638-4486. Registrar: Marjorie Stephens. Offers ceramics 3 times annually for 18 students; stained glass 3 times annually for 16 students; jewelry and weaving 3 times annually for 15 students. Course length is 15 weeks; summer session is 8 weeks. Fee: $100/course for fall or spring; $75/course summer session, includes registration and tuition. Write for application.

CEDAR ART CENTER, 171 Cedar St., Corning NY 14830. (607)936-4448. Director: Claire Benedict. Estab. 1968. Basic and advanced workshops in technique offered 4 times annually to 6-10 students for sessions ranging from 1 day-10 weeks. Emphasizes batik; ceramics; glass art; leatherworking; quilting; soft sculpture; weaving; spinning and dyeing; and metal and other sculpture. Fee: $5-6/day; includes registration, some materials; major equipment. Write, call, or visit for application.
Purpose: "This varies according to level of student, instructor, and subject or field covered. All beginners or those new to a craft would cover basic techniques and materials on a high artistic level."

CENTER FOR BOOK ARTS, 15 Bleecker St., New York NY 10012. (212)260-6860. Executive Director: Richmond Minsky. Estab. 1975. Basic and advanced workshops in book arts instruction offered to 7 students for 1 semester. Emphasizes bookbinding; printing; papermaking; and hand engraving. Fee: $150/semester includes registration and some materials. Write for more information.

CHAUTAUQUA INSTITUTION, Schools Office, Box 28, Chautauqua NY 14722. (716)357-4411, 357-5635. Administrative Assistant: Virginia Rodes. Offers batik; ceramics; jewelry; metalsmithing; needlecrafts; quilting; tole painting; and weaving. Credit recommendation approved by New York State Department of Education through student's school. Write.

CLAY CRAFTS COMMUNITY, 222 W. 79th St., New York NY 10024. (212)595-2222. Contact: Deena Kolbert. Estab. 1973. All levels of workshops in marketing; technique; and everything related to pottery offered several times a month in sessions varying from 1 day to 1 week. Emphasizes ceramics. Fee: $50/workshop, includes registration; materials; lodging; and meals. Write for brochure of activities. Sometimes requests slides or photos by mail. SASE.
Purpose: "Information about the specific subject being discussed; slide presentations; demonstrations; sometimes follow up with museum trips."

CLAY WORKSHOP, Box 300, Rt. 1, Otego NY 13825. (607)783-2476. Contact: Elizabeth Nields. Offers pottery and sculpture annually the month of August for 15 students; 3 summer sessions of 8 lessons in pottery for 15 students; and children's pottery annually for 10 students. Fee: $550/August workshop, includes registration; materials; lodging; and meals. $325/August workshop for local people; $50/8 week session. Credit can be arranged in advance through Hofstra University at extra cost. To apply write to above address; $75 deposit for August workshop.
Purpose: "Proficiency with wheel, understanding of clay bodies and glaze. Development of sense of form in pottery and sculpture, and hopefully a very good time."

COLLEGE OF NEW ROCHELLE, Art Department, New Rochelle NY 10801. (914)632-5300, ext. 229. Contact: Chairman, Art Department. Offers Jewelry 1-2 first semester and summer session for 20 beginning students; Ceramics 1 each semester and summer session for 18 beginning students; Ceramics 2-3 each semester and summer session for 18 advanced potters; Clay and Glaze Calculation once in 4 semesters for 15 advanced potters; Weaving 1-2 each semester and summer session for 15 beginning students. Loomless Weaving; Pattern Drafting; and Spinning/Dyeing alternate semesters and Jewelry 3 or enameling offered second semester. Length of semester is 13 weeks; summer session is 4 weeks. Fee: $75/credit, includes registration. Materials fee: $35-45. Credit available. Apply to Academic Dean. Submit actual work for advanced courses. SASE.
Purpose: "Good craftsmanship; skills in the media under research; knowledge of the current trends in the field as well as exposure to the best in historic cultures. We are an art department that sits within a liberal arts framework so that it has this integrating dimension."

COOPER-HEWITT MUSEUM, 2 E. 91st St., New York NY 10028. (212)860-6868. Director of Programs: Jane Clark. Offers 10 1-day embroidery classes per semester for 15 novice-intermediate students; 5 craft workshops (batik, candlemaking, ceramics, decoupage, glass art, jewelry, leatherworking, metalsmithing, needlecrafts, quilting, soft sculpture, tole painting, and weaving) each semester. Fee: $17/members; $20/nonmembers, includes registration and materials. Write Programs Office.

CRAFT SKELLAR, Neperan Rd., Tarrytown NY 10591. (914)631-3200. Director: Sister Bianca Haglich. Offers weaving workshops 2-10 days throughout the year for beginning and advanced students; quilting workshop throughout the year for 3 days; and needlecraft for 3 evenings throughout the year. Fee: $15-100/workshop. Write for more information.

CRAFT STUDENTS LEAGUE, YWCA, 610 Lexington Ave., New York NY 10022. (212)755-4500. Secretary: Reeva Cohen. Offers ceramics 4 times annually for 20 students; bookbinding 4 times annually for 9 students; decoupage; stained glass; jewelry; and woodworking 4 times annually for 15 students. Course length is 12 weeks. Fee: $75/2 hours; $93/2½ hours; $111/3 hours, includes registration. Materials fee: $5-25. "Send for brochure or come in person to Registration Department. Full fee plus $15 YWCA membership must be paid in advance."

DAEMEN COLLEGE, 4380 Main St., Buffalo NY 14226. (716)839-3600. Art Department Chairman: Dr. Margaret Bacon. Offers Ceramics 1 fall and spring semesters for 18 students; Ceramics 2 fall and spring semesters for 10 students; Advanced Ceramics alternating semesters for 5 students; and Fiber 1 alternating semesters for 18 students. Semester length is 15 weeks. Fee: $82/credit hour, includes registration. Shop fee: $25/ceramics; $15/fibers. Credit available; offers BA, BS, or BFA in art. Courses conducted by artists with their masters; all have regional and/or national reputations.

Applications: Write to Office of Admissions. $15 application fee. Submit slides and photos for ceramics. Slides, photos or actual 2-dimensional work for fibers. SASE.

DASH SCHOOL OF ART, 654 Rt. 9W, Upper Grandview NY 10960. (914)359-2151. Director: Harvey D. Dash. Offers pottery; prints; ceramics; and jewelry 3 times annually for 6 students. Course length is 10-12 weeks; summer sessions is 6 weeks, double time. Fee: $70/course part time; $1,200 full time, includes registration and tuition. "Our courses have been given credit by all colleges and art schools where students have requested transfer credit." Write requesting a part time or full time application. $25 application fee for full time.

EARTHWORKS AND ARTISANS, 251 W. 8th St., New York NY 10024. (212)874-8245. Director: Claire DesBecker. Estab. 1940. Basic and advanced workshops in technique offered quarterly to 130 students in small groups of 8 for 3 months. Advanced students must have previous experience. Emphasizes ceramics. Fee: $84/3 month sessions. Materials fee: 1.5c per cubic inch. Write or call for application. Submit slides or present actual work for advanced classes. SASE. Workshop provides "technical guidance; professional milieu; fun; sense of accomplishment; and creativity."

EARTHWORKS POTTERY, LTD., 255 E. 74th St., New York NY 10021. (212)650-9337. President: Stephen Marx. Estab. 1977. Basic and advanced workshops in technique offered annually to 8 students for 10 weeks. Emphasizes ceramics. Fee: $80/workshop, includes registration and materials. Firing fee: 1½c/cubic inch. Write or call for application.

FIBRE CONCEPTS, 127 Greene St., New York NY 10012. Director: Linda Daly. Estab. 1972. Basic and advanced workshops in technique offered to maximum of 8-12 students for 6 weeks. Emphasizes macrame and weaving. Fee: $50/beginning workshop, $75/advanced workshop, includes registration and beginning materials. Write for application. Submit slides, photos, or actual work for advanced workshop. SASE.

Purpose: "In depth study into technical and design areas of fibre forms and analysis of product for production if desired by student."

GLASS ROOTS STUDIOS, 1190 Lexington Ave., New York NY 10028. (212)472-1424. President: Chester Gelband. Offers copper foil/stained glass throughout the year for 10 students. Course length is 6 weeks. Fee: $95/course, includes registration, use of studio tools, and some materials. Materials fee: varies with project. Write or call for application.

THE GREAT SEW-CIETY, 731 King St., Port Chester NY 10573. (914)939-3605. Contact: Virginia Avery. Offers quilting; patchwork; and applique throughout the year for 6-10 week and all day workshops. Fee: $70/10 week course; $42/6 week course; $15-20/workshops. Write or call.

GREENWICH HOUSE POTTERY, 16 Jones St., New York NY 10014. (212)242-4106. Director: Jane Hartsook. Offers ceramics twice annually for 14 students for 15 weeks in fall and spring and 6 weeks in June-July. $100 for 15 classes, includes registration and materials. Firing charges: 1½c/cubic inch. Write for application. $5 registration fee.

JOHN HARRA WOODWORKING STUDIO, 39 W. 19th St., New York NY 10011. (212)741-0290. Contact: Harvey Karp. Estab. 1972. Basic and advanced workshops in technique offered 7 times annually for 10-20 students. Emphasizes all crafts. Fee: $95-190, includes instruction and shop use. Write for application.

THE HIRED HAND, 1324 Lexington Ave., New York NY 10028. (212)722-1355. Contact: Tullah Kellman or Fran Stein. Offers patchwork 6-7 times annually for 10 students for 6 weeks. Fee: $50/course, includes registration. Students supply own materials. Call or visit for application.

Purpose: "Will learn to piece shapes together in PW designs; develop greater color sense; draft designs; hand pieces; and hand applique."

HOFSTRA UNIVERSITY, Long Island Craftsmen's Guild Inc., Hempstead NY 11550. (516)560-3313, 673-0543. Director: Judith Gloston. Offers batik; ceramics; glass art; jewelry;

leatherworking; metalsmithing; needlecrafts; quilting; soft sculpture; and weaving. Fee: $50-95/course. "Credit for our courses is being negotiated. If granted it will be through Hofstra University." Apply to Long Island Craftsmen's Guild.

JAMESTOWN COMMUNITY COLLEGE, 525 Falconer St., Jamestown NY 14701. (716)665-5220. Chairman, Visual and Performing Arts Division: William Disbro. Offers ceramics twice annually for 25 students for 16 weeks plus 6 week summer session. Fee: $60/tuition, includes registration. Materials fee: $14. $5 Faculty-Students Association fee. Credit available. Write Admissions Office.
Purpose: "May take individual courses for academic credit or may enroll in sequence of courses leading to a 60 hour Associate of Arts Degree."

JEWISH COMMUNITY CENTER, 1200 Edgewood Ave., Rochester NY 14618. (716)461-2000. Assistant Arts Director: Jill Reitzfeld. Offers Beginning Ceramics; Advanced Ceramics; batik; copper enameling; sculpture; and jewelry 3 times annually for 10 students. Course length is 8 weeks. Fee: $20/course, JCC members; $30/course, others. Materials fee varies. Register at Jewish Community Center.

THE KNOWHOW WORKSHOP, 17 E. 16th St., New York NY 10003. (212)741-1194. President: Guy Alland. Estab. 1972. Basic workshops in technique offered throughout the year for 12 students for 12 week sessions. Emphasizes carpentry; woodworking; dollhouse construction; woodcarving; and calligraphy. Fee: $95-180/workshop, includes registration and materials. Materials fee: $10-75. Write for application.
Purpose: "The aim of the workshops is to enable the student to achieve self-sufficiency in everyday life by developing a knowledge of how things work and how they can be maintained, repaired, or constructed."

KULICKE-STARK, Academy of Jewelry Art, 2231 Broadway, New York NY 10024. (212)362-8633. Director: Margot Bachmann. Estab. 1970. All levels of workshops in classical technique offered throughout the year to 18 students. Emphasizes jewelry. Fee: $165/10-3 hour sessions. Write for brochure. Workshop provides knowledge of classical technique and history of jewelry.

LAKE PLACID SCHOOL OF ART, Saranac Ave., Lake Placid NY 12946. (518)523-2591. Dean of Students: Lesley Cadman. Offers basic ceramics and advanced ceramics twice annually for 15 weeks; production pottery, throwing workshop, kiln building, porcelain, and papermaking once in summer for 12 advanced students for 1 week. Fee: $95-125/workshop; $855/full time tuition, includes registration and materials. Credit available. Write or call for application. Submit 6-12 slides for Advanced Lithography Workshop. SASE.
Purpose: "The workshops are designed to be intensive, information-sharing situations in which students will work cooperatively with master craftspersons. Students will also have access to all the programs at The Center for music, drama, and art."

MARYMOUNT COLLEGE, Tarrytown NY 10591. (914)631-3200. Chairman, Art Department: Sister Bianca Haglich. Offers Ceramics 1 twice annually for beginning students; Ceramics 2 twice annually for advanced students. Course length is 14-15 weeks. Fee includes registration, some materials, and use of equipment. Credit available. Write for further information.

MAVROS WORKSHOP, 49 W. 28th St., New York NY 10001. (212)689-1097. Director: Donald Mavros. Offers continuous classes for 18 students in pottery; clay sculpture; glaze chemistry; and mold making. Fee: $30/month for up to 120 hours of studio and instruction time, includes registration and materials; 1½c/cubic inch firing fee. Write for details.

MINI MUNDUS SCHOOL, 970 Lexington Ave., New York NY 10021. (212)288-5855. Contact: Kathryn Falk. Offers Miniature Furniture Making and Electrifying Dollhouse throughout the year; Dollhouse Building twice annually for 5 students for 6 weeks. Write for information.

MUSEUM OF AMERICAN FOLK ART, Craft Classes, 49 W. 53rd St., New York NY 10019. (212)581-2474. Contact: Class Administrator. Estab. 1973. Basic and advanced workshops and classes in technique offered 3 times annually to 5-15 students for 1 class per week for 5 weeks. Emphasizes needlecrafts; quilting; weaving; rug hooking and braiding; basketry; and whittling. Fee: $50/workshop, includes registration. Write or call for application. Purpose: basic/advanced instruction in the craft studied.

MUSEUMS AT STONY BROOK CRAFT CENTER, Christian Ave., Stony Brook NY 11790. (516)751-0440. Education Assistant: Elizabeth Reuter. Offers weaving 4 times annually for 26 students; calligraphy for 20 beginners and 10 advanced; and silversmithing. Course length is 10 weeks; various 1-2 day workshops offered throughout the year. Fee: varies according to courses; $10 materials fee. Credit available.
Purpose: "A craftsperson can expect to gain knowledge in the basic mechanics of a course, then go on to explore and create in depth as they wish. Beginners and intermediates are encouraged to be as creative and innovative as possible."
Application: Write Education Assistant. "A file is kept up to date on craftworker's profile; resume; and; where possible, photos or slides of their work."

NAPLES MILL SCHOOL OF ARTS AND CRAFTS, Box 567, Naples NY 14512. (717)374-6386. Contact: Director. Estab. 1972. Basic, advanced, and resident artist professional workshops in technique offered 3 times annually to 10-18 students for sessions ranging from 3 days-8 weeks. Emphasizes batik; ceramics; glass art; metalsmithing; needlecrafts; quilting; and weaving. Fee: $125-150/week, includes registration, lodging and meals. Write or call for application. Slides and an interview required prior to acceptance as resident artists.

NEW MUSE COMMUNITY MUSEUM OF BROOKLYN, 1530 Bedford Ave., Brooklyn NY 11216. (212)774-2884. Cultural Arts Director: Gaylord Hassan. Basic and advanced workshops in marketing and technique offered 3 sessions annually to 50 students for 8 weeks. Emphasizes batik; ceramics; needlecrafts; soft sculpture; and weaving. Fee: $10, includes registration and materials. Write or call for application.

THE NEW SCHOOL, Crafts Department, 66 W. 12th St., New York NY 10011. (212)741-5614. Chairman: Deborah Aguado. Offers batik; glass art; jewelry; leatherworking; metalsmithing; needlcrafts; quilting; soft sculpture; weavings; basic design; plastic instruction. All classes held 3 semesters annually for 15 students. Semester equals 12 sessions. Fee: $100-150/course, includes registration and tuition; students purchase their own materials. Call or write for current catalog and registration dates. Credit available.
Purpose: Courses are to promote "development; technical assistance and direction; critiques; and technical tutoring."

NEW SCHOOL FOR SOCIAL RESEARCH, Parson's School of Design Bldg., 2 W. 13th, New York NY 10011. (212)741-5690. Estab. 1975. Basic and advanced workshops in technique offered twice annually and in the summer to maximum of 15 students for 12 sessions. Emphasizes leatherworking. Write for fee information. Students supply own materials. Write for application. "Prefer students with some background in basic techniques for Sculptural Leather."

NEW YORK STATE COLLEGE OF CERAMICS AT ALFRED UNIVERSITY, Division of Art and Design, Alfred NY 14802. Head of Division: T. Hepburn. Offers ceramics; glass art; sculpture; cold and hot glass; and wood design. All courses offered in 2 semester program September-December and February-May with minimester in January. "We also have an excellent summer program in ceramics." Fee: varies according to residency. Credit available; offers BFA and MFA.
Application: To apply for the undergraduate program write Admissions Office, Alfred University. To apply for graduate program write Graduate Admissions, Alfred University. "We require a portfolio of work from all applicants. For freshman applicant flat work; photos; and slides are accepted." SASE.

NEW YORK STATE HISTORICAL ASSOCIATION, Seminars on American Culture, Cooperstown NY 13326. (607)547-2534. Assistant in Education: Kathie A. Kent. Offers needlecrafts; quilting; woodworking; printing; blacksmithing; painting on tin; and furniture. Fee: $105/course, includes registration and meals. Materials fee: $10. "We give in-service credit for courses." Write for more information.

NEW YORK UNIVERSITY, Department of Art and Art Education, 735 East Building, Washington Square, New York NY 10003. (212)598-3482. Director, Craft Shop: Professor Carl Podrus. Offers Advanced Crafts 3 times annually; Introduction to Jewelry, Intermediate Jewelry, Wood and Leather once annually; and Weaving twice annually. Courses are for 15-20 students. Course length is 15 weeks. Credit available. Write Admissions Office. Submit samples of work for advanced crafts. SASE.

THE NIDDY NODDY, 416 Albany Post Rd., Croton-on-Hudson NY 10520. (914)271-9724. Contact: Irene Miller. Offers spinning, dyeing, and machine knitting throughout the year; basketry and sweater design 3 times annually. Fee: $8/session. "Student must arrange college credit." Write or call for application.

NORTH COUNTRY COMMUNITY COLLEGE, Crafts Management Program of the Malone Extension Center, 101 E. Main St., Malone NY 12953. (518)483-4550. Director: Douglas Kelley. Offers 1 year of instruction in pottery, weaving, and wood carving (3 credits per semester for 2 semesters); and 1 semester of instruction in blacksmithing and quilt-making. Fee: $22/credit; $325/semester for 12-16 credits, includes registration. Materials fee: $5-20. Credit available. Write for application.

NORTH SHORE COMMUNITY ARTS CENTER, 236 Middle Neck Rd., Great Neck NY 11021. (516)466-3636. School Director: Charlotte Rabb. Offers pottery 3 times annually for 15 sessions for 12 students; silver jewelry and enameling 3 times annually for 8 sessions for 12 students; and batik 3 times annually for 10 sessions for 12 students. Fee: $85/pottery; $50/- jewelry; $85/batik, includes some materials. Request a school brochure.

C.W. POST CENTER OF LONG ISLAND UNIVERSITY, Crafts Center, Greenvale NY 11548. (516)299-2203. Director: Joan Harrison. Offers pottery; weaving; and jewelry/enameling spring, fall, 3 summer sessions, and an intensive Dean's semester and weekend college for 20 students per class. Length of course varies. Fee: $270/3 credit course; $135/noncredit audit. Materials fee: $25. Credit available. Write or call for application.

PRATT INSTITUTE, 215 Ryerson St., Brooklyn NY 11205. (212)636-3600. Assistant Dean: Andrew Phelan. Offers ceramics; stained glass; and jewelry twice annually for 10 weeks for 30 students. Fee: $93/credit, includes registration. Credit available.
Application: Write Admissions, School of Art and Design, Dekalb Hale, Pratt Institute. $15 application fee. Slide portfolio must be presented at interview.

RISING POTTERY, 1903 Palmer Ave., Larchmont NY 10538. (914)834-8827. Contact: Dick or Jan Rising. Estab. 1974. Basic and advanced workshops in technique offered weekly for 10 sessions to 8 students over 16 years. Emphasizes ceramics and macrame. Fee: $60/workshop, includes registration and materials. Firing fee. Write or call for application. Workshop provides proficiency in technique.

ROBERSON CENTER FOR THE ARTS AND SCIENCES, 30 Front St., Binghamton NY 13905. (607)772-0660. Class Coordinator: Terri Shea. Offers pottery 3 times annually for 15 beginning, 15 intermediate, and 15 advanced students for 15 weeks; and stained glass twice annually for 15 students for 10 weeks. Fee: $70/course, includes registration and some materials. "Credit can be earned through Empire State College of State University of New York." Write or call for application.

ROCHESTER INSTITUTE OF TECHNOLOGY, 1 Lomb Dr., Rochester NY 14623. Associate Dean: Peter Giopulos. Basic and advanced courses in technique and aesthetics offered in the summer to 18 students per class for 5 weeks. Requires high school diploma. Emphasizes ceramics; jewelry; metalsmithing; weaving; and woodcrafting. Fee: Institute's tuition. Materials fee: varies. Write Summer Session.

ROCKLAND CENTER FOR THE ARTS, 27 S. Greenbush Rd., West Nyack NY 10944. (914)358-0877. Offers ceramics; glass art; jewelry; soft sculpture; and weaving twice annually. Course length is 10-12 weeks. Fee: $70-80. Credit available through St. Thomas Aquinas College and Empire State College. Write requesting catalog. "A few advanced classes may require discussion with the instructor for proper placements."

ROCKLAND COMMUNITY COLLEGE, 145 College Rd., Suffern NY 10901. (914)356-1527. Executive Assistant to Dean, Adult Continuing Education: S. Zistler. Offers stained glass twice annually for 25 students for 10 weeks. Fee: $29/course, includes registration. Materials fee: $27. Credit available for day program. Write for application.

ROPE GALLERY, 213 Thompson St., New York NY 10012. (212)254-7315. Contact: Stanley Postek. Offers macrame (includes rope sculpture and woodwork) twice annually for 8 students for 4 weeks. Fee: $50/course, includes registration. Materials fee: average $20. Write or call for application.

RYE ART CENTER, Box 582, Rye NY 10580. (914)967-0072. Executive Director: Ellen McDermott. Offers jewelry; pottery; quilting; vegetable dying and weaving twice annually for 10 beginning or intermediate students. Course length is 10 weeks. Also offers many individual quilting workshops. Fee: $50-75/course, includes registration. Materials fee: varies; students usually supply own materials. Write for application.
Purpose: "For beginning or intermediate students an opportunity to have an excellent grounding in basic crafts from experienced instructors in a small class situation."

SARA'S CENTER, 781 Middle Neck Rd., Great Neck NY 11024. (516)482-1550. Director: Marion Berliner. Offers creative arts experiences for the handicapped. "Our program is on an ongoing basis and all center participants may join any group at any time provided they are capable of dealing with the activity. We are developing a program with a University working towards a credit degree." Write or call for information.

ELIZABETH SETON COLLEGE, 1060 N. Broadway, Yonkers NY 10701. (914)969-4000. Contact: Sister Regina Kraft. Offers ceramics twice annually plus summer session for 12 students; jewelry and enameling once annually for 12 students. Course length is 15 weeks; summer session is 7 weeks. Fee: $60/credit, includes tuition. Materials fee: $13/ceramics; $6/-jewelry. Credit available. Program stresses "knowledge of technical skills and instruction in design."
Application: Write or call Admissions Office. "To enroll as an art major in full time program a portfolio with a variety of media is required." SASE.

78TH STREET POTTERY, 169 W. 78th St., New York NY 10024. (212)787-9696. Manager: Howard Budin. Offers Ceramics/Wheel for 40 students, all levels; Ceramics/Handbuilding and Ceramics/Glaze 3 times annually for 10 students, all levels; and Ceramics/Advanced Wheel 3 times annually for 10 advanced throwers. Course length is 12 weeks. Fee: $90/course, includes registration. Materials fee: $4.75/25 pounds of clay and 1c/cubic inch firing fee. Write or call for application.
Purpose: "The craftworker will learn techniques of wheel and handbuilt pottery; aesthetics of form; and knowledge of glazing. He or she will work with different clay bodies and use slips and oxides in decoration."

SKIDMORE COLLEGE, Summer "Six" Art Program, Saratoga Springs NY 12866. (518)584-5000, ext. 373. Director: Regis C. Brodie. Estab. 1968. Basic, advanced, and graduate workshops in art studio offered annually for 6 weeks in the summer to 15 students with high school diploma. Emphasizes ceramics; jewelry; metalsmithing; and weaving. Fee: $250/workshop plus $20 application fee, includes registration and tuition. Write for application.

STUDIO WORKSHOP, 3 W. 18th St., New York NY 10011. (212)243-0219. Director: Richard D. Rapaport. Estab. 1967. Basic and advanced workshops in marketing, technique, and ideas offered annually to 12 students for sessions of 1 day-2 months. Emphasizes ceramics; jewelry; and soft sculpture. Fee: $85-95 includes registration. Materials fee: $3.50/25 pounds of clay. Write or call for application.

SUNY AT PURCHASE, Purchase NY 10577. (914)253-5077. Offers Beginning Jewelry once or twice annually for 20 students for 12-15 weeks; Cloth as Art Medium once annually for 25 students for 12-15 weeks; Bronze Casting and Silkscreen 3 times annually for 20 students for 15 weeks; Woodcarving twice annually for 20 students for 15 weeks; and glass/metal once annually for 20 students for 15 weeks. Fee: $60-125/course, includes registration. Credit available. Write and ask for catalog.

VILLAGE WEAVING CENTER, 434 6th Ave., New York NY 10011. (212)260-2100. Estab. 1974. Basic and advanced workshops in technique, design, and drafting offered to 4-15 students for sessions of 1 day-1 weekend. Emphasizes needlecrafts and weaving. Materials fee: $10 maximum. Write for application.

WAVE HILL CENTER FOR ENVIRONMENTAL STUDIES, 675 W. 252nd St., Bronx NY 10471. (212)549-2055. Program Director: Cyrus Bryant. Basic and some intermediate workshops in technique offered throughout the year to a maximum of 20 students for sessions of 1 day-2 weekends. Emphasizes batik; candlemaking; leatherworking; needlecrafts; weaving; natural dyes and spinning. Fee: minimum of $3, includes registration and materials. Call for application. Instructors are always the most experienced available. Workshops provide a basic working knowledge.

THE WEAVER'S STUDIO, 69A 7th Ave., Brooklyn NY 11217. (212)857-0221. Contact: Judith Shangold. Offers 4-Harness Weaving 4 times annually for 7 beginning-intermediate students for 10 weeks; 2-Harness Weaving every 6 weeks for 6 beginning-intermediate students for 6 weeks; basketry 4 times annually for 6 beginning students for 3 weeks. Also offers macrame; creative crochet; needlecrafts; spinning; natural dyeing; and needlepoint. Fee: $12-85/course, includes registration and materials. Write for application.

WEST SIDE YMCA, 5 W. 63rd St., New York NY 10023. (212)787-4400, ext. 1549. Assistant Program Director: A. Warshaw. Estab. 1973. Basic classes and workshops in technique offered 4+ times annually to 15-25 students for sessions ranging from 1 day to 8-10 weeks. Emphasizes ceramics; glass art; needlecrafts; quilting; weaving; basketry; crochet; and calligraphy. Fee: $10-20/workshop; $50-80/classes; includes registration, materials, and tuition. Write or call for brochure. Workshops provide instruction, constructive criticism, and creative support.

THE WOODSMITH'S STUDIO, INC., 142 E. 32nd St., 3rd Flr., New York NY 10016. (212)684-3642. President: Jerry Gerber. Estab. 1974. Basic and advanced workshops in technique offered 5 times annually for 10 week sessions. Emphasizes wood. Write or call for application.

YM-YWHA OF MID-WESTCHESTER, 999 Wilmot Rd., Scarsdale NY 10583. (914)472-3300. Art Director: Wayne Kartzinel. Offers ceramics; leatherworking; needlecrafts; and weavings. Fee: $200/course, includes registration. Program provides beginning through advanced instruction. Send resume for application.

North Carolina

APPALACHIAN STATE UNIVERSITY, Boone NC 28607. (704)262-2220. Contact: Marianne S. Suggs. Offers 2 sections of ceramics 4 times annually for 60 students; 2 sections of jewelry 4 times annually for 60 students; and 3 sections of fibers 5 times annually for 75 students. Course length varies. Credit available.

Application: Must be admitted as undergraduate or graduate student. Contact Admissions Office. Slides must be submitted for graduate students. Contact Sherry Waterworth, Art Department. SASE.

ASHEVILLE ART MUSEUM LEARNING CENTER, Asheville Art Museum, Civic Center Complex, Asheville NC 28801. (704)253-3227. Educational Curator: Sara Sagar. Estab. 1970. Basic workshops in technique offered twice annually for 8-10 weeks. Emphasizes ceramics; needlecrafts; weavings; and wood carving. Fee: $30-35/workshop, includes registration and materials for some courses. Materials fee: varies, seldom over $15. Write for application.

ATLANTIC CHRISTIAN COLLEGE, Art Department, Wilson NC 27893. (919)237-3161. Chairman, Art Department: Edward Brown. Offers pottery 3 times annually for 12 students; and weaving once annually for 12 students. Course length is 15 weeks. Fee: $150/course, includes registration. Materials fee: $12. Credit available. Write Admissions Office. $10 application fee.

THE JOHN C. CAMPBELL FOLK SCHOOL, Rt. 1, Brasstown, NC 28902. (704)837-2775. Director: Esther H. Hyatt. Offers pottery 9 times annually for 7 students; weaving and wood carving 9 times annually for 10 students; wood working 4 times annually for 5 students; blacksmithing 6 times annually for 6 students; and enameling 9 times annually for 8 students. Course length is 12 weeks. Fee: $60/week tuition, includes registration. "Room and board available, fee charged according to accomodation, i.e. single, double or dorm room. "Materials fee: $12. Credit available through Western Carolina University, Cullowhee, North Carolina. Write for application. $25 pre-registration fee which will later be applied toward tuition.

EAST CAROLINA UNIVERSITY, Ceramics Department, School of Art, Greenville NC 27834. (919)757-6665. Chairman, Ceramics Department: Charles F. Chamberlain. Offers 16 levels of ceramics twice annually, beginning through graduate thesis work. Registration limit depends on course level. Course length is 14 weeks. Credit available. Write Registrar. Submit 20 slides of work or present actual work at personal interview. SASE. $10 application fee.

MARS HILL COURSE, Mars Hill NC 28754. (704)689-1200. Head, Art Department: Joe C. Robertson. Offers pottery 3 times annually for 14 students. Course length is 15 weeks. Enameling offered for 3 weeks in January. Fee: $40/course audit; $130/course part time student;

$1,050/course full time student, includes registration, materials, lodging, meals, and tuition. Materials fee: $15-20 for audit only. Credit available. Write Registrar.

SACRED HEART COLLEGE, Main St., Belmont NC 28012. (704)825-5146. Chairman, Department of Art: Sister Theophane. Offers Ceramics Handbuilding and Ceramics Throwing twice annually for 15 students; Jewelry Fabrication and Jewelry Casting once annually for 15 students. Course length is 16 weeks. Fee: $65/credit hour part time; full time covered by tuition, includes registration. Lab fee: $25, some materials extra. Credit available. Apply to Director of Admissions requesting admission to Art Department. $10 application fee.

SOUTHERN HIGHLAND HANDICRAFT GUILD, Box 9545, Asheville NC 28805. (704)298-7928. Assistant Director: James Gentry. Estab. 1976. Basic and advanced workshops in technique and design offered annually for 1 week in the summer to 200 adults 18 years and up and open to children 5 years and up when accompanied by parent. Emphasizes (Appalachian crafts) ceramics; needlecrafts; quilting; soft sculpture; weaving; basketry, wood carving; chair bottoming; and classes for children. Fee: $150/workshop; includes registration, materials, lodging and meals. Materials fee: $8. Write for application.
Purpose: "Basic knowledge for individuals interested in learning a craft; new skills and knowledge for individuals who wish to expand their work toward combining media. Inspiration of working with people of like interest. Pace of workshop is relaxed; enrichment activities are planned for the week; recreational activities offered; and child care provided for reasonable fee."

UNIVERSITY OF NORTH CAROLINA AT GREENSBORO, Art Department, Greensboro NC 27412. (919)379-5248. Head: Dr. Joan Gregory. Offers ceramics twice annually for 20 students; jewelry, soft sculpture, and weaving (fibers) twice annually for 15 students. Course length is 18 weeks. Fee: $78.50/course, residents; includes registration, academic fee, and activities fee. Credit available. Write to Admissions Office, Foust Building.

WESTERN CAROLINA UNIVERSITY, Department of Industrial Education, Cullowhee NC 28723. (704)293-7368. Director of Craft Instruction: Don C. Wood. Offers stained glass twice annually for 20 students. Fee: $70/course, includes materials. Credit available. Write Director of Craft Instruction. $10 application fee.

North Dakota

UNIVERSITY OF NORTH DAKOTA, Visual Arts Department, Box 8134, Grand Forks ND 58202. (701)777-2257. Chairman: Ron Schaefer. Offers Batik on request once annually for 30 students; 3 sections of Beginning Ceramics twice annually for 30 students; 2 sections of Throwing Ceramics twice annually for 20 advanced students; Beginning Ceramics once each summer for 30 students; and Beginning Jewelry twice annually for 12 beginning and advanced students. Course length is 16 weeks; summer session is 8 weeks. Fee: $5 lab fee plus tuition, includes chemicals and equipment. Materials fee: $5-100. Credit available; offers BA and BFA in Ceramics.
Application: Contact Chairman, Visual Arts Department. Prerequisites of Design 1-2 and presentation of slides or actual work for admittance into jewelry. SASE.

Ohio

AKRON UNIVERSITY, Akron OH 44325. (216)375-7010. Department Head: Warren A. Wolf. Offers ceramics and jewelry/metals every semester for 15 students for 4 years; weaving every semester for 15 students for 2 years. Fee: $90/course, includes registration. Credit available. Write Registrar.

BOWLING GREEN UNIVERSITY, School of Art, Bowling Green OH 43403. (419)372-2787. Director, School of Art: Dr. Joesph R. Spence. Offers Beginning Ceramics; Advanced Ceramics; Beginning Jewelry; Jewelry Design/Metal; Enameling; and Weaving/Fibers 3 times annually for 20 students. Course length is 10 weeks. Fee: $29.50/credit hour, Ohio undergraduate; $40/credit hour, nonresident undergraduate; $36.50/credit hour, Ohio graduate; $76.50/credit hour, nonresident graduate. Materials fee: $75. Credit available. Write Admissions Office. $25 application fee. Submit slides for graduate programs. SASE.
Purpose: 'Excellent instruction; challenging atmosphere; good facilities and equipment. A University with many exciting programs located in a rural setting but close to Toledo, Detroit, Cleveland and Chicago."

CRAFTSUMMER, Miami University, 31 Hiestand Hall, Oxford OH 45056. (513)529-6010. Director: Peter Dahoda. Offers batik; ceramics; decoupage; jewelry; metalsmithing; soft sculpture; weaving; direct dye on fabric; fabric printing; enameling; wood construction; Japanese metal work; and porcelain. Holds intensive 1-2 week workshops during summer. Fee: $68.25/week for in state undergraduate; $79.50/week for in state graduates, includes instruction and basic materials. Students must be at least 18 years old. Contact Director.
Purpose: "Craftsummer is a concentration of craft workshops. Its philosophy centers around the dedication of craftspeople searching with tools and materials to seriously develop techniques in an effort to provide opportunities for affecting the human imaginations toward greater responsiveness. Another major concern is to create visual art forms which possess the inherent qualities of the craftsperson."

DAYTON ART INSTITUTE, Box 941, Dayton OH 45401. (513)223-5272. Contact: Studio Coordinator. Offers pottery twice annually for 30 students. Course length is 10 weeks. Fee: $55/course, includes registration and materials. Materials fee: $15. Write for more information.

KENT STATE UNIVERSITY, School of Art, Kent OH 44242. (216)672-2192. Coordinator, Crafts Division: Jack D. Smith. Offers batik; ceramics; glass art; jewelry; metalsmithing; needlecrafts; quilting; soft sculpture; weaving; fiber arts; and printed and dyed enameling. Credit available; offers BFA, MA, and MFA. Send for catalog describing courses. Write to William Quinn, Assistant Director, School of Art.
Purpose: "A four year craft major, a l year Master of Arts or 2 year Master of Fine Arts degree in programs tailored to the needs and interests of the student. Certification for public school teaching is available."

LAKE ERIE COLLEGE, 391 W. Washington, Painesville OH 44077. (216)352-3361, ext. 415. Art Department, Coordinating Head: Clinton Kuopus. Offers ceramics 3 times annually for 18 students; raku once annually for 18 students; jewelry/metalsmithing twice annually for 18 students; introduction to fibers twice annually for 15 students; advanced fibers once annually; and soft sculpture once annually for 18 students. Course length is 10 weeks. Fee: tuition plus $25 lab fee, includes registration, partial materials, and equipment. Credit available. $10 application fee.
Purpose: "Our craft courses are oriented to explore fine arts objects and concepts. Besides receiving technical instruction the student solves aesthetic and design problems."

MALONE COLLEGE, 515 25th St. NW, Canton OH 44709. (216)454-3011. Contact: Mary Louise Robson. Offers ceramics; applied design (metal section and soft goods section-weaving, batik, needlecrafts, sometimes quilting and leather) once annually for 12 students. Course length is 9½ weeks. Fee: $78/credit hour. Materials fee: $25. Credit available; offers BA in Art. Write Admissions Office. $10 application fee. Submit slides or actual work. SASE.

OHIO UNIVERSITY, School of Art, Athens OH 45701. (614)594-5667. Director: Erik Forrest. Offers all levels of ceramics; weaving; glass and metal throughout the year. Course length is 10 weeks. Fee: $25 approximately, includes registration. Materials fee: $15 approximately, includes registration. Credit available, offers BFA. Write Director.

OHIO WESLEYAN UNIVERSITY, Fine Arts Department, Delaware OH 43015. Contact: Betty Heald. Offers ceramics 3 times annually; fiber arts once annually; metalsmithing and casting twice annually. Course length is 10 weeks. Fee: application to college program, includes registration, lodging, and meals. Credit available; offers BFA in Art with a concentration in desired craft area. Write to Art Department or Admissions Office. "Slides of work are helpful to place students and introduce them to art faculty." SASE.

RIVERBEND ARTS COUNCIL, Riverbend Art Center, 142 Riverbend Dr., Dayton OH 45405. (513)225-5479. Director, Riverbend Art Center: Pat Shoop Lowry. Estab. 1975. Basic and advanced workshops in technique offered annually for 1 week. Emphasizes batik; jewelry; metalsmithing; weaving; faceting; lapidary; stained glass; and raku. Fee: $50-65, includes tuition; materials; and Arts Council membership. Write for summer brochure.

YELLOW SPRINGS STRINGS, INC., Box 107, Yellow Springs OH 45387. (513)767-1116. President: Corinne Whitesell. Estab. 1976. Basic and advanced workshops in technique offered annually to 20 students for 2 weeks. Emphasizes weaving. Fee: $125/week includes lodging and meals. Materials fee: $75. Write for application.

YOUNGSTOWN STATE UNIVERSITY, Bliss Hall, Art Department, 410 Wick Ave., Youngstown OH 44555. (216)746-1851. Chairman: Jon Naberezny. Estab. 1977. Basic workshops in technique, art and personal growth offered annually to 18 students for 10 days. Emphasizes ceramics and weaving. Fee: $126/out-of-state; $69/resident, includes registration and ceramic materials. Students supply own materials for weaving. Write for application.

Oklahoma

NORTHEASTERN OKLAHOMA STATE UNIVERSITY, Grand Ave., Tahlequah OK 74464. (918)456-5511, ext. 532. Contact: Dr. C. L. Lombardi. Offers jewelry and metalsmithing twice annually for 30 students. Course length is 18 weeks; summer session is 9 weeks. Credit available. Write Registrar, Office of Admissions.

OKLAHOMA STATE UNIVERSITY, 104 Industrial Building, Stillwater OK 74074. (405)624-7414. Contact: Dr. John B. Tate. Offers an industrial crafts course which includes ceramics; decoupage; jewelry; leatherworking; and metalsmithing. Fee: $35/class in-state; $101.50/nonresident. Students supply own materials. Credit available. Program provides "a broad knowledge of crafts by demonstration and practice." Write Registrar.

PHILBROOK ART CENTER MUSEUM SCHOOL, 2727 S. Rockford Rd., Tulsa OK 74114. (918)749-7945. Museum School Director: Nancy Godsey. All levels of workshops in technique including aesthetic and art value judgments offered semiannually plus a summer session for 150 Philbrook members for 9 weeks. Emphasizes ceramics/pottery; jewelry; needlecrafts. Fee: $35/workshop, includes registration. Materials fee: $10-15. Write or call Museum School Director.

THE UNIVERSITY OF TULSA, 600 S. College, Tulsa OK 74104. (918)939-6351. Contact: Virgil Lampton. Offers Arts and Crafts and pottery 3 times annually for 25 students. Course length is 18 weeks; summer session is 4 weeks. Fee: $65/credit hour, includes registration. Credit available. Write Registrar.

Oregon

CASA DEL SOL, 82 N. Main St., Ashland OR 97520. (503)482-5443. Contact: John Connors. Estab. 1967. Basic and advanced workshops in technique offered to a maximum of 15 students for 1-6 weeks. Emphasizes ceramics. "Workshops are usually advertised in *Ceramics Monthly and West Art*." Workshops provide skill and understanding of process taught.

CREATIVE ARTS COMMUNITY, Menucha, Box 8887, Portland OR 97208. (503)223-5360. President: Charles Knapp. Offers sculpture; pottery; and weaving once annually for beginners through advanced students, no registration limit. Course length is 2 weeks. Fee: $200-350, includes registration, lodging, and meals. Credit available through Portland State University. Write for brochure.
Purpose: "The best way I can describe this is an 'art-vacation.' Participants range in age from 14-70. Some are beginners, others have much experience in their field. This is an opportunity for the novice or the professional to share, to participate, to become a part of this community. In addition to the classes there is a swimming pool, tennis courts, badminton, and 90 acres for jogging, walking and terrific scenery for painting."

LEWIS AND CLARK COLLEGE, SW Palatine Hill Rd., Portland OR 97219. Basic and advanced workshops in technique and aesthetic considerations offered quarterly to 18 students for 10 weeks. Emphasizes ceramics and weaving. Write for application. Workshops provide college credit and skills in producing craft articles.

OREGON STATE UNIVERSITY, Department of Art, Corvallis OR 97331. (503)754-4745. Head Advisor: Berkley Chappell. Offers batik 1-2 terms annually for 12 students; ceramics 4 terms annually for 30 beginning students and 30 advanced students; jewelry/metalsmithing 4 terms annually for 36 beginning students and 18 advanced students; and weaving (fiber) 3-4 terms annually for 15 beginning and 15 advanced students. Course length is 10 weeks. Fee: $10-30/course plus University tuition, includes materials. Credit available; offers BA, BS, or BFA. Write Director of Admissions.

HAL PAINTER OREGON WORKSHOP, Star Rt. 2, Box 570-D, Chiloqwuin OR 97624. (503)783-2507. Contact: Hal Painter or Jim Brown. Estab. 1971. Basic and advanced workshops in technique (marketing is discussed) offered anually in July and August for a maximum of 15 students for 1-2 weeks. Emphasizes weaving; spinning; plant dyeing. Fee: $46/week. Fee: $5/2

week dyeing lab chemicals. Write for a free brochure. Offers a scholarship.
Purpose: "The experience of relaxing way out in the pine woods and working in an informal situation with plenty of projects to keep one busy according to your desires."

SCHOOL OF THE ARTS AND CRAFTS SOCIETY, 616 NW 18th, Portland OR 97209. (503)228-4741. Registrar: Jon Ziady. Offers ceramics; glass art; jewelry; metalsmithing; weaving; spinning and dyeing; and woodworking. "We offer 40-50 specific courses on a 10 week quarter basis. Enrollment is limited to 15 students per class or less." Fee: $67/course plus $8 annual membership and variable lab fee, includes registration and use of studio space. Students supply own materials. Write for application.

Pennsylvania

CLARION STATE COLLEGE, Wood St., Clarion PA 16214. (814)226-6000. Department Head: Dr. Robert Hobbs. Offers ceramics and advanced ceramics for 20 students; arts and crafts for 30 students; combined jewelry and advanced jewelry for 16 students. Course length is 18 weeks. All courses except jewelry also taught 5 weeks at summer school. Fee: $110/3 credit course, includes registration; materials; and tools. Some additional materials required. Credit available. Apply to Dean of Admissions or Dean of Continuing Education.

THE CLAY PLACE, 5600 Walnut St., Pittsburgh PA 15232. (412)441-3799. Director: Elvira L. Peake. Offers pottery 4 times annually for 4 students. Course length is 10 weeks. Fee: $50/course, includes registration and materials. Write or call for application.

THE COMMUNITY ARTS CENTER OF WALLINGFORD, 414 Plush Mill Rd., Wallingford PA 19086. (215)566-1713, 566-1714. Executive Secretary: Elizabeth Baker. Offers batik; ceramics; decoupage; jewelry; leatherworking; needlecrafts; soft sculpture; weaving; and wood carving 3 times annually. Course length is 12-15 weeks. Fee: $45-60/course. Materials fee: $2.50-5. Write or call. "Membership in Potter's Guild has advanced requirements."
Purpose: "For the beginner an opportunity to get a grounding; test aptitude; and develop knowledge and skill. For the advanced complicated techniques; chance to work on own; opportunities for selling and showing; and association with others in the field."

EVERYDAY PEOPLE, 6th St. and Reed Ave., Monessen PA 15062. (412)684-3450. Director: Carol E. Burrows. Estab. 1974. Basic and advanced workshops in technique offered throughout the year to 4-12 low income, handicapped students for 1 day. Emphasizes batik; candlemaking; glass art; jewelry; leatherworking; needlecrafts; quilting; and weaving. Fee: $1/workshop, includes registration and materials. Call for registration. Sample of actual work should be presented in person. Instructors have BA or MS in Arts or are experienced craftworkers. Workshops provide instruction of new arts and determining of costs.

HUNT INSTITUTE, Carnegie-Mellon University, Pittsburgh PA 15213. (412)578-2436. Contact: Jean Gunner. Estab. 1973. Basic and advanced workshops in technique offered semiannually for 8 students once a week for 10 weeks. Emphasizes fine and rare books. Fee: $180/workshop, includes registration. Write for application.

LYCOMING COLLEGE, Williamsport PA 17701. (717)326-1951. Department of Art Chairman: Roger D. Shipley. Offers Ceramics 1-2 twice annually for 10-25 students for 15 weeks. Fee: $340/course, includes materials. Credit available. $15 application fee. Submit slides of work. SASE.

MOUNT ALOYSIUS JUNIOR COLLEGE, Rt. 22, Cresson PA 16630. (814)886-4131. Chairman: Hettie Osborne. Offers ceramics once annually for 12 students; and weaving/fabrics once annually for 12 students. Course length is 15 weeks. Fee: $210/course. Materials fee: $30. Credit available.
Application: Write to Admissions Director. $15 application fee. Submit slides and letter of intent or arrange personal interview and present actual work. SASE.

NATIONAL STANDARDS COUNCIL OF AMERICAN EMBROIDERERS CORRESPONDENCE SCHOOL, Box 4594, Pittsburgh PA 15205. (412)279-0299. Director: Sally Schreiber. Estab. 1970. Basic; intermediate; advanced; and teachers' training workshops in technique offered throughout the year. Emphasizes needlecrafts. Write for brochure.

PENNSYLVANIA STATE UNIVERSITY, 256 Chambers Building, Department of Art Education, University Park PA 16802. (814)865-6570. Director of Division: Dr. Harlan Hoffa. Offers fiber art, ceramics, and metals 3 times annually for 20 students; plus a summer workshop in each for 20 students. Course length is 10 weeks; summer workshop is 3 weeks. Fee: $171/course instate undergraduate; $345/course out-of-state undergrad; $180/course instate grad; $354/course out-of-state grad, includes registration. Materials fee: none except ceramics. Credit available.
Application: "During the year, because of preregistration, it is very difficult for nondegree students to obtain a place in the courses." Prerequisite: 6 credits of art at accredited college or university. For summer workshops write Pat Bodman, 410 Keller Center, Pennsylvania State University, University Park PA 16802.

TEMPLE UNIVERSITY, Tyler School of Art, Beech and Penrose Aves., Elkins Parks PA 19117. (215)224-7575. Contact: Stanley Lechtzin. Workshops in ceramics; glass art; jewelry; metalsmithing; and weaving for the high school graduate.

Rhode Island

MARKEY AND ASPLUND INC., 131 Washington St., Providence RI 02903. (401)421-9277. President: Daniel G. Knowlton. Estab. 1958. Basic and advanced workshops offered in technique to 15 students 3 hours weekly for 12 sessions. Emphasizes hand bookbinding, rare book restoration, marble papers, and book repair. Fee: $75, includes registration. Materials fee: $20/tool kit. Write for application. Offers certificate after each course and a diploma after 6 semesters.

South Carolina

FLORENCE MUSEUM, 558 Spruce St., Florence SC 29501. (803)662-3351. Museum Director: Dr. William A. Burns. Estab. 1975. Basic and advanced 1 week workshops in marketing and technique offered to a maximum of 6 students with demonstrated manual dexterity plus artistic or creative talent as evidenced by work. Emphasizes all crafts. Fee: $15-60, includes registration and materials. Write in April for application. Submit color slides or actual work. SASE.

THE GIBBES ART GALLERY SCHOOL, 135 Meeting St., Charleston SC 29401. (803)577-7275. Supervisor: Barbara Karesh. Offers pottery 3 times annually for 64 beginning students for 10 weeks; weaving 3 times annually for 7-12 students for 6-8 weeks; batik 3 times annually for 7-12 students for 6 weeks; furniture 3 times annually for 12-15 students for 10 weeks; and basketmaking 3 times annually for 12-15 students for 6 weeks. Fee: $50/10 week course; $35/6 week course, includes registration. Materials fee: $10. Negotiating for credit with the Citadel or the College of Charleston. Write or call Registrar.
Purpose: "These courses are designed for the beginner. A professional craftsperson would be most interested in a teaching position at the school."

MUSEUM SCHOOL OF ART, 420 College St., Greenville SC 29601. (803)271-7570. Registrar: Anne-Marie Hardin. Offers Pottery 7-10 times annually for 60-100 students; Jewelry/Casting twice annually for 20 students; Jewelry/Fabrication and Enameling once annually for 10 students; and Weaving 4 times annually for 40-50 students. Course length is 13 weeks and 2 weeks. Fee: $75/course, includes registration and materials. Credit available; offers 2-year Associate Degree in Applied Arts or Fine Arts. Write or call the school. "Examples of work are required for continuance after the first semester if the student wants to be in the Associate Degree Program."
Purpose: "A good solid understanding of the techniques involved in the discipline; sufficient expertise to set up a small working studio; involvement with faculty and students with similar interests; and a beginning toward a personal aesthetic."

South Dakota

BLACK HILLS STATE COLLEGE, Industrial Arts Division, Spearfish SD 57783. (605)642-4385. Chairman, Industrial Arts Division: Dr. L. D. Edwards. Offers leathercraft twice annually for 30 students; plastics and Industrial Crafts once annually for 20 students; and Art Metals once annually for 18 students. Course length is 18 weeks. $16.50/semester hour, residents; $36/semester hour, nonresident, includes registration. Credit available. Write Director of Admissions.

MOUNT MARTY COLLEGE, Art Department, Yankton SD 57078. (605)668-1011. Head, Art Department: S. Kathleen Hickenbotham. Offers pottery twice annually for 10 students and offers crafts (decoupage; jewelry; and needlecrafts) biennially with unlimited registration. Course length is 1 semester. Fee: $60/credit hour; $10 materials fee. Credit available; offers degree in art with an emphasis in pottery. Write Registrar.

NORTHERN STATE COLLEGE, Box 667, Aberdeen SD 57401. (605)622-2571. Contact: Dr. Terry Richardson. Offers ceramics; candlemaking; leathercrafts; lapidary; jewelry; metalsmithing; plastics; and decoupage twice annually for 48 students. Course length is 18 weeks. Fee: $53/course, includes registration. Materials fee: $10-20. Credit available. Write Admissions and Records.

SOUTH DAKOTA STATE UNIVERSITY, Art Department, Solberg Hall, Brookings SD 57007. (605)688-4103. Head, Art Department: Dr. Fred Bunce. Offers Ceramics 1-2 twice annually for 15 students; Weaving 1-2 twice annually for a total of 18 students; and Textile Design once annually for 18 students. Course length is 18 weeks. Fee: $52.50/course, includes registration. Materials fee: $15-20. Credit available. Write Art Department. Submit slides of work. SASE.

Tennessee

THE ARROWMONT SCHOOL OF ARTS AND CRAFTS, Box 567, Gatlinburg TN 37738. (615)436-5860. Director: Ray Pierotti. Estab. 1945. Basic and advanced workshops in technique and design offered annually to 120-150 students for 1-2 weeks. Emphasizes batik; ceramics; glass art; jewelry; metalsmithing; quilting; soft sculpture; weaving; dyeing; textile printing; enameling; and woodworking. Fee. $75/week plus $75-100 for food and lodging.
Purpose: "Contact with the nation's leading artists; technical and social exchange of information between other members of the faculty and student body; a sound foundation in visual arts design coupled with professional and exceptional craftsmanship."
Application: Write for application. "In the case of desiring graduate credit through the craftworker's home university or through the University of Tennessee, Knoxville, which will offer credit through Arrowmont, a portfolio or letter of recommendation is required."

EAST TENNESSEE STATE UNIVERSITY, Southeast Regional American Crafts Council, Department of Art, Box 23740 A, Johnson City TN 37601. (615)929-4247. Workshop Coordinator: Debra Lynn Gold. Estab. 1978. Basic and advanced workshops offered semiannually for 300 or more students in 6 separate workshops for 1 day. Emphasizes ceramics; jewelry; soft sculpture; enameling; and basketry. Fee: $15/day, includes registration and banquet. Materials fee: $6 maximum. Write for application. Workshops offer exchange of ideas; experience; and technical information with other craftworkers.

MIDDLE TENNESSEE STATE UNIVERSITY, Box 125, Murfreesboro TN 37132. (615)898-2781. Contact: Dr. M. R. Bachler. Basic and advanced workshops in technique offered annually to a maximum of 20 students for 18 week semester. Emphasizes jewelry; leatherworking; metalsmithing; lapidary; plastics; and enameling. Write Office of Admissions and Records for application. Workshops offer basic skills in 8 craft areas.

UNION UNIVERSITY, Hwy. 45 Bypass, Jackson TN 38301. (901)663-1818. Art Department Chairman: Grove Robinson. Pottery offered to 15 students 4 times a year (3 15-week courses; 1 5-week course); jewelry offered to 10 students once a year for 15 weeks. Fee: $15/credit to audit, includes registration and some materials. Call or write Art Department. Instructors hold MFA degrees and have 6-13 years teaching experience. Credit available.

UNIVERSITY OF TENNESSEE, 13th at Cumberland, Knoxville TN 37916. (615)974-2369. Head of Crafts, Interior Design: Robbie G. Blakemore. Offers batik; ceramics; jewelry; soft sculpture; weavings; wood design; and textile design 3 times annually for 20 students. Course length is 10 weeks. Fee: $16-22/quarter hour, includes registration. Credit available. Submit slides of work. SASE. $10 application fee.

Texas

STEPHEN F. AUSTIN STATE UNIVERSITY, Department of Art, Box 3001, SFA Station, Nacogdoches TX 75962. (713)569-4804. Department Head: Jon D. Wink. Offers Art Metal/Jewelry twice annually for 20 students; Ceramics 1-2 twice annually for 16 students; and Fiber Design once annually for 20 students. Course length is 15 weeks. Fee: depends on number of hours and if state resident. Credit available. Write Director of Admissions. Slide presentation required for graduate students.

MARY HARDIN BAYLOR, Belton TX 76513. (817)939-5811. Contact: Maurine Burks. Offers ceramics, jewelry and fabrics 3 times annually. Fee: tuition plus $2.50. Students supply own materials. Credit available. Write Admissions Office.

CORPUS CHRISTI STATE UNIVERSITY, Box 6010, Corpus Christi TX 78911. (512)991-6810. Dean, Arts/Humanities: Dean Wagenschein. Offers ceramics twice annually for 20 students; ceramics twice during summer session for 20 students; weaving once annually for 10 students; jewelry once annually for 15 students; and metals twice annually for 15 students. Course length is 15 weeks; summer session is 5½ weeks. Fee: $70/course, includes registration. Materials fee: $15. Credit available. Write Director of Admissions.

CRAFT COMPOUND, 6617 Snider Plaza, Dallas TX 75205. (214)528-3767. Contact: Mrs. John W. Rhea. Offers pottery throughout the year for 6 students for 8 weeks; Off Loom Weaving throughout the year for 6 students for 5 weeks; macrame throughout the year for 6 beginning students for 4 weeks; and basketry throughout the year for 6 students for 2 days. Fee: $20-35/course, includes registration. Write for more information.

EAST TEXAS STATE UNIVERSITY, Department of Industry and Technology, E.T. Station, Commerce TX 75428. (214)468-2268. Contact: Dr. Leon T. Harney. Offers ceramics; jewelry; leatherworking; metalsmithing; plastics; and crafts for elementary teachers twice annually for 25 students. Course length is 16 weeks; summer session is 6 weeks. Fee: $80-90/course resident; $150-200/course nonresidents, includes registration. Materials fee: varies. Credit available; offers BS; MS; MED; and DED. Write for application.

HILL COUNTRY ART FOUNDATION, Box 176, Ingram TX 78024. (512)367-5710. Contact: Art Chairman. Offers jewelry, stitchery, weaving and macrame once annually for 25 students for 1 week. Offers soft sculpture and ceramics; pottery; and Theory of Weaving once annually for 25 students for 2 weeks. Fee: $45/1 week; $80/2 weeks; includes registration. Some classes have materials fee. Write for registration form. Basically a summer school.

SAM HOUSTON STATE UNIVERSITY, Art Department, Huntsville TX 77340. (713)295-9406. Contact: Evelyn E. Anderson. Offers Beginning Ceramics 2-4 times annually for 24 students; Advanced Ceramics 3 times annually for 20 students; Graduate Ceramics 2-3 times annually for 10 students; jewelry and fabric design twice annually for beginning, advanced, and graduate students. Course length is 15 weeks; summer program is 5 weeks. Fee: $75/1 course to $135/4 or more courses, includes registration. Students purchase all materials. Credit available. **Application:** Write Chairperson, Department of Art. Slides are necessary for graduate MFA program only. SASE.

McMURRAY COLLEGE, Art Department, Abilene TX 79605. (915)692-4130. Contact: Bob Howell. Offers ceramics twice annually for 20 students; Advanced Ceramics twice annually for 10 students; and Jewelry twice annually for 8 students. Course length is 16 weeks. Fee: $54/credit hour, includes registration. Materials fee: $20. Credit available. Write to Registrar's Office. $10 application fee.
Purpose: "A student will gain a thorough knowledge of the materials and aesthetics of the art he is working in."

THE MUSEUM OF FINE ARTS, School of Art, Box 6826, Houston TX 77005. (713)529-7659. Administrative Dean: Clem Barron. Offers Beginning and Advanced Ceramics; Beginning and Advanced Jewelry; Beginning and Advanced Sculpture 2 semesters and 1 summer session annually, unlimited registration. Course length is 16 weeks; summer session is 6 weeks. Fee: $115/course plus $30-35 lab fee, includes registration and some basic materials. Credit available. Program provides "foundation for professional career." Enrollment prior to semester beginning; no pre-application necessary.

NARANJO'S AMERICAN INDIAN ARTS, 10001 Westheimer 20A, Houston TX 77042. (713)783-0833. Manager: Stella Naranjo. Estab. 1977. Basic and advanced workshops in technique offered to 6-10 students for 8 week sessions. Emphasizes silversmithing and jewelry. Fee: $75/workshop; includes registration, some materials, and use of tools. Materials fee: $35. Write for application.
Purpose: Finer techniques in jewelry making.

NORTH TEXAS STATE UNIVERSITY, Box 5098, N.T. Station, Denton TX 76203. (817)788-2398. Contact: Co-ordinator of Undergraduate Studies. Offers ceramics; weaving; and jewelry both semesters and 2 summer sessions. Fee: $4/semester hour, resident; $40/semester hour, nonresident. Fee includes registration, medical fee, building fee, student service fee, and union building fee. Credit available; offers graduate and undergraduate degree in ceramics, weaving or jewelry. Write to Registrar. Submit work samples for graduate level.

SAN ANTONIO COLLEGE, 1300 San Pedro Ave., San Antonio TX 78284. (512)734-7311. Contact: John W. Ingle. Offers ceramics and metalsmithing twice annually for 20 students; and lapidary twice annually for 15 students. Course length is 16 weeks. Fee: $4/hour plus $8 lab fee, includes materials. Credit available. Write for more information.

TEXARKANA COLLEGE, 2500 N. Robison Rd., Texarkana TX 75501. Director, Community Services: John Ferguson. Offers ceramics 3 times annually; tole painting and macrame twice annually; and leathercraft once annually. Registration limit: 20 beginning and advanced students. Course length is 6 weeks. Fee: average $25, includes registration. Credit available for ceramics. Write Evening and Continuing Education Division.

TEXAS WOMAN'S UNIVERSITY, Department of Art, TWU Station, Box 22995, Denton TX 76201. (817)382-8923. Chairman: Dr. Donald E. Smith. Offers Begining Ceramics; Beginning Fibers; jewelry; and metalsmithing 4 times annually, unlimited registration. Courses are offered twice for 16 weeks and twice for 6 weeks. Materials fee: $10-50. Credit available. Write Department of Art. Submit slides for master's program. SASE.

WHARTON COUNTY JUNIOR COLLEGE, Boling Hwy., Wharton TX 77488. (713)532-4560, ext. 52. Department Chairman: Dr. Bruce Turner. Offers ceramics once annually for 20 students for 1 semester. Credit available. Program provides solid foundation in hand built ceramics. On campus registration.

Utah

SALT LAKE ART CENTER, 54 Finch Lane, Salt Lake City UT 84102. (801)328-4201. Curator of Education: Mark Anderson. Offers Beginning through Advanced Ceramics 4 times annually for 16 students; jewelry, stained glass, and weaving 4 times annually for 16 students. Course length is 9 weeks. Fee: $45/course, includes registration. Materials fee: $7.50-10. Write for information.

UTAH STATE UNIVERSITY, Art Department, Logan UT 84322. (801)752-4100, ext. 7538. Head, Art Department: Dr. Ray W. Hellberg. Offers ceramics 6 classes per term for 20-25 students; textile design 5 classes per term for 20-25 students; and jewelry 2 classes annually for 30 students. Course length is 10 weeks. Fee: $54/3 credit course (out of state student higher), includes registration. Materials fee: $5-20. Credit available. Write Admissions and Records.

UTAH STATE UNIVERSITY, Vinta Potters Guild, Vernal UT 84078. Resident Potter: Ronald Kovatch. Basic and Advanced workshops in technique; taste; and history for students who have at least 1 Utah State University ceramics class credit or equivalent for annual sessions ranging from 1 day-1 weekend-2 weeks. Emphasizes ceramics. Fee: $150/workshop; includes registration and materials. Write for application.

WEBER STATE COLLEGE, 3750 Harrison Blvd., Department of Art, Ogden UT 84408. (801)399-5941, ext. 462. Chairman, Art Department: Richard Van Wagoner. Offers Beginning Ceramics every quarter for 18 students; Intermediate Ceramics every quarter for 10 students; Advanced Ceramics every quarter for 6 students; 2 sections of Beginning Weaving every quarter for 18 students per section; Intermediate and Advanced Weaving every quarter for 6 students; Beginning Jewelry and Beginning Metal Arts every quarter and evening for 16 students; and Intermediate and Advanced Jewelry and Intermediate and Advanced Metal Arts every quarter and evenings for 4 students. Also offers Craft Seminar/Studio Practice for 3-8 students. Course length is 10 weeks. Fee: $53.50/3 unit course, resident; $103.50/3 unit course, nonresident; includes registration. Lab fee: $12/ceramics. Credit available. Write Art Department Chairman or Registrar. Not required but encourages presentation of slides; photos and actual work also accepted. SASE.

Vermont

BENNINGTON COLLEGE, Bennington VT 05201. (802)442-5401. Director Special Projects: C. Graham. Offers ceramics (sometimes varies) summers for 15 students per faculty. Summer session is 4 weeks. Fee: $706/course; includes registration, lodging, meals, and course credit. Credit available. Write for information on summer programs. Submit slides and photos of work; no samples.

MICHAEL COFFEY SCHOOL OF FINE WOODWORKING, Rt. 2, Poultney VT 05764. (802)287-4091. Contact: Michael Coffey. Offers woodworking and furniture making starting each September for 3 new students and 3 advanced students. Course length is 2 years. Fee:

$3,000/year, includes tuition. Students supply own materials. Program provides "professional competence in custom furniture making." Write for course outline and application. $5 application fee. Resume of Michael Coffey sent on request.

JUDY FOX SCHOOL OF WEAVING, Box 123A Rt. 1, Waitsfield VT 05673. (802)496-2402. Contact: Judy Fox. Estab. 1965. Basic workshops in technique and use of color and texture in weaving offered annually to 4 students by the week for 3 weeks maximum. Emphasizes weavings. Fee: $60/week, includes registration and individual instruction. Students supply own materials. Write for application.
Purpose: 4-harness loom with some advanced projects on 8 harnesses; other techniques include frame loom weaving for tapestry and off-the-loom techniques for sculptural pieces.

GODDARD COLLEGE, Plainfield VT 05667. (802)454-8311. Department Head, Ceramics and Glass: William Happel. Offers ceramics twice annually for 25 students; Advanced Ceramics twice annually for 10 students; blown glass twice annually for 18 students; and Advanced Glass twice annually for 4 students. Course length is 13 weeks. Fee: $275/course, includes registration. Materials fee: $40. Credit available.
Purpose: "A total experience in glass and ceramics covering aesthetics; current trends chemistry; equipment fabrication; basic and advanced techniques. In glass: blowing; free and mold; pressing; casting; cutting and polishing. In clay: history; aesthetics; methods; throwing; casting; hand building; glaze chemistry and application; stoneware and local earthenware technology; gas, electric, and wood fired kiln technology; primitive firing; and refractory technology."
Application: Write Admissions Department. For direct inquiry and portfolios contact Glass and Ceramics Department. Submit slides of recent work and/or portfolio of related work and statement of intent.

SHELBURNE SPINNERS, 2 Howard St., Burlington VT 05401. (802)862-7107. Contact: Linda Towler. Estab. 1977. Basic workshop in wool preparation and hand spinning on a drop spindle offered monthly to 10 students for 1 day. Emphasizes hand spinning. Fee: $20/workshop, includes registration and materials. Write or call for information on latest workshop.
Purpose: "All basic knowledge of wool sorting; washing; and carding with instruction in spinning so that student can follow the whole process at home."

SOCIETY OF VERMONT CRAFTSMEN, Fletcher Farm Craft School, Ludlow VT 05149. Director: Merle Larsen. Estab. 1948. Basic and advanced workshops in technique offered to 40 students for spring and fall weekend workshops and 65 students for 2 week summer sessions. Emphasizes ceramics; jewelry; needlecrafts; tole painting; weaving; woodcarving; stained glass; spinning and dyeing; rosemaling; basketry; rug hooking; and calligraphy. Fee: $60/weekend workshop; $110/2 week summer session tuition. Write for brochure and application. SASE.

VERMONT STATE CRAFT CENTER AT WINDSOR HOUSE, Box 110, Windsor VT 05089. (802)674-6729. Director: Cornelis Pietersen. Offers classes in arts and crafts 4 times annually. Offers advanced classes for craftworkers exclusively. Sponsors a Gallery/Shop exhibiting work of 250 Vermont craftworkers. Write for information.

Virginia

ART LEAGUE OF NORTHERN VIRGINIA, Art League Workshop, 101 N. Union St., Alexandria VA 22314. (703)683-2323. Workshop Director: Kay Allardice. Estab. 1937. All levels of workshops in technique offered 3 semesters to 15-20 students for 15 weeks, 1 day a week. Emphasizes ceramics and glass art. Fee: $80/workshop plus registration fee.

EASTERN MENNONITE COLLEGE, Harrisonburg VA 22801. (703)433-2771. Assistant Professor: Jerry Lapp. Offers Pottery 1-2 annually for 10½ weeks (3 credit hours) for 20-25 students and continuing education ceramics twice annually for 10 weeks (1-2 credit hours) for 20-25 students. Fee: $10/credit hour, includes registration and materials. Credit offered. Write Director of Admissions. $10 admission fee. "The program is good introduction to ceramics arts."

FALL FESTIVAL OF NEEDLEWORK, Woodlawn Plantation, Box 37, Mount Vernon VA 22121. Staff Assistant: Margaret Davis. Sponsor: Woodlawn Plantation, National Trust Historic Preservation. Estab. 1976. Offers annual needlework seminar 1 week in October for 40-45 students. Fee: $20/day. Stresses "all phases of needlework."

HOLLY STUDIO, INC., Rt. 2, Box 351, Lancaster VA 22503. (804)462-2973. President: Kay Healy. Offers ceramics and glass art throughout the year. Fee: $60-90, includes registration and materials. Continuing education units awarded by Montclair State College, New Jersey, for all courses. Write for application.
Purpose: Higher degree of proficiency in advanced ceramic techniques; more thorough knowledge of materials used; and college level recognition of continuing development.

JAMES MADISON UNIVERSITY, Art Department, Harrisonburg VA 22801. (703)433-6216. Department Chairman: Dr. David Diller. Offers 2 sections of weaving and textiles; ceramics; metal and jewelry 3 times annually for 15-20 students per section. Offers graduate level weaving and textiles; ceramics; metal and jewelry 3 times annually for 5-10 students. Course length is 16 weeks; summer session is 8 weeks. Fee: $55/part time resident; $107/part time nonresident; $400/full time resident; $650/full time nonresident, includes registration. Students supply own materials. Credit available; offers 4 year BFA program with concentration in any of the craft areas listed.
Application: Write Admissions Office for catalog and application. $15 application fee. For graduate level submit slides of work and past transcripts to Dr. David Diller, Art Department.

RADFORD COLLEGE, Art Department, Box 5791, Radford VA 24142. (703)731-5475. Chairman, Art Department: Dr. Lynn Gordon. Offers ceramics, jewelry, crafts, and fiber techniques 4 times annually for 15 students; Advanced Ceramics, Advanced General Crafts, Advanced Jewelry, and Advanced Fiber Techniques 4 times annually for 8-10 advanced students. Course length is 10 weeks. Fee: $25/quarter hour, resident; $42/quarter hour, nonresident; includes registration. Credit available. Write to Admissions Office. $15 application fee.

STRASBURG MUSEUM POTTERY, Strasburg Museum, E. King St., Strasburg VA 22657. (703)465-3175. Contact: Ruth Dryer. Offers pottery 8 weeks during summer for 20 potters. Fee: $20/course, includes registration; instruction; use of wheels and kiln. Materials fee: clay and glaze available at extra cost. Write for application. Museum open May-October.

THE VATEN SCHOOL OF CRAFTS, INC., Loomis Lane, Bristol VA 24201. Director: Penny Jessee. Estab. 1967. Basic and advanced workshops in technique offered quarterly to 5-12 students once or twice a week for 6-12 weeks. Emphasizes ceramics; jewelry; needlecrafts; soft sculpture; weaving; and calligraphy. Fee: $32.50/workshop, includes registration. Materials fee: $5-10. Write for application. "For advanced work student must show some assurance that he can work on the level being taught."

VIRGINIA STATE COLLEGE, Box 26, VSC, Petersburg VA 23803. (804)520-6328. Chairman, Department of Fine Arts: Dr. A. D. Macklin. Offers ceramics and jewelry for 20 students. Course length is 15 weeks; summer session is 6 weeks. Fee: $105/course, includes registration and materials. Credit available. Program stresses "individual attention, excellent facilities." Write Director of Admissions. $10 application fee.

VIRGINIA WESLEYAN COLLEGE, Wesleyan Dr., Norfolk VA 23501. (804)461-3232. Contact: Neil Britton. Offers Beginning Ceramics twice annually for 24 students; Intermediate Ceramics once annually for 20 students; Advanced Ceramics twice annually for 15 students; Crafts/Macrame and Fabric, Crafts/Jewelry, and Crafts/Weaving once annually for 24 students. Course length is 1 semester. Fee: $105/credit hour, includes registration. Materials fee: $25.50. Credit available. Write Department of Admissions.

Washington

BIG BEND COMMUNITY COLLEGE, Art Department, Moses Lake WA 98837. (509)762-5351. Contact: Stephen Tse. Offers pottery 3 times annually for 20 students. Course length is 10-11 weeks. Fee: $36, includes registration. Materials fee: $20. Credit available. Write for application.

CENTRAL WASHINGTON UNIVERSITY, Art Department, Randall Hall, Ellensburg WA 98926. (509)963-2665. Offers glassblowing twice annually for 18 students; and jewelry 4 times annually for 18 students. Course length is 10 weeks. Fee. $20/credit (average credits 3/course), includes registration and some materials. Credit available. Write Admissions Office. Requires work samples for advanced courses. SASE.

EASTERN WASHINGTON UNIVERSITY, Department of Art, Cheney WA 99004. (509)359-2493. Chairman: Dr. Gregory Hawkins. Offers ceramics; weaving; jewelry; and metals for 15-20 students. Course length is 10 weeks. Fee: $19/credit hour, includes registration. Credit available. Apply to Department of Art. For admision to BFA program submit slides/portfolio. SASE.

FACTORY OF VISUAL ART, 4649 Sunnyside N., Seattle WA 98103. (206)632-8177. Director: Mickey Gustin. Offers beginning, intermediate, and advanced batik; ceramics; glass art; jewelry; metalsmithing; quilting; soft sculpture; weaving; textile printing; and spinning/dyeing 4 times annually for 15 students. Course length is 11 weeks. Fee: $132/course, includes registration. Materials fee: $5-30. "Classes are college level and sometimes can be transferred to degree-granting insititutions." Write or call for catalog.

SKAGIT VALLEY COLLEGE, 2405 College Way, Mt. Vernon WA 98273. (206)424-1031. Head of the Art Department: Orville Chatt. Offers pottery 3-4 times annually and night classes for 20 students; jewelry 7 times annually and night classes for 20 students; weaving 3 times annually for 20 students; and general crafts 3 times annually for 24 students. Course length is 10 weeks; summer session is 6 weeks. Fee: $8.30/credit, residents; $22.70/credit, nonresidents (most classes are 3 credits), includes registration. Students supply own materials. Credit available; offers AA degree. Write for application.

HELLA SKOWRONSKI STUDIO, 740 94th NE, Bellevue WA 98004. (206)454-1589. Contact: Hella Skowronski. Offers weaving and sprang throughout the year for 6 students. Course length is 8 weeks. Fee: $40/course, includes registration. Materials fee: $5 loom rental. Write or call for application.

SPOKANE FALLS COMMERCIAL COLLEGE, W. 3410 Ft. George Wright Dr., Spokane WA 99204. (509)456-6100. Offers 3 sections of Art Media/Enameling annually for 18 students; 27 sections of ceramics annually for 18 students; 6-8 sections of Volume Design annually for 18 students; 2 sections of Leaded Glass annually for 18 students; 6 sections of weaving annually for 12 students; and 3 sections of Jewelry Design annually for 18 students. Course length is 12 weeks. Fee: $10/credit hour (ceramics and Volume Design are 4 credits; the rest are 3 credits), includes registration. Credit available. Write to Creative Art Department.
Purpose: "Depending on his prior knowledge, a student can gain a new perspective at the least, and basic and advanced techniques at the most. We have well equipped studios."

UNIVERSITY OF WASHINGTON, Division of Textiles: Weaving Department, 203 Raitt, DL-10, Seattle WA 98195. (206)543-1730. Offers Beginning Weaving 3 times annually for 12-15 students; Intermediate and Advanced Weaving twice annually for 12-15 students; and Off Loom Processes 1-2 times annually for 12-15 students. Course length is 11 weeks. Credit available; offers BA and MA. For program information packet on undergraduate or graduate level write Textiles Division, School of Nutritional Sciences and Textile. Submit slides of work. SASE.

WASHINGTON STATE UNIVERSITY, Pullman WA 99164. (509)335-3823. Chairman of Clothing, Interior Design, and Textiles: Mignon Perry. Offers weaving twice annually for 32 students. Course length is 15 weeks. Fee: $27.50/credit hour, summer session; includes registration. Students supply own materials. Credit available. Write Office of Admissions. Also contact Tom Hale, Rm. 57, Cleveland Hall, Pullman WA 99164. (509)335-4845. Offers basic and advanced workshops in technique twice annually to 20 students of sophomore standing for 1 semester. Emphasizes glass art, leatherworking and metalsmithing. Write for application.

WENATCHEE VALLEY COMMUNITY COLLEGE, 1300 5th St., Wenatchee WA 98801. (509)662-1651. Contact: Gary Baskett. Offers pottery 3 times annually for 38 students; jewelry 3 times annually for 28 students; and sculpture 3 times annually for 25 students. Course length is 8-10 weeks. Fee: $11/credit, includes registration. Materials fee: $15-20. Credit available. To apply write Registrar.
Purpose: Quality work is expected. Pride in performance; varying concepts and techniques; individual instruction; remodeled facilities; and enthusiasm plus.

WESTERN WASHINGTON UNIVERSITY, Art Department, Bellingham WA 98225. (206)676-3660. Offers batik; ceramics; glass art; jewelry; soft sculpture; weaving; and fabric design. For specifics write for University catalog. Fee: $23/credit, includes registration. Materials fee varies with each class. Credit available; BA or BFA offered. For application write Office of Admissions, Old Main, Western Washington University, Bellingham WA 98225.

Washington DC

THE SILVER SHUTTLE, 1301 35th St. NW, Washington DC 20007. (202)338-3789. President: Miss J. Anderson. Estab. 1964. Basic workshops in technique offered to 8-14 students for 30 hours. Emphasizes spinning and specialized weaving techniques. "We are a business catering to handweavers and spinners and offering instruction."

West Virginia

AUGUSTA HERITAGE ARTS WORKSHOP, Box 1878, Elkins WV 26241. (304)636-0006. Director: K. Gillispie. Estab. 1973. Basic and advanced workshops in technique and appreciation of Appalachian culture offered to 15-20 students 14 years or older for 1-4 weeks. Emphasizes ceramics; glass art; needlecrafts; quilting; tole painting; weaving; general crafts; musical instrument construction; woodcarving; and basketry. Fee: $30/1 week, state resident; $40/1 week, nonresident; includes registration. Materials fee: maximum of $75. Write for brochure.

CRAFT CENTER, Cedar Lakes, Ripley WV 25271. (304)372-6263. Crafts Coordinator: Tim Pyles. Estab. 1975. Basic and advanced workshops in fundamentals; technique; and design offered 4 times annually to 90-100 students for 1 week or 1 weekend. Some advanced classes require previous experience. Emphasizes batik; quilting; soft sculpture; weaving; wood sculpture; furniture making; and basketry. Fee: $75; includes registration, lodging and meals. Materials fee: $5-40. Write to be put on mailing list.

DAVIS AND ELKINS COLLEGE, Elkins WV 26241. (304)636-1900. Contact: Admissions Office. Offers pottery 2 semesters and summer session for 36 students; weaving 2 semesters and summer session for 15 students; quilting; basketry, and stained glass summer session only. Semester is 14 weeks; summer session is 4 weeks. Fee: $90/semester hour, includes materials. Credit available. Write Admissions Office.

GLENVILLE STATE COLLEGE, Department of Art, Pottery Workshop, Glenville WV 26351. (304)462-7186. Contact: Charles C. Scott. Estab. 1968. Basic and advanced workshops in technique offered annually to 20 students (high school seniors or older) for 1-9 weeks. Emphasizes ceramics. Fee: $60/week, in state; $95/week, out of state; includes registration, materials, lodging, and meals. Write to the College Art Department for information. Purpose: Fundamental skill in throwing; glazes; and kiln firing.

SALEM COLLEGE, Fort New Salem, Heritage Arts Program, Salem WV 26426. (304)782-5245, 782-5233. Director of Public Information: Carol Ann Schweiker. Offers basketry; chair bottoming; blacksmithing; candlemaking; needlework; quilting; spinning; weaving; bookbinding; and woodworking throughout the year. Fee: "varies greatly with individual need; fee information furnished with specific request." Credit available.

Purpose: "Fort New Salem is an historically based craft program whose purpose is to preserve the culture and arts and crafts of Appalachia as found in West Virginia. The craft courses offered here are derived from the daily life subsistence efforts of the early settlers. The academic program is therefore historically oriented. The public workshops and special projects which may be had need not be concerned with historical background but do emphasize traditional methods. The areas of competence that may be attained are professional craftworker, capable of earning a living in their craft; art education degree with emphasis on the heritage crafts; craft therapy or use of craft teaching in public programs; occupation in various areas of professional historical reconstruction and living museum situations; supplement as a minor or associate college degree; and brief experience in a wide variety of traditional crafts."

Application: "Any request for information only would be followed up with information geared to the requested interest of the craftsperson. If application is made for the college degree that request is sent through the admissions office. In either case final registration or application fee is $10. Interview required (may be by phone) for apprenticeship or advanced study. Slides, photos, or actual work are all acceptable for presentation. The Heritage Arts Committee would also require a written statement of purpose and past experience. SASE; insured if sample."

Wisconsin

THE CLEARING, Box 65, Ellison Bay WI 54210. (414)854-4088. Resident Manager: Donald Buchholz. Offers stained glass once annually for 16 students; weaving twice annually for 12 students; nature crafts, woodcarving, and fiber sculpture once annually for 16 students; and natural dyeing once annually for 14 students. Course length is 1 week. "Not all of these classes are offered every year as we vary each season." Fee: $145/dormitory; $165/twin-bedded room; includes registration, lodging, and meals. Write for brochure. $25 application fee.

Purpose: "This is a week of quiet to learn a new craft or to spend a week of uninterrupted work. The philosophy of The Clearing is 'One must get back to nature to find oneself and for self expression.' We offer 128 acres of natural environment for inspiration."

CONCORDIA COLLEGE, 3201 W. Highland, Milwaukee WI 53208. (414)344-3400. Chairman, Art Department: William L. Chandler. Offers Fundamental Crafts every semester for 18 students. Fee: $60/credit, includes registration. Materials fee: $15. Credit available; offers AA degree. Write or call Admissions Department. $15 application fee.

LAWRENCE UNIVERSITY, Appleton WI 54510. (414)739-3681. Chairman, Art Department: E. Dane Purdo. Offers pottery twice annually for 10 beginning students and art metal twice annually for 10 beginning students. Course length is 10 weeks. "Student must be enrolled in degree program." Credit available. Write Admissions. "Only requirement is Art 1 and 2, Introduction to Studio Art."

MILWAUKEE AREA TECHNICAL COLLEGE, 1015 N. 6th St., Milwaukee WI 53203. (414)278-6432. Acting Associate Dean: Harold A. Milbrath. Offers ceramics evenings twice annually for 16-18 students for 12 weeks; jewelry and silversmithing evenings and days twice annually for 16 students for 15-17 weeks; leathercraft and art metal evenings and days twice annually for 16 students for 12-17 weeks. Fee: $7/tuition fee per credit and $5/course fee per credit, includes registration. Write for application.

UNIVERSITY OF WISCONSIN, Art Department, River Falls WI 54022. (715)425-3266. Department Chairperson: Mary Barrett. Offers clay 4 times annually for 10 weeks (summer school 4-8 weeks) for 15-30 advanced potters; fibers 4 times annually for 10 weeks (summer school 3 weeks) for 50 students; glass 3 times annually for 10 weeks for 30 students; and metals-jewelry 3 times annually, sometimes 4, for 10 weeks (summer school 4 weeks) for 30 students. Fee: $71.64/3 credit hours, Wisconsin and Minnesota residents; $215.64/3 credit hours, nonresident; includes registration and materials. Credit available; offers specialized instruction as Special Student or BFA, BA or BS.
Application: Write Admissions or Director of Summer School. Slides; photos; or actual work should be presented for advanced placement. SASE.

UNIVERISTY OF WISCONSIN/PARKSIDE, Kenosha WI 53140. (414)553-2457. Contact: J. Murphy. Offers ceramics twice annually for 25 students; jewelry and fabrics once annually for 25 students. Course length is 16 weeks. "Regular University tuition for 1 course." Students supply own materials. Credit available; offers art degree or option for art degree with certification K-12. Write for catalog. Submit slides of work. SASE.

UNIVERSITY OF WISCONSIN/PLATTEVILLE, Art Department, Platteville WI 53818 (608)342-1228. Contact: Bud Wall. Offers woodworking twice annually for 2 advanced students for 2 years; ceramics 3 times annually for 20 students for 1 semester; jewelry twice annually for 10 students for 1 semester. Materials fee: $50, jewelry. Credit available. "The University of Wisconsin/Platteville Art Department is now offering credit in weaving through The Looms Weaving School and Museum, Mineral Point, Wisconsin.

Wyoming

NORTHWEST COMMUNITY COLLEGE, Powell WY 82435. (307)754-6507. Contact: Ken Fulton or John Banks. Offers pottery twice annually for 30 students; jewelry twice annually for 15 students; general crafts twice annually for 20 students; and design twice annually for 25 students. Course length is 18 weeks. Fee: $11/semester hour resident; $33/semester hour nonresident, includes registration. Students supply own materials and tools. Credit available. "Depending on the course you may get graduate credit through the University of Wyoming or undergraduate credit from Northwest Community College." Write to Dean of Students and request application. "Individualized attention in small classes; new facilities; well equipped work area; pollution free environment; variety of instructional methods; and qualified staff."

A TOUCH OF CLASS, Stained Glass Studio, Art Museum Bldg., 104 Rancho Rd., Casper WY 82601. (307)234-4758. Contact: Barbara Harris. Estab. 1975. Basic and advanced workshops in technique offered 4 times annually to 30 students for 1 weekend. Emphasizes glass art. Fee: $30/individual, includes registration and individual instruction. Materials fee: $60. Write for application. Purpose: how to work in the art of stained glass; design; and glass cutting (glazing, soldering, and fabricating).

Canada

ARTISTS' WORKSHOP, 296 Brunswick Ave., Toronto, Ontario Canada M5S 2M7. (416)920-8370. Public Relations: E. Durno. Estab. 1964. Basic and advanced workshops in technique offered twice annually to 10-20 students for 1 day or 1 weekend. "Sometimes we have part time courses running for 6-11 weeks. Experience is necessary for the advanced courses." Emphasizes ceramics; jewelry; needlecrafts; quilting; soft sculpture; weaving; dyeing; basket making; paper making; and book binding. Fee: $15-75, includes registration. Materials fee: usually under $10. For more information and to be put on mailing list write Three Schools, 296 Brunswick Ave., Toronto, Ontario Canada M5S 2M7.

Purpose: "Usually the craftworker will learn techniques and perhaps some history or background of the craft. Examples of various crafts are brought in and the construction techniques and design of article are discussed."

ECOLE DE TEXTILES LECLERC, C. P. 244 Lislet-Sur-Mer, Lislet-Sur-Mer, Quebec, Ontario Canada F0B 3B0. (418)247-3116. Director: France Cote. Offers all levels of dyeing; tapestry; weaving; and spinning throughout the year for 1-2 weeks. Fee: up to $160/50 hours of classes; includes registration and materials. Write for application. Submit work samples or curriculum vitae. SASE.

MOHAWK COLLEGE, 135 Fennell Ave. W., Hamilton, Ontario Canada L8N 3T2. (416)389-4461, ext. 209. Workshop Administrator: Lauren Chapman. Estab. 1973. Basic and advanced workshops in technique offered 3 terms annually to 10-20 students for 1 weekend during the summer or 1 weekend. Emphasizes batik; ceramics; glass art; jewelry; leatherworking; metalsmithing; needlecrafts; quilting; soft sculpture; and weaving. Write or call for Creative Arts Workshops brochure. "If applying as instructor submit slides or photos of work. We pay instructor's fee; travel; and living expenses."

Purpose: To learn more about his/her media and meet others with the same goals.

NEW BRUNSWICK CRAFT SCHOOL, Woodstock Rd., Fredericton, New Brunswick Canada. (506)453-2305. Contact: Philip Salmon. Estab. 1971. Offers creative problem solving and design workshop 4 times annually or whenever asked to a maximum of 15 practicing craftworkers for 1 day/week for 6 weeks or 1 week each day except Sunday. "Will travel for craft groups and associations." Emphasizes all craft areas. Fee: $35/workshop, includes registration and some materials. Write for application.

Purpose: Greater awareness of design and creativity.

NOVA SCOTIA DESIGNER CRAFTSMEN, Box 3355, Halifax, Nova Scotia Canada B3J 3J1. (902)423-3837. Estab. 1976. All levels of workshops in marketing; technique; and a variety of areas to meet the variety of interests offered annually to 80-100 students in sessions of 15 students for 1 weekend. Emphasizes ceramics; jewelry; leatherworking; and weaving. Fee: varies but usually $10/day or sometimes $30/weekend, includes registration. Write for dates and brochures.

VISUAL ARTS CENTRE, 350 Victoria Ave., Montreal, Quebec Canada H3Z 2N4. (514)488-9559. Assistant Director: Suzanne Sauvage. Basic and advanced workshops in technique and Exploration of Different Approaches offered to 15 students with interest and some experience in the medium for 2-3 days. Emphasizes ceramics; glass art; quilting; soft sculpture; and weaving. Fee: $25-35, includes registration. Materials fee: $5-25. Write for application.

Purpose: "To discover new dimensions in the specific media. The Centre also offers special workshops for teachers to broaden the scope of their teaching methods."

Publications of Interest

The listings in this book and introductory materials have been designed to help the craftworker sell his/her work. But, it would be impossible for them to cover every market and every marketing technique. New ideas and outlets pop up every day. The listings in this section are here to help steer you to additional sources of markets and information. Included are magazines, newsletters, books and publishing sources.

AMERICAN ARTIST, 1515 Broadway, New York NY 10036. Editor: Susan E. Meyer. Estab. 1937. Circ. 140,000. Monthly magazine; approximately 100 pages/issue. "Amateur and professional artists [readers] are provided with features and departments describing and displaying technical, professional and motivational aspects of being a successful artist." Material aimed at the average-level ceramicist, glass artist, jeweler, macrame designer, metal sculptor, miniature artist, potter and other sculptors (although main emphasis is on drawing, painting, printmaking and design). Includes announcements of upcoming craft shows; upcoming workshops; classified advertising; features on craftworkers; health information; articles on technique; marketing advice; legal information; legislative news; letters to the editor; and "artist-craftspeople interviews and display of works."
Columns: "Art Mart," new products; "Art Books," reviews; "Bulletin Board," shows; "Directory of Art Schools & Workshops," in March issue; "Forum," topical essays; "Professional Page," on taxes, government, marketing, business matters; "Quick Tips," technical by Ralph Mayer; "Looking at Paintings," tips from readers; "Technical Page," advice on painting techniques by Bernard Dunstan; "Footnotes," background on material and contributors in issue.

AMERICAN INDIAN ART MAGAZINE, 7333 E. Monterey Way, Suite 5, Scottsdale AZ 85251. (602)994-5445. Editor: Pamela Forbes McLane. Estab. 1975. Circ. 15,000. Quarterly magazine; 96 pages. "*American Indian Art Magazine* appeals to scholars and collectors of American Indian material; its wide-ranging and handsomely illustrated articles discuss all Native American art forms — jewelry, basketry, textiles, painting, ceramics, sculpture — in an informative and comprehendable style. Teachers and craftworkers (average-level) find the magazine an excellent reference source for styles and techniques." Emphasizes announcements of new galleries/shops and features on craftworkers. Regular columns include Museums and Galleries, a listing of events throughout the country; Museum Feature, featuring museum with American Indian art collection; Conservation Series, describes techniques for conservation of American Indian artifacts for both laymen and professionals; and Book Reviews.

ART EDUCATION, 1916 Association Dr., Reston VA 22091. (703)860-8000. Editor: Dr. John J. Mahlmann. Estab. 1947. Circ. 11,000. Monthly September-April magazine; 32 pages. "Our readers are art teachers and art educators at all levels in visual art education — elementary and secondary school through university and adult education. The journal offers articles on current trends; problems; and issues in education through and in the visual arts. Crafts are an integral part of this education. We rarely have articles relating specifically to crafts education, but the crafts are often incorporated in the material discussed in various articles. The educational issues involved are very pertinent to craftspersons and craft educators." Also publishes *Art Teacher*, magazine of elementary and secondary art education which often includes articles specifically on craft approaches.

ART LETTER, 850 3rd Ave., New York NY 10022. (212)593-2100. Monthly newsletter; 6 pages. Readers are artists; craftspersons; museum personnel; and other arts professionals. "Contains listings of grant programs and opportunities to show and sell as well as detailed reports on news developments and issues affecting visual artists and craftspersons."

THE ART OF WINNING FOUNDATION GRANTS, The Vanguard Press, 424 Madison Ave., New York NY 10017. Authors: Howard Hillman/Karin Abarbanel. 104-page book. Deals with choosing and applying to a foundation for a grant.

ARTIST AND HANDCRAFTER INFORMATION SERVICE, Box 253, Burke VA 22015. Editor: Eugene H. Fichter. Estab. 1975. Bimonthly newsletter; 20 pages. Provides readers with craft marketing information. For artists and handcrafters seeking show dates and places.

THE ARTISTS & CRAFTSPEOPLE DIRECTORY, 905 Grant Place, North Bellmore NY 11710. Annual directory listing craftworkers who are interested in selling their work. Write for a questionnaire and information for possible inclusion.

ARTISTS EQUITY NEWS, 3726 Albemarle St. NW, Washington DC 20016. (202)244-0209. Contact: *Artists Equity Association, Inc.* Editorial Board. Estab. 1947. Circ. 7,000+. Quarterly newsletter; approximately 8 pages/issue. "Readership consists of professionals in the visual arts, arts administrators, educators, congressional and other federal agency personnel, and state arts councils. The major emphasis is advocacy issues and legislative news. One technical article is included in each issue." For average and advanced craftpersons ("although most members are in 'fine arts' i.e., painters, sculptors, printmakers").
Columns: Each issue includes an interview with a figure with major responsibility for arts policy and programs; "Open Forum," a health hazards column by Dr. Michael McCann; an editorial; and legislative update.

THE ARTS JOURNAL, 324 Charlotte St., Asheville NC 28801. (704)255-7888. Editor: Martha Abghire. Estab. 1975. Circ. 3,000. Monthly tabloid; 24 pages. "*The Arts Journal* serves as a forum for artists (covers all levels of all crafts) and as a communication between the arts and the arts supportive community. We view our purpose as educational and inspirational. By representing quality within a quality format we hope to help our audience become all that they can be." Emphasizes announcements of upcoming craft shows, upcoming workshops, personnel changes in the craft field, and new galleries/shops; classified advertising; features on craftworkers; marketing articles; legal information; legislative news; and letters to the editor. Regular columns include Profiles; Opportunities, Shows, Job Openings, Etc.; Preservation: Book Reviews; Plants; Gourmet Cooking; Dance; Photos; and Visual Arts.

ARTS MANAGEMENT, 408 W. 57th St., New York NY 10019. (212)245-3850. Editor: Alvin H. Reiss. Estab. 1962. Newsletter published 5 times annually; 4 pages. Readers are managers and directors of cultural institutions or programs of every size and type including those in crafts. "The newsletter is a trade journal with information on developments; advice on funding; management techniques and promotion and case histories of successful programs." Emphasizes technique and marketing articles; legal information; and legislative news. Regular columns include checklist of significant articles; how-to briefs; and round-up of developments.

ARTWEEK, 1305 Franklin St., Oakland CA 94612. (415)763-0422. Editor: Cecile N. McCann. Estab. 1970. Circ. 13,000. Tabloid published weekly September-May and biweekly June-August; 16-20 pages. "Of interest to the broadest possible art community. We function as a trade publication covering art activity on the West Coast and Texas, including all areas of fine arts; crafts and photography as art; video and performance; legislation; and other news important to our community. Also extensive listings of competitions and festivals/sales plus classifieds and a screened guide to West Coast and Texas galleries." Covers all professional level crafts. Emphasizes announcements of upcoming craft shows, shops/galleries needing crafts, and upcoming workshops; classified advertising; legal information; legislative news; and letters to the editor.

BLACK SHEEP NEWSLETTER, 28068 Ham Rd., Eugene OR 97405. (503)344-9964. Sachiye Jones. Estab. 1974. Circ. 800. Newsletter published 5 times annually; 24 pages. Readers are small farmers; growers of black sheep who raise them primarily for handspinning; handspinners; and weavers. Emphasizes announcements of upcoming workshops; classified advertising; features on craftworkers; and handspinning articles related to wool or small sheep production.

CALENDAR OF SUMMER ARTS FAIRS, c/o Iowa Arts Council, State Capitol Bldg., Des Moines IA 50319. (515)281-4451. Editor: Ann Larsen. Estab. 1974. Circ. 3,000. Annual newsletter; 12 pages. "*The Calendar* is used primarily by craftspeople in Iowa, Wisconsin, Minnesota, and Illinois but is available on request to anyone at no charge. Provides specific vital data for all fairs included plus additional information that may be available and of interest to craftspeople. This is the only comprehensive list of Iowa art fairs. Information is carefully compiled and checked for accuracy and is a reliable annual source for this type of information. Its primary purpose is to make craftspeople aware of Iowa summer crafts markets." Covers all crafts; hobbyist to advanced.

CANADA CRAFTS, 380 Wellington St. W., Toronto, Ontario Canada M5V 1E3. Editor: Gwenn P. Dempsey. Circ. 10,000. Bimonthly magazine; 56 pages. "*Canada Crafts* is a periodical of interest to craftspeople; craft educators; craft collectors; and people who just like crafts. While we are interested in profiles of Canadian artists and their works and new processes in any media, we welcome any opinions succinctly expressed about any crafts oriented subject." Covers all crafts; average to advanced. Emphasizes announcements of upcoming craft shows and workshops; features on craftworkers; technique and marketing articles; and legislative news. Regular columns include Craft Calendar (shows, exhibitions, sales workshops); Craft Connections (lectures, competitions, and scholarships) and Book Reviews.

CANADA QUILTS, 360 Stewart Dr., Sudbury, Ontario Canada P3E 2R8. (705)522-9211. Editor: Mary M. Conroy. Estab. 1973. Circ. 2,500. Newsletter published 5 times annually; 32 pages. Readers "are mostly women who quilt as a hobby, who teach quilting, or who make quilts and quilted items for sale. The 'slant' is towards the upgrading of quilting as an art and the exchange of information and ideas. Two-thirds of readers are Canadian; remainder are from US; UK; New Zealand; West Germany; and Australia." Emphasizes announcements of upcoming craft shows, shops/galleries needing crafts, upcoming workshops, personnel changes in the craft field, and new galleries/shops; classified advertising; features on craftworkers; health information; technique and marketing articles; legal information; legislative news; and letters to the editor. Regular columns included are Book Review; Teacher's Page (teachers describe how they teach, techniques, etc.); The Patchworks, editorial; and Readers' Quilts, photos and description of quilts by readers. Also publishes 2 annuals, brochures, and patterns.

CASTING AND JEWELRY CRAFT, 507 5th Ave., New York NY 10017. (212)867-5212. Editor: Nick Frank. Estab. 1976. Circ. 4,000. Bimonthly magazine; 28 pages. "Informative articles on every aspect of creating jewelry for hobbyists; students; instructors; professionals and jewelers." Emphasizes announcements of upcoming craft shows and workshops, new galleries/shops; and technique articles. Regular columns include Response (question and answer column written on problems or difficulties encountered by our readers).

CERAMIC SCOPE, Box 48643, Los Angeles CA 90048. (213)939-4821. Editor: Mel Fiske. Estab. 1964. Circ. 6,300. Monthly magazine; 64 pages. "We provide business information to owners and operators of ceramic hobby shops and teaching studios. Articles deal with ceramic studio management and with stories about successful studio operation." Covers ceramics and glass for business people. Emphasizes announcements of upcoming ceramic shows and workshops, personnel changes in the ceramic hobby field, and new shops; features on ceramic studio owners; health information; class projects for teachers; marketing articles; legal information; legislative news; and letters to the editor. Regular columns include Glady's Gallery and Kay's Kaleidescope. Also publishes *Ceramic Scope Buyers Guide*, the only compendium and directory in the ceramic hobby industry with buying sources; listings of distributors; associations; shows; and teachers.

CERAMICS MONTHLY, Box 12448, Columbus OH 43212. (614)488-8236. Editor: Spencer L. Davis. Estab. 1953. Circ. 45,000. Monthly (except July and August) magazine; 100 pages. Readers are studio potters; professionals and amateurs; schools; universities; and colleges. "We cover current exhibitions (contemporary and historic ceramics); feature studio potters in interview style articles; have an on-going school series featuring the ceramics departments of colleges and universities; and give technical information through how-to articles, Questions and Answers, and Suggestions." Covers ceramics and occasionally glass; hobbyist to advanced. Emphasizes announcements of upcoming craft shows and workshops, personnel changes in the craft field, new galleries/shops; features on craftworkers; health information; technique and marketing articles; legal information; legislative news; and letters to the editor. Regular columns include Itinerary; Where to Show; Answers to Questions; Suggestions from Our Readers; and Ceramic Activities. Also publishes 9 different how-to ceramics handbooks.

CHICAGO ARTISTS' COALITION NEWSLETTER, 1515 W. Howard, Chicago IL 60626. (312)262-4067. Editor: George A. Jarvis Jr. Estab. 1975. Circ. 600. Monthly newsletter; 12 pages. "Readership is the Chicago artist community. The purpose of the newsletter is to dispense information pertinent to being an artist in Chicago and survival as a professional." Covers all advanced crafts and visual arts. Emphasizes announcements of upcoming craft shows, shops/galleries needing crafts, upcoming workshops, and new galleries/shops; health information; legal information; legislative news; and letters to the editor. Regular items include Art Law Briefs and Queries and Elucidations.

CHIP CHATS, 7424 Miami Ave., Cincinnati OH 45243. (513)561-9051. Editor: Edward F. Gallenstein. Estab. 1953. Circ. 13,500. Bimonthly magazine; 40-48 pages. Readers are amateur and professional woodcarvers and whittlers. "We try to supply information on what is going on in the carving world; let members know of new sources of supply; where they can sell their work; book reviews; news of shows and exhibitions; and spread good fellowship among carvers." Emphasizes announcements of upcoming craft shows, shops/galleries needing crafts, workshops, personnel changes in the craft field, and new galleries/shops; features on craftworkers and how-to articles.

CHRONICLE OF THE EARLY AMERICAN INDUSTRIES ASSOCIATION, Old Economy, Ambridge PA 15009. (412)266-4500. Editor: Daniel B. Reibel. Estab. 1933. Circ. 2,-500. Quarterly magazine; 16 pages. "Readers are primarily interested in technology of old tools. Most collect tools. We provide a wide range of articles on tools and technology for rank amateur through very sophisticated academic." Covers old crafts and industries. Emphasizes antique tools; crafts; and craftworkers. Regular columns include Tools in Art; Collection of (collector); book review; Interesting and Unusual Tools; and What It Is (unidentified tools). Also publishes a line of books on antique American tools.

COBBLESTONE, Box 1128, Los Alamitos CA 90720. (213)438-3424. Editor: Janet Valentine. Estab. 1975. Circ. 5,000. Quarterly magazine; 64 pages. "Our readers are all artists, and we provide information on all the arts." Emphasizes features on craftworkers.

CONTEMPORARY CRAFTS MARKET PLACE, R. R. Bowker Co., 1180 Avenue of the Americas, New York NY 10036. Compiled by the American Crafts Council. Biennial crafts directory containing listings of shops and galleries, shows, organizations, courses, audiovisual materials, suppliers, packers, shipping companies, insurers and publications.

CRAFT HORIZONS, American Crafts Council, 44 W. 53rd St., New York NY 10019. (212)977-8980. Editor: Rose Slivka. Estab. 1941. Circ. 40,000. Bimonthly magazine; 70 pages. Readers are professional and amateur craftspeople, artists, teachers, architects, designers, decorators, collectors, connoisseurs and the general public. Offical publication of the American Crafts Council. "It is the only magazine today devoted entirely to contemporary handcraft. Covers all crafts and discusses the technology, the materials, and the ideas of the artists who do the work wherever it is being done throughout the world." Emphasizes announcements of upcoming craft shows and workshops; shops/galleries needing crafts; personnel changes in the craft field, new galleries/shops; classified advertising; features on craftworkers; health information; technique and marketing articles; legal information; legislative news; and letters to the editor. Regular columns include Film; Health Issues; Money Matters; and Books.

CRAFT MARKET NEWS, 521 5th Ave., Suite 1700, New York NY 10017. (212)575-0140. Editor: Arleen M. Landi. Estab. 1975. Monthly newsletter; 12 pages. Readers are "professional craftspeople looking for craft shops, galleries and department stores which are ready to buy their work. Readers also include owners of craft shops and galleries and department store buyers." Provides listings and articles on business techniques for craftspeople and shops, ranging from pricing and shipping to promotion, display, bookkeeping, etc. "CMN is a monthly marketing service in newsletter form." Covers all crafts. Emphasizes announcements of shops/galleries needing crafts; personnel changes in the craft field; new galleries/shops; classified advertising; features on craftworkers; health information; marketing articles; legal information; and legislative news. Regular columns include Marketing Seminar-in-Print; CMN Craft Showcase; Management and Marketing Clinic; and My Way, craftspeople share their marketing techniques. Also publishes *Craft Marketing Manual*, a basic guide to marketing crafts.

CRAFTNEWS, 346 Dundas St. W., Toronto, Ontario Canada M5T 1G5. (416)366-3551. Editor: Elizabeth Dingman. Estab. 1976. Circ. 3,000. Bimonthly newsletter; 8 pages. Readers are professional and amateur craftworkers. "The intention is to convey practical information which will advance their skills and their careers." Covers all crafts; hobbyist to advanced. Emphasizes announcements of upcoming craft shows and personnel changes in the craft field; features on craftworkers; health information; marketing articles; legal information; legislative news; and letters to the editor. Regular columns include Festival Fairs Shows, upcoming events; Whowhatwherewhen, news of craftworkers and craft organizations; Books and Other Publications, reviews and notices of new books; and announcements of Ontario Crafts Council Craft Resource Centre published by Ontario Crafts Council.

CRAFTS, Crafts Advisory Committee, 12 Waterloo Place, London England SW1Y 4AU. Bimonthly magazine; approximately 68 pages. Includes announcements on upcoming gallery shows and features on craftworkers. Regular columns include In Brief and Notes and Reviews.

THE CRAFTS BUSINESS ENCYCLOPEDIA, Harcourt Brace Jovanovich, Inc., 757 3rd Ave., New York NY 10017. Author: Michael Scott. 320-page handbook for anyone who makes crafts for sale. Organized in alphabetical order, it discusses everything from accounting to zoning, including necessities such as balance sheets, consignment sales, overhead and portfolios. Also included are basic business know-hows such as finance, insurance, marketing, bookkeeping, credit, taxes, and sales promotions. (Michael Scott is the author of "Keeping Records" and "Copyrights and Patents" in this book.)

THE CRAFTS FAIR GUIDE, Box 262, Mill Valley CA 94941. Editor: Lee Spiegel. Estab. 1973. Circ. 1,100. Published quarterly. 60 pages. Readers are craftworkers who sell at crafts fairs on the West Coast who use it to decide which fairs to do. "The CFG is basically a review/critique of the fairs." Covers all advanced crafts. Emphasizes announcements and reviews of upcoming West Coast craft shows; health information; marketing articles; and letters to the editor. Also publishes monthly supplement.

THE CRAFTS REPORT, 700 Orange St., Wilmington DE 19801. (302)656-2209. Editor: Michael Scott. Estab. 1975. Circ. 3,800+. Monthly newspaper/tabloid; 8-12 pages. Readers are professional craftspeople; educators; administrators; etc. "We furnish news and information related to marketing, management and money matters as they affect craftspeople who produce to sell." Covers all professional crafts. Emphasizes announcements of upcoming craft shows; shops/galleries needing crafts; upcoming workshops; personnel changes in the craft field; and new galleries/shops; classified advertising; features on craftworkers; health information; marketing articles; legal information; legislative news; letters to the editor; business; accounting; promotion; and advertising. Regular columns include craft photography column. Also publishes *Consignment Selling — Pro and Con* with other publications in preparation on health and safety; government impact on crafts; apprenticeships; etc.

CRAFTSMEN IN BUSINESS: A GUIDE TO FINANCIAL MANAGEMENT & TAXES, American Crafts Council, 44 W. 53rd St., New York NY 10019. Author: Howard W. Connaughton, C.P.A. 73-page book. Deals with the financial aspects of running a crafts business, from accounting to taxes.

CREATIVE CRAFTS, Box 700, Newton NJ 07860. (201)383-3355. Editor: Sybil C. Harp. Estab. 1967. Circ. 65,000. Bimonthly magazine; 84 pages. "Readers are serious, adult hobbyists, usually women over 35 with some advanced skills. They are not looking for 'far out' designs but want challenge for their technical abilities. Very heavy on scale dollhouse miniatures." Covers all hobbyist crafts. Emphasizes announcements of upcoming craft shows; classified advertising; technique and marketing articles; and letters to the editor. Regular columns include Going Places, places of interest to craftworkers; Backroom Workshop, readers' assistance; Craft News; Who's Who and What's What in Fibers; Product and Book Review; and Quick and Easy, projects using craft shop products. Also publishes *The Minature Magazine* and several books of reprinted articles from past issues of *Creative Crafts*.

DE NOVO, Box 12758, New Brighton MN 55112. Editor: Jill Hanna. Estab. 1977. Published quarterly. "Our publication has been aimed at anyone interested in the visual arts from either a customer or patron aspect to those working in different medias; teaching; and running supply stores, galleries, studios, and museums." Covers all crafts; beginner to advanced. Emphasizes announcements of upcoming craft shows, shops/galleries needing crafts, upcoming workshops, personnel changes in the craft field, and new galleries/shops; classified advertising; features on craftworkers; health information; marketing articles; legal information; legislative news; and letters to the editor. Regular columns include Health Hazards; Rambling; Publisher's Corner; and Show Listings.

DECORATIVE ARTS NEWSLETTER, c/o Kenneth Ames, Winterthur Museum, Winterthur DE 19735. (302)656-8591. Editor: Kenneth Ames. Estab. 1975. Circ. 550. Quarterly magazine; 28-36 pages. Readers are involved in museums or educational institutions working professionally with any aspects of decorative arts including crafts. "Hope to provide platform for critical reviews of exhibitions; publications; and other endeavors as well as medium for new dissemination." Covers all advanced crafts. Emphasizes announcements of upcoming craft shows and workshops and reviews of exhibitions and publications.

DIRECTORY OF ART SCHOOLS & WORKSHOPS, c/o American Artist, 1515 Broadway, New York NY 10036. Editor: Sheila Ward. Published in each March issue of *American Artist*, and available separately at $1.50 each. Includes craft courses.

THE DULCIMER PLAYERS NEWS, Box 157, Front Royal VA 22630. (703)635-3811. Estab. 1975. Circ. 1,500. Quarterly magazine/newsletter; 40 pages. "Our publication is written by dulcimer people for dulcimer people and is a simple sharing of information." Covers woodworking; hobbyist to advanced. Emphasizes announcements of upcoming craft shows, workshops and new galleries/shops; features on craftworkers; technique articles; letters to the editor; music; and songs. Regular columns include Feedback; Mountain Dulcimer Section; Hammer Dulcimer Section; booklist; and record list. Also publishes *How to Build A Hammer Dulcimer.*

EARLY AMERICAN LIFE MAGAZINE, Box 1831, Harrisburg PA 17105. (717)234-2674. Editor: Robert G. Miner. Estab. 1970.Circ. 299,000. Bimonthly magazine; 100 pages. "The *Early American Life* readers are energetic folks whose interests lie mainly in restoring and creating early American style in their lives. The magazine carries articles on decorating; history; arts and crafts; historic places of interest for travel; and regular columns in each issue. We carry a do-it-yourself project in each issue, usually a woodworking project, and also regular craft features (hooking rugs, stenciling, scherenschnitte, weaving, making your own pewter molds are a few of the most recent)." Covers all levels of candlemaking; decoupage; dollmaking; fibers; jewelry; metal; miniatures; pottery; sculpture; tole painting; and woodworking. Emphasizes announcements of upcoming craft shows and sometimes workshops; classified advertising; features on craftworkers; technique articles and letters to the editor. Regular columns include Merit Awards, parchment certificates given readers for outstanding craftsmanship announced in the magazine; Calendar of Events; and Readers' Exchange, helps readers locate items they are having difficulty in obtaining (could be crafts, restoration, etc.).

FARMER COOPERATIVE INFORMATION, Rm. 1474, South Building, US Department of Agriculture, Washington DC 20250. Write for a list of their publications on starting a craft cooperative.

FIBERARTS, 3717 4th NW, Albuquerque NM 87107. (505)345-2530. Editor: Rob Pulleyn. Estab. 1975. Circ. 15,000. Bimonthly tabloid. Readers are seriously involved in fiber (weaving, dyeing, soft sculpture, stitchery, clothing, basketry, etc.) from amateurs to full time professionals. We try to give our readers a feeling for what others are doing; how to get more out of their own work; and give them ideas and information." Covers advanced weaving; batik; fibers; knotting; dyeing; soft sculpture; clothing; basketry; and stitchery. Emphasizes announcements of upcoming craft shows, shops/galleries needing crafts, and up coming workshops; classified advertising; features on craftworkers; health information; sophisticated technique articles; marketing articles; legal information; legislative news; and letters to the editor. Regular columns include Tips; Hangups, short articles with photos on recent shows and exhibitions; Gallery, short articles with photos on new or unique artists; and Book Review.

FINE WOODWORKING, The Taunton Press, Inc., 52 Church Hill Rd., Box 355, Newtown CT 06470. (203)426-8171. Editor: John Kelsey. Estab. 1975. Circ. 100,000. Bimonthly magazine; 84 pages. "Emphasizes design and shop technique in all areas of woodworking. Written and edited for the serious amateur craftsman, teachers, and professional cabinetmakers. Regular columns include letters; Methods of Work, brief tips on shop procedures; Questions/Answers, readers ask about cabinetmaking and finishing; Woodcraft Scene, success stories about woodworking businesses; Sources of Supply, where to find tools and materials; and book reviews." Also publishes *Biennial Design Book.* "We invite readers to send photos of their best work. We select and publish 600 photos with name and address of maker."

GEMS AND MINERALS, 1979 Capri Ave., Mentone CA 92359. (714)794-1173. Editor: Jack R.Cox. Estab. 1948. Circ. 40,000. Monthly magazine; 95 pages. Readers "are interested in jewelry making; rock collecting; lapidary; and rock hobby crafts. Articles are written to provide how-to projects; collecting areas; product reviews, etc." Emphasizes announcements of upcoming rock shows, upcoming workshops, and new galleries/shop; classified and display advertising; and how-to articles. Regular columns include Mineral Notes and News; Lapidary Tips; News Notes of Collecting Areas; What's New; and Coming Events.

THE GOODFELLOW CATALOG OF WONDERFUL THINGS, Box 4520, Berkeley CA 94704. (415)845-7645. Editor: Christopher Weills. Estab. 1974. Circ. 50,000. Paperback book/catalog; 418 pages. Readers are "both craftspeople and shoppers. We provide listings of crafts and the people who make them with photographs of each craft and the name, address, and philosophy of the craftsperson. Also included are lists of schools, craft organizations, craft-funding agencies and reference books of interest to folks engaged in producing and selling crafts."

THE GOODFELLOW REVIEW OF CRAFTS, Box 4520, Berkeley CA 94704. (415)845-7645. Editor: Christopher Weills. Estab. 1973. Circ. 10,000. Bimonthly publication. Readers are "active craftspeople, both professional and part time, as well as members of general public appreciative of American crafts." Covers all crafts, beginning to advanced. Emphasizes announcements of upcoming craft shows, shops/galleries needing crafts, upcoming workshops, personnel changes in the craft field, new galleries/shops; classified advertising; features on craftworkers; health information; technique; marketing; legal information; legislative news; and letters to the editor. Regular columns include informative columns of specific crafts; a calendar of events; book reviews; current craft news; several pages covering business aspects of crafts; and regular columnists.

GUILD OF BOOK WORKERS JOURNAL, 1059 3rd Ave., New York NY 10021. President: Mary C. Schlosser. Estab. 1962. Circ. 400. Magazine published 3 times yearly (no deadlines, dates vary); 36 pages. "Published as a service to members of the Guild of Book Workers. Individual subscriptions not available except to institutions (about 75 libraries subscribe). Reports on Guild activities; catalogs its exhibitions; solicits technical articles on hand binding and restoration; reprints articles of interest; and generally covers matters relating to the hand book crafts." Covers all levels of handbookbinding; restoration; calligraphy; and hand decorated papers. Emphasizes features on craftworkers; technique articles; reprints; and translations. Also publishes for members annual membership list; biannual supply list; quarterly newsletter; and booklet *Opportunities for Study in Hand Bookbinding and Calligraphy*, $1, available to public.

HANDWEAVING WITH ROBERT AND ROBERTA, Box 287, Center Sandwich NII 03227. (603)284-6915. Editor: Robert Ayotte. Estab. 1977. Published 4 times annually. 36 pages. A step by step home study course for beginning-average weavers interested in making progress. Emphasizes work assignments and weaving projects. Regular columns include Our Story, Question and Answer.

HOW TO MAKE MONEY WITH YOUR CRAFTS, William Morrow and Company, Inc., 105 Madison Ave., New York NY 10016. Author: Leta Clark. 240-page book on selling crafts. Deals with financing, bookkeeping, legal problems, advertising, mail order and other marketing subjects.

HOW TO SELL YOUR ART AND CRAFTS, Charles Scribner's Sons, 597 5th Ave., New York NY 10017. Author: Loretta Holz. 267-page book. Deals with ways to sell work and the advantages of each; legal obligations of partnerships; employer-employee arrangements; tax returns; handling public relations; and how to set up a business.

INTERWEAVE, 2938 N. Country Rd. 13, Loveland CO 60537. (303)667-7936. Editor: Linda C. Ligon. Estab. 1975. Circ. 5,000. Quarterly magazine. "*Interweave* is a general interest magazine for people in weaving and related fiber crafts. We try to strike a balance between features on individuals doing interesting work and informational articles on technique, history, and marketing. Articles for all levels of expertise." Includes announcements of upcoming craft shows and workshops; classified advertising; features on craftworkers; technique and marketing articles; legal information; and letters to the editor. Regular columns include In the Beginning, for the novice weaver; Home Brew, natural dyes; Coverlet Information, research on historical American coverlets; and regular features on handspinning. Also publishes annual *Spin-off* and a series entitled *A Portfolio of American Coverlets*.

LADY'S CIRCLE PATCHWORK QUILTS, 21 W. 26th St., New York NY 10010. (212)689-3933. Editorial Director: Ms. Carter G. Houck. Estab. 1973. Circ. 200,000. Quarterly magazine; 75 pages. Readers are "the growing number, women and men, who quilt for pleasure and/or profit, who show their work and who attend shows." Covers patchwork and applique. Emphasizes announcements of upcoming craft shows and shops/galleries needing crafts; classified advertising; features on craftworkers; technique articles; and full size patterns. Regular columns include Patchwork Book Roundup.

MAKE IT WITH LEATHER, Box 1386, Fort Worth TX 76101. (214)335-8500. Editor: Earl Warren. Estab. 1956. Circ. 55,000. Bimonthly magazine; 68 pages. "Readers are cross-section of all levels of education, income, and skills. 60% men and 40% women. Large number of young people below 17 years of age. Average subscriber is above average in dollar amount spent on craft supplies." Covers all levels of leatherworking. Emphasizes articles on technique; patterns; and feature articles on dyeing, tooling, pricing, and old patterns.

THE MALLET, National Carvers Museum, Woodcarver Park, Monument CO 80132. (303)481-2656. Editor: Pat Lind. Estab. 1976. Circ. 10,800. Monthly magazine. "Provides marketing; technique; hobby and educational material for woodcarvers." Covers all levels of sculpture; woodworking; carving; and whittling. Emphasizes classified advertising; features on craftworkers; technique and marketing articles; and letters to the editor.

MIDWEST ART FARE, 1056 56th, Des Moines IA 50311. (515)274-0675. Editor: Manfred Kiess. Estab. 1975. Circ. 300. Monthly newsletter; 5-6 legal size pages, average. "Our purpose is to provide artists and craftworkers with a marketplace for their work and also to report to them show information provided by field auditors." Covers all crafts; average to advanced. Emphasizes announcements of upcoming craft shows, shops/galleries needing crafts, upcoming workshops, and new galleries/shops; marketing articles; legislative news; and show critiques.

NATIONAL CALENDAR OF INDOOR/OUTDOOR ART FAIRS, 5423 New Haven Ave., Fort Wayne IN 46803. Editor: Henry Niles. Estab. 1969. Quarterly show listing; 32-48 pages (summer issues larger). "Entry and contact information for participation in art/craft shows. Benefiting many persons in making a living; providing info for the hobbyist to sell and display their creations." Emphasizes announcements of upcoming art/craft shows.

NATIONAL CALENDAR OF OPEN COMPETITIVE ART EXHIBITIONS, 5423 New Haven Ave., Fort Wayne IN 46803. Editor: Henry Niles. Estab. 1970. Quarterly show listing. "Directed to the professional/advanced artist and craftsperson. Museum and gallery type shows for those persons wanting recognition and competing for awards and prize money."

NATIONAL CARVERS REVIEW, Drawer 693, Chicago IL 60642. Editor: Lawrence F. Martin. Estab. 1970. Circ. 12,000. Quarterly magazine; 44 pages. Readers are woodcarvers ranging from the beginner to the master. Emphasizes announcements of upcoming craft shows and workshops, personnel changes in the craft field, and new galleries/shops; classified advertising; features on craftworkers; health information; technique articles; letters to the editor; book reviews; product evaluation; and patterns.

THE NATIONAL DIRECTORY OF GRANTS AND AID TO INDIVIDUALS IN THE ARTS, Washington International Arts Letter, Box 9005, Washington DC 20003. Annual directory listing most grants, prizes and awards for professional work in the US and abroad, and information about universities and schools that offer special aid to students.

NATIONAL GUIDE TO CRAFT SUPPLIES, Van Nostrand Reinhold, 450 W. 33rd St., New York NY 10001. Author: Judith Glassman. Lists more than 600 sources of craft supplies and more than 600 additional listings for craft bookstores, societies and organizations, galleries and museums, places of instruction, fairs and publications.

NATIONAL NEEDLEWORK NEWS, 171 Guadalupe Dr., Sonoma CA 90476. Publisher: Sherry Baker. Estab. 1975. Circ. 10,865. Quarterly newspaper; 11-20 pages. Readers are needlework shop owners and buyers; buyers and managers of needlepoint departments of major stores; fabric and yarn shops; craft shops; and consumers interested in needlework. "Provides hint for running successful shops and needlework technique." Covers almost exclusively needlework but some dollmaking, fibers, and macrame; all levels. Emphasizes announcements of upcoming needlework shows and workshops, and personnel changes in the needlework field; classified advertising; features on needlework designers, shops, and teachers; and technique articles. Regular columns include Designer's Gallery; Shop Talk, pictures and stories on successful shop operations; Book Marks; Stitch Wizardry, patterns with biographies of designers; Original Knits; and Creative People.

NEEDLE ARTS, 6 E. 45th St., 15th Flr., New York NY 10017. (212)986-0460. Executive Editor: Judith Leibman. Estab. 1970. Circ. 16,000. Quarterly magazine; 32 pages. "Published by Embroiderers' Guild of America, Inc. Subscriptions to members only but membership open to anyone. Educational organization to promote the design, execution, and appreciation of the art of embroidery." Covers all levels of fibers. Emphasizes announcements of upcoming craft shows and workshops; classified advertising; features on craftworkers; techniques articles; and information on collections and historical items.

NEEDLEPOINT BULLETIN, 50 S. US 1, Suite 200, Jupiter FL 33458. Editor: Sharlene Weldon Krenkel. Estab. 1974. International circulation. Bimonthly newsletter; 32 pages. "*Needlepoint Bulletins* is for all those who needlepoint from the beginner to the advanced and the professional. Pertinent, relevant text. A source of information for those who needlepoint and for those who want to needlepoint but don't know how to go about it or even where to get supplies or help." Emphasizes announcements of upcoming needlepoint shows, shops/galleries needing crafts, upcoming workshops, personnel changes in the craft field, and new galleries/shops; features on needleworkers; technique and marketing articles; legal information; legislative news; and newsworthy items affecting needlepoint. Regular columns include Bookshelf and Where To Buy Needlepoint Supplies By Mail. Also publishes information sheets available to subscribers at no charge.

NEWSLETTER, League of New Hampshire Craftsmen, 205 N. Main St., Concord NH 03301. Editor: Robert Miner. Estab. 1934. Circ. 5,000. Bimonthly newsletter; 8 pages. Readers are members of the League of New Hampshire Craftsmen. Covers all crafts; all levels. Emphasizes announcements of upcoming craft shows, shops/galleries needing crafts, upcoming workshops, personnel changes in the craft field and new galleries/shops; features on craftworkers; health information; legal information; legislative news; and letters to the editor.

OCULAR, 1549 Platte St., Denver CO 80202. (303)458-6064. Editor: Eric Schwartz. Estab. 1976. Circ. 2,000. Quarterly magazine; 88 pages. Readers are visual artists in all media. "Provides opportunities and information for the visual artist. Covers all visual arts. Emphasizes announcements of upcoming craft shows and workshops; health information; marketing articles; legal information; and legislative news. Regular columns include Art Hazards News; Legal Byline; Grants and Fellowships; Employment Opportunities; Competitions; Exhibits; and Workshops.

OPENING YOUR OWN RETAIL STORE, Henry Regnery Co., 180 N. Michigan Ave., Chicago IL 60601. Author: Lyn Taetzsch. Discusses what kind of a store you should open; legal and capital requirements; packaging; sales slip; financial backing and other aspects of retail sales.

THE ORIGINAL ART REPORT, Box 1641 Chicago IL 60690. Editor: F. Salantrie. Estab. 1967. Monthly newsletter. Readers are art critics, museum trustees, collectors, artists, craftworkers and gallery owners. Covers all crafts. Emphasizes legislative news and commentary and news of the art condition.

THE OZARKS MOUNTAINEER, Star Rt. 3, Branson MO 65616. (417)546-5390. Editor: Clay M. Anderson. Estab. 1952. Circ. 26,000. Monthly (except January) magazine; 42 pages. "Dedicated to the advancement of the Ozark region, covering a variety of subjects. One of the more important is the tradition and revival of crafts." Covers candlemaking; dollmaking; fibers; leather; pottery; sculpture; woodworking; and traditional crafts such as basketry, soap making and natural dyes. Emphasizes announcements of upcoming craft shows and workshops; classified advertising; features on craftworkers; technique articles; and letters to the editor. Regular columns include Ozark Arts and Crafts and Bookshelf.

PHOTOGRAPHING CRAFTS, American Crafts Council, 44 W. 53rd St., New York NY 10019. 66-page book. Deals with photographing your work to its best advantage.

PHOTOGRAPHY FOR ARTISTS AND CRAFTSMEN, Van Nostrand Reinhold Co., 450 W. 33rd St., New York NY 10001. Author: Claus-Peter Schmid. Deals with amateur photography pertaining specifically to craftworkers who want to photograph their work.

REGIONAL ART FAIR LIST, Rt. 1, Box 136, Stockholm WI 54769. Editor: Nelson Brown. Estab. 1972. Circ. 500-700. Quarterly newsletter; 2-8 pages. "Readers are artists, craftworkers, art councils, schools, libraries, fair committees, and art patrons that are interested in the date, location, and basic information about a fair. Speculation (rating) helps determine a choice as to whether or not to attend. Also mentions pertinent books and periodicals and addresses that expand the possibilities of market for these people." Covers all crafts. Emphasizes announcements of upcoming craft shows, shops/galleries needing crafts, and upcoming workshops; limited classified advertising; reviews; brief comments about fairs; and pertinent suggestions.

THE RUG HOOKER, News and Views, North St., Kennebunkport ME 04046. (207)967-3711. Editor: Joan Leith Moshimer. Estab. 1972. Circ. 5,000. Bimonthly magazine; 28 pages. "This is the only magazine directed at the early American craft of rug-hooking (as opposed to punch and latchet) in which cut strips of wool flannel are used. Many rug-hookers wishing to design their own, or dye their own wool, find practical, down-to-earth help in *The Rug Hooker.* We also publish news and pictures of exhibits, rug-camps, guilds, etc. Free designs in every issue." Covers traditional rug-hooking, including dyeing of the wool; beginner to advanced. Emphasizes announcements of upcoming craft shows and workshops, and new galleries/shops; classified advertising; features on craftworkers; technique articles; and letters to the editor. Regular columns include Swatch Gossip, tips and amusing anecdotes; Editorial; Quotes and Questions; Memo from Maggie; From Our Mailbag, photos; Cook's Corner; and Ask Anne, dye problems. Also publishes manuals. SASE. Free sample copy.

SHELBURNE SPINNERS NEWSLETTER, 2 Howard St., Burlington VT 05401. (802)862-7107. Editor: John Ennis. Estab. 1977. Circ. 2,000. Bimonthly newsletter; 4-6 pages. "Our readers are interested in wool, spinning, and natural dyeing. We provide them with background information on sheep and the making of wool into yarn. Also events at Shelburne Spinners and new products." Covers fibers; all levels. Emphasizes announcements of upcoming craft shows and workshops; features on craftworkers; technique articles; and informative articles about wool, spinning and dyeing.

SHUTTLE, SPINDLE, AND DYEPOT, 65 La Salle Rd., Box 7-374, West Hartford CT 06107. (203)233-5124. Editor: Kevin Chase. Estab. 1969. Circ. 20,000. Quarterly magazine; 107 pages. Readers are primarily handweavers, spinners, and dyers. "Provides beginning, intermediate, and advanced how-to's; histories; profiles; show information; properties of fibers; marketing of fiber art; guild news; and scholarship awards. Published by the Handweavers Guild of America." Emphasizes announcements of upcoming craft shows, workshops, and personnel changes in the craft field; classified advertising; features on craftworkers; health information; technique and marketing articles; legal information; legislative news; and letters to the editor. Regular columns include Calendar; Bookshelf; Test and Report; and Volunteer Activities. Also publishes *Education Directory* and *Suppliers Directory.*

SOUTHERN CRAFTS AND ART NEWS, Box 446, Greenville Hwy., Flat Rock NC 28731. (704)693-4570. Editor: Jack Day. Estab. 1972. Circ. 350. Bimonthly magazine; 48 pages. Readers are primarily professional crafts and art exhibitors. "Provides a very thorough listing of shows." Covers all crafts; average. Emphasizes announcements of upcoming craft shows and shops/galleries needing crafts; features on craftworkers; marketing articles; and letters to the editor.

STAINED GLASS, 753 Hawthorne Dr., Valparaiso IN 46383. (219)462-8177. Editor: Norman Temme. Estab. 1906. Circ. 4,500. Quarterly magazine; 76-84 pages. Readers are members; architects; libraries; educators; craftworkers; hobbyists; and small shop/studio owners in the stained glass craft. It is the publication of the Stained Glass Association of America. Emphasizes announcements of upcoming craft shows, shops/galleries needing crafts; upcoming workshops; personnel changes in the craft field, and new galleries/shops; classified advertising; features on craftworkers; health information; technique and marketing articles; legal information; legislative news; letters to the editor; new briefs; and obits. Regular columns include Focus on Yesteryears; Names in the News; Browzing in the Books; Mining the Magazines; The Editor's Page; The Reader's Page; Sources of Supply; Stained Glass Mart; and SGAA at Hoosuck Training Programs.

STRAW INTO GOLD NEWSLETTER, 5533 College Ave., Oakland CA 94618. (415)652-SPIN. Editor: Susan C. Druding. Estab. 1977. Circ. 4,000. Quarterly newsletter/tabloid; 16-32 pages. "Provides news of textile events; reviews; technical information; classes offered; and classifieds. Covers average batik; fibers; weaving; spinning; and dyeing. Emphasizes announcements of upcoming craft shows, shops/galleries needing crafts, upcoming workshops, and new galleries/shops; classified advertising; features on craftworkers; health information and safety; technique articles; and letters to the editor. Regular columns include special programs in textiles; textile book reviews; and a technical column. Also publishes books on spinning.

SUNSHINE ARTISTS, USA, Box 426, Fern Park FL 32730. (301)645-3155, no collect calls. Editor: Joan L. Wahl. Estab. 1972. Circ. 15,312. Monthly magazine; 68 pages. "We do provide the largest art and craft show list in the country along with show reports and reports regarding state markets for all 50 states plus Canada." Covers all crafts. Emphasizes announcements of 700-900 upcoming craft shows each month, shops/galleries needing crafts, and new galleries/shops; classified advertising; features on craftworkers; health information; marketing articles; legal information; legislative news; letters to the editor; and articles on how to display, merchandise, prepare work for sale including costing and pricing. Regular columns include 2-3 editorials; 20-25 state reports; 2 craft columns; a show review column; a market philosophy column plus incidental health columns.

SURFACE DESIGN JOURNAL, 25879 Center School Rd., Halsey OR 97348. (503)466-5991. Editor: Stephen Blumrich. Estab. 1976. Circ. 750. Quarterly magazine; 32 pages. Readers are students; educators; designers; artist/craftworkers involved in surface design techniques, on pre-woven fabrics. Batik; screen-printing; tie-dye; photo techniques; etc. Emphasizes announcements of upcoming craft shows, shops/galleries needing crafts, upcoming workshops, and personnel changes in the craft field; classified advertising; features on craftworkers; health information; articles on technique and marketing; legal information; legislative news; letters to the editor; news on membersip activities; book reviews; and display advertising. Regular columns include safety; regional reports; and 2 editorials.

U.S. SMALL BUSINESS ADMINISTRATION, Rm. 3100, 26 Federal Plaza, New York NY 10007. Write for a full list of their publications on management assistance.

WASHINGTON INTERNATIONAL ARTS LETTER, Box 9055, Washington DC 20003. (202)488-0800. Editor: Daniel Millsaps. Estab. 1962. Circ. 15,000+. Monthly (except July and December) newsletter. "Financial information for all arts. Sources of grants and new developments in patronage patterns." Covers all advanced crafts.

THE WEAVER'S JOURNAL, 1900 55th St., Boulder CO 80301. (303)449-1170. Editor: Clotilde Barrett. Estab. 1976. Circ. 2,500. Quarterly magazine; 48 pages. "Our readers are fiber craftworkers of varied abilities. We give them clear how-to articles on weaving, dyeing and spinning to stimulate them to try new things and to explore traditional weaves more thoroughly. We include ethnic weaving, construction of useful tools, and ways of finishing woven articles. Each issue includes a project for nonloom weavers. Our magazine is a technical magazine for fiber craftworkers and handweavers." Regular columns include book reviews.

WEAVER'S NEWSLETTER, Box 259, Homer NY 13077. Editors: Cyril and Ora Koch. Estab. 1976. Circ. 5,300. Monthly (September-May) newsletter; 8 pages. Readers are average-advanced weavers; spinners; and fiber artists. "Provides news of trends in the field; notices of exhibits and competitions; major commissions; guild events; marketing information; legislation; and government activities; research; equipment; and book reviews." Emphasizes announcements of upcoming craft shows and workshops; display and classified advertising; features on craftworkers; health information; legislative news; and letters to the editor. Regular columns include Book Review and The Weaving Experience.

WESTART, Box 1396, Auburn CA 95603. (916)885-3242, 855-0969. Editor: Jean L. Couzens. Estab. 1962. Circ. 7,700+. Semimonthly publication. Readers are artists; artist/craftsmen; teachers; students; and patrons of the arts. "We provide an overview of the West Coast art scene — current art news; information on competitions; and some features." Covers all crafts; beginning to advanced. Emphasizes announcements of upcoming craft shows, occasionally shops/galleries needing crafts, upcoming workshops as space permits, and new galleries/shops; classified advertising; occasional features on craftworkers; some health information; some legal information and legislative news; and letters to the editor. "Our treatment of crafts is usually from a general view point and we only use features of exceptional interest."

WOMEN ARTISTS NEWSLETTER, Box 3304, Grand Central Station, New York NY 10017. (212)666-6990. Editor: Cynthia Navaretta. Estab. 1975. Circ. 3,500. Monthly newsletter; 12 pages. Readers are teachers, historians, art writers and arts/craftswomen. "Our focus is on women in the visual arts — articles, news, and current information." Covers all advanced crafts. Emphasizes announcements of upcoming craft shows, shops/galleries needing crafts, and upcoming workshops; classified advertising; features on craftworkers; technique articles; legal information; legislative news; and letters to the editor.

WOOL GATHERING, Babcock WI 54413. Editor: Elizabeth Zimmerman. Estab. 1969. Circ. 800. Semiannual (March and September) newsletter; 8 pages. Readers are all handknitters. Provides 1-3 original designs (all levels) in every issue along with news on knitting books; materials; tools; and techniques. Most designs are for circular needles. Back issues indefinitely available.

THE WORKING CRAFTSMAN, Box 42, 1290 Shermer, Northbrook IL 60062. (312)498-0073. Editor: Marilyn Heise. Estab. 1971. Circ. 10,000. Quarterly magazine; 44 pages. Readers are professional and part time craftworkers; art and craft teachers; craft shop owners; suppliers; and others seriously involved in crafts. Covers all crafts; beginning to advanced. Emphasizes announcements of upcoming craft shows, shops/galleries needing crafts, upcoming workshops, personnel changes in the craft field, and new galleries/shops; classified advertising; features on craftworkers; health information; marketing articles; legal information; legislative news; letters to the editor; and book reviews. Regular columns include A Professional Sounds Off; Fair Share; and Hazards in the Arts. Also publishes annual *Source Directory.*

Glossary

AA. Associate of Arts degree.

Artists-in-Schools Program. Funded by the National Endowment for the Arts and administered by individual states, the program offers visual and performing artists salaried residencies at colleges and universities.

Biennial. Every 2 years.

Bimonthly. Every 2 months.

Biweekly. Every 2 weeks.

Commission. Percentage of retail price taken by a sponsor/salesperson (go-between) on work sold.

Consignment. Arrangement by which the craftworker leaves his work with a retailer and does not get paid for the work until it is sold. A commission is almost always charged for this service.

Exclusive Representation. Requirement that a craftworker's work appear in only one gallery/shop within a defined geographical area.

Finished Crafts. Those works made by a designer-craftworker who has total control over design and styling and has complete creative involvement. Means of production varies from handmade to the use of power tools. These crafts are of the highest quality.

First Rights. The craftworker gives the purchaser permission to reproduce a work once in a copyrighted medium, and the craftworker agrees not to permit additional publication of the work elsewhere for a specified amount of time.

One-time Rights. The craftworker sells the rights to use his/her work 1 time in any copyrighted medium. The rights transfer back to the craftworker on his/her request after the work's use.

Photocopy. Inexpensive and commonly used photographic reproduction process.

Prejudging. Process by which a committee or designated individual reviews one's work prior to acceptance.

Primitive Crafts. Those works made usually by an artisan (a person who rarely has creative input into the production of a work). This individual usually has some home training in a traditional manner or may be self-taught. The work is produced by hand-powered tools and techniques or is created by hand. Several individuals may be involved in producing 1 product. We commonly refer to these crafts as folk or traditional crafts.

Purchase Prize. Awarded for an entry which has been purchased by the sponsor of a competition.

Repousse. Technique by which craftworkers can work in relief in metal.

Retail Price. Amount of money charged to the ultimate consumer by the retailer.

Retailer. Person or outlet that sells goods to the ultimate consumer. Retailers in this book include shops, galleries, museums and department stores.

Royalty. An agreed percentage paid by the salesperson to the craftworker for each copy of his/her work sold.

Semiannual. Two times each year.

Semimonthly. Two times monthly.

Simultaneous Submissions. Submissions of the same work to more than 1 potential buyer at the same time.

Wholesaler. Person or outlet who sells work in large amounts to retailers or jobbers rather than directly to consumers.

Index

A &A Trophy Manufacturers 53
Abacus Gallery 135
Abbey School of Jewelry and Design 532
Academy of the Arts 362
Acadian Crafts Association 135, 485
Acadiana Arts Council 484
Acorn 171
Act I, Gallery 210
ADA Gifts and Crafts 220
Adamy's Plastics and Mold-Making 533
Added Touch, The 81
ADI (Ashworth Designs, Inc.) 42
ADI Gallery 81
Adirondack Lakes Center for the Arts 533
Adrian College 44
Adventures in Crafts 533
Adventures in Crafts Decoupage Sales and Exhibit 394
Advocates for the Arts 478
After the Gold Rush 81
Agricultural Heritage Museum 241
Akron Society of Artists (see Boston Mills Invitational Art Festival 411)
Akron University 541
Alabama Assembly of Community Arts Councils 476
Alabama State Council on the Arts 476
Alabama-Coushatta Indian Arts & Crafts 246
Alameda County Fair 294

Alaska Ceramic Supply, Inc. 74
Alaska Native Arts & Crafts 74
Albair, Steve 472
Albany Arts Festival 332
Albany Holiday Market 417
Albany League of Arts, Inc. 491
Albany Park Arts and Crafts Fair 336
Albany Spring Arts Festival 418
Albany Winter Carnival, Invitation Crafts Show 394
Albatross Gallery 98
Albion College 525
Alderson-Broaddus College Arts & Crafts Fair 451
Alena Jewelers-Designers 102
Aletta 472
Alexandria Bicentennial Museum Shop 258
Algonac Art Fair 371
Algonac Sponsors of the Arts 486
Ali Baba 145
All American Indian Days Arts and Crafts Show 461
All Arts Festival 367
All By Hand 188
All Crafts Fair 371
Allard's Flathead Indian Trading Post, Doug 168
Allegany Indian Arts and Crafts Co-op 491
Allentown Outdoor Art Festival 394
Alliance Museum Shop, The 123

Allied Artists of America Exhibition 395

Allied Arts Street Fair 449

Alnico Gallery 188

Alonzo Gallery, Inc. 188

Alpha Double Plus 261

Alrod Enterprises 133

Altamonte Mall 319

Alumnae Arts and Crafts Show of Rosary High School 336

American Artist 555

American Artists and Artisans 336

American Celebration, An 346

American Concern for Artistry and Craftsmanship (see Festival of American Craftsmanship 397)

American Council for the Arts 491

American Craft Enterprises, Inc. (see Pacific States Crafts Fair 303, Winter Market of American Crafts 367, Northeast Craft Fair 401)

American Crafts Council 491

American Crafts Expositions 68 (also see Farmington Crafts Expo 313)

American Fairs, Inc. 68

American Folk Arts Festival 294

American Folklife Center 503

American Indian Art Magazine 555

American International College 44

American Miniatures 53

American Scandinavian Foundation 491

American Society of Artists, Inc. 68, 114, 482 (also see 336, 337, 339, 341, 342, 345, 346)

Americana Day Celebration 436

Amish Farm Market 115

Anacortes Arts and Crafts Festival 449

Ancient Art Updated, An 294

Anderson County Arts Council 240, 449 (also see Arts in the Park 430)

Anderson Gallery 258

Andersonville Festival Art Fair 336

Androgyny Crafts Gallery 226

Angeles Arts in Action 449

Angelique Jewelry 54

Ann Arbor Art Associaton (see Holiday Gift Show 373)

Ann Arbor Street Art Fair, The 372

Ann Arbor Winter Art Fair 372

Annapolis Arts Festival 362

Antelope Valley Arts Council 478

Antioch 45

Antique, Quilt & Craft Show 417

Antique Show and Collectors Flea Market 381

Antiques and Uniques Festival 444

Apollos Art 130

Appalachia: American Mountain Crafts and Culture 81

Appalachian Arts and Crafts Festival 451

Appalachian Festival 40

Appalachian House 102

Appalachian State University 540

Appalachiana 141

Appalshop Inc. 484

Apple Basket, The 220

Apple Blossom Art & Crafts Fair 54

Apple Blossom Festival Arts and Crafts Fair 449

Apple Harvest Arts & Crafts Festival 445

Apple Harvest Festival 419

Johnny Appleseed Day 301

April Arts and Crafts Fair 436

Arabia's Art Gallery 267

Arabis, Contemporary American Design 145

Arachne 214

Arc en Ciel 533

Arc en Ciel Stained Glass 189

Arcosanti 507

Arcosanti Festival 289

Area Artists Annual 410

Argyle Craft Gallery, The 102

Arizona Commission On The Arts and Humanities 477

Arkansas Arts Center, The 508 (also see Delta Art Exhibition 291, Prints, Drawings & Crafts Exhibition 293, Toys Designed by Artists Exhibition 293)

Arkansas Arts Center Art Rental-Purchase Gallery 78

Arkansas River Valley Arts & Crafts Fair & Sale 290

Arkansas State Arts and Humanities 478

Arkwright and His Friends, The 115

Armstrong County League of Arts 498

Army Arts and Crafts Program, HQDA (DAAG-MSA) 503

"Around The Table" 381

Arrowcraft Shop and Gallery 243

Arrowmont School of Arts and Crafts, The 546

Art Affaire, The (see Mud in Your Eye Pottery Studio 90)

Art and Craft Expo 410

Art and Flower Festival 372
Art Association of Columbus (see Calico Fair 380)
Art Barn, The 269
Art Center 270
Art Center Association 484
Art Center Museum Shop 123
Art Center, The 246
Art Centre of New Jersey, The 388
Art Crate, Inc. 270
Art-Design-Craft Center 246
Art Education 555
Art Enterprise 68 (also see Down Town Fulton Show 297, Down Town Novato Center 298, Santa Cruz County Fair 306, Sonoma County 306)
Art Fair 455
Art Fair USA 455
Art Festival in the Village, The 319
Art For Fun(d)'s Sake Craft Fair 294
Art Gallery, The 168
Art Glass Alcove, The 154
Art Guild Burlington, Inc. (see Snake Alley Art Fair 355)
Art in All Media 295
Art in Architecture 508
Art in Park (New York) 395
Art in the Park (Clarinda, Iowa) 353
Art in The Park (Clinton, Iowa) 353
Art in the Park (Kansas 355)
Art in the Park (Mississippi) 379
Art in the Park (Ohio) 410
Art Independent Gallery 270
Art Information Center, Inc. 492
Art Institute At The Depot 487
Art Institute of Boston, The 523
Art Jamboree 436
Art League of Northern Virginia 549
Art Lease and Sales Gallery 173
Art Letter 555
Art Merchant, The 223
Art of Winning Foundation Grants, The 555
"Art On The Green" 335
Art-On-The-Lake Show 284
Art On The Rockes 284
Art Palette, The 267
Art Sales and Rental Society 276
Art Shop & Studio of J. Van Huesen, The 74
Art Shows by Murray 68

Art Studios, The 515
Art Unlimited 168
Artarama 455
Art-Craft Associates 68
Artesans Gallery 226
Artesian Well, The 470
Arthritis Art Committee 361
Artifactrie, The 81
Artifacts Galleries, Ltd. 168
Artisan Fair, Boston Mills 410
Artisan House 189
Artisan Shop and Gallery 115
Artisan, The 189
Artisans' Alley, Inc. 82
Artisan's Cooperative (Boston) 145
Artisan's Cooperative (Nantucket Island, Massachusetts) 145
Artisan's Cooperative (Chads Ford, Pennsylvania) 227
Artisans Cooperative (Philadelphia) 227
Artisans Gallery (Michigan) 154
Artisan's Gallery, The (New Jersey) 173
Artisan's Studio 276
Artisan's Workshop 171
Artist and Craftsmen's Guild of Jackson 500
Artist and Handcrafter Information Service 556
Artist Exhibition and Registry Series 115
Artist-Craftsmen School and Gallery 533
Artists Access Library 270
Artists Alpine Holiday 309
Artists & Artisans at Work 336
Artists & Craftspeople Directory, The 556
Artists Co-op 68
Artists' Co-op Gallery 180
Artists Equity Association 504
Artists Equity News 556
Artists in Wood 115
Artists' Market 103
Artists' Workshop 554
Artpark Store 186
Arts Alive Festival 405
Arts & Activities 464
Arts and Crafts Bazaar 336
Arts & Crafts by the Handicapped 455
Arts and Crafts Fair (Arkansas) 291
Arts & Crafts Fair (Connecticut) 311
Arts and Crafts Fair (Kansas) 355
Arts and Crafts Fair (Texas) 436
Arts & Crafts Fair (Wisconsin) 455

Arts & Crafts Fair of the Southwest 393
Arts & Crafts Fall Festival Show & Sale 381
Arts & Crafts Festival (Connecticut) 311
Arts & Crafts Festival (Florida) 319
Arts and Crafts Festival (Kentucky) 357
Arts & Crafts Festival (Minnesota) 378
Arts & Crafts Festival (Texas) 436
Arts & Crafts Festival of Southeastern North Carolina 405
Arts and Crafts; Fine Arts; Hobby Crafts; Country Crafts 411
Arts and Crafts in Action 337
Arts & Crafts in the Park 347
Arts and Crafts Market 455
Arts & Crafts Mart 432
Arts and Crafts Show (Iowa) 353
Arts & Crafts Show (Tennessee) 432
Arts & Craft Show & Sale 432
Arts Association of Alamance County, The 495
Arts Community Association of Arizona 477
Arts Council of Bakersfield 478
Arts Council of Fayetteville 495 (also see Sunday on the Square 407)
Arts Council of Oklahoma City 497
Arts Council of Spartanburg County, Inc. 499
Arts Council of the Mid-Columbia Region 503
Arts Council of Wilson, Inc. 210
Arts Council of Windham County 501
Arts Development Services, Inc. 492
Arts Festival 319
Arts Festival At The Laundry 337
Arts Festival of Atlanta 332
Arts in Action 437
Arts in the Park (South Carolina) 430
Arts in the Park (Virginia) 445
Arts International Ltd. 115
Arts Journal, The 556
Arts Management 556
Arts 'n Crafts by the Sea 295
Arts/Objects 141
Arts Potpourri in the Park 319
Arts Unlimited 69
Arts Workshop at the Newark Museum 531
ArtsAffair 411
Artspace, Ltd. 270
Artweek 464, 556

Artworks 189
Artworks, Inc. 270
Artworks, The 74
Asbury College 521
Asheville Art Museum Learning Center 540
Ashkar, Faris Abdullah 472
ASID International Exposition of Designer Sources 395
Association of Artists & Craftsmen of Porter County 347
Association of Community Arts Council of Kansas 483
Astabula Arts Center 215
Atchafalaya Crafters (see Shrimp & Petroleum Craft Show 360)
Atlantic Christian College 540
Atlantic City Art Center (see Indian Summer Art Show 390)
Atmore Council of Fine Arts 476
Auburn University Department of Consumer Affairs 506
Augusta Heritage Arts Workshop 552
Austin State University, Stephen F. 45, 546
Autumn Art Festival 395
Autumn Leaves 111
Autumn Leaves Festival 405
Auxiliary to the Art Museum of South Texas, The (see Art Jamboree 436)
Avantaos 180
Averett College 45
Ayn's Shuttle Shop 145
Ayottes' Designery 171

B aldwin Artist's Showplace, Betty 69
Baldwin Pottery, Inc. 189
Baltimore Museum of Art 141
Baltimore Winter Market (see Winter Market of American Crafts 367)
Banana Box at Ybor Square, The 108
Banff Centre, The 277
Barclay Gallery 112
Bare Wall Gallery 227
Barron Fibre Creations, Barbara 190
Barry's: A Unique Alternative 163
Barry's Originals 129
Bartel Interior Design 82
Barter Day 380
Bates & Son, C.J. 54
Batesville Annual Art Mart 380
Baulines Craftsman's Guild 508

Bay Area Art Association (see Waterfront Art Fair 377)
Bay Studio Crafts 135
Baylor, Mary Hardin 546
Bayly Museum Shop, University of Virginia 258
Bazaar Del Mundo Gallery 82
B.C. and Western Craft Shows 69
Bea Hive, The 173
Beadery, The 54
Bearpaw Leather Shop 173
Beautiful Things (Scotch Plains, New Jersey) 173
Beautiful Things (Summit, New Jersey) 174
Beautiful Woods, Inc. 190
Beaux Arts Festival of Art 320
Beaux Arts Gift Shop of Fresno Arts Center 82
Beckerhoff in Stowe, Ltd. 252
Becky's Country Nook 141
Bedford/Downing Glass 190
Bee Skep, The 190
Bella Vista Arts & Crafts Festival 291
Bellardo Ltd. 190
Belle of the Bend 353
Belleville Area College 517
Bellfort Frame and Art Center 246
Beloit & Vicinity Exhibition 456
Benchmark Gallery 131
Bencsik Gallery 266
Bennett Folk Festival, Sue 357
Bennett Spring Hillbilly Days 382
Bennington Christmas Craft Show, The 444
Bennington College 45, 548
Benson Gallery 190
Benton County Arts & Crafts Show 433
Berea College (see Log House Sales Room 132)
Bergen, Wesley 191
Bergstrom Art Center (see The Bergstrom Museum Shop 270)
Bergstrom Museum Shop, The 270
Berkshire Crafts Fair, The 367
Bernat & Sons Co., Emile 54
Bernier Studio 171
Berry College 45, 516
Berry Patch Arts and Craft Festival, The 333
Bersted's Hobby Craft Inc. 54
Beverly Hills Affaire in the Gardens Art Show 295
BGI Crafts International 55

Big Anvil Forge School of Blacksmithing 528
Big Bend Community College 550
Big Thicket Museum 246
Bindery, The (Los Angeles) 508
Bindery, The (Connecticut) 514
Bird, Animal, Wild Flowers and Decoy Show 362
Bird in the Hand, Inc. 227
Bishop Museum 113
Bishop Museum, Bernice P. 517
Bits & Pieces, Inc. 163
Bitterroot Pottery 169
Bittersweet Farm 65
Black Diamond Woodworks 527
Black Expo & Bazaar 312
Black Eyed Pea Jamboree Arts and Crafts Show 437
Black Fox Festival (see Pikeville Arts & Crafts Show 435)
Black Hawk College 517
Black Hills State College 545
Black Sheep Newsletter 556
Black's Art Glass Studio 247
Blackhawk Indian Valley Arts and Crafts Show 456
Blackston Chamber of Commerce Annual Arts & Crafts Festival 445
Blair Galleries Ltd. 180
Blanchet School 521
Blount County Arts & Crafts Guild (see Midland Center Arts and Crafts Festival 434)
Blown Glass II 337
Blue Door Gallery/Gift Shop 180
Blue Duck, The 275
Blue Grass Art and Hobby Center 126
Blue Ridge Hearthside Crafts 210
Blue Sky Gallery, The 227
Boardwalk Art and Craft Show 445
Bodycraft Galleries 210
Bogalusa Chamber of Commerce Arts, Crafts, & Antique Mart 358
Boin Arts and Crafts Company 531
Boise Gallery of Art 114
Bond's Alley Art and Craft Fair 437
Bonneville Gallery 261
Borger Fine Arts Festival 437
Bosque County Run 437
Boston Area Spinners and Dyers 485
Boston Athenaeum Gallery 145
Boston Baked Beads 145

Boston Center for Adult Education 523
Boston Mills Invitational Art Festival 411
Boston University 523
Bounty Shop 108
Boutz Family Glassblowers 243
Bowling Green State University 541
Boynton Beach Annual Festival of the Arts 320
Bradford College 45, 523
Bradley University 517
Brandywine Arts Festival 318
Braxton County Arts and Crafts Show 452
Brecksville Fine Arts Council 496
Brentwood Commons Art and Craft Festival 337
Brevard Mall Festival of Arts & Crafts 320
Bridgton Art Show 361
Briggs Silversmithing and Jewelry, Nancy 533
Brigham City Museum-Gallery 252
Bristol Mum Festival Art Show 312
Bristol Women's College Club Craft Fair 312
British Columbia Forest Museum 277
Brockman Gallery Christmas Crafts Show 295
Brockman Gallery Productions 82
Brody Miniatures, Molly 103
Brook High School Arts & Crafts Festival, The 284
Brook Things Unlimited, Allen 191
Brookfield Craft Center, Inc. 514
Brookings Summer Folk Arts Festival 431
Brookline Art Society (see Fall Arts and Crafts Market 368)
Brookline Arts Center 523
Brooklyn Artists Annual Rose Festival, Fine Arts and Crafts Show and Sale 372
Brooklyn Center Community Center 159
Brooklyn Museum Art School, The 533
Brookneal Department Store 62
Brooks Memorial Art Gallery (see Mississippi River Craft Show 434)
Brotman Forge, The 530
Broussard Memorial Galleries, Jay R. (see Louisiana State Art Exhibition for Professional Artists 359)
Brown Studio, Ken 55
"B. Rugged" 189, 533
Brunswick Craft League 522
Bryant College 45
Buckroe Beach Art Show 446

Bucks County Guild of Craftsmen 498
Buffalo Gap Art Festival 437
Burgett's Myrtlewood Shops 223
Burien Arts Gallery 262
Burke Arts Council 495
Burlington County Cultural and Heritage Commission 490
Burlington Mall Children's Hour Show 367
Burlington Mall Professional Craft and Sculpture Show 367
Bush Foundation Fellowship for Artists 487
Bushwhacker Arts & Crafts Festival 382
Busyhaus/Papermaking Workshops 522
Butler Institute of American Art (see Ceramic, Sculpture and Craft Show 412)
Butterfly, The 240
By Hand — A Gallery of Mind Over Metal 124
By Hand Fine Craft Gallery 174

C abarrus County Agricultural Fair Arts & Crafts Show 405
Cabin Craft Shoppes 271
Cabin Creek Quilts (New Jersey) 197
Cabin Creek Quilts (Cabin Creek, West Virginia) 267
Cabin Creek Quilts (Charleston, West Virginia) 268
Cabin Creek Quilts Cooperative 504
Cable Cookhouse 277
Cakewalk: A Handworks Gallery 135
Calendar of Summer Arts Fairs 556
Calico Art Festival 296
Calico Cat 142
Calico Cottage Gifts and Interiors 133
Calico Fair 380
Calico Fort Arts & Crafts Fair 284
California Artists and Craftsmen's Guild 82
California Clothing Co. 163
California Crafts 296
California Craftsman, The 296
California Lutheran College 508
California Polytechnic State University 508
California State/San Bernardino 508
California State University 509
California 3-Dimensional Regional Exhibition and Competition 296
Calle de Crafts — Arcade of Artisans 65
Camille Maher Antiques and Gifts 134
Campbell Folk School, The John C. 210, 540

Campbell River and District Museum 277
Campus Martius Museum 215
Canaan Craftsmen's Christmas Fair 386
Canada Council, The 505
Canada Crafts 557
Canada Crafts Magazine 464
Canada Quilts 464, 567
Canandian Craft Show LTD., The 461
Candle in the Night, A 252
Candlelite House 509
Candles Created by Martin 531
Candlestock 191
Candlewic Company 227
Candling Mill, The 159
Cannon Shop 262
Canton Flea Market Arts & Crafts Show, The 380
Canyon Gallery Two 82
Cape Henlopen Craft Fair & Folk Life Festival 318
Cape May County Art League Boardwalk Art Show 388
Capital City Art and Craft Show 452
Capital Expo 357
Capital Woodcarvers Association Show 296
Caravan Gallery, Ltd. 220
Carbondale Council on Arts & Humanities 479
Carbondale Mountain Fair 309
Cards and Shards 146
Cargo Hold, Inc., The 240
Caribou Sidewalk Arts and Crafts Festival 361
Carlson's Art Room 277
Carmel Work Center Shop 83
Carolina Mountain Arts & Crafts 210
Carolista Jewelry Designers 211
Carousel Crafts Company 55
Carrie Weaves Studio 514
Carrizo Art and Craft Courses 532
Carroll Sidewalk Art Show 353
Casa Blanca Weavers 180
Casa de Colores 180
Casa Del Sol 223, 543
Cass County Log Cabin Festival 382
Casting and Jewelry Craft 557
Catalina Festival of Art 297
Catalyst, The 75
Catawba College 46
Cat's Cradle 146
Cavalier Gallery of Art, Inc. 108
Cave House, The 258
Cedar Art Center 533

Cedar Chest, The 275
Cedar Creek Festival of Arts and Crafts 456
Cedar Point, Inc. 215
Cedar Points' Craft Show 411
Celebrate Weekend (see Lawrence University 48)
Celebration of the Arts 297
Center for Book Arts 533
Center for the History of American Needlework 228
Center for The Visual Arts 478
Center of Things, The (see April Arts and Crafts Fair 436)
Central Madison Council 65
Central Michigan University 525
Central Missouri State University 528
Central New York Community Arts Council (see Greater Utica Summer Festival Craft Show 399)
Central Pennsylvania Festival of the Arts Sidewalk Sale 419
Central Texas Arts and Crafts Sale 438
Central Washington University 550
Central Wyoming Museum of Art (see A Touch of Glass, Stained Glass Studio 276)
Centralia Community College 503
Centre for Anti Gravity 507
Centre Square Art Fair 419
Ceramic Hut 247
Ceramic Industry 465
Ceramic League of Miami School 515
Ceramic Scope 465, 557
Ceramic, Sculpture and Craft Show 412
Ceramic Studio's 191
Ceramics Monthly 465, 557
Cermak Road Business Association 69 (also see Spring Arts and Craft Fair 345)
Chadron State College 529
Chalaka Arts and Crafts Festival 284
Changing Scene, The 271
Chaparral 247
Chapman Galleries Ltd. 277
Chase Gallery, Gail 262
Chastain Arts and Crafts Center 516
Chatauqua of the Arts 347
Chatham Festival of the Arts 368
Chattahoochee Art Association (see Holiday Happening 334)
Chautauqua Institution 534
Chemung Valley Arts Council 492
Cherokee Strip Living Museum 129
Cherries Jubilee Craft Show 419
Cherry Creek Festival of the Arts 309

Cherry Hill Mall Arts Festival 388
Cherry Hill Mall Craft and Sculpture Show 388
Cherry Hill Mall Professional Craft and Sculpture Show 388
Chicago Artists' Coalition Newsletter 557
Chickasaw Council House Museum 221
Chillicothe Art and Craft Show 337
Chip Chats 558
Chitimacha Craft 133
Chmielewski Gallery 228
Chocolate and Vanilla Ltd. 55
Chocorua Potters 171
Choice Incorporated 83
Christmas Art & Craft Sale 297
Christmas Arts and Crafts (Abilene, Kansas 355)
Christmas Arts and Crafts (Topeka, Kansas 355)
Christmas Arts and Crafts (Wichita, Kansas 356)
Christmas Arts and Crafts Fair (see Lawrence University 48)
Christmas Arts and Crafts Show 395
Christmas Arts Festival 312
Christmas Craft & Art Show 430
Christmas Craft and Hobby Show 372
Christmas Craft Bazaar 382
Christmas Craft Fair 418
Christmas Craft Fair, The 361
Christmas Craft Market 462
Christmas Crafts Fair 284
Christmas Fair at Project, The 368
Christmas Gift & Hobby Show 347
Christmas In September Festival 452
Christmas Show 335
Christmas Stocking Craft Show 312
Chronicle of the Early American Industries Association 558
Cintas Fellowship Program 492
Cir-Kit Concepts, Inc. 527
Citrus County Festival of the Arts 320
City of Las Vegas Cultural and Community Affairs 489
Clarion State College 544
Clark County Fair 449
Clarke Area Arts Council 483
Classical Glass 154
Clay and Fiber Gallery 181
Clay Crafts Community 191, 534
Clay Gallery, The 154
Clay Place Gallery, The 228
Clay Place, The 544

Clay Pot, The 191
Clay Workshop 534
Clear Light Studio 191
Clearing, The 552
Clemson University 46
Cleveland Area Arts Council 496
Cleveland County Historical Society (see Pioneer Craft Festival 293)
Clinton Historical Museum Village 174 (also see Craft Day in the Park 388)
Cloth and Clay, Inc 277
Clothesline Exhibit 419
Clouds 192
Coast Guard Festival Crafts Fair 372
Coastal Crafters Expo 430
Coastal Crafters, Inc. 69
Coastland Center Invitational Winter Festival of Art 320
Cobblestone 465, 558
Cob-Web Hall 75
Coco Plum Woman's Club Jeweled Egg Show 320
Coe College 520
Coffee Cantata 83
Coffee County Arts Alliance 476
Coffeetrees at Stewart's 131
Coffey School of Fine Woodworking, Michael 548
Coffeyville Community Junior College 520
Cohn Co., M.M. 62
Collaborative, The 228
Collage Boutique 278
Collage, The 214
Collection, The 228
Collector's Corner, Huntington Galleries 268
Collectors Shop 192
Collectors' Showroom 116
College of Dupage 517
College of Fine and Applied Arts 482
College of Great Falls 529
College of New Rochelle 534
College of St. Catherine 46
College of Santa Fe 532
College of Wooster (see Functional Ceramics 412)
College Port Sidewalk Art Festival 321
Colonial Charter 228
Colonial Craftsmen, Inc. 55
Colonial Vermont, Inc. 253
Colorado Mountain College 512
Colorado River Indian Tribes Museum 76
Colorado State University 512

Colorado Women's College 513
Columbia Art Gallery 223
Columbia Mall Professional Arts Festival 362
Columbus Art-Craft-Hobby-Miniature Fair 412
Columbus Arts Guild Inc. (see Fair on the Square 348)
Columbus College 516
Combined Effort, A 192
Commission of Arts and Humanities 502
Common Ground Artists Co-operative 83
Common Place 124
Commonwealth of Pennsylvania 499
Community Arts Center of Wallingford, The 544
Community Craft and Art Co-op, Inc. 271
Community Crafts & Art Co-op 505
Community Free School 513
Company Store, The 83
Complex, The 243
Comstock Lode, The 116
Concordia College 553
Conestoga Valley Chapter, Pennsylvania Guild of Craftsmen (see Fall Craft Market at Park City Mall 420, Spring Craft Market 427)
Confederation Centre of the Arts (see Gallery Gift Shop 279)
Connecticut Commission on the Arts 480
Connecticut Craft Professionals (see Spring Market 317)
Connecticut Guild of Craftsmen, Inc. 480
Contemporary Art Glass Gallery 192
Contemporary Art Workshop 65, 116
Contemporary Crafts Association 224
Contemporary Crafts Expo 321
Contemporary Crafts Market Place 558
Contemporary Craftsman, The 181
Contemporary Gallery 247
Contemporary Quilt, The 116
Contra Costa County Fair 297
Cook Forest Sawmill Craft Shop 229
Cook Workshop, Mary Lou 532
Cooper and French, Ltd. 239
Cooperative Artisanale de Cheticamp LTEE 278
Cooperative Arts Council of Clark County 503
Cooperative Extension Service 485
Cooper-Hewitt Museum 534
Cooperstown Annual National Art Exhibition 395

Coos Art Museum 224
Coos Art Museum Craft Show 418
Coppertone Workshop 103
Coqui Galleries 103
Coral Gables Miracle Mile Sidewalk Art Show 321
Corcoran Shop, The 266
Corn Hill Arts Festival 395
Cornerhouse Gallery and Frame 126
Cornwall Crafts 253
Coronado School of Fine Arts 509
Corpus Christi Arts Council 501
Corpus Christi State University 547
Cortland Art League (see Park Art Festival 402)
Coshocton Canal Festival 412
Coss Gallery 146
Costello Craft Shows, Linn 69
Cothran's Art Galleries (Cedar Rapids, Iowa) 127
Cothran's Art Galleries (Czech Village, Iowa)
Cottage Crafts of Vermonth 253
Cottonlandia Foundation 162
Council of Arts 479
Country Art Store, The 133
Country Bazaar 103
Country Crafts 271
Country Craftsmen, The 262
Country Cupboard, The 79
Country Fair and Auction 337
Country Gallery, The 192
Country Manor Interiors 114
Country Roads 333
Country Store, The 241
Countryside Mall Starving "American" Arts and Crafts 337
Countryside Village Art Fair 385
Countrywide Crafts 83
Courthouse Arts Festival 362
Couturier Galerie (see International Guest Exhibition of Painting, Sculpture & Graphics 315)
Coweta Festivals, Inc. (see Power's Crossroads Country Fair and Art Festival 335)
Coyne Galleries, Elaine 112
Craft Adventure 368
Craft Alliance, The 134, 521
Craft Alliance Gallery 163 (also see "Around the Table" 381)
Craft, Art, and Hobby Show 372
Craft Barn, The 192

Craft Career Center 516
Craft Center (Massachusetts) 146, 524
Craft Center (West Virginia) 552
Craft Clocks and Gifts 116
Craft Compound 547
Craft Connection 465
Craft Connection, Ltd. 116
Craft Connection, Ltd., The 229
Craft Cranny, The 244
Craft Day in the Park 388
Craft Days 396
Craft Designs Unlimited 193
Craft Exhibition of the Central Pennyslvania Festival of the Arts 420
Craft Fair (Connecticut) 313
Craft Fair (Andover, Massachusetts) 368
Craft Fair (Boxborough, Massachusetts) 368
Craft Fair at Bromey Mountain, The 444
Craft Fair at Riverfront 347
Craft Festival 396
Craft Gallery 338
Craft Gallery Ltd., The 142
Craft Gallery of the Ontario Crafts Council, The 278
Craft Gallery, The 84
Craft Guild of Greater Cincinnati, The 496
Craft Horizons 465, 558
Craft Industries 247
Craft Market News 558
Craft People's Cooperative 193
Craft Products Companies (Elmhurst, Illinois) 116
Craft Products Companies (St. Charles, Illinois) 116
Craft Professionals of Vermont 501
Craft Publications, Inc. 465
Craft Shop Crafts Fair 338
Craft Shows and Promotions 69
Craft Skellar 534
Craft Store 229
Craft Street, Inc. 84
Craft Students League 534
Crafters' Gallery 258
Craftnews 466, 558
Craftpeople's Guild of Federick County 485
Craftproducers Craft Fair at Mount Snow 444
Craftproducers Incorporated 69
Crafts (England) 559
Crafts (New Jersey) 389
Crafts and Creations 396
Crafts and Things 108

Crafts Barn, The 193
Crafts Business Encyclopedia, The 559
Crafts Exhibition 318
Crafts Fair 396
Crafts Faire (see Texas Christian University 51)
Crafts Incredible, Inc. 129
Crafts Ltd. 55
Crafts Marketplace 428
Crafts Report, The 466
Crafts Village at Kerrville Music Festivals 438
Craftsman 466
Craftsman's Corner 174
Craftsman's Fair of the Southern Highlands 405
Craftsman's Gallery Ltd., The 193
Craftsman's Gallery of Carmel 84
Craftsman's Hand, The 244
Craftsmen Corner, Inc. 193
Craftsmen in Business: A Guide to Financial Management & Taxes 559
Craftsmen of Chelsea Court 266
Craftsmen's Fair 386
Craftsmen's Fair at Delaware Art Museum 319
Craftsmens Guild of Pittsburgh (see A Fair in the Park 420)
Craftsummer 542
Craftworks (New Jersey) 174
Craftworks (Virginia) 259
Crafty Fox, The 216
Crafty Lady Shop, The 174
Crafty Peddlers, The 211
Cranbrook Institute of Science 154
Creation Art & Craft Center 216
Creations and Crafts Co. 194
Creative Art Studio 271
Creative Artist Group (see Peach Tree Mall 303)
Creative Artists Group (see Marysville Mall Art & Craft Show 386)
Creative Artists Public Service Program 492
Creative Arts Community 543
Creative Arts Group 509
Creative Arts League, The 503
Creative Craft Show n Sell 431
Creative Crafts 389
Creative Clutter by Vergene 216
Creative Crafts (Washington) 262
Creative Crafts (New Jersey) 466, 559
Creative Crafts Fair 313
Creative Education Program 522

Creative Faires, Ltd. 69 (also see Harvest Crafts Festival 399)
Creative Gift Studio, Inc. 117
Creative Hands 229
Creative Jewelry 194
Creative Papers 55
Creative Women's Collective 194
Creatively Yours Studio 117
Crewel Elephant, The 98
Crocker Art Gallery, E.B. (see California Crafts 296)
Critters and Cohorts 338
Crochet Association International 481
Crockett Arts and Crafts Festival, David 433
Cross County Mall Art and Craft Show 338
Croton Crafts Fair 397
Cuelenaere Library, John M. 65
Culver-Stockton College 528
Cumberland County Fair 389
Cumberland Mountain Craft Association 500
Cumberland Valley Exhibition 363
Curbstone Craft Festival 397
Curiosity Shop, The 131
Current Crafts 104
Custom Crafts 127
Custom Handweavers 84, 509
Custom House 163
Custom House of Needle Arts and Design, Inc. 55
Custom-Foam Crafts, Inc. 55
Cystic Fibrosis Arts and Crafts Fair 313

D aemen College 534
Dakin Farm 253
Dakota State College 46
Dalton, Ken and Kathleen 472
Danbury Amateur Art Show 313
Dancing Deer, The 136
Dandelion 2 229
Dane County Humane Society Animal Art Fair 456
Danforth Museum Shop 146
Danish Festival Arts and Crafts Show 372
Dash School of Art 535
David (see Light Opera 84)
David County Arts Council (see Arts Alive Festival 405)
Daviess Martin County Art Festival 348
Davis and Elkins College 552
Davis Art Center (see Christmas Art & Craft Sale 297)
Dawntreader 259
Day & Associates Landscape Architects & Planners ASLA, A. Dewitt 42
Day In The Country, A 338
Dayton Art Institute 412, 542
De Anza College 509
De Vargas Arts and Crafts Fair 181
De Vargas Summer Arts and Crafts Show 393
De Young Museum Art School, The 509
Deadwood Gulch Art Gallery 242
Decatur Art Guild 476
Decatur Civic Chorus Annual Arts & Crafts Fair 333
Decorating and Craft Ideas 466
Decorative Arts Newsletter 559
Deepwood Crafts Gallery 229
Deerfield Commons Arts and Selected Crafts Fair 338
Dekalb Council for the Arts, Inc. 481
Del Sol, Inc. 181
Deland Outdoor Art Festival 321
Delaware Art Museum 480, 515 (also see Crafts Exhibition 318)
Delta Art Exhibition 291
Delta State University 527
DeNovo 466, 559
Department of Conferences and Institutes 507
Department of Crafts Design 480
Deparment of Tourism, City of Petersburg 65
Depke Inc., Pat 466
Deptford Mall Patriots Art Brigade 389
Derrevere, William R. 472
Des Moines Art Center 520
Des Moines Symphony Guild (see Needlework 354)
Deshane Miniature Galleries 56
Design and Concepts in Stained Glass in Charters, France 509
Design Division — Regency/Century Greetings 56
Designer/Craftsman 297
Designs in Silver, Etcetera 194
DeSota Caverns (see Fallfest 285, Indian Crafts Festival & Pioneer Fair 286)
Detailed Look, National Metalsmithing and Jewelry Invitational, A 456
Detroit Artists Market 154
Dewey— Kofron Gallery 181
Dexterity, Ltd. 175

Dezign House III 42
Diablo Alliance for the Arts 479
Dickinson County Council for the Arts (see Midwest Arts and Crafts Show 374)
Different Drummer, A 108
Dinjii Zhuu Enjit Museum 75
Directory of Art Schools & Workshops 560
"Discover Ravinia Day" 339
Discovery 155
Disney Shopping Village, Walt (see The Art Festival in the Village 319)
DJM Proudctions (see Art and Craft Expo 40)
Dodge House Art Gallery 146
Dogwood Arts Festival State Crafts Fair 433
Doll House, Inc., The 112
Dollhouse World 216
Door Knob, Inc., The 247
Dorchester County Arts Commission (see Edisto River Fun Festival 430)
Doris' Craft Fair 84
Double D Enterprises 69
Doubletree Gallery 175
Douglas Gallery, Inc., The 104
Dovetail 84
Down on the Farm, Ltd. 104
Down Town Fulton Show 297
Down Town Novato Center 298
Downstairs Downtown 131
Downtown Bay City Sidewalk Days 373
Drumm Studios and Gallery, Don 216
Drury College 528
Drutt Gallery, Helen 230
Ducks Unlimited Midwest Wildlife Art Show 382
Dulcimer Players News, The 560
Dulcimer Shoppe, The 79
Dunconor Design Workshops 513
Dundee Arts and Crafts Club Outdoor Exhibit 373
Dunlap Co., The 62
Durham Art Guild Annual Juried Exhibit 405
Durham Arts Council (see Triangle Festival of Crafts 408)
Dyeco 117

E ager Weavers 194
Eagle Ceramics Inc. 522
Eagle Creek Arts and Folk Music Festival 348
Earlham College 519
Early American Life 466
Early American Life Magazine 560
Earnest, Lynn 472
Earth, Air, Fire, Water 509
Earth and Fire Ceramic Studio and Gallery 175, 531
Earth Glass Studio, Inc. 117
Earth Muse 279
Earth To Stone 129
Earthworks and Artisans 535
Earthworks Headshop 266
Earthworks Pottery 194
Earthworks Pottery, Ltd. 535
East Carolina University 540
East End Arts and Humanities Council 492
East Hartford Fine Arts Commission 480
East Tennessee Crafts Inc. 244
East Tennessee State University 546
East Texas State University 547
Eastern Illinois University 517 (also see Festival 339)
Eastern Illinois University (Art Department) 518
Eastern Maine Crafts Co-op 136
Eastern Mennonite College 549
Eastern Michigan University 525
Eastern Montana College 529
Eastern New Mexico University 532 (also see Peanut Valley Festival 393)
Eastern States Exposition (see Craft Adventure 368)
Eastern Upper Peninsula Craftsmen 486
Eastern Washington University 550
Eastfield Mall Arts Festival 368
Ebenezer Allen Country Store & Gift Shop (Burlington, Vermont) 253
Ebenezer Allen Country Store & Gift Shop (South Hero, Vermont) 254
Eckerd College 515
Ecole De Textiles LeClerc, C. P. 554
Edens Plaza Arts & Craft Fair 339
Edgemont Yarn Service, Inc. 131
Edisto River Fun Festival 430
Edmonds Art Festival 450
Edward Dean Museum of Decorative Arts (see Summer Outdoor Art Show 308)
Eggorama 420
Ehrman Mansion Art Show & Fair 298
Eight Hands at the Farm Women's Market, The 142
8-State Annual 357
El Diez y Seis de September 310

El Gringo 182
El Paso Museum of Art Gift Shop 247
El Rincon 182
Elder Craftsmen of Philadelphia 230
Elder Craftsmen, The (New York) 194
Electrum Festival of the Arts 385
Electrum Jewelry 195
Ellsworth Community College 520
Elmhurst Outdoor Art Fair 339
Elpa Marketing Industries (see Thorens Music Boxes 61)
Elvehjem Art Center 272
Embroiderers' Guild of America, Inc., The 492
Embroiderers Guild of Pittsburgh (see Stitchery '79 428)
Emergency Workshop 131
Emerson Gallery, The 85
Emmons, Wesley 230
Emporium, The 231
Enamel Guild West (see An Ancient Art Updated 294)
Enamel Guild: West 479
Enamels 446
Enchanted Doll House, The 254
Encounter, The 99
Endicott College 524
Endion Station 159
Erie Art Center (see Spring Show 427)
Especially Maine 136
Estudios Rio, Gallery of Contemporary Arts and Crafts 248
Etgen Fine Jewelry, Beth and Bill 85
Ethan Allen Gift Shoppe 254
Evans Farm Country Store 259
Evans Farm Festival, Bob 412
Evansville Arts & Education Council 483 (also see Craft Fair at Riverfront 347, Walkway Festival 352)
Evansville Museum of Arts and Science (see Mid-States Craft Exhibition 350)
Everett Waterfront Show 450
Everhart Museum Sales Shop 231
Everyday People 231, 544
Everything Creative By Susie Sells 117
Evolution Art Institute 510
Exhibition 280 452

F actory of Visual Art 551
Fair In The Park, A 420
Fair November 462
Fair on the Square 348
Fair, The 62
Faith Workshop 268
Fall Arts and Crafts Market 368
Fall Arts & Crafts Show 321
Fall Arts Fair 378
Fall Craft Market at Park City Hall 420
Fall Craft Show 285
Fall Festival of Arts 339
Fall Festival of Needlework 549
Fall Foliage Festival 420
Fall for Art 321
Fallfest 285
Family and Friends 85
F&T Associates (see Southern California Powwow 307)
Fanshawe Pioneer Village 279
Fantasma Productions (see South Florida Spring Arts & Crafts Festival 329, South Florida Winter Arts & Crafts Festival 329)
Fantasy Creations 56
Far Country Craft Fair 442
Farian, Babette S. 472
Farmer Cooperative Information 560
Farmington Crafts Expo 313
Farmington Valley Arts Center 66, 514
Farmington Valley Arts Center, Inc. 104
Farnsworth Library and Art Museum, William A. 136
Favell Museum of Western Art & Indian Artifacts 224
Favorite Things 142
Fayerweather Craft Center 239
Feast of The Hunters' Moon 348
Feather Your Nest 164
Federal Establishment, The 254
Federal Smallwares Corp. 56
Feldman Fine Arts, Arthur L. 216
Felician College Arts & Crafts Fair 339
Fells Point Fun Festival 363
Ferrum Craft Shop 259
Festival 339
Festival Arts & Crafts Fair 289
Festival in the Park (Alabama) 285
Festival in the Park (North Carolina) 405
Festival In The Park (Virginia) 446
Festival of American Craftsmanship 397
Festival of Arts (Connecticut) 313
Festival of Arts & Crafts 298
Festival of Leaves 446
Festival of the Arts (California) 299
Festival of the Arts (Florida) 322
Festival of the Arts (New York) 397
Festival of the Arts (see Hood College 47)

Festival of the Arts Market 462
Festival of the Elms-Craft Fair 340
Festival of the Fish 412
Fiber Show 299
Fiber to Fabric Shop 127
Fiberarts 467, 560
Fiberfolk, Ltd. 195
Fiberworks 85
Fibrations Weaving Studio and Gallery 109
Fibre Concepts 535
Fibrous Beginnings 85
Fiesta 349 (Indiana)
Fiesta 438 (Texas)
Fiesta del Artes 299
Fifth Avenue Gallery 262
57th Street Art Fair 340
Filley Department Store, George 62
Fine Arts Center of Clinton 177
Fine Arts Center of Kershaw County, Inc. 240
Fine Arts Council of Trumbull County (FACT) 496
Fine Arts Show 382
Fine Arts Society of the Cayuga Museum of History and Art 492
Fine Woodworking 467, 560
Finger Lakes Craftsmen (see Christmas Arts and Crafts Show 395, Summer Indoors Arts & Crafts Show 403, Thanksgiving Weekend Christmas Arts & Craft Show 403)
Fire on the Mountain Glass Shop (see Sonora Christmas Fair 306)
Fire Works, The 118
Firehouse Arts and Crafts Festival 333
Firmee, Judith 472
First Additions 470
First Impressions 259
First Monday's Art Sunday 285
First National Bank 272
First Sunday in the Park 299
Fitchburg State College Campus Center 46
Fitzgerald Enterprises, Inc. 56
Five Ninety Three 76
Flathead Lake Galleries 169
Flathead Valley Art Festival 385
Flint Art Fair 373
Flint Institute of Arts (see Flint Art Fair 373)
Florence Museum 545
Florida Folk Festival 322
Florida Forest Festival Arts & Crafts Show & Sale 322

Florida State University (Center for Participant Education) 515
Florida State University (Craft Design Program) 515
Florida Technological University 46
Flo-Sculpt Studios, Inc. 56
Floyd County Museum 124
Flushing Art League Outdoor Exhibition 397
Focus Crafts and Furnishings, Inc. 195
Following Sea 113
Folk Art Fair 456
Folk Arts 525
Folk Arts & Music Festival 349
Folk Music & Crafts Festival 383
Folklorica 147
Fond Du Lac Artists Association Annual Arts and Crafts Fair 457
Fontana Gallery 231
Foo-Fa-Rah 85
Foothills Art Center (see Threads Unlimited 311)
Foothills Craft Guild Show & Sale 433
Forest Mall Arts & Crafts Fair 457
Forest Mall's Arts and Crafts Fair/Sale 457
Forge Patio Art Gallerie, Associations 86
Forms and Foliage, Ltd. 195
Fort Armstrong Folk Festival 420
Fort Edmonton Park 279
Fort Lauderdale Museum of the Arts Gift Shop 109
Fort Ouiatenon Blockhouse Trading Post 124
Fort Wayne Museum of Art Gift Shop 124
Fortress of Louisbourg Reproductions 279
Foster Center, Stephen (see Celebration & Open Air Crafts Fair 322, Forida Folk Festival 322, Suwanee River Crafts Show-Sale 330)
Foster Museum, The Ralph 164
Fountain Festival 290
4 Arts Gallery 118
Four Corners Navajo Arts & Crafts Cooperative 491
Fourth of July Carnival 446
Fourth of July Celebration & Open Air Crafts Fair 322
Fourth Street Artists Gallery, Inc. 127
Fowler House Museum (see Tippecanoe County Historical Association, Fowler House Museum 125)
Fox River Grove Lions Arts and Crafts 340
Fox School of Weaving, Judy 549

Fox Valley Center (see Wonderful World of Crafts 346)
Fragile Art Competition 418
Francis Park Art and Craft Show 340
Frankenmuth Bavarian Festival 373
Frankenmuth Historical Museum 155
Franklin Gallery, The 76
Franklin Street Mall 66
Frederick Craft Fair 363
Fredericksburg Gallery of Art 259
Fredonia Arts Council, Inc. 129
Free Air Arts Fair 450
Free Art Fair 417
Freelands National Arts & Crafts Shows 69 (also see Altamonte Mall 319, Great Lakes Mall 413, Richmond Mall 415, Southern Park Mall 415, Summit Mall 416, Woodville Mall 417)
Freeport Community Arts Council 492
Freeport Art Museum (see Plaza Art Fair 344)
Fresno City Parks and Recreation Department 510
Friedman, Ken 473
Friends of the Free Library Gift Shop 231
Friends of the Middle Border Museum 242
Friends of the Museum, Inc. 109
Frishman Gallery, Daniel 147
From Trash to Treasures 373
Front Room, The 76
Frontiersmen Gift Shop 217
Fulton County Arts Council, Inc. 493
Fulton County Street Arts Festival 398
Fun Festival 291
Functional Ceramics 412

G ail Moore Quilters (see Quilt Faire 304)
Gainesville Cultural Commission 481
Galerie De Tours 86
Galerie Internationale 195
Galerie Paula Insel 195
Gales Creek Enterprises of Oregon Limited 66
Galleria Internazionale, Ltd. 155
Gallerie of Fine Arts 248
Gallery at the Southwest Craft Center, The 248
Gallery 8 86
Gallery 18 106
Gallery 84 Inc. 195
Gallery 500 231
Gallery 501— Mint Museum of Art 211

Gallery Gift Shop 279
Gallery House Sol 279
Gallery in the Park 398
Gallery North 196
Gallery North Outdoor Art Show 398
Gallery of World Art, Inc. 147
Gallery on Main Street, The 217
Gallery on the Park 142
Gallery Shop, Albright-Knox Art Gallery, The 196
Gallery Shop at Jamaica Arts Center 196
Gallery Shop, The (Michigan) 155
Gallery Shop, The (Utah) 252
Gallery 10 Ltd. 266
Gallery, The (Kentucky) 132
Gallery, The (Ohio) 217
Gallery, The (South Carolina) 240
Gallery 3 (Arizona) 76
Gallery III (Tennessee) 244
Gallery Three Twenty Three, Inc. 275
Gallery 2W0 175
Gallery Yolanda 118
Gallo Manufacturing Co. 56
Gamekeeper, Inc., The 136
Garden Grove Artisan's Guild 86
Garendo Gallery 87
Garret, The 242
Garrison Art Center Arts and Crafts Fair 398
Gasparilla Sidewalk Art Festival 323
Gaspee Day (see Pawtuxet Village Arts & Crafts Festival 429)
Gathering, The (Arizona) 76
Gathering, The (Missouri) 164
Gavilan College 510
Gays Mills Pace Club Arts & Crafts Fair 457
Gazebo, Ltd., The 221
GCAH Crafts Program 66
Geauga County Historical Society, Crossroads Country Store 217
Gems and Minerals 560
General Expositions Company (see American Folk Arts Festival 294, Sacramento Harvest Festival 304, San Diego Harvest Festival 305, San Francisco Harvest Festival 305, San Jose Harvest Festival 305)
Genessee Guild, The 493
Geneva's Gift Shoppe 127
Georgia Council for the Arts and Humanities 481
Georgia Designer Craftsmen, Inc. 481

Georgia Jubilee 333

Georgia Mountain Arts Association 112, 481

Georgia Mountain Fair 334

Georgia Volunteer Lawyers for the Arts 482

German Alps Festival 398

German American Day 363

Ghetzler Productions 70

Gibbes Art Gallery School, The 66, 545

Gibson House Museum 280

Gift Festival 300

Gift Haus 196

Gilcrease Museum Gift Shop 221

Gillary Gallery 196

Giraffe 118

Glad Hand 87

Glass Art Society 486

Glass Ballet, Ltd. 196

Glass Eye, The 524

Glass Lantern, Ltd., The 99

Glass magazine (see Fragile Art Competition 418)

Glass Masters, Inc. 197

Glass Roots Studios 535

Glass Workbench, Inc., The 164

Glastonbury Art Guild (see On the Green 316)

Glen Echo Park 485

Glens Falls Farmer's Market 398

Glenview Art Fair 340

Glenville State College 552

Go Fly a Kite Inc. 56

Goddard College 549

Godston, Joel 473

Gold and Silversmiths of Vail, The 99

Gold Coast Art Fair 340

Gold Hill Art Festival 386

Gold Hill Pottery and Art Gallery (see Gold Hill Art Festival 386)

Golden Door Gallery 232

Golden Hobby Shop 217

Golden Toad, The 172

Goldenbells Festival Art & Craft Market 313

Goldmann's & Sons, A. 63

Goldsboro Art Center 211

Goldsmith Shop, The 232

Goldsmith, The 147

Good Stuff Gifts 254

Goodfellow Catalog of Wonderful Things, The 560

Goodfellow Review of Crafts, The 467, 561

Goody Shoppe, The 143

Goucher College 46

Goundie House Museum Shop 232

Gourley's Olde Shoppe 125

Gra Wun Jewelers, Ltd. 77

Grabill Country Fair 349

Graham Gallery 197

Grand Central Mall Arts Festival 452

Grand Irish Jubilee 421

Grand Prairie Festival of Arts 291

Grand Teton Lodge Co. 276

Grand Valley State College 526

Grandma's Folly 164

Grandma's House 170

Grandmothers Trunk 147

Granny's Attic 128

Granny's Loft, Inc. 175

Grants for Graduate Study Abroad 493

Graphic Ideas 56

Grassroots Handcrafts 106

Gray Gallery, Inc., Lenore 239

Great Chase, The 143

Great Gulfcoast Festival 323

Great Lakes Mall 413

Great River Festival of Traditional Music and Crafts 457

Great River Roads Craft Fair, The 380

Great Sew-Ciety, The 535

Great West Fair 442

Greater Birmingham Arts Alliance 73, 476

Greater Harrisburg Arts Festival 421

Greater Hartford Civic & Arts Festival 314

Greater Malone Community Council's Arts Committee (see Northern New York Crafts Festival 401)

Greater Milwaukee Council of Arts for Children 505

Greater Milwaukee Craft Fair 457

Greater Utica Summer Festival Craft Show 399

Greater Westbury Arts Council, Inc., The 493

Greater Woodlands Artisan Fair, The 438

Green Apple Gallery 170

Green Country Art Center 221

Green Hill Art Gallery, Inc. 211

Green Hills Pottery (see Madison Chautauqua of the Arts 350)

Green Mountain Sugar House 254

Green River 99

Green Spring Farm Gallery 259

Greenbaer Metal Works 99

Greenup Old Fashioned Days Arts & Crafts Show 358

Greenwich Arts Council 480
Greenwich Handcraft Show and Sale 315
Greenwich House Pottery 493, 535
Greenwood Arts and Crafts Fair 446
Greenwood Handweavers' Guild 500
Grey's the Batik Art Place, Robin 511
Griffin, Bea 70
Grinders Switch Arts & Crafts Fair 433
Grist Mill General Store on the River, The 197
Gromosiak, John and Diane 70
Group Showing of American Artists 323
Grove House, Inc. 109
Grove House School of Arts and Crafts 515
Guild of Book Workers Exhibition 399
Guild of Book Workers Journal 561
Guild of Ohio Dollmakers 496
Guild of Strawberry Banke 172
Guild Store, The 87
Guilford Handcraft Center 514
Guilford Handcrafts Exposition 315
Guilderland Annual Fall Arts Festival 39 3
Guiyermo Galleries 182

H. A.S. Bin Gift Shoppe, The 73
H.O.M.E. Fair 361
H.O.M.E. Learning Center 524
Habitat Institute for the Enviroment 524
Hackley Art Museum (see Regional 375)
Hager Frontier Craft Day, Jonathan 363
Hahn Gallery, The 232
Haines Township Dutch Fall Festival 421
Haleyville Merchants Association Arts & Crafts Show 286
Half Moon Bay Art & Pumpkin Festival 300
Halfpenny Playhouse, The (see West Hudson Community Arts Festival 392)
Halifax Historical Society, Inc. 109
Hallandale Civic Center Fund Arts, Crafts, & Plants Festival 323
Hallandale Fall Art Festival 323
Hallie's Alley Jewelry School 510
Hallie's West Gallery 87
Hamlet, The 217
Hampton Arts and Humanities 260
Hancock Park Festival of Art 300
Hand and the Spirit Crafts Gallery, The 77
Hand Feats 176
Hand Made USA, Inc. 182
Hand Maiden 182
Hand of the Craftsman 197

Hand Work Shop, Inc. 260
Handcrafter, The 148
Handcrafter's Cottage, Ltd. 197
Handcrafters Gallery 136
Handcrafts Shop, The 254
Handmaids 176
Hands of Man 143
"Hands of Man" Show & Sale (New Hampshire) 364
"Hands of Man" Show & Sale (Philadelphia) 421
"Hands of Man" Show & Sale (Pittsburgh) 421
Handscapes 148
Handweavers Guild of America 480
Handweavers of Houston, Inc. 248
Handweaving with Robert and Roberta 561
Handworks 149
Hanna's Town Folk Festival, The 421
Happy Hands Craft Shoppe 172
Happy Peasant Gallery 276
Harbinger — Huntress Stained Glass 182
Harbour Town Crafts 241
Harcourt Bindery 524
Harlan Gallery (see Seton Hill College 50)
Harra Woodworking Studio, John 535
Harris Shows, Inc., Jinx 70 (also see 362, 364, 367-371, 387, 388, 390-393, 424-427, 429)
Hartford Art School of the University of Hartford 514
Harvest Arts and Crafts Fair 290
Harvest Crafts Festival 399
Hattiesburg Civic Arts Council 488
Haven House 197
Hayloft, The 272
Hazleton Art League (see Regional Art Exhibition 426)
Hazleton Creative Arts Festival Sidewalk Sale 422
Head House Crafts Fair 422
Heard Museum Guild (see Indian Artists and Craftsmen of North America 290)
Heikes, Grete Bodogaard 473
Helena Arts Council (see Electrum Festival of the Arts 385)
Hemphill-Wells Co. 63
Henry Folk Festival, John 452
Herbie Productions 70
Heritage Days 452
Heritage Galleries Ltd. 280
Heritage House 232
Heritage Metalcraft, Inc. 137

Hermosa Beach Chamber of Commerce (see Arts 'n Crafts by the Sea 295)
Heron Point Gallery 137
Hickman County Art Guild (see Grinders Switch Arts & Crafts Fair 433)
Hicks Gallery, Henry 197
Hide 'n' Freak Leather Workshop and Crafts Bazaar 87
High Point Glass & Decorative Co. 42
High Street of Boston 149
Highland Area Arts Council 482 (also see Plaza Art Fair 344)
Hill Country Art Foundation 547
Hill Skills 430
Hillcrest Park Lively Arts Festival 300
Hill's Gallery of Contemporary Crafts 182
Hillsborough County Museum (see Friends of the Museum, Inc. 109)
Hillside Selected Crafts Festival 340
Hillside Starving "American" Arts and Crafts 340
Hinckley School of Crafts 522
Hired Hand, The 198, 535
Historic Camden Crafts Festival 430
Historic Hoosier Hills Guild Festival 349
Historical Association of Southern Florida, Inc. 109
Hobbit House 137
Hobbs Place 198
Hobby Shop (Missouri) 165
Hobby Shop, The (see New Hampshire College 48)
Hobe Cie. Ltd. 57
Hockaday Center for the Arts Gift Shop 169
Hockaday Center for the Arts (see Flathead Valley Art Festival 386)
Hoffman, David 473
Hoffman's This 'N That Shoppe 241
Hofstra University 535
Holden Arboretum, The 218
Holden Gallery 143
Hole In The Wall Gallery, The 232
Holiday Arts & Crafts Fair 399
Holiday Crafts Fair 400
Holiday Faire 300
Holiday Festival of Arts and Crafts 341
Holiday Gift Show 373
Holiday Happening 334
Holland Day Art Fair "On The Green" 458
Holland Fine Arts Show 374
Holly Day Fair 458

Holly Studio, Inc. 550
h-o-m-e Inc. 137
Homeplace 112
Honeycomb, The 159
Honolulu Academy of Arts 517
Hood College 47
Hoonah Arts Fair 289
Hoosuck Institute, The 524
Hoot Owl, The 155
Hopi Arts & Crafts Cooperative Guild 77
Horner Museum Gift Area 224
Horse Feathers of Nyack 198
Hot Springs Art Council 500
Houby Festival Arts and Craft Fair 341
House and Table 183
House of Bernard 176
House of Fine Art, Inc. 110
Houston Designer Craftsmen 501
Houston State University, Sam 547
How to Make Money with Your Crafts 561
How to Sell Your Art and Crafts 561
Howard Galleries, Ltd. 110
Howard-Western Craft & Sculpture Fair 341
Huachuca Historical Society 77
Hudson County Cultural and Heritage Affairs Division 490
Hudson Valley Art Association, Inc., The 315
Hudson Valley Crafts Co-op 198
Haguette Fisher Gallery, Inc. 155
Hunt Institute 544
Hunter Publishing Co. 467
Huntington Dogwood Arts and Crafts Festival 453
Huntsville Art League & Museum Association (see Spring Celebration of the Arts 288)
Hutchinson Area Chamber of Commerce (see Arts & Crafts Festival 378)

I.M.U. Craft Center 520
I and We 233
Ice House Arts Festival 341
Idaho Commission on the Arts and Humanities 482
Ides of March Arts & Crafts Fair 290
Idyllwild School of Music and the Arts 510
Illinois Railway Museum 118
Illinois State University 518
Image Gallery 149

Images — A Festival of the Arts 323
Images Gallery 218
Independence Arts Council (see Art in the Park 355)
Independent Art Council (see Parsons Outdoors Arts and Crafts 356)
Indialantic Seaside Art Show 324
Indian Artists and Craftsmen of North America 290
Indian Arts and Crafts Development Program 504
Indian Crafts Festival & Pioneer Fair 286
Indian Head Art Fair 458
Indian Hills Trading Co. 156
Indian Museum of the Carolinas 211
Indian Summer Art Show 390
Indian Summer Arts and Crafts Festival 413
Indiana Artist-Craftsmen, Inc. (see Talbot Street Art Fair 351)
Indiana Arts Commission 483
Indiana Crafts 349
Indiana Department of Natural Resources Division of Museums and Memorials (see The Museum Shop 125)
Indiana University South East 519
Indianapolis Museum of Art (see The Alliance Museum Shop 123, Indiana Crafts 349)
Indoor Art and Craft Fair — County Faire 458
Indoor Handcraft Show 390
Ink & Clay 301
Insel Annual Exhibition, Paula 401
International Art Gallery 233
International Christmas Exhibition From Around the World 315
International Craft Show 400
International Fine Arts Exhibit 301
International Folk Festival 390
International Guest Exhibition of Painting, Sculpture & Graphics 315
International Guild of Craft Journalists, Authors, and Photographers 503
Interweave 467, 561
In the Children's Room 171
Interarc Planning Corp. 43
Invitational Ann Arbor Spring Art Fair 374
Invitational Ann Arbor Winter Art Fair 374
Invitational Columbus Spring Art Fair 413
Invitational Craft Fair 383

Invitational Crafts Show 431
Iowa Designer Craftsmen 483
Iris 87
Iron County Museum 156
Island Store, The 137
Iszard Co., S.F. 63
Ithac House Gallery 198
I-Ye-Quee Gift Shop 87

J. D. Enterprises 57
Jackson County Arts Council (see First Monday's Art Sunday 285)
Jacksonville Art Museum Shop 110
Jacksonville State University 506
Jacksonville University 515
Jacqu Min Inc. 57
Jamestown Community College 536
Janesville Mall Art and Craft Show 341
J&R Productions 70
Jane-Gray Shoppe 138
Jan's Gallery 128
Jaro Jewelry Galleries, Inc. 198
Jean Johnson Miniatures 177
Jeannine's Ceramics 118
Jefferson Unitarian Church Annual Juried Art Show 310
Jeffersonville Arts & Crafts Festival 349
Jellybeans 183
Jenkins, Dennis L. 473
Jenkintown Festival of the Arts 423
Jenks Jewelry 255
Jewish Community Center 536
Jewish Community Center's Craft Sale 364
Jewish Museum Shop 199
Jo-Han Models, Inc. 57
Johns, Phyllis 473
Johnson Gallery, Helen 248
Johnson, Meadow-Jerome 473
Johnstown Area Arts Council (see Spring Arts Festival 427)
Joliet Ceramic Arts and Crafts, Inc. 118
Jolly Trolly, Ltd., The 212
Jorice Designs, Inc. 199
Journeyman, Inc. 149
J-P's Gallery 199
Julie: Artisan's Gallery 199
Junction City Art in the Park 356
Juniata College 47
Jupp, Christopher M. 473
Juried Craft Show 423
Juried Crafts Exhibition of the Central

Pennsylvania Festival of the Arts 423
Just Accessories, Inc. 199

K agan Studio and Gallery, Richard 233
Kaill Fine Crafts 75
Kakie's Goldmine 177
Kalamazoo Nature Center 156
Kaleidoscope (New York) 199
Kaleidoscope (Texas) 438
Kalico Korner 159
Kalkaska Arts and Crafts Festival 374
Kamm's Brewery Arts and Crafts Festival 350
Kansas City Art Institute (see Renaissance Festival 384)
Kathy Kay Shop, The 125
Kauri Shell Gallery 88
Kearnery State College 529
Keene State College 47, 530
Keffeler's Jubilant Jewelry 88
Kelley, Judy (see Chillicothe Art and Craft Show 337, Cross County Mall Art and Craft Show 338, Francis Park Art and Craft Show 340, Janesville Mall Art and Craft Show 341, Sandburg Mall Art and Craft Show 344, Times Square Mall Arts and Crafts Show 345, Village Mall Art and Craft Show 346)
Kenan Craft Festival 400
Kenosha Art Fair 458
Kent State University 542
Kentuck Arts and Crafts Festival 286
Kentucky Arts Commission 484
Kentucky Guild of Artists and Craftsmen's Fair 358
Kentucky Hills Industries, Inc. 132
Kenyon College 47
Kermerzaar 438
Kerns Art Center, Maude J. 224, 497
Ketchikan Arts and Crafts Guild 477
Kettle Moraine Art and Crafts 458
Kettle Moraine Christmas Fair 458
Key Biscayne Art Festival 324
KFOR Arts and Crafts 386
Kidd Associates, Robert L. 526
Kilicke-Stark 536
Killmaster, John H. 474
King County Arts Commission 503
King Richard's Faire — A Return to the Renaissance 458
Kingdom Come Swappin' Meetin' 358

Kingpitcher Gallery 233
Kingsdale Recreation Center (see Bella Vista Arts & Crafts Festival 291)
Kinston Arts Council 212
Kipp Gallery 233
Kirbus, Frank Andrew 474
Kirk-Lamothe Gallery 172
Kirkland Art Center 199
Kittery Art Association Sidewalk Sale 361
Kittery Art Association's Weekend Exhibits 361
Kiva: Artisan's Gallery, The 200
Klein Art Gallery 88
Klein, Iris G. 70 (also see Group Showing of American Artists 323, Edens Plaza Arts & Crafts Fair 339, Felician College Arts & Crafts Fair 339, Randhurst Autumn Art Festival 344)
Knock on Wood 200
Knotty Pine, The 260
Knowhow Workshop, The 536
Knox Campbell Galleries 77
Knox College 47
Koehnline Gallery 119
Kohler Arts Center, John Michael 272
Kolache Day 409
Kondos Art Galleries, Peter J. 272
Kornbluth Gallery 177
Kouts Annual Arts & Crafts Show 350
Kruger Gallery 200
Kudzu Kuntry Bluegrass Celebration 287

L a Fontaine Arts Council 483
La Galeria 77
La Galerie Rouge 200
La Paloma Gallery 183
La Porte Jaycees Art Show 350
La Roche College 47
La Salle College 47
Lady Bug Gallery 244
Lady's Circle Patchwork Quilts 561
Lafayette Art Association (see Fiesta 349, Tippecanoe Regional Painting, Print and Sculpture Biennial Exhibition 352)
Lafayette Art League (see Fiesta 349)
Lafayette Arts and Crafts Center 516
Lafayette Natural History Museum and Planetarium 134
Lafayette Natural History Museum Association 484 (also see Louisiana

Native Crafts Festival 359)
Laguna Beach School of Art 510
Laguna Gloria Art Museum 248
Lake Country Craftsman, Inc. 493
Lake Erie College 542
Lake Lanier Stoneware Potters 517
Lake of Ozarks Arts & Crafts Show & Sale 384
Lake Placid School of Art 536
Lake Tahoe Art and Craft Fair 301
Lake Wales Sidewalk Art Show 325
Lakeland College 47
Lakeside Gallery School of Art 114
Lakewinds Gallery 156
Lamb to Loom Weavers' Guild 493
Lambda Rising 267
Lamoureux Designs 110
Lamp Post Craft Shop, The 138
Langman Gallery 233
Las Novedades 183
Laurentian University Museum and Arts Centre 280
Lawbre Co. 57
Lawrence Arts Center 483, 520
Lawrence County Arts Commission (see Arts & Crafts Show 432, David Crockett Arts and Crafts Festival 433)
Lawrence Gallery 224
Lawrence University 48, 553
Lawton Fort Sill Annual Art Show 417
Lawyers Artshop 143
Lawyers for the Arts 485
Lawyers for the Creative Arts 482
LBW Community Arts Council (see Kudzu Kuntry Bluegrass Celebration 287)
Leader Art Gallery 249
League of New Hampshire Craftsmen 489 (also see Craftsmen's Fair 386)
League of New Hampshire Craftsmen (Concord, New Hampshire) 172
League of New Hampshire Craftsmen (Wolfeboro, New Hampshire) 173
League of New Hampshire Craftsmen, Hanover Shop 172
Lea's Hallmark Shop 221
Leather Gallery, The 183
Leather Shed 149
Leather Stuff 143
Leaves 'n' Weaves 156
Lebanon County Historical Society Museum Store 234
Lebowitz Designs, Jack 200

Lee County Alliance of the Arts (see Arts Festival 319)
Lee Shop, The 200
Lee Sidewalk Arts & Crafts Show 325
Legacy, Ltd., The 263
Lehigh Valley Crafts Association 499
Lehigh Valley Mall Arts Festival 423
Lehner, Mary 70
Leisure Supplies Inc. 57
Leisure Time Publishing 467
Lemmon Chamber of Commerce Christmas Fair 431
Leverett Craftsmen and Artists 522
Leverett Craftsmen & Artists, Inc. 150
Lewis and Clark College 543
Lewis Corporation 57
Lewisburg Craft Fair 423
Lewiston Council On The Arts Craft and Sale Show 400
Lewittes Design Gallery, Esther 88
Liberty Gifts 276
Liberty Tree Mall Children's Hour Show 369
Life-Like Products Inc. 58
Light Opera 88
Light Through Yonder Window, The 510
Lilac Festival Decorated Egg Show 400
Lima Area Arts Council (see Square Fair 415)
Lima Art Association (see Spring Show 415)
Limited Unlimited 200
Lions Club Spring Arts & Crafts Show 434
Little Art Gallery 212
Littleton Gallery 150
Living Desert Reserve 88
Livonia Arts and Crafts Festival 374
Loch Haven Art Center Shop 110
Lockport Old Canal Days Folk Art and Craft Show 341
Lodi Grape Festival & National Wine Show (see Gift Festival 300)
Log House Sales Room 132
Lollie Shop, The 73
London Venturers 150
Londonderry Faire 369
Long Island Craftsmen's Guild 493
Longpre Gallery 88
Loom Room Gift Shop 157
Loom Room, Inc. 134, 521
Loom Room, The 119, 518
Looms and Lessons 518

Looms, The 272
Loon Mountain Arts & Crafts Show 386
Loon's Nest, The 280
Los Arboles Artisans Co-op (see Mama's Folk Art Festival 301)
Louisiana Crafts Council 134, 485
Louisiana Fur & Wildlife Festival 358
Louisiana Native Crafts Festival 359
Louisiana State Art Exhibition for Non-Professionals and/or Art Students 359
Louisiana State Art Exhibition for Professional Artists 359
Louisville School of Art 484, 521 (also see Paper & Felt Redefined 358)
Louisville School of Art Gallery 132
Love and Let Love 201
Love-Built Toys and Crafts 58
Loveland's Annual Arts & Crafts Festival 310
Lowe Art Museum (see Beaux Arts Festival of Art 320)
Lowell's Annual Arts and Crafts Festival 350
Lower Adirondack Regional Arts Council 66, 493
Lower Adirondack Regional Arts Council Arts and Crafts Festival 400
Loyola University 48
Lubbock Garden & Arts Center "Fiesta" 439
Lubec Crafts Council, Inc., The 138
Ludington Arts & Crafts Fair 374
Lumbertown USA 159
Luminere Creations, Inc. 201
Luta Studios 104
Lycoming College 544

M abee-Gerrer Museum, The 221
McGuffey Arts Association, Inc. 502
McGuire Art Shows, Nancy 70
MACHA Market — Chicago Craft-Hobby Industry Show 342
MacIvor Reddie Gallery 150
McKendree Collaborative 157
McMinnville Association of the Arts 497
McMurry College 547
McNeal Gallery and Framing 212
Maco Crafts, Inc. 212
Mad Money Boutique 159
Mad Monk, The 201

Mad Woofer, The 89
Madison Art Center, Inc. 272
Madison Chatauqua of the Arts 350
Madison County Historical Society (see Craft Days 396)
Madison Square Park Fair 401
Madison University, James 550
Magic Mushroom Gallery, The 169
Magnes Museum Gift Shop, Judah 89
Main Line Center of the Arts 234
Maine Craft Store 138
Maine Scene, The 201
Maine State Commission on the Arts and Humanities 485
Make it with Leather 467, 561
Mall of New Hampshire Professional Craft and Sculpture Show 387
Mallet, The 562
Malone College 542
Mama's Folk Art Festival 301
Man Clothing & Jewelry Co. 63
Manchester Institute of Arts & Sciences (see The Yuletide Fair 388)
Mannings National Juried Show, The 423
Manos Maravillosas 89
Many Hands Creative Arts Cooperative 89
Maple Hill Pottery Craft Gallery 138
Mapleshade Pottery 234
Marathon County Historical Society 272
Marblehead Chamber of Commerce Craft Show 369
Marche Enterprises, Inc. 71
Marge's Back Porch 218
Mari Galleries of Westchester, Ltd. 201
Marietta College 48
Marietta College Crafts National 414
Marietta National, The 414
Marigold Festival's "Art in the Park" 342
Marinaccio Doll House Furniture and Accessories, Mary Anne 177
Marion College 48
Mark of the Potter, Inc. 113
Market Square Fair 447
Market, The 183
Marketplace, Inc., The 138
Markey and Asplund Inc. 545
Marks Studio/Gallery 157
Marlborough Creative Arts Festival 316
Mars Hills College 48, 540
Marshall Museum Store, George 139
Marson Ltd. 143
Martha's Vineyard Craftsmen Fair 369

Martis Jr., Architects, James A. 43
Marv-Paul Inc. 58
Maryland Craft Festival 365
Maryland Institute College of Art, The 522
Maryland Oktoberfest Inc. 365
Marymount College 536
Marysville Mall Art & Craft Show 386
Massachusetts Arts and Humanities Foundation, Inc. 486
Massachusetts Audubon Society Gift Shop 150
Massachusetts College of Art 524
Massillon Museum Sidewalk Show, The 414
Massillon Museum, The 218 (also see Ohio Artists and Craftsmen Show 415)
Match Box, The 129
Mathis Gallery 273
Matsqui-Sumas-Abbotsford Museum 280
Mattoon Arts Festival 369
Mavros Workshop 536
Maxwell House Miniature Show and Sale 423 (also see Maxwell House Miniatures 58)
Maxwell House Miniatures 58
Maxwell International Ltd. 58
Maxwell Museum Gift Shop 184
May Show 414
Mayfest 439
ME Enterprises 58
Meet the Artists 316
Melting Point Glassworks and Pottery, The 184
Memorial Hall Museum (see Old Deerfield Craft Fair 370)
Memphis Music Heritage Festival 434
Mendocino Art Center 511
Mendocino Art Center Gallery 89
Mercer Museum Shop 234
Merchant's Association of Brookfield Square Shopping Center 71
Meridian Junior College 527
Meridian Museum of Art Bi-State Show 381
Merkel's Department Store 63
Merrill Chase Galleries, Ltd. 119
Merritt Square Festival of Arts & Crafts 325
Mesa College 513
Metro Art & Craft Festival 342
Metropolitan Sertoma Club (see Arts & Crafts Mart 432)
Metropolitan State College 513

Miami Beach Festival of the Arts 325
Miami Dade Community College 516
Micanopy Fall Harvest Festival 325
Michigan Council for the Arts 486
Michigan State University 526
Mid-America Craft-Hobby Associaton (see MACHA Market — Chicago Craft-Hobby Industry Show 342)
Mid-American Metalcrafts 384
Middle Tennessee State University 546
Middlesex County College 531
Middlesex County Cultural and Heritage Commission 490 (also see International Folk Festival 390)
Midland Center Arts and Crafts Festival 434
Midland Crafters 212
Midnight Sun, The 267
Mid-South Arts and Crafts Show/Sale 434
Mid-South Crafts Fair 434
Mid-States Craft Exhibition 350
Mid-Summer Festival of Arts and Crafts 342
Midwest Art Fare 562
Midwest Art Show & Sale 378
Midwest Artists Association 71
Midwest Artists' Guild Festival of the Arts 378
Midwest Arts and Crafts Show 374
Midwest Craft Festival 342
Midwest Old Settlers and Threshers Association, Inc. 353
Mifflin County Goose Day Celebration 424
Mifflin-Juniata Arts Festival 424
Mikolas, Karel 474
Milan Art Fair 374
Miles Community College 529
Milford Pottery, The 218
Mill Valley Arts Guild (see Fiber Show 299)
Mill Valley Arts Guild Winter Festival 302
Miller Gallery 218
Miller-Goldsmith, Gary W. 474
Miller's Thumb, The 255
Million Dollar Mile Art Show 365
Million Pines Arts and Crafts Festival 334
Milwaukee Area Techinical College 553
Milwaukee Art Center Wisconsin Gallery 273
Mindscape Gallery and Studio 119 (also see Blown Glass II 337, Critters and Cohorts 338)
Mineola Arts and Crafts Fair 439

Mini Gallery 273
Mini Mundus School 536
Mini Mundus Shop 201
Miniature Makers Society (see Fantasy Creations 56)
Miniature Reflections 58
Miniatures by Elnora 157
Minis by Me 58
Minnesota Crafts Council 487
Minnesota Landscape Arboretum Gift Shop 160
Minnesota State Arts Board 487
Minot Art Association (see North Dakota Art Exhibition 409)
Minot Art Association Art Fair 409
Minot Art Gallery 215
Minot Art Gallery Artfest 409
Mint Museum of Art (see Piedmont Crafts Exhibition 406)
Mintz Company, Stephen A. 58
Miss Boutique Inc. 58
Mississippi Gulf Coast Craftsmen's Guild, Inc. 488
Mississippi River Craft Show 434
Mississippi State University 528
Mississippi University for Women 488, 528
Missouri Arts Council 488
Missouri River Trading Company 165
Missouri Southern State College 528
Mizpah Art Gallery 263
Moffat County Council for the Arts and Humanities (see Spring Art Gala 311)
Mohave Community College 507
Mohawk College 554
Mon-Dak Historical & Arts Society (see J.K. Ralston Museum & Art Center Juried Exhibit 385)
Monford Stop Gallery 99
Monroeville Mall Arts Festival 424
Monroeville Mall Children's Hour Show 424
Montana Arts Council 489
Montana State University 529
Montclair State College 490, 531
Monterey County Fair 302
Monterey Peninsula Museum of Art (see The California Craftsman 296)
Montgomery College 523
Montgomery Kiwanis Sidewalk Art Show 414
Montgomery Mall Craft and Sculpture Show 424

Montreal Military and Maritime Museum, The 280
Monument Square Art Fair 459
Moonshell Galleries 249
Moorestown Mall Arts Festival 390
Moorestown Mall Children's Hour Show 390
Moorestown Mall Craft and Sculpture Show 390
Moorhead State University 527
Moorpark College Festival of the Arts 302
Moravian College 48
Morehead State University 521
Morgan Loom Factory 59
Morgan State University 523
Morgantown Art Association 504
Morgie's 165
Morningside College 520
Morris Museum Shop 177
Morristown Craftmarket 390
Morrow and Grant R. Hartsock, Constance E. 71
Morton Grove Art Guild Fair 342
Mossy Creek Pottery and Gallery 225
Mosteller's, Inc. 63
Mostly Handmade, Inc. 120
Mother Lode Art Show 302
Mott Community College, C. S. 526
Mount Aloysius Junior College 544
Mount Dora Art Festival 325
Mount Holyoke College Peddler's Fair 369
Mount Marty College 545
Mt. Mitchell Craftsmen's Fair 406
Mt. Prospect Plaza Fall Art and Craft Fair 342
Mt. Prospect Plaza Summer Art and Craft Fair 343
Mount Snow Craft Fair, The 444
Mount Vernon College 48
Mountain Aire 303
Mountain Craft Days 424
Mountain Craft Shop 268
Mountain Heritage Art and Crafts Festival 453
Mountain Laurel 470
Mountain State Arts and Craft Fair 453
Mountain Weaver 90
Muckenthaler Cultural Center (see Holiday Faire 300)
Muckle's Ridge Festival 287
Mud Dauber's Nest, The 113
Mud in Your Eye Pottery Studio 90

Mueller's Wrought Iron Shop 120

Mundelein College 518

Muriel Originals 158

Murray Art Guild (see Arts & Crafts Festival 357)

Murray State University 521

Muscoda Arts and Crafts Fair 459

Museum Art Education Council, The 506

Museum of Afro American History 151

Museum of American Folk Art Craft Classes 536

Museum of Anthropology Sales Desk, University of Missouri— Columbia 165

Museum of Arts and Sciences 110

Museum of Fine Arts Shop 110

Museum of Fine Arts, The 547

Museum of International Folk Art (see New Mexico Crafts Biennial 393, Southwest Crafts Biennial 394)

Museum of Northern Arizona 77

Museum of Northern British Columbia, Museum Art Gallery 281

Museum School of Art 545

Museum Shop at the International Folk Art Museum, The 184

Museum Shop, Bowdoin College Museum of Art 139

Museum Shop of the Arkansas Arts Center 79

Museum Shop — Palace of the Governor 184

Museum Shop, Philadelphia Museum of Art 234

Museum Shop, The (Indiana) 125

Museum Shop, The (Texas) 249

Museums at Stony Brook Craft Center 537

Mushroom Gallery, The 263

Musical Museum, The 202

My House Gallery 90

My Sister 202

Myford, James C. 474

Mystic Outdoor Art Festival 316

Mystic Seaport Museum Store 104

N ancy's Corner 222

Nantucket School of Needlery 524

Naples Mill School of Arts and Crafts 537

Naranjo's American Indian Arts 249, 547

Nashco Products, Inc. 59

Nashville Hobby & Craft Christmas Market 435

Natcol Crafts, Inc. 59

Natick Mall Children's Hour Show 370

Natick Mall Craft and Sculpture Show 370

National April Art Exhibit 443

National Artists Tour 71

National Calendar of Indoor/Outdoor Art Fairs 562

National Calendar of Open Competitive Art Exhibitions 562

National Carvers Museum 100

National Carvers Museum Foundation 480

National Carvers Review 562

National Craft Fair 365

National Crafts Festival (Missouri) 384

National Crafts Festival (Tennessee) 435

National Crafts Ltd. (see Rocky Mountain Craft Fair 311, Frederick Craft Fair 363, National Craft Fair 365)

National Directory of Grants and Aid to Individuals in the Arts, The 562

National Drawing and Small Sculpture Show 439

National Enamelists' Guild 504 (also see Enamels 446)

National Guide to Craft Supplies 562

National Guild of Decoupeurs 487

National Invitational Fibers and Fabric and Ceramic Exhibition 343

National Needlework News 468, 562

National Postal Museum 281

National Raku Exhibition 391

National Rosemaling Exhibition 354

National Standards Council of American Embroiderers Correspondence School 544

National Standards Council of American Embroiderers, The 477

Natural Leather 202

Natural Selection 120

Nature Loft, The 165

NCAA Juried Show 316

Nebraska Arts Council 489

Nebraska Wesleyan University 530

Necessities, Inc. 213

Needle Arts 562

Needle Nook, The 90

Needlepoint Bulletin 563

Needlework 354

Nehalem Arts Festival 418

Neshaminy Mall Arts Festival 424

Neshaminy Mall Professional Craft and Sculpture Show 425

Nevada State Council on the Arts 489

New Beginnings Festival Arts and Crafts 356

New Brunswick Craft School 554

New Carlisle Historical Days 351

New England Artists and Craftsmen's Guild, Inc. 480

New England Buyers' Market Place 370

New England Painting and Sculpure Exposition 316

New Hampshire Arts Festival 387

New Hampshire College 48

New Hampshire Commission on the Arts 490

New Harmony Gallery of Contemporary Art 125, 519

New Holstein Kiwanis Arts and Crafts Fair 459

New Jersey Designer-Craftsmen (see Morristown Craftmarket 390)

New Jersey State Council on the Arts 490

New Market Arts & Crafts Show 447

New Mexico Art League 184

New Mexico Arts & Crafts Fair 393

New Mexico Crafts Biennial 393

New Mexico State University 532

New Morning Gallery 213 (also see Village Art & Craft Fair 408)

New Muse Community Museum of Brooklyn 537

New Orleans Jazz & Heritage Festival Crafts Fair 359

New Orleans Museum of Art, Artists Biennial 359

New Salem Mountain Festival 334

New School for Social Research 537

New School, The 537

New Visions Gallery, Inc. 274

New World Resource and Supply Co. 90

New York State College of Ceramics at Alfred University 537

New York State Crafts, Home Arts and Fine Arts Competition 401

New York State Craftsmen, Inc. 494 (also see International Craft Show 400)

New York State Fair (see New York State Crafts, Home Arts and Fine Arts Competition 401)

New York State Historical Association 537

New York State University (see Festival of the Arts 397)

New York University 537

Newmarket North Arts & Crafts Show 447

Newsletter 563

Newton County Arts and Crafts Show 291

Nicholas Press 59

Niddy Noddy, The 202, 538

Niknac Gallery, Inc./DBA Sophisticat 225

Niles Art Guild Art Fair 351

9 Artisans, Inc. 202

Normandale College Gallery 160

North Carolina Artists Exhibition 406

North Carolina Arts Council 495

North Carolina Department of Cultural Resources 474

North Carolina League of Creative Arts and Crafts, Inc. 213

North Carolina Museum of Art (see North Carolina Artists Exhibition 406)

North Country Arts & Crafts 401

North Country Community College 538 (also see Northern New York Crafts Festival 401)

North Dakota Art Exhibition 409

North End-Waterfront Arts Council 486

North Park College 49

North Point Pier 66

North Shore Art Fair 378

North Shore Art League (see Midwest Craft Festival 342)

North Shore Community Arts Center 538

North Star Arts & Crafts Festival 378

North Tahoe Art Guild (see Ehrman Mansion Art Show & Fair 298)

North Texas State University 547

Northbrook Arts & Crafts Show & Sale 379

Northeast Alabama Craftsmen's Association 477

Northeast Craft Fair 401

Northeast Louisiana University 522

Northeastern Illinois University 518

Northeastern Oklahoma State University 543

Northeastern Wisconsin Art Annual 459

Northern Adirondack Craft Guild, The Crafts Barn 494

Northern Appalachian Festival 425

Northern Arizona University 507

Northern Illinois University 518

Northern Indiana Art Association 483 (also see Wicker Park Art Fair 352)

Northern Kentucky University 49

Northern Kingdom Printworks 474

Northern Michigan University 526

Northern Nevada Community College 530

Northern New York Crafts Festival 401

Northern State College 546

Northern Virginia Woodcarver Association 502

Northfield Arts Guild (see Fall Arts Fair 378)

Northpoint Arts and Selected Crafts Festival 343

Northshore Plaza Arts Festival 370

Northshore Plaza Children's Hour Show 370

Northwest Community College 553

Northwest Craft Center 263

Northwest Crafts Exhibition 450

Northwest Kansas Area Art Show & Sale 356

Northwest Missouri State University 528

Northwestern Connecticut Art Association (see NCAA Juried Show 316)

Northwestern Craftsmen 432

Northwestern Michigan Artists and Craftsmen (see Traverse Bay Outdoor Art Fair 376)

Northwestern Mid College (see Traverse Bay Outdoor Art Fair 376)

Northwoods Annual Craft Show 343

Norwegian-American Museum (see National Rosemaling Exhibition 354)

Nor'wester and Loyalist Museum 281

Nova Scotia Designer Craftsmen 554

O ak Grove Country Fair 334

Oak Park Village Mall Art and Craft Festival 343

Oak Ridge Community Art Center 500

Oakbrook Invitational Crafts Exhibition 343

Oakland Museum Art Department, The 479

Oakton Community College (see Starving Artists Arts & Crafts Fair 345)

Oates Gallery 244

OCA Crafts Co. 59

Occasion for the Arts, An 447

Ocean City Cultural Arts Center (see Crafts 389)

Ocean East Mall Festival of Arts & Crafts 326

Octagon Art Center Shop, The 128

Octagon Art Center's Clay and Fiber Show, The 354

Octagon Shop 120

Octoberfest Art Craft and Antique Show & Sale 303

Ocular 468, 563

Offray & Son Inc., C.M. 59

Oglebay Institute Craft Festival 453

Oglebay Institute Upper Ohio Valley Art Show 454

Ohio Artists and Craftsmen Show 415

Ohio Arts Council 496

Ohio State University 49

Ohio University 542

Ohio Wesleyan University 542

Ojai Crafts Festival 303

Okaloosa-Walton Junior College 516

Okefenokee Festival Arts and Craft Show 334

Oklahoma Arts & Humanities Council 497

Oklahoma City Festival of the Arts 417

Oklahoma Designer Craftsmen 497

Oklahoma Indian Arts and Crafts Co-operative 222

Oklahoma State University 543

Oktoberfest 291

Olathe Area Chamber of Commerce Annual Olathe Art Fair and Crafts Show 356

Old Bedford Village 234

Old Bronte Post Office Gallery, The 281

Old Country Store and Museum 165

Old Deerfield Craft Fair 370

Old Home Day 387

Old Mill Crafts 166

Old Mill, The 268

Old Saratoga Historical Association Art Show 402

Old Sash Mill 66

Old Slave Mart Museum and Gallery 241

Old Store Gallery 75

Old Town Art Fair 344

Old World Craft Show 444

Olde Foren Gallery 518

Olde Town Gallery 120 (also see Toy Show 346)

Oldebrooke Spinnery Inc. 531

Oleary Library and Museum Association 281

Olney Fall Festival of Arts and Crafts 344

Omaha Summer Arts Festival (Arts Festival on the Mall 386)

On The Green 316

One Art Service 470

One Manz Family Arts & Crafts 166

1 of a Kind 184

One Step Up Gifts 132

100 American Craftsmen Craft Festival (see Kenan Craft Festival 400)

Only Originals 177
Ontario Crafts Council 281
Ontario Potters Associaton 505
Oomingmak 477
Opelika Arts Festival 287
Open Door Art Shop, The 235
Open Door, Ltd., The 274
Opening Your Own Retail Store 563
Orange Park Mall Festival of Art 326
Orange Park Mall Olde Tyme Arts & Crafts Faire 326
Orange Park Mall Winter Craft Show 326
Orange Peel, The 245
Oregon Arts Commission 497
Oregon State University 543
Original Art Report, The 468, 563
Orlando Gallery 90
OSAS Art Services 202
Osceola Art Festival 326
Other Delights 281
Otis Art Institute of Los Angeles County 479
Ottawa Christmas Craft Sale 462
Ottumwa Heights Family Art Festival 354
Ouachita County Arts & Crafts Fair 292
Outdoor Art Fair 375
Outdoor Arts and Crafts Fair 303
Outdoor Arts Festival (Ohio) 415
Outdoor Arts Festival (Wisconsin) 459
Outdoor Crafts Festival 326
Outdoor Fine Arts Gallery & All Crafts Fair 351
Overly-Raker Village 235
Owensboro Area Museum 132
Owensboro Museum of Fine Art 132
Owl's Nest, The 185
Own Your Own Art Show 310
Oxford Gallery 202
Oxford Valley Mall Children's Hour Show 425
Ozark Craft Festival 384
Ozark Folk Center Sales Shop, The 79
Ozark Foothills Arts and Crafts Association 478
Ozark Foothills Craft Guild 79 (also see The Store, Arkansas Territorial Restoration 80)
Ozark Foothills Craft Guild Spring Show & Sale 292
Ozark Frontier Trail Festival and Craft Show 292
Ozarks Arts & Crafts Fair 292

Ozarks Mountaineer, The 563
Ozarks Whittlers & Woodcarvers 489

P acific Basin School of Textile Arts 511
Pacific Basin Textile Arts 90
Pacific Center of the Arts and Crafts 263
Pacific Northwest Arts and Crafts Fair 450
Pacific States Crafts Fair 303
Packard's Indian Trading Co. 185
Paddlewicker 151
Painter Oregon Workshop, Hal 543
Paley, Albert 474
Palm Springs Desert Museum Shop 91
Palmyra Canaltown Days 402
Palos Verdes Community Arts Association (see Art for Fun(d)'s Sake 294)
Panama Art Association (see Fall Arts & Crafts Show 321)
Paper and Felt Redefined 358
Paraffinalia 202
Paris Art Fair 439
Park Art Festival (New York) 402
Park Arts Festival (Maryland) 365
Park City Art Festival 443
Park Shore Plaza Festival of Arts & Crafts 327
Park West Galleries 158
Parlour, The 249
Parsons Outdoors Arts and Crafts 356
Partridge, Irene "Rae" 71 (also see Countryside Mall Starving "American" Arts and Crafts 337, Deerfield Commons Arts and Selected Crafts Fair 338, Hillside Starving "American" Arts and Crafts 340, Hillside Selected Crafts Festival 340, Northpoint Arts and Selected Crafts Festival 343)
Pasadena City College 511
Paseo Design Center 222
Patchwork Derby 287
Patchwork Factory, Inc., The 219
Patriots Art Brigade 391
Patriots Art Festival 327
Patty's Place 263
Paula Insel Annual Exhibition 463
Paula's Place 178, 531
Pavilion, The 77
Pawtuxet Village Arts & Crafts Festival 428
Peach Tree Mall 303

Peanut Patch, The 260
Peanut Valley Festival 393
Pearsall Fall Arts and Crafts Festival 439
Pearson Handicrafts, Hazel 59
Peasant Shop, The 235
Peddler's Cart Gallery 185
Peddlers Cellar, The 178
Peddlers, The 170
Pema Browne Ltd. 470
Pembroke Arts Festival 370
Pendleton Arts Council (see Christmas Craft Fair 418)
Pendleton Fabric Craft School 507
Pendleton Shop, The 78
Penn Museum Shop, William 235
Pennsylvania Council on the Arts 499
Pennsylvania Guild of Craftsmen, Inc. and Craft Artists of Pennsylvania, Inc., The 499
Pennsylvania Guild of Craftsmen's Market 425
Pennsylvania Handicrafts 236
Pennsylvania Maple Festival 425
Pennsylvania State University 545
Pensacola Arts Council (see Great Gulfcoast Festival 323)
Pensacola Museum of Art 110
People's and Cultures Gift Shop — In the Flats 219
Peoria Art Guild 121
Pera's Summer Resort 67
Perceptions, Inc. 151
Performers' Outlet 203
Perryopolis Area Historical Society Inc. Pioneer Days 425
Persimmon Seed, The 222
Peru State College 530
Peters Valley Craft Fair 391
Peters Valley Craftsmen 178, 490, 531 (also see National Raku Exhibition 391)
Petersham Craft Center 486, 525
Petersham Craft Center & Craft Shop 151
Peyton Originals 105
Phelps Annual Saurkraut Festival 402
Philadelphia Art Alliance, The 236
Philadelphia Craft Show, The 426
Philadelphia Museum of Art (see The Philadelphia Craft Show 426)
Philbrook Art Center Museum School 543
Phoenix Art Museum Shop 78
Phoenix Gallery 203
Phoenix Shop 91

Phoenix Workshops 530
Photographing Crafts 563
Photography for Artists and Craftsmen 563
Piedmont Crafts Exhibition 406
Piedmont Craftsmen, Inc. 495
Pierre National Bank, The 242
Pik Place, The 274
Pikeville Arts & Crafts Show 435
Pima County Parks & Recreation Dept. 477
Pinchpenny Gallery 203
Pine Tree Kiln 139
Pink Corral Gift Shop 276
Pink Petunia, The 111
Pinkstenfest Summer 'Minifest' 402
Pioneer Day of Pocahontas County 454
Pioneer Craft Festival 293
Pittsburgh State University 49
Place des Arts 282
Placer County Museum 91
Placerville Arts Association (see Mother Lode Art Show 302)
Plains Art Museum 160 (also see Red River Annual 379)
Planters Craftsmen 406
Plaster Unlimited 250
Platte Technical Community College 530
Plaza Art Fair 344
Plaza Arts and Crafts Show 393
Pleasure Faire of the Renaissance and Summer Marketplace 402
Plebian, The 91
Pletcher Village Art Festival 351
Plum Dandy 139
Plum Nelly Shop, The 245
Plymouth Meeting Mall Craft and Sculpture Show 426
Poko, Inc. 264
Polich's Desert Products and Manufacturing 59
Pomfret Shop, The 255
Pontiac Annual Art Fair-Heritage Festival 375
Pontiac Art Center 158
Poor Richard's Gallery 152
Popovi da Indian Arts & Crafts 185
Port City Craftsmen, Inc. 477 (also see Fall Craft Show 285, Spring Craft Show 288)
Porter County Arts Commission (see Outdoor Fine Arts Gallery & All Crafts Fair 351)
Portland Harvest Festival 418

Portsmouth National Seawall Art Show 447

Post Center of Long Island University, C. W. 538

Pot Farm, The 511

Pot 'N Stuff 169

Pot Shop, The/Art Gallery 128

Potomac Craftsmen, Inc. 504

Pot-Pourri Gallery of American Crafts 203

Potpourri, Inc. 219

Potter's Guild of Balto, Inc. 144

Potters Studio 91

Pottery & South 4th 203

Pottery Classes & Workshop 511

Pottery Guild 483

Pottery Northwest 264

Pottery Workshop 525

Powers' Crossroads Country Fair and Art Festival 335

Powhatan Arts and Crafts Show and Sale 447

Prairie Flower Crafts 130

Prairie House 121

Prairie Peoples Handicraft Market, Inc. 242

Prater's Mill Country Fair 335

Pratt Institute 538

Preakness Festival 366

Pre-Christmas Pottery Show 355

Prema Productoins (see Contemporary Crafts Expo 321)

Preservation Shops 267

Prestige Galleries Inc. 121

Pricketts Fort Memorial Foundation, Inc. 268

Priehs Department Store 63

Primitives and Contemporaries 185

Princess Angeline Gallery 264

Prints, Drawings & Crafts Exhibiton 293

Prism Crescents 91

Professional Arts, Crafts and Indoor Plants Show 304

Project, Inc. 525

Promenades Shopping Center Festival of Arts & Crafts 327

Providence Art Club Exhibitions 71

Prudential Center Children's Hour Show 370

Prudential Center Craft and Sculpture Show 371

Pumpkin Patch, The 139

Putnam Area Chamber of Commerce Sidewalk Art Exhibit 316

Putnam Arts Council (see Crafts and Creations 396)

Q uaigh Design Centre, Inc. 255

Quaker Bridge Mall Arts Festival 391

Quaker Bridge Mall Children's Hour Show 391

Qualla Arts and Crafts Mutual, Inc. 213

Queens College 49

Queens Museum, The 203

Quest for Handcrafts, The 105

Quilt Country 166

Quilt Country Enterprises, Inc. 166

Quilt Faire 304

Quilter's Haven 245

Quiltery, The 236

Quincy College 518

Quincy Society of Fine Arts, The 482

Quinebaug Valley Cultural Center (see All Arts Festival 367)

Quittacus Workshop Originals 152

Quivira Shop 185

R &R Promotions 71 (also see E.J. Thomas Christmas Art and Crafts Show 416)

R & S Associates 71

Raach's Plaza Gallery Inc. 166

Racine Christmas Gift Market 459

Radford College 550

Rainbow Enterprises 71 (also see Crafts Marketplace 428)

Raintree Book and Art Shop 204

Ralston Museum and Art Center Gift Shop, J.K. 169

Ralston Museum & Art Center Juried Exhibit, K.K. 385

Ramnad Corporation — D/B/A Pink Flamingo 121

Randhurst Autumn Art Festival 344

Rare Discovery Collectables 114

Readey, J.J. (see Coastland Center Invitational Winter Festival of Art 320, Ocean East Mall Festival of Arts & Crafts 326, Orange Park Mall Festival of Art 326, Orange Park Mall Olde Tyme Arts & Crafts Faire 326, Orange Park Mall Winter Craft Show 326, Park Shore Plaza Festival of Arts & Crafts 327,

Promenades Shopping Center Festival of Arts & Crafts 327, University Mall Winter Craft Show 330, Rivergate Mall Summer Festival of Arts & Crafts 435)
Readey Promotions, J.J. 71
Red Barn, The 121
Red Cloud Indian Art Show 432
Red Cock Craftsmen's Outlet, The 225
Red Cross Craft Market 426
Red Geranium, The 121
Red Oak, The 121
Red River Annual 379
Red River Revel, A Celebration of the Arts 360
Red River Street Fair 409
Red-Horse, Wayne 92
Reedcraft Weavers 158
Regional 375
Regional Art Exhibition 426
Regional Art Fair List 563
Regional Craftsmen's Fair 387
Regis College 525
Reiter Promotions, Inc. 71 (also see Midwest Art Show & Sale 378, Northbrook Arts & Crafts Show & Sale 379)
Renaissance Arts Faire 310
Renaissance Celebration 327
Renaissance Festival 384
Replica Sea Craft Studios 59
Return 186
Revolutionary War Days 366
Reynolds, William 474
Rhinebeck Show (see Northeast Craft Fair 401)
Rhode Island State Council on the Arts 499
Rhododendron State Outdoor Art and Craft Festival 454
Richmond Art Center (see Designer/Craftsman 297)
Richmond Craft Fair 448
Richmond Mall 415
Ricker Blacksmith Shop 140
Ridge Art Association's Exhibit and Fair at Evergreen Plaza 344
Ridgeway Gallery 245
Ringling Museum's Annual Crafts Festival (see Outdoor Crafts Festival 326)
Ris Galleries, William (New Jersey) 178
Ris Galleries, William (Camp Hill, Pennsylvania) 236
Ris Galleries, William (Hershey, Pennsylvania) 236

Rising Pottery 538
Ritasue Siegel Agency 470
River Arts Festival 439
River Gallery 225
Riverbend Arts Council 496, 542
Riverfront Market Day 287
Rivergate Mall Summer Festival of Arts & Crafts 435
Riverside Art Center and Museum 92
Riverside County Summer Outdoor Art Show 304
Riverside Downtown Saturday Market 304
Roach Galleries, J. 166
Roads Galleries 204
Roanoke Craft Festival, The 448
Roberson Center For The Arts and Sciences 538
Robinsons' Red Door Gallery 92
Rochester Institute of Technology 538
Rockhound Round-Up 463
Rockland Arts Day 402
Rockland Center for the Arts 538
Rockland Community College 538
Rock 'N Chair Productions (see Mountain Aire 303)
Rocky Mountain College 529
Rocky Mountain Craft Fair 311
Rocky Mountain Park Co. 100
Rohnert Park Cultural Arts Corporation 479
Rome Historical Society Ft. Stanwix Museum 204
Rome Prize Fellowship 494
Ronbach Shop 274
Rooftop Gallery 111
Rope Gallery 538
Rosary College Art Department 519
Roscoe Craft Center 204
Rosser's Arts and Crafts Center 242
Rotary Crafts Festival 361
Royal Oak Outdoor Art Fair 375
Rubicon Gallery 92
Rubidoux Arts & Crafts Fair, Joseph 384
Rug Crafters 92
Rug Hooker, The 563
Rug Hooker, News and View, The 468
Rumbling Waters Arts & Crafts Show & Sale 287
Running Water Draw Arts and Crafts Festival 440
Rustic Shoppe, The 92
Ruybalid's Indian Shop & Santa Fe Arts & Crafts 186

Rye Art Center 539

S and A Ceramics 122
Sabal Chase Outdoor Art and Artisans Fair 327
Sacramento Harvest Festival 304
Sacred Heart College 541
Salt Lake Art Center 548
St. Andrews Presbyterian College 49
St. Charles Artists Guild 166
St. Clair Art Fair 375
St. Cloud Annual Art Festival 328
St. Cloud State University 49, 527
St. Francis College (Indiana) 50
Saint Francis College (Pennsylvania) 50
St. Joseph Art Association's Outdoor Art Fair 375
St. Joseph College Arts & Crafts Fair 317
St. Mary's College 50
St. Mary's College of Maryland 50
St. Tammany Art Association 485
Salado Art Fair 440
Salem Art Association 497
Salem College 552
Salem Craftsmen's Guild, The 532
Sales, Paul H. 474
Salibello, Anna 475
Salz Tannery Annual Leather As Art Contest 304
Samara 255
San Antonio Artists' Exhibition 440
San Antonio College 548
San Diego Harvest Festival 305
San Diego Potters' Guild 511
San Diego State University 511
San Francisco Annual Arts Festival 305
San Francisco Harvest Festival 305
San Francisco Museum of Modern Art School 511
San Gabriel Arts and Crafts Show 440
San Jose Art League Center 92 (also see California 3-Dimensional Regional Exhibit and Competition 296)
San Jose Harvest Festival 305
San Mateo County Fair Crafts Exhibition 306
Sandalmaker 93
Sandburg Mall Art and Craft Show 344
Sande Gallery, Rhoda 204
Sandeen's Scandinavian Gift Shop 160
Sandie's Showcase 250

Sanford-Seminole Art Association (see Fall for Art 321)
Sanibel Shell Fair 328
Santa Barbara Museum of Art Shop 93
Santa Barbara Museum of Natural History 93
Santa Cruz Association of Artists and Craftspeople 479
Santa Cruz County Fair 306
Santa Fe Community College (see Spring Arts Festival 329)
Santa Fe Festival of the Arts 393
Santa Fe Workshops of Contemporary Art 491
Santa-Cali-Gon Days 384
Santa's Christmas Gift Show 306
Santa's Treasure House Arts and Crafts Bazaar 440
Santaville Arts and Crafts Fair 460
Sappa Valley Arts Club (see Northwest Kansas Area Art Show & Sale 356)
Sara's Center 539
Saturday Market 419
Sauk County Art Festival 460
Sawdust Festival 306
Schelu Artisans 186
Schenectady Museum (see Craft Festival 396)
Schiefer, C. R. 475
Schlitz Brewing Co., Joseph (see Memphis Music Heritage Festival 434)
School Arts 468
School of the Arts and Crafts Society 544
School of the Arts and Crafts Society — Bookstore/Sales Gallery 226
School of the Ozarks, The 529
Scott, Charles C. 475
Scottsdale Arts Festival 290
Schweig Gallery, Martin 167
Sea Crafters, The 140
Sea, The 93
Seacoast Crafts Fair 362
Seas National 328
Seattle Harvest Festival 450
Seaview Square Mall Craft and Sculpture Show 392
Sebastian-Moore Gallery 100
Seidel Shops, Betty 236
Selexor Displays Inc. 60
Self Expressions 100
Sensemaya 93
Serendipity 162

Serendipity Arts and Crafts Shop, The 268
Serendipity Galleries 245
Serkin Co., L. J. 256
Sermon-Anderson, Inc. 167
Seton Hill College 50
Seton College, Elizabeth 539
7 Live Arts Festival, Incorporated, Art Show 328
Seven Springs Crafts Shop 79
1770 Crafts 204
Seventeenth Colony House 219
78th Street Pottery 539
Shaker Museum, The 204
Shalako Shop 187
Sharon Arts Center 530
Shasta College 511
Shawano Arts and Crafts Fair 460
Shawnee Arts and Crafts Center 222
Shaw-Rimmington Gallery 282
Shed, Inc., The (Warwana, Houston, Texas) 250
Shed, The (Blalock, Houston, Texas) 250
Shelburne Spinners 549
Shelburne Spinners Newsletter 564
Sheridan Village Shopping Center 345
Sherman Corporate Art, Liza 43
Sherrymike Pottery/Gallery 140
Shetani Gallery 282
Sheyenne Valley Arts and Crafts Festival 409
Shippensburg Fair Crafts-Arts-Antique Show 426
Shoop, Charles E. 236
Shop, Adirondack Lakes Center for the Arts, The 205
Shop, Albany Institute of History and Art, The 205
Shop at the Gallery (Nevada Art Gallery), The 171
Shop— Guilford Handcraft Center, The 105
Shop of the Rainbow Man, Inc. 187
Shop, The (California) 94
Shop, The (West Virginia) 269
Short Grass Arts Festival 432
Show and Sell 454
Show of Hands, A 205
Show of the Craft Guild of Greater Cincinnati 415
Shreveport Art Guild National 360
Shrimp & Petroleum Craft Show 360
Shuttle, Spindle, and Dyepot 564
Side Street, The 122
Sidewalk Arts and Crafts Fair 379

Sidewalk Show 451
Siena Heights College 526
Sign of the Acorn 130
Sign of the Copper Lantern, The 158
Signal Mountain Fall Festival of Arts & Crafts 435
Silo, The 105
Silver Dollar City Craft Guild 489
Silver Dollar City, Inc. 167
Silver Shuttle, The 552
Silverdale's Whaling Days 451
Silvermine Guild of Artists (see Christmas Arts Festival 312, New England Painting and Sculpture Exhibition 316)
Simply Natural 205
Sioux City Art Center (see Pre-Christmas Pottery Show 355)
Skagit Valley College 551
Sketch Box, The 250
Skidmore College 539
Skowronski Studio, Hella 551
Skylight Gallery 264
Slater Memorial Museum 317
Slater Mill Museum Shop 239
Smith Silversmith Shop, C. Leslie 237
Smith-Mason Gallery Museum 267
Smull Gallery, A. D. 144
Snaggy Hollow Craftsmen 213
Snake Alley Art Fair 355
Sneak Box Studio, The 152
Society of Connecticut Craftsmen 105
Society of Craft Designers 499
Society of North American Goldsmiths, The 486
Society of the Arts' Annual Festival of the Arts 328
Society of Vermont Craftsmen 549
Soft Touch, Ltd., The 256
Some Place 94
Some Place Textile Studio 512
Somerset Invitational 376
Something Special in Sierra City 94
Sonnenberg Gardens, Garden Gifts 205
Sonoma County Fair 306
Sonora Christmas Fair 306
Sophienburg Museum Shop 251
Source Gallery (California) 94
Source Gallery, The (Pennsylvania) 237
South Bear School 520
South Carolina Arts Commission (Charleston, South Carolina) 500
South Carolina Arts Commission (Columbia, South Carolina) 500

South Carolina Arts Commission Exhibition 431

South County Art Annual 429

South Dakota Arts Council 500

South Dakota Memorial Art Center 243 (also see Northwestern Craftsmen 432)

South Dakota State University 546

South Florida Fairs & Expositions, Inc. 329

South Florida Spring Arts & Crafts Festival 329

South Florida Winter Arts & Crafts Festival 329

South Hills Village Arts Festival 426

South Hills Village Children's Show 427

South Hills Village Professional Arts Festival 427

South Lake Festival of the Arts 306

South Parkersburg Band Boosters Christmas Arts and Craft Show 454

South Shore Plaza Children's Hour Show 371

South Shore Plaza Fiber Fair 371

South Shore Plaza Wooden Way Show 371

South Tahoe Art Festival 307

Southeast Community College (see Kingdom Come Swappin' Meetin' 358)

Southeast Missouri Council on the Arts, Inc. (see Christmas Craft Bazaar 382)

Southeast Missouri State University 529

Southeastern Hobby Fair 431

Southeastern North Carolina Arts Council 495 (also see Arts & Crafts Festival of Southeastern North Carolina 405)

Southeastern-Northgate Art Show 406

Southern Berkshire Leather Works 152

Southern California Expositions 307 (also see Art in All Media 295)

Southern California Powwow 307

Southern Christmas Show 407

Southern Connecticut State College 514

Southern Crafts and Art News 564

Southern Highland Handicraft Guild 495, 541

Southern Illinois University 50 (also see Craft Shop Crafts Fair 338)

Southern Illinois University/Edwardsville 519

Southern Kentucky Guild of Artists and Craftsmen, Inc. 484

Southern Living Show 407

Southern Park Mall 415

Southern Tier Arts Association Inc. (see Art in Park 395)

Southern Vermont Craft Fair, The 445

Southland Art Show 307

Southwest Arts, Inc. (see De Vargas Summer Arts and Crafts Show 393)

Southwest Georgia Art Association (see Albany Arts Festival 332)

Southwest Minnesota Arts and Humanities Council 487

Southwestern Association on Indian Affairs (see SWAIA Indian Market 394)

Southwestern Craft and Hobby Show 440

Southwest Crafts Biennial 394

Southwestern Indian Arts 187

Spartanburg County Art Association (see Invitational Crafts Show 431)

Special Studies in Wood Work (Furniture) 512

Spectra Productions, Inc. 72 (also see Christmas Show 335)

Spectrum of American Artists and Craftsmen, Inc., The (Brewster, Massachusetts) 152

Spectrum of American Artists and Craftsmen, Inc., The (Hyannis, Massachusetts) 152

Spectrum of American Artists and Craftsmen, Inc., The (Rhode Island) 239

Speed Art Museum, J.B. (see 8-State Annual 357)

Spencer Pottery 264

Spertus Museum of Judaica, Museum Store 122

Spiegl Gallery and Gift Shop 94

Spinster Shop, The 130

Spirit of the Earth 237

Spokane Falls Commercial College 551

Sports Art 135

Sportsman's Gallery 251

Spot Arts and Crafts Shop, Inc. 205

Sprecher, Stanley 475

Spring Arbor College 50

Spring Art and Crafts Show and Sale 441

Spring Art Gala 311

Spring Arts and Craft Fair (Illinois) 345

Spring Arts & Crafts Fair (Maryland) 366

Spring Arts & Crafts Festival 360

Spring Arts & Crafts Show (New York) 403

Spring Arts/Crafts Show (Wisconsin) 460

Spring Arts Festival (Florida) 329

Spring Arts Festival (Illinois) 345

Spring Arts Festival (Pennsylvania) 427

Spring Arts Potpourri In The Park 330

Spring Celebration of the Arts 288

Spring Craft Fair 460
Spring Craft Festival 366
Spring Craft Market at Park City Mall 427
Spring Craft Show 288
Spring Fest of Arts and Crafts 345
Spring Fling 441
Spring Market 317
Spring National Crafts Festival 385
Spring Show (Ohio) 415
Spring Show (Pennsylvania) 427
Spring Street Pottery, The 79
Springfield Art Associaton 122 (also see National Invitational Fibers and Fabric and Ceramic Exhibition 343)
Springfield Art Museum (see Invitational Craft Fair 383)
Springfield College 525
Springfield Mall Children's Hour Show 427
Springfield Mall Craft and Sculpture Show 427
Springs Folk Festival 428
Springville Quilt and Fiber Show 443
Spurgeon Mercantile Co. 63
Square Fair 415
Square Nail, The 206
Squires Street Square Association 487
Stained Glass 564
Stained Glass Associates 213
Stained Glass Club 494
Stanley, Architects, Duffy B. 43
Starving Artists Art Show 441
Starving Artists Arts & Crafts Fair 345
Starving Artist's Sale 441
State Historical Society of Wisconsin, The 274
Station Gallery 125
Stencil-Magic 60
Stephens County Historical Museum 222
Sterling House Community Center (see Christmas Stocking Craft Show 312)
Stitchery '79 428
Stone Mountain Crafts, Inc. 213
Stone Mountain Park (see Yellow Daisy Festival 335)
Stone Soldier Pottery 256
Stoneflower 160
Stoner, Karen L. 475
Stonewall Jackson Jubilee 454
Store, Arkansas Territorial Restoration, The 80
Store, Ltd., The 144
Store, The 237
Storehouse, Inc. (Apple Valley Rd., Atlanta) 113
Storehouse, Inc. (Early St., Buckhead, Atlanta) 113
Storehouse, Inc. (Lenox Square, Atlanta) 113
Storehouse, Inc. (Northlake 2, Atlanta) 113
Storehouse, Inc. (Sand Springs Plaza, Atlanta) 113
Storehouse, Inc. (Tennessee) 245
Storehouse, Inc. (Austin, Texas) 251
Storehouse, Inc. (Carillon Plaza, Dallas) 251
Storehouse, Inc. (Center Plaza, Dallas) 251
Storehouse, Inc. (San Antonio) 251
Storrowton Village Museum 152
Stowe Art Barn 256
Strasburg Museum 260
Strasburg Museum Pottery 550
Stratton Arts Festival 445
Straw into Gold Newsletter 564
Strawberry Patch, The 94
Streets of Taos 187
Studio for the Lapidary Arts 532
Studio Gallery, The 187
Studio, Inc., The 206
Studio S. Gallery 246
Studio Suenaga 95
Studio Workshop 539
Strong Craft Gallery 140
Stroy Book Crafts 219
Studio, The 94
Studio Workshop 494
Studios West — Encinitas 95, 475
Stuffed Stocking, The 167
Sturgis Newcomers Club Arts and Crafts Fair 376
Sugar Creek Craft Shop 80
Sugarloaf Mountain Works, Inc. (see Maryland Craft Festival 365, Spring Arts & Crafts Fair 366, Spring Craft Festival 366)
Suggin Folklife Art Show 293
Summer Craft Show & Bazaar 317
Summer Outdoor Art Show 308
Sun Shop, The 237
Sun Sign 100
Sunbow Gallery 226
Sunbury Shores Arts and Nature Center, Inc. 67
Sunflower Shop 158
Sunnyvale Creative Arts Center 95
Sunrise of Santa Fe 187
Sunshine Factory, The 105

Sunshine Store 95
Sutter Street Art Festival 308
Suburban Fine Arts Center 122
Summer Arts Festival 360
Summer Fest of Arts and Crafts 345
Summer Indoor Arts & Crafts Show 403
Sumerfair Inc. 415
Summerfest 460
Summit Mall 416
Sun Valley Center for Arts and Humanities 517
Sunbonnet Festival 407
Sunbury Shores Arts and Nature Centre 282
Sunday on the Square 407
Sunrise Shops 269
Sunshine Artists, USA 564
Sunshine Hollow 130
Sunshine Shoppe, The 178
Sunshine Snowy Day 257
Sunshine Unlimited, Inc. 122
Suny at Purchase 539
Suny College of Environmental Science and Forestry 51
Surface Design Association 483
Surface Design Journal 565
Sutter's Mill 153
Sutton-Hoo Goldsmith 101
Suwanee River Crafts Show-Sale 330
Suzuki Gallery 206
SWAIA Indian Market 394
Swamp John's 140
Sweet Earth Shop 95
Swope Art Gallery, Sheldon (see Wabash Valley Exhibition 352)
Sylamore Creek Craft Shop 80
Symmography, Inc. 60
Syndicate, The (Dallas) 251
Syndicate, The (Mesquite, Texas) 251
Synergy 220

T albot Street Art Fair 351
Talent Tree, The 130
Talisman Gallery 223
Talladega Square Arts & Crafts Show & Sale 288
Tama County Fair 403
Tamarind Tree, The 96
Tanana Valley Fair Mosquito Market 289
Tanana Valley State Fair Craft Market 289
Taos Festival of the Arts 394

Tapestry 101
Tapestry Associates 43
Tarbox Gallery 96
Tarpon Springs Arts and Crafts Show 330
Tawas Bay Waterfront Art Fair 376
Taylor-London's Old Curiousity Shop 252
Teasel Crafts 237
Tehachapi Mountain Festival Art Faire 308
Temple Mound Museum 111
Temple of Good Things 96
Temple University 545
Tennessee Crafts Enterprises, Inc. 501
Texarkana College 548
Texas Area Artists at Valley View Center 441
Texas Christian University 51
Texas Commission on the Arts and Humanities 501
Texas Folklife Festival 441
Texas State Arts and Crafts Fair 442
Texas Woman's University 548
Tex-Craft Co. Inc. 61
Textile Workshops Inc. 532
Textiles by Design 96
Textured Yarn Arts, Inc. 61
Thanksgiving Weekend Christmas Arts & Crafts Show 403
Theatre by the Sea Street Fair 387
Thendara Studio 514
Things for Living 101
Thistledown Handspinners Guild 494
Thomas Christmas Art and Crafts Show, E.J. 416
Thompson Gallery, The 78
Thorens Music Boxes 61
Threadbare Unlimited 206
Threads Unlimited 311
3-Arts Club (see First Monday's Art Sunday 285)
Three Crowns, The 206
Three Rivers Arts Festival 428
Three Rivers Festival Arts and Craft Show 352
3 Rooms Up 161
Thumb Fun Amusement Park 67
Thumb Print, The 251
Tidepool Gallery (California) 96
Tidepool Gallery (Minnesota) 161
Tifanee Tree, The 144
Times Square Mall Arts and Crafts Show 345
Tippecanoe County Historical Association,

Fowler House Museum 125
Tippecanoe Regional Painting, Print and Sculpture Biennial Exhibition 352
Titusville Art League Annual Show 330
Todorof Galleries 206
Toledo Festival of the Arts 416
Tomlinson Craft Collection, The 144
Tompkins County Quilters' Guild 494
Tomtegard, Inc., Scandinavian Design Interiors 140
Tool and Talent 178
Topeka Public Library Gallery of Fine Arts 130
Toperzer Visual Arts Consultant, Tom R. 67
Touch of Glass, A 553
Touch of Glass, Stained Glass Studio, A 276
Touch of Whimsy, A 207
Tower Gallery 123
Towle Company, E.J. 61
Towson State University 523
Toy Show 346
Toys Designed by Artists Exhibition 293
Trading Company, The 188
Traditional Glassworks Studio 519
Trail of Tears Crafts Center 80
Traverse Bay Outdoor Art Fair 376
Traverse City Arts Council Inc. 487
Treasures of Yesterday, Today, Tomorrow 403
Tregre and Miller Associates, Inc. (see Madison Square Park Fair 401, Tama County Fair 403, Treasures of Yesterday, Today, Tomorrow 403)
Trenton Cultural Arts Commission 487
Trial Balloon 238
Triangle Festival of Crafts 408
Trias Gallery 207
Trilogy Gallery Inc. 126
Trinity College 51
Triton Museum of Art 96
Troy State University 506
Truckee Outdoor Arts and Crafts Fair 308
Truro Center for the Arts at Castle Hill Inc. 525
Tuckaleechee Cove Arts, Crafts & Music Festival 435
Tulane University 522
Tuscarora Pottery School 530
Tuttles Seahorse Shell Shop 111
Twelmeyer Galleries 274

Twenty Four Collection, The 111
Twenty-nine Palms Artists Guild (see Southland Art Show 307)
26 East Art Center, Inc. 223
Two Flags Festival Outdoor Show 290
2 + 2 Ltd. Gallery 135
Two Rivers Gallery/Roberson Center for the Arts and Sciences 207

U. F.O. and Plants 114
UFM-Monterey's Free University Arts & Crafts Show 308
Ulster County Council for the Arts Showcase 403
Uncommon, The 207
Unfinished Universe, The 133
Unicorn City Corporation, The 207
Union College 51
Union Street Spring Festival & Crafts Fair 308
Union University 546
Unique Shop 261
Unique, The 101
Universal Galleries, Inc. 179
University Gallery of Chicago State University, The 123
University Mall Winter Craft Show 330
University of Alabama 51
University of Alaska 507
University of Arizona 507
University of California, Davis 512
University of California, San Diego 512
University of Central Arkansas 51
University of Delaware 515
University of Evansville Art Workshops 519
University of Illinois 519
University of Kansas 520
University of Maine at Farmington 51
University of Maryland 523
University of Miami 516
University of Michigan 526
University of Michigan Artists and Crafstmen Guild Christmas Art Fair 376
University of Michigan Artists and Craftsmen Guild Fall Art Fair 377
University of Michigan Artists and Craftsmen Guild Farmington County Art Fair 377
University of Michigan Artists and

Craftsmen Guild Summer Arts Festival 377
University of Minnesota 527
University of North Alabama 506
University of North Carolina 51
University of North Carolina at Greensboro 541
University of North Dakota 541
University of North Dakota Art Galleries 215
University of Northern Colorado 513
University of Notre Dame 519
University of Southern California 52
University of Southern California Craft Center 309
University of Southern Colorado 513
University of Tennessee 546
University of the Pacific 52
University of Tulsa, The 543
University of Washington 551
University of West Florida, The 516
University of Wisconsin 553
University of Wisconsin/Parkside 553
University of Wisconsin/Platteville 553
Unusual Shop, The 167
Up Country Crafts Catalog 67
Up In Central Park Craft Fair 377
Up North Handcrafts/Lady Slipper Designs 161, 488
Upper Catskill Community Council of the Arts 494
Upper Echelon 96
Upper Peninsula Crafts Council 487
Upstairs Gallery, The 133
Upstairs Pottery 106
Upstate New York Craftsmen's Guild (see Holiday Arts & Crafts Fair 399)
Uptown Art Fair 379
Uriah Heeps 101
US Customs 102
US Small Business Administration 565
USL Union Craft Shop 135
Usquepaugh Johnny Cake Festival, The 429
USS Alabama Battleship 73
Utah State University (Logan, Utah) 548
Utah State University (Vernal, Utah) 548

V aldosta Junior Service League Arts and Crafts Show 335
Valley Art Center, Inc. 264

Valley Art Gallery 97
Valley Beth Shalom Temple's Annual Community Arts & Crafts Faire 309
Valley Craft Guild Christmas Show 309
Valley, The 64
Van Doren Gallery 97
Vassar College 52
Vaten School of Crafts, Inc., The 550
Venice Place Arts Center 97
Verde Valley Art Gallery, Inc. 78
Verde-Mont Gifts 257
Vermont Artisans, Inc. 502
Vermont Council on the Arts, Inc. 502
Vermont Crafts Market, Inc. 257
Vermont Historical Society 257
Vermont Lumber Specialties 257
Vermont Maple Art & Craft Show 445
Vermont State Center at Frog Hollow 502
Vermont State Craft Center at Windsor House 257, 549
Vero Beach Art Club Winter Art Show 330
Verzyl Gallery 207
Victorian Craft Festival 379
Viets — Creative Promotions, Jay 72
Village Art & Craft Fair 408
Village Art Fair 346
Village Artists and Craftsmen 494
Village Artists' and Craftsmen's Art and Craft Fair 403
Village Crafts 246
Village Crafts and Curios 207
Village Craftsman 126
Village Craftsmen (New York) 208
Village Craftsmen (North Carolina) 214
Village Leather Shop, The 144
Village Mall Art and Craft Show 346
Village Miniatures 168
Village Silversmith, The 208
Village Weaving Center 539
Virgin Islands Council on the Arts 505
Virginia Beach Folk Arts Festival 448
Virginia Crafts Council 502
Virginia Crafts Council Craft Fair 448
Virginia Handcrafts, Inc. 261
Virginia Mountain Crafts Guild 502
Virginia Museum 261, 503
Virginia Polytechnic Institute & State University Art Gallery 261
Virginia State College 550
Virginia Wesleyan College 550
Visual Arts Centre 554
Vitti Artisans Gallery 179

Vlada 153
Volksfest Of The Arts 461
Voltaire's Shop and Gallery 106
Volunteer Lawyers for the Arts 494

W a Yah' Sti Indian Traditions 214
Wabash Valley Exhibition 352
Wakefield Flowers and Gifts, Don 97
Walkway Festival 352
Wall Gallery, The 179
Walnut Creek Civic Arts Gallery 97
Walnut Street Theatre Gallery, The 67
Walnut Valley National Flat-Picking Championship and Folk Arts and Crafts Festival 356
Walser's Decor Encounter 97
Ward Productions, Lydia 72
Ward-Nasse Gallery 208
Ware Gallery 108
Ware Gallery, Gifts 108
Warren Festival of Arts 377
Warwick Mall Children's Hour Show 429
Warwick Mall Professional Craft and Sculpture Show 429
Washington Art Association 106
Washington County Arts Council, Inc. (see Park Arts Festival 365)
Washington International Arts Letter 565
Washington State University 551
Water Tower Art and Craft Festival 346
Water Wheel, The 102
Waterfront Art Fair 377
Waterfront Art Festival 404
Watkins, Inc. 64
Watts Towers Arts Center 512
Wave Hill Center for Environmental Studies 208, 539
Wayne County Historical Museum 126
Waynesboro Studio Club (see Clothesline Exhibit 419)
Waynesboro's Craft Day 428
Weavers Guild Fiber Fair 379
Weavers Guild of Greater Cincinnati, The 497
Weavers Guild of Minnesota, Inc. 488
Weaver's Journal, The 565
Weaver's Newsletter 468, 565
Weaver's Place, The 523
Weavers' Store, The 168
Weaver's Studio, The 540
Weaver's Web 257

Weaving Workshop 123
Web, Inc., The 111
Webb and Parsons 208
Webb's School Art and Craft Festival 436
Weber State College 548
Wee Littles Shoppe 275
Weed Lady and Other Wondrous Wares and Gingham Gallery, The (Bellevue, Washington) 264
Weed Lady and Other Wondrous Wares and Gingham Gallery, The (Edmonds, Washington) 265
Weiss Studio and Craft Workshops 532
Weissner Designs, Inc., Helene 43
Welcome Rood Studio 239
Wenatchee Valley Community College 551
West Boggs Art Festival 352
West Hartford Spring Arts & Crafts Fair 317
West Hudson Community Arts Festival 392
West Mobile Arts & Crafts Show 288
West Nebraska Arts Center 170
West Plains Council on the Arts (see Folk Music & Crafts Festival 383)
West Shore Art League (see Ludington Arts & Crafts Fair 374)
West Side YMCA 540
West Virginia Department of Culture and History 505
West Virginia Oil and Gas Festival 455
Westart 468, 565
Westbury Annual Outdoor Art & Crafts Festival 404
Westchester Home Furnishings Art & Craft Show 404
Westerly Art Festival 429
Western Carolina University 541
Western Heritage Gallery 169
Western Kentucky University 521
Western Maryland College 52
Western North Carolina Craft Federation 470
Western State College of Colorado 513
Western Washington Fair Art Show 451
Western Washington University 551
Western Woodcarvings 243
Westerville Musical and Arts Festival 416
Westfield Arts & Crafts Festival 404
Westheimer Colony Art Festival, The 442
Westland Arts and Crafts Show 416
Westport Creative Arts Festival 317
Westport Handcrafts Fair 317
Westport-Weston Arts Council 480

Westville Historic Handicrafts, Inc. 113
Westwood Ceramic Supply Company Gallery 97
Westwood Ceramic Supply Company Gallery Shows 309
Wewoka Trading Post 223
Whale's Tale 179
Wharton County Junior College 548
What's New 471
Whatsmenot? 188
Wheaton Village 179
Wheelbarrow, The 208
Wheelwright Museum, The 188
Whickerbill Contemporary 102
Whifferdill, The 275
Whimsey Craftshop and Gallery, The 208
Whistle Shop, The 163
Whistlin' Jack Arts and Crafts 451
White Bird Gallery, The 226
White Hall State Shrine's Annual Labor Day Shoot 358
Wholly Cow 97
Whoopsie Daisy 98
Wicker Garden, Inc., The 209
Wicker Park Art Fair 352
Wickford Art Festival 429
Widen Gallery, Ross 220
Wiita Decorator Crafts, Inc., Betty 61
Wildwood Carvers 81
Wilkes Gallery, Inc. 209
Will-O-The-Wick, Ltd. 209
Willowbrook Mall Art Show 392
Willowbrook Mall Wooden Way Show 392
Wimberley Country Arts and Crafts Fair 442
Wind River Valley National Show 461
Window on Main Street 209
Windsor Gallery 161
Windward Crafts 74
Winfield House 238 (also see Lewisburg Craft Fair 423)
Winnipeg Folk Festival 463
Winona County Historical Society Museum Shop, The 161
Winona Trading Post 188
Winter Market of American Crafts 367
Winter Park Mall Craft Show 331
Winter Park Sidewalk Art Festival 331
Winthrop Gallery 126
Wisconsin Arts Board 505
Wisconsin Festival of Arts 461
Wisconsin Rural Artists Association, Inc. 505

Wishing Well Arts & Crafts Festival, The 436
Wistariahurst Museum 153
Witte Museum Shop 251
Wohali Traders 214
Womankraft 478
Woman's Workshop 512
Women Artists Newsletter 565
Womencrafts, Inc. 153
Wonderful Things, Inc. 153
Wonderful World of Crafts 346
Wonderful World of Ohio Mart 416
Wondrous Things, Inc. 209
Wood Carving School, The 527
Wood 'N Thread 269
Wood Shop, The 265
Woodbridge Center Craft and Sculpture Show 393
Woodcarver's Weekend 515
Woodchop 64
Woodmere Museum Shop 238
Wood's Gallery 265
Woodshop 512
Woodsmith's Studio, Inc., The 540
Woodsy Junction 126
Woodville Mall 417
Woodville Museum of Southern Decorative Arts 163
Wool Gathering 565
Worcester Art Museum 154
Worcester Polytechnic Institute 52
Worcester State College 52
Working Craftsman, The 468, 566
Works Craft Gallery, The 239
Works Gallery East, Inc., The 209
Wo-Zha-Wa Days Art Fair 461
Wurlitzer Foundation of New Mexico, Helene 67
Wustum Museum of Fine Arts (see Mini Gallery 273)

X avier University 52

Y AAF Exhibition of Fine Art 318
Yab Yum 98
Yadkin Arts Council (see Sunbonnet Festival 407)
Yakima Mall Christmas Show 451
Yaley Enterprises 61
Yancey County Country Store 214
Yankee Artisan 141

Yankee Peddler Festival 417
Yarn and Weavers Things 98
Yarn Bazaar 261
Ybor Square Christmas Crafts Carnival 331
Ybor Square Fall Arts & Crafts Fiesta 331
Ybor Square Spring Arts & Crafts Fiesta 332
Ybor Square Summer Crafts Carnival 332
Ye Olde Huff N Puff 61
Ye Old Town Shoppe 251
Ye Wise Owl Shoppe Ltd. 282
Yellow Daisy Festival 335
Yellow Door, The 179
Yellow Springs Strings, Inc. 542
Yellowstone Art Center 170
Yesteryear Toy Company, Inc. 269
YM-YWHA of Mid-Westchester 540
Young Gallery 98
Youngstown State University 543
Your Adventure in Art 346
Yuletide Fair, The 388
Yuma Art Center 78

Z ara Gallery 98
Zeeland Arts Festival 378
Zero Wampum 240
Zjay Gallery 252

Books of Interest From Writer's Digest

Artist's Market, edited by Betsy Wones. Lists 4,000 places where you can show and sell your art. Galleries, art shows, magazines, ad agencies, pr firms, dealers, shops — they're all there. Complete with names, addresses, submission requirements, payment rates and more! 624 pp. $10.95.

The Beginning Writer's Answer Book, edited by Kirk Polking, Jean Chimsky, and Rose Adkins. "What is a query letter?" "If I use a pen name, how can I cash the check?" These are among 567 questions most frequently asked by beginning writers — and expertly answered in this down-to-earth handbook. Cross-indexed. 270 pp. $7.95.

The Cartoonist's and Gag Writer's Handbook, by Jack Markow. Longtime cartoonist with thousands of sales reveals the secrets of successful cartooning — step by step. Richly illustrated. 157 pp. $7.95.

A Complete Guide to Marketing Magazine Articles, by Duane Newcomb. "Anyone who can write a clear sentence can learn to write and sell articles on a consistent basis," says Newcomb (who has published well over 3,000 articles). Here's how. 248 pp. $6.95.

The Confession Writer's Handbook, by Florence K. Palmer. A stylish and informative guide to getting started and getting ahead in the confessions. How to start a confession and carry it through. How to take an insignificant event and make it significant. 171 pp. $6.95.

The Craft of Interviewing, by John Brady. Everything you always wanted to know about asking questions, but were afraid to ask — from an experienced interviewer and editor of *Writer's Digest*. The most comprehensive guide to interviewing on the market. 244 pp. $9.95.

Craftworker's Market, edited by Lynne Lapin. Here are 3,000 places where you can sell your crafts. Tells you exactly who to contact and where, payment rates, special requirements and more. 672 pp. $10.95.

The Creative Writer, edited by Aron Mathieu. This book opens the door to the real world of publishing. Inspiration, techniques, and ideas, plus inside tips from Maugham, Caldwell, Purdy, others. 416 pp. $6.95.

The Greeting Card Writer's Handbook, by H. Joseph Chadwick. A former greeting card editor tells you what editors look for in inspirational verse . . . how to write humor . . . what to write about for conventional, studio and juvenile cards. Extra: a renewable list of greeting card markets. Will be greeted by any freelancer. 268 pp. $6.95.

A Guide to Writing History, by Doris Ricker Marston. How to track down Big Foot — or your family Civil War letters, or your hometown's last century — for publication and profit. A timely handbook for history buffs and writers. 258 pp. $8.50.

Handbook of Short Story Writing, edited by Frank A. Dickson and Sandra Smythe. You provide the pencil, paper, and sweat — and this book will provide the expert guidance. Features include James Hilton on creating a lovable character; R. V. Cassill on plotting a short story. 238 pp. $8.95.

Law and the Writer, edited by Kirk Polking and Leonard S. Meranus. Don't let legal hassles slow down your progress as a writer. Now you can find good counsel on libel, invasion of privacy, fair use, plagiarism, taxes, contracts, social security, and more — all in one volume. 249 pp. $9.95.

Magazine Writing Today, by Jerome E. Kelley. If you sometimes feel like a mouse in a maze of magazines, with a fat manuscript check at the end of the line, don't fret. Kelley tells you how to get a piece of the action. Covers ideas, research, interviewing organization, the writing process, and ways to get photos. Plus advice on getting started. 220 pp. $9.95.

The Mystery Writer's Handbook, by the Mystery Writers of America. A howtheydunit to the whodunit, newly written and revised by members of the Mystery Writers of America. Includes the four elements essential to the classic mystery. A comprehensive handbook that takes the mystery out of mystery writing. 273 pp. $8.95.

One Way to Write Your Novel, by Dick Perry. For Perry, a novel is 200 pages. Or, two pages a day for 100 days. You can start *and finish* your novel, with the help of this step-by-step guide taking you from blank sheet to polished page. 138 pp. $8.95.

Photographer's Market, edited by Melissa Milar and William Brohaugh. Contains what you need to know to be a successful freelance photographer. Names, addresses, photo requirements, and payment rates for 3,000 markets. 624 pp. $12.95.

The Poet and the Poem, by Judson Jerome. A rare journey into the night of the poem — the mechanics, the mystery, the craft and sullen art. Written by the most widely read authority on poetry in America, and a major contemporary poet in his own right. 482 pp. $7.95 ($4.95 paperback).

Songwriter's Market, edited by William Brohaugh. Lists 1,500 places where you can sell your songs. Included are the people and companies who work daily with song-writers and musicians. Features names and addresses, pay rates and other valuable information you need to sell your work. 384 pp. $9.95.

Stalking the Feature Story, by William Ruehlmann. Besides a nose for news, the newspaper feature writer needs an ear for dialog and an eye for detail. He must also be adept at handling off-the-record remarks, organization, grammar, and the investigative story. Here's the "scoop" on newspaper feature writing. 310 pp. $9.95.

A Treasury of Tips for Writers, edited by Marvin Weisbord. Everything from Vance Packard's system of organizing notes to tips on how to get research done free, by 86 magazine writers. 174 pp. $5.95.

Writer's Digest. The world's leading magazine for writers. Monthly issues include timely interviews, columns, tips to keep writers informed on where and how to sell their work. One year subscription, $15.

The Writer's Digest Diary. Plan your year in it, note appointments, log manuscript sales, be prepared for the IRS. With advice such as the reminder on March 21 to "plan your Christmas story today." It will become a permanent annual record of writing activity. Durable cloth cover. 144 pp. $8.95.

Writer's Market, edited by Bruce Joel Hillman. The freelancer's bible, containing 4,500 places to sell what you write. Includes the name, address and phone number of the buyer, a description of material wanted and rates of payment. 984 pp. $14.95.

Writer's Yearbook, edited by John Brady. This large annual magazine contains how-to articles, interviews and special features, along with analyses of 500 major markets for writers. $2.50.

Writing and Selling Non-Fiction, by Hayes B. Jacobs. Explores with style and know-how the book market, organization and research, finding new markets, interviewing, humor, agents, writer's fatigue and more. 317 pp. $9.95.

Writing and Selling Science Fiction, compiled by the Science Fiction Writers of America. A comprehensive handbook to an exciting but oft-misunderstood genre. Eleven articles by top-flight sf writers on markets, characters, dialog, "crazy" ideas, world-building, alien-building, money and more. 191 pp. $7.95.

Writing for Children and Teen-agers, by Lee Wyndham. Author of over 50 children's books shares her secrets for selling to this large, lucrative market. Features: the 12-point recipe for plotting, and the Ten Commandments for writers. 253 pp. $8.95.

Writing Popular Fiction, by Dean R. Koontz. How to write mysteries, suspense thrillers, science fiction, Gothic romances, adult fantasy, Westerns and erotica. Here's an inside guide to lively fiction, by a lively novelist. 232 pp. $7.95.

(1-2 books, add $1.00 postage and handling; 3 or more, additional 25c each.
Allow 30 days for delivery. Prices subject to change without notice.)

Writer's Digest Books, Dept. B, 9933 Alliance Road, Cincinnati, Ohio 45242